Handbook
of
Research
Design
and
Social
Measurement

To
Social and Behavioral
Students, Scholars, and Practitioners

To the Students:

   —Seeking Teaching, Organizational, or Practitioner Careers

To the Scholars:

   —In the Liberal Arts Colleges
   —In the Small Universities
   —In the Major Research Universities

To the Practitioners:

   —With Their Own Practices
   —In Business and Government Organizations
   —In Research and Service Organizations

In this book the author and the many writers are trying to talk with you.
Whether all of you out there realize it or not, your orientation to research and to
the research method ties you together. Your command of the tools of research
opens the door to new knowledge. This book seeks to give you new leverage
toward your various research and career goals.

Handbook
of
Research
Design
and
Social
Measurement

Fifth Edition

Delbert C. Miller

SAGE PUBLICATIONS
The International Professional Publishers
Newbury Park   London   New Delhi

For information address:

SAGE Publications, Inc.
2455 Teller Road
Newbury Park, California 91320
E-mail: order@sagepub.com

SAGE Publications Ltd.
6 Bonhill Street
London EC2A 4PU
United Kingdom

SAGE Publications India Pvt. Ltd.
M-32 Market
Greater Kailash I
New Delhi 110 048 India

Printed in the United States of America

Library of Congress Cataloging-in-Publication Data

Miller, Delbert Charles, 1913-
    Handbook of research design and social measurement / Delbert C.
Miller. — 5th ed.
    p.   cm.
Includes bibliographical references and index.
    ISBN 0-8039-4219-2 — ISBN 0-8039-4220-6 (Pbk).
    1. Social sciences — Research. 2. Sociometry. I. Title.
H62.M44   1991
302′.072—dc20

                                                              91-15047
                                                                 CIP

        99   00   12   11   10   9

Sage Production Editor: Michelle R. Starika

Contents

Preface

This fifth edition of the *Handbook of Research Design and Social Measurement* remains a carefully designed sourcebook for all the research steps in social research investigation. It seeks to provide guidance for research in the social sciences and such applied professions as journalism, education, social work, and business. Some researchers in hotel administration, hospital administration, and police administration may also find it applicable to their problems.

With this edition the *Handbook* celebrates 26 years of service to social researchers. It has been used in three different ways.

1. It has been used as an independent handbook for all social researchers who have wanted a professional sourcebook. As a reference work, this volume includes every digest of useful knowledge that behavioral science researchers need as a guide to their research requirements. For that reason the contents cover searches of periodicals, useful sourcebooks, bibliographies, computer programs, many of the most important scales and sources of scales, sources of funding and publication—and much more. The purpose is to place in the *Handbook* enough information so that older researchers can find digests of material not taught in the days of their graduate training or information that may be used for review by any researcher.

This revision has a significantly new orientation. From the beginning there is a recognition of the three major research activities of social scientists. The activities and objectives of basic, applied, and evaluation research are delineated. These three fields have emerged because the importance of basic research has been maintained and the demand for the services of applied and evaluation researchers has greatly expanded in business, government, and social services generally.

2. It has served as a supplement to social methods texts for teachers who wanted to provide their students with basic information about social science research and how it is organized. Much of the book is concerned with professional education. Grantsmanship, professional organizations, research institutes, and professional writing and communication are the stuff that careers are made of.

3. As a text, the book provides step-by-step instructions for students' research training. It begins where every basic researcher, student or professional, begins—in finding a creative idea, a middle-range theory, and initial hypotheses. It proceeds through design, proposal, collection and analysis of data, and finally writing, reporting, publication, and utilization of research skills.

For applied and evaluation researchers, an orientation to the practical problems to be faced in their research assignments is outlined. The activities and objectives of basic, applied, and evaluation research are delineated. The way that such problems may be handled by theory and methodological tools is described.

Teachers usually supplement the textual guide with appropriate lectures or other books and photocopied material. The world of behavioral research is big and fast moving; no single book can cover it all or keep up with advances. Certainly social research has changed greatly since the introduction of this book in 1964, when it had 332 pages and sold for $3.50. The computer has appeared and opened possibilities only dreamed about in the early 1960s. The period of the IBM card sorter and the mechanical calculator is gone. Increased funding has made large-scale research possible and lengthened the time span of investigation. At one point Guttman-type scales became so popular that they reached faddish proportions. At the present time the vogue is for each researcher to produce his or her own individual item scales. In accordance with insistence on the importance of replication and accumulation of research knowledge, I have refused to honor any scale with inclusion in this volume unless it has passed rigorous tests of reliability, validity, and utility. Such scales as have won repeated usage are given major consideration.

Besides the standard and often "classic" contents preserved from the previous editions, this revised fifth edition contains much new material, including the following:

- an inside look at a microcomputer, with a description of the types of networks around which computers may be arranged
- descriptions of the newest software for social science research
- a computer bibliography of general books, software, networks, artificial intelligence, and computer periodicals
- additions to the dictionary of newer statistical tools and methodological techniques, including event history analysis, Delphi technique, communication network analysis, meta-analysis, and probit and logit models
- a history of evaluation research and an updated evaluation bibliography
- discussion of problems encountered by the applied researcher
- an updated bibliography of methods guides, with new methods of conversation analysis and secondary analysis
- the follow-up inventory of measures utilized in the *American Sociological Review*, 1981-87
- thoroughly revised guides to federal and private funding
- career utilization for students with B.A., M.A., and Ph.D. degrees
- new or updated listings of sociological and related-field journals that serve as publication outlets to behavioral scientists
- a review and critique of the usage of sociometric scales

In addition to the above, Schuessler's Social Life Feelings Scales are presented for the first time. Also, revised Nam-Powers Socioeconomic Status Scores are made available, and new scales of marital adjustment are presented.

I continue to be grateful to behavioral science researchers everywhere, especially to the users of and contributors to previous editions of the *Handbook*. There is an intellectual kinship across the social and applied social sciences that is knit by our common adherence to scientific methods and the methodological and statistical techniques that guide our work. For this reason the book's dedication to all behavioral science researchers seems fitting. The reader is directed to examine the perspective that places behavioral scientists among all contemporary scientists. (See "The Behavioral Scientist Market in the United States," Section 7.E.2.)

I am especially grateful for the secretarial services of Jane Railsback, Susan Duke, Lorene Fox, and Eleanor Schloesser at Indiana University. The Research and Graduate Development Office of the university provided the funds that made possible the inventory of measures utilized in the *American Sociological Review*, 1981-87.

I am indebted to Charles Zoltac and Jiangong Lei for their assistance with the inventory. Sociology colleagues have always provided a guiding hand when I sought help, and subtle additions that have resulted from intellectual osmosis are beyond measurement.

In the years behind me are three teachers of sociology who inspired me with the same thought: *Social data are natural data. Their study can and should follow the contours of the scientific method.* After two years of high school teaching as an instructor of physical science and mathematics, I became a student of the social sciences. I went back to the university to learn about social research. I must now salute Read Bain, my M.A. mentor at Miami University; F. Stuart Chapin, my Ph.D. mentor at the University of Minnesota; and his student, George A. Lundberg, who became my teacher and department head at the University of Washington. All carried the vision of the sociometric scale as a crucial element in social measurement. This book itself was born with that vision in a classroom during a course in social measurement at Pennsylvania State University. It has been nurtured by me for 31 years at Indiana University. Every research article in the *American Sociological Review*, official organ of the American Sociological Association, has been examined for the scales used and classified as to type, frequency, and trend from 1951 to 1987. The Summary Notes can be found in this and previous editions of the *Handbook*.

The books and personal vitae of research from which this book was compiled may be found in the D. C. Miller Book Collection of Research Design and Social Measurement, which is housed at Purdue University in the Library of Humanities, Education, and Social Science.

Delbert C. Miller

Acknowledgments

Permission to reprint from the following is gratefully acknowledged:

From *Career Patterns of Liberal Arts Graduates*, by Robert Calvert, Jr. Copyright © 1973 by The Carroll Press. Reprinted by permission of The Carroll Press, Cranston, Rhode Island.

From *Mail and Telephone Surveys*, by Don A. Dillman. Copyright © 1978 by John Wiley & Sons, Inc. Reprinted by permission of John Wiley & Sons, Inc.

From *Concepts, Theory, and Explanation in the Behavioral Sciences*, edited by Gordon J. DiRenzo. Copyright © 1967 by Random House, Inc. Reprinted by permission of Random House, Inc.

From *Surveys by Telephone* (New York: Academic Press, 1979), by Robert M. Groves and Robert L. Kahn. Reprinted by permission of the publisher and Robert M. Groves.

From "Urban Friendships: Qualitative and Quantitative Aspects of Primary-Relations in an Urban Setting," unpublished dissertation by Lea Hagoel. Copyright © 1982 by Lea Hagoel. Reprinted by permission of the author.

From *Process of Stratification* (New York: Academic Press, 1977), by Robert M. Hauser and David L. Featherman. Reprinted by permission of Academic Press and David L. Featherman.

From "Factors Affecting Response Rate to Mailed Questionnaires: A Quantitative Analysis of the Published Literature," by Thomas A. Heberlein and Robert Baumgartner in *American Sociological Review* 43 (August 1978). Reprinted by permission of the American Sociological Association and the authors.

From *Community Power Succession: Atlanta's Policy-Makers Revisited*, by Floyd Hunter. Copyright © 1980 by the University of North Carolina Press. Reprinted by permission of the publisher.

From *Organizational Stress: Studies in Role Conflict and Ambiguity*, by Robert L. Kahn et al. Copyright © 1964 by John Wiley & Sons, Inc. Reprinted by permission of the publisher.

From *The Conduct of Inquiry* (pp. 30-33), by Abraham Kaplan (Chandler Publishing Co.). Copyright © 1964 by Harper & Row, Publishers, Inc. Reprinted by permission of the publisher.

From *Handbook of Survey Research* (New York: Academic Press, 1982), edited by Peter Rossi, James D. Wright, and Andy Anderson. Reprinted by permission of the publisher and Don A. Dillman.

From *A Methodology for Social Research* (New York: Harper & Row, 1968), by Gideon Sjoberg and Roger Nett. Copyright held by Sjoberg and Nett; reprinted by permission of the authors.

From *Social Sciences Index* for 1982. Copyright © 1982 by the H. W. Wilson Company. Material reproduced by permission of the publisher.

From "Recording Changes" to "Reliability of Results" (pp. 217-218) in *Say It with Figures*, 4th edition, by Hans Zeisel. Copyright © 1947, 1950, 1957 by Harper & Row Publishers, Inc. Reprinted by permission of the publisher.

From *Annual Review of Sociology* (Volume 20, 1984) by Peter Rossi and James D. Wright. Copyright © 1984 by Annual Reviews, Inc., Palo Alto, California. Reprinted by permission of Annual Reviews, Inc.

From *Data Systems and Management*, 3rd edition (Englewood Cliffs, NJ: Prentice-Hall, 1985), by Alton R. Kindred. Reprinted by permission of the publisher.

From *Doing Research That Is Useful for Theory and Practice* (San Francisco: Jossey-Bass, 1985), by Edward E. Lawler III and Associates. Copyright by Jossey-Bass, Inc. Reprinted by permission of the publisher.

From *Writing Documented Papers*, rev. 1941 (pp. vii-viii) (Totowa, NJ: Barnes & Noble Books), by George Sheldon Hubbell. Reprinted by permission of the publishers.

From *Inside a Microcomputer*, by Eric Schlene. University Computing *Times* (September-October 1990): 14-17. Indiana University Computing Center. Reprinted by permission of Eric Schlene.

Part 1

General Description of the Guides to Research Design and Sampling: Basic, Applied, and Evaluation Research

PART 1 EXHIBITS the defining characteristics of basic, applied, and evaluation research. The orientations and commitments of the three types of researchers are spelled out. The opportunities and problems inherent in basic, applied, and evaluation research are described.

RESEARCH COMES IN THREE PATTERNS: DEFINING CHARACTERISTICS OF BASIC, APPLIED, AND EVALUATION RESEARCH

Behavioral or organizational problems focus research inquiries in three different directions. These are generally called *basic, applied,* and *evaluation,* although each can be found under other names. For example, basic research is often called *pure research.* Applied research has been transformed as *policy research, action research,* and *useful research.* Evaluation research may be found as *assessment* or *appraisal research,* and sometimes as *social accounting.*

Table 1.1 seeks to sort out the differences among the three patterns. Note the defining characteristics are set out as (a) nature of the problem, (b) goal of the research, (c) guiding theory, and (d) appropriate techniques.

A careful reading of Table 1.1 will reveal a connecting thread. Basic research seeks the new knowledge needed to understand social phenomena; applied research hopes to provide useful knowledge that can be applied to a pressing problem; and evaluative research strives to give a social accounting of ongoing action programs. Each type of research needs the help of the others. Yet an increasing number of researchers find themselves in different camps. The variant research patterns—basic, applied, and evaluation—cannot be taken lightly. The divergent goals commit researchers to differing research orientations. And researchers feel strongly about the worth of their own kinds of research.

The research mind can be likened to a computer searching its way through many arrays of data to find the most significant bits required to answer a question put to it. So, likewise, the greater mastery the researcher has of basic knowledge, theory, design, and methodological techniques, the greater are the options available. This is true whether the task is problem discovery and definition, design possibilities, collection and treatment of data, or final validation or rejection of a hypothesis. Greatness in creative research begins here, and whether the problem falls in the focus of basic, applied, or evaluative research, the same rule applies.

All researchers, whatever their bent, must master the discipline of basic research. This handbook is oriented precisely to this discipline, but references will be made to that growing area of applied and evaluation research where social practitioners live and are tested daily. Rossi and Wright have defined the reciprocal relationship between the research fields:

We also anticipate that basic research will continue to benefit from the substantive and technical advances made by applied researchers as the latter attempt to tackle even more complicated applied research tasks. There is no doubt that much technical and substantive knowledge flows the other way as well. A discipline that does not have an applied side loses a certain richness of theory and method. An applied field that loses touch with its basic discipline also runs a risk of parochialism and overly narrow attention to policy-makers' definitions of social problems and their most feasible solutions.[1]

TABLE 1.1 Research Design Orientations

Defining Characteristic	Basic (pure) [a]	Applied (policy-action-useful) [b]	Evaluation (assessment-appraisal) [c]
Nature of the problem	Basic scientific investigation seeks new knowledge about social phenomena, hoping to establish general principles with which to explain them.	Applied scientific investigation seeks to understand a demanding social problem and to provide policymakers well-grounded guides to remedial action.	Evaluative research seeks to assess outcomes of the treatment applied to a social problem or the outcome of prevailing practices.
Goal of the research	To produce new knowledge including discovery of relationships and the capacity to predict outcomes under various conditions.	To secure the requisite knowledge that can be immediately useful to a policymaker who seeks to eliminate or alleviate a social problem.	To provide an accurate social accounting resulting from a treatment program applied to a social problem.
Guiding theory	Selection of theory to guide hypothesis testing and provide reinforcement for a theory under examination.	Selection of a theory, guidelines, or intuitive hunches to explore the dynamics of a social system.	Selection of a theory to fit the problem under assessment. Watch for ways to hook findings to a new theory or an established one.
Appropriate techniques	Theory formulation, hypothesis testing, sampling, data collection techniques (direct observation, interview, questionnaire, scale measurement), statistical treatment of data, validation or rejection of hypotheses.	Seek access to individual actions and inquire what actors are feeling and thinking at the time; elicit the attributions and evaluation made about self, other, or situational factors; regard crucial explanations as hypotheses to be tested.	Use all conventional techniques appropriate to the problem.

a. Abraham Kaplan, *The Conduct of Inquiry* (San Francisco: Chandler, 1964; Robert Dubin, *Theory Building* (New York: Free Press, 1969).
b. J. S. Coleman, *Policy Research in the Social Sciences* (Morristown, NJ: General Learning Press, 1972); Chris Argyris, Robert Putnam, and Diana McLain Smith, *Action Science* (San Francisco: Jossey-Bass, 1985); Edward E. Lawler III and Associates, *Doing Research That Is Useful for Theory and Practice* (San Francisco: Jossey-Bass, 1985); Howard E. Freeman, Russell R. Dynes, Peter H. Rossi, and William Foote Whyte, eds., *Applied Sociology: Roles and Activities of Sociologists in Diverse Settings* (San Francisco: Jossey-Bass, 1983).
c. Armand Lauffer, *Assessment Tools*, vol. 30 (Beverly Hills, CA: Sage; Thomas J. Luck, *Personnel Audit and Appraisal* (New York: McGraw-Hill, 1955); F. Thomas Juster and Kenneth C. Land, eds., *Social Accounting Systems: Essays on the State of the Art* (New York: Academic Press, 1982).

1.2　THE ORIENTATION AND COMMITMENT OF THE BASIC RESEARCHER

Basic investigators define their goal as that of advancing knowledge. Any immediate utility is irrelevant. Basic researchers assert that the primary objective of science is to describe the world as it exists, not to change it. There is general acceptance that all knowledge, whether it validates a hypothesis or not, will be useful in the short or long run. It is always useful to know what is true and what is not true. Hans Selye once said, "I've always felt that many great scientists who have made many valuable contributions were not primarily motivated by curiosity or a great desire to serve humanity, but an emotional reluctance to accept defeat."

In the real world a large number of social variables are found to be highly interrelated. Causes and effects are hard to disentangle. In social science itself, many theories and explanations abound for the same phenomena. Individual biases and ideological differences reside in the very methodological approaches that are advised by various "experts."

So why do young social researchers commit themselves to working with such uncertain, shifting, confusing, and exasperating phenomena? Many students welcome the challenge of working in new scientific fields, where the origins are only a scant century old. Others just like the social sciences because they address what they consider the most important problems of our time. Some respect the criteria of the scientific method and the mathematical tools that demand intellectual discipline and integrity. All of those who get research "in their blood" find challenges and satisfactions that sustain them through all difficulty.[2]

Committed social researchers never give up! Whatever the outcome, researchers have a responsibility both to themselves and to other researchers to search for better ways to handle data. Researchers seek causal statements. They often seek relationships to fit such generic propositions as this: Under conditions *A, B,* and *C,* if *X* were increased (or decreased), then *Y* can be expected to increase (or decrease) by a determined magnitude. This is commonly expressed in probability terms, but the effort is always to increase that probability. Researchers would like "overwhelming results." They attempt replication to affirm findings. With each increase in predictive power, the value of the knowledge and of the discipline increases. When the policymaker demands social science data and finds them indispensable, social science moves forward and research is enhanced. When theory and data intertwine and research strengthens theory, social study becomes social science.

Notes

1. Peter H. Rossi and James D. Wright, "Evaluation Research: An Assessment," in *Evaluation Studies Review Annual*, vol. 10, ed. Linda H. Aiken and Barbara H. Kehrer (Beverly Hills, CA: Sage, 1985), 76.

2. See John B. Williamson, *The Research Craft* (Boston: Little Brown, 1977); P. B. Medawar, *Advice to a Young Scientist* (New York: Harper Colophon, 1981).

How do scientists go about making discoveries, propounding "laws," or otherwise enlarging human understanding? How can I tell if I am cut out to be a scientific research worker? Sir Peter Medawar, Nobel laureate and one of the most erudite of contemporary scientists, answers these and related questions and offers useful advice to both young and older scientists and to nonscientists "who may for any reason be curious about the delights and vexations of being a scientist, or about the motives, moods, and mores of members of the profession."

James D. Watson, *The Double Helix: A Personal Account of the Discovery of the Structure of DNA.* (New York: New American Library, 1969); Phillip E. Hammond, ed., *Sociologists at Work* (New York: Basic Books, 1964).

THE VALIDITY OF RESEARCH METHODOLOGY   1.3

George Shelton Hubbell[1]

The validity of research as a way of study is based upon certain characteristics of the method:

1. *It is thorough.* The researcher seeks to find out about all aspects and backgrounds of his subject. He gets access to all available knowledge about it. If the task of learning so much proves too great, he limits the subject. But within the more restricted field, he still looks for all that has been contributed, using the resources of a good modern library, which helps enormously by supplying indexes, abstracts, and huge compendiums of information. Thus the researcher, when he has done his task properly, is not ignorant—as most of us without special study are bound to be—of various little points which might invalidate the conclusions reached. And even a little unit of research which a beginner can do in a few weeks, imperfect as it must be and not really thorough, has many advantages over a hit-or-miss study by an unsound method.

2. *Research is responsible.* By the system of bibliography and footnotes, it checks up on each step of progress. Any unsupported statement is challenged by the writer himself. Exaggerations, prejudices, wish thinking are likely to be detected and set right. This does not mean that imagination and individual opinion are ruled out. They are in fact used extensively in all good research. But they are checked by facts and evidence. And if the evidence does not support them, they stand apart as especially disputable matters for which the author does not presume to require acceptance.

3. *Research is a system of world-wide collaboration.* The "learned" periodicals appear at their stated intervals, making research studies simultaneously available all over the world so that this month a Japanese scholar may find the answer to a problem which an American scholar stated last month. Perhaps this collaborative feature of research accounts, more fully than any other one cause, for the phenomenal spread of modern learning, and its astonishing results in transforming man's life. Such collaboration would be greatly impaired, of course, if it were not for the system of bibliography and footnotes, which makes available everything needful to a reader who would be more than a mere reader—who would work upon the problem himself and perhaps contribute to its solution.[2]

Notes

1. This section is reprinted from George Shelton Hubbell, *Writing Documented Papers*, rev. ed. (New York: Barnes & Noble, 1941), viii.
2. See David Brinberg and Joseph E. McGrath, *Validity and Research Process* (Beverly Hills, CA: Sage, 1985).

1.4   THE ORIENTATION AND COMMITMENT OF THE APPLIED RESEARCHER

Applied researchers seek to create knowledge that can be used to solve pressing social and organizational problems. This knowledge must be valid, descriptive of the problem, and informative of how change may be accomplished. Those who call themselves policy or action researchers claim that much of the social science research knowledge of today does not have the proper methodological foundation to interpret the dynamic behavior of the social systems in ongoing organizations. But all applied researchers would accept the "applied mind-set" described in Section 1.5. What is set out for application to social work can be related to any organizational system.

RESEARCH UTILIZATION

An illustration of an "applied mind-set" can be clearly seen
professors of the School of Social Work at the University of Mich
Tony Tripodi, and Henry J. Meyer. They set forth the questions to
utilization of any experimental research relevant to social work:[1]

Utilization

1. What objects of social work interest are addressed by the research (recipients, the process of serving, purveyance of services)?
2. To what extent is the research relevant to the social work purposes of treatment, enhancement, and prevention?
3. On what levels does the research view the objects of social work interest? Is it concerned with individuals, groups, organizations, communities, or society?
4. Is the level of knowledge achieved by the research useful to social work primarily as empirical findings ("facts" or empirical generalizations), conceptual contributions (concepts, hypotheses, theories), or methods (for diagnostic or treatment procedures) potentially applicable to practice?
5. After evaluation, how valid is the research judged to be?
6. How engineerable are the variables identified in the research?
   a. How available (accessible and manipulable) are the variables for possible control by practitioners?
   b. How much difference in the practice situation will it make if the variables are manipulated?
   c. How feasible is it to manipulate variables of the research in the practice situation (economic feasibility, ethical suitability, organizational constraints)?
7. What types of use can be made of the research (direct application, indirect or complementary application, general stimulation of ideas)?

Rubin has developed a typology of applied social researchers that he depicts as follows:[2]

	Focus upon Policy Implications	Focus upon Data Gathering and Data Interpretation
Concern with Social Processes	policy analyst	evaluation researcher
Concern with Social Outcomes	social monitor	data analyst

These four research types are defined in order:

- A *policy analyst* studies social processes and describes what policy alternatives exist for solving an existing problem.
- An *evaluation researcher* studies social processes to determine if a program or project is accomplishing what it is intended to accomplish.
- A *social monitor* examines outcome data to discover patterns that require some organizational or government action.

analyst uses and refines methodological tools to interpret outcome data. Advanced statistical procedures are often indicated.

Two major tasks confront all applied researchers: All bear a responsibility for understanding research methodology and all must determine the cost of gathering information versus its value for decision making. An applied researcher may be called upon to fill any one or all of the roles, depending upon the call of an administrator who is seeking help. In this book a distinction is made between applied and evaluative research because the applied researcher is often intimately involved in the policy and formulation of a program whereas the evaluation researcher is called upon only after the program is in place.

Notes

1. Phillip Fellin, Tony Tripodi, and Henry J. Meyer, eds., *Exemplars of Social Research* (Itasca, IL: F. E. Peacock, 1969), 16-17.
2. Herbert J. Rubin, *Applied Social Research* (Columbus, OH: Charles E. Merrill, 1983).

1.6 DESIGN OPPORTUNITIES FOR APPLIED RESEARCH

Many opportunities for performance effectiveness of an organization have been outlined by J. Richard Hackman:

First, we can watch for occasions when unexpected or unintended changes in authority structures, technologies, and human resource strategies do occur and be prepared to exploit the learning opportunities these occasions provide. When a crisis occurs, for example, an organization may temporarily operate in ways that management would find wholly unacceptable during normal operations. If we are present, prepared, and not already fully occupied with evaluating the latest productivity program, we may be able to capitalize on such occurrences—and just might generate findings showing that "unacceptable" ways of operating actually result in improved performance effectiveness.

Second, we can seek out organizations that go about their business in ways that differ markedly from standard corporate practice. We have much to learn from public and nonprofit organizations, for example. And of special interest are work organizations that have chosen a deliberately democratic model of governance, such as worker cooperatives. Some of these organizations manage the productive work of the firm using interesting, nontraditional structures and systems. They can serve as a kind of laboratory for examining the impact on performance effectiveness of ways of operating that are quite unlikely to appear spontaneously in more traditional businesses.

Finally, we can prepare ourselves to help create nontraditional organizational forms when opportunities present themselves and carefully document what happens and what is learned in the process. Creation of new plants, for example, has provided some valuable opportunities to learn about alternative ways of improving productivity, even in corporations whose headquarters operate quite traditionally (Lawler, 1978). This option may be the most engaging and promising alternative to evaluation research on productivity improvement programs. It is also the most challenging, in that it requires not only a model of the conditions that foster work effectiveness but also a theory of action to guide implementation and management of the innovative system (Argyris, 1980). It is hard to deal with "What is to be done" and "How and when should we do it" questions at the same time. It surely is worth the trouble to try.

Yet we may have to go even further. If we seek to do research that can have a significant impact on organizational performance, we may have to start dealing explicitly with the assumptions and values held by managers in the organizations where the research is conducted. And to ask managers to examine their unstated assumptions and values requires that we be aware of our own—and be willing to make them explicit. If our research is intended to generate knowledge useful in improving productivity, for example, then we must be prepared to assert that we believe improved productivity to be a positive outcome, something worth espousing and supporting.

One can, of course, take the contrary position, that research and practice aimed at productivity improvement are not desirable for this society at this time in history. But if we choose the view that higher productivity is beneficial and involve ourselves in research or action intended to promote it, then it seems to me we are obligated to do that work as well and with as much impact as possible. And this will, on occasion, require us to confront managers directly about what is and what is not open to change in an organization.[1]

Universities offer some courses in applied research, but the most likely place to learn is in the research activity of many social science institutes. And there learning will take place through internships, apprenticeships, and staff entry-level positions. Professional schools such as schools of business, social work, and education are receptive to applied research that is "useful in theory and practice." Many individual professors can be found in the midst of "practical" research in those schools.

Note

1. J. Richard Hackman, in Edward E. Lawler III and Associates, *Doing Research That Is Useful for Theory and Practice* (San Francisco: Jossey-Bass, 1985), 145-46; see also Herbert J. Rubin, "Organizational Research and Ethical Dilemmas," in *Applied Social Research* (Columbia, OH: Charles E. Merrill, 1983), 24-48.

APPLIED RESEARCH REQUIRES COPING WITH DEFENSIVE BEHAVIOR 1.7

The researcher is an agent of intervention in a relatively closed social system. Everyone is curious about why the researcher is looking around and asking questions. Employees start asking questions, too. "What do you expect to find?" "What are you trying to do?" "Are you going to put us on a couch, Doc?" "Is management trying to speed us up?"

Supervisors may refuse to cooperate or may cooperate with sullen indifference. If top management is not wholeheartedly in support of the research there will be endless difficulty.

Any researcher who has not weathered a hostile environment may find coping very difficult. The researcher carries the single thought: "I am trying to help improve the well-being of the employees and the economic success of the organization. Why are the employees and supervisors so defensive? Why are they so suspicious of my research?"

These questions should alert all applied researchers who go into organizations to gain the full approval of representatives of employees (labor unions, if they exist) as well as management. However, confronting these difficulties within the research site does not end all the concerns that may face the researcher.

1.8   FUTURE TRAINING NEEDS FOR APPLIED RESEARCHERS

The American Sociological Association (ASA) is fully aware of the need to reassess the capability of sociology to make knowledge available that relates to productive goals and to furnish knowledge valuable to evaluation and policy-making. The ASA sponsors workshops on directions in applied sociology. For eligibility standards, consult the ASA about specific programs.

In one ASA study, a questionnaire was mailed to 119 American Ph.D.-granting departments in sociology.[1] A total of 89 department chairs responded to the question, "In this decade what curriculum changes and/or requirements do you anticipate being introduced to make our Ph.D.'s more competitive for positions in the public and private sectors of our economy?" The results were as follows:[2]

applied research training, 55
evaluative analysis, 30
data- and word-processing skills, 15
interdiscipline outreach experience, 10
increased statistical sophistication, 8
field internships, 6

Methodological training now stresses skills in computer analysis, with mastery of the required software necessary for treatment of data calculations. Evaluation and policy-making research have high priority.[3]

It must be remembered that applied research training does not stand in opposition to basic research training. Quite the contrary—the best applied researchers will always possess basic research training. Essentially, the only difference is the goal orientation. Most federal funding will go toward the training of applied behavioral scientists and applied researchers. It is hoped that a core of basic research funds will still come from federal funds and private foundations.

Notes

1. *Footnotes* of the American Sociological Association 9 (October 1981): 1.
2. Most respondents gave only one answer, a few gave more. See Edward C. McDonagh and Kent P. Schwirian, in *Footnotes* of the American Sociological Association 9 (October 1981): 8.
3. Ibid.

APPLIED RESEARCH ORGANIZATIONS ARE MUSHROOMING 1.9

The growing interest in applied research and sociological practice is evidenced by the growth in numbers of sociological practitioners, sociological practice organizations, and applied research itself. At the annual meeting of the American Sociological Association in New York City in August 1986, 13 organizations interested in sociological practice were brought together for a celebration by the Sociological Practice Association, a professional association of clinical and applied sociologists. Participating organizations included the following:

- Society for the Study of Social Problems
- Society for Applied Sociology
- Sociological Practice Section of ASA
- New Jersey Sociological Society
- Texas Sociological Practice Association
- D.C. Sociological Society
- Chicago Sociological Practice Association
- American University Department of Sociology
- North Texas State University Department of Sociology
- Social Oncology Network
- ASA Sociological Practice Committee
- Alpha Kappa Delta Chapter of American University
- Clinical and Applied Sociological Student Association

The Council of the American Sociological Association has approved an association-sponsored journal to be called *Sociological Practice Review*. It is reported that this action is taken in recognition of the number of sociological practitioners, which "increased dramatically since the late 1970's and will continue to do so throughout the 1980's."[1]

Note

1. Bettina J. Huber, "ASA Establishes Practice Journal," *Footnotes* of the American Sociological Association 15 (March 1987), 1.

THE ORIENTATION AND COMMITMENT OF THE EVALUATION RESEARCHER 1.10

Evaluation researchers are called in when a policymaker wishes an action program assessed. A judgment must be made as to whether a goal-directed activity was worthwhile. Edward Suchman writes:

In actuality, when the evaluation process begins, activities may be, and usually are, already going on. The evaluator may come in at any point. A crucial question in evaluative research is, "What do we mean by a successful result?" All programs will have some effects, but how do we measure these effects and how do we determine whether they are the particular effects we are interested in producing? As in the case of the independent program variables, we note a multiplicity and interdependence of effect variables. Again, our main problem is one of selecting from among the myriad of possible effects, those most relevant to our objectives.

We have already noted five major criteria for determining relevance: (1) effort or activity; (2) performance or accomplishment; (3) adequacy or impact; (4) efficiency or output relative to input; and (5) process or specification of conditions of effectiveness. In a sense we may classify the first two criteria as *evaluative,* that is, concerned with the determination of the relationship between activities and effects; the second two as *administrative,* dealing with a judgment about the size and cost of the effort relative to the effects; while the last one is really a *research* criterion, concerned with increased knowledge or understanding irrespective of effect.

Indices for the first two, effort and performance, are likely to be defined by the public service worker in terms of professional standards; the next two, adequacy and efficiency, are more likely to be determined by the administrator in terms of basic knowledge. To a large extent, the formulation of the objectives and design of an evaluative research project will depend upon who is conducting the project and what use will be made of the results.[1]

Evaluation researchers must have good human relations skills and be adept at communication. They must adapt to the needs of organizations as interpreted by the policymakers with whom they work. Evaluation researchers must be ready to grapple with all five major criteria for determining relevance.

Note

1. Edward A. Suchman, *Evaluative Research, Principles and Practice in Public Service and Social Action Programs* (New York: Russell Sage Foundation, 1967). Reprinted by permission.

Part 2

Basic Research Design

PART 2 EMPHASIZES the discipline of basic research as the common denominator of all research, whether it is basic, applied, or evaluative. Guides are set out to accompany the first five steps in the sequence of a planned research proposal: selection and definition of a sociological problem, description of the relationship of the problem to a theoretical framework, formulation of working hypotheses, design of the experiment or inquiry, and sampling procedures. The brief treatments of these subjects may be enriched by use of the bibliography.

Part 2

Basic Research Design

Instructions for Use of Guide 2.1

This outline for the design of social research lists the essential considerations in designing a research project.[1] It is recommended that all steps be planned before fieldwork or laboratory work is undertaken. Each of the guides in Part 2 has been selected to aid in planning the first five steps shown in the outline. Other guides, in Parts 3, 4, and 5, are available to assist the researcher in most of the steps shown.

I. The Sociological Problem
   A. Present a clear, brief statement of the problem, with concepts defined where necessary.
   B. Show that the problem is limited to bounds amenable to treatment or test.
   C. Describe the significance of the problem with reference to one or more of the following criteria:
      1. Is timely.
      2. Relates to a practical problem.
      3. Relates to a wide population.
      4. Relates to an influential or critical population.
      5. Fills a research gap.
      6. Permits generalization to broader principles of social interaction or general theory.
      7. Sharpens the definition of an important concept or relationship.
      8. Has many implications for a wide range of practical problems.
      9. May create or improve an instrument for observing and analyzing data.
      10. Provides an opportunity for gathering data that is restricted by the limited time available for gathering particular data.
      11. Provides the possibility for a fruitful exploration with known techniques.

II. The Theoretical Framework
   A. Describe the relationship of the problem to a theoretical framework.
   B. Demonstrate the relationship of the problem to previous research.
   C. Present alternate hypotheses considered feasible within the framework of the theory.

III. The Hypotheses
   A. Clearly state the hypotheses selected for test. (Null and alternate hypothesis should be stated.)
   B. Indicate the significance of test hypotheses to the advancement of research and theory.
   C. Define concepts or variables (preferably in operational terms).
      1. Independent and dependent variables should be distinguished from each other.
      2. The scale upon which variables are to be measured (quantitative, semiquantitative, or qualitative) should be specified.
   D. Describe possible mistakes and their consequences.
   E. Note seriousness of possible mistakes.

IV. Design of the Experiment or Inquiry
   A. Describe ideal design or designs with particular attention to the control of interfering variables.
   B. Describe selected operational design.
      1. Describe stimuli, subjects, environment, and responses with the objects, events, and properties necessary for their specification.

          2. Describe how control of interfering variables is achieved.

      C. Specify statistical tests including dummy tables for each test.

          1. Specify level of confidence desired.

  V. Sampling Procedures

      A. Describe experimental and control samples.

          1. Specify the population to which the hypotheses are relevant.

          2. Explain determination of size and type of sample.

      B. Specify method of drawing or selecting sample.

          1. Specify relative importance of type I and type II error.

          2. Estimate relative costs of the various sizes and types of samples allowed by the theory.

  VI. Methods of Gathering Data

      A. Describe measures of quantitative variables showing reliability and validity when these are known. Describe means of identifying qualitative variables.

      B. Include the following in description of questionnaires or schedules, if these are used.

          1. Approximate number of questions to be asked of each respondent.

          2. Approximate time needed for interview.

          3. The schedule as it has been constructed to this time.

          4. Preliminary testing of interview and results.

      C. Include the following in description of interview procedure, if this is used.

          1. Means of obtaining information (i.e., by direct interview, all or part by mail, telephone, or other means).

          2. Particular characteristics interviewers must have or special training that must be given them.

      D. Describe use to be made of pilot study, pretest, or trial run.

          1. Importance of and means for coping with unavailables, refusals, and response error.

  VII. Working Guide

      A. Prepare working guide with time and budget estimates.

          1. Planning.

          2. Pilot study and pretests.

          3. Drawing sample.

          4. Preparing observational materials.

          5. Selection and training.

          6. Trial plan.

          7. Revising plans.

          8. Collecting data.

          9. Processing data.

          10. Preparing final report.

      B. Estimate total person-hours and cost.

  VIII. Analysis of Results

      A. Specify method of analysis.

          1. Use of tables, calculator, sorter, computer, and so on.

          2. Use of graphic techniques.

          3. Specify type of tables to be constructed.

  IX. Interpretation of Results

      A. Discuss how conclusions will be fed back into theory.

  X. Publication or Reporting Plans

      A. Write these according to department and graduate school requirements.

      B. Select for journal publication the most significant aspects of the problem in succinct form (probably no more than 15 typewritten pages, double-spaced). Follow style and format specified by the journal to which the article will be submitted.

Note

1. This outline is based on Russell L. Ackoff, *The Design of Social Research* (Chicago: University of Chicago Press, 1953). Adapted by Delbert C. Miller.

A GENERAL STATEMENT TO GUIDE THE BASIC RESEARCHER IN THE FORMULATION OF RESEARCH PROBLEMS

2.2

Instructions for Use of Guide 2.2

The first step in the design of research is the selection of a fruitful problem. The range of potential topics for social research is as broad as the range of social behavior. This fact does not aid the researcher in making a *choice*, however, and the choice is the most important step. Selection of a problem represents a commitment of time, money, and energy. It is not unusual for a researcher to give six months to a year to finding a specific problem and formulating it for research study; it may take many years to conduct and publish the research.

The significance of a problem rests upon its probable contribution to knowledge. How can this significance be foreseen for research not yet undertaken and tested? The answer is that this is, to a great extent, an art; but there is little mystery about it. The master researcher knows the research literature and where the cutting edges of current research are. A rich array of theory and methodology is available against which to cast the proposed problem. To this is added a creative imagination, which provides the master contribution.[1]

The student is led through this process during training and can develop mastery by finding a personal path. Progress can be charted; the following list provides suggestions for maximizing effectiveness in finding a dissertation topic and research design:

1. Choosing begins with the first course.
   a. The art of raising questions is cultivated.
   b. The research implications of these questions are explored.
2. In choosing a field, consider the following:
   a. your interest
   b. your capacity
   c. your potential growth and future career
   d. the ability of the professor
   e. your ability to work with the professor

As you continue course work, take these steps:

3. Grow through seminars.
   a. Examine carefully how others have tackled research problems.
   b. Initiate small research projects in the direction of your interests.
4. Begin discussion and work on a given topic.
   a. *Which* large, unexplored areas of the field should be studied?
   b. Define and delineate specific areas.
   c. Investigate previous research in one or more areas.

    d. Make a review of pertinent theory as it bears upon the specific areas.

    e. Set up hypotheses. Formulate theoretical background. Review all pertinent research.

    f. Explore the feasibility of testing hypotheses:

      i. time required

      ii. money required

      iii. availability of data

      iv. promise of fruitful contribution to general field

    g. Fix experimental design.

      i. Create a progress chart with time schedule.

    h. "Pretest" design by setting up dummy tables.

      i. Check scales of measurement, statistics.

    i. Prepare your dissertation proposal by following the outline guide in Section 2.1, above.[2]

It is well to recognize that this plan rests on the assumption that the student is planning for a future career and not simply to "knock out a thesis" (a plan of short-run expediency). From a thesis may emerge published articles that will provide the base for the researcher's reputation in the field and the springboard for future growth and contributions.

For the young researcher seeking to be a master researcher there are no shortcuts to this process except that he or she may perform an important role by replicating some outstanding research models on different populations and in different settings. Social science needs this kind of research badly in acquiring cumulative evidence. The student may utilize secondary data (see Section 4.18, "Guide to Bodies of Collected Data for the Social Science Researcher: Data References and Data Archives") to enrich research and to minimize time and money problems.

A few suggestions of value for selecting important problems may be found in some books written especially for students.[3] The final formulation of the problem determines its potential for the growth of knowledge.

A preliminary assessment of the worth of a problem can be gauged by using the suggested criteria for research problems that follow.

Suggested Criteria for Research Problems[4]

1. A concern with basic concepts and relationships of concepts, as distinguished from local, particularized, or exclusively applied research, to the end that the knowledge produced may be cumulative with that from other studies.

2. The development, refinement, and testing of theoretical formulations. At present the theories appropriate as research guides will be more limited in scope than the comprehensive, speculative systems prominent in the early history of social science.

3. Superior research design, including careful specification of the variables involved and use of the most precise and appropriate methods available.

4. A probable contribution to methodology by the discovery, development, or refinement of practicable tools, techniques, or methods.

5. Full utilization of relevant concepts, theories, evidence, and techniques from related disciplines.

6. The integration of any single study in a planned program of related research to the end that the results become meaningful in a broad context.

7. Adequate provision to train additional research scientists.

8. Provision, wherever feasible, to repeat or check related research of other persons in order to provide a check on the generality of conclusions. A special aspect of this characteristic would be the repetition of studies in more than one culture group.

Decisions Ahead: Some Alternatives of Sociological Research Design

Even in the choosing of the problem, there must be some evaluation of the total research design. Obviously, no problem, however valuable, is a good choice if the required research cannot be carried out. Some considerations may be classified and used as a preliminary checklist:[5]

type of underlying theory	general theory middle-range theory suppositions
study design	experimental group after experimental group before and after experimental and control group after experimental and control group before and after (See Section 2.3, "The Choice of Research Design.")
access to organization and respondents	requires permission of individual respondents only requires permission of organizational officials requires permission of organizational and labor officials requires permission of organizational and labor officials and respondents
researcher control over the social system to be studied	no control partial control complete control
data for test of hypotheses	case and observational studies only quantitative analysis only quantitative supplemented with case and observational studies other (historical, cross-cultural, etc.)
type of datum	personal (fact predicated about single individual) unit (fact predicated about aggregate of persons)
temporal dimension	cases from a single society at a single period (cross-sectional) cases from a single society at many periods (time series or longitudinal) cases from many societies at a single period (comparative cross-cultural) cases from many societies at different periods (comparative longitudinal)
sample or universe to be studied	individual in a role within a group pair of interrelated group members (dyad) primary group (30 or less) secondary group (31 or more) tertiary group (crowd, public, etc.) state, nation, or society
number of cases	single or few cases small sample of selected or random cases (under 30) large sample of selected or random cases (31-5,000 or more)
source of data	new data collected specifically by researcher secondary data to be secured secondary data already in hand
method of gathering data	direct observation with researcher as observer participant observation with researcher as participant interviewing by personal contact of researcher

	interviewing by use of assistants or agents mailed questionnaire combined observation and interviewing other
number of variables involved	one two more than two
type of variables involved	nominal ordinal interval
selection of scales for measurement	none available; researcher must construct scales available but relatively untested scales of proved utility with high reliability and validity
character of distribution of variables	normal (allowing for parametric statistics) nonnormal (requiring nonparametric statistics)
treatment of data	hand calculation machine calculation computer
time required for study	less than one year two years more than two years
funding required	personal funds sufficient partial support required full support required
availability of funds	funds assured local funds available requiring competitive application national funds available requiring competitive application

In the pages that follow, guides are provided for many of these design decisions. The choice of a research design is most important because this decision influences greatly all the outcomes of the study.

Notes

1. John P. Campbell, Richard L. Daft, and Charles L. Hulin, *What to Study: Generating and Developing Research Questions* (Beverly Hills, CA: Sage, 1982); Lawrence F. Locke, Waneen Wyrick Spiriduso, and Stephen J. Silverman, *Proposals That Work: A Guide for Planning Dissertations and Grant Proposals*, 2nd ed. (Newbury Park, CA: Sage, 1987).

2. See also Harris M. Cooper, *Integrating Research: A Guide for Literature Review*, 2nd ed. (Newbury Park, CA: Sage, 1989).

3. For example, see Jacqueline P. Wiseman and Marcia S. Aron, *Field Projects for Sociology Students* (Cambridge, MA: Schenkman, 1970); Editors of Arco Books, *1000 Ideas for Term Papers for Sociology Students* (New York: Arco Books, 1970); Shulamit Reinharz, *On Becoming a Social Scientist* (San Francisco: Jossey-Bass, 1979).

4. From *Report of the Study for the Ford Foundation on Policy and Program* (Detroit: Ford Foundation, 1949).

5. I am indebted to Matilda White Riley for the idea of "alternatives of sociological research design." See her treatment on the cover page of *Sociological Research: A Case Approach* (New York: Harcourt, Brace & World, 1963).

THE CHOICE OF RESEARCH DESIGN   **2.3**

Instructions for Use of Guide 2.3

Empirical research in social science proceeds in a variety of settings and contexts. The choice of a design setting for any research project is generally a vital concern of the researcher, who seeks to determine the validity of a hypothesis and how best to discover evidence to either accept or reject it. Social phenomena are usually interlaced with numerous variables, and control of variables is difficult at best. What design will best ascertain associations or causal paths among the variables under study? How that question is answered may well determine the future outcome of the study. It will most certainly determine the time and money required for the study.

The guideline "Start strong" supersedes any other consideration. It specifies that every effort be made to select a design setting with a population in which *large variations* of both independent and dependent variables may be found. And for any research project, *insurance* is important and may be secured by combining case analysis with any other research design. Failure to find statistical relations spurs the need for case study. In the intense probing, especially of *extreme cases at the tails of a distribution*, may be found polarized relationships that suggest new hypotheses, new designs, and new analyses of the data.

Look at the various designs, their characteristics, and prospective outcomes.

Type of Research Design Setting	Central Characteristics	Prospective Outcomes
1. Descriptive survey *Admin data* a. Cross-sectional study. *Examples:* U.S. decennial census; James A. Davis, *Undergraduate Career Decisions;* Peter M. Blau and O. D. Duncan, *The American Occupational Structure.*	Concerned with information generally obtained by interview or mailed questionnaire. Other sources include official reports or statistics. Occasionally, data banks of other researchers provide appropriate information. Requires an effort to procure 100% enumeration of the population under study.	A sizable volume of information that can be classified by type, frequency, and central tendency. Expense of survey will be very large if population is substantial. Final yield: data that may be analyzed for numerous relationships.
b. Longitudinal study. *Example:* Greg J. Duncan and James N. Morgan, eds., *Five Thousand American Families,* vol. 8, *Eleven Years of the Panel Study of Income Dynamics.*	Time series are produced showing social or behavioral changes over varying periods of time.	Standardized data capable of comparative analysis over successive time intervals.

(continued)

Type of Research Design Setting	Central Characteristics	Prospective Outcomes
2. Sample survey. *Examples:* Gallup, Harris, and Roper polls of public opinion; Current Population Surveys of the Bureau of the Census; William H. Sewell and Robert M. Hauser, *Education, Occupation, and Earnings.*	Deals with only a fraction of a total population (universe). Sampling methods employed to provide a sample that is an accurate representation of the total population. Test hypotheses may be established. To ensure validity, researcher will utilize techniques for scaling, careful attention to questionnaire wording, inclusion of personal background data, etc.	Data may be analyzed for simple relationships between two variables. Multivariate analysis may involve factor analysis, matrix, and multiple discriminant analysis. Both quantitative and qualitative data analyzed with appropriate parametric or nonparametric statistics.
3. Field studies. *Examples:* Robert and Helen Lynd, *Middletown* and *Middletown in Transition;* August S. Hollingshead, *Elmstown's Youth;* William F. Whyte, *Street Corner Society;* Phillip E. Hammond, ed., *Sociologists at Work.*	Concerned primarily with processes and patterns under investigation of a single group, family, institution, organization or community. Emphasis is on the social structure, i.e., interrelationships of parts of the structure and social interaction taking place. Attempts observations of social interactions or investigates thoroughly the reciprocal perceptions and attitudes of people playing interdependent roles. Direct and participant observation, interview, and scaling techniques employed.	Data gathered enable many hypotheses to be tested that were not amenable to survey data. Greater control achieved by focusing on subgroup of larger population. Sociological products such as processes, patterns, roles, attitudes, and values made available.
4. Case studies of persons. *Examples:* Elizabeth Eddy, *Becoming a Teacher: The Passage to Professional Status;* Irwin O. Smigel, *The Wall Street Lawyer;* W. F. Cottrell, *The Railroader.*	Usually refers to relatively intensive analysis of a single instance of a phenomenon being investigated. Investigator interviews individuals or studies life history documents to gain insight into behavior. Attempts to discover unique features and common traits shared by all persons in a given classification. Cases may be grouped by type to discover uniformities.	Data can be assembled to throw light on conditioning relationships and causative factors. Personality and socialization processes can be identified. Concepts can be tested; concepts can be discovered. Cases may be coded and statistical tests applied to classifications providing associations between variables.
5. Combined survey and case study. *Examples:* E. W. Burgess and Leonard S. Cottrell, Jr., *Predicting Success or Failure in Marriage;* Alfred C. Kinsey and Associates, *Sexual Behavior in the Human Male* and *Sexual Behavior in the Human Female.*	Survey methodology is combined with study of specific cases to illuminate relationships first portrayed in a correlational pattern and then interpreted through case study to display processes and patterns. Cases selected after survey reveals those that are high or low on a criterion variable or those that display significant characteristics.	Relationships accompanied by process and pattern data revealing personal socialization in greater depth. Two data banks assembled: statistical data and case analysis data.

multimethod

Type of Research Design Setting	Central Characteristics	Prospective Outcom
6. Prediction studies. *Examples:* Sheldon and Eleanor Glueck, *Predicting Delinquency and Crime;* Paul Horst, *The Prediction of Personal Adjustment* (see especially Paul Wallin, "The Prediction of Individual Behavior from Case Studies"). *econometric study*	Aim is to estimate, in advance of participation, the level of an individual's performance in a given activity. Search is made on a population to find factors to serve as basis of prediction for such outcomes as success or failure in marriage, degree of success on parole, finding potential delinquents at an early age, school success, criminal behavior. A dichotomous dependent variable is always sought: stable marriage vs. broken (divorced) marriage; law abiding vs. criminal behavior; delinquent vs. nondelinquent boys and girls. Academic achievers vs. nonacademic achievers.	Relationships between factors and a predict determined. Selected factors weigh as few as five or six ....g...st relationship with the criterion) in the construction of prognostic tables. Prognostic tables utilized to make predictions.
7. Controlled experiments. Major types are laboratory, "natural," and field experiment. a. Laboratory. *Example:* Robert Bales, *Personality and Interpersonal Behavior.*	Investigator creates a situation with the exact conditions wanted and in which he or she controls some and manipulates other variables. Investigator observes and measures effect of manipulation of independent variables on dependent variables in a situation where other relevant factors are held to a minimum.	Relationships found can be considered more precise as a result of control of other "interfering" variables.
b. "Natural" experiments (cross-sectional or ex post facto). Example: F. S. Chapin, Experimental Designs in Social Research; see also Stouffer, Section 2.8, this volume. *quasi-experimental one group after only design*	Researcher capitalizes on some ongoing changes in normal community setting and studies their effect in an experimental design. A treatment or social program may be given to one group of persons and their personal adjustment compared with a group of persons without such a program. Matching of groups makes the two groups homogeneous when selected factors are held constant by individual or frequency matching.	Discovers and exposes causal complexes under controlled conditions. Statements of greater rigor made possible and increased validity of social treatments or programs demonstrated.
c. Field experiment. *Example:* J. G. Miller, *Experiments in Social Process.*	Involves manipulation of conditions by the experimenter in order to determine causal relations. Maximum variation in the independent and dependent variables are built into structure of design. Experimental and control groups established, holding constant factors believed to interfere with relationship under study.	Independent variable (treatment) is capable of wide variation; sensitive or definitive criterion variable is found. Matching data provide strongest possible control. A causal pattern may be inferred with high confidence.

24

2.4

experimental pre-post

HOW SCIENCE IS BUILT

Instructions for Use of Guide 2.4

This guide sets forth the canons of science as seen by the behavioral researcher. Treat the guide as a signpost that points the direction and possible difficulties ahead. Call it a digest of the philosophy that researchers carry in their heads, use in their work, and live by amid the ups and downs of research life.

The three statements that follow describe (a) the importance of conceptual definition and theory formulation in the construction of scientific knowledge, (b) assumptions underlying the application of the scientific method, and (c) dilemmas of the researcher and the distinctiveness of behavioral science.

Importance of Conceptual Definition and Theory Formulation

Gordon J. DiRenzo[1]

Scientific investigation seeks to explain the phenomena it studies in our world of experience; by establishing general principles with which to explain them, hopefully, science can predict such phenomena. The principles of science are stated ultimately in what are known as theories. To explain the facts of reality, scientists require an organized system of concepts. A "science without concepts" is an impossibility— as unthinkable as any form of rational activity without concepts would be. Yet, to say that concepts are indispensable to science is merely to presuppose or to make possible the problems, namely, the definition and formation of the required scientific elements.

Initially, in scientific inquiry, description of phenomena may be stated in a non-technical vocabulary. The growth of a discipline soon involves the development of a system of speculation, more or less abstract, of concepts and corresponding terminology. Nevertheless, even after decades of definition, and redefinition, many of the fundamental terms in the sciences are far from being distinguished by a universally accepted definition—as much within as outside of particular disciplines. For example, to name just three of the pivotal concepts of the behavioral sciences, there are several denotations for "society," "culture," and "personality." How scientific and technical concepts are introduced and how they function in the scientific process are the central questions here.

Conceptual definition and theory formulation go hand in hand as necessary steps in one unified process of scientific research. The analysis of concepts is but one phase—a fundamental requisite—of that complex process of scientific inquiry which culminates in theory. Concepts, thus, are the irreducible elements of theory or theoretical systems, as the term "theory" has come to be understood more particularly in the behavioral sciences. The more precise and refined the conceptual elements, the more precise and refined the theory.

The question to which we are addressing ourselves is a fundamental one for all areas of scientific inquiry.

Assumptions Underlying the Application of the Scientific Method

Gideon Sjoberg and Roger Nett[2]

A minimum set of assumptions (often left unstated) which underlie the application of the scientific method are (1) that there exists a definite order of recurrence of events, (2) that knowledge is superior to ignorance, (3) that a communication tie, based upon sense impressions, exists between the scientist and "external reality" (the so-called "empirical assumption"), and (4) that there are cause-and-effect relationships within the physical and the social orders. Moreover, (5) there are certain "observer" assumptions: (a) that the observer is driven to attain knowledge by his desire to ameliorate human conditions, (b) that the observer has the capacity to conceptually relate observations and impute meanings to events, and (c) that society will sustain the observer in his pursuit of knowledge. These assumptions, which the scientist more or less takes for granted, are in the last analysis largely understandable as "functional fictions." Their usefulness in the acquisition of knowledge is the primary raison d'être.

The Assumption of Order in the "Natural" World

Science, insofar as it seeks to generalize and predict, depends upon the existence of some degree of order in the physical or social world under study. That which it cannot describe as a manifestation of regularity it must define as some describable departure from regularity. Such reasoning assumes that events are ordered along certain dimensions. To be sure, all systems of knowledge rest upon the assumption of order in the universe, but this may be of greater significance for science than for other systems of knowledge. After all, scientists spend most of their time differentiating among classes of relative uniformity and relating these one to another. Even within a rapidly changing, revolutionary system there is a degree of order. And change itself displays patterns that can be described and analyzed.

The assumption of order leads the social scientist, if he is to remain a scientist, to eschew historicism. Those who advocate the historicist position in its extreme form assume that every cultural system must be studied as a separate entity and that, moreover, no regularities obtain across cultures. Of course, even the historicist admits there is a uniformity of sorts, for he recognizes that each system has its own laws of development.

The notion of order is closely related to the concept of a "natural universe." In our sketch of the history of science, we observed that a major breakthrough occurred when scholars were able to conceive of the physical and social environments in naturalistic terms, that is, as functioning independently of factors in the spiritual realm. This was an essential step in modern man's development of the means to manipulate and positively control aspects of the social and physical spheres.

In light of the evidence, it would be a mistake to confuse scientifically based knowledge with wisdom, as did some of the utopian thinkers of the nineteenth century. Wisdom involves sound ethical direction, the exercise of good taste, and distinguishing the worthwhile from the not so worthwhile.

The scientific method (in the narrow sense) does not tell us how to use empirically verified knowledge other than to further the ends of science; however, by utilizing more of the empirically validated knowledge and less of the unverified and often flat knowledge of other epistemologies the cause of humanity may be advanced.

Dilemmas of the Researcher and the Distinctiveness of Behavioral Science

Abraham Kaplan [3]

Dilemmas

In the conduct of inquiry we are continuously subjected to pulls in opposite directions: to search for data or to formulate hypotheses, to construct theories or to perform experiments, to focus on general laws or on individual cases, to conduct molar studies or molecular ones, to engage in synthesis or in analysis. It is seldom of much help, in the concrete, to be told that we must do both. In the constraints of specific problematic situations these are genuine dilemmas. But they are a species of what have come to be known as existential dilemmas: not characteristic of some special historical situation but intrinsic to the pursuit of truth. We do not make a choice of the lesser of two evils and abide by the unhappy outcome. The problems which the existential dilemmas pose cannot be solved at all, but only coped with; which is to say, we learn to live with them. "We need hard workers and empiricism, not inspiration," it is urged with good reason. But equally good reason can also be given for the converse. The fact is, we need all we can get. This state of affairs is in no way peculiar to behavioral science. Its methodology, as I see it, is not different from that of any other science whatever. If this identity is contemplated in speaking of "the scientific method," I warmly approve of the usage.

The Specialty of Behavioral Science

What is distinctive of behavioral science, therefore, is basically its subject-matter; the techniques that the subject-matter permits or demands are only derivative. If some single discriminant of this subject-matter is called for, I believe the most generally applicable one is that suggested by C. W. Morris: the use of "signs." Behavioral science deals with those processes in which symbols, or at any rate meanings, play an essential part. Just how broadly "meaning" is to be construed, and how much of animal behavior it comprises even in its broadest construction, are questions which need not trouble us here. There is no doubt that behavioral science spills over into biology however we choose to circumscribe its limits. But this difficulty is more administrative (for foundations, librarians, and deans) than methodological.

What is significant here is that the data for behavioral science are not sheer movements but actions—that is, acts performed in a perspective which gives them meaning or purpose. Plainly, it is of crucial importance that we distinguish between the meaning of the act to the actor (or to other people, including ourselves, reacting with him) and its meaning to us as scientists, taking the action as subject-matter. I call these, respectively, act meaning and action meaning. I shall return to this distinction later; for the present, we may note that behavioral science is involved in a double process of interpretation, and it is this which is responsible for such of its techniques as are distinctive. The behavioral scientist must first arrive at an act meaning, that is, construe what conduct a particular piece of behavior represents; and then he must search for the meaning of the interpreted action, its interconnections with other actions or circumstances. He must first see the act of marking a ballot or operating a machine as the action of casting a vote, and then pursue his study of voting behavior.

Now although interpretation for act meanings usually involves special techniques, these are subject to the same methodological norms that govern interpretation for action meanings (and thereby other sciences as well). We interpret speech-acts (in our own language) without any special effort—indeed, usually without any awareness at all of the acts as acts (we do not hear the words, but what is said). Yet every such interpretation is a hypothesis, every reply an experiment—we may, after all, have misunderstood. When it comes to interpreting foreign languages, and in general to interpreting the patterns of another culture, the situation becomes clearer, though it is essentially no different. Some implications of this state of affairs will be explored in connection with the role of "verstehen" in behavioral science. The point I am making here is that the behavioral scientist seeks to understand behavior in just the same sense that the physicist, say, seeks to understand nuclear processes. The difference is not that there are two kinds of understanding but that the behavioral scientist has two different things to understand: for instance, a psychiatrist needs to understand why a patient makes certain noises (to tell his therapist how much he hates him), and why he says the things he does (because he has not yet worked through the transference). Admittedly, we have special ways of understanding noises, because we are ourselves human; but for the same reason, we also have special ways of interpreting light waves, but need quite other techniques for radio waves. The point is that even what we see is not always to be believed. Every technique is subject to validation, and the same norms apply to all of them.

Notes

1. Reprinted with permission from Gordon J. DiRenzo, ed., *Concepts, Theory, and Explanation in the Behavioral Sciences* (New York: Random House, 1967), 66.
2. Reprinted with permission from Gideon Sjoberg and Roger Nett, *A Methodology for the Social Researcher* (New York: Harper & Row, 1968), 30-31.
3. Reprinted with permission from Abraham Kaplan, *The Conduct of Inquiry* (San Francisco: Chandler, 1964), 30-33.

THE BEARING OF SOCIOLOGICAL THEORY ON EMPIRICAL RESEARCH   2.5

Instructions for Use of Guide 2.5

Robert K. Merton describes the bearing of theory on empirical research. He says that the "notion of directed research implies that, in part, empirical inquiry is so organized that if and when empirical discoveries are made, they have direct consequences for a theoretic system." Note the functions of theory that he sets forth. The researcher must often formulate "middle-range" or miniature theories that will link hypotheses to a more inclusive theory. Zetterberg has written that miniature theories delineate convenient research problems: "Granted that our intimate purpose is a general theory and that this general theory will in part be made up by means of miniature theories, experimental evidence supporting a miniature theory will support also the inclusive theory of which the miniature theory is a special case." [1]

Milton Friedman has listed the following criteria for significant theory:

A theory is "simpler" the less initial knowledge is needed to make a prediction within a given field of phenomena; it is the more "fruitful" the more precise the resulting prediction, the wider the area within which the theory yields predictions, and the more additional lines for further research it suggests. . . . The only relevant test of the validity of a hypothesis is comparison of prediction with experience. [2]

Notes

1. Hans L. Zetterberg, *On Theory and Verification in Sociology* (New York: Tressler, 1954), 15.
2. Milton Friedman, "The Methodology of Positive Economics," in *Essays in Positive Economics* (Chicago: University of Chicago Press, 1953), 10.

Empirical Generalizations in Sociology

Robert K. Merton [1]

Not infrequently it is said that the object of sociological theory is to arrive at statements of social uniformities. This is an elliptical assertion and hence requires clarification. For there are two types of statements of sociological uniformities that differ significantly in their bearing on theory. The first of these is the empirical generalization: an isolated proposition summarizing observed uniformities of relationships between two or more variables. [2] The sociological literature abounds with such generalizations that have not been assimilated to sociological theory. Thus, Engel's "laws" of consumption may be cited as examples. So, too, the Halbwachs' finding that laborers spend more per adult unit for food than white-collar employees of the same income class. [3] Such generalizations may be of greater or less precision, but this does not affect their logical place in the structure of inquiry. The Groves-Ogburn finding, for a sample of American cities, that "cities with a larger percentage engaged in manufacturing also have, on the average, slightly larger percentages of young persons married" has been expressed in an equation indicating the degree of this relationship. Although propositions of this order are essential in empirical research, a miscellany of such propositions only provides the raw materials for sociology as a discipline. The theoretic task, and the orientation of empirical research toward theory, first begins when the bearing of such uniformities on a set of interrelated propositions is tentatively established. The notion of directed research implies that, in part, [4] empirical inquiry is so organized that if and when empirical uniformities are discovered, they have direct consequences for a theoretic system. Insofar as the research is directed, the rationale of findings is set forth before the findings are obtained.

Sociological Theory

The second type of sociological generalization, the so-called scientific law, differs from the foregoing inasmuch as it is a statement of invariance derivable from a theory. The paucity of such laws in the sociological field perhaps reflects the prevailing bifurcation of theory and empirical research. Despite the many volumes dealing with the history of sociological theory and despite the plethora of empirical investigations, sociologists (including the writer) may discuss the logical criteria of sociological laws without citing a single instance that fully satisfies these criteria.[5]

Approximations to these criteria are not entirely wanting. To exhibit the relations of empirical generalizations to theory and to set forth the functions of theory, it may be useful to examine a familiar case in which such generalizations were incorporated into a body of substantive theory. Thus, it has long been established as a statistical uniformity that, in a variety of populations, Catholics have a lower suicide rate than Protestants.[6] In this form the uniformity posed a theoretical problem. It merely constituted an empirical regularity that would become significant for theory only if it could be derived from a set of other propositions, a task that Durkheim set himself. If we restate his theoretic assumptions in formal fashion, the paradigm of his theoretic analysis becomes clear:

1. Social cohesion provides support to group members subjected to acute stresses and anxieties.
2. Suicide rates are functions of *unrelieved* anxieties and stresses to which persons are subjected.
3. Catholics have greater social cohesion than Protestants.
4. Therefore, lower suicide rates should be anticipated among Catholics than among Protestants.[7]

This case serves to locate the place of empirical generalizations in relation to theory and to illustrate the several functions of theory.

1. It indicates that theoretic pertinence is not inherently present or absent in empirical generalizations but appears when the generalization is conceptualized in abstractions of higher order (Catholicism-social cohesion-relieved anxieties-suicide rate) that are embodied in more general statements of relationships.[8] What was initially taken as an isolated uniformity is restated as a relation, not between religious affiliation and behavior, but between groups with certain conceptualized attributes (social cohesion) and the behavior. The *scope* of the original empirical finding is considerably extended, and several seemingly disparate uniformities are seen to be interrelated (thus differentials in suicide rates between married and single persons can be derived from the same theory).

2. Once having established the theoretic pertinence of a uniformity by deriving it from a set of interrelated propositions, we provide for the *cumulation* both of theory and of research findings. The differentials-in-suicide-rate uniformities add confirmation to the set of propositions from which they—and other uniformities—have been derived. This is a major function of *systematic theory*.

3. Whereas the empirical uniformity did not lend itself to the drawing of diverse consequences, the reformulation gives rise to various consequences in fields of

conduct quite remote from that of suicidal behavior. For example, inquiries into obsessive behavior, morbid preoccupations, and other maladaptive behavior have found these also to be related to inadequacies of group cohesion.[9] The conversion of empirical uniformities into theoretic statements thus increases the *fruitfulness* of research through the successive exploration of implications.

4. By providing a rationale, the theory introduces a *ground for prediction* that is more secure than mere empirical extrapolation from previously observed trends. Thus, should independent measures indicate a decrease of social cohesion among Catholics, the theorist would predict a tendency toward increased rates of suicide in this group. The atheoretic empiricist would have no alternative, however, but to predict on the basis of extrapolation.

5. The foregoing list of functions presupposes one further attribute of theory that is not altogether true of the Durkheim formulation and which gives rise to a general problem that has peculiarly beset sociological theory, at least, up to the present. If theory is to be productive, it must be sufficiently *precise* to be *determinate*. Precision is an integral element of the criterion of *testability*. The prevailing pressure toward the utilization of statistical data in sociology, whenever possible, to control and test theoretic inferences has a justifiable basis, when we consider the logical place of precision in disciplined inquiry.

The more precise the inferences (predictions) that can be drawn from a theory, the less the likelihood of *alternative* hypotheses that will be adequate to these predictions. In other words, precise predictions and data serve to reduce the *empirical* bearing upon research of the *logical* fallacy of affirming the consequent.[10] It is well known that verified predictions derived from a theory do not prove or demonstrate that theory; they merely supply a measure of confirmation, for it is always possible that alternative hypotheses drawn from different theoretic systems can also account for the predicted phenomena.[11] But those theories that admit of precise predictions confirmed by observation take on strategic importance since they provide an initial basis for choice between competing hypotheses. In other words, precision enhances the likelihood of approximating a "crucial" observation or experiment.

The internal coherence of a theory has much the same function, for if a variety of empirically confirmed consequences are drawn from one theoretic system, this reduces the likelihood that competing theories can adequately account for the same data. The integrated theory sustains a larger measure of confirmation than is the case with distinct and unrelated hypotheses, thus accumulating a greater weight of evidence.

Both pressures—toward precision and logical coherence—can lead to unproductive activity, particularly in the social sciences. Any procedure can be abused as well as used. A premature insistence on precision at all costs may sterilize imaginative hypotheses. It may lead to a reformulation of the scientific problem in order to permit measurement with, at times, the result that the subsequent materials do not bear on the initial problem in hand.[12] In the search for precision, care must be taken to see that significant problems are not thus inadvertently blotted from view. Similarly, the pressure for logical consistency has at times invited logomachy and sterile theorizing, inasmuch as the assumptions contained in the system of analysis are so far removed from empirical referents or involve such high abstractions as not to permit of empirical inquiry.[13] But warrant for these criteria of inquiry is not vitiated by such abuses.

Notes

1. Reprinted with permission of the publisher from Robert K. Merton, "The Bearing of Sociological Theory on Empirical Research," in *Social Theory and Social Structure*, rev. ed. (Glencoe, IL: Free Press, 1957), 95-99. Copyright 1949 by The Free Press, copyright 1957 by The Free Press, A Corporation.

2. This usage of the term "empirical" is common, as Dewey notes. In this context, "*empirical* means that the subject-matter of a given proposition which has existential inference, represents merely a set of uniform conjunctions of traits repeatedly observed to exist, without any understanding of *why* the conjunction occurs; without a theory which states its rationale." John Dewey, *Logic: The Theory of Inquiry* (New York: Henry Holt, 1938), 305.

3. See a considerable collection of such uniformities summarized by C. C. Zimmerman, *Consumption and Standards of Living* (New York: Van Nostrand, 1936), 55ff.

4. "In part," if only because it stultifies the possibilities of obtaining fertile new findings to confine researches *wholly* to the test of predetermined hypotheses. Hunches originating in the course of the inquiry that may not have immediately obvious implications for a broader theoretic system may eventuate in the discovery of empirical uniformities that can later be incorporated into a theory. For example, in the sociology of political behavior, it has been recently established that the larger the number of social cross-pressures to which voters are subjected, the less interest they exhibit in a presidential election (P. F. Lazarsfeld, Bernard Berelson, and Hazel Gaudet, *The People's Choice* [New York: Duell, Sloan & Pearce, 1944], 56-64). This finding, which was wholly unanticipated when the research was first formulated, may well initiate new lines of systematic inquiry into political behavior, even though it is not yet integrated into a generalized theory. Fruitful empirical research not only tests theoretically derived hypotheses; it also originates new hypotheses. This might be termed the "serendipity" component of research, i.e., the discovery, by chance or sagacity, of valid results that were not sought for.

5. E.g., see the discussion by George A. Lundberg, "The Concept of Law in the Social Sciences," *Philosophy of Science* 5 (1938): 189-203, which affirms the possibility of such laws without including any case in point. The book by K. D. Har, *Social Laws* (Chapel Hill: University of North Carolina Press, 1930), does not fulfill the promise implicit in the title. A panel of social scientists discussing the possibility of obtaining social laws finds it difficult to instance cases. Herbert Blumer, *An Appraisal of Thomas and Znaniecki's The Polish Peasant in Europe and America* (New York: Social Science Research Council, 1939), 142-50.

6. It need hardly be said that this statement assumes that education, income, nationality, rural-urban residence, and other factors that might render this finding spurious have been held constant.

7. We need not examine further aspects of this illustration, e.g. (1) the extent to which we have adequately stated the premises implicit in Durkheim's interpretation; (2) the supplementary theoretic analysis that would take these premises not as given but as problematic; (3) the grounds on which the potentially infinite regression of theoretic interpretations is halted at one rather than another point; (4) the problems involved in the introduction of such intervening variables as social cohesion that are not directly measured; (5) the extent to which the premises have been empirically confirmed; (6) the comparatively low order of abstraction represented by this illustration; and (7) the fact that Durkheim derived several empirical generalizations from this same set of hypotheses.

8. Veblen has put this with typical cogency: "All this may seem like taking pains about trivialities. But the data with which any scientific inquiry has to do are trivialities in some other bearing than that one in which they are of account." Thorstein Veblen, *The Place of Science in Modern Civilization* (New York: Russell & Russell, 1961), 42.

9. See, e.g., Elton Mayo, *Human Problems of an Industrial Civilization* (New York: Macmillan, 1933), 113 and passim. The theoretical framework utilized in the studies of industrial morale by Whitehead, Roethlisberger, and Dickson stemmed appreciably from the Durkheim formulations, as the authors testify.

10. The paradigm of "proof through prediction" is, of course, logically fallacious: If A (hypothesis), then B (prediction).

B is observed.

Therefore, A is true.

This is not overdisturbing for scientific research, inasmuch as other than formal criteria are involved.

11. As a case in point, consider that different theorists had predicted war and internecine conflict on a large scale at midcentury. Sorokin and some Marxists, for example, set forth this prediction on the basis of quite distinct theoretic systems. The actual outbreak of large-scale conflicts does not in itself enable us to choose between these schemes of analysis, if only because the observed fact is consistent with both. Only

if the predictions had been so *specified,* had been so precise, that the actual occurrences coincided with the one prediction and not with the other, would a determinate test have been instituted.

12. Stuart A. Rice comments on this tendency in public opinion research; see *Eleven Twenty-six: A Decade of Social Science Research,* ed. Louis Wirth (Chicago: University of Chicago, 1940), 167.

13. It is this practice to which Walker refers, in the field of economics, as "theoretic blight." E. Ronald Walker, *From Economic Theory to Policy* (Chicago: University of Chicago, 1943), chap. 4.

2.6   BRIDGING THE GAP BETWEEN THE LANGUAGES OF THEORY AND RESEARCH

Hubert M. Blalock, Jr. [1]

1. Owing to the inherent nature of the scientific method, there is a gap between the languages of theory and research. Causal inferences belong on the theoretical level, whereas actual research can only establish covariations and temporal sequences.

2. As a result, we can never actually demonstrate causal laws empirically. This is true even where experimentation is possible. Causal laws are working assumptions of the scientist, involving hypothetical statements of the if-then variety.

3. One admits that causal thinking belongs completely on the theoretical level and that causal laws can never be demonstrated empirically. But this does not mean that it is not helpful to think causally and to develop causal models that have implications that are indirectly testable. In working with these models it will be necessary to make use of a whole series of untestable simplifying assumptions, so that even when a given model yields correct empirical predictions, this does not mean that its correctness can be demonstrated.

Reality, or at least our perception of reality, admittedly consists of ongoing processes. No two events are ever exactly repeated, nor does any object or organism remain precisely the same from one moment to the next.[2] And yet, if we are ever to understand the nature of the real world, we must act and think as though events are repeated and as if objects do have properties that remain constant for some period of time, however short. Unless we permit ourselves to make such simple types of assumptions, we shall never be able to generalize beyond the simple and unique event.

4. The point we are emphasizing is that no matter how elaborate the design, certain simplifying assumptions must always be made. In particular, we must at some point assume that the effects of confounding factors are negligible. Randomization helps to rule out some of such variables, but the plausibility of this particular kind of simplifying assumption is always a question of degree. We wish to underscore this fact in order to stress the underlying similarity between the logic of making causal inferences on the basis of experimental and nonexperimental designs.

Notes

1. Reprinted with permission from Hubert M. Blalock, Jr., *Causal Inferences in Non-experimental Research* (Chapel Hill: University of North Carolina Press, 1964), 172-73, 6-7, 26.

2. This particular point is emphasized in Karl Pearson's classic, *The Grammar of Science* (New York: Meridian, 1957), chap. 5.

CRITERIA FOR JUDGING USABLE HYPOTHESES

Instructions for Use of Guide 2.7

The formulation of usable hypotheses is of central importance. The entire study rests upon the potential significance of the hypotheses. In this guide, William J. Goode and Paul K. Hatt prescribe step-by-step methods for evaluating hypotheses against criteria. Note again the emphasis given to the criterion that a hypothesis should be related to a body of theory. It is also important to anticipate the verification problem. Zetterberg has stated three criteria for the acceptance of a working hypothesis: (a) that the empirical data were found to be arranged in the manner predicted by the working hypothesis, (b) that we have disproved the null hypothesis with a certain probability, and (c) that we have disproved alternate hypotheses to the one tested.

From *Methods in Social Research*

William J. Goode and Paul K. Hatt[1]

1. The *hypotheses must be conceptually clear*. The concepts should be clearly defined, operationally if possible. Moreover, they should be definitions that are commonly accepted and communicable rather than the products of a "private world."

What to do: One simple device for clarifying concepts is to write out a list of the concepts used in the research outline. Then try to define them (a) in words, (b) in terms of particular operations (index calculations, types of observations, etc.), and (c) with reference to other concepts to be found in previous research. Talk over each concept with fellow students and other researchers in the field. It will often be found that supposedly simple concepts contain many meanings. Then it is possible to decide which is the desired referent.

2. *Hypotheses should have empirical referents*. It has also been previously pointed out that scientific concepts must have an ultimate empirical referent. No usable hypothesis can embody moral judgments. Such statements as "criminals are no worse than businessmen," "women should pursue a career," or "capitalists exploit their workers" are no more usable hypotheses than is the familiar proposition that "pigs are well named because they are so dirty" or the classical question, "How many yards of buttermilk are required to make a pair of breeches for a black bull?" In other words, while a hypothesis may involve the study of value judgments, such a goal must be separated from a moral preachment or a plea for acceptance of one's values.

What to do: First, analyze the concepts that express attitudes rather than describe or refer to empirical phenomena. Watch for key words such as "ought," "should," "bad," etc. Then transform the notions into more useful concepts. "Bad parents" is a value term, but the researcher may have a definite description in mind: parents who follow such practices as whimsical and arbitrary authoritarianism, inducing psychic insecurity in the child, failure to give love, etc. "Should" is also a value term, but the student may simply mean, "If women do not pursue a career, we can predict emotional difficulties when the children leave home, or we can predict that the society will not be able to produce as much goods," etc. When, instead, we find that our referent is simply a vague feeling and we cannot define the operations needed to observe it, we should study the problem further and discover what it is that we really wish to investigate.

3. *The hypotheses must be specific.* That is, all the operations and predictions indicated by it should be spelled out. The possibility of actually testing the hypothesis can thus be appraised. Often hypotheses are expressed in such general terms, and with so grandiose a scope, that they are simply not testable. Because of their magnitude, such grand ideas are tempting because they seem impressive and important. It is better for the student to avoid such problems and instead develop his skills upon more tangible notions.

By making all the concepts and operations explicit is meant not only conceptual clarity but a description of any indexes to be used. Thus, to hypothesize that the degree of vertical social mobility is decreasing in the United States requires the use of indexes. [At present there are many operational definitions of the status levels that define mobility. Therefore, the hypothesis must include a statement of the index that is to be used; see Part 6 for available indexes.]

Such specific formulations have the advantage of assuring that research is practicable and significant, in advance of the expenditure of effort. It furthermore increases the validity of the results, since the broader the terms the easier it is to fall into the trap of using selective evidence. The fame of most prophets and fortune-tellers lies in their ability to state predictions so that almost any occurrence can be interpreted as a fulfillment. We can express this in almost statistical terms: the more specific the prediction, the smaller the chance that the prediction will actually be borne out as a result of mere accident. Scientific predictions or hypotheses must, then, avoid the trap of selective evidence by being as definite and specific as possible.

What to do: Never be satisfied with a general prediction, if it can be broken into more precise subhypotheses. The general prediction of war is not enough, for example: we must specify time, place, and participants. Predicting the general decline of a civilization is not a hypothesis for testing a theory. Again, we must be able to specify and measure the forces, specify the meaning and time of decline, the population segments involved, etc. Often this can be done by conceptual analysis and the formulation of related hypotheses: e.g., we may predict that urbanization is accompanied by a decline in fertility. However, we gain in precision if we attempt to define our indexes of urbanization; specify which segments will be affected, and how much (since in the United States the various ethnic and religious segments are affected differently); specify the amount of fertility decline, and the type (percentage childless, net reproduction rate, etc.). Forming subhypotheses (1) clarifies the relationship between the data sought and the conclusions; and (2) makes the specific research task more manageable.

4. *Hypotheses should be related to available techniques.* Earlier, the point was repeatedly made that theory and method are not opposites. The theorist who does not know what techniques are available to test his hypotheses is in a poor way to formulate usable questions.

This is not to be taken as an absolute injunction against the formulation of hypotheses that at present are too complex to be handled by contemporary technique. It is merely a sensible requirement to apply to any problem in its early stages in order to judge its researchability.

There are some aspects of the impossible hypothesis that may make its formulation worth while. If the problem is significant enough as a possible frame of reference, it may be useful whether or not it can be tested at the time. The socioeconomic hypotheses of Marx, for example, were not proved by his data. The necessary techniques were not available either then or now. Nevertheless, Marxian frameworks are an important source of more precise, smaller, verifiable propositions. This is true for much of Emile Durkheim's work on suicide. His related formulations concerning social cohesion have also been useful. The work of both men has been of paramount importance to sociology, even though at the time their larger ideas were not capable of being handled by available techniques.

Furthermore, posing the impossible question may stimulate the growth of technique. Certainly some of the impetus toward modern developments in technique has come from criticisms against significant studies that were considered inadequate because of technical limitations. In any serious sociological discussion, research frontiers are continuously challenged by the assertion that various problems "ought" to be investigated even though the investigations are presently impossible.

What to do: Look for research articles on the subject being investigated. Make a list of the various techniques that have been used to measure the factors of importance in the study. If you are unable to locate any discussion of technique, you may find it wiser to do a research on the necessary research techniques. You may, instead, decide that this lack of techniques means your problem is too large and general for your present resources.

Some items, such as stratification or race attitudes, have been studied by many techniques. Try to discover why one technique is used in one case and not in another. Note how refinements in technique have been made, and see whether one of these may be more useful for your purposes. Look for criticisms of previous research, so as to understand the weaknesses in the procedures followed.

Again, other problems may have been studied with few attempts at precise measurement. Study the literature to see why this is the case. Ascertain whether some subareas (for example, of religious behavior) may be attacked with techniques used in other areas (for example, attitude measurement, stratification measures, research on choice making, etc.).

5. *The hypothesis should be related to a body of theory.* This criterion is one which is often overlooked by the beginning student. He is more likely to select subject matter that is "interesting," without finding out whether the research will really help to refute, qualify, or support any existing theories of social relations. A science, however, can be cumulative only by building on an existing body of fact and theory. It cannot develop if each study is an isolated survey.

Although it is true that the clearest examples of crescive theoretical development are to be found in the physical and biological sciences, the process can also be seen in the social sciences. One such case is the development of a set of generalizations concerning the social character of intelligence. The anthropological investigations at the end of the nineteenth century uncovered the amazing variety of social customs in various societies, while demonstrating conclusively that there were a number of common elements in social life: family systems, religious patterns, an organization of the socialization process, etc.

The French school of sociology, including Lucien Lévy-Bruhl, Emile Durkheim, Marcel Mauss, Henri Hubert, and others, formulated a series of propositions, at the turn of the century, which suggested that the intellectual structure of the human mind is determined by the structure of the society. That is, perception and thought are determined by society, not alone by the anatomical structure of our eyes, ears, and other senses. Modes of thought vary from society to society. Some of these formulations were phrased in an extreme form that need not concern us now, and they were often vague. Nevertheless, the idea was growing that the intelligence of a Polynesian native could not be judged by European standards; his thinking was qualitatively, not merely quantitatively, different.

At the same time, however, better techniques were being evolved for measuring "intelligence," which came to be standardized in the form of scores on various IQ tests. When these were applied to different groups it became clear that the variation in IQ was great; children of Italian immigrants made lower grades on such tests, as did Negroes. Northern Negroes made higher grades than whites from many Southern states. American children of Chinese and Japanese parents made rather high scores. Since it was generally assumed that these tests measured "innate intelligence," these data were sometimes generalized to suggest that certain "racial" groups were by nature inferior and others superior.

However, such conclusions were opposed on rational grounds, and liberal sentiments suggested that they be put to the test. There were, then, two major sets of conclusions, one suggesting that intelligence is in the main determined by social experience, the other suggesting that the IQ is innately determined. To test such opposing generalizations, a research design was needed for testing logical expectations in more specific situations. If, for example, it is true that the intelligence of individuals who are members of "inferior" groups is really determined biologically, then changes in their environments should not change their IQ. If, on the other hand, the social experience is crucial, we should expect that such changes in social experience would result in definite patterns of IQ change.

Further deductions are possible. If identical twins are separated and are placed in radically different social experiences at an early age, we might expect significant differences in IQ. Or, if a group of rural Negro children moves from the poor school and social experience of the South to the somewhat more stimulating environment of the North, the group averages would be expected to change somewhat. Otto Klineberg, in a classic study, carried out the latter research. He traced Negro children of various ages after they had moved to the North and found that, in general, the earlier the move to the North occurred, the greater the average rise in the IQ. The later the move, the smaller the increase. Even if one assumes that the "better," more able, and more daring adult Negroes made this move, this does not explain the differences by time of movement. Besides, of course, the subjects were children at the time of the migration.[2]

In this research design a particular result was predicted by a series of deductions from a larger set of generalizations. Further, the prediction was actually validated. In justice to the great number of scholars who have been engaged in refining and developing IQ tests, it should be mentioned that other tests and investigations of a similar order have been carried out by many anthropologists, sociologists, and social psychologists. They do not invalidate the notion that IQ is based in part on "innate" abilities, but they do indicate that to a great extent these abilities must be stimulated by certain types of experience in order to achieve high scores on such tests.

From even so sketchy an outline of a theoretical development as the foregoing is, it can be seen that when research is systematically based upon a body of existing theory, a genuine contribution in knowledge is more likely to result. In other words, to be worth doing, a hypothesis must not only be carefully stated, but it should possess theoretical relevance.

What to do: First, of course, cover the literature relating to your subject. If it is impossible to do so, then your hypothesis probably covers too much ground. Second, try to abstract from the literature the way in which various propositions and sets of propositions relate to one another (for example, the literature relating to Sutherland's theory of differential association in criminology, the conditions for maximum morale in factories, or the studies of prediction of marital adjustment). Third, ascertain whether you can deduce any of the propositions, including your own hypothesis, from one another or from a small set of major statements. Fourth, test it by some theoretical model, such as Merton's "Paradigm for Functional Analysis in Sociology" (*Social Theory and Social Structure*, pp. 50-54), to see whether you have left out major propositions and determinants. Fifth, especially compare your own set of related propositions with those of some classic author, such as Weber on bureaucracy or Durkheim on suicide. If you find this task of abstraction difficult, compare instead with the propositions of these men as explained by a systematic interpreter such as Talcott Parsons in his *Structure of Social Action*. What is important is that, whatever the source of your hypothesis, it must be logically derivable from and based upon a set of related sociological propositions.

Notes

1. Reprinted by permission from William J. Goode and Paul K. Hatt, *Methods in Social Research* (New York: McGraw-Hill, 1952), 68-73. Copyright 1962 by McGraw-Hill Book Company, Inc.
2. Otto Klineberg, *Negro Intelligence and Selective Migration* (New York: Columbia University Press, 1935).

SCIENCE: OBSERVATIONAL, EXPERIMENTAL, HISTORICAL | 2.8

Instructions for Use of Guides to Study Design: Guides 2.8, 2.9, 2.10

The study design involves such decisions as whether historical analysis, statistical sampling, qualitative structured observation, or controlled experimentation is needed. In the following, Raymond Siever, a physical scientist, describes varieties and styles of science and stresses the importance of the problem and its relation to scientific method.

Science: Observational, Experimental, Historical

Raymond Siever[1]

A question that has concerned many scientists for about as long as sciences started to differentiate from each other is, "Are there different sciences or is there just one science?" A related question can be put, "Is there *a* scientific method, or are there many scientific methods?" Discussion of these points is usually obfuscated by the speaker's background, in particular, what science he happens to be doing at the moment. It also, of course, is characteristically confused by mixing subject matter with the way in which an investigation is carried out. I will give my idea of how the different conventional groupings of sciences relate to each other and propose some answers to the question of whether there is just one science or many. It is not that these ideas are new. It is more that we need to remind ourselves of our philosophical underpinnings, especially now that branches of science have become more specialized and yet at the same time have joined together in attacks on complex systems.

TABLE 2.1 Words That Have Been Used in Characterizing Differences Among the Sciences

Analytical	Descriptive
Experimental	Observational
Soft	Hard
Nonmathematical	Mathematical
Good	Bad
Interesting	Dull
"Stamp collecting"	Crucial experimentation
Classical	Modern
The general equation	The encyclopedic monograph
Rigorous	Inexact
Easy	Difficult
Exploding	Mined-out

Observational Versus Experimental

The distinction between an observational science and an experimental science is often made. In this context in some people's language, the word "observational" is associated with the thought "solely descriptive" and the word "experimental" is usually associated with an analytical approach. There is an extension of these associations by which some scientists, thereby qualifying themselves as superior, imply that there is "good" or "bad" science by linking observational with bad and experimental with good. This choice of terms is dictated by diplomacy within the scientific community, for it is not good policy to refer to work that one's colleagues in another field are doing as bad; it is much better simply to call it "descriptive." We all know that there are appropriate uses for the words bad and good, but properly only as applied to an individual piece of work.

There are, of course, other terms that we are familiar with. There are the "hard" sciences and, by implication I suppose, the "soft" sciences. We also know that a good many other words have been juxtaposed to distinguish between "two cultures" within science (Table 2.1). Without trying to wreck diplomacy, it is worthwhile to point out just how these words, observational, descriptive, experimental, analytical, are being used.

It must be taken as given, I think, that all sciences observe and describe. An example is one product of science that has been with us for a long time, the heat flow equation, an equation that is fundamentally based on simple observation. The laws that Newton first formulated for heat flow are simpler than the more elegant mathematical statements that we now use. But this elegant formulation with which we are able to do so much rests on rather elementary kinds of observations. So it is silly to speak of a nonobservational or a nondescriptive science.

There are said to be scientists who describe things and do not wish to make any analysis of them. They say description for its own sake is worthwhile science. It is true, of course, that many sciences in their early stages of development are characterized by an extraordinarily high ratio of data collecting to data analysis. This rarely implies that those who accumulate the data are not thinking about what they are describing or trying to integrate it into some pattern. It is obvious that those who describe are making a choice of what to describe and that analysis is involved in the selection of the object to be described. We ordinarily do not consider it science for somebody to observe everything that could be catalogued about a particular process, phenomenon, object, or other, though the point may be argued, and probably will be when the first man lands on the moon.

There is no denying that the scientific population includes some who do describe for its own sake, who admit that description is their only goal. As such they bear the same relationship to science as the inventory-taker does to business. But most who solely describe will say that they are only temporarily so engaged, that they are always working toward the goal of analysis (usually put off to some future time).

If it is true that description for its own sake, without any analysis of what to describe or how to integrate it after description, is not what we usually call science, then we really cannot speak of a descriptive or nondescriptive science. When some scientists say of another scientist's work or of another field within science, "It's descriptive," they really mean that it is not science.

The kind of statement made above may also be interpreted to mean, with good grace, that the proportion of description of analysis is high compared to those in some other field. The proportion varies, of course, with the stage of development of the field and it varies, obviously, with the person. Even within a field that is largely beyond the stage where description is in a high ratio to analysis, the invention of a new instrument can lead to new kinds of observations, temporarily producing a great abundance of data relative to analysis.

If one of the major objects of scientific endeavor is to make general laws from specific observation, then it must also be granted that the endeavor is more or less difficult. Physics has come to be, by and large, the domain of those who work where generalizations are relatively easy to make from limited data (though no one would claim physics as an easy field in terms of mental effort). Another way to put it is that the data have small variance and the generalizations are very good. It is also true that in certain fields, of which perhaps the social sciences are the most obvious example, the data have such high variance that the generalizations are either difficult or almost impossible to make. This inevitably leads to differences in the overall logical structure of disciplines. A great many parts of physics are tied together with a strong interconnecting network of fundamental physical theory from which all other parts can be derived, so-called first principles. On the other hand we have fields, such as some areas of engineering, where empiricism is the order of the day simply because there is no generally valid group of first principles from which to operate.

Experiment and Science

Experiments have always been associated with science, and have rightly been considered the most powerful tools of science. Our vision of experiment is largely based on those that have been done in physics and chemistry. But there are a number of ways in which one can look at experiments. They can be divided into controlled and uncontrolled experiments. Alternatively, we can formulate experimentation as either natural or artificial. The artificial experiment we all know about; one chooses the starting materials and conditions of the experiment, then one observes the process in action or the final results.

The natural experiment we are somewhat less familiar with, except for those of us whose primary interest lies in biology, the earth sciences, or astronomy. We may ask what would have happened had Newton one day seen the mythical apple on the ground, somewhat overripe, partly eaten, and decayed. From such an observation, could he have extracted a generalization on gravity? I think it not improbable that he might have, but perhaps at a much greater cost in time and effort and with much less assurance. Many geochemists, for example, have to go about analyzing chemical processes on the earth in a special way. It would be as if someone who wanted to find out what was going on in an elementary chemistry laboratory would go to the laboratory when no one was in it, analyze what he found in the sink, and analyze what he found in the sewer leading from the laboratory. Noting how the laboratory is equipped he could make some deductions as to the experiments that were performed and guess what the starting reagents might have been. So natural experimentation has built into it restricted control and limited information on the nature of the starting materials. Natural experimentation, of course, has the same restrictions as artificial experimentation; one must pick the right observational parameters.

The natural experiment can be refined by looking at separable parts of it or by choosing the chance event that has resulted in a specially controlled or restricted experiment. In a multivariate situation we look for the occasional place or time when the variables are fewer. Those who have spent a good deal of time looking for controlled natural experiments can speak with feeling about the rarity or impossibility of finding the perfectly controlled natural experiment. They all have defects. And so those who work with such data seem always to be trying to draw some generalizations from rather poor experiments.

Restrictions on artificial experimentation possibilities in science are many. The first restriction is the largeness of some systems. Scaling factors are not always available or adequate to reduce the system in size for examination in the laboratory. The two most notable sciences in this regard are astronomy and geology. Here again, restricted bits and pieces of these large systems can be removed and taken to the laboratory, but the interrelatedness of the system itself cannot be reproduced.

The complexity and interrelatedness of some systems restrict the experiment. Warren Weaver (1955) applied the words "strongly coupled" and "weakly coupled" to the sciences. Weaver applied these terms to differentiate the natural from the social sciences, but I think the point can equally be taken to differentiate among the natural sciences. Some aspects of the study of the oceans, for example, the general oceanic circulation, appear to be relatively weakly coupled, in that one considers a few interactions between the motion of the planet, its atmosphere, and the heat budget of the earth and the oceans. Another branch of oceanography, ecology, is a very strongly coupled science. Ecology in the ocean is so strongly coupled that it is difficult even to distinguish the variables from each other. It appears that most natural phenomena of large scale on the earth's surface are rather strongly coupled in the sense that the variables are not separable either for experimental or analytical purposes.

There are, of course, large-scale artificial experiments that have been done and have revealed a great deal of information. I would class the modern air and water pollution disaster as an obvious, though socially evil, experiment. I can offer more examples: Bomb-C^{14} spread through the atmosphere and exchanged with the ocean to give us a much better picture of the circulation of CO_2 and its equilibrium between the ocean and the atmosphere than we had had previously. Attempts to counter the current pollution of the Great Lakes may be an experiment in reversibility; we have the social hope but scientific uncertainty that the Lakes can be cleaned up. Whether reversible or not, the pollution and the counter measures are certainly giving us a good deal of scientific (or engineering?) information.

In the past, social taboos have prevented a whole class of experiments, but it now seems that even these have broken down at some times, most notably with Nazi so-called "experimentation" in some concentration camps. There have been suggestions that warfare in Viet Nam involves certain experimental tests of new equipment and ideas. But it is still largely true that, for scientists, areas considered important in biological experimentation are taboo for what we consider good and sufficient social reasons.

Simulated or "hypothetical" experiments and systems analysis have been used to circumvent social control or for large systems that cannot be taken to the laboratory. But such "experiments" are only as good as the first principles that allow them to be carried on in the mind alone. Theoretical physics is a clear choice for the field in which such experiments have great value. But in most of the world of scientific practice, scientists use hypothetical experiments as a prelude to actual experimentation or further observation. One does not perform hypothetical experiments for their own sake. We grant that as teachers we have frequent recourse to such devices. As research workers in science they are of little value of and for themselves.

It appears then, that experimental science is of many different kinds, that though the nature of experiment is the same no matter where one sees it, the controls may vary and the ability to observe different parts of the experiment may be limited, and finally that there are experiments that simply cannot be done for social reasons.

Historical Versus Nonhistorical Science

This topic, a recurring theme in the dialogue on the nature of science (Nagel, 1952), has been explored recently by G. G. Simpson (1963) and R. A. Watson (1966). It appears to me that there is no fundamental difference between historical and nonhistorical science except as it may be economically profitable or culturally desirable to determine as exactly as possible what happened at a certain place and time. Thus we really do not care, as Watson puts it, exactly how the Grand Canyon of the Colorado River was formed. We only care how the generic class of Grand Canyons forms and has formed in the past, assuming that canyon-cutting was not a unique event. This is true in the same way that a chemist does not care what the particular numbers of an individual experiment are. His only concern is in repeating and generalizing that experiment so that the results from his or anybody else's operation of the same kind will fall into the same pattern. In fact, one rarely sees the particular numbers of any experiment. The raw data are of little interest except as an intermediate stage in the calculation of the quantities that are usually of true interest, quantities the significance of which has been established by earlier scientific studies. So, though we measure a particular mass and volume, we quote the important number as the density.

We may differentiate the historical sciences from the so-called nonhistorical sciences by the time scale of the processes involved. Though a chemical reaction has a "history," that history is usually faster than most processes we consider "historical." Even slow chemical reactions are extraordinarily fast compared to geological processes. In astronomy, too, a great many processes are very slow, although there are others that are fast. But even the history of a chemical reaction can be of major importance, for the study of chemical kinetics is just this. Again, though it is a historical event, the chemist studying the course of a reaction is rarely interested in any particular one performed at any particular time in his laboratory, but rather in the general repeatable experiment that anyone can do.

What is different about historical sciences is that many times only one natural experiment is observable, or so few that generalization is difficult if not impossible. We have on this earth, apparently, only one example of organic macroevolution. The general appearance of oxygen in the earth's primitive atmosphere probably happened only once. In modern times, the change in our lives caused by the development of the atomic bomb could happen only once. If the essence of experiment, whether artificial or natural, is that it be repeatable and that one needs at least one degree of freedom in order to make an average or to generalize, then we are destroyed by the uniqueness of some events. That is not to say, of course, that they are unique in the universe; they are only unique as far as our observational capabilities are concerned. It is for this reason that there is interest among biologists about the possibilities of some form of life on the moon or on Mars. They are simply seeking the additional experiment. Almost worse than the unique experiment is the availability of a very few experiments with a high variance. We have on the Earth only a few continents. In the development of the structure of the North American continent there have been only a few major evolutionary patterns of geosynclines and mountain chain evolution on the borders of the continent. There are only a few terrestrial planets. The social sciences to some extent are plagued by the same. There are as yet only a few nations that have atomic bombs.

Styles in Science

Each scientist selects the discipline he works in for a variety of reasons, but many styles can be found in all. I use the word "style" because, as has already become apparent, I reject the notion that there are different kinds of science, or scientific disciplines. There are many different personalities that go into science, and each of these personality types has his own way of doing things, as pointed out by Kurie (1953) and Eiduson (1962). Though there may be some correlation between personality and the discipline selected, I do not wish to discuss that issue.

Style is a word that has many meanings, ranging from a particular historical "school" in any subject (for example, "classical style") to a designation of a particular approach to any intellectual effort that is the product of the interaction of a personality with his time and his subject. It is the latter meaning of the word that I will use exclusively. Styles are probably related to personality, but they are always modified by the field in which that person works. An obvious recent example of different styles is that given by the contrast in the addresses of two recent Nobel laureates in physics, Richard Feynman (1966) and Julian Schwinger (1966). Here two men working in the same field of physics reveal very different styles of tackling the same kind of problem and writing about it.

We can recognize and tag some of the more distinctive styles that are common to all fields. We recognize that some of these are cross-coupled and one may indulge in several styles at different periods or as the mood strikes:

the rigorous formalist

the brilliant phenomenologist

the painstaking laboratory methodologist and his equivalent, the careful, detailed field observer

the quick and dirty cream skimmer

the niche-lover or horizontal monopolist

the subgeneralist or vertical monopolist

the dilettante and his brother, the versatile virtuoso, separated by the difference between success and failure

the older, wiser generalist

This is a parlor game that anyone can play and apply to his friends and colleagues.

Value judgments are usually made about the relative worth of various stylists' contributions. But it is probably so that all of these styles are necessary for science to advance, for everyone leans on everyone else. There is some danger at the present time that there will be too much emphasis on certain styles in picking the leaders of science, and that style will be confused with discipline and with fundamental ability of the individual to make advances in science. Pluralism and diversity make for more interest in science as they do elsewhere in life. But let us have differences in style and subject and recognize that invidious distinctions between "kinds" of science serve only to build hierarchies of position and privilege.

Note

1. Reprinted from Raymond Siever, "Science: Observational, Experimental, Historical," *American Scientist* 56, no. 1 (1968): 70-77. Copyright by *Sigma Xi,* Princeton, NJ.

References

Eiduson, Bernice T. *Their Psychological World.* New York: Basic Books, 1962.

Feynman, Richard P. "The Development of the Space-Time View of Quantum Electrodynamics." *Science* 153 (1966): 699-708.

Kurie, L. S. "Problems of the Scientific Career." *Scientific Monthly* 74 (1953). (Reprinted in *Readings in the Philosophy of Science,* edited by H. Feigle and M. Brodbeck, 688-700. New York: Appleton-Century-Crofts, 1953.)

Schwinger, Julian. "Relativistic Quantum Field Theory." *Science* 153 (1966): 949-53.

Simpson, G. G. "Historical Science." In *The Fabric of Geology,* edited by C. C. Albritton, Jr., 24-27. Reading, MA: Addison-Wesley, 1963.

Watson, R. A. "Is Geology Different: A Critical Discussion of 'The Fabric of Geology.' " *Philosophy of Science* 33 (1966): 172-85.

Weaver, Warren, "Science and People." *Science* 122 (1955): 1255-59.

Guides for Design, Model Building, and Large-Scale Research

At this point one must decide the nature of proof desired, taking into consideration the level of one's hypotheses, the size of one's budget, the amount of personnel and their skills, the time required, and so on. It is now generally accepted that the model of the controlled experiment is always a valuable guide even if, in practice, deviation is necessary. "Some Observations on Study Design" (Section 2.9) by Samuel A. Stouffer is regarded as the single most useful statement of design requirements for social investigation.

Hans L. Zetterberg explains the problems facing the researcher who wishes to use controlled observation and how alternative hypotheses can be tested with pseudo-experimental designs. See Section 2.10, an excerpt from Zetterberg's *On Theory and Verification in Sociology.*

Model building has become an integral part of scientific work. "The Role of Models in Research Design" (Section 2.11) describes various types of models in current use.

Edward Suchman, in Section 2.12, "General Considerations of Research Design," lists some realistic appraisals often needed when ideal plans must be compromised. Professional researchers keep these guides before them.

Factors affecting the validity of the research design are described in Section 2.13. Large-scale group research has grown in volume and in scope. In Part 3, "The Shaping of Research Design in Large-Scale Group Research" (Section 3.A.5) provides a case study for the team research proposal. The breaking down of the problem into manageable parts is illustrated and the importance of individual differences among researchers is highlighted. Note also the progression of research stages. This guide applies to design in large-scale research only.

2.9   SOME OBSERVATIONS ON STUDY DESIGN

Samuel A. Stouffer[1]

We must be clear in our own minds what proof consists of, and we must, if possible, provide dramatic examples of the advantages of relying on something more than plausibility. And the heart of our problem lies in study design *in advance,* such that the evidence is not capable of a dozen alternative interpretations.

Basically, I think it is essential that we always keep in mind the model of a controlled experiment, even if in practice we may have to deviate from an ideal model. Take the simple accompanying diagram.

	Before	After	After–Before
Experimental Group	x_1	x_2	$d = x_2 - x_1$
Control Group	x_1'	x_2'	$d' = x_2' - x_1'$

The test of whether a difference d is attributable to what we think it is attributable to is whether d is significantly larger than d'.

We used this model over and over again during the war to measure the effectiveness of orientation films in changing soldiers' attitudes. These experiences are described in Volume III of our *Studies in Social Psychology in World War II.* [2]

One of the troubles with using this careful design was that the effectiveness of a single film when thus measured turned out to be so slight. If, instead of using the complete experimental design, we simply took an unselected sample of men and compared the attitudes of those who said they had seen a film with those who said they had not, we got much more impressive differences. This was more rewarding to us, too, for the management wanted to believe the films were powerful medicine. The gimmick was the selective fallibility of memory. Men who correctly remembered seeing the films were likely to be those most sensitized to their message. Men who were bored or indifferent may have actually seen them but slept through them or just forgot.

Most of the time we are not able or not patient enough to design studies containing all four cells as in the diagram above. Sometimes we have only the top two cells, as in the accompanying diagram.

x_1	x_2	$d = x_1 - x_2$

In this situation we have two observations of the same individuals or groups taken at different times. This is often a very useful design. In the army, for example, we could take a group of recruits, ascertain their attitudes, and restudy the same men later. From this we could tell whose attitudes changed and in what direction. (It was almost always for the worse, which did not endear us to the army!) But exactly what factors in the early training period were most responsible for deterioration of attitudes could only be inferred indirectly.

The panel study is usually more informative than a more frequent design, which might be pictured thus:

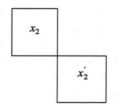

Here at one point in time we have one sample, and at a later point in time we have another sample. We observe that our measure, say, the mean, is greater for the recent sample than for the earlier one. But we are precluded from observing which men or what type of men shifted. Moreover, there is always the disturbing possibility that the populations in our two samples were initially different; hence the differences might not be attributable to conditions taking place in the time interval between the two observations. Thus we would study a group of soldiers in the United States and later ask the same questions of a group of soldiers overseas. Having matched the two groups of men carefully by branch of service, length of time in the army, rank, etc., we hoped that the results of the study would approximate what would be found if the same men could have been studied twice. But this could be no more than a hope. Some important factors could not be adequately controlled, for example, physical conditions. Men who went overseas were initially in better shape on the average than men who had been kept behind; but, if the follow-up study was in the tropics, there was a chance that unfavorable climate already had begun to take its toll. And so it went. How much men overseas changed called for a panel study as a minimum if we were to have much confidence in the findings.

A very common attempt to get the result of a controlled experiment without paying the price is with the design that might be as shown in the accompanying diagram. This is usually what we get with correlation analysis. We have two or more groups of men whom we study at the same point in time.

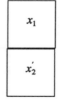

Thus we have men in the infantry and men in the air corps and compare their attitudes. How much of the difference between x_2' and x_2 we can attribute to experience in a given branch of service and how much is a function of attributes of the men selected for each branch we cannot know assuredly. True, we can try to rule out various possibilities by matching; we can compare men from the two branches with the same age and education, for example. But there is all too often a wide-open gate through which other uncontrolled variables can march.

Sometimes, believe it or not, we have only one cell:

When this happens, we do not know much of anything. But we can still fill pages of social science journals with "brilliant analysis" if we use plausible conjecture in supplying missing cells from our imagination. Thus we may find that the adolescent today has wild ideas and conclude that society is going to the dogs. We fill in the dotted cell representing our own yesterdays with hypothetical data, where x_1 represents us and x_2 our offspring. The tragicomic part is that most of the public, including, I fear, many social scientists, are so acculturated that they ask for no better data.

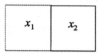

I do not intend to disparage all research not conforming to the canons of the controlled experiment. I think that we will see more of full experimental design in sociology and social psychology in the future than in the past. But I am well aware of the practical difficulties of its execution, and I know that there are numberless important situations in which it is not feasible at all. What I am arguing for is awareness of the limitations of a design in which crucial cells are missing.

Sometimes by forethought and patchwork we can get approximations that are useful if we are careful to avoid overinterpretation. Let me cite an example:

In Europe during the war the army tested the idea of putting an entire platoon of Negro soldiers into a white infantry outfit. This was done in several companies. The Negroes fought beside white soldiers. After several months we were asked to find out what the white troops thought about the innovation. We found that only 7 percent of the white soldiers in companies with Negro platoons said that they disliked the idea very much, whereas 62 percent of the white soldiers in divisions without Negro troops said they would dislike the idea very much if it were tried in their outfits. We have:

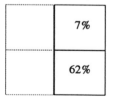

Now, were these white soldiers who fought beside Negroes men who were naturally more favorable to Negroes than the cross section of white infantrymen? We did not think so, since, for example, they contained about the same proportion of southerners.

The point was of some importance, however, if we were to make the inference that actual experience with Negroes reduced hostility from 62 to 7 percent. As a second-best substitute, we asked the white soldiers in companies with Negro platoons if they could recall how they felt when the innovation was first proposed. It happens that 67 percent said they were initially opposed to the idea. Thus we could tentatively fill in a missing cell and conclude that, under the conditions obtaining, there probably had been a marked change in attitude.

Even if this had been a perfectly controlled experiment, there was still plenty of chance to draw erroneous inferences. The conclusions apply only to situations closely approximating those of the study. It happens, for example, that the Negroes involved were men who volunteered to leave rear-area jobs for combat duty. If other Negroes had been involved, the situation might have been different. Moreover, they had white officers. One army colonel who saw this study and whom I expected to ridicule it because he usually opposed innovations, surprised me by offering congratulations. "This proves," he said, "what I have been arguing in all my thirty years in the army—that niggers will do all right if you give 'em white officers!" Moreover, the study applied only to combat experiences. Other studies would be needed to justify extending the findings to noncombat or garrison duty. In other words, one lone study, however well designed, can be a very dangerous thing if it is exploited beyond its immediate implications.

Now experiments take time and money, and there is no use denying that we in social science cannot be as prodigal with the replications as the biologist who can run a hundred experiments simultaneously by growing plants in all kinds of soils and conditions. The relative ease of experimentation in much—not all—of natural science goes far to account for the difference in quality of proof demanded by physical and biological sciences, on the one hand, and social scientists, on the other.

Though we cannot always design neat experiments when we want to, we can at least keep the experimental model in front of our eyes and behave cautiously when we fill in missing cells with dotted lines. But there is a further and even more important operation we can perform in the interest of economy. That lies in our choice of the initial problem.

Note

1. Reprinted from Samuel A. Stouffer, "Some Observations on Study Design," *American Journal of Sociology* 55 (January 1950): 356-59. Copyright 1950 by the University of Chicago.

2. Carl I. Hovland, Arthur A. Lumsdaine, and Fred D. Sheffield, *Experiments on Mass Communication* (Princeton, NJ: Princeton University Press, 1949).

ON THE DECISIONS IN VERIFICATIONAL STUDIES   2.10

Hans L. Zetterberg[1]

The advantages of the experimental design, however, rest with the possibility of a random assignment of cases to the experimental and control groups and on the possibility of producing what the working hypothesis terms the cause. Unfortunately, in sociology we rarely have these possibilities.

Certainly many factors are intentionally introduced into society by politicians, educators, welfare agencies, etc. But these phenomena are seldom or never produced, because they are termed causes in a scientific social theory. Furthermore, when compulsory education, socialized medicine, public housing projects, etc., are introduced into a society, the very complexity of the new phenomena does not make them suitable as indicators of concepts of a theory.

In the second place, we can rarely introduce randomization of the persons supposed to enjoy these intentionally produced phenomena without violating strong moral sentiments. As to the social programs of the welfare state Chapin makes the comment:

> The conventional method of equalizing factors that are known and also unknown (by R. A. Fisher's design of experiment) is to select at random both the experimental group that receives treatment and the control group that serves as a reference group for comparison. In social research the program of social treatment cannot be directed toward a randomly selected group because the prevailing mores require that this treatment be directed to a group of individuals who are eligible because of greater *need*. Thus precise control of unknown is impossible and the only factors that can be controlled are factors that are known to be in the particular social situation because of previous studies.[2]

It seems that this inability to study the conditions for a profitable use of the experimental design would definitely curtail the sociologist's prospect to verify his theories. However, the situation is by no means disastrous: sciences like meteorology and astronomy have verified theories without the employment of the experimental method.

For control of alternative hypotheses, the sociologist is to a large extent dependent on what might be called *pseudoexperimental* designs. These designs control propositions known as alternative ones, but, unlike the experimental designs, these designs cannot control unknown alternatives.

The most commonly used method in sociology for control of known alternative propositions is multivariate analysis, which has been formalized by Paul Lazarsfeld.[3] Skill in its use has become essential for most sociological research; those who know how to use it deserve to be called "modern sociologists." The technique controls alternative propositions by testing the hypothesis in subsamples that are homogeneous with respect to the determinants specified by the alternative propositions. It can be used to control all known alternative determinants provided the sample used is large enough.

The simplest relation between two variates X and Y is a fourfold table:

	X	non-X	
Y			
non-Y			

To discover whether a third variable, Z, accounts for any of the relations found in such a table, we break it into two parts:

	X	non-X			Z: X	non-X			non-Z: X	non-X	
Y				Y				Y			
			=				+				
non-Y				non-Y				non-Y			

If the relation between X and Y still holds in all subclasses of Z, we may retain, for the time being, our trust in the proposition that X affects Y. To this kind of design many new alternative determinants can be added, and it works equally well for qualitative and quantitative varieties.

However, the advantages do not end here. We can tabulate:

	X	non-X			Y: X	non-X			non-Y: X	non-X	
Z				Z				Z			
			=				+				
non-Z				non-Z				non-Z			

and also:

	Y	non-Y			X: Y	non-X			non-X: Y	non-Y	
Z				Z				Z			
			=				+				
non-Z				non-Z				non-Z			

The purpose of these tabulations is to discover the actual linkage between the three variables. It would carry us far to review all the rules of interpretation involved here. However, if certain assumptions about the time lag between the variates can be made, it is possible to use such tabulations to disentangle a wide variety of causal chains, as shown in the diagram (below) adapted from Dahlström.[4]

(1) $X \rightarrow Y \rightarrow Z$ (2) $X \rightarrow Z \rightarrow Y$

(3) $Z \rightarrow X \rightarrow Y$ (4)
$$\begin{array}{c} X \searrow \\ \quad\quad Y \\ Z \nearrow \end{array}$$

(5)
$$\begin{array}{c} X \searrow \\ \updownarrow \quad Y \\ Z \nearrow \end{array}$$
(6)
$$\begin{array}{c} X \searrow \\ \downarrow \quad Y \\ Z \nearrow \end{array}$$
(7)
$$\begin{array}{c} X \searrow \\ \uparrow \quad Y \\ Z \nearrow \end{array}$$

(8)
$$\begin{array}{c} X \\ \updownarrow \quad Y \\ Z \nearrow \end{array}$$
(9)
$$\begin{array}{c} X \searrow \\ \updownarrow \quad Y \\ Z \end{array}$$
(10)
$$\begin{array}{c} X \\ \quad\quad Y \\ Z \nearrow \end{array}$$

(11)
$$\begin{array}{c} X \searrow \\ \downarrow \quad Y \\ Z \end{array}$$
(12)
$$\begin{array}{c} X \\ \downarrow \quad Y \\ Z \nearrow \end{array}$$
(13)
$$\begin{array}{c} X \\ \updownarrow \quad Y \\ Z \nearrow \end{array}$$

Another method of pseudoexperimental control is that of *matching*, advocated by F. S. Chapin.[5] An experimental group and a control group are made equal on some criteria by discarding cases in one group for which no "twin" can be found in the other group. One disadvantage of this procedure is that the matched groups so obtained are not representative of the original groups. When this way of matching is employed, we do not quite know to what population the results can be generalized.

Control in pseudoexperimental design can be obtained through the use of other statistical adjustments. Various applications of the *multiple regression* approach can be made, provided variables fitting the rather rigid assumptions are used. The most common methods are those of partial correlation and analysis of covariance. These methods become rather laborious if the number of factors to be controlled is more than three or four.

Experimental designs and pseudoexperimental designs may be cross-sectional or longitudinal. We have already pointed out that longitudinal designs are more effective than cross-sectional designs and that experimental designs are more effective than pseudoexperimental designs. We can now reach a typology of designs:

		The Test of the Null Hypothesis	
		Cross-Sectional	Longitudinal
The Control of Alternative Hypotheses	No control		
	Pseudoexperimental		
	Experimental		

The closer a design comes to the longitudinal experimental, the better it is. However, we know little or nothing about how to evaluate crosswise combinations of the two criteria. We have no way in which to tell whether a pseudoexperimental longitudinal design (such as a panel with multivariable analysis) is as effective as the cross-sectional experimental design (the conventional laboratory experiment).

Notes

1. From H. L. Zetterberg, *On Theory and Verification in Sociology*, 2nd ed., rev. (Totowa, NJ: Bedminster, 1963), 61-66. Reprinted by permission.

2. F. Stuart Chapin, "Experimental Designs in Social Research," *American Journal of Sociology 55* (1950): 402.

3. Paul F. Lazarsfeld, "Interpretation of Statistical Relations as a Research Operation," in *The Language of Social Research*, ed. Paul F. Lazarsfeld and Morris Rosenberg (Glencoe, IL: Free Press, 1955), 115-25.

4. Edmund Dahlström, "Analys av surveymaterial," in *Sociologiska metoder*, ed. Georg Karlsson et al. (Stockholm: Svenska Bokförlaget, 1961), 193.

5. F. Stuart Chapin, *Experimental Designs in Sociological Research* (New York: Harper, 1947). For further reading, the advanced student should see F. Stuart Chapin, *Experimental Designs in Sociological Research*, rev. ed. (New York: Harper, 1955); Ernest Greenwood, *Experimental Sociology: A Study in Method* (New York: King's Crown, 1945); Claire Selltiz, Marie Jahoda, Morton Deutsch, and Stuart W. Cook, *Research Methods in Social Relations*, rev. ed. (New York: Henry Holt, 1959), chap. 4; Russell L. Ackoff, *The Designs of Social Research* (Chicago: University of Chicago Press, 1953), chap 3; Abraham Kaplan, *The Conduct of Inquiry* (San Francisco: Chandler, 1964).

THE ROLE OF MODELS IN RESEARCH DESIGN 2.11

Instructions for Use of Guide 2.11

Model building has been an integral part of social science for a long time. The work of Herbert Spenser and his followers based on a biological model of society would fill a small library. Physics has also served to encourage social scientists to seek social analogues. August Comte often used the term *social physics* to describe modern sociology.

Model building has been accentuated and accelerated by many forces in contemporary life. Models seem appropriate to the new world of computers, automation, and space terminology; and they have conferred new status on the scientist in government, industry, and the military. Model building has become "modeling," and the language of social science now includes such terms as *game models* (*gaming*), *simulation models, mathematical models, trend models, stochastic models, laboratory models, information* and *cybernetic models, causal* and *path models*, and many more. Even theory itself is being fractionalized into *theoretical models*. All these terms stand for a closed system from which are generated predictions (or hypotheses) that, when made, require some kind of empirical test.

In trying to bring some order out of the variety of models, one soon discovers that there is a great deal of overlap, and that widely different usages exist. There is no common agreement on the classification of models. In the following description, five categories of models and their variants are set out.[1] Researchers should not hesitate to use models if they assist in identifying significant variables in such a way that tests of hypotheses can be defined more sharply. Whenever possible, the researcher should be guided by the following rules:

1. We must first understand as completely as possible the system to be modeled.
2. Only the important parts of a system, and their controls, can be modeled.
3. Wherever possible, constants, rates, and relationships in the model must be measured and not taken from the literature.
4. The modeling exercise and the resultant simulations are regarded as tools to be used to further our understanding of how the system works.[2]

Physical Models

A physical model is a concrete object fashioned to look like the represented phenomenon. These objects incorporate static or structural properties. Examples include skeletons, organs, molecules, atoms, small-scale buildings, airplanes, and air tunnels. Perhaps the most famous model in contemporary science is the double-helix model showing the structuring of the DNA code gene that governs human reproduction. Pilot operating models introduce dynamic system patterns to represent functioning mechanisms in many fields.

A cognitive function is performed by the physical model in almost every field of science and branch of technology from sewing to architecture and aeronautical engineering. Sociology has made limited use of physical models, but F. S. Chapin has experimented with models to demonstrate institutions and social space and D. C. Miller with models of group and power relations. Many possibilities present themselves.

Basic Reading

Chapin, F. S. "A Theory of Social Institutions." In *Contemporary American Institutions*, 319-52. New York: Harper & Bros., 1935.
Miller, Delbert C. "The Research, Administrative, and Teaching Uses of Sociological Models in Depicting Group Relations." *Proceedings of the Pacific Sociological Society* 19 (June 1951): 98-102.

Theoretical Models

The term *model* is often used loosely to refer to any scientific theory phrased in symbolic, postulational, or formal styles. If there is any value in using *theory* and *model* as synonymous, it probably exists when a theory is set forth as a set of postulations with the relations among the parts clearly specified or exhibited. Thus Talcott Parsons and Charles Ackerman argue that the "social system is a theoretical device which maximizes analytical attention to its connectedness and it does so in a disciplined manner." [3]

Basic Reading

Dubin, Robert. *Theory Building: A Practical Guide to the Construction and Testing of Theoretical Models.* New York: Free Press, 1969.
Land, Kenneth C. "Formal Theory." In *Sociological Methodology 1971*, edited by Herbert L. Costner. San Francisco: Jossey-Bass, 1971.
Lave, Charles A., and James G. March. *An Introduction to Models in the Social Sciences.* New York: Harper & Row, 1975.

Mathematical Models

Applied in the social sciences, the term *mathematical model* refers to the use of mathematical equations to depict the behavior of persons, groups, communities, states, or nations. Common use of mathematics can be observed in trend, causal, path, and stochastic models.

Trend model refers to the fitting of time-series data to equations or curves postulated as change principles or laws.

Research Examples

Bartos, Otomar J. *Simple Models of Group Behavior.* New York: Columbia University Press, 1967.
Coleman, James S. *The Mathematics of Collective Action.* Chicago: Aldine, 1973.
Dodd, Stuart Carter. "Testing Message Diffusion in Controlled Experiments: Charting the Distance and Time Factors in the Interactance Hypothesis." *American Sociological Review* 18 (August 1952): 410-16.
Dunteman, George M. *Introduction to Linear Models.* Beverly Hills, CA: Sage, 1984.
Hart, Hornell. "Logistic Social Trends." *American Journal of Sociology* 50 (March 1945): 337-52.
Henry, Louis. *Population Analysis and Models.* New York: Academic Press, 1977.
Hernes, Gudmund. "The Process of Entry into First Marriage." *American Sociological Review* 37 (April 1972): 173-82.
Kemp, William F., and Bruno H. Repp. *Mathematical Models for Social Psychology.* New York: John Wiley, 1977.
Long, J. Scott. *Covariance Structure Models: An Introduction to LISREL.* Beverly Hills, CA: Sage, 1983.
Restle, Frank. *Mathematical Models in Psychology.* Baltimore: Penguin, 1971.
Stouffer, Samuel A. "Intervening Opportunities: A Theory Relating Mobility and Distance." *American Sociological Review* 5 (December 1940): 845-67.

Causal and path models involve the construction of a simplified model of social reality in which variables are presumed to act in a causal or processual sequence. The most important variables affecting some dependent (outcome) variable or criterion are sought and arranged according to their influence or impact. All other variables entering into the causal system are regarded as residuals.[4]

Research Examples

Asher, Herbert B. *Causal Modeling.* 2nd ed. Beverly Hills, CA: Sage, 1983.
Berry, William D. *Nonrecursive Causal Models.* Beverly Hills, CA: Sage, 1984.
Duncan, O. D. "Path Analysis: Sociological Examples." *American Journal of Sociology* 72 (July 1966): 1-16.
———— and Peter Blau. "The Process of Stratification." In *The American Occupational Structure*, 163-77. New York: John Wiley, 1967.
Sewell, William H., Archibald O. Haller, and George W. Ohlendorf. "The Educational and Early Occupational Status Attainment Process: Replication and Revision." *American Sociological Review* 35 (December 1970): 1014-27.

The term *stochastic model* refers to a probability construction in which a sequence of behavioral events occurs in time and to which are assigned probabilities for the joint occurrence of such events. Such models deal with "stochastic processes."

Research Examples

Dodd, S. C. "Diffusion Is Predictable: Testing Probability Models for Laws of Interaction." *American Sociological Review* 20 (August 1955): 392–401.
Galaskiewicz, Joseph, and Stanley Wasserman. "A Dynamic Study of Change in a Regional Corporate Network." *American Sociological Review* 46 (August 1981): 475–84.
Hunter, Albert. "Community Change: A Stochastic Analysis of Chicago's Local Communities, 1930-60." *American Journal of Sociology* 39 (January 1974): 923–47.

Basic Reading

Bartholomew, D. J. *Stochastic Models for Social Processes.* 2nd ed. New York: Wiley-Interscience, 1974.
Coleman, James S. *Introduction to Mathematical Sociology.* New York: Free Press, 1964.
Doreian, Patrick, and Norman Hummon. *Modeling Social Processes.* New York: Elsevier, 1976.
Fararo, Thomas J. *Mathematical Sociology.* New York: Wiley-Interscience, 1973.
Kemeny, John G., and Laurie Snell. *Mathematical Models in the Social Sciences.* Cambridge: MIT Press, 1962.
Lazarsfeld, Paul F. *Mathematical Thinking in the Social Sciences.* Glencoe, IL: Free Press, 1954.
Newbold, Paul, and Theodore Bos. *Stochastic Parameter Regression Models.* Beverly Hills, CA: Sage, 1985.
Tufte, Edward R. *Data Analysis for Politics and Policy.* Englewood Cliffs, NJ: Prentice-Hall, 1974.

Mechanical Models

In social science mechanical models use concepts from physics to provide analogues for social behavior. Mathematics was to be the handmaiden for building the field and bringing new rigor and validity. Increasingly, interest has grown in machine models; these are an extension of the concern with mathematical models, since they are based on mathematical language and symbolic logic. The computer is the focus of the machine model, and the terms *computer-simulated model* and *electronic-simulated model* are current. The game model is clearly related.

The *computer-simulated model* is focused on the use of a computer program to provide a test of a set of constructs that are internally consistent and have presumed explanatory power in order to derive generalizable propositions from the coded empirical data. Electronic computers are increasingly used to substitute for mathematical derivations in formal models. The postulates of the model can be programmed onto the computer (making the computer program the theory), and the computer will calculate the behavior that the program (i.e., theory) dictates. Herbert Simon reports that recent computer-simulation models have shown how a research problem can be pursued through sequences of experiments, and progress is now being made in modeling the construction of representations. The simulation models are tested by comparison with historical data on important scientific discoveries.

Research Examples

Beshers, James M. *Computer Methods in the Analysis of Large Scale Social Systems.* Cambridge: MIT Press, 1965.
Cohen, Kalman J., and Richard M. Cyert. "Simulation of Organizational Behavior." In *Handbook of Organizations,* edited by James G. March, 305-34. Chicago: Rand McNally, 1965.
Guetzkow, Harold, Philip Kotler, and Randall R. Schultz. *Simulation in Social and Administrative Science.* Englewood Cliffs, NJ: Prentice-Hall, 1972.

Gulahorn, John T., and Jeanne E. Gulahorn. "Some Compute. *Sociological Review* 30 (June 1965): 363-65.

Hanneman, Robert. *Computer-Assisted Theory Building: Mod.* Park, CA: Sage, 1988.

Hare, Paul A., R. Richardson, and Hartman Scheiblechner. "Comp. sions." Vienna: Institute for Higher Studies, 1968.

Langley, Pat, Herbert Simon, et al. *Scientific Discovery: Computation.* Cambridge: MIT Press, 1987.

Roby, Thornton B. "Computer Simulation Models for Organization Theo. *Research*, edited by Victor H. Vroom, 171-211. Pittsburgh: Univers.

Microanalytic simulation models are used to examine the e of policies on the demographic structure of the population, sav income security during retirement, social class differences in hea numerous other aspects of the population and its well-being. simulation system (MASS) was originally developed by Guy Orcu. University. It is a computer approach to capturing many of the complexit.s of a nation's social and economic structure. It is sophisticated enough to handle research problems as complex as the real-life events that affect the economic lives of whole populations of human beings: marrying and divorcing, giving birth, changing residence, becoming unemployed and finding new jobs, retiring, and dying. Research involving general simulation modeling to capture very large sets of human behaviors is still rare. A research leader in this work is Dr. James D. Smith at the Institute for Social Research, University of Michigan, Ann Arbor (see his book cited below).

Research Examples

Haveman, Robert H., and Kevin Hollenbeck, eds. *Microeconomic Simulation Models for Public Policy Analysis.* 2 vols. New York: Academic Press, 1980.

House, Peter W., and John McLeod. *Large Scale Models for Policy Evaluation.* New York: John Wiley, 1977.

Smith, James D. *Modeling the Distribution and Intergenerational Transmission of Wealth.* Chicago: University of Chicago Press, 1980.

Basic Reading

Brier, Alan, and Ian Robinson. *Computers and the Social Sciences.* London: Hutchinson, 1974.

Dyke, Bennett, and Jean Walters MacCluer, eds. *Computer Simulation in Human Population Studies.* New York: Academic Press, 1974.

Schrodt, Philip A. *Microcomputer Methods for Social Scientists.* Newbury Park, CA: Sage, 1987.

Game models rest on a mathematical theory that pertains to the determination of optimum strategies in a competitive situation (game of strategy) involving two or more individuals or parties. Games of strategy, in contrast to games in which the outcome depends only on chance, are games in which the outcome depends also, or entirely, on the moves chosen by the individual players.

Research Examples

Feld, Allan G. *CLUG: Community Land Use Game.* New York: Free Press, 1972.

Gamson, William A. *SIMSOC: Simulated Society.* 2nd ed. New York: Free Press, 1972.

Valadez. *Simulated International Processes: Theories and Research in Global* rly Hills, CA: Sage, 1981.

and Anne Cleaves, eds. *The Guide to Simulations and Games for Education and Training.* . Beverly Hills, CA: Sage, 1980.

. Gary. *Star Power.* La Jolla, CA: Simile II, 1969.

bick, Martin. *The Uses and Methods of Gaming.* New York: Elsevier, 1975.

Singleton, Robert R., and William F. Tyndall. *Games and Programs: Mathematics for Modeling.* San Francisco: Freeman, 1974.

Winters, P. R. *The Carnegie Tech Management Game: An Experiment in Business Education.* Homewood, IL: Irwin, 1964.

Yates, David Jules. *Community Interaction Game.* Cambridge, MA: Simulmatics, 1967.

Zagare, Frank C. *Game Theory: Concepts and Applications.* Beverly Hills, CA: Sage, 1984.

Basic Reading

Barton, Richard F. *A Primer on Simulation and Gaming.* Englewood Cliffs, NJ: Prentice-Hall, 1970.

Duke, Richard. *Gaming: The Future's Language.* New York: Halsted, 1974.

Gibbs, G. Ian. *Dictionary of Gaming, Modeling, and Simulation.* Beverly Hills, CA: Sage, 1978.

Greenblat, Cathy. *Designing Games and Simulations: An Illustrated Handbook.* Newbury Park, CA: Sage, 1987.

——— and R. Duke, eds. *Gaming-Simulation: Rationale, Designs, and Applications.* Rev. ed. New York: Halsted, 1981.

Inbar, Michael, and Clarence S. Stoll. *Simulation and Gaming in Social Science.* New York: Free Press, 1972.

Shubick, Martin. *Games for Society, Business, and War.* New York: Elsevier, 1975.

Simulation & Gaming (journal). An interdisciplinary forum for scholarly communication on all aspects of theory, design, and research bearing on the use of human, human-machine, and machine simulations of social processes. Editor: David Crookall, University of Alabama. Publisher: Sage Publications, Inc., 2455 Teller Rd., Newbury Park, CA 91320; published quarterly (March, June, September, December).

Symbolic Interactionist Models

Symbolic interactionist models address themselves to the meanings that actors give to the symbols they use or encounter. In social interaction, cues to behavior are transmitted by word and gesture. Behavior is constantly changing as transactions occur. There are many nuances of meaning too subtle to be treated as mechanical phenomena. Some symbolic interactionist models are simple constructs involving few persons; others are more elaborate and use computers to seek out patterns and generalizations. All models tend to be simulation models; that is, they are based on contrived situations or structured concepts that are isomorphic to reality situations.

Laboratory models involve contrived situations simulating groups or organizations in which actors play roles that are either structured or unstructured according to the design of the researcher. Generally, such behavior is observed in a closed environment where observation and recording devices can be employed. Well-known examples can be cited from the small group laboratory. Somewhat less attention has been given to the organization in the laboratory, but research is increasing rapidly.

Research Examples

Bales, Robert F. *Interaction Process Analysis: A Method for the Study of Small Groups.* Cambridge, MA: Addison-Wesley, 1950.

Burke, Peter J. "The Development of Task and Social-Emotional Role Differentiation." *Sociometry* 30 (December 1968): 379-92.

Slater, Philip E. "Role Differentiation in Small Groups." *American Sociological Review* 20 (June 1955): 300-310.
Weick, Karl E. "Laboratory Experimentation with Organizations." In *Handbook of Organizations*, edited by James G. March, 194-260. Chicago: Rand McNally, 1965.
———. "Organizations in the Laboratory." In *Methods of Organizational Research*, edited by Victor H. Vroom, 1-56. Pittsburgh: University of Pittsburgh Press, 1967.

Basic Reading

Bales, Robert F. "Interaction Process Analysis." In *International Encyclopedia of Social Sciences*, edited by D. L. Sills. New York: Free Press & Colliers Encyclopedia, 1968.
———. *Personality and Interpersonal Behavior.* New York: Holt, Rinehart & Winston, 1970.
Hare, Paul A. *Handbook of Small Group Research.* 2nd ed. New York: Free Press, 1975.

Information and cybernetic models depict information inputs, flows, and outputs within communication systems.[5] Models may range from mechanical to symbolic interactionist, where meaning becomes more significant. The computer may or may not be a useful adjunct. Models may treat with noise, redundancy, looping, and feedback. The most common analogue is human intelligence and the functioning of the brain. The scientific base is the information-scientific principle of intelligence as explained by Pieter J. van Heerden:

We have a black box with an input signal $f(t)$ which is a function of the time t only, and an output signal $g(t)$; both are binary time series:

input $f(t)$ → Black Box → output $g(t)$
. . . 1011010100   . . . 1100101110

Figure 1. Basic Model of Artificial Intelligence

The black box is the analogy of living intelligent beings. The input signal forms the analogy of the psychological drives, while the output is analogous to the command, from the brain, through the nerves, to the muscles of hands, feet, mouth, etc. In a machine, the input series would be any information with which we want to disturb the machine and cause it to react; the output would operate any physical means we may wish to make available to it. A simple example would be an intelligent machine which operates a number of elevators, and the input would be formed by the buttons people push, and the complaints they utter, translated in a binary code.[6]

Research Examples

DeFleur, Melvin L., and Otto N. Larsen. *The Flow of Information: An Experiment in Mass Communication.* New York: Harper, 1958.
Dodd, S. C. "Diffusion Is Predictable: Testing Probability Models for Laws of Interaction." *American Sociological Review* 20 (August 1955): 392-401.
Singer, Benjamin D. *Feedback and Society.* Lexington, MA: D. C. Heath, 1973.

Basic Reading

Fuchs, Walter R. *Cybernetics for the Modern Mind.* New York: Macmillan, 1971.

Klír, Jiri, and Miroslav Valach. *Cybernetic Modeling.* Princeton, NJ: Van Nostrand, 1967.
McKay, Donald. *Information, Mechanism, and Meaning.* Cambridge: MIT Press, 1969.
Weiner, Norbert. *Cybernetics.* New York: John Wiley, 1948.

Notes

1. See Charles A. Lave and James G. March, *An Introduction to Models in the Social Sciences* (New York: Harper & Row, 1975); see also Lyndhurst Collins, ed., *The Use of Models in the Social Sciences* (Boulder, CO: Westview, 1976); R. Robert Huckfeldt, C. W. Kohfeld, and Thomas W. Likens, *Dynamic Modeling: An Introduction* (Beverly Hills, CA: Sage, 1982).

2. James E. Hobbie, ed., *Lymnology of Tundra Ponds, Barrow, Alaska* (Stroudsburg, PA: Hutchinson & Ross, 1980), 2.

3. Gordon J. DiRenzo, ed., *Concepts, Theory, and Explanation in the Behavioral Sciences* (New York: Random House, 1967), 6-27.

4. See David Knoke, "A Path Analysis Primer," in *A Handbook of Social Science Methods*, vol. 3, ed. Robert B. Smith (New York: Praeger, 1985), 390-407.

5. These concepts are often used interchangeably. Information theory is concerned with the making of representations (i.e., symbolism in its most general sense) and measuring changes in knowledge. Norbert Wiener, often called the father of cybernetics, said the term *cybernetics* would be used to cover "the entire field of control and communication theory whether in the machine or in the animal." Norbert Weiner, *Cybernetics* (New York: John Wiley, 1948), 8.

6. Pieter J. van Heerden, *The Foundation of Empirical Knowledge with a Theory of Artificial Intelligence* (Wassenar, Netherlands: N. V. Uitoererij Wistik, 1968).

2.12   GENERAL CONSIDERATIONS OF RESEARCH DESIGN

Edward A. Suchman[1]

1. It seems to us futile to argue whether or not a certain design is "scientific." The design is *the plan of study* and, as such, is present in all studies, uncontrolled as well as controlled and subjective as well as objective. It is not a case of scientific or not scientific, but rather one of good or less good design. The degree of accuracy desired, the level of "proof" aimed at, the state of existing knowledge, etc., all combine to determine the amount of concern one can have with the degree of "science" in one's design.

2. The proof of hypotheses is never definitive. The best one can hope to do is to make more or less plausible a series of alternative hypotheses. In most cases multiple explanations will be operative. Demonstrating one's own hypotheses does not rule out alternative hypotheses and vice versa.

3. There is no such thing as a single "correct" design. Different workers will come up with different designs favoring their own methodological and theoretical predispositions. Hypotheses can be studied by different methods using different designs.

4. All research design represents a compromise dictated by the many practical considerations that go into social research. None of us operates except on limited time, money, and personnel budgets. Further limitations concern the availability of data and the extent to which one can impose upon one's subjects. A research design must be *practical*.

5. A research design is not a highly specific plan to be followed without deviation, but rather a series of guideposts to keep one headed in the right direction. One must be prepared to discard (although not too quickly) hypotheses that do not work out and to develop new hypotheses on the basis of increased knowledge. Furthermore, any research design developed in the office will inevitably have to be changed in the face of field considerations.

Note

1. From Edward A. Suchman, "The Principles of Research Design," in *An Introduction to Social Research*, ed. John T. Doby, with the assistance of Edward A. Suchman, John C. McKinney, Roy G. Francis, and John P. Dean (New York: Stackpole, 1954), 254-55. By permission of Edward A. Suchman and the Stackpole Company.

FACTORS JEOPARDIZING INTERNAL AND EXTERNAL VALIDITY OF RESEARCH DESIGNS

2.13

Campbell and Stanley list 12 factors jeopardizing the validity of various experimental designs.

From *Experimental and Quasi-Experimental Designs for Research*

Donald T. Campbell and Julian C. Stanley[1]

Fundamental to this listing is a distinction between *internal validity* and *external validity*. *Internal validity* is the basic minimum without which any experiment is uninterpretable: Did in fact the experimental treatments make a difference in this specific experimental instance? *External validity* asks the question of generalizability: To what populations, settings, treatment variables, and measurement variables can this effect be generalized? Both types of criteria are obviously important, even though they are frequently at odds in that features increasing one may jeopardize the other. While *internal validity* is the *sine qua non*, and while the question of *external validity*, like the question of inductive inference is never completely answerable, the selection of designs strong in both types of validity is obviously our ideal.

Relevant to *internal validity,* eight different classes of extraneous variables will be presented; these variables, if not controlled in the experimental design, might produce efforts confounded with the effect of the experimental stimulus. They represent the effects of:

1. *History*, the specific events occurring between the first and second measurement in addition to the experimental variable.
2. *Maturation*, processes within the respondents operating as a function of the passage of time per se (not specific to the particular events), including growing older, growing hungrier, growing more tired, and the like.
3. *Testing,* the effects of taking a test upon the scores of a second testing.

4. *Instrumentation*, in which changes in the calibration of a measuring instrument or changes in the observers or scores used may produce changes in the obtained measurements.
5. *Statistical regression*, operating where groups have been selected on the basis of their extreme scores.
6. Biases resulting in differential *selection* of respondents for the comparison groups.
7. *Experimental mortality*, or differential loss of respondents from the comparison groups.
8. *Selection-maturation interaction*, etc., which in certain of the multiple-group quasi-experimental designs is confounded with, i.e., might be mistaken for, the effect of the experimental variable.

The factors jeopardizing *external validity* or *representativeness* are:

9. The *reactive* or *interaction effect of testing*, in which a pretest might increase or decrease the respondent's sensitivity or responsiveness to the experimental variable and thus make the results obtained for a pretested population unrepresentative of the effects of the experimental variable for the unpretested universe from which the experimental respondents were selected.
10. The *interaction* effects of *selection* biases and the *experimental variable*.
11. *Reactive effects of experimental arrangements*, which would preclude generalization about the effect of the experimental variable upon persons being exposed to it in nonexperimental settings.

The value of such a list is that it gives the researcher some cautions before finalizing a design. To increase the degree of accuracy desired, these factors cannot be ignored. What is put into a research design directs what will come out after the data are collected and analyzed.

Note

1. Reprinted from Donald T. Campbell and Julian C. Stanley, *Experimental and Quasi-Experimental Designs for Research* (Chicago: Rand McNally, 1966), 5-6. By permission of the American Educational Research Association.

2.14   THE SAMPLING CHART

Instructions for Use of Guide 2.14

A sample is a smaller representation of a larger whole. The use of sampling allows for more adequate scientific work by making the time of scientific workers count. Instead of spending much of their time analyzing a large mass of material from one point of view, they can use that time to make a more intensive analysis from many points of view. Researchers can also save time and money by sampling, thus making possible investigations that could not otherwise be carried out.

Sampling problems may be divided into those that affect (a) the definition of the population, (b) the size of the sample, and (c) the representativeness of the sample.

In regard to the definition of the population, the important problem is to decide the group about which the researcher wishes to generalize his or her findings. In regard to size of sample, consideration must be given to the persistent disappearance of cases in a breakdown analysis. This disappearance should be foreseen as clearly as possible. Dummy tables help provide for such planning. The third and perhaps most intricate sampling problem arises in connection with the method of securing a representative sample. The essential requirement of any sample is that it is as representative as possible of the population or universe from which it is taken.

Three methods of sampling are commonly used: *random sampling, stratified sampling,* and *judgmental* or *purposive sampling.*

Random sampling. A random sample is one that is drawn in such a way that every member of the population has an equal chance of being included. The most rigorous method of random sampling employs a table of random numbers. In this method, a number is assigned to each member of the population. Those members are included in the sample whose numbers are taken from the table of random numbers in succession until a sample of predetermined size is drawn. A more common method is to write the names or numbers of the members of a population on cards or disks, shuffle these, and then draw. A convenient method, known as systematic sampling, which is not exactly equivalent to random sampling but is often close enough for practical purposes, is to take every *n*th item in the population, beginning at some random member in the population.

Stratified sampling. The aforementioned methods assume that the composition of the total group is not known, and that a representative sample will be best approximated by a strictly random selection or a selection by regular intervals. In some cases the more or less exact composition of the total group with respect to some significant characteristics is known before the sample is selected. For example, we may know the exact ratio of men to women in the population and that sex differences are related to the variables we wish to test. In such cases researchers can increase the chances of selecting a representative sample by selecting subsamples proportionate in size to the significant characteristics of the total population. Thus they can select a sample that is mathematically absolutely representative with regard to some significant characteristics. There are numerous forms of stratified random sampling techniques, as shown in the Ackoff Sampling Chart.

Judgmental or purposive sampling. When practical considerations preclude the use of probability sampling, researchers may seek a representative sample by other means. They may look for a subgroup that is typical of the population as a whole. Observations are then restricted to this subgroup, and conclusions from the data obtained are generalized to the total population. An example would be the choice of a particular state or country as a barometer of an election outcome, relying upon the results of past elections as evidence of the representativeness of the sample for the nation or state. Sampling errors and biases cannot be computed for such samples. For this reason judgmental sampling should be restricted to the following situations: (a) when the possible errors are not serious and (b) when probability sampling is practically impossible. Data from judgmental samples at best suggest or indicate conclusions, but in general they cannot be used as the basis of statistical testing procedures.

Sampling Chart *

Type of sampling	Brief description	Advantages	Disadvantages
A. Simple random	Assign to each population member a unique number; select sample items by use of random numbers	1. Requires minimum knowledge of population in advance 2. Free of possible classification errors 3. Easy to analyze data and compute errors	1. Does not make use of knowledge of population which researcher may have 2. Larger errors for same sample size than in stratified sampling
B. Systematic	Use natural ordering or order population; select random starting point between 1 and the nearest integer to the sampling ratio (N/n); select items at interval of nearest integer to sampling ratio	1. If population is ordered with respect to pertinent property, gives stratification effect, and hence reduces variability compared to A 2. Simplicity of drawing sample; easy to check	1. If sampling interval is related to a periodic ordering of the population, increased variability may be introduced 2. Estimates of error likely to be high where there is stratification effect
C. Multistage random	Use a form of random sampling in each of the sampling stages where there are at least two stages	1. Sampling lists, identification, and numbering required only for members of sampling units selected in sample 2. If sampling units are geographically defined, cuts down field costs (i.e., travel)	1. Errors likely to be larger than in A or B for same sample size 2. Errors increase as number of sampling units selected decreases
1. With probability proportionate to size	Select sampling units with probability proportionate to their size	1. Reduces variability	1. Lack of knowledge of size of each sampling unit before selection increases variability
D. Stratified 1. Proportionate	Select from every sampling unit at other than last stage a random sample proportionate to size of sampling unit	1. Assures representativeness with respect to property which forms basis of classifying units; therefore yields less variability than A or C 2. Decreases chance of failing to include members of population because of classification process 3. Characteristics of each stratum can be estimated, and hence comparisons can be made	1. Requires accurate information on proportion of population in each stratum, otherwise increases error 2. If stratified lists are not available, may be costly to prepare them; possibility of faulty classification and hence increase in variability
2. Optimum allocation	Same as 1 except sample is proportionate to variability within strata as well as their size	1. Less variability for same sample size than 1	1. Requires knowledge of variability of pertinent characteristic within strata
3. Disproportionate	Same as 1 except that size of sample is not proportionate to size of sampling unit but is dictated by analytical considerations or convenience	1. More efficient than 1 for comparison of strata or where different errors are optimum for different strata	1. Less efficient than 1 for determining population characteristics; i.e., more variability for same sample size

Sampling Chart—Continued

Type of sampling	Brief description	Advantages	
E. Cluster	Select sampling units by some form of random sampling; ultimate units are groups; select these at random and take a complete count of each	1. If clusters are geo-graphically defined, yields lowest field costs 2. Requires listing only individuals in selected clusters 3. Characteristics of clusters as well as those of population can be estimated 4. Can be used for subse-quent samples, since clusters, not individuals, are selected, and substi-tution of individuals may be permissible	...uster, inability to do so may result in duplica-cation or omission of individuals
F. Stratified cluster	Select clusters at random from every sampling unit	1. Reduces variability of plain cluster sampling	1. Disadvantages of strati-fied sampling added to those of cluster sampling 2. Since cluster properties may change, advantage of stratification may be re-duced and make sample unusable for later re-search
G. Repetitive: multiple or sequential	Two or more samples of any of the above types are taken, using results from earlier samples to design later ones, or determine if they are necessary	1. Provides estimates of population characteristics which facilitate efficient planning of succeeding sample, therefore reduces error of final estimate 2. In the long run reduces number of observations required	1. Complicates adminis-tration of fieldwork 2. More computation and analysis required than in nonrepetitive sampling 3. Sequential sampling can only be used where a very small sample can ap-proximate representative-ness and where the num-ber of observations can be increased conveniently at any stage of the re-search
H. Judgment	Select a subgroup of the population which, in the basis of available information, can be judged to be represen-tative of the total population; take a com-plete count or sub-sample of this group	1. Reduces cost of pre-paring sample and field-work, since ultimate units can be selected so that they are close together	1. Variability and bias of estimates cannot be mea-sured or controlled 2. Requires strong as-sumptions or consider-able knowledge of popu-lation and subgroup selected
I. Quota	Classify population by pertinent properties; determine desired pro-portion of sample from each class; fix quotas for each observer	1. Same as above 2. Introduces some strati-fication effect	1. Introduces bias of ob-servers' classification of subjects and nonrandom selection within classes

The three forms of sampling discussed above do not exhaust the range of sampling procedures. The Ackoff Sampling Chart lists such types as multistage random sampling, cluster, stratified cluster, and repetitive sampling. Ackoff writes:

> From practical as well as purely scientific purposes it is necessary to use selection procedures whose errors are measurable. A procedure should be capable of characterization relative to bias and variability. The fundamental procedure satisfying these conditions is simple random sampling, a method in which each individual has an equal chance of being selected. Simple random sampling is performed with the aid of random numbers, while systematic sampling is a variation which proceeds from a random start to select elements at a preset interval.
>
> By breaking the population into subgroups, we may select a sample in stages. If a random sample is selected at each stage, we have a multistage random sample. If a complete count of sampling units is taken at one stage other than the last, we have a stratified sample. If a complete count is made at the last stage, we have a cluster sample. The probability of selecting any subgroup may be made proportionate to some function of the size of the subgroup, and the number of units selected from any subgroup may also be made proportionate to some such function. Proportionate sampling tends to reduce sampling errors. Stratification and clustering can be combined to yield efficient samples, particularly where stratification and/or clustering is based on geographic properties (i.e., in area sampling). Area sampling reduces the complexity of preparing sampling lists and permits the clustering of subjects so that they come in bunches.
>
> In double sampling a first sample can be used to provide information which can in turn be used to design an efficient second sample. Such sampling can also be used to reduce the number of observations required, on the average, for coming to a conclusion. When double sampling is generalized, it yields sequential sampling, a method of drawing one item or set of items at a time and using the data obtained to decide whether to continue sampling or not.
>
> The ultimate basis for selecting a sampling procedure should be minimization of the cost of getting the sample and the expected cost of errors which may result from using the method. Expert assistance should be employed in making such evaluations.
>
> The sampling chart summarizes in a very brief way the description, advantages, and disadvantages of the various sampling procedures discussed.[1]

Note

1. Russell Ackoff, *The Design of Social Research* (Chicago: University of Chicago Press), 123-26.

2.15 A SELECTED BIBLIOGRAPHY ON RESEARCH DESIGN

Ackoff, Russell L. *The Design of Social Research.* Chicago: University of Chicago Press, 1953.
———— and Fred E. Emery. *On Purposeful Systems.* Chicago: Aldine, 1972.
Alwin, Duane F., ed. *Survey Design and Analysis.* Beverly Hills, CA: Sage, 1978.
Armer, Michael, and Allen Grimshaw, eds. *Comparative Social Research: Methodological Problems and Strategies.* New York: John Wiley, 1973.
Blalock, Hubert M., Jr. *Theory Construction.* Englewood Cliffs, NJ: Prentice-Hall, 1969.
————. *Causal Inferences in Non-Experimental Research.* New York: Norton, 1972.
————, ed. *Measurement in the Social Sciences: Theories and Strategies.* Chicago: Aldine, 1974.
————. *Conceptualization and Measurement in the Social Sciences.* Beverly Hills, CA: Sage, 1982.
————. *Basic Dilemmas in the Social Sciences.* Beverly Hills, CA: Sage, 1984.

Blau, Peter M., and Joseph E. Schwartz. *Crosscutting Social Circles: Treating a Macrostructural Theory of Intergroup Relations.* New York: Academic Press, 1984.

Bohrnstedt, G. W., and E. F. Borgatta, eds. *Social Measurement: Current Issues.* Beverly Hills, CA: Sage, 1981.

Brinberg, David, and Joseph E. McGrath. *Validity and the Research Process.* Beverly Hills, CA: Sage, 1985.

Campbell, John P., Richard L. Daft, and Charles L. Hulin. *What to Study: Generating and Developing Research Questions.* Beverly Hills, CA: Sage, 1982.

Collins, Randall. *Sociology Since Midcentury: Essays in Theory Accumulation.* New York: Academic Press, 1981.

Carroll, John S., and Eric Johnson, Jr. *Decision Research: A Field Guide.* Newbury Park, CA: Sage, 1990.

Diesing, Paul. *Patterns of Discovery in the Social Sciences.* Hawthorn, NY: Aldine, 1971.

Fielding, Nigel G. *Actions and Structure: Research Methods and Social Theory.* Newbury Park, CA: Sage, 1988.

Fisher, R. A. *The Design of Experiments.* 7th rev. ed. New York: Hafner, 1960.

Forcese, Dennis P., and Stephen Richer, eds. *Stages of Social Research: Contemporary Perspectives.* Englewood Cliffs, NJ: Prentice-Hall, 1970.

In this volume 41 authors describe such stages as the scientific approach, conceptualization, measurement, research format, sampling, data collection, and data analysis and interpretation.

Greer, Scott. *The Logic in Inquiry.* Chicago: Aldine, 1969.

Hakim, Catherine. *Research Design.* Winchester, MA: Allen & Unwin, 1987.

Hanson, N. R. "Theories." Chap. 4 in *Patterns of Discovery: An Inquiry into the Conceptual Foundations of Science.* Cambridge: Cambridge University Press, 1958.

Hempel, Carl G., and P. Oppenheim. "Studies in the Logic of Explanation." *Philosophy of Science* 15 (1948): 135-75.

James, Lawrence R., Stanley A. Mulaik, and Jeanne M. Brett. *Causal Analysis: Assumptions, Models, and Data.* Beverly Hills, CA: Sage, 1982.

Kaplan, Abraham. "Theories." Chap. 8 in *The Conduct of Inquiry: Methodology for Behavioral Science.* San Francisco: Chandler, 1964.

Kave, Charles A., and James G. March. *An Introduction to Models in the Social Sciences.* New York: Harper & Row, 1975.

Kratochwill, Thomas R., ed. *Single Subject Research: Strategies for Evaluating Change.* New York: Academic Press, 1978.

Lieberson, Stanley. *Making It Count: The Improvement of Social Research and Theory.* Berkeley: University of California Press, 1985.

McGrath, Joseph E., Joanne Martin, and Richard A. Kulka. *Judgment Calls in Research.* Vol. 2. Beverly Hills, CA: Sage, 1982.

Morgan, Gareth, ed. *Beyond Method: Strategies for Social Research.* Beverly Hills, CA: Sage, 1983.

Namboodiri, Krishnan, Lewis F. Carter, and Hubert M. Blalock, Jr. *Applied Multivariate Analysis and Experimental Design.* New York: McGraw-Hill, 1975.

Oyen, Else. *Comparative Methodology: Theory and Practice in International Social Research.* Newbury Park, CA: Sage, 1990.

Rabinow, Paul, and William G. Sullivan, eds. *Interpretive Social Science: A Second Look.* Berkeley: University of California Press, 1987.

Roloff, Michael E., and Gerald R. Miller. *Persuasion: New Directions in Theory and Research.* Beverly Hills, CA: Sage, 1980.

Saxe, Leonard, and Michelle Fine. *Social Experiments: Methods for Design and Evaluation.* Beverly Hills, CA: Sage, 1981.

Sjoberg, Gideon, and Roger Nett. *A Methodology for the Social Sciences.* New York: Harper & Row, 1968.

Skidmore, William. *Theoretical Thinking in Sociology.* Cambridge: Cambridge University Press, 1975.

Smith, Robert B., ed. *A Handbook of Social Science Methods.* Vol. 3. New York: Praeger, 1982.

This volume bridges qualitative and quantitative methods. It focuses on public opinion research, quantitative survey research, and statistical methods for evaluative research. Part 1 discusses focused survey research and Part 2 discusses causal modeling. Volumes 1 and 2 of the *Handbook* (both published by Ballinger) are *An Introduction to Social Research* and *Qualitative Methods.*

Spector, Paul E. *Research Designs.* Beverly Hills, CA: Sage, 1981.

Stephens, William N. *Hypotheses and Evidence.* New York: Crowell, 1968.

Stouffer, Samuel. *Social Research to Test Ideas.* New York: Free Press, 1962.

Strauss, Anselm, and Juliet Corbin. *Basics of Qualitative Research: Grounded Theory Procedures and Techniques.* Newbury Park, CA: Sage, 1990.

Turner, Jonathan H., ed. *Theory Building in Sociology: Assessing Theoretical Accumulation.* Newbury Park, CA: Sage, 1988.

Van Maanen, John, James M. Dabbs, Jr., and M. Faulkner. *Varieties of Qualitative Research.* Beverly Hills, CA: Sage, 1982.

Westie, Frank R. "Toward Closer Relations Between Theory and Research: A Procedure and an Example." *American Sociological Review* 22 (April 1957): 149-54.

Whitehead, Alfred N. *A Philosopher Looks at Science.* New York: Philosophical Library, 1965.

Williams, Bill. *A Sampler on Sampling.* New York: John Wiley, 1978.

Zeller, Richard A., and Edward G. Carmines. *Measurement in the Social Sciences: The Link Between Theory and Data.* New York: Cambridge University Press, 1980.

Zetterberg, Hans L. *On Theory and Verification in Sociology.* 3rd ed., rev. Totowa, NJ: Bedminster, 1965.

Part 3

Applied and Evaluation Research

PART 3 DESCRIBES how applied and evaluation researchers both confront operational or policy-making problems. Unlike in basic research, the research problem is not chosen by the researcher; it is given to the researcher by an administrator or legislator who needs help now.

The applied researcher moves in to confront the problem head-on; the evaluation researcher must evaluate the end product of a program or process. Both types of research offer very important research challenges. In this part we look at the technical and social considerations with which applied and evaluation researchers must grapple. Cost and effectiveness are constant criteria by which their work is judged.

Part 3

Applied and Evaluation Research

Section A

Applied Research

APPLIED SOCIOLOGY AND POLICY-MAKING

3.A.1

Applied sociology has received greatly renewed interest because of the growth of employment opportunities outside universities combined with a tight academic market. Moreover, over the past two decades social science has been found to be increasingly useful in applied social science research in support of social programs of a wide variety. Otto Larsen, director of Social and Economic Sciences at the National Science Foundation, explains the role of social scientists in policy-making:

> Scientists do not make public policies, elected officials do. Research from social and behavioral research can and does inform the decision-making process through a variety of mechanisms. For example, the National Research Council of the National Academy of Sciences is regularly consulted for advice on policy matters. Its committees and panels draw heavily on the research of the social and behavioral sciences as they evaluate programs and deal with such concerns as energy, taxation, biomedical technologies, environmental monitoring, alcohol abuse, protection of individual privacy, aging, noise abatement, child development, and changes in fertility and mortality. The same is true of the many Presidential Commissions such as those dealing with violence, obscenity, population, or crime. Organizations outside government also use social science data to inform and advise the policy process. For example, under the auspices of the Hoover Institution at Stanford University, a distinguished set of scholars, mainly economists and political scientists, provides a review and analysis of major domestic and international issues in a book, *The United States in the 1980's*, edited by Peter Duignan and Alvin Rabushka.[1]

Peter Rossi believes social science departments have a major opportunity to serve as suppliers of social science expertise through bidding on applied social science contracts: "As an organized discipline, we have to build linkages to the applied social science world, apprising the contracting agencies and the research industry that sociology has something to offer and to our own colleagues and students that applied social research is a career that is exciting and interesting."[2]

Writing as chairman of the Committee on Professional Opportunities in Applied Sociology (American Sociological Association), Howard E. Freeman points to the current status of applied sociology:

Applied sociology has long roots in the discipline; certainly since the 1930's there have been numerous declarations by outstanding sociologists about the need to apply the findings of social research, conferences about the importance of applied work, and books documenting the utility of sociological studies. Further, applied sociology has been growing within the discipline as evidenced by the increase in extra university employment and career opportunities, possibilities for research support, and graduate training opportunities. The 1980 Guide to Graduate Departments of Sociology lists over 100 departments offering courses and special programs in applied sociology; some of the larger profit and nonprofit research organizations employ more sociologists than many sociology departments; and Federal support for basic research is only a small fraction of current applied research funding.[3]

All applied social science training programs must teach that to influence policymakers a number of factors must be taken into account. Leonard Saxe writes:

> Successful use of social science by policymakers is dependent on a host of factors. these include how problems are defined, the credibility of the researchers, the nature of the argument developed by the researchers, the quality and availability of the research evidence, the ability of analysts to communicate their ideas and research findings, and the timeliness of the policymakers' interest in the issue.[4]

Notes

1. Otto Larsen, "Need for Continuing Support for Social Sciences," *Footnotes* of the American Sociological Association (March 1981): 8.
2. *Footnotes* of the American Sociological Association (August 1980): 20.
3. *Footnotes* of the American Sociological Association (December 1980): 1. See Study Project of Social Research and Development, *Study Project Report*, vol. 1, *The Federal Investment in Knowledge of Social Problems* (Washington, DC: National Academy of Sciences, 1978), especially pp. 66-67 and the excellent bibliography.
4. Leonard Saxe, "Policymakers' Use of Social Science Research," in *Evaluation Studies Review Annual*, vol. 12, ed. William R. Shadish, Jr., and Charles S. Reichardt (Newbury Park, CA: Sage, 1987), 226; Ann Majchrzak, *Methods for Policy Research* (Beverly Hills, CA: Sage, 1984); Jack McKillip, *Need Analysis: Tools for the Human Services and Education* (Newbury Park, CA: Sage, 1987).

3.A.2   APPLIED RESEARCH DESIGN

In contrast with basic research, applied behavioral research has many important differences, with new rules and demands.

1. The applied researcher must address a pressing problem presented by some client. The client may be the researcher's boss in a business, government, or service organization, or the client may be an outside organization seeking the services of a professor or a consulting management or research agency. The client is often a government or private funding agency. Each wants the same thing: useful knowledge serving to answer a question that is being faced by policymakers.
2. The researcher must be a translator between the academic discipline in which he or she works and the world of action. Major demands come from the world of action, including concern with timeliness, action, use of everyday language and concepts, ever-present involvement of special interests, conflict, and struggle over resources.[1]

3. The researcher must decide whether it is important to find a relationship between action findings and theory. Academic researchers are usually under rather heavy pressures to publish their work with scientific standing. Patterns of hypothesis testing based on a guiding theory must then be followed. This requirement will influence the design toward *basic* research standards. But the demand for practical policy guidance will always be a strong opposing pull.
4. The researcher is paid by the client and the work is evaluated by the results obtained in solving or alleviating the management (as policy) problem.

The late Professor Samuel Stouffer of Harvard University, who directed large-scale research on the American soldier for the U.S. Army in World War II, used to say, "If I get the chance to do ten percent basic research while carrying out the operational research for the U.S. Army, I shall be happy." His success with both types of research was certified by the commendation of General George Marshall of the U.S. Army as well as the praise of American sociologists and psychologists for the superb four volumes known as *The American Soldier.*[2] For this bridging of basic and applied research, *The American Soldier* is a model.

All researchers, basic and applied, need funds. More funds can usually be secured for applied research than for basic research. Ability to provide research designs that capitalize on combinations of basic and practical goals is desirable.

Notes

1. James S. Coleman, *Policy Research in the Social Sciences* (Morristown, NJ: General Learning Press, 1972).
2. Samuel A. Stouffer, *Studies in Social Psychology: The American Soldier*, 4 vols. (Vol. 1, *Adjustment During Army Life*; Vol. 2, *Combat and Its Aftermath*; Vol. 3, *Experiments in Mass Communication*; Vol. 4, *Measurement and Prediction.*) (Princeton NJ: Princeton University Press, 1947, 1949).

FITTING AN APPLIED RESEARCH DESIGN TO A PROBLEM   3.A.3

An applied research design must be able to interpret behavior embedded in a complex social system. The researcher begins by trying to conceptualize the parts of the system under investigation, its boundaries, its interface with other systems, the feedback loops, and other subsystems to which it may be connected. The key questions become:

- How do we achieve specific ends in the system?
- What key causal factors are involved?

Analysis begins with location of situational factors. It progresses to a definition of existing psychological and behavioral responses. Interpersonal factors such as perceptions, norms, values, evaluations, and goals must be mapped as participants interact. Now a theory of intervention must be designed to manipulate situational factors through policy and structural changes. After intervention, evaluation should be undertaken.

Chris Argyris has pointed out that practitioners need to consider what kind of knowledge individuals require and use while acting. People make sense of their world by organizing data into patterns, storing them in their heads, and retrieving them whenever they need them. Social scientists can help ensure that the knowledge they produce will be usable by organizing these behavioral patterns in the form of maps for action.

Argyris fashions action maps that set out factors in a given problem situation and traces the participants as they cooperate and conflict. The sequence of steps includes the pressures the participants report with their successes and failures as they try to cope, and their outcome behavior.[1]

Note

1. See Chris Argyris in Edward E. Lawler III and Associates, *Doing Research That Is Useful for Theory and Practice* (San Francisco: Jossey-Bass, 1985), 79-125; Chris Argyris, Robert Putnam, and Diana McLain Smith, *Action Science* (San Francisco: Jossey-Bass, 1985), 225-265.

3.A.4   THE MOOD OF THE ACADEMIC RESEARCHER ENGAGED IN APPLIED RESEARCH

Academics in applied research seem to get caught up in ambivalent feelings. Again, Hackman says it well:

> First, despite my intellectual confidence that new conceptual and methodological approaches are required in organizational behavior, experimenting with those approaches occasionally makes me feel as if my deviations from traditional ways of pursuing scientific values were somehow heretic and sinful. Second, when one is trying to do something which one does not know how to do and for which there are no ready models, failure is always a real possibility and is probably more likely than success. Such ambivalence tends to be accompanied by anxiety, which, in turn, can block intellectual work and make it hard to get anything done, let alone something new and possibly interesting. But ambivalence and anxiety are also reputed to be the precursors of creativity, so there is always hope that something worthwhile will emerge if one sticks with it long enough.
>
> These, then, are the kinds of questions and issues, both emotional and intellectual, that I am wrestling with these days as I continue to try to develop practical theories of individual and group performance effectiveness. I am finding the challenges—to my imagination and to my courage—substantial.[1]

Successful Applied Research Can Be Developed

None of the obstacles to applied research is insuperable. Researchers learn to take all difficulties in their stride. The following article is a description of action research. The steps designating movement from exploration of the human relations problems to experimental study are pointed out. And in the midst of it all can be found many of the human relations problems confronting the research team, among its own members.

Note

1. J. Richard Hackman in Edward E. Lawler III and Associates, *Doing Research That Is Useful in Theory and Practice* (San Francisco: Jossey-Bass, 1985), 148-49.

THE SHAPING OF RESEARCH DESIGN IN LARGE-SCALE GROUP RESEARCH

3.A.5

Delbert C. Miller[1]

This paper examines some of the problems and opportunities in the shaping of research design posed by a large-scale group research project undertaken by the University of Washington for the U.S. Air Force.

The project began in June 1951 under a contract with the Human Resources Research Institute calling for an exploration of human relations problems of air force personnel manning isolated Air Defense radar stations "with reference to job requirements, morale factors, and leadership under stressful noncombat conditions and to develop methods for improving effectiveness." The contract was concluded in December 1953. During the thirty-two months of active research, the project moved from exploration to descriptive and diagnostic study. Some cross-sectional experimental studies were undertaken in the final phase. The full research program included a national survey of the U.S. Air Defense Command Aircraft Control and Warning Stations, a study of the Japan Air Defense Command (A.C. and W.), and numerous investigations in the 25th Division of the Pacific Northwest. All these undertakings centered on personnel problems and squadron efficiency.

It is the theme of this paper that research design in a group project is a product of a social process. That process is influenced by a number of organizational demands as well as by the dynamic interplay of personalities and experiences that are encountered by the group as research penetration continues. It is believed that it is entirely fallacious to consider group research as individual research simply grown big.

Research design for group research must be sensitive to needs of individual researchers, to organizational demands, and to research growth through contact with the problem. Indeed, it should be clearly recognized that individual researchers do not become group researchers merely by joining group research. The problem of research design becomes one of wedding the logic of scientific method to the social pressures of many internal and external considerations. Four major factors affected research design on the Air Site Project. These were: (I) the characteristic imperatives of group research, (II) the personal wants of researchers, (III) the demands of education, and (IV) the accumulation of empirical and theoretical knowledge.

I. The Characteristic Imperatives of Group Research

A. *The Restrictions of Interdependent Research Relationships.* The individual researcher confronting group research is asked to change many research habits that he may value highly. The change in habits may be experienced as a set of onerous restrictions. He may find that he cannot choose his problem, and the problem assigned to him may require collaboration with others that reduces still further his area of free movement. He discovers that he has come to live in a web of interrelationships in which his work is intertwined. His own methods of work undergo close scrutiny of the group. He is subordinate to the final approval of a research director. Status and craft comparisons may clearly become causes of interpersonal conflict.[2] If the researcher does not or cannot adjust to this new social environment, conflict processes are intensified and spread to the group. In this atmosphere, even interpretation of words can become a serious source of wrangling.[3] Learning to live together in close interdependence does not come easy. And in group research for a client, many additional pressures are added.

B. *The Demands of a Time Schedule.* Group research for a client usually has a number of deadlines. Our military client required quarterly, interim, and final reports on given dates. No longer could researchers regard as indefinite the date for concluding a study. The demand for a report often meant intensified work, and this brought to some workers a sense of frustration that quality had been sacrificed for lack of time to do one's best.

C. *Conciliation of Other Pressures.* The client—or, as in our project, the monitoring agent—may offer suggestions and instructions as the research proceeds. These are usually accepted as persuasions to modify or intensify work in a given direction. These come to the project director and are transmitted through his actions or instructions to the group researchers. Sometimes the reason is not understood, or it may be understood but resented as an outside idea, foreign to the group process, and emotionally rejected.

Scientific canons of rigor may be opposed by demands for exploratory or applied research on problems for which hypotheses and measurement tools cannot be readied. A researcher whose pride system has incorporated strict and rigid standards of craftsmanship may quail before problems whose solution requires simple exploration or vulgar practicality (especially if he does not see how he can get a published paper from it).

The requirements of expense accounts, security clearances, permission for entry to the research field, "logistic support," and numerous matters of red tape are often further irritations—a headache to researchers and director alike.

The airmen and officers in the research field also exert subtle pressure on the researchers. The questions, "What's this all about? What are you trying to find out?" are continuous and require some kind of answer. The challenge, "You won't be able to do any good" is even more difficult to meet. It can undermine the feeling of acceptance and make fieldwork a resented rather than a welcome experience.

All these new elements call for personal adjustments. It is apparent that a number of strains must be borne by group researchers who have not confronted these factors before. Who are these researchers that come into the group and what do they want?

II. The Personal Wants of Researchers

A. *Motivations of Researchers.* Young researchers are attracted to group research. If they are graduate students, the prospect of funds and a thesis presents an opportunity both to do research and to eat. Young Ph.D.s see opportunity for publication, promotion, and freedom from teaching. Both of these groups are seeking to build research reputations through publication. This motive serves to make the burdens of fieldwork sufficiently acceptable to get the necessary data collecting done, but marriage, parenthood, and sedentary proclivities all contrive to make absence from the home an increasing burden.

B. *Security Needs of Researchers.* Research staffs are often recruited from among those persons who are seeking permanent employment. When contracts are on a year-to-year basis with no fixed guarantee as to their duration, a job insecurity is added to the social influences that bear upon the researchers' morale and productivity. As individual contracts begin to approach termination, personal insecurities mount and are intensified by group interaction. The feelings of insecurity are expressed in many different ways, which may include demands for more say in both policy and administrative decisions, safeguards for individual publication rights, and almost single-minded preoccupation with the acquisition of the *next* research contract.

A research design is under the stress of individual wants, for group thinking is colored every step of the way by these personal concerns. Each person wants to know what part of the design he can claim for his research publications. Each person wants to have an opportunity to guide his fieldwork in such a way as to minimize its burdens. Each wants the maximum opportunity to determine his working conditions.

C. *Role of the Research Director.* The research director takes his place in the center of all the forces that have been described. His role is to direct group processes, ascertain group sentiment, and make decisions so that research can be designed and executed with harmony and efficiency. He must see that role definitions for each member are clearly outlined. He must interpret the external demands on the project and relate them to his research personnel so that appropriate action is taken. He must come to recognize that he will get little opportunity to do field research himself. And he must accept the fact that some interpersonal friction will accompany his most valiant efforts to make group research palatable, especially during the early period when a number of individual researchers are learning to live together as group researchers. He will come to understand that each member of the group is concerned with his reputation as the result of his membership. He wants to have his say as to what others do when he feels his own standards are being violated. This is at once a source of group power and of group conflict. The director will often be challenged as to how these group motivations can be channeled.

A research director who wishes to manage by the use of democratic methods must know the dilemmas of leadership in the democratic process and find his own way to cope with them.[4] Softhearted, inexperienced democratic leadership rivals autocratic blindness in creating poor conditions for efficiency and morale.

III. The Demands of Education

The major problem facing organization of group research within a university is to secure opportunity for each researcher to have maximum freedom to apply his talents to a project whose major problems have been outlined in a contract for him. This is no little task. A professional researcher, we have said, wants to choose his problem, be given the proprietary right of publication for his work, and have control over his working conditions. The university is concerned that graduate students receive broad research training and not be employed at mere clerical tasks. The research design must be constructed in recognition of these concerns and the staff organized in optimum-size working groups so that the best combination of professional staff and graduate students may be obtained.

The basic research unit of the Air Site Project was made up of a professional sociologist and two graduate students; in 1952-53, there were four such units in the

Project. Graduate students alternated fieldwork and classwork so that both types of training were secured. In the close association of professional sociologist and graduate student, both educational and research functions were served.

IV. The Accumulation of Empirical and Theoretical Knowledge

Research progress on a central problem usually proceeds through stages—first, exploration of the social setting of the problem, the factors involved, and the criteria that may be used to measure or appraise the problem; then descriptive and diagnostic study may be possible. Hypotheses are set up, factors are isolated, measured, and relationships ascertained. Still later, experimental studies may be undertaken. Research design keeps changing as hypotheses are modified, eliminated, and substituted. Each stage of research requires the use of new skills, the recasting of theory, the introduction of new revised factors, and perhaps reinterpretation of results.[5]

A. *Exploratory Study.* The Air Site Project began as a military requirement to investigate the morale and personnel problems of air force personnel in radar squadrons. We agreed to go to the research field and discover the personnel problems and personnel needs. At the same time we were to find the most significant problems for basic research into morale and motivation. Three professional sociologists developed a plan of sampling and interviewing and devoted three months between July and October 1951 to field visits and analysis of seven squadrons in one Air Defense division.[6] Detailed interviews were held with a representative sample of air force personnel in each squadron. We lived with and observed the operations and leisure activities of each squadron for a number of days. From our interviews and notes a common record was prepared by the research team for each squadron. This record ranked the major personnel problems as reported to us in each squadron, the needs as expressed by air force personnel, and research clues that we determined through our experiences in the field. Table 3.1 gives a record of major personnel needs and research clues for one air force squadron.

Interviews were coded and an analysis of major personnel problems was made to determine possible associations with age, marital status, education, length of service, and isolation of site. Various tables were constructed to show analyses of interview data—Analysis of Management Problems, Impact of Isolation on Operating Problems, and Personnel Needs as Defined by Site Personnel. All these tables were prepared especially for top military leaders and were presented in briefing sessions to them for their guidance. On the basis of these facts and others, new facilities were subsequently made available to the squadrons.

Meanwhile, research clues were combed to find the most significant research problems. General clusters of factors that we called research sectors were set forth as the ones we believed to be most directly related to the adjustment of air force personnel.[7] We selected (1) The Job and the Career, (2) Organization and Communication, (3) Leadership, and (4) Morale and Motivation. We pressed forward without an overall theory;[8] rather, research teams were formed and these teams selected a research sector, set up hypotheses, and began field research in the fall of 1951.

B. *Descriptive and Diagnostic Study.* In January 1952, six months after the initiation of the project, the research design was composed of the parts shown in Figure 3.1. The central problem had become the adjustment of the person to a military organization. Morale, motivation, and management or personnel problems had been chosen as the principal objects of study. Guttman scaling techniques were being applied to the study of various attitude areas. Nonverbal indices, such as rate of

TABLE 3.1 Major Personnel Needs and Research Clues for One Air Force Squadron

Problems encountered
1. Recreational outlets on the base.
2. Access to city or large town.
3. Degree of supervision.
4. Housing for the married man and his family.
5. Living on Indian reservation and adjustment to Indian people.
6. Restrictions imposed on minors.
7. Career misassignment.
8. Pressures from division and group commands.
9. Irritations from GI regulations.
10. Inequities in promotions and advancements.
11. Supply problems.
12. Access to weapon and monotony of tracking.
13. Organizational change to larger unit.
14. Relative deprivation.
15. Organizational cleavages.

Basic research clues for possible future study
1. Study of relationship between humor and tension. Compare a tense and relaxed site, watching for differences.
2. Study of emotional outbursts as manifested in attitude and in behavior such as AWOL, chewing out, or fighting.
3. Time sampling study of a group of highly motivated and poorly motivated personnel.
4. A study of newcomers over an extended time period to watch acculturation.
5. A study of the effect of increasing size on organizational and morale changes.
6. Relations of age, marital status, military experience, and residence and education to adjustment of highly and poorly adjusted persons.
7. A validation of relative deprivation.
8. A study of language functions, especially jargon and argot.
9. Socialization of the civilian to military culture.
10. Description of military culture.
11. The relation of job satisfaction to civilian training, experience, and goals.
12. Extent to which realization alone of choice of job is related to job satisfaction.

Observation clues for possible future measurement
1. Evaluate condition of uniform and military bearing at spot point.
2. Number of persons found in various places—barracks, dayroom, mess hall (goldbricking).
3. Count number who leave camp every day—check those who leave on two-day-off periods.
4. Turnover as a generalized aspect of military organizations.
   —among officers (upward mobility involves spatial mobility)
   —among airmen (stay only 18 months in a site)
5. What is relation of high turnover to problem of morale, organization, and leadership, to identification with the site, fellows, CO?

promotion, were being developed. Later, as a squadron efficiency rating system was developed by the officers of one air division (assisted by the Air Site Project), this criterion was introduced. Against these criteria we sought to determine the relationship of many social and social psychological variables.

The illustration presented as Figure 3.1, Basic Generalities of Social Organization, became our overall design. It was based essentially on the importance of studying certain difficult sociological problems *intensively* while ascertaining the full scope of other problems *extensively*. The six research sectors that received intensive study were those of Personal History, Job Adjustment, Group Integration, Leadership, Organization, and Family and Community. In these sectors researchers attempted to find relationships in areas where it was difficult to secure the relevant data and in which understanding could come only through patient, skillful, and persistent study. Such study was usually confined to one or two sites.[9] As crucial variables were

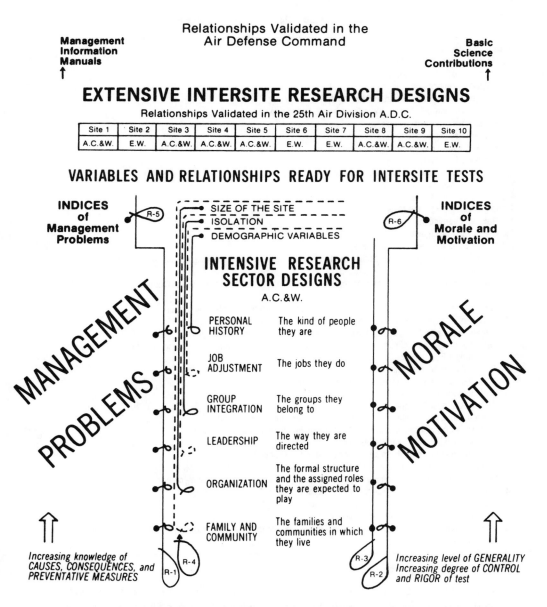

Figure 3.1 Basic Generalities of Social Organization. This figure depicts the general research design of large-scale investigation into the human factors affecting morale, motivation, and efficiency of radar sites.

identified and quantitative measures were developed, these variables were considered ready for extensive intersite test. The intersite design called for a testing of variables on a selected sample of air force men in all (or representative sample of all) sites in the population studied. Here, the criteria of morale, personnel problems, and efficiency were measured by the most refined measures that could be constructed or utilized. Selected social, demographic, and ecological variables were employed as independent variables to determine significant relationships to criteria measures.

Intersite questionnaires were administered in twelve sites of one division[10] (May 1952), and in the Japan Air Defense Command[11] (August-September 1952), and a national survey of the Air Defense Command was executed in April and May 1953.

The design reflects the twofold objectives: (1) to carry on basic research in morale (or personal adjustment) at the descriptive level, and (2) to work on personnel problems at the diagnostic level. The design thus reflects both the canons of basic research and the requirements of the client for operational results. The balance between these two foci was often beset by subtle pressures deriving from professional standards, on the one hand, and the practical concerns of the military officials, on the other. The research director who seeks to advance knowledge must see that the research work is so designed that the long-run concerns of basic science are carried along and, at the same time, good diagnostic studies of operational problems are produced that convince his client that research can be of service to him on the problems he faces *now*. He must persuade his staff of the importance of these twin demands, and he must protect them so that there is ample opportunity to achieve both basic and operational research. The basic research design of the Air Site Project grew out of these pressures, and it sought to satisfy them.

But more than this, the design must be understood as an expression of the researcher's desire for freedom to attack his problem in his own way. Some researchers took to the field at once to explore their problem. Others began to devise measuring instruments and to work out sampling plans. Some planned much observational work in the field; others planned fieldwork only to make pretests of questionnaires and scales. These differences seemed to be explained sometimes by differences in research approach (interactionists versus statistical testers) and sometimes by different adjustments to fieldwork. The deprivations of fieldwork and the new role relationships of a fieldworker (in contrast to those of the classroom teacher and library researcher) presented adjustment problems to all staff members. Some found field contact exciting and satisfying; others found absence from home and from customary routines of office a deprivation and sought to center their research in the university. It has already been suggested that the home plays an influential role in shaping the attitudes of the field researcher and thus indirectly the research work itself.

C. *Experimental Study.* Samuel Stouffer has written that "the necessary condition for dealing with a collection of variables is to isolate and identify them and, in addition, it is useful if they can also be measured. Until the relevant variables can be identified, empirical tests of a conceptual scheme involving these variables hardly can be expected." [12]

In the Air Site Project we identified the objects of study and were able to measure some of them. We ascertained many relationships between our criteria and social, demographic, and ecological factors. Many hypotheses were tested by field teams. Experimental work of a cross-sectional type was carried out.[13] Perhaps one of the most important relationships tested was that between morale in a squadron and the efficiency of the squadron. It is widely believed that good human relations are related positively to high efficiency. However, only a few tests have been made under experimental conditions involving a control group.[14]

The assignment of air force men is made according to the training specialty of available personnel and according to organizational needs. The assignment of men who are drawn out to fill quotas results in near stratified-random selection. As a result it is possible to find squadrons that have almost identical characteristics as to mean age, length of service, marital status, education, rank structure, degree of isolation, work conditions, and living conditions. In one division we studied twelve squadrons. Efficiency ratings of these squadrons were made each quarter by the responsible division officials. We constructed Guttman-type scales or items measuring such areas of morale as satisfaction with air site, satisfaction with air force, job satisfaction, and acceptance of mission goals. The relationship of morale to efficiency under controlled conditions was ascertained in our population. Because of the randomization in the squadron populations, control by frequency distribution could be employed. Squadrons were selected from the total universe (one division) and matched on variables believed to affect efficiency. The significance of differences between means was determined. Replication of this design was made on our larger universe of squadrons from all divisions.[15]

D. *Projected Experimentation*. Plans had been made for moving to the stage of true experimental study by taking before and after measures of experimental and control groups under controlled conditions. This would have consummated the direction of research movement. Unfortunately, the sharp curtailment of funds for human relations research in 1953 made it impossible to proceed into this type of experimentation. Projected experiments were not undertaken earlier because needed measures of morale, leadership, and efficiency had to be constructed first. Moreover, a high degree of confidence and cooperation from line military officers had to be earned before such work would have been possible. This is a hard social fact that cannot be ignored.

Four major factors influenced the shaping of research design on one large-scale group research project. These were: the characteristic imperative of group research, the personal wants of researchers, the demands of education, and the accumulation of empirical and theoretical knowledge.

These factors created both problems and opportunities. Problems have been considered in much of this paper, but opportunities were also abundant. Adequate financing of research brings professional, clerical, and technical assistance, permitting a rapid increase in the quantity and quality of research. Access to the research field and cooperation within it opens a new wealth of social data. A long-standing weakness of social science research has been the inability to get enough individual cases or organizational units so that relationships could be validated through replication. This is possible in large-scale group research. These opportunities can be capitalized, but only as the social processes of group research are marshaled. Social processes ever blend with scientific thinking to mold research design. As an end product of group research, it is a precipitate of personal feelings, thoughts, habits, and hopes.

Notes

1. Reprinted from Delbert C. Miller, "The Shaping of Research Design in Large-Scale Group Research," *Social Forces* 33 (May 1955): 383-90. This paper is based on the conclusions of the writer as director of the Air Site Project. Other members of the project have contributed in many different ways to the experiences described. Appreciation is acknowledged to Orvis F. Collins (Southern Illinois University), Edward Gross (University of Washington), F. James Davis (Illinois State University at Normal), Glenn C. McCann (North Carolina State College), Nahum Z. Medalia (Oakland University at Rochester, Michigan), Charles D. McGlamery (University of Alabama at Birmingham), professional sociologists; David S. Bushnell, Donald L. Garrity, Robert Hagedorn, John Hudson, Harold Kant, Alvin S. Lackey, Robert Larson, Herman Loether, Duane Strinden, Wes Wager, Shirley Willis, and David Yaukey, research fellows; all are now professional sociologists in the United States.

The research was supported in part by the U.S. Air Force under contract number AF-33-038-26823, monitored by the Human Resources Research Institute, Air Research and Development Command, Maxwell

Air Force Base, Alabama. Permission is granted for reproduction, translation, publication, and disposal in whole and in part by or for the U.S. government.

I am especially indebted to the continuous encouragement of Dr. Raymond V. Bowers, director of the Institute from 1949 to 1952, and to Dr. Abbott L. Ferris, chief of the Human Relations Division, whose administration efforts made possible our access to many research fields.

2. Joseph W. Eaton, "Social Process of Professional Teamwork," *American Sociological Review* 16 (October 1951): 707-13; Alfred M. Lee, "Individual and Organizational Research in Sociology," *American Sociological Review* 16 (October 1951): 701-7.

3. Urie Bronfenbrenner and Edward C. Devereux, "Interdisciplinary Planning for Team Research on Constructive Community Behavior," *Human Relations* 5 (1952): 187-203; William Caudill and Bertram H. Roberts, "Pitfalls in the Organization of Interdisciplinary Research," *Human Organization* 10 (Winter 1951): 12-15.

4. Chester I. Barnard, "Dilemmas of Leadership in the Democratic Process," in *Organization and Management* (Cambridge, MA: Harvard University, 1949), 24-50.

5. Robert K. Merton, "The Bearing of Empirical Research upon the Development of Social Theory," *American Sociological Review* 13 (October 1948): 505-15.

6. Squadrons varied in size from approximately 100 to 300 men, depending on type and function of the station.

7. For a full report of this exploratory survey, see F. James Davis, Edward Gross, and Delbert C. Miller, *Survey Report on Military Management Problems in Aircraft Control and Warning Stations in the Air Defense Command* (Maxwell Air Force Base, AL: Human Resources Research Institute, Air University, 1951).

8. This was a source of much concern to some of our researchers, and we held many staff meetings groping for such a theory. Some members of the staff believed we should not set out at all until a fully developed theory was in hand. Others believed theory should wait until the research and field experience were more advanced.

9. For published reports of this work, see F. James Davis, "Conceptions of Official Leader Roles in the Air Force," *Social Forces* 32 (March 1954): 253-58; F. James Davis and Robert Hagedorn, "Testing the Reliability of Systematic Field Observations," *American Sociological Review* 19 (June 1954): 345-48; F. James Davis, Robert Hagedorn, and J. Robert Larson, "Scaling Problems in the Study of Conceptions of Air Force Leader Roles," *Public Opinion Quarterly* 18 (Fall 1954): 279-86; Edward Gross, "Some Functional Consequences of Primary Controls in Formal Work Organizations," *American Sociological Review* 18 (August 1953): 368-73; Edward Gross, "Primary Functions of the Small Group," *American Journal of Sociology* 60 (July 1954): 24-29; Herman J. Loether, "Propinquity and Homogeneity as Factors in the Choice of Best Buddies in the Air Force," *Pacific Sociological Review* 3 (Spring 1960): 18-22; C. D. McGlamery, "Developing an Index of Work Group Communications," *Research Studies, State College of Washington* 21 (1953): 225-30; Nahum Z. Medalia, "Unit Size and Leadership Perception," *Sociometry* 17 (February 1945): 64-67; Nahum Z. Medalia, "Authoritarianism, Leader Acceptance, and Group Cohesion," *Journal of Abnormal and Social Psychology* 51 (September 1955): 207-13.

10. The Human Resources Research Institute published interim reports in 1952.

11. A final report has been prepared for the Human Resources Research Institute by Edward Gross and Orvis Collins, *American Air Sites in Japan: An Analysis of Human Relations in A. C. & W. Detachment Within the Japan Air Defense Force* (Maxwell Air Force Base, AL: Human Resources Research Institute, Air University, 1953).

12. Samuel A. Stouffer et al., *The American Soldier*, vol. 1, *Adjustment During Army Life* (Princeton, NJ: Princeton University Press, 1949), 34.

13. Stouffer writes, "I would trade a half dozen army-wide surveys on the attitudes toward officers for one good controlled experiment. Keeping the model of the controlled experiment as an ideal, it is sometimes possible for one to approximate it. . . . Ingenuity in locating ready-made situations is much needed. In any program of future research, I would put far more emphasis on this than ever has been done in the past." Quoted in Robert K. Merton and Paul F. Lazarsfeld, eds., *Studies in the Scope and Method of "The American Soldier"* (Glencoe, IL: Free Press, 1950), 211.

14. See Daniel Katz, Nathan Maccoby, and Nancy C. Morse, *Productivity, Supervision and Morale in an Officer Situation*, pt. 1 (Ann Arbor: University of Michigan, Institute for Social Research, 1950); Daniel Katz, Nathan Maccoby, Gerald Gurin, and Lucretia G. Floor, *Productivity, Supervision, and Morale Among Railroad Workers* (Ann Arbor: University of Michigan, Survey Research Center, 1951); Irving R. Wechsler, Murray Kahane, and Robert Tannenbaum, "Job Satisfaction, Productivity and Morale: A Case Study," *Occupational Psychology* 1 (January 1952): 1-14; Gunner Westerlund, *Group Leadership: A Field Experiment* (Stockholm: Nordisk Rotogravyr, 1952).

15. This research is described by Nahum Z. Medalia and Delbert C. Miller, "Human Relations Leadership and the Association of Morale and Efficiency in Workgroups: A Controlled Study with Small Military Units," *Social Forces* 33 (May 1955): 348-52. See also D. C. Miller and N. Z. Medalia, "Efficiency, Leadership, and Morale in Small Military Organizations," *Sociological Review* 3 (July 1955): 93-107; Edward Gross and D. C. Miller, "The Impact of Isolation on Worker Adjustment in Military Installations of the United States and Japan," *Estudios de Sociologia* (Buenos Aires) 1 (Fall 1961): 70-86; Glenn C. McCann, Nahum Z. Medalia, and Delbert C. Miller, "Morale and Human Relations Leadership as Factors in Organizational Effectiveness," in *Studies of Organizational Effectiveness,* ed. R. V. Bowers (Washington, DC: Air Force Office of Scientific Research, 1962), 85-114.

3.A.6   BIBLIOGRAPHY ON APPLIED SOCIOLOGY, KNOWLEDGE UTILIZATION, AND POLICY-MAKING

Abt, Clark C., ed. *Perspectives on the Costs and Benefits of Applied Social Research.* Cambridge, MA: Abt, 1979.

Over the last decade the United States has spent almost a billion dollars on applied social research. In this book, leading social researchers from government, academia, and the private research community examine the complex analytical problems and issues involved in effective cost-benefit measurement of their work.

———, ed. *Problems in American Social Policy Research.* Cambridge, MA: Abt, 1980.

In this volume, 38 contributors identify crucial problems faced by social researchers today, including overemphasis on data collection and data analysis to the detriment of new social program design.

Allen, T. Harrell. *New Methods in Social Science Research Policy and Futures Research.* New York: Praeger, 1978.

Describes new methods of social science research suited to the analysis of complex problems. Argues that researchers have been relying on survey methods and that many new methods that attack the whole system rather than its separate parts are better suited to solving increasingly interrelated social issues. This approach is especially relevant to the fields of policy science and future research. Case studies explain the methodologies.

Arrow, Kenneth, Clark C. Abt, and Stephen J. Fitzsimmons, eds. *Applied Research for Social Policy: The United States and the Federal Republic of Germany Compared.* Cambridge, MA: Abt, 1979.

A unique attempt on the part of leading German and American social scientists to exchange information, review major social science research efforts that have influenced political decision making in their countries, and define ways in which applied social research can contribute to better political decision making.

Berg, David N., and Kenwyn K. Smith, eds. *Exploring Clinical Methods for Social Research.* Beverly Hills, CA: Sage, 1985.

Brenner, M. Harvey. *Assessing the Contributions of the Social Sciences to Health.* Boulder, CO: Westview, 1980.

American Association for the Advancement of Science selected symposium.

Bulmer, Martin, and Associates. *Social Science and Social Policy.* Winchester, MA: Allen & Unwin, 1986.

Cherns, Albert. *Using the Social Sciences.* Boston: Routledge & Kegan Paul, 1979.

A collection of papers published over the last 10 years that brings together the extraordinarily wide-ranging contribution made by Albert Cherns to the study of the role of the social sciences in policy-making.

DeNeafville, Judith Innes. *Social Indicators and Public Policy.* New York: Elsevier, 1975.

Etzioni, Amatai, ed. *Policy Research.* Leiden: Brill, 1978.

Research papers and discussions of the application of the social sciences to policy.

Glaser, Edward M., Harold H. Abelson, and Kathalee N. Garrison. *Putting Knowledge to Use: Facilitating the Diffusion of Knowledge and the Implementation of Planned Change.* San Francisco: Jossey-Bass, 1983.

Draws on more than 2,000 reports, articles, case studies, and other sources to bring together a wealth of detail in one convenient volume. The authors consolidate, organize, and analyze this material to provide comprehensive, up-to-date information on how knowledge is used to bring about beneficial change. They present the most important findings from psychology, organizational behavior, sociology, economics, education, evaluation research, and other fields on ways to assess the readiness of organizations to change, overcome resistance to change, improve interpersonal and written communication, enhance collaboration between researchers and practitioners, overcome problems in transferring technology to developing countries, and assess the effects of psychological, political, and economic factors on planned change.

Hakel, Milton D., Melvin Sorcher, Michael Beer, and Joseph L. Moses. *Making It Happen: Designing Research with Implementation in Mind.* Beverly Hills, CA: Sage, 1982.

Isolates and discusses key behaviors and constraints in the design and execution of research when implementation is the explicit goal. Offers numerous ideas and exercises on how to conduct research that can make a constructive difference in organizational life.

Havelock, Ronald G., et al. *Planning for Innovation Through Dissemination and Utilization of Knowledge.* Ann Arbor: University of Michigan, Institute for Social Research, 1969.

Provides an understanding of how knowledge is disseminated and utilized. Brings together the research and theory from more than 1,000 studies on the planning of change, the diffusion of innovations, and the transfer and utilization of scientific knowledge.

Horowitz, Irving L. *Constructing Policy: Dialogues with Social Scientists in the National Political Arena.* New York: Praeger, 1979.

Perceptive, in-depth interviews with 12 leading U.S. social science policymakers present insights into the ideological and intellectual stances of such important figures as Sar Levitan, Eli Ginsberg, Seymour Martin Lipset, and Frank Reissman. Thoughtful questions and comments by Horowitz bring forth each individual's premises, principles, expertise, orientation, and role, as well as wide-ranging discussions of his or her work, experiences, and views on historical events. From these interviews, Horowitz ponders such areas of the social scientist policy-making process as expertise versus political stance, success in government, and equity versus equality.

—— and James E. Katz. *Social Science and Public Policy in the United States.* New York: Praeger, 1975.

A very worthwhile book about the interaction among social scientists, social science, public policymakers, and public policy in the United States.

Judd, Charles M., and David A. Kenny. *Estimating the Effects of Social Interventions.* New York: Cambridge University Press, 1981.

Methods for measuring the impact of social interventions of all sorts; the strengths and weaknesses of various research designs—experimental, quasi-experimental, and nonexperimental—with a systematic and critical review of statistical measures for analyzing data.

Lazarsfeld, Paul F., and Jeffrey G. Reitz. *An Introduction to Applied Sociology.* New York: Elsevier, 1975.

See especially Chapter 4, "Translating a Practical Problem into Research" (pp. 66-97).

Lewin, Arle Y., and Melvin F. Shakun. *Policy Sciences: Methodologies and Cases.* Oxford: Pergamon, 1976.

Presents a pragmatic, descriptive/normative methodology for policy analysis within which different disciplines can be integrated for policy analysis and formulation. Part 1 presents the framework within which components of policy science may be integrated and applied to real decision problems, Part 2 focuses on methodologies, and Part 3 presents a number of cases that apply methodologies to real-world problems. Designed as a text for courses in policy sciences and interorganizational decision making or for similar courses at the advanced undergraduate or graduate level, this book is also suitable as a basic reference for practicing policy scientists and policymakers.

Lewis, Michael, ed. *Research in Social Problems and Policy: A Research Annual.* Greenwich, CT: JAI, 1979, 1981.

Presents original analyses of contemporary social issues and the policy responses they elicit. This book is informed by an editorial philosophy that holds that the value of sociology must ultimately be measured by its power to provide an analytic basis for maximizing human serviceability in society. Each contribution was selected because it breaks new ground and promises to provide fresh premises for policy discourse. On the assumption that the nature of the problem to be studied should determine the method of its study, the papers appearing in this annual series will represent a variety of analytic approaches extant in contemporary society.

Locke, Edwin A., ed. *Generalizing from Laboratory to Field Settings.* Lexington, MA: Lexington, 1988.

Research findings from industrial-organizational psychology, organizational behavior, and human resource management.

Majchrzak, Ann. *Methods for Policy Research.* Beverly Hills, CA: Sage, 1984.

Misra, Girishwar, ed. *Applied Social Psychology in India.* New Delhi: Sage, 1990.

Nord, Walter R., and Sharon Tucker. *Implementing Routine and Radical Innovations.* Indianapolis: Lexington, 1987.

Much research has been done on the initiation of changes—on the decision to develop or adopt a new product, service, technological process, or organizational structure. Considerably less is known about how organizations implement innovations effectively. This important book is a major contribution to the theoretical understanding of innovation and, since its conclusions are directly applicable, it provides practical guidelines for managers.

Olsen, Marvin E., and Michael Micklin. *Handbook of Applied Sociology: Frontiers of Contemporary Research.* New York: Praeger, 1981.

This book is divided into sections on developing applied techniques, improving social institutions, reducing social inequities, providing human services, and ensuring human survival.

Price, Richard H., and Peter E. Politser. *Evaluation and Action in the Social Environment.* New York: Academic Press, 1980.

This volume begins with the presentation of a conceptual and methodological framework for doing evaluation and action research. Examples of evaluation and action strategies in a wide range of contexts are presented, including family settings, hospital settings, personal social networks, residential treatment settings, human service organizations, community groups, and architectural environments. Each chapter describes the relevant research literature, an analytical framework used to assess the setting, a rationale for translating the assessment into proposals for action, and a description of the evaluation method used to assess the impact of the change strategy. (For further information on evaluation research, see Section 3.B of this volume.)

Rothman, Jack. *Using Research in Organizations: A Guide to Successful Application.* Beverly Hills, CA: Sage, 1980.

Isolates and discusses key behaviors and constraints in the design and execution of research when implementation is the explicit goal. Offers numerous ideas and exercises on how to conduct research that can make a constructive difference in organizational life.

Saks, Michael J., and Charles H. Baron, eds. *The Use/Nonuse/Misuse of Applied Social Research in the Courts.* Cambridge, MA: Abt, 1980.

A significant step toward cooperation between the legal community and the social science community.

Scott, Robert A., and Arnold Shaw. *Why Sociology Does Not Apply: A Study of the Use of Sociology in Public Policy.* New York: Elsevier, 1979.

An analysis of problems in the application of sociology to public policy.

Segall, Marshall H. *Human Behavior and Public Policy: A Political Psychology.* Oxford: Pergamon, 1976.

Based on the conviction that existing knowledge of human behavior contains important lessons for policymakers, this book aims to demonstrate that important social and political implications are inherent in social psychological research findings. What social psychologists know, or know how to find out, is of crucial relevance to the real world. Knowledge as to why and under what conditions people behave as they do permits evaluation of social policy alternatives. Written primarily for undergraduates, the book contains illustrations of the implications of existing social psychological findings for such problems as intergroup relations, educational innovations, relations between the sexes, and the control of violence in a free society. The work contains most of what is included in a traditional social psychology course, but embeds it in a context of relevance.

Smithsonian Science Information Exchange. *Research Information Packages.* Washington, DC: Smithsonian Science Information Exchange, 1980.

The Exchange is the national registry for providing current research information in all the sciences, including sociology, political science, and economics. The *Research Information Packages* contain up-to-date knowledge about research in progress. Each package is a collection of one-page descriptions of social science projects relevant to the title. Classifications of packages include criminology, environmental social sciences management and methodology, social welfare, sociology of population, and urban sociology.

Study Project on Social Research and Development. *Assembly of Behavioral and Social Sciences.* 6 vols. (Vol. 1, *Knowledge and Policy: The Uncertain Connection*; Vol. 2, *The Funding of Social Knowledge Production and Application: A Survey of Federal Agencies*; Vol. 3, *The Uses of Basic Research: Case Studies in Social Science*; Vol. 4, *Studies in the Management of Social R&D: Selected Issues*; Vol. 5, *Case Studies in the Management of Social R&D: Selected Policy Areas*; Vol. 6, *Understanding Crime.*) Washington, DC: National Academy of Sciences, 1977-80.

All of these volumes are concerned with social science and policy relevance. They explore means of improving the linkage between social research and public policy.

Thomas, Edwin J. *Designing Interventions for the Helping Professions.* Beverly Hills, CA: Sage, 1984.

Trela, James E., and Richard O'Toole. *Roles for Sociologists in Service Organizations.* Kent, OH: Kent State University Press, 1974.

Tropman, John E., Milan Dluhy, Wayne Vasey, and Tom A. Croxton, eds. *Strategic Perspectives in Social Policy.* Oxford: Pergamon, 1976.

The development of social policy by administrators requires an assessment of goals, elements of social change, and the politics of policy-making. Emphasis is on the process of intervention in developing a policy for practical ends. Strategic points of intervention within the policy system are examined from the point of view of policymakers, policy conceptualizers, and students of government. Included are guides for both social policy and social program analyses of interest to students of public administration, policy science, social work, urban and regional planning, and political science.

Wildavsky, Aaron. *Speaking Truth to Power: The Art and Craft of Policy Analysis.* Boston: Little, Brown, 1979.

A political scientist describes policy analysis in terms of political processes and procedures.

Specialized Journal

Evaluation Review: A Journal of Applied Social Research. Editors: Richard A. Berk and Howard E. Freeman.

Published bimonthly by Sage Periodicals Press, Sage Publications, Inc., 2455 Teller Rd., Newbury Park, CA 91320. This journal, which first appeared in 1976, is devoted to all aspects of applied social research, theory, method, data collection and analysis, application, intervention, and evaluation.

Section B

Evaluation Research

3.B.1   EVALUATION RESEARCH AS A PROCESS

Every attempt to reduce or eliminate a social problem involves a theory, a program, and usually a large amount of money. The effectiveness of programs to reduce crime and delinquency, combat drug addiction, conquer health problems, and improve neighborhoods and communities and the quality of life generally—all pose problems of evaluation. Because these problems are so important to national and community life and are so costly, evaluation has been give a high priority and evaluation research is increasing.

Edward Suchman has written:

It may be helpful to visualize the evaluation process as a circular one, stemming from and returning to the formation of value, as shown in Figure 1.

Figure 1. Evaluation Process

Evaluation always starts with some value, either explicit or implicit—for example, it is good to live a long time; then a goal is formulated derived from this value. The selection of goals is usually preceded by or concurrent with *"value formation."* An example of "*goal-setting*" would be the statement that fewer people should develop coronary disease, or that not so many people should die from cancer. Goal-setting forces are always in competition with each other for money, resources, and effort.

There next has to be some way of "*measuring goal attainment.*" If we set as our goal that fewer people should die from cancer, then we need some means of discovering how many are presently dying from cancer (for example, vital statistics). The nature of the evaluation will depend largely on the type of measure we have available to determine the attainment of our objective.

The next step in the process is the identification of some kind of "goal-attaining activity." In the case of cancer, for example, a program of cancer-detection activities aimed at early detection and treatment might be considered. Then the goal-attaining activity is put into operation. Diagnostic centers are set up and people urged to come in for check-ups.

Then, at some point, we have the *assessment* of this goal-directed operation. This stage includes the evaluation of the degree to which the operating program has achieved the predetermined objectives. As stated previously, this assessment may be scientifically done or it may not.

Finally, on the basis of the assessment, a *judgment* is made as to whether the goal-directed activity was worthwhile. This brings us back to value formation. Someone now may say that it is "good" to have cancer diagnostic centers. At the end of the evaluation process, we may get a new value, or we may reaffirm, reassess, or redefine an old value. For example, if the old value was "it is good to live a long time," the new value might be, "it is good to live until 100 if you remain healthy; but if you can't remain healthy it's better not to live past eighty." [1]

Note

1. From Edward A. Suchman, *Evaluative Research, Principles and Practice in Public Service and Social Action Programs* (New York: Russell Sage Foundation, 1967). © 1967 by the Russell Sage Foundation. Reprinted by permission.

EVALUATION RESEARCH: AN ASSESSMENT   3.B.2

Peter H. Rossi and James D. Wright[1]

Evaluation research came into prominence as an applied social scientific activity during the Great Society programs of the mid-1960s. The distinctive feature of the past 25 years is the explicit recognition among policymakers and public administrators that evaluations could be conducted systematically using social scientific research methods and could produce results that had more use and validity than the judgmental approaches used previously. During the Great Society era, Congress authorized many new programs and systematic evaluations were mandated in several of the more important pieces of legislation.[2]

The new administrative agencies set up to implement many of these programs were partially staffed by social scientists who had strong interests in applied work. The entire gamut of the social scientific disciplines was involved. Economists had a strong foothold in the Office of Economic Opportunity; sociologists, psychologists, and educators were ensconced in the Office of Education (later the Department of Education); the Department of Health, Education and Welfare (now Health and Human Services) was big enough to accommodate members of all of the social scientific disciplines in critical positions; and the Department of Labor's Manpower Research Division was also generous, providing opportunities for all.

The interdisciplinary character of this new social scientific activity was especially noteworthy. Economists, sociologists, psychologists, and educational researchers often found themselves bidding on the same contracts in competition with each other, a process that facilitated the transfer of knowledge, craft lore, and mutual respect across disciplinary boundaries. Research firms and institutes previously dominated by one discipline broadened their outlooks by hiring professionals from other social sciences, mainly in order to increase their competitive edge. Interdisciplinary professional societies were also founded, e.g., the Evaluation Research Society and the Evaluation Network.[3]

University-based social scientific researchers were slow to take advantage of the new opportunities for research funding, even though the topics involved were often of central interest, a reflection of the indifference (even hostility) to applied work that has characterized the academic social science departments until very recently (Raizen & Rossi 1981, Rossi & Wright 1983, Rossi et al. 1978). Private entrepreneurs, however, were quicker to notice and exploit the new emphasis on evaluation. Some existing firms that had not been particularly interested in the social sciences opened subsidiaries that could compete for social research contracts (e.g., Westinghouse). Others greatly expanded their social science research sections (e.g., the Rand Corporation). In addition, literally hundreds of new firms appeared on the scene, a handful of which became spectacular successes during the "golden years" (e.g., Abt Associates).[4]

By the middle of the 1970s, some 500-600 private firms existed primarily to bid on contracts for applied social research. As in other areas of corporate activity, a few firms garnered the majority of the available funds. For example, in the period 1975-1980, 6 large research firms received over 60% of the evaluation funds expended by the Department of Education (Raizen & Rossi 1981).

An additional large number of firms sprang up to bid on contracts for evaluation and other applied social research activities at the state and local levels. These research opportunities were neither as well funded as those on the federal level nor were the tasks as intellectually or technically challenging. There was (and continues to be) enough evaluation "business" on the state and local levels, however, to provide the essential "bread and butter" for a very large number of small-scale job shops.

Some of the existing university-based research institutes with histories of large-scale social research also prospered during this period. The National Opinion Research Center at the University of Chicago and the Survey Research Center at the University of Michigan both grew enormously in size. Their staffs eventually came to dwarf most academic departments in the relevant fields. New academic research organizations also were started to take advantage of the funding opportunities offered through the grant and contract mechanism.

A corresponding growth took place on the conceptual side of evaluation research. The publication in 1966 of Donald T. Campbell and Julian Stanley's seminal work on research designs useful in the evaluation of educational programs created an entirely new vocabulary for the taxonomy of research designs and for the discussion of validity issues. It also made the randomized, controlled experimental paradigm the method of choice for causal analyses. Both of these emphases came to dominate large portions of the evaluation field for the next decade.

Evaluation research was initially seen as, quintessentially, the assessment of programs' net effects. Correspondingly, the main problem in designing evaluation research was to specify appropriate *ceteris paribus* conditions that would permit valid estimates of these net effects. Within this framework, the randomized, controlled experiment became the ruling paradigm for evaluation research. The conceptual foundations had been developed many decades earlier, and this approach had been the ruling research paradigm in both psychology and biology for many years. The special contribution made during the period under current review was that the paradigm was taken out of the laboratory and into the field, and it was combined with the sample survey in studies designed to test the effects of the proposed programs. To many social scientists of a technocratic bent, the randomized field experiment promised to replace our bumbling trial-and-error approaches to forging social policy with a more self-consciously rational "experimenting society" (Campbell 1969).

By the early 1970s, an impressive number of large-scale field experiments had been funded and started. These experiments covered a wide variety of topics: income maintenance plans intended to replace the existing welfare benefits system: housing allowances that might stimulate the market to produce better housing for the poor; health insurance plans that would not create perverse medical-care price effects; and so on through a veritable laundry list of field experiments. Ironically, most of them were designed and run by economists, members of a field not noted for its tradition of experimental work.

The realization quickly emerged, however, that randomized, controlled experiments could only be done correctly under very limited circumstances and that the demand for evaluation covered many programs that simply could not be assessed in this way. Not only were there frequent ethical and legal limitations to randomization, but many existing programs that had full (or almost full) coverage of their intended beneficiary populations could not be assessed using controlled experiments because there was no way to create appropriate control groups. It also turned out that field experiments took a long time—3 to 5 years or more—from design to final report, a delay that was simply intolerable given the much shorter time horizons of most policymakers and public administrators.

Campbell & Stanley (1966) had provided one possible solution to this dilemma by coining the term quasi-experiments and using it to cover evaluation research designs that do not rely on randomization to form controls. Although they explicitly recognized the inferior validity of data generated in this way, they also discussed the conditions under which valid causal inferences could be drawn from evaluation studies using such designs. Their treatment of quasi-experimental research designs certainly stimulated the use of such designs in evaluation studies, sometimes under conditions that Campbell & Stanley explicitly stated were potentially fatal. Indeed, the vast majority of the evaluations that have been carried out have been quasi-experiments, rather than randomized, "true" experiments, mainly because the latter have proven difficult, if not impossible, to implement in real world settings.

But even quasi-experimental designs have their limitations. For one thing, while not as expensive or time-consuming as "true" experiments, a well-conducted quasi-experiment may demand more funds, time and talent than are available. Another problem is that many of the more sophisticated quasi-experimental designs (in particular, interrupted time series designs) require long time series of data—ideally, series that contain a long run of observations prior to the introduction of a policy intervention and that continue for several years after that. Concerning the first, the necessary data often do not exist; and, concerning the second, the old problem of timeliness reappears. A final problem, of course—one Campbell & Stanley discussed in detail—is that there are potential threats to the validity of *any* quasi-experimental design. In using such designs, one always runs some risk of mistaking various artifacts for true program effects. Hence, quasi-experiments are almost always vulnerable to critical attack; witness the rancorous controversies surrounding some of the major educational evaluations (e.g., McLaughlin 1975, Mosteller & Moynihan 1972, Rossi & Wright 1982).

Due to the many evident problems of both experimental and quasi-experimental approaches to evaluation research, the need for methods of evaluation that were timely, relatively inexpensive, and responsive to many program administrators' and officials' fears that evaluations would somehow "do them in" quickly became apparent. This statement applies especially to evaluations that were mandated by Congress and that the program agencies themselves were supposed to conduct. Indeed, Congress—coupling its newfound enthusiasm for evaluations with a seriously flawed understanding of the time, talent and funding needed to carry out evaluations of even minimum quality—often imposed evaluation tasks on program agencies that far exceeded the agencies' research capacities and then provided funds that were grossly inadequate to accomplish them.

The need for evaluations that could be carried out by technically unsophisticated persons and that would be timely and useful to program administrators fueled a strong interest in qualitative approaches to evaluation research (Patton 1980, Scriven 1977, Guba & Lincoln 1981, House 1980). Qualitative research methods have always had some following in all of the social sciences, especially in sociology. Their special attraction in sociology is their presumed ability to stay close to reality and to promote an understanding of social processes through intimate familiarity with field conditions. In addition, for evaluation purposes, qualitative methods seemed to have the attractive triple advantages of being inexpensive, timely, and responsive to administrators' needs.

These approaches were especially attractive to program sponsors and operators because they appeared to be flexible enough to cope with social programs that, once implemented, tend to vary sharply from one locale to another not only in their goals but also in the benefits and services that are actually delivered. The goals for some broad-spectrum programs (e.g., Model Cities) were not clearly defined by Congress or the administering agencies. Each operating agency thus defined its own goals and often changed them frequently (Kaplan 1973, Williams 1980). The appeal, at least initially, of qualitative approaches to evaluation is that they apparently had the potential to be sensitive to the nuances of ill-defined and constantly evolving program goals.

The great boom in evaluation ended in 1981 when the Reagan administration began to dismantle the social programs that had been developed over the previous 20 years. The extensive manpower research program of the Department of Labor was reduced to almost nothing and there were similar (although less drastic) cuts in the Departments of Health and Human Services, Education, and Agriculture, among others. The immediate consequence was a drastic reduction in the amount of federal money available for applied social research.

Ironically, the Reagan cutbacks occurred just as more and more academic departments began to discover that there was a nonacademic market for newly minted PhDs. Openings for evaluation researchers were a large component of this market. The American Sociological Association held an extremely well-attended conference in Washington, D.C., in 1981 (Freeman et al. 1983) on the appropriate training for careers in applied sociology. Many graduate departments throughout the country began programs to train applied researchers of all kinds, and there was an evident interest among at least some prominent sociologists. Indeed, both presidents of the American Sociological Association in 1980 and 1981 devoted their presidential addresses to applied work (Rossi 1981, Whyte 1982).

The Intellectual Harvest of the Golden Years of Evaluation

The frenzied growth of evaluation research during the 1960s and 1970s produced a real increment in our knowledge about the relevant social problems and a decided increase in the technical sophistication of research in the social sciences. Both of these developments have already had some impact on the social sciences and will be increasingly valuable to our fields in the future.

The Large-Scale Field Experiments of the "Golden Age"

Perhaps the most impressive substantive and technical achievements of the entire Golden Age were those of the large-scale field experiments. Most of these experiments were initially funded by the Office of Economic Opportunity and, upon the demise of that agency, by the Department of Health, Education and Welfare.

On the technical side, these experiments combined both sample survey techniques and classical experimental designs. Experimental and control groups were created by sampling open communities and then randomly allocating sampled households to experimental and control groups. Interviews with experimental and control households were then undertaken, using traditional sample survey techniques to measure responses to the experimental treatments. Looked upon as surveys, these experiments were long-term panels with repeated measurements of the major dependent (i.e., outcome) variables. Measures were taken as often as once a month in some of the experiments and extended over periods of up to five years. Viewed as experiments, the studies were factorial ones in which important parameters of the treatments were systematically varied.

Perhaps the best-known of the field experiments during the Golden Age were those designed to test various forms of the "negative income tax" (NIT) as a means of maintaining a reasonable income floor for poor households. All told, there were five such experiments in the United States and one in Canada.

Fixing Up Nonexperimental Designs

The discussion so far has been fairly narrowly focused on randomized experimental designs for impact assessment because (a) the technically most successful impact assessments were carried out using that design and therefore (b) the randomized, controlled experimental paradigm has dominated the evaluation scene for the last two decades. As detailed above, however, there are good reasons at least to modify the experimental paradigm, chief among them being that for most social programs evaluation must perforce use nonexperimental methods.

There are many reasons why randomized experimental designs cannot be used in some evaluation studies. First, ongoing programs that cover most or all of their intended target populations simply do not admit of believable controls. For example, an estimated 5-10% of the persons eligible for Old Age and Survivors Insurance (Social Security) benefits have not applied for them. These nonapplicants cannot realistically serve as controls for estimating the effects of social security benefits, however, because the self-selection factors are undoubtedly strong. Comparing persons receiving social security benefits with those who are eligible but, for whatever reasons, have not applied for them violates the *ceteris paribus* condition.

Second, some programs, such as Head Start, fail to reach significantly large proportions of the eligible population—perhaps as much as 25% of the Head Start example. These children are not reached by the Head Start program because parents have not allowed their children to enroll or because the school systems involved have too few poor children to support Head Start projects. Clearly, strong self-selection factors are at work, and hence, contrasting Head Start participants with eligible nonparticipants would not hold constant important differences between the two groups.

Finally, it would be ethically unthinkable to use randomization in the evaluation of some programs. For example, a definitive way of estimating the relative effectiveness of private and public high schools would be to assign adolescents to one or the other randomly and observe the outcome over an extended period of time. Obviously, there is no way that either policymakers or parents would allow such an evaluation to take place.

Thus, many of the evaluation studies of the past two decades have employed something other than classical randomized experimental designs. Unfortunately, these evaluations have not been technically successful on the whole. Each of the major nonexperimental evaluations has been shrouded in controversy—controversy that arises out of the political implications of the findings but that often centers on the technical inadequacies of the designs employed. Thus, Coleman's (1966) attempt to sort out schools' effects on achievement by analyzing a cross-sectional survey of thousands of students from hundreds of high schools was criticized mainly because of the statistical models he used (Mosteller & Moynihan 1972). Similarly, an evaluation (Westinghouse Learning Corporation 1969) of the long-lasting effects of participating in Head Start came under fire (Campbell & Erlbacher 1970) because the researchers compared youngsters who had attended Head Start preschools with "comparable" children who had not. According to the study's critics, confounding self-selection factors were undoubtedly at work that made the two groups incomparable in important respects.

The problem of administrative or self-selection of program participants and nonparticipants is at the heart of nonexperimental evaluation designs' vulnerability to criticism. To illustrate this point, we can consider Coleman and his associates' (1982) recent study of academic achievement in public and private (mostly Catholic) high schools. The critical comparisons in such a study are clearly plagued by self-selection factors: whether a child attends the Catholic parochial high schools or the public high schools cannot by any stretch of the imagination be considered a random choice. Parents often make the choice alone, although they sometimes consult the child; they make their education decisions on the basis of factors such as their anticipated income, their commitment to their religious group and its ideology, their assessments of their child's intellectual capabilities, the relative reputations of the local high schools, and so on. Nor are parents and child the only forces involved. Parochial high schools exercise judgment about whom they want to admit, selecting students on the basis of factors like their previous educational experience, the kind of curriculum the child or parents want, and the child's reputation as a behavioral problem. Some of these factors are probably related to high school achievement; the extent to which these factors independently affect such achievement would confound any *simple* comparisons between the achievement scores of parochial and public high school students.

Obviously, one way out of the problem is to hold constant stati~~s~~ relating both to achievement and to school choice. The diffic~~ulties~~ however, are also obvious. First, it is necessary to specify t~~he~~ correctly, a task that is usually difficult because of the abser~~ce of~~ grounded theory to aid in that specification. Secondly, if the eleme~~nts~~ of those factors (as in this example), it *cannot* be held constant si~~nce~~ for one group but not for the other; in the present case, that is, non~~-Catholics~~ not have the option of sending their children to parochial school~~. See~~ Wright (1982) for a more detailed critique of Coleman along these l~~ines.~~

A potentially fruitful solution to this problem has recently bee~~n sugg~~ested by the econometricians (Goldberger 1980, Barnow et al. 1980, Berk & Ray 1982). They propose that researchers construct explicit models of the decision process and incorporate these models into structural equation systems as a means of holding constant the self-selection process. Although these proposals are somewhat more attractive than the usual approach of adding independent variables to a regression equation, they are still largely irrelevant because the appropriate decision models cannot be constructed except in special circumstances.

Another important development in the methodology used in nonexperimental evaluations has been the application of time series models to the assessment of the net effects of large-scale programs. [These models were originally developed in economic forecasting (Pindyck & Rubinfeld 1976) and subsequently applied specifically to evaluation problems (McCleary & Hay 1980, Cook & Campbell 1979).] First suggested by Campbell & Stanley (1966) as "interrupted time series" designs, the application of time series models has made it possible to assess the impact of new large-scale programs or the effects of modifying existing ones without recourse to classical randomized experiments. This approach is limited to programs that have long time series of data on their outcomes available and whose onset can be definitely located in time as, for example, with the enactment of new legislation.

Among the best-known interrupted time series evaluations are the various assessments of the Massachusetts Bartley-Fox gun law (G. L. Pierce & Bowers 1979, Deutsch & Alt 1977, Hay & McCleary 1979). This law imposed a mandatory penalty for carrying guns without a license, with the objective of reducing the use of guns in crimes. Using time series models, the researchers modeled the trends in gun-related crimes before the Bartley-Fox law went into effect and compared the resulting projections with the trends observed after the law was enacted. The findings suggest that the law led to only a slight reduction in the use of guns in crimes. The times series models used (Box-Jenkins models) are composed of a family of frameworks, each differing from the others in its assumptions about the kinds of time-dependent processes at work. To some degree, the choice among models is a judgment call, a condition that has led to polemical exchanges among independent researchers about the law's true effects (e.g., Hay & McCleary 1979, Deutsch 1979).

The two developments just discussed have implications for sociology that go considerably beyond evaluation research per se. The conceptualization of the self-selection problem in evaluation research has direct applications to most sociological research that relies on cross-sectional studies. The data analysis problems encountered are identical, so solutions developed in the evaluation field have immediate applications in the many sociological studies in which self-selection issues complicate the interpretation of findings.

...e series of critical data are available on many of the substantive areas of interest ...sociologists. Aggregate data on crime rates go back almost 50 years; unemployment rates have been available on a monthly basis for almost 40 years; and so on.

Research on program implementation is primarily research in public administration. Although good examples are rare, in principle it is no more difficult to test several alternative ways of delivering a program than to test several alternative programs; indeed, the two problems are formally identical. That implementation issues are often critical is widely recognized (Williams & Elmore 1976, Pressman & Wildavsky 1973, W. S. Pierce 1981), but the importance of research on the issues involved has not received the attention it deserves.

The Future of Evaluation Research: An Addendum by Delbert C. Miller

Since the above assessment of evaluation research was written by Rossi and Wright in 1984, evaluation research has suffered a decline in fiscal support. The decline began to be evident as early as 1980, in the political climate imposed by the Reagan administration. Personnel of the U.S. General Accounting Office recently reported the following:

1. Between 1980 and 1984, the number of professional staff in all agency evaluation units decreased by 22%, from about 1,500 to about 1,200. In contrast, the total number of staff in these agencies decreased by only 6% during this period.
2. Between 1980 and 1984, funds for program evaluation were reduced by 37%, compared with a 4% increase for the agencies as a whole.
3. Information loss and distortion of findings were reported as the result of lack in assessment. These failures were shown to be most serious in the areas of defense, the environment, and labor and personnel (Chelimsky et al. 1989).

The future of evaluation research, in spite of recent declines, is promising:

Reducing the federal deficit and promoting public confidence in the federal government are two top concerns the incoming Congress and administration must face. Crucial to both is the availability of timely, technically sound information for *legislative oversight,* for *program management,* and for *public awareness.* Information for the first audience—Congress—answers questions about how money is being spent and managed, and what results have been achieved. Information for the second audience—program managers—answers questions about what needs to be done to comply with the law and to achieve greatest effectiveness and efficiency of operations. Information for the third audience—the public—answers questions about what it is getting for its money.

Program evaluation is an essential tool in providing information to all three audiences. (Chelimsky et al. 1989, p. 25)

These needs will not go away. If anything, as old social demands increase in severity and new social needs arise, and as budgets rise by the multibillions of dollars, evaluation research becomes ever more important to Congress, to program managers, and to the public. And the need for evaluation is not limited to the federal government; it is equally important for state and city governments.

Evaluation appears to have become part of the tools of government. Private research agencies will continue to receive important contracts for program assessment. Therefore, there will probably be a continuing need for personnel well trained in the social sciences to staff the research projects that will be undertaken, and sociologists may continue to find employment in evaluation research.

The accompanying list of the literature cited by Rossi and Wright is an outstanding compilation of both evaluation methodology and evaluation studies of social programs. An additional bibliography follows, but the reader should be warned that a complete bibliography is not feasible because of space constraints. The reader must select those writings that come closest to his or her own personal needs.

Notes

1. From Peter H. Rossi and James D. Wright, "Evaluation Research: An Assessment," in *Annual Review of Sociology*, vol. 10, ed. Ralph H. Turner and James F. Short, Jr. (Palo Alto, CA: Annual Reviews, 1984), 332-52. Reprinted by permission.

2. Especially important were the evaluations mandated in the 1964 Elementary and Secondary School Education Act (McLaughlin 1975), in the Housing and Urban Development budget authorization of 1970 calling for the experimental evaluation of a proposed housing allowance program (Struyck & Bendick 1981), and in the enabling legislation for the Department of Labor's Comprehensive Employment Training Program (Rossi et al. 1980). Evaluation research is found today in all major fields of social intervention, including health, mental health, criminal justice, housing, and handicapped children and their families. The Department of Defense has used evaluation research increasingly.

3. A tabulation of the primary disciplines of the members of the Evaluation Research Society (Evaluation Research Society 1979) nicely illustrates the interdisciplinary character of the evaluation research field. Herewith, the breakdown of membership by field: psychology 47%; sociology 10%; economics 4%; political science 6%; education 15%; and other 18%.

4. Some of the spectacular successes of those prosperous times, of course, have been greatly diminished by the reverses of today's harder times. At its height, Abt Associates employed more PhDs in the social sciences than any one of the Boston area universities and more than most combinations of universities. In the past few years, its PhD workforce has been reduced by almost 50%.

Literature Cited

American Institutes for Research. 1977. *Evaluation of the Impact of the EASA Title 7 Spanish/English Bilingual Education Program.* Vols. 1-3, Palo Alto, CA: Am. Inst. Res.
American Institutes for Research. 1980. *The National Evaluation of the PUSH for Excellence Project.* Washington, DC: Am. Inst. Res.
Barnow, B. S., Cain, G. G., Goldberger, A. S. 1980. Issues in the analysis of selectivity bias. In *Evaluation Studies Review Annual*, vol. 5, ed. E. W. Stormsdorfer, G. Farkas, 43-59. Beverly Hills, CA: Sage.
Bawden, D. L., Harrar, W. S., eds. 1978. *Rural Income Maintenance Experiment: Final Report.* 6 vols. Madison, WI: Inst. Res. Poverty.
Berk, R. A., Ray, S. C. 1982. Selection biases in sociological data. *Soc. Sci. Res.* 11(4): 352-98.
Bernstein, I., Freeman, H. 1975. *Academic and Entrepreneurial Research.* New York: Russell Sage Found.
Bradbury, K., Downs, A., eds. 1981. *Do Housing Allowances Work?* Washington, DC: Brookings Inst.
Campbell, D. T., Erlebacher, A. 1970. How regression artifacts in quasi-experiments can mistakenly make compensatory education look harmful. In *The Disadvantaged Child.* ed. J. Helmuth, 185-210. New York: Brunner-Mazel.
Campbell, D. T., Stanley, J. C. 1966. *Experimental and Quasi-Experimental Designs for Research.* Skokie, IL: Rand McNally.
Chelimsky, E. C., Cordray, D., Datta, L. 1989. Federal evaluation: The pendulum has swung too far. *Eval. Practice* 10(2):24-28.
Chen, H., Rossi, P. H. 1983. Evaluating with sense: The theory driven approach. *Eval. Rev.* 7(3):283-302.
Coleman, J. C. 1966. *Equality of Educational Opportunity.* Washington, DC: USGPO.
Coleman, J. C., Hoffer, T., Kilgore, S. 1982. *High School Achievement: Public, Catholic and Private Schools Compared.* New York: Basic.
Cook, T. D., Campbell, D. T. 1979. *Quasi-Experimentation: Design and Analysis Issues for Field Settings.* Chicago: Rand McNally.

Cronbach, L. J. 1982. *Designing Evaluations of Educational and Social Programs.* San Francisco: Jossey-Bass.

Cronbach, L. J., Ambron, S. R., Dornbusch, S. M., Hess, R. D., Hornik, R. C., Phillips, D. C. 1980 *Toward Reform of Program Evaluation.* San Francisco: Jossey-Bass.

Davidson, W. S., et al. 1981. *Evaluation Strategies in Criminal Justice.* New York: Pergamon.

Deutsch, S. J. 1979. Lies, damned lies and statistics: A rejoinder to the comment by Hay and McCleary. *Eval. Q.* 3(2):315-28.

Deutsch, S. J., Alt, F. B. 1977. The effect of Massachusetts' gun control law on gun-related crimes in the city of Boston. *Eval Q.* 1(3):543-67

Deutscher, I. 1977. Toward avoiding the goal trap in evaluation research. In *Readings in Evaluation Research.* ed. F. G. Caro, 108-23. New York: Russell Sage Found.

Evaluation Research Society. 1979. *Membership Directory.* Columbus, OH: Eval. Res. Soc.

Fairweather, G. W., Tornatzky, L. G. 1977. *Experimental Methods for Social Policy Research.* New York: Pergamon.

Freeman, H., Dynes, R., Rossi, P. H., Whyte, W. F., eds. 1982. *Applied Sociology.* San Francisco: Jossey-Bass.

Friedman, J., Weinberg, D., eds. 1983. *The Great Housing Experiment.* Beverly Hills, CA: Sage.

Friesema, H. P., Caporaso, J., Goldstein, G., Lineberry, R., McCleary, R. 1979. *Aftermath.* Beverly Hills, CA: Sage.

Goldberger, A. S. 1980. Linear regression after selection. *J. Economet.* 15(12):357-66.

Gramlich, E. M., Koshel, P. P. 1975. *Educational Performance Contracting: An Evaluation of an Experiment.* Washington, DC: Brookings Inst.

Guba, E. G., Lincoln, Y. S. 1981. *Effective Evaluation.* San Francisco: Jossey-Bass.

Hamilton, W. L. 1979. *A Social Experiment in Program Administration: The Housing Allowance Administrative Agency Experiment.* Cambridge, MA: Abt.

Hay, R., Jr., McCleary, R. 1979. Box-Tiao time series models for impact assessment: A comment on the recent work of Deutsch and Alt. *Eval. Q.* 3(2):277-314.

House, E. 1980. *Evaluating with Validity.* Beverly Hills, CA: Sage.

Kaplan, M. 1973. *Urban Planning in the 1960's: A Design for Irrelevancy.* New York: Praeger.

Kelling, G. L., Pate, T., Dieckman, D., Brown, C. E. 1974. *The Kansas City Preventive Patrol Experiment: A Technical Report.* Washington, DC: Police Found.

Kershaw, D., Fair, J. 1975. *The New Jersey-Pennsylvania Income Maintenance Experiment.* Vol. 1. New York: Academic Press.

Manderscheid, R. W., Greenwald, M. 1983. Trends in employment of sociologists. In *Applied Sociology,* ed. H. E. Freeman, R. R. Dynes, P. H. Rossi, W. F. Whyte, 51-63. San Francisco: Jossey-Bass.

Manpower Demonstration Research Corporation Board of Directors. 1980. *Summary and Findings of the National Supported Work Demonstration.* Cambridge, MA: Ballinger.

McCleary, R., Hay, R. A., Jr. 1980. *Applied Time Series Analysis.* Beverly Hills, CA: Sage.

McLaughlin, M. W. 1975. *Evaluation and Reform: The Elementary and Secondary Education Act of 1965.* Cambridge, MA: Ballinger.

Moffitt, R. A. 1979. The labor supply response in the Gary experiment. *J. Hum. Resour.* 14(4):477-87.

Mosteller, F., Moynihan, D. P., eds. 1972. *On Equality of Educational Opportunity.* New York: Vintage.

Nathan, R., Cook, R. F., Rawlins, V. L. 1981. *Public Service Employment: A Field Evaluation.* Washington, DC: Brookings Inst.

Newhouse, J. P., Rolph, J. E., Mori, B., Murphy, M. 1980. The effects of deductibles on the demand for medical care services. *J. Am. Stat. Asso.* 75(371):525-33.

Patton, M. 1980. *Qualitative Evaluation Methods.* Beverly Hills, CA: Sage.

Pierce, G. L., Bowers, W. J. 1979. *The Impact of the Bartley-Fox Gun Law on Crime in Massachusetts.* Boston: Cent. Appl. Soc. Res., Northeastern Univ.

Pierce, W. S. 1981. *Bureaucratic Failure and Public Expenditures.* New York: Academic.

Pindyck, R. S., Rubinfeld, D. L. 1976. *Econometric Models and Economic Forecasts.* New York: McGraw-Hill.

Pressman, J., Wildavsky, A. 1973. *Implementation.* Berkeley: Univ. Calif. Press.

Raizen, S., Rossi, P. H. 1981. *Program Evaluation in Education.* Washington, DC: Nat. Acad. Sci.-Nat. Res. Counc.

Robins, P. K., Spiegelman, R. G., Weiner, S., Bell, J. G., eds. 1980. *A Guaranteed Annual Income: Evidence from a Social Experiment.* New York: Academic.

Rossi, P. H. 1978. Issues in the evaluation of human services delivery. *Eval. Q.* 2(3):573-99.

Rossi, P. H. 1981. Presidential address: The challenge and opportunities of applied social research. *Am. Sociol. Rev.* 45(6):889-904.

Rossi, P. H. 1983. Pussycats, Weasels, or Percherons? Current Prospects for the Social Sciences Under the Reagan Regime. *Eval. News* 40(1):12-27.

Rossi, P. H., Berk, R. A., Lenihan, K. 1980. *Money, Work and Crime.* New York: Academic.

Rossi, P. H., Berk, R. A., Lenihan, K. 1983. Saying it wrong with figures. *Am. J. Sociol.* 88(2):390-93.

Rossi, P. H., Freeman, H. E. 1982. *Evaluation: A Systematic Approach.* 2nd ed. Beverly Hills, CA: Sage.

Rossi, P. H., Lyall, K. 1974. *Reforming Public Welfare.* New York: Russell Sage Found.

Rossi, P. H., Wright, J. D. 1982. Best schools—Better discipline or better students? *Am. J. Educ.* 91 (1):79-89.

Rossi, P. H., Wright, J. D. 1983. Applied social science. *Contemp. Sociol.* 12(2):148-51.

Rossi, P. H., Wright J. D., Wright, S. R. 1978. The theory and practice of applied social research. *Eval. Q.* 2(2):171-91.

Scriven, M. 1977. *Evaluation Thesaurus.* 3rd ed. Inverness, CA: Edgepress.

Struyk, R. J., Bendick, M., Jr. 1981. *Housing Vouchers for the Poor.* Washington, DC: Urb. Inst.

Tornatzky, L., Fergus, E., Avellar, J., Fairweather, G., Fleischer, M. 1980. *Innovation and Social Process: A National Experiment in Implementing Social Technology.* New York: Pergamon.

Watts, H. W., Rees, A. 1976. *The New Jersey Income-Maintenance Experiment.* Vols. 2, 3. New York: Academic.

Watts, H. W., Skidmore, F. 1981. A critical review of the program as social experiment. In Bradbury & Downs 1981, pp. 33-65.

Weiss, R., Rein, M. 1970. The evaluation of broad-aimed programs: Experimental design, its difficulties, and an alternative. *Admin. Sci. Q.* 15(1):97-109.

Westinghouse Learning Corporation. 1969. *The Impact of Head Start.* Athens, OH: Westinghouse Learn. Corp. & Ohio Univ.

Whyte, W. F. 1982. Presidential address: Social questions of resolving human problems. *Am. Sociol. Rev.* 47(1):1-13.

Williams, W. 1980. *Government by Agency: Lessons from the Social Program Grants-in-Aid Experience.* New York: Academic.

Williams, W., Elmore, R. F. 1976. *Social Program Implementation.* New York: Academic.

Williams, W., Elmore, R., Hall, J., Jung, R., Kirst, M., Machmanus, S. 1982. *Studying Implementation: Methodological and Substantive Issues.* New York: Chatham.

Wright, J. D., Rossi, P. H., Wright, S. R., Weber-Burdin, E. 1979. *After the Clean-Up: Long Range Effects of Natural Disasters.* Beverly Hills, CA: Sage.

Zeisel, H. 1983. Evaluation of an experiment. *Am. J. Sociol.* 88(2):378-89.

SELECTED REFERENCES TO EVALUATION RESEARCH   3.B.3

Evaluation: How to Do It

Sage Publications has made a very active publication effort in the field of evaluation, with coverage of theory, method, and utilization. Sage has three major programs addressed to researchers who wish to learn how to do evaluation research:

- The *Program Evaluation Kit* (described below)
- *An Evaluation Primer* and accompanying *Workbooks*
- The Sage Research Progress Series in Evaluation (addresses specific problems in evaluation)

The student or researcher interested in operational aspects of evaluation research should first examine these, and then continue with the readings listed in this section for other selected examples of evaluation research focused on specific problems. The "general references" are directed to the student who seeks a fuller understanding of theory, method, and research advances. Interest in evaluation research is exploding, both in scope and in publication.

Program Evaluation Kit: Series Editor, Joan L. Herman

This kit, first published in 1978, has now been released in a second edition.[1] It purports to provide every technique necessary to evaluate any program.

- Volume 1: *Evaluator's Handbook*, Joan L. Herman, Lynn Lyons Morris, and Carol Taylor Fitz-Gibbon
- Volume 2: *How to Focus on Evaluation*, Brian M. Stecher and W. Alan Davis
- Volume 3: *How to Design a Program Evaluation*, Carol Taylor Fitz-Gibbon and Lynn Lyons Morris
- Volume 4: *How to Use Qualitative Methods in Evaluation*, Michael Quinn Patton
- Volume 5: *How to Assess Program Implementation*, Jean A. King, Lynn Lyons Morris, and Carol Taylor Fitz-Gibbon
- Volume 6: *How to Measure Attitudes*, Marlene E. Henerson, Lynn Lyons Morris, and Carol Taylor Fitz-Gibbon
- Volume 7: *How to Measure Performance and Use Tests*, Lynn Lyons Morris, Carol Taylor Fitz-Gibbon, and Elaine Lindheim
- Volume 8: *How to Analyze Data*, Carol Taylor Fitz-Gibbon and Lynn Lyons Morris
- Volume 9: *How to Communicate Evaluation Findings*, Lynn Lyons Morris, Carol Taylor Fitz-Gibbon, and Marie E. Freeman

An Evaluation Primer and Workbooks

An Evaluation Primer takes the reader—student, human services practitioner, or program administrator—step by step through the process of designing, implementing, and reporting an evaluation. The primer is supplemented by two workbooks—*Practical Exercises for Health Professionals* and *Practical Exercises for Educators*—that make the set ideal for use both as a classroom text and as a self-teaching tool for the evaluator of small-scale community programs. The primer and the workbook that is right for your needs as a health professional or as an educator will provide an invaluable resource to demystify the evaluation process, focusing on these crucial steps:

- formulating credible evaluation questions
- constructing evaluation designs
- planning and collecting evaluation information
- planning and conducting information analysis activities
- reporting evaluation information
- managing an evaluation

An Evaluation Primer. Arlene Fink and Jacqueline Kosecoff (Forewords by Charles E. Lewis and Wilson Riles), 1980.
An Evaluation Primer Workbook: Practical Exercises for Educators. Arlene Fink and Jacqueline Kosecoff, 1980.
An Evaluation Primer Workbook: Practical Exercises for Health Professionals. Arlene Fink and Jacqueline Kosecoff, 1980.

Sage Research Progress Series in Evaluation

Utilizing Evaluation: Concepts and Measurement Techniques. Edited by James A. Ciarlo, Mental Health
  Systems, Evaluation Project, and Department of Psychology, University of Denver, 1981.
Qualitative and Quantitative Methods in Evaluation Research. Edited by Thomas D. Cook, Northwestern
  University, and Charles S. Reichardt, University of Denver, 1979.
Evaluator Intervention Pros and Cons. Edited by Robert Perloff, Graduate School of Business, University
  of Pittsburgh, 1979.
Translating Evaluation into Policy. Edited by Robert F. Rich, Woodrow Wilson School of Public and
  International Affairs, Princeton University, 1979.
Evaluating Victim Services. Edited by Susan E. Salasin, Chief, Research Diffusion and Utilization Section,
  Mental Health Services Development Branch, National Institute of Mental Health, 1981.
The Evaluation of Management. Edited by Herbert C. Schulberg and Jeanette M. Jerrell, both at Western
  Psychiatric Institute and Clinic, University of Pittsburgh School of Medicine, 1979.
Methods for Evaluating Health Services. Edited by Paul M. Wortman, School of Public Health, University
  of Michigan, 1981.
Evaluation in Legislation. Edited by Franklin M. Zweig, Committee on Human Resources, U.S. Senate
  (Foreword by Senator Harrison A. Williams, Jr.), 1979.
Educating Policymakers for Evaluation: Legislation. Edited by Franklin M. Zweig, Director, Center for
  Public Services, University of Rhode Island, and Keith E. Marvin, Associate Director, Institute for
  Program Evaluation, U.S. General Accounting Office, 1981.

Selected Examples of Evaluation Research

Abt, Clark C., ed. *The Evaluation of Social Programs.* Beverly Hills, CA: Sage, 1977.
Abt, Wendy Peter, and Magidson, Jay. *Reforming Schools: Problems in Program Implementation and
  Evaluation.* Beverly Hills, CA: Sage, 1980.
Alkin, Marvin, C. Daillak, and Peter White. *Using Evaluations: Does Evaluation Make a Difference?*
  Beverly Hills, CA: Sage, 1979.
Argyris, Chris. *Diagnosing Human Relations in Organizations: A Case Study of a Hospital.* New Haven,
  CT: Yale University Press, 1956.
Braskamp, Larry A., Dale C. Brandenburg, & John C. Ory. *Evaluating Teaching Effectiveness: A Practical
  Guide.* Beverly Hills, CA: Sage, 1984.
Comrey, A. L., J. M. Pfifner, and H. P. Beem. *Studies in Organizational Effectiveness I.* Los Angeles: U.S.
  Forest Survey, University of California, 1951.
Filsinger, Erik E., and Robert A. Lewis. *Assessing Marriage: New Behavioral Approaches.* Beverly Hills,
  CA: Sage, 1981.
Finsterbusch, Kurt, *Understanding Social Impacts: Assessing the Effects of Public Projects.* Beverly Hills,
  CA: Sage, 1980.
Guba, Egon G., and Yvonna S. Lincoln. *Fourth-Generation Evaluation.* Newbury Park, CA: Sage, 1989.
Hamilton, William L. *A Social Experiment in Program Administration: The Housing Allowance Adminis-
  trative Agency Experiment.* Cambridge, MA: Abt, 1979.
Johnston, Jerome, ed. *Evaluating the New Information Technologies.* San Francisco: Jossey-Bass, 1984.
Katz, Daniel, Barbara A. Gutek, Robert L. Kahn, and Eugenia Barton. *Bureaucratic Encounters: A Pilot
  Study in the Evaluation of Government Services.* Ann Arbor: University of Michigan, Institute for
  Social Research, 1975.
Katzer, Jeffrey, Kenneth H. Cook, and Wayne W. Crouch. *Evaluating Information: A Guide to Users of
  Social Science Research.* Reading, MA: Addison-Wesley, 1979.
Lipton, Douglas, Robert Martinson, and Judith Wilks. *The Effectiveness of Correctional Treatment: A
  Survey of Evaluation Treatment Studies.* 2 vols. New York: Praeger, 1975.
Meyer, Henry J., and Edgar F. Borgatta. *An Experiment in Mental Patient Rehabilitation.* New York: Russell
  Sage Foundation, 1959.
Price, Richard, and Peter Politser, eds. *Evaluation and Action in the Social Environment.* New York:
  Academic Press, 1980.
Price, Richard H., and Sallie S. Smith. *A Guide to Evaluating Prevention Programs in Mental Health.*
  Washington, DC: Government Printing Office, 1985.

Robins, Philip K., Robert G. Spiegelman, and Samuel Weiner, eds. *A Guaranteed Annual Income: Evidence from a Social Experiment.* New York: Academic Press, 1980.

Rothman, Jack. *Using Research in Organizations: A Guide to Successful Application.* Beverly Hills, CA: Sage, 1980.

Rutman, Leonard, ed. *Evaluation Research Methods: A Basic Guide.* 2nd ed. Beverly Hills, CA: Sage, 1984.

Sarri, Rosemary C., and R. John Lawrence, eds. *Issues in the Evaluation of Social Welfare Programs.* Sydney: New South Wales University Press, 1980.

Salmen, Lawrence F. *Listen to the People: Participant-Observer Evaluation of Development Projects.* Washington, DC: World Bank, 1987.

Schierer, Mary Ann. *Program Implementation: The Organizational Context.* Beverly Hills, CA: Sage, 1981.

Shadish, William R., Thomas D. Cook, and Laura C. Leviton. *Foundations of Program Evaluation: Theories of Practice.* Newbury Park, CA: Sage, 1990.

Spiro, Shimon E., and Ephraim Yuchtman-Yaar. *Evaluating the Welfare State, Social and Political Perspectives.* New York: Academic Press, 1983.

Stern, Paul C. *Evaluating Social Science Research.* New York: Oxford University Press, 1979.

Williams, Walter, and Richard R. Elmore, eds. *Social Programs Implementation.* New York: Academic Press, 1976.

Wilner, Daniel M., Rosabelle P. Walkley, Thomas C. Pinkerton, and Matthew Tayback. *The Housing Environment and Family Life.* Baltimore: Johns Hopkins University Press, 1962.

Wortman, Paul, ed. *Methods for Evaluating Health Services.* Beverly Hills, CA: Sage, 1981.

Wright, James D., Peter H. Rossi, and Sonia R. Wright. *After the Clean-Up: Long-Range Effects of Natural Disaster.* Beverly Hills, CA: Sage, 1979.

Zusman, Jack. *Program Evaluation: Alcohol, Drug Abuse, and Mental Health Services.* Lexington, MA: Lexington, 1975.

General References to Evaluation Research

Abert, James G., and Murray Kamrass, eds. *Social Experiments and Social Program Evaluation.* Cambridge, MA: Ballinger, 1974.

Alkin, Marvin C. *A Guide for Evaluation Decision Makers.* Beverly Hills, CA: Sage, 1985.

——— and Lewis C. Solomon. *The Costs of Evaluation.* Beverly Hills, CA: Sage, 1983.

Bernstein, Ilene N., and Howard E. Freeman. *Academic and Entrepreneurial Research: The Consequences of Diversity in Federal Evaluation Studies.* New York: Russell Sage Foundation, 1975.

    Provides data about "high"- and "low"-quality evaluation research and contains recommendations for restructuring the entire evaluation research enterprise.

Bernstein, Ilene N., ed. *Validity Issues in Evaluative Research.* Beverly Hills, CA: Sage, 1975.

Burstein, Leigh, Howard E. Freeman, and Peter H. Rossi. *Collecting Evaluation Data: Problems and Solutions.* Beverly Hills, CA: Sage, 1985.

Ciarlo, James A., ed. *Utilizing Evaluation: Concepts and Measurement Techniques.* Beverly Hills, CA: Sage, 1981.

Cook, Thomas D., and Charles S. Reichardt. *Qualitative and Quantitative Methods in Evaluation Research.* Beverly Hills, CA: Sage, 1979.

Conner, Ross F., ed. *Methodological Advances in Evaluation Research.* Beverly Hills, CA: Sage, 1981.

Dolbeare, Kenneth M., ed. *Public Policy Evaluation.* Beverly Hills, CA: Sage, 1975.

    See especially Chapter 1 by James S. Coleman, "Problems of Studying Policy Impacts."

Epstein, Irwin, and Tony Tripodi. *Research Techniques for Program Planning, Monitoring, and Evaluation.* New York: Columbia University Press, 1977.

Fitz, Gordon F., and Jack McKillip. *Decision Analysis for Program Evaluators.* Beverly Hills, CA: Sage, 1984.

Franklin, Jack L., and Jean H. Thrasher. *Introduction to Program Evaluation.* New York: Wiley-Interscience, 1976.

Guba, Egon G., and Yvonna S. Lincoln. *Effective Evaluation.* San Francisco: Jossey-Bass, 1983.

Guttentag, Marcia, and Elmer L. Struening, eds. *Handbook of Evaluation Research.* 2 vols. Beverly Hills, CA: Sage, 1975.

Helpman, Elhanan, Assaf Razin, and Efraim Sadka. *Social Policy Evaluation: An Economic Perspective.* New York: Academic Press, 1983.

House, Ernest R. *Evaluating with Validity.* Beverly Hills, CA: Sage, 1983.

Levin, Henry M. *Cost-Effectiveness: A Primer.* Beverly Hills, CA: Sage, 1983.

Levine, Robert A., Marian A. Solomon, Gerd-Michael Hellstern, and Helmut Wallman. *Evaluation Research and Practice: Comparative and International Perspective.* Beverly Hills, CA: Sage, 1980.

Livingstone, John Leslie, and Sanford C. Gunn. *Accounting for Social Goals: Budgeting and Analysis of Non-Market Projects.* New York: Harper & Row, 1974.

Moos, Rudolf H. *Evaluating Treatment Environments: A Social Ecological Approach.* New York: Wiley-Interscience, 1974.

Compares and evaluates treatment milieus in hospital-based and community-based programs.

Morehouse, Thomas A. *The Problem of Measuring the Impacts of Social-Action Programs.* Fairbanks, AK: Institute of Social Economic and Government Research, 1972.

Moursund, Janet. *Evaluation: An Introduction to Research Design.* Monterey, CA: Brooks/Cole, 1973.

National Research Council. *Policy and Program Research in a University Setting: A Case Study Report.* Washington, DC: National Academy of Sciences, 1971.

Nachmias, David, ed. *The Practice of Policy Evaluation.* New York: St. Martin's, 1980.

Patton, Michael Quinn. *Qualitative Evaluation and Research Methods.* 2nd ed. Newbury Park, CA: Sage, 1990.

Patton, Michael Quinn. *Utilization-Focused Evaluation.* 2nd ed. Beverly Hills, CA: Sage, 1986.

Posavac, Emil J., and Raymond G. Carey. *Program Evaluation: Methods and Case Studies.* 2nd ed. Englewood Cliffs, NJ: Prentice-Hall, 1985.

Riecken, Henry W., and Robert F. Boruch. *Social Experimentation: A Method for Planning and Evaluating Social Intervention.* New York: Academic Press, 1974.

Rivlin, Alice M. *Systematic Thinking for Social Action.* Washington, DC: Brookings Institution, 1971.

Roesch, Ronald, and Raymond H. Corrado. *Evaluation and Criminal Justice Policy.* Beverly Hills, CA: Sage, 1981.

Rossi, Peter H., and Howard E. Freeman *Evaluation: A Systematic Approach.* 4th ed. Newbury Park, CA: Sage, 1989.

Rutman, Leonard. *Evaluation Research Methods: A Basic Guide.* 2nd ed. Beverly Hills, CA: Sage, 1984.

——— and M. Mowbray. *Understanding Program Evaluation.* Beverly Hills, CA: Sage, 1983.

Schierer, Mary Ann. *Program Implementation: The Organizational Context.* Beverly Hills, CA: Sage, 1981.

Seidman, Edward., ed. *Handbook of Social Intervention.* Beverly Hills, CA: Sage, 1983.

Smith, Nick L., ed. *New Techniques for Evaluation.* Beverly Hills, CA: Sage, 1981.

———. *Communication Strategies in Evaluation.* Beverly Hills, CA: Sage, 1982.

Struening, Elmer L., and Marilyn B. Brewer, eds. *The University Edition of the Handbook of Evaluation Research.* Beverly Hills, CA: Sage, 1983.

Symposium Proceedings at Fordham University. *Evaluation of Social Intervention.* San Francisco: Jossey-Bass, 1972.

The most comprehensive survey available for the entire evaluation process. A panel of 50 expert consultants offers guidance on program types and content, strategies and methods of evaluation, reviews of relevant literature, data aggregation across program parameters, determination of program effects, obstacles, and errors.

Thompson, Mark S. *Benefit-Cost Analysis for Program Evaluation.* Beverly Hills, CA: Sage, 1980.

Trochim, W. M. K. *Research Design for Program Evaluation.* Beverly Hills, CA: Sage, 1984.

Weiss, Carol H. *Evaluation Research: Methods for Assessing Program Effectiveness.* Englewood Cliffs, NJ: Prentice-Hall, 1972.

———, comp. *Evaluating Action Programs: Readings in Social Action and Education.* Boston: Allyn & Bacon, 1972.

Williams, Walter. *The Capacity of Social Science Organizations to Perform Large Scale Evaluative Research.* Seattle: Institute of Governmental Research, 1971.

———. *Social Policy Research and Analysis: The Experience in the Federal Agencies.* New York: Elsevier, 1971.

The Exploding Research Frontier of Evaluation: For the Researcher Who Tries to Keep Up with Contemporary Developments

Evaluation Studies Review Annuals, published by Sage Publications, have traced the dramatic growth in the concerns of the evaluation specialist from the beginning to the issues of today: integration rather than production of data, the validity of data aggregations, and the utilization of evaluation research in policy decisions. The ground-breaking articles contained in these volumes are prepared by the interdisciplinary editorial board drawn from universities, government agencies, and independent research firms. In addition to studies on evaluation method and theory, articles are included on evaluation research in the fields of education, mental health and public health services, welfare and social services, and criminal justice.

- Volume 1: edited by Gene V Glass (1976, 704 pages)
- Volume 2: edited by Marcia Guttentag with Shalom Saar (1977)
- Volume 3: edited by Thomas D. Cook and Associates (1978, 783 pages)
- Volume 4: edited by Lee Sechrest and Associates (1979, 768 pages)
- Volume 5: edited by Ernst W. Stromsdorfer and George Farkas (1980, 800 pages)
- Volume 6: edited by Howard E. Freeman and Marian A. Solomon (1981, 769 pages)

Drawing on the rich and varied literature on evaluation that appeared in 1980, the editors of Volume 6 present a book that focuses on the emerging issues of the decade: the increasing concerns with pre- and postevaluation process (with evaluability assessment or exploratory evaluations on the one hand and utilization on the other); the challenges (and uncertainties) evaluators will face in an era of budgetary restraint; the attempts to bring evaluation efforts closer to operational activities and policy decision making through a greater emphasis on implementation and via growing sophistication in both the procurement and monitoring of evaluation research. These concerns are illustrated in the areas of education, human resources, social services, law, public safety, health, mental health, and substance abuse. The following volumes described the emergent issues:

- Volume 7: edited by Ernest R. House and Associates (1982, 752 pages)
- Volume 8: edited by Richard J. Light (1983, 672 pages)
- Volume 9: edited by R. Conner, D. G. Altman, and C. Jackson (1984, 752 pages)
- Volume 10: edited by Linda H. Aiken and Barbara H. Kehrer (1985, 650 pages)
- Volume 11: edited by David S. Cordray and Mark W. Lipsey (1986, 1987, 757 pages)
- Volume 12: edited by William R. Shadish, Jr., and Charles S. Reichardt (1988, 704 pages)

Specialized Evaluation Journals

Evaluation & the Health Professions. Editor: R. Barker Bausell, University of Maryland.
Evaluation Review: A Journal of Applied Social Research. Editors: Richard A. Berk, Howard E. Freeman, both at University of California, Los Angeles.

Both of these journals are published by Sage Periodicals Press, Sage Publications, Inc.

Note

1. All nine volumes of the *Program Evaluation Kit* were published as a second edition in 1988 by Sage Publications. For further information on these books or any of the other evaluation materials published by Sage, write to Sage Publications, Inc., 2455 Teller Rd., Newbury Park, CA 91320.

Section C

Organizational Effectiveness

EFFECTIVENESS INDICES AS EVALUATION RESEARCH CRITERIA   **3.C.1**

Effectiveness may be defined as the degree to which a social system achieves its goals. For example, a drug addiction center that has a therapeutic goal that successfully reduces addiction in a high proportion of its treatment population would be considered an effective center.

Effectiveness must be distinguished from efficiency. Efficiency is mainly concerned with cost relative to output. Effectiveness is directly concerned with goal attainments. The social researcher may be asked to make a cost-benefit analysis, but such a request would be supplementary to any effectiveness assessment.

Evaluation of organizational effectiveness is a task best performed by sociological or social psychological researchers. Economists are best prepared to provide cost-benefit analyses.

The organization goals most commonly set by their leaders are high productivity and employee will to work. How these goals are translated within different organizations varies greatly. Organizations functioning in the market sector must achieve a level of productivity sufficient to maintain profitability. Those private and public organizations that dispense services must maintain a level of efficiency that continues to attract funds from their contributors (donors or taxpayers). In all cases the quality of the good or service must satisfy the needs of the consumer.

A general appraisal of an organization is based on some concept of the interaction of employees with the organization. The most commonly accepted assumption is that effective teamwork is related to productivity and morale and that both goals should be appraised. Two superior efforts are represented in Rensis Likert's *The Human Organization* and E. Wight Bakke's *Bonds of Organization.*[1]

Likert describes many years of research conducted at the Institute for Social Research of the University of Michigan on the effect on performance of four kinds of management systems. He calls these (a) exploitive-authoritative, (b) benevolent-authoritative, (c) consultative, and (d) participative group. Each involves a particular cluster of motivating and decision-making beliefs and behaviors. Likert demonstrates that as management moves from the first kind of system to the last, higher productivity, lower costs, more favorable attitudes, and excellent labor relations result.

Bakke, in his appraisal of effective teamwork, assesses the adequacy of five elements that he regards as most important in achieving high productivity and will to work: *functional specifications*, which weld people together as partners in productions; *the status system*, which designates them as directors and directed employees; *the communication system*, which divides them into givers and receivers of information; *the reward and penalty system*, which designates them as agents of reward and penalty; and *the organization charter*, which conceives of organization members as sharers of a conception of the organization as a whole.

The researcher seeking general criteria for assessment of organizational effectiveness will find yardsticks in both these books that may be applied to almost any organization, private or public. Likert's Profile of Organizational Characteristics is reproduced in Section 3.C.2. It is a well-tested set of rating scales that may be applied to probe the motivating facets of relevant organizational variables. Productivity measures themselves must usually be devised by operating officials in the given organization. Appraisals have been conducted in many different kinds of organizations: hospitals, schools, government agencies, banks, voluntary organizations, and the like. Special criteria have been formulated to deal with the different qualities of these organizations. The selected bibliography presented in Section 3.C.3 provides suggestions to the researcher.

Researchers may wish to compare the Profile of Organizational Characteristics with the Survey of Organizations developed by James C. Taylor and David G. Bowers.[2] This is a machine-scored questionnaire that taps certain critical dimensions of organizational climate, managerial leadership, peer behavior, group processes, and satisfaction. The manual traces the origin, concepts, development, methodology, and administrative procedure of the survey. The 1970 questionnaire is composed of 92 items, about half of which probe attitudes using the Likert scale response set. The items are drawn from numerous studies made at the Institute for Social Research, including many from the Profile of Organizational Characteristics. The survey has been administered to more than 20,000 respondents in many different organizations. It takes from 30 to 45 minutes to complete. Numerous tests of reliability and validity are reported. For further information, write to the Organizational Development Research Program, Institute for Social Research, P.O. Box 1248, Ann Arbor, MI 48106.

The Profile of Organizational Characteristics is a set of rating scales used in interviewing managers in the organization. They are applicable for any group of supervisory heads in any organization. The form can be used to measure the management system of any unit within an organization, as well as that of the total organization.

Data gathered by the researcher through observation and records may be assembled, if desired, to validate further the dominant system of the organization as exploitive-authoritative, benevolent-authoritative, consultative, or participative group. Likert has prepared a chart of the organizational and performance characteristics of different management systems based on a comparative analysis.[3] Responses to the profile indicate that leadership styles and related organizational characteristics display a remarkably consistent set of interrelationships. In Appendix I of *The Human Organization*, Pearsonian coefficients of correlation are shown that measure the extent to which answers to one item are consistent with answers to another. Apart from the performance items, all correlations between an item and the total score are greater than +.73.[4]

Notes

1. Rensis Likert, *The Human Organization: Its Management and Value* (New York: McGraw-Hill, 1967); E. Wight Bakke, *Bonds of Organization* (New York: Harper & Row, 1950).

2. James C. Taylor and David G. Bowers, *Survey of Organizations* (Ann Arbor: University of Michigan, Institute for Social Research, 1974).

3. See Likert, *The Human Organization*, 14-24; or see Rensis Likert, *New Patterns of Management* (New York: McGraw-Hill, 1961).

4. For the validation of the high relationship between productivity and the consultative and participative group systems, see the results reported on the Weldon Plant, Plan L, and Company H. For an excellent critique, see Dale G. Lake et al., *Measuring Human Behavior* (New York: Teachers College Press, 1973), 262-64.

PROFILE OF ORGANIZATIONAL CHARACTERISTICS[1]

3.C.2

Instructions (for managers to be interviewed)

1. On the lines below each organizational variable (item), please place an *n* at the point which, *in your experience*, describes your organization at the present time (*n* = now). Treat each item as a continuous variable from the extreme at one end to that at the other.

2. In addition, if you have been in your organization one or more years, please also place a *p* on each line at the point which, *in your experience*, describes your organization as it was one to two years ago (*p* = previously).

3. If you were not in your organization one or more years ago, please check here _____ and answer as of the present time, i.e., answer only with an *n*.

Organizational variable					Item no.
1. Leadership processes used					
a. Extent to which superiors have confidence and trust in *subordinates*	Have no confidence and trust in subordinates	Have condescending confidence and trust, such as master has in servant	Substantial but not complete confidence and trust; still wishes to keep control of decisions	Complete confidence and trust in all matters	
					1
b. Extent to which subordinates, in turn, have confidence and trust in *superiors*	Have no confidence and trust in superiors	Have subservient confidence and trust, such as servant has to master	Substantial but not complete confidence and trust	Complete confidence and trust	
					2
c. Extent to which superiors display supportive behavior toward others	Display no supportive behavior or virtually none	Display supportive behavior in condescending manner and situations only	Display supportive behavior quite generally	Display supportive behavior fully and in all situations	
					3

(Continued)

d. Extent to which superiors behave so that subordinates feel free to discuss important things about their jobs with their immediate superior	Subordinates feel completely free to discuss things about the job with their superior	Subordinates feel rather free to discuss things about the job with their superior	Subordinates do not feel very free to discuss things about the job with their superior	Subordinates do not feel at all free to discuss things about the job with their superior	4
e. Extent to which immediate superior in solving job problems generally tries to get subordinates' ideas and opinions and makes constructive use of them	Always gets ideas and opinions and always tries to make constructive use of them	Usually gets ideas and opinions and usually tries to make constructive use of them	Sometimes gets ideas and opinions of subordinates in solving job problems	Seldom gets ideas and opinions of subordinates in solving job problems	5
2. Character of motivational forces *a.* Underlying motives tapped	Physical security, economic needs, and some use of the desire for status	Economic needs and moderate use of ego motives, e.g. desire for status, affiliation, and achievement	Economic needs and considerable use of ego and other major motives, e.g. desire for new experiences	Full use of economic, ego, and other major motives. as, for example, motivational forces arising from group goals	6
b. Manner in which motives are used	Fear, threats, punishment, and occasional rewards	Rewards and some actual or potential punishment	Rewards, occasional punishment, and some involvement	Economic rewards based on compensation system developed through participation; group participation and involvement in setting goals, improving methods, appraising progress toward goals, etc.	7
c. Kinds of attitudes developed toward organization and its goals	Attitudes are strongly favorable and provide powerful stimulation to behavior implementing organization's goals	Attitudes usually are favorable and support behavior implementing organization's goals	Attitudes are sometimes hostile and counter to organization's goals and are sometimes favorrable to the organization's goals and support the behavior necessary to achieve them	Attitudes usually are hostile and counter to organization's goals	8
d. Extent to which motivational forces conflict with or reinforce one another	Marked conflict of forces substantially reducing those motivational forces leading to behavior in support of the organization's goals	Conflict often exists; occasionally forces will reinforce each other, at least partially	Some conflict, but often motivational forces will reinforce each other	Motivational forces generally reinforce each other in a substantial and cumulative manner	9

e. Amount of responsibility felt by each member of organization for achieving organization's goals

Personnel at all levels feel real responsibility for organization's goals and behave in ways to implement them	Substantial proportion of personnel, especially at higher levels, feel responsibility and generally behave in ways to achieve the organization's goals	Managerial personnel usually feel responsibility; rank and file usually feel relatively little responsibility for achieving organization's goals	High levels of management feel responsibility; lower levels feel less; rank and file feel little and often welcome opportunity to behave in ways to defeat organization's goals

10

f. Attitudes toward other members of the organization

Favorable, cooperative attitudes throughout the organization with mutual trust and confidence	Cooperative, reasonably favorable attitudes toward others in organization; may be some competition between peers with resulting hostility and some condescension toward subordinates	Subservient attitudes toward superiors; competition for status resulting in hostility toward peers; condescension toward subordinates	Subservient attitudes toward superiors coupled with hostility; hostility toward peers and contempt for subordinates; distrust is widespread

11

g. Satisfaction derived

Relatively high satisfaction throughout the organization with regard to membership in the organization, supervision, and one's own achievements	Some dissatisfaction to moderately high satisfaction with regard to membership in the organization, supervision, and one's own achievements	Dissatisfaction to moderate satisfaction with regard to membership in the organization, supervision, and one's own achievements	Usually dissatisfaction with membership in the organization, with supervision, and with one's own achievements

12

3. Character of communication process

a. Amount of interaction and communication aimed at achieving organization's objectives

Very little	Little	Quite a bit	Much with both individuals and groups

13

b. Direction of information flow

Downward	Mostly downward	Down and up	Down, up, and with peers

14

c. Downward communication
(1) Where initiated

Initiated at all levels	Patterned on communication from top but with some initiative at lower levels	Primarily at top or patterned on communication from top	At top of organization or to implement top directive

15

(2) Extent to which superiors willingly share information with subordinates

Provide minimum of information	Gives subordinates only information superior feels they need	Gives information needed and answers most questions	Seeks to give subordinates all relevant information and all information they want

16

(Continued)

(3) Extent to which communications are accepted by subordinates

| Generally accepted, but if not, openly and candidly questioned | Often accepted but, if not, may or may not be openly questioned | Some accepted and some viewed with suspicion | Viewed with great suspicion |

17

d. Upward communication

(1) Adequacy of upward communication via line organization

| Very little | Limited | Some | A great deal |

18

(2) Subordinates' feeling of responsibility for initiating accurate upward communication

| None at all | Relatively little, usually communicates "filtered" information and only when requested; may "yes" the boss | Some to moderate degree of responsibility to initiate accurate upward communication | Considerable responsibility felt and much initiative; group communicates all relevant information |

19

(3) Forces leading to accurate or distorted upward information

| Virtually no forces to distort and powerful forces to communicate accurately | Occasional forces to distort along with many forces to communicate accurately | Many forces to distort; also forces for honest communication | Powerful forces to distort information and deceive superiors |

20

(4) Accuracy of upward communication via line

| Accurate | Information that boss wants to hear flows; other information may be limited or cautiously given | Information that boss wants to hear flows; other information is restricted and filtered | Tends to be inaccurate |

21

(5) Need for supplementary upward communication system

| No need for any supplementary system | Slight need for supplementary system: suggestion systems may be used | Upward communication often supplemented by suggestion system and similar devices | Great need to supplement upward communication by spy system, suggestion system, and similar devices |

22

e. Sideward communication, its adequacy and accuracy

| Usually poor because of competition between peers, corresponding hostility | Fairly poor because of competition between peers | Fair to good | Good to excellent |

23

f. Psychological closeness of superiors to subordinates (i.e., friendliness between superiors and subordinates)

| Usually very close | Fairly close | Can be moderately close if proper roles are kept | Far apart |

24

(1) How well does superior know and understand problems faced by subordinates?

| Knows and understands problems of subordinates very well | Knows and understands problems of subordinates quite well | Has some knowledge and understanding of problems of subordinates | Has no knowledge or understanding of problems of subordinates |

25

(2) How accurate are the perceptions by superiors and subordinates of each other?

Often in error	Often in error on some points	Moderately accurate	Usually quite accurate

26

4. Character of interaction-influence process
   a. Amount and character of interaction

Extensive, friendly interaction with high degree of confidence and trust	Moderate interaction, often with fair amount of confidence and trust	Little interaction and usually with some condescension by superiors; fear and caution by subordinates	Little interaction and always with fear and distrust

27

   b. Amount of cooperative teamwork present

Very substantial amount throughout the organization	A moderate amount	Relatively little	None

28

   c. Extent to which subordinates can influence the goals, methods, and activity of their units and departments
   (1) As seen by superiors

None	Virtually none	Moderate amount	A great deal

29

   (2) As seen by subordinates

None except through "informal organization" or via unionization	Little except through "informal organization" or via unionization	Moderate amount both directly and via unionization (where it exists)	Substantial amount both directly and via unionization (where it exists)

30

   d. Amount of actual influence which superiors can exercise over the goals, activity, and methods of their units and departments

Believed to be substantial but actually moderate unless capacity to exercise severe punishment is present	Moderate to somewhat more than moderate, especially for higher levels in organization	Moderate to substantial, especially for higher levels in organization	Substantial but often done indirectly, as, for example, by superior building effective interaction-influence system

31

   e. Extent to which an effective structure exists enabling one part of organization to exert influence upon other parts

Highly effective structure exists enabling exercise of influence in all directions	Moderately effective structure exists; influence exerted largely through vertical lines	Limited capacity exists; influence exerted largely via vertical lines and primarily downward	Effective structure virtually not present

32

5. Character of decision-making process
   a. At what level in organization are decisions formally made?

Bulk of decisions at top of organization	Policy at top, many decisions within prescribed framework made at lower levels but usually checked with top before action	Broad policy decisions at top, more specific decisions at lower levels	Decision making widely done throughout organization, although well integrated through linking process provided by overlapping groups

33

(Continued)

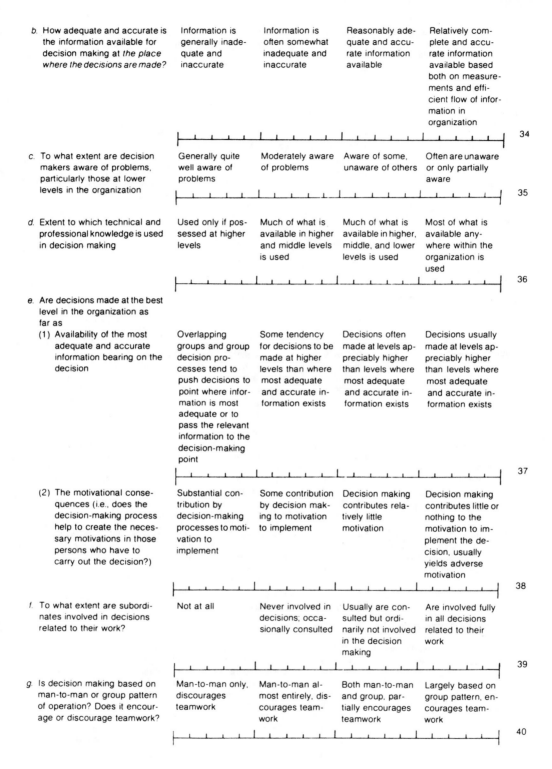

b. How adequate and accurate is the information available for decision making at *the place where the decisions are made?*	Information is generally inadequate and inaccurate	Information is often somewhat inadequate and inaccurate	Reasonably adequate and accurate information available	Relatively complete and accurate information available based both on measurements and efficient flow of information in organization	34
c. To what extent are decision makers aware of problems, particularly those at lower levels in the organization	Generally quite well aware of problems	Moderately aware of problems	Aware of some, unaware of others	Often are unaware or only partially aware	35
d. Extent to which technical and professional knowledge is used in decision making	Used only if possessed at higher levels	Much of what is available in higher and middle levels is used	Much of what is available in higher, middle, and lower levels is used	Most of what is available anywhere within the organization is used	36
e. Are decisions made at the best level in the organization as far as					
(1) Availability of the most adequate and accurate information bearing on the decision	Overlapping groups and group decision processes tend to push decisions to point where information is most adequate or to pass the relevant information to the decision-making point	Some tendency for decisions to be made at higher levels than where most adequate and accurate information exists	Decisions often made at levels appreciably higher than levels where most adequate and accurate information exists	Decisions usually made at levels appreciably higher than levels where most adequate and accurate information exists	37
(2) The motivational consequences (i.e., does the decision-making process help to create the necessary motivations in those persons who have to carry out the decision?)	Substantial contribution by decision-making processes to motivation to implement	Some contribution by decision making to motivation to implement	Decision making contributes relatively little motivation	Decision making contributes little or nothing to the motivation to implement the decision, usually yields adverse motivation	38
f. To what extent are subordinates involved in decisions related to their work?	Not at all	Never involved in decisions; occasionally consulted	Usually are consulted but ordinarily not involved in the decision making	Are involved fully in all decisions related to their work	39
g. Is decision making based on man-to-man or group pattern of operation? Does it encourage or discourage teamwork?	Man-to-man only, discourages teamwork	Man-to-man almost entirely, discourages teamwork	Both man-to-man and group, partially encourages teamwork	Largely based on group pattern, encourages teamwork	40

6. Character of goal setting or ordering

   a. Manner in which usually done

Except in emergencies, goals are usually established by means of group participation	Goals are set or orders issued after discussion with subordinates of problems and planned action	Orders issued, opportunity to comment may or may not exist	Orders issued

   41

   b. To what extent do the different hierarchial levels tend to strive for high performance goals?

High goals sought by all levels, with lower levels sometimes pressing for higher goals than top levels	High goals sought by higher levels but with occasional resistance by lower levels	High goals sought by top and often resisted moderately by subordinates	High goals pressed by top, generally resisted by subordinates

   42

   c. Are there forces to accept, resist, or reject goals?

Goals are overtly accepted but are covertly resisted strongly	Goals are overtly accepted but often covertly resisted to at least a moderate degree	Goals are overtly accepted but at times with some covert resistance	Goals are fully accepted both overtly and covertly

   43

7. Character of control processes

   a. At what hierarchial levels in organization does major or primary concern exist with regard to the performance of the control function?

At the very top only	Primarily or largely at the top	Primarily at the top but some shared feeling of responsibility felt at middle and to a lesser extent at lower levels	Concern for performance of control functions likely to be felt throughout organization

   44

   b. How accurate are the measurements and information used to guide and perform the control function, and to what extent do forces exist in the organization to distort and falsify this information?

Strong pressures to obtain complete and accurate information to guide own behavior and behavior of own and related work groups; hence information and measurements tend to be complete and accurate	Some pressure to protect self and colleagues and hence some pressures to distort; information is only moderately complete and contains some inaccuracies	Fairly strong forces exist to distort and falsify; hence measurements and information are often incomplete and inaccurate	Very strong forces exist to distort and falsify; as a consequence, measurements and information are usually incomplete and often inaccurate

   45

   c. Extent to which the review and control functions are concentrated

Highly concentrated in top management	Relatively highly concentrated, with some delegated control to middle and lower levels	Moderate downward delegation of review and control processes; lower as well as higher levels perform these tasks	Review and control done at all levels with lower units at times imposing more vigorous reviews and tighter controls than top management

   46

(Continued)

d. Extent to which there is an informal organization present and supporting or opposing goals of formal organization	Informal organization present and opposing goals of formal organization	Informal organization usually present and partially resisting goals	Informal organization may be present and may either support or partially resist goals of formal organization	Informal and formal organization are one and the same; hence all social forces support efforts to achieve organization's goals

47

e. Extent to which control data (e.g., accounting, productivity, cost, etc.) are used for self-guidance or group problem solving by managers and nonsupervisory employees, or used by superiors in a punitive, policing manner	Used for policing and in punitive manner	Used for policing coupled with reward and punishment, sometimes punitively; used somewhat for guidance but in accord with orders	Used for policing with emphasis usually on reward but with some punishment; used for guidance in accord with orders; some use also for self-guidance	Used for self-guidance and for coordinated problem solving and guidance; not used punitively

48

8. Performance goals and training

a. Level of performance goals which superiors seek to have organization achieve	Seek to achieve extremely high goals	Seek very high goals	Seek high goals	Seek average goals

49

b. Extent to which you have been given the kind of management training you desire	Have received no management training of kind I desire	Have received some management training of kind I desire	Have received quite a bit of management training of kind I desire	Have received a great deal of management training of kind I desire

50

c. Adequacy of training resources provided to assist you in training your subordinates	Training resources provided are excellent	Training resources provided are very good	Training resources provided are good	Training resources provided are only fairly good

51

The table above can be used for other purposes by appropriate modifications in the instructions. The table was used to obtain from managers their descriptions of particularly high- and low-producing organizations. The directions below indicate other uses:

Form S Instructions

On the line below each organizational variable (item), please indicate the kind of organization you are trying to create by the management you are providing. Treat each item as a continuous variable from the extreme at one end to that at the other. Place a check mark on each line to show the kind of management you are using and the kind of organization you are creating.

Form D Instructions

On the line below each organizational variable (item), please indicate by a check mark where you would *like* to have your organization fall with regard to that item. Treat each item as a continuous variable from the extreme at one end to that at the other.

Note

1. From Rensis Likert, *The Human Organization.* Copyright © 1967 by McGraw-Hill, Inc. Reprinted by permission.

SELECTED REFERENCES TO ASSESSMENT OF ORGANIZATIONAL EFFECTIVENESS

3.C.3

American Institute for Research. *Evaluating the Performance of Research Personnel.* Pittsburgh: University of Pittsburgh, 1951.

Andrews, Fred M., ed. *Scientific Productivity: The Effectiveness of Research Groups in Six Countries.* New York: Cambridge University Press and UNESCO, 1979.

Argyris, Chris. *Organization of a Bank.* New Haven, CT: Yale University, Labor and Management Center, 1954.

Bakke, E. Wight. *Bonds of Organization.* New York: Harper & Row, 1950.

Becker, Selwyn W., and Duncan Neuhauser. *The Efficient Organization.* New York: Elsevier, 1975.

Braskamp, Larry, A. Brandenburg, and John C. Ory. *Evaluating Teaching Effectiveness: A Practical Guide.* Beverly Hills, CA: Sage, 1984.

Brinkerhoff, Robert O., and Dennis E. Dressler. *Productivity Measurement: A Guide for Managers and Evaluators.* Newbury Park, CA: 1989.

Corson, John T., and George A. Steiner. *Measuring Business Social Performance: The Corporate Social Audit.* New York: Committee for Economic Development, 1974.

Cummings, Larry L., and Donald P. Schwab. *Performance in Organizations: Determinants and Appraisal.* Glenview, IL: Scott, Foresman, 1973.

Georgopoulos, Basil S., and Floyd C. Mann. *The Community General Hospital.* New York: Macmillan, 1962.

Ghorpade, Jaisingh, ed. *Assessment of Organizational Effectiveness: Issue, Analysis and Readings.* Pacific Palisades, CA: Goodyear, 1971.

See especially the chapters by A. W. Gouldner, A. Etzioni, D. Katz and R. L. Kahn, B. S. Georgopoulos, and A. S. Tannenbaum et al.

Harrison, Michael L. *Diagnosing Organizations: Methods, Models and Processes.* Newbury Park, CA: Sage, 1987.

Jones, Michael Owen, Michael Dane Moore, and Richard Christopher Snyder. *Inside Organizations: Understanding the Human Dimension.* Newbury Park, CA: Sage, 1988.

Lawler, Edward E., III, David Nadler, and Cortlandt Camman. *Organizational Assessment: Perspectives on the Measurement of Organizational Behavior and Quality of Working Life.* New York: Wiley-Interscience, 1980.

Levin, Henry M. *Cost-Effectiveness: A Primer.* Beverly Hills, CA: Sage, 1983.

Likert, Rensis. *The Human Organization: Its Management and Value.* New York: McGraw-Hill, 1967.

Luck, Thomas J. *Personnel Audit and Appraisal.* New York: McGraw-Hill, 1955.

Munday, Leo A. *Toward a Social Audit of Colleges: An Examination of College Student Outcomes in Terms of Admission Information.* ACT Research Report No. 75. Iowa City: American College Testing Program, Research and Development Division, 1976.

National Industrial Conference Board. *Measuring Company Productivity.* Studies in Business Economics No. 89. New York: National Industrial Conference Board, 1965.

Office of Personnel Management. *Measuring Federal Productivity.* Washington, DC: Government Printing Office, 1978.

Price, James. *Organizational Effectiveness: An Inventory of Propositions.* Homewood, IL: Irwin, 1968.

Rossi, Peter H., and Howard E. Freeman. *Evaluation: A Systematic Approach.* 4th ed. Newbury Park, CA: Sage, 1990.

See especially Chapter 8 on measuring efficiency, an excellent summary of cost-benefit and cost-effectiveness analysis.

Schoorman, F. David, and Benjamin Schneider, eds. *Facilitating Work Effectiveness.* Indianapolis: Lexington, 1988.

Seashore, Stanley S., Edward E. Lawler III, and Philip H. Mirvis. *Assessing Organizational Change: A Guide to Methods, Measures, and Practices.* New York: John Wiley, 1983.

Wickert, Frederick R., and Dalton E. McFarland, eds. *Measuring Executive Effectiveness.* New York: Appleton-Century-Crofts, 1967.

An Annotated Bibliography

Franklin, Jerome L. *Organization Development: An Annotated Bibliography.* Ann Arbor: University of Michigan, Institute for Social Research, 1974.

Abstracts of books and articles that focus on the improvement of organizational performance. Each abstract contains a summary description of the major ideas, a listing of major topics, a table of contents, and a list of contributing authors.

Part 4

Guides to Methods and Techniques of Collecting Data in Library, Field, and Laboratory: Social Science Data Libraries and Research Centers

THE COLLECTION OF DATA is the crucial operation in the execution of a good research design. The quality of the research rests upon the quality of the data. In this part the methods and techniques of social research are presented according to their common situses of research: library, field, and laboratory. Advantages and disadvantages of principal methods are pointed out. Guides to the construction of questionnaires, interviews, and scales are described.

A listing of social science data libraries is given. These social science archives are available to research scholars and offer many excellent opportunities for research. The collection of data is expensive, and the ability to use data previously collected offers the possibility of superior research at a greatly lowered cost. The guide to the U.S. Census and Bureau of Labor Statistics is especially thorough, to make known and usable the rich mine of data available to social researchers.

Finally, directories of social science research centers in the United States, England, and throughout the world are presented to aid the researcher. A list of important research associations and institutes affiliated with the International Sociological Association may provide valuable contact points for determining the status of current research and comparative research advances in various fields.

The collection of data occurs in a designed inquiry only after a long series of steps, including the following:

1. the definition of the problem
2. the construction of the theoretical framework
3. the stating of hypotheses
4. the establishment of the design of inquiry
5. the determination of sampling procedures

This section introduces the most common methods of social science research and presents a brief set of instructions for the construction of questionnaires, interviews, and scales. These instructions will assist the researcher in evaluating the appropriate method for his or her particular problem; he or she should consult methods books for a thorough explanation of each method or technique.

Methods are handmaidens of designed inquiry. It is important to distinguish carefully among four terms: methodology, situs, method, and technique.

Methodology is a body of knowledge that describes and analyzes methods, indicating their limitations and resources, clarifying their presuppositions and consequences, and relating their potentialities to research advances. In this part the methods of social science are first examined in order to set forth the advantages and disadvantages of each method. The aim is to help researchers to understand the process of gathering data and what their choices of methods entail.

Situs refers to the place in which the data are gathered. For most sciences, the most used situses are the library, the field, and the laboratory.

Method refers to the means of gathering data that are common to all sciences or to a significant part of them. Thus methods include such procedures as the making of observations and measurements, performing experiments, building models and theories, or providing explanations and making predictions. The social sciences use documentary analysis, the mailed questionnaire, and the personal interview most frequently.

Technique refers to specific procedures that are used in a given method. For example, the field method worker may employ such techniques as use of sociometric scales to measure social variables and personality inventories to identify personal traits. The research worker such as a demographer may draw heavily on statistical documents and use various statistical techniques to describe relationships or gain statistical control over the data.

Wise counsel is offered by Muzafer Sherif:

No procedure and no technique for data collection are powerful or effective in their own right. The theory should be the *guide* for fruitful research. The techniques are powerful tools for data collection, if—and only if—they are appropriate in terms of the nature and characteristics of the *problems*. And *significant problems* can be formulated only *after* gaining substantial familiarity with the universe of discourse and not before.[1]

TABLE 4.1 Outline of Common Research Methods and Techniques in Three Situses

Situs	Methods	Techniques
Library	1. Analysis of historical records: primary records—letters, diaries, etc.; secondary interpretations of events	Recording of notes Content analysis Tape and film listening and analysis
	2. Analysis of documents: statistical and nonstatistical records of formal agencies	Statistical compilations and manipulations Reference and abstract guides Microfilm, microfiche searches
	3. Literature search for theory and previous research in books, journals, and monographs	Computer information probes
Field	1. Mail questionnaire	Identification of social and economic background of respondents Use of sociometric scales to ascertain such variables as social status, group structure, community and social participation, leadership activity, and family adjustment Use of attitude scales to measure morale
	2. Personal interview Structured interview schedule	Interviewer uses a detailed schedule with open and closed questions Sociometric scales may be used
	3. Focused interview	Interviewer focuses attention upon a given experience and its effects; knows in advance what topics or questions he or she wishes to cover
	4. Free story interview	Respondent is urged to talk freely about the subjects treated in the study
	5. Group interview	Small groups of respondents are interviewed simultaneously; any of the above techniques may be used
	6. Telephone survey	Used as a survey technique for information and for discerning opinion May be used for follow-up of a questionnaire mailing to increase return
	7. Case study and life history	For case study, cross-sectional collection of data for intensive analysis of a person emphasizing personal and social factors in socialization For life history, longitudinal collection of data of intensive character also emphasizing socialization over an extended period of time
	8. Nonparticipant direct observation	Use of standard score cards and observational behavior scales
	9. Participant observation	Interactional recording; possible use of tape recorders and photographic techniques
	10. Mass observation	Recording mass or collective behavior by observation and interview using independent observers in public places
Laboratory	Small group study of random behavior, play, problem solving, or stress behavior of individuals and/or groups; organizational and role analysis	Use of contrived and nonconstructed situations, use of confederates; use of audiovisual recording devices; use of observers behind one-way mirror

Table 4.1 presents an outline of methods and techniques as employed in the three situses: library, field, and laboratory. Aids are presented for the most common methods and techniques. Later in this part, a list of reference books is given that describes various methods and techniques in detail.

Robert and Barbara B. Sommers have developed some rules of thumb for selecting among these methods.[2] Table 4.2 shows these rules. Note that these authors begin

TABLE 4.2 Choosing Among Research Techniques

Problem	Approach	Research Technique
To obtain reliable information under controlled conditions	Test people in a laboratory	Laboratory experiment, simulation
To find out how people behave in public	Watch them	Natural observation
To find out how people behave in private	Ask them to keep diaries	Personal documents
To learn what people think	Ask them	Interview, questionnaire, attitude scale
To find out where people go	Chart their movements	Behavioral mapping, trace measures
To identify personality traits or assess mental abilities	Administer a standardized test	Psychological testing
To identify trends in verbal material	Systematic tabulation	Content analysis
To understand an unusual event	Detailed and lengthy investigation	Case study

SOURCE: Robert Sommers and Barbara B. Sommers, *A Practical Guide to Behavioral Research,* 2nd ed. (New York: Oxford University Press, 1986), 8.

with a brief inventory of research inquiries and describe appropriate approaches and research techniques. They point out that

> observation is well suited for what people do in public. For private behavior, the personal diary is more appropriate. The experiment is an immensely powerful tool for deciding between alternative explanations of a phenomenon. It is less useful, however, for studying natural behavior or opinions. With opinions and attitudes the questionnaire and interview are very efficient.[3]

Standardized tests and scales have a unique role to play because they can make comparative rankings of persons, groups, and organizations.

The Central Research Activity

Surveys have come to dominate the landscape of empirical research in the United States. Opinion polling did not begin until the 1930s. It has grown to the extent that from 1971 to 1976, 100 million survey interviews were conducted in the United States; in 1980, 28 million people were interviewed on the telephone alone.[4]

Notes

1. Muzafer Sherif, in *Concepts, Theory, and Explanation in the Social Sciences*, ed. Gordon J. DiRenzo (New York: Random House, 1967), 55-56.

2. Robert Sommers and Barbara B. Sommers, *A Practical Guide to Behavioral Research*, 2nd ed. (New York: Oxford University Press, 1986).

3. Ibid., 8.

4. Eleanor Singer, "Researchers Told to Be Wary of How Surveys Are Used," *Chronicle of Higher Education* 35 (September 7, 1988): A-10.

4.2   SEARCHING THE SCIENTIFIC LITERATURE FOR PUBLISHED RESEARCH REPORTS IN THE AREAS OF INTEREST TO SOCIAL SCIENTISTS

The research question that motivates research generally comes first in the history of any research project. Then a search of the scientific literature becomes paramount. Social scientists often minimize this step. Sometimes they mistakenly believe that their problems are so novel that past literature will not apply. But all too often they simply do not give enough importance to the way in which their work will help build on past research to validate a test hypothesis or theory and thus make a growing accumulation of findings. They underestimate past work and sell short the future requirements of their science.

Physical and biological scientists dare not take such risks because they know that fellow scientists will quickly detect these faults in scientific work. Social scientists have to learn that they cannot do so with impunity.

The resources for conducting a literature search are great and marvelous. They fall into four categories: indexes to periodical literature, computer-assisted reference services, microfilm-microfiche-microprint media, and specialized sourcebooks.

Indexes to Periodical Literature

The following indexes are of most value to social scientists and are described in the order in which they are usually consulted:

1. *Social Sciences Index* is a cumulative index to English-language periodicals. The main body of the index consists of author and subject entries to periodicals in the fields of anthropology, area studies, economics, environmental sciences, geography, law and criminology, medical sciences, political sciences, psychology, public administration, sociology, and related subjects. In addition, there is an author listing of citations to book reviews following the main body of the index. This index, which is published quarterly with bound cumulation each year, has a fairly long history. It began in 1907 as the *International Index*; in 1955 its name was changed and it continued as the *Social Science and Humanities Index*. The growing body of knowledge necessitated a division of the index into a separate *Social Sciences Index* and a *Humanities Index* (1974). This division continues today. The periodicals listed below are indexed; all data reflect the latest information available.[1]

Periodicals Indexed

Academy of Political Science, Proceedings. $22. q. Academy of Political Science, 619 W. 114th St., Ste. 500, New York, NY 10025

Acta Sociologica. $38. q. Universitetsforlaget, P.O. Box 7508, Skillebekk, Oslo 2, Norway

Adolescence. $25. q. Libra Publishers Inc., P.O. Box 165, 391 Willets Rd., Roslyn Heights, LI, NY 11577

Advances in Thanatology. $60. 4 times a yr. Arno Press, 3 Park Ave., New York, NY 10016

Africa Today. $15. q. Africa Today Associates, c/o Graduate School of International Studies, University of Denver, Denver, CO 80208

African Studies. R20. bi-ann. Witwatersrand University Press. Jan Smuts Ave., Johannesburg 1002, South Africa

African Studies Review. $45. 3 times a yr. African Studies Assn., Subscription Department, 255 Kinsey Hall, University of California, Los Angeles, CA 90024

The American Anthropologist. American Anthropological Assn., 1703 New Hampshire Ave., NW, Washington, DC 20009

The American Behavioral Scientist. $45. bi-m. Sage Publications, Inc., 2455 Teller Rd., Newbury Park, CA 91320

American Economic Review. $43. 5 times a yr. Rendings Fels, 1313 21st Ave. South, Nashville, TN 37212 (May number has added title: *Papers and Proceedings of the Annual Meeting of the American Economic Association*)

The American Economist. $6. 2 times a yr. University of Alabama, Department of Economics, P.O. Drawer AS, AL 35486

American Journal of Correction. See *Corrections Today*

American Journal of Economics and Sociology. $10. q. 50 E. 69th St., New York, NY 10021

American Journal of International Law. $47. 4 times a yr. American Society of International Law. 2223 Massachusetts Ave., NW, Washington, DC 20008

American Journal of Nursing. $15. m. Subscription Department, 555 W. 57th St., New York, NY 10019

American Journal of Orthopsychiatry. $22. q. AOA Publications Sales Office, 49 Sheridan Ave., Albany, NY 12210

American Journal of Physical Anthropology. $214. 8 times a yr. Alan R. Liss, Inc., 150 5th Ave., New York, NY 10011

American Journal of Political Science. $30. q. University of Texas Press, Box 7819, Austin, TX 78712

American Journal of Psychiatry. $27. m. American Psychiatric Assn., Circulation Department, 1700 18th St., NW, Washington, DC 20009

American Journal of Psychology. $30. q. University of Illinois Press, 54 E. Gregory Dr., Box 5081, Station A, Champaign, IL 61820

American Journal of Public Health. $40. m. American Public Health Assn., 1015 18th St., NW, Washington, DC 20036

American Journal of Sociology. $40. bi-m. University of Chicago Press, 5801 Ellis Ave., Chicago, IL 60637

American Opinion. $18. m. (Ag-Je) R. Welch, Inc., 395 Concord Ave., Belmont, MA 02178

American Planning Association Journal. $22. q. American Planning Assn., 1776 Massachusetts Ave., NW, Washington, DC 20036

American Political Science Review. $50. q. American Political Science Assn., 1527 New Hampshire Ave., NW, Washington, DC 20036

American Psychologist. $25. m. American Psychological Assn., Inc., Subscription Section, 1200 17th St., NW, Washington, DC 20036

American Society for Psychical Research Journal. $20. q. American Society for Psychical Research, Inc., 5 W. 73rd St., New York, NY 10023

American Sociological Review. $30. bi-m. American Sociological Assn., 1722 N St. NW, Washington, DC 20036

Annals of the American Academy of Political and Social Science. $36. bi-m. Sage Publications, Inc., 2455 Teller Rd., Newbury Park, CA 91320

Anthropological Quarterly. $18. q. Catholic University of America Press, Washington, DC 20064

Anthrops: International Review of Ethnology and Linguistics. Swiss Fr 140. 3 times a yr. Editors Saint-Paul, 1700 Fribourg, Switzerland

Archaeology and Physical Anthropology in Oceania. $15. 3 times a yr. Mackie Building, University of Sydney, New South Wales, Australia 2006

Asia. $10. bi-m. Asia Society, P.O. Box 379, Fort Lee, NJ 07024

Asian Affairs: Journal of the Royal Society for Asian Affairs. $20. 3 times a yr. Royal Society for Asian Affairs, 42 Devonshire St., London, W1N 1LN, England

Asian Survey. $37.50. m. University of California Press, Berkeley, CA 94720

Association of American Geographers, Annals. $30. q. Assn. of American Geographers, 1710 16th St., NW, Washington, DC 20009

Atlantic Community Quarterly. $15. q. Atlantic Council of the United States, 1616 H St., NW, Washington, DC 20006

Aztlan: International Journal of Chicano Studies Research. $20. 3 times a yr. Chicano Studies Centers, 405 Hilgard Ave., Los Angeles, CA 90024

Bell Journal of Economics. free. semi-ann. American Telephone & Telegraph Co., 195 Broadway, New York, NY 10007

The Black Scholar: Journal of Black Studies and Research. $16. bi-m. P.O. Box 908, Sausalito, CA 94965

Boston College Environmental Affairs Law Review. $20. q. Boston College Law School, 885 Centre St., Newton Centre, MA 02159

British Journal of Criminology: Delinquency and Deviant Social Behavior. $37.50. q. Fred B. Rothman & Co., 57 Leuning St., S. Hackensack, NJ 07606

British Journal of Political Science. $99. q. Cambridge University Press, 32 E. 57th St., New York, NY 10022

British Journal of Psychology. $100. q. Distribution Center, Blackhorse Road, Letchworth, Herts SG6 1HN, United Kingdom

British Journal of Sociology. $50. q. Routledge Journals, 9 Park St., Boston, MA 02108

Brookings Papers on Economic Activity. $15. 3 times a yr. 1775 Massachusetts Ave., NW, Washington, DC 20036

Bulletin on Narcotics. $10. q. United Nations Sales Section, New York, NY 10017

Business and Society Review. $38. q. Warren, Gorham & Lamont, Inc., 870 7th Ave., New York, NY 10019

Business History Review. $20. q. Harvard Graduate School of Business Administration, 215 Baker Library, Soldiers Field, Boston, MA 02163

Canadian Forum: An Independent Journal of Opinion and the Arts. $15. m. 70 The Esplanade, 3rd floor, Toronto, Ontario, Canada M5E 1A6

The Canadian Geographer. $25. q. Canadian Assn. of Geographers, Burnside Hall, McGill University, 805 Sherbrooke St., W. Montreal, Canada H3A 2KG

Canadian Geographic. $17. bi-m. Royal Canadian Geographical Society, 488 Wilbrod St., Ottawa, Ontario, Canada K1N 6MB

Canadian Journal of Economics. $36. q. University of Toronto Press, 5201 Dufferin St., Downsview, Ontario, Canada M3H 5T8

Canadian Journal of Political Science. $35. q. Wilfrid Laurier University Press, Waterloo, Ontario, Canada N2L 3C5

Canadian Journal of Psychology/Revue Canadienne de Psychologie. $35. q. Canadian Psychological Assn., King Edward Ave., Ottawa, Ontario, Canada K1N 7N6

Caribbean Studies. $8. q. University of Puerto Rico, Institute of Caribbean Studies, Box BM, University Station, Rio Piedras, Puerto Rico 00931

Center Magazine. $5. bi-m. Fund for the Republic, Inc., 2056 Eucalyptus Hill Rd., Santa Barbara, CA 93017

Child Development. $50. q. University of Chicago Press, 5801 Ellis Ave., Chicago, IL 60637

China Quarterly: An International Journal for the Study of China. $30. q. Contemporary China Institute, School of Oriental and African Studies, Malet St., London, WC1E 7HP, England

Civil Rights Digest. See *Perspectives: The Civil Rights Quarterly*

Civil Service Journal. $5.75. q. Superintendent of Documents, Government Printing Office, Washington, DC 20402 (ceased publication with v. 19, no. 4)

Community Development Journal: An International Forum. $17.50. 3 times a yr. Journals Manager, Oxford University Press, Press Rd., Neasden, London, NW 10, England

Community Mental Health Journal. $50. q. Human Sciences Press, 72 5th Ave., New York, NY 10011

Comparative Political Studies. $35. q. Sage Publications, Inc., 2455 Teller Rd., Newbury Park, CA 91320

Comparative Politics. $25. q. Subscription Fulfillment, Transaction Periodicals Consortium, Rutgers University, New Brunswick, NJ 08903

Contemporary Drug Problems. $24. q. Federal Legal Publications, Inc., 157 Chambers St., New York, NY 10007

Crime & Delinquency. $38. q. Sage Publications, Inc., 2455 Teller Rd., Newbury Park, CA 91320

Corrections Today. $18. bi-m. American Correction Assn., Inc., 4321 Hartwick Rd., Ste. L-208, College Park, MD 20740 (formerly *American Journal of Correction*; name changed with v. 41, no. 1, January 1980)

Criminology: An Interdisciplinary Journal. $25. q. American Society of Criminology, 1314 Kinnear Rd., Columbus, OH 43212

The Crisis: A Record of the Darker Races. $6. 10 times a yr. 1790 Broadway, New York, NY 10019

Current Anthropology: A World Journal of the Sciences of Man. $44. 6 times a yr. University of Chicago Press, 5801 Ellis Ave., Chicago, IL 60637

Demography. $35. q. Business Manager, Population Assn. of America, P.O. Box 14182, Benjamin Franklin Station, Washington, DC 20044

Development/The International Development Review.* $15. q. Society for International Development, 1346 Connecticut Ave., NW, Washington, DC 20036

Developmental Psychology. $36. bi-m. American Psychological Assn., Inc., Subscription Section, 1200 17th St., NW, Washington, DC 20036

Dissent. $17. q. Foundation for the Study of Independent Social Ideas, 505 5th Ave., New York, NY 10017

East European Quarterly. $12. q. 1200 University Ave., Boulder, CO 80302

Econometrica. $63. bi-m. Tieto Ltd., 4 Bellevue Mansions, Bellevue Rd., Clevedon, Avon, BS21 7NU, England

Economic Development and Cultural Change. $40. q. University of Chicago Press, 5801 Ellis Ave., Chicago, IL 60637

Economic Geography. $18.50. q. Business Manager, Clark University, Worcester, MA 01610

Economic History Review. $30. q. Titus Wilson & Son Ltd., 28 Highgate, Kendal Cumbria, LA9 4TB, England

Economic Inquiry. $65. q. Western Economic Assn. Executive Office, Department of Economics, California State University, Long Beach, CA 90840

Economic Journal. $72. q. Cambridge University Press, 32 E. 57th St., New York, NY 10022

Economica. $32. q. Tieto Ltd., 5 Elton Rd., Clevedon, Avon, BS21 7RA, England

The Economist. $85. w. Subscription Department, P.O. Box 190, 23a St. James St., London, SW1A 1HF, England

Education and Urban Society. $36. q. Corwin Press, Sage Publications, Inc., 2455 Teller Rd., Newbury Park, CA 91320

Ekistics: The Problems and Science of Human Settlements. $36. 10 times a yr. Athens Center of Ekistics, P.O. Box 471, Athens, Greece

Environment. $22. 10 times a yr. Scientists' Institute for Public Information, 4000 Albemarle St., NW, Washington, DC 20016

Environment and Behavior. $51. bi-m. Sage Publications, Inc., 2455 Teller Rd., Newbury Park, CA 91320

Environmental Research. $61. bi-m. Academic Press, Inc., 111 5th Ave., New York, NY 10003

Ethics: An International Journal of Social, Political, and Legal Philosophy. $30. q. University of Chicago Press, 5801 Ellis Ave., Chicago, IL 60637

Ethnic Groups: An International Periodical of Ethnic Studies. $67.50. q. Gordon and Breach Science Publishers, Inc., 42 William IV St., London, WC2, England

Ethnohistory. $10. q. American Society for Ethnohistory, c/o Arizona State Museum, University of Arizona, Tucson, AZ 85721

Ethnology: An International Journal of Cultural and Social Anthropology. $17. q. Department of Anthropology, University of Pittsburgh, PA 15260

European Economic Review. $172.50 for 2 volumes. 3 times a yr. North Holland Publishing Co., Box 211, Amsterdam, The Netherlands

European Journal of Sociology*/Archives Européennes de Sociologie. $53.50. 2 times a yr. Cambridge University Press, 32 E. 57th St., New York, NY 10022

Far Eastern Economic Review. $62. w. Datamovers, Inc., 28 W. 36th St., New York, NY 10018

Federal Probation. free. q. Administrative Office of the U.S. Courts, Supreme Court Building, Washington, DC 20544

Foreign Affairs. $18. 5 times a yr. Subscription Department, P.O. 2615, Boulder, CO 80322

Foreign Policy. $12. q. P.O. Box 984, Farmingdale, NY 11735

Freedomways. $4.50. q. Freedomways Associates, 799 Broadway, New York, NY 11737

Futures: The Journal of Forecasting and Planning. $67. bi-m. IPC Business Press, Ltd., 205 E. 42nd St., New York, NY 10017

The Futurist: A Journal of Forecasts, Trends and Ideas about the Future. $21. bi-m. World Future Society, P.O. Box 30369, Bethesda Branch, Washington, DC 20014

Geographical Journal. $55. 3 times a yr. Royal Geographical Society, 1 Kensington Gore, London, SW7 2AR, England

Geographical Magazine. $35.20. m. IPC Business Press Ltd., Oakfield House, Perrymount Rd., Haywards Heath, West Sussex, RH16 3DH, England

Geographical Review. $40. q. American Geographical Society, Broadway & 156th St., New York, NY 10032

Geography. $15. q. George Philip & Son Ltd., 12-14 Long Acre, London, WC2E 9LP, England

The Gerontologist. $25. bi-m. Gerontological Society. 1835 K St., NW, Washington, DC 20006

Government and Opposition. $60. q. London School of Economics and Political Science, Houghton St., London, WC2A 2AE, England

History of Political Economy. $28. q. Duke University Press, 6697 College Station, Durham, NC 27708

Human Ecology. $65. q. Plenum Press, 227 W. 17th St., New York, NY 10011

Human Organization. $25. q. Society for Applied Anthropology, 1703 New Hampshire Ave., NW, Washington, DC 20009

Human Relations: A Journal of Studies Towards the Integration of the Social Sciences. $115. m. Plenum Press, 227 W. 17th St., New York, NY 10011

Impact of Science on Society. French Fr 40. q. UNIPUB, Box 433, Murray Hill Station, New York, NY 10016

The Indian Historian. $7. q. 1451 Masonic Ave., San Francisco, CA 94117

Inter-American Economic Affairs. $20. q. Box 181, Benjamin Franklin Station, Washington, DC 20044

International Affairs. $25. q. Oxford University Press, Press Rd., London, NW10 0DD, England

International Economic Review. $46. 3 times a yr. Department of Economics, McNeil Building CR, University of Pennsylvania, Philadelphia, PA 19104

International Journal of Comparative Sociology. $42.77. q. E. J. Brill, Leiden, The Netherlands

International Journal of Middle East Studies. $95. 8 times a yr. Cambridge University Press, 32 E. 5th St., New York, NY 10022

International Journal of Offender Therapy and Comparative Criminology. $28. 3 times a yr. 199 Gloucester Place, London, NW1 6BU, England

International Journal of Social Psychiatry. $50. q. Avenue Publishing Co., 18 Park Ave., London, NW11 7SJ, England

International Organization: A Journal of Political and Economic Affairs. $30. q. Journals Department, University of Wisconsin Press, 114 N. Murray St., Madison, WI 52701

International Review of Social History. $26.15. 3 times a yr. Royal VanGorcum, Assen, The Netherlands

International Social Science Journal. French Fr 70. q. UNIPUB, Inc., P.O. Box 433, New York, NY 10016

International Studies Quarterly. $70. q. Butterworth Publishers, 80 Montvale Ave., Stoneham, MA 02180

JEI*/Journal of Economic Issues. $20. q. Assn. for Evolutionary Economics, Fiscal Office, Department of Economics, University of Nebraska, Lincoln, NE 68588

Jewish Social Studies: A Quarterly Journal Devoted to Contemporary and Historical Aspects of Jewish Life. $25. q. Conference on Jewish Social Studies. 250 W. 57th St., New York, NY 10019

Journal of Abnormal Psychology. $34. bi-m. American Psychological Assn., Inc., Subscription Section, 1200 17th St., NW, Washington, DC 20036

Journal of Anthropological Research. $16. q. Subscription Manager, University of New Mexico, Albuquerque, NM 87131

Journal of Applied Behavior Analysis. $22. q. University of Kansas, Department of Human Development, Lawrence, KS 66045

Journal of Applied Behavioral Science. $23. q. NTL Institute for Applied Behavioral Science, P.O. Box 9155, Rosslyn Station, Arlington, VA 22209

Journal of Asian and African Studies. $26.52. q. E. J. Brill, Leiden, The Netherlands

Journal of Black Studies. $39. q. Sage Publications, Inc., 2455 Teller Rd., Newbury Park, CA 91320

Journal of Common Market Studies. $57. q. Basil Blackwell, 108 Cowley Rd., Oxford, OX4 1JF, England

Journal of Conflict Resolution: Journal of The Peace Science Society (International). $42. q. Sage Publications, Inc., 2455 Teller Rd., Newbury Park, CA 91320

Journal of Consulting and Clinical Psychology. $50. bi-m. American Psychological Assn., Inc., Subscription Section, 1200 17th St., NW, Washington, DC 20036

Journal of Contemporary Asia. $26. q. P.O. Box 49010, Stockholm 49, Sweden

Journal of Contemporary Ethnography. $38. q. Sage Publications, Inc., 2455 Teller Rd., Newbury Park, CA 91320 (formerly *Urban Life*)

Journal of Counseling Psychology. $30. bi-m. American Psychological Assn., Inc., Subscription Section, 1200 17th St., NW, Washington, DC 20036

Journal of Creative Behavior. $9. q. Managing Editor, State University College at Buffalo, 1300 Elmwood Ave., Buffalo, NY 14222

Journal of Criminal Law & Criminology. $25. q. Northwestern University School of Law, 357 E. Chicago Ave., Chicago, IL 60611

Journal of Development Studies. $49.50. q. Frank Cass & Co., Ltd., 11 Gainsborough Rd., London, E11 1RS, England

Journal of Economic History. $25. q. Eleutherian Mills Historical Library, Wilmington, DE 19807

Journal of Economic Theory. $138. bi-m. Academic Press, 111 5th Ave., New York, NY 10003

Journal of Experimental Psychology: Animal Behavior Processes. $14. q. American Psychological Assn., Inc., Subscription Section, 1200 17th St., NW, Washington, DC 20036

Journal of Experimental Psychology: General. $16. q. American Psychological Assn., Inc., Subscription Section, 1200 17th St., NW, Washington, DC 20036

Journal of Experimental Psychology: Human Learning and Memory. $30. bi-m. American Psychological Assn., Inc., Subscription Section, 1200 17th St., NW, Washington, DC 20036

Journal of Experimental Psychology: Human Perception and Performance. $20. q. American Psychological Assn., Inc., Subscription Section, 1200 17th St., NW, Washington, DC 20036

Journal of Experimental Social Psychology. $53. bi-m. Academic Press, Inc., 111 5th Ave., New York, NY 10003

Journal of General Psychology. $54. q. 2 Commercial St., Provincetown, MA 02657

Journal of Gerontology. $35. bi-m. Gerontological Society, 1835 K St., NW, Washington, DC 20006

Journal of Health and Social Behavior. $16. q. American Sociological Assn., 1722 N St., NW, Washington, DC 20036

Journal of Housing. $33. 11 times a yr. National Assn. of Housing and Redevelopment Officials, Watergate Building, 2600 Virginia Ave., NW, Washington, DC 20037

Journal of Human Resources: Education, Manpower, and Welfare Policies. $28. q. Journals Department, University of Wisconsin Press, 114 N. Murray St., Madison, WI 53715

Journal of Humanistic Psychology. $36. q. Sage Publications, Inc., 2455 Teller Rd., Newbury Park, CA 91320

Journal of Interamerican Studies and World Affairs. $26. q. Jaime Suchlicki, Editor, Box 24-8134, University of Miami, Coral Gables, FL 33124

Journal of International Affairs. $12. semi-ann. Columbia University, 420 W. 118th St., New York, NY 10027

Journal of International Economics. $117. q. North-Holland Publishing Co., P.O. Box 211, Amsterdam-C, The Netherlands

Journal of Latin American Studies. $33. 2 times a yr. Cambridge University Press, 32 E. 57th St., New York, NY 10022

Journal of Law and Economics. $20. 2 times a yr. University of Chicago Law School, 1111 E. 60th St., Chicago, IL 60637

Journal of Leisure Research. $15. q. National Recreation & Park Assn., 1601 N. Kent St., Arlington, VA 22209

Journal of Marriage and the Family. $30. q. National Council on Family Relations, 1219 University Ave., SE, Minneapolis, MN 55414

Journal of Modern African Studies: A Quarterly Survey of Politics, Economics and Related Topics in Contemporary Africa. $46.50. q. Cambridge University Press, 32 E. 57th St., New York, NY 10022

Journal of Money, Credit and Banking. $17.50. q. Ohio State University Press, 2070 Neil Ave., Columbus, OH 43210

Journal of Parapsychology. $15. q. Box 6847, College Station, Durham, NC 27708

Journal of Peace Research. $28. q. P.O. Box 258, Irvington-on-Hudson, NY 10533

Journal of Personality and Social Psychology. $80. m. American Psychological Assn., Inc., Subscription Section, 1200 17th St., NW, Washington, DC 20036

Journal of Police Science and Administration. $25. q. International Assn. of Chiefs of Police, 11 Firstfield Rd., Gaithersburg, MD 20760

Journal of Political Economy. $30. bi-m. University of Chicago Press, 5801 Ellis Ave., Chicago, IL 60637

Journal of Politics. $19. q. Manning J. Dauer, Managing Editor, University of Florida, Gainesville, FL 32611

Journal of Psychedelic Drugs. $30. q. Student Assn. for the Study of Hallucinogens, 118 S. Bedford St., Madison, WI 53703

Journal of Psychology: The General Field of Psychology. $54. 6 times a yr. 2 Commercial St., Provincetown, MA 02657

Journal of Research in Crime and Delinquency. $39. q. Sage Publications, Inc., 2455 Teller Rd., Newbury Park, CA 91320

Journal of Social History. $25. q. Carnegie-Mellon University, Pittsburgh, PA 15213

Journal of Social Issues. $32. q. Society for the Psychological Study of Social Issues, P.O. Box 1248, Ann Arbor, MI 48106

Journal of Social Psychology. $54. bi-m. Box 543, 2 Commercial St., Provincetown, MA 02657

Journal of Studies on Alcohol. $50. m. Publications Division, Center of Alcohol Studies, P.O. Box 969, Piscataway, NJ 08854

Journal of Verbal Learning and Verbal Behavior. $72. bi-m. Academic Press, Inc., 111 5th Ave., New York, NY 10003

Kyklos: International Review for Social Sciences. Swiss Fr 70. q. Kyklos-Verlag, Postfach 524, CH-4000, Basel 2, Switzerland

Latin American Research Review. $30. 3 times a yr. LARR Subscription, 316 Hamilton Hall, University of North Carolina, Chapel Hill, NC 27514

Law and Contemporary Problems. $20. q. Duke University Press, Box 6697, College Station, Durham, NC 27708

Law and Society Review. $35. q. Law and Society Assn., Executive Office, University of Denver College of Law, 200 W. 14th Ave., Denver, CO 80204

Man: The Journal of the Royal Anthropological Institute. $52. q. Royal Anthropological Institute, 56 Queen Anne St., London, W1M 9LA, England

Manchester School of Economic and Social Studies. $37.50. q. Manchester University, Department of Economics, Dover St., Manchester, M13 9PL, England

Mankind. $18. 2 times a yr. Anthropological Society of NSW, c/o Department of Anthropology, University of Sydney, Sydney, Australia

Middle East Journal. $15. q. 1761 N St., NW, Washington, DC 20036

Middle Eastern Studies. $71.85. q. Frank Cass & Co., Ltd., Gainsborough House, Gainsborough Rd., London, E11 1RS, England

Modern Age. $10. q. Intercollegiate Studies Institute, Inc., 14 S. Bryn Mawr Ave., Bryn Mawr, PA 19010

Modern Asian Studies. $95. q. Cambridge University Press, American Branch, 32 E. 57th St., New York, NY 10022

Monthly Review: An Independent Socialist Magazine. $24. 11 times a yr. 62 W. 14th St., New York, NY 10011

National Wildlife. $7.50. bi-m. National Wildlife Federation, Inc., 1412 16th St., NW, Washington, DC 20036

New Left Review. $35. bi-m. 7 Carlisle St., London, W1V 6NL, England

New Statesmen. $44. w. 10 Great Turnstile, London, WC1V 7HJ, England

Nursing Outlook. $71. m. 555 W. 57th St., New York, NY 10019

Oceania: A Journal Devoted to the Study of the Native Peoples of Australia, New Guinea and the Islands of the Pacific Ocean. $71.50. q. University of Sydney, New South Wales, Australia 2006

Oceans. $15. bi-m. Oceanic Society, Fort Mason, San Francisco, CA 94123

Orbis: A Journal of World Affairs. $25. q. 3508 Market St., Ste. 350, Philadelphia, PA 19104

Oxford Economic Papers. $30. 3 times a yr. Oxford University Press, Walton St., Oxford, OX2 6DP, England

Parliamentary Affairs. $34. q. Oxford Journals, Press Rd., Neasden, London, NW10 0DD, England

Perspectives: The Civil Rights Quarterly. $15. q. Commission on Civil Rights, 1121 Vermont Ave., NW, Washington, DC 20425 (formerly *Civil Rights Digest;* name changed with v. 12, no. 1, Spring 1980)

Phylon: The Atlanta University Review of Race and Culture. $12. q. Atlanta University, Atlanta, GA 30314

Political Quarterly. $41.50. q. 4 Bloomsbury Sq., London, WC1, England

Political Science Quarterly. $24. q. Academy of Political Science, 619 W. 114th St., Ste. 500, New York, NY 10025

Political Studies. $44. q. Political Studies Assn. of the United Kingdom, Oxford University Press, Press Rd., Neasden, London, NW10 0DD, England

Politics and Society. $28. q. Geron-X, Inc., Publishers, Box 1108, Los Altos, CA 94022

Population Bulletin. $25. bi-m. Population Reference Bureau, Inc., Circulation Department, 1337 Connecticut Ave., Washington, DC 20036

Problems of Communism. $10. bi-m. Superintendent of Documents, Government Printing Office, Washington, DC 20402

The Professional Geographer. $19. q. Assn. of American Geographers, 1710 16th St., NW, Washington, DC 20009

Psychiatry: Journal for the Study of Interpersonal Processes. $24. q. 1610 New Hampshire Ave., NW, Washington, DC 20009

Psychological Record. $21.50. q. Kenyon College, Gambier, OH 43022

Psychological Reports. $112. bi-m. Box 9229, Missoula, MT 59807

Psychological Review. $26. bi-m. American Psychological Assn., Inc., Subscription Section, 1200 17th St., NW, Washington, DC 20036

Public Administration Review. $35. bi-m. American Society for Public Administration, 1225 Connecticut Ave., NW, Washington, DC 20036

The Public Interest. $12. q. Box 542, Old Chelsea Post Office, New York, NY 10011

Public Management. $15. m. International City Management Assn., 1140 Connecticut Ave., NW, Washington, DC 20036

Public Opinion Quarterly. $28. q. Elsevier North-Holland, Inc., 52 Vanderbilt Ave., New York, NY 10017

Public Polity. $25. q. John Wiley & Sons, Inc., 605 3rd Ave., New York, NY 10158

Quarterly Journal of Economics. $30. q. John Wiley and Sons, Inc., 605 3rd Ave., New York, NY 10016

Quarterly Review of Economics and Business. $17. q. 428 Commerce West, Urbana, IL 61801

Review of Black Political Economy. $15. q. Rutgers University, New Brunswick, NJ 08903

Review of Economic Studies. $67. 5 times a yr. Longman Group Ltd., Journals Division, 43-45 Annandale St., Edinburgh, EH7 4AT, Scotland

Review of Economics and Statistics. $56. q. North-Holland Publishing Co., P.O. Box 211, Amsterdam, The Netherlands

Review of Politics. $10. q. University of Notre Dame, IN 46556

Review of Social Economy. $18. 3 times a yr. Assn. for Social Economics, DePaul University, 25 E. Jackson Blvd., Chicago, IL 60604

The Round Table: The Commonwealth Journal of International Affairs. $30. q. Professional & Scientific Publications, Tavistock House East, Tavistock Sq., London, WC1H 9JR, England

Rural Sociology. $28. q. Rural Sociological Society, 325 Morgan Hall, University of Tennessee, Knoxville, TN 37916

Scandinavian Review. $15. q. American-Scandinavian Foundation, 127 E. 73rd St., New York, NY 10021

Science & Society: An Independent Journal of Marxism. $20. q. John Jay College, CUNY, 445 W. 59th St., New York, NY 10019

Simulation & Gaming: An International Journal of Theory, Design, & Research. $39. q. Sage Publications, Inc., 2455 Teller Rd., Newbury Park, CA 91320

Social and Economic Studies. $15. q. University of the West Indies, Institute of Social and Economic Research, Mona, Jamaica

Social Biology. $35. q. University of Wisconsin, 1180 Observatory Dr., Madison, WI 53706

Social Casework: The Journal of Contemporary Social Work. $25. m. (S-Je) Family Service Assn. of America, 44 E. 23rd St., New York, NY 10010

Social Forces: An International Journal of Social Research. $15.60 q. University of North Carolina Press, Box 2288, Chapel Hill, NC 27514

Social Policy. $15. bi-m. Room 1212, 33 W. 42nd St., New York, NY 10036

Social Problems: Official Journal of the Society for the Study of Social Problems. $35. 5 times a yr. 208 Rockwell Hall, State University College, 1300 Elmwood Ave., Buffalo, NY 14222

Social Psychology Quarterly. $16. q. American Sociological Assn., 1722 N St., NW, Washington, DC 20036

Social Research: An International Quarterly of the Social Sciences. $20. q. New School for Social Research, 66 W. 12th St., New York, NY 10011

Social Science Quarterly. $30. q. University of Texas Press, Box 7819, Austin, TX 78712

Social Service Review. $22. q. University of Chicago Press, 5801 Ellis Ave., Chicago, IL 60637

Social Theory and Practice. $21. 3 times a yr. Florida State University, Department of Philosophy, Tallahassee, FL 32306

Social Work: Journal of the National Association of Social Workers. $30. bi-m., 49 Sheridan Ave., Albany, NY 12210

Sociological Quarterly. $15. q. Southern Illinois University, Department of Sociology, Carbondale, IL 62901

The Sociological Review: New Series. $30. q. University of Keele, Staffordshire, ST5 5BG, England

Sociology and Social Research: An International Journal. $30. q. University of Southern California Press, University Park, Los Angeles, CA 90007

Sociology of Education: A Journal of Research in Socialization and Social Structure. $16. 4 times a yr. American Sociological Assn., 1722 N St., NW, Washington, DC 20036

Sociology: The Journal of the British Sociological Association. $50.26. 3 times a yr. 10 Portugal St., London, WC2A 2HD, England

Southern Economic Journal. $30. q. Hanes Hall 019-A, Chapel Hill, NC 27514

Soviet Review: A Journal of Translations. $25. q. M. E. Sharpe, Inc., 901 N. Broadway, White Plains, NY 10603

State Government. $12. q. P.O. Box 11910, Lexington, KY 40578

Studies in Comparative Communism: An International Interdisciplinary Journal. $22. q. Editorial and Business Offices, VKC 330, School of International Relations, University of Southern California, University Park, Los Angeles, CA 90007

Survey: A Journal of East and West Studies. $27. q. Oxford University Press, Subscription Department, Press Rd., Neasden, London, NW10 0DD, England

Technology and Culture. $27. q. University of Chicago Press, 5801 Ellis Ave., Chicago, IL 60637

Town and Country Planning. $20. 11 times a yr. Town and Country Planning Assn., 17 Carlton House Terrace, London, SW1Y 5AS, England

Town Planning Review. $36. q. Liverpool University Press, 123 Grove St., Liverpool, 17 7AF, England

Trial: The National Legal Newsmagazine. $18. n. Assn. of Trial Lawyers of America, P.O. Box 3717, 1050 31st St., NW, Washington, DC 20007

Urban Affairs Quarterly. $38. q. Sage Publications, Inc., 2455 Teller Rd., Newbury Park, CA 91320

Urban Studies. $38. 3 times a yr. Longman Group, Ltd., Journals Division, 43-45 Annandale St., Edinburgh, EH7 4AT, Scotland

Washington Monthly. $20. 11 times a yr. 1611 Connecticut Ave., NW, Washington, DC 20009

Western Political Quarterly. $20. q. D. W. Hanson, Editor, University of Utah, Salt Lake City, UT 84112

World Marxist Review: Problems of Peace and Socialism. $7.50. m. Progress Subscription Service, 71 Bathurst St., Toronto, Ontario, Canada M5V 2P6

World Politics: A Quarterly Journal of International Relations. $22.50. q. Princeton University Press, Princeton, NJ 08540

The World Today. $27. m. Oxford University Press, Press Rd., Neasden, London, NW10 0DD, England

2. *Sociological Abstracts* is an index that describes briefly every research article published in 24 major information areas: methodology and research technology; sociology—history and theory; social psychology; group interactions; culture and social structure; complex organizations (management); social change and economic development; mass phenomena; political interactions; social differentiation; rural sociology and agricultural economics; urban structures and ecology; sociology of the arts; sociology of education; sociology of religion; social control; sociology of science; demography and human biology; the family and socialization; sociology of health and medicine; social problems and social welfare; sociology of knowledge; community development; and planning, forecasting, and speculation.

It is indexed by subject and by author. A cumulative index for each volume is published as the last (eighth) issue of the year and includes a table of contents, a subject index, a periodical index, a monograph index, an author index, and a list of abbreviations. Abstracts of the papers of the annual meetings of the American Sociological Association are published annually as a supplement that includes a table of contents, abstracts, and an author index.

Sociological Abstracts has been published since 1952 and is especially valuable after an article has been identified as of interest to the researcher. The abstract conveys the findings and enables the researcher to decide whether the original article has significance for the work pursued. Eight issues are published each year.

Sociofile on CD-ROM is a computerized data base now available on compact disc. It contains the same information as *Sociological Abstracts*, 1974 to the present. Check in the reference department of the main college library.

3. *Social Sciences Citation Index* (SSCI) is a calendar-year index begun in 1966 that continues currently. The items covered in SSCI are taken from more than a thousand of the world's most important social science journals in the following disciplines: anthropology, archaeology, area studies, business and finance, communication, community health, criminology and penology, demography, economics, educational research, ethnic group studies, geography, history, information and library sciences, international relations, law, linguistics, management, marketing, philosophy, political science, psychiatry, psychology, sociology, statistics, and urban planning and development.

Undertaking a search in the SSCI. Using SSCI is a relatively simple affair. In a citation index the subject of a search is symbolized by the starting reference rather than by a word or subject heading. Consequently, searching is independent of special nomenclatures or artificial languages. The searcher starts with a reference or an author he or she has identified through a footnote, book, encyclopedia, or conventional word or subject index. He or she then enters the Citation Index section of the SSCI and searches for the particular author's name. After locating the author's name, the searcher checks to see which of several possible references best fits his or her particular interest. Under the year, journal, volume, and page number of the selected reference, the searcher then looks to see who has currently cited this work. After noting the bibliographic citations of authors citing the work, the searcher then turns to the Source Index section and obtains complete bibliographic data for the works found.

The fundamental question one can answer quickly through the SSCI is, Where and by whom has this paper been cited in the literature? The SSCI is also used by scientists to determine whether their work has been applied or criticized by others. It can facilitate feedback in the communication cycle. Any author may choose to ignore citations to his or her own work and still use the index to retrieve publications that cite works by other social scientists. The SSCI can be used to identify researchers currently working on special problems or to determine whether a paper has been cited, whether there has been a review of a subject, or whether a concept has been applied, a theory confirmed, or a method improved. Because indications of corrections are published in the SSCI, it is also useful as an aid in following particular articles. Only the user's imagination limits the extent to which the SSCI can be a useful tool for the scientist and librarian. Among the many questions that the SSCI can answer are these:

- Has this paper been cited?
- Has there been a review on this subject?
- Has this theory been confirmed?
- Has this work been extended?
- Has this method been improved?
- Has this suggestion been tried?
- Is this idea really original?
- Was this "to be published" paper published, and where?

- Where is the full paper for this preliminary communication?
- Has this technical report been published in a journal?
- Have subsequent errata and correction notes been published?
- Where are the data for an introduction to this paper?
- Where are the raw data for a review article on this subject?
- Is there sufficient new information to warrant updating a chapter in a book?
- What are the raw data for an analytical historical network diagram?
- Who else is working in this field?
- Are there data to delineate this field of study?
- What are some potential new markets for this product?
- Has this theory or concept been applied to a new field?
- What published work originated from this organization?
- Has this article been abstracted in primary journals?
- What are all the current works in which this person is primary author?
- What are all the current works in which this person is secondary author?
- What other works has this person written?
- Has this person's work been compiled?

Current Information About Published Work

4. *Current Contents in the Social Behavioral Sciences* is a weekly listing of the contents of journals and some books in the social and behavioral sciences. It also includes an index by first author and principal words in the titles of articles.

Related Indexed Areas of Interest to the Social Science Researcher

5. *Psychological Abstracts* does for psychology what *Sociological Abstracts* does for the wider field of social science. Social scientists often work in similar areas. In *Psychological Abstracts* there are 16 major content classifications, including general psychology, psychometrics, experimental psychology (human and animal), physiological psychology, physiological intervention, communication systems, developmental psychology, social processes and social issues, experimental social psychology, personality, physical and psychological disorders, treatment and prevention, professional personnel and professional issues, educational psychology, and applied psychology. There is a subject index and an author index. This index service goes back to 1927.

6. *Resources in Education* is a monthly abstract journal published by the Educational Resources Information Center (ERIC) of the National Institute of Education (NIE). *Resources in Education* announces research reports and other nonjournal literature of interest to the educational community. These documents are cataloged, abstracted, and indexed by subject, author or investigator, and responsible institution.

Resources in Education started publication in November 1966 and can be purchased in single copies or by subscription from the Superintendent of Documents, U.S. Government Printing Office, Washington, DC 20402. Annual cumulative sets have been reprinted and can be obtained from Macmillan Information, 216R Brown St., Riverside, NJ 08075. Macmillan Information also publishes *Current Index to Journals in Education* (CIJE), which indexes articles in more than 700 journals. These journals represent the core of the periodical/serial literature in the field of education.

Individual monthly volumes and yearly cumulations of *Resources in Education* and CIJE are available in many college and university libraries, as well as in some special libraries. Most of these libraries are open to the public for on-site reference, and many also have complete ERIC microfiche collections. *Resources in Education* is also available in the offices of many school systems at the state and local levels. All routine searches for documentary material should begin with *Resources in Education*.

All of the indexes—the *Social Science Index, Sociological Abstracts, Social Sciences Citation Index, Psychological Abstracts,* and *Resources in Education*—are housed in almost all college libraries and in many larger public libraries. The same information is available on computer-assisted reference services in major university libraries. These same reference data are also commonly on microfilm or microfiche in major libraries. Interlibrary loans from major universities make everything available to the smallest college anywhere in the United States and to many parts of the world.

Computer-Assisted Reference Service

Many major libraries provide searches by computer of bibliographic citations. More than 400 university libraries in the United States are currently on-line. Topics best suited for computer-assisted reference service (CARS) searches include the following:

1. searches on topics so new or specialized that they may not appear as subject headings in printed indexes (examples: cognitive mapping, splinter skills in children)
2. searches that require the coordination of two or more separate concepts (example: effect of parental divorce on children's self-concepts)
3. searches on topics for which there are so many synonyms that a manual search of a key-word-in-context index would take an extremely long time (example: adolescents, teenagers, juveniles, youth, young adults, students)
4. searches that are relatively narrow in scope and are likely to result in a fairly small number of citations (example: PCBs in Indiana)

The advantages of computer-assisted searches are many:

1. They are quick. CARS can often locate appropriate citations in minutes, while a search of printed indexes might take several days.
2. They are comprehensive. CARS can search several sets of sources, which is probably more than the researcher would have time to do manually.
3. They are precisely focused. Printed indexes restrict the number of index terms more than a machine-readable data base does. CARS gives the searcher many additional access points to a given article.
4. They provide good copy. Citations may be printed on-line during the search for immediate delivery, or they can be printed off-line (usually a cheaper option) to be mailed for delivery within three to four days. An average search usually costs between $15 and $30, depending on the data base(s) used and the extent of the search, as well as the number of citations ordered.

Data bases are numerous. For a full list, see Martha E. Williams et al., eds., *Computer-Readable Data Bases: A Directory and Data Source Book* (Washington, DC: American Society for Information Science, 1980). The most important for the social scientist include the following:

- Sociological Abstracts
- Social Scisearch
- Psychological Abstracts
- Population Bibliography

- U.S. Political Science Documents
- American Statistics Index (CIS, Inc.)
- SSIE Current Research (Smithsonian Science Information)
- CIS/Index (Congressional Information Services)
- GPO Monthly Catalog (U.S. Government Printing Office)
- ERIC[2]

Specialized Indexes of Interest to Social Scientists

Population Index attempts to cover the bibliography of demographic research for demographers. To this end, the editors scan as much as possible of the world literature and select some 2,500 titles a year. These are presented in a scheme of topics, with titles translated into English and with annotations or indicative abstracts of varying length provided for the majority. The material indexed consists of publications in 20 Western and Slavic languages, as well as the maximum feasible coverage in Oriental languages. The index includes government documents, periodical articles, books, monographs, and pamphlets. Excluded are unpublished materials, maps and other graphics, and newspaper articles. Selection favors the citation of primary source material and substantive studies of primary data by analytical methods. *Population Index* is based in the offices of Population Research at Princeton University.

Population Bibliography (1966-present, 47,500 records, bimonthly updates; University of North Carolina Population Center, Chapel Hill) is the world's largest single computer data base covering monographs, journals, technical reports, government documents, conference proceedings, dissertations, and many unpublished reports on population. The bibliography is a principal source for information on abortion, demography, migration, family planning, fertility studies, and general areas of population research such as population policy and law, population education, and population research methodology.

The *International Population Census Bibliography: Revision and Update, 1945-1977*, compiled by Doreen S. Goyer (University of Texas, Austin, 1980), has more than 13,000 citations of reports from population censuses taken from 1945 through 1977, almost as many publications in the past 32 years as there were in the preceding period of more than 200 years. No other reference work in the field duplicates exactly the scope of these publications. The *Revision and Update* is a reference tool to aid the researcher and guide the librarian through the maze of census publications. For the researcher it presents the results of a country's census production in a logical manner, using familiar bibliographic descriptions. It tells where a copy of almost every item listed may be found in the United States for consultation in person or via interlibrary loan. On the surface it may seem to have many more conveniences for the librarian, but if the librarian has control of the literature, the researcher reaps the benefits.

American Statistics Index is a comprehensive index of the statistical publications from more than 400 central or regional issuing agencies of the U.S. government. Statistical data include population and economic censuses, foreign trade data, Consumer Price Index reports, unemployment statistics, agricultural data, vital statistics, educational data, and much more. A computer data base covering the same material is available.

Statistical Reference Index is a new index offering information on state government publications, statistical studies by universities, independent research organizations, and business organizations and associations.

PAIS on CD-ROM. A major index to public policy literature, PAIS, is now available on compact disc. PAIS (*Public Affairs Information Service Bulletin*) contains information about journal articles, government reports and documents, and books pertaining to political science, international relations, economics, government, law, business, demography, and public affairs. Check in the reference department of the main college library.

Religion Index on CD-ROM. The Religion Index is the computerized version of four American Theological Library Association publications, and covers publications from 1975 to the present. It contains over 350,000 citations to books, monographs, journal articles, theses, doctoral projects, and book reviews on all aspects of religion and theology. Subjects covered in the index include church history, biblical literature, theology, history of religions, and sociology and psychology of religion, as well as related areas in the humanities and social sciences, and current events. Check the reference desk in the main college library.

Microfilm-Microfiche-Microprint Services[3]

These services provide reproductions of books, newspapers, magazines, scientific journals, and doctoral dissertations. Because it is relatively cheap to acquire and reproduce, use of microfiche especially is growing rapidly. It packs a lot of information in an incredibly small space. Most librarians call it the medium of the future—at least until the computer takes over all reference work. Today many journals are acquired in microfiche to save money and space.

Major newspapers are available generally on microfilm. Such newspapers include the *New York Times, Washington Post, Christian Science Monitor, Los Angeles Times, Manchester Guardian, London Times, Observer,* and *Chicago Tribune.*

Microprint was developed earlier than the other two services. It is a positive print, in contrast to the negative prints of microfilm and microfiche. It holds fewer data, is more expensive, and is more difficult to store.

What is significant for the research scholar is that major indexes such as *Sociological Abstracts* are available on microfiche. This means a missing page in or volume of the printed book need not delay research; it is available with high reliability on microfiche. Interlibrary loan can fill researchers' needs anywhere in the United States.

University Microfilms International (UMI) makes available journal articles and issue reprints of nearly 10,000 magazines and journals, by article or issue and in single or multiple copies. All of the major journals in sociology and the social sciences generally can be obtained for a fee. Every periodical cited in the UMI catalog is available either on paper or in microform (microfilm or microfiche). For further information, contact the UMI Article Reprint Department, 300 North Zeeb Rd., Ann Arbor, MI 48106. In England the address is 18 Bedford Row, London WCIR4EJ.

Online Computer Library Center (OCLC) operates a computer network used by more than 2,400 libraries in the United States and Canada, of which more than 300 are U.S. federal libraries. Founded in 1967 as the Ohio College Library Center, it has grown rapidly into an international center for library automation. To reflect its broadened geographic scope, the name was changed in 1977 to OCLC, Inc., the acronym by which it had already become known throughout the world. More than 3,800 remote computer terminals in the network are linked to OCLC's computer center in Dublin, Ohio. Libraries use the OCLC system to catalog books, order custom-printed catalog cards, maintain location information on library materials, and arrange for interlibrary lending of materials. The files contain more than 6 million records of books and other library materials such as U.S. government documents.

The researcher can use a terminal to check bibliographic information (author, title, and so on), find out whether his or her library owns the item, or locate items in other libraries. Most college and university libraries do not charge for these services. This is the super card catalog of the future, operating now.

Notes

1. This list of periodicals is adapted from a list provided by H. W. Wilson Co., publishers of the *Social Sciences Index*. Reprinted by permission.

2. ERIC was originally conceived in the U.S. Office of Education in the mid-1960s as a system for providing ready access to recent educational research and other education-related literature. The ERIC Processing and Reference Facility is a centralized information processing facility serving Central ERIC and 16 decentralized clearinghouses, each specializing in a branch of knowledge. For further information, write ERIC Processing and Reference Facility, 4833 Rugby Ave., Ste. 303, Bethesda, MD 20014; telephone (301) 656-9723.

3. For a full list of available microforms, see *Microforms in Print, Incorporating International Microforms in Print*. This is an annual publication listing author, subject, price, type of microform, and publisher. It is available from Microform Review, Inc., 520 Riverside Ave., Westport, CT 06880. Johnson Associates have complete sets of 80 sociological journals available in microfiche; if not in your library, they may be purchased by set or volume. For further information, write for the catalog *A Selection of Journals in Sociology Available in Microfiche*, JAI Press, Inc., 165 W. Putnam Ave., Greenwich, CT 06830.

DESCRIPTION OF IMPORTANT DOCUMENTARY RESOURCES AVAILABLE IN THE LIBRARY[1]

4.3

Social science researchers commonly use reference books, bibliographies, data bases, and other materials to assist them. Some of the most useful of these are listed below.

Statistical Sourcebooks

U.S. Bureau of the Census. *Statistical Abstract of the United States, 1981*. 102nd ed. Washington, DC: Government Printing Office, 1981.

Arranged in 33 sections: population; vital statistics, health, and nutrition; immigration and naturalization; education; law enforcement; federal courts and prisons; area, geography, and climate; public lands, parks, recreation, and travel; labor force, employment, and earnings; national defense and veterans' affairs; social insurance and welfare services; income, expenditures, and wealth; prices; elections; federal government finances and employment; state and local government finances and employment; banking, finance, and insurance; business enterprise; communications; power; science; transportation—land; transportation—air and water; agriculture—farms, land, and finances; agriculture—production, marketing, and trade; forests and forest products; fisheries, mining and mineral products; construction and housing; manufactures; distribution and services; foreign commerce and aid; outlying areas under the jurisdiction of the United States; comparative international statistics. Three appendixes; index of names and subjects. Clothbound.

U.S. Census of Population by States. Washington, DC: Government Printing Office, 1981.

Contains the following information for most urban places of population 2,500 or more: size of population by sex; major occupation groups by sex; income for stated year of total families and unrelated individuals; major industry groups by sex; color of population by sex; age of population by sex; years of school completed; marital status of males and females, 14 years and above; country of birth of foreign-born whites (a decennial publication).

U.S. Bureau of the Census. *Historical Statistics of the United States: Colonial Times to 1970.* Washington,
   DC: Government Printing Office, 1975.
Historical data on population; vital statistics and health and medical care; migration; labor; prices and price
   indexes; national income and wealth; consumer income and expenditures; social statistics; land,
   water, and climate; agriculture; forestry and fisheries; minerals; construction and housing; manufactures; transportation; communication; power; distribution and services; foreign trade and other
   international transactions; business enterprise; productivity and technological development; banking
   and finance; government; colonial statistics. Index of names and subjects. Clothbound.
City Directories

   Often useful in giving a wide range of information about industries and social organizations of the community. These
directories typically contain alphabetical lists of persons in a community, listing occupation and address of each adult.

The County and City Data Book. Washington, DC: Government Printing Office.

   Lists numerous tables for each county and cities of 25,000 or more. Contains such tables as labor force, income,
elections, banking and finance, business enterprises, and education.

A Comparative Atlas of America's Great Cities, by John S. Adams and Ronald Abler. Minneapolis:
   University of Minnesota Press, 1977.

   A comparative analysis of the nation's 20 largest cities.

The Municipal Year Book. Chicago: International City Managers' Association. Issued yearly.

   Authoritative reference book on municipal governments. Facts available about the role of city governments,
including education, housing, welfare, and health, make it possible to compare any city with other cities on hundreds
of items.

   For specialized purposes, consult the following publications:

> *U.S. Census of Manufacturers, Area Statistics*
> *U.S. Census of Population, Census Tract Bulletin*
> *Poor's Register of Directors and Executives*
> *Rand McNally's International Bankers' Directory*
> *Moody's Industrial Manual*
> *Editor and Publisher Market Guide*
> *Sales Management, Survey of Buying Power*
> *Fortune Magazine Directory of 500 Largest Corporations*
> *The Economic Almanac*
> *Labor Fact Book*
> *Directory of National and International Labor Unions in the United States*
> *Directory of Scholars, Social and Behavioral Sciences*
> *Who's Who in America* (see also *Who's Who in the East, Who's Who in the Midwest, Who's Who in the South
>   and Southwest, Who's Who on the Pacific Coast*)
> *Who's Who in Commerce and Industry*
> *Who's Who in Labor*

*America's Governments: A Fact Book on Census Data on the Organization, Finances, and Employment of
   Federal, State, and Local Governments*, compiled by Richard P. Nathan and Mary M. Nathan. New
   York: John Wiley, 1979.

   Contains data compiled from U.S. Bureau of the Census documents that describe the form, functions, and finances
of the more than 80,000 governments in the United States. Text, tables, and charts enable the researcher to find out
how a particular large government is organized and financed and how its major characteristics compare with other
governments in the nation.

World Handbook of Political and Social Indicators, by Bruce M. Russett, Haywood R. Alker, Jr., Karl W.
   Deutsch, and Harold D. Lasswell. New Haven, CT: Yale University Press, 1964. (Revised 2nd ed. by
   Charles Lewis Taylor and Michael C. Hudson, 1972.)

   An extensive compilation of 75 variables for 133 states and colonies based on indices covering human resources,
government and politics, communication, wealth, health, education, family and social relations, distributions of wealth
and income, and religion. A matrix of intercorrelation is presented for the 75 variables and an analysis of trends and
patterns is presented, showing how the data can be used to investigate a wide variety of political and social questions.

UNESCO Statistical Yearbook. New York: UNIPUB, 1981.

   Topics covered worldwide include the following:

Population: Tables outline population by area and density from 1960 through 1976, and estimate major areas from
   1970-2000.

Education: Summary tables for all levels of education are cited; public expenditure on education is given at the current market prices and by level of education.

Science and Technology: Manpower is inventoried by research and experimental development; expenditures in the field are totaled.

Libraries: Summarizes libraries and their holdings by category of library, collections, borrowers, works loaned out, current expenditures, personnel.

Publishing: Book production is delineated by number of titles published, language, number of copies, subject groups, translations, and authors; totals of newspapers and other periodicals, paper production, and consumption are aggregated.

Media: Seating capacity and annual attendance at cinema is given; radio/TV tables provide statistical information on transmitters, receivers, and programs.

Basic Statistical References for Education: Elementary, Secondary, and Adult Education; American and World Universities

Standard Education Almanac, 1980-81. Chicago: Marquis Academic Media.

Compiled from latest government and private statistics, this unique almanac provides the most complete coverage of elementary, secondary, and adult education in the United States today. Completely updated, this edition includes statistical information ranging from historical to current, plus projection, in some cases, through the year 2000. A substantial body of information on current trends is presented through articles, reports, and evaluative studies. For coverage of special education and adult education, see *Yearbook of Special Education* and *Yearbook of Adult and Continuing Education* (Chicago: Marquis).

Yearbook of Higher Education, 1980. Chicago: Marquis Academic Media.

This directory provides both statistical and descriptive data about higher education. Part 1 provides essential information about more than 3,400 two- and four-year colleges and universities in the United States and Canada. Part 2 provides updated statistics relating to such areas as enrollment, faculty/staff, income, expenditures, degrees, and the role of the federal government in higher education. Part 3 provides information on higher education associations and accrediting bodies, statewide agencies for postsecondary education, ERIC clearinghouses, and more. (For more reference books published by Marquis Academic Media, see below.)

International Handbook of Universities and Other Institutions of Higher Education. 7th ed. Edited by H. M. R. Keyes and D. J. Aitkew. Paris: International Association of Universities, 1977.

Commonwealth Universities Yearbook, 1980. 4 vols. London: Association of Commonwealth Universities.

Directory of Educational Research Institutions (U1074). New York: UNESCO, 1980.

This first edition of the *Directory* was compiled by UNESCO on the basis of feedback from a preliminary version circulated in late 1979 to the institutions concerned. It is intended to familiarize educational researchers with such institutions and to serve as a link between institutions and researchers, helping to breach the isolation that too often prevents cross-fertilization between them. Its 208 pages contain over 550 entries and cover 117 regions and countries.

Reference Books Published by Marquis Academic Media, Chicago

Annual Register of Grant Support
Consumer Protection Directory
Current Audiovisuals for Mental Health Education
Directory of Certified Psychiatrists and Neurologists
Directory of Publishing Opportunities
Directory of Registered Lobbyists and Lobbyist Legislation
Environmental Protection Directory
Family Factbook
Grantsmanship: Money and How to Get It
Mental Health in America: The Years of Crisis
NASA Factbook
NIH Factbook
NSF Factbook
The Selective Guide to Audiovisuals for Mental Health and Family Life Education
The Selective Guide to Publications for Mental Health and Family Life Education
Sourcebook of Equal Educational Opportunity

Sourcebook on Aging
Sourcebook on Food and Nutrition
Sourcebook on Mental Health
Standard Education Almanac
Standard Medical Almanac
Yearbook of Adult and Continuing Education
Yearbook of Higher Education
Yearbook of Special Education
Worldwide Directory of Computer Companies
Worldwide Directory of Federal Libraries

Abstracts

Abstracts of the Papers of the Annual Meetings of the American Sociological Association. Sociological Abstracts, Inc., 2315 Broadway, New York, NY 10024.

1961. Annually. Table of contents. Abstracts. Author index. Published as a supplement to *Sociological Abstracts.*

Catholic University of America Studies in Sociology Abstract Series. Catholic University of America Press, 620 Michigan Ave., NW, Washington, DC 20017.

1950. Irregularly. Abstracts of dissertations in sociology from the Catholic University of America.

Sociological Abstracts. Sociological Abstracts, Inc., 2315 Broadway, New York, NY 10024.

For full description, refer to Section 4.2.

Communication Abstracts. Sage Publications, Inc., 2455 Teller Rd., Newbury Park, CA 91320.

1978. Bimonthly. Provides in-depth abstracts of recent communication-related literature from publishers, research institutions, universities, and information services; 60 professional journals are searched regularly.

Sociology of Education Abstracts. School of Education, University of Liverpool, 19 Abercromby Sq., Liverpool 7, England.

1965. Quarterly. Education study areas index. Sociological study areas index. List of abstractors.

Almanacs

Brittain, J. Michael, and Stephen A. Roberts. *Inventory of Information Resources and the Social Sciences.* Lexington, MA: D. C. Heath, 1975.

This book provides a detailed list of specialized information resources and services in the social sciences and related fields in Western Europe, Scandinavia, Canada, and Japan. The inventory covers query answering and referral centers, bibliography sources, and ongoing research into information systems. For each resource listed, details are given—full name and address, range of subjects covered and information handled, availability of services, and relevant changes. Comprehensive title, subject, and geographical indexes are provided; these, together with headings in the text and the editorial introduction, are given in French and English.

Gendell, Murray, and Hans L. Zetterberg, eds. *A Sociological Almanac for the United States.* 2nd ed. New York: Scribner's, 1964.

This volume is made up of three essays—"The United States Summed Up by Browsing in a Sociological Almanac," "The Organization of a Sociological Almanac," and "How to Read a Table"—and 96 tables about American society organized in terms of nine major topics: human resources, nonhuman resources, polity and order, economy and prosperity, science and knowledge, religion and sacredness, art and beauty, ethics and virtue, and community—local and national. Paperbound, 109 pages.

Bibliography

International Bibliography of the Social Sciences—Sociology. Hawthorne, NY: Aldine.

1952-54, volumes 1-4, published in *Current Sociology*; 1955-59, volumes 5-9, published as *International Bibliography of Sociology, 1960.* Published annually. List of periodicals consulted. Classification scheme. Bibliography. Author index. Subject index.

Dictionaries and Glossaries

Bogardus, Emory S. "Selected Sociological Concepts for Beginning Students in Sociology," *Sociology and Social Research* 44 (January-February 1960): 200-208.

A brief definition of and discussion about 52 sociological concepts recommended to beginning sociology students.

Fairchild, Henry Pratt, ed. *Dictionary of Sociology*. New Students Outline Series. Paterson, NJ: Littlefield, Adams, 1961.

This is a reprint, unchanged from the original edition that appeared in 1944. Paperbound, 350 pages.

Gould, Julius, and William L. Kolb, eds. *A Dictionary of Social Science*. New York: Free Press, 1964.

Each entry outlines a brief history of usage and discusses the variations in current usage. Foreword by the Secretariat of UNESCO. Clothbound, 777 pages.

Mihanovich, Clement S., Robert J. McNamara, and William N. Tome, eds. *Glossary of Sociological Terms*. Milwaukee, WI: Bruce, 1957.

40 pages.

Mitchell, G. Duncan, ed. *A Dictionary of Sociology*. Hawthorne, NY: Aldine, 1968.

Especially prepared to introduce students to the language of the discipline. 232 pages.

Mitchell, G. Duncan, ed. *A New Dictionary of the Social Sciences*. Hawthorne, NY: Aldine, 1979.

Updated and expanded edition of above to cover all social sciences.

Reading, Hugh R. *A Dictionary of the Social Sciences*. Boston: Routledge & Kegan Paul, 1977.

Designed for students of the social sciences, public administration, social administration, and social work, this dictionary is also useful to those who work in specialized agencies and international organizations. Defines more than 7,500 terms.

Theodorson, George A., and Achilles G. Theodorson, eds. *Modern Dictionary of Sociology*. New York: Crowell, 1969.

Encyclopedias

Boudon, Raymond, and Francois Bouricand. *A Critical Dictionary of Sociology*. Chicago: University of Chicago Press, 1989.

Kuper, Adam, and Jessica Kuper. *The Social Science Encyclopedia*. London: Routledge & Kegan Paul, 1985.

Seligman, Edwin R. A., and Alvin Johnson, eds. *Encyclopedia of the Social Sciences*. 15 vols. New York: Macmillan, 1930-35.

The original 15 volumes are now issued in an 8-book set. Volume 1, in addition to regular articles, includes 23 essays in two introductory sections: "The Development of Social Thought and Institutions" and "The Social Sciences as Disciplines." Volume 15, in addition to regular articles, includes a complete index.

Sills, David L., ed. *International Encyclopedia of the Social Sciences* (Foreword by Alvin Johnson). 17 vols. New York: Macmillan, 1968.

Volume 17 is a complete index. Comprehensive, thorough, authoritative. Succinct information on all important subjects in one source.

Guides to the Literature

Blau, Peter M., and Joan W. Moore. "Sociology." In *A Reader's Guide to the Social Sciences*, rev. ed., edited by Bert F. Hoselitz, 158-87. Glencoe, IL: Free Press, 1975.

Arranged in two major sections. The first section, "The Development of Sociology," includes early social philosophy, the separation of state and society, inevitable evolutionary forces, concern with social reform, history and sociology, the scientific study of social facts, implications, and reactions. The second section, "Contemporary Sociological Literature in Selected Areas," includes social theory, interviewing surveys, social psychology, demography and human ecology, social differentiation in community and nation, formal and informal organization.

Bottomore, T. B. *Sociology: A Guide to Problems and Literature*. 2nd ed. New York: Pantheon, 1971.

Lewis, Peter R. "Sociology." Chap. 10 in *The Literature of the Social Sciences: An Introductory Survey and Guide*. London: Library Association, 1960.

Arranged in five parts: bibliographies, guides, and reference books; sociological theory; sources on social conditions; social services; libraries and library problems.

Lu, Joseph K. *U.S. Government Publications in the Social Sciences: An Annotated Guide.* Beverly Hills, CA: Sage, 1975.

Library of Congress. *A Dictionary of Information Resources in the United States: Social Sciences.* Washington, DC: Government Printing Office, 1973.

Mukherjee, A. K. "Sociology, Social Psychology, and Allied Topics." In *Annotated Guide to Reference Materials in the Human Sciences*, 177-256. London: Asia Publishing House, 1962.

Chapter 4 is arranged in 8 parts: dictionary, encyclopedia, yearbook, directory, handbook, bibliography, abstract and index, historical material. Chapter 5 covers specialized journals. Chapter 6 is arranged in 16 parts: basic source material and standard treatise—sociology, rural and urban sociology, social change, social problems, family and kinship, social survey and methodology, social casework, race problems, social psychology, culture and personality, personality study, ethnopsychology, somat-psychology, author index, subject index.

UNESCO. *Main Trends of Research in the Social and Human Sciences.* Pt. 1, *The Social Sciences.* New York: Mouton, 1980.

An examination of the present state as well as the perspectives for development of various social science disciplines and inter- and multidisciplinary dimensions of research in these fields.

White, Carl M., and Associates. *Sources of Information in the Social Sciences: A Guide to the Literature.* 2nd ed. Chicago: American Library Association, 1973.

Zetterberg, Hans L. "Sociology." In *Sources of Information in the Social Sciences: A Guide to the Literature*, edited by Carl M. White (with an annotated bibliography by Thompson M. Little and Carl M. White), 183-228. Totowa, NJ: Bedminster, 1964.

Zetterberg's essay is arranged in 20 parts, organized under five major headings: general orientation, sociological theory, topics of sociology, methods of sociology. Little and White's bibliography is organized under the following 14 heading: guides to the literature; reviews of the literature; abstracts and digests; bibliographies—current; bibliographies—retrospective; dictionaries; encyclopedias and encyclopedic sets; directories and biographical information; atlases and pictorial works; handbooks, manuals, compendia; yearbooks; statistical sources; sources of scholarly contributions; sources of unpublished information.

Handbooks, Sourcebooks, and Reviews

Bart, Pauline, and Linda Frankel. *The Student Sociologist's Handbook.* 2nd ed. Morristown, NJ: General Learning Press, 1975.

Berger, Charles R., and Steven H. Chaffee. *Handbook of Communication Science.* Newbury Park, CA: Sage, 1987.

Berry, William D., and Michael S. Lewis-Beck, eds. *New Tools for Social Scientists: Advances and Applications in Research Methods.* Beverly Hills, CA: Sage, 1986.

Borgatta, Edgar F., and Karen S. Cook. *The Future of Sociology.* Newbury Park, CA: Sage, 1988.

Bunker, Barbara B., Howard B. Pearlson, and Justin W. Schultz. *Student's Guide to Conducting Social Research.* New York: Human Sciences Press, 1975.

Collins, Randall. *Sociology Since Mid-Century: Essays in Theory Cumulation.* New York; Academic Press, 1981.

This volume discusses major intellectual developments in sociology.

Dubin, Robert, ed. *Handbook of Work, Organization, and Society.* Skokie, IL: Rand McNally, 1976.

Experts describe research areas of industrial sociology.

Filsinger, Erik E., ed. *Marriage and Family Assessment: A Sourcebook for Family Therapy.* Beverly Hills, CA: Sage, 1983.

Contains a wide array of scales, inventories, and other proven assessment techniques.

Goslin, David A., ed. *Handbook of Socialization Theory and Research.* Chicago: Rand McNally, 1969.

Gouldner, Alvin, and S. M. Miller, eds. *Applied Sociology: Opportunities and Prospects.* Glencoe, IL: Free Press, 1964.

Experts describe application of sociology to numerous fields of activity.

Handy, Rollo, and Kurtz, Paul. "Sociology." In *A Current Appraisal of the Behavioral Sciences*, 25-34. Great Barrington, MA: Behavioral Research Council, 1964.

Arranged under nine headings: working specification of the field; other specifications of the field; schools, methods, techniques; results achieved; contemporary controversy; problems of terminology; comment and evaluation; selected bibliographies; germane journals.

Hare, Paul A. *Handbook of Small Group Research.* 2nd ed. New York: Free Press, 1976.

Hauser, Philip M., ed. *Handbook for Social Research in Urban Areas.* Paris: UNESCO, 1964.

Hoselitz, Bert F., ed. *A Reader's Guide to the Social Sciences.* Rev. ed. New York: Free Press, 1975.

General introduction and guide to the literature of the social sciences. Covers historical development of sociology, psychology, anthropology, geography, and economics with appraisals of the classics in the field, systematic review of current output, and critical comments on present trends and directions. Bibliography.

Janovitz, Morris. *The Last Half-Century: Societal Change and Politics in America.* Chicago: University of Chicago Press, 1978.

Comprehensive systematic analysis of the major trends in American society during the first half of the twentieth century; compare with Randall Collins as cited above.

Lazarsfeld, Paul F., William H. Sewell, and Harold L. Wilensky, eds. *The Uses of Sociology.* New York: Basic Books, 1967.

Introduction and 31 articles written especially for this volume and arranged in six parts: sociological perspectives, the uses of sociology in the professions, the uses of sociology in establishments, social problems and formal planning, rapid social change, institutional problems in applied sociology. Index of names, index of subjects. Clothbound, 913 pages.

Lindzey, Gardner, and Elliot Aronson, eds. *Handbook of Social Psychology.* 5 vols. Reading, MA: Addison-Wesley, 1968-70.

Lipset, Seymour Martin, and Neil J. Smelser, eds. *Sociology, the Progress of a Decade: A Collection of Articles.* Englewood Cliffs, NJ: Prentice-Hall, 1961.

Introduction and 64 articles arranged in four parts; the discipline of sociology; the major boundaries of social systems; the production and allocation of wealth, power, and prestige; the balance between stability and change in society. Clothbound, 646 pages.

March, James G., ed. *Handbook of Organizations.* Chicago: Rand McNally, 1965.

McInnis, Raymond G., and Scott, James W. *Social Science Research Handbook.* New York: Barnes & Noble, 1974.

Madge, John. *The Origins of Scientific Sociology.* New York: Free Press, 1962.

A review of selected work by outstanding sociologists who have contributed to the building of a scientific sociology.

Merton, Robert K., Leonard Broom, and Leonard S. Cottrell, Jr., eds. *Sociology Today: Problems and Prospects.* New York: Basic Books, 1959.

Introduction and 25 articles written especially for this volume and arranged in five parts; problems in sociological theory and methodology, problems in the sociology of institutions, the group and the person, problems in demographic and social structure, selected applications of sociology. Index of names and subjects. Clothbound, 658 pages. Also available in a two-volume paperbound set from Harper & Row, New York.

Merton, Robert K., and Matilda White Riley, eds. *Sociological Tradition from Generation to Generation: Glimpses into the American Experience.* Norwood, NJ: Ablex, 1980.

Mitchell, G. Duncan. *A Hundred Years of Sociology.* Chicago: Aldine, 1968.

A concise history of the major ideas, figures, and schools of sociological thought.

Mohan, Raj P., and Don Martindale. *Handbook of Contemporary Developments in World Sociology.* Westport, CT: Greenwood, 1975.

This collection brings together a number of notable sociologists, all of whom were asked to examine how sociology, a transnational discipline, has been and continues to be shaped by the individual nation-states of the world. Differences in methodology, viewpoint, and emphasis are apparent throughout the work. The split in French sociology between a global, humanistic sociology and a historical microsociology is explored, as is the impact of an outmoded university system, religion, and regional divisions on the development of sociology in Italy. The complex and often contradictory effects of American sociological thought on the Western Hemisphere and Russian thought on Eastern Europe are detailed. The receptivity of Japan and Australia to Western empirical methods is analyzed.

Nesselroade, John R., and Raymond B. Cattell. *Handbook of Multivariate Experimental Psychology.* 2nd ed. New York: Plenum, 1988.

Presents methodological breakthroughs in multivariate method and theory construction, multivariate modeling and data analysis, and domains of applications.

Olson, David H., ed. *Inventory of Marriage and Family Literature.* 7 vols. Beverly Hills, CA: Sage, 1977-81.
Systematic, comprehensive listing of current literature.

Parsons, Talcott, ed. *American Sociology: Perspective, Problems, Methods.* New York: Basic Books, 1968.
Introduction and 24 essays especially prepared for this volume and arranged in six parts and a conclusion: components of social systems; methods of investigation; functional subsystems; sociology of culture; strain, deviance, and social control; total societies and their change; conclusion, index of names of subjects. Clothbound, 368 pages.

Seidman, Edward. *Handbook of Social Intervention.* Beverly Hills, CA: Sage, 1983.

Shils, Edward K. *The Calling of Sociology and Other Essays on the Pursuit of Learning.* Chicago: University of Chicago Press, 1980.

Short, James F., Jr., ed. *The State of Sociology: Problems and Prospects.* Beverly Hills, CA: Sage, 1981.
Assessments of accomplishments in methodology, theory, empirical knowledge, and application of sociology over the last 25 years.

Smelser, Neil J., ed. *Handbook of Sociology.* Newbury Park, CA: Sage, 1988.
Essays cover theoretical and methodological issues, bases of inequality in society, major institutional and organizational settings, and social processes and change.

Stogdill, Ralph M. *Handbook of Leadership, Theory, and Research.* New York: Free Press, 1974.

Sussman, Marvin B., and Suzanne K. Steinmetz, eds. *Handbook of Marriage and the Family.* New York: Plenum, 1987.

Van Hasselt, Vincent B., Randall L. Morrison, and Michel Hersen. *Handbook of Family Violence.* New York: Plenum, 1988.

Wakefield Washington Associates. *Family Research: A Source Book, Analysis, and Guide to Federal Funding.* Westport, CT: Greenwood, 1980.

Note

1. This guide was originally assembled by John Pease, University of Maryland; I have made additions and changes in revised editions, with much assistance by Herman Loether.

4.4   GUIDES FOR SELECTION AND CONSTRUCTION OF QUESTIONNAIRES AS UTILIZED IN FIELD RESEARCH

The mail questionnaire is a list of questions for information or opinion that is mailed to potential respondents who have been chosen in some designated manner. The respondents are asked to complete the questionnaire and return it by mail.

This means of gathering information is very popular because it promises to secure data at a minimum of time and expense. The popularity of the method is often defeated because many respondents are overburdened by the number of questionnaires that reach them. In the competition for their time, respondents increasingly examine the purpose of the study, the sponsorship, the utility of findings to them, the time required to fill out the questionnaire, the quality and readability of the type, and perhaps the quality of the paper.

Decision-making criteria. Every researcher who chooses the mail questionnaire should consider its value in a highly competitive environment in which the majority of respondents will probably not complete and return the questionnaire. The researcher should examine carefully the advantages and disadvantages described below. The disadvantages are shown first to emphasize their importance. If the advantages override these disadvantages, and if the method fits the study, then the questionnaire is appropriate. A guide to questionnaire construction follows that should prove useful. Also note the guide to techniques for increasing percentage of returns.

Disadvantages of the Mail Questionnaire[1]

1. The problem of nonreturns must be addressed.
   a. Response rates to mail questionnaires usually do not exceed 50% when conducted by private and relatively unskilled persons.
   b. Intensive follow-up efforts are required to increase returns.
2. Those who answer the questionnaire may differ significantly from nonrespondents, thereby biasing the sample.
   a. Nonrespondents become a collection of individuals about whom virtually nothing is known.
   b. Special efforts must be made (registered letters, telephone calls, personal interviews, and so on), to assess how nonrespondents compare with respondents.
   c. The most thorough of follow-up efforts bring the researcher up against persons who cannot be located, who may be inaccessible, or who are unreachable. The residual group of "no response" or "refuse to answer" can be considerable.

Advantages of the Mail Questionnaire

1. Permits wide coverage for minimum expense, both in money and in effort.
2. Affords wider geographic contact.
3. Reaches people who are difficult to locate and interview.
4. Greater coverage may yield greater validity through larger and more representative samples.
5. Permits more considered answers.
6. More adequate in situations in which the respondent has to check information.
7. More adequate in situations in which group consultations would give more valid information.
8. Greater uniformity in the manner in which questions are posed.
9. Gives respondent a sense of privacy.
10. Affords a simple means of continual reporting over time.
11. Lessens interviewer effect.

Guide to Questionnaire Construction[2]

Reclarify the relation of the method to the problem and hypotheses. Obtain a thorough grasp of the area to be studied and a clear understanding of the objectives of the study and the nature of the data needed.

In a *descriptive* inquiry the investigator is seeking to estimate as precisely and comprehensively as possible a problem area; in an *explanatory* inquiry of a theoretical type, the investigator is seeking to test some particular hypothesis about the determinants of a dependent variable or factor. In either type, economy and efficiency are important criteria. The rule is, Gather the data you need but not more than is needed. Know how you will use and analyze your data. Make your dummy tables now if possible and challenge their adequacy for describing the possible distributions or relationships that are related to your problem or hypotheses.

Formulate questions. Take the following points into account in building your questionnaire.

1. Keep the language pitched to the level of the respondent.

   Interviews given only to specialized respondents can use the terminology with which they are familiar, but interviews given to the general public must use everyday language.

2. Try to pick words that have the same meaning for everyone.

   For instance, a questionnaire involving American and British respondents might ask, "How often do you have tea?" Americans would probably think of tea as a drink. The British would likely think of *tea* in this question as referring to a light afternoon meal.

3. Avoid long questions.

   When questions are too long they often become ambiguous and confusing.

4. Do not assume a priori that your respondent possesses *factual* information or firsthand opinions.

   A mother may be able to report what books her child reads, but the child must be questioned to find out how he or she feels about reading those books.

5. Establish the frame of reference you have in mind.

       Don't ask: How many magazines do you read?

             Ask: Which magazines do you read?

6. In forming a question, either suggest all possible alternatives to the respondent or don't suggest any.

       Don't ask: Do you think the husband should help with dressing and feeding the small children when he's home?

             Ask: Do you think the husband should help with dressing and feeding the small children when he's home, or do you think it's the wife's job in any case?

             Or: Who should dress and feed the children when the husband is home?

7. Protect your respondent's ego.

       Don't ask: Do you know the name of the chief justice of the Supreme Court?

             Ask: Do you happen to know the name of the chief justice of the Supreme Court?

8. If you are after unpleasant orientations, give your respondent a chance to express positive feelings first, so that he or she is not put in an unfavorable light.

             Ask: What do you like about X?

           Then: What don't you like about X?

9. Decide whether you need a direct question, an indirect question, or an indirect question followed by a direct one.

           Direct: Do you ever steal on the job?

         Indirect: Do you know of anyone ever stealing on the job?

     Combination: Do you know of anyone ever stealing on the job? Have you ever taken anything from the job?

10. Decide whether the question should be open or closed.

            Open: It is believed that some people in this community have too much power. Do you think this is true? Who are they?

          Closed: It is believed that some people in this community have too much power. Is this statement ☐ True. ☐ False.

                 ☐ Don't know. If true, who are they?

                 ☐ Negroes. ☐ Jews. ☐ Poles. ☐ Italians.

11. Decide whether general or specific questions are needed.

          It may be enough to ask: How well did you like the book?

    It may be preferable also to ask: Have you recommended the book to anyone else?

12. Avoid ambiguous wording.

        Don't ask: Do you usually work alone?

              Ask: ☐ No, I never work alone.

☐ Yes, I work alone less than half the time.

☐ Yes, I work alone most of the time.

13. Avoid biased or leading questions.

    Don't ask: Did you exercise your right as an American citizen to vote in the last election?

    Ask: Did you vote in the last election?

14. Phrase questions so that they are not unnecessarily objectionable.

    Don't ask: Did you graduate from high school?

    Ask: What is the highest grade in school you completed?

15. Decide whether a personal or impersonal question will obtain the better response.

    Impersonal: Are working conditions satisfactory or not satisfactory where you work?

    Personal: Are you satisfied or dissatisfied with working conditions in the plant where you work?

16. Questions should be limited to a simple idea or a single reference.

    Don't ask: Do you favor or oppose increased job security and the guaranteed annual wage?

    Ask: Do you favor or oppose increased job security?

    And: Do you favor or oppose the guaranteed annual wage?

Organize the questionnaire. The order in which questions are asked is very important. Take the following into account in organizing your questions:

1. Start with easy questions that the respondent will enjoy answering.
   a. Don't start with age, occupation, or marital status.
   b. Ask questions to arouse interest.
2. Don't condition answers to subsequent questions by preceding ones.
   a. Go from the general to the specific.

    Ask: How do you think this country is getting along in its relations with other countries?

    Then: How do you think we are doing in our relations with the Soviet Union?

    b. Go from easier questions to more difficult ones.
3. Use the sequence of questions to protect the respondent's ego. Save personal questions, such as those about income, for later.
4. Decide whether one or several questions will best obtain the information for a given objective.
5. With free-answer questions, it is sometimes helpful to have the questions in pairs, asking for the pros and cons of a particular issue.
6. Open-ended questions, which require most thought and writing, should be kept to a minimum. Generally, these should be placed at the end to assure that the closed questions will be answered.
7. Topics and questions should be arranged so that they make the most sense to the respondent. The aim is to secure a sequence that is natural and easy for the respondent.

Pretest the questionnaire.

1. Select a number of respondents representative of those you expect to survey and interview them. Encourage them to ask any questions that they have as they respond to your items. Watch for misunderstanding, ambiguity, and defensiveness. Ask them how they would restate questions that are difficult to understand or to answer.
2. Never omit pretesting!

TABLE 4.3 Techniques for Increasing Percentage of Returns

Method	Possible Increase of Total % of Returns	Optimal Conditions
Follow-up	50%	More than one follow-up may be needed. If possible, returns may be increased by using double postcards with the most important questions on follow-ups. The telephone can often be used effectively for follow-up. Researcher should find out if respondent needs another copy of the questionnaire (it may have been destroyed or misplaced). Sewell and Shaw report an 87.2% return on 9,007 from parents of Wisconsin high school students using three waves of mailed questionnaires and final telephone interview. *American Sociological Review* 33 (April 1968): 193.
Sponsor	17%	John K. Norton found that people the respondent knew produced the best results. A state headquarters received the second best rate. Others following in order were a lower-status person in a similar field, a publishing firm, a college professor or student, and a private association or foundation.
Length	22%	If a questionnaire is short, then the shorter the better. A double postcard should produce the best results. However, if the questionnaire is over 10 pages at the minimum, length may cease to be a factor. Sewell and Shaw used a double post-card in the study reported.
Introductory letter	7%	An altruistic appeal seems to have better results than the idea that the respondent may receive something good from it.
Type of questions	13%	Questionnaires asking for objective information receive the best rate, and questionnaires asking for subjective information receive the worst.

Select paper and typeface carefully. The use of a good-quality typeface can produce a mimeographed questionnaire on good paper that looks like a printed copy.

Consider how you can present the strongest possible sponsorship. The person, persons, or group that will support your efforts through a covering letter is important. Note the increase of 17% return reported in the technique guide for increasing percentage of returns (see Table 4.3).

Examine each of the techniques discussed in Section 4.9 for increasing return of the questionnaire, and decide which will maximize returns for you.

Refer to the examples of question wording above. Note how open and closed questions are phrased.

Experiences of Researchers with the Mail Questionnaire: Guides 4.5, 4.6, 4.7, and 4.8

The records that follow were selected from a large universe of mail questionnaires. Guide 4.5 is a compilation of return rates from many different populations with different content in the questionnaires. This record shows the wide range of returns that may be expected. Guide 4.6 is a model of outcomes from a long questionnaire mailed to more than 18,000 college graduates from different colleges across the United States. This record shows how the problems of eligibility, location, accessibility, and acceptability diminish returns. Guide 4.7 is an analysis of returns from a study of top leaders on the East Coast of the United States. This compilation displays the importance of occupational type and indicates how the geocultural character of a city can diminish returns. Guide 4.8 is a summary of response rates based on 183 published studies that used mail questionnaires. This guide displays the wide variation in response rates and highlights the successful use of follow-up mailings.

Notes

1. See David Wallace, "A Case For—and Against—Mail Questionnaires," *Public Opinion Quarterly* 18 (1954): 40-52.
2. See Paul F. Lazarsfeld, *Qualitative Analysis: Historical and Critical Essays* (Boston: Allyn & Bacon, 1972), chap. 8; see also Don A. Dillman, "Writing Questions," chap. 3 in *Mail and Telephone Surveys* (New York: Wiley-Interscience, 1978).

A RECORD OF RETURN RATES FROM MANY DIFFERENT MAIL QUESTIONNAIRES

4.5

Instructions for Use of Guide 4.5

The compilation shown in Table 4.4 is based on a selection of questionnaires to show the range of returns that follow a mailing of questionnaires. Note that there are populations representing the general public, adult women, and powerful eastern urban leaders from business, labor, government, religious, and civic and civil rights groups. These populations yield returns varying from 3% to 71%.

The populations following these are those of college and high school graduates; note that these yield a range of 24-90% return. The succeeding populations are as various as members of the American Sociological Association, deans of professional schools in the United States, women cafeteria employees, and women faculty members. Returns range from 24.5% to 65%.

A MODEL OF OUTCOMES FROM A LONG MAIL QUESTIONNAIRE

4.6

Instructions for Use of Guide 4.6

This guide reports on a study made in 1963 by Robert Calvert, Jr., of male liberal arts graduates from a wide selection of colleges and universities across the United States.[1] The years sampled are for graduates in 1948, 1953, and 1958. This means that 15, 10, and 5 years had elapsed since graduation for the respective classes. The questionnaire was long—20 pages. The population consisted of highly educated

TABLE 4.4 A Record of Return from Many Different Mail Questionnaires

Population	Aim and Date of Questionnaire	Length	Number Sent	Number Returned	Percentage Returned	Number of Follow-Ups	Research Agent
Statewide samples of general public in Arizona, Indiana, North Carolina, and Washington (see Section 4.10 for details, including published sources)	To find views about living in communities of various sizes, 1970–71–73	12 pages (8 pages in Indiana)	Washington, 4,137; North Carolina, 4,470; Arizona, 2,021; Indiana, 7,558	Washington, 3,103; North Carolina, 3,116; Arizona, 1,441; Indiana, 5,360	Washington, 75; North Carolina, 69.7; Arizona, 71.3; Indiana, 70.9	3 in all states	Independent researchers Don A. Dillman, Edwin H. Carpenter, James A. Christensen, and Ralph M. Brooks
Adult women who were given or wrote in for questionnaire; reached through N.Y. Chapter of NOW and ads in newspapers, magazines, and church bulletins	To study the sexual conduct of females, 1972–73	5 pages (60 items)	100,000	3,000	3	None	Independent researcher Shere Hite (published in *The Hite Report*)
Key and top leaders in urban affairs in Boston-Washington, D.C., region (see Section 4.7 for details)	To find out how leaders functioned in solving urban problems and in working with other business, labor, government, religious, and civic leaders (1968–69) as well as with organizations	12 pages	200 key leaders and 200 top leaders	100 key leaders and 78 top leaders	50 for key leaders and 39 for top leaders	3 plus new appeal and another questionnaire	Delbert C. Miller, *Power and Leadership in Bos-Wash Megalopolis*
High school students from 10 Illinois high schools 15 years after graduation	To discover achievements and problems in the transition to adulthood, especially sex differences in educational attainment and age at marriage (1972)	Not known	Original (1957) sample of 8,617	6,498	75 (44 by mail, 31 by shorter telephone interview)	1 (telephone)	Margaret Mooney Marini, "The Transition to Adulthood: Sex Differentials in Educational Attainment and Age at Marriage," *American Sociological Review* 43 (August 1978)

Population	Purpose	Length	Number sent	Number returned	Response rate (%)	Follow-ups	Conducted by
June graduates from 135 colleges and universities; sample designed to be representative of June 1961 graduates receiving degrees from accredited colleges and universities	To discover intended career field and plans for graduate study; reactions to various aspects of college life (1961)	19 pages	42,209, of which 2,231 subsequently declared ineligible	33,982 eligible returns	85	Not known	National Opinion Research Center; James A. Davis, study director (published as *Undergraduate Career Decisions*)
Liberal arts graduates of a national sample (see Section 4.6 for details)	To survey activities of graduates, November 1963–June 1964	20 pages	17,449	10,877	62.3	2 mailings with copy of questionnaire	Survey Research Center, University of California at Berkeley; Charles Y. Glock, director
Graduates, arts and sciences, Miami University	To survey activity of the class of 1976 one year after graduation (1977); to survey activity of class of 1978 one year after graduation	1 page each	792 in 1977; 700 in 1978	572 in 1977; 532 in 1978	72 in 1977; 76 in 1978	None	Office of Dr. C. K. Williamson, dean of college of A&S, Miami University (published in *Miami: Alumnus*, January 1980)
Graduates, Miami University, Oxford, Ohio, 1893–1971	To secure information about employment and activities (1971)	3 pages	6,158 (one to every sixth alumni in pool of 45,000)	2,958	48	None	Douglas M. Wilson, director of Alumni Affairs, Miami University (published in *Miami University Alumni News*, September 1971)
Graduates, all campuses, Indiana University	Survey of present background and activities of class of 1970, 10 years later	3 pages with covering letter from president	9,200	2,676	29.2 (no return postage)	None	Indiana University Alumni Association (published in university alumni association magazine, January 1980)
Short supplementary study of graduates of Indiana University	Survey of present background and activities of class of 1970, 10 years later	1½ pages with letter from alumni secretary	9,200	2,172	23.6 (no return postage)	None	I.U. Alumni Association

(Continued)

TABLE 4.4 (Continued)

Population	Aim and Date of Questionnaire	Length	Number Sent	Number Returned	Percentage Returned	Number of Follow-Ups	Research Agent
Doctoral graduates, Indiana University	Survey of background and activities of class of 1970, 10 years later	3 pages with letter from president	570	228	40 (no return postage)	None	I.U. Alumni Association
Graduates of DePauw University, 1975 and 1976	To secure information about employment, 1976 and 1977	1 page	407 (1975 class); 465 (1976 class)	367 (1975 class); 421 (1976 class)	90 (1975 class); 90 (1976 class)	None	President's Office, DePauw University, Greencastle, Indiana
Members of the American Sociological Association	To find out if respondents thought ASA should publish a nontechnical journal; 1979	1 page	2,000	489	24.5	None	ASA Committee on Publication (see Footnotes of ASA, October 1979)
Deans of professional schools in the United States	To secure a ranking of outstanding schools; 1977	3 pages	1,180	621	53	Shortened questionnaire increased return to 76%	Peter M. Blau, professor of sociology, Columbia University; financed by NSE
Women employees of cafeterias in Indiana University dormitories	To secure information about satisfaction with work, personal life, and husband's attitudes; June 1977	2 pages	80 (handed a questionnaire to fill out during coffee break)	52	65	None	Susie Holly, independent journalist (published in Indiana Daily Student, June 17, 1977)
Women faculty and staff members in telephone directory of Indiana University	As above; June 1977	2 pages	145 (randomly chosen from population of 921; mailed questionnaires through campus mailing system)	72	50	None	Holly, as above

TABLE 4.5 Response to Mail Questionnaire

Outcome	Number	Percentage
Returned, complete, and eligible	10,877	60.4
Returned, ineligible[a]	277	1.4
Unlocatable[b]	1,312	7.2
Inaccessible[c]	5	negligible
No response or refused to answer[d]	5,583	31.0
Total mailed	18,004	100.0

a. *Ineligible:* A subject was considered ineligible if his returned questionnaire or letter from him or a relative indicated that he was not a male U.S. citizen or foreign citizen residing in the United States who graduated from one of the sample schools with a liberal arts major in 1948, 1953, or 1958.

b. *Unlocatable:* A graduate was counted as unlocatable if questionnaires mailed to him were returned as undeliverable by the post office and no new address could be obtained from the post office or from his college or university.

c. *Inaccessible:* A graduate was classified as inaccessible if he was locatable but unable to answer because of illness or a similar legitimate reason.

d. *No response:* Residual group not meeting the criteria for classification in the above categories of the 5,583 included here. Of the group, 161 wrote letters stating that they refused to answer or returned blank questionnaires.

persons. Two follow-up mailings were made. This guide will alert the researcher to the difficulties of follow-up studies under the conditions of this model.

The questionnaire was prepared by the Survey Research Center of the University of California (Charles Y. Glock, director). The study was financed by the U.S. Office of Education and the Carnegie Foundation.

In November 1963 the 20-page booklet was mailed to each of 18,004 liberal arts male graduates, with a covering letter and a prepaid envelope. A second mailing was made in January 1964 and a third in March 1964, with a cutoff date of June 1964. Each mailing included a copy of the questionnaire and a prepaid return envelope. The response to the mail questionnaire is shown in Table 4.5.

All questionnaires were sent with a return request. When a questionnaire was returned without a forwarding address, the college was contacted and asked for a more current address for the graduate or his parents. More than 3,000 address corrections were obtained, and an additional 1,250 mailings were made.

A follow-up study was undertaken to gain additional information about the 5,583 who did not respond and to ascertain how they differed from the respondents. A systematic random sample of 55 was drawn, and various approaches were taken to reach them. A registered letter was first mailed to each member of the sample, asking for his completion of a brief questionnaire. Those not responding were next contacted by telephone if telephone numbers could be obtained for them. At least three calls were made to each subject at his home or office before he was considered unreachable for the follow-up study. Subjects without known telephone numbers were mailed a second registered letter asking for their cooperation. The outcomes of these activities are presented in Table 4.6.

Calvert concludes:

There is a group of non-respondents about whom virtually nothing is known. These are the graduates who proved totally unlocatable, either because their college had no address for them or because they were unreachable through their last known address. Such graduates comprised approximately 14 percent of all graduates of the cooperating institutions who

TABLE 4.6 Response to Follow-Up Study

Outcome	Number	Percentage
Unlocatable (registered letter undeliverable)	47	8.5
Contacted by phone or mail	420	75.7
Eligible and completed follow-up questionnaire	360	64.9
Found ineligible	24	4.3
Refused ineligible	36	6.5
Inaccessible (hospitalized, abroad for extended period or classified assignment, etc., as reported by person at last address)	17	3.0
Unreachable (registered letter unanswered, no telephone number available)	71	12.8
Total follow-up sample	555	100.0

might have been included in the survey. They must remain a potential and essentially unassessable bias in the results presented.

This study should alert the researcher to the persistent problems of (a) getting the questionnaire to its desired destination (7.2% not locatable or accessible in this study), (b) lack of response (31.0%), (c) ineligible respondents (1.4%), (d) the importance of conducting a special effort (registered letters, telephone calls, and so on) to assess how nonrespondents compare with respondents (note that 64.9% of the follow-up sample finally completed questionnaires), and (e) the almost impossible task of removing all bias of findings because of the difficulty of securing all respondents in the sample (14% in this study).

Note

1. Robert Calvert, Jr., *Career Patterns of Liberal Arts Graduates*, rev. ed. (Cranston, RI: Carroll, 1973).

4.7 VARIABILITY OF RESPONSE RATE BY OCCUPATION AND CITY OF RESIDENCE FOR POWERFUL LEADERS AS SHOWN BY THE BOS-WASH MEGALOPOLIS LEADERSHIP STUDY

This study shows how wide variations in questionnaire returns are correlated with occupational group and city of residence. The returns in this study were secured by three mailings of a 12-page questionnaire. The first mailing was sent to all 200 key leaders and 200 top leaders (April 11, 1969). A follow-up mailing 18 days later (April 29) went to those leaders who had not answered. A third mailing was made 15 days later (May 14). In each follow-up a short appeal for a return was attached to another copy of the questionnaire. The final record of returned questionnaires shows 100 returned by key leaders (50%) and 78 returned by top leaders (39%).

TABLE 4.7 Variability of Response Rate by Occupation and City of Residence

Questionnaire returns by Occupational Type and Influence Rating of Leader	Key (N = 200)	Top (N = 200)	Questionnaire Returns by Northeastern City and Influence Type of Leader	Key (N = 200)	Top (N = 200)
Religion	67%	47%	Baltimore	67%	73%
Business	51	27	Boston	67	27
Labor	51	51	Philadelphia	60	54
Civic	43	45	Washington, DC	37	43
Political government	43	23	New York	37	20

SOURCE: From Delbert C. Miller, *Leadership and Power in the Bos-Wash Megalopolis* (New York: John Wiley, 1975), 380.

Key leaders were those judged by panels of experts to be the most influential leaders in urban affairs in the Boston to Washington, D.C., region (Bos-Wash); top leaders were those judged as influential but not as much so as the key leaders.

The final returns are drawn from a population of leaders judged most important in the Bos-Wash megalopolis and probably the busiest. The questionnaires reached persons who could not have been interviewed easily. All had offices at some central point, but many were likely to be away for various periods of time. Busy people can sandwich mail questionnaires into their schedules (probably when they answer their mail) when they cannot (or will not) yield valuable interview time. This was the researchers' experience after many attempts to conduct interviews with key leaders.

Table 4.7 shows widely varying responses based on occupational types of leaders, influence ratings of leaders, and residence of respondent leaders. Note that highest returns came from *religious, business,* and *labor* leaders of key influence living in *Baltimore, Boston,* and *Philadelphia.* Lowest returns came from civic and political leaders of key and top influence living in Washington, D.C., and New York.

These findings should alert researchers to the disparity that may be expected based on occupation, influence, and place of residence. Of special significance is the impact of the names of all respondents appearing on the questionnaire. Key leaders responded to sociometric questions pertaining to 200 other key leaders named on the questionnaire. Top leaders saw the names of key leaders but not their own names. A reduction in response seems to have followed as a result of this difference. (It will be recalled that 50% of the key leaders returned questionnaires, whereas only 39% of the top leaders did so.) Researchers should list *all* respondents on questionnaires if this is feasible. This gives the respondent a feeling of identity with a given population.

SUMMARY OF RESPONSE RATES BASED ON A LARGE NUMBER OF MAIL QUESTIONNAIRES WITH A WIDE VARIETY OF STUDIES   4.8

Heberlein and Baumgartner conducted a study on factors that affect response rates to mailed questionnaires; some of their findings are displayed in Table 4.8. The following observations can be made:

TABLE 4.8 Summary of Response Rates Based on Mail Questionnaires

				Percentiles				
Percentage Response from	*N*	*Mean*	*SD*	*5*	*25*	*Median*	*75*	*95*
Initial mailing	183	48.1	19.9	18.6	30.1	47.4	62.1	82.4
Follow-up 1	58	19.9	7.7	7.5	14.0	19.5	25.6	31.6
Follow-up 2	40	11.9	6.2	3.0	7.8	10.7	15.5	24.5
Follow-up 3	25	10.0	5.1	2.8	6.8	8.1	14.3	19.3

SOURCE: Based on the report of Thomas A. Heberlein and Robert Baumgartner, "Factors Affecting Response Rate to Mailed Questionnaires," *American Sociological Review* 43 (August 1978): 451. Permission to reprint granted by the American Sociological Association and the authors.

1. The table presents response rates from 183 studies where *on the average* 48% of those who received one mailing of the questionnaire returned it. Note the wide deviation in response from these 183 studies.
2. A follow-up mailing nets, *on the average*, nearly 20% of the initial sample as reported in 58 studies. Again, observe the wide deviation reported.
3. Second (*N* = 40 studies) and third (*N* = 25 studies) follow-ups, *on the average*, yield about 12% and 10% returns, respectively. There is again substantial variation in effectiveness, which makes simple generalizations difficult.
4. Not shown in Table 4.8 are 31 studies that had four follow-up contacts, but the response rate for these studies was not significantly better than for three contacts (83.9%, compared with 80.6%).
5. Finally, Table 4.9 reports on 214 studies that utilized one or more follow-ups.

TABLE 4.9

				Percentiles				
	N	*Mean*	*SD*	*5*	*25*	*Median*	*75*	*95*
Final response rate percentage based on studies utilizing one or more follow-ups	214	60.6	24.3	21.2	40.9	60.8	82.9	96.6

TECHNIQUES FOR INCREASING PERCENTAGE OF QUESTIONNAIRE RETURNS   **4.9**

Method	Possible Increase of Total % of Returns	Optimal Conditions
Follow-up contacts	40% to 50%.	See sections 4.9 and 4.10, which show conclusively that follow-up mailings pay off.
1. By mail	Based on a large number of studies, *one follow-up* nets, on the average, 20% more responses. A *second* and *third follow-up,* on the average, yield about 12% and 10% higher return, respectively.[a]	In the Calvert study, after a registered letter was mailed with the first questionnaire, the telephone was used if the questionnaire was not returned. Three calls were made to each subject at his home or office before he was considered unreachable for follow-up study (75.7% final return).
2. By telephone	Increase in returns depends on whether the telephone is used solely or as a supplement to mail follow-ups. As a supplement, another 15% to 30% may be obtained.	Sewell and Shaw report an 87.2% return from a population of 9,007 parents of Wisconsin high school students using three waves of mailed questionnaires and a final telephone interview (*American Sociological Review* 33 [April 1968]: 193). A 15-year follow-up of high school students gave a 44% return to a mailed questionnaire; there was a 31% increase with a telephone follow-up. (See M. M. Marini in Table 4.4.)
Type of population surveyed	Response varies with education, income, occupation, and geographic location of respondent populations. (See section 4.7, which reports variations ranging from 23% to 67% for different occupational groups and from 20% to 73% for city of residence.)	1. The better educated are more likely to return questionnaires; among them, professionals are more likely to return questionnaires. One of the highest returns reported in the research literature is that by Rensis Likert. In a study of the League of Women Voters (commissioned by the League) a cross-sectional sample of 2,905 League members and officers showed the following percentages of return: 79% of members, 95% of board members, 100% of chapter presidents. 2. Remember: Nonreaders and nonwriters are excluded from participation automatically.
Salience of content	30% to 40%.	Questionnaires are more likely to be returned if they are judged as salient to the respondent. Heberlein and Baumgartner report that 43 surveys with nonsalient questionnaires averaged a 42% return, while 26 questionnaires judged to be salient for the respondent obtained a 77% return.[b]

(Continued)

Method	Possible Increase of Total % of Returns	Optimal Conditions
Nature of sponsor and covering letter	Not well known, but range could be considerable.	The sponsor and letter describing importance of questionnaires are seldom self-evident. Sponsor and appeal are very important. The most prestigious and respected person to make the appeal is one who can most influence returns, all other factors held constant. An altruistic appeal seems to get better results than the idea that the respondent may receive something of personal value. The Bureau of Social Science Research, Inc., 1200 17th St., NW, Washington, DC 20036, has compiled completion rates in mail surveys undertaken by BSSR. Data compiled by Lenore Reid. They report a 65% to 90% return with as many as four follow-ups. *Covering letter from institutional sponsor believed very important.*
Sensitive areas of inquiry	Not well known, but range can be very wide. More sophistic approaches are now being utilized to increase returns. Among these are the randomized response technique and the multiplicity technique.[c]	Substantial drop in response if questions probe areas regarded by the respondent as private and/or a threat to him or his immediate group (family, company, neighborhood, church, political party, etc.). A promise of complete confidentiality may help. If respondent does not need to place his or her name on the questionnaire, some fear may be dispelled. Personal sexual behavior is often one of the most sensitive areas. Note that Shere Hite received only 3% return of her questionnaire to 100,000 adult women seeking information about their sexuality. Often questions about income of education dampen the return. Important variations can occur between respondents of different nations because of varying cultural "sensitivities."
Inducements	Not clearly established.	Response Analysis, a private research organization, reports that a monetary incentive raises response by 40%. Response Analysis mailed questionnaires to a random sample of 700 Delaware residents in March 1980. The sample was divided into four groups of 175 each: monetary incentive, sponsor letterhead; monetary incentive, Response Analysis letterhead; no monetary incentive, sponsor letterhead; no monetary incentive, Response Analysis letterhead. Completion rates varied from 76% for the first group to 35% for the fourth group.[d] Research reviews of the literature show that relatively few studies have used monetary incentives. Two studies paid $1.00 and had 80% returns; nine paid $.50 and had 66% returns; seven paid $.25 and had 45% returns (all using only one contact). Most studies ($N = 187$) used no incentives and averaged a 62% response. There is a suggestion that incentives have a linear trend effect, but there is no significant zero-order effect.[e] University sponsorship, type of population, and type of questionnaire could make such inducements unnecessary. Consider promise of report to respondent as inducement; appeal to advancement of knowledge.
Method of return	Not known.	Special techniques include use of registered letter, double postcards, sending respondent another copy of the questionnaire, and inclusion of stamped addressed envelope. A regular stamped envelope produces better results than business reply envelope.
Time of arrival	Not known.	The questionnaire, if sent to the home, should arrive near the end of the week.

Method	Possible Increase of Total % of Returns	Optimal Conditions
Format	Not known.	Sletto found a need for an aesthetically pleasing cover, a title that would arouse interest, an attractive page format, a size and style of type easily readable under poor illumination and for people with poor vision, and photographs to illustrate the questionnaire. (See section 4.10 for further information.)
Length of ques- tionnaire	Not significant.	In their study of 214 mailed questionnaires Heberlein and Baumgartner found no significant correlation between any of the length measures and overall responses. Length varied from a single page to 22 pages.[f]

a. Thomas A. Heberlein and Robert Baumgartner, "Factors Affecting Response Rates to Mailed Questionnaires," *American Sociological Review* 43 (August 1978): 460.
b. Ibid., 451.
c. The randomized response technique places a random device such as a coin in the hands of the respondent and asks that he or she select by chance one of two questions: a sensitive question related to the topic under study or a nonsensitive question. For example, in a study of abortion, two questions might be (a) I had an abortion during the past year; (b) I was born in the month of April. The respondent would be instructed to reply merely yes or no to the selected statement without telling the interviewer which question was being answered. The interviewer can point out that the interviewer will *never know* which question was asked and answered, and the respondent can then answer without fear of embarrassment or reprisal. The researcher knowing the percentage of women born in April can deduce the desired finding.
c. The multiplicity technique allows respondents to avoid a self-report by asking them to report anonymously on the behavior of specified individuals such as close friends or relatives. This approach has its highest utility when the behavior being studied is likely to be denied by a considerable portion of respondents (e.g., in the case of illegal or stigmatized behavior, as in drug use). For further information, write Dr. Patricia Fishburne, Research Director, Response Analysis, Research Park, Route 206, Princeton, NJ 08540.
d. Results from the 1980 study almost duplicate those from a 1977 research project conducted with the same design. Completion rates in the 1977 study ranged from 78% for the first group to 39% for the fourth group (no monetary incentive group). There was a consistent favorable bias when the sponsor's letterhead was used. This verifies the importance of the sponsor, as indicated earlier. The results favoring a monetary incentive may be due to an identification with a private research organization. University sponsorship may explain the conflicting evidence reported in previous research studies. See *The Sampler from Response Analysis* (Research Park, Princeton, NJ), no. 19 (Winter 1981): 1–2.
e. Heberlein and Baumgartner, "Factors Affecting Response Rates," 453.
f. Ibid., 452.

GUIDE FOR INCREASING RETURNS OF MAIL QUESTIONNAIRES, EXPECTED RESULTS, AND COSTS

4.10

Response rates to mail questionnaires are typically low, usually not exceeding 50%. Recent research indicates that much better return rates can be achieved by skilled use of questionnaire construction and follow-up procedures. Four particular researchers are so sure of their methods that they assert that "with a mail methodology available which will consistently provide a high response, poor return rates can no more be excused than can inadequate theory or inappropriate statistics." [1]

The effectiveness of a particular method for eliciting response to lengthy questionnaires (85-165 items) was tested on large statewide samples of the general public in Arizona, Indiana, North Carolina, and Washington. The methods utilized produced response rates of 69.7% to 75.2%. They were equally effective in rural and urban regions. The quality of the data was uniformly high throughout the items.

Increasing Returns of Mail Questionnaires

The method of achieving such results can be detailed in successive steps:

TABLE 4.10 Cumulative Response Rates to Four Mailings Used in Each Study (in percentages)

Mailing	Time	Washington 1970 (N = 4,137)[a]	Washington 1971 (N = 4,175)[a]	North Carolina 1973 (N = 4,470)[a]	Arizona 1973 (N = 2,021)[a]	Indiana 1973 (N = 7,558)[a]	Overall Mean
1. First mailing	Week 1	27.0	26.3	20.6	26.5	18.6	23.8
2. Postcard follow-up	Week 2	45.7	51.1	35.1	41.6	36.5	42.0
3. First replacement questionnaire	Week 4	59.2[b]	67.6	53.0	60.1	55.3	59.0
4. Second replacement questionnaire sent by certified mail	Week 7	75.0	75.2	69.7	71.3	70.9	72.4

SOURCE: From Don A. Dillman, James A. Christensen, Edwin H. Carpenter, and Ralph M. Brooks, "Increasing Mail Questionnaire Response: A Four State Comparison," *American Sociological Review* 39 (October 1974). Used by permission of the authors and the American Sociological Association.
a. *N* = number of *potential* respondents. This is slightly less than the original mailing. Those dropped included persons (a) who had moved from the state so were no longer eligible, (b) to whom a questionnaire could not be delivered (usually because of moving and either leaving no forwarding address or leaving one that expired), (c) who had died, or (d) who were physically incapable of responding (usually due to infirmities of old age). The first two categories accounted for approximately three-fourths of the drops. The numbers (and percentages of the original mailing) dropped in each state are as follows: Washington 1970, 363 (8.1%); Washington 1971, 325 (7.2%); North Carolina, 612 (12.0%); Arizona, 229 (10.2%); Indiana, 479 (5.9%).
b. In this study the third mailing did not include a replacement questionnaire.

1. Prepare the questionnaire as a booklet, through photo reduction and multilithing. (This makes it seem less formidable.)
2. Make the cover page attractive and eye-catching.
3. Use straightforward, unambiguous questions, carefully ordered and presented in a visually attractive manner. (See Section 4.4 for examples of question wording and suggestions for question order.) Questions on the first pages should be designed largely to attract respondents' interest in order to increase the likelihood that important questions of limited interest and appeal will be answered.
4. Prepare a cover letter emphasizing the social usefulness of the study and the importance of each individual respondent to the success of the study.
5. Make full use of personalization procedures.[2] Address respondents by name—that is, do not use *Dear Sir* or *Dear Madam* as a salutation—sign your name, and so on.
6. Send questionnaires via first-class mail.
7. Use postcard follow-up one week later.
8. Prepare letters with replacement questionnaires and send them to nonrespondents at the end of the third week.
9. Send final letters with replacement questionnaires by certified mail to nonrespondents after seven weeks.[3]

Table 4.10 shows the cumulative response rates of the four mailings used in each study.[4]

Expected Results

Note that the final response rates for the four states vary just over five percentage points from highest to lowest. Since there was high similarity in content, there is evidence that the topic per se made no difference.

Table 4.10 also reveals the importance of intensive follow-ups. Without the final two mailings, the probable final response rates would have been less than 50% for four of the five studies. The third mailing increased returns by an average of 17.0%. The fourth mailing (the final mailing) was only slightly less productive, with a 13.4% return.

Cost of Data Collection Process

Low cost is one of the major advantages of the mail survey compared with personal interviews. Costs are incurred in such categories as labor, postage, printing, and supplies. What researchers have at their disposal can make a big difference in unit costs. Needless to say, costs do not stabilize; they continue to rise. (For further information on research costing, see Part 7, Section C.)

A Research Follow-Up on the Total Design Method for Mail Surveys

Don A. Dillman [5]

Forty-eight mail surveys have been reported by Dillman since the first mail survey was described by him and his co-workers. Each of these were conducted by what Dillman calls the Total Design Method (pp. 160-98) and as spelled out in the previous article. The surveys were done by a large number of investigators under 37 different projects most of which were of populations in Washington State. Surveys have been conducted in nine different states, and six were national in scope. Most have been conducted from college and university settings. No nationwide survey has been undertaken by the TDM, nor have any surveys been conducted in the largest metropolitan centers.

With this note of caution, the results of the 48 surveys show an average response rate of 74 percent. No survey obtained less than a 50 percent response rate. Results from some of the studies exhibit response rates near 90 percent.

References to Factors Affecting Response Rates to Questionnaires

Alwin, Duane F., ed. "Survey Design and Analysis" (special issue). *Sociological Methods and Research* 6 (November 1977).

   Articles included are as follows: Duane F. Alwin, "Making Errors in Surveys: An Overview"; Howard Schuman and Stanley Presser, "Question Wording as an Independent Variable in Survey Analysis"; Seymour Sudman, Norman Bradman, Ed Blair, and Carol Stocking, "Modest Expectations: The Effects of Interviewers' Prior Expectations on Responses"; Lloyd Lueptow, Samuel A. Mueller, Richard R. Hammes, and Lawrence S. Master, "Response Rate and Response Bias Among High School Students Under the Informed Consent Regulations"; Gideon Vigderhous, "Analysis of Patterns of Response to Mailed Questionnaires"; Jae-on Kim and James Curry, "The Treatment of Missing Data in Multivariate Analysis"; William T. Bielby and Robert M. Hauser, "Response Error in Earnings Functions for Nonblack Males."

American Statistical Association Conference on Surveys of Human Population. "Report on the ASA Conference on Surveys of Human Populations." *American Statistician* 28 (February 1974): 30-34.

Armstrong, J. Scott. "Monetary Incentives in Mail Surveys." *Public Opinion Quarterly* 39 (Spring 1975): 111-16.

Bachrach, Stanley D., and Harry M. Scoble. "Mail Questionnaire Efficiency: Controlled Reduction of Non-Response." *Public Opinion Quarterly* 31 (Summer 1967): 264-71.

Berdie, Douglas R. "Questionnaire Length and Response Rate." *Journal of Applied Psychology* 58 (October 1973): 278-80.

Boek, Walter E., and James H. Lade. "A Test of the Usefulness of the Postcard Technique in a Mail Questionnaire Study." *Public Opinion Quarterly* 27 (Summer 1963): 303-6.

Carpenter, Edwin H. "Personalizing Mail Surveys: A Replication and Reassessment." *Public Opinion Quarterly* 38 (Winter 1974-75): 614.

Champion, Dean J., and Alan M. Sear. "Questionnaire Response Rates: A Methodological Analysis." *Social Forces* 47 (March 1969): 335-39.

Dillman, Don A. "Increasing Mail Questionnaire Response in Large Samples of the General Public." *Public Opinion Quarterly* 36 (Summer 1972): 254-57.

———. *Mail and Telephone Surveys: The Total Design Method.* New York: Wiley-Interscience, 1978.

An 18-page bibliography on mail and telephone surveys may be found on pages 299-318.

———, James A. Christenson, Edwin H. Carpenter, and Ralph M. Brooks. "Increasing Mail Questionnaire Response: A Four State Comparison." *American Sociological Review* 39 (October 1974): 744-56.

Dillman, Don A., and James H. Frey. "The Contribution of Personalization to Mail Questionnaire Response as an Element of a Previously Tested Method." *Journal of Applied Psychology* 59 (1974): 297-301.

Dunning, Bruce, and Don Calahan. "By Mail vs. Self-Administered Questionnaires." *Public Opinion Quarterly* 37 (Winter 1973-74): 618-24.

Ferriss, Abbott L. "A Note on Stimulating Response to Questionnaires." *American Sociological Review* 16 (April 1951): 247-49.

Kerlinger, Fred. *Foundations of Behavioral Research.* New York: Holt, 1973.

Leik, Robert K. *Methods, Logic and Research of Sociology.* Indianapolis: Bobbs-Merrill, 1972.

Leuthold, David A., and Raymond J. Scheele. "Patterns of Bias in Samples Based on Telephone Directories." *Public Opinion Quarterly* 35 (Summer 1961): 296-99.

Maclean, Mavis. *Methodological Issues in Social Surveys.* Atlantic Highlands, NJ: Humanities Press, 1979.

National Research Council Panel on Privacy and Confidentiality. *Privacy and Confidentiality as Factors in Survey Response.* Washington, DC: National Academy of Sciences, 1979.

Perry, Joseph, Jr. "A Note on the Use of Telephone Directories as a Sample Source." *Public Opinion Quarterly* 32 (Fall 1968): 691-95.

Potter, Dale R., Kathryn Sharpe, John C. Hendee, and Roger N. Clark. *Questionnaires for Research: An Annotated Bibliography on Design, Construction and Use.* USDA Forest Service Research Paper, PNW-140. Portland, OR: Pacific Northwest Forest and Range Experiment Station, 1972.

Rosenberg, Milton J. "The Conditions and Consequences of Evaluation Apprehension." In *Artifact in Behavioral Research,* edited by R. Rosenthal and R. Rosnow, 279-341. New York: Academic Press, 1969.

Rosenthal, Robert, and Ralph L. Rosnow. "The Volunteer Subject." In *Artifact in Behavioral Research,* edited by R. Rosenthal and R. Rosnow, 61-118. New York: Academic Press, 1969.

Schuman, Howard, and Johnson, Michael P. "Attitudes and Behavior." In *Annual Review of Sociology,* edited by Alex Inkeles, vol. 2, 161-207. Palo Alto: Annual Reviews, 1976.

Schwartz, Shalom H. "Normative Influences on Altruism." In *Advances in Experimental Social Psychology,* edited by L. Berkowitz, vol. 10, 222-79. New York: Academic Press, 1977.

Sletto, Raymond F. "Pretesting of Questionnaires." *American Sociological Review* 5 (April 1940): 193-200.

Slocum, W. L., L. T. Empey, and H. S. Swanson. "Increasing Response to Questionnaires and Structured Interviews." *American Sociological Review* 21 (April 1956): 221-25.

Sudman, Seymour, and Norman Bradburn. *Response Effects in Surveys.* Chicago: Aldine, 1974.

Vincent, Clark E. "Socioeconomic Status and Familiar Variables in Mail Questionnaire Responses." *American Journal of Sociology* 69 (May 1964): 647-53.

Notes

1. Don A. Dillman, James A. Christensen, Edwin H. Carpenter, and Ralph M. Brooks, "Increasing Mail Questionnaire Response: A Four State Comparison," *American Sociological Review* 39 (October 1974): 755.

2. Don A. Dillman and James H. Frey, "The Contribution of Personalization to Mail Questionnaire Response as an Element of a Previously Tested Method," *Journal of Applied Psychology* 59, no. 3 (1974): 297-301. See also Edwin H. Carpenter, "Personalizing Mail Surveys: A Replication and Reassessment," *Public Opinion Quarterly* 38 (Winter 1974-75).

3. Adapted from Dillman et al., "Increasing Mail Questionnaire Response," 746.

4. Ibid., 748.

5. From Don A. Dillman, *Mail and Telephone Surveys: The Total Design Method.* (New York: Wiley-Interscience, 1978). For a list of the 48 mail surveys and the response rates, see pp. 22-24.

GUIDES FOR SELECTION AND USE OF PERSONAL INTERVIEWS AS UTILIZED IN FIELD RESEARCH

4.11

The interview represents a personal contact between an interviewer and a respondent, usually in the home or office of the respondent. The interview can range from a highly structured situation with a planned series of questions to a very informal talk with no structure except for some areas of discussion desired by the interviewer. The degrees of freedom represent opportunity and danger: opportunity to explore many subjects with intensity, but with the danger that the interview may not yield the appropriate data. It is often not susceptible to codification and comparability.

The researcher may not appreciate that every open-ended question will take considerable interview time. The analysis of open-ended questions requires a code guide and careful independent observers to establish the validity and reliability of the coding for each question. If the researcher must employ open-ended questions, he or she should choose a few with care and with the precise aims of the study in mind. If hypotheses are to be tested, the researcher should make sure that the questions bear directly upon them. Open-ended questions are appropriate and powerful under conditions that require probing of attitude and reaction formations and ascertaining information that is interlocked in a social system or personality structure.

In general, interviews should be kept within a 45-minute time span. Public opinion interviewers have reported that most respondents begin to weary and show less interest in the interview at this point. It is true that some respondents will "wake up" as the interview proceeds, and there are examples of six- and eight-hour interviews in the literature. (Robert Dahl with community leaders in New Haven, Connecticut, and Neal Gross in planned interviews with Massachusetts school superintendents in Cambridge, Massachusetts).[1] These long interviews are exceptional and can occur only under specially prepared conditions.

Interviews may take three forms: the *structured interview schedule*, the *focused interview*, and the *free story*. These forms and their characteristics are shown in Table 4.1 (see Section 4.1). Common techniques that may be employed include the use of scales to measure social factors, attitudes, and personality traits. Secret ballots and panel techniques are often employed.

The guide that follows lists advantages and disadvantages of the personal interview. It is recommended for use as a checklist; the researcher can mark those advantages that are important or essential with a plus sign and those that will negatively affect his or her use of the interview with a minus. This can provide an adequate base for choosing or rejecting the personal interview.

Other field methods are available, including the group interview, telephone interview, case study and life history, direct observation, participant observation, and mass observation. Guides have not been prepared for these methods, but a list of reference books is appended to this part describing in detail all the methods and techniques.

Guide for Appraisal of the Personal Interview for Data Collection

The researcher should check the advantages important for his or her study, check the disadvantages that cannot be overcome, and appraise the choice. He or she should then reconsider documentary analysis, mail questionnaire, telephone interview, observation, or other methods suggested in Table 4.1 (see Section 4.1).

Advantages of the Personal Interview

1. Personal interviews usually yield a high percentage of returns, for most people are willing to cooperate.
2. Personal interviews can be made to yield an almost perfect sample of the general population because practically everyone can be reached by and can respond to this approach.
3. The information secured is likely to be more correct than that secured by other techniques, because the interviewer can clear up seemingly inaccurate answers by explaining the questions to the informant. If the latter deliberately falsifies replies, the interviewer may be trained to spot such cases and use special devices to get the truth.
4. The interviewer can collect supplementary information about the informant's personal characteristics and environment that is valuable in interpreting results and evaluating the representativeness of the persons surveyed.
5. Scoring and test devices can be used, the interviewer acting as experimenter to establish accurate records of the subject.
6. Visual material to which the informant is to react can be presented.
7. Return visits to complete items on the schedule or to correct mistakes can usually be made without annoying the informant. Thus greater numbers of usable returns are assumed than when other methods are employed.
8. The interviewer may catch the informant off guard and thus secure more spontaneous reactions than would be the case if a written form were mailed out for the informant to mull over.
9. The interviewer can usually control which person or persons answer the questions, whereas in mail surveys several members of the household may confer before questions are answered. Group discussions can be held with the personal interview method if desired.
10. The personal interview may take long enough to allow the informant to become oriented to the topic under investigation. Thus recall of relevant material is facilitated.
11. Questions about which the informant is likely to be sensitive can be carefully sandwiched in by the interviewer. By observing the informant's reactions, the investigator can change the subject if necessary or explain the survey problem further if it appears that the interviewee is about to rebel. In other words, a delicate situation can usually be handled more effectively in a personal interview than by other survey techniques.
12. More of the informant's time can be taken for the survey than would be the case if the interviewer were not present to elicit and record the information.
13. In cases where a printed schedule is not used (compare disadvantage 2, below), the language of the survey can be adapted to the ability or educational level of the person interviewed. Therefore, it is comparatively easy to avoid misinterpretations or misleading questions.
14. The length of the interview does not affect refusal rates.[2]

Disadvantages of the Personal Interview

Especially in large metropolitan areas, two factors have had an especially great impact on personal interviewing: higher costs and lower response rates than were encountered previously.

1. Higher costs have been encountered in all phases of the interview operation. Salaries both in the field and in the central offices of survey agencies have followed the

inflationary spiral. Travel costs for visiting sample households have spiraled, along with the price of gasoline, which has more than doubled in recent years.[3]

2. Lower response rates are being reported in all quarters, especially in large metropolitan areas, where increases in personal and property crimes have altered the life-styles of residents. Locked central entrances to apartment buildings and a greater concern among residents about opening their doors to strangers prevent interviewing in many multiunit dwellings. There is also an increasing reticence to admit strangers in single-family dwellings in areas with high crime rates. Some interviewers refuse to enter areas perceived to be dangerous. In large metropolitan areas the final proportion of respondents who are located and consent to an interview is declining to a rate close to 50%.[4]

3. The above disadvantages have focused more attention on the telephone survey (to be described in the following section). Consideration is also being given to a combination of data collection methods utilizing the mail questionnaire, telephone survey, and personal interview where indicated. For example, if the largest possible return is sought, a personal interview may be required as the follow-up to round out the sample after telephone and mail inquiries have exhausted their usefulness.

4. Unless personal interviewers are properly trained and supervised, data may be inaccurate and incomplete. A few poor enumerators may make a much higher percentage of returns unusable than if informants filled out the interview forms and mailed them to survey headquarters.

5. The personal interview usually takes more time than the telephone interview, providing the persons who can be reached by telephone are a representative sample of the population to be covered by the survey. For a sample of the general public, however, a telephone inquiry is no substitute for a personal interview. Members of the lowest-income groups often do not have telephones.[5]

6. If the interview is to be conducted in the home during the day, the majority of informants will be housewives. If a response is to be obtained from a male member of the household, most of the fieldwork has to be done in the evenings or on weekends. Since only an hour or two can be used for evening interviewing, the personal interview method requires a large staff if studies need contacts with the working population.

7. The human equation may distort the returns. Interviewers with a certain economic bias, for example, may unconsciously ask questions so as to secure confirmation of their views. In opinion studies especially, such biases may operate. To prevent such coloring of questions, most opinion surveyors instruct their interviewers to ask questions exactly as they are printed in the schedule.

8. Researchers should be aware that funding agencies may be reluctant to make grants to projects relying heavily on the personal interview. Given all the disadvantages, especially those associated with higher costs and lower response rates, the applicant for a grant may be placed on the defensive.

Notes

1. Robert A. Dahl, *Who Governs* (New Haven, CT: Yale University Press, 1961), 334. Neal Gross, Ward S. Mason, and Alexander W. McEachern, *Explorations of Role Analysis: The Superintendency Role* (New York: Wiley, 1958), 85.

2. In a study of 500 adults testing 25-minute and 75-minute interviews, no relationship was found between interview length and overall item response. *BSSR: Newsletter of the Bureau of Social Science Research* 14, no. 3 (Fall 1980): 1-2.

3. See Part 7, Section C, for a more detailed description of costs for the personal interview, mailed questionnaire, and telephone survey.

4. Robert M. Groves and Robert L. Kahn, *Surveys by Telephone: A National Comparison with Personal Interviews* (New York: Academic Press, 1979), 3.

5. This is true, but telephone availability has grown; more than 90% of all residences in the United States now possess telephones. Many persons can be reached on business telephones.

4.12 DESCRIPTION AND INSTRUCTIONS FOR PREPARATION OF A TELEPHONE INTERVIEW SURVEY

Description

With increasing frequency, social science researchers are utilizing the telephone for social investigation. There are a number of reasons for this, including the following:

1. Almost all residences in the United States now have telephones. It is estimated that at least 90% of all persons in a cross-sectional sample can be reached by telephone. The probability of social class bias stemming from telephone availability has greatly diminished.[1]
2. Personal interview costs have risen greatly, and telephone surveys can be made for only 45% to 65% of personal interview costs.[2] (For further information on costing, see Part 7, Section C.)
3. Personal interviews are incurring falling response rates in large cities, and telephone interviewing is competitive in response rate achieved on national populations. Telephone survey response rates are running only 5-10% lower than those of comparable in-person surveys.[3]
4. A comparison of response rates for mail surveys with telephone surveys favors the telephone. Dillman reports an average response of 91% for 31 surveys, a full 17 percentage points higher than the average for 48 mail surveys. The difference persists for both specialized and general populations. These results were obtained in the state of Washington.[4]
5. The rapid emergence of the telephone as a survey research tool means that the social science community has little information about telephone surveys. Among the unknowns may be listed the following: (a) what response rates to expect for various populations, (b) how long different people will stay on the telephone, and (c) the unique requirements of telephone interviews in contrast with the familiar mail and personal interview survey.

It is believed that most surveyors have adapted their normal interviewing procedures to the telephone and are simply conducting "face-to-face interviews" by telephone. This procedure is not recommended.[5] Groves and Kahn contend that "the transition from personal interview methods to telephone methods requires a total reorganization for collecting data."[6]

Groves believes that surveys in the future may combine telephone and personal interviews so that the two modes can complement each other and perhaps provide greater precision than is possible with either one alone. It is known that proportionately more telephone respondents feel uneasy about discussing some topics, especially financial status and political attitudes. Yet in large metropolitan areas respondents feel more comfortable about answering questions on the telephone than about inviting strangers into their homes. A combination of telephone and personal interviewing would take advantage of the lower costs of telephone interviews and maintain representation of households without telephones at the same time.[7]

Instructions for the Telephone Interview[8]

The telephone interview contrasts sharply with the mail questionnaire. Telephone interviews depend entirely on verbal communication, and the interviewer must build rapport with the respondent in an interchange during which neither sees the other. Unlike in face-to-face interviews, the telephone interviewer cannot use visual aids to help explain questions, and cannot observe respondents' facial expressions for hints that something is misunderstood.

The design of the telephone questionnaire must be shaped to meet the needs of three audiences: respondents, interviewers, and coders.

Respondents. Responding to a telephone interview is difficult. Respondents may be called to the telephone unexpectedly and asked to do something they do not fully understand. They may be in the midst of another activity, such as preparing dinner, playing a game, reading the newspaper, listening to the radio, or watching TV. Their feelings may range from frustration, suspicion, and anxiety to downright hostility. Subtle ways must be found to discourage respondents from beginning or continuing with other activities that may distract their attention from the interview. "Getting through" may mean that the respondent needs time to get used to the interviewer's way of speaking, understanding different words and the meanings of questions, and so on. Being interviewed by telephone is a new experience, and the respondent may need time to think through answers. Most respondents need support and encouragement.

Interviewers. The interviewer must secure completion of a telephone questionnaire with information that is accurate and that can be accurately recorded. The interviewer must determine who of the household is eligible to respond and get this person on the phone. The first few seconds are all-important in determining whether or not a successful interview will take place. The interviewer may be faced with such questions as: How do I know you are who you say you are? What are you trying to sell? I don't know anything about you or your product—why don't you call someone else? I have a call that I am expecting—you will have to hang up now. Can you call later?

Interviewers must "prove" *their* legitimacy and the *worth* of their projects, and must stimulate respondents to begin. As the interview proceeds, the interviewer must move the conversation from question to question, write answers while mentally preparing to ask the next question, listen intently for any changes of mood, record unsolicited comments, hold the telephone receiver, and turn the pages of the questionnaire.

Coders. Methods of facilitating rapid data compilation are important. Precoding identifies the computer card columns and punches for each response category on the questionnaire. Precoding marks and additional instructions for coders usually do not interfere with the requirements of the interviewer. Some important steps include the following:

1. Prepare the telephone questionnaire so that all questions are straightforward, unambiguous, and carefully ordered. Begin the questionnaire with items central to the topic that seem easy to answer, interesting, and socially important. All topical questions should be asked before questions relating to personal characteristics.
2. A well-constructed questionnaire will maximize the probability that interviewers will administer it in exactly the same fashion to each respondent. Each response category is assigned an identifying number that is used to represent it on a computer punch. The final version should be carefully pretested, and interviewers might role-play the interviewer-respondent interchange.
3. The most difficult part of conducting telephone surveys is combining all elements in the research design for administration. Each act of preparation is oriented to the single critical act of the initial interviewing. Use of the following list of activities that must be completed before interviewing begins, prepared by Dillman, will help prevent oversights and organizational failures.

Countdown List of Activities That Must Be Done Prior to the Start of Interviews [9]

Draw Sample

___Names, street addresses, and telephone number drawn from directories typed onto gummed labels and attached to cover page of questionnaire
[*or*]

___Random number generated by computer (or manually from table) and printed on lists for distribution to interviewers

Facilities and Equipment

___Access to telephones arranged

___Telephones checked to be sure they are in working order

___Access to leased lines arranged (if needed)

___Chairs and tables assembled (if needed)

___Labeled boxes for sorting questionnaires into appropriate categories (e.g., refusals, completions, and callbacks)

Computer Related Needs (if immediate data processing is planned)

___Arrange access to computer

___Arrange access to computer equipment (e.g., keypunch, and sort reproducer)

___Decide analysis programs to be used and set up format statements for their use

___Do preliminary computer runs with "dummy" data to check for errors in analysis programs

Materials

___Questionnaires

___Duplicated

___Assembled

___Cover page and selection procedures (if any) added

___Directory listing attached to cover page (if applicable)

___Randomized for distribution to interviewers

___"What the Respondent Might Like to Know" duplicated

___"Rules Book" duplicated

___Special dialing instruction duplicated (if needed)

___Pencils and note pads, thumbtacks, rubber bands, and other miscellaneous supplies

___All of the above placed at each interviewing station

Advance Letter

___Printed, personalized, and stuffed into envelopes

___Each letter is mailed three to five days before call is likely to be made

Personnel

___Interviewers

___Hired

___Trained

___Scheduled

___Supervisory personnel scheduled

___Persons to check questionnaires for completeness scheduled

___Coders and/or keypunchers

___Hired

___Trained

___Scheduled

___Persons to "troubleshoot" disconnected numbers and other problem calls scheduled

Other Resources
___Telephone directories that cover study area (to aid in checking possible errors)
___Notify relevant officials that survey is in process

Dillman has created an 18-page reference bibliography on mail and telephone surveys, which is coded as follows: *M* = an explicit treatment of mail surveys; *T* = an explicit treatment of telephone surveys; *G* = an explicit treatment of either mail or telephone surveys, but has implications for conducting them.[10]

Notes

1. Don A. Dillman, *Mail and Telephone Surveys: The Total Design Method* (New York: Wiley-Interscience, 1978), 10.
2. Robert M. Groves, "Telephone Helps Solve Survey Problems," *Newsletter of the Institute of Social Research* (University of Michigan) 6, no. 1 (1980): 3.
3. Ibid.
4. Dillman, *Mail and Telephone Surveys*, 28.
5. Ibid., 11
6. Robert M. Groves and Robert L. Kahn, *Surveys by Telephone* (New York: Academic Press, 1979), 4.
7. Groves, "Telephone Helps Solve Survey Problems," 3.
8. This section is based on Dillman, *Mail and Telephone Surveys*, 200-281. Users of the telephone survey should consult his thorough treatment, which includes constructing telephone questionnaires and administering the survey.
9. This list is reprinted with permission of the publisher from Don A. Dillman, *Mail and Telephone Surveys: The Total Design Method* (New York: Wiley-Interscience, 1978), 274. Copyright © 1978 by John Wiley and Sons, Inc. See also Paul J. Lavrakas, *Telephone Survey Methods: Sampling, Selection, and Supervision* (Newbury Park, CA: Sage, 1987).
10. See Dillman, *Mail and Telephone Surveys*, 299-318.

A COMPARISON OF TELEPHONE SURVEYS WITH PERSONAL INTERVIEWS

4.13

The development of telephone interviews and procedures for sampling households by means of random-digit dialing may be the most important innovations in survey research since the introduction of multistage probability sampling. But comparisons of telephone surveys with personal interviews raise many questions:

1. *Are telephone responses as reliable and as valid as those given in personal interviews?*

There is no simple answer to this question, even when all conditions of sample and survey content are held constant—and that is almost impossible. However, hard data are available in regard to such important matters as sample coverage, selection of respondents in households, overall rates of response and nonresponse, and validity of response.

On sample coverage. With more than 90% of all households in the United States reachable by telephone, the overall coverage of telephone samples begins to approach the levels typically obtained by personal interviews of an area probability sample of households. For some subpopulations, however, households not covered by telephone are crucial. These include poor households, where there are more nonsubscribers; rural households, which tend to have lower incomes than urban households; elderly people, who tend to have lower incomes and experience more hearing difficulties; and households of young adults, who are more transient and possess lower incomes than middle-aged adults.

One cannot assume that nonsubscribers are like subscribers, but the proportion of nonsubscribers continues to shrink. The bias in statistics linked to the absence of nonphone households depends on the nature of measurements taken.

On selection of respondents in households. The selection of respondents within sample households must be done at the time of the interview. In personal interview surveys, household selection is done by using a full listing of household members. In telephone surveys, the procedure can be simplified by using a grid corresponding to different numbers of male and female adults. The telephone interviewer determines the total number of adults in the household and the number of them who are women. Use of the grid then indicates the individual selected as respondent. Use of this procedure showed it yielded an error in selection in about 10% of the sample households! [1]

On different rates of response. The response rate of national telephone surveys remains at least five percentage points lower than that expected in personal surveys. This has been a rather stable comparison despite numerous changes in training interviewers, monitoring and feedback procedures, and techniques of introducing the survey to the respondent.[2]

On validity of response. Later studies using validity checks find small, generally negligible differences between telephone and personal interviews on reports of embarrassing events such as personal bankruptcy and arrests for drunken driving.[3]

> 2. *Are there systematic differences in the content or depth of the answers people give by telephone and those they give in person?*

Consistent differences in interviewing speed between telephone and personal modes have been noted by researchers. The faster pace of telephone interviews is associated with differences both in the number and type of responses to open-ended items. Some people begin telephone interviews but do not complete them. A lower response rate (5% lower) has already been noted for the telephone interview. In spite of these differences, very few response discrepancies have been found between the two sets of data that were large enough to be considered statistically significant.[4]

Many studies have concentrated on reports of embarrassing or sensitive data. These studies have generally found no or only slight differences between telephone and personal interviews. Most results vary because of differences in research design, populations studied, or kinds of data collected. A general statement is inappropriate.[5]

There is a real concern about rapport between respondent and interviewer in the telephone survey. Nonresponse rates suggest that respondents find the telephone interview to be a less rewarding experience and more of a chore than the personal interview. A first priority for future research must be given to telephone techniques to establish motivation and trust equal to the face-to-face survey.[6]

> 3. *Are there large gains in efficiency when sample households are interviewed by telephone?*

Personnel needs for a national telephone survey are smaller than those for an equivalent personal interview survey. Take the case of a personal interview survey requiring 200 interviewers, each conducting 7 or 8 interviews. National telephone surveys are often conducted in the same amount of time using 30-40 interviewers, each doing 40-50 interviews. Supervisory and coordinating staff are similarly reduced.[7] Clearly, cost advantages exist for telephone interviewing. (For a comparative analysis of costs for mail questionnaire, personal interview, and telephone surveys, see Part 7, Section C.)

Efficiency results by having questionnaires of the telephone survey coded soon after they are taken. Interviewer errors discovered during coding are quickly detected and corrected. Feedback to interviewers on interview behavior and results obtained can be quickly reported.

Increasingly, sampling is done by random-digit dialing (RDD), which involves direct selection of numbers listed in telephone books. Generally, a set of randomly chosen digits corresponds to a working telephone number. This means a random sample can be quickly and easily located. A detailed description of the RDD procedure is clearly stated by Klecka and Tuchfarber.[8] Stratified random design and cluster designs are often employed.[9]

Notes

1. Robert M. Groves and Robert L. Kahn, *Surveys by Telephone* (New York: Academic Press, 1979), 217.
2. Ibid., 219.
3. Ibid., 8-9.
4. Ibid., 231.
5. Ibid., 9.
6. Ibid., 222-23.
7. Ibid., 8.
8. W. Klecka and A. Tuchfarber, "Random-Digit Dialing: A Comparison to Personal Surveys," *Public Opinion Quarterly* 41 (1978): 105-14. For further information about a study design for a statewide survey program, see Alan Booth, Lynn White, David R. Johnson, and Joan Litze, "Combining Contract and Sociological Research: The Nebraska Annual Social-Indications Survey," *American Sociologist* 15 (November 1980): 226-32.
9. For a discussion of these, see Groves and Kahn, *Surveys by Telephone*, 215-16.

CHOOSING AMONG THE MAIL QUESTIONNAIRE, PERSONAL INTERVIEW, AND TELEPHONE SURVEY   4.14

The choice of a mode of collecting data involves many factors. The projection of results expected is speculative, because in one sense every sample and the conditions surrounding it are unique. Even changes in world events during administration can make a difference. If the researcher is prepared to utilize many follow-ups or a combination of methods, then a prediction of higher response can be projected.

Table 4.11 presents an evaluation of the modes of field operation covering eight important factors. The researcher must determine what is most important among these factors for the design selected and choose accordingly.

Cost is of high priority. It can be seen that the mailed questionnaire is the cheapest, the telephone survey is of intermediate cost, and the personal survey is the most

TABLE 4.11 Choosing Among the Mail Questionnaire, Personal Interview, and Telephone Survey

Factors Influencing Coverage and Information Secured	Mailed Questionnaire	Personal Interview	Telephone Survey
Lowest relative cost	1	3	2
Highest percentage of return	3	1	2
Highest accuracy of information	2	1	3
Largest sample coverage	3	1	3
Completeness, including sensitive material	3	1	2
Overall reliability and validity	2	1	3
Time required to secure information	3	2	1
Ease of securing information	1	3	2
Total number of rankings, 1, 2, 3	2, 2, 4	5, 1, 2	1, 5, 1

SOURCE: Based on author's evaluation of findings for cross-sectional samples of student and adult populations. All evaluations are based on "average" determinations.
NOTE: 1 = most favorable ranking; 2 = intermediate ranking; 3 = least favorable ranking.

expensive. If the telephone survey involves substantial long-distance calling, however, the cost figures change quickly to give telephoning a less favorable position in comparison with the personal survey. (For a full description of comparative costs, see Part 7, Section C.)

Note that cost is in inverse relation to almost all the other factors when comparing the mailed questionnaire with the personal interview. The personal interview, unless placed among the most vulnerable conditions of dangerous sections in large urban environments, easily leads in desirable factors. The telephone survey yields a very consistent set of rankings in the intermediate range; this accounts for its growing popularity.

4.15   THE PANEL TECHNIQUE AS A RESEARCH INSTRUMENT

Social scientists are currently giving a great deal of attention to methods for analyzing time data. It has been noted that all the social science disciplines have moved from static to dynamic models. The panel technique is an important research instrument. So much attention is now being given to it that it seems almost to have been rediscovered.

Definition. The panel technique involves interviewing the *same* group of people on *two or more occasions*. It is mainly used for studying changes in behavior or attitudes through repeated interviews ("waves"). Most panel studies contain a set of core questions or observations that are repeated on all or nearly all the waves. Considerable supplementary material may be obtained at each wave or in different waves to be used in interpreting changes found in the core questions.

Uses. The panel is used in many areas of investigation, such as political polls, occupational and income movements, consumer habits, and mass communications. We can distinguish two major kinds of panels: those that focus mainly on attitudes and opinions, and those that deal mainly with factual material regarding economic, consumption, and communications behavior.

Panel studies focusing on opinion and attitude changes generally have a limited number of waves, usually ranging from two to four, and rarely exceeding seven. Since they seek specifically to pin down a particular fact or a reason that accounts for the changes noted, they are ordinarily restricted to the study of short-range changes of specific attitudes.

Advantages of the Panel Technique

The researcher has two options in searching for short-range changes of specific attitudes. First, information can be obtained involving facts or experiences during the course of time from a *single* contact with the respondent. Such questions as "For whom did you intend to vote one month ago?" or "Have you recently made a change in your job?" may be asked. Such information may be inaccurate because the memory of the respondent is inadequate for the question, it may be deceptive, or both. Second, based as it is on repeated contact, the panel technique can be trusted to be more reliable and valid, with a number of distinct advantages. Zeisel has listed these advantages; they are presented in Table 4.12.

Difficulties Inherent in the Panel Technique

There are two basic difficulties in the use of the panel technique: panel mortality and reinterviewing bias.

1. Mortality is the loss of panel members as a percentage of the difficulty of reaching the same person for two or more contacts, or because of the respondent's refusal of continuous cooperation. Since different sections of the panel may show different mortality rates, some danger of a biased sample arises.
2. Reinterviewing bias is the effect of repeated discussions on certain topics on the respondent's behavior or attitude toward these very topics. Thus the fact of being repeatedly interviewed may in itself induce changes of opinion.

Panel Mortality

There is bound to be a loss of panel members over time—and the longer the time, the greater the loss. The main reason for failure to reinterview is the respondent's temporary absence from the original place of interview or a complete change of address. This problem can be partly overcome by recording both home and business addresses at the time of the first interview and by persistent efforts to reach the respondent at the time of repeat interviews. If telephone interviewing has been the manner of contact, then the mailed questionnaire or a personal interview may be tried. A certified letter may increase response.

Mortality bias is a concern that increases with the loss of panel members. This is particularly true because mortality does not occur at random. It is well known that younger people and people in large cities, as well as people in the lower-income brackets, have higher mobility than older, small-town, and upper-class respondents.[1] The researcher must find out in each case whether such a bias exists. Most efforts to do this center on nonrespondents. A vigorous effort is made to secure as many reinterviews as possible, using different approaches and persistence. When returns

TABLE 4.12 Repeated Cross-Sections Versus Panel Technique

Cross-Sections Technique	Panel Technique
1. Recording changes	
In comparing, for example, the "proportion of users of XX-branded soap" at two different periods, one obtains the difference in the total proportion of users at each interview: the net change.	In addition to the net change, one obtains an accurate picture of the number and direction of individual shifts, which, when added together, account for the net change.
2. Reasons for observed changes	
For instance, whether or not a certain type of propaganda has influenced a person's political attitude. This is difficult to ask and to answer.	By analyzing separately those who were exposed to a certain piece of propaganda and those who were not, the panel can ascertain whether the number and direction of attitude changes are different for the two groups.
3. Amount of collected information	
Since the respondents differ from survey to survey, one does not know more about each respondent than can be gathered in any one interview.	Repeated interviews with the same respondents yield an ever-increasing amount of information. In a three-interview panel study we can get two or three hours' worth of information about each member of our panel.
4. Data referring to time periods	
One-interview surveys will yield accurate results if the question refers to the time instant at which the interview takes place. If the respondent is to recall events that extend over a time period, one must rely on memory. Such data are most always required if certain research concepts are to be defined: If we want to find out a person's "reading habits" or whether he is a "regular listener" to a certain radio program, we must rely entirely on the respondent's memory and judgment.	Only through the panel can one avoid reliance on the respondent's memory if one aims at data that refer to an extended period of time. Repeated interviews yield objective data on the consistency and fluctuations of habits and attitudes. Such distinctions as that of "regular" vs. "nonregular" listener can be made with accuracy and reliability.
5. Reliability of results	
The statistical significance of observed changes from survey to survey depends upon the size and structure of the particular sample.	In most cases an observed change in a panel will be of higher statistical significance than a change of equal size observed in repeated cross sections that equal the panel in size and structure.

SOURCE: Hans Zeisel, *Say It with Figures*, 4th ed. (New York: Harper & Row, 1957), 217–18. Copyright © 1957 by Harper & Row. Reprinted by permission of Harper & Row.

are secured from the previously nonrespondent group, the researcher carefully analyzes to see if mortality bias has been introduced and how serious it may be for interpreting the findings.

A consumer panel study made by Response Analysis in 1986 indicates that the panel technique can be effective in securing replies of at least 67% of the respondents from wave one to wave two in a given sample. The study was made of consumers in a worldwide chain of retail stores operated by the U.S. Navy for military personnel and their dependents. The research involved four interviewing periods in two locations during the first eight months of 1986. Two research questions were posed: How willing are the customers to participate as panelists? What percentage of panelists complete their assignments through three waves of interviewing?

Specially trained interviewers went to two store locations and sought consumers willing to participate. Some 94% of those asked agreed to be panelists. A total of 2,190 mail questionnaires were sent in the first wave; 1,989 completed and returned the questionnaires, a 57% return. A second wave showed that once panelists completed the first questionnaire they were more likely to remain in the study. A return rate of 78% was received on the second wave. For wave three a $10 gift certificate was offered to customers who completed all three waves. Wave three respondents posted an 89% return. Senior Vice President Al Vogel of Response Analysis, who designed and directed the study, believes that the completion rate at any stage in the study could have been dramatically affected by changes in the incentive.[2]

Reinterviewing Bias

Bias may be introduced by reinterviewing simply because the first interview may have heightened the respondent's attention. He or she may have then given more thought to the topic, and the ultimate effect may be a bias. The increasing familiarity gained by reinterviewing may add to the biasing of respondents' opinions.

To detect the presence of such bias, the researcher may interview a control group that is parallel to the panel. At the time of the first panel interview, a field sample that matches the structure of the panel is interviewed on the same topic. Again, at the time of second panel interview, a different field sample is interviewed. In this way, any resulting bias can be discovered by comparing any changes within the panel with changes between the two field samples.

These two principal sources of error in panel studies, mortality and reinterviewing bias, must receive attention. Nevertheless, studies have shown that neither of these two factors seriously endangers the use of the panel; it is a highly promising and powerful tool in the field of social research.[3]

There are a number of important decisions to be made in designing a panel study. Each of these is briefly described in Table 4.13.

General References

Hyman, Martin D. "Panel Analysis." In *Handbook of Social Sciences*. Vol. 2, *Quantitative Social Research*, edited by Robert B. Smith. New York: Irvington, 1980.

Jahoda, Marie, Morton Deutsch, and Stuart W. Cook, eds. *Research Methods in Social Relations*. New York: Dryden, 1951.

Kessler, Ronald C., and David E. Greenberg. *Linear Panel Analysis: Models of Quantitative Change*. New York: Academic Press, 1981.

Lazarsfeld, Paul F., Ann K. Pasanella, and Morris Rosenberg, eds. *Continuities in the Language of Social Research*. New York: Free Press, 1975. (Rev. ed. of *Language of Social Research*.)

Wiggins, Lee M. *Panel Analysis: Latent Probability Models for Attitude and Behavior Processes*. San Francisco: Jossey-Bass, 1973.

Zeisel, Hans. *Say It with Figures*. 5th ed. New York: Harper & Row, 1965.

Methodological References for Advanced Students

Clarridge, Brian R., Linda L. Sheehy, and Tarissa S. Hauser. "Tracing Members of a Panel: A 17-Year Follow-Up." In *Sociological Methodology 1978*, edited by Karl F. Schuessler. San Francisco: Jossey-Bass, 1978.

Duncan, Greg J., Richard D. Coe, Mary E. Corcoran, Martha S. Hill, Saul D. Hoffman, and James N. Morgan. *Years of Poverty, Years of Plenty: The Changing Economic Fortunes of American Workers and Families*. Ann Arbor: University of Michigan, Institute for Social Research, 1984.

TABLE 4.13 Problems of Administration and Suggestions for Dealing with Them

Administration Problem	Suggestion
1. Number of waves	
The number of waves must consider the extent of co-operativeness on the part of respondents. They may become bored, annoyed, or irritated by repeated interviews. Repeated interviewing is also expensive. Like energy, cheap interviewing is gone.	The number of waves should usually be reduced to the minimum.
2. Interval between waves	
Deciding on the interval between waves is governed by the factors of freshness of memory, type of information desired, and the speed with which a situation changes. If too long an interval elapses the panel member may suffer a loss of memory of previous events and may distort the answer.	The type of information desired is the most important factor in determining the appropriate interval. Consumer panels: ordinarily run waves at intervals of one or two weeks. Political panels: ordinarily, waves of one to two months apart are about right. In an exciting political campaign or a political crisis, short intervals are preferable.
3. Sample size	
Sampling error can be reduced with larger samples but this increases cost. A larger sample size can compensate for dropout mortality anticipated prior to first wave (1,200 set up in the original sample so that a desired 1,000 is available for interview). The problem here is that the original mortality may differ from the group that is interviewed.	Check sampling error associated with different sample sizes. Within the limitations imposed by cost, the researcher can either try to reduce the original mortality by repeated callbacks or try to obtain a sample of the original mortality.
4. Sample type—quota vs. area	
Quota samples have the advantage of being easier and cheaper to use than area samples. If respondents could be selected on the streets according to specific quota requirements, the speed and cost would be very desirable. After obtaining respondents' names and addresses, they could conduct interviews next time in their homes. This has not proved feasible as much of the original sample is lost for various reasons. The area sample is subject to considerably less mortality.	Whenever possible, personal interview panels should be conducted on an area basis in the home.
5. Incentives	
An incentive of some sort is needed to obtain the respondent's cooperation and participation. This is especially true in a panel study involving respondent's cooperation over fairly long periods and many waves of reinterviewing. The researcher faces the problem of first securing and then sustaining cooperation.	Two major incentives are usually effective depending on type of sponsor and the panel respondents. These are tangible (money, premiums, etc.) or prestigious (sponsorship, ego enhancement) incentives. Consumer panels: Use some sort of tangible reward such as points redeemable for premiums. Consider a small monetary payment. Government and educationally sponsored panels: Stress prestige and duty as citizen in advancing knowledge or improving society.

Administration Problem	Suggestion
6. Type of interview: personal, telephone, mail	
Personal interviews have been most common in panel studies, but this is the most expensive form of interview and is becoming more expensive. Telephone interviewing is becoming more common since the telephone is almost universally available at the home or work address. It is more difficult to get many kinds of sensitive information and attitudinal data by telephone.	The telephone interview is gaining in popularity as expenses of personal interviewing rise. New techniques and interview skills are making telephone interviewing more reliable and valid.
The mail interview involves two problems not present in personal or telephone interviews: a. Mail interviews become impractical when the interval between waves is important since there is no control over the time factor. b. Mail interviews are open to the very real possibility of a bias introduced by a discussion of answers with family members or neighbors.	Avoid the mail interview unless the telephone or personal interview is not feasible. The mail interview has some merit where it is not safe to enter areas of the city or where sensitive data is difficult to secure.

Draws upon ISR's ongoing Panel Study of Income Dynamics to identify patterns of economic change (see entries for Morgan et al., below.)

Duncan, Otis Dudley. "Unmeasured Variables in Linear Models for Panel Analysis." In *Sociological Methodology 1972*, edited by Herbert L. Costner. San Francisco: Jossey-Bass, 1972.

————. "Testing Key Hypotheses in Panel Analysis." *Sociological Methodology 1980*, edited by Karl F. Schuessler. San Francisco: Jossey-Bass, 1980.

Goodman, Leo A. "Causal Analysis of Data from Panel Studies and Other Kinds of Survey." *American Journal of Sociology* 78 (March 1973): 1135-91.

————. "A Brief Guide to the Causal Analysis of Data from Surveys." *American Journal of Sociology* 84 (March 1979): 1078-95.

Hanman, Michael T., and Alice A. Young. "Estimation in Panel Models: Results on Pooling Cross-Sections and Time Series." In *Sociological Methodology 1977*, edited by David R. Heise. San Francisco: Jossey-Bass, 1977.

Morgan, James N., Greg Duncan, and the Staff of the Economic Behavior Program. *Five Thousand American Families—Patterns of Economic Progress: Analyses of the Panel Study of Income Dynamics.* Vols. 1-7. Ann Arbor: University of Michigan, Institute for Social Research, 1974-79.

The analyses in these seven volumes constitute an intensive investigation into the factors that affect changes in the economic well-being of families over time. For 10 years this massive, pioneering study has documented the lives of a large and representative sample of the entire U.S. population. More than 15,000 families were studied in 1968 and more than 2,000 new families have been added to the panel as members of the original households split off to form new households. Volume 1, *Analyses of the First Five Years* (1974, 436 pages); Volume 2, *Special Studies of the First Five Years* (1974, 376 pages); Volume 3, *Analyses of the First Six Years* (1975, 490 pages); Volume 4, *Analyses of the First Seven Years* (1976, 520 pages); Volume 5, *Analyses of the First Eight Years* (1977, 534 pages); Volume 6, *Analyses of the First Nine Years* (1978, 528 pages); Volume 7, *Analyses of the First Ten Years* (1979, 392 pages).

————. *A Panel Study of Income Dynamics: Documentation for Interviewing Years 1968 to 1977.* Vols. 1-2. Ann Arbor: University of Michigan, Institute for Social Research.

These volumes present complete documentation for this ongoing study of factors affecting family economic well-being over time. Data tape available (no. 7439). Volume 1, *Study Design, Procedures, Available Data* (1968-72, 400 pages); Volume 2, *Tape Codes and Indexes* (1968-72, 1,100 pages); Supplements 1973-78.

Pelz, Donald C., and Frank M. Andrews. "Detecting Causal Priorities in Panel Study Data." *American Sociological Review* 29 (December 1964): 836-54.

Wheaton, Blair, Bergt Muthén, Duane F. Alwin, and Gene F. Summers. "Assessing Reliability and Stability in Panel Models." In *Sociological Methodology 1979*, edited by David R. Heise. San Francisco: Jossey-Bass, 1977.

Notes

1. See Hans Zeisel, *Say It with Figures*, 4th ed. (New York: Harper & Row, 1957), 246.
2. "Sampler," *Response Analysis* 47 (September 1987), 2. The address of the Response Analysis Corporation is Research Park, P.O. Box 158, Princeton, NJ 08542.
3. See Lee Wiggins, *Panel Analysis: Latent Probability Models for Attitude and Behavior Processes* (San Francisco: Jossey-Bass, 1973).

4.16   GUIDES FOR THE SELECTION AND CONSTRUCTION OF SOCIAL SCALES AND INDICES

Scaling techniques play a major role in the construction of instruments for collecting standardized, measurable data. Scales and indices are significant because they provide quantitative measures that are amenable to greater precision, statistical manipulation, and explicit interpretation. However, before constructing a new scale, it is exceedingly important that a very careful survey of the literature be made to ascertain if an appropriate scale is already available to measure the dependent or independent variables in a given study. The general rule is this: The available scale should be used if it has qualities of validity, reliability, and utility (and in that order of priority). With such a scale, comparative and accumulative research is possible. The need to develop a new scale can almost be considered a disciplinary failure unless the variable represents a factor never before considered as open to measurement. This discussion begins, therefore, at the point at which the literature has not revealed an appropriate scale and the researcher decides to construct an index or scale.

How does one "think up" a number of indicators to be used in empirical research? This question is answered by Paul F. Lazarsfeld and Morris Rosenberg as follows:

> The first step seems to be the creation of a rather vague image or construct that results from the author's immersion in all the detail of a theoretical problem. The creative act may begin with the perception of many disparate phenomena as having some underlying characteristic in common. Or the author may have observed certain regularities and is trying to account for them. In any case, the concept, when first created, is some vaguely conceived entity that makes the observed relations meaningful. Next comes a stage in which the concept is specified by elaborate discussion of the phenomena out of which it emerged. We develop "aspects," "components," "dimensions," or similar specifications. They are sometimes derived logically from the overall concept, or one aspect is deduced from another, or empirically observed correlations between them are reported. The concept is shown to consist of a complex combination of phenomena, rather than a simple and directly observable item. In order to incorporate the concept into a research design, observable indicators of it must be selected.[1]

The terms *indices* and *scales* are often used interchangeably to refer to all sorts of measures, absolute or relative, single or composite, the product of simple or elaborate techniques of measurement.

Indices may be very simple. For example, one way to measure morale is to ask the direct question, "How would you rate your morale? Very good, good, fair, poor, very poor." This might be refined slightly so that the responses are placed on a numerical scale. Note that there are nine points on the following scale.

How Would You Rate Your Morale?								
very good		good		fair		poor		very poor
1	2	3	4	5	6	7	8	9

The basis for construction is logical inference, and the use of a numerical scale requires the assumption of a psychological continuity that the respondent can realistically act upon in self-rating. Face validity is usually asserted for such a scale, although it would be possible to make tests of relations with criteria such as work performance, absenteeism, lateness, amount of drinking, and hours of sleep.

A composite index is one of a set of measures, each of which is formed by combining simple indices. For example, morale may be considered as a composite of many dimensions.

Four measures can be combined by such questions as the following:

How satisfied are you with your job?
How satisfied are you with your company or organization?
How satisfied are you in your personal life?
How satisfied are you with your community?

Response choices of very good, good, fair, poor, and very poor may be offered for each question, with respective weights of 5, 4, 3, 2, and 1. A range from 4 to 20 points is possible. Such a composite index may improve precision, reliability, and validity.

Rigor is introduced as greater attention is paid to tests of validity and reliability. At a certain point a given means of measurement reaches its limit of improvement and a more refined technique becomes necessary for greater precision. Many scaling techniques concern themselves with linearity and equal intervals or equal-appearing intervals. This means that the scale follows a straight-line model and that a scoring system is devised, preferably based on interchangeable units and subject to statistical manipulation. This is a major attribute of the Thurstone attitude scaling technique.

Unidimensionality or homogeneity is another desired attribute assuring that only one dimension is measured and not some mixture of factors. This is a prime concern of the Guttman scaling technique. Reproducibility is a characteristic that enables the researcher to predict the pattern of a respondent's answers by knowing only the total scale score. This attribute is built into Guttman scaling techniques.

The intensity of feeling is introduced in the Likert technique. The respondent is usually asked to indicate his or her feelings on a 5-point scale ranging from "strongly agree" to "strongly disagree." Tests of item discrimination are applied.

There is no single method that combines the advantages of all of these techniques;[2] it is therefore important that we understand their respective purposes and the differences between them.

Notes

1. Paul F. Lazarsfeld and Morris Rosenberg, eds., *The Language of Social Research: A Reader in the Methodology of Social Research* (Glencoe, IL: Free Press, 1962), 15.

2. The scale discrimination technique developed by Allen Edwards represents an excellent attempt to secure a combination of the Thurstone, Likert, and Guttman features. See the following pages as well as

Allen L. Edwards and Kathryn Claire Kenney, "A Comparison of the Thurstone and Likert Techniques of Attitude Scale Construction," *Journal of Applied Psychology* 30 (1946): 72-83.

4.16.a Thurstone Equal-Appearing Interval Scale

Nature: This scale consists of a number of items whose positions on the scale have been determined previously by a ranking operation performed by judges. The subject selects the responses that best describe how he or she feels.

Utility: This scale approximates an interval level of measurement. This means that the distance between any two numbers on the scale is of known size. Parametric and nonparametric statistics may be applied. See Section 5.5 of this handbook.

Construction:

1. The investigator gathers several hundred statements conceived to be related to the attitude being investigated.
2. A large number of judges (50-300) independently classify the statements in 11 groups, ranging from most favorable to neutral to least favorable.
3. The scale value of a statement is computed as the median position to which it is assigned by the group of judges.
4. Statements that have too broad a spread are discarded as ambiguous or irrelevant.
5. The scale is formed by selecting items that are evenly spread along the scale from one extreme to the other.

Example: Brayfield and Roethe's Index of Job Satisfaction, which is reproduced in Section 6.H.4 of this volume, is an example of this kind of scale. The Thurstone technique is used in the initial development of the scale to provide equal-appearing intervals. The full scale contains 18 items, with Thurstone scale values ranging from 1.2 to 10.0 with approximately .5 step intervals. Some items from the scale representing the job satisfaction continuum are as follows:

My job is like a hobby to me.
I am satisfied with my job for the time being.
I am often bored with my job.
Most of the time I have to force myself to go to work.

Research applications: Scales have been constructed to measure attitudes toward war, the church, capital punishment, the Chinese, blacks, whites, and institutions.

4.16.b Likert-Type Scale

Nature: This is a summated scale consisting of a series of items to which the subject responds. The respondent indicates agreement or disagreement with each item on an

intensity scale. The Likert technique produces an ordinal scale that g
nonparametric statistics. See Section 5.5 of this handbook.

Utility: This scale is highly reliable when it comes to a rough or
with regard to a particular attitude or attitude complex. The score in
of intensity as expressed on each statement.

Construction:

1. The investigator assembles a large number of items considered rele
   being investigated and either clearly favorable or unfavorable.
2. These items are administered to a group of subjects representative of those with whom
   the questionnaire is to be used.
3. The responses to the various items are scored in such a way that a response indicative of
   the most favorable attitude is given the highest score.
4. Each individual's total score is computed by adding his or her item scores.
5. The responses are analyzed to determine which items differentiate most clearly between
   the highest and lowest quartiles of total scores.
6. The items that differentiate best (at least six) are used to form a scale.

Example: The Rundquist and Sletto Scales of Morale and General Adjustment are
representative of the Likert attitude scale technique, as are their scales measuring
inferiority, family, law, and economic conservatism. A significant characteristic is
that each selected statement has been carefully researched to determine its discrimination through a criterion of interval consistency. A second feature is the addition of
the intensity dimension to each statement, as follows:

The future looks very black.
    strongly agree (5), agree (4), undecided (3), disagree (2), strongly disagree (1)

Most people can be trusted.
    strongly agree (1), agree (2), undecided (3), disagree (4), strongly disagree (5)

4.16.c Guttman Scale Analysis

Nature: The Guttman technique attempts to determine the unidimensionality of a
scale. Only items meeting the criterion of reproducibility are acceptable as scalable.
If a scale is unidimensional, then a person who has a more favorable attitude than
another should respond to each statement with equal or greater favorableness than
the other.[1]

Utility: Each score corresponds to a highly similar response pattern or scale type.
It is one of the few scales where the score can be used to predict the response pattern
to all statements. Only a few statements (5 to 10) are needed to provide a range of
scalable responses. Note the analysis presented in Table 4.14, which shows how 14
subjects responded (yes) to several statements and how scores reflect a given pattern
of response.

LE 4.14

Respondent	Item 7	Item 5	Item 1	Item 8	Item 2	Item 4	Item 6	Item 3	Score
7	yes	yes	yes	yes	yes	yes	yes	—	7
9	yes	yes	yes	yes	yes	yes	yes	—	7
10	yes	yes	yes	yes	yes	yes	—	—	6
1	yes	yes	yes	—	yes	yes	—	yes	6
13	yes	yes	yes	yes	yes	yes	—	—	6
3	yes	yes	yes	yes	yes	—	—	—	5
2	yes	yes	yes	yes	—	—	—	—	4
6	yes	yes	yes	yes	—	—	—	—	4
8	yes	yes	yes	—	—	yes	—	—	4
14	yes	yes	yes	yes	—	—	—	—	4
5	yes	yes	yes	—	—	—	—	—	3
4	yes	yes	—	—	—	—	—	—	2
11	—	—	—	—	yes	—	—	—	1
12	yes	—	—	—	—	—	—	—	1

Construction

1. Select statements that are felt to apply to the measurable objective.
2. Test statements on a sample population (about 100).
3. Discard statements with more than 80% agreement or disagreement.
4. Order respondents from most favorable responses to fewest favorable responses. Order from left to right.
5. Order statements from most favorable responses to fewest favorable responses. Order from left to right.
6. Discard statements that fail to discriminate between favorable respondents and unfavorable respondents.
7. Calculate coefficient of reproducibility.
   a. Calculate the number of errors (favorable responses that do not fit pattern)
   b. $$\text{Reproducibility} = 1 - \frac{\text{number of errors}}{\text{number of responses}}$$
   c. If reproducibility equals .90, a unidimensional scale is said to exist.
8. Score each respondent by the number of favorable responses or response patterns.

Example

This volume reproduces one scale constructed by the Guttman scaling technique, Wallin's scale for measuring women's neighborhood practices (see Section 6.F.3).

When attitudes are measured, the statements must permit a range of opinions and evoke a definite feeling. Note the statements scaled on air force personnel reflecting their satisfaction with the air force:

I have a poor opinion of the air force most of the time.
Most of the time the air force is not run very well.
I am usually dissatisfied with the air force.
The air force is better than any of the other services.
If I remain in military service I would prefer to remain in the air force.[a]

a. From Delbert C. Miller and Nahum Z. Medalia, "Efficiency, Leadership and Morale in Small Military Organizations," *Sociological Review* 3 (July 1955): 93–107.

Note

1. An excellent manual on how to construct and apply a unidimensional scale in social research is now available for novice researchers. See Raymond L. Gordon, *Unidimensional Scaling of Social Variables* (Riverside, NJ: Free Press, 1977). For a critical analysis, see Nan Lin, *Foundations of Social Research* (New York: McGraw-Hill, 1976), 189.

4.16.d Scale Discrimination Technique

Nature: This technique seeks to develop a set of items that meet the requirements of a unidimensional scale, possess equal-appearing intervals, and measure intensity. Aspects of the construction of Thurstone's equal-appearing intervals, Likert's summated scales, and Guttman's scale analysis are combined in this technique developed by Edwards and Kilpatrick.

Utility: Three distinct advantages of separate scaling techniques are combined. The interval scale quality of the Thurstone technique can be achieved. The discriminability between respondents and the addition of an intensity measure are derived from the Likert technique, and unidimensionality from the Guttman technique. Caution: Item analysis will eliminate items in the middle of the scale.

Construction:

1. The investigator selects a large number of statements that are thought to apply to the attitude being measured.
2. Items that are ambiguous or too extreme are discarded.
3. The statements are given to judges, who judge the favorableness of each statement and place it in 1 of 11 categories.
4. Half of the items with the greatest scatter or variance are discarded.
5. Scores are assigned to the remaining items as the median of the judges' scores.
6. The statements are formulated in the form of a summated scale and given to a new set of judges.
7. An item analysis is performed to determine which questions discriminate best between the lowest and highest quartiles.
8. Twice the number of items that are wanted in the final scale are selected. From each scale interval, the statements that discriminate best are selected.
9. These statements are divided in half, and the halves are submitted to separate test groups.
10. Coefficients of reproducibility are determined for each test group; those that are .90 or above are used.

4.16.e Rating Scales

Nature: This technique seeks to obtain an evaluation or a quantitative judgment of personality, group, or institutional characteristics based upon personal judgments. The rater places the person or object being rated at some point along a continuum or in one of an ordered series of categories; a numerical value is attached to the point or the category.

Utility: Rating scales can be used to assess attitudes, values, norms, social activities, and social structural features.

Construction:

1. The continuum to be measured is divided into an optimal number of scale divisions (approximately five to seven).

2. The continuum should have no breaks or divisions.
3. The positive and negative poles should be alternated.
4. Each trait is introduced with a question to which the rater can give an answer.
5. Descriptive adjectives or phrases are used to define different points on the continuum.
6. The investigator should decide beforehand upon the probable extremes of the trait to be found in the group in which the scale is to be used.
7. Only universally understood descriptive terms should be used.
8. The end phrases should not be so extreme in meaning as to be avoided by the raters.
9. Descriptive phrases need not be evenly spaced.
10. During pretesting, the investigator asks respondents to raise any questions they have about the ratings and the different points on the continuum if they are unclear.
11. To score, assigned numerical values are used.

Example: Miller's Scale Battery of International Patterns and Norms, reproduced in Section 6.I.3, contains 20 rating scales to ascertain important norms and patterns within national cultures. The significant feature is the meaningful continuum that can be developed with approximately worded statements or adjectives for each point on the continuum. The scale can be designed so that the researcher or the respondent may make the rating. An example of a rating scale is Item 7, Moral Code and Role Definitions of Men and Women, taken from the Miller Scale Battery of International Patterns and Norms:

7. Moral Code and Role Definitions of Men and Women

1	2	3	4	5	6

| Single code of morality prevails for men and women. Separate occupational and social roles are not defined for men and women. Similar amounts and standards of education prevail. | | Variations between moral definitions for men and women exist for certain specified behaviors. Occupational and social role definitions vary in degree. Varying educational provisions for the sexes. | | Double code of morality prevails. Separate occupational and social roles for men and women exist and are sharply defined. Amount and standards of education vary widely between the sexes. | |

4.16.f   Latent Distance Scales

Nature: This is a technique for scalogram analysis based on a probability model that attempts to apply to qualitative data the principles of factor analysis providing ordinal information. The basic postulate is that there exists a set of latent classes such that the manifest relationship between any two or more items on a questionnaire can be accounted for by the existence of these latent classes and by these alone.

The study of latent class analysis has become a rapidly developing methodology for analyzing categorical data. Latent class analysis provides a description of categorical latent (unobserved) variables from an analysis of the structure of the relationships among several categorical manifest (observed) variables. This method is commonly called *categorical data analogue to factor analysis.*

For beginning students, the simplest statement is found in Stouffer's "Scaling Concepts and Scaling Theory." [1] The reader is advised to go next to Allan L. McCutcheon's *Latent Class Analysis.* [2] More advanced treatments may be found

TABLE 4.15 Complete Analysis of Latent Distance Scale on Neurotic Inventory

Response Pattern 1 2 3 4	Percentage of Each Pattern in Latent Class							
	n_I	n_{II}	n_{III}	n_{IV}	n_V	Total	Fitted Total	Actual Total
+ + + +	94.9	4.2	0.8	0.1	0.0	100	76.8	75
+ + − +	90.0	3.9	0.7	4.6	0.8	100	14.6	10
+ + + −	90.4	4.0	0.7	0.1	4.8	100	5.8	8
+ − + +	66.8	2.9	24.5	5.0	0.8	100	16.3	14
− + + +	2.5	79.3	14.7	3.0	0.5	100	108.3	110
− − + +	0.3	8.8	73.5	14.9	2.5	100	145.4	141
− + − +	1.3	38.9	7.2	45.1	7.5	100	39.7	49
+ − − +	24.5	1.1	9.0	56.1	9.3	100	8.0	11
− − − +	0.0	1.4	11.9	74.3	12.4	100	169.9	161
+ + − −	36.7	1.6	0.3	1.9	59.5	100	2.6	3
− + + −	1.3	40.7	7.6	1.5	48.9	100	15.2	11
+ − + −	25.9	1.2	9.5	1.9	61.5	100	3.0	8
− − + −	0.1	1.5	12.8	2.6	83.0	100	60.2	64
− + − −	0.1	2.5	0.5	2.9	94.0	100	44.0	41
+ − − −	1.3	0.0	0.5	3.0	95.2	100	10.9	9
+ + + +	0.0	0.1	0.5	3.0	96.4	100	287.3	285
Total in Each Class	109.9	129.5	161.3	181.4	417.9		1,000.0	1,000

SOURCE: The above items were taken from a neurotic inventory presented by Samuel A. Stouffer. *The American Soldier: Measurement and Prediction* (Princeton, NJ: Princeton University Press, 1949), 4: 445. Consult the book for instruction in this technique or see Section 4.9 of this handbook. The bibliography on index and scale construction will prove useful. Paul F. Lazarsfeld developed latent structure analysis. See Lazarsfeld, "Recent Developments in Latent Structure Analysis," *Sociometry* 18 (December 1955): 647–59.

in Paul F. Lazarsfeld and Neil W. Henry's *Latent Structure Analysis* and Rolf Langeheine and Jürgen Rost's *Latent Trait and Latent Class Models*.[3] Both of these books include extensive bibliographies. Few latent distance scales have yet found their way into the research literature.

Utility: Unlike scalogram analysis, this technique includes imperfect scale types in the analysis without considering them as mistakes.

Construction:[4]

1. The investigator lists questions believed to be related to the latent attitude.
2. Answers to questions are dichotomized in terms of positive-negative, favorable-unfavorable, and so on.
3. The proportion of respondents who demonstrate latent attitude in each response is calculated.
4. Items are arranged in terms of their manifest marginals.
5. The latent class frequencies are computed through inverse-probability procedures.
6. Response patterns are ranked in terms of average latent position, or an index is used to characterize each response pattern.

Example: The Latent Distance Scale on the Neurotic Inventory provides an example of this kind of scale (Table 4.15).

1. Have you ever been bothered by pressure or pains in the head?
     Positive answer: Yes, Often or Yes, Sometimes or No
     Answer: 13.8%

2. Have you ever been bothered by shortness of breath when you were not exercising or working hard?

> Positive answer: Yes, Often or Yes, Sometimes or No
> Answer: 30.7%

3. Do your hands ever tremble enough to bother you?

> Positive answer: Yes, Often or Yes, Sometimes or No
> Answer: 43.1%

4. Do you often have trouble in getting to sleep or staying asleep?

> Positive answer: Very Often or No
> Answer: 57.1%

Notes

1. Samuel A. Stouffer, "Scaling Concepts and Scaling Theory," in Marie Jahoda, Morton Deutsch, and Stuart W. Cook, eds., *Research Methods in Social Relations*, Part 2, *Selected Techniques* (New York: Dryden, 1951), 691-705.

2. Allan L. McCutcheon, *Latent Class Analysis* (Newbury Park, CA: Sage, 1987).

3. Paul F. Lazarsfeld and Neil W. Henry, *Latent Structure Analysis* (Boston: Houghton Mifflin, 1968); Rolf Langeheine and Jürgen Rost, eds., *Latent Trait and Latent Class Models* (New York: Plenum, 1988).

4. See Lazarsfeld and Henry, *Latent Structure Analysis*; Langeheine and Rost, *Latent Trait and Latent Class Models*.

4.16.g Paired Comparisons

Nature: This technique seeks to determine psychological values of qualitative stimuli without knowledge of any corresponding respondent values. By asking respondents to select the more favorable of a pair of statements or objects over a set of several pairs, an attempt is made to order the statements or objects along a continuum. This is sometimes called the *forced-choices technique.* Note how it is applied in Neal and Seeman's Powerlessness Scale, reproduced in Section 6.I.3.

Utility: Ordering by paired comparisons is a relatively rapid process for securing a precise and relative positioning along a continuum. Comparative ordering generally increases reliability and validity over arbitrary rating methods.

Construction:

1. The investigator selects statements that relate to the attribute being measured.
2. The statements are combined in all possible combinations of pairs: $\dfrac{N(N-1)}{2}$
3. Judges are asked to select which statement of each pair is the more favorable.
4. The proportion of judgments each statement received over every other statement is calculated.
5. The proportions are totaled for each statement.
6. The proportions are translated into standardized scale values.
7. An internal consistency check is applied by computing the absolute average discrepancy.
8. Statements are presented to respondents, who are asked to indicate favorableness or unfavorableness of each statement.
9. Respondent's score is the median of his or her favorable responses.

TABLE 4.16

Item Set Favorable to U.S. Involvement in Korea	Paired Comparison Scale Score
1. I suppose the United States has no choice but to continue the Korean war.	0.00
2. We should be willing to give our allies in Korea more money if they need it.	0.74
3. Withdrawing our troops from Korea at this time would only make matters worse.	0.98
4. The Korean war might not be the best way to stop communism, but it was the only thing we could do.	1.07
5. Winning the Korean war is absolutely necessary whatever the cost.	1.25
6. We are protecting the United States by fighting in Korea.	1.46
7. The reason we are in Korea is to defend freedom.	1.71

Example: Hill's Scale of Attitudes Toward Involvement in the Korean War (Table 4.16) is representative of this kind of scale.[1]

Note

1. From Richard J. Hill, "A Note on Inconsistency in Paired Comparison Judgments," *American Sociological Review* 18 (October 1953): 564-66. Richard Ofshe and Ronald E. Anderson have translated Hill's Korea items to Vietnam; the Vietnam scale is described in "Testing a Measurement Model," in *Sociological Methodology 1969,* ed. Edgar F. Borgatta (San Francisco: Jossey-Bass, 1969).

4.16.h   Semantic Differential

Nature: The semantic differential seeks to measure the meaning of an object to an individual. The subject is asked to rate a given concept (e.g., "Negro," "Republican," "wife," "me as I would like to be," "me as I am") on a series of 7-point, bipolar rating scales. Any concept, whether a political issue, a person, an institution, or a work of art, can be rated. The 7-point scales include such bipolar scales as the following: (a) fair-unfair, clean-dirty, good-bad, valuable-worthless; (b) large-small, strong-weak, heavy-light; and (c) active-passive, fast-slow, hot-cold (Table 4.17). The rating is made according to the respondent's perception of the relatedness or association of the adjective to the word concept. Osgood and his colleagues have inferred that the three subgroups measure the following three dimensions of attitude:

    a: the individual's *evaluation* of the object or concept being rated, corresponding to the favorable-unfavorable dimension of more traditional attitude scales

    b: the individual's perception of the *potency* or power of the object or concept

    c: the individual's perception of the *activity* of the object or concept

TABLE 4.17 A Sample of a Semantic Differential Scale

Fifteen concepts: Love, Child, My Doctor, Me, My Job, Mental Sickness, My Mother, Peace of Mind, Fraud, My Spouse, Self-Control, Hatred, My Father, Confusion, Sex.
Each concept was rated on the following 10 scales:

valuable	____ : ____ : ____ : ____ : ____ : ____ : ____	worthless
clean	____ : ____ : ____ : ____ : ____ : ____ : ____	dirty
tasty	____ : ____ : ____ : ____ : ____ : ____ : ____	distasteful
large	____ : ____ : ____ : ____ : ____ : ____ : ____	small
strong	____ : ____ : ____ : ____ : ____ : ____ : ____	weak
deep	____ : ____ : ____ : ____ : ____ : ____ : ____	shallow
fast	____ : ____ : ____ : ____ : ____ : ____ : ____	slow
active	____ : ____ : ____ : ____ : ____ : ____ : ____	passive
hot	____ : ____ : ____ : ____ : ____ : ____ : ____	cold
tense	____ : ____ : ____ : ____ : ____ : ____ : ____	relaxed

SOURCE: This sample semantic differential scale was used in a study reported by Charles E. Osgood and Zella Luria, "A Blind Analysis of a Case of Multiple Personality Using the Semantic Differential," *Journal of Abnormal and Social Psychology* 49 (1954): 579–91. For detailed information, see James G. Snider and Charles E. Osgood, eds., *Semantic Differential Technique: A Sourcebook* (Hawthorne, NY: Aldine, 1969).

These authors suggest that the measuring instrument is not grossly affected by the nature of the object being measured or by the type of persons using the scale.[1]

Utility: A 100-item test can be administered in about 10 to 15 minutes. A 400-item test takes about an hour. The semantic differential may be adapted through choice of concepts and scales to the study of numerous phenomena. It may be useful in constructing and analyzing sociometric scales.

Construction:

1. The investigator prepares a list of concepts appropriate to the theory guiding the variable to be measured.
2. Pairs of polar adjectives are selected on a priori grounds.
3. Selection of adjectives is determined empirically by asking different groups (comparative or experimental-control design) to take prescribed orientations in responding to an adjective-rating task. For example, members of one group of respondents are asked to rate as they believe a person would rate the concept if he or she held a positive attitude; other respondents are asked to rate as they believe a person would rate the concept if he or she held a strong negative attitude. Respondents are given the standard instructions for using the semantic differential form.[2] Data are analyzed, and adjective pairs are selected that distinguish clearly between the groups.
4. New groups of respondents are selected who take prescribed orientations in rating the concepts. Data are analyzed.[3]

Notes

1. For further information, see the work of the developers of the semantic differential: Charles E. Osgood, George J. Suci, and Percy H. Tannenbaum, *The Measurement of Meaning* (Urbana: University of Illinois Press, 1957).
2. Ibid.
3. For guidance, again see Osgood et al., ibid.

4.16.i   Generalized Scales Versus Specific Scales

Daniel J. Mueller[1]

All of the attitude scales that have been studied result in a single score, which seems to imply a unidimensional conceptualization. What is more, in all attitude-scaling techniques, some effort has been made to achieve internal consistency. In some techniques, most notably Guttman scaling, extreme emphasis is placed specifically upon unidimensionality. At the same time, in an effort to achieve content and construct validity, constructors of Likert and Thurstone scales are urged to collect a broad array of opinion statements representing the entire universe of opinions about the attitudinal object. Gordon Allport recognized this dilemma in 1935 when he noted that two individuals may have the same degree of affect toward an object yet differ "qualitatively" in their attitudes toward it.[2] For example, two people may both have a moderately positive attitude toward the church, but one may be attracted to the church primarily for its spiritual qualities (associated with God, heaven, morality, and so forth), whereas the other may like the church primarily as an instrument for the fulfillment of social needs.

This line of reasoning leads us to examine the complexity of attitudinal objects. Simple attitudinal objects such as toothbrushes, watermelons, and parking lots don't seem to raise suggestions of multidimensionality. These are relatively simple, single-function objects. To the extent that they fulfill that function well, they are liked; to the extent that they don't, they are disliked. More complex objects, though, engender more diverse opinions and thus more complex attitudes. I may like an automobile for its power, luxury, handling, and status but dislike its lack of economy, size, and country of origin. Or I may feel that a particular automobile is fine for delivering pizza but not for delivering dignitaries.

In part, the problem of multidimensionality of attitude toward complex objects can be resolved by dividing the object into smaller and less complex elements on the basis of component parts, specific functions, or particular contexts. I may, for instance, have a positive attitude toward a particular automobile as a pizza-delivery vehicle, but a negative attitude toward the same automobile as a limousine. Or I may like the economic policies of the president but not his moral policies.

Exactly when to subdivide complex objects into components for purposes of measurement is not an easy decision. In general, psychological research is facilitated by the use of tightly defined, unidimensional constructs. Scores on unidimensional scales have a clear and precise psychological meaning. But in real life people must often deal with objects, no matter how complex, as integral entities. If I don't have the luxury to allow both the purchase of a pizza-delivery vehicle and a limousine, I must develop an overall attitudinal position toward every prospective vehicle and purchase the one that best fulfills my combined needs. Likewise, I must decide either to vote for the president in the next election or to vote against him. In order to make this decision, my separate attitudinal positions toward components of "the president" must be combined to effect a single, composite attitudinal position. In fact, our attitudes toward persons constitute one of the clearest examples of the formation of global or summary attitudes toward highly complex attitudinal objects. As Newcomb concludes, after a thorough and insightful discussion of the attitude-dimensionality issue, "it is likely that we form meaningful generalized attitudes about any object, however complex." [3]

Further evidence for the existence of meaningful generalized attitudes is the fact that separate attitude scales toward the same attitudinal object, constructed either by the same or by different scaling methods, tend to intercorrelate highly—sometimes nearly as highly as their respective reliabilities will permit.

Summary (by Delbert C. Miller)

The researcher seeking guidance between the conflicting foci of specific or generalized attitudes must make decisions that speak to the demands of the research problem. Few researchers are willing to go all the way with Sherif's dictum that a single score is "a most inadequate indicator of an individual's attitude." [4] However, most researchers would agree that a generalized scale is inappropriate for an attitude that is to be focused on a very specific function. A large majority would insist that appropriate social scales with high reliability and validity are essential. Cumulative research that throws light on a prevailing theory is the goal. Replication that brings acceptance or rejection of hypotheses is the process. Put your research problem against these criteria. Consider multidimensional scaling.

Multidimensional Scaling

Multidimensional scaling is a technique that is increasingly of interest to the social sciences. In psychophysics multidimensional scaling has been utilized for some time.[5] In the study of attitudes, however, there is a dearth of satisfactory methods, but there is nothing to prevent the adoption of the multidimensional method to the attitude domain. The key concept involved is that of social or psychological distance. Social distance is well known; see, for example, the Bogardus scale and the research cited in Part 6 of this volume. Psychological distance is a concept employed in approach and avoidance gradient theory[6] and in Lewin's field theory.[7]

If social or psychological distance can be analyzed as though it were physical distance, it would be possible to draw a "map" of the way in which an individual structures the similarities and differences among attitudes (or behavioral or organizational characteristics) in a given domain. On such a map, short distances would represent similarity or agreement, and long distances would represent dissimilarity or disagreement. Multidimensional scales based upon the interpretation of dissimilarities or disagreements as distances have already been constructed with nonpsychological stimuli.[8]

For students interested in multidimensional scaling, a good model is Abelson's "A Technique and a Model for Multi-Dimensional Attitude Scaling." [9] Students interested in applying multidimensional scaling to social characteristics should see Joel H. Levine's "The Sphere of Influence." [10] Levine describes an analysis of a network of interlocking directorates, specifically the network in which the boards of major banks interact with the boards of major industrials in the United States. He constructs maps showing "spheres of influence." The sectors of the sphere represent similarly linked corporations, and the relations among the sectors represent the relations among bank industrial communities. Smallest-space analysis is utilized.

Another very interesting application of multidimensional scaling can be found in Edward O. Laumann's "The Social Structure of Religious and Ethnoreligious Groups in a Metropolitan Community." [11] The relatively new technique of smallest-space analysis is used to analyze the formation of friendship relations among 15 religious and 27 ethnoreligious groups. Indexes of Dissimilarity of friendship choices are computed, and three dimensional solutions are mapped.

Good treatments of multidimensional scaling for advanced students can be found in Clyde H. Coombs's *A Theory of Data*, Warren S. Torgerson's *Theory and Methods of Scaling*, and Susan S. Schiffman, M. Lance Reynolds, and Forrest W. Young's *Introduction to Multidimensional Scaling.*[12]

Notes

1. The first part of this section is from Daniel J. Mueller, *Measuring Social Attitudes* (New York: Teachers College Press, Columbia University, 1986), 101-102. Reprinted by permission.

2. Gordon W. Allport, "Attitudes," in C. Murchison, ed., *Handbook of Social Psychology* (Worchester, MA: Clark University Press, 1935), 798-884.

3. Newcomb, T. M., R. H. Turner, and P. E. Converse, *Social Psychology: The Study of Human Interaction* (New York: Holt, Rinehart & Winston, 1965).

4. Carolyn W. Sherif, Muzafer Sherif, and Roger E. Nebergal, *Attitude and Attitude Change* (Philadelphia: W. B. Saunders, 1965), 24-27.

5. M. W. Richardson, "Multidimensional Psychophysics," *Psychological Bulletin* 35 (1938): 659-60.

6. N. Miner, "Comment on Theoretical Models," *Journal of Personality* 20 (1951): 82-100.

7. Kurt Lewin, *Principles of Topological Psychology* (New York: McGraw-Hill, 1936).

8. F. L. Klingberg, "Studies in Measurement of the Relations Among Sovereign States," *Psychometrika* 6 (1941): 335-52; C. E. Osgood and G. J. Suci, "A Measure of Relations Determined by Both Mean Difference and Profile Information," *Psychological Bulletin* 49 (1952): 251-62. For other applications, see Roger N. Shepard, A. Kimball Romney, and Sarah Beth Nerlove, eds., *Multidimensional Scaling: Theory and Applications in the Behavioral Sciences*, 2 vols. (New York: Academic Press, 1972).

9. Robert P. Abelson, "A Technique and a Model for Multi-Dimensional Attitude Scaling," *Public Opinion Quarterly* (Winter 1954-55): 405-18. Also reprinted in Martin Fishbein, ed., *Readings in Attitude Theory and Measurement* (New York: John Wiley, 1967), 147-56.

10. Joel H. Levine, "The Sphere of Influence," *American Sociological Review* 37 (February 1972): 14-27.

11. Edward O. Laumann, "The Social Structure of Religious and Ethnoreligious Groups in a Metropolitan Community," *American Sociological Review* 3 (April 1969): 182-97.

12. Clyde H. Coombs, *A Theory of Data* (New York: John Wiley, 1967), 444-95; Warren S. Torgerson, *Theory and Methods of Scaling* (New York: John Wiley, 1960) 247-97; Susan S. Schiffman, M. Lance Reynolds, and Forrest W. Young, *Introduction to Multidimensional Scaling* (New York: Academic Press, 1981).

GUIDE TO THE POSITION PAPERS ON SCALING   4.17

Most of the significant position papers on scaling can be found in *Scaling: A Sourcebook for Behavioral Scientists*, edited by Gary M. Maranell.[1] The table of contents to that volume follows:

Part I. Measurement and Scaling
  1. Ernest Nagel, "Measurement"
  2. S. Smith Stevens, "Measurement"
  3. Cletus J. Burke, "Measurement Scales and Statistical Models"

Part II. Thurstonian Methods
  4. Louis L. Thurstone, "Psychophysical Analysis"
  5. Louis L. Thurstone, "A Law of Comparative Judgment"

For a brief history of scaling after 1974, see Karl Schuessler's "Causes for the Lack of Standard Scales in Behavioral Research" (Section 6.L.3).

Note

1. Gary M. Maranell, ed., *Scaling: A Sourcebook for Behavioral Scientists* (Chicago: Aldine, 1974).

GUIDE TO BODIES OF COLLECTED DATA FOR THE SOCIAL SCIENCE RESEARCHER: DATA REFERENCES AND DATA ARCHIVES

4.18

Instructions for Use of Guide 4.18

Two major kinds of information resources are important to the researcher. The first contains bibliographic *references* to documents that contain data; the second consists of *collected data* such as population characteristics, public opinion, or voting records. The modern researcher explores both sources before embarking on the expensive task of collecting new data. Today great stores of data are available, often at no cost or limited cost. Data seldom are exhaustively analyzed by the original research effort, although the initial collection may have cost hundreds of thousands of dollars. There may be an unexplored gold mine of data available for the problem a researcher wishes to investigate. A review of data sources is now as important as a review of the research literature.

Data References

Directory of Data Bases in the Social and Behavioral Sciences, edited by Vivian Sessions. Science Associates/International, Inc., 23 E. 26th St., New York, NY 10010. 1974.

Contains references for some 1,500 groups of data files from more than 60 organizations throughout the world, representing the data holdings of government, academic, and commercial organizations. Information on data files includes major subject field, title, time frame of data, geographic coverage, data sources, and data collection agency. Also contains profiles of reporting organizations. Completely indexed; 300 pages.

The National Archives and Statistical Research, edited by Meyer H. Fishbein. Ohio University Press, Athens, OH 45701. 1973.

Proceedings of a conference held May 27 and 28, 1968, cosponsored by the National Archives and Records Service and the National Academy of Science. Examines statistical data available in the records of the National Archives; discusses uses by economists, historians, geographers, political scientists, sociologists, and statisticians; and discusses current production of conventional and electronic statistical source records as well as criteria for preserving records for future research. 255 pages.

1975 Directory of Computerized Data Files and Related Software Available from Federal Agencies. National Technical Information Service, Springfield, VA. 1975.

This directory is a product of the National Technical Information Service (NTIS) of the U.S. Department of Commerce. It is essentially a bibliographic project. A few of the 72 subject fields are consumer affairs, elections, immigration, price statistics and price indexes, state and local government finance, and international relations. Although originally weak in the "soft sciences," the system is now more heavily committed to the social sciences, and to the urban area in particular. NTIS offers numerous bibliographic information services: a weekly index to documents wholly or partially funded by federal money in just about every aspect of human endeavor, a weekly abstract service for the most significant documents in specialty areas, information retrieval services either in batch mode through direct query to NTIS or on-line through both the Lockheed and the Systems Development dial-up systems, and physical access to the documents themselves in either microform or hard copy. Each NTIS reference to a data file has an identifying title, a date, name of the generating agency, the distributing agency (if different), notes about the number of tapes in each file, the density of the tapes, the number of tracks, and the coding structure. There is also an abstract of about 100 words describing the contents of the file—subject, kinds of variables, and the number of records in the file. The subject index, in addition to providing subject access to the contents of the 530 computerized data files listed in this edition of the *Directory,* is also a good source of terminology for those faced with the problem of analyzing the contents of data files. (This description is drawn from Vivian S. Sessions, *Public Data Use* 3 [January 1975]: 3.) Of special interest to the social scientist is the weekly *Behavior and Society,* containing government abstracts of social research projects.

The Review of Public Data Use. Data Use and Access Laboratories (DUALabs), 1601 N. Kent St., Ste. 900, Arlington, VA 22209.

This is an interdisciplinary journal published by a nonprofit corporation and devoted to the spectrum of intellectual activity associated with public data access and use. It publishes primary articles and current awareness information on social science research and methodology using publicly available bases as well as planning and research in state and local government fields. In addition, it covers computer software for accessing statistical data files, information technology, technical problems of data file use, legislation and administrative actions affecting public access, and foreign developments.

S.S. Data. Newsletter of Social Science Archival Acquisitions, 321A Schaffer Hall, University of Iowa, Iowa City, IA 52242.

This quarterly was published by the Laboratory for Political Research of the University of Iowa; it ceased publication with the summer 1981 issue. Its purpose was to communicate information on the current acquisitions of social science data archives to social science researchers. More than 40 archives cooperated in providing information about the original data collection agency and principal investigator, the time period of the data, the population covered, and a paragraph describing the substance of the study. (A list of cooperating archives appears in the following pages.) The information was classified in the categories of sociology, political science, history, public opinion surveys, and miscellaneous. The newsletter also published descriptions of the archives participating in the project and information on new technical developments that enhance the use of machine-readable data for research and instruction.

University On-Line Computer Searches for Social Scientists

An increasing number of universities are providing their own on-line bibliographic search facilities. For example, Indiana University has a contract with Dialog Information Retrieval Services, Inc. This service has nearly 300 data bases from a broad scope of disciplines. The Dialog system contains in excess of 152 million records. Records include bibliographic information, abstracts of journal articles, and conference papers. The *Dialog Data Base Catalog* is published annually by Dialog Information Services, Inc., Marketing Department, 3460 Hillview Ave., Palo Alto, CA 94304.

Among data bases most important to social scientists are the following:

Sociological Abstracts On-Line

More than 1,200 journals and other publications are scanned each year to provide coverage of original research, reviews, discussions, monographic publications, conference reports, panel discussions, and case reports. Coverage is from 1963 to the present. File is updated quarterly.

Social Scisearch On-Line

This is equivalent to the printed *Social Sciences Citation Index.* It covers journal literature and books in the social and behavioral sciences from 1972 to the present. The file is updated monthly; growth is 80,000 items per year.

SSIE Current Research On-Line

SSIE (Smithsonian Science Information Exchange) provides a data base covering all fields of research (both government-funded and privately funded research) initiated or completed from 1972 through 1982. Updated information may be obtained on federally funded research.

Social Science Data Archives in the United States[1]

The Inter-university Consortium for Political and Social Research (ICPSR) is essentially a vast archive of machine-readable data. The results of numerous studies and a huge number of facts are available to potentially every researcher in the world. The ICPSR is a federation of more than 300 colleges and universities worldwide. Each makes available data that are often not fully explored by the researchers who collect them, and through the Consortium they are made available for continuing study by others. Many of the major studies of the Institute for Social Research, University of Michigan, are in the ICPSR archive. Major studies of the National Opinion Research Center's General Social Survey are also available. Frequently requested data sets in the huge archive are those from the decennial Census of the

United States from the beginning of its history until 1990. ICPSR has both the National Archive for Computerized Data on Aging and the Criminal Justice Archive and Information Network.

ICPSR also has a vast array of data sets on social phenomena occurring in more than 130 countries. These data sets are relevant to political science, sociology, economics, education, history, mass communication, psychology, and the full range of social science disciplines. ICPSR publishes *A Guide to Research*.

Inquiries about ICPSR and its data holdings and services should be addressed to Executive Director, Inter-university Consortium for Political and Social Research, P.O. Box 1248, Ann Arbor, MI 48106.

Because the full list of ICPSR archives is too large to publish, two smaller but very significant archive confederations are shown here. The first lists members of the original Council of Social Science Data Archives (see Table 4.18, pp. 194-195). The type of data and subject matter are shown. The second list contains those archives currently cooperating with the Laboratory for Political Research, University of Iowa. There is some overlap, but together the two lists represent a fairly exhaustive bibliography of social data. For employment of data banks, the research described by Hyman demonstrates how productive use can be made of such archival data.[2] Deutsch's statement about comparisons across time, space, concepts, and methods illustrates that the surface of prospects for data bank use is barely scratched.[3]

List of Archives Cooperating with the Laboratory for Political Research, University of Iowa [4]

Project TALENT Data Bank
American Institute for Research
P.O. Box 1113
Palo Alto, CA 94302

Alfred J. Tuchfarber, Jr., Director
Behavioral Sciences Laboratory
University of Cincinnati
Cincinnati, OH 45221

Phillippe Laurent
Belgian Archives for the Social Sciences
Place Montesquieu, 1 Boite 18
B-1348 Louvain-la-Neuve, Belgium

**Celade Latin American Population
    Data Bank**
United Nations Latin American Demographic
    Center (CELADE)
Casilla 91
Santiago, Chile

Librarian, Information Documentation Center
DUALabs, Inc.
1601 N. Kent St., Ste. 900
Arlington, VA 22209
Data Information Service

European Consortium for Political Research
Fantoftvegen 38
N-5036 Fantoft-Bergen
Norway

Thomas Atkinson, Director, Data Bank
Institute for Behavioral Research
York University
4700 Keele St.
Downsview, Ontario
Canada

Social Science Data Librarian
Center for Social Analysis
State University of New York
Binghamton, NY 13901

**Center for Quantitative Studies in
    Social Sciences**
117 Savery Hall
DK-45
University of Washington
Seattle, WA 98195

Per Nielsen
Danish Data Archives
Odense University
Niels Bohrs Alle 25
DK-5230 Odense M.
Denmark

Alice Robbin
Data and Program Library Service
4451 Social Science Bldg.
University of Wisconsin
Madison, WI 53706

Laine Ruus
Data Library
6356 Agricultural Rd., Rm. 206
University Campus
Vancouver, British Columbia
Canada V6T 1W5

Data Librarian, Data Library
Survey Research Center
University of California
Berkeley, CA 94720

Drug Abuse Epidemiology Data Center
Institute of Behavioral Research
Texas Christian University
Fort Worth, TX 76129

Stuart J. Thorson
Polimetrics Laboratory
Department of Political Science
Ohio State University
Columbus, OH 43210

Political Science Data Archive
Department of Political Science
Michigan State University
East Lansing, MI 48823

Russell Hanson, Director
Political Science Laboratory and Data Archive
Department of Political Science
215 Woodburn Hall
Indiana University
Bloomington, IN 47401

Assistant Director for Member Services
**Inter-university Consortium for Political and
    Social Research**
P.O. Box 1248
Ann Arbor, MI 48106

E. M. Avedon
Leisure Studies Data Bank
University of Waterloo
Waterloo, Ontario
Canada N2L 3G1

Reference Service
Machine-Readable Archives Division (NNR)
National Archives and Records Service
Washington, DC 20408

Patrick Bova
National Opinion Research Center
University of Chicago
6030 S. Ellis Ave.
Chicago, IL 60637

Lorraine Borman
Northwestern University Information Center
Vogelback Computing Center
Northwestern University
Evanston, IL 60201

Norwegian Social Science Data Services
Universiteet i Bergen
Hans Holmboesgt. 22
N-5014 Bergen-Univ.
Norway

Robert Darcy
Oklahoma Data Archive
Center for the Application of the Social
    Sciences
Oklahoma State University
Stillwater, OK 74074

Everett C. Ladd, Jr.
Social Science Data Center
University of Connecticut
Storrs, CT 06268

James Pierson
Social Science Data Center
University of Pennsylvania
353 McNeil Bldg. CR
3718 Locust Walk
Philadelphia, PA 19104

Sue A. Dodd
Social Science Data Library
University of North Carolina
Manning Hall, Rm. 10
Chapel Hill, NC 27514

David K. Miller, Director
Project Impress
Dartmouth College
Hanover, NH 03755

Machine-Readable Archives
Public Archives Canada
395 Wellington St.
Ottawa, Ontario
Canada K1A ON3

Roper Center, Inc.
Box U-164R
University of Connecticut
Storrs, CT 06268

Social Data Exchange Association
229 Waterman St.
Providence, RI 02906

**Social Science Computer Research
    Institute**
621 Mervis Hall
University of Pittsburgh
Pittsburgh, PA 15260
James Grifhorst

Social Science Data Archive
Laboratory for Political Research
321A Schaeffer Hall
University of Iowa
Iowa City, IA 52242

JoAnn Dionne
Social Science Data Archive
Social Science Library
Yale University
Box 1958 Yale Station
New Haven, CT 06520

Social Science Data Archives
Department of Sociology and
    Anthropology
Carleton University
Colonel By Drive
Ottawa, Ontario
Canada K1S 5B6

Judith S. Rowe
Social Science User Service
Princeton University Computer
    Center
87 Prospect Ave.
Princeton, NJ 08540

Patricia Meece
SRL Data Archive
Survey Research Laboratory
1005 W. Nevada St.
University of Illinois
Urbana, IL 61801

Director
SSRC Survey Archive
University of Essex
Wivenhoe Park, Colchester
Essex, England

Jack Citrin, Director
State Data Program, Survey Research Center
2538 Channing Way
University of California
Berkeley, CA 94720

Robert M. deVoursney
State Government Data Base
Council of State Governments
Iron Works Pike
Lexington, KY 40578

Steinmetzarchief
Herengracht 410-412
1017 BX Amsterdam
Netherlands

**Zentral Archive für Empirische Sozial
    Forschung**
Universitat zu Koln
Bachemer str. 40
D-5000 Koln 41
West Germany

Base for Archives of Institutional Change

An organization has been formed in Washington, D.C., to survey the social responses of institutions devoted to the advancement and application of knowledge. The Archives of Institutional Change is a nonprofit documentation center that collects reports and published findings of studies of educational and research institutions, libraries, learned and professional societies, museums, experimental social services, and comparable establishments, primarily in North America. In cooperation with Acropolis Books of Washington, D.C., the Archives has published a number of institutional studies in a series with the overall title of *Prometheus*. The titles of the first four books were as follows: *The Bankruptcy of Academic Policy*; *Scientific Institutions of the Future*; *Talent Waste—How Institutions of Learning Misdirect Human Resources*; and *Documenting Change in the Institutions of Knowledge—A Prometheus Bibliography*.

Inquiries are invited and may be addressed to the Archives of Institutional Change, Georgetown Office Service Center, 3160 O St., NW, Washington, DC 20007.

Major Data Sources of Political Statistics for the United States

The Almanac of American Politics, 1988. Michael Barone and Grant Ujifusa. Washington, DC: National Journal, 1988.

Published yearly.

American Public Opinion Index. Louisville, KY: Opinion Research Service, 1981-1988 and continuing.

An exhaustive attempt to include both the questions asked and responses given in all nonproprietary public opinion polls conducted for local, state, and national samples.

TABLE 4.18 Members of the Council of Social Science Data Archives

Name of Data Library	Address	Type of Data	Subject Matter
Archive on Political Elites in Eastern Europe	Dept. of Political Science 1028 H Cathedral of Learning University of Pittsburgh Pittsburgh, PA 15123	Biographical information	Political elites in Eastern Europe
Archive on Comparative Political Elites	Dept. of Political Science University of Oregon Eugene, OR 97403		
Bureau of Applied Social Research	Columbia University 605 W. 115th St. New York, NY 10025	Sample surveys	Health and welfare occupations and professions, mass communications, politics, education, organizations
Bureau of Labor Statistics[a]	United States Department of Labor		
Carleton University, Social Science Data Archive	Dept. of Political Science Carleton University Colonel By Drive, Ottawa 1, Canada	Sample surveys, biographies, election statistics, census data	Politics and public opinion
Center for International Studies Data Bank	Massachusetts Institute of Technology E53-365, Herman Bldg. Cambridge, MA 02139	Sample surveys	Politics, social behavior, public opinion
Columbia University School of Public Health and Administrative Medicine Research Archives	630 W. 168th St. New York, NY 10032	Sample surveys, operational data	Administrative medicine, public health
Council for Inter-Societal Studies	Northwestern University 1818 Sheridan Rd. Evanston, IL 60201		
National Opinion Research Center	University of Chicago 6030 S. Ellis Ave. Chicago, IL 60637	Sample surveys	Health and welfare, mass communication, community problems
Political Science Research Library and Political Data Program	Yale University 89 Trumbell St. New Haven, CT 06520	Sample surveys	Studies from Roper ICPR in political science
Public Opinion Survey Unit	Research Center, School of Business & Public Administration University of Missouri Columbia, MO 65201	Sample surveys	Politics and public opinion in Missouri
Project Talent Data Bank	132 N. Bellefield Ave. Pittsburgh, PA 15213	Sample surveys	High school student attitudes surveys, career plans, aptitude tests

Name of Data Library	Address	Type of Data	Subject Matter
Roper Public Opinion Research Center[a]	Williams College Williamstown, MA 01267	Sample surveys	Politics, economics, business, education, public opinion
Social Science Data and Program Library Service[a]	Social Systems Research Institute Rm. 4451 Social Science Bldg. University of Wisconsin Madison, WI 53703	Sample surveys	Economics, demography
Survey Research Laboratory	437 David Kinley Hall University of Illinois Urbana, IL 61801	Sample surveys, statistics	Politics, economics, public opinion
UCLA Political Behavior Archive	Dept. of Political Science University of California Los Angeles, CA 90024		
Yale Growth Center	Yale University 52 Hillhouse Ave. New Haven, CT 06520	National accounts	Country analysis of underdeveloped nations
Graduate School of Industrial Administration	Carnegie Institute of Technology Pittsburgh, PA 15213	Ecological statistics, sample surveys	French cantons; election and demographic statistics
Human Relations Area Files	Yale University P.O. Box 2054 Yale Station New Haven, CT 06520	Some machine-readable data, reports, bibliographies, texts	Social structure, organization; diet practices, kinship
International Data Library and Reference Service[a]	Survey Research Center 2220 Piedmont Ave. University of California Berkeley, CA 94720	Sample surveys	Politics, communication, social behavior; emphasis on Asia, Latin America
International Development Data Bank	Michigan State University 322 Union Bldg. East Lansing, MI 48823		
Intervention-University Consortium for Political Research[a]	University of Michigan P.O. Box 1248 Ann Arbor, MI 48106	Sample surveys	Political behavior, public opinion
Laboratory for Political Research	Dept. of Political Science University of Iowa Iowa City, IA 52240	Sample surveys, voting studies	Politics; biography data on American and Argentine legislators
Louis Harris Political Data Center[a]	Dept. of Political Science University of North Carolina Cardwell Hall Chapel Hill, NC 27514	Public opinion surveys	Politics in individual states in U.S.

NOTE: This is not an exhaustive list of data archives, as it contains only those that affiliated with the Council of Social Science Data Archives. The council itself is not currently active. The list of archives cooperating with the Laboratory for Political Research, University of Iowa, provides names of archives cooperating in political research.
a. General purpose, service-oriented libraries. Materials in these libraries are routinely available to the entire community of social scientists.

Congressional District Atlas: Districts of the 100th Congress of the United States. Washington, DC: Government Printing Office, 1985.

Congressional Information Service Congressional Masterfile, 1789-1969. Bethesda, MD: CIS, 1987.

A CD-ROM product covering 200 years of Congress, this disk allows one to search the U.S. Congressional Committee Hearings Index (1822-1969), the U.S. Serial Set Index (1789-1969), the U.S. Congressional Committee Prints Index (1833-1969), and the Unpublished Senate Committee Hearings Index (1824-1964). It provides all the information available in the print copy but with more ways to locate topics and at a fraction of the time.

Congressional Information Service Statistical Masterfile. Bethesda, MD: CIS, continuing.

This is a CD-ROM set of searchable data bases containing bibliographic records for statistical publications issued by U.S. federal and state governments, international organizations, professional and trade associations, business organizations, commercial publishers, and university and independent research organizations. It is available on compact disc. Check the government publications in your main college library.

County and City Data Book, 1988. U.S. Bureau of the Census. Washington, DC: Government Printing Office, 1988.

Directory of Congressional Voting Scores and Interest Group Ratings. J. Michael Sharp. New York: Facts on File, 1988.

The Gallup Opinion Index 1965-1983 and Yearly Gallup Report 1984-1988. Princeton, NJ: The Gallup Report, 1988.

The Gallup Poll: Public Opinion 1935-1971. George H. Gallup. New York: Random House, 1972.

Guide to U.S. Elections. Edited by Robert A. Diamond. Washington, DC: Congressional Quarterly Press, 1975.

Historical Atlas of the United States Congressional Districts, 1789-1983. Kenneth C. Martis, Ruth A. Rawles, and Associates. New York: Free Press, 1982.

National Inventory of Documentary Sources in the United States. Alexandria, VA: Chadwyck-Healey, 1984 and continuing.

This is a microfiche collection providing immediate access to detailed descriptions of archives and manuscript collections throughout the country.

Official Congressional Directory: 100th Congress (1987-1988). Washington, DC: Government Printing Office, 1988.

Party Strength in the United States, 1872-1970. Paul T. David. Charlottesville: University of Virginia Press, 1972.

The Political Marketplace. Edited by David L. Rosenbloom. New York: Quadrangle, 1972.

The Representative Vote in the Twentieth Century. Edward Franklin Cox. Bloomington: Indiana University, Department of Political Science, 1981.

State and National Voting in Federal Elections, 1910-1970. Edward Franklin Cox. Hamden, CT: Archon, 1972.

Statistical Abstract of the United States, 1988. U.S. Department of Commerce, Bureau of the Census. Washington, DC: Government Printing Office, 1986.

Voting and Registration in the Election of November 1984. U.S. Department of Commerce, Bureau of the Census. Washington, DC: Government Printing Office, 1986.

The Human Relations Area Files

Any student or research scholar interested in a question involving cross-cultural and comparative material will find the Human Relations Area Files useful. These files have been called a vast ethnographic encyclopedia. They contain information on more than 300 cultural groups around the world, divided into 888 different categories of cultural and natural information. The material may be found on 5 × 8-inch paper slips or 3 × 5-inch microfilm cards, depending on the institution. These have accumulated by the tens of thousands, with more than a thousand items added yearly.

Most major universities house these files. For more than a quarter of a century, the Human Relations Area Files Inc. (HRAF), a nonprofit research organization sponsored by 25 major universities, has served the educational community by making available primary research materials and by encouraging systematic cross-cultural research. Useful publications of HRAF include the following:

Lagace, Robert O. *Nature and Use of the HRAF Files.* New Haven, CT: Human Relations Area Files, 1974.
   49 pages; $1.00 paperbound.
———, ed. *Sixty Cultures: A Guide to the HRAF Probability Sample Files.* New Haven, CT: Human Relations Area Files, 1977.
   507 pages; $10.00 clothbound.
Naroll, Raoul, Gary L. Michik, and Frada Naroll. *Worldwide Theory Testing.* New Haven, CT: Human Relations Area Files, 1976.
   138 pages; $5.00 paperbound. For further information on the above three works, write Human Relations Area Files, 755 Prospect St., Box 2054, Yale Station, New Haven, CT 06520.

Following are representative examples of published research drawing on HRAF files, listed in order of publication.

Murdock, George Peter. *Social Structure.* New York, 1949.
Freedman, Lawrence Z., and Vera M. Ferguson. "The Question of 'Painless Childbirth' in Primitive Cultures." *American Journal of Orthopsychiatry* 20 (1950).
Ford, Clellan S., and Frank A. Beach. *Patterns of Sexual Behavior.* New York, 1951.
Whiting, John W. M., and Irving L. Child. *Child Training and Personality: A Cross-Cultural Study.* New Haven, CT, 1953.
Sprio, M. E., and Roy D'Andrade. "A Cross-Cultural Study of Some Supernatural Beliefs." *American Anthropologist* 60 (1958).
Udy, Stanley. *Organization of Work.* New Haven, CT, 1959.
Robert, J. M., M. J. Arth, and R. R. Bush. "Games in Culture." *American Anthropologist* 61 (1959).
Naroll, Raoul. "A Tentative Index of Culture Stress." *International Journal of Social Psychiatry* 5 (1959).
Nag, Moni. *Factors Affecting Human Fertility in Nonindustrial Societies: A Cross-Cultural Study.* YUPA No. 66, 1962.
Stephens, William N. *The Family in Cross-Cultural Perspective.* New York, 1963.
Textor, Robert B. *A Cross-Cultural Summary.* New Haven, CT, 1967.

Notes

   1. Assembled and described by David Nasatir, assistant research sociologist, Survey Research Center, University of California, Berkeley, *American Sociologist* 2 (November 1967): 207-12.
   2. Herbert Hyman, *Secondary Analysis of Sample Surveys* (New York: John Wiley, 1972).
   3. Karl W. Deutsch, "The Impact of Complex Data Bases on the Social Sciences," in *Data Bases, Computers and the Social Sciences,* ed. Ralph Bisco (New York: John Wiley, 1970), 19-41.
   4. This list is from *S.S. Data: Newsletter of Social Science Archival Acquisitions* 10 (Spring 1981): 7-8. This periodical discontinued publication with the summer issue of 1981, and I have been unable to verify address changes since 1983.

GUIDE TO THE U.S. CENSUS AND BUREAU OF LABOR STATISTICS: DATA REFERENCES AND DATA ARCHIVES

4.19

Instruction for Use of Guide 4.19

   The U.S. Census is one of the richest sources of primary data available to the social scientist. The data are collected at 10-year intervals as a national enumeration of the U.S. population. Various survey samples of many different kinds are taken at intervals between the decennial censuses. Because of its magnitude and importance, this special section has been prepared. Data references are first shown and then the character of the data bank is described. Almost every field of sociology can draw upon this magnificent collection, and the U.S. Census staff are anxious to help researchers.

The Bureau of Labor Statistics in the Department of Labor is an excellent complement to the U.S. Census. It gathers a large amount of information on occupations and the changes affecting them. It is a major source of data about cost of living, wages, strikes, and industrial relations generally. The Bureau will cooperate with researchers seeking data relevant to the responsibilities of the office.

Data References: A Primer on 1980 Census References and Guides

1980 Census User's Guide.

This is the primary guide for serious users of 1980 census data. This is the reference source to turn to for more information on all aspects of the 1980 census, from collection and processing methodology to products and services. The guide is issued on a subscription basis, so users automatically receive occasional updates and supplementary material.

Data User News.

This is the Census Bureau's monthly newsletter for data users. It reports on new publications and computer tapes, developments in services to users, upcoming conferences and training courses, and related matters. It includes the quarterly supplement, *1980 Census Update.*

Bureau of the Census Catalog.

Issued quarterly with monthly supplements, the *Catalog* provides a comprehensive listing of all new publications, computer tape files, and special tabulations.

1980 Census Indexes.

These are comprehensive subject matter and geographic indexes to data tables from both published reports and computer tape files from the 1980 Census.

There are a number of specialized guides, which are fully listed in *Census '80: Continuing the Factfinding Tradition*, a text written by Charles P. Kaplan and Thomas L. Van Valey for the U.S. Department of Commerce.[1]

U.S. Census Data Files and Special Tabulations

The Bureau of the Census publishes only essential and widely useful data in its printed reports of censuses and surveys, but much more information is available to the public. The Bureau maintains data files that can be processed to provide almost unlimited subject cross-classifications and area tabulations. Some of these tape and punchcard files, which do not contain confidential individual records, may be purchased and used by the purchaser for making tabulations. All files, under appropriate circumstances, can be used by the Bureau to prepare tabulations specified by customers. Special tabulations can also be prepared directly from files on filled-in questionnaires. Tabulations made from individual records are subject to review to make certain that the results are in such summary form that no individual information is disclosed. Some unpublished nonstatistical information is also available, including maps, computer programs, and address directories of public officials.

The materials are arranged according to major subject field. Within each field, the items generally are separated into two groups, Data Files and Selected Special Tabulations, with the occasional use of a third category, Other Materials. Under Data Files are listed the large machine-readable files that have become available during the period covered by this issue of the *Catalog*; the contents of each are described, and the description indicates whether the files are for sale or may be used only by the

Census Bureau to prepare tabulations for individual customers. Under Selected Special Tabulations are listed examples of tabulations prepared during the current period for individual users. Under Other Materials are maps and computer programs as well as materials that have become available during the period covered by this issue of the *Catalog*.

A section describing available machine-readable materials first appeared in the 1964 *Catalog*. It provided information on many data files of the 1960 Censuses of Population and Housing, the 1959 Census of Agriculture, the 1958 Census of Business and Manufactures, the 1962 Census of Governments, the *County and City Data Book,* and other series that have not been repeated in later issues of the *Catalog*. The 1969 edition of *Guide to Census Bureau Data Files and Special Tabulations* provides a cumulative inventory of items still available for the period 1958 through 1968.

For detailed information about any item listed, write to the chief of the division named at the beginning of each section. When inquiring about a file or special tabulation, specify the catalog item number.

The Bureau's data files are of two basic types: (a) those containing basic records on individual respondents (i.e., the returns for each person, establishment, and the like), and (b) those containing statistical totals (i.e., summarizations for small areas or for detailed subject classifications). The description of each file indicates whether it is for sale or may be used only by the Census Bureau for preparation of special tabulations for the buyer.

Basic record tapes. The tapes containing basic individual records are in nearly all cases confidential; therefore the Bureau cannot sell them but can prepare special tabulations from them. However, certain sets of nonconfidential individual records on tapes and punchcards (as described in the *Guide to Census Bureau Data Files and Special Tabulations* mentioned above) can be purchased from the Bureau. The Bureau has prepared for sale tape files containing 1/100, 1/1,000, and 1/10,000 samples of individual records from the 1960 and 1970 Censuses of Population and Housing by removing all information that might make possible identification of any person, household, or housing unit. The Bureau also makes available the nonconfidential returns from some of the public agencies that report on their activities for the Bureau's surveys; for example, information from each building permit-issuing jurisdiction is available on computer tapes.

Summary tapes. Many summary tapes are available; these contain small-area totals that were subsequently added together by the computer to obtain the results required for the published tables. Summary tapes are generally useful for further machine processing to obtain totals for areas not shown separately in the published reports or for preparing derived measures (averages, rations, and so on) for specific geographic areas. The data on these tapes can also be obtained as printouts of the tape content. Such displays are accompanied by technical memoranda explaining the content and organization of the display and supplying identification for the totals.

In addition to the data described above, some files contain the same statistics found in published reports; these files are made available for users who wish to summarize further or to rearrange the published data. Examples of such data files are the computer tape copies of all editions of the *County and City Data Book,* which are also available on punchcards on a special-order basis.

Documentation furnished with tapes. Furnished with all purchases of computer tapes are descriptions of the data, a layout of the record format, the code structure used, and other needed technical documentation.

TABLE 4.19 Population and Housing Items: 1980 Census Items Compared with 1970

Population Items	1980	1970	Housing Items	1980	1970
Household relationship	100	100	Coverage questions	100	100
Sex	100	100	Access to unit	100	100
"Race"	100	100	Complete plumbing facilities	100	100
Age	100	100	Number of rooms	100	100
Marital status	100	100	Tenure (whether unit is owned	100	100
Spanish/Hispanic origin			or rented)		
or descent	100	5	Condominium	100	—
School enrollment	21	15	Acreage and presence of		
Educational attainment	21	20	commercial establishment	100	100
Place of birth	21	20	Value of home	100	100
Citizenship and year of			Monthly rent	100	100
immigration	21	5	Occupancy and vacancy status	100	100
Current language	21	—	Description of building	21	20
Ancestry	21	—	Stories, elevator in structure	21	5
Place of residence 5 years ago	21	15	Source of water	21	15
Activity 5 years ago	21	20	Sewage disposal	21	15
Veteran status	21	15	Year built	21	20
Disability	21	5	Year present occupant		
Children ever born	21	20	moved into house	21	15
Marital history	21	5	Heating equipment	21	21
Employment status	21	20	Fuels	21	5
Hours worked last week	21	20	Cost of utilities and fuels	21	20
Place of work	21	15	Complete kitchen facilities	21	100
Travel time to work	21	—	Number of bedrooms	21	5
Mode of transportation to			Number of bathrooms	21	15
work	21	15	Telephone	21	100
Carpooling	21	—	Air conditioning	21	15
Year last worked	21	20	Number of automobiles	21	—
Industry, occupation, class			Number of light trucks and		
of worker	21	20	vans	21	—
Work and weeks looking	21	20	Basement	—	100
for work previous year	21	20	Clothes washing machine	—	5
Income last year	21	20	Clothes dryer	—	5
Birthplace of parents	—	15	Dishwasher	—	5
Mother tongue	—	15	Home food freezer	—	5
Vocational training	—	5	Television	—	5
Industry, occupation, and class			Radio	—	5
of worker 5 years ago	—	5	Second home	—	5

NOTE: The sample percentages population and housing items included in the 1980 census in comparison with the items in the 1970 census are shown. Please note that as new items have been added to the census questionnaire, others have had to be dropped. The 1980 census added more products and services that were formulated in response to needs for more racial, ethnic group, and small area data. For information about these changes, see David E. Silver and Lucille D. Catherton, "1980 Census Data Products and Coverage Improvements," *Statistical Reporter* (August 1979), 279–88.

Maps. Maps are generally published as part of the corresponding reports. Some of the computer tape products are available on microfiche.

Data Archive: The U.S. Census as a Data Bank

The U.S. Census is a gold mine of data for the social science researcher.[2] The 1980 census content and coverage shown in Tables 4.19 and 4.20 indicates the scope of information compared with the 1970 census gathered in the decennial census on population and housing.

TABLE 4.20 Published Census Tract Report—Population Data

Table P-1. General Characteristics of Persons	*Table P-2. Social Characteristics of Persons: 1980[a]*
Census Tracts	**Census Tracts**
AGE	**NATIVITY AND PLACE OF BIRTH**
Total persons	**Total persons**
Under 5 years	Native
5 to 9 years	Born in State of residence
10 to 14 years	Born in different State
15 to 19 years	Born abroad, at sea, etc.
20 to 24 years	Foreign born
25 to 34 years	**LANGUAGE SPOKEN AT HOME AND**
35 to 44 years	**ABILITY TO SPEAK ENGLISH**
45 to 54 years	Persons 5 to 17 years
55 to 64 years	Speak a language other than English at
65 to 74 years	home
75 years and over	Percent who speak English not well
3 and 4 years	or not at all
16 years and over	Persons 18 years and over
18 years and over	Speak a language other than English at
21 years and over	home
60 years and over	Percent who speak English not well
62 years and over	or not at all
Median	**SCHOOL ENROLLMENT AND TYPE OF SCHOOL**
Female	**Persons 3 years old and**
Under 5 years	**over enrolled in school**
5 to 9 years	Nursery school
10 to 14 years	Private
15 to 19 years	Kindergarten
20 to 24 years	Private
25 to 34 years	Elementary (1 to 8 years)
35 to 44 years	Private
45 to 54 years	High school (1 to 4 years)
55 to 64 years	Private
65 to 74 years	College
75 years and over	
3 and 4 years	**YEARS OF SCHOOL COMPLETED**
16 years and over	
18 years and over	**Persons 25 years old and over**
21 years and over	Elementary: 0 to 4 years
60 years and over	5 to 7 years
62 years and over	8 years
	High School: 1 to 3 years
Median	4 years
	College: 1 to 3 years
HOUSEHOLD TYPE AND	4 or more years
RELATIONSHIP	Percent high school graduates
Total persons	
In households	**FERTILITY**
Householder	Women 35 to 44 years
Family householder	Children ever born per 1,000 women
Nonfamily householder	
Living alone	**RESIDENCE IN 1975**
Spouse	
Other relatives	**Persons 5 years and over**
Nonrelatives	Same house

(Continued)

TABLE 4.20 (Continued)

Table P-1.   General Characteristics of Persons

Inmate of institution
Other, in group quarters
Persons per household
Persons per family

Persons 65 years and over
In households
  Householder
    Nonfamily householder
      Living alone
  Spouse
  Other relatives
  Nonrelatives
Inmate of Institution
Other, in group quarters

FAMILY TYPE BY PRESENCE OF OWN CHILDREN
  Families
With own children under 18 years
  Number of own children under 18 years
    Married-couple families
With own children under 18 years
  Number of own children under 18 years
    Female householder, no husband present
With own children under 18 years
  Number of own children under 18 years

MARITAL STATUS
  Male, 15 years and over
Single
Now married, except separated
Separated
Widowed
Divorced
  Female, 15 years and over
Single
Now married, except separated
Separated
Widowed
Divorced

Table P-2.   Social Characteristics of Persons: 1980[a]

Different house in United States
  Same county
  Different county
    Same State
    Different State
      Northeast
      North Central
      South
      West
  Abroad

JOURNEY TO WORK

  Workers, 16 years and over
Private vehicle: Drive alone
  Carpool
Public transportation
  Bus or streetcar
  Subway, elevated train, or railroad
Walked only
Other means
Worked at home
Persons per private vehicle
Mean travel time to work   Minutes
Worked in county of residence
Worked outside county of residence
Place of work not reported

Table P-3.   Labor Force and Disability Characteristics of Persons: 1980

Census Tracts

LABOR FORCE STATUS
  Persons 16 years and over
Labor force
  Percent of persons 16 years and
    over
Civilian labor force
  Employed

Table P-4.   Income and Poverty Status in 1979: 1980

Census Tracts

INCOME IN 1979
  Households
Less than $5,000
$5,000 to $7,499
$7,500 to $9,999
$10,000 to $14,999
$15,000 to $19,999

Table P-3. Labor Force and Disability
Characteristics of Persons: 1980

Table P-4. Income and Poverty Status
in 1979: 1980

Unemployed
    Percent of civilian labor force
Female, 16 years and over
Labor force
    Percent of female, 16 years and
    over
    Civilian labor force
    Employed
    Unemployed
        Percent of civilian labor force
With own children under 6 years
    in labor force
Married, husband present
    in labor force
Civilian persons 16 to 19 years
Not enrolled in school
    Not high school graduate
        Employed
        Unemployed
        Not in labor force

**OCCUPATION AND SELECTED
INDUSTRIES**
    **Employed persons 16 years and
    over**

Managerial and professional specialty oc-
    cupations
    Executive, administrative, and manage-
    rial occupations
    Professional specialty occupations
Technical, sales, and administrative support
    occupations
    Technicians and related support occu-
    pations
    Sales occupations
    Administrative support occupations, in-
    cluding clerical
Service occupations
    Private household occupations
    Protective service occupations
    Service occupations, except protective
    and household
Farming, forestry, and fishing occupations
Precision production, craft, and repair oc-
    cupations
Operators, fabricators, and laborers
    Machine operators, assemblers, and in-
    spectors
    Transportation and material moving oc-
    cupations
    Handlers, equipment cleaners, helpers
    and laborers

Manufacturing
Wholesale and retail trade
Professional and related services

$20,000 to $24,999
$35,000 to $49,000
$50,000 or more
Median
Mean
Owner-occupied households
    Median income
    Mean income
Renter-occupied households
    Median income
    Mean income
Families
    Median income
    Mean income
Unrelated individuals 15 years and over
    Median income
    Mean income
Per capita income

INCOME TYPE IN 1979
    Households
With earnings
    Mean earnings
With Social Security income
    Mean Social Security income
With public assistance income
    Mean public assistance income

MEAN FAMILY INCOME IN 1979 BY FAMILY TYPE
Families
    With own children under 18 years
    Without own children under 18 years
Married-couple families
    With own children under 18 years
    Without own children under 18 years
Female householder, no husband present
    With own children under 18 years
    Without own children under 18 years

ALL INCOME LEVELS IN 1979
    Families
Householder worked in 1979
    With related children under 18 years
Female householder, no husband present
    Householder worked in 1979
    With related children under 18 years
        With related children under 6 years
Householder 65 years and over

    **Unrelated individuals for whom
    poverty status is determined**
65 years and over

    **Persons for whom poverty status
    is determined**
Under 18 years
    Related children under 18 years
        Related children 5 to 17 years

(Continued)

TABLE 4.20 (Continued)

Table P-3. Labor Force and Disability Characteristics of Persons: 1980	*Table P-4. Income and Poverty Status in 1979: 1980*

Class of worker
Private wage and salary workers
Government workers
  Local government workers
Self-employed workers

LABOR FORCE STATUS IN 1979

Persons 16 years and over, in labor force
  in 1979
Percent of persons 16 years and over
  Worked in 1979
    40 or more weeks
      Usually worked 35 or more hours
        per week
    50 to 52 weeks
      Usually worked 35 or more hours
        per week
With unemployment in 1979
  Percent of those in labor force in
    1979
  Unemployed 15 or more weeks
  Mean weeks of unemployment

**DISABILITY STATUS OF
NONINSTITUTIONAL PERSONS
  Male, 16 to 64 years**
With a work disability
Not in labor force
Prevented from working

Female, 16 to 64 years
(Repeat as Male, 16 to 64)

Persons 16 to 64 years
With a public transportation disability
With a work disability

Persons 65 years and over
With a public transportation disability

WORKERS IN FAMILY IN 1979

No workers
  Mean family income
1 worker
  Mean family income
2 workers
  Mean family income
3 or more workers
  Mean family income

18 to 59 years
60 years and over
  65 years and over

**INCOME IN 1979 BELOW POVERTY LEVEL
  Families**
Percent below poverty level
Householder worked in 1979
With related children under 18 years
Female householder, no husband present
  Householder worked in 1979
    With related children under 18 years
      With related children under 6 years
Householder 65 years and over
    Unrelated individuals for whom
      poverty status is determined
Percent below poverty level
65 years and over

**Persons for whom poverty status
  is determined**
Percent below poverty level
Under 18 years
  Related children under 18 years
  Related children 5 to 17 years
18 to 59 years
60 years and over
  65 years and over

**INCOME IN 1979 BELOW SPECIFIED
POVERTY LEVEL**

Percent of persons for whom poverty sta-
tus is determined:
  Below 75 percent
  Below 125 percent
  Below 150 percent
  Below 200 percent

a. Peter A. Bounpane, acting chief, Decennial Census Division Memorandum, PHC80-2 Census Tracts, U.S. Bureau of the Census (January 21, 1982).

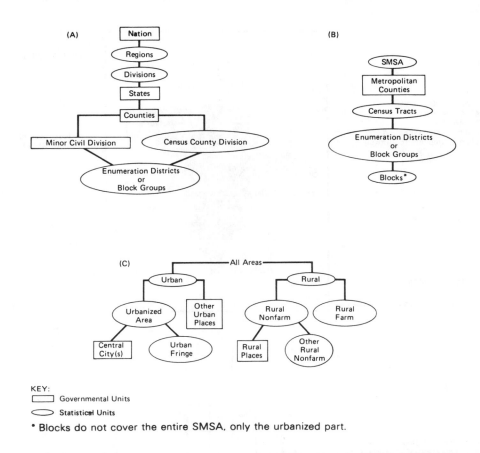

Figure 4.1. Hierarchical Relationships of Census Bureau Geographic Units. This figure illustrates hierarchical or "nesting" relationship among census geographic areas. Note that the hierarchies overlap; for example, counties are subdivided into minor civil divisions or census county division (a), into urban and rural components (C), and, inside SMSAs, into census tracts (B). Note also the relationship among governmental and statistical units as data summary areas.

Geographic Areas

The 1980 census provides data for more geographic areas than any other census. These areas are classified as either governmental or statistical areas. Figure 4.1 lists all Census Bureau geographic units and the hierarchical relationships for which census data are available. Figure 4.2 shows the subdivisions of a standard metropolitan statistical area as they appeared in the 1970 census. These divisions are all continued in the 1980 census, including census regions and divisions of the United States and ZIP code areas.

The Bureau initiated a Neighborhood Statistics Program in 1980. Certain summary statistics are tabulated for officially designated neighborhoods in municipalities of 10,000 or more population that chose to take part in the voluntary program. The neighborhoods were defined by local officials in terms of census tracts and blocks.

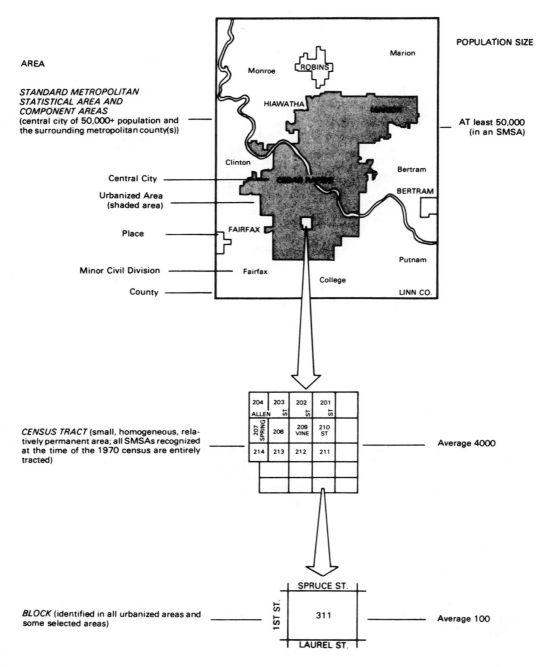

Figure 4.2. Geographic Areas in 1980 Census Reports

New data were tabulated for 269 federal and state Indian reservations. This is the first decennial census for which the Bureau has systematically identified the boundaries of Indian reservations.

Potential users of the 1980 census now have tabulated data available for 43,000 census tracts, 300,000 block groups and enumeration districts, and more than 2.5 million blocks. In addition, government geography data have been tabulated for 3,136 counties; 20,000 legally incorporated villages, towns, and cities; and 35,000 minor civil divisions or census county divisions.[3]

These geographical areas show how data are summarized in many different ways. For example, summary tape file (STF) 1 (1982) provides 321 cells of complete-count population and housing data. Data are summarized for the United States, regions, divisions, states, SCSAs, SMSAs, urbanized areas, congressional districts, counties, county subdivisions, places, census tracts, enumeration districts in unblocked areas, and blocks and block groups in blocked areas. These tape data are in a file set that will appear in printed reports PHC80-1, PHC80-3, and PC80-1-A.

Of all these geographical units, the census tract is often the most valuable. As shown in Figure 4.2, it is a small, homogeneous, relatively permanent area. Because it has many common social and economic characteristics, it offers many comparative study opportunities for community research.

The information on population items is generally of most interest to the social scientist. Tables 4.19 and 4.20 have been selected from the census tract data to show items of some social and labor force characteristics of the United States population. Statistics for most of the population and housing subjects included in the 1980 census are presented for census tracts in SMSAs and in other tracted areas in the final printed report series PHC80-2 (1983).

Also available are other census tract tables that include breakdowns of general characteristics; social and labor force characteristics for white persons, 1980, and black persons, 1980; and occupation, income in 1979, and poverty status in 1979 of white persons and black persons. The same data sets can be secured for American Indian, Eskimo, and Aleut persons, 1980; Asian and Pacific Islander persons, 1980; and Spanish-origin persons, 1980. Other tables include information on structural, equipment, and household characteristics of housing units, total population, 1980. All of these items are then broken down for the white householder, the black householder, the American Indian, Eskimo, and Aleut householder, Asian and Pacific householder, and householders of Spanish origin. Additional information by census tract is available on financial characteristics of housing units, each in turn broken down by the same racial and geographic units specified above.

General and Specialized Summaries of U.S. Census Data

Congressional District Data Book.
   Population and housing data with maps for each district; votes cast for president and Congress.
County and City Data Book.
   Demographic, social, and economic data for states, counties, cities, and unincorporated places of 25,000 or more, and for metropolitan and urbanized areas.
Historical Statistics of the United States, Colonial Times to 1970—Bicentennial Edition, 1975.
   Demographic, social, and economic trends. Analytical text and detailed source notes. Comprehensive index.
Pocket Data Book, U.S.A.
   A condensation of the *Statistical Abstract*, simplified for ready reference, with charts on current trends. Index and glossary of terms.
Statistical Abstract of the United States.

The standard annual summary of statistics on the social, political, and economic characteristics of the nation. Extensive guide to public and private sources. Comprehensive index.

Subject and U.S. Area Reports.

U.S. summaries for specific censuses.

Public Use Samples of the U.S. Census could prove especially valuable to social scientists who want to perform detailed analyses that would exhaust samples of the usual size of 1,500 to 3,000.[4] For example, detailed cross-tabulation of race, sex, and occupation become quite feasible with the public use sample (PUS). The U.S. Bureau of the Census has released a collection of samples of the U.S. population as of April 1, 1970, that contains data on individuals and their households. The *Public Use Samples of Basic Records* from the 1970 census come from the sample questionnaires administered to the population as part of the decennial census. No names, addresses, or other identifying details are included in the data, but all other data collected through the sample questionnaire are coded onto computer-readable magnetic tapes. These individual and household data are a major resource for social science research, for they provide flexibility in analysis that the aggregate (tabulated) data released by the Bureau cannot provide. PUS is a collection of six statistically independent samples, each reporting data from a 1% sample of households permitting a pooling of approximately 12 million observations (or 6% of households). An interesting application of the PUS has been described by Richard C. Rockwell.[5]

For users of small-area statistics, *Data User News* is valuable. This publication is issued monthly by the Social and Economic Statistics Administration of the Department of Commerce, Washington, DC. For information, write to the Editor, Data User Services Division, Bureau of the Census, Washington, DC 20233.

Community leaders will find *Census Data for Community Action* suitable for their use. Several examples are provided of the types of community problems that might be solved by beginning with analysis of census statistics. In one, the census results are used to evaluate the impact of alternate routes for an expressway on various neighborhoods in a community. Another shows how census data on age, education, and other population characteristics can establish the need for adult education programs. A third indicates how census data can help in assessing a community's need for day-care centers. Income figures, numbers of female-headed households, and number of children under 5 years of age are all utilized in this analysis. Copies of the booklet may be obtained from the Publications Distribution Section, Social and Economic Statistics Administration, Washington, DC 20233.

For more detailed research activity in the local area, the *Census Use Study* is the required resource. The *Census Use Study* was established by the U.S. Bureau of the Census to explore the current uses and future needs for small-area data, and data handling and display techniques in local, state, and federal agencies. There is a growing need to improve the system for relating census data with local agency data. Linking of data from census and local sources is essential for enhancing the analysis of various urban problems and trends of change. For example, in the study of crime and delinquency statistics, agencies are interested in linking incident reports prepared by law enforcement agencies with neighborhood socioeconomic data available from the Census Bureau. Similarly, in transportation planning, local data on land use and travel patterns must be related to specific demographic and social characteristics for small areas such as traffic zones. Trip-generation rates as related to the socio-economic characteristics of study areas can then be computed and used to estimate future transportation facility requirements. Other areas of interest include educational planning, health planning, housing and redevelopment planning, public safety planning, and various subjects of concern to commerce and industry, such as studies of telephone and bank service users in relation to the socioeconomic characteristics of small groups of the population.

Data Access Descriptions are intended as a means of access to unpublished data of the Bureau of the Census for persons with data requirements not fully met by the published reports. These are published as occasional reports when various kinds of data become available. Address inquiries to *Data Access Description,* U.S. Bureau of the Census, Washington, DC 20233.

Data Access News is published by the Clearinghouse and Laboratory for Census Data (CLCD) six to eight times a year. The CLCD also publishes the quarterly *Review of Public Data Use.* The CLCD is operated by Data Use and Access Laboratories (DUALabs) with a grant from the National Science Foundation. CLCD offices: 1601 N. Kent St., Ste. 900, Arlington, VA 22209. These are significant references for current information about research and data for behavioral sciences.

Current Population Reports represents a data resource of great value to demographers and social scientists generally. In addition to the findings of the Census of Population, conducted every few years, the Bureau of the Census publishes continuing and up-to-date statistics on population counts, characteristics, and other special studies on the American people. Data are issued under eight subject areas and released under the general title *Current Population Reports.* The eight categories are as follows:

P-20 Population Characteristics

P-23 Special Studies

P-25 Population Estimates and Projections

P-26 Federal-State Cooperative Program for Population Estimates

P-27 Farm Population

P-28 Special Census

P-60 Consumer Income

P-65 Consumer Buying Indicators

Of these, P-20 Population Characteristics and P-23 Special Studies have most general utility to the social scientist. The P-20 series began in September 1947. Since then, approximately 10 reports a year have been issued, covering current national and, in some cases, regional data on geographic residence and mobility, fertility, education, school enrollment, marital status, numbers and characteristics of households and families, and so on. Almost 300 reports have appeared.

Census Bureau Methodological Research is available to researchers interested in methodological problems centered on census surveying and data processing. This annual publication is an annotated list of papers and reports on the status of methodological research within the Bureau of the Census. The first list covered the years 1963-66; the list has been issued annually since then. Sections include "Statistical Theory and Sampling Methods," "General Planning and Procedures for Censuses and Surveys," "Measurement of Coverage and Response Error," "Census of Population and Housing Evaluation Projects," "Data Processing," "Concepts and Techniques of Analysis," "Data Access and Use," "Other Documents of Methodological Interest," and "Selected Methodological Reports Conducted in Past Years."

Where to Find Census Reports

Most college and university libraries contain census reports. Many public libraries obtain the principal census reports for their communities; if your branch library does not, try the main library. The city planning office, city government library, mayor's office, chamber of commerce, or similar public and private agencies also often have census reports on hand.

Community action groups may discover that they have frequent need to refer to census reports. If so, copies are available at a reasonable cost. Department of Commerce field offices in 43 cities stock many of the reports for their cities and surrounding areas, or orders may be sent directly to the U.S. Superintendent of Documents. Order forms may be obtained by writing to the Publications Services Division, Social and Economic Statistics Administration, Washington, DC 20233. Table 4.21 provides further information on the data user services available from the Bureau of the Census.

Bureau of Labor Statistics

The Bureau of Labor Statistics is a fact-finding agency engaged in the collection, interpretation, and dissemination of economic information. It conducts research on employment, human resources, prices, wages and industrial relations, productivity, safety and health, and economic growth. In many of these areas the Bureau has experience dating back to 1884. A description of the Bureau's current activity may be found in *Major Programs* (published annually), U.S. Department of Labor, Bureau of Labor Statistics, Washington, DC 20212.

Publications include the *Monthly Labor Review, Occupational Outlook Quarterly, Handbook of Labor Statistics* (annual), *BLS Handbook of Methods,* and *Publications of the Bureau of Labor Statistics,* a semiannual annotated catalog listing all current Bureau publications.

Of particular interest to social scientists are the Special Labor Force Reports. Copies of individual reports in this series may be obtained from the Bureau of Labor Statistics in Washington, DC, or at any of its regional offices. In libraries these reports are filed under U.S. Bureau of Labor Statistics, Special Labor Force Reports, Government Classification No. L.2.98. The titles of some of these reports follow:

Long Hours and Premium Pay, May 1976 (No. 196)

New Labor Force Projections to 1990 (No. 197)

The Labor Force Patterns of Divorced and Separated Women, March 1975 (No. 198)

Employment and Unemployment in 1976 (No. 199)

Students, Graduates, and Dropouts in the Labor Market, October 1976 (No. 200)

Work Experience of the Population, 1976 (No. 201)

The Extent of Job Search by Employed Workers, May 1976 (No. 202)

Year-Round Full-Time Earnings in 1975 (No. 203)

Going Back to School at 35 and Over, October 1976 (No. 202)

Children of Working Mothers, March 1976 (No. 205)

Marital and Family Characteristics of the Labor Force in March 1976 (No. 206)

Absence from Work—Measuring the Hours Lost, May 1973-76 (No. 207)

TABLE 4.21 Where to Find Research Assistance: A Primer on Data User Services

Specialists at the Census Bureau's Washington headquarters and 12 regional offices can provide answers to questions concerning census data products and services:

Is the information I need available?

In what media is it available—on computer tape, in a printed report, on microfiche?

If it is on computer tape, who can I get to print out tabulations for me?

For what geographical areas can I get the data?

How do I order the maps, tapes, or reports I need?

Workshops, conferences, training courses, and seminars are conducted at locations throughout the country. These educational and training activities introduce users in businesses, academic institutions, and government to Census Bureau programs, products, and services.

Washington contact: Data User Services Division, Bureau of the Census, Washington, DC 20233; (301) 763-2400

Regional office contacts: Data User Services Officer, Bureau of the Census

Atlanta, GA 1365 Peachtree St., NE, Rm. 638, 30309; (404) 881-2274

Boston, MA 441 Stuart St., 8th Flr., 02116; (617) 223-0668

Charlotte, NC 230 S. Tryon St., Ste. 800, 28202; (704) 371-6144

Chicago, IL 55 E. Jackson Blvd., Ste. 1304, 60604; (312) 353-0980.

Dallas, TX 1100 Commerce St., Rm. 3C54, 75242; (214) 767-0625.

Denver, CO 575 Union Blvd., 80225; (303) 234-5825

Detroit, MI Federal Bldg. & U.S. Courthouse, Rm. 565, 231 W. Lafayette, 48226; (313) 226-4675

Kansas City, KS One Gateway Center, 4th & State Sts., 66101; (816) 374-4601

Los Angeles, CA San Vicente Blvd., 8th Flr., 90049; (213) 824-7291

New York, NY 26 Federal Plaza, Federal Office Bldg., Rm. 37-130, 10007; (212) 264-4730

Philadelphia, PA 600 Arch St., Rm. 9226, 19106; (215) 597-8314

Seattle, WA 915 2nd Ave., Rm. 312, 98174; (206) 442-7080

Labor Force Trends: A Synthesis and Analysis; and a Bibliography, October 1977 (No. 208)

Educational Attainment of Workers, March 1977 (No. 209)

Job Search of the Unemployed, May 1976 (No. 210)

Multiple Jobholders in May 1977 (No. 211)

Employment and Unemployment Trends During 1977 (No. 212)

Women Who Head Families: A Socioeconomic Analysis, March 1977 (No. 213)

Long Hours and Premium Pay, May 1977 (No. 214)

Students, Graduates, and Dropouts in the Labor Market, October 1977 (No. 215)

Marital and Family Characteristics of Workers, March 1977 (No. 216)

Children of Working Mothers, March 1977 (No. 217)

Employment and Unemployment During 1978: An Analysis (No. 218)

Marital and Family Characteristics of Workers, 1970-78 (No. 219)

Divorced and Separated Women in the Labor Force—An Update, October 1978 (No. 220)

Multiple Jobholders in May 1978 (No. 221)

Job Search of Recipients of Unemployment Insurance, February 1979 (No. 222)

Students, Graduates, and Dropouts in the Labor Market, October 1978 (No. 223)

Work Experience of the Population in 1977 (No. 224)

Educational Attainment of Workers—Some Trends from 1973 to 1978 (No. 225)

Long Hours and Premium Pay, May 1978 (No. 226)

Back to School at 35 and Over, October 1978 (No. 227)

Labor Force Patterns of Single Women, August 1979 (No. 228)

Absent Workers and Lost Hours, May 1978 (No. 229)

Median Earnings in 1977 Reported for Year-Round Full-Time Workers, June 1979 (No. 230)

Occupational Mobility During 1977 (No. 231)

Workers on Late Shift in a Changing Economy (No. 232)

Young Workers and Families: A Special Section (No. 233)

Employment and Unemployment During 1979: An Analysis (No. 234)

Job Tenure Declines as Work Force Changes (No. 235)

Work Experience of the Population in 1978 (No. 236)

Marital and Family Characteristics of the Labor Force, March 1979 (No. 237)

Percent Working Long Hours Show First Post-Recession Decline (No. 238)

Women's Share of Moonlighting Nearly Doubles During 1969-79 (No. 239)

Educational Attainment of Workers, March 1979 (No. 240)

School and Work Among Youth During the 1970s (No. 241)

Women in Domestic Work: Yesterday and Today (No. 242)

The Employment Situation for Military Wives (No. 243)

Employment and Unemployment: A Report on 1980 (No. 244)

The Department of Labor has a unique set of longitudinal data on labor force behavior and work attitudes, which is available to interested users for a fee. The opportunities have been described by Herbert S. Parnes.[6] The Department of Labor may support research using data from the tapes through either small grants for dissertation research by doctoral candidates on manpower-related subjects or contracts or grants for research that is likely to have significant implications for manpower policies or programs. Write Howard Rosen, director, Office of Manpower Research and Development, Patrick Henry Bldg., 601 D St., NW, Washington, DC 20213.[7]

Notes

1. Charles P. Kaplan and Thomas L. Van Valey, *Census '80: Continuing the Factfinding Tradition* (U.S. Department of Commerce, Bureau of the Census) (Washington, DC: Government Printing Office, 1980), 351-59.

2. For excellent descriptions of census applications in urban and regional planning in business, use of population and housing by geographers and by social demographers, see Kaplan and Van Valey, *Census '80*, 363-432.

3. Ibid., 128-57.

4. U.S. Bureau of the Census, *Public Use Samples of Basic Records from the 1970 Census: Description and Technical Documentation* (Washington, DC: Government Printing Office, 1972).

5. Richard C. Rockwell, "Applications of the 1970 Census Public Use Samples in Affirmative Action Programs," *American Sociologist* 19 (February 1975): 41-46.

6. Herbert S. Parnes, "The National Longitudinal Surveys: New Vistas for Labor Market Research," *American Economic Review* 65 (May 1975): 244-49.

7. Challenging problems in this area may be found in Willard Wirtz, *The Boundless Resource: A Prospectus for an Educational/Work Policy* (Washington, DC: New Republic).

GUIDE TO PRIVATE PROFESSIONAL SERVICES FOR THE SOCIAL RESEARCHER

4.20

This guide is not a complete directory, but rather a selected compilation of certain services that are available at various prices. They are services rendered by universities, government, and private companies. Perhaps the National Opinion Research Center (NORC) General Social Survey (GSS) is the most valuable commercial social data service, bringing to fruition an idea long nurtured by researchers, that is, to provide a nationwide sample of data available on an annual basis such that time-series analysis might be possible. Such a sample was also needed by sociologists to make selected data available that, for various reasons, could not be delivered by the U.S. Census.

Other services provide research in progress within specified fields, such as designing a sample, developing questionnaires or interview schedules, collecting data by mail or personal interview, and completing analysis. The researcher can even get help on budgeting and funding.

NORC also provides a variety of services for the social survey researcher. These include sample design, questionnaire construction, pretesting of questionnaires, coding, data processing, and analyses. NORC has had 25 years' experience in data collection, maintaining a national probability sample and a staff of trained and experienced interviewers. For information, write to the National Opinion Research Center, University of Chicago, 6030 S. Ellis Ave., Chicago, IL 60637.

The NORC General Social Survey

This is a program of social indicators research and a data diffusion system. The data come from annual personal interviews administered to national cross sections of about 1,500 adults, using a standard questionnaire repeated each year. The questionnaire content covers a broad spectrum of sociological interests.

With the completion of the 1988 General Social Survey the combined surveys, 1972-88, include nearly 1,100 variables and cover 23,000 respondents. It is now possible to study social trends and consistencies. A social indicator series is in place. The survey covers a full range of demographics: behavioral items on such topics as organizational membership, voting, gun ownership, smoking, and drinking; attitudinal items in such areas as abortion, crime and punishment, governmental spending preferences, race relations, violence, and women's rights; and personal evaluations of happiness, satisfaction, and anomie.

The 1988 General Social Survey has many important new research opportunities. There is a major section containing more than 70 new items designed to explore political knowledge and participation. There are new items about religious contributions. In all, 450 variables offer an immense variety of lines of analysis. Another 1,819 cases are added to the cumulative files for drawing population subsets such as ethnic groups, denominations, supporters of "other" political parties, and the like.

Mainframe tapes containing the GSS can be ordered from the Roper Center for Public Opinion Research, Storrs, CT 06268. Copies in the exclusive Micro Case format provide complete question wordings and category labels on diskette for $95.00. University departments that have membership in the Show Case Curriculum plan have received the 1988 GSS. For information about the Micro Case format, contact Show Case Forum, Cognitive Development, Inc., 12345 Lake City Way, NE, Ste. 141, Seattle, WA 98125.

The basic idea of GSS is to provide a nationwide sample of data so that time-series data of high quality are available on an annual basis. The rationale for the enterprise stems from NORC's opinion that the field of sociology shows a number of research weaknesses when compared with other social science disciplines. An unhealthy division exists between a handful of investigators associated with major research institutes and the great majority of sociologists, who can obtain national data only on a hand-me-down basis after the original investigation or when Uncle Sam is tired of the materials. It is hoped this resource will stimulate research and make available high-quality national data that now can be analyzed even on small personal computers.

Given the scope of the questionnaire, a variety of analyses can be performed. For example:

1. The researcher can replicate findings from previous studies, perhaps introducing variables that were not available to the original author.
2. The researcher can test his or her own hypotheses.
3. The researcher can study small population groups by merging studies across years (possible because of the repetition of questions).
4. The researcher can study trends over time by comparing current results with those in the various baseline studies. The codebooks give references to the original study for each item drawn from a previous national sampling.
5. Because respondent age is reported to the year, the researcher can use the cohort method in studying age trends for variables reported by age in the original study.

The data can also be used in class work in a number of ways:

1. Students can use the data to test hypotheses derived from readings and lectures.
2. Methods classes can use the data for practice in analyses. Many content areas have enough items for exercises on scale and index construction.
3. Teachers can run data to bring their lectures up to date.

References

Citro, Constance F., with the assistance of James A. Davis. "The NORC General Social Survey." *Public Data Use* 2 (October 1974): 28-31.
National Opinion Research Center. "The NORC General Social Survey: Questions and Answers." Chicago: National Opinion Research Center, 1974.
   All questionnaire items classified by broad content type and causal stage. Revised and updated.

Broadly speaking, the measures of the GSS survey fall into the following content scheme:

1. ecology
2. family and life cycle
   a. age
   b. marriage and family structure
   c. sex (gender, behavior, and roles, especially employment)
   d. children and fertility
   e. miscellaneous
3. socioeconomic status
   a. occupational level
   b. education
   c. income
   d. class consciousness
4. primordial groups
   a. ethnicity
   b. religion
   c. race
   d. politics
5. social psychology
   a. interaction
   b. social integration
   c. other
6. miscellaneous
   a. deviance
   b. health
   c. other

An *Annotated Bibliography of Papers Using the General Social Surveys* has been completed by the National Data Program for the Social Sciences. This bibliography cites more than 16,001 scholarly papers, articles, government reports, and books that use the GSS as a data source. Each citation includes a list of the variables and surveys used and an abstract. In addition, there is a mnemonic index that allows the user to locate literature quickly using variables of interest. The bibliography can be ordered from Patrick Bova, Library, National Opinion Research Center, 6030 S. Ellis Ave., Chicago, IL 60637.

Response Analysis

This organization, like NORC, offers a full range of research services. It will collect data, design a sample, consult on questionnaire development, or do analysis. Response Analysis advertises the advantages of its services as follows:

> We can undertake any kind of study, anywhere. We have developed our own national probability sample and also possess expertise in the design and implementation of local and regional studies. We have a national resident staff of over 500 personally trained interviewers, including specially trained elite interviewers.
>
> We are cost-efficient. We insist on quality work, but we do it efficiently for reasonable budgets.
>
> We get the job done when you need it, and have developed a special field control system toward that end.

For further information, write to Response Analysis, Research Park, P.O. Box 158, Princeton, NJ 08540.

Smithsonian Science Information Exchange (Research Retrieval)

The SSIE is a nonprofit corporation of the Smithsonian Institution. It calls itself the "national source for information on research in progress." By maintaining a data base of information about ongoing or recently completed research projects, the SSIE has been serving research investigators and managers in the social sciences since 1963. The SSIE receives project information from more than 1,300 federal and other organizations that support research, indexes it, and stores it in a computerized file. Exchange scientists conduct searches of this file upon requests from users in government agencies and research laboratories in universities and private industry. Information is collected at the time a project is funded and is usually available for retrieval well before reports are made at professional meetings or articles appear in the published literature.

The current data base, which covers ongoing research and research initiated and completed between July 1973 and the present, contains information on more than 8,000 projects in all areas of the social sciences. This research is sponsored by organizations such as the National Science Foundation; the U.S. Department of Health, Education and Welfare; the Social Science Research Council; and many other public and private groups. For further information, write to Ann Riordan, chief, Social Sciences Branch, Smithsonian Science Information Exchange, 1730 M St., NW, Rm. 300, Washington, DC 20036.

NEXUS, a Baker and Taylor Information Service (Literature Retrieval)

NEXUS is a data storage and retrieval firm specializing in research tools to serve the academic community throughout the English-speaking world. The word *nexus* means *link*, and in this context it refers to a link between modern computer technology and traditional research methods to furnish speedy, efficient access to large bodies of published scholarly source materials.

NEXUS promises an individually tailored resource list and describes its services as follows:

> *Preliminary Bibliographies with Enlightening Speed.* We have on computer the authors and abstracted titles of all articles ever printed in any of 534 history, political science and sociology journals . . . published the world over, obscure and well-known both, since these journals began—more than 350,000 articles in all, going back to 1834. We'll search the file by computer on any topic you select, furnishing a bibliography individually tailored to your needs. The computer will dig out citations either by a specific author *or* about a specific subject (your choice).
>
> *Periodical Guide.* In effect, we're a computerized periodical literature guide covering pertinent (sometimes esoteric) journals of most interest to the serious researcher. Based on your own "key word" choices, our bibliography homes in directly on your specific research target. With one search, it can cover the entire 140-year archive. In the handy form of computer printouts, our source lists are easily tucked into a notebook or pocket and carried along with you.

For further information, write to NEXUS, P.O. Box 1517, Costa Mesa, CA 92705.

Institute for Scientific Information (Literature Retrieval)

The Institute for Scientific Information offers an individualized weekly service of reporting on any of 68 topics in the social and behavioral sciences as they appear in the world's leading professional journals. ASCATOPICS is the computer system used to locate articles relevant to the topics the researcher selects. For further information, write to the Institute for Scientific Information, 325 Chestnut St., Philadelphia, PA 19106.

Academic Media (Literature Search)

This organization searches directories, fact books, almanacs, and other sources for information desired by the researcher. For further information, write to Academic Media, 14852 Ventura Blvd., Sherman Oaks, CA 91403.

Inventory Services Available in Public Institutions

Following are some examples of available inventories and of their great variety in format and content:

A Guide to Resources and Services of the Inter-university Consortium for Political Research, 1972-73. Ann Arbor: University of Michigan, Institute for Social Research, 1974.
Canadian Social Science Data Catalog. Toronto: York University, Institute for Behavioral Research, 1974.
Latin American Data Bank: File Inventory. Gainesville: University of Florida, Center for Latin American Studies, 1974.

Clearinghouses Offer Sociologists a Variety of Services

Several clearinghouses operating in the United States can be usefully employed by sociologists to keep posted on research projects, to conduct literature searches, to maintain currency with the existing information, and to circulate their products.

Contents of clearinghouses range from broad, general topics such as mental health to narrow, limited topics such as commuting students.

Among the services provided by clearinghouses are computer-generated bibliographies tailored to specific requests; notification of new literature in the field through the mailing of concise summaries of abstracts; specialized bibliographies on selected subjects of wide interest; a variety of publications, including books, monographs, newsletters, digests, and directories; and referrals to other sources that have more complete information. Many services are provided free of charge. For more information, write to the clearinghouses listed below.

Association for the Development of Religious Information Systems, Department of Sociology and Anthropology, Marquette University, Milwaukee, WI 53233

Child Abuse and Neglect Clearinghouse Project, Herner and Company, 2100 M St., NW, Ste. 316, Washington, DC 20037

Clearinghouse, Bureau of Research and Training (MH), Eastern Pennsylvania Psychiatric Institute, Henry Ave. and Abbottford Rd., Philadelphia, PA 19129

National Agricultural Library, 10301 Baltimore Blvd., Beltsville, MD 20705

National Clearinghouse for Alcohol Information, P.O. Box 2345, Rockville, MD 20852

National Clearinghouse for Commuter Programs, 1211 Student Union, University of Maryland, College Park, MD 20742

National Clearinghouse for Drug Abuse Information, P.O. Box 1908, Rockville, MD 20852

National Clearinghouse for Mental Health Information, 5600 Fishers Ln., Rockville, MD 20852

National Clearinghouse on Revenue Sharing, 1785 Massachusetts Ave., NW, Washington, DC 20036

National Criminal Justice Reference Service, Law Enforcement Assistance Administration, U.S. Department of Justice, Washington, DC 20530

National Female Offender Resource Center, 1705 DeSales St., NW, Washington, DC 20036

National Library of Medicine, 8600 Rockville Pike, Bethesda, MD 20014

4.21   DIRECTORIES OF SOCIAL RESEARCH CENTERS IN THE UNITED STATES, ENGLAND, AND THE WORLD

Research Centers in the United States

Research Centers Directory, 6th ed. Gale Research Co., Detroit, MI 48226, 1979. Updated supplements.

Lists 3,200 research centers specializing in the following areas:

1. agriculture, home economics, and nutrition
2. astronomy
3. business, economics, and transportation
4. conservation
5. education
6. engineering and technology
7. government and public affairs
8. labor and industrial relations
9. law
10. life sciences
11. mathematics
12. physical and earth sciences
13. regional and area studies
14. social sciences, humanities, and religion (376 centers listed, including centers for research in anthropology, communications, human development, population, religion, sociology, history, ethnic folklore, linguistics, journalism, creativity, family studies, behavior, race relations)
15. multidisciplinary programs
16. research coordinating offices

This typical entry shows the information given:

2750 Columbia University
    Center for the Social Sciences (1976)
    (formerly Bureau of Applied Science)
    Founded 1937
    8th Level, 420 West 118th St.
    New York, New York 10027
    Dr. Jonathan R. Cole, Director; Phone (212) 280-3093

Integral unit of graduate faculties of Columbia University. Supported by parent institution, U.S. Government, state and local agencies, foundations, non-profit social organizations, and industry. Staff: 41 research professionals, 7 supporting professionals, 20 graduate research assistants, 15 others, plus research fellows, interns, and part-time student interviewers, coders, and statistical clerks.

Principal Fields of research: Public and elite opinion formation; political behavior; international comparative studies; manpower and populations; sociology of professions; formal organizations; community studies and evaluation of social programs. Also collects cases of application of social research to practical problems, codifies social research methods, develops new methods for study of aggregate aspects of mass social behavior, and provides empirical social science research training for graduate students and visiting foreign scholar. Maintains its own IBM data processing equipment.

Research results published in books, monographs, professional journals, project reports, and graduate student doctoral dissertations. Publication: *CSS Newsletter* (tri-annually). Also a Preprint Series, a Reprint Series and Impact on Policy Monograph Series. Holds periodic seminars on social and political problems and applications of social science research methodology.

World Directory of Research Institutes

The World of Learning, 31st ed. Europe Publications, Ltd., 18 Bedford Square, London, England, 1980-81.

A compilation, for all countries of the world, of academies, learned societies, research institutes, libraries, museums, art galleries, and universities (including lists of faculty) in all fields of knowledge. This coverage is excellent for most purposes but often fails to include research organizations within academic departments and the university generally.

In the United States the *Gale Research Centers Directory* is superior. For additional information, consult the Social Science Research Council, 230 Park Ave., New York, NY 10017.

World Directory of Social Science Institutions. UNESCO, UNIPUB, Box 433, Murray Hill Station, New York, NY 10016, 1977.

This comprehensive reference tool is based on collections of the UNESCO Social Science Documentation Centre, which systematically acquires social science data relating to social science research, social scientists, research projects, research publications, and social science periodicals.

LIST OF IMPORTANT RESEARCH ASSOCIATIONS AND INSTITUTES AFFILIATED WITH THE INTERNATIONAL SOCIOLOGICAL ASSOCIATION

4.22

This guide should assist research scholars who wish to communicate with other sociological researchers around the world. The list is not definitive. Not all research organizations are affiliated with the International Sociological Association. Many members belong to the older International Institute of Sociology, and scholars should try to contact that group's members as well to have a more complete channel of communication. *The World of Learning* cited in the previous guide will be helpful.

Collective Members Directory of the International Sociological Association

Members in Category A:
National Sociological Associations

Africa

Egypt
Egyptian Sociological Association
National Center for Sociological & Criminological
    Research
Gezira P.O., Cairo

Ghana
Ghana Sociological Association
Department of Sociology
University of Ghana
Legon, Accra

Morocco
Centre Universitaire de la Recherche
    Scientifique
Université du Marco
Avenue Ibn Batota
B.P. 447
Rabat

Nigeria
Nigerian Anthropological and Sociological
    Association
Department of Sociology
University of Ibadan
Ibadan

Tunisia
Institut de Planification Statistique et d'Etudes
    Juridiques, Economiques et Sociales
23, rue d'Espagne
Tunis

Asia

Cyprus
Cyprus Sociological Association
P.O. Box 4688
Nicosia

India
Indian Sociological Society
Centre for the Study of Social Systems
Jawaharlal Nehru University
New Delhi 110057

Iran
Institute for Social Studies and Research
Faculty of Social Sciences and Cooperative
    Studies
University of Tehran
P.O. Box 13
1155 Tehran

Asia (Continued)

Israel
Israel Sociological Society
Department of Sociology
Hebrew University
Jerusalem

Korea
Korean Sociological Association
Department of Sociology
Korea University
Seoul

Japan
Japan Sociological Society
Department of Sociology
Faculty of Letters
University of Tokyo
Bunkyo-ku, Tokyo

Mongolia
Academy of Sciences of the Mongolian
    People's Republic
Institute of Philosophy, Sociology and Law
Str. Peace, Bldg. B 54
Ulan-Bator

Taiwan
Chinese Sociological Association
Department of Agricultural Extension
National Taiwan University
Taipei

Australia and New Zealand

Australia and New Zealand
Sociological Association of Australia and
    New Zealand
Department of Sociology
La Trobe University
Bundoora, Victoria 3083

Eastern Europe

Bulgaria
Bulgarian Sociological Association
27B Moskowaska St.
Sofia

Czechoslovakia
Czechoslovak Sociological Society
Ul. 1, Listopadu
Nouzove stavby cp. 804
Praha 4—Nusle

Eastern Europe (Continued)

DDR
Nationalkomitee für Soziologische Forschung
　　bei der Akademie der Wissenschaften
　　der Deutschen Demokratischen Republik
Otto-Nuschke-strasse 22/23
108 Berlin

Hungary
Institute of Sociology
Hungarian Academy of Sciences
Uri Utca 49
Budapest 1

Poland
Polish Sociological Association
Warsaw University
Department of Sociology
72 Nowy Swiat
Warsaw 00 330

Rumania
Comitetul National de Sociologie
Academy of Social and Political Sciences
Str. Onesti Nr. 11, Sectorul 1
Bucharest

USSR
Soviet Sociological Association
Novocheremushkinskaya 46
Moscow 117418

Western Europe

Austria
Österreichische Gesellschaft für Soziologie
Fleischmarkt 3-5
A-1010 Wien

Belgium
Belgian Sociological Society
Van Evenstraat 2C
B-3000 Louvain

Denmark
Danish National Institute of Social Research
Borgergade 28
DK-1300 Copenhagen K

FRG
Deutsche Gesellschaft für Soziologie
Universität Mannheim
Lehrstuhl für Soziologie
Schloss, 68 Mannheim 1

Finland
The Westermarck Society
PL 85
00511 Helsinki 51

Western Europe (Continued)

France
Société Française de Sociologie
82 rue Cardinet
75017 Paris

Great Britain
British Sociological Association
13, Endsleigh St.
Skepper House
London W.C. 1

Greece
Hellenic Sociological Association
"Alexander Papanastassiou"
1, Pesmajoglou Str.
Athens 121

Ireland
Economic and Social Research Institute
4 Burlington Rd.
Dublin 4

Italy
Asociazione Italiana di Scienze Sociali
Istituto di Sociologia
Facolta di Magistero
Universita di Torino
10100 Torino

Netherlands
Nederlandse Sociologische en Antropologische
　　Vereniging
Mauritsweg 26A
Rotterdam 3002

Norway
Norsk Sosiologforening
P.O. Box 41
Blindern
Oslo 3

Sweden
Sveriges Sociologforbund
Sociologiska Institutionen
Drottninggatan 1A
S-752 20 Uppsala

Switzerland
Société Suisse de Sociologie
Case 152
1000 Lausanne 24

Yugoslavia
Yugoslav Sociological Association
Studentski trg. 1
11000 Beograd

Latin America[1]

Cuba
Universidad de la Habana
Relaciones Internacionales
La Habana

Mexico
Asociacion Mexicana de Sociologia
Providencia 330
Col. del Valle
Mexico 12, D.F.

Venezuela
Asociacion Venezolana de Sociologia
Apdo. 80044
Caracas 108

North America

Canada
Canadian Sociology and Anthropology
    Association
P.O. Box 878
Montreal, P.Q.

Association Canadienne des Sociologues
    et Anthropologues de Langue Française
Dépt. de Sociologie
Université de Montréal
Montréal, P.Q.

United States
American Sociological Association
1722 N St., NW
Washington, DC 20036

Society for the Study of Social Problems
Executive Office: Social Problems
P.O. Box 533
Notre Dame, IN 46556

Members in Category B: International and Multinational Regional Associations of Sociologists

Western Europe

France
International Council for Research in
    Cooperative Development
7, avenue Franco-Russe
Paris 7

Association Internationale des Sociologues de
    Langue Française
17, rue de la Sorbonne
Paris 5

Western Europe (Continued)

European Association of Experimental Social
    Psychology
Université de Provence
13100 Aix-en-Provence

FRG
Arbeitsgemeinschaft Sozialwissenschaftliches
    Institut
Plittersdorfer Str. 21
53 Bonn-Bad Godesberg

European Society for Rural Sociology
Nussallee 21
Bonn

Switzerland
Institut International de Sociologie
Palais Wilson
C.P. 7
1211 Genève 14

Africa

South Africa
Association for Sociology in Southern Africa
Center for Intergroup Studies
University of Cape Town
Rondebosch 7700

Members in Category C: Research Institutes and University Departments

Africa

Mozambico
Course of Economics
University of Laurenço
Marques
Lourenço Marques

Dahomey
Département de Sociologie
Centre de Recherches Appliquées du Dahomey
B.P. 6
Porto-Novo

Republique du Niger
Institut de Recherche en Sciences Humaines
Université de Niamey
B.P. 318
Niamey

Sudan
Department of Social Anthropology and
    Sociology
Faculty of Economic and Social Studies
University of Khartoum
Khartoum

Africa (Continued)

Economic and Social Research Council
P.O. Box 1166
Khartoum

South Africa
Centre for Intergroup Studies
c/o University of Cape Town
Rondebosch 7700

Department of Sociology and Criminology
University of Fort Hare
Private Bag 314
Alice 5700

School of Social Sciences
University of Cape Town
Department of Sociology
Private Bag
Rondebosch, C.P.

New Zealand

New Zealand
Department of Sociology
University of Auckland
Private Bag
Auckland

Asia

Cyprus
Social Research Centre
Charalambides Building
Grivas Dighenis Ave.
Nicosia

Hong Kong
Social Research Centre
Chinese University of Hong Kong
545 Nathan Rd., On Lee Bldg., 10/F
Kowloon

India
Indian Statistical Institute
203, Barrackpore Trunk Rd.
35 Calcutta

Western Europe

Austria
Institut für Musiksoziologie und
    Musikpädagogische Forschung
Lothringerstrasse 18
A-1030 Wien

Belgium
Sociologische Onderzoeksinstituut
Katholieke Universiteit Leuven
Van Evenstraat 2B
3000 Louvain

Western Europe (Continued)

Centre de Recherches Sociologiques
Université Catholique de Louvain
Van Evenstraat 2B
3000 Louvain

France
Centre d'Etudes Sociologiques
Centre National de la Recherche Scientifique
82, rue Cardinet
75017 Paris

Centre de Recherches Sociologiques de
    Toulouse
Faculté des Lettres et des Sciences Humaines
56, chemin du Mirail
31 Toulouse

FRG
Forschungsinstitut für Soziologie der Universität
    Köln
Zulpicher strasse 182
5 Köln-Sulz

Institut für Marxistische Studien und Forschungen
Liebigstrasse 6
6 Frankfurt/Main
Zentralarchiv für Empirische Sozialforschung
    der Universität zu Köln
D-5000 Koln 41 (Lindenthal)
Bachemer Strasse 40

Institut für Soziologie der Rheinisch-
    Westfälischen Technischen
    Hochschule
Kopernikusstrasse 16
51 Aachen

Greece
Centre National de Recherches Sociales
1, rue Sophocleous
Athens 122

Italy
Istituto di Sociologia
Facolta di Magistero
Via S. Ottavio 20
10123 Torino

Instituto di Studi Sociali
Facolta di Scienze Politiche
Universita degli Studi di Perugia
06100 Perugia

Centro Nazionale di Prevenzione e Difesa
    Sociale
Piazza Castello 3
20121 Milano

Istituto per gli studi di servizio sociale
Via Arno 2
Roma 00198

Western Europe (Continued)

Istituto di Sociologia
Facolta di Scienze Politiche
Universita degli Studi di Milano
Via Conservatorio 7
20122 Milano

Dipartimento di Sociologia e de Scienze
    Politica
Universita della Calabria
Arcavacata
87100 Cosenza

Servizio Richerche Sociologiche e Studi sull'
    Org. della Ing. C. Olivetti & Co
Via Jervis 24
10015 Ivrea

Spain
Instituto "Balmes" de Sociologia
4 Duque de Medinaceli
Madrid 14

Instituto de Estudios Politicos
Plaza de la Marina Espanola 8
Madrid 13

Switzerland
Département de Sociologie
Université de Genève, C.P. 141
1211 Genève 24

Latin America

Argentina
Centro de Investigaciones
Sociales del Instituto Torcuato di Tella
Superi 1502
Buenos Aires

Asociacion de Graduados en Sociologia de la
    Facultad de Ciencias Sociales
Universidad del Salvador
Callao 542
Buenos Aires

Brazil
Departmento de Ciencias Sociales e Filosofia
Universidade Federal do Ceara
C.P. 1257
Fortaleza 60000
Ceara

Chile
Instituto de Sociologia
Universidad Catolica de Chile
Casilla 1114-D
Santiago

Latin America (Continued)

Dominican Republic
Escuela de Sociologia
Universidad Nacional Pedro Henrquez Urena
Santo Domingo

Haiti
Centre Haïtien d'Investigation en Sciences
    Sociales
rue Bonne Foi, 23
B.P. 1294
Port-au-Prince

Paraguay
Centro Paraguayo de Estudios Sociologicos
Eligio Ayala 973
Asuncion

Venezuela
Centro de Investigaciones en Ciencias Sociales
Apartado 12863
Caracas 101

West Indies
Department of Sociology
Faculty of Social Sciences
University of the West Indies
St. Augustine
Trinidad

Department of Economics
University of the West Indies
Cave Hill Campus
G.P.O. Box 64
Barbados

North America

Canada
Queen's University
Department of Sociology
Kingston, Ontario

United States
Rural Sociology Society
306A Comer Hall
Auburn University
Auburn, AL 36830

Sociological Abstracts, Inc.
P.O. Box 22206
San Diego, CA 92122

*Members in Category E: Supporting
Organizations and Institutions*

FRG
Forschungsgruppe für Gerontologie
Am Bergwerkswald 16
3 Giessen

Lehrstuhl für Betriebswirtschaftslehre
Universität München
Amalienstrasse 73
8 München 73

Great Britain
National Documentation Centre for Sport,
 Physical Education and Recreation
University of Birmingham
P.O. Box 363
Birmingham B15 2TT

Note

1. For further information on Latin America, see Gunther Remmling, *South American Sociologists: A Directory* (Austin: University of Texas, Institute of Latin American Studies, 1966).

A BIBLIOGRAPHY OF METHODS GUIDES   4.23

Documents

Allport, Gordon. *The Use of Personal Documents in Psychological Science.* New York: Social Science
 Research Council, 1942.
Gottschalk, L., C. Kluckhorn, and R. Angell. *The Use of Personal Documents in History, Anthropology,
 and Sociology.* New York: Social Science Research Council, 1945.
Plummer, Ken. *Documents of Life: An Introduction to the Problems and Literature of a Humanistic Method.*
 Winchester, MA: Allen & Unwin.
Thomas, W. I., and F. Znaniecki. *The Polish Peasant in Europe and America.* New York: Dover, 1958.
Webb, Eugene J., Donald T. Campbell, Richard D. Schwartz, and Lee Sechrest. *Unobtrusive Measures:
 Nonreactive Research in the Social Sciences.* Chicago: Rand McNally, 1966.
  See especially Chapters 3 and 4.

Content Analysis

Berelson, Bernard. *Content Analysis in Communication Research.* New York: Free Press, 1952.
Holsti, Ole R. *Content Analysis for the Social Sciences and Humanities.* Reading, MA: Addison-Wesley,
 1969.
Krippendorff, Klaus. *Content Analysis: An Introduction to Its Methodology.* Beverly Hills, CA: Sage, 1980.
Rosengren, Karl Erik, ed. *Advances in Content Analysis.* Beverly Hills, CA: Sage, 1981.
Stone, Phillip J., et al. *The General Inquirer: A Computer Approach to Content Analysis.* Cambridge: MIT
 Press, 1966.
Weber, Robert Philip. *Basic Content Analysis.* Beverly Hills, CA: Sage, 1985.

Conversation Analysis

Bossard, James H. S. "Family Table Talk: An Area for Sociological Study." *American Sociological Review*
 8 (1944): 295-301.
Sanders, William B. *The Sociologist as Detective: An Introduction to Research Methods.* Rev. ed. New
 York: Praeger, 1976.
  See Chapter 12, "Conversation Analysis."

Questionnaire Construction

Hogarth, Robin M., ed. *Question Framing and Response Consistency.* San Francisco: Jossey-Bass, 1982.

Laban, Patricia. *Advanced Questionnaire Design.* Cambridge, MA: Abt, 1980.

Lazarsfeld, Paul F., and Allen Barton. "Some General Principles of Questionnaire Classification." In *The Language of Social Research,* edited by Paul Lazarsfeld and Morris Rosenberg, 83-92. Glencoe, IL: Free Press, 1962.

Oppenheim, A. N. *Questionnaire Design and Attitude Measurement.* New York: Basic Books, 1966.

See Chapters 2 and 3.

Schuman, Howard, and Stanley Presser. *Questions and Answers in Attitude Surveys.* New York: Academic Press, 1981.

Sudman, Seymour and Norman M. Bradburn. *Asking Questions: A Practical Guide to Questionnaire Design.* San Francisco: Jossey-Bass, 1982.

Interview

Bradburn, Norman M., Seymour Sudman, and Associates. *Improving Interview Method and Questionnaire Design.* San Francisco: Jossey-Bass, 1979.

Cannell, Charles F., Sally A. Lawson, and Doris L. Hausser. *A Technique for Evaluating Interviewer Performance: A Manual for Coding and Analyzing Interviewer Behavior from Tape Recordings of Household Interviews.* Ann Arbor: University of Michigan, Institute for Social Research, 1975.

Cannell, Charles F., Lois Oskenberg, and Jean M. Converse. *Experiments in Interviewing Techniques: Field Experiments in Health Reporting, 1971-1977.* Ann Arbor: University of Michigan, Institute for Social Research, 1979.

Douglas, Jack D. *Investigative Social Research: Individual and Team Field Research.* Beverly Hills, CA: Sage, 1976.

——— . *Creative Interviewing.* Beverly Hills, CA: Sage, 1984.

Frey, James H. *Survey Research by Telephone.* Beverly Hills, CA: Sage, 1983.

Gordon, Raymond L. *Interviewing: Strategy, Techniques, and Tactics.* Rev. ed. Homewood, IL: Dorsey, 1975.

Guenzel, Pamela J., Tracy F. Berckmans, and Charles F. Cannell. *General Interviewing Techniques: A Self-Instructional Workbook for Telephone and Personal Interview Training.* Ann Arbor: University of Michigan, Institute for Social Research, 1983.

Audiocassette available.

Hyman, Herbert H., et al. *Interviewing in Social Research.* Chicago: University of Chicago Press, 1954; reissued 1975.

Kahn, Robert L., and Charles F. Cannell. *The Dynamics of Interviewing.* New York: John Wiley, 1957.

Merton, Robert K., et al. *The Focused Interview: A Manual of Problems and Procedures.* Glencoe, IL: Free Press, 1956.

Staff of the Survey Research Center. *Interviewer's Manual.* Rev. ed. Ann Arbor: University of Michigan, Institute for Social Research, 1976.

Stewart, David W., and Prem N. Sham Dasani. *Focus Groups: Theory and Practice.* Newbury Park, CA: Sage, 1990.

Index and Scale Construction

Bauer, Raymond A., ed. *Social Indicators.* Cambridge: MIT Press, 1966.

Carley, Michael. *Social Measurement and Social Indicators.* London: Allen & Unwin, 1981.

Combs, Clyde H., Robin M. Dawes, and Amos Iversky. "Scaling and Data Theory." In *Mathematical Psychology: An Elementary Introduction.* Englewood Cliffs, NJ: Prentice-Hall, 1970.

Edwards, Allen. *Technique of Attitude Scale Construction.* New York: Appleton-Century-Crofts, 1957.

Land, Kenneth C., and Seymour Spilerman, eds. *Social Indicator Models.* New York: Russell Sage Foundation, 1975.

Maranell, Gary M., ed. *Scaling: A Sourcebook for Behavioral Scientists.* Chicago: Aldine, 1974.

Oppenheim, A. N. *Questionnaire Design and Attitude Measurement.* New York: Basic Books, 1966.

See Chapter 5.

Riley, Matilda W., John W. Riley, and Jackson Toby. *Sociological Studies in Scale Analysis.* New Brunswick, NJ: Rutgers University Press, 1954.

Shaw, Marvin E., and Jack M. Wright. *Scales for the Measurement of Attitudes.* New York: McGraw-Hill, 1967.

Sheldon, Eleanor B., and Wilbert E. Moore. *Indicators of Social Change: A Symposium of Concepts and Measures.* New York: Russell Sage Foundation, 1968.

Stouffer, Samuel, et al. *The American Soldier.* Vol. 4, *Measurement and Prediction.* Princeton, NJ: Princeton University Press, 1949.

See the chapters on scaling and on latent structure analysis.

Torgerson, W. *Theory and Methods of Scaling.* New York: John Wiley, 1958.

The Sample Survey (Vehicle for Data Collection)

Alwin, Duane F., ed. *Survey Design and Analysis: Current Issues.* Beverly Hills, CA: Sage, 1978.

Bateson, Nicholas. *Data Construction in Social Surveys.* Winchester, MA: Allen & Unwin, 1984.

Converse, Jean M. *Survey Research in the United States: Roots and Emergence, 1890-1960.* Berkeley: University of California Press, 1987.

Dijkstra, W., and J. Van Der Zouwen. *Response Behavior in the Survey-Interview.* New York: Academic Press, 1982.

Fink, Arlene, and Jacqueline Kosecoff. *How to Conduct Surveys: A Step-by-Step Guide.* Beverly Hills, CA: Sage, 1985.

Hess, Irene. *Sampling for Social Research Surveys, 1947-1980.* Ann Arbor: University of Michigan, Institute for Social Research, 1985.

Hoinville, Roger J., and Associates. *Survey Research Practice.* Exeter, NH: Heinemann, 1978.

Hyman, Herbert. *Survey Design and Analysis: Principles, Cases, and Procedures.* Glencoe, IL: Free Press, 1955.

——— . *Secondary Analysis of Sample Surveys: Principles, Procedures and Potentialities.* New York: John Wiley, 1972.

Jensen, Raymond. *Statistical Survey Techniques.* New York: John Wiley, 1978.

Marsh, Catherine. *The Survey Method: The Contribution of Surveys to Sociological Explanation.* Winchester, MA: Allen & Unwin, 1982.

Namboodiri, N. Krishnan, ed. *Survey Sampling and Measurement.* New York: Academic Press, 1978.

Rosenberg, Morris. *The Logic of Survey Analysis.* New York: Basic Books, 1968.

Rossi, Peter H., James D. Wright, and Andy B. Anderson. *Handbook of Survey Research.* New York: Academic Press, 1983.

Schuman, Howard and Stanley Presser. *Questions and Answers in Attitude Surveys: Experiments on Question Form, Wording, and Context.* New York: Academic Press, 1981.

Sudman, Seymour, and Norman M. Bradburn. *Response Effect in Surveys: A Review and Synthesis.* Chicago: Aldine, 1974.

Vaus, David de. *Surveys in Social Research.* Winchester, MA: Allen & Unwin, 1986.

Warwick, Donald P. *The Sample Survey.* New York: McGraw-Hill, 1975.

Direct Observation

Bales, Robert F. *Interaction Process Analysis.* Reading, MA: Addison-Wesley, 1949.

See also his revised work, *Personality and Interpersonal Behavior* (New York: Holt, Rinehart & Winston, 1970).

Dunphy, Dexter C. *The Primary Group: A Handbook for Analysis and Field Research.* New York: Appleton-Century-Crofts, 1972.

Hartmann, Donald P., ed. *Using Observers to Study Behavior.* San Francisco: Jossey-Bass, 1982.

Kahle, Lynn R., ed. *Methods for Studying Person-Situation Interactions.* San Francisco: Jossey-Bass, 1979.

Riley, Matilda, and Edward E. Nelson, eds. *Sociological Observation: A Comparative Strategy for New Social Knowledge.* New York: Basic Books, 1974.

In this volume, 28 observation research studies are critically evaluated.

Sechrest, Lee, ed. *Unobtrusive Measurement Today.* San Francisco: Jossey-Bass, 1979.

Webb, Eugene J., Donald T. Campbell, Richard D. Schwartz, and Lee Sechrest. *Unobtrusive Measures: Nonreactive Research in the Social Sciences.* Chicago: Rand McNally, 1966.

See Chapters 5 and 6.

Historical and Theoretical Methods in Research

Erickson, Kai I., Charles Tilly, and Anthony F. C. Wallace. "Essays on Social Historical Research."
    Contemporary Sociology 9 (March 1980): 1985-94.
Freese, Lee, ed. *Theoretical Methods in Sociology: Seven Essays.* Pittsburgh: University of Pittsburgh Press,
    1981.
Outhwaite, William. *Understanding Social Life: The Method Called Verstehen.* New York: Holmes &
    Meier, 1976.
Tilly, Charles. *As Sociology Meets History.* New York: Academic Press, 1981.

Participant Observation

Bruyn, Severyn T. *The Human Perspective in Sociology: The Methodology of Participant Observation.*
    Englewood Cliffs, NJ: Prentice-Hall, 1966.
Friedricks, J., and H. Ludtke. *Participant Observation Theory and Practice.* Lexington, MA: D. C. Heath,
    1975.
Jacobs, Glenn, ed. *The Participant Observer.* New York: Braziller, 1970.
Jorgensen, Danny L. *Participant Observation: A Methodology for Human Studies.* Newbury Park, CA:
    Sage, 1989.
Powdermaker, Hortense. *Stranger and Friend: The Way of an Anthropologist.* New York: Norton, 1966.
Spradley, James P. *Participant Observation.* New York: Holt, Rinehart & Winston, 1980.

Secondary Research Analysis

Jacob, Herbert. *Using Published Data: Errors and Remedies.* Beverly Hills, CA: Sage, 1984.
Kiecolt, K. Jill, and Laura E. Nathan. *Secondary Analysis of Survey Data.* Beverly Hills, CA: Sage, 1985.
Stewart, David W. *Secondary Research: Information Sources and Methods.* Beverly Hills, CA: Sage, 1984.

Use of Panels

For references and instructions in the use of panels, see Section 4.15.

Use of Informants

Seidler, John. "On Using Informants: A Technique for Collecting Quantitative Data and Controlling
    Measurement Error in Organizational Analysis." *American Sociological Review* 39 (December 1974):
    816-31.

Field Methods for Studying Social Organizations

Adler, Patricia A., and Peter Adler. *Membership Roles in Field Research.* Newbury Park, CA: Sage, 1987.
Burgess, Robert G. *In the Field: An Introduction to Field Research.* Winchester, MA: Allen & Unwin, 1984.
Feldman, Elliot J. *A Practical Guide to the Conduct of Field Research in the Social Sciences.* Boulder, CO:
    Westview, 1981.
Glazer, Myron. *The Research Adventure: Promise and Problems of Field Work.* New York: Random House,
    1972.
Gubrium, Jaber F. *Analyzing Field Reality.* Newbury Park, CA: Sage, 1988.
Habenstein, Robert W., ed. *Pathways to Data: Field Methods for Studying Ongoing Social Organizations.*
    Chicago: Aldine, 1970.
Hammond, Phillip E., ed. *Sociologists at Work.* Garden City, NY: Anchor/Doubleday, 1970.
Punch, Maurice. *The Politics and Ethics of Fieldwork.* Beverly Hills, CA: Sage, 1985.
Schein, Edgar H. *The Clinical Perspective in Fieldwork.* Newbury Park, CA: Sage, 1987.
Shaffir, William B., ed. *Fieldwork Experience: Qualitative Approaches to Social Research.* New York: St.
    Martin's, 1980.

Warren, Carol A. B. *Gender Issues in Field Research.* Newbury Park, CA: Sage, 1988.
Whyte, William Foote. *Learning from the Field.* Beverly Hills, CA: Sage, 1984.
————, ed. *Participatory Action Research.* Newbury Park, CA: Sage, 1990.

HUMAN RELATIONS SKILLS IN SOCIAL RESEARCH   4.24

Interviewing and field research require social skills of rapport, participation, involvement, and communication. The researcher who seeks to be effective in personal contact would be well advised to read some of the works listed below, which grew out of the efforts of researchers who learned through the hard lessons of experience.

Bain, Robert K. "The Researcher's Role: A Case Study." *Human Organization* 9 (Spring 1950): 23-28.

Bellack, Alan S., and Michel Hersen, eds. *Research and Practice in Social Skills Training.* New York: Plenum, 1979.

Beauchamp, Tom L., et al., eds. *Ethical Issues in Social Science Research.* Baltimore: Johns Hopkins University Press, 1982.

Covers major areas of controversy over experimentation in the social sciences: harm and benefit, informed consent and deception, privacy and confidentiality, and government regulation.

Berg, David N., and Kenwyn K. Smith, eds. *The Self in Social Inquiry: Researching Methods.* Beverly Hills, CA: Sage, 1985.

Discusses the multiple interests of individuals participating in research and the underlying bias problems that plague field research.

Form, William H. "The Sociology of Social Research." In *The Organization, Management, and Tactics of Social Research*, edited by Richard O'Toole, 3-42. New York: Schenkman, 1971.

Describes human relations and social dimensions that surround research activity.

Georges, Robert A., and Michaelo Jones. *People Studying People: The Human Element in Field Work.* Berkeley: University of California Press, 1980.

Reports of fieldworkers' experiences.

Gouldner, Alvin W. *Patterns of Industrial Bureaucracy.* New York: Free Press, 1954.

See especially the appendix, "Field Work Procedures: The Social Organization of a Student Research Team."

Hammond, Phillip E., ed. *Sociologists at Work: The Craft of Social Research.* Garden City, NY: Doubleday, 1967.

Relates research experiences of skilled social investigators, including Peter M. Blau, James C. Coleman, Melville Dalton, James A. Davis, Renee C. Fox, Herbert Hyman, Seymour Lipset, David Reisman, Jeanne Watson, and Robert N. Bellah. Especially useful for the beginning researcher is Blanche Greer's "First Days in the Field" (pp. 372-98).

Hollingshead, A. B. *Elmtown's Youth.* New York: John Wiley, 1949.

See especially field procedures as utilized in this community-based research.

Johnson, John M. *Doing Field Research.* New York: Free Press, 1975.

Excellent chapters on developing trust, gaining and managing entree in field research, personal relations, and data collection.

Madan, T. N., ed. *Encounter and Experience: Personal Accounts of Fieldwork.* Honolulu: University Press of Hawaii, 1975.

Good statement stressing importance of personal relations in the field.

Mann, Floyd C. "Human Relations Skills in Social Research." *Human Relations* 4, no. 4 (1951): 341-54.

This article provides an outstanding description. Mann outlines a *field* of study.

Reinharz, Shulamit. *On Becoming a Social Scientist: From Survey Research and Participant Observation to Experiential Analysis.* San Francisco: Jossey-Bass, 1979.

This book seeks to prepare the student for the human relations problems encountered in research. Contents: "Encountering the World of Sociology," "The Ritual of Survey Empiricism," "Dilemmas of Participant Observation," The Stress of Detached Fieldwork," "Reclaiming Self-Awareness as a Source of Insight," "Analysis of the Team Fieldwork Experience," "Dimension of an Experiential Sociological Method," "The Integration of Person, Problem, and Method."

Reynolds, Paul Davidson. *Ethical Dilemmas and Social Science Research: Moral Issues Confronting Investigators in Research Using Human Participants.* San Francisco: Jossey-Bass, 1979.

Individual investigators are now being held accountable for deception of research participants, failure to secure informed consent, physical discomfort and psychic stress experienced by volunteers, invasions of privacy, and other effects of their studies.

4.25   GENERAL BIBLIOGRAPHY ON THE UNDERSTANDING OF RESEARCH PROCESSES AND METHODS

Allen T. Harrell. *New Methods in Social Science Research.* New York: Praeger, 1978.

Bailey, Kenneth D. *Methods of Social Research.* 3rd ed. New York: Free Press, 1987.

Andrich, David. *Rasch Models for Measurement.* Newbury Park, CA: Sage, 1988.

Berg, David N., and Kenwyn K. Smith, eds. *Exploring Clinical Methods for Social Research.* Beverly Hills, CA: Sage, 1985.

Berry, William D., and Michael S. Lewis-Beck, eds. *New Tools for Social Scientists: Advances and Applications in Research Methods.* Beverly Hills, CA: Sage, 1986.

Brinberg, David, ed. *Forms of Validity in Research.* San Francisco: Jossey-Bass, 1982.

Eichler, Margrit. *Nonsexist Research Methods: A Practical Guide.* Winchester, MA: Allen & Unwin, 1987.

Fichter, Joseph H. *One-Man Research: Reminiscences of a Catholic Sociologist.* New York: Wiley-Interscience, 1973.

Fielding, Nigel G., and Jane L. Fielding. *Linking Data.* Beverly Hills, CA: Sage, 1986.

Kazdin, Alan E., ed. *Single Case Research Designs.* San Francisco: Jossey-Bass, 1982.

Kirk, Jerome, and Marc L. Miller. *Reliability and Validity in Qualitative Research.* Beverly Hills, CA: Sage, 1986.

Marsden, P. V., ed. *Linear Models in Social Research.* Beverly Hills, CA: Sage, 1981.

McCleary, Richard, and Richard A. Hay, Jr. *Applied Time Series Analysis for the Social Sciences.* Beverly Hills, CA: Sage, 1980.

McKeown, Bruce, and Dan Thomas. *Methodology.* Newbury Park, CA: Sage, 1988.

Moyser, George, and Margaret Wagstaffe, eds. *Research Methods for Elite Studies.* Winchester, MA: Allen & Unwin, 1986.

O'Toole, Richard, ed. *The Organization, Management, and Tactics of Social Research.* Cambridge, MA: Schenkman, 1971.

Rose, Gerry. *Deciphering Sociological Research.* Beverly Hills, CA: Sage, 1983.

Rosenthal, Robert, ed. *Quantitative Assessment of Research Domains.* San Francisco: Jossey-Bass, 1980.

Rossi, P. H., and S. L. Nock. *Measuring Social Judgments: The Factorial Survey Approach.* Beverly Hills, CA: Sage, 1982.

Saxe, L., and M. Fine. *Social Experiments: Methods for Design and Evaluation.* Beverly Hills, CA: Sage, 1981.

Schwartz, Howard, and Jerry Jacobs. *Qualitative Sociology: A Method to the Madness.* New York: Free Press, 1979.

Van Maanen, John, ed. *Qualitative Methodology.* Beverly Hills, CA: Sage, 1983.

Part 5

Guides to Statistical Analysis and Computer Resources

THIS PART INCLUDES guides that should prove useful to researchers as they seek statistical tools and computer resources to test hypotheses. Researchers may find it necessary to reformulate initial hypotheses in order to use the most powerful statistical test. There is a reciprocal relationship between research design and statistical analysis. Superior designs are developed when the researcher has a command of both the required research knowledge and the full scope of statistical treatments available. Imaginative research questions require the fullest possible weighing of research implementation. When the twin conditions are realized, research options of maximum effectiveness open to stir the creative imagination.

Qualitative and quantitative variables require appropriate statistics to provide tests of association or of significant differences between groups. In this part statistical tests are organized to deal with both kinds of variables. In addition, the question of the probability of normal distribution of the data forces the researcher to make a distinction between parametric and nonparametric statistics in drawing inferences from samples. These distinctions are presented with the descriptions of the statistics.

Computations being done in the social sciences today increasingly use high-speed computers through user terminals that resemble typewriters or television screens. User terminal clusters are located in universities or in organizations such as banks and insurance offices. The hardware is found in some central location. Since the 1970s the explosion of mini- and microcomputer technology has generated mini- and microcomputers in almost every department of the university. Home computers are also increasingly available.

For smaller sets of data and more limited analysis, there are punchcard sorters, counter sorters, and various types of scanners. Desk calculators are becoming more sophisticated and less expensive. Electronic calculators are noiseless and more reliable than the earlier models and often contain storage and program keys that greatly increase their usefulness.

All this hardware makes possible complex and sophisticated statistical analyses, and important scientific questions can be researched as never before. The computer can swallow masses of data and organize their relationships at split-second speed.

With these tools available, the student is challenged to develop statistical knowledge and a creative imagination. Computers can be used for generating formal models of social systems; for simulating the behavior of persons, groups, or nations; and for retrieving large amounts of documentary material such as abstracts of journal articles (as explained in Part 4). The cost of computer time requires more attention than ever before to research design, especially statistical planning.

Statistical planning is an integral part of designed research. The sooner attention can be given to this part of research, the better. After the problem, theory, study design, and hypotheses are chosen, the time for statistical planning has arrived. Researchers should not wait until they are in the process of gathering or analyzing data. This caveat applies especially to young researchers wishing to avoid mistakes, but all researchers will have better research designs if their statistical planning is done before fieldwork begins.

Causal analysis refers to the depiction of the causal relationships of the variables. Zetterberg lists 13 possible causal chains for three variables.[1] The selection of an appropriate chain is an important first step in designing statistical analysis.

Example: Two major determinants influencing the productivity or effectiveness of a work group are leadership behavior and the morale of workers. The causal relationship is often assigned to the chain that identifies leadership behavior as the independent variable (x), morale as an intervening variable (y), and productivity as the outcome (or dependent) variable (z). The causal chain can be diagrammed as $x \to y \to z$. The statistical tests of hypotheses now are given form, and appropriate techniques are applied. Alternate assumptions about the causal relationships of these three variables would call for different treatments.

A multivariate problem with many interacting variables poses more elaborate constructions. A *path model* is important if many independent and intervening variables are involved in measuring relationships with a dependent variable.

Example: Path analysis is discussed in Section 5.14, where a path diagram is shown. This model diagrams the interrelationships of variables believed to influence the son's current occupation. Father's occupation and father's education are shown as independent variables, with son's education and son's first job as intervening variables. The algebraic representation of the causal scheme now rests on a system of equations rather than on the single equation often employed in multiple regression analysis.

Dummy statistical tables become the statistical plan for qualitative data. These tables represent the actual tables to be used for analysis when data are collected and frequencies or values are inserted within them. By setting up dummy tables in advance, the researcher can make a careful appraisal of the appropriate statistics, and then can select the best technique. If the researcher wants help from a statistician, these tables are a necessity. With them, decisions can be made as to the statistic, techniques, and confidence that may be entertained. Perhaps a recasting of the data collection process may be called for, or different types of data are needed. This is the

TABLE 5.1 Example of a Skeletal Primary Table

Product-Moment Correlations Between Socioeconomic Status and Sentence Length for Crime Categories in Three States

	New York			Colorado			Mississippi		
	r	r^2	N	r	r^2	N	r	r^2	N
2nd degree murder	—	—	—	—	—	—	—	—	—
Forcible rape	—	—	—	—	—	—	—	—	—
Burglary	—	—	—	—	—	—	—	—	—
Embezzlement	—	—	—	—	—	—	—	—	—
Drug offenses	—	—	—	—	—	—	—	—	—

SOURCE: The suggestion for this table is drawn from Theodore G. Chiricos and Gordon P. Waldo, "Socioeconomic Status and Criminal Sentencing: An Empirical Assessment of a Conflict Proposition," *American Sociological Review* 40 (December 1975): 760.

stage at which the researcher needs this kind of information. Later it may not be possible, and valuable time and money may be lost.

Example: Note how Allen Barton, in Section 5.2, has prepared dummy tables for dichotomous and trichotomous attributes in two-, three-, and four-dimensional space. The variables involve relationships of father's occupation, father's political party with son's occupation, and political party. The dummy tables are particularly useful in permitting the effects of the various background variables to be compared, holding the others constant in each case.

Skeleton primary tables are tables proposed for future display of published data. The scientific worth of the tables depends upon the soundness of the reasoning underlying the classifications and associations of the data. The originator of a set of tables should ask the following questions:

- What important fact or facts should this table emphasize?
- How can these facts be made most evident?
- Is the form adapted for the vehicle of publication?[2]

An example of a skeletal primary table is presented as Table 5.1. This table will show the product-moment correlation (Pearsonian *r*) between the socioeconomic status level of defendants and the sentences received for specific crimes within three states. Also to be shown is the proportion of variance (r^2) in one variable that is explained by the other, as well as the sample size (*N*) for each crime category. Levels of statistical significance for computed correlation coefficients will be shown where relevant.[3]

Reluctance to take these steps in statistical design means that the research is placed under greater risk. The execution of these steps means the heart of the completed product is projected in advance for appraisal and evaluation. Improvements can be made and risks of failure minimized.

No limited set of guides can replace a good text in statistics. However, the researcher can find an array of concepts so organized that he or she may be able to survey the dimensions of the problem. Computation guides have been included for the most commonly used statistical measures.

A section on causation and multivariate analysis includes an introduction to the computer, path analysis, and factor analysis.

The bibliography at the end of this part has been selected to provide additional information on statistics, tables, and graphic presentation. Each reference enables the reader to follow step-by-step explanations. A brief dictionary of some newer statistical tools and methodological techniques has been prepared in order to acquaint the uninformed reader with the general meaning of the terms.

Notes

1. See Hans L. Zetterberg, "On the Decisions in Verificational Studies," Section 2.10 of this volume.

2. For further information about construction of such tables, see Mary Louise Mark, *Statistics in the Making*, Bureau of Business Research Publication 92 (Columbus: Ohio State University, College of Commerce and Administration, 1958), 156-79.

3. For presentation of the data in graphic form, see Calvin F. Schmid, *Handbook of Graphic Presentation* (New York: Ronald, 1954). For a brief description of graphic presentation, see Pauline V. Young, *Scientific Social Surveys and Research*, 3rd ed. (Englewood Cliffs, NJ: Prentice-Hall, 1956), 360-405.

5.1   THE IMPERTINENT QUESTIONER: THE SCIENTIST'S GUIDE TO THE STATISTICIAN'S MIND

Instructions for Use of Guide 5.1

This article should sharpen researchers' awareness of the dimensions of their hypotheses as they prepare to test them. As Lurie puts it:

> It is the scientist's responsibility to decide exactly what his hypotheses are, what these hypotheses are about, and how sure he wants to be of their correctness. . . . And the more the scientist becomes aware of his responsibilities, and takes them into account in his work, so much more accurate and valid will his conclusions be, and so much more properly related to the reality with which he deals.

The Impertinent Questioner: The Scientist's Guide to the Statistician's Mind

William Lurie [1]

Prologue

It has become fashionable to ornament science with statistical embellishments. No equation is complete without at least a double summation sign somewhere in it, sub-ij's attach themselves to familiar Xs, Ys, and Zs; and phrases like "polymodal distribution," "inverse reciprocal correlation," and "multivariate deviations" now can be seen on practically every other page of "The Journal of the Society for Thus-and-So," "The Transactions of the Association for Such-and-Such," and "The Proceedings of the Symposium on Etc., Etc."

But in addition to providing mathematical and linguistic ornamentation for these publications, the statistician, if he is really to assist the scientist, must perform a necessary, but irritatingly annoying task: he must ask the scientist impertinent questions. Indeed, the questions, if bluntly asked, may appear to be not only impertinent but almost indecently prying—because they deal with the foundations of the scientist's thinking. By these questions, unsuspected weaknesses in the foundations may be brought to light, and the exposure of weaknesses in one's thinking is a rather unpleasant occurrence.

The statistician will, then, if he is wise in the ways of human beings as well as learned in statistics, ask these questions diplomatically, or even not ask them as questions at all. He may well guide the discussion with the scientist in such a way that the answers to the questions will be forthcoming without the questions having been even explicitly asked.

And if happily the scientific and statistical disciplines reside within one mind, and it is the scientist's statistical conscience that asks him these questions, instead of impertinent questioning there is valid scientific soul-searching.

Regardless, then, of whether these questions arise inside or outside the scientist's own mind, what are they? These:

1. With respect to the experiment you are performing, just what are your ideas?
2. With respect to the scientific area to which these ideas refer, just what are they about?
3. How sure do you want to be of the correctness of these ideas?

In order to understand the statistician's reasons for asking these questions, let us first see how the scientist's activities look to the statistician.

From the statistician's point of view, what the scientist does, is: performs experiments and/or makes observations to obtain data relating to *an idea he has* about the organization of *that portion of the world he is interested in*, so that he can decide *whether his idea was correct or not*.

For each of these italicized aspects of the scientist's activity, there is a corresponding question.

Let us, then, examine each of these aspects of the scientist's activities, and the purpose for and consequences of the question concerning it.

An Idea He Has

The impertinent questioner must take the risk of appearing to imply that the scientist is not thinking clearly. And, of course, even an implication to this effect is not calculated to endear the implier to the heart of the implyee. But it is exactly this implication that, perhaps innocently, is associated with the question, "Just what are your ideas?"

Why does the statistician ask this impertinent question? Because it is a precondition for the statistician's being able to help the scientist accomplish his objective. A hazily formulated idea not only can be discussed, at best, with difficulty, but further, it is practically impossible to test its correctness. Therefore, the statistician has a rule, his name for which is: EXPLICIT HYPOTHESIZATION. This rule expresses the requirement that the idea, whose correctness is to be determined by the experiment, should be stated in as clear, detailed, and explicit form as possible, preferably before the experiment is conducted. This idea can relate either to the influence of one factor or to the influence of several factors, or to the numerical characterization of a property (or properties) of whatever is being experimented on. In the early stages of an investigation, where what are being sought are the influential factors (i.e., those which, when they are at varying levels, give rise to sufficiently varied results), the idea (or hypothesis) need not be specific, but it must be explicit. The hypothesis can be broad, but it must be explicitly broad—that is, even though it is not a hypothesis about details, its boundary must be sharply delineated.

For example, "Factors A, B, C, and D individually influence the results," "Factors A and B, acting in conjunction, influence the results differently than would be expected from the effects of A alone and B alone," "Factors A, B, and C, acting in conjunction, etc., etc." Or later in the investigation, and more specifically, "The measurement of the effect of factor A at level a_1, will result in the numerical value $N \pm n$."

To emphasize unmistakably the requirement for explicit hypothesization, let us use an obviously exaggerated example dealing with a particular subject: the task of an industrial psychologist who has been given the job of finding out why the accounting clerks are making too many errors in addition. (The problem of deciding how many errors are "too many" is another statistical problem, which will not be considered here.)

The psychologist, for the purposes of this example, may say to himself: "My training as a psychologist tells me that the situation in which a person operates affects his behavior. So let me find out what the situation is that is causing the clerks to make these errors." If the formulation of the psychologist's idea goes no further than this, he can obviously continue to attempt to find out what the situation is, from now on forever, since "The Situation" has no boundaries.

It might, for example, not only include the working circumstances of the clerks, but their home circumstances, their childhood histories, their dream life; and it is seen that the possibilities are unlimited. As then is obvious, the hypothesis has not been sufficiently explicitly formulated, nor the situation covered by it clearly enough delineated, for a decision to be able to be arrived at as to the correctness of the hypothesis.

But now, let the psychologist's statistical conscience awaken, and his ideas begin to crystallize out of their original diffuseness. "The Situation?—Well, to be more specific, let's just consider the office situation. And within the office situation, I'll pick three factors that I believe affect the performance of the clerks. The factors I'm selecting to study for their effects are: Temperature, Humidity, and Noise. And now, my explicit hypothesis: It makes a difference what the levels of temperature, humidity, and noise are with respect to the number of errors in addition made by the accounting clerks." The hypothesis could (and probably should) have been even more explicitly formulated (e.g., including as factors Illumination Level, Desk Space per employee, etc.) but the direction of the path to statistical virtue has been pointed out, and further travel along that path is left to the reader.

Now, assuming that the hypothesis has been sufficiently explicitly formulated, the scientist and statistician can together review the plan (or design) of the experiment, and assure themselves that such data will be obtained as will be sufficient to determine the correctness (or noncorrectness) of the scientist's idea.

That Portion of the World He Is Interested In

Again, the impertinent questioner must be careful in asking: "Just what are your ideas about?" Even though one may admit that his ideas are not as clearly and explicitly formulated as he would like, the question "Just what are your ideas about?" carries with it, to the person being asked, the implication that he isn't clear about the subject-matter of his ideas, surely not a flattering implication. The statistician has a reason for his implied aspersion on the basis of the scientist's self-esteem. The statistician's reason can be stated to the scientist thus: "It's for your own good. If I am to help you decide, on the basis of the experimental facts, whether your ideas are correct or not, I have to know, as explicitly as possible, not only what your ideas are, but *what they are about*. My name for this requirement is: MODEL FORMULA-TION." Technically, model formulation establishes the requirement that a clear differentiation be made as to whether the scientist's ideas are intended to be applicable only to the conditions of the experiment (the narrower range of application) or to conditions (i.e., levels of the factors) other than those specific ones under which the experiment is being conducted (the broader range of application). Why the necessity for this differentiation? Because, when the experimental data have been obtained, the analysis of the data is carried on in different ways, depending on· whether the hypotheses are intended to have the broader or narrower range of application.

Let us again, for exemplification, return to our industrial psychologist. And, let us say, his experimental conditions are, for temperature, 40°, 55°, and 70°F.; for humidity, 40, 55, and 70 percent; and for noise level, 40, 55, and 70 decibels.

It may well make a difference in the way the experimental data are analyzed to arrive at conclusions (i.e., decisions as to correctness of ideas), and whether any conclusions can be arrived at, and, if so, what they are, depending on whether the scientist wants his conclusions to apply only to the three levels of temperature, humidity, and noise level that have been used in the experiment, or also to other (unspecified) temperature, humidity, and noise levels. Data that support narrow conclusions may not be sufficient to support broader conclusions. Therefore, the scientist must have clearly in mind what his hypotheses are about, and whether, consequently, his conclusions will be broad or narrow; and the statistician's effort to assure that the scientist does have this clearly in mind, may well, to the scientist, appear to be impertinent.

Whether His Idea Was Correct or Not

The statistician's third question—"How sure do you want to be of the correctness of your ideas?"—is the least important of the three. This question, unlike the other two, does not probe the foundations of the scientist's thinking, but rather requests him to quantify a previously unquantified aspect of it. (In fact, the request is in accordance with the scientist's own predilection for quantitative data.) This aspect is that dealing with levels of assurance, for which ordinary language supplies us with qualitatively descriptive terms (somewhat sure, rather sure, quite sure, extremely sure). But these terms are not sufficiently explicit for scientific use. Therefore, the statistician asks the scientist to decide upon and express his desired level of assurance in quantitative terms, so that it can be determined, by analysis of the quantitative data, whether the desired level of assurance of the conclusions has been achieved. The statistician's name for the choice and quantitative expression of the desired level of assurance is: SIGNIFICANCE LEVEL SELECTION. And how does the statistician help the scientist choose the desired level of assurance? By bringing to the forefront of the scientist's consciousness his already unconscious awareness of the inherent variability of events (i.e., that, because of chance alone, no repetition of an experiment will give exactly the same results); by helping the scientist decide what assurance is desired that the hypothesis has not been "confirmed" just by the operation of chance alone; and by furnishing the mathematical tools to decide, on the basis of the experimental data, whether the desired level of assurance has been attained. Say, for example, in the temperature-humidity-noise level experiment, when all the data have been accumulated, and the scientist is preparing them for analysis so that he may decide whether his hypotheses were correct or not, the statistician will then say to him: "You know, of course, that if you did the experiment over, under as near the same conditions as possible, you'd get slightly, or even somewhat different results. The results might even, just by chance, be different enough to lead you to believe that temperature does affect accuracy, even though it really doesn't. Or even if you didn't do the experiment over again, the particular experiment you've just done might be the one in which the data are such that you'd believe temperature has an effect though it really doesn't. *But I can test these data of yours.* I can assure you that when you state the conclusion, say, that temperature does affect accuracy, you'll have only a 5 percent, or 1 percent, or 1/10th of 1 percent chance of being wrong, as a result of that off chance I told you about. Now—what chance do you want to take? If you select a very small chance of being wrong in saying there is a temperature effect when there really isn't you're taking a bigger chance of saying there isn't a temperature effect when there really might be. I can figure this out for you also. So again, what chance do you want to take?"

When the scientist has selected the chance he is willing to take of being wrong (or what is equivalent, how sure he wants to be that he is correct) in his conclusions, the statistician can analyze the data and tell the scientist what conclusions he can validly draw (i.e., what decisions he can make about the correctness of his ideas).

Epilogue

One final word. *It is the statistician's responsibility to ask these questions, not to answer them.* It is the scientist's responsibility to decide exactly what his hypotheses are, what these hypotheses are about, and how sure he wants to be of their correctness.

The statistician, in asking his impertinent questions, is just explicitly bringing to the scientist's attention responsibilities that the scientist may not have been aware that he had. And the more the scientist becomes aware of his responsibilities, and takes them into account in his work, so much more accurate and valid will his conclusions be, and so much more properly related to the reality with which he deals.

Note

1. From William Lurie, "The Impertinent Questioner: The Scientist's Guide to the Statistician's Mind," *American Scientist* 46 (March 1958): 57-61. Reprinted by permission of the author and publisher.

5.2　THE IDEA OF PROPERTY-SPACE IN SOCIAL RESEARCH

Instructions for Use of Guide 5.2.

This guide presents a technique of classifying qualitative data so that associations may be discovered. Arranging data in "property-space" is particularly useful in permitting the effects of various background variables to be compared, while other variables are held constant in each case. The concept of property-space is valuable because it becomes a way of thinking about qualitative data and the way in which relations may be ascertained. Hans Zeisel has presented a more elaborate description of causal analysis and the role of cross-tabulation for the reader who wishes additional knowledge.[1] The more advanced student should consult Herbert Hyman's *Survey Design and Analysis.*[2] See also the selected readings on causal models and multivariate analysis in the bibliography at the end of this part.

The Idea of Property-Space in Social Research

Allen H. Barton [3]

Everyone is familiar with the idea of indicating location in space by means of coordinates. Every point on this page can be described by two numbers: its distance from the left-hand side and its distance from the bottom (or from any other pair of axes we choose). The location of any point on the earth's surface can be indicated by giving its latitude and longitude, using as base lines the equator and the Greenwich meridian.

Other properties besides location in physical space can likewise be indicated by coordinates. A man can be characterized by his scores on tests of mathematical and linguistic ability, just as by his latitude and longitude. These two scores locate him in a "property-space" with the two dimensions of mathematical ability and linguistic ability. We can chart this property-space on paper by using mathematics score as one axis and linguistic score for the other, just as we can chart the earth's surface. Of course in the latter case we are making a special representation of actual spatial dimensions, only on a smaller scale. In the former our distances on paper represent the numbers of correct answers to questions given by people taking tests, or in a larger sense, the ability of their minds to perform certain tasks.

The dimensions on which we "locate" people in property-space can be of different kinds. Most psychological test scores are for all practical purposes *continuous variables,* but they usually do not have equal intervals or a meaningful zero point. They provide only a relative ordering of people. Once we have located a representative sample of the United States population in our mathematical-linguistic property-space, we can say that a man is in the fifth percentile of the population in mathematical ability and in the fortieth in linguistic ability. Sometimes social scientists do work with continuous variables that do have a zero-point and equal intervals, at least formally: age, income, size of community, number of hours spent watching television.

More often, probably, the dimensions will be qualitative properties, which locate cases in one of a number of classes, like "state of birth," "military rank," or "occupation." State of birth locates everyone born in the continental U.S. in one of 51 *unordered classes* (counting District of Columbia). Military rank locates members of the armed forces in what is by definition a set of *rank-ordered classes,* ranging from buck private up to five-star general. Occupations in themselves do not necessarily form a set of ranked classes, although some of them are specifically defined in terms of degree of "skill." We might simply list them arbitrarily, as in alphabetical order. Or we might draw upon outside information about them—for example average income, as known from census data, or prestige status, as discovered through surveys—to arrange them in one or another rank-order.

The simplest type of property by which an object can be characterized is a *dichotomous attribute,* such as voter/nonvoter, white/nonwhite, male/female, or

TABLE 5.2 A Qualitative Property-Space of Political Position

		USUAL PARTY AFFILIATION		
		Republican	Democratic	Independent
	High			
Degree of Political Intent	Medium			
	Low			

Democrat/Republican. It is always possible to simplify a more complex property by reducing the number of classes that are distinguished. A continuous variable can be cut up to form a set of ranked classes, like income brackets or age levels. A set of ranked classes, in turn, can be simplified by combining all those above a certain point into one class and all those below into a second class, forming a dichotomy. This is done when we reduce the military hierarchy to the distinction between officers and enlisted men, or the income brackets to above or below a certain amount. By picking out one aspect of a set of unordered classes we can sometimes order them into a dichotomy, as when we classify states as east or west of the Mississippi, or occupations as manual or nonmanual.

When we chart the property-space formed by two qualitative characteristics the result is not, of course, a continuous plane, but an array of cells each representing one combination of values on two properties. For example, a study of the 1952 election described people's "political position" in October 1952 in terms of the two dimensions of "usual party affiliations" and "degree of political interest." If one asks Americans what their usual party affiliation is almost everyone falls into three categories: Republicans, Democrats, and independents. These are natural divisions. Degree of interest on the other hand can be divided into any number of ranked categories we please, depending on the alternatives we offer the respondent. In the present case they could rate themselves as having high, medium, or low interest. These two trichotomous dimensions then define a ninefold property-space as shown in Table 5.2.

We can locate a person within this property-space by giving as coordinates his usual party affiliation and his degree of political interest.

There is no reason why we cannot characterize objects by as many properties as we want. We can add a test in historical knowledge to tests in mathematics and language, and characterize our subjects by three coordinates. These can still be presented in the form of a physical model, by using a box in which everyone is located by distance from the left-hand side, from the front, and from the bottom. If we add a fourth test, for instance, of reading speed, we can give our subjects four coordinates and locate them in a four-dimensional property-space. Thus we can say that someone is in the fifth percentile of the U.S. population in mathematics, the fortieth in language skill, the sixtieth in historical knowledge, and the twenty-ninth in reading speed. We can no longer represent this by a physical model, but we can perform mathematical operations on the four coordinates just as well as on two or three.

TABLE 5.3 A Three-Dimensional Attribute-Space Laid Out in Two Dimensions

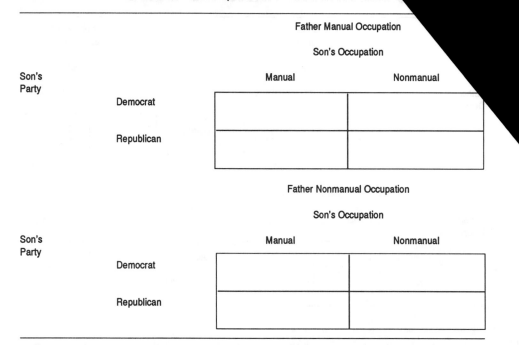

In dealing with qualitative property-spaces which have limited numbers of categories on each dimension, we can still chart the property-space on paper even though it is three-dimensional or even higher-dimensional. Let us take the two dimensions of occupation, dichotomized as manual/nonmanual, and political preference, dichotomized as Democratic/Republican. These give us a fourfold table. If we add the dimension of father's occupation, again dichotomized as manual/nonmanual, we now have a "two-story" fourfold table: occupation and party of sons of manual workers and occupation and party of sons of nonmanually employed people. This can be physically represented by a cube with eight cells, with the original fourfold table repeated on both the "first floor" and the "second floor." If we want to represent this cube on a flat piece of paper, all we have to do is to lay the two "stories" side by side, as an architect would two floor plans. (See Table 5.3.)

Now suppose that we ask a fourth question, for example, the father's usual party, again dichotomized as Democratic/Republican. Our property-space then becomes a four-dimensional "cube." But we can still lay out each level on this fourth dimension on paper as we did those on the third. (See Table 5.4.)

The combination of dichotomous attributes produces a type of property-space that may be labeled "dichotomous attribute-space." [4] Position in a dichotomous attribute-space can be indicated as a response-pattern of plus and minus signs, where we have assigned these values (arbitrarily or otherwise) to the two sides of each dichotomy and arranged the dimensions in some order. Thus a Democratic manual worker, whose father was a Democratic manual worker, might be indicated by the coordinates (++++). A Republican nonmanually employed person, whose father was a Democratic manual worker, would have the coordinates (– – ++), and so on. (This system of notation is often used in "political score-sheets" that show how congressmen voted

ttribute-Space Laid Out in Two Dimensions

er Manual
upation

Father Nonmanual
Occupation

cupation

Son's Occupation

241

	Nonmanual			Manual	Nonmanual
			Son Democrat		
			Republican		

	Son's Occupation				Son's Occupation	
Father Republican	Manual	Nonmanual			Manual	Nonmanual
Son Democrat				Son Democrat		
Republican				Republican		

on a series of bills, a plus sign showing a "correct" vote and a minus sign a "wrong" vote, in terms of a given political viewpoint or economic interest.)

If we are particularly interested in one of the dimensions as a criterion or dependent variable, we may present a dichotomous attribute-space in abbreviated form by showing only the "background" factors as dimensions in the chart, and filling in each cell with a figure showing the percent who are "positive" on the criterion behavior. No information is lost since the attribute is a dichotomy, and all those not positive are classified as "negative" on the attribute. It is as if we had raised three-dimensional bars from the two-dimensional chart of background characteristics with a height proportional to the positive answers on the criterion behavior, and then replaced them with figures indicating their height just as altitudes are shown on a flat map. Thus Table 5.4 could be presented as an eightfold table showing the dimensions of father's occupation, father's party, and son's occupation; the cells would be filled in with figures showing "percent Democrat" (or vice versa). (See Table 5.5.)

Such tables are particularly useful in permitting the effects of the various background variables to be compared, holding the others constant in each case.[5]

To suggest how far the use of very high-dimension property-spaces has actually developed in social research, we need only note that the results of each interview in a survey are normally punched on an IBM card containing 80 columns, each with 12 rows. Such a card provides for an 80-dimensional property-space, with each property having 12 classes. In practice one never uses all 80 dimensions simultaneously to characterize a respondent; however, they are all available to use in whatever smaller combinations we select. If we consider each position in the 80 by 12 matrix as representing a dichotomous attribute (each can either be punched or not punched), we have the possibility of locating each respondent in a dichotomous attribute-space of 960 dimensions.

TABLE 5.5 Abbreviated Presentation of a Four-Dimensional Attribute-Space

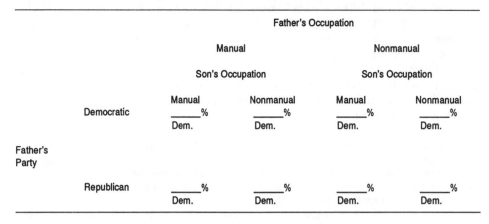

		Father's Occupation			
		Manual		Nonmanual	
		Son's Occupation		Son's Occupation	
		Manual	Nonmanual	Manual	Nonmanual
Father's Party	Democratic	_____% Dem.	_____% Dem.	_____% Dem.	_____% Dem.
	Republican	_____% Dem.	_____% Dem.	_____% Dem.	_____% Dem.

Notes

1. Hans Zeisel, *Say It with Figures*, 5th ed., rev. (New York: Harper, 1968).

2. Herbert Hyman, *Survey Design and Analysis: Principles, Cases, and Procedures* (Glencoe, IL: Free Press, 1966).

3. From Allen H. Barton, "The Idea of Property-Space in Social Research," in *The Language of Social Research*, ed. Paul F. Lazarsfeld and Morris Rosenberg (Glencoe, IL: Free Press, 1955), 40-44. Copyright 1955 by The Free Press, A Corporation. Reprinted by permission.

4. This has special characteristics that are used in latent-structure analysis, but this will not be discussed here. A dichotomous system is also equivalent to a binary number system, or an "off/on" system of information, as used in computing machines and in communication theory.

5. Many concrete examples can be found in Zeisel, *Say It with Figures*, chap. 10.

SUMMARY OF COMMON MEASURES OF ASSOCIATION   5.3

Instructions for Use of Guide 5.3

Statistical methods enable us to study and to describe precisely averages, differences, and relationships. The number of statistical tests available has risen considerably in the last 30 years and has become so large that not even professional statisticians can keep all of them at their fingertips. As these tests have become more numerous, so have the kinds of hypotheses that can be tested by statistical procedures. Common questions researchers often ask include the following:

- Is there a significant difference between these two (or more) groups on this variable?
- What confidence can I have that observed differences did not occur by chance?
- Is there an association between these two (or more) variables? If so, how close is the association?

To ascertain the significance of differences between two or more groups on a given variable, the most common statistics used include the *t* test, χ^2, and *F*. A summary of the more common measures of association would include Pearson's product-moment

r, with its increasing display in correlation matrices, the correlation ratio eta, gamma G, Spearman's rank difference coefficient rho, lambda λ, and the multiple correlation R.[1] Consult the bibliography in Section 5.11 for a statistical text describing these measures. Note that computation guides have been included in this handbook for the very useful statistics t, r, χ^2, and r_s.

The following list summarizes common measures of association. Since a major object of scientific inquiry is to discover relationships, these measures become standard equipment in the training of the scientist who uses statistical tests to ascertain relationships.[2]

Pearson product-moment r: For measuring relationships between two variables when both are continuous and the relationship is rectilinear. The coefficient of correlation is most reliable when based upon a large number of pairs of observations.

The correlation ratio eta: For measuring relationships between two continuous variables that are related in a curvilinear fashion.

Spearman's rank difference coefficient rho r_s: For measuring the association between two rankings. The measure is based on the difference between ranks. It is primarily used where rankings of individual cases on two variables are available so that rankings range from 1 to N for each variable. Rho will have a value of $+1.0$ for a perfect match of ranks, to a value of -1.0 if the ranks are exactly opposite.

Gamma G: For measuring the association between two ordinal variables, each of which is arranged in rank order. Gamma can always achieve the limiting values of -1.0 or $+1.0$ regardless of the number of ties between the pairs in the data.

Lambda λ: For measuring the association between two bivariate distributions where both variables are interpreted to be nominal variables. Lambda simply reverses the role of two variables predicting x from information about y.

Multiple correlation coefficient R: For measuring the maximum relationship that may be obtained between a combination of several continuous (independent) variables and some other continuous (dependent) variable.

Partial correlation coefficient $r_{12.3}$: For measuring the relationship between two continuous variables with the effects of a third continuous variable (or several others) held constant.

Biserial r: For measuring relationships when one variable is recorded in terms of a dichotomy and the other is continuous. Biserial r assumes that the individuals in each of the two categories represent a complete distribution (i.e., not just the two extremes), that the dichotomized variable is really continuous and normally distributed, and that the relationship between the two variables is rectilinear.

Point biserial r: For measuring the relationship between a truly dichotomous variable and a continuous variable.

Contingency coefficient c: For measuring the association between two variables that can be classified in two or more categories, but when the categories themselves are not quantitative.

Phi coefficient ϕ: For measuring the association between two variables that are truly dichotomous. Compare with Yule's Q for appropriate use.

Kendall coefficient of concordance N: For measuring the degree of agreement among m sets of n ranks. If we have a group of n objects ranked by each of m judges, the coefficient of concordance tells us the degree of agreement among the m sets of ranks.[3]

Notes

1. Based on tests of association used in journal articles in *ASR, AJS,* and *SF,* as compiled by Kenneth J. Pollinger.

2. See Herman J. Loether and Donald G. McTavish, *Descriptive Statistics for Sociologists* (Boston: Allyn & Bacon, 1974). Note especially pp. 256-57 for a table listing current measures with formulas and guides to the selection of the measure appropriate to the dimensions of different problems.

3. For a good treatment of this coefficient, see Sidney Siegel, *Nonparametric Statistics for the Behavioral Sciences* (New York: McGraw-Hill, 1956), 229-38.

FOUR LEVELS OF MEASUREMENT AND THE STATISTICS APPROPRIATE TO EACH LEVEL   5.4

Instructions for Use of Guide 5.4

In Part 6 of this volume, many sociometric scales are included to measure social variables. These scales may be *nominal, ordinal, interval,* or *ratio* types.

- *Nominal or classificatory scales* use numbers or other symbols simply to classify an object, person, or characteristic (e.g., folkways, mores, laws).
- *Ordinal or ranking scales* involve a level of measurement in which objects in various categories of a scale stand in some kind of *relation* to the categories. Given a group of equivalence classes, if the relation *greater than* holds between some but not all pairs of classes, we have a partially ordered scale. If the relation *greater than* holds for all pairs of classes so that a complete rank ordering of classes arises, we have an ordinal scale (e.g., socioeconomic status as conceived by Warner in his ranking from Lower Lower to Upper Upper).
- *Interval scales* have all the characteristics of ordinal scales, and in addition the distances between any two numbers on the scale are of known size. Measurement considerably stronger than ordinality can be achieved with interval scales. Thurstone's equal-appearing interval scale is an example.
- *Ratio scales* have all the characteristics of interval scales, and in addition have true zero points as their origins. The ratio of any two scale points is independent of the unit of measurement (e.g., the Centigrade temperature scale).

Each of these types of scales has defining relations that make particular statistical tests appropriate. Nominal and ordinal scales require nonparametric tests; only interval and ratio scales may permit use of parametric tests. Since most indexes and scales are ordinal, the nonparametric test is of especial importance. It is necessary to match the appropriate statistic with the defining characteristics of the scale. Table 5.6 summarizes these relations between type of scale and appropriate statistic.

NONPARAMETRIC STATISTICAL TESTS APPROPRIATE TO VARIOUS TYPES OF SCALES   5.5

Instructions for Use of Guide 5.5

In the development of modern statistical methods, the first techniques of inference that appeared were those that made many assumptions about the nature of the population from which the scores were drawn. Since population values are "parameters," these statistical techniques are called *parametric*. For example, a technique of inference may be based on the assumption that the scores were drawn from a normally distributed population, or the technique of inference may be based on the assumption that both sets of scores were drawn from populations having the same variance (σ^2) or spread of scores. Such techniques produce conclusions that contain qualifications;

TABLE 5.6 Four Levels of Measurement and the Statistics Appropriate to Each Level

Scale	Defining Relations	Examples of Appropriate Statistics	Appropriate Statistical Tests
Nominal	1. Equivalence	Mode Frequency Contingency coefficient	Nonparametric test
Ordinal	1. Equivalence 2. Greater than	Median Percentile Spearman r_S Kendall T Kendall W	Nonparametric test
Interval	1. Equivalence 2. Greater than 3. Known ratio of any two intervals	Mean Standard deviation Pearson product-moment correlation Multiple product-moment correlation	Nonparametric and parametric tests
Ratio	1. Equivalence 2. Greater than 3. Known ratio of any two intervals 4. Known ratio of any two scale values	Geometric mean Coefficient of variation	Nonparametric and parametric tests

SOURCE: From Sidney Siegel, *Nonparametric Statistics for the Behavioral Sciences* (New York: McGraw-Hill, 1956). Copyright 1956 by McGraw-Hill Book Co., Inc. Reprinted by permission.

for instance, "If the assumptions regarding the shape of the population(s) are valid, then we may conclude that . . . ."

In recent years a large number of techniques of inference have been developed that do not make stringent assumptions about parameters. These newer nonparametric techniques are "distribution free," so that conclusions do not require qualifications: "Regardless of the shape of the population(s), we may conclude that . . . ."

In the computation of parametric tests, we add, divide, and multiply the scores from samples. When these arithmetic processes are used on scores that are not truly numerical, they naturally introduce distortions in those data and thus throw doubt on conclusions from the test. Thus it is permissible to use parametric techniques only with scores that are truly numerical. The mean and standard deviation are the central concepts of position and dispersion. Many nonparametric tests, on the other hand, focus on the order or ranking of the scores, not on their "numerical" values. The advantages of order statistics for data in the behavioral sciences are especially pronounced because so many "numerical" scores are numerical in appearance only.

Table 5.7 presents a wide range of various nonparametric statistical tests. Note that each row divides the tests into those appropriate for nominal, ordinal, and interval scales. The first column contains those tests that may be used when one wishes to determine whether a single sample is from a specified sort of population. Columns 2 and 3 contain tests that may be used when one wishes to compare the scores obtained from two samples—one set considers tests for two related samples, while the other considers tests for two independent samples. Columns 4 and 5 are devoted to significance tests for k (three or more) samples; one of these presents tests for k related

TABLE 5.7 Nonparametric Statistical Test

Level of Measurement	One-Sample Case (Chap.4) [1]	Two-Sample Case: Related Samples (Chap. 5) [2]	Two-Sample Case: Independent Samples (Chap. 6) [3]	k-Sample-Case: Related Samples (Chap. 7) [4]	k-Sample-Case: Independent Samples (Chap. 8) [5]	Nonparametric Measure of Correlation (Chap. 9) [6]
Nominal	Binomial test, pp. 36–42; χ^2 one-sample test, pp. 42–47	McNemar test for the significance of changes, pp. 63–67	Fisher exact probability test, pp. 96–104; χ^2 test for two independent samples, pp. 104–11	Cochran Q test, pp. 161–66	χ^2 test for k independent samples, pp. 175–79	Contingency coefficient: C, pp. 196–202
Ordinal	Kolmogorov-Smirnov one-sample test, pp. 47–52; One-sample runs test, pp. 52–58	Sign test, pp. 68–75; Wilcoxon matched-pairs signed-ranks test, pp. 75–83[a]	Median test, pp. 111–16; Mann-Whitney u test, pp. 116–27; Kolmogorov-Smirnov two-sample test, pp. 127–36; Wald-Wolfowitz runs test, pp. 136–45; Moses test of extreme reactions, pp. 145–52	Friedman two-way analysis of variance by ranks, pp. 166–72	Extension of the median test, pp. 179–84; Kruskal-Wallis one-way analysis of variance by ranks, pp. 184–93	Spearman rank correlation coefficient: r_s, pp. 202–13; Kendall rank correlation coefficient: r, pp. 213–23; Kendall partial rank correlation coefficient: r_{xyz}, pp. 223–29; Kenda[...]
Interval		Walsh test, pp. 83–87; Randomization test for matched pairs, pp. 88–92	Randomization test for two independent samples, pp. 152–56			

NOTE: Each column lists, cumulatively downward, the tests applicable to the given level of measurement. For example, in the case of k related samples, when ordinal measurement [...] analysis of variance and the Cochran Q test are applicable. For use of this table, consult Sidney Siegel, *Nonparametric Statistics for the Behavioral Sciences* (New York: McGraw-Hill, 1[...] refer to that book.

a. The Wilcoxon test requires ordinal measurement not only within pairs, as is required for the sign test, but also of the differences between pairs. See the discussion on pp. 75–76 of Sie[...]

ples and the other presents tests for k independent samples. Column 6 gives nonparametric measures of association and the tests of significance that are useful with some of these.

The field of statistics has developed to the extent that we now have, for almost all research designs, alternative statistical tests that might be used in order to come to a decision about a hypothesis. Having alternative tests, researchers have two choices—to read carefully about criteria to follow in choosing among various tests applicable to a given research design, or to get advice from a professional statistician. Preferably, they should do both. In order to use the information in Table 5.7 intelligently, researchers should note where their problems fall within the table and then consult Siegel's *Nonparametric Statistics for the Behavioral Sciences.*[1]

Researchers at the Institute for Social Research, University of Michigan, have prepared a guide for selecting statistical techniques for both parametric and nonparametric statistics. The core of the guide—a "decision tree"—consists of 16 pages of sequential questions and answers that lead the user to the appropriate technique. It presents a systematic but highly condensed overview of more than 100 currently used statistics and statistical techniques and their uses. These are indexed for the decision tree, which is built around two major questions:

How many variables does the problem involve?
ONE VARIABLE____ TWO VARIABLES____ MORE THAN TWO VARIABLES____
How do you want to treat the variables with respect to scale of measurement?
NOMINAL____ ORDINAL____ INTERVAL____
(including all possible combinations for two- and three-variable measurements)

Appendices cite major references to each statistic, programs of the OSIRIS III computer software system that compute given statistics, and new or rarely used statistical techniques.[2] The new edition contains expanded coverage of multivariate analysis.

Notes

1. Sidney Siegel, *Nonparametric Statistics for the Behavioral Sciences* (New York: McGraw-Hill, 1956).
2. Frank M. Andrews, Laura Klem, Terrence N. Davidson, Patrick M. O'Malley, and Willard L. Rodgers, *A Guide for Selecting Statistical Techniques for Analyzing Social Science Data*, 2nd ed. (Ann Arbor: University of Michigan, Institute for Social Research, 1981).

5.6 COMPUTATION GUIDES

Instructions for Use of Guide 5.6

The computation guides that follow describe procedures for computing four statistics commonly needed by research workers in the behavioral sciences. (It should be understood that computer programs exist for all common statistical measures. These guides are used by researchers working with small samples or when a computer is not available.) Statistics t and r are parametric statistics, assuming randomness and normality of the populations; χ^2 and r_s are nonparametric or "distribution free," only randomness is generally assumed.

The computation design for the *t* test of the significance of the difference between two means is for the case of two independent samples. This is the test commonly used to test the difference between two means because we are often dealing with small samples, and we cannot assume that our data and values of *t* derived from them are normally distributed as are the parameters of large samples of 500 or more observations. However, it is assumed that the observations are drawn from normally distributed populations. The computation design for *r*, Pearson's product-moment coefficient of correlation, is useful when the number of cases is relatively large and the correlation chart is desired as a substitute for machine calculation. Pearson's *r* is for measuring relationships between two variables when both are continuous and the relationship is rectilinear. Both *t* and *r* may be used when the scores under analysis result from measurement in the strength of at least an *interval scale*.

The computation design for χ^2 is for testing significance of association between two attributes: for the general $r \times s$ case and for the special 2×2 table. This is the most widely used statistic for use with qualitative variables. The Spearman rank order coefficient r_s is the nonparametric statistic corresponding to the parametric Pearsonian *r*. This statistic is based on two sets of rankings of the same set of items. The Spearman rank order coefficient is not limited by the restrictions of normality and linearity imposed upon the Pearsonian product-moment *r*. While χ^2 is a test of the *existence* of a possible association, r_s provides a measure of the *degree of relationship* between two sets of rankings. Both χ^2 and r_s may be used when the scores under analysis result from measurements of *ordinal* or *nominal scales*.

5.6.a *t* Test of Significance Between Two Means of Independent Samples

Computation Design for *t* Test of the Difference Between Two Means, for Two Independent Samples[1]

$$from\ S_1:\ \overline{X}_1 = \Sigma X_{1i}/N_1$$

$$\Sigma x_1^2 = \Sigma X_{1i}^2 - (\Sigma X_{1i})^2/N_1$$

$$from\ S_2:\ \overline{X}_2 = \Sigma X_{2i}/N_2$$

$$\Sigma x_2^2 = \Sigma X_{2i}^2 - (\Sigma X_{2i})^2/N_2$$

1. H_0: (See below for instructions.)

2. $s_{\overline{x}1 - \overline{x}2} = \sqrt{\left(\dfrac{\Sigma x_1^2 + \Sigma x_2^2}{N_1 + N_2 - 2}\right)\left(\dfrac{1}{N_1} + \dfrac{1}{N_2}\right)}$

   $=$

3. $t = \dfrac{\overline{X}_1 - \overline{X}_2}{s_{\overline{x}1 - \overline{x}2}} =$

4. d.f. $= N_1 + N_2 - 2 =$

5. $P =$

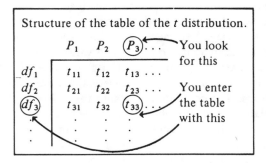

1. Formulate the null hypothesis you wish to test. This will determine whether you are to make a two-sided or one-sided test. The chief null hypotheses are $\mu_1 = \mu_2$ (two-sided), $\mu_1 \leq \mu_2$, or $\mu_1 \geq \mu_2$ (both one-sided). Write the hypothesis on line 1.

2. Compute the standard error of the difference by pooling estimates of the sums of squares. Enter on line 2.

3. Assume that both samples are normally and independently distributed; assume also that they have equal variances; then the distribution of t, which is the difference between the means divided by the estimated standard error of the difference, follows the t distribution with $N_1 + N_2 - 2$ degrees of freedom. Enter t on line 3 and d.f. on line 4.

4. With the value of t and d.f. you enter the table of t. You are looking for P, the probability that a value of t this large or larger would have been obtained by chance if the null hypothesis were true. P will be shown along the head of the table, d.f. down the side, and the values of t will be shown in the body of the table. The probability shown will be two-tailed (i.e., the *sum* of the probability to the right of t and to the left of $-t$); if the hypothesis is one-sided, use one-half the tabled probability.

5. If P is equal to, or less than, 0.05, reject the null hypothesis. (Set the level of significance at 0.01 if you prefer greater certainty.) If P is greater than 0.05, accept the null hypothesis.

Note

1. From Morris Zelditch, Jr., *A Basic Course in Sociological Statistics* (New York: Holt, 1959), 245. For further discussion, see Theodore R. Anderson and Morris Zelditch, Jr., *A Basic Course in Statistics: With Sociological Applications*, 3rd ed. (New York: Holt, 1975), 272-77.

5.6.b   Pearsonian *r* to Measure Linear Correlation
Between Two Variables

A scatter diagram should be prepared and carefully observed. If the distribution is judged to be rectilinear, proceed to analyze for the strength of the correlation.

Product-Moment Correlation for Ungrouped Data

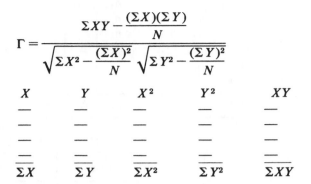

$$\Gamma = \frac{\Sigma XY - \dfrac{(\Sigma X)(\Sigma Y)}{N}}{\sqrt{\Sigma X^2 - \dfrac{(\Sigma X)^2}{N}}\ \sqrt{\Sigma Y^2 - \dfrac{(\Sigma Y)^2}{N}}}$$

X	Y	X^2	Y^2	XY
—	—	—	—	—
—	—	—	—	—
—	—	—	—	—
ΣX	ΣY	ΣX^2	ΣY^2	ΣXY

1. List X and Y scores in adjacent columns.
2. Compute each X^2, Y^2, and XY.
3. Obtain ΣX, ΣY, ΣX^2, ΣY^2, ΣXY, and N.
4. Substitute in formula. Compute standard error of r.

$$\sigma r = \frac{1 - r^2}{\sqrt{N}}. \text{ Evaluate.}$$

See interpretation of r, below.

Interpretation of r

1. .00–.20 little or no relationship.
   .20–.40 some slight relationship
   .40–.60 substantial relationship
   .60–.80 strong useful relationship
   .80–1.00 high relationship
2. The usefulness of a correlation is determined by its size. The sign has no bearing on the strength of the relationship. It determines only the direction of the relationship: direct or inverse.
3. A significant correlation means that the population from which the data were drawn probably does not have a zero correlation.

5.6.c χ^2 Test of Association

Computation Design for χ^2 for Testing Significance of Association Between Two Attributes for the General $r_1 \times s$ Case and for the Special 2×2[1]

n_{11}	n_{12}	n_{13}	$\cdots$	n_{1s}	$n_{1\cdot}$
n_{21}	n_{22}	n_{23}	$\cdots$	n_{2s}	$n_{2\cdot}$
n_{31}	n_{32}	n_{33}	$\cdots$	n_{3s}	$n_{3\cdot}$
$\cdot$	$\cdot$	$\cdot$		$\cdot$	$\cdot$
$\cdot$	$\cdot$	$\cdot$		$\cdot$	$\cdot$
$\cdot$	$\cdot$	$\cdot$		$\cdot$	$\cdot$
n_{r1}	n_{r2}	n_{r3}	$\cdots$	n_{rs}	$n_{r\cdot}$
$n_{\cdot 1}$	$n_{\cdot 2}$	$n_{\cdot 3}$	$\cdots$	$n_{\cdot s}$	N

1	2	3	4	5
O	E	$O - E$	$(O - E)^2$	$(O - E)^2/E$
n_{11}	$n_{1\cdot}n_{\cdot 1}/N$			
n_{12}	$n_{1\cdot}n_{\cdot 2}/N$			
n_{13}	$n_{1\cdot}n_{\cdot 3}/N$			
$\cdot$	$\cdot$			
$\cdot$	$\cdot$			
$\cdot$	$\cdot$			
n_{rs}	$n_{r\cdot}n_{\cdot s}/N$			

$$\chi^2 = \Sigma \left[(O - E)^2/E \right]$$
$$\text{d.f.} = (r - 1)(s - 1)$$

1. Enter the observed frequencies in column 1.

2. Calculate the expected values, E, as follows: Find the marginal in the rows containing the cell ij and the marginal in the column containing the cell, and multiply them together, giving $n_{i\cdot}n_{\cdot j}$; then divide by N, the total number of observations in the table, giving $n_{i\cdot}n_{\cdot j}\ /N$, and enter in column 2.

3. Subtract the expected values from the observed, column 2 from 1, and enter the result in column 3.

4. Square the differences obtained and enter in column 4.

5. Divide each entry in column 4 by the expected values in column 2 and enter in column 5.

6. Add up column 5. This gives you χ^2.

7. To find the number of degrees of freedom with which you enter the table, take one less than the number of rows times one less than the number of columns $(r - 1)(s - 1)$.

Interpretation of χ^2 as a Test of Relationship Between Variables

As reported by David Gold in "A Note on Statistical Analysis in the American Sociological Review," "qualitative data are by far the most common data with which the sociologist concerns himself.—It is evident that, on the most elementary descriptive level, there is markedly inadequate statistical analysis of qualitative data."

These statements should alert the social science researcher to the importance of the correct use and interpretation of χ^2. It is this coefficient that appears most frequently in social science research as a test of association and significance. The following article by Thomas J. Duggan and Charles W. Dean should be "must" reading for all social scientists.

Note

1. From Morris Zelditch, Jr., *A Basic Course in Sociological Statistics* (New York: Holt, 1959), 290. See also Theodore R. Anderson and Morris Zelditch, Jr., *A Basic Course in Statistics: With Sociological Applications*, 3rd ed. (New York: Holt, Rinehart & Winston, 1975), 256-64.

5.6.d   Common Misinterpretations of Significance Levels in Sociological Journals

Thomas J. Duggan and Charles W. Dean [1]

Periodically, the uses and misuses of probability statistics in social and behavioral science research have been reviewed. For instance, in 1949 Lewis and Burke pointed to several misuses of the chi-square test[2] and in 1959 an article by Selvin stimulated discussion on the general question of using statistics in social surveys.[3] Most recently, Skipper, Guenther, and Nass reviewed the discussion of substantive interpretation associated with significance levels.[4] While such discussions have served to clarify some of the technical requirements and have corrected some of the misunderstandings often associated with the use of statistical tests, one crucial matter has received relatively little attention. This concerns the substantive interpretation of significance tests and the consequences of such interpretations.

The frequently used chi-square test, and the interpretation given to data analyzed by this statistic, will serve to illustrate the problem. This statistic can be used to test goodness of fit or independence although it is the latter which is more frequently used in reporting research. Since this is a test of the independence of variables, significant values of chi-square are often taken to indicate a dependence or relationship between variables. In interpreting such relationships, there are two serious problems which are often overlooked. The first concerns the strength of relationship and the second the form of relationship.

Strength of Relationship

As to the first problem, if the chi-square is significant at the chosen level, then the investigator routinely rejects the null hypothesis of independence and tentatively accepts the alternate hypothesis that the variables are dependent or are related. Regardless of how low the probability associated with the obtained value of chi-square, nothing can be inferred about the strength or degree of that relationship. However, in practice, this point is often overlooked.

Consider Table 5.8, which was reported in a major sociological journal within the last year.[5] According to the author's interpretation, the significance level of the chi-square test was so high that if variables X and Y were not clearly separate measures, "We would suspect the relationship to be tautological." Since the author failed to report the degree of association, Goodman and Kruskels' gamma was

TABLE 5.8

Variable Y	Variable X			
	Very High	High	Low	Very Low
High	5	24	17	9
Moderate	12	18	9	3
Low	19	22	16	2

NOTE: $\chi^2 = 14.0$; $p < .05$; $G = -.30$.

computed. In this instance, gamma equaled –.30, which suggests a relationship which is far from tautological. The difference in the interpretation based on chi-square and gamma should be noted and emphasized. In contrast to these data, consider Table 5.9, which was presented in the same article.

In this case, the probability is such that the sociologist normally would accept the null hypothesis of independence. However, gamma was computed for these data and G equaled .22. Here, data non-significant according to chi-square has a relationship only slightly lower than that of the preceding example, where it was concluded that the variables were highly related. To further demonstrate the need for sensitivity to the difference between significance level and strength of association, Table 5.10 was constructed.[6]

Table 5.10 clearly demonstrates that while chi-square, properly used, may be sensitive to the dependence of variables, after dependence is shown the usefulness of this statistic is exhausted. As the data of Table 5.10 show, significance at the .001 level could mean that the relationship between the variables could be less than .09 or more than .80. At the .001 level, the distribution of the strength of association appears to approach randomness. While these data do show that non-significance, or significance at or about the arbitrary .05 level, will usually result in a relationship which is consistently weaker, the relationship is as likely to be above .10 at the .30 level as at the .05 level. Still, all three tables reporting significance above the .30 level had gammas ranging between .10 and .19. In contrast, of the seven tables reporting significance at .05, only three had gammas in the .10 to .19 range, while four tables had gammas below .10. If more non-significant tables were reported in the journals, the distribution of measures of association would probably be even broader. Generally, the lower the significance level, the greater the probability of a low relationship, but this cannot be assumed. These data emphatically demonstrate that a measure of strength of association is necessary before statements about strength of relationship can be made.

TABLE 5.9

Variable Y	Variable X		
	High	Moderate	Low
High	24	18	10
Moderate	19	12	7
Low	19	18	21

NOTE: $\chi^2 = 6.2$; $p < .20$; $G = .22$.

TABLE 5.10 A Comparison of Level of Significance and Strength of Relationship (*n* = 45 articles)

Level of Significance	.00 to .09	.10 to .09	.20 to .29	.30 to .39	.40 to .49	.50 to .59	.60 to .69	.70 to .79	.80 to .89
.001	3	2	2	8	..	1	..	2	3
.01	1	..	6	..	2	..	..	..	..
.05	4	3	..	..	..	..	..	..	..
.10	1	..	1	..	..	..	..	..	..
.20	1	1	1	..	..	..	..	..	..
.30+	..	3	..	..	..	..	..	..	..

These data illustrate the serious problem in interpreting significance levels of the chi-square test of independence and indicate the need for a reminder that statistical significance is not equitable with practical significance. A significant chi-square value, at best, permits one to say that *probably* there is some dependence between variables in the population, but the extent of dependence may be virtually zero *regardless of the significance level.* The consequences for understanding the phenomena under investigation and for the construction of theories require constant awareness of the limited interpretations which can be given to statistical significance.

Form of Relationship

The second problem refers to the form of relationship between variables. In using tables three by three or larger, users of the chi-square are often prone to think and interpret results in terms of linear relationships, but the contingency table and the chi-square statistic are not sensitive to and provide no basis for assuming the existence of this form of relationship.

The data of Table 5.11, also presented in a major sociological journal within the last year, illustrate the error in interpreting the direction of the relationship in linear terms. The author stated that the data of this table confirmed the hypothesis that the greater the degree of variable *X*, the greater the degree of variable *Y*. An inspection of the table reveals that this is not the case. As Table 5.11 indicates, the largest number of subjects ranking in the "frequent" category of variable *X* rank in the low category of variable *Y*. However, the largest number of subjects in the "occasional" and "infrequent" categories of variable *X* rank in the "moderate" category of variable *Y*. Only those ranking "low" on variable *Y* are distributed in the expected pattern.

TABLE 5.11

Variable Y	Variable X Frequent	Variable X Occasional	Variable X Infrequent
High	3	9	6
Moderate	14	30	12
Low	17	12	6

NOTE: χ^2 (4 *df*) = 8.51; *p* < .05.

Another team of authors in a recent edition of another sociological journal presented data similar to that of Table 5.11 to test the hypothesis that the greater the degree of variable *A*, the higher the degree of variable *B*. They computed chi-square values for their data table and stated, "The relationship shown is significant beyond the .001 level; therefore, the hypothesis is accepted." Throughout the article, the authors made similar statements from similar data about linear relationships.

While the above authors did not attempt to disguise their acceptance of linearity, frequently, other researchers state a linear hypothesis, present the data, table, accept the hypothesis on the basis of the chi-square probability and then discuss only those proportions of the table which fit the linear model. This more subtle but equally erroneous procedure appears frequently in the sociological literature.

A linear relationship exists only if the pattern of concentration of subjects lies along a diagonal of the table. If this is not the case, the relationship cannot be interpreted as a linear one. If the phenomenon of possible nonlinearity is not taken into account or if the implication of linearity is made in interpreting chi-square, serious consequences again arise in interpreting data and in developing explanatory theories. This problem can be averted by inspecting the data table, outlining the pattern of concentration and describing the pattern.

Conclusion

To avoid these errors of confusing significance with strength of association and of misinterpreting form of relationship, two elementary safeguards can be exercised in reporting results. One is routinely to compute and report a measure of degree of association in addition to the statistical test whenever this is possible. The second safeguard is the introduction of care and caution in the verbal interpretation of data tables and the inferred association of variables.[7]

In this day when computer technology is so drastically improving the analytical tools of the sociologist, it seems paradoxical that there is a need to remind researchers of such basic rules of interpretation.

Notes

1. From Thomas J. Duggan and Charles W. Dean, "Common Misinterpretations of Significance Levels in Sociological Journals," *American Sociologist* 3 (February 1968): 45-46. Reprinted by permission.

2. Don Lewis and C. J. Burke, "The Use and Misuse of the Chi-square Test," *Psychological Bulletin* 46 (1949): 433-89.

3. Hanan Selvin, "A Critique of Tests of Significance in Survey Research," *American Sociological Review* 22 (October 1957): 519-27.

4. James K. Skipper, Anthony L. Guenther, and Gilbert Nass, "The Sacredness of .05: A Note Concerning the Uses of Statistical Levels of Significance in Social Science," *American Sociologist* 2 (February 1967): 16-18.

5. Since the purpose of these tables is to illustrate peculiarities in the use of chi-square rather than to criticize individual research, no tables will identify author, journal, or original variables actually treated. However, all tables were reported in refereed sociological journals within a year prior to the writing of this piece.

6. These data were derived from major sociological journals published between 1955 and 1965 in a systematic search for three by three tables, both variables ordinal.

7. For detailed information see Denton E. Morrison and Ramon E. Henkel, *The Significance Test Controversy: A Reader* (Hawthorne, NY: Aldine, 1970).

5.6.e　Spearman's Rank Order Correlation

Computation Design for Spearman Rank Order Coefficient, r_s[1]

K_i designates an ordered position. K_{xi} designates the position of the ith observation in an array of the X variable; K_{yi} designates the position of the *same* observation in the Y array. If, for example, the first observation, O_1, is first in the X array and fourth in the Y array, the first row of the layout form below should read

$$K_{x1} = 1, K_{y1} = 4, K_{x1} - K_{y1} = -3, (K_{x1} - K_{y1})^2 = 9$$

(1) O_i	(2) K_{xi}	(3) K_{yi}	(4) d	(5) d^2
O_1	K_{x1}	K_{y1}	$K_{x1} - K_{y1}$	$(K_{x1} - K_{y1})^2$
O_2	K_{x2}	K_{y2}	$K_{x2} - K_{y2}$	$(K_{x2} - K_{y2})^2$
.	.	.	.	.
.	.	.	.	.
.	.	.	.	.
O_N	K_{xN}	K_{yN}	$K_{xN} - K_{yN}$	$(K_{xN} - K_{yN})$

$$\Sigma(K_{xi} - K_{yi})^2 = \Sigma d^2 =$$

$$r_s = 1 - \frac{6\Sigma d^2}{N(N^2 - 1)} =$$

$$t = r_s \sqrt{\frac{N - 2}{1 - r_s^2}} = \qquad\qquad , \text{d.f.} = N - 2.$$

1. Form an array of the observations on the X variable. (Start with the "best," "smallest," "highest." You may choose the starting point at will, but you must be consistent on both X and Y, or the sign of r_s will be meaningless.) Order the observations on the variable Y in the same manner.

2. Replace the X value of each observation by its rank in the X array and the Y value of each observation by its rank in the Y array. In column 2 at the right enter ranks of the observations on the X variable and in column 3 enter ranks of the observations on the Y variable. Ranks in the same row must be for the *same* observation.

3. Take the difference between ranks and enter in column 4.

4. Square these differences, enter in column 5, and sum column 5.

5. Compute r_s from the formula shown above.

6. For $N > 10$, to test $H_0: \rho_s = 0$, use t, computed from the formula shown above with $(N - 2)$ d.f. (ρ_s [read "rho sub-s"] is the population parameter corresponding to r_s.)

Note

1. From Morris Zelditch, Jr., *A Basic Course in Sociological Statistics* (New York: Holt, 1959), 326. See also Theodore R. Anderson and Morris Zelditch, Jr., *A Basic Course in Statistics: With Sociological Applications*, 3rd ed. (New York: Holt, 1975), 126-32.

5.7   CAUSATION AND MULTIVARIATE ANALYSIS

From Univariate and Bivariate Problems to Multivariate Analysis of Social Behavior

It was once generally thought that for every effect there existed only one cause; if several causes were discovered, it was assumed there must really be more than one effect. The history of social theory is largely a series of statements asserting that one factor is the sole cause of social change. These notions have been called "determinisms"; they include geographic, physical, racial, psychological, religious, political, economic, technological, and familial determinism, and there are many more.

It is characteristic of all these notions of determinism to assert that the sole factor operates according to its own inherent laws, independently of all factors, including human will and desires. These single-factor theories were relatively simple to understand and appealed to scholars and laypersons alike. They seemed to draw truth from the complex phenomena presented by social problems. But in their oversimplification the single-factor theories distorted reality and foisted a great amount of mischief and misery on people. For example, racial determinism bred prejudice and discrimination in every country of the world. In Hitler's Germany, it brought humankind's most cruel inhumanity.

Modern humans know better, although single-factor theories still abound. The contemporary approach involves allowing for and expecting a number of different causes for a single effect.

Four Manifestations of Causes

Causes may manifest themselves in a *sequence,* as a *convergence* or cluster, as producing *dispersion* effects, or as a *complex network.*

1. Causes may occur in a sequence, like the links on a chain. Some of these causes are direct and immediate, others are indirect and remote. Thus a decline in worker motivation and sense of personal responsibility may be due to the direct fact that much labor is performed in the large corporation on highly repetitive jobs; the remote causes are the factory system and mass market, which in turn were brought about by the steam engine, the electric motor, and machine tools.
2. Several causes may converge to produce a change. Thus electric power and several transportation and communication inventions have converged to augment the decentralization of industry. These converging causes are often called a cluster.
3. The effects of a single cause may be dispersed outward into many different sectors of a society. Thus the average increase of formal education that is being acquired by Americans has many different effects on family, church, community, military organization, and labor relations.

4. The phenomena of convergence and of dispersion may be tied in with the phenomena of sequence to produce a complex network of causes. This is a very common manifestation, but the complexity can be simplified by recognizing that causes vary in importance, and important causes may be identified that account for a large part of the effects observed.

Future Developments

New technology is ready to deal with these more complex notions of causation. Loether and McTavish have written about future developments in theory, research methods, and statistics, stressing the importance of multivariate analysis:

The increasing availability of computers has shifted the emphasis in sociology from the study of univariate and bivariate problems to the study of multivariate problems. To be efficient predictors, sociological theories generally need to be stated in multivariate terms. Before computers, multivariate statistical techniques were so tedious that they were not commonly used. The computer has now made these techniques accessible and practical. In response to this breakthrough, sociological theories are increasingly becoming multivariate in form. It is becoming increasingly important for the sociologist to be a knowledgeable computer user. Computer technology is racing forward at a breathtaking pace, and the potential uses of computers for sociological analysis stagger the imagination.

Another very promising development in sociology is the gradual but dramatic disappearance of the chasm separating theory and research. Sociology appears to be moving forward by returning to the model which Durkheim set for us in the nineteenth century. The effect of this long overdue marriage of theory and research is the development of theory that is researchable and the appearance of more theory-oriented research. The advent of the computer in sociology and the increasing emphasis upon multivariate analysis have done much to facilitate this development.

There is a third important development that promises to have a significant impact on sociology and on the academic preparation of future sociologists. Traditionally, sociologists have used a structure rather than a process to theorizing and researching. Social behavior has been viewed in static terms, and much research has focused on single points in time, much like stopping a movie and studying a single frame. Sociologists are now beginning to realize that what is orderly about social behavior may be the way in which it changes rather than the way in which it resists change. This perspective focuses attention on time series and longitudinal analysis. The shift in statistics is toward the increasing use of stochastic processes and techniques of time series analysis. This emphasis will make the understanding of calculus an important requirement in the academic training of future sociologists. It seems inevitable that process models involving the use of calculus will appear with increasing frequency in the sociological literature.

Obviously sociology is coming of age. The public and our public leaders are beginning to realize that the pressing problems of today and the foreseeable future are those for which solutions are encouched in a knowledge of social behavior. Sociology is in a position to contribute that knowledge. This is an exciting time in which to be a part of it. We believe that those students of sociology who will make important contributions to that knowledge will be those who are well versed in theory, research methods, and statistics.[1]

Note

1. Herman J. Loether and Donald G. McTavish, *Inferential Statistics for Sociologists* (Boston: Allyn & Bacon, 1974), 283-84.

5.7.a   The Statistical World of Multivariate Analysis

Multivariate analysis has now developed techniques for dealing with more than three variables or attributes at a time. The type of analysis to use in attempting to unravel a complex of variates in a real-life situation depends on what will best bring out the essential relationships under scrutiny. Multivariate analysis may give increased precision to prediction problems (the relation of a number of predictor variables to a criterion), offer greater control of interfering or confounding variables (holding more variables constant), and furnish guiding principles in the development of attitude scales, rating scales, psychological tests, and criterion measures (finding dimensions of behavior). Some of the most important multivariate techniques include the following:

- multiple correlation and classification analysis
- path analysis
- factor analysis
- partial correlation analysis
- analysis of variance and covariance
- multiple discriminant analysis

Full descriptions of these techniques are beyond the scope and purpose of this volume. Nevertheless, computer technology is advancing at a rapid rate and is an indispensable adjunct to multivariate analysis. An introduction to the computer is presented in Section 5.8 for those who are seeking guidance in using computer programs. Descriptions of multiple correlation and classification analysis (Section 5.7.b), path analysis (Section 5.14), and factor analysis (Section 5.15) are also set out to provide an introduction to these forms of multivariate analysis now so common to sociological research.

5.7.b   Multiple Correlation and Classification Analysis

R as a Coefficient

The multiple correlation ($R_{1.234}$) is simply the correlation between the actual scores on a single dependent variable and the scores derived from any linear combination of independent variables. The multiple correlation, like the simple product-moment correlation (r), varies on a scale from 0 to +1. The smaller the coefficient, the poorer the correlation; the larger the coefficient, the stronger the correlation. The multiple correlation can be interpreted by squaring it. R^2 is called the coefficient of multiple determination and expresses the proportion of the variation in the dependent variable that is explained by the regression equation.

Scope of Application

The utility of R has been known for some time, but it was originally cumbersome to calculate when more than four or five independent variables (predictors) were introduced. The computer erased that limitation, but a second limitation intervened. The coefficient was adaptable only when the variables were continuous. Modern methods of *multiple classification analysis* have removed this limitation. There are computer techniques that can handle predictors with no better than nominal measurement and interrelationships of any form among predictors or between predictors or between a predictor and the dependent variable. Many of the most interesting analysis problems involve the simultaneous consideration of several predictor variables (i.e., "independent" variables) and their relationships to a dependent variable. Sometimes one wants to know *how well* all the variables together explain variation in the dependent variable. Other times it is necessary to look at each predictor separately to see how it relates to the dependent variable, either considering or neglecting the effects of other predictors. A criterion generally used is its contribution to reduction in unexplained variance or "error." Another is the extent to which its class means differ from the grand mean.

A different but related concern is the matter of predicted relations. Instead of asking *how well* one can predict, one sometimes asks *what level* (i.e., what particular value or score) would one predict for a person or other unit having a certain combination of characteristics. This is the classic problem to which multiple regression has frequently been applied.

Finally, one sometimes wants to know whether one's ability to predict is significantly better than chance.

The multiple classification analysis devised by Frank M. Andrews, James N. Morgan, John A. Sonquist, and Laura Klem (reported in Section 5.7.b) implements a multivariate technique that is relevant for all the above problems and that may be applied to many kinds of data for which the simpler forms of the traditional techniques would be inappropriate. Its chief advantage over conventional dummy variable regression is a more convenient input arrangement and understandable output that focuses on sets of predictors, such as occupation groups, and on the extent and direction of adjustments made for intercorrelations among the sets of predictors.

Research Examples of Multivariate Analysis

Duncan, Otis Dudley. "A Socioeconomic Index for All Occupations." In *Occupations and Social Status*, edited by Albert J. Reiss, 109-38. New York: Free Press, 1961.

Hodge, Robert W., Paul M. Siegel, and Peter H. Rossi. "Occupational Prestige in the United States, 1925-1963." *American Journal of Sociology* 70 (November 1964): 286-302.

House, James S., and William M. Mason. "Political Alienation in America, 1952-68." *American Sociological Review* 40 (April 1975): 123-47.

Ladinsky, Jack L. "Occupational Determinants of Geographic Mobility Among Professional Workers." *American Sociological Review* 32 (April 1967): 253-64.

Scott, Joseph W., and Mohamed El-Assal. "Multiversity, University Size, University Quality, and Student Protest: An Empirical Study." *American Sociological Review* 34 (October 1969): 702-9.

Brief Treatments of Multiple Correlation and Regression

Loether, Herman J., and Donald G. McTavish. *Descriptive Statistics for Sociologists: An Introduction.* Boston: Allyn & Bacon, 1974, 306-40.

Schuessler, Karl. *Analyzing Social Data.* Boston: Houghton Mifflin, 1971, 10-30.

General References

Anderson, T. W. *An Introduction to Multivariate Statistical Analysis*. New York: John Wiley, 1958.

Bennett, S., and Donald W. Bowers. *An Introduction to Multi-Variate Techniques for the Social and Behavioral Sciences*. New York: Halsted, 1976.

Blalock, Hubert M., Jr. *Social Statistics*. 2nd ed. New York: McGraw-Hill, 1972.

Coleman, James S. "Multivariate Analysis." In *Introduction to Mathematical Sociology*, 189-240. New York: Free Press, 1964.

Cooley, William W., and Paul R. Lohnes. *Multivariate Procedures for the Behavioral Sciences*. New York: John Wiley, 1962.

See Chapter 3, "Multiple and Canonical Correlation."

Costner, Herbert L., ed. *Sociological Methodology, 1971*. San Francisco: Jossey-Bass, 1971.

See especially Chapter 5, by George Bohrnstedt and T. Michael Carter, "Robustness in Regression Analysis"; also Chapter 6, by Morgan Lyons, "Techniques for Using Ordinal Measures in Regression and Path Analysis."

Draper, Norman R., and Harry Smith. *Applied Regression Analysis*. New York: John Wiley, 1966.

Dubois, Philip H. *Multivariate Correlation Analysis*. New York: Harper & Row, 1957.

Ezekial, Mordecai, and Karl A. Fox. *Methods of Correlation Analysis*. 3rd ed. New York: John Wiley, 1959.

Gordon, Robert A. "Issues in Multiple Regression." *American Journal of Sociology* 73 (March 1968): 592-616.

Hellevik, Ottar. *Introduction to Causal Analysis*. Winchester, MA: Allen & Unwin, 1984.

Jöreskog, Karl G., and Marielle van Thillo. *LISREL: A General Computer Program for Estimating a Linear Structural Equation System Involving Multiple Indicators of Unmeasured Variables*. Princeton, NJ: Educational Testing Service, 1972.

Kendall, M. G. *A Course in Multivariate Analysis*. London: Griffin, 1961.

Lazarsfeld, Paul F., Ann K. Pasanella, and Morris Rosenberg, eds. *Continuities in the Language of Social Research*. New York: Free Press, 1975.

This is a revised edition of *Language of Social Research*. See the section on multivariate analysis for articles and selected examples.

For additional references, see Section 5.17.

5.8   AN INTRODUCTION TO THE COMPUTER

Purpose

The purpose of any process of data analysis is to condense information contained in a body of data into a form that can be easily comprehended and interpreted. Sometimes this process is used simply to describe a body of empirical data, but it is far more common for social science data analysis to involve a search for meaningful patterns of relationships among sets of variables, that is, a means to test empirical social theory. Computers are extremely useful for the routine processing of large quantities of data. Indeed, the need for large-scale processing led directly to the development of the computer. Such processing includes the classification, sorting, storing, and retrieval of data that have been presented to the computer in a suitable coded form. These routine tasks, termed *data processing*, constitute the most important use of computers at present.

But the computer is also a *communication device*. Computers can talk to computers, and the ability of a computer to hook into other information storage systems and retrieve information is an extremely valuable asset. It does this by providing access to incredibly wide worlds of information, some of which include instruction on how best to use this information in a given circumstance. It is predicted that the computer of the future will not use a typewriter but will respond to the human voice.

The trend from maxi- to mini- to microcomputers extends over the 10-year period beginning approximately in the mid-1960s and progressing into the mid-1970s. The minis and micros now have processing and storage capabilities greater than most of the commercial computers in use in the mid-1960s. The components and subsystems have not changed functionally; all that has changed is that they have become significantly smaller. The decreases in size and price have not changed one basic fact about computers: No matter what its size, any digital computer is made up of five basic subsystems or components. Step inside a microcomputer with Eric Schlene, senior technical communications specialist, Computing Support Center, Indiana University, Bloomington, Indiana.

5.8.a   Inside a Microcomputer

Eric J. Schlene [1]

What makes a microcomputer tick? If you ask that question of 10 people, you'll probably get 10 different answers. After years of trying on explanations, my favorite analogy distills the answer to this: microcomputers are electronic libraries.

On the surface, it may be hard to see the connection between the box on your desk and your campus library. Still, look at a library in very general terms for a moment. The function of a library is to manipulate the library's principal commodity—information. It takes three key resources to do this: bookshelves, a circulation desk, and a librarian. The bookshelves serve as a storage area for the information, while the circulation desk is the gateway for moving information in and out of the library. Central to the operation is the librarian. This key player catalogs the information, coordinates the orderly, temporary storage of the information on the bookshelves, and oversees the distribution and retrieval of information via the circulation desk.

Similarly, the principal commodity of a microcomputer is data. The microcomputer, too, can be divided into three basic elements: memory chips, input/output devices, and a central processor. Much like a librarian, the central processor controls the operation of the computer. It manipulates the data it receives, coordinates the orderly temporary storage of data within the memory chips, and controls the flow of data in and out of the machine via input/output devices such as monitors, disk drives, keyboards, and printers. In a macro view, it's quite simple.

So what makes these "little libraries" so confusing? Many people are bewildered by the torrent of computing buzzwords and acronyms. It's easy to sympathize. To help us all, the *Times* developed this brief glossary of common microcomputing terms computer users are likely to encounter.

The System

The term "system" generally refers to the microcomputer and all connected peripheral equipment dedicated to its use. For example, a microcomputer, monitor, dedicated printer, and modem all combine to make one system. To be effective, all

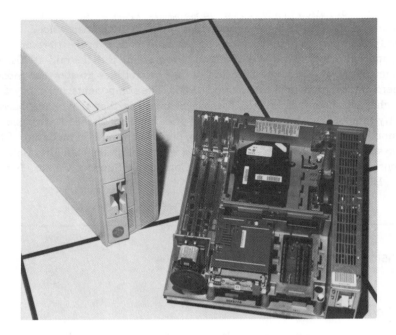

Figure 5.1 IBM PS/2 Model 50Z

components of the system must function together to met the needs of the software programs, or "applications," the microcomputer executes. Key system variables include the central processor unit (CPU), a quantity of temporary internal random-access memory (RAM), a quantity of stable data storage (disk space), dedicated peripherals (devices that are attached to the computer, such as modems, bar label readers, and printers), and optional network connections to the shared resources of local or wide-area networks.

Before you select a microcomputer system, define the work you want to perform, explore the software and hardware required to do the work, and examine the level of support available for each alternative. A great place to get advice about your options is the ACCESS MicroCenter, IMU 059.

Chip

A generic term for an integrated circuit (IC), a "chip" is a complex assemblage of ultraminiature electronic circuits, constructed on a tiny flat square of silicon. Packaged in ceramic or plastic, these integrated circuits are wired to metallic legs that can be either soldered in place on a circuit board or plugged into a matching IC socket.

Many types of chips perform the various functions in a microcomputer. Some chips help to control such devices as monitors (see "Monitor"). Memory chips have the sole purpose of "remembering" pieces of information (see "Memory"), while microprocessor chips (see "Central Processing Unit") are used to execute program instructions.

Memory

A microcomputer cannot function without memory. Microcomputer memory is usually present in the form of chips. The two types of memory chips are read-only memory (ROM) and random-access memory (RAM). ROM chips are stable; once data are written to ROM they cannot be lost, even if the power to the computer is turned off. Programmed by the computer manufacturer, ROM chips typically house the data that execute CPU instructions (see "Central Processing Unit") and invoke the software needed to operate the system from disk storage.

Most memory in a microcomputer is RAM. RAM chips are not stable; any data stored in RAM are lost when power to the computer is turned off. The computer uses its RAM to store program code and data, much like a vast temporary scratchpad, while it executes programs. The computer stores this data using electrical charges, which it can place or remove at predefined locations within the RAM chip. Because the computer can also detect the presence or absence of these charges, it can use a series of memory locations to create a sequential binary code, then later retrieve that code.

The binary code used to store data is represented, for the purpose of discussion only, by the digits 1 and 0. It takes eight of these binary digits, or "bits," to create a single character, or "byte." For example, the character "A" is represented in computer memory as 01000001, a sequence of eight bits, or a single byte.

Memory is measured in units called "kilobytes," "K" for short. Each kilobyte of memory can hold 1,024 characters of information. One thousand twenty-four kilobytes is called a "megabyte," "MB" for short. Memory sizes in early microcomputers ranged from 16K to 640K. Memory in today's microcomputers has expanded greatly, with machines commonly boasting two, four, or even eight megabytes of RAM. Computer manufacturers are now bundling memory into single online memory modules (SIMMs), each containing several ICs. The most common SIMMs typically hold 1 megabyte of memory. Some specially configured systems can be equipped with as much as 64 megabytes of memory. Many popular programs now require that the computer have at least one megabyte of memory.

Central Processing Unit (CPU)

The CPU is a specialized chip that is the focal point of a microcomputer. Also called a "microprocessor," or simply "processor," the CPU interprets and executes software instructions.

A CPU can vary from other CPUs both in the number of bits it can process at one time, also known as "register width," and in the length of time the CPU requires to process those bits, also known as a "cycle." The bits processed by the CPU are a binary code that represents data and/or CPU instructions. In comparison with other microprocessor models, a CPU that has either an increase in register width or a decrease in cycle time will provide improved performance because it will be able to process more bits in the same amount of time.

Adapter Board

This is a general term for an auxiliary circuit board that typically plugs into a microcomputer main circuit board to provide the computer with additional functionality. Some adapter boards are used to increase system memory, while others allow you to attach optional input and output devices such as printers, modems, disk drives,

Figure 5.2 Hewlett-Packard Laser Jet Series II. This printer is typical of the new generation of relatively low-cost laser printers.

and digitizers. Among other common terms for an adapter board are "interface board," "expansion card," and "add-on board."

Installing an adapter board generally requires you to open your machine. You may occasionally also need to change interval switch settings inside the machine. The socket that the adapter board plugs into is called the "bus port" or "expansion slot." "Bus" refers to the circuitry and signal method by which data are moved in and out of the CPU. Buses vary among computer brands and models; be sure the adapter board you purchase is correct for the bus of your machine.

Printer

A wide variety of printers fills today's market. Dot-matrix printers and laser printers are most common. All but extinct are the expensive, slow, thundering daisy-wheel printers of the early 1980s.

The print quality of today's dot-matrix printers has improved dramatically over what was available just a few years ago. Almost all provide near-letter-quality print.

The introduction of relatively low-cost (under $2000) laser printers such as the Hewlett-Packard LaserJet has made near-typeset-quality text and graphics more widely affordable.

Printers have long been oriented to specific system architectures (e.g., Apple, IBM). However, these lines are being blurred by advances in networking, interfaces, and printing software protocols.

Monitor

This term refers to the display device (usually similar to a television) through which the computer relays information to the operator. Most systems require a monitor-specific display adapter board (see "Adapter Board") to connect the monitor to the computer.

Figure 5.3 Monochrome Monitor

Microcomputers typically use one of two monitor types: monochrome or color. The simpler monitors are monochrome and project a single color, usually white, green, or amber. These general-purpose display devices provide, for a reasonable price, text and graphics display. They come in a wide range of sizes.

As software and operating systems have become more powerful and sophisticated, color monitors that can make better use of their graphics capabilities have grown in popularity. Considerably more expensive than monochrome monitors, color monitors can be purchased in a variety of sizes and resolution levels.

Keyboard

The keyboard serves as the primary input device by which the operator enters data into the computer. The keys on modern keyboards are organized in the traditional typewriter configuration. Often called a QWERTY keyboard, this arrangement derives its name from the six letter keys in the upper left corner of the keyboard. Other, less common, key arrangements are also available. Most keyboards also include several additional function keys and numeric keypads similar to those found on adding machines.

The location of function keys, those keys that computer programs can program to serve as multi-step "quick keys," is becoming standardized among many microcomputer manufacturers. Although this standardization causes keyboards to appear identical across computer brand lines, keyboards are not interchangeable. The electronics that create the signal sent to the computer are usually specific to one brand of computer.

Disk Drives

Unlike microcomputer system RAM chips that lose all stored data the moment you switch off the power, disks provide stable, long-term storage of data files. The disk drive, the device that spins disks to read and write information on them, falls into three categories: floppy, fixed (or hard), and optical.

Figure 5.4 QWERTY Keyboard

Floppy disks are typically used for moving software and data between machines. They can also be used strictly for data storage. Common to all floppy disks is a thin plastic disk with a magnetic coating on which the disk drive stores information. Although flexible 5.25-inch floppy disks were popular for many years, 3.5-inch hard-cased floppy disks have become standard for most modern microcomputers. In general, floppy disks can be used only on machines that use the same operating system as the machine on which they were formatted. However, even this line is blurring: some manufacturers are introducing disk drives and software that can read disks formatted by otherwise incompatible systems.

Fixed disk drives evolved from the need for larger volumes of data storage. A fixed disk drive is a self-contained unit that holds at least one metal "platter" upon which data can be stored. This platter is encased in an airtight chamber to prevent contamination by dust and moisture. Early fixed disk drives offered 10 to 20 megabytes of data storage; today fixed disk drives for microcomputers can store as much as 600MB.

Optical disk drives, which use laser technology to store data on a removable disk, much like an audio compact disc, are becoming common in the microcomputer market. Optical drives combine the portability of a floppy disk with the mass storage capability of a fixed disk drive.

Modems

Modems allow digital computer signals to be converted to analog audio tones (and vice versa), enabling two or more computers to exchange data over telephone wires. Modems derive their name from their function: they modulate and demodulate signals. They can be incorporated into microcomputer systems either as external devices or as internal add-on boards.

The speed at which a modem can send and receive data is referred to as its "baud rate." Early modems operated at 300 baud, a speed regarded as painfully slow by today's standards. Today speeds between 1,200 and 9,600 baud are common. However, as speeds increase, so do prices.

Figure 5.5 Modem

Diskettes

Most microcomputers have a method of storing information for later retrieval. Diskettes commonly used range in size from 3.5 to 8 inches in diameter. The amount of information stored on a diskette is dependent upon the particular computer with which it is used. The typical capacity of a diskette is 350,000 to 1.5 million characters. The most common type in use today is the 5.25-inch double-sided disk, but the coming standard is 3.5 inches.

Figure 5.6 Diskette

Diskettes fresh from the factory are not usable by a microcomputer; they must first be "formatted," a process which is performed by the microcomputer. After being formatted the diskette is then unique to the brand of the micro that did the formatting. Herein lies one of the major obstacles to compatibility among microcomputers: each micro has its own disk format, causing its diskettes to be virtually useless to another micro.

Note

1. Eric J. Schlene, "Inside a Microcomputer," *University Computing Times* (September-October 1990), 14-17. Wrubel Computing Center, Indiana University, Bloomington, IN 47405. Reprinted by permission.

5.8.b   The Structure of a Modern General-Purpose Computer

The social scientist does not have to have complete technical knowledge of computers, but a limited degree of familiarity is essential to understanding what computers can do. Within a large access network the possibilities are very great.

The heart of the computer network is the central processing unit. Everything else depends on it (see Figure 5.7). In the CPU all communication is two-way, but many other connections operate in only one direction. The all-time classic beginner's mistake is to put input on an output device or vice versa.

Equipment in the local computer system can also be operated remotely. Generally this is done over the public phone system. This means a researcher on one part of the campus can work with a computer elsewhere on campus or anywhere in the world. The only limits to this are the price of the phone call, cost of computer time, and accessibility to the line.

5.8.c   Types of Networks

Alton R. Kindred[1]

Terminals, modems, lines, and central processors may be arranged in many different ways. Three such arrangements are (1) star networks, (2) ring networks, and (3) distributed networks.

Star Networks

A star network consists of a central host computer connected to one or more terminals, resembling a star (Figure 5.8). A *pure star network* contains only point-to-point lines between the terminals and the host system. A *modified star network* (Figure 5.9) may provide multipoint lines along with or instead of point-to-point lines.

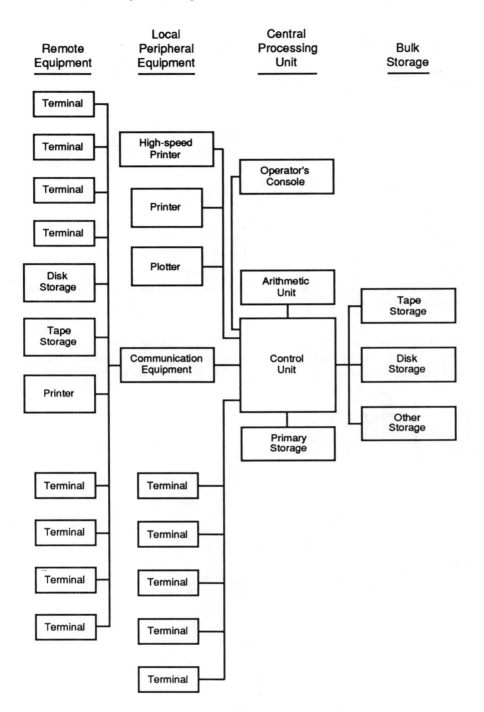

Figure 5.7 The Structure of a Modern General-Purpose Computer

SOURCE: I am indebted to Douglas M. Klieger for this version of a general-purpose computer. See his *Computer Usage for Social Scientists* (Boston: Allyn & Bacon, 1984), 20.

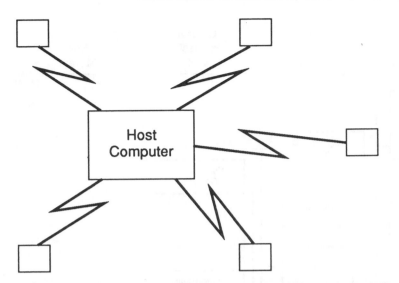

Figure 5.8 A star network has a single line to each terminal. Modems are required as usual at each end of the line but are omitted from this drawing.

The central host computer contains all programs and the data base for a star network. Terminals carrying heavy volumes of work can be provided with point-to-point lines, while those with lighter traffic can share lines with a multipoint system.

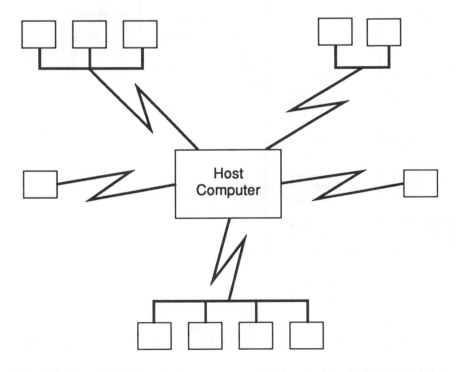

Figure 5.9 The modified star network may use a combination of point-point lines to reach the terminals.

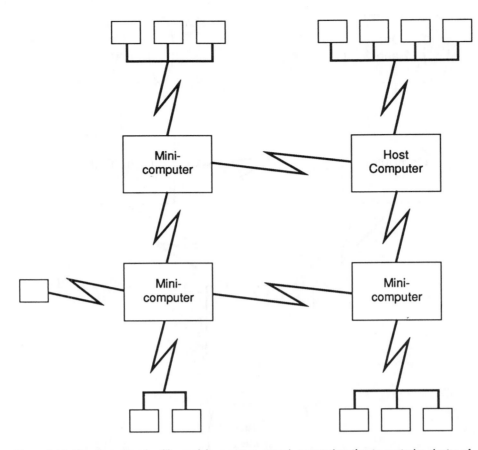

Figure 5.10 The ring network utilizes minicomputers at each remote location to control a cluster of terminals and take over certain functions that would otherwise have to be done by the host computer.

Ring Networks

Ring networks consist of several computer systems that can communicate with one another. A large mainframe is usually host to the entire system, while mini- or microcomputers are hosts to each cluster of terminals. The smaller hosts can communicate with the central host and perhaps with one another. The data base is at the central site (see Figure 5.10).

Distributed Networks

Distributed networks are extensions of ring networks. They are sometimes called *distributed* or *dispersed* data processing. Each smaller processor in the network not only can communicate with the host processor as any terminal might do but also can perform many functions on a stand-alone basis.

In a true distributed system not only processing functions but portions of the data base itself are located with the smaller processors. Part or all of the distributed data base might be a copy of that available at the central host processor. The data base is

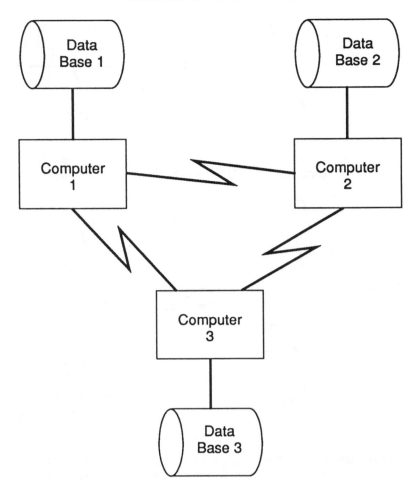

Figure 5.11 The distributed data base provides a separate data base as well as a separate processor at each remote location. Ideally, any terminal on the entire network has access to the resources in any data base at any location.

distributed wherever it is of most use. The processor at one location has access to data bases at the central station or even at other locations. Figure 5.11 shows a distributed data base.

The smaller processors at remote stations can perform many functions locally and reduce the amount of data that must be transmitted over long distance lines. The large central host can be freed from many tasks in supervising individual terminals and increase total system production.

Network Design Considerations

Certain problems arise in online systems that are not met in batch processing. First, there is no effective way to determine from an inquiry how much information will be required for the answer. Thus a question from a terminal might result in many pages of output data, which are too long to be returned over the terminal. One possible solution is to return an estimate of response time and give the user an option as to whether the answer should be typed out via terminal or printed out to be sent to the user via messenger or mail. Many users, accustomed to voluminous, detailed print-outs, feel slighted when they receive back only highly concise, digested information.

A second problem concerns the number of online stations that can be accommo-dated. It is desirable to make the system serve the maximum number of users, but overloading the system means that some user inevitably will have to wait for information. The longer she (or he) must wait, the less likely she will be to use the terminal. After a while the volume of work waiting in the queue to be processed will be reduced, not because there is no demand, but because the system is not adequately responsive to the demand.

Even if it were financially possible to have unlimited terminals, the multiplexing capacity of the systems input channels poses a third problem. The user may be able to get to a terminal, but if she always receives a busy signal she will be discouraged from trying to gain access to the system.

A fourth problem arises from the sheer size of the system's auxiliary storage. If the user must wait for the operator to mount additional tapes or disk packs before she can access the desired file, she will find the system less useful and will be more likely to seek her answers in other ways.

There were about 15 million computer terminals in use in the United States in 1988. By 1990, an estimated 40 million workers will use a computer terminal every day on the job.

Note

1. From Alton R. Kindred, *Data Systems and Measurement: An Introduction to Systems Analysis and Design*, 3rd ed. (Englewood Cliffs, NJ: Prentice Hall, 1985), 348-51. Reprinted by permission.

THE INDIANA UNIVERSITY DEPARTMENT OF SOCIOLOGY COMPUTING SYSTEM

5.9

Louie Miller, III (1989) [1]
Revised by David Jones (June 1990) [2]

The Department of Sociology at Indiana University offers a sophisticated comput-ing system that includes approximately 100 microcomputers available to faculty, staff, and students engaged in teaching, research, and administration. All of these computers are linked to the department's local area network (LAN), to university mainframes, and beyond. The department's LAN, which is housed in its Institute for Social Research, is supported by two powerful computers that function as network servers. Both are 80386 computers with 8 and 10 megabytes of memory (RAM) respectively, and both have a hard disk storage capacity of 600 megabytes. A staff of five full- and part-time computer professionals maintains this system and assists in its use.

Each faculty member has at least one microcomputer. Most have an IBM XT or equivalent, but several have 80386-based machines and the department is in the process of upgrading the rest to the 80386 standard. Each faculty workstation is well equipped. All have hard disks, printers, and either modems or network cards. Many also have math co-processors. Standard faculty software includes word processing and communication programs. Also, depending upon individual needs, faculty members may have a variety of other programs including statistical and mathematical packages, database systems, and spreadsheets. In addition, faculty members may utilize one of five laptop computers made available for research conducted at remote locations. Three computer display projectors, too, are available for use in the classroom or for making presentations elsewhere. The department currently has nine laser printers, one of which is operated by a secretary to whom faculty members may deliver documents for printing. Finally, a graphics workstation equipped with a plotter, a scanner, a digitizer, a laser printer, and advanced graphics software currently is in the planning stages.

Each faculty member also has a minimum of eight megabytes of disk storage on campus mainframes, a quantity that is readily expandable in response to research and other needs. To facilitate the analysis of very large data sets, the department also maintains an additional 1.2 gigabytes of its own mainframe disk storage space.

In addition, the department supports the Center for Survey Research, which facilitates research and the teaching of research methods. The Center has a PC-based Computer Assisted Telephone Interviewing (CATI) system. This system consists of 33 networked PCs, 25 of which are individual interviewing stations. Interviews can be overseen by supervisors located at any of four monitoring stations. Moreover, four other computers enable programmers and administrative staff members to oversee and modify all aspects of CATI system operations.

Department of Sociology staff and students have excellent computer facilities as well. Each staff member has his or her own personal computer. Staff computers are equipped much like faculty machines, with the exception that most do not have math co-processors.

The department supports two post-doctoral programs and a large graduate program. Post-doctoral students have their own cluster of five AT-class and two XT-class computers. All have hard disks and math co-processors. Two dot-matrix printers and a laser printer are attached to this cluster as well. Finally, the department provides a cluster of seven computers in a separate graduate student cluster. It includes five AT and two 80386sx machines, the latter equipped with math co-processors and hard disks. This cluster also includes both dot-matrix and laser printers. Finally, both of these clusters are connected to the departmental LAN to the larger university network.

Notes

1. Dr. Louie Miller III, University of Texas, Austin, Burdine Hall 436, Austin, Texas 78712-1088.
2. Dr. David Jones, Assistant Scientist in Sociology and Coordinator of Sociology Computing, Sociology Department, Indiana University, Bloomington, Indiana 47405.

5.10   PRINCIPAL PROGRAMS FOR THE COMPUTER

The term *software* refers to the detailed instructions or programs that are fed into a computer to tell it what to do. The software makes a computer useful. No computer system can be truly effective without good software. The listing that follows pertains to software that has proved most useful to social scientists.

The Institute for Social Research at Indiana University in Bloomington has the following programs currently running on the Indiana University Computer Network System. All programs except SAS run on VAX.

- SPSS^X: Statistical Package for the Social Sciences
- BMD: Biomedical Computer Programs
- SAS: Statistical Analysis System, currently running on the IBM4341 at IUPUI in Indianapolis, Indiana
- LISREL: Analysis of Linear Structural Relationships by the Method of Maximum Likelihood, version 4
- RATE: continuous time, discrete state Markov models for events data

SPSS^X

SPSS^X is a comprehensive, integrated system for managing, analyzing, and displaying information. It incorporates all of the proven advantages of the SPSS^X Batch System, including report writing and more than 40 major statistical procedures and state-of-the-art file and data management capabilities as well as expanded data displays. Presentation-ready summaries and reports are produced automatically.

SPSS^X User's Guide. 2nd ed. Chicago: SPSS Inc., 1986.
SPSS^X Introductory Statistics Guide. Marija J. Norusis. Chicago: SPSS Inc.

This text features an introduction to statistics with instructions for performing sample analyses with SPSS^X. It is intended as a supplementary guide for teaching and for personal use. It carries the reader from basic statistics through multiple regression.

SPSS^X Advanced Statistics Guide. Marija J. Norusis. Chicago: SPSS Inc.

Designed for researchers and use in the multivariate statistics course, the text covers regression, discriminant factor, and cluster analysis; multivariate and repeated measures analysis of variance; and log-linear models. It includes a reference section on SPSS^X commands and a brief introduction to data definition and management.

The Institute for Social Research at Indiana University relies mainly on the SPSS^X computer program write-ups maintained in the University Computer Center. These include the following:

"Frequency Distributions and Descriptive Statistical" (mean, median, mode, range, variance, measures of skewness and kurtosis, and percentiles; bar charts and frequency tables can be displayed; histograms available)
"Tabular Descriptions of Relationships Among Several Variables"
"Correlation Coefficients and Scatterplots"
"Multiple Regression Analysis"
"Factor Analysis"
"Discriminant Analysis"
"Survival Analysis"
"Analysis of Additive Scales"
"Nonparametric Statistics"
"Univariate and Multivariate Comparisons of Means"
"Log-Linear Models" (includes hiloglinear, probit, cluster, and quick cluster procedures)
"Multidimensional Sampling"
"Box-Jenkins Analysis of Time Series Data"
"Color Graphic Options"
"Report Writing Options"

SCSS Program

Norman H. Nie et al.'s *SCSS: A User's Guide to the SCSS Conversational System* (New York: McGraw-Hill, 1980) refers to a sister program to SPSS. Nevertheless, SCSS is not just an extension or modified version of SPSS, but a new package with a somewhat different language. The major parallel to SPSS is that both packages encompass approximately the same statistical procedures.

Conversational, or interactive, computing allows users to obtain immediate feedback while retaining step-by-step control over the computational process. For researchers, SCSS would be most useful for purposeful and theoretically guided model building and testing. Promising avenues of investigation can be quickly distinguished from dead ends. For teachers, SCSS might provide a means for students to explore empirically a substantive area using basic cross-tabulation techniques on a carefully limited data set.

IDA is an option to SCSS. See the following.

IDA, Conversational Statistics: An Introduction to Data Analysis and Regression. Harry V. Roberts and Robert F. Ling. New York: McGraw-Hill, 1982.

Oriented to interactive data analysis: the formulation, fitting, checking, and validation of statistical models that attempt to capture what is going on in a set of data. The word "conversational" in the title of the book refers primarily to interactive statistical computation, in which a statistical analysis is developed in easy steps as part of a friendly conversation between the user and computer.

LISREL VI. Karl Jöreskog and D. Sörbom. Chicago: SPSS Inc.

Now available as a new option to the SPSS[X] Information Analysis System, this software program has powerful capabilities, including fitting causal path models; estimating linear structural relations among econometric variables; studying time-dependent relations in longitudinal data; performing confirmatory factor analysis and covariance structure analysis; and performing standard multivariate techniques, such as principal components and canonical correlation analysis.

LISCOMP. 2nd ed. Bengt O. Muthén. Mooresville, IN: Scientific Software, Inc., 1987.

LISCOMP is a structural equation modeling program especially well suited for categorical and other nonnormal data. Analyses include multiple regression, path analysis, latent variable modeling, factor analysis, structural equation modeling, and Monte Carlo studies. The program has special features that make it particularly useful for advanced uses and for research on statistical issues related to structural equation modeling.

OSIRIS

OSIRIS is another widely used package of computer programs designed for the analysis of social science data. The statistical analysis capabilities include a variety of multivariate and nonparametric analysis programs. Potential users should read *Computer Processing of Social Science Data using OSIRIS IV* by Judith Rattenbury, Paula Pelletier, and Laura Klem (Ann Arbor: University of Michigan, Institute for Social Research, 1984).

OSIRIS is intended to guide researchers and their assistants in the field of social science through all the stages necessary for processing data with a computer. No previous knowledge of computers is assumed, although at least theoretical knowledge of data collection and analysis is expected.

The monograph describes procedures and strategies geared to studies involving relatively large bodies of data. Discussed are the basic components of computers and the different kinds of software necessary for using a computer, different types of data and analysis, the various steps of the processing stages, and the kinds of errors commonly made when using a computer for data processing and how they can be avoided.

OSIRIS IV: Statistical Analysis and Data Management Software System, by the Computer Support Group, Survey Research Center (Ann Arbor: University of Michigan, Institute for Social Research, 1981), is the latest update of the OSIRIS IV software system. The volume describes the major features basic to the system and includes a general description of the program, special terminology, command features, printed output, data input and output, restrictions, examples, and keywords as appropriate.

5.10.a Other Computer Languages

COBOL: The COBOL language is well suited for handling large amounts of data and is the most frequently chosen language for business applications. Topics include basic program structure, file manipulation (sort/merge), the report writer, and features unique to the CDC COBOL compiler.

FORTRAN: Topics covered are an introduction to computer organization, algorithms and flowcharts, FORTRAN language statements and syntax, and program debugging.

Advanced FORTRAN: Designed for researchers and students who are experienced FORTRAN programmers. Topics include learning how to interpret an exchange package, speedy input/output procedures, representation of data on CDC machines, buffering overlays, the segment loader, basic data structures, and Advanced FORTRAN Syntax.

Pascal: Intended for persons with little or no programming experience. Topics include the advantages of programming in Pascal, how to prepare a Pascal program, and solving problems via computer programs. Includes the most basic statements of Pascal: assignment, conditionals, iteratives, declarations, types, case statements, procedures, functions, and using arrays.

5.10.b Specialized Computer Programs

The Institute for Social Research at the University of Michigan currently offers the following works on computer techniques in social science research:

Andrews, Frank M., and Robert C. Messenger. *Multivariate Nominal Scale Analysis: A Report on a New Analysis Technique and a Computer Program.* 1975.

This monograph describes a powerful new technique for conducting multivariate analysis of categorical dependent variables. It applies the most common analytic model—the additive one—to categorical dependent variables and arrives at answers to the usual questions addressed by multivariate analysis. It is uniquely useful in exploring the interrelationships of theoretical concepts involving categorical dependent variables and substantial numbers of independent variables at various levels of measurement.

Andrews, Frank M., James N. Morgan, John A. Sonquist, and Laura Klem. *Multiple Classification Analysis: A Report on a Computer Program for Multiple Regression Using Categorical Predictors.* 1967; rev. ed., 1974.

Multiple classification analysis is a technique for examining the interrelationship between several predictor variables and a dependent variable within the context of an additive model. The program will handle missing data on both the dependent and predictor variables.

Morgan, James N., and Robert C. Messenger. *THAID: A Sequential Analysis Program for the Analysis of Nominal Scale Dependent Variables.* 1973.

Like its companion volume, *Multivariate Nominal Scale Analysis*, this monograph describes a recently developed technique for conducting multivariate analyses of categorical dependent variables. Although common in social research, such variables have, until now, been difficult to handle with available statistical techniques. THAID describes a searching process that provides an efficient and effective means for sorting through a variety of analytic models to find the most able to produce useful predictions. The program searches for subgroups that differ maximally as to their distribution; it assumes neither additivity nor linearity, so requires substantial samples of 1,000 or more cases.

Rattenbury, Judith. *Introduction to the IBM 360 Computer and OS/JCL (Job Control Language).* 1971; rev. ed., 1974.

This monograph will be of value to both the complete novice and those who have used other computers. It not only gives details of the most used subset of the IBM 360 job control language but also attempts to make it meaningful by describing the physical characteristics of tapes and disks and by explaining how the operating system works.

Sonquist, John A. *Multivariate Model Building: The Validation of a Search Strategy.* 1970; reprint, 1971.

This book undertakes the validation of the automatic interaction detection (AID) technique. It uses computer techniques for data generation to produce models in which the actual structure of the relationship between variables is completely known. Then, applying both AID and multiple classification analysis (MCA) techniques to the data, it explores the ability of each algorithm to lead the analyst to a correct assessment of the structure of the predictive model implicit in the data. The conclusion leads to further developments in a strategy for the back-to-back use of AID and MCA in the task of multivariate building.

Sonquist, John A., Elizabeth Lauh Baker, and James N. Morgan. *Searching for Structure.* 1971; rev. ed., 1974.

This report presents an approach to analysis of substantial bodies of microdata and documentation for a computer program. The new computer program—AID 111—is a descendant of the original automatic interaction detector program that started the application of search strategy; several new features have been added to the new program.

The Community and Family Study Center of the University of Chicago has the following monographs on computer techniques available:

Donald J. Bogue. *Techniques of Making Population Projections: How to Make Age-Sex and Functional Projections by Electronic Computer*, Manual No. 12.

This manual presents the basic methodology of population forecasting and the techniques necessary for forecasting the future size of functional subgroupings of the population.

Donald J. Bogue and Elizabeth J. Bogue. *Techniques of Pregnancy History Analysis.*

This manual systematizes data collection, computerizes data processing, and codifies the steps involved in adjusting and interpreting the data of pregnancy histories. Computer programs for use on small computers are included.

Donald J. Bogue, Scott Edmonds, and Elizabeth J. Bogue. *An Empirical Model for Demographic Evaluation of the Impact of Contraception and Marital Status on Birth Rates with Computerized Applications to the Setting of Targets and Quotas for Family Planning Programs*

This manual attempts to solve the practical problem of the valid projection of family-planning targets. It develops an empirical model that links birthrates to contraceptive behavior in a new form able to yield realistic results. A "packaged" computer program for small computers is included.

Donald J. Bogue and James Nelson. *The Fertility Components and Contraceptive History Techniques for Measuring Contraceptive Use-Effectiveness.*

A contribution to the methodology for measuring and interpreting the implications of contraceptive use-effectiveness for fertility areas, this manual includes techniques for a new system of measurement, practical procedures for data collection, and a "packaged" computer program for small computers.

Henry G. Elkins. *Mini-Tab Edit, Mini-Tab Frequencies and Mini-Tab Tables: A Set of Three Interrelated Statistical Programs for Small Computers.*

A set of simplified and versatile programs written in basic FORTRAN to tabulate social data where large computers and more elaborate programs are not readily available.

Maurice J. Moore. *Mini-Regression: A Small Computer Program for Performing Multiple Regression Analysis*, Manual No. 14.

Basic principles of multiple regression analysis are presented. A computer program for calculating regression coefficients and related statistics is included.

Thomas Mossberg. *ADDLIB: A Computer Program for Addressing Mail and Indexing Libraries.* Family Planning Research and Evaluation Manual No. 13.

ADDLIB is a computer program that performs two important functions: First, it addresses labels for all mailings; names and addresses written on ordinary punched cards can be selected, sorted, and printed on labels with respect to any desired combinations of up to five criteria of selection. Second, it prints out bibliographies of items contained in a library, permitting selection by subject for any desired combinations of up to five subject-matter classifications. Written for small (32K) computers, it eliminates costly addressing equipment and permits rapid information retrieval at many additional sites throughout the world.

5.10.c   New Data Bases Available: Cendata and Newsworks II[1]

The CENDATA data base, the Census Bureau's on-line data base available through DIALOG Information Services, has expanded considerably since its inception in mid-1984. It now offers the most current economic statistics in the areas of manufacturing, business, foreign trade, and construction as well as selected historic economic data. Demographic statistics include the most recent population estimates for U.S. states and counties; detailed national-level information in income, poverty, and household composition; and a very detailed demographic profile of the United States. The data base also has demographic profiles for each country in the world and detailed statistics for each state including a ranking among all states for each of more than 50 demographic/economic data items. CENDATA can be accessed by any terminal, word processor, or personal computer with communications capability. For more information about CENDATA, contact the CENDATA staff at (301) 763-2074 or DIALOG Customer Services at (800) 334-2564.

NEWSWORKS II is a social science data base designed by *Newsweek* magazine for high school and lower-division college audiences. Each diskette contains three data files: fundamental themes in geography, the causes and effects of military conflicts, and the spending priorities of the U.S. budget. NEWSWORKS II is designed for Apple IIe and IIc microcomputers using the data base manager in AppleWorks. The lessons come with an instructor's manual with ideas about how to use the exercises in class. The program can be purchased for $29.95 with 15 subscriptions to *Newsweek.* For more information, call (800) 526-2595. Dan Cover, Furman University, is interested in knowing about this data set and how sociologists have used it at the college level.

Note

1. Reported in *Footnotes* of the American Sociological Association (February 1988): 6.

5.11 BIBLIOGRAPHY OF GENERAL BOOKS ON COMPUTERS

Brownell, Blaine A. *Using Microcomputers: A Guidebook for Writers, Teachers, and Researchers in the Social Sciences.* Beverly Hills, CA: Sage, 1985.
Chen, Milton, and William Paisley. *Children and Microcomputers: Research on the Newest Medium.* Beverly Hills, CA: Sage, 1985.
Cozby, Paul C. *Using Computers in the Behavioral Sciences.* Palo Alto, CA: Mayfield, 1984.
Day, John C., Thomas H. Athey, and Robert W. Zmud. *Microcomputers and Applications.* Boston: Scott, Foresman, 1988.
Dewdney, A. K. *The Armchair Universe: An Exploration of Computer Worlds.* New York: Freeman, 1988.
Feinstein, David L., Carl Feingold, and Fritz H. Grupe. *Computers, Concepts, and Applications.* 4th ed. Dubuque, IA: Wm. C. Brown, 1990.
Frude, Neil. *The Intimate Machine: Close Encounters with Computers and Robots.* New York: North American Library, 1983.
Graham, Neil. *The Mind Tool: Computers and Their Impact on Society.* 4th ed. St. Paul, MN: West, 1986.
Hallam, Teresa A., Stephen F. Hallam, and James Hallam. *Micrometer Use.* New York: Harcourt Brace Jovanovich, 1988.
Hanneman, Robert. *Computer-Assisted Theory Building.* Newbury Park, CA: Sage, 1987.
Heise, David R., ed. *Microcomputers in Social Research.* Beverly Hills, CA: Sage, 1981.
Kershner, Helene G. *Introduction to Computer Literacy.* Lexington, MA: D. C. Heath, 1990.
Klieger, Douglas M. *Computer Usage for Social Scientists.* Boston: Allyn & Bacon, 1984.
Langley, Pat, Herbert Simon, et al. *Scientific Discovery: Computational Explorations of the Creative Process.* Cambridge: MIT Press, 1987.
Lombardi, John V. *Computer Literacy: The Basic Concepts and Language.* Bloomington: Indiana University Press, 1983.
Lu, Cary, and Ellen W. Chu. *The Apple Macintosh Book.* 3rd ed., rev. Redmond, WA: Microsoft, 1988.
Moreau, R. *The Computer Comes of Age: The People, the Hardware, the Software.* Cambridge: MIT Press, 1984.
Nagel, Stuart S. *Microcomputers, Evaluation Problems, and Policy Analysis.* Beverly Hills, CA: Sage, 1986.
Nickerson, Raymond S. *Using Computers.* Cambridge: MIT Press, 1986.
Patterson, David, Denise S. Kiser, and Neil D. Smith. *Computing Unbound: Using Computers in the Arts and Sciences.* New York: W. W. Norton, 1989.
Pfaffenberger, Bryan. *Microcomputer Applications in Qualitative Research.* Newbury Park, CA: Sage, 1988.
Savage, John E., Susan Magidson, and Alex M. Stein. *The Mystical Machine: Issues and Ideas in Computing.* Reading, MA: Addison-Wesley, 1986.
Schellenberg, Kathryn, ed. *Computers in Society.* 2nd ed. Guildford, CT: Dushkin, 1988.
Shelly, Gary B., and Thomas J. Cashman. *Computer Fundamentals for an Information Age.* Brea, CA: Anaheim, 1984.
Walsh, Myles E. *Understanding Computers: What Managers and Users Need to Know.* New York: John Wiley, 1981.
Willis, Jerry, and Merl Miller. *Computers for Everybody.* 2nd ed. Beaverton, OR: Dilithium, 1983.

5.12 BIBLIOGRAPHY OF COMPUTER SOFTWARE, COMPUTER NETWORKS, AND ARTIFICIAL INTELLIGENCE

Connell, John L., and Linda Shafer. *The Professional User's Guide to Acquiring Software.* New York: Van Nostrand Reinhold, 1987.
Editors of *The Scientific American. Computer Software.* New York: Freeman, 1984.

Foehr, Theresa, and Thomas B. Cross. *The Softside of Software: A Management Approach to Computer Documentation.* New York: John Wiley, 1986.

Hearn, Donald, and M. Pauline Baker. *Computer Graphics.* Englewood Cliffs, NJ: Prentice-Hall, 1986.

Ledgard, Henry, and John Tauer. *Programming Practice: Professional Software.* Vol. 3. Reading, MA: Addison-Wesley, 1987.

Lehman, M. M., and L. A. Belady. *Program Evolution: Processes of Software Change.* New York: Academic Press, 1985.

Marcotty, Michael, and Henry Ledgard. *The World of Programming Languages.* New York: Springer-Verlag, 1986.

Mitrani, I. *Modeling of Computer and Communication Systems.* New York: Cambridge University Press, 1987.

Rattenbury, Judith, Paula Pelletier, and Laura Klem. *Computer Processing of Social Science Data Using OSIRIS IV.* Ann Arbor: University of Michigan, Institute for Social Research, 1984.

Reardon, Ray, ed. *Networks for the 1990s.* New York: John Wiley, 1988.

Tannenbaum, Andrew S. *Operating Systems: Design and Implementation.* Englewood Cliffs, NJ: Prentice-Hall, 1987.

Artificial Intelligence

Berk, A. A. *LISP: The Language of Artificial Intelligence.* New York: Van Nostrand Reinhold, 1985.

Charmiak, Eugene, and Dres McDermont. *Artificial Intelligence.* Reading, MA: Addison-Wesley, 1987.

Michie, Donald. *On Machine Intelligence.* 2nd ed. New York: John Wiley, 1986.

Osherson, Daniel M., Michael Stob, and Scott Weinstein. *Systems That Learn.* Cambridge: MIT Press, 1986.

Partridge, D. *Artificial Intelligence: Applications in the Future of Software Engineering.* New York: John Wiley, 1986.

This is only one in a series of more than 40 books in the Ellis Horwood Series in Artificial Intelligence. Researchers with further interest should write either John Wiley and Sons, 605 Third Ave., New York, NY 10158 or Ellis Horwood Ltd., Market Cross House, Cooper Street, Chichester, West Sussex, P.O. 19, 1EB, England.

Computer Dictionary

Rosenberg, Jerry M. *Computers, Information Processing, and Telecommunications.* 2nd ed. New York: John Wiley, 1987.

Guide to Personal Computing

Digital Equipment Corporation. *Guide to Personal Computing.* Maynard, MA: Digital Equipment Corporation, 1982.

Keep in touch with the company for revised editions: Digital Equipment Corporation, New Products Marketing, 1298 Parker St., Maynard, MA 01754.

Reader's Guide to Microcomputer Books

Nicita, Michael, and Ronald Petrusha. *The Reader's Guide to Microcomputer Books.* New York: Golden-Lee, 1983.

Publisher's full address: Golden-Lee Books, 1000 Dean St., Brooklyn, NY 11238.

Scholarly Journals

Social Science Computer Review. (Incorporating the *Social Science Microcomputer Review* and *Computers and the Social Sciences.*)

Published quarterly by the Duke University Press, 6697 College Station, Durham, NC 27708.

Other Journals Reporting Applications

Behavior Research Methods, Instruments and Computers.
  Published bimonthly by the Psychonomic Society, 1710 Fortview Rd., Austin, TX 78704.
Computers in Human Behavior: Use of Computers from a Psychological Perspective.
  Published quarterly by Pergamon Press, Elmsford, NY 10523.

5.13 A GUIDE TO COMPUTER PERIODICALS

Fred D. Hanson[1]

Computer magazines can tell you how computers work, what computers can do, how a computer might be of personal use, and what experts think about certain system components.

The number of computing magazines is overwhelming. You can find computer magazines practically everywhere: grocery stores, bookstores, computer stores, and libraries. How do you decide which type of magazine to purchase and read?

First of all, you need to select a magazine that fits your level of technical understanding. If you are a beginner, you should start with magazines which have frequent articles on computing fundamentals. Avoid magazines aimed at experienced computer users or programmers. Your frustration in trying to understand information that is too technical can blind you to very practical applications which require little technical knowledge.

Following is a selected list of periodicals which have been grouped by category. Those under "general" would be of special interest to beginners, but most will also be of value to more advanced readers. The "advanced" group is for individuals interested in programming, technical issues of hardware and software, or hardware construction projects. The remaining categories are for magazines dedicated to specific brands. Those magazines designated with an asterisk (*) are thought by this author to be especially good.

While this list is not exhaustive, it should get you started.

General

Personal Computing
Compute!
*Infoworld**
PC-Week
MISweek
COMPUTERWORLD

Advanced/Programming

*Byte**
Microsystems
*Dr. Dobb's Journal**
Programmer's Journal
Personal Publishing
MICRO CORNUCOPIA
Microsoft Systems Journal
CD-ROM review
COMPUTER LANGUAGE

Apple MacIntosh

MacUser
MACazine
HPER LINK
MacWeek
*MacWorld**

DEC

*digital review**
DEC Professional
VAX Professional

IBM

PC-World
*PC-Magazine**
PC-Tech Journal
Compute!'s PC
PC-Computing

Note: The above is not a complete listing of all the journals available, but represents those commonly found at local book and computer stores (revised listing, October 1988).

Addendum (by Delbert C. Miller)

Patricia Galloway recommends three general magazines:

Personal Computing
Portable Computer
Whole Earth Software Review

For programmers, she lists the following:

BYTE
Microsystems
Dr. Dobb's Journal

Note that there is high agreement between Galloway and Fred Hanson on magazines recommended.

Galloway's book list has only three entries:

Writing in the Computer Age, by Andrew Fluegelman and Jeremy Joan Hewed
The Word Processing Book, by Peter McWilliams
Database: A Primer, by C. J. Date

For more advice, see Galloway's article "Computers for Professors." [2]

Notes

1. Extracted from Fred D. Hanson, "A Guide to Periodicals." *On Line: Personal Computing* (Fall 1984). Available from Bloomington Academic Computing Services, 1125 Atwater, Bloomington, IN 47405.
2. Patricia Galloway, "Computers for Professors: A Guide for the Perplexed." *Academe* 70, no. 4 (1984): 9-16.

5.14   PATH ANALYSIS

Path Analysis as Causal Analysis

Path analysis has become a popular form of data analysis because it provides possibilities for causal determination among sets of measured variables. A principal objective of science is to build theoretical explanations of social phenomena. Kaplan has said:

> Science is a search for constancies, for invariants. It is the enterprise of making those identifications in experience which prove to be most significant for the control of appreciation of the experience to come. The basic scientific question is "what the devil is going on around here?" [1]

When the underlying assumptions of path analysis are met, theory and data may be related in situations where many variables are to be handled simultaneously. Path analysis is essentially a data-analytic technique using standardized multiple regression equations in examining theoretical models.

Extravagant hopes for causal explanations should not be entertained—at least not yet. The inability to deal with all variables in a social system, to measure and plot their exact interactions, makes the results in most problems only first approximations to causality. But the power of the technique continues to challenge researchers, and its use is proliferating.

A researcher commonly wishes to discover the relationship of independent factors to a dependent variable. Simple and multiple correlations are utilized and often yield important relationships, yet they never demonstrate causality. For example, if we wish to relate father's occupational status to son's occupational status, then, using correlational techniques, their correlational relationship can be determined, but causality can only be inferred. Using path analysis it is possible to postulate that such independent factors as father's educational attainment and occupational status are causal factors in the son's subsequent educational attainment, the status of the first job achieved, and the status of the current job.

Six Steps in the Application of Path Analysis

1. Develop a causal scheme or model.
2. Establish a pattern of associations between the variables in the sequence.
3. Depict a path diagram.
4. Calculate path coefficients for the basic model.
5. Test for "goodness of fit" with the basic model.
6. Interpret the result.

Step 1: Develop a causal scheme. Path analysis allows the social theorist to state a theory in the form of a linear causal model. The crucial question has to do with the order of priority for the variables in the system in a causal or processual sequence. Causal models involve the construction of an oversimplified model of social reality in the sense that the model takes into account only a very limited number of variables that are of interest in the specific research area. The most important variables are

TABLE 5.12 Simple Correlations for Five Status Variables

Variable	Z	Y	X	B	A
Z Son's current occupational status	—	.541	.596	.405	.322
Y Son's first-job status		—	.538	.417	.332
X Son's education			—	.438	.453
B Father's occupational status				—	.516
A Father's education					—

sought; all others are regarded as "residual." The social scientist represents the process assumed to be in operation among the variables based upon the results of past research and current theory.

Let us suppose that we utilize stratification theory and research. We postulate that status changes in the life cycle of a cohort of males indicate that father's educational attainment (A) and father's occupational attainment (B) will determine the subsequent educational attainment of the son (S), his first job (Y), and his current job (Z). This is the linear statement or temporal order and may be written as follows:

$$(A \rightarrow B) \rightarrow X \rightarrow Y \rightarrow Z$$

The earlier variables may affect a later one not only through intervening variables but also directly.

Step 2: Establish a pattern of associations between the variables in the sequence. The conceptual framework must be translated into quantitative estimates. This is done by establishing the pattern of association of the variables in the sequence. A correlation matrix is developed utilizing the simple correlations for the five status variables in the model. An adaptation of Blau and Duncan shows the matrix of their occupational mobility study (see Table 5.12).[2] Simple correlation measures the gross magnitude of the effect of an antecedent variable upon the consequent variable. The current job status is the expected outcome of all the other four antecedent variables. Reading across the first row, it is observed that all four antecedent variables show significant correlation to current job status, the highest being for the son's education ($r = .596$) and the next being his first job status ($r = .541$). As expected, father's occupational status and father's education are related in somewhat diminished magnitude ($r = .405$ and $r = .322$, respectively). The second row reports correlations with first-job status, and again the same pattern of relationship with father's occupation and education appears. The third row repeats expected relationships of son's education to father's occupation and education. The fourth row demonstrates the high correlation of father's occupation and education ($r = .516$).[3]

Step 3: Depict a path diagram. Path diagrams are generally illustrated, as in Figure 5.12, by means of one-headed arrows connecting some or all of the variables included in the basic model. Variables are distributed from left to right, depending upon their theoretical ordering. The first independent variables are placed at the extreme left. In this case, these are father's education and father's occupation, and the link is shown as an arrowhead at both ends to distinguish it from other paths of influence. Intercorrelations (zero-order) between variables not influenced by other variables in the model are called *exogenous* variables, which refer to all variables prior to and outside the model.

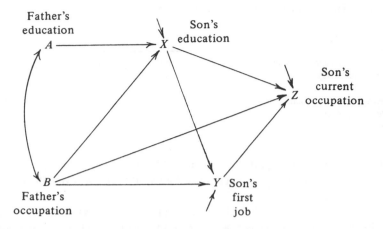

Figure 5.12 Basic Model of the Process of Stratification. The algebraic representation of the causal scheme now shown in the path model rests on a system of equations rather than the single equation more often employed in multiple regression analysis. This feature permits a flexible ordering of the inferred influences. Each line represents a search and a determination of direct (or net) influences. Note how much emphasis Blau and Duncan have given to the father's occupation as a causative factor as path coefficients are traced to son's education, first job, and current job. Father's education, on the other hand, is traced only through the son's education.

SOURCE: Adapted from Blau and Duncan, *American Occupational Structure* (New York: John Wiley, 1967); used by permission.

The remaining subset of variables (which may consist of only one variable) is taken as dependent, and these variables are called *endogenous* (*X, Y,* and *Z*). As contrasted with the exogenous variables, this subset is considered totally determined by some combination of the variables in the system. The straight lines above running from one measured variable to another represent the direct influences of one variable upon another. There are also indirect influences, as illustrated in the diagram under analysis. Variables recognized as effects of certain antecedent factors may, in turn, serve as causes for subsequent variables. For example, *X* is caused by *A* and *B*, which in turn influences *Y* and *Z*, thus *Y* and *Z* are affected indirectly by both *A* and *B*, in addition to any direct effects.

Finally, residual paths must be drawn. These are the lines with no source indicated carrying arrows to each of the endogenous or effect variables. Residuals are represented as the arrows coming from outside the system to *X, Y,* and *Z,* and are due to causes not recognized or measured, errors of measurement, and departures of the true relationships from additivity and linearity, properties that are assumed throughout the analysis.

Step 4: Calculate path coefficients. Path coefficients reflect the amount of direct contribution of a given variable on another variable when effects of other related variables are taken into account. Path coefficients are identical to partial regression coefficients (the betas) when the variables are measured in standard form. Two ways of computing path coefficients are frequently employed. The first uses regression programs that take raw data and compute partial coefficients from standardized input data. Both path coefficients and multiple correlation coefficients are generally provided by standard computer regression programs.[4] The second method uses only

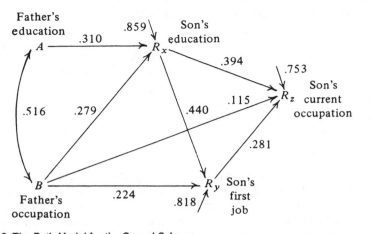

Figure 5.13 The Path Model for the Causal Scheme

SOURCE: Adapted from Blau and Duncan, *American Occupational Structure* (New York: John Wiley, 1967), 170; used by permission.

zero-order correlations among variables; a researcher can employ the "basic theorem" to compute the path coefficients.[5]

In Figure 5.13, the path coefficients have been entered on the path diagram with the exception of antecedent variables *A* and *B*. The path basic model is now complete and awaits evaluation.

Step 5: Test for "goodness of fit" with basic model. The crux of the analysis is the test for goodness of fit between the observed data and the basic model. Three general approaches may be made:

1. examining the amount of *variation* in dependent variables that is *explained* by variables linked as specified in the model
2. examining the *size of path coefficients* to see whether they are large enough to warrant the inclusion of a variable or path in the model
3. evaluating the ability of the model to *predict correlation coefficients* that were not used in computation of the path coefficients themselves[6]

An investigator usually contrasts the usefulness of the model in these three respects with alternative models. This is the heart of explanatory progress in any science.

The partial regression coefficients in standard form and the coefficients of determination for specified combinations of variables are essential for applying the first goodness-of-fit criterion. Table 5.13 is an adaptation of the Blau and Duncan data. This table shows that the coefficient of determination for father's occupation, father's education, and son's education is .26, which is to say that 26% of the variation in son's education may be accounted for by the father's occupation and education.

Similarly, 33% of the variation in son's first job may be accounted for by father's occupation, father's education, and son's education. Finally, 43% of the variation in son's current occupation is due to father's occupation, father's education, son's education, and son's first job. Note that father's education is not helpful in explaining this variance. The unexplained variation $1 - R^2_{4.123} = .57$. The model leaves unexplained 57% of the variance in son's current job. This is not as satisfactory as might

TABLE 5.13 Partial Regression Coefficients in Standard Form (Beta Coefficients) and Coefficients of Determination, for Specified Combinations of Variables

Dependent Variable	First Job	Son's Education	Father's Occupation	Father's Education	Coefficient of Determination (R^2)
Son's education			.279	.310	.26
First job		.433	.214	.026	.33
Current occupation	.282	.397	.120	−.014	.43

be hoped. The "unexplained" variation is due to variables or measurement error not included in the model and, for sake of completeness, the square root of these $1 - R^2$ values are ascribed to the residual variables, R_x, R_y, and R_z as shown in Figure 5.13. These "residual" paths are large, and the investigator must reexamine his or her causal scheme. However, it must not be assumed that the size of the residual is necessarily a measure of success in explaining the phenomenon under study. "The relevant question about the residual is not really its size at all, but whether the unobserved factors it stands for are properly represented *as being uncorrelated* with the measured antecedent factors." [7]

In terms of the second criterion of goodness of fit, the model fares well. Most of the path coefficients are significant. It turned out that the net regressions of both father's occupation and son's first job on father's education were so small as to be negligible. Hence father's education could be disregarded without loss of information.[8] One might consider eliminating father's education as a factor because of its low coefficients and recompute path coefficients.

Third, one could examine the "fit" between observed correlations not previously used in formulas for calculating path coefficients and predictions of correlation coefficients that would be derived from the model. In this instance the correlation between father's education and son's first job (as well as current job) was not used to estimate path coefficients.

The question of testing an alternative model involves a thorough reexamination of the basic mode. Two possibilities present themselves: (a) substituting factors in the basic model believed to be more important, and (b) adding new factors to the basic model. Whether a path diagram or the causal scheme it represents is adequate depends on both theoretical and empirical considerations. The causal scheme must be complete in the sense that all causes are accounted for. Unmeasured causes presumed to be uncorrelated with the dependent variable must be represented.

Step 6: Interpret the result. The variables in the causal scheme may be studied for their direct and indirect effects. The direct effect of father's occupation on son's education, first job, and current occupation is shown by path coefficients of .279, .224, and .115, none of which is particularly large. Nevertheless, the cumulative indirect effects are significant. Father's occupation and education do influence son's education, and this in turn influences the son's first job, which in turn influences the son's current occupation. At the same time, many other factors of even greater influence are clearly operating to determine this last dependent variable of interest.

The technique of path analysis is not a method of discovering causal laws but a procedure for giving a quantitative interpretation of an assumed causal system as it operates within a given population.

Nygreen has reported a program called the Interactive Path Analyzer (IPA) to increase the practical power of path analysis. He describes on-line path analysis for those who have access to computer facilities:

In many locations, social science researchers are beginning to gain access to computer facilities via remote typewriter-like "time-sharing" terminals. The increasing ubiquity of such "on-line" computer resources has given many social scientists access to the computational power of digital computers in a much more convenient form than has been the case in the past. Time-sharing computers are becoming increasingly commonplace on college campuses either in addition to or in lieu of the more conventional "batch" processing techniques.

In a time-sharing environment, the analyst can "talk" with the computer by specifying different input criteria to his problem and observing the results immediately. These characteristics of the "conversational" environment provide an advantageous setting in which path analyses can be performed. Specifically, the researcher can think through and then specify his causal model, but the computer can do the numerical calculations, displaying the coefficients for inspection almost immediately. The sociologist is able to postulate alternative theoretical causal formulations, modify his current model[9] and again have the lengthy computations performed in milliseconds, with the results arrayed on the typewriter before him. Properly utilized, the time-sharing computer environment increases the practical power of path analyses, reducing turn-around time literally to seconds.[10]

IPA has been tested in this on-line environment, with very favorable results. The availability of the time-shared computer and the Interactive Path Analyzer lends flexibility and convenience to an otherwise tedious procedure in calculating path coefficients.

Notes

1. Abraham Kaplan, *The Conduct of Inquiry* (San Francisco: Chandler, 1964), 85.

2. Peter M. Blau and Otis Dudley Duncan, *The American Occupational Structure* (New York: John Wiley, 1967), 169.

3. Ibid.

4. For explanations of this procedure in the most understandable terms, see one of the following: Blau and Duncan, *American Occupational Structure*, 171-77; Herman J. Loether and Donald C. McTavish, *Descriptive Statistics for Sociologists* (Boston: Allyn & Bacon, 1974), 321-28. Other references are appended.

5. G. T. Nygreen, "Interactive Path Analysis," *American Sociologist* 6 (February 1971): 37-43.

6. Kenneth C. Land, "Principles of Path Analysis," in *Sociological Methodology 1969*, ed. Edgar F. Borgatta (San Francisco: Jossey-Bass, 1969).

7. Blau and Duncan, *American Occupational Structure*, 175.

8. Ibid., 173.

9. Evaluation procedures that require reformulation of the causal model and recomputation of the path coefficients will not be dealt with here.

10. Nygreen, "Interactive Path Analysis," 41; requests for copies of this program should be directed to Ms. Judith Rowe, Office for Survey Research and Statistical Studies, O-S-17 Green Hall, Princeton University, Princeton, NJ. Source decks and listings with documentation are available for $10.00.

Brief Treatments of Path Analysis

Boyle, Richard P. "Path Analysis and Ordinal Data." *American Journal of Sociology* 75 (January 1970): 461-80.

Duncan, Otis Dudley. "Path Analysis: Sociological Examples." *American Journal of Sociology* 72 (July 1966): 1-16.

> Traces history of path analysis and provides many examples.

Loether, Herman J., and Donald G. McTavish. *Descriptive and Inferential Statistics.* 3rd ed. Boston: Allyn & Bacon, 1988.

> See pp. 340-70.

Nygreen, G. T. "Interactive Path Analysis." *American Sociologist* 6 (February, 1971): 37-43.

Research Examples of Path Analysis

Blau, Peter M., and Otis Dudley Duncan. *The American Occupational Structure.* New York: John Wiley, 1967.

> See pp. 163-205.

Featherman, David L. "Achievement Orientations and Socioeconomic Career Attainments." *American Sociological Review* 37 (April 1972): 131-43.

Kelley, Jonathan. "Causal Chain Models for the Socioeconomic Career." *American Sociological Review* 38 (August 1973): 481-93.

Land, Kenneth C. "Path Models of Functional Theories of Social Stratification as Representations of Cultural Beliefs on Stratification." *Sociological Quarterly* 11 (Fall 1970): 474-84.

Robinson, Robert V., and Jonathan Kelley. "Class as Conceived by Marx and Dahrendorf: Effects on Income Inequality and Politics in the United States and Great Britain." *American Sociological Review* 44 (February 1979): 38-58.

Sewell, William H., Archibald O. Haller, and George W. Ohlendorf. "The Educational and Early Occupational Status Attainment Process: Replication and Revision." *American Sociological Review* 35 (December 1970): 1014-27.

General References for Path Analysis

Blalock, Hubert M., Jr. *Causal Inferences in Nonexperimental Research.* Chapel Hill: University of North Carolina Press, 1964.

Boudon, Raymond. "A Method of Linear Causal Analysis: Dependence Analysis." *American Sociological Review* 30 (June 1965): 365-74.

Costner, Herbert L., and Robert K. Leik. "Deductions from 'Axiomatic Theory.' " *American Sociological Review* 29 (December 1964): 819-35.

Forbes, H. D., and E. R. Tufte. "A Note of Caution in Causal Modelling." *American Political Science Review* 62 (December 1968): 1258-64.

Heise, D. R. "Problems in Path Analysis and Causal Inference." In *Sociological Methodology 1969*, edited by Edgar F. Borgatta, 38-71. San Francisco: Jossey-Bass, 1969.

Li, C. C. *Population Genetics.* Chicago: University of Chicago Press, 1955.

Simon, Herbert A. *Models of Man.* New York: John Wiley, 1957.

Stinchcombe, Arthur. *Construction of Social Theories.* New York: Harcourt, Brace & World, 1968.

> See Chapter 3 and Appendix for application of path analysis to tests of sociological theories.

Wright, Sewell. "The Method of Path Coefficients." *Annals of Mathematical Statistics* 5 (1934): 161-215.

——— . "Path Coefficients and Path Regressions: Alternative or Complementary Concepts?" *Biometrics* 16 (June 1960): 189-202.

——— . "The Treatment of Reciprocal Interaction, with or without Lag in Path Analysis." *Biometrics* 16 (September 1960): 423-45.

For additional references, see Section 5.17.a.

FACTOR ANALYSIS

Explaining Relations Among Numerous Variables in Simpler Terms

The purpose of this introduction is to provide sociological researchers with a working knowledge of the basic concepts of factor analysis without burdening them with statistical details. It will be assumed in the following discussion, however, that the user has some grasp of the meaning of correlation and regression coefficients. Factor analysis is a procedure for investigating the possibility that a large number of variables have a small number of factors in common that account for their inter-correlations. As Schuessler explains, "We observe that pupils who score high in reading tend to score high in spelling and arithmetic. We ascribe this consistency, or correlation, in pupils' marks to the general factors of intelligence." [1] Thus it can be seen in brief that this principle holds that a circumstance common to a succession of categorically identical events, which otherwise have nothing in common, may be regarded as a cause of that event. Therefore, to discover the cause of an event, we search for the lone circumstance that is always present when the event occurs. In a similar manner, by means of factor analysis, we seek to isolate those common elements that are present in two or more variables and to which the intercorrelations among these variables may be attributed. It can be seen, then, that factor analysis is an arithmetical procedure for determining whether the intercorrelations among many variables could be due to a few common factors.

C may be considered as either a cause of both X and Y or simply an element present in both variables (see Figure 5.14). Factor analysis considers the possibility that X and Y are indicators of the same thing. From the observed correlation between X and Y, the inference can be drawn that they were produced by the same cause or that they are, in varying degrees, different aspects of the same thing.

Finding Underlying Factors

To distinguish the observed variables, which are manipulated, from the common variables, which are hidden components in them, it is customary to speak of the latter as factors rather than variables. Thus for the simplest case of two variables, Z_1 and Z_2, where each is the sum of the two parts, one part common (A) and one part distinct to each variable (B_i), where

$$Z_1 = A + B_1$$
$$Z_2 = A + B_2$$

Z is conventionally spoken of as a variable and A and B_i as factors. Before proceeding any further, it should be emphasized that factors are statistical variables in the usual sense in all respects: Factors possess both a mean and a variance, they may be symmetrically distributed, and they may also be correlated with other factors. The special term *factor* serves to maintain the distinction between the composite variable, which is observed, and its component parts, which are hypothetical.

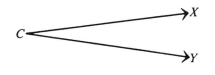

Figure 5.14

Data-Reduction Capability of Factor Analysis

The single most distinctive characteristic of factor analysis is its data-reduction capability. This means that given an array of correlation coefficients for a set of variables, factor-analytic techniques enable the researcher to see whether some underlying pattern of relationships exists such that the data may be "rearranged" or reduced to a smaller set of factors that may be considered source variables accounting for the observed interrelations in the data. There are multiple uses for this statistical capability, but the most frequent applications of the method fall into one of the following three categories: (a) exploratory uses, the exploration and detection of patterning of variables with a view to the discovery of new concepts and a possible reduction of data; (b) confirmatory uses, the testing of hypotheses about the structuring of variables in terms of the expected number of significant factors and factor loadings; or (c) uses as a measuring device, the construction of indices to be used as new variables in later analysis.[2]

Factor Analysis as Research Design

Factor analysis presents one of the few methods capable of teasing out what *would* happen through manipulation where manipulation is impossible. It seeks conclusions through statistical techniques rather than through the more traditional experimental route of manipulative control.

Three Major Steps in Factor Analysis Procedure

Factor analysis includes a fairly large variety of statistical techniques, but there are basically three steps in a factor analysis procedure:

1. preparation of a correlation matrix
2. extraction of the initial factors—the exploration of possible data reduction
3. rotation to a terminal solution—the search for simple and interpretable factors

Major options at each of these three stages may be summed up by three dichotomies: *R*-type versus *Q*-type factor analysis in step 1, defined versus inferred factors in step 2, and orthogonal versus oblique in step 3. These are defined in detail in the treatments of factor analysis listed in the following bibliography.

Notes

1. Karl Schuessler, *Analyzing Social Data* (Boston: Houghton Mifflin, 1971), 44.
2. N. H. Nie et al., *Statistical Package for the Social Sciences* (New York: McGraw-Hill, 1970).

Research Examples of Factor Analysis

Bales, Robert F., and Arthur S. Couch. "The Value Profile: A Factor Analytic Study of Value Statements."
Sociological Inquiry 39 (Winter 1969): 3-17.

Crew, Robert E. "Dimensions of Public Policy: A Factor Analysis of State Expenditures." *Social Science Quarterly* 50 (September 1969): 381-88.

McRae, Duncan, Jr. *Issues and Parties in Legislative Voting*. New York: Harper & Row, 1970.

Neal, Arthur, and Solomon Rettig. "On the Multidimensionality of Alienation." *American Sociological Review* 32 (February 1967): 54-63.

Schuessler, Karl F. *Measuring Social Life Feelings*. San Francisco: Jossey-Bass, 1982.

Brief Treatment of Factor Analysis

Comrey, Andrew L. *A First Course in Factor Analysis*. New York: Academic Press, 1973.

Cottrell, Raymond F. "Factor Analysis: An Introduction to Essentials. I. The Purpose and Underlying Models." *Biometrics* 21 (March 1965): 190-215.

———. "Factor Analysis: An Introduction to Essentials. II. The Role of Factor Analysis in Research." *Biometrics* 21 (June 1965): 405-35.

Kim, Jae-on, and Charles W. Mueller. *Introduction to Factor Analysis: What It Is and How to Do It*. Beverly Hills, CA: Sage, 1978.

Rummel, Rudolph J. "Understanding Factor Analysis." *Journal of Conflict Resolution* 11 (December 1967): 444-80.

Schuessler, Karl. *Analyzing Social Data*. Boston: Houghton Mifflin, 1971.

See pp. 44-84.

General References for Factor Analysis

Fruchter, Benjamin. *Introduction to Factor Analysis*. Princeton, NJ: Van Nostrand, 1954.

Cattell, Raymond B. *Factor Analysis: An Introduction and Manual for the Psychologist and Social Scientist*. New York: Harper & Row, 1952.

Harman, Harry H. *Modern Factor Analysis*. 2nd ed. Chicago: University of Chicago Press, 1967.

Horst, Paul. *Factor Analysis of Data Matrices*. New York: Holt, Rinehart & Winston, 1965.

Jöreskog, K. G. *Advances in Factor Analysis and Structural Equation Models*. Cambridge, MA: Abt, 1979.

Kim, Jae-on, and Charles W. Mueller. *Factor Analysis: Statistical Methods and Practical Issues*. Beverly Hills, CA: Sage, 1978.

Nie, N. H., D. H. Bent, and C. H. Hull. *Statistical Package for the Social Sciences*. New York: McGraw-Hill, 1970.

Rummel, Rudolph J. *Applied Factor Analysis*. Evanston, IL: Northwestern University Press, 1970.

Recent applications of factor analysis in political and social research are listed in a special chapter.

Thurstone, Louis L. *Multiple Factor Analysis*. Chicago: University of Chicago Press, 1947.

A BIBLIOGRAPHY OF STATISTICAL METHODS   5.16

The writing of introductory statistics is as prolific as the writing of introductory sociology texts—perhaps more so since many departments of a university teach introductory courses. It is difficult to find the "best" text for a given class. Royce Singleton, Jr., of Holy Cross College was asked to review the following introductory texts:

Daniel, Wayne W. *Introductory Statistics with Applications.* Boston: Houghton Mifflin, 1977. 475 pp.

Levin, Jack. *Elementary Statistics in Social Research.* 2nd ed. New York: Harper & Row, 1977. 293 pp.

Malec, Michael A. *Essential Statistics for Social Research.* Philadelphia: Lippincott, 1977. 235 pp.

Pine, Van-Derlyn R. *Introduction to Social Statistics.* Englewood Cliffs, NJ: Prentice-Hall, 1977. 415 pp.

Runyon, Richard P. *Winning with Statistics: A Painless First Look at Numbers, Ratios, Percentages, Means, and Inference.* Reading, MA: Addison-Wesley, 1977. 210 pp.

Schutte, Jerald G. *Everything You Always Wanted to Know About Elementary Statistics (But Were Afraid to Ask).* Englewood Cliffs, NJ: Prentice-Hall, 1977. 230 pp.

Singleton's approach to this problem of assessment is instructive to all who must make a choice among introductory statistics books. To begin with, he identified the first four listed books as "texts." The last two he regarded as textbook supplements. He describes his method of judging as follows:

For a summary comparison of the textbooks, I rated each in six areas: adequacy and effectiveness of presentation of (1) Univariate Description (frequency distributions and their graphs; central tendency; variability), (2) Bivariate Description (contingency table analysis, including nominal and ordinal measures of association; correlation and regression), (3) Probability (fundamental laws, definitions, and calculus; sampling distributions), and (4) Inferential Statistics (logic of; hypothesis testing; estimation; ANOVA), (5) Communication Effectiveness (readability; use and explanation of symbols; use of illustrations, drawings, tables, graphs, etc.) and (6) Use of Examples, and Exercises (number and pedagogical value). A 1 to 4 scale with pluses and minuses was used, in which 1 is inadequate, 2 is adequate, 3 is good, and 4 is superior. These ratings are found in table 1. It is apparent that I judged none of these texts to be superior. Indeed, in my judgment, all four are much inferior to Blalock's *Social Statistics* and Mueller, Schuessler, and Costner's *Statistical Reasoning in Sociology.*[1]

TABLE 1. Summary Ratings of Four Introductory Statistics Textbooks

	Daniel	Levin	Malec	Pine
Univariate description	1	3	3	3−
Bivariate description	1+	2	3+	2+
Probability	3+	2	2	2
Inferential statistics	3+	2+	2	2−
Communication effectiveness	2	3	3+	3−
Use of examples & exercises	3	4−	2	3

The following books are especially valuable when the researcher is seeking a readable step-by-step explanation or procedure. The selections are based on the simplicity of the description and the inclusion of illustrative examples.

Anderson, Theodore R., and Morris Zelditch, Jr. *A Basic Course in Statistics: With Sociological Applications.* 3rd ed. New York: Holt, Rinehart & Winston, 1975.
Step-by-step computation guides for all basic statistics; well illustrated.

Bernstein, Allen L. *A Handbook of Statistical Solutions for the Behavioral Sciences.* New York: Holt, Rinehart & Winston, 1964.
Presents solutions to typical problems.

Besag, Frank P., and Peter L. Besag. *Statistics for the Helping Professions.* Beverly Hills, CA: Sage, 1985.
Good application to nursing and social work.

Bohrnstedt, George W., and David Knoke. *Statistics for Data Analysis in the Social Sciences.* 2nd ed. Itasca, IL: Peacock, 1987.

Current applications of statistics to data analysis. See Chapter 12 for "path analysis."

Blalock, Hubert M., Jr. *Social Statistics.* Rev. ed. New York: McGraw-Hill, 1979.

Well-written book introducing the student to modern developments.

Child, Dennis. *The Essentials of Factor Analysis.* New York: Holt, Rinehart & Winston, 1973.

Elementary treatment with examples and application to psychology, sociology, and the medical sciences.

Conway, Freda. *Sampling: An Introduction for Social Sciences.* New York: Humanities Press, 1967.

Lucid, neatly organized book on statistics using large-sample theory.

Coombs, Clyde H., Robyn M. Dawes, and Amos Tversky. *Mathematical Psychology: An Elementary Introduction.* Englewood Cliffs, NJ: Prentice-Hall, 1970.

An elementary treatment with applications to psychology.

Crowley, Francis J., and Martin Cohen. *Basic Facts of Statistics.* New York: Collier, 1963.

Digests elementary statistics in a very brief and comprehensive manner within 62 pages.

Edwards, Allen. *Statistical Methods.* 2nd ed. New York: Holt, Rinehart & Winston, 1967.

Statistical techniques and methods presented for the student with a minimum amount of mathematical knowledge. Parametric and nonparametric methods are integrated into the text.

Freund, John E., Paul E. Livermore, and Irvin Miller. *Manual of Experimental Statistics.* Englewood Cliffs, NJ: Prentice-Hall, 1960.

Presents in outline form the most frequently used statistical techniques, including appropriate computing formulas and completely worked out examples of each method.

Hanushek, Eric A., and John E. Jackson. *Statistical Methods for Social Scientists.* New York: Academic Press, 1977.

Contemporary methods of quantitative analysis as used in sociology, economics, and political science. Good coverage of telephone surveys.

Kenny, David A. *Statistics for the Social and Behavioral Sciences.* Boston: Little, Brown, 1987.

For students majoring in social and behavioral sciences. Covers both descriptive and inferential statistics with appropriate examples. Writing is in an informal style.

Krishef, Curtis H. *Fundamental Statistics for Human Services and Social Work.* Boston: Duxbury, 1987.

Especially designed for students with a minimum background in mathematics.

Loether, Herman J., and Donald G. McTavish. *Descriptive Statistics and Inferential Statistics.* 3rd ed. Boston: Allyn & Bacon, 1988.

Careful treatment of statistical techniques that sociologists commonly use and illustrations showing how sociologists make use of them. *Inferential Statistics* focuses attention on statistical techniques that make inferences possible from samples.

Mansfield, Edwin. *Basic Statistics with Applications.* New York: W. W. Norton, 1986.

Practical exercises from psychology, political science, business, health care, and other.

Mendenhall, William. *Introduction to Probability and Probability Statistics.* Boston: Duxbury, 1987.

Excellent treatment of statistical inference, statistical design, variance, and nonparametric statistics.

Moore, David S. *Statistics: Concepts and Controversies.* 2nd ed. New York: Freeman, 1987.

Emphasizes ideas rather than techniques.

Mueller, John H., Karl F. Schuessler, and Herbert Costner. *Statistical Reasoning in Sociology.* 3rd ed. Boston: Houghton Mifflin, 1977.

Emphasizes reasons for each statistical procedure.

Schmid, Calvin F. *Handbook of Graphic Presentation.* New York: Ronald, 1954.

Methods for presenting social statistics in a visual manner.

Smith, Gary. *Statistical Reasoning.* Boston: Allyn & Bacon, 1985.

According to the author, "You will learn how to use probability and statistical reasoning, how to recognize the abuses of others, and how to compare claims of advertisers and politicians."

Tanur, Judith M. *Statistics: A Guide to Political and Social Issues.* San Francisco: Holden-Day, 1977.

Statistics applied to current political and social issues.

———, Frederick Mosteller, William H. Kruskul, Richard F. Link, Richard S. Pieters, and Gerald R. Rising. *Statistics: A Guide to the Unknown.* San Francisco: Holden-Day, 1972.

Everyday use of statistics.

Weiss, Robert S. *Statistics in Social Research.* New York: John Wiley, 1968.

The traditional topics are treated from the point of view of someone guiding a student through the research process.

Wike, Edward L. *Data Analysis: A Statistical Primer for Psychology Students.* Chicago: Aldine-Atherton, 1971.

A "how to do it" text that illustrates the use of statistics in data obtained from small samples. Intended for students who are conducting experiments for the first time. Organized around types of experimental designs.

Wright, Susan E. *Social Science Statistics.* Boston: Allyn & Bacon, 1986.

Traditional skills but with emphasis on understanding evaluation, interpretation, and communication.

Zeisel, Hans. *Say It with Figures.* 5th ed. New York: Harper & Row, 1968.

A guide to the assembly and interpretation of social statistics.

Zeller, Richard A., and Edward G. Carmines. *Statistical Analysis of Social Data.* Chicago: Rand McNally, 1978.

Good applications for the political scientist student.

Note

1. Royce Singleton, Jr., *Contemporary Sociology* 8 (January 1979): 114-16.

5.17   A SPECIALIZED BIBLIOGRAPHIC SECTION FOR THE ADVANCED STUDENT

5.17.a   Selected Readings on Causal Models and Multivariate Analysis

Bishop, Y. M. M., S. E. Fineberg, and P. W. Holland. *Discrete Multivariate Analysis.* Cambridge: MIT Press, 1975.

Blalock, Hubert M., Jr., ed. *Measurement in the Social Sciences: Theories and Strategies.* Chicago: Aldine, 1974.

———. *Causal Inferences in Non-Experimental Research.* Chapel Hill: University of North Carolina Press, 1964.

———, A. Aganbegian, F. M. Borodkin, Raymond Boudon, and Vittorio Capecchi, eds. *Quantitative Sociology: International Perspectives on Mathematical and Statistical Modelling.* New York: Academic Press, 1975.

Blalock, Hubert M., Jr., and Ann B. Blalock, eds. *Methodology in Social Research.* New York: McGraw-Hill, 1968.

Bohrnstedt, George W., and Edgar F. Borgatta, eds. *Social Measurement: Current Issues.* Beverly Hills, CA: Sage, 1981.

Cooley, William W., and Paul R. Lohnes. *Multivariate Data Analysis.* New York: John Wiley, 1971.

Coombs, Clyde H. *A Theory of Data.* New York: John Wiley, 1964.

Costner, Herbert L., ed. *Sociological Methodology.* San Francisco: Jossey-Bass, 1974.

Duncan, Otis Dudley. *Introduction to Structural Equation Models.* New York: Academic Press, 1975.

Dunteman, George H. *Introduction to Linear Models.* Beverly Hills, CA: Sage, 1984.

———. *Introduction to Multivariate Analysis.* Beverly Hills, CA: Sage, 1984.

Goldstein, Mathew, and William R. Dillon. *Discrete Discriminant Analysis.* New York: John Wiley, 1978.

Grawoig, Dennis E. *Decision Mathematics.* New York: McGraw-Hill, 1967.

Haberman, Shelby J. *Analysis of Qualitative Data.* Vol. 2. *New Developments.* New York: Academic Press, 1979.

Heise, David R. *Causal Analysis.* New York: John Wiley, 1975.

Kerlinger, Fred N., and Elazar J. Pedhazur. *Multiple Regression in Behavioral Research.* New York: Holt, Rinehart & Winston, 1973.

Leik, Robert K., and Barbara F. Meeker. *Mathematical Sociology.* Englewood Cliffs, NJ: Prentice-Hall, 1975.

Lieberman, Bernhardt. *Contemporary Problems in Statistics: A Book of Readings for the Behavioral Sciences.* New York: Oxford University Press, 1971.

McCleary, Richard, Richard A. Hay, Jr., and Associates. *Applied Time Series Analysis for the Social Sciences.* Beverly Hills, CA: Sage, 1980.

Morrison, Donald F. *Multivariate Statistical Methods.* New York: McGraw-Hill, 1967.

Nowak, S. "Some Problems of Causal Interpretation of Statistical Relationships." *Philosophy of Science* 27 (January 1960): 23-38.

Polk, Kenneth. "A Note on Asymmetric Causal Models." *American Sociological Review* 27 (August 1962): 539-42.

Robinson, W. S. "Asymmetric Causal Models: Comments on Polk and Blalock." *American Sociological Review* 27 (August 1962): 545-48.

Schuessler, Karl. *Analyzing Social Data.* Boston: Houghton Mifflin, 1971.

Simon, Herbert A. "Causal Ordering and Identifiability." In *Studies in Econometric Methods,* edited by W. C. Hood and T. C. Koopmans, 49-74. New York: John Wiley, 1953.

———. "Spurious Correlation: A Causal Interpretation." *Journal of the American Statistical Association* 49 (September 1954): 467-79.

———. *Models of Man: Social and Rational.* New York: John Wiley, 1957.

    See pp. 37-49.

Tabachnick, Barbara G., and Linda S. Fidell. *Using Multivariate Statistics.* New York: Harper & Row, 1983.

    Features comparison of SPSS and BMD programs, canonical correlation, discriminant function analysis, factor analysis, linear models, matrix algebra.

Tufte, Edward R. *Data Analysis for Politics and Policy.* Englewood Cliffs, NJ: Prentice-Hall, 1974.

5.17.b   Selected Readings on the Application of Mathematics to Social Analysis and Special Problems

Aigner, D. J., and A. S. Goldberger, eds. *Latent Variables in Socioeconomic Models.* Amsterdam: North-Holland, 1977.

Achew, Christopher H. *The Statistics Analysis of Quasi-Experiments.* Berkeley: University of California Press, 1987.

Bijnen, E. *Cluster Analysis.* Tilburg, Netherlands: Tilburg University Press, 1973.

    A sociologist describes cluster analysis and its social applications.

Boudon, Raymond. *Mathematical Structures of Social Mobility.* San Francisco: Jossey-Bass, 1973.

Box, G. E. P., and G. M. Jenkins. *Time Series Analysis: Forecasting and Contract.* San Francisco: Holden-Day, 1976.

Coleman, James S. *Introduction to Mathematical Sociology.* Glencoe, IL: Free Press, 1964.

    The emphasis in this book is on mathematics as a tool for the elaboration of sociological theory.

Coleman, James S. *The Mathematics of Collective Action.* Chicago: Aldine, 1973.

    A theory relating the decisions and actions of social growth with instrumental powers to the specific interests and resources of group members.

Dodd, Stuart C., and Stefan C. Christopher. "The Reactants Models." In *Essays in Honor of George Lundberg,* 143-79. Great Barrington, MA: Behavioral Research Council, 1968.

    A search for laws of communicative behavior by fitting curves to diffusion data as item moves through a population.

Doreian, Patrick. *Mathematics and the Study of Social Relations.* New York: Schocken, 1971.

Goldberg, Samuel. *Introduction to Difference Equations.* New York: John Wiley, 1958.

Revised edition of monograph on difference equations written in 1954 at the invitation of the SSRC Committee on the Mathematical Training of Social Scientists.

Hamlin, Robert L., R. Brooke Jacobsen, and Jerry L. Miller. *A Mathematical Theory of Social Change.* New York: John Wiley, 1973.

Harman, Harry H. *Modern Factor Analysis.* 2nd ed. Chicago: University of Chicago Press, 1967.

Hayes, Patrick. *Mathematical Methods in Social and Managerial Sciences.* New York: Wiley-Interscience, 1975.

Horst, Paul. *Factor Analysis of Data Matrices.* New York: Holt, Rinehart & Winston, 1967.

Jackson, David J., and Edgar F. Borgatta, eds. *Factor Analysis and Measurement: A Multidimensional Perspective.* Beverly Hills, CA: Sage, 1981.

Kemeny, John G., and Laurie J. Snell. *Mathematical Models in the Social Sciences.* Boston: Blaisdell, 1962.

This book is for a mathematics course, not a social science course; the problems in the social sciences are introduced only as an incentive to learn mathematics.

Kish, Leslie. *Statistical Design for Research.* New York: John Wiley, 1986.

Lazarsfeld, Paul F. "Notes on the History of Quantification in Sociology: Trends, Sources, and Problems." In *Quantification,* edited by Harry Woolf. Indianapolis: Bobbs-Merrill, 1961.

———, ed. *Mathematical Thinking in the Social Sciences.* Glencoe, IL: Free Press, 1954.

Lundberg, George A. "Statistics in Modern Social Thought." In *Contemporary Social Theory,* edited by Harry Elmer Barnes, Howard Becker, and Francis Bennett Becker, 110-40. New York: Appleton Century, 1940.

Historical account of the rise of social statistics.

Johnson, Dallas E., and George A. Milliken. *Analysis of Messy Data.* Vol. 1. *Designed Experiment.* New York: Van Nostrand Reinhold, 1984.

Long, J. Scott. *Confirmatory Factor Analysis: A Preface to LISREL.* Beverly Hills, CA: Sage, 1983.

Lorr, Maurice. *Cluster Analysis for Social Scientists: Techniques for Analyzing and Simplifying Complex Blocks of Data.* San Francisco: Jossey-Bass, 1983.

Martindale, Don. "Limits to the Uses of Mathematics in the Study of Sociology." In *Mathematics and the Social Sciences,* edited by James C. Charlesworth, 95-121. Philadelphia: American Academy Political and Social Science, 1963.

McGinnis, Robert. *Mathematical Foundations for Social Analysis.* Indianapolis: Bobbs-Merrill, 1965.

Provides an introduction to mathematical procedures increasingly employed in sociology: sets, relations, real numbers, matrices, and limits.

Merton, Robert K., James C. Coleman, and Peter H. Rossi, eds. *Qualitative and Quantitative Social Research: Papers in Honor of Paul F. Lazarsfeld.* New York: Free Press, 1979.

Mokken, R. J. A. *Theory and Procedure of Scale Analysis.* The Hague: Mouton, 1971.

Theoretical and practical issues of Guttman scale techniques.

Morrison, Denton E., and Ramon E. Henkel, eds. *The Significance Test Controversy: A Reader.* Chicago: Aldine, 1970.

Pollard, W. E. *Bayesian Statistics for Evaluation Research: An Introduction.* Beverly Hills, CA: Sage, 1985.

Rashevsky, Nicholas. *Mathematical Biology of Social Behavior.* Chicago: University of Chicago Press, 1950.

Application of mathematical methods to study of social stratification.

Solomon, Herbert, ed. *Mathematical Thinking in the Measurement of Behavior.* Glencoe, IL: Free Press, 1960.

Includes contributions by James S. Coleman on mathematics and small group research, Ernest W. Adams on utility theory, and Herbert Solomon on factor analysis.

Stone, Richard. "Mathematics in the Social Sciences." *Scientific American* 211 (September 1964): 168-86.

Stouffer, Samuel A., Louis Guttman, Edward A. Suchman, Paul F. Lazarsfeld, Shirley A. Star, and John A. Clausen. *Measurement and Prediction.* Princeton, NJ: Princeton University Press, 1950.

Theoretical and empirical analysis of scales and problems of prediction.

White, Harrison. "Uses of Mathematics in Sociology." In *Mathematics and the Social Sciences,* edited by James C. Charlesworth, 77-94. Philadelphia: American Academy of Political and Social Science, 1963.

————. *An Anatomy of Kinship.* Englewood Cliffs, NJ: Prentice-Hall, 1963.

Attempt to analyze logic underlying kinship systems by mathematical methods.

Zipf, George Kingsley. *Human Behavior and the Principle of Least Effort.* Reading, MA: Addison-Wesley, 1949.

Quantitative Applications in the Social Sciences

Brief, clearly articulated explanations of advanced methodological concepts have been developed by research specialists and published as a series by Sage Publications, 2455 Teller Rd., Newbury Park, CA 91320. A list of titles follows:

1. *Analysis of Variance* (2nd ed.), by Gudmund Iversen and Helmut Norpoth
2. *Operations Research Methods,* by Stuart Nagel with Marian Neef
3. *Causal Modeling* (2nd ed.), by Herbert B. Asher
4. *Tests of Significance,* by Ramon E. Henkel
5. *Cohort Analysis,* by Norval D. Glenn
6. *Canonical Analysis and Factor Comparison,* by Mark S. Levine
7. *Analysis of Nominal Data* (2nd ed.), by H. T. Reynolds
8. *Analysis of Ordinal Data,* by David K. Hildebrand, James D. Laing, and Howard Rosenthal
9. *Time Series Analysis: Regression Techniques* (2nd ed.), by Charles W. Ostrom, Jr.
10. *Ecological Inference,* by Laura Irwin Langbein and Allan J. Lichtman
11. *Multidimensional Scaling,* by Joseph B. Kruskal and Myron Wish
12. *Analysis of Covariance,* by Albert R. Wildt and Olli T. Ahtola
13. *Introduction to Factor Analysis: What It Is and How to Do It,* by Jae-on Kim and Charles W. Mueller
14. *Factor Analysis: Statistical Methods and Practical Issues,* by Jae-on Kim and Charles W. Mueller
15. *Multiple Indicators: An Introduction,* by John L. Sullivan and Stanley Feldman
16. *Exploratory Data Analysis,* by Frederick Hartwig with Brian E. Dearing
17. *Reliability and Validity Assessment,* by Edward G. Carmines and Richard A. Zeller
18. *Analyzing Panel Data,* by Gregory B. Markus
19. *Discriminant Analysis,* by William R. Klecka
20. *Log-Linear Models,* by David Knoke and Peter J. Burke
21. *Interrupted Time Series Analysis,* by David McDowall, Richard McCleary, Errol E. Meidinger, and Richard A. Hay, Jr.
22. *Applied Regression: An Introduction,* by Michael S. Lewis-Beck
23. *Research Designs,* by Paul Spector
24. *Unidimensional Scaling,* by John P. McIver and Edward G. Carmines
25. *Magnitude Scaling: Quantitative Measurement of Opinions,* by Milton Lodge
26. *Multiattribute Evaluation,* by Ward Edwards and J. Robert Newman
27. *Dynamic Modeling: An Introduction,* by R. Robert Huckfeldt, C. W. Kohfeld, and Thomas W. Likens
28. *Network Analysis,* by David Knoke and James H. Kuklinski
29. *Interpreting and Using Regression,* by Christopher H. Achen
30. *Test Item Bias,* by Steven J. Osterlind
31. *Mobility Tables,* by Michael Hout
32. *Measures of Association,* by Albert M. Liebetrau
33. *Confirmatory Factor Analysis: A Preface of LISREL,* by J. Scott Long
34. *Covariance Structure Models: An Introduction to LISREL,* by J. Scott Long
35. *Introduction to Survey Sampling,* by Graham Kalton

CONTENTS OF *SOCIOLOGICAL METHODOLOGY* 1969-1987

5.18

Sociological Methodology is an official publication of the American Sociological Association. It is an annual series that began in 1969 and was designed to keep social scientists abreast of methodological changes and innovations in all areas of sociological inquiry. Because of its importance in defining the cutting edge of the discipline, the contents are reproduced to provide a ready reference for the researcher. All volumes are published by Jossey-Bass, Inc., 615 Montgomery St., San Francisco, CA 94111.

1969: Edgar F. Borgatta and George W. Bohrnstedt, eds.

Part One: Path Analysis, Causal Inferences, and the Measurements of Change
1. "Principles of Path Analysis," Kenneth C. Land
2. "Problems in Path Analysis and Causal Inference," David R. Heise
3. "Contingencies in Constructing Causal Models," Otis Dudley Duncan
4. "Observations on the Measurement of Change," George W. Bohrnstedt

Part Two: General Papers
5. "Logic and Levels of Scientific Explanation," John T. Dody
6. "Ecological Variables," Desmond S. Cartwright
7. "Covariance Analysis in Sociological Research," Karl Schuessler
8. "Stochastic Processes," Thomas J. Fararo

Part Three: Shorter Papers and Notes
9. "Testing a Measurement Model," Richard Ofshe and Ronald E. Anderson
10. "Use of Ad Hoc Definitions," Jeffrey K. Hadden
11. "Probabilities from Longitudinal Records," Peter A. Morrison

1970: Edgar F. Borgatta and George W. Bohrnstedt, eds.

Part One: Theory Building and Causal Models
1. "Causal Inference from Panel Data," David R. Heise
2. "Heise's Causal Model Applied," Donald C. Pelz and Robert A. Lew
3. "Partials, Partitions, and Paths," Otis Dudley Duncan
4. "Evaluating Axiomatic Theories," Kenneth D. Bailey

Part Two: Measurement, Reliability, and Validity
5. "Statistical Estimation with Random Measurement Error," H. M. Blalock, Caryll S. Wells, and Lewis F. Carter
6. "Validity, Invalidity, and Reliability," David R. Heise and George Bohrnstedt
7. "Effect of Reliability and Validity on Power of Statistical Tests," T. Anne Cleary, Robert L. Linn, and G. William Walster
8. "Bivariate Agreement Coefficients for Reliability of Data," Klaus Krippendorff
9. "Validity and the Multitrait-Multimethod Matrix," Robert P. Althauser and Thomas A. Heberlein
10. "Validation of Reputational Leadership by the Multitrait-Multimethod Matrix," Gene F. Summers, Lauren H. Seiler, and Glenn Wiley

Part Three: Statistical Techniques
11. "Statistics According to Bayes," Gudmund R. Iversen
12. "Uncertainty Analysis Applied to Sociological Data," Doris R. Entwisle and Dennis Knepp
13. "Multivariate Analysis for Attribute Data," James S. Coleman
14. "Statistical Significance as a Decision Rule," G. William Walster and T. Anne Cleary

Part Four: Mathematical Sociology
15. "Mathematical Formalization of Durkheim's Theory of Division of Labor," Kenneth C. Land
16. "Status Dynamics," Thomas J. Fararo
17. "Structure of Semantic Space," Andy B. Anderson

1971: Herbert L. Costner, ed.

Part One: Strategies of Data Production
1. "Systematic Observation of Natural Social Phenomena," Albert J. Reiss, Jr.
2. "Detection Theory and Problems of Psychosocial Discrimination," Darrell K. Adams and Z. Joseph Ulehla
3. "Coding Responses to Open-Ended Questions," Kenneth C. W. Kammeyer and Julius Roth

Part Two: Measurement Error in Regression and Path Analysis
4. "The Treatment of Unobservable Variables in Path Analysis," Robert M. Hauser and Arthur S. Goldberger
5. "Robustness in Regression Analysis," George W. Bohrnstedt and T. Michael Carter
6. "Techniques for Using Ordinal Measures in Regression and Path Analysis," Morgan Lyons

Part Three: Path and Process Models
7. "Formal Theory," Kenneth C. Land
8. "Key Variables," Phillip Bonacich and Kenneth D. Bailey
9. "Coleman's Process Approach," Martin Jaeckel

Part Four: Association and Prediction of Variables
10. "Integrated Approach to Measuring Association," Robert K. Leik and Walter R. Grove
11. "Continuities in Social Prediction," Karl Schuessler

1972: Herbert L. Costner, ed.

1. "Strategies for Meaningful Comparison," Ronald Schoenberg
2. "Unmeasured Variables in Linear Models for Panel Analysis," Otis Dudley Duncan
3. "Polythetic Reduction of Monothetic Property Space," Kenneth Bailey
4. "The Generation of Confidence: Evaluating Research Findings by Random Subsample Replication," Bernard M. Finifter
5. "Technique for Analyzing Overlapping Memberships," Phillip Bonacich
6. "Retest of a Measurement Model," Cynthia J. Flynn and Lewis F. Carter
7. "Using Monotone Regression to Estimate a Correlation Coefficient," Lawrence S. Mayer

1973-74: Herbert L. Costner, ed.

"Prologue," Herbert L. Costner
1. "Some Issues in Sociological Measurement," David R. Heise
2. "Theta Reliability and Factor Scaling," David J. Armor

3. "Construction of Composite Measures by the Canonical-Factor-Regression Method," Michael Patrick Allen
4. "Approaches to the Interpretation of Relationships in the Multitrait-Multimethod Matrix," Duane F. Alwin
5. "Inferring Validity from the Multitrait-Multimethod Matrix: Another Assessment," Robert P. Althauser
6. "Correlation of Ratios or Difference Scores Having Common Terms," Glenn V. Fuguitt and Stanley Lieberson
7. "Alternative Approaches to Analysis-of-Variance Tables," Peter J. Burke and Karl Schuessler
8. "Hierarchical Models for Significance Tests in Multivariate Contingency Tables: An Exegesis of Goodman's Recent Papers," James A. Davis
9. "Questions About Attitude Survey Questions," Howard Schuman and Otis Dudley Duncan
10. "Problems of Statistical Estimation and Causal Inference in Time-Series Regression Models," Douglas A. Hibbs, Jr.
11. "Spectral Analysis and the Study of Social Change," Thomas F. Mayer and William Ray Arney
12. "Social Mobility Models for Heterogeneous Populations," Burton Singer and Seymour Spilerman

1975: David R. Heise, ed.

1. "Toward the Integration of Content Analysis and General Methodology," John Markoff, Gilbert Shapiro, and Sasha R. Weitman
2. "Cluster Analysis," Kenneth D. Bailey
3. "Scaling Replicated Conditional Rank-Order Data," Forrest W. Young
4. "Method for Classifying Interval-Scale and Ordinal-Scale Data," Kenneth R. Bryson and David P. Phillips
5. "Multiple Indicators and the Relationship Between Abstract Variables," Lawrence S. Mayer and Mary Sue Younger

1976: David R. Heise, ed.

1. "Local Structure in Social Networks," Paul W. Holland and Samuel Leinhardt
2. "Comparing Causal Models," David A. Specht and Richard D. Warren
3. "The Relationship Between Modified and Usual Multiple-Regression Approaches to the Analysis of Dichotomous Variables," Leo A. Goodman
4. "Analyzing Contingency Tables with Linear Flow Graphs," D. Systems and James A. Davis
5. "Predictive-Logic Approach to Causal Models of Qualitative Variates," David K. Hildebrand, James D. Laing, and Howard Rosenthal
6. "Effects of Grouping on Measures of Ordinal Association," Roland K. Hawkes
7. "Can We Find a Genuine Ordinal Slope Analogue?" H. M. Blalock, Jr.
8. "Using Assumptions of Linearity to Establish a Metric," Phillip Bonacich and Douglas Kirby
9. "Monotonic Regression Analysis for Ordinal Variables," Richard K. Leik
10. "Causal Models with Nominal and Ordinal Data," Richard K. Leik
11. "Rank-Sum Comparisons Between Groups," Stanley Lieberson

1977: David R. Heise, ed.

1. "The Epistemological Bases of Social Order: Toward Ethnoparadigm Analysis," Allen W. Imershein

2. "Estimation in Panel Models: Results on Pooling Cross-Sections and Time Series," Michael T. Hannan and Alice A. Young
3. "Assessing Reliability and Stability in Panel Models," Blair Wheaton, Bengt Muthén, Duane F. Alwin, and Gene F. Summers
4. "On Analyzing the Effects of Policy Interventions: Box-Jenkins and Box-Tiao Versus Structural Equation Models," Douglas A. Hibbs, Jr.
5. "Estimates for Differential Equation Models of Social Phenomena," Patrick Doreian and Norman P. Hummon
6. "Estimating Rates from Retrospective Questions," Aage B. Sørensen
7. "Network Time Series from Archival Records," Ronald S. Burt and Nan Lin
8. "An Examination of CONCOR and Related Methods for Blocking Sociometric Data," Joseph E. Schwartz
9. "Statistical Inference and Statistical Power in Applications of the General Linear Model," William T. Bielby and James R. Kluegel

1978: Karl F. Schuessler, ed.

1. "Understanding World Models," Nathan Keyfitz
2. "Forecasting Sociological Phenomena: Application of Box-Jenkins Methodology to Suicide Rates," Gideon Vigderhous
3. "Analyzing Political Participation Data with a MIMIC Model," David C. Stapleton
4. "The Allocation of Time Among Individuals," Christopher Winship
5. "Using Boolean Algebra to Analyze Overlapping Memberships," Phillip Bonacich
6. "Parametrizing Age, Period, and Cohort Effects: An Application to U.S. Delinquency Rates, 1964-1973," Thomas W. Pullum
7. "Measures of Association for Multiple Regression Models with Ordinal Predictor Variables," Lawrence S. Mayer and Jeffrey A. Robinson
8. "Multiple Regression with a Categorical, Interval-Level Control Variable: The Between-Groups Component," Robert H. Somers
9. "Tracing Members of a Panel: A 17-Year Follow-Up," Brian R. Clarridge, Linda L. Sheehy, and Tarissa S. Hauser
10. "Statistical Analysis of Qualitative Variation," Alan Agresti and Barbara F. Agresti
11. "The Reliability of Variables Measured as the Number of Events in an Interval of Time," Paul D. Allison
12. "The Reliability of Products of Two Random Variables," George W. Bohrnstedt and Gerald Marwell

1979: Karl F. Schuessler, ed.

1. "Identification and Estimation of Age-Period-Cohort Models in the Analysis of Discrete Archival Data," Stephen E. Fienberg and William M. Mason
2. "Multiway Contingency Analysis with a Scaled Response or Factor," Otis Dudley Duncan and James A. McRae, Jr.
3. "On the Design Matrix Strategy in the Analysis of Categorical Data," Mark Evers and N. Krishnan Namboodiri
4. "A Note on Fitting and Interpreting Parameters in Models for Categorical Data," Stephen E. Fienberg
5. "The Utility of Systems of Simultaneous Logistic Response Equations," Stephen S. Brier
6. "Simultaneous Equation Models and Two-Stage Least Squares," John Fox
7. "Detection of Specification Errors in Linear Structural Equation Models," W. E. Saris, W. M. de Pijper, and P. Zegwaart
8. "Clustering on the Main Diagonal in Mobility Matrices," Burton Singer and Seymour Spilerman

9. "Approaches to the Censoring Problem in Analysis of Event Histories," Nancy Brandon Tuma and Michael T. Hannan
10. "The Assessment of 'No Opinion' in Attitude Surveys," Howard Schuman and Stanley Presser
11. "Some Problems of Inference from Chain Data," Bonnie H. Erickson
12. "A Note on Classifying Ordinal-Scale Data," Nan M. Laire
13. "Exploratory Data Analysis: An Introduction to Selected Methods," Samuel Leinhardt and Stanley S. Wasserman

1980: Karl F. Schuessler, ed.

1. "The Welfare Approach to Measuring Inequality," Joseph Schwartz and Christopher Winship
2. "The Continuing Debate over the Use of Ratio Variables: Facts and Fiction," Susan B. Long
3. "Measurement Models for Response Errors in Surveys: Issues and Applications," Duane F. Alwin and David J. Jackson
4. "Binary Variables and Index Construction," Jae-On Kim and James Rabjohn
5. "Assessing the Reliability of Linear Composites," Vernon L. Greene and Edward G. Carmines
6. "The Interpretation of Net Migration Rates," Stanley Lieberson
7. "Multidimensionality in Population Analysis," Nathan Keyfitz
8. "Modeling Macro Social Change," Kenneth C. Land
9. "Testing Key Hypotheses in Panel Analysis," Otis Dudley Duncan
10. "A Reexamination of Selection and Growth Processes in the Nonequivalent Control Group Design," David A. Kenny and Steven H. Cohen
11. "Maximum-Likelihood Estimation in Panel Studies with Missing Data," Margaret Mooney Marini, Anthony R. Olsen, and Donald B. Rubin
12. "When Can Interdependence in a Dynamic System of Qualitative Variables Be Ignored?" Nancy Brandon Tuma
13. "A Stochastic Model for Directed Graphs with Transition Rates Determined by Reciprocity," Stanley S. Wasserman
14. "Some Exploratory Methods for Modeling Mobility Tables and Other Cross-Classified Data," Robert M. Hauser
15. "The Measurement and Decomposition of Causal Effects in Nonlinear and Nonadditive Models," Ross M. Stolzenberg
16. "The Algebra of Blockmodeling," Phillip Bonacich and Maureen J. McConaghy
17. "The Application of Bayesian Techniques in Randomized Response," John D. Spurrier and W. J. Padgett
18. "Quantitative Coefficients for Selecting a Measure of Central Location," Jean D. Gibbons and Gordon R. Stavig

1981: Samuel Leinhardt, ed.

1. "Production Markets as Induced Role Structures," Harrison C. White
2. "Structural Models for Discrete Data: The Analysis of Discrete Choice," Charles F. Manski
3. "A Survey of Statistical Methods for Graph Analysis," Ove Frank
4. "Categorical Data Analysis of Single Sociometric Relations," Stephen E. Fienberg and Stanley S. Wasserman
5. "Three Elementary Views of Log Linear Models for the Analysis of Cross-Classifications Having Ordered Categories," Leo A. Goodman
6. "A Comparison of Alternative Models for Analyzing the Scalability of Response Patterns," Clifford C. Clogg and Darwin O. Sawyer

7. "Two Faces of Panel Analysis: Parallels with Comparative Cross-Sectional Analysis and Time-Lagged Association," Otis Dudley Duncan
8. "Estimation of Nonstationary Markov Chains from Panel Data," Burton Singer
9. "Spectral Decomposition as a Tool in Comparative Mobility Research," David D. McFarland
10. "Estimating Linear Models with Spatially Distributed Data," Patrick Doreian
11. "Research on Interviewing Techniques," Charles F. Cannell, Peter V. Miller, and Lois Oksenberg.

1982: Samuel Leinhardt, ed.

1. "Nonparametric and Partially Parametric Approaches to Event-History Analysis," Nancy Brandon Tuma
2. "Discrete-Time Methods for the Analysis of Event Histories," Paul D. Allison
3. "New Methods for Analyzing Individual Event Histories," Christopher J. Flinn and James J. Heckman
4. "Applied Nonlinear Smoothing," Paul F. Velleman
5. "Candidate Ordering and Issue Circles: Structural Analysis of the 1980 Presidential Primary Campaign," James R. Beniger
6. "Structural Analysis of Multivariate Data: A Review," Harri Kiiveri and T. P. Speed
7. "Asymptotic Confidence Intervals for Indirect Effects in Structural Equation Models," Michael E. Sobel
8. "Criticism and Influence Analysis in Regression," R. Dennis Cook and Sanford Weisberg

1983-84: Samuel Leinhardt, ed.

1. "Methods for Large-Scale Surveys and Experiments," Judith M. Tanur
2. "Contextual Analysis Through the Multilevel Linear Model," William M. Mason, George Y. Wong, and Barbara Entwisle
3. "Linearity in Log-Linear Analysis," Arthur L. Stinchcombe
4. "Power Transformations for Data Analysis," Michael A. Stoto and John D. Emerson
5. "Some Large-Sample Standard Errors for Components of a Mean Difference Under a Linear Model," Michael E. Sobel
6. "Durations in Social States: Concepts of Inertial and Related Comparisons in Stochastic Models," Yigal Gerchak
7. "Impermeability and Distance: A Method for the Analysis of Some Structural Characteristics Underlying Social Processes," Kazuo Yamaguchi
8. "Information-Theoretic Scales for Measuring Cultural Rule Systems," Jonathan L. Gross
9. "Local Blockmodel Algebras for Analyzing Social Networks," Lawrence L. Wu
10. "Roles and Positions: A Critique and Extension of the Blockmodeling Approach," Christopher Winship and Michael Mandel

1985: Nancy Brandon Tuma, ed.

1. "Measures of Segregation," David R. James and Karl E. Taeuber
2. "An Elaboration of Guttman Scaling with Rasch Models for Measurement," David Andrich
3. "Simultaneous Latent Structure Analysis in Several Groups," Clifford C. Clogg and Leo A. Goodman
4. "On the Dimensions of Political Alienation in America," William M. Mason, James S. House, and Steven S. Martin

5. "Use of Null Models in Evaluating the Fit of Covariance Structure Models," Michael E. Sobel and George W. Bohrnstedt
6. "The Deviant Dynamics of Death in Heterogeneous Populations," James W. Vaupel and Anatoli I. Yashin
7. "Latent Variables in the Analysis of Limited Dependent Variables," Ronald Schoenberg
8. "Correcting for Unmeasured Heterogeneity in Hazard Models Using the Heckman-Singer Procedure," James Trussell and Toni Richards
9. "A Continuous-Time Multivariate Gaussian Stochastic Model of Change in Discrete and Continuous Variables," Kenneth G. Manton and Max A. Woodbury
10. "Robust M-Estimation of Location and Regression," Lawrence L. Wu

1986: Nancy Brandon Tuma, ed.

1. "Direction-of-Wording Effects in Dichotomous Social Life Feeling Items," Mark Reiser, Michael Wallace, and Karl Schuessler
2. "Techniques for Disaggregating Centrality Scores in Social Networks," Mark S. Mizruchi, Peter Mariolis, Michael Schwartz, and Beth Mintz
3. "A Methodological Analysis of Intergroup Marriage," Robert Schoen
4. "A General Reliability Model for Categorical Data Applied to Guttman Scales and Current-Status Data," Joseph E. Schwartz
5. "Statistical Power in Covariance Structure Models," Ross L. Matsueda and William T. Bielby
6. "Some New Results on Indirect Effects and Their Standard Errors in Covariance Structure Models," Michael E. Sobel
7. "Linear Stochastic Differential Equation Models for Panel Data with Unobserved Variables," Gerhard Arminger
8. "Alternative Approaches to Unobserved Heterogeneity in the Analysis of Repeatable Events," Kazuo Yamaguchi
9. "Heterogeneity and Interdependence: A Test Using Survival Models," Christopher Winship
10. "Simulation Methods for Analyzing Continuous Time Event-History Models," Douglas A. Wolf

1987: Clifford C. Clogg, ed.

1. "A Methodological Framework for the Sociology of Culture," Wendy Griswold
2. "Total, Direct, and Indirect Effects in Structural Equation Models," Kenneth A. Bollen
3. "Estimation of Linear Models with Incomplete Data," Paul D. Allison
4. "The Detection and Correction of Specification Errors in Structural Equation Models," Willem E. Saris, Albert Satorra, and Dag Sörbom
5. "Logit-Based Interval Estimation for Binomial Data Using the Jeffreys Prior," Donald B. Rubin and Nathaniel Schenker
6. "Association and Heterogeneity: Structural Models of Similarities and Differences," Michael Hout, Otis Dudley Duncan, and Michael E. Sobel
7. "Evaluating Census Data Quality Using Intensive Reinterviews: A Comparison of U.S. Census Bureau Methods and Rasch Methods," Robert A. Johnson and Henry F. Woltman
8. "Scaling Via Models for the Analysis of Association: Social Background and Educational Careers in France," Herbert L. Smith and Maurice A. Garnier
9. "Using Goodness of Fit and Other Criteria to Choose Among Competing Duration Models: A Case Study of Hutterite Data," James J. Heckman and James R. Walker
10. "Grade-of-Membership Techniques for Studying Complex Event History Processes with Unobserved Covariates," Kenneth G. Manton, Eric Stallard, Max A. Woodbury, H. Dennis Tolley, and Anatoli I. Yashin

11. "Effect Displays for Generalized Linear Models," John Fox
12. "Making It Count Even More: A Review and Critique of Stanley Lieberson's *Making It Count: The Improvement of Social Theory and Research*," Gerhard Arminger and George W. Bohrnstedt
13. "Advancing Social Research: An Essay Based on Stanley Lieberson's *Making It Count*," Burton Singer and Margaret Mooney Marini

---

5.19   DICTIONARY OF NEWER STATISTICAL TOOLS AND METHODOLOGICAL TECHNIQUES

The concepts in this section are among those that commonly appear in the sociological research writing found in major journals. The explanations given are attempts to state as simply as possible what these concepts mean. References are given after the discussion of each concept to indicate research applications. The aim is to provide the reader with understanding but not to formulate operational procedures. This latter kind of information can be found in the various statistical bibliographies cited previously.

Bayesian Methods: Bayesian Inference, Bayesian Statistics

Bayesians believe that scientists should qualify their opinions as probabilities before performing their experiments, do the experiment so as to collect data bearing on these opinions, and then use a Bayesian theorem formally to revise prior probabilities to yield new posterior probabilities. Posterior probabilities are scientists' revised opinions in the light of information provided by the data. That is the key idea behind all Bayesian methods.

Statistically, a Bayesian inference is simply a conditional probability. It gives the probability of a cause (hypothesis) on condition that the effect (evidence) has occurred. The usual ordering of reasoning is reversed: from effect to cause rather than the other way around. In its emphasis on subjective beliefs, a Bayesian inference has the distinctive characteristic of refining one's probability.

Bayesian methods are seldom used in sociology, although they have been used advantageously in economics and psychology. A Bayesian approach would seem to have value to sociology whenever the social analyst works backward from effect to causes, as indicated in the method of analytical induction. In this method the cause must be present whenever the effect is present; it must be absent whenever the effect is absent. The body of statistics dealing with Bayesian inferences is called Bayesian statistics. Such statistical methods utilize prior information (objective or subjective) about parameters. The term has also been applied to statistical methods based on the concept of subjective or personal probability.

References

Foschi, Martha, and Ricardo Foschi. "Bayesian Model for Performance Expectations." *Social Psychology Quarterly* 42 (1979): 232-42.
Lindley, D. V. *Introduction to Probability and Statistics from a Bayesian Viewpoint.* Parts 1-2. Cambridge: Cambridge University Press, 1965.

Phillips, Lawrence D. *Bayesian Statistics for Social Scientists.* London: Thomas
Pollard, William E. *Bayesian Statistics for Evaluation Research: An Introduction.* B
   1986.
Schmitt, Samuel A. *Measuring Uncertainty: An Elementary Introduction to Bayesian Sta*
   MA: Addison-Wesley, 1969.
Schuessler, Karl F. "Prologue." In *Sociological Methodology 1980.* San Francisco: Jossey-Bass,

Canonical Correlation

The canonical correlation is the maximum correlation between two sets of independent and dependent variables. It can be compared to the simpler coefficient of multiple correlation, which provides the maximum correlation between a number of independent variables with a single dependent variable.

The basic idea of canonical correlation is that, through least squares analysis, two linear composites are formed, one for the independent variables, X_J, and one for the dependent variables, Y_N. The correlation between these two composites is the canonical correlation R_c. The square of the canonical correlation, R_c^2, is an estimate of the variance shared by the two composites.

References

Kerlinger, Fred N., and Elazar J. Pedhazur. *Multiple Regression in Behavior Research.* New York: Holt,
   Rinehart & Winston, 1973, 341-49.
Levine, Mark S. *Canonical Analysis and Factor Comparison.* Beverly Hills, CA: Sage, 1977.
Reeve, Vannemar, and Fred C. Pampel. "The American Perception of Class and Status." *American Sociological Review* 42 (June 1977): 432-37.

Causal Analysis

Causal analysis is given high priority in all branches of social science. Causal judgments are made to *explain* the occurrence of events to understand *why* particular events occur. With causal knowledge it is often possible to predict events—and to exercise some measure of control over them. The article by Marini and Singer shown in the following references contains an excellent bibliography.

Richard A. Berk provides an excellent review of causal influence in sociology in his essay "Causal Inference for Sociological Data" (in Smelser's *Handbook of Sociology*; see following references), which is followed by an extensive bibliography. Berk points out that increased attention was focused on causality when Hubert M. Blalock and Otis Dudley Duncan introduced "structural equations" to serve as a model from which causal inferences could be drawn when experimental methods could not be employed. The description of path analysis as causal analysis is made in Part 3 of the Smelser volume. The promises and limitations are pointed out. Bernett has observed, in his 70-year survey of causal terminology in American sociology, "Causality in sociology has proved to be a fragile core concept."

References

Berk, Richard A. "Causal Inference for Sociological Data." In *Handbook of Sociology*, edited by Neil J.
   Smelser, 155-71. Newbury Park, CA: Sage, 1988.
Bernett, Christopher. "The Career of Causal Analysis in American Sociology." *British Journal of Sociology* 34, no. 2 (1983): 230-54.
Kish, Leslie. *Statistical Design for Research.* New York: John Wiley, 1987.

ausality in the Social Sciences." In *Sociological Methodology*
7-409. Washington, DC: American Sociological Association,

Nelson & Sons, 1973.
verly Hills, CA: Sage,
stics. Reading,
981.

311

ch the researcher identifies items that "cluster"
orrelation, is called *cluster analysis*. For example,
s because of such factors as the ability to exercise
vork with people and the desire to earn a substantial
operty. If various questions about job characteristics
esearcher might find that items would fall into three
uld include items that are more highly intercorrelated
with items outside that cluster.

e developed and rows and columns of the matrix
rearranged so that the more highly intercorrelated items form triangular "bunches"
at different points along the diagonal. In this way, the nature of interacting forces can
be revealed with precision.

References

Anderberg, Michael R. *Cluster Analysis for Applications*. New York: Academic Press, 1973.
Everitt, Brian. *Cluster Analysis*. London: Heinemann, 1974.
Loether, Herman J., and Donald G. McTavish. *Descriptive and Inferential Statistics: An Introduction*. 3rd ed. Boston: Allyn & Bacon, 1988, 380-84.

Cohort Analysis

The term *cohort* refers to persons of similar age or other selected characteristics matched so that the defining characteristic can be held constant. A cohort analysis is the study of one or more cohorts in which designated variables are assessed. Such analysis is very valuable for occupational and industrial sociology because cohorts in the labor force are studied both in cross-sectional and longitudinal designs. Population, health sciences, criminology, gerontology, and many other fields frequently use cohort analysis.

References

Glenn, Norval D. *Cohort Analysis*. Beverly Hills, CA: Sage, 1977.
Lane, Angela. "The Occupational Achievement Process, 1940-1949: A Cohort Analysis." *American Sociological Review* 40 (August 1975): 472-82.
Riley, Matilda W. "Aging and Cohort Succession: Interpretations and Misinterpretations." *Public Opinion Quarterly* 37 (1973): 35-49.

Communication Network Analysis

This is a method of research for identifying the communication network in a system. Much human behavior occurs in the interaction through which one individual exchanges information with one or more other individuals. A communication network depicts the interconnected individuals who are linked by patterned communication flows. Analysis includes various research procedures, including identification of cliques, specialized communication roles (liaisons, bridges, and isolates), and communication structural indices such as communication connectedness for individuals, dyads, personal networks, cliques, or entire systems.

References

Burt, Ronald S., Michael J. Minor, and Associates. Applied Network Analysis: A Methodological Introduction. Beverly Hills, CA: Sage, 1983.

Holland, Paul W., and Samuel Leinhardt, eds. *Perspectives on Social Network Research.* New York: Academic Press, 1979.

Marsden, Peter V., and Nan Lin, eds. *Social Structure and Network Analysis.* Beverly Hills, CA: Sage, 1982.

Rogers, Everett M., and D. Lawrence Kincaid. *Communication Networks: Toward a New Paradigm for Research.* New York: Free Press, 1981.

Decomposition of a Dependent Variable

Many social variables are composites. For example, population growth is the sum of natural increase and net migration; each of the latter may be further decomposed. Natural increase can be calculated as births minus deaths; net migration is the difference between in- and out-migration. When such decomposition is possible, it is of interest (a) to compute the relative contributions of the components to variation in the composite variable and (b) to ascertain how causes affecting the composite variables are transmitted through the respective components.

Reference

Duncan, Otis Dudley. "Path Analysis: Sociological Examples." *American Journal of Sociology* 72 (July 1966).

Decomposition of Effects in Causal Modeling

It is important to interpret patterns of direct and indirect causation in path models and other structural equation models. Such interpretation helps answer questions of the form: How does variable X affect variable Y? How much does mechanism Z contribute to the effect of X or Y? Does mechanism Z contribute as much to explaining the effect of X on Y in population A as in population B?

Causal modeling usually entails decomposing the total effect of the antecedent variable into direct and indirect components. The direct effect of one variable on another is simply that part of the total effect not transmitted via intervening variables. Indirect effects are those parts of a variable's total effect transmitted or mediated by variables intervening between the cause and effect interest in a model. *Decomposition* here means calculating total, direct, and indirect effects in multiequation models.

References

Alwin, Duane F., and Robert M. Hauser. "The Decomposition of Effects in Pattern Analysis." *American Sociological Review* 40 (February 1975): 37-47.

Parcel, Toby L. "Race, Regional Labor Markets, and Earnings." *American Sociological Review* 44 (April 1979): 262-79.

Schlaifer, Robert. "The Relay Assembly Test Room: An Alternative Statistical Interpretation." *American Sociological Review* 45 (December 1980): 995-1005.

See especially p. 997, "Importance of Explanatory Variables and Decomposition of R^2."

The Delphi Technique

The Delphi technique is a forecasting methodology for generating expert opinion on any given subject. It was developed in the early 1950s by the RAND Corporation as an attempt to eliminate interpersonal feelings and actions as the controlling variables, as commonly happens when experts interact in meetings. Delphi uses written answers rather than placing experts in a face-to-face meeting or conference. The written anonymity prevents domination by certain individuals in a group meeting. It is especially helpful when the experts are widely scattered and cannot get together physically. It can also be useful in situations where respondents are hostile to one another.

References

Allen, T. Harrell. *New Methods in Social Science Research: Policy Sciences and Futures Research.* New York: Praeger, 1978, 119-31.

Dalkey, Norman, and D. Rourke. *Experimental Assessment of Delphi Procedures with Group Value Judgments.* R-612-ARPA. Santa Monica, CA: RAND Corporation, 1971.

Delbecq, Andre. *Group Techniques for Program Planning.* Glenview, IL: Scott, Foresman, 1975.

Discriminant (Function) Analysis

The discriminant function was originally proposed by R. A. Fisher (see following references). It was designed to aid in the classification of an individual observation into one of two groups. The discriminant function has been defined as a linear combination of a set of n variables that will classify into two different classes (or groups) the events or items for which the measurements of the n variables are available, and will do so with the smallest possible proportion of misclassifications. It is useful, for example, in the problem of classifying persons into two social groups, such as culturally assimilated and culturally alienated. (See also "Multiple Discriminant [Function] Analysis.")

References

Fisher, R. A. "The Use of Multiple Measurements in Taxonomic Problems." *Annals of Eugenics* 7 (1936): 179-88.

Klecka, William R. *Discriminant Analysis.* Beverly Hills, CA: Sage, 1978.

Van de Geer, John P. *Introduction to Multivariate Analysis for the Social Sciences.* San Francisco: Freeman, 1971, 243-72.

Vanneman, Reeve, and Fred C. Pampel. "The American Perception of Class and Status." *American Sociological Review* 42 (June 1977): 422-37.

Dummy Variable: Dummy Variable Regression Analysis

Dummy variables are dichotomous variables employed when the researcher is working with categorical or nominal variables. The binary nature of the computer is happy with dummy variables that indicate the presence (scored 1) or absence (scored 0) of a certain characteristic for each individual respondent. For qualitative variables it is especially useful. For example, marital status can be coded using four dummy variables:

currently married: 1 = yes; 0 = no

never married: 1 = yes; 0 = no

widowed: 1 = yes; 0 = no

separated: 1 = yes; 0 = no

divorced: pattern of 0, 0, 0, 0 would indicate a person is divorced; no dummy variable needed

If a person were widowed, rather than having a score of 3, he or she would have four scores, one on each of the four dummy variables: 0010.

These dummy variables are all included in the usual multiple regression analysis. When a zero score appears for an individual on one of the dummy variables, that is the regression weight placed in the regression equation. Otherwise, the regression weight becomes the value assigned by the researcher to a particular status.

Dummy variables can be used as independent variables in standard score or raw score form, and they can be used in path analysis. Dummy variables are useful if a researcher wishes to "score" specific combinations of values of variables to search for expected statistical interaction in a multiple regression equation when otherwise the model would assume an additive relationship among variables. These efforts are called *dummy variable regression analysis.*

References

Koo, Hagen, and Doo-Seung Houg. "Class and Income Inequality in Korea." *American Sociological Review* 45 (August 1980): 610-26.

Loether, Herman J., and Donald G. McTavish. *Descriptive Statistics for Sociologists.* Boston: Allyn & Bacon, 1974, 333-34.

Rindfuss, Ronald R., Larry Bumpass, and Craig St. John. "Education and Fertility: Implications for the Roles Women Occupy." *American Sociological Review* 45 (June 1980): 431-47.

Event History Analysis

Event history analysis uses methods for analyzing data on the number, timing, and sequencing of events experienced by persons and entities. Essentially, an event is a change of state, such as the change from being single to being married. Events are separated by time intervals. Marriage serves as an episode until divorce or death occurs. Events can also be analyzed for such entities as firms or nations, which experience firm failures, national wars, depressions, and revolutions.

The potential utility of event analysis for sociology is great. The procedures that have been developed make use of data on the order of the occurrence of events instead of exact dates. Sociologists and economists have found event analysis useful in the study of work histories and various problems of labor force dynamics. Sequential data are available for the study of annual fertility, the number of children in integrated schools, yearly costs of criminal victimization, and so on.

The general analytic approach for both persons and entities involves positing a stochastic model that relates the probability of no change in state, or a change in state, or movement among various states. A sample of event histories is used to estimate the population parameters.

References

Allison, Paul D. *Event History Analysis: Regression for Longitudinal Event Data.* Beverly Hills, CA: Sage, 1985.

Cox, D. R., and P. A. W. Lewis. *The Statistical Analysis of Series of Events.* London: Methuen, 1966.

Karlin, S., and H. M. Taylor. *A First Course on Stochastic Processes.* New York: Academic Press, 1975.

Flinn, Christopher J., and James J. Heckman. "New Methods for Analyzing Individual Event Histories." In *Sociological Methodology 1982*, edited by Samuel Leinhardt. San Francisco: Jossey-Bass, 1982.
Supplemented with an excellent bibliography.

Log-Linear Modeling and Analysis

A recent development in contingency table analysis, log-linear modeling applies new techniques to analyzing multidimensional tables. In the past, purely categorical data have been difficult to analyze, especially in the construction of multivariate models. Leo A. Goodman has said that log-linear models not only help one find bivariate relationships and higher-order interactions in complex tables but can be viewed as analogous to the analysis of simultaneous equations. The promise is that the exploration of polls and surveys may have caught up with causal and path analysis. Some researchers caution that the same concepts they employ in studying interval-level data may not apply unambiguously in interpreting cross-classifications of categorical data.

Essential to log-linear modeling is building a model for the expected frequencies in a multidimensional population cross-classification by introducing so-called main and interaction effects. It is sometimes more convenient to work with the natural logarithms of the expected frequencies. A model is to be described by the set of "fitted marginals" tables used in estimating the expected frequencies under the model.

References

Goodman, Leo A. "Causal Analysis of Data from Panel Studies and Other Kinds of Surveys." *American Journal of Sociology* 79 (March 1973): 1135-91.

——— . *Analyzing Qualitative Categorical Data: Log-Linear Models and Latent Structure Analysis.* Cambridge, MA: Abt, 1978.

Knoke, David, and Peter J. Burke. *Log-Linear Models.* Beverly Hills, CA: Sage, 1980.

Reynolds, H. T. "Some Comments on the Causal Analysis of Surveys with Log-Linear Models." *American Journal of Sociology* 83 (July 1977): 127-43.
See excellent bibliography.

Swafford, Michael. "Three Parametric Techniques for Contingency Table Analysis." *American Sociological Review* 45 (August 1980): 664-90.

Markov Chains

Markov chains are models predicting changes taking place over time. Imagine a problem predicting the outcomes over time as some persons move from job to job while others stay on the same job. When the data consist of a chain of M-1 turnover tables (see "Turnover Tables"), it is natural to wonder whether the observed frequencies might be accounted for by a simple probability law. Markov's law (simple) would account for a stationary, but not necessarily equal, division of movers and stayers toward the end of the time sequence. A Markov chain might be found for all kinds of change behavior stated in dichotomous terms: those who change their minds before election day, those who never change their minds; those whose morale changes daily, those whose morale remains fixed; and so on.

References

Blumen, I., M. Kogan, and P. J. McCarthy. *The Industrial Mobility of Labor as a Probability Process*. Ithaca, NY: Cornell University Press, 1955.

Suresh, L., M. Konda, and Shelby Stewman. "An Opportunity Labor Demand Model and Markovian Labor Supply Models Comparative Tests in an Organization." *American Sociological Review* 45 (April 1980): 276-301.

See excellent bibliography.

Matrix Algebra

This branch of mathematics provides one of the most powerful tools for conceptualizing and analyzing psychological, sociological, and educational research data. Matrix algebra is a system of notations that relates to vectors and matrices using sums, sums of squares, and cross products. The need for such calculations occurs repeatedly in multivariate analysis. Matrix algebra notation and thinking fit in nicely with the conceptualization of computer programming and use.

References

Kerlinger, Fred N., and Elazar J. Pedhazur. *Multiple Regression in Behavioral Research*. New York: Holt, Rinehart & Winston, 1973, 454-66.

Van de Geer, John P. *Introduction to Multivariate Analysis for the Social Sciences*. San Francisco: Freeman, 1971.

See Part I, "Introduction to Matrix Algebra," pp. 3-82.

Meta-Analysis

This term refers to analytical procedures for the cumulation of evidence on organizations—both within single research studies and across studies of the same phenomena—done at different times by different researchers.

References

Glass, Gene V, Barry McGaw, and Mary Lee Smith. *Meta-Analysis in Social Research*. Beverly Hills, CA: Sage, 1981.

Hunger, John E., Frank C. Schmidt, and Gregg B. Jackson. *Meta-Analysis: Cumulating Research Findings Across Studies*. Beverly Hills, CA: Sage, 1984.

Wolf, Fredric M. *Meta-Analysis: Quantitative Methods for Research Synthesis*. Beverly Hills, CA: Sage, 1986.

Multicollinearity Problem

Multicollinearity is a term used to describe a common situation in multiple regression analysis where there is such a high degree of correlation between two or more explanatory (independent) variables that it is impossible to measure their individual effects on the explained (dependent) variable. In a matrix many important theoretical variables are highly intercorrelated, and the empirical associations among them may be underestimated due to random measurement errors. It is suggested that a correction of this multicollinearity problem will require a combination of large samples and good measurement.

Reference

Blalock, Hubert M., Jr. "Measurement and Conceptualization Problems: The Major Obstacle to Integrating Theory and Research." *American Sociological Review* 44 (December 1979): 881-94.

Multiple Discriminant (Function) Analysis

The discriminant function technique has been extended by Fisher to include more than two groups (see Fisher reference below). With the computer it is now possible to study a large number of groups simultaneously across many variables.

Multiple discriminant function analysis provides three kinds of information:

1. It determines whether in fact certain groups are really distinct with respect to selected characteristics.
2. It tells on what factors the groups may be best discriminated.
3. It indicates whether an individual is like other individuals in the group to which he or she has been assigned. That is, it indicates the extent to which individuals have been theoretically misclassified.

References

Fisher, R. A. "The Statistical Utilization of Multiple Measurements." *Annals of Eugenics* 13 (1938): 376-86.

Hoel, P. G. *Introduction to Mathematical Statistics.* 3rd ed. New York: John Wiley, 1962.

Klecka, William R. *Discriminant Analysis.* Beverly Hills: Sage, 1980.

Loy, John W., Jr. "Social Psychological Characteristics of Innovators." *American Sociological Review* (February 1969): 73-82.

Rao, C. R. *Advanced Statistical Methods in Biometric Research.* New York: John Wiley, 1952.

Rettig, Solomon. "Multiple Discriminant Analysis: An Illustration." *American Sociological Review* 29 (June 1964): 398-402.

Rulon, Phillip J. "Distinctions Between Discriminant and Regression Analysis and a Geometric Interpretation of the Discriminant Function." *Harvard Educational Review* 21 (Spring 1951): 80-90.

Tiedeman, David V. "The Utility of the Discriminant Function in Psychological and Guidance Investigations." *Harvard Educational Review* 21 (Spring 1951): 71-80.

Van de Geer, John P. *Introduction to Multivariate Analysis for the Social Sciences.* San Francisco: Freeman, 1971, 267-70.

Probit and Logit Models

These models are nonlinear regressions used as alternatives to the ordinary multivariate linear regression model for estimating a dichotomous dependent variable. Common examples of such dichotomous dependent variables are "succeeds" or "fails," "occurring" or "not occurring," "maintained parole" or "violated parole," "remained in school" or "dropped out," voted "Republican" or "Democratic." Both probit or logit are used because the ordinary least squares regression estimates with a dichotomous variable are misleading. A key assumption of the ordinary least squares model—constant variance of the error term across all observations—is violated.

References

Aldrich, John H., and Forrest Nelson. *Linear Probability, Logit, and Probit Models.* Beverly Hills, CA: Sage, 1984.
    References to research development and applications can be found on pp. 93-94.

Finney, D. J. *Probit Analysis.* Cambridge: Cambridge University Press, 1971. (Originally published 1947)

Smallest Space Analysis

This is a mapping technique, developed by James C. Lingoes and Louis F. Guttman, that depicts social phenomena in graphic terms. The social objects are graphed according to their proximity on selected social characteristics. One-, two-, and three-dimensional space solutions may be applied.

References

Laumann, Edward O. "The Social Structure of Religious and Ethno-Religious Groups in a Metropolitan Community." *American Sociological Review* 34 (April 1969): 182-97.
—— and Louis Guttman. "The Relative Associational Contiguity of Occupations in an Urban Setting." *American Sociological Review* 31 (April 1966): 169-78.
Laumann, Edward O., and Peter V. Marsden. "The Analysis of Oppositional Structures in Political Elites: Identifying Collective Actors." *American Sociological Review* 44 (October 1979): 713-32.
Lingoes, James C. "An IBM-7070 Program for Guttman-Lingoes Smallest Space Analysis." *Behavioral Science* 10 (April 1965): 183-84.
——. *The Guttman-Lingoes Non-metric Program Series.* New York: Academic Press, 1973.
Mortimer, John T. "Patterns of Intergenerational Occupational Movements: A Smallest-Space Analysis." *American Journal of Sociology* 79 (March 1974): 1278-99.

Stochastic Processes

In the study of random processes one is generally concerned with sequences of random variables with special reference to their interdependence and limiting behavior. Random processes are governed at least in part by some random mechanism and may be expressed by a corresponding mathematical model.

Examples of random processes in physical nature are provided by the growth of populations such as bacterial colonies. Similarly, stochastic probability processes may be considered as models of human mobility, population growth, and migration.

References

Fararo, Thomas J. "Stochastic Processes." In *Sociological Methodology 1969*, edited by Edgar F. Borgatta and George W. Bohrnstedt. San Francisco: Jossey-Bass, 1970.
McGinnis, Robert. "A Stochastic Model of Social Mobility." *American Sociological Review* 33 (October 1968): 712-22.
Parzen, Emanuel. *Stochastic Processes.* San Francisco: Holden-Day, 1962.

Structural Equations and Structural Equation Models

Structural equations are equations that relate a dependent variable to various structural components believed to have causal influence on the dependent variable. Various *structural equation models* may be developed. Each "dependent" variable must be regarded explicitly as completely determined by some combination of variables in the system. In problems in which complete determination by measured variables does not hold, a residual variable uncorrelated with other determining variables must be introduced.

For example, let us posit a stratification system in which rewards assure the placement and motivation of persons in various occupational positions within a social structure. Rewards may include prestige, income, leisure, and other amenities. Prestige may be designated dependent variable X_3 and other rewards such as income, leisure, and amenities may be designated as a second dependent variable, X_4. Now suppose we postulate the theorem that the rated functional importance of an occupation X_1 and required skill X_2 will deliver appropriate rewards of prestige, income, and leisure, and will draw the aspiring incumbent into an achieved status position.

Using X to stand for the standard score of a given variable, one could express the relationship as a path of influence in which

prestige $X_3 = p_{31} X_1 + p_{32} X_2 + p_{3a} X_a$
other rewards $X_4 = p_{41} X_1 + p_{42} X_2 + p_{4b} X_b$

These structural equations correspond to multiple regression equations. In these equations, p is a path coefficient[1] and the subscripts indicate the variable it connects. X_a and X_b are included to reflect variables external to prestige (X_3) and income (X_4) and measurement errors that may influence the dependent variables. These are sometimes called *residual variables*. This is a "fully" recursive model because all the possible one-way arrows are drawn between four explicit variables: X_1, X_2, X_3, and X_4.

The term *recursive* refers to a system of equations (as above) in which correlations between any pair of variables can be written in terms of paths leading from common antecedent variables. In path diagrams this is represented by one-way arrows leading from each determining variable to each variable dependent upon it.

Nonrecursive systems involve instantaneous reciprocal action of variables; thus no path of influence can be plotted for such systems.

Note

1. Path coefficients are identical to beta coefficients in the standard multiple regression equation.

References

Berk, Richard A., Kenneth J. Lenihan, and Peter H. Rossi. "Crime and Poverty: Some Experimental Evidence from Ex-Offenders." *American Sociological Review* 45 (October 1980): 766-86.
This work presents an example of a nonrecursive model.
Duncan, Otis Dudley. "Path Analysis: Sociological Examples." *American Journal of Sociology* 72 (July 1966): 1-12.
———. *Introduction to Structural Equation Models.* New York: Academic Press, 1975.
Goldberger, Arthur S., and Otis Dudley Duncan, eds. *Structural Equation Models in the Social Sciences.* New York: Academic Press, 1973.
Many different applications are presented.
Hodge, Robert W., and Donald J. Treiman. "Social Participation and Social Status." *American Sociological Review* 33 (October 1968): 722-40.
Judd, Charles M., and Michael M. Milburn. "The Structure of Attitude Systems in the General Public: Comparisons of a Structural Equations Model." *American Sociological Review* 45 (August 1980): 627-43.
An example of a fully recursive model.
Loether, Herman J., and Donald G. McTavish. *Descriptive and Inferential Statistics.* 3rd ed. Boston: Allyn & Bacon, 1988, 340-77.

Turnover Tables (Panel Analysis)

When the same persons (panel) are cross-classified on the same dichotomy, y, at two points in time, the result is a 2×2 turnover table; when the same persons are cross-classified on two dichotomies, y and x, at two points in time, the result is a 4×4 turnover table; when the same persons are cross-classified on the same dichotomy at three or more (m) points in time, the result is a chain of m-1 turnover tables.

Reference

Schuessler, Karl. "Quantitative Methodology in Sociology." *American Behavioral Scientist* 23 (July/August 1980): 850-52.

RECENT TRENDS IN SOCIOLOGICAL METHODOLOGY
5.20

Recent trends in sociological methodology reported by Schuessler include the following:

1. increasing use of the language of causal modeling
2. development of methods for analyzing categorical or qualitative data
3. increased application of statistical mathematics to theory building and theory testing
4. growing interest in methods for analyzing time data
5. building and testing structural equation theory
6. increasing dependence of theory building and theory testing on the high-speed computer[1]

Bohrnstedt has reviewed methodology employed by the social sciences generally over the last 25 years and concludes that five common themes can be distinguished:

1. All social science disciplines have moved from rather crude description to the development of a set of more or less precise mathematical models.
2. The social sciences have rather freely borrowed methods from one another.
3. All social science disciplines have moved from static to dynamic models.
4. As the disciplines have matured, the models have become increasingly complex.
5. The final commonality is the apparent failure of most models to do much more than account for the observed data in the sample on which the models were developed. Most models are rather precise mathematical descriptions of a set of observations bound by time and culture rather than powerful predictive instruments.[2]

A major driving force behind the development—of new methodological procedures—is the rapid evolution of computing. Three factors of the computing environment seem most important:

The continuing drop in computation cycle cost; the increasing availability of microcomputers, minicomputers, and computer terminals, and the dissemination of reliable software packages.[3]

Notes

1. For a detailed look at these trends, see Karl F. Schuessler, "Quantitative Methodology in Sociology: The Last 25 Years," *American Behavioral Scientist* 23 (July/August 1980): 835-60.

2. George Bohrnstedt, "Social Science Methodology: The Past 25 Years," *American Behavioral Scientist* 23 (July/August 1980): 781-87.

3. Samuel Leinhardt, "Prologue, in *Sociological Methodology 1982*, ed. Samuel Leinhardt. San Francisco: Jossey-Bass, 1983.

Part 6

Selected Sociometric Scales and Indexes

THERE ARE LITERALLY THOUSANDS of scales and indexes to measure social variables. Social scientists have often elected to construct new measures even when scales of high reliability and validity have been available. This practice is wasteful of time, energy, and money. In addition, it makes replication and accumulation of research findings difficult if not impossible. The selection of scales to be found in this handbook was based on such criteria as validity, reliability, and utility. The variables most commonly used in social measurement were studied, and measures for them were sought. Those with the highest reliability and validity were selected. It is hoped that his handbook will encourage greater use of these scales or stimulate the search for better ones.

In general, three groups of variable factors need to be observed and measured in any research design that seeks to test a basic hypothesis or social relationship. First, there is the dependent variable, the effect we wish to observe and describe. Second, there is the independent variable (or variables) that has been designated as the causal factor. Sometimes this factor must be broken down into component parts, which operate more or less as a unit pattern. Third, there are intervening or other independent variables that must be controlled lest they obscure the relationship we wish to measure by use of experimental design.

Sociometric scales have been constructed in substantial numbers to permit quantitative description of these factors in human relations. Three areas of social measurement can be identified. These are as follows:

1. *Psychometric and social psychological scales:* These include intelligence scales, personality tests and scales, and attitude tests and scales. Examples of such scales included in this part are the Minnesota Multiphasic Personality Inventory, the Authoritarian Personality (F) Scale, Morale and Job Satisfaction Scales, as well as attitude scales to measure leisure satisfactions, community attitudes, achievement orientation, and alienation.
2. *Demographic scales:* These scales measure the forms or results of social behavior in large units such as the community, state, or nation. Examples in this part include

community rating scales, scales of community services activity and citizen political activity, and a community solidarity index.
3. *Sociometric scales:* These are used to measure the social structure and process. Examples in this part include sociometric tests to measure informal friendship constellations, measurements of social participation, of social distance, and of group cohesiveness. Other scales are provided to assess marital adjustment and group dimensions. The measurement of social status is of such crucial importance that a number of scales are included, such as Duncan's Socioeconomic Index, Siegel's Prestige Scores, Nam-Powers Socioeconomic Status Scores, Hollingshead's Two Factor Index of Social Position, Alba Edwards's Socioeconomic Scale, and Warner's Revised Occupational Scale for Social Class.

If you do not find a scale that fits your particular research interest, consult the inventory of measures used by researchers represented in the *American Sociological Review* during 1986-87 (see Section 6.L.1). Introducing this inventory is a listing of major sources for scale information and appraisal. One very important source consists of the occupational, political, and social psychological scales carefully selected and appraised by John P. Robinson and his coworkers at the Institute for Social Research of the University of Michigan (a complete listing is shown in Section 6.L.6).

Also presented (in Section 6.L.7) is the list of attitude scales from Marvin E. Shaw and Jack M. Wright, *Scales for the Measurement of Attitudes* (New York: McGraw-Hill, 1967). The complete scale can be found in their book.

Scale construction yields four types of scales: the *nominal* scale, consisting simply of distinguishable categories with no implication of "more" or "less"; the *ordinal* scale, on which positions can be identified in a rank order with no implication as to the distance between positions; the *interval* scale, which has equal distance between any two adjacent positions on the continuum; and the *ratio* scale, which has not only equal intervals but an absolute zero.

The ideal scale is a ratio scale, but with the possible exception of the procedures for measuring certain psychophysical phenomena, none of the measurement techniques currently used fits the requirements for a ratio scale. The nominal scale permits neither rank ordering nor a metric scale. It is so elemental as a classification scheme that such scales are generally regarded as first approximations toward the quantification of a social variable. The result is that ordinal and interval scales are the most frequent types in use. There is considerable disagreement over whether an ordinal or interval scale provides the most appropriate model for social data. Some writers have taken the view that few, if any, of the techniques now in use provide data that can be considered appropriate to more than ordinal scales. Others believe that various types of scales may properly be treated as conforming to interval scales. Still others have taken the position that, although most of the measurements used do not go beyond ordinal scales, little harm is done in applying statistics to them that are appropriate to interval scales.

The result is that statistics appropriate to interval scales continue to be widely used in the analysis of social data, whether the assumptions are met or not. However, there is also an increasing use of statistics that are specifically appropriate to ordinal scales. The statistical tools included in Part 5 of this volume are for the use of the ordinal and interval scales included in this section.

The selection of a good scale involves weighing a number of criteria. Frequency of use is one useful criterion for choice of a scale because of the possibility of maximizing accumulated research in the test of hypotheses. In the selection of scales for the revised edition this frequency criterion has been utilized. However, it is not the only determinant. Frequency can be misleading. New and better scales are constantly appearing. Moreover, use of a scale by others does not guarantee that they have chosen the "best" scale as described by rigorous criteria. For this reason some of the scales selected for this section may not be high on frequency count, but it is believed that they are the scales the researcher should use *now.* The most important single consideration is validity. Does the scale measure what it purports to measure? How much and what kind of evidence is available? Does the scale fit the problem selected for study?

Other considerations include reliability, precision, simplicity, and ease of administration. In recent years there has been considerable emphasis on unidimensionality. The Guttman technique enables the researcher to identify the construct scales of a single dimension. This may be very important in increasing the precision and predictability of a given variable. However, two qualifications must be kept in mind. Such a scale may not be the most effective either for measuring attitudes toward complex objects or for making predictions about behavior in relation to such objects. It must also be remembered that a given scale may be unidimensional for one group of individuals but not for another.

The scales assembled in this part include those constructed by arbitrary or judgmental ranking, by item analysis techniques, by Thurstone's equal-appearing interval method, by Guttman's technique of scale analysis, and by factor analysis. Regardless of the method used in construction, what the researcher seeks is the scale that best fits his or her problem, has the highest reliability and validity, is precise, and is relatively easy to apply.[1] When the researcher has made a selection, he or she must be aware of the statistical techniques that will subsequently be applied. Generally, nonparametric statistics will be used for ordinal scales and parametric statistics for interval scales and for those ordinal scales that do not deviate too far from the assumptions of randomness and normal distribution.

Note

1. For an excellent discussion of these criteria, see Paul F. Lazarsfeld and Morris Rosenberg, *The Language of Social Research* (Glencoe, IL: Free Press, 1955); Hans Zeisel, *Say It with Figures,* 5th ed., rev. (New York: Harper, 1968), 76-102. See also George W. Bohrnstedt, "A Quick Method for Determining the Reliability and Validity of Multiple-Item Scales," *American Sociological Review* 34 (August 1969): 542-48. For a critique of Likert, Thurstone, and Guttman scales, see Nan Lin, *Foundations of Social Research* (New York: McGraw-Hill, 1976), 182-92.

Section **A**

Social Status

Social class or status is one of the most important variables in social research. The socioeconomic position of a person affects his or her chances for education, income, occupation, marriage, health, friends, and even life expectancy. The variable has proved difficult to measure in a pluralistic, egalitarian, and fluid society such as exists in the United States. Nevertheless, many researchers have tried to identify the social strata and to measure variables associated with them. Nearly 30% of all research articles in major sociological journals are devoted to social stratification. Occupation has been shown to be the best single predictor of social status, and overall occupational prestige ratings have been found to be highly stable. A number of factors act in close relationship between occupation and social status. Both individual income and educational attainment are known to be correlated with occupational ranks. Education is a basis for entry into many occupations, and for most persons, income is derived from occupation. House type and dwelling area constitute other highly correlated factors.

Seven scales are presented here for the researcher's choice. They vary in length and in the number of factors included in the scale.

1. O. D. Duncan's Socioeconomic Index
2. Siegel's (NORC) Prestige Scores
3. Treiman's Standard International Occupational Prestige Scale
4. Nam-Powers Socioeconomic Status Scores
5. August B. Hollingshead's Two-Factor Index of Social Position
6. The Revised Occupational Rating Scale from Warner, Meeker, and Eell's Index of Status Characteristics.
7. Alba M. Edwards's Social-Economic Grouping of Occupations

Of the seven, the standard Duncan Socioeconomic Index (SEI) is most widely used and is generally considered to be superior for most survey and large-sample situations. It takes into account income, education, and occupational prestige. Siegel's (NORC) Prestige Scores are based on respondents' subjective rankings to establish the standing of a large number of occupations. It represents an effort to secure a "pure" prestige rating. Treiman has a prestige scale that is superior for studying international comparisons of occupational status.

Nam-Powers, which is based on the 1970 U.S. Census, has used socioeconomic status scores for occupations listed in that census. Scores are based on average levels of education and income for U.S. males and females in 1970. Researchers have the option of choosing the Nam-Powers Socioeconomic Scores if they wish to employ a measurement without prestige weights. A correlation of .97 is reported between the Duncan Socioeconomic Index and Nam-Powers Socioeconomic Status Scores.

Hollingshead's Two Factor Index of Social Position is based on occupation and education. The occupation scale differentiates among kinds of professionals and size and economic strength of business. The 7-point educational scale is premised upon the assumption that men and women who possess similar educations will tend to have similar tastes and similar attitudes and will exhibit similar behavior patterns. The Hollingshead and Duncan indices have been shown to be moderately correlated. When they differ, it is usually because Duncan has had to use one of the grosser census categories. Researchers concerned especially about the professional and business personnel in their sample may elect to use Hollingshead's index.

The researcher might choose Warner, Meeker, and Eell's Revised Occupational Rating Scale if a short scale is desired. This 7-point occupation scale is probably the most sophisticated short classification available. Occupation is one measure in the Index of Status Characteristics. Other measures include source of income, house type, and dwelling area. If these data are available, somewhat greater precision can be obtained. The scale provides scores ranging from 12 to 84, but occupations are grouped into 7 classifications. The scale is comparable to Edwards's socioeconomic groupings, but the Warner scale obtained greater rigor by increased homogeneity of its classifications.

If a relatively broad classification is satisfactory for the research problem, the researcher might choose Edwards's Social-Economic Grouping of Occupations. This grouping makes it possible to use the U.S. Census for many kinds of comparative purposes. This nominal scale has been used widely in research on occupational mobility and occupational trends generally. The most often cited criticisms of the Edwards classifications concern the lack of homogeneity of the categories and the weak scale properties of hierarchical grouping.

Two questions concern the researcher: What is the relative validity of the available social status scales? Can social status be regarded as unidimensional and measurable by a single socioeconomic index? Some tentative answers are possible.

The Relative Validity of Social Status Scales

The researcher will probably find that the problem under study indicates a choice among Duncan's SEI, Siegel's (NORC) Prestige Scores, and Nam-Powers Socio-economic Status Scores. A summary of the relative measures is shown in Table 6.1.

The small range of possible score values marks the Hollingshead Two Factor Index of Social Position, Warner's Index of Status Characteristics, and Edwards's Social-Economic Grouping of Occupations. As the range of possible score values decreases, the scales seem to approach what should be called ordinal scales—in contrast to the interval scales of Duncan, Siegel, and Nam-Powers. This reduction of range blunts the precision of coding and the validity of any given score, but there is no denying that limited-range scales are easier to code and manipulate statistically.

Specific problems beset all current measures. Haug has said that all of the major occupational stratification schemes indicated in the scales presented have a common parent in government census classification: "Given that occupations provide the best

TABLE 6.1 Summary of Relative Measures

Duncan's SEI	Siegel's Prestige Scores	Nam-Powers Socioeconomic Status Scores
Combines education, income, and prestige in a multi-item index.	Prestige index only.	Combines education, income, and occupation in a multi-item index.
Provides a composite socioeconomic and prestige measure.	Provides a direct subjective measure of prestige.	Provides a direct, objective measurement of SES.
Underrates clergymen, farmers, and certain blue-collar workers (e.g., machinists, carpenters); overrates entertainers, newspaper personnel, and sanitation workers.	Respondents who judged occupations biased some scores because of respondents' own status and familiarity with various occupations in the middle of the status scale.	Will underrate some occupations and overrate others where income and education are not principal factors in social status.
Provides scores for men only.	Provides scores for men only.	Provides combined scores for men and women.

or at least the most feasible single indicator of relative standing in a societal system, the problem still remains of defining them, deciding on the most valid way to order them, and determining the most theoretically sound way to group and utilize them." [1]

Haug elaborates on this issue by pointing out that in the framework of the Weberian dimensions of class, status, and power, researchers developing methods of ordering occupations hierarchically have selected the first two dimensions as guidelines, but have not always kept them conceptually distinct. There is, moreover, a neglect of the power dimension. Updating is constantly needed because changes are constantly jeopardizing validity of the measures. Haug pleads that "overcoming measurement shortcomings in the fundamental sociological concept of stratification calls for top scientific priority for the whole discipline." [2] Haug and Sussman mention the need for a valid index based on the theoretical distinction between class (economic position) and social status (prestige) and adapted to current structural realities.[3] They express concern over the changes in income and education in various age cohorts since the construction of the scales. Nevertheless, remarkable stability in occupational stratification has been reported by Hodge, Siegel, and Rossi, who found only small changes in prestige ratings and conclude that "there have been no substantial changes in occupational prestige in the United States since 1925." [4]

These reassuring facts about stability do not resolve some difficulties that are inherent in the differing social repute assigned to education and income. Because status variables are only loosely intertwined, the vast majority of individuals in modern societies are able to advance some legitimate claims to recognition and the other rewards of society. Those with little education may still achieve ample incomes, and those with modest incomes may land prestigious jobs. At the moment the only way to weigh the merits of a scale is for the researcher to examine the data on occupations among his or her respondents and compare the categories incorporated in the scales.

The researcher is urged to consider the second question: Can socioeconomic status be considered unidimensional? Caplow and Hatt say no;[5] Hodge goes still further and urges a multidimensional approach, claiming that different indicators of social participation and psychological well-being are in fact associated with different indicators of socioeconomic status. "Any attempt to combine these indicators—educational attainment, occupational pursuit, family income or occupational origins—into a single index of socioeconomic status will prove unsatisfactory because its component parts have different consequences for the same variables." [6]

Researchers have options. Regression, factor analysis, and path analysis all offer an opportunity to use socioeconomic characteristics as independent variables when seeking correlations with a dependent variable. When appropriate, the "best" indexes of social status should be utilized. With all their shortcomings, there is good evidence that the socioeconomic indexes described in this section are among the most valid and useful scales used as sociological instruments. If your problem so indicates, employ them; they will permit your research findings to be cumulative and therefore valuable to the advancement of social knowledge.

Notes

1. Marie R. Haug, "Measurement in Social Stratification," *Annual Review of Sociology* 3 (1977): 73.

2. Ibid., 75. See the brief statement of this article under "Bibliography of Assessments."

3. Marie R. Haug and Marvin B. Sussman, "The Indiscriminate State of Social Class Measurement," *Social Forces* 49 (June 1971): 549-63. See the commentary by Hollingshead, defending his index, on pp. 563-67.

4. Robert W. Hodge, Paul M. Siegel, and Peter H. Rossi, "Occupational Prestige in the United States, 1925-1963," *American Journal of Sociology* 70 (November 1964): 296.

5. Theodore Caplow, *Sociology of Work* (Minneapolis: University of Minnesota Press, 1954), 33-57; Paul K. Hatt, "Occupation and Social Stratification," *American Journal of Sociology* 55 (May 1950): 538-43.

6. Robert W. Hodge, "Social Integration, Psychological Well-Being, and Their SES Correlates," in *Social Stratification: Research and Theory for the 1970's*, ed. E. O. Laumann (Indianapolis: Bobbs-Merrill, 1970), 182-206.

Assessments of Status Scales

Haller, Archibald O., and David B. Bills. "Occupational Prestige Hierarchies: Theory and Evidence." *Contemporary Sociology* 8 (September 1979): 721-34.

Excellent review of Treiman's Standard International Occupational Prestige Scale; brief history of prestige measurement; discussion of prestige hierarchies; good bibliography.

Haug, Marie R. "Measurement in Social Stratification." *Annual Review of Sociology* 3 (1977): 51-77.

Reviews Hollingshead, Duncan, Siegel, Canadian and British measures, Treiman, and Edwards. Critical judgment is excellent.

Hauser, Robert M., and David L. Featherman. *The Process of Stratification: Trends and Analysis*. New York: Academic Press, 1977.

Excellent analysis of Duncan, Siegel, and Treiman scales. Uses research demonstrations to show differences among the three scales.

Nam, Charles B., and E. Walter Terrie. "Measurement of Socioeconomic Status from United States Census Data." In *AAAS Selected Symposium 81*, edited by Mary G. Powers, American Association for the Advancement of Science. Boulder, CO: Westview, 1981.

Rainwater, Lee, and Richard Coleman. *Social Standing in America: New Dimensions of Class*. New York: Basic Books, 1978.

Assessment of measures of class; presents original status scales with sophisticated interview techniques to capture the many complexities of our social class system.

Robinson, John B., Robert Athanasiou, and Kendra B. Head. *Measures of Occupational Attitudes and Occupational Characteristics*. Ann Arbor: University of Michigan, Institute for Social Research, 1969.

See pp. 335-76. Evaluations of Socio-Economic Status Scale (Duncan, 1961), Socio-Economic Status Scores (Bureau of Census 1963), Occupational Ratings (North and Hatt, 1947, 1965), Index of Status Characteristics (Warner et al., 1949), Index of Social Position (Hollingshead and Redlich, 1958), Class Identification (Centers et al., 1949-66), Facets of Job Evaluation (Guttman, 1965), Occupation Scale (Warner et al., 1949).

Standard Works and Bibliographies of Stratification Research

Blau, Peter, and Otis Dudley Duncan. *The American Occupational Structure.* New York: John Wiley, 1967.
Featherman, David L., and Robert M. Hauser. *Opportunity and Change.* New York: Academic Press, 1978.
    (Replication in 1973 of Blau and Duncan study of 1962.)
Glenn, Norval D., Jon P. Alston, and David Weiner. *Social Stratification: A Research Bibliography.*
    Berkeley, CA: Glendessary, 1970.
Laumann, E. O., ed. *Social Stratification: Research and Theory for the 1970's.* Indianapolis: Bobbs-Merrill,
    1970.
————, P. M. Siegel, and Robert W. Hodge. *The Logic of Social Hierarchies.* New York: Markham, 1970.
Stratification and Inequality Essays. *Contemporary Sociology* 9 (January 1980): 1-63.
Tumin, M. M. *Social Stratification.* Englewood Cliffs, NJ: Prentice-Hall, 1967.

DUNCAN'S SOCIOECONOMIC INDEX

6.A.1

Variable measured: A socioeconomic index relating such basic characteristics as occupational prestige, education, and income.

Description: This measure was developed to secure two objectives: (a) to extend the North-Hatt (NORC) occupational prestige scores from 90 to 446 occupations in the detailed classification of the 1950 Census of Population, and (b) to obtain a socioeconomic index in terms of the relationship between the NORC prestige ratings and socioeconomic characteristics of the population. This index has been developed and has face validity, in terms of its constituent variables, and sufficient predictive efficiency with respect to the NORC occupational prestige ratings.

The Duncan index differs from NORC Prestige Scores in that NORC scores rely solely on subjective occupational ratings of representative samples of respondents. Duncan constructed the occupational socioeconomic index in terms of the relationship between the NORC prestige ratings X_1 and socioeconomic characteristics of the occupations, such as education X_2 and income X_3 with a multiple correlation of R_{123} = 0.91. Each occupation was given an education weight (X_2) based on the prestige of those in the occupation who were high school graduates. Income weights (X_3) were determined by those in each occupation reporting $3,500 or more in 1949. Occupational scores on each of these indicators were compared with NORC Prestige Scores (X_1) for the 45 occupations on the NORC list that were reasonably equivalent to U.S. Census titles. In addition to specific socioeconomic scores, a population decile scale was constructed permitting the researcher the option of arranging the data in a 10-point ranking order. For more information on the construction of the index, the researcher is referred to the following citations.

Where published: Initial scale, 1961: Albert J. Reiss, with O. D. Duncan, Paul K. Hatt, and C. C. North, *Occupations and Social Status* (Glencoe, IL: Free Press, 1961).

Revised scale, 1975: Robert M. Hauser and David L. Featherman, *The Process of Stratification: Trends and Analysis* (New York: Academic Press, 1977). Appendix A contains new socioeconomic indices based on the 1970 Census Classification of Occupations.

TABLE 6.2

	Father's Occupation		Current Occupation	
	Australia	United States	Australia	United States
Duncan-Siegel	.7904	.7224	.8585	.9013

Revised scale, 1982: David L. Featherman and Gillian Stevens made another updating of the Duncan Socioeconomic Index using more recent measures of income and educational attainments of the labor force, providing a better approximation of the prestige measure, and considering attributes of both the male and total labor force. Researchers should examine this revision, titled "A Revised Socioeconomic Index of Occupational Status: Application in Analysis of Sex Differences in Attainment," Chapter 7 in *Social Structure and Behavior: Essays in Honor of William Hamilton Sewell* (New York: Academic Press, 1982).

Reliability: Reliability problems emerge as respondent's description of his or her occupation is translated into an occupational code number using the U.S. Census Index of Occupations and Industries or the *Dictionary of Occupational Titles* published by the U.S. Department of Labor. For increasing reliability or expediting of clerical labor, see Donald G. McTavish's "A Method for More Reliable Coding Detailed Occupations into Duncan's Socio-Economic Categories" [1] and Robert F. Winch, Samuel A. Mueller, and Lois Godiksen's "The Reliability of Respondent-Coded Occupational Prestige." [2]

Validity: The prestige variable is rather highly related to each predictor: With education, $r = 0.84$; with income, 0.85. The multiple correlation among the three variables, $R_{1(23)} = 0.91$. Overall occupational ratings have been found to be highly stable over time ($r = .99$ from 1947 to 1963) and across social systems.[3]

Hauser and Featherman present many validating coefficients between Duncan SEI scores with father's education, father's occupation, son's education, son's first job, and son's current occupation. Interscale correlations over major occupation groups, Duncan (1961) SEI scores, and Siegel Prestige Scores (1971) show correlations as presented in Table 6.2 for Australian men aged 20 and over in 1965 and U.S. men aged 20-64 in 1962.[4]

A moderate correlation ($r = .74$) has been found between the Hollingshead and Duncan indices. However, these scales are constructed differently, and the correlation can be explained.[5] It is of consequence, however, that the two "leading" measures of social status express such a variance.

Certain anomalies appear. For example, since clergymen typically earn small salaries, their Duncan scores are considerably below those found by more subjective procedures. In the blue-collar world, large differences are found among semiskilled workers in various industries. Important regional differences are not expressed. For these reasons Duncan does not recommend that the scale be used for comparisons within certain regions of the country or within certain segments of the status hierarchy, such as skilled workers. The researcher concerned with these discrepancies should consult Haug and Sussman's "The Indiscriminate State of Social Class Measurement." [6]

Utility: The basic data required are subjects' descriptions of their occupations. These must then be translated into occupational codes by the researcher, and the occupational titles then converted into preexisting Duncan SEI scores (or NORC transformed Prestige Scores if desired). There are many subtleties in the art of occupation coding, especially for blue-collar occupations. The researcher should reserve adequate time for training and cross-checking. Anyone planning detailed occupation coding should heed the sound recommendations of McTavish and Winch et al. For codes and decile scores, see John B. Robinson et al.'s *Measures of Occupational Attitudes and Occupational Characteristics.*[7]

Research applications:

Blau, Peter M. "The Flow of Occupational Supply and Recruitment." *American Sociological Review* 30 (August 1965): 475-90. (See p. 476)

Clark, John P., and Eugene P. Wenninger. "Socioeconomic Class and Areas as Correlates of Illegal Behavior Among Juveniles." *American Sociological Review* 27 (December 1962): 826-34. (See p. 828)

——— . "Goal Orientations and Illegal Behavior Among Juveniles." *Social Forces* 42 (October 1963): 49-59. (See p. 51)

Eckland, Bruce K. "Academic Ability, Higher Education, and Occupational Mobility." *American Sociological Review* 30 (October 1965): 735-46. (See p. 739)

——— . "Social Class and College Graduation: Some Misconceptions Corrected." *American Journal of Sociology* 70 (July 1964): 36-50. (See p. 43)

Erbe, William. "Social Involvement and Political Activity: A Replication and Elaboration." *American Sociological Review* 29 (April 1964): 198-215. (See p. 203)

Reiss, Ira L. "Social Class and Premarital Sexual Permissiveness: A Reexamination." *American Sociological Review* 30 (October 1965): 747-56. (See p. 749)

For more recent research use, see all references in the period 1981-87 in the *American Sociological Review* inventory presented in Section 6.L.1 under Duncan's Socioeconomic Index.

Notes

1. Donald G. McTavish, "A Method for More Reliable Coding Detailed Occupations into Duncan's Socio-Economic Categories," *American Sociological Review* 29 (June 1964): 402-6.

2. Robert F. Winch, Samuel A. Mueller, and Lois Godiksen, "The Reliability of Respondent-Coded Occupational Prestige," *American Sociological Review* 34 (April 1969): 245-51.

3. See Robert W. Hodge, Paul M. Siegel, and Peter H. Rossi, "Occupational Prestige in the United States, 1925-1963," *American Journal of Sociology* 70 (November 1964): 296.

4. See Robert M. Hauser and David L. Featherman, *The Process of Stratification: Trends and Analysis* (New York: Academic Press, 1977), 18-19.

5. See August B. Hollingshead, "Commentary on 'The Indiscriminate State of Social Class Measurement,'" *Social Forces* 49 (June 1971): 567.

6. Marie R. Haug and Marvin B. Sussman, "The Indiscriminate State of Social Class Measurement," *Social Forces* 49 (June 1971): 549-63.

7. John B. Robinson et al., *Measures of Occupational Attitudes and Occupational Characteristics* (Ann Arbor: University of Michigan, Survey Research Center, 1969), 342-58.

6.A.2   SIEGEL'S (NORC) PRESTIGE SCORES

Social Prestige as a Social Variable

Occupations can be differentiated with respect to the knowledge or skill required to perform them. So, too, they can be differentiated with respect to the economic power their incumbents will wield. All of the attributes attached to occupational roles give rise to corresponding differences in privilege. Privilege begets *prestige*. Prestige is seen as a symbolic definition of an occupational role based on deference entitlements. It is on the basis of knowledge, skill, power, and privilege that persons grant deference to themselves and claim it from others. It is on the basis of simultaneous assessments of their own and others' deference that they regulate their conduct toward others and anticipate the deferential responses of others.

Power and privilege are universally valued. Treiman contends that the prestige ordering of occupations is fundamentally invariant in all complex societies, past or present.[1] He bases this generalization on a comparative analysis of some 85 studies of occupational prestige conducted in nearly 60 countries throughout the world, ranging from highly industrialized countries such as the United States to traditional peasant societies in India, Thailand, Nigeria, and New Guinea.[2]

What is the difference between social status and prestige? When should the researcher use a social status scale and when a prestige scale? Can the researcher use Duncan's Socioeconomic Index of Occupations to measure either social status or prestige?

Researchers working closely with prestige insist that social status and prestige are not identical dimensions, although the correlations between the underlying factors are high.[3] (Prestige with education, $r = 0.84$, and with income, $r = 0.85$. The multiple correlation among the three variables 0.91 indicates that about 83% of the variance in the prestige of individual occupations can be attributed to a combination of the education and income of the incumbents.) It is asserted that "a socioeconomic index is a better indicator than a prestige index of the way occupations serve as *resources* that facilitate the transmission of advantage from one generation to the next or the conversion of one form of advantage into another. On the other hand, prestige as a major occupational reward may be a better indicator of occupational attainment." [4]

Duncan's SEI and the NORC Prestige Scores reflect approximately equivalent prestige and socioeconomic status for most occupations, but for a substantial number they do not. This can be seen in the category "farmers" (owners and tenants); they have average prestige but very low socioeconomic status (because of limited education and low reported monetary returns). Because of numerous disparities like this, the Duncan scale cannot be adequate for prestige scores. Socioeconomic factors are the main determinants of prestige; but prestige is determined by other factors as well.[5]

What, then, are appropriate criteria for choosing between a prestige and a socioeconomic scale of occupational status? One answer: Use a prestige measure if the dependent variable is "status attainment"; use a socioeconomic index if the dependent variable is "occupational mobility." [6] Another answer is to code occupations in alternative ways and investigate the results obtained. Duncan's Socioeconomic Index of Occupations has become the most widely used occupational status scale in research carried out on American data. Siegel's (NORC) Prestige Scores are most commonly used in prestige measurement in the United States. It is useful to compare the two scales for occupations included in a research sample. For cross-national comparability, the Standard International Occupational Prestige Scale (Treiman) should be used.

Notes

1. Donald J. Treiman, *Occupational Prestige in Comparative Perspective* (New York: Academic Press, 1977), 5.

2. Ibid., 25.

3. Frank D. Bean and Gray Swicegood, "Intergenerational Occupational Mobility and Fertility: A Reassessment," *American Sociological Review* 44 (August 1974): 608-19. See also Aage B. Sørensen, "A Model and a Metric for the Analysis of the Intergenerational Status Attainment Process," *American Journal of Sociology* 85 (September 1979): 361-84.

4. Treiman, *Occupational Prestige*, 212.

5. Ibid., 208.

6. Robert M. Hauser and David L. Featherman, *The Process of Stratification: Trends and Analyses* (New York: Academic Press, 1977). Hauser and Featherman have made the most careful investigation of the relative efficacy of the Duncan Socioeconomic Index and the Siegel (NORC) and Treiman prestige scales. They conclude: "Occupational socioeconomic status captures the major axis of occupational preference, aspiration, and inter- and intragenerational mobility. A socio-economic index for occupations is substantively, and statistically, preferable to prestige indexes in stratification research" (p. xxiii).

Similarly, they warn: "A socioeconomic status is a more valid status index *only* with reference to occupational *mobility*; other occupational processes may be less responsive to the purely socioeconomic hierarchy of these roles than is mobility and may be more responsive to other desirable 'prestigious' but non-socioeconomic occupational dimensions. Therefore 'prestige' is indeed a multidimensional concept and one needs to be quite specific about the occupational process one is discussing in identifying the most salient or valid dimension of status" (p. 50).

Siegel's (NORC) Prestige Scores

Variable measured: An index measuring the prestige of a stratification system.

Description: The North-Hatt NORC study of occupational prestige appeared in 1947 and thereafter was widely used in research on prestige. Prestige scores were obtained for 90 occupations by a national sample of the American adult population.[1] In 1963, under a National Science Foundation grant to the National Opinion Research Center, a replication was undertaken to provide definitive prestige scores for a more representative sample of occupations and in order to uncover some of the characteristics of occupations that generate their prestige scores. As in the 1947 study, occupational ratings were elicited by asking respondents to judge an occupation as having excellent, good, average, somewhat below average, or poor standing (along with a "don't know" option) in response to the item: "For each job mentioned, please pick out the statement that best gives your own personal opinion of the general standing that such a job has."

One indicator of prestige position is the proportion of respondents (among those rating an occupation) giving either an "excellent" or a "good" response. Another measure can be derived from a matrix of ratings by occupation by weighting the various responses with arbitrary numerical values. Assigning to an "excellent" rating a numerical average of these arbitrarily assigned values over all respondents rating the occupation yields the NORC prestige score. This latter measure has received rather widespread use, despite arbitrariness in the numerical weights assigned to the five possible ratings.

The NORC Occupational Prestige Ratings of 1963 were limited to 90 occupations (compared with the more than 500 occupation scores available in the Duncan SEI). By 1970 this limitation was removed, as Hodge, Siegel, and Rossi established prestige scores on more than 400 occupations. More recently, Wisconsin researchers have transformed the 1964-65 NORC Prestige Scores (reported in Siegel for the 1960 census detailed occupational titles) into the 1970 Classification System. These scores are shown below, in Section 6.A.5.

Where published: P. M. Siegel, "Prestige in the American Occupational Structure" (Ph.D. dissertation, University of Chicago, Department of Sociology, 1971); David L. Featherman, Michael Sobel, and David Dickens, *A Manual for Coding Occupations and Industries into Detailed 1970 Categories and a Listing of 1970-Basis Duncan Socioeconomic and NORC Prestige Scores,* Working Paper 75-1 (Madison: University of Wisconsin, Center for Demography and Ecology, 1975); Robert M. Hauser and David L. Featherman, *The Process of Stratification: Trends and Analyses* (New York: Academic Press, 1977), Appendix B, 319-29.

Reliability: The respondent's own social status and familiarity with various occupations have been found to affect scores. Lowered reliability has also been found for occupations in the middle of the status scale. Guttman scale analysis of Hatt's data (1950) failed to find a single underlying prestige dimension. However, Hatt did find internally homogeneous scales with eight occupational groups: political, professional, business, recreation, agriculture, manual, military, and service.

Validity: A correlation of 0.87 is reported by Siegel (1971) between Duncan's SEI scores (1960) and NORC Prestige Scores. The correlation between NORC Prestige Scores and Treiman's Standard International Occupational Prestige Scale scores is 0.95. The Duncan SEI seems to underrate clergy, farmers, and certain blue-collar workers (e.g., machinist, carpenter) while overrating entertainers, newspaper personnel, and sanitation workers. NORC scores show discrepant ratings of these occupations when compared with Duncan ratings, and the researcher may prefer to substitute NORC ratings for these occupations.[2]

Because of the way they were created (weights used in combining income and education were those that maximized scale scores with prestige), Duncan's scores have often been treated as estimates of the relative prestige of occupations, but in fact the correlations between Duncan scores and actual prestige scores are far from perfect. Some significant discrepancies have been pointed out, but the best demonstrated finding is that prestige scores in toto are less valid indicators of the dimension of status that underlies occupational mobility than are Duncan SEI scores. Prestige measures may be more responsive to nonsocioeconomic occupational dimensions.[3]

Utility: The best strategy is to code occupations in alternative ways and investigate differences in the results obtained. If the researcher wishes to settle on a single occupational status index for American data, there are two advantages to the Duncan index: It is the most widely used and offers opportunities for comparative analysis, and it will capture more joint variance with education and income than would a prestige scale. When other information on socioeconomic status is available for individuals, the NORC prestige ratings will avoid artificially inflated correlations with income and education.[4]

Research applications:

Alexander, C. Norman. "Status Perceptions." *American Sociological Review* 37 (December 1972): 767-73.

Hodge, Robert W., Paul M. Siegel, and Peter H. Rossi. "Occupational Prestige in the United States, 1925-63." *American Journal of Sociology* 70 (November 1964): 286-302.

Labovitz, Sanford. "The Assignment of Numbers to Rank Order Categories." *American Sociological Review* 35 (June 1970): 515-24.

Lane, Angela. "The Occupational Achievement Process, 1940-1949: A Cohort Analysis." *American Soci-ological Review* 40 (August 1975): 472-82.

Parcel, Toby L. "Race, Regional Labor Markets and Earnings." *American Sociological Review* 44 (April 1979): 262-79.

Simmons, Roberta G., and Morris Rosenberg. "Functions of Children's Perceptions of the Stratification System." *American Sociological Review* 30 (April 1971): 235-49.

Snyder, David, and Paula M. Hudis. "Occupational Income and the Effects of Minority Competition and Segregation: A Re-Analysis and Some New Evidence." *American Sociological Review* 41 (April 1976): 209-34.

Vanneman, Reeve, and Fred C. Pampel. "The American Perception of Class and Status." *American Sociological Review* 42 (June 1977): 422-37.

See use of the NORC Occupational Prestige Scale by Christine Bose and Peter Rossi in the *American Sociological Review* inventory (Section 6.L.1).

Notes

1. See Albert J. Reiss, Jr., et al., *Occupations and Social Status* (New York: Free Press, 1961).

2. See John P. Robinson, Robert Athanasiou, and Kendra B. Head, *Measures of Occupational Attitudes and Occupational Characteristics* (Ann Arbor: University of Michigan, Institute for Social Research, 1969), 337.

3. See Robert M. Hauser and David L. Featherman, *The Process of Stratification: Trends and Analysis* (New York: Academic Press, 1977), 37, 50.

4. See Donald J. Treiman, *Occupational Prestige in Comparative Perspective* (New York: Academic Press, 1977), 311-12. See also Edward O. Laumann, P. M. Siegel, and Robert W. Hodge, *The Logic of Social Hierarchies* (New York: Markham, 1970).

TREIMAN'S STANDARD INTERNATIONAL OCCUPATIONAL PRESTIGE SCALE   6.A.3

Variable measured: A standardized prestige measure that can be used to code occupations in any country and to make cross-national comparisons.

Description: The scale consists of prestige scores for 509 occupations, 288 unit groups, 84 minor groups, and 11 major categories. The scale has a range of 92 points, from "chief of state" with a score of 90 to "gatherer" with a score of –2. The mean scale score computed over the 509 occupations is 43.3.

Where published: Donald J. Treiman, *Occupational Prestige in Comparative Perspective* (New York: Academic Press, 1977).

Reliability: The scale has been shown to be highly reliable. The average intercountry correlation based on seven countries is .97.

Validity: The Standard Scale is extremely highly correlated with prestige hierarchies of 55 countries. The mean correlation of intercountry correlations with the Standard Scale is .91 computed over the 55 countries with pure prestige data. Of the 55 countries only 7 exhibit correlations with the Standard Scale smaller than .87. For the United States and Great Britain the correlations exceed .96.

Utility: Because of the basic similarity of prestige evaluations in all societies, Donald Treiman has been able to produce the first prestige scale that can be validly used to assign prestige scores to occupations in any country.

Research applications:

Treiman, Donald J. "Correlations of (60) Individual Country Prestige Scores with the Standard Scale and with Version of Standard Scale Excluding Scores for the Country in Correlation." In *Occupational Prestige in Comparative Perspective*, 175-77. New York: Academic Press, 1977.
  Determination of Prestige Scores for each country in the analysis, pp. 318-493.
────── and Kermit Terrell. "Sex and the Process of Status and Attainment: A Comparison of Working Women and Men." *American Sociological Review* 40 (April 1975): 174-200.
────── . "The Process of Status Attainment in the United States and Great Britain." *American Journal of Sociology* 81 (November 1975): 563-83.

Because of its length, the Standard International Occupational Prestige Scale is not reproduced. For the complete scale, see Appendix A in *Occupational Prestige in Comparative Perspective*, pp. 235-60. Standard Scale scores for the 1960 U.S. Census, Detailed Occupational Classification, are on pp. 299-315. See use of the Treiman scales in the *American Sociological Review* inventory, Section 6.L.1.

6.A.4 NAM-POWERS SOCIOECONOMIC STATUS SCORES

Variable measured: A multiple-item measure derived by averaging scores for the component items of occupation, education, and family income. A companion measure of status consistency is also available.

Description: In the 1960s, Charles B. Nam, Mary G. Powers, and their associates worked at the U.S. Bureau of the Census, where they devised socioeconomic status scores for occupations (without use of prestige ratings) based on 1960 census data for income and education. There was interest at that time in constructing an occupational status index that was more detailed and homogeneous than the Alba Edwards classification scheme, which, since about 1930, had permitted arrangement of occupations into major groupings that formed a crude social scale. The Census Bureau's group decided that homogeneity could best be achieved not only by stratifying occupations per se but by developing a multiple-item index of socioeconomic status that combined independent ratings of education and income with ratings of occupations.

The procedure employed to compute the scores is similar to that used by Duncan, but with these differences: (a) median education and income, rather than percentages of specified education and income levels, were used; (b) Duncan indirectly standardized scores by age; and (c) Duncan used the 1947 NORC prestige ratings in deriving rights for census characteristics. The similarity between the census and Duncan's index is attested to, however, by the Pearsonian coefficient of .97, as previously reported.

In planning for the 1970 census, the Census Bureau decided to drop the practice of generating socioeconomic scores using any procedure.

Nam and Powers take cognizance of the controversy between the pure prestige approach (Siegel's [NORC] Prestige Scores) and those of SES determination of prestige of occupations. They believe a third option, the direct measurement of SES without reference to prestige, deserves a more careful assessment. This approach was used in the work of August B. Hollingshead and Frederick C. Redlich[1] and that of Peter M. Blau and Otis Dudley Duncan.[2] This orientation begins with the notion that often one wants a measure of class or life chances or objective status conditions; any of these criteria for valuing occupations leads one to pure socioeconomic indicators of occupational rankings. This third, purely socioeconomic approach has been evident in work produced by the U.S. Bureau of the Census for the past century.

Nam and Terrie have continued to generate new Nam-Powers occupational status scores based on 1980 census data. A rationale for their "pure" socioeconomic multiple-item measure is presented in Nam and Powers's *The Socioeconomic Approach to Status Measurement.*[3]

Where published: Initial work on 1960 census data appears in U.S. Bureau of the Census, *Methodology and Scores of Socioeconomic Status*, Working Paper No. 15 (Washington, DC: Government Printing Office, 1963); U.S. Bureau of the Census, *U.S. Census of Population, 1960, Socioeconomic Status*, Final Report PC(2)-5C (Washington, DC: Government Printing Office, 1967).

Work on the 1970 census incorporated SES scores for males, females, full-time year-round female workers, and both sexes. These scores are shown in Charles B. Nam, John LaRocque, Mary G. Powers, and Joan Holmberg, "Occupational Status Scores: Stability and Change," *Proceedings of the American Statistical Association, Social Statistics Section* (1975), 570-75. More recent work on 1980 census data incorporates identical SES scores for both sexes. See Charles B. Nam and E. Walter Terrie, "1980 Based Nam-Powers Occupational Status Scores," Working Paper Series 88-148 (Tallahassee: Florida State University, Center for the Study of Population).

Reliability: When Nam and Powers compared the full list of detailed occupations for men for 1950 and 1960, they calculated a correlation coefficient between the two sets of scores of .96. The 1950-60 correlation coefficient using the 126 occupations is .95. The calculation for men in the 126 occupations in 1960 and 1970 provides a correlation coefficient of .97, indicating that an extremely high degree of stability in status scores has been maintained. Even the correlation coefficient between scores for men in 1950 and 1970 is .91. For all women, the coefficient for 1960-70 was .85, reasonably high but much lower than for men. In 1980 an increasing similarity of scores for men and women was observed such that a single set of scores for men and women combined is now indicated.

Validity: Measured against prestige measures (Duncan or Siegel), very high correlations are reported. While these two dimensions, socioeconomic status and prestige, are highly associated, there is a tendency for occupational status to vary more over time than occupational prestige.[4]

Utility: Women have become increasingly involved in the labor force, and labeling occupations as exclusively men's or women's is disappearing. Scores for both men and women are shown in Section 6.A.5.

Research applications:

Broman, Sarah H., Paul L. Nichols, and Wallace A. Kennedy. *Preschool IQ: Prenatal and Early Developmental Correlates*. New York: John Wiley, 1975.

Chiricos, Theodore G., and Gordon P. Waldo. "Socioeconomic Status and Criminal Sentencing: An Empirical Assessment of a Conflict Proposition." *American Sociological Review* 40 (December 1975): 753-72.

Myrianthopoulos, N. C., and K. S. French. "An Application of the U.S. Bureau of the Census Socioeconomic Index to a Large, Diversified Patient Population." *Social Science and Medicine* 2 (1968).

Nam, Charles B. "Changes in the Relative Status Level of Workers in the United States, 1950-1960." *Social Forces* 47 (December 1968): 167-70.

—— and Mary G. Powers. "Variations in Socioeconomic Structure by Race, Residence, and the Life Cycle." *American Sociological Review* 30 (February 1965): 97-103.

TABLE 6.3 Group Occupational Status Scores for Men

Occupation Group	Scales Duncan (1970)	Siegel (1970)	Treiman (1960)	Nam-Powers (1970)
Professional, technical, and kindred	75	60	57	85
Managers, officials, proprietors	57	50	64	79
Clerical and kindred	45	39	44	56
Sales and kindred	49	34	40	66
Craft and kindred	31	39	41	49
Operatives	18	29	33	33
Service	17	25	31	25
Nonfarm labor	7	18	19	15
Farmers and farm managers	14	41	47	20
Farm laborers	9	19	27	4

SOURCES: Duncan, Siegel, and Treiman scale scores are drawn from Robert Hauser and David Featherman. *The Process of Stratification* (New York: Academic Press, 1977), 17. Nam-Powers scores appear in Mary G. Powers and Joan J. Holmberg, "Occupational Status Scores: Changes Introduced by the Inclusion of Women." *Demography* 15 (May 1978): 188. Nam and Powers report that major occupational groupings of the 1960 census are not at all homogeneous and constitute too crude a status scale to be useful in socioeconomic analysis. Among males, half of the detailed occupations under the category "Professional, technical, and kindred workers" have status scores between 90 and 100 and two-thirds have status scores between 80 and 100; but one-third have scores less than 80, several scores ranging between 40 and 59. The status scores for clerical occupations are widely distributed, with over one-fourth below 45 and one-third 65 or above. Some service occupations have status scores of near zero, while others have scores near 70 or above. These variations are common for women as well as for men.

—— and Paul C. Glick. "Socioeconomic Characteristics of the Population: 1960." *Current Population Reports*, Series P-23, no. 12 (1964).

Powers, Mary G., and Joan J. Holmberg. "Occupational Status Scores: Changes Introduced by the Inclusion of Women." *Demography* 15: (May 1978): 183-204.

In Table 6.3, the Duncan, Siegel, and Nam-Powers scores are shown for the occupational group codes developed for the 1970 census. The Duncan and Nam-Powers SEI scores can take values approximately between 0 and 100 on both indexes, but since they are constructed somewhat differently, it is not appropriate to make direct comparisons. The Siegel Prestige Scores have a much smaller range, with bootblacks at 09.3 and various college and university teachers at 78.3. When wide variations appear on any of the indexes, caution should be used in interpreting the status of individual occupations. This is especially true in comparisons of men and women workers.

Table 6.3 shows socioeconomic index scores for major occupation groups by Duncan's SEI (weighted prestige, education, income), Siegel's and Treiman's Prestige Scores (subjective weighting of judges), and by Nam-Powers "pure" multiple-item Socioeconomic Scores (based on simple average of scores for occupation, education, and income for both sexes of all ages in civilian labor force in 1980).

Notes

1. See August B. Hollingshead and Frederick C. Redlich, *Social Class and Mental Illness: A Community Study* (New York: John Wiley, 1958).

2. See Peter M. Blau and Otis Dudley Duncan, *The American Occupational Structure* (New York: John Wiley, 1967).

3. Charles B. Nam and Mary G. Powers, *The Socioeconomic Approach to Status Measurement* (Houston: Cap & Gown, 1983).

4. See Ronald M. Pavalko, *Sociology of Occupations and Professions* (Itasca, IL: Peacock, 1971), 132, 140.

OCCUPATIONAL CLASSIFICATION SYSTEM OF THE U.S. BUREAU OF THE CENSUS WITH PARALLEL LISTINGS OF STEVENS AND CHO'S 1980 UPDATE OF DUNCAN'S SEI SCORES AND NAM-POWERS' 1980 STATUS SCORES

6.A.5

Occupation code	Occupational category	1980 Duncan SEI Score[a]	1980 Nam-Powers Score[a]
A. Managerial and Professional Specialty Occupations			
I. Executive, administrative, and managerial occupations			
003	Legislators	57	90
004	Chief executives and general administrators, public administration	57	75
005	Administrators & officials, public administration	54	89
006	Administrators, protective services	35	80
007	Financial managers	59	92
008	Personnel and labor relations managers	60	89
009	Purchasing managers	49	91
013	Managers, marketing, advertising, and public relations	58	91
014	Administrators, education and related fields	82	96
015	Managers, medicine and health	62	86
016	Managers, properties and real estate	42	64
017	Postmasters and mail superintendents	40	74
018	Funeral directors	60	81
019	Managers and administrators, NEC	47	82
	Management-related occupations		
023	Accountants and auditors	65	84
024	Underwriters	54	73
025	Other financial officers	62	80
026	Management analysts	70	95
027	Personnel, training, and labor relations specialists	60	79
028	Purchasing agents and buyers, farm products	35	64
029	Buyers, wholesale and retail trade, except farm products	46	70
033	Purchasing agents and buyers, NEC	54	77
034	Business and promotion agents	50	74
035	Construction inspectors	36	74
036	Inspectors and compliance officers, except construction	44	78
037	Management related occupations, NEC	52	82
II. Professional specialty occupations			
	Engineers, architects, and surveyors		
043	Architects	80	95
	Engineers		
044	Aerospace engineers	84	96
045	Metallurgical and materials engineers	79	96
046	Mining engineers	75	95
047	Petroleum engineers	82	96
048	Chemical engineers	87	96
049	Nuclear engineers	83	97
053	Civil engineers	77	95
054	Agricultural engineers	79	95
055	Electrical and electronic engineers	79	95
056	Industrial engineers	71	91
057	Mechanical engineers	77	95
058	Marine engineers and naval architects	78	90
059	Engineers, NEC	76	95
063	Surveyors and mapping scientists	39	72
	Mathematical and computer scientists		
064	Computer system analysts and scientists	73	94
065	Operations and systems researchers and analysts	65	93
066	Actuaries	80	95
067	Statisticians	65	85
068	Mathematical scientists, NEC	84	98
	Natural scientists		
069	physicists and astronomers	87	99

Occupation code	Occupational category	1980 Duncan SEI Score[a]	1980 Nam-Powers Score[a]
073	Chemists, except biochemists	78	94
074	Atmospheric and space scientists	75	94
075	Geologists and geodesists	87	97
076	Physical scientists, NEC	80	94
077	Agricultural and food scientists	68	84
078	Biological and life scientists	77	89
079	Forestry and conservation scientists	50	84
083	Medical scientists	77	95
	Health diagnosing occupations		
084	Physicians	88	100
085	Dentists	90	100
086	Veterinarians	87	99
087	Optometrists	86	99
088	Podiatrists	83	99
089	Health diagnosing practitioners, NEC	80	96
	Health assessment and treating occupations		
095	Registered nurses	46	73
096	pharmacists	81	95
097	Dieticians	43	64
	Therapists		
098	Inhalation therapists	60	66
099	Occupational therapists	60	73
103	Physical therapists	60	78
104	Speech therapists	60	77
105	Therapists, NEC	60	70
106	Physicians' assistants	59	65
	Teachers, postsecondary		
113	Earth, environmental, and marine science teachers	85	97
114	Biological science teachers	84	96
115	Chemistry teachers	85	90
116	Physics teachers	84	98
117	Natural science teachers, NEC	82	97
118	Psychology teachers	86	97
119	Economics teachers	87	97
123	History teachers	84	96
124	Political science teachers	85	97
125	Sociology teachers	82	96
126	Social science teachers, NEC	85	90
127	Engineering teachers	85	97
128	Mathematical science teachers	82	85
129	Computer science teachers	82	67
133	Medical science teachers	82	99
134	Health specialties teachers	81	85
135	Business, commerce, and marketing teachers	83	85
136	Agriculture and forestry teachers	86	97
137	Art, drama, and music teachers	80	79
138	Physical education teachers	81	74
139	Education teachers	86	92
143	English teachers	81	79
144	Foreign language teachers	79	70
145	Law teachers	90	99
146	Social work teachers	85	96
147	Theology teachers	81	89
148	Trade and industrial teachers	69	85
149	Home economics teachers	73	83
153	Teachers, postsecondary, NEC	82	81
154	Postsecondary teachers, subject not specified	77	91
	Teachers, except postsecondary		
155	Teachers, prekindergarten and kindergarten	59	49
156	Teachers, elementary school	71	78
157	Teachers, secondary school	75	82
158	Teachers, special education	52	67
159	Teachers, NEC	53	56
163	Counselors, educational and vocational	77	85
	Librarians, archivists, and curators		
164	Librarians	65	72
165	Archivists and curators	61	77

Occupation code	Occupational category	1980 Duncan SEI Score[a]	1980 Nam-Powers Score[a]
	Social scientists and urban planners		
166	Economists	78	95
167	Psychologists	82	89
168	Sociologists	78	88
169	Social scientists, NEC	74	80
173	Urban planners	80	91
	Social, recreation, and religious workers		
174	Social workers	66	75
175	Recreation workers	54	46
176	Clergy	66	76
177	Religious workers, NEC	57	55
	Lawyers and judges		
178	Lawyers	88	99
179	Judges	77	99
	Writers, artists, entertainers, and athletes		
183	Authors	71	70
184	Technical writers	60	86
185	Designers	49	67
186	Musicians and composers	46	51
187	Actors and directors	52	76
188	Painters, sculptors, craft-artists, and artist printmakers	54	63
189	Photographers	43	64
193	Dancers	30	37
194	Artists, performers, and related workers, NEC	56	50
195	Editors and reporters	67	77
197	Public relations specialists	67	82
198	Announcers	55	55
199	Athletes	49	52

B. Technical, Sales, and Administrative Support Occupations

III. Technicians and related support occupations

Occupation code	Occupational category	1980 Duncan SEI Score	1980 Nam-Powers Score
	Health technologists and technicians		
203	Clinical laboratory technologists and technicians	55	70
204	Dental hygienists	67	68
205	Health record technologists and technicians	51	67
206	Radiologic technicians	39	68
207	Licensed practical nurses	25	54
208	Health technologists and technicians, NEC	45	57
	Technologists and technicians, except health, engineering and related technologists and technicians		
213	Electrical and electronic technicians	46	75
214	Industrial engineering technicians	45	75
215	Mechanical engineering technicians	49	83
216	Engineering technicians, NEC	45	74
217	Drafting occupations	48	73
218	Surveying and mapping technicians	39	64
	Science technicians		
223	Biological technicians	39	63
224	Chemical technicians	50	76
225	Science technicians, NEC	46	66
	Technicians, except health, engineering, and science		
226	Airplane pilots and navigators	68	93
227	Air traffic controllers	50	85
228	Broadcast equipment operators	35	58
229	Computer programmers	66	84
233	Tool programmers, numerical control	59	87
234	Legal assistants	42	66
235	Technicians, NEC	51	76

IV. Sales occupations

Occupation code	Occupational category	1980 Duncan SEI Score	1980 Nam-Powers Score
243	Supervisors and proprietors, sales occupations	48	66
	Sales representatives, finance, and business services		
253	Insurance sales occupations	53	81
254	Real estate sales occupations	52	77
255	Securities and financial services sales occupations	71	94
256	Advertising and related sales occupations	59	74
257	Sales occupations, other business services	46	75

Occupation code	Occupational category	1980 Duncan SEI Score[a]	1980 Nam-Powers Score[a]
	Sales representatives, commodities except retail		
258	Sales engineers	78	94
259	Sales representatives, mining, manufacturing, and wholesale	50	81
	Sales workers, retail and personal services		
263	Sales workers, motor vehicles and boats	35	65
264	Sales workers, apparel	25	26
265	Sales workers, shoes	25	25
266	Sales workers, furniture and home furnishings	32	53
267	Sales workers, radio, television, hi-fi, and appliances	33	49
268	Sales workers, hardware and building supplies	29	46
269	Sales workers, parts	39	55
274	Sales workers, other commodities	26	29
275	Sales counter clerks	26	26
276	Cashiers	21	20
277	Street and door-to-door sales workers	29	28
278	News vendors	20	3
	Sales-related occupations		
283	Demonstrators, promoters and models, sales	26	28
284	Auctioneers	34	61
285	Sales support occupations, NEC	25	56
V.	*Administrative support occupations, including clerical*		
	Supervisors, administrative support occupations		
303	Supervisors, general office	37	70
304	Supervisors, computer equipment operators	40	88
305	Supervisors, financial records processing	37	81
306	Chief communications operators	26	83
307	Supervisors: distribution, scheduling, and adjusting clerks	30	71
	Computer equipment operators		
308	Computer operators	37	60
309	Peripheral equipment operators	24	52
	Secretaries, stenographers, and typists		
313	Secretaries	35	49
314	Stenographers	30	59
315	Typists	25	39
	Information clerks		
316	Interviewers	36	42
317	Hotel clerks	25	36
318	Transportation ticket and reservation agents	39	73
319	Receptionists	29	38
323	Information clerks, NEC	33	37
	Records processing occupations, except financial		
325	Classified ad clerks	25	49
326	Correspondence clerks	33	59
327	Order clerks	29	49
328	Personnel clerks, except payroll and timekeeping	32	51
329	Library clerks	45	38
335	File clerks	25	32
336	Records clerks	32	45
	Financial records processing occupations		
337	Bookkeepers, accounting and auditing clerks	30	45
338	Payroll and timekeeping clerks	27	52
339	Billing clerks	25	41
343	Cost and rate clerks	32	54
344	Billing, posting, and calculating machine operators	24	39
	Duplicating, mail, and other office machine operators		
345	Duplicating machine operators	26	39
346	Mail preparing and paper handling machine operators	24	31
347	Office machine operators, NEC	24	36
	Communications equipment operators		
348	Telephone operators	22	42
349	Telegraphers	28	65
353	Communications equipment operators, NEC	25	33
	Mail and message distributing occupations		
354	Postal clerks, except mail carriers	30	75
355	Mail carriers, postal service	28	75

Occupation code	Occupational category	1980 Duncan SEI Score[a]	1980 Nam-Powers Score[a]
356	Mail clerks, except postal service	26	34
357	Messengers	24	29
	Materials recording, scheduling, and distributing clerks, NEC		
359	Dispatchers	31	63
363	Production coordinators	34	63
364	Traffic, shipping, and receiving clerks	23	43
365	Stock and inventory clerks	25	43
366	Meter readers	24	56
368	Weighers, measures, and checkers	24	40
369	Samplers	28	44
373	Expediters	36	55
374	Material recording, scheduling, and distributing clerks, NEC	33	32
	Adjusters and investigators		
375	Insurance adjusters, examiners, and investigators	56	64
376	Investigators and adjusters, except insurance	46	64
377	Eligibility clerks, social welfare	35	66
378	Bill and account collectors	35	55
	Miscellaneous administrative support occupations		
379	General office clerks	29	41
383	Bank tellers	29	40
384	Proofreaders	35	47
385	Data-entry keyers	23	45
386	Statistical clerks	31	56
387	Teachers' aides	32	36
389	Administrative support occupations, NEC	32	59

C. Service Occupations

VI. Private household occupations

403	Launderers and ironers	16	6
404	Cooks, private household	15	6
405	Housekeepers and butlers	15	3
406	Child care workers, private household	18	5
407	Private household cleaners and servants	15	2

VII. Protective service occupations

	Supervisors, protective service occupations		
413	Supervisors, firefighting and fire prevention occupations	33	83
414	Supervisors, police and detectives	38	88
415	Supervisors, guards	30	74
	Firefighting and fire prevention occupations		
416	Fire inspection and fire prevention occupations	41	72
417	Firefighting occupations	33	75
	Police and detectives		
418	Police and detectives, public service	38	79
423	Sheriffs, bailiffs, and other law enforcement officers	33	72
424	Correctional institution officers	24	63
	Guards		
425	Crossing guards	17	9
426	Guards and police, except public service	24	40
427	Protective service occupations, NEC	29	27

VIII. Service occupations, except protective and household

	Food preparation and service occupations		
433	Supervisors, food preparation and service occupations	21	31
434	Bartenders	24	33
435	Waiters and waitresses	19	15
436	Cooks, except short order	18	8
437	Short-order cooks	18	3
438	Food counter, fountain, and related occupations	21	3
439	Kitchen workers, food preparation	18	7
443	Waiters'/waitresses' assistants	19	2
444	Miscellaneous food preparation occupations	18	3
	Health service occupations		
445	Dental assistants	27	44
446	Health aides, except nursing	26	36
447	Nursing aides, orderlies, and attendants	24	27

Occupation code	Occupational category	1980 Duncan SEI Score[a]	1980 Nam-Powers Score[a]
	Cleaning and building service occupations except household		
448	Supervisors, cleaning and building service workers	21	46
449	Maids and housemen	16	7
453	Janitors and cleaners	18	15
454	Elevator operators	17	23
455	Pest control occupations	19	43
	Personal service occupations		
456	Supervisors, personal service occupations	28	54
457	Barbers	20	33
458	Hairdressers and cosmetologists	19	29
459	Attendants, amusement and recreation facilities	29	26
463	Guides	26	42
464	Ushers	25	5
465	Public transportation attendants	46	78
466	Baggage porters and bellhops	23	31
467	Welfare service aids	27	27
468	Child care workers, except private household	24	27
469	Personal service occupations, NEC	28	21

D. Farming, Forestry, and Fishing Occupations

IX. Farming, forestry, and fishing

Occupation code	Occupational category	1980 Duncan SEI Score[a]	1980 Nam-Powers Score[a]
	Farm Operators and Managers		
473	Farmers, except horticultural	24	40
474	Horticultural specialty farmers	23	49
475	Managers, farms, except horticultural	35	54
476	Managers, horticultural specialty farms	48	35

Other agricultural and related occupations

Occupation code	Occupational category	1980 Duncan SEI Score[a]	1980 Nam-Powers Score[a]
	Farm occupations, except managerial		
477	Supervisors, farm workers	26	43
479	Farm workers	17	6
483	Marine life cultivation workers	20	46
484	Nursery workers	17	11
	Related agricultural occupations		
485	Supervisors, related agricultural occupations	26	54
486	Groundskeepers and gardeners, except farm	19	15
487	Animal caretakers, except farm	23	27
488	Graders and sorters, agricultural products	17	3
489	Inspectors, agricultural products	21	46
	Forestry and logging occupations		
494	Supervisors, forestry and logging workers	33	60
495	Forestry workers, except logging	36	28
496	Timber cutting and logging occupations	18	16
	Fishers, hunters, and trappers		
497	Captains and other officers, fishing vessels	32	55
498	Fishers	22	30
499	Hunters and trappers	21	57

E. Precision Production, Craft, and Repair Occupations

X. Precision production, craft, and repair

Occupation code	Occupational category	1980 Duncan SEI Score[a]	1980 Nam-Powers Score[a]
	Mechanics and repairers		
503	Supervisors, mechanics and repairers	31	72

Mechanics and repairers, except supervisors

Occupation code	Occupational category	1980 Duncan SEI Score[a]	1980 Nam-Powers Score[a]
	Vehicle and mobile equipment mechanics and repairers		
505	Automobile mechanics	21	42
506	Automobile mechanic apprentices	21	18
507	Bus, truck, and stationary engine mechanics	22	51
508	Aircraft engine mechanics	31	76
509	Small engine repairers	25	37
514	Automobile body and related repairers	22	37
515	Aircraft mechanics, except engine	31	65
516	Heavy equipment mechanics	23	58
517	Farm equipment mechanics	20	42
518	Industrial machinery repairers	22	53
519	Machinery maintenance occupations	20	50

Occupation code	Occupational category	1980 Duncan SEI Score[a]	1980 Nam-Powers Score[a]
	Electrical and electronic equipment repairers		
523	Electronic repairers, communications and industrial equipment	29	60
525	Data processing equipment repairers	49	82
526	Household appliance and power tool repairers	24	54
527	Telephone line installers and repairers	28	73
529	Telephone installers and repairers	33	75
533	Miscellaneous electrical and electronic equipment repairers	27	60
534	Heating, air conditioning, and refrigeration mechanics	26	57
	Miscellaneous mechanics and repairers		
535	Camera, watch, and musical instrument repairers	27	57
536	Locksmiths and safe repairers	25	50
538	Office machine repairers	33	67
539	Mechanical controls and valve repairers	24	58
543	Elevator installers and repairers	24	70
544	Millwrights	26	66
547	Specified mechanics and repairers, NEC	24	52
549	Not specified mechanics and repairers	26	55
	Construction trades		
	Supervisors, construction occupations		
553	Supervisors: brickmasons, stonemasons, and tile setters	23	67
554	Supervisors, carpenters and related workers	23	66
555	Supervisors, electricians and power transmission installers	31	76
556	Supervisors, painters, paperhangers, and plasterers	21	60
557	Supervisors, plumbers, pipefitters, and steamfitters	27	71
558	Supervisors, NEC	42	72
	Construction trades, except supervisors		
563	Brickmasons and stonemasons	23	37
564	Brickmason and stonemason apprentices	23	40
565	Tile setters, hard and soft	23	41
566	Carpet installers	23	38
567	Carpenters	23	42
569	Carpenter apprentices	21	36
573	Drywall installers	24	36
575	Electricians	31	66
576	Electrician apprentices	31	54
577	Electrical power installers and repairers	28	69
579	Painters, construction and maintenance	21	29
583	Paperhangers	23	48
584	Plasterers	22	35
585	Plumbers, pipefitters, and steamfitters	27	58
587	Plumber, pipefitter, and steamfitter apprentices	27	49
588	Concrete and terrazzo finishers	21	31
589	Glaziers	25	48
593	Insulation workers	28	44
594	Paving, surfacing, and tamping equipment operators	22	30
595	Roofers	20	19
596	Sheetmetal duct installers	26	57
597	Structural metal workers	28	55
598	Drillers, earth	21	40
599	Construction trades, NEC	21	34
	Extractive occupations		
613	Supervisors, extractive occupations	39	72
614	Drillers, oil well	21	45
615	Explosive workers	20	48
616	Mining machine operators	20	51
617	Mining occupations, NEC	20	52
	Precision production occupations		
633	Supervisors, production occupations	34	70
	Precision metal working occupations		
634	Tool and die makers	32	69
635	Tool and die maker apprentices	33	59
636	Precision assemblers, metal	18	53
637	Machinists	24	57
639	Machinist apprentices	24	52
643	Boilermakers	26	66
644	Precision grinders, fitters, and tool sharpeners	20	56
645	Patternmakers and modelmakers, metal	31	71

Occupation code	Occupational category	1980 Duncan SEI Score[a]	1980 Nam-Powers Score[a]
646	Layout workers	24	56
647	Precious stones and metals workers (jewelers)	26	39
649	Engravers, metal	27	40
653	Sheet metal workers	26	59
654	Sheet metal worker apprentices	26	44
655	Miscellaneous precision metal workers	33	40
	Precision woodworking occupations		
656	Patternmakers and modelmakers, wood	31	71
657	Cabinetmakers and bench carpenters	21	40
658	Furniture and wood finishers	20	17
659	Miscellaneous precision woodworkers	24	40
	Precision textile apparel, and furnishings machine workers		
666	Dressmakers	18	13
667	Tailors	19	21
668	Upholsters	18	24
669	Shoe repairers	18	14
673	Apparel and fabric patternmakers	17	40
674	Miscellaneous precision apparel and fabric workers	21	14
	Precision workers, assorted materials		
675	Handmolders and shapers, except jewelers	20	34
676	Patternmakers, layout workers, and cutters	38	59
677	Optical goods workers	29	54
678	Dental laboratory and medical appliance technicians	33	57
679	Bookbinders	20	32
683	Electrical and electronic equipment assemblers	18	28
684	Miscellaneous precision workers, NEC	22	39
	Precision food production occupations		
686	Butchers and meat cutters	21	43
687	Bakers	19	24
688	Food batchmakers	19	20
	Precision inspectors, testers, and related workers		
689	Inspectors, testers, and graders	24	60
693	Adjusters and calibrators	18	32
	Plant and system operators		
694	Water and sewage treatment plant operators	27	56
695	Power plant operators	33	74
696	Stationary engineers	28	71
699	Miscellaneous plant and system operators	22	66

F. Operators, Fabricators, and Laborers

XI. Machine operators, assemblers, and inspectors

Machine operators and tenders, except precision

	Metal working and plastic working machine operators		
703	Lathe and turning machine setup operators	23	49
704	Lathe and turning machine operators	22	56
705	Milling and planing machine operators	22	57
706	Punching and stamping press machine operators	18	38
707	Rolling machine operators	23	57
708	Drilling and boring machine operators	19	45
709	Grinding, abrading, buffing, and polishing machine operators	19	37
713	Forging machine operators	21	50
714	Numerical control machine operators	19	66
715	Miscellaneous metal, plastic, stone, and glass working machine operators	21	54
717	Fabricating machine operators, NEC	18	36
	Metal and plastic processing machine operators		
719	Molding and casting machine operators	19	34
723	Metal plating machine operators	20	38
724	Heat treating equipment operators	22	51
725	Miscellaneous metal and plastic processing machine operators	19	32
	Woodworking machine operators		
726	Wood lathe, routing, and planing machine operators	21	34
727	Sawing machine operators	17	18
728	Shaping and joining machine operators	19	20
729	Nailing and tacking machine operators	16	11
733	Miscellaneous woodworking machine operators	19	29

Occupation code	Occupational category	1980 Duncan SEI Score[a]	1980 Nam-Powers Score[a]
	Printing machine operators		
734	Printing machine operators	26	51
735	Photoengravers and lithographers	31	66
736	Typesetters and compositors	28	53
737	Miscellaneous printing machine operators	26	40
	Textile, apparel, and furnishings machine operators		
738	Winding and twisting machine operators	14	14
739	Knitting, looping, taping, and weaving machine operators	15	20
743	Textile cutting machine operators	18	14
744	Textile sewing machine operators	15	10
745	Shoe machine operators	15	11
747	Pressing machine operators	15	8
748	Laundering and dry cleaning machine operators	17	10
749	Miscellaneous textile machine operators	15	16
	Machine operators, assorted materials		
753	Cementing and gluing machine operators	19	24
754	Packaging and filling machine operators	18	22
755	Extruding and forming machine operators	19	44
756	Mixing and blending machine operators	19	42
757	Separating, filtering, and clarifying machine operators	20	62
758	Compressing and compacting machine operators	19	28
759	Painting and paint spraying machine operators	18	34
763	Roasting and baking machine operators, food	19	38
764	Washing, cleaning, and pickling machine operators	19	28
765	Folding machine operators	19	14
766	Furnace, kiln, and oven operators, except food	21	53
768	Crushing and grinding machine operators	19	36
769	Slicing and cutting machine operators	18	28
773	Motion picture projectionists	33	45
774	Photographic process machine operators	29	41
777	Miscellaneous machine operators, NEC	19	37
779	Machine operators, not specified	19	33
	Fabricators, assemblers, and handworking occupations		
783	Welders and cutters	21	46
784	Solderers and brazers	16	24
785	Assemblers	18	32
786	Hand cutting and trimming occupations	19	17
787	Hand molding, casting, and forming occupations	19	27
789	Hand painting, coating, and decorating occupations	24	39
793	Hand engraving and printing occupations	19	47
794	Hand grinding and polishing occupations	21	22
795	Miscellaneous hand working occupations	19	19
	Production inspectors, testers, samplers, and weighers		
796	Production inspectors, checkers, and examiners	22	42
797	Production testers	22	53
798	Production samplers and weighers	19	31
799	Graders and sorters, except agricultural	16	13
	XII. Transportation and material moving occupations		
	Motor vehicle operators		
803	Supervisors, motor vehicle operators	35	67
804	Truck drivers, heavy	21	42
805	Truck drivers, light	23	38
806	Driver, salesworkers	23	57
808	Bus drivers	21	30
809	Taxicab drivers and chauffeurs	22	28
813	Parking lot attendants	23	18
814	Motor transportation occupations, NEC	21	40
	Transportation occupations, except motor vehicles		
	Rail transportation occupations		
823	Railroad conductors and yardmasters	36	71
824	Locomotive operating occupations	31	71
825	Railroad brake, signal, and switch operators	26	70
826	Rail vehicle operators, NEC	25	71
	Water transportation occupations		
828	Ship captains and mates, except fishing boats	33	66
829	Sailors and deckhands	22	41

Occupation code	Occupational category	1980 Duncan SEI Score[a]	1980 Nam-Powers Score[a]
833	Marine engineers	24	57
834	Bridge, lock, and lighthouse tenders	17	49
	Material moving equipment operators		
843	Supervisors, material moving equipment operators	33	71
844	Operating engineers	22	47
845	Longshore equipment operators	23	49
848	Hoist and winch operators	21	45
849	Crane and tower operators	22	55
853	Excavating and loading machine operators	22	42
855	Grader, dozer, and scraper operators	21	33
856	Industrial truck and tractor equipment operators	18	38
859	Miscellaneous material moving equipment operators	20	39
XIII. Handlers, equipment cleaners, helpers and laborers			
863	Supervisors: handlers, equipment cleaners, and laborers, NEC	35	68
864	Helpers, mechanics and repairers	19	15
	Helpers, construction and extractive occupations		
865	Helpers, construction trades	19	16
866	Helpers, surveyor	27	36
867	Helpers, extractive occupations	21	42
869	Construction laborers	18	25
873	Production helpers	19	28
	Freight, stock and material handlers		
875	Garbage collectors	17	16
876	Stevedores	23	44
877	Stock handlers and baggers	20	8
878	Machine feeders and offbearers	18	26
883	Freight, stock, and material handlers, NEC	20	34
885	Garage and service station related occupations	20	8
887	Vehicle washers and equipment cleaners	17	9
888	Hand packers and packagers	16	16
889	Laborers, except construction	19	24

Note: I am indebted to Gillian Stevens and Joo Hyun Cho for permission to reprint the update of Duncan SEI scores for 1980, as published in "Socioeconomic Indexes and the New 1980 Census Occupational Classification Scheme," *Social Science Research* 14, 142-168 (1985); and to Charles B. Nam and E. Walter Terrie for permission to reprint "1980-Based Nam-Powers Occupational Status Scores," Working Paper Series 88-48, Center for the Study of Population, Florida State University, 1988.
a. Stevens-Cho estimates for 1980 were provided for males and for both sexes combined. The Nam-Powers scores for 1980 were prepared only for both sexes combined. Both sets of scores are shown for both sexes combined, which other research has shown to be preferable for analysis involving both males and females, to facilitate comparisons.
NEC = not elsewhere classified

HOLLINGSHEAD'S TWO-FACTOR INDEX OF SOCIAL POSITION   6.A.6

Variable measured: Positions individuals occupy in the status structure.

Description: There are two- and three-factor forms of the index that have been used extensively. The two-factor index is composed of an occupational scale and an educational scale. The three-factor index includes a residential scale. Since the residential scale was based on sociological analysis previously made by Davis and Myers in New Haven, many communities would not be amenable until residential areas were mapped into a six-position scale. The two-factor index requires only knowledge of occupation and education.

The occupational scale is a 7-point scale representing a modification of the Edwards system of classifying occupations into socioeconomic groups. The Edwards system does not differentiate among kinds of professionals or the size and economic strength of businesses. The Hollingshead index of social position ranks professions into different groups and business by their size and value.

The educational scale is also divided into seven positions. In the two-factor index, occupation is given a weight of 7 and education is given a weight of 4. If one were to compute a score for the manager of a Kroger store who had completed high school and one year of business college, the procedure would be as follows:

Factor	Scale Score ×	Factor Weight	= Partial Score
Occupation	3	7	21
Education	3	4	<u>12</u>
Index of Social Position Score			33

The range of scores in each of five social classes (of New Haven, Connecticut) are as follows:

Class I: 11-17

Class II: 18-31

Class III: 32-47

Class IV: 48-63

Class V: 64-77

Where published: August B. Hollingshead, *Two Factor Index of Social Position* (copyright 1957), privately printed 1965, Yale Station, New Haven, CT. August B. Hollingshead and Frederick C. Redlich, *Social Class and Mental Illness: A Community Study* (New York: John Wiley, 1958), 387-97.

The researcher will find Hollingshead's account of the background and rationale for the two-factor scale in August B. Hollingshead, "Commentary on 'The Indiscriminate State of Social Class Measurement,' " *Social Forces* 49 (June 1971): 563-67.

Reliability and validity of Index of Social Position: High correlation is reported between the Hollingshead and Redlich measure and the index of class position devised by Ellis, Lane, and Olesen.[1]

Various combinations of the scale score for occupation and education are reproducible in the Guttman sense, for there is no overlap between education-occupation combinations. If an individual's education and occupation are known, one can calculate his or her score; if one knows an individual's score, one can calculate both occupational and educational level.

Hollingshead and Redlich report a correlation between judged class with education and occupation as $R_{1(23)}$ = .906. Judged class with residence, education, and occupation, $R_{.(234)}$ = .942.

Hollingshead and others have made extensive studies of the reliability of scoring and validity of the index on more than 100 variables.

Slomczynski, Miller, and Kohn report that "the use of the Hollingshead index of occupational status for research in the U.S. is validated by longitudinal measurement models that show the Hollingshead index to be as strong an indicator of occupational status as is Treiman's International Prestige Scale, the Hodge-Siegel Index, or the Duncan Socio-Economic Index."[2]

Utility: Because of the difficulty in obtaining residential information where adequate ecological maps do not exist, the two-factor variation of the Index of Social Position has been used widely. Only occupation and education are needed, and these data are relatively easy to obtain. The scale score can be quickly computed and individual social position established.

Research applications:

Bell, Gerald D. "Processes in the Formation of Adolescents' Aspirations." *Social Forces* 42 (December 1963): 179-86. (See p. 182)

Ellis, Robert A. "Social Stratification and Social Relations: An Empirical Test of the Disjunctiveness of Social Classes." *American Sociological Review* 22 (October 1957): 570-78. (See p. 571)

Hollingshead, August B., and Frederick C. Redlich. "Social Stratification and Psychiatric Disorders." *American Sociological Review* 18 (April 1953): 163-69. (See p. 165)

―――. "Social Stratification and Schizophrenia." *American Sociological Review* 19 (June 1954): 302-6. (See p. 302)

―――. "Social Mobility and Mental Illness." *American Journal of Psychiatry* 112 (September 1955): 179-85. (See pp. 180-82)

―――. *Social Class and Mental Illness: A Community Study.* New York: John Wiley, 1958. (See pp. 390-91)

―――, Robert Ellis, and E. Kirby. "Social Mobility and Mental Illness." *American Sociological Review* 19 (October 1954): 577-84. (See p. 579)

Hollingshead, August B., Frederick C. Redlich, and L. Z. Freeman. "Social Class and the Treatment of Neurotics." In *The Social Welfare Forum*, 194-205. New York: Columbia University Press, 1955. (See pp. 195)

Hunt, Raymond G., Orville Gursslin, and Jack L. Roach. "Social Status and Psychiatric Science in a Child Guidance Clinic." *American Sociological Review* 23 (February 1958): 81-83. (See p. 81)

Kohn, Melvin L. "Social Class and Parental Values." *American Journal of Sociology* 64 (January 1959): 337-51. (See p. 338)

―――and Eleanor E. Carroll. "Social Class and the Allocation of Parental Responsibilities." *Sociometry* 23 (December 1960): 372-92. (See p. 374)

Lawson, Edwin D., and Walter E. Bock. "Correlations of Indexes of Families' Socio-Economic Status." *Social Forces* 39 (December 1960): 149-52. (See p. 150)

Lefton, Mark, Shirley Angrist, Simon Dintz, and Benjamin Pasamanick. "Social Class, Expectations, and Performance of Mental Patients." *American Journal of Sociology* 68 (July 1962): 79-87. (See p. 82)

Leslie, Gerald R., and Kathryn P. Johnsen. "Changed Perceptions of the Maternal Role." *American Sociological Review* 28 (December 1963): 919-28. (See p. 923)

Levinger, George. "Task and Social Behavior in Marriage." *Sociometry* 27 (December 1964): 433-48. (See pp. 442, 446)

Lewis, Lionel S. "Knowledge, Danger, Certainty, and the Theory of Magic." *American Journal of Sociology* 69 (July 1963): 7-12. (See p. 9)

──── and Joseph Lopreato. "Arationality, Ignorance, and Perceived Danger in Medical Practices." *American Sociological Review* 27 (August 1962): 508-14. (See p. 508)

Mizruchi, Ephraim H. "Social Structure and Anomia in a Small City." *American Sociological Review* 25 (October 1960): 645-54. (See p. 647)

Psathas, George. "Ethnicity, Social Class and Adolescent Independence from Parental Control." *American Sociological Review* 22 (August 1957): 415-23. (See p. 417)

Rosen, Bernard C. "The Achievement Syndrome: A Psychocultural Dimension of Social Stratification." *American Sociological Review* 21 (April 1956): 203-11. (See p. 204)

────. "Race, Ethnicity, and the Achievement Syndrome." *American Sociological Review* 24 (February 1959): 47-60. (See p. 48)

────. "Family Structure and Achievement Motivation." *American Sociological Review* 26 (August 1961): 574-85. (See p. 576)

────. "Socialization and Achievement Motivation in Brazil." *American Sociological Review* 27 (October 1962): 612-24. (See p. 613)

────. "The Achievement Syndrome and Economic Growth in Brazil." *Social Forces* 42 (March 1964): 341-54. (See p. 345)

──── and Roy d'Andrade. "The Psychosocial Origins of Achievement Motivation." *Sociometry* 22 (September 1959): 185-218. (See p. 189)

Slomczynski, Kazimierz M., Joanne Miller, and Melvin L. Kohn. "Stratification, Work, and Values." *American Sociological Review* 46 (December 1981): 720-44. (See p. 727)

Smith, Bulkeley, Jr. "The Differential Residential Segregation of Working Class Negroes in New Haven." *American Sociological Review* 24 (August 1959): 529-33. (See p. 530)

Strodtbeck, Fred L., Margaret R. McDonald, and Bernard C. Rosen. "Evaluation of Occupations: A Reflection of Jewish and Italian Mobility Differences." *American Sociological Review* 22 (October 1957): 546-53. (See p. 547)

Wechsler, Henry. "Community Growth, Depressive Disorders, and Suicide." *American Journal of Sociology* 67 (July 1961): 9-16. (See p. 15)

Yarrow, Marian R., Phyllis Scott, Louise deLeeuw, and Christine Heinig. "Child-Rearing in Families of Working and Nonworking Mothers." *Sociometry* 25 (June 1962): 122-40. (See p. 124)

Notes

1. R. Ellis, W. Lane, and V. Olesen, "The Index of Class Position: An Improved Intercommunity Measure of Stratification," *American Sociological Review* 28 (April 1963): 271-77.

2. Slomczynski, Kazimierz M., Joanne Miller, and Melvin L. Kohn. "Stratification, Work, and Values," *American Sociological Review* 46 (December 1981): 727.

Hollingshead's Two-Factor Index of Social Position

The following two scales are reprinted by permission from Hollingshead and Redlich, *Social Class and Mental Illness: A Community Study* (New York: John Wiley, 1958). Copyright 1958 by John Wiley and Sons, Inc.

The Occupational Scale

1. Higher Executives of Large Concerns, Proprietors, and Major Professionals

A. *Higher Executives (Value of corporation $500,000 and above as rated by Dun and Bradstreet)*

Bank
    Presidents
    Vice-Presidents
    Assistant vice-presidents

Business
    Vice-Presidents
    Assistant vice-presidents
    Executive secretaries
    Research directors
    Treasurers

B. Proprietors (Value over $100,000 by Dun and Bradstreet)

Brokers
  Contractors
  Dairy owners

Farmers
Lumber dealers

C. Major Professionals

Accountants (CPA)
Actuaries
Agronomists
Auditors
Architects
Artists, portrait
Astronomers
Bacteriologists
Chemical engineers
Chemists
Clergymen (professional trained)
Dentists
Economists
Engineers (college graduates)
Foresters
Geologists

Judges (superior courts)
Lawyers
Metallurgists
Military: commissioned officers,
  major and above
Officials of the executive branch of
  government, federal, state, local:
  e.g., Mayor, City manager, City plan
  director, Internal Revenue director
Physicians
Physicists, research
Psychologists, practicing
Symphony conductor
Teachers, university, college
Veterinarians (veterinary surgeons)

2. Business Managers, Proprietors of Medium-Sized Businesses, and Lesser Professionals

A. Business Managers in Large Concerns (Value $500,000)

Advertising directors
Branch managers
Brokerage salesmen
Directors of purchasing
District managers
Executive assistants
Export managers, international
  concerns
Government officials, minor, e.g.,
  Internal Revenue agents

Manufacturer's representatives
Office managers
Personnel managers
Police chief; Sheriff
Postmaster
Production managers
Sales engineers
Sales managers, national concerns
Store managers

B. Proprietors of Medium Businesses (Value $35,000-$100,000)

Advertising
Clothing store
Contractors
Express company
Farm owners
Fruits, wholesale
Furniture business

Jewelers
Poultry business
Real estate brokers
Rug business
Store
Theater

C. Lesser Professionals

Accountants (not CPA)
Chiropodists
Chiropractors
Correction officers
Director of Community House

Military: commissioned officers,
  lieutenant, captain
Musicians (symphony orchestra)
Nurses
Opticians

Engineers (not college graduate)
Finance writers
Health educators
Labor relations consultants
Librarians

Optometrists, D.O.
Pharmacists
Public health officers (MPH)
Research assistants, university
(full-time)
Social workers

3. Administrative Personnel, Owners of Small Businesses, and Minor Professionals

A. Administrative Personnel

Advertising agents
Chief clerks
Credit managers
Insurance agents
Managers, departments
Passenger agents, railroad
Private secretaries
Purchasing agents
Sales representatives

Section heads, federal, state and
local governmental offices
Section heads, large businesses and
industries
Service managers
Shop managers
Store managers (chain)
Traffic managers

B. Small Business Owners ($6,000-$35,000)

Art gallery
Auto accessories
Awnings
Bakery
Beauty shop
Boatyard
Brokerage, insurance
Car dealers
Cattle dealers
Cigarette machines
Cleaning shops
Clothing
Coal businesses
Contracting businesses
Convalescent homes
Decorating
Dog supplies
Dry goods
Engraving business
Feed
Finance companies, local
Fire extinguishers
Five and dime
Florist
Food equipment
Food products
Foundry
Funeral directors

Furniture
Garage
Gas station
Glassware
Grocery, general
Hotel protection
Jewelry
Machinery brokers
Manufacturing
Monuments
Music
Package stores (liquor)
Paint contracting
Poultry
Real estate
Records and radios
Restaurant
Roofing contractor
Shoe
Signs
Tavern
Taxi company
Tire shop
Trucking
Trucks and tractors
Upholstery
Wholesale outlets
Window shades

C. Semiprofessionals

Actors and showmen
Army, master sergeant
Artists, commercial
Appraisers (estimators)

Navy, chief petty officer
Oral hygienists
Physiotherapists
Piano teachers

Clergymen (not professionally
    trained)
Concern managers
Deputy sheriffs
Dispatchers, railroad
Interior decorators
Interpreters, courts
Laboratory assistants
Landscape planners
Morticians

Publicity and public relations
Radio, TV announcers
Reporters, court
Reporters, newspapers
Surveyors
Title searchers
Tool designs
Travel agents
Yard masters, railroad

D. Farmers

Farm owners ($20,000-$35,000)

4. Clerical and Sales Workers, Technicians, and Owners of Little Businesses
     (Value under $6,000)

A. Clerical and Sales Workers

Bank clerks and tellers
Bill collectors
Bookkeepers
Business machine operators,
    offices
Claims examiners
Clerical or stenographic
Conductors, railroad
Factory storekeepers

Factory supervisors
Post Office clerks
Route managers
Sales clerks
Sergeants and petty officers, military
    services
Shipping clerks
Supervisors, utilities, factories
Supervisors, toll stations

B. Technicians

Dental technicians
Draftsmen
Driving teachers
Expediter, factory
Experimental tester
Instructors, telephone company,
    factory
Inspectors, weights, sanitary,
    railroad, factory
Investigators
Laboratory technicians

Locomotive engineers
Operators, PBX
Proofreaders
Safety supervisors
Supervisors of maintenance
Technical assistants
Telephone company supervisors
Timekeepers
Tower operators, railroad
Truck dispatchers
Window trimmers (stores)

C. Owners of Little Businesses ($3,000-$6,000)

Flower shop
Grocery

Newsstand
Tailor shop

D. Farmers

Owners (Value $10,000-$20,000)

5. Skilled Manual Employees

Auto body repairers
Bakers
Barbers
Blacksmiths
Bookbinders
Boilermakers
Brakemen, railroad
Brewers
Bulldozer operators
Butchers
Cabinet makers
Cable splicers
Carpenters
Casters (founders)
Cement finishers
Cheese makers
Chefs
Compositors
Diemakers
Diesel engine repair and
  maintenance (trained)
Diesel shovel operators
Linoleum layers (trained)
Masons
Masseurs
Mechanics (trained)
Millwrights
Moulders (trained)
Painters
Paperhangers
Patrolmen, railroad
Pattern and model makers
Piano builders
Piano tuners
Plumbers
Policemen, city
Postmen
Printers
Radio, television maintenance
Repairmen, home appliances

Electricians
Engravers
Exterminators
Firemen, city
Firemen, railroad
Fitters, gas, steam
Foremen, construction, dairy
Gardeners, landscape (trained)
Glass blowers
Glaziers
Gunsmiths
Gauge makers
Hair stylists
Heat treaters
Horticulturists
Linmen, utility
Linotype operators
Lithographers
Locksmiths
Loom fixers
Machinists (trained)
Maintenance foremen
Rope splicers
Sheetmetal workers (trained)
Shipsmiths
Shoe repairmen (trained)
Stationery enginers (licensed)
Stewards, club
Switchmen, railroad
Tailors (trained)
Teletype operators
Tool makers
Track supervisors, railroad
Tractor-trailer trans.
Typographers
Upholsterers (trained)
Watchmakers
Weavers
Welders
Yard supervisors, railroad

Small Farmers
Owners (Value under $10,000)

Tenants who own farm equipment

6. Machine Operators and Semiskilled Employees

Aides, hospital
Apprentices, electricians, printers,
  steam fitters, toolmakers
Assembly line workers
Bartenders
Bingo tenders
Bridge tenders
Building superintendents
  (construction)

Practical nurses
Pressers, clothing
Pump operators
Receivers and checkers
Roofers
Setup men, factories
Shapers
Signalmen, railroad
Solderers, factory

Bus drivers
Checkers
Coin machine fillers
Cooks, short order
Deliverymen
Dressmakers, machine
Elevator operators
Enlisted men, military services
Filers, sanders, buffers
Foundry workers
Garage and gas station attendants
Greenhouse workers
Guards, doorkeepers, watchmen
Hairdressers
Housekeepers
Meat cutters and packers
Meter readers
Operators, factory machines
Oilers, railroad

Sprayers, paint
Steelworkers (not skilled)
Standers, wire machines
Strippers, rubber factory
Taxi drivers
Testers
Timers
Tire moulders
Trainmen, railroad
Truck drivers, general
Waiters–waitresses ("better placed")
Weighers
Welders, spot
Winders, machine
Wiredrawers, machine
Wine bottlers
Wood workers, machine
Wrappers, stores and factories

Farmers
Smaller tenants who own little equipment

7. Unskilled Employees

Amusement park workers
   (bowling alleys, pool rooms)
Ash removers
Attendants, parking lots
Cafeteria workers
Car cleaners, railroad
Carriers, coal
Countermen
Dairy workers
Deck hands
Domestics
Farm helpers
Fishermen (clam diggers)
Freight handlers
Garbage collectors
Gravediggers
Hod carriers
Hog killers
Hospital workers, unspecified
Hostlers, railroad
Janitors (sweepers)
Laborers, construction

Laborers, unspecified
Laundry workers
Messengers
Platform men, railroad
Peddlers
Porters
Relief, public, private
Roofer's helpers
Shirt folders
Shoe shiners
Sorters, rag and salvage
Stage hands
Stevedores
Stock handlers
Street cleaners
Struckmen, railroad
Unemployed (no occupation)
Unskilled factory workers
Waitresses ("hash houses")
Washers, cars
Window cleaners
Woodchoppers

Farmers
Sharecroppers

The Educational Scale

The educational scale is premised upon the assumption that men and women who possess similar educations will tend to have similar tastes and similar attitudes, and they will also tend to exhibit similar behavior patterns.

The educational scale is divided into seven positions:

1. *Graduate professional training:* Persons who completed a recognized professional course that led to the receipt of a graduate degree were given scores of 1.
2. *Standard college or university graduation:* All individuals who had completed a four-year college or university course leading to a recognized college degree were assigned the same scores. No differentiation was made between state universities and private colleges.
3. *Partial college training:* Individuals who had completed at least one year but not a full college course were assigned this position.
4. *High school graduation:* All secondary school graduates, whether from a private preparatory school, public high school, trade school, or parochial school, were given this score.
5. *Partial high school:* Individuals who had completed the tenth or eleventh grades, but had not completed high school were given this score.
6. *Junior high school:* Individuals who had completed the seventh grade through the ninth grade were given this position.
7. *Less than seven years of school:* Individuals who had not completed the seventh grade were given the same scores irrespective of the amount of education they had received.

REVISED OCCUPATIONAL RATING SCALE FROM WARNER, MEEKER, AND EELLS'S INDEX OF STATUS CHARACTERISTICS   6.A.7

Variable measured: Social class position according to a 7-point rating.

Description: The rating of occupations is one measure included in the Index of Status Characteristics. The index is composed of four status characteristics: occupation, source of income, house type, and dwelling area. Each of these is rated on a 7-point scale, and this rating is then weighted according to its separate contributions to the total index. The weighted ratings are totaled to yield the scores that are appropriate to the various classes. The scores on the Index of Status Characteristics range from 12 to 84. The ranges are calculated by validating preliminary scores using the evaluated participation method of determining social class position. Occupation is the single measure most highly correlated with class position.

Where published: W. Lloyd Warner, Marcia Meeker, and Kenneth Eells, *Social Class in America* (Chicago: Science Research Associates, 1949), 121-59. The occupational rating scale is shown on pp. 140-41.

Validity of Index of Status Characteristics:

1. Accuracy in prediction: 85% of the Old Americans in "Yankee City" were placed correctly or within one point. Not as valid for ethnics.
2. Correlation with the evaluative participation method as reported by Warner et al. on p. 168.

   occupation: $r = .91$
   source of income: $r = .85$
   house type: $r = .85$
   dwelling area: $r = .82$
   ISC (all four measures): $r = .97$

3. Comparative study by John L. Haer: Five indexes of social stratification were compared and evaluated by examining their capacities for predicting variables shown in previous

studies to be related to measures of stratification. These five indexes include Center's class identification question, an open-ended question, occupation, education, and Warner's Index of Status Characteristics. An overall comparison reveals that coefficients are higher for the Index of Status Characteristics than for other indexes in 18 out of 22 comparisons. Its greater efficiency may be due to the fact that it is a composite index that provides a continuous series of ranks. These features make it possible to discern minute variations in relation to other variables.[1]

Validity of the Occupation Scale: Joseph A. Kahl and James A. Davis selected 19 single measures of socioeconomic status and measured their intercorrelations. They report a product-moment correlation of .74 between occupation (Warner) and status of friends: "Our data agree with Warner's that occupation (as he measures it) is the best predictor of either social participation or the whole socioeconomic cluster represented by the general factor identified by factor analysis."[2]

Stanley A. Hetzler reports the following coefficients between seven rating scales and ratings of social class and social position:

rating scales	social class	social position
occupational prestige	.69	.57
residential area	.54	.46
family background	.53	.48
personal influence	.49	.52
dwelling unit	.47	.39
family wealth	.45	.45
personal income	.34	.44

The four rating scales showing the highest coefficients were occupational prestige, family background, residential area, and personal influence. The multiple correlation of these four scales with social class is .75; with social position it is .68.[3]

Utility: The Index of Status Characteristics presents a comparatively objective means of determining social class position. The limits defined for the various 7-point ratings are sufficiently precise to eliminate to a great degree any subjective judgment. All one needs to know is a person's name, occupation, and address; the source of income can generally be derived from the occupation, and the house type and dwelling area can be evaluated through the address. This eliminates extensive, time-consuming interviewing.

The Occupation Scale is the best single predictor of social class position within a 7-point range. The high correlation it exhibits with the evaluative participative method of social class position ($r = .91$) commends occupation as a single dimension. Researchers will achieve a high degree of predictive efficiency by use of the one scale. Robinson and his coworkers call Warner's index "the most sophisticated short classification of occupational status available."[4]

Research applications:

Freeman, Howard E., and Ozzie G. Simmons. "Social Class and Post-Hospital Performance Levels." *American Sociological Review* 24 (1959): 345-51.

Goffman, Irwin W. "Status Consistency and Preference for Change in Power Distribution." *American Sociological Review* 22 (June 1957): 275-81. (See p. 277)

Kanin, Eugene, Jr., and David H. Howard. "Postmarital Consequences of Premarital Sex Adjustments." *American Sociological Review* 23 (October 1958): 556-62. (See p. 557)

Havighurst, Robert J., and Allison Davis. "A Comparison of the Chicago and Harvard Studies of Social Class Differences in Child Rearing." *American Sociological Review* 20 (August 1955): 438-42. (See p. 439)

TABLE 6.4 Warner, Meeker, and Eells's Revised Scale for Rating Occupation

Rating Assigned to Occupation	Professionals	Proprietors and Managers	Businessmen	Clerks and Kindred Workers, etc.	Manual Workers	Protective and Service Workers	Farmers
1	Lawyers, doctors, dentists, engineers, judges, high-school superintendents, veterinarians, ministers (graduated from divinity school), chemists, etc., with postgraduate training, architects	Businesses valued at $75,000 and over	Regional and divisional managers of large financial and industrial enterprises	Certified public accountants			Gentlemen farmers
2	High-school teachers, trained nurses, chiropractors, undertakers, ministers (some training), newspaper editors, librarians (graduate)	Businesses valued at $20,000 to $75,000	Assistant managers and office and department managers of large businesses, assistants to executives, etc.	Accountants, salesmen of real estate and insurance, postmasters			Large farm owners, farm owners
3	Social workers, grade school teachers, optometrists, librarians (not graduate), undertaker's assistants, ministers (no training)	Businesses valued at $5,000 to $20,000	All minor officials of businesses	Auto salesmen, bank clerks and cashiers, postal clerks, secretaries to executives, supervisors of railroad, telephone, etc., justices of the peace	Contractors		
4		Businesses valued at $2,000 to $5,000		Stenographers, bookkeepers, rural mail clerks, railroad clerks, railroad ticket agents, sales people in dry goods stores, etc.	Factory foremen, electricians, plumbers, carpenters, watchmakers (own business)	Dry cleaners, butchers, sheriffs, railroad engineers and conductors	

TABLE 6.4 (Continued)

Rating Assigned to Occupation	Professionals	Proprietors and Managers	Businessmen	Clerks and Kindred Workers, etc.	Manual Workers	Protective and Service Workers	Farmers
5		Businesses valued at $500 to $2,000		Dime-store clerks, hardware salesmen, beauty operators, telephone operators	Carpenters, plumbers, electricians (apprentice), timekeepers, linemen, telephone or telegraph, radio repairmen, medium-skilled workers	Barbers, firemen, butcher's apprentices, practical nurses, policemen, seamstresses, cooks in restaurants, bartenders	Tenant farmers
6		Businesses valued at less than $500			Moulders, semi-skilled workers, assistants to carpenter, etc.	Baggage men, night policemen and watchmen, taxi and truck drivers, gas station attendants, waitresses in restaurants	Small tenant farmers, laborers
7					Heavy laborers, migrant workers, odd-job men, miners	Janitors, scrubwomen, newsboys	Migrant farm laborers

Lawson, Edwin D., and Walter E. Bock. "Correlations of Indexes of Families' Socioeconomic Status." *Social Forces* 39 (December 1960): 149-52.

Littman, Richard A., Robert C. A. Moore, and John Pierce-Jones. "Social Class Differences in Child-Rearing: A Third Community for Comparison with Chicago and Newton." *American Sociological Review* 22 (December 1957): 694-704. (See p. 695)

Morland, J. Kenneth. "Racial Recognition by Nursery School Children in Lynchburg, Virginia." *Social Forces* 37 (December 1958): 132-41. (See p. 132)

——— . "Educational and Occupational Aspirations of Mill and Town School Children in a Southern Community." *Social Forces* 39 (December 1960): 169-75.

Salisbury, W. Seward. "Religion and Secularization." *Social Forces* 36 (March 1958): 197-205. (See p. 198)

Scudder, Richard, and Arnold C. Anderson. "Range of Acquaintance and of Repute as Factors in Prestige Rating Methods of Studying Social Status." *Social Forces* 32 (March 1954): 248-53. (See p. 252)

——— . "Migration and Vertical Occupational Mobility." *American Sociological Review* 19 (June 1954): 329-34. (See p. 330)

Stone, Gregory P., and William H. Form. "Instabilities in Status: The Problem of Hierarchy in the Community Study of Status Arrangements." *American Sociological Review* 18 (April 1953): 149-62.

——— . "The Local Community Clothing Market: A Study of the Social and Social Psychological Contexts of Shipping." Technical Bulletin No. 247. East Lansing: Michigan State University, 1955.

Swinehart, James W. "Socioeconomic Level, Status Aspiration, and Maternal Role." *American Sociological Review* 28 (June 1963): 391-99.

Warner, W. Lloyd, et al. *Democracy in Jonesville.* New York: Harper & Brothers, 1949.

Westie, Frank R., and David H. Howard. "Social Status Differentials and the Race Attitudes of Negroes." *American Sociological Review* 19 (October 1954): 584-91. (See p. 587)

White, Martha Sturm. "Social Class, Child Rearing Practices and Child Behavior." *American Sociological Review* 22 (December 1957): 704-12.

For more recent research use, see the *American Sociological Review* inventory presented in Section 6.L.1.

Notes

1. John L. Haer, "Predictive Utility of Five Indices of Social Stratification," *American Sociological Review* 22 (October 1957): 541-46.

2. Joseph A. Kahl and James A. Davis, "A Comparison of Indexes of Socio-Economic Status," *American Sociological Review* 20 (June 1955): 317-25.

3. Stanley A. Hetzler "An Investigation of the Distinctiveness of Social Classes," *American Sociological Review* 18 (October 1953): 493-97. See also J. L. Haer, "A Test of the Unidimensionality of the Index of Status Characteristics," *Social Forces* 34 (1955): 56-58.

4. See John B. Robinson, Robert Athanasiou, and Kendra B. Head, *Measures of Occupational Attitudes and Occupational Characteristics* (Ann Arbor: University of Michigan, Institute for Social Research, 1969), 338, 362-66.

ALBA M. EDWARDS'S SOCIAL-ECONOMIC GROUPING OF OCCUPATIONS   6.A.8

Variable measured: Socioeconomic position.

Description: Occupations are classified into six major groups, with each group purported to have a somewhat distinct economic standard of life and to exhibit intellectual and social similarities. The two major dimensions for the ranking order are income and education.

Where published: Alba M. Edwards, *Comparative Occupation Statistics for the United States* (Washington, DC: Government Printing Office, 1934), 164-69; U.S.

TABLE 6.5

Occupational Group	Men		Women	
	Mean School Years Completed 25 Years and Over (1970) [a]	Mean Earnings 25–64 Years (1969) [b]	Mean School Years Completed 25 Years and Over 1970) [a]	Mean Earnings 25–64 Years (1969) [b]
Professional, technical, and kindred workers	16.5	$16,007	16.1	$6,366
Managers and administrative workers, except farm	12.9	13,733	12.5	6,430
Sales workers	12.8	11,537	12.2	3,290
Clerical and kindred workers	12.5	8,461	12.5	4,605
Craftsmen, foremen, and kindred workers	11.8	8,749	11.8	5,048
Operatives and kindred workers	10.7	7,376	10.3	3,810
Laborers, except farm and mine	9.3	6,089	10.6	3,466

a. 1970 U.S. Census of Population, *Educational Attainment*, PC (2)-5B (Washington, DC: Government Printing Office, March 1973), table 11, 213–14.
b. 1970 U.S. Census of Population, *Earnings by Occupation and Education*, PC (2)-8B (Washington, DC: Government Printing Office, January 1973), tables 1 and 7.

Bureau of the Census, *1960 Census of Population: Classified Index of Occupations and Industries* (Washington, DC: Government Printing Office, 1960).

Reliability: Occupational grouping shows high comparability with similar occupational ranking systems such as Barr-Taussig, Beckman Goodenough and Anderson, and Centers.

Validity: Major occupational groups can be ranked on the two dimensions of income and education with relatively high correspondence, as shown for the occupational groups listed in Table 6.5.

Utility: This has been a widely used scale of social-economic groupings of gainful workers in the United States. It is the basis on which the U.S. Census has grouped workers since 1930 in the decennial census.

The universe of gainful workers is fully enumerated every 10 years. Any research worker can check his or her sample against enumeration parameters and can draw generalizations with high confidence.

Research applications:

Anderson, H. Dewey, and Percy E. Davidson. *Occupational Trends in the United States.* Stanford, CA: Stanford University Press, 1940.
———. *Occupational Mobility in an American Community.* Stanford, CA: Stanford University Press, 1937.

Blau, Peter M., and Otis Dudley Duncan. *The American Occupational Structure in the United States.* New York: John Wiley, 1967.

Davidson, Percy E., and H. Dewey Anderson. *Ballots and the Democratic Class Struggle.* Stanford, CA: Stanford University Press, 1943.

Glenn, Norval D., and John P. Alston. "Cultural Distances Among Occupational Categories." *American Sociological Review* 33 (June 1968): 365-82.

Jaffe, A. J., and R. O. Carleton. *Occupational Mobility in the United States, 1930-1960.* New York: Columbia University Press, 1954.

Lipset, Seymour Martin, and Reinhard Bendix. *Social Mobility and Industrial Society.* Berkeley: University of California Press, 1959.

Taussig, F. W., and C. S. Joslyn. *American Business Leaders.* New York: Macmillan, 1932.

Warner, W. Lloyd, and James C. Abegglen. *Occupational Mobility in American Business and Industry, 1928-1952.* Minneapolis: University of Minnesota Press, 1955.

For an extensive list of applications, see Charles M. Bonjean, Richard J. Hill, and S. Dale McLemore, *Sociological Measurement* (San Francisco: Chandler, 1967), 423-37.

Social-Economic Grouping of Occupations (After Alba M. Edwards)

Current U.S. Census classification of occupational groups:

1. professional, technical, and kindred workers
2. business managers, officials, and proprietors
   a. nonfarm managers, officials, and proprietors
   b. farm owners and managers
3. clerical and sales workers
   a. clerical and kindred workers
   b. sales workers
4. craftsmen, foremen, and kindred workers
5. operatives and kindred workers
6. unskilled, service, and domestic workers
   a. private household workers
   b. service workers, except private household
   c. farm laborers, unpaid family workers
   d. laborers, except farm and mine

Comment on Diverse Use of Occupational Classifications and Miscellaneous Measures as Status, Mobility, and Prestige Measures

Sociologists continue to use or modify occupational classifications to fit their definitions of the problems they wish to examine. In the 1981-87 *American Sociological Review* inventory in Section 6.L.1 of this volume, 15 articles are presented by their authors as author-constructed or -adapted measures of different occupational classifications. Five author-constructed measures are used to determine prestige; various measures of income are used in five articles as a status or mobility measure; highly individual efforts to measure status are demonstrated in three articles.

Section **B**

Group Structure and Dynamics

This section contains five scales, each of which measures a different variable relating to group structure and dynamics. Hemphill's Index of Group Dimensions, which ascertains 13 dimensions of a group, is the most ambitious attempt to measure the structural properties of groups. Bales's International Process Analysis is a nominal scale widely used to assess the characteristics of personal interaction in problem-solving groups. Seashore's Group Cohesiveness Index provides a measure of the strength of a group to maintain its identity and to persist. The Sociometry Scales of Spontaneous Choice and Sociometric Preference reveal the interpersonal attractions of members in groups. These scales may be widely adapted to suit many different situations. They are useful not only to researchers seeking basic relationships but also to action researchers or social workers. New groupings of individuals can be quickly arranged and new measurements of morale or productivity can be made. The Bogardus Social Distance Scale may also be adapted to many different purposes. The social distance between two persons, between person and group, or between groups can be measured in such diverse situations as that involving an out-group member and a country, a community, or an organization.

No articles in the 1981-87 *American Sociological Review* inventory (Section 6.L.1) have used any of these measures, but 29 articles appear! A survey of these articles reveals that the authors are seeking many new and, in many cases, highly individualized variables. They attempt to measure status integration, conversational ties, perceptions of social distance, behavioral tolerance measures, antisocial measures, and more. A professional trade-off keeps occurring: New ground is explored, but continuity is denied.

6.B.1   HEMPHILL'S INDEX OF GROUP DIMENSIONS

Variable measured: The index is designed to measure group dimensions of characteristics.

Description: The index is built upon 13 comparatively independent group dimensions: autonomy, control, flexibility, hedonic tone, homogeneity, intimacy, participation, permeability, polarization, potency, stability, stratification, and viscidity. The 150 items are answered on a 5-point scale. The dimensions were selected from a list of group adjectives used by authorities. Items were suggested from a free-response-type questionnaire administered to 500 individuals, and five judges then put the items into the dimensional categories.

Where published: John K. Hemphill, *Group Dimensions: A Manual for Their Measurement*, Research Monograph No. 87 (Columbus: Ohio State University, Bureau of Business Research, 1956).

Reliability: Split-half reliabilities range from .59 to .87. The relationship between an item and high-low categories ranges from .03 to .78, with a median of .36 on the keyed items and from .01 to .36 with a median of .12 on the randomly selected items. Intercorrelation of dimension scores ranges from –.54 to .81, with most within +.29 (which has a .01 significance level). Agreement between different reporters of the same group ranges from .53 to .74.

Validity: The dimension scores describing the characteristics of two quite different groups vary accordingly, while those describing the characteristics of two similar groups are quite similar. A careful critique of reliability and validity is available in Lake, Miles, and Earle's *Measuring Human Behavior.*[1]

Utility: The index can be useful in studying the relationships between the behavior of leaders and characteristics of groups in which they function. Although fairly long, it is comparatively easy to administer and score.

Research applications: Validation and reliability studies on 200 descriptions of 35 groups.

Bentz, V. J. "Leadership: A Study of Social Interaction." Unpublished report, Bureau of Business Research, Ohio State University.

Hemphill, John K., and Charles M. Westie. "The Measurement of Group Dimensions." *Journal of Psychology* 29 (April 1950): 325-42.

———. "The Measurement of Group Dimensions." In *The Language of Social Research*, rev. ed., edited by Paul F. Lazarsfeld and Morris Rosenberg. Glencoe, IL: Free Press, 1975.

Note

1. Dale G. Lake, Mathew B. Miles, and Ralph B. Earle, Jr., *Measuring Human Behavior* (New York: Teachers College Press, 1973), 91.

Group Dimensions Descriptions Questionnaire

Directions

Record your answer to each of the items on the answer sheet for the group you are describing. Make no marks on the question booklet itself.

In considering each item go through the following steps:

1. Read the item carefully.
2. Think about how well the item tells something about the group you are describing.
3. Find the number on the answer sheet that corresponds with the number of the item you are considering.

4. After each number on the answer sheet you will find five pairs of dotted lines lettered A, B, C, D, or E.

If the item you are considering tells something about the group that is definitely true, blacken the space between the pair of dotted lines headed by A.

If the item you are considering tells something that is mostly true, blacken the space between the pair of lines headed by B.

If the item tells something that is to an equal degree both true and false, or you are undecided about whether it is true or false, blacken the space between the pair of lines headed by C.

If the item you are considering tells something that is mostly false, blacken the space between the pair of lines headed by D.

If the item you are considering tells something about the group that is definitely false, blacken the space between the pair of dotted lines headed by E.

5. When blackening the space between a pair of lines, fill in all the space with a heavy black line. If you should make an error in marking your answer, erase thoroughly the mark you made and then indicate the correct answer.

6. In rare cases where you believe that an item does not apply at all to the group or you feel that you do not have sufficient information to make any judgment concerning what the item tells about the group, leave that item blank.

7. After you have completed one item, proceed to the next one in order.

You may have as long as you need to complete your description. Be sure the number on the answer sheet corresponds with the number of the item being answered in the booklet.

Questions

The questions that follow make it possible to describe objectively certain characteristics of social groups. The items simply describe characteristics of groups; they do not judge whether the characteristic is desirable or undesirable. Therefore, in no way are the questions to be considered a "test" either of the groups or of the person answering the questions. We simply want an objective description of what the group is like.

1. The group has well understood but unwritten rules concerning member conduct.
2. Members fear to express their real opinions.
3. The only way a member may leave the group is to be expelled.
4. No explanation need be given by a member wishing to be absent from the group.
5. An individual's membership can be dropped should he fail to live up to the standards of the group.
6. Members of the group work under close supervision.
7. Only certain kinds of ideas may be expressed freely within the group.
8. A member may leave the group by resigning at any time he wishes.
9. A request made by a member to leave the group can be refused.
10. A member has to think twice before speaking in the group's meetings.
11. Members are occasionally forced to resign.
12. The members of the group are subject to strict discipline.
13. The group is rapidly increasing in size.
14. Members are constantly leaving the group.
15. There is a large turnover of members within the group.
16. Members are constantly dropping out of the group but new members replace them.
17. During the entire time of the group's existence no member has left.
18. Each member's personal life is known to other members of the group.

19. Members of the group lend each other money.
20. A member has the chance to get to know all other members of the group.
21. Members are not in close enough contact to develop likes or dislikes for one another.
22. Members of the group do small favors for one another.
23. All members know each other very well.
24. Each member of the group knows all other members by their first names.
25. Members are in daily contact either outside or within the group.
26. Members of the group are personal friends.
27. Certain members discuss personal affairs among themselves.
28. Members of the group know the family backgrounds of other members of the group.
29. Members address each other by their first names.
30. The group is made up of individuals who do not know each other well.
31. The opinions of all members are considered as equal.
32. The group's officers hold a higher status in the group than other members.
33. The older members of the group are granted special privileges.
34. The group is controlled by the actions of a few members.
35. Every member of the group enjoys the same group privileges.
36. Experienced members are in charge of the group.
37. Certain problems are discussed only among the group's officers.
38. Certain members have more influence on the group than others.
39. Each member of the group has as much power as any other member.
40. An individual's standing in the group is determined only by how much he gets done.
41. Certain members of the group hold definite office in the group.
42. The original members of the group are given special privileges.
43. Personal dissatisfaction with the group is too small to be brought up.
44. Members continually grumble about the work they do for the group.
45. The group does its work with no great vim, vigor, or pleasure.
46. A feeling of failure prevails in the group.
47. There are frequent intervals of laughter during group meetings.
48. The group works independently of other groups.
49. The group has support from outside.
50. The group is an active representative of a larger group.
51. The group's activities are influenced by a larger group of which it is part.
52. People outside the group decide on what work the group is to do.
53. The group follows the examples set by other groups.
54. The group is one of many similar groups that form one large organization.
55. The things the group does are approved by a group higher up.
56. The group joins with other groups in carrying out its activities.
57. The group is a small part of a larger group.
58. The group is under outside pressure.
59. Members are disciplined by an outside group.
60. Plans of the group are made by other groups above it.
61. The members allow nothing to interfere with the progress of the group.
62. Members gain a feeling of being honored by being recognized as one of the group.
63. Membership in the group is a way of acquiring general social status.
64. Failure of the group would mean little to individual members.
65. The activities of the group take up less than ten percent of each member's waking time.
66. Members gain in prestige among outsiders by joining the group.
67. A mistake by one member of the group might result in hardship for all.
68. The activities of the group take up over ninety percent of each member's waking time.
69. Membership in the group serves as an aid to vocational advancement.
70. Failure of the group would mean nothing to most members.

71. Each member would lose his self-respect if the group should fail.
72. Membership in the group gives members a feeling of superiority.
73. The activities of the group take up over half the time each member is awake.
74. Failure of the group would lead to embarrassment for members.
75. Members are not rewarded for effort put out for the group.
76. There are two or three members of the group who generally take the same side on any group issue.
77. Certain members are hostile to other members.
78. There is constant bickering among members of the group.
79. Members know that each one looks out for the other one as well as for himself.
80. Certain members of the group have no respect for other members.
81. Certain members of the group are considered uncooperative.
82. There is a constant tendency toward conniving against one another among parts of the group.
83. Members of the group work together as a team.
84. Certain members of the group are responsible for petty quarrels and some animosity among other members.
85. There are tensions among subgroups that tend to interfere with the group's activities.
86. Certain members appear to be incapable of working as part of the group.
87. There is an undercurrent of feeling among members that tends to pull the group apart.
88. Anyone who has sufficient interest in the group to attend its meetings is considered a member.
89. The group engages in membership drives.
90. New members are welcomed to the group on the basis "the more the merrier."
91. A new member may join only after an old member resigns.
92. A college degree is required for membership in the group.
93. A person may enter the group by expressing a desire to join.
94. Anyone desiring to enter the group is welcome.
95. Membership is open to anyone willing to further the purpose of the group.
96. Prospective members are carefully examined before they enter the group.
97. No applicants for membership in the group are turned down.
98. No special training is required for membership in the group.
99. Membership depends upon the amount of education an individual has.
100. People interested in joining the group are asked to submit references which are checked.
101. There is a high degree of participation on the part of members.
102. If a member of the group is not productive he is not encouraged to remain.
103. Work of the group is left to those who are considered most capable for the job.
104. Members are interested in the group but not all of them want to work.
105. The group has a reputation for not getting much done.
106. Each member of the group is on one or more active committees.
107. The work of the group is well divided among members.
108. Every member of the group does not have a job to do.
109. The work of the group is frequently interrupted by having nothing to do.
110. There are long periods during which the group does nothing.
111. The group is directed toward one particular goal.
112. The group divides its efforts among several purposes.
113. The group operates with sets of conflicting plans.
114. The group has only one main purpose.
115. The group knows exactly what it has to get done.
116. The group is working toward many different goals.

117. The group does many things that are not directly related to its main purpose.
118. Each member of the group has a clear idea of the group's goals.
119. The objective of the group is specific.
120. Certain members meet for one thing and others for a different thing.
121. The group has major purposes which to some degree are in conflict.
122. The objectives of the group have never been clearly recognized.
123. The group is very informal.
124. A list of rules and regulations is given to each member.
125. The group has meetings at regularly scheduled times.
126. The group is organized along semimilitary lines.
127. The group's meetings are not planned or organized.
128. The group has an organization chart.
129. The group has rules to guide its activities.
130. The group is staffed according to a table of organization.
131. The group keeps a list of names of members.
132. Group meetings are conducted according to "Robert's Rules of Order."
133. There is a recognized right and wrong way of going about group activities.
134. Most matters that come up before the group are voted upon.
135. The group meets at any place that happens to be handy.
136. The members of the group vary in amount of ambition.
137. Members of the group are from the same social class.
138. Some members are interested in altogether different things than other members.
139. The group contains members with widely varying backgrounds.
140. The group contains whites and Negroes.
141. Members of the group are all about the same ages.
142. A few members of the group have greater ability than others.
143. A number of religious beliefs are represented by members of the group.
144. Members of the group vary greatly in social background.
145. All members of the group are of the same sex.
146. The ages of members range over a period of at least 20 years.
147. Members come into the group with quite different family backgrounds.
148. Members of the group vary widely in amount of experience.
149. Members vary in the number of years they have been in the group.
150. The group includes members of different races.

Scoring Key and Directions for Scoring

A subject's score for a particular dimension is the sum of the item scores for that dimension. For example, the raw score for the dimension "Control" is the sum of the scores for items 1 to 12 inclusive. The total (raw) score for this dimension can range from 12 to 60.

Occasionally a respondent may fail to indicate an answer. Such omissions are scored as C responses (neither true nor false). However, if the number of omitted items exceeds half the total number of items assigned to a given dimension, no score for that dimension is assigned. In general, experience has shown that few respondents deliberately omit items.

The answers are marked on a separate answer sheet (IBM Answer Sheet No. 1100 A 3870). A separate blank answer sheet may be used for preparing a scoring key for each dimension.

Scoring Keys

Control	A	B	C	D	E
1	5	4	3	2	1
2	5	4	3	2	1
3	5	4	3	2	1
4	1	2	3	4	5
5	5	4	3	2	1
6	5	4	3	2	1
7	5	4	3	2	1
8	1	2	3	4	5
9	5	4	3	2	1
10	5	4	3	2	1
11	5	4	3	2	1
12	5	4	3	2	1
Stability	A	B	C	D	E
13	1	2	3	4	5
14	1	2	3	4	5
15	1	2	3	4	5
16	1	2	3	4	5
17	5	4	3	2	1
Intimacy	A	B	C	D	E
18	5	4	3	2	1
19	5	4	3	2	1
20	5	4	3	2	1
21	1	2	3	4	5
22	5	4	3	2	1
23	5	4	3	2	1
24	5	4	3	2	1
25	5	4	3	2	1
26	5	4	3	2	1
27	5	4	3	2	1
28	5	4	3	2	1
29	5	4	3	2	1
30	1	2	3	4	5
Stratification	A	B	C	D	E
31	1	2	3	4	5
32	5	4	3	2	1
33	5	4	3	2	1
34	5	4	3	2	1
35	1	2	3	4	5
36	5	4	3	2	1
37	5	4	3	2	1
38	5	4	3	2	1
39	1	2	3	4	5
40	5	4	3	2	1
41	5	4	3	2	1
Hedonic tone	A	B	C	D	E
43	5	4	3	2	1
44	1	2	3	4	5
45	1	2	3	4	5
46	1	2	3	4	5
47	5	4	3	2	1
Autonomy	A	B	C	D	E
48	5	4	3	2	1
49	1	2	3	4	5

	1	2	3	4	5
50	1	2	3	4	5
51	1	2	3	4	5
52	1	2	3	4	5
53	1	2	3	4	5
54	1	2	3	4	5
55	1	2	3	4	5
56	1	2	3	4	5
57	1	2	3	4	5
58	1	2	3	4	5
59	1	2	3	4	5
60	1	2	3	4	5
Potency	A	B	C	D	E
61	5	4	3	2	1
62	5	4	3	2	1
63	5	4	3	2	1
64	1	2	3	4	5
65	1	2	3	4	5
66	5	4	3	2	1
67	5	4	3	2	1
68	5	4	3	2	1
69	5	4	3	2	1
70	1	2	3	4	5
71	5	4	3	2	1
72	5	4	3	2	1
73	5	4	3	2	1
74	5	4	3	2	1
75	1	2	3	4	5
Viscidity	A	B	C	D	E
76	1	2	3	4	5
77	1	2	3	4	5
78	1	2	3	4	5
79	5	4	3	2	1
80	1	2	3	4	5
81	1	2	3	4	5
82	1	2	3	4	5
83	5	4	3	2	1
84	1	2	3	4	5
85	1	2	3	4	5
86	1	2	3	4	5
87	1	2	3	4	5
Permeability	A	B	C	D	E
88	5	4	3	2	1
89	5	4	3	2	1
90	5	4	3	2	1
91	1	2	3	4	5
92	1	2	3	4	5
93	5	4	3	2	1
94	5	4	3	2	1
95	5	4	3	2	1
96	1	2	3	4	5
97	5	4	3	2	1
98	5	4	3	2	1
99	1	2	3	4	5
100	1	2	3	4	5

Participation	A	B	C	D	E
101	5	4	3	2	1
102	5	4	3	2	1
103	1	2	3	4	5
104	1	2	3	4	5
105	1	2	3	4	5
106	5	4	3	2	1
107	5	4	3	2	1
108	1	2	3	4	5
109	1	2	3	4	5
110	1	2	3	4	5
Polarization	A	B	C	D	E
111	5	4	3	2	1
112	1	2	3	4	5
113	1	2	3	4	5
114	5	4	3	2	1
115	5	4	3	2	1
116	1	2	3	4	5
117	1	2	3	4	5
118	5	4	3	2	1
119	5	4	3	2	1
120	1	2	3	4	5
121	1	2	3	4	5
122	1	2	3	4	5
Flexibility	A	B	C	D	E
123	5	4	3	2	1
124	1	2	3	4	5
125	1	2	3	4	5
126	1	2	3	4	5
127	5	4	3	2	1
128	1	2	3	4	5
129	1	2	3	4	5
130	1	2	3	4	5
131	1	2	3	4	5
132	1	2	3	4	5
133	1	2	3	4	5
134	1	2	3	4	5
135	5	4	3	2	1
Homogeneity	A	B	C	D	E
136	5	4	3	2	1
137	1	2	3	4	5
138	1	2	3	4	5
139	1	2	3	4	5
140	1	2	3	4	5
141	5	4	3	2	1
142	1	2	3	4	5
143	1	2	3	4	5
144	1	2	3	4	5
145	5	4	3	2	1
146	1	2	3	4	5
147	1	2	3	4	5
148	1	2	3	4	5
149	1	2	3	4	5
150	1	2	3	4	5

Group Dimensions Profile and Face Sheet

Name _____ Age _____ Date _____

Name of group _____

Length of your membership _____ No. of group members _____

General purpose of the group _____

Dimension		Stanine score								
		1	2	3	4	5	6	7	8	9
A	Autonomy	.	.	.	.	.	.	.	.	.
B	Control	.	.	.	.	.	.	.	.	.
C	Flexibility	.	.	.	.	.	.	.	.	.
D	Hedonic Tone	.	.	.	.	.	.	.	.	.
E	Homogeneity	.	.	.	.	.	.	.	.	.
F	Intimacy	.	.	.	.	.	.	.	.	.
G	Participation	.	.	.	.	.	.	.	.	.
H	Permeability	.	.	.	.	.	.	.	.	.
I	Polarization	.	.	.	.	.	.	.	.	.
J	Potency	.	.	.	.	.	.	.	.	.
K	Stability	.	.	.	.	.	.	.	.	.
L	Stratification	.	.	.	.	.	.	.	.	.
M	Viscidity	.	.	.	.	.	.	.	.	.

BALES'S INTERACTION PROCESS ANALYSIS   6.B.2

Variable measured: Group interaction.

Description: This index consists of 12 categories—shows solidarity, shows tension release, agrees, gives suggestion, gives opinion, gives orientation, asks for orientation, asks for opinion, asks for suggestion, disagrees, shows tension, shows antagonism. Scoring is made by designating each person in the group with a number. All interaction is analyzed according to the category and marked in the fashion of 1-5 or 1-0 as the interaction takes place. After observation, a summary or profile can be constructed and inferences made to describe the underlying workings of the group.

A slightly revised version of the categories has been developed by Bales.[1] A new interpersonal behavior rating system is organized around the dimensions of "up/down," "forward/back," and "positive/negative." Category 1 is now labeled "Seems Friendly" and category 12 "Seems Unfriendly"; category 2 is now "Dramatizes," and categories 6 and 7 are "Gives Information" and "Asks for Information." Contents of other categories (except 3, 8, and 10) have also been changed.

While Bales's scheme is not widely used today in its original form, it remains the model in its field. It did much to aid early development of small group analysis. The new form is somewhat simpler and easier to use. New norms are not available, but Bales provides estimates of how the changes may influence percentage distributions.

Where published: R. F. Bales, *Interaction Process Analysis: A Method for the Study of Small Groups* (Cambridge, MA: Addison-Wesley, 1950). See also John Madge, *The Origins of Scientific Sociology* (New York: Free Press, 1967), 424-77.

Reliability: With competent and trained observers, an interobserver correlation of between .75 and .95 can be obtained.

Validity: Face validity. Consult the critique by Lake, Miles, and Earle.[2]

Utility: This is a general-purpose, standard set of categories well suited for the observation and analysis of small groups. The chief disadvantage is that the training of observers requires a great deal of practice. Frequent retraining is also necessary.

Research applications:

Bales, Robert F. *Personality and Interpersonal Behavior.* New York: Holt, Rinehart & Winston, 1970. (See pp. 532-42)

Burke, Peter J. "Participation and Leadership in Small Groups." *American Sociological Review* 39 (December 1974): 832-43.

Hare, Paul A. *Handbook of Small Group Research.* 2nd ed. Glencoe, IL: Free Press, 1975.

———, Edgar F. Borgatta, and Robert F. Bales, eds. *Small Groups: Studies in Social Interaction.* Rev. ed. New York: Knopf, 1965.

See the bibliography on small group research.

Smith, H. W. "Some Developmental Interpersonal Dynamics Through Childhood." *American Sociological Review* 38 (October 1973): 543-52.

For additional references, check *Social Psychology Quarterly*, published by the American Sociological Association.

1	SHOWS SOLIDARITY, raises others' status, gives help, reward:					
2	SHOWS TENSION RELEASE, jokes, laughs, shows satisfaction:					
3	AGREES, shows passive acceptance, understands, concurs, complies:					
4	GIVES SUGGESTION, direction, implying autonomy for other:					
5	GIVES OPINION, evaluation, analysis, expresses feeling, wish:					
6	GIVES ORIENTATION, information, repeats, clarifies, confirms:					
7	ASKS FOR ORIENTATION, information, repetition, confirmation:					
8	ASKS FOR OPINION, evaluation, analysis, expression of feeling:					
9	ASKS FOR SUGGESTION, direction, possible ways of action:					
10	DISAGREES, shows passive rejection, formality, withholds help:					
11	SHOWS TENSION, asks for help, withdraws "Out of Field":					
12	SHOWS ANTAGONISM, deflates other's status, defends or asserts self:					

Notes

1. R. F. Bales, *Personality and Interpersonal Behavior* (New York: Holt, Rinehart & Winston, 1970); see Appendix 4 for a description of the changes.

2. Dale G. Lake, Mathew B. Miles, and Ralph B. Earle, *Measuring Human Behavior* (New York: Teachers College Press, 1973).

SEASHORE'S GROUP COHESIVENESS INDEX 6.B.3

Index of Group Cohesiveness

"Do you feel that you are really a part of your work group?"

- ☐ Really a part of my work group
- ☐ Included in most ways
- ☐ Included in some ways, but not in others
- ☐ Don't feel I really belong
- ☐ Don't work with any one group of people
  - ☐ Not ascertained

"If you had a chance to do the same kind of work for the same pay, in another work group, how would you feel about moving?"

- ☐ Would want very much to move
- ☐ Would rather move than stay where I am
- ☐ Would make no difference to me
- ☐ Would rather stay where I am than move
- ☐ Would want very much to stay where I am
  - ☐ Not ascertained

"How does your work group compare with other work groups at Midwest on each of the following points?"

	Better than most	About the same as most	Not as good as most	Not ascertained
The way people get along together	☐	☐	☐	☐
The way people stick together	☐	☐	☐	☐
The way people help one another on the job	☐	☐	☐	☐

Variable measured: The index measures group cohesiveness, defined as attraction to the group or resistance to leaving.

Description: The test consists of three questions: "Do you feel that you are really a part of your work group?" "If you had a chance to do the same kind of work for the same pay, in another work group, how would you feel about moving?" and "How does your work group compare with other work groups at Midwest on each of the following points?"—the way people get along together, the way people stick together, and the way people help each other on the job. The first two questions can be answered by five degrees, while the three items of the third question are answered by four degrees.

Where published: Stanley E. Seashore, *Group Cohesiveness in the Industrial Work Group* (Ann Arbor: University of Michigan, Institute for Social Research, Survey Research Center, 1954).

Reliability: Intercorrelations among mean scale values for the groups on scales constituting the index of cohesiveness ranged from .15 to .70.

Validity: The variance found among groups on this scale was significant beyond the .001 level.

Utility: As the questions are phrased, the index is especially set up for an industrial situation. It can probably, with a few changes, be adapted to almost any situation where an index of group cohesiveness is required. The test takes very little time to administer. The subject should be assured that replies will be kept confidential.

Research applications: The study of 228 section-shift groups in a company manufacturing heavy machinery, described in the aforementioned Seashore monograph.

6.B.4   SOCIOMETRY SCALES OF SPONTANEOUS CHOICE AND SOCIOMETRIC PREFERENCE

Variable measured: The degree to which individuals are accepted in a group, interpersonal relationships that exist among individuals, and structure of the group.

Description: Results are most satisfactory for small cohesive groups. The sociometric technique consists of asking each individual in a group to state with whom among the members of the group he or she would prefer to associate for specific activities or in particular situations. Criteria (selected areas that should include different aspects of possible association: work, play, visiting) range in number from 1 to 8 or more; choices, from 1 to as many as desired by the researcher.

Where published: J. L. Moreno, *Who Shall Survive? A New Approach to the Problem of Human Relationships* (Beacon, NY: Beacon House, 1934).

Reliability:

Loeb's correlation between odd-even items: $r = .65$ to $.85$
Loeb's correlation between split-halves: $r = .53$ to $.85$
Mary L. Northway between general criteria: $r = .64$ to $.84$
Mary L. Northway between skill criteria: $r = .37$ to $.50$
correlations between scores on tests given at different times: $r = .74$
constancy of choice (actual preference on first test repeated later on): $r = .69$

Validity: Eugene Byrd's comparison of sociometric choice with actual choice and then an eight-week interval retest shows $r = .76, .80, .89$.[1] Gronlund's comparison of judgment of teachers versus testing shows $r = .59$.[2]

For further discussion of reliability and validity, see Northway's *A Primer of Sociometry* and Merl E. Bonney's "A Study of Constancy of Sociometric Ranks Among College Students over a Two-Year Period."[3]

Standard scores: None.

Research applications:

Bronfenbrenner, Urie. *The Measurement of Sociometric Status, Structure and Development.* Sociometry Monograph No. 6. Beacon, NY: Beacon House, 1945.

Holland, Paul W., and Samuel Leinhardt. "A Method of Detecting Structure in Sociometric Data." *American Journal of Sociology* 76 (November 1970): 492-513.

Jacobs, John H. "The Applications of Sociometry to Industry." *Sociometry* 8 (May 1945): 181-98.

Jennings, Helen H. *Leadership and Isolation: A Study of Personality in Interpersonal Relations.* 2nd ed. New York: McKay, 1950.

Leinhardt, Samuel. "Developmental Change in the Sentiment Structure of Children's Groups." *American Sociological Review* 37 (April 1972): 202-12.

Lundberg, George A., and Lenore Dickson. "Inter-Ethnic Relations in a High School Population." *American Journal of Sociology* 57 (July 1952): 1-10.

Massarik, Fred, Robert Tannenbaum, Murray Rahane, and Irving Weschler. "Sociometric Choice and Organizational Effectiveness: A Multi-Relational Approach." *Sociometry* (August 1953): 211-38.

——— . *Leadership and Organization.* New York: McGraw-Hill, 1961, 346-70.

Moreno, J. L. *Who Shall Survive? A New Approach to the Problem of Human Relationships.* Beacon, NY: Beacon House, 1934.

——— . *Sociometry and the Science of Man.* Beacon, NY: Beacon House, 1956.

White, Harrison. "Management Conflict and Sociometric Structure." *American Journal of Sociology* 67 (September 1961): 185-99.

Zeleny, Leslie D. "Selection of Compatible Flying Partners." *American Journal of Sociology* 52 (March 1947): 424-31.

For an excellent review of the literature on measures of sociometric structure, see M. Glanzer and R. Glaser, "Techniques for the Study of Group Structure and Behavior: I. Analysis of Structure," *Psychological Bulletin* 56 (September 1959): 317-32. See also J. L. Moreno, "Contributions of Sociometry to Research Methodology in Sociology," *American Sociological Review* 12 (June 1947): 287-92; Jacob L. Moreno et al., *The Sociometry Reader* (Glencoe, IL: Free Press, 1959). For more recent work, check *Social Psychology Quarterly*.

Spontaneous Choice Test

Opposite each name, check how you feel about persons in your group.

	Like	Dislike	Indifferent
Mary J.			
James F.			
John J.			
Etc.			

Sociometric Preference Test

Choose five persons you would most like to work with.[a] Mark 1st, 2nd, 3rd, 4th, 5th choice.

Mary J.			
James F.			
John J.			
Sam E.			
Etc.			

a. Many criteria may be employed. For example, to have in a discussion group, to have in your neighborhood, to play bridge with, to work on a project with, etc.

Notes

1. Eugene Byrd, "A Study of Validity and Constancy of Choices in a Sociometric Test," *Sociometry* 9 (1946): 21.

2. N. Gronlund, *Accuracies of Teachers' Judgments Concerning the Sociometric Status of Sixth Grade Pupils,* Sociometry Monograph No. 25 (Beacon, NY: Beacon House, 1951).

3. Mary L. Northway, *A Primer of Sociometry* (Toronto: University of Toronto, 1952), 16-20; Merl E. Bonney, "A Study of Constancy of Sociometric Ranks Among College Students over a Two-Year Period," *Sociometry* 18 (December 1955): 531-42.

6.B.5   BOGARDUS'S SOCIAL DISTANCE SCALE

Variable measured: The social distance or degree of social acceptance that exists between given persons and certain social groups. The scale may be adapted to measure the social distance between two persons or between two or more social groups. The method has been applied to racial distance, regional distance, sex distance, age distance, parent-child distance, educational distance, class distance, occupational distance, religious distance, and international distance.

Description: Typically, a group of persons is asked to rank a series of social types with respect to the degrees of social distance on 7 attributes, starting with "acceptance to close kinship by marriage" and concluding with "would exclude from my country." A group of 100 people acting as judges have identified these 7 attributes among 60 as those ordered on a continuum of social distance.

Where published: Best source is Emory S. Bogardus, *Social Distance* (Yellow Springs, OH: Antioch, 1959). See also Emory S. Bogardus, *Immigration and Race Attitudes* (Boston: Heath, 1928); E. S. Bogardus, "A Social Distance Scale," *Sociology and Social Research* 17 (January-February 1933): 265-71. Excellent instructions may be found in William J. Goode and Paul K. Hatt, *Methods in Social Research* (New York: McGraw-Hill, 1952), 26, 245-49.

Reliability: Split-half reliability coefficient reported at .90 or higher in repeated tests by Eugene L. Hartley and Ruth E. Hartley.

Validity: Theodore Newcomb reports high validity if one uses "agreement with other scales that in certain particulars are more exact." Application of the known-group method is advocated in determination of validity. This involves finding groups known to be favorable toward some of the ethnic types and unfavorable toward others. If the responses of these groups fit the requisite pattern, evidence for validity may be accepted. For full discussion, see Bogardus's *Social Distance* (pp. 92-95).

Scoring: Several scoring methods have been used. A simple method that has been found to be as reliable as more complex ones is that of counting the numbers of the "nearest column" that is checked. That is, if the racial distance quotient (RDQ) of a number of persons is desired, then the arithmetic mean of the total number of the "nearest columns" that are checked by all the subjects for each race is obtained. If the RDQ of a person is sought, then the arithmetic mean of the total numbers of the "nearest column" for each race is obtained.

Standard scores: RDQs given to racial groups in 1956 by 2,053 selected persons throughout the United States:

1. Americans (U.S. White)	1.08	16. Jews	2.15
2. Canadians	1.16	17. Czechs	2.22
3. English	1.23	18. Armenians	2.33
4. French	1.47	19. Japanese Americans	2.34
5. Irish	1.56	20. Indians (American)	2.35
6. Swedish	1.57	21. Filipinos	2.46
7. Scots	1.60	22. Mexican Americans	2.51
8. Germans	1.61	23. Turks	2.52
9. Hollanders	1.63	24. Russians	2.56
10. Norwegians	1.56	25. Chinese	2.68
11. Finns	1.80	26. Japanese	2.70
12. Italians	1.89	27. Negroes	2.74
13. Poles	2.07	28. Mexicans	2.79
14. Spanish	2.08	29. Indians (from India)	2.80
15. Greeks	2.09	30. Koreans	2.83

Arithmetic mean of 61,590 racial reactions: 2.08.

Utility: The Bogardus scale may be used to estimate the amount of potential and real conflict existing between any cultural groups, anywhere in industrial, political, racial, religious, and other phases of life. It also helps to determine the extent of the trend toward conflict or toward cooperation between groups. The test is easy to administer and to score. It can be adapted easily to other problems of social distance.

A good illustration of such an adaptation is to be found in the Mock Table for a Scale to Measure the Attractiveness of Different Communities in William J. Goode and Paul K. Hatt, *Methods in Social Research* (New York: McGraw-Hill, 1952), 248. The fullest description of applications is to be found in Bogardus's *Social Distance.*

Research applications:

Barber, Bernard. *Social Stratification.* New York: Harcourt, Brace, 1957.
Bardis, Panos D. "Social Distance Among Foreign Students." *Sociology and Social Research* 41: 112-15.
———. "Social Distance in a Greek Metropolitan City." *Social Science* 37 (April 1962): 108-11.
Best, W. H., and C. P. Sohner. "Social Distance Methodology in the Measurement of Political Attitudes." *Sociology and Social Research* 40: 266-70.
———. "Social Distance and Politics." *Sociology and Social Research* 40: 339-42.
Biesanz, J., and M. Biesanz. "Social Distance in the Youth Hostel Movement." *Sociology and Social Research* 25: 237-45.
Binnewies, W. G. "A Method of Studying Rural Social Distance." *Sociology and Social Research* 10: 239-42.
Bogardus, Emory S. See articles in *Sociometry* 10: 306-11; *International Journal of Opinion and Attitude Research* 1: 55-62; *American Sociological Review* 16: 48-53; *Journal of Educational Sociology* 3: 497-502; *Survey Graphic* 9: 169-70, 206, 208; *Journal of Applied Sociology* 9: 216-26; *Sociology and Social Research* 12: 173-78; 13: 73-81; 13: 171-75; 14: 174-80; 17: 167-73; 17: 265-61; 18: 67-73; 20: 473-77; 22: 462-76; 24: 69-75; 32: 723-27; 32: 798-802; 32: 882-87; 33: 291-95; 36: 40-47; 43: 439-41; *The Urban Community,* edited by E. W. Burgess, 48-54. Chicago: University of Chicago Press, 1927.
Bradway, John S. "Social Distance Between Lawyers and Social Workers." *Sociology and Social Research* 14: 516-24.
Briggs, Arthur E. "Social Distance Between Lawyers and Doctors." *Sociology and Social Research* 13: 156-63.
Brooks, Lee M. "Racial Distance as Affected by Education." *Sociology and Social Research* 21: 128-33.
Campbell, Donald T. "The Bogardus Social Distance Scale." *Sociology and Social Research* 36: 322-25.
Catapusan, Benicio T. "Social Distance in the Philippines." *Sociology and Social Research* 38: 309-12.
Dodd, Stuart C. "A Social Distance Test in the Near East." *American Journal of Sociology* 41 (September 1935): 194-204.

—— and J. Nehnevajsa. "Physical Dimensions of Social Distance." *Sociology and Social Research* 38: 287-92.

Duncan, W. L. "Parent-Child Isolations." *The Family* 10: 115-18.

DuVall, Everett W. "Child-Parent Social Distance." *Sociology and Social Research* 21: 458-63.

Eisenstadt, S. N. *From Generation to Generation: Age Groups and the Social Structure*. Glencoe, IL: Free Press, 1956.

Ellefsen, J. B. "Social Distance Attitudes of Negro College Students." *Phylon* 17: 79-83.

Ellis, Robert A. "Social Status and Social Distance." *Sociology and Social Research* 40: 240-46.

Franklin, Clay. "The Effect of the Format upon the Scale Values of the Bogardus Social Distance Scale." *Research Studies of the State College of Washington* 18: 117-20.

Gleason, George. "Social Distance in Russia." *Sociology and Social Research* 17: 37-43.

Grace, H. A., and J. O. Neuhaus. "Information and Social Distance as Predictors of Hostility Toward Nations." *Journal of Abnormal and Social Psychology* 47 (1952): 540-45.

Greifer, Julian L. "Attitudes to the Stranger." *American Sociological Review* 10 (December 1945): 739-45.

Gurnee, H., and E. Baker. "Social Distances of Some Common Social Relationships." *Journal of Abnormal and Social Psychology* 33 (1938): 265-69.

Halbwachs, M. *The Psychology of Social Classes*. Glencoe, IL: Free Press, 1958.

Hamren, Vandyce. "Social Farness Between the A.F. of L. and the C.I.O." *Sociology and Social Research* 24: 442-52.

——. "Social Nearness Between the A.F. of L. and the C.I.O." *Sociology and Social Research* 26: 232-40.

Hartley, Eugene L. *Problems in Prejudice*. New York: Columbia University Press, 1946.

—— and Ruth E. Hartley. *Fundamentals of Social Psychology*. New York: Knopf, 1952, 431-43.

Hunt, Chester L. "Social Distance in the Philippines." *Sociology and Social Research* 40: 253-60.

Hypes, E. L. "The Social Distance Score Card as a Teaching Device." *Social Forces* 7 (December 1928): 234-37.

Jameson, S. H. "Social Distance Between Welfare Organizations." *Sociology and Social Research* 5: 230-43.

——. "Social Nearness Among Welfare Organizations." *Sociology and Social Research* 15: 322-33.

Kahl, Joseph A. *The American Class Structure*. New York: Rinehart, 1957.

Koch, H. L. "Study of Some Factors Conditioning the Social Distance between the Sexes." *Journal of Social Psychology* 20: 79-107.

Krout, M. H. "Periodic Change in Social Distance: A Study in the Shifting Bases of Perception." *Sociology and Social Research* 27: 339-51.

Lambert, W. E. "Comparison of French and American Modes of Response to the Bogardus Social Distance Scale." *Social Forces* 31: 115-60.

Martin, R. R. "Sudden Change in Social Distance." *Sociology and Social Research* 22: 53-56.

McDonagh, Edward C. "Social Distance Between China and Japan." *Sociology and Social Research* 22: 131-36.

——. "Asiatic Stereotypes and National Distance." *Sociology and Social Research* 22: 474-78.

——. "Military Social Distance." *Sociology and Social Research* 29: 289-96.

McKenzie, R. D. "Spatial Distance and Community Organization Pattern." *Social Forces* 5: 623-27.

——. "Spatial Distance." *Sociology and Social Research* 13: 536-44.

McMath, Ella M. "A Girl Without a Country." *Journal of Applied Sociology* 11: 65-71.

Mitchell, Roy. "An Ethnic Distance Study in Buffalo." *Sociology and Social Research* 40: 35-40.

Mowrer, E. R. *Domestic Discord*. Chicago: University of Chicago Press, 1928, chap. 3.

Neprash, J. A. "Minority Group Contacts and Social Distance." *Phylon* 14: 207-12.

Newcomb, Theodore M. *Social Psychology*. Rev. ed. New York: Holt, Rinehart & Winston, 1955, 154-75.

Nimkoff, M. F. "Parent-Child Conflict." *Sociology and Social Research* 12: 446-58.

——. "Parent-Child Conflict." *Sociology and Social Research* 14: 135-50.

North, C. C. *Social Differentiation*. Chapel Hill: University of North Carolina Press, 1926.

Owen, John E. "Social Distance in England." *Sociology and Social Research* 30: 460-65.

Parish, Helen R. "Social Nearness Between Latin America and the United States." *Sociology and Social Research* 19: 253-58.

Park, R. E. "The Concept of Social Distance." *Journal of Applied Sociology* 8: 339-44.

Pettigrew, Thomas F. "Social Distance Attitudes of South African Students." *Social Forces* 38 (March 1960): 246-53.

Poole, W. C., Jr. "Distance in Sociology." *American Journal of Sociology* 33: 99-104.

――――. "Social Distance and Social Pathology." *Sociology and Social Research* 12: 268-72.

――――. "Social Distance and Personal Distance." *Journal of Applied Sociology* 11: 114-20.

――――. "The Social Distance Margin Reviewed." *Sociology and Social Research* 13: 49-54.

―――― and Harriet K. Poole. "Laws of Social Distance." *Journal of Applied Sociology* 11: 365-69.

Prothro, E. T., and O. K. Miles. "Social Distance in the Deep South as Measured by a Revised Bogardus Scale." *Journal of Social Psychology* 37: 171-74.

Runner, Jessie R. "Social Distance in Adolescent Relationships." *American Journal of Sociology* 43: 428-39.

Sartain, A. I., and Harold V. Bell, Jr. "An Evaluation of the Bogardus Scale of Social Distance by the Method of Equal-Appearing Intervals." *Journal of Social Psychology* 29: 85-91.

Sarvis, Guy W. "Social Distance in Religion." *Christian Century* 49: 1331-33.

Schenk, Q. F., and A. K. Romney. "Some Differential Attitudes Among Adolescent Groups as Revealed by Bogardus' Social Distance Scale." *Sociology and Social Research* 35: 38-45.

Schnetz, Alfred. "The Stranger." *American Journal of Sociology* 49: 499-508.

Schroff, Ruth. "Charting Social Distance." *Sociology and Social Research* 14: 567-70.

Seymour, J. G. "Rural Social Distance of Normal School Students." *Sociology and Social Research* 14: 238-48.

Sherif, Muzafer, and Carolyn W. Sherif. *An Outline of Social Psychology.* New York: Harper & Brothers, 1956, 659-78.

Shideler, Ernest. "The Social Distance Margin." *Sociology and Social Research* 12: 243-52.

Sorokin, P. *Social Mobility.* New York: Harper & Brothers, 1927, chap. 6.

Stephenson, C. M., and Carol G. Wilcox. "Social Distance Variations of College Students." *Sociology and Social Research* 39: 240-41.

Turbeville, Gus. "A Social Distance Study of Duluth, Minnesota." *Sociology and Social Research* 18: 420-30.

Van den Berghe, Pierre L. "Distance Mechanisms of Stratification." *Sociology and Social Research* 44 (January-February 1960): 155-64.

Westie, F. R. "Negro-White Status Differentials and Social Distance." *American Sociological Review* 17 (October 1952): 550-58.

―――― and Margaret L. Westie. "The Social Distance Pyramid: Relationships Between Caste and Class." *American Journal of Sociology* 63 (September 1957): 190-96.

――――. "Social Distance Scales: A Tool for the Study of Stratification." *Sociology and Social Research* 43: 251-58.

Wood, Margaret Mary. *Paths of Loneliness.* New York: Columbia University Press, 1953.

Zeligs, Rose, and G. Hendrickson. "Checking the Social Distance Technique Through Personal Interviews." *Sociology and Social Research* 18: 420-30.

Ziegler, George H. "Social Farness Between Hindus and Moslems." *Sociology and Social Research* 33: 188-95.

Interesting adaptations of the social distance scale are found in the following works:

DeFleur, M. L., and Frank R. Westie. "Verbal Attitudes and Overt Acts: An Experiment on the Salience of Attitudes." *American Sociological Review* 23 (December 1958): 667-73.

Jackson, Elton F. "Status Consistency and Symptoms of Stress." *American Sociological Review* 27 (August 1962): 469-80.

Longworthy, Russell L. "Community Status and Influence in a High School." *American Sociological Review* 24 (August 1959): 537-39.

Martin, James G., and Frank R. Westie. "The Tolerant Personality." *American Sociological Review* 24 (August 1959): 521-28.

Photiadis, John D., and Jeanne Biggar. "Religiosity, Education, and Ethnic Distance." *American Journal of Sociology* 67 (May 1962): 666-73.

Photiadis, John D., and Arthur L. Johnson. "Orthodoxy, Church Participation, and Authoritarianism." *American Journal of Sociology* 69 (November 1963): 244-48.

Westie, Frank R. "A Technique for the Measurement of Race Attitudes." *American Sociological Review* 18 (February 1953): 73-78.

――――. "Note to Prospective Users of the Summated Differences Technique." In *Sociological Measurement*, edited by Charles M. Bonjean, Richard J. Hill, and Dale McLemore, 158-62. San Francisco: Chandler, 1976.

Bogardus's Racial Distance Scale

Race is defined here largely as a cultural group.

Directions

1. Remember to give your *first feeling reactions* in every case.
2. Give your reactions to each race as a *group*. Do not give your reactions to the best or to the worst members that you have known, but think of the picture or stereotype that you have of the whole race.
3. Put a cross after each race in as many of the seven rows as your feeling dictate.

Category	English	Swedes	Poles	Koreans	Etc.
1. To close kinship by marriage					
2. To my club as personal chums					
3. To my street as neighbors					
4. To employment in my occupation					
5. To citizenship in my country					

6.B.6   HAGOEL'S FRIENDSHIP VALUE SCALES

Variable measured: This instrument measures four dimensions of friendship: (a) Intensity—feeling of closeness, sharing secrets; (b) Homophily—similarity of background, with items for religious, ethnic, racial background, political views, marital status, age differences; (c) Emotionality/Instrumentality—tests polar concepts, friendship as an emotional, affectional experience or friendship as important in gaining personal goals; (d) Intimacy—sharing of intimate personal information about oneself and others.

Description: The four dimensional scales were developed to measure the values people attach to friendship relations in general and to their friends in particular. The friendship relation is shown to be multidimensional; the dimensions can be distinguished from one another, and they vary at different rates. The four scales are made up of 32 items. Statements are presented in random order. There is no mention of number or nature of the four dimensions when the scales are administered. A scoring code for the researcher follows the presentation of the scales.

Where published: Lee Hagoel, "Friendship Values and Intimacy Patterns in an Urban Community," paper presented at the annual meeting of the American Sociological Association, New York, August 1980; Lee Hagoel, "Qualitative and Quantitative Aspects of Primary-Relations in an Urban Community Context" (Ph.D. dissertation, University of Minnesota, Minneapolis, 1980).

Reliability: Alpha scores on the reliability test are as follows: Intensity, 6 items, .736; Homophily, 12 items, .850; Emotionality/Instrumentality, 8 items, .680; Intimacy, 6 items, .587.

Validity: Factor analysis indicates that the four dimensions are not directly related to one another. The internal consistency of each dimension has been demonstrated. The scales were applied in a study of dyad relations among residents in a suburban area of the Minneapolis-Saint Paul metropolitan area (the South Dale Cluster). Friendship patterns characterized the entire sample (in a cosmopolitan type of interaction), while friendship values significantly distinguished among subgroups by age and sex in the same sample.

Standard scores: Scores of the 57 residents in the South Dale study for the four dimensions of the friendship scale are as follows:

Dimension	Score Range	Mean Score	Standard Deviation
A. Intensity	6-36	17.82	3.12
B. Homophily	12-72	55.74	6.65
C. Emotionality/instrumentability	8-14	17.84	4.00
D. Intimacy	6-36	20.14	2.78

Friendship Value Scales

The following is a copy of the scales as they were applied in the study. Note that statements are presented in random order. There is no mention of number or nature of the four dimensions or of the scales. Respondents are presented with this instrument as a single scale.

DIRECTIONS: The following statements are meant to explore some of your feelings toward friends and friendships. There are no right or wrong answers. We are interested in what *you* think. Please read each item carefully and decide whether you agre

Very strongly agree (VSA)	Strongly agree (SA)	Agree (A)	Disagree (D)	Strongly disagree (SD)	Very strongly disagree (VSD)

1. Friends ought to know what one another is doing most of the time. (VSA) (SA) (A) (D) (SD) (VSD)
2. Friends are important because one can borrow money from them. (VSA) (SA) (A) (D) (SD) (VSD)
3. The understanding of my friends is more important to me than their material help.
4. Friends ought to help and support one another in bad times. (VSA) (SA) (A) (D) (SD) (VSD)
5. Friends are people we feel very close to. (VSA) (SA) (A) (D) (SD) (VSD)
6. I would like to have friendships last a life-time. (VSA) (SA) (A) (D) (SD) (VSD)
7. I would never make friends with people of different religious beliefs than mine. (VSA) (SA) (A) (D) (SD) (VSD)
8. Friends ought to know as much as possible about one another's past lives. (VSA) (SA) (A) (D) (SD) (VSD)
9. Good friends do not necessarily have to feel close. (VSA) (SA) (A) (D) (SD) (VSD)
10. I want to feel close to my friends. (VSA) (SA) (A) (D) (SD) (VSD)
11. I would not like to make friends with people who are much older than I am. (VSA) (SA) (A) (D) (SD) (VSD)
12. I want my friends to feel close to me. (VSA) (SA) (A) (D) (SD) (VSD)
13. I feel that friends should know as much about each other's lives as possible. (VSA) (SA) (A) (D) (SD) (VSD)
14. Single people cannot be good friends with married people. (VSA) (SA) (A) (D) (SD) (VSD)
15. Friends should share their secrets with me. (VSA) (SA) (A) (D) (SD) (VSD)
16. A good friend is someone who understands my problems. (VSA) (SA) (A) (D) (SD) (VSD)
17. Blacks and whites do not make the best of friends. (VSA) (SA) (A) (D) (SD) (VSD)
18. I won't be friends with people who don't return favors. (VSA) (SA) (A) (D) (SD) (VSD)
19. Close friends should probably be of the same religious belief. (VSA) (SA) (A) (D) (SD) (VSD)
20. Friendships exist in the here and now, and have no reference to the past or future. (VSA) (SA) (A) (D) (SD) (VSD)
21. I could not make friends with people of different political views than mine. (VSA) (SA) (A) (D) (SD) (VSD)
22. A good friend will provide me with advice when I need it. (VSA) (SA) (A) (D) (SD) (VSD)
23. A man and a woman can be good friends. (VSA) (SA) (A) (D) (SD) (VSD)
24. An important thing about friends is that they can relax in each other's company. (VSA) (SA) (A) (D) (SD) (VSD)
25. Whether or not a friend is married is unimportant. (VSA) (SA) (A) (D) (SD) (VSD)
26. Friends are important because of the "connections" they provide. (VSA) (SA) (A) (D) (SD) (VSD)
27. I would not like to make friends with people who are much younger than I am. (VSA) (SA) (A) (D) (SD) (VSD)
28. Friends ought to have a pretty clear idea of one another's plans for the future. (VSA) (SA) (A) (D) (SD) (VSD)
29. Good friends should hold the same political views. (VSA) (SA) (A) (D) (SD) (VSD)
30. Blacks and whites should not be friends. (VSA) (SA) (A) (D) (SD) (VSD)
31. Good friends can be of different ethnic (national) backgrounds. (VSA) (SA) (A) (D) (SD) (VSD)
32. I expect my friends to return the favors I've done for them as soon as they possibly can. (VSA) (SA) (A) (D) (SD) (VSD)

Researcher's Scoring Code

A. The scoring of each statement.
B. Summation—by dimension (scale) only.

A. The following statements (numbers match the form used in data collection)—
1,3,4,5,6,7,8,10,11,12,13,14,15,16,17,19,21,22,24,27,28,29,30—are scored in this way:

very strongly agree	= 1
strongly agree	= 2
agree	= 3
disagree	= 4
strongly disagree	= 5
very strongly disagree	= 6

The following statements (numbers match the form used in data collection)—
2,9,18,20,23,25,26,31,32—are scored in this way:

very strongly agree	= 6
strongly agree	= 5
agree	= 4
disagree	= 3
strongly disagree	= 2
very strongly disagree	= 1

B. Summation is done for all the statements in a *given dimension*. Thus each respondent has 4 scores.

The code for the statements in each dimension is as follows:

Dimension A (Intensity) consists of these statements: 9,10,12,15,16,22.
Dimension B (Homophily) consists of these statements: 7,11,14,17,19,21,23,25,27,29,30.
Dimension C (Instrumentality/Emotionality) consists of these statements:
2,3,4,5,18,24,26,32.
Dimension D ("completeness") consists of these statements: 1,6,8,13,20,28.

Section C

Social Indicators

The role of social indicators known as *social reporting, social systems accounting, and social intelligence* is set forth in the following definition: Social indicators—statistics, statistical series, and all other forms of evidence—are summary measures that enable policymakers and other decision makers to assess various social aspects of an ongoing society and to evaluate specific programs and determine their impacts. Social indicators help experts and laypersons alike to understand better their own and other societies with respect to values and goals and the nature of social change. Stuart Rice has provided a most compact statement:

> Social Indicators, the tools, are needed to find pathways through the maze of society's interconnections. They delineate *social states*, define *social problems*, and trace *social trends*, which by *social engineering* may hopefully be guided toward *social goals* formulated by *social planning*.[1]

The potential scope of social indicators is very broad. The question of goals must be resolved before the appropriate scope can be determined. The final answer may best be given by the needs of a society and the requests of policymakers for information about problems they must meet and solve. On February 17, 1974, the U.S. Office of Management and Budget released a pioneering study in the field of social reporting: *Social Indicators, 1973*. This study began by identifying widely held basic social objectives: good health and long life, freedom from crime and the fear of crime, sufficient education to take part in society and make the most of one's abilities, the opportunity to work at a job that is satisfying and rewarding, income sufficient to cover the necessities of life, with opportunities for improving one's income, housing that is comfortable within a congenial environment, and time and opportunity for discretionary activities. For each identified social concern, one or more indicators—statistical measures of important aspects of the concerns—were identified.

In 1977 *Social Indicators II* appeared,[2] and this was followed in December 1980 by *Social Indicators III*. Like its predecessors, *Social Indicators III* is restricted almost entirely to data about objective conditions. It details both the current status of American society and some of the trends and developments that may presage the nature of changes to come. Eleven major subject areas are treated in separate chapters. The indicators are primarily time series showing national totals. The list of the indicators is reproduced on the following pages and may be compared with the economic indicators that follow in Section 6.C.2. Social indicators have not yet been institutionalized as have economic indicators, which were mandated by the Employment Act of 1946. The legislation necessary to enact the development of a social report was first presented in 1967 and called for a Council of Social Advisers and the publication of an annual social report. Senator Walter Mondale of Minnesota was not able to muster sufficient votes for its enactment, but the idea has been planted. Meanwhile, research on and use of social indicators continue to be vigorous, as can be seen by the abundant bibliographies in *Social Indicators III*.

Notes

1. Stuart A. Rice, "Social Accounting and Statistics for the Great Society," *Public Administration Review* 27 (June 1967): 173.
2. *Social Indicators II* included three new areas: family, social welfare and security, and social mobility and stratification.

NATIONAL SOCIAL INDICATORS, 1980   **6.C.1**

Following is the table of contents from *Social Indicators III: Selected Data on Social Conditions and Trends in the United States* (Washington, DC: Government Printing Office, 1980). The information in each chapter is presented in three parts: text, charts, and statistical tables.

Introduction

NATIONAL ECONOMIC INDICATORS

6.C.2

**Monthly Report Prepared for the Joint Economic Committee
by the Council of Economic Advisers**

Contents

6.C.3 SOCIAL INDICATORS AT THE STATE LEVEL

The social indicator movement has not neglected the state level. The U.S. Department of Labor has developed state economic and social indicators. The public welfare load, infant mortality, crime, and educational deficiency are cited as problem areas to provide the clues to social problems requiring social action to resolve. Indicators are presented under education, aid to families with dependent children, infant mortality rates under one year, and crime rates.

The Midwest Research Institute has devised the Social-Economic-Political Scale, which measures "the good life" of a state. The S-E-P index is designed to reflect both a state's general economic health and its willingness to provide services essential to continual well-being. The study uses nine areas for measurement:

1. *status of the individual:* enhancing personal dignity and widening areas of choice
2. *equality:* efforts to end discrimination
3. *democratic process:* informed and involved citizenry, good public administration
4. *education:* improving quantity and quality of education at all levels
5. *economic growth:* public capital investment, improved standard of living, education for a better-trained work force
6. *technological change:* research and availability of manpower and facilities for economic growth
7. *agriculture:* seeking efficient-size farm sector and helping excess farm workers relocate
8. *living conditions:* alleviation of poverty and improvement of decayed urban areas
9. *health and welfare:* improving level of welfare assistance, vocational rehabilitation, and provision of good public and private medical services[1]

California ranks first and Mississippi fiftieth on the S-E-P index.[2]

Notes

1. U.S. Department of Labor, *State Economic and Social Indicators*, Bulletin No. 328 (Washington, DC: Government Printing Office, 1973); $1.00 per copy.
2. Other publications providing information about quality-of-life indicators for the states developed by the Midwest Research Institute include the following: Ben-Chieh Liu, *The Quality of Life in the United States, 1970: Index, Rating and Statistics* (Kansas City: Midwest Research Institute, 1973); Ben-Chieh Liu, "Variations in the Quality of Life in the United States by State, 1970," *Review of Social Economy* 32 (October 1974): 131-47; Ben-Chieh Liu, "Quality of Life: Concept, Measure and Results," *American Journal of Economics and Sociology* 34 (January 1975): 1-13; Ben-Chieh Liu, *Quality of Life Indicators in U.S. Metropolitan Areas, 1970: A Summary* (Kansas City: Midwest Research Institute, 1975); Ben-Chieh Liu, *Quality of Life Indicators in U.S. Metropolitan Areas: A Statistical Analysis* (New York: Praeger, 1976).

6.C.4 SOCIAL INDICATORS AT THE COMMUNITY LEVEL

Community social indicators should meet the same criteria as do national and state indicators. They should demonstrate *measurability*, tap *social importance and shared goals*, have *policy importance*, and *fit into a model* that explicates the most important relationships between the indicator and empirically associated variables.[1]

Clark suggests a focus on policy outputs and policy impact as the two types of phenomena important for an understanding of community dynamics. He indicates that development of community indicators is at an early stage, but suggests that policy outputs may be measured by fiscal indicators such as "funds spent for given activities" and by performance indicators such as "tons of refuse collected." A comparative measure of policy outputs in various communities would allow a community to evaluate on a relative basis the services it is getting.

Policy outputs can be contrasted with *policy impacts*. Policy impacts are "changes resulting in a social system as a consequence of policy outputs." Policy impacts can be considered in terms of these criteria on (a) citizen preferences, (b) community leader preferences, (c) extracommunity actor preferences, (d) professional criteria, and (e) social scientific criteria. Suggestions for indicators are developed in the cited article.

Clark and his coworkers have completed a study of 54 American cities, ranking them on 29 fiscal strain indicators. Factors associated with fiscal strain have been identified and policy recommendations have been set forth.[2]

A tested community indicator is an index called Social Vulnerability, developed by John C. Maloney of the Community Service Council of Metropolitan Indianapolis, Inc. (July 1973).[3] This index was constructed "to measure the relative extent to which persons residing in specified geographic areas of the community were vulnerable to experiencing adverse social and physical strains beyond their ability to cope without help." It consists of eight sufficient but not exhaustive variables determined by factor analysis:

1. median family income
2. percentage of families below poverty level
3. percentage of families with both husband and wife
4. percentage of housing without some or all plumbing facilities
5. percentage of the civilian labor force unemployed
6. percentage of households lacking an available automobile
7. rate of ambulance runs per 1,000 population
8. rate of tuberculosis per 1,000 population

This index has identified areas in Marion County "most urgently requiring the investment of both human and capital social resources" in order to mitigate adverse conditions. Scores are available for all census tracts of Marion County. Listings of the scores for each census tract are shown on each of the eight variables listed above.

The city stress index created by Robert Levine ranks 286 American cities by their degree of "psychological health." [4] Levine says "there are reliable data for four important indicators of psycho-social pathology: rates of alcoholism, suicide, divorce, and crime." These measures were chosen because they are both causes and effects of social stress. State College, Pennsylvania, which had the best record, is socially and economically built around Pennsylvania State University, which dictates a highly educated, predominantly middle- and upper-middle-class population. There are no major unresolved social problems and no explosive uncontrolled growth. At the other extreme, Reno and Las Vegas, Nevada, were ranked last based on alcoholism, suicide, and divorce rates higher than those in the rest of the country.

For the student or researcher who wishes to examine the use of social indicators in other cities, the excellent bibliography on pages xxxii-xxxiv in *Social Indicators III* provides extensive information. Among the cities using social indicators are Albuquerque, Kansas City, Charlotte, New York City, Denver, San Diego, Austin, Detroit, Baltimore, Tampa, Phoenix, and Washington, DC.

Notes

1. Terry N. Clark, "Community Social Indicators: From Analytical Models and Policy Applications," *Urban Affairs Quarterly* (September 1973): 5-7. See also Peter H. Rossi, "Community Social Indicators," in *The Human Meaning of Social Change*, ed. A. Campbell and P. E. Converse (New York: Russell Sage, 1972), 87-126.

2. Terry N. Clark, Irene S. Rubin, Lynne C. Pettler, and Erwin Zimmerman, *How Many New Yorks? The New York Fiscal Crisis in Comparative Perspective*, Comparative Study of Community Decision Making, Research Report No. 72 (Chicago: University of Chicago, Sociology Department, 1976).

3. For further information, write Research Department, Community Service Council of Metropolitan Indianapolis, Inc., 615 N. Alabama St., Indianapolis, IN 46204.

4. Robert Levine, "City Stress Index: 25 Best, 25 Worst," *Psychology Today* 22 (November 1988): 52-58; ratings for all 286 cities are shown on pp. 55-57.

6.C.5 RANGE OF SOCIAL INDICATORS AND CURRENT DEVELOPMENTS

The number of social indicators currently available to measure social trends is large. The potential is huge. Scholars and decision makers differ on their choices of important social areas or facets of society. In Table 6.6, three writers exhibit social areas in which they suggest a broad range of indicators. Their ideas can be compared with the indicators in the latest (1980) national edition of *Social Indicators*.

Current Developments in Social Indicators Research

In the United States

Russell Sage Foundation. This foundation has had a long interest in social indicators as a part of its study of social change. It has supported research on indicators of social trends by developing a general orientation as shown by *Indicators of Social Change: Concepts and Measurements*, edited by Eleanor B. Sheldon and Wilbert E. Moore (1968). A number of specific research volumes published by the Russell Sage Foundation are listed in the bibliography of social indicators in Section 6.C.6.

Social Science Research Council. This is an interdisciplinary organization that maintains several research committees, one of which is the Committee on Social Indicators. The Social Science Research Council's Center for Social Indicators has added a planning staff to the program it has had in place since 1972. In October 1977 the Center was urged by a site visit team appointed by the National Science Foundation (NSF) to prepare explicit guidelines for research on social indicators for the United States over the next decade. In 1979 the Center began full-scale work on this project, with support from the NSF. Over the next few years, SSRC's Advisory and Planning Committee on Social Indicators, which provides intellectual guidance for the Center, sought the views of a wide community of scholars, staff in statistical

TABLE 6.6 Comparative List of Social Areas with Compilation of Indicators

O. D. Duncan [a]	U.S. Department of Health, Education and Welfare [b]	Raymond A. Bauer [c]	Social Indicators III [d]
1. Occupational changes	1. Health and illness	1. Population	1. Population and the family
2. Conditional probabilities for attending college (SES and mental ability)	2. Social mobility	2. Technological advances	2. Health and nutrition
3. Air-pollution index	3. Physical environment	3. Education	3. Housing and the environment
4. Incidence of victimization by criminal acts	4. Income and property	4. Military appropriations	4. Transportation
5. Educational opportunity	5. Public order and safety	5. Utilities and transportation	5. Public safety
6. Political participation	6. Learning, science, and art	6. Governmental growth	6. Education and training
7. Voluntary association membership	7. Participation and alienation	7. Natural resources	7. Work
8. Tolerance of political dissent		8. Welfare	8. Social security and welfare
9. Mental health			9. Income and productivity
10. Alienation			10. Social participation
11. Time budgets			11. Culture, leisure, and use of time
12. Income and assets			
13. Value change			
14. Religious affiliation and belief			

a. Otis Dudley Duncan, *Toward Social Reporting: Next Steps* (New York: Russell Sage Foundation, 1959).
b. U.S. Department of Health, Education and Welfare (now the Department of Health and Human Services), *Toward a Social Report* (Ann Arbor: University of Michigan Press, 1970).
c. Raymond A. Bauer, ed., *Social Indicators* (Cambridge: MIT Press, 1969).
d. U.S. Bureau of the Census, *Social Indicators III* (Washington, DC: Government Printing Office, 1980).

agencies and research institutes, and others who have an interest in the future of social indicators.[1]

During the 1970s, much was accomplished by the replication of selected existing studies. These include the following:

- A project was undertaken at the University of Wisconsin to produce public use samples from the U.S. Censuses of 1940 and 1950 that will afford researchers a decennial series of public use samples from 1940 through 1980.
- The 1962 Occupational Changes in a Generation Study was replicated in 1973.
- The cohorts of the National Longitudinal Survey of Labor Market Experience were refreshed by the addition of cohorts of men and women aged 14-21 in 1978, and by a new longitudinal study, "High School and Beyond," which was fielded in 1980 to follow that year's sophomore and senior classes.

In addition to development of the data base, both substantive research and methodology advanced in the 1970s in ways that have contributed to fundamental research on social change. There have been important analytical advances in the study of longitudinal data, including log-linear models for the analysis of categorical data and solutions (e.g., maximum likelihood) for systems of linear structural equations. These latter methods are proving especially important because they permit the researcher to bring a theory of measurement and a concern for error structures to the final stages of statistical analysis. Journal articles frequently report quantitative studies of social change, many of which use social indicators time series. People involved in this research are to be found in disciplines as varied as historical demography, life-span developmental psychology, labor economics, social history, and sociology.

Considerable effort is being made to identify some of the issues that should be the foci of planning for social indicators in the 1980s. Central to the planning effort is an assessment of the condition of social measurement in the United States—what is going well, where some revision is needed, and where no measurement work is being undertaken. Linked to this interest in the improvement of measurement is a concern with ensuring the integrity of the time series that are fundamental to social indicators research. The integrity of these time series is problematic due to a basic tension between the desire to maintain continuity and the need to respond to opportunities for improvement and innovation.

One area in which innovation may be called for concerns social indicators of change in social organization, structure, conflict, and integration. The majority of social indicators are derived from survey observations of individual behavior or attitudes, while much of the theoretical emphasis of the social sciences has been at collective levels of social organizations, culture, and conflict. It is clear that many central research questions cannot be addressed by today's data base. The planning report will outline ways in which to broaden the content of social indicators beyond the present focus on the individual and family.

The Center issues a *Social Indicators Newsletter* on research in the field, and via its library is assisting the journal *Social Indicators Research*. Communications may be sent to the Center at 1785 Massachusetts Ave., NW, Washington, DC 20036.

National Science Foundation. The NSF's major role in social indicators-oriented activities has been the funding of research projects in various areas, such as objective measurement of social and urban conditions, developing goals accounting systems, and trend analyses of political, economic, and social changes. Although funds were cut after 1981, the NSF continued to give high priority to measurement methods and data resources. Support for the NORC General Social Survey (National Opinion Research Center, Chicago) and for the Center for Coordination of Research on Social Indicators (Social Science Research Council, New York) was steady.

After 11 fruitful years of supporting "cutting-edge" social indicators research, the National Science Foundation program was discontinued in 1984. Support still is available for typical social indicators research—social accounting, social reporting, social forecasting, and the like—but submissions now are to the most appropriate disciplinary program. Interested scholars should contact Murray Aborn, head of the Social Measurement and Analysis Section of NSF, Washington, DC.

U.S. Bureau of the Census. The Center for Demographic Studies in the Census Bureau published *Social Indicators III* in December 1980. This continues the pioneering efforts of 1973 and 1976 in providing a comprehensive overview of current social conditions and trends in the United States.

U.S. Department of Labor. In 1974 the U.S. Department of Labor organized the Working Group on Indicators of the Quality of Employment. This group has been clarifying conceptual issues involved in developing measures of the quality of employment to be used in an accounting system of national social indicators. See the bibliography in Section 6.C.6 for published work.

Institute for Social Research, University of Michigan. On a general level, the Institute is continuing its wide interest in social indicators. It has done several studies to measure social changes in consumer behavior, economic well-being, youth in transition, residential mobility, and early retirement. Studies of attitudes and values have included such areas as drugs, violence, racial behavior, and discrimination. Note the work of Angus Campbell and his associates shown in the bibliography in Section 6.C.6.

Survey Research Center, University of California (Berkeley), Bank of America, General Motors, State and Local Governments, et al. Numerous organizations are active in social indicators research as part of long-range planning programs. Each accumulates data and is concerned with social indicators research generally in order to make comparisons useful to its specific goals.

On the International Level

Organization for Economic Cooperation and Development. This is an international program consisting of 15 member states concerned with developing measurement instruments related to the quality of living across several countries. The program is designed to last several years, looking at such "agreed-upon" primary goal areas as personal health and safety, time and leisure, and the physical, social, and political environments.

United Nations Research Institute for Social Development. This institute has been established as a result of government grants from both the United States and the Netherlands. The agency is concerned with studying problems from an international viewpoint, one not often examined by national universities and institutes. According to a 1971 statement, some of its activity areas are the "quantitative analysis of socio-economic development, methods of decision-making, preparation of the child for economic and technological modernization and measurement of real progress at the local level."

The World Bank. This institution monitors world development indicators regularly. The World Bank has recently published *World Development Indicators 1988.* These indicators comprise 33 statistical tables that provide comprehensive, up-to-date data on social and economic development in 129 countries. New tables in the 1988 edition include the structure of consumption, health and nutrition, and women in development. For information, write World Bank Publications, 1818 H St., NW, Washington, DC 20433.

Note

1. For a more complete description, see *Footnotes* of the American Sociological Association (April 1981): 3.

6.C.6   SELECTED BIBLIOGRAPHY STRESSING HISTORY, THEORY, AND ROLE OF SOCIAL INDICATORS

Annals of the American Academy of Political and Social Science 453 (January 1981). Special issue: *Social Indicators: American Society in the Eighties.*

Bauer, Raymond A., ed. *Social Indicators.* Cambridge: MIT Press, 1966.

———. *Social Measurement and Social Indicators.* London: Allen & Unwin, 1981.

Carley, Michael. *Rational Techniques in Policy Analysis.* London: Heinemann, 1980.

Duncan, Otis Dudley. *Toward Social Reporting: Next Steps.* New York: Russell Sage Foundation, 1969.

Fox, Karl A. *Social Indicators and Social Theory: Elements of an Operational System.* New York: John Wiley, 1974.

Harrison, Daniel P. *Social Forecasting Methodology: Suggestions for Research.* New York: Russell Sage Foundation, 1977.

Juster, E. Thomas, and Kenneth C. Land, eds. *Social Accounting Systems: Essays on the State of the Art.* New York: Academic Press, 1981.

Land, Kenneth C., and Seymour Spilerman, eds. *Social Indicator Models.* New York: Russell Sage Foundation, 1975.

Neufville, Judith Innes de. *Social Indicators and Public Policy.* New York: Elsevier, 1975.

Bibliography of Special Indicators

Andrews, Frank M., ed. *Research on the Quality of Life.* Ann Arbor: University of Michigan, Institute for Social Research, 1986.

Biderman, Albert D., and Thomas F. Drury, eds. "The Quality of Employment Indicators." *American Behavioral Scientist* 17 (January-February 1975): 299-432.

     The volume includes the following papers: "Introduction," Albert D. Biderman; "The Role of Quality Employment Indicators in General Social Reporting Systems," Kenneth C. Land; "Job Satisfaction Indicators and Their Correlates," Stanley E. Seashore and Thomas D. Taber; "Going Beyond Current Income: A Preliminary Appraisal," E. Thomas Juster and Greg Duncan; "Equity Concepts and the World of Work," Lester Thurow; "Evaluating Changes in the Occupational Distribution and the Occupational System," Arthur L. Stinchcombe.

———, eds. *Measuring Work Quality for Social Reporting.* New York: John Wiley, 1976.

     A collection of papers dealing with problems of matching concepts and indicators of work in relation to health criteria, psychic values, general well-being, life careers, positive and negative aspects of job mobility, social and moral qualities of jobs, responsiveness to workers of employment systems, and the dynamics of the occupational system.

Campbell, Angus. *The Sense of Well-Being in America: Recent Patterns and Trends.* New York: McGraw-Hill, 1981.

———, Philip E. Converse, and Willard L. Rodgers. *The Quality of American Life: Perceptions, Evaluations, and Satisfactions.* New York: Russell Sage Foundation, 1976.

Converse, Philip E., Jean D. Dotson, Wendy J. Hoag, and William H. McGee III. *American Social Attitudes Data Sourcebook, 1947-1978.* Cambridge, MA: Harvard University Press, 1980.

     Selected attitudinal data gathered from 1947 to 1978 to generate a portfolio of long-term indicators of the nature and quality of American life. Areas covered include attitudes toward self and others, blacks and whites, women, family living, work and retirement, personal economic outlook, national economic outlook, and government spending.

Davis, Louise E., and Albert B. Cherns. *The Quality of Working Life.* Vol. 1. New York: Free Press, 1975.

     See especially Chapter 2, "Defining and Measuring the Overall Quality of Working Life."

Ferriss, Abbott L. *Indicators of Trends in American Education; Indicators of Change in the American Family; Indicators of Trends in the Status of American Women.* 3 vols. New York: Russell Sage Foundation, 1970, 1971.

Strumpel, Burkhard. *Economic Means for Human Needs: Social Indicators of Well-Being and Discontent.* Ann Arbor: University of Michigan, Institute for Social Research, 1976.

United Nations. *Social Indicators for Housing and Urban Development.* New York: UNIPUB, 1973.

Comprehensive Annotated Bibliographies

Gilmartin, Kevin J., et al. *Social Indicators: An Annotated Bibliography of Current Literature.* New York: Garland, 1979.

Wilcox, Leslie D., et al. *Social Indicators and Social Monitoring: An Annotated Bibliography.* New York: Elsevier, 1974.

Handbook of Social Indicators

Rossi, Robert J., and Kevin J. Gilmartin. *The Handbook of Social Indicators: Sources, Characteristics, and Analysis.* New York: Garland STPM, 1980.

Specialized Research Journal

Social Indicators Research: An International and Interdisciplinary Journal of Quality of Life Measurement. Editor: Alex C. Nichalos, University of Guelph, Department of Philosophy, Guelph, Ontario, Canada. Established 1974. Publisher: D. Reidel Publishing, Dordrecht, Netherlands.

News

Social Indicators Network News. Editor: Abbott L. Ferris, P.O. Box 24064, Emory University Station, Atlanta, GA 30322. Established 1984.

Section D

Measures of Organizational Structure

There are a number of basic facts about organizational measurement:

1. A very large number of structural attributes and interpersonal relationships exist within the same and different organizations.
2. The development of organizational measurement has come a long way in recent years, but serious shortcomings remain.
3. There is little standardization of the measures used in studying organizations. The lack of standardization hinders the development of organizational theory; it forces the researcher to use a high degree of judgment in selecting an organizational measure.
4. While the measurement and description of structure is an interesting process and exercise in its own right, important research problems are centered about the correlation of various structural arrangements in organizations.
5. Correlates will range from such internal factors as morale and decision making to the impact of structure on external relationships such as cooperative, defensive, and competitive postures vis-à-vis other organizations. Interrelationships of structural relationships themselves reveal a great deal about the character of the organization as a collective unit.
6. Some consensus about the most important structural variables is emerging. These include size, formalization, and centralization. Whatever else may be of interest, these variables usually cannot be ignored in research designs.
7. There is high interest in many other variables, including absenteeism, administrative staff, alienation, autonomy, communication, complexity, consensus, coordination, dispersion, distributive justice, effectiveness, innovation, mechanization, motivation, bases of power, routinization, satisfaction, span of control, specialization, and succession.
8. Two different sets of measures exist to assess many of these variables. One set represents the institutional approach, which relies on documents and informants; the other set relies on the survey approach, which is characterized by the use of questionnaire and interview schedules.
9. The best available guide for the selection of an organizational measure is James L. Price's *Handbook of Organizational Measurement* (Lexington, MA: D. C. Heath, 1972). The researcher will save time by using it for immediate reference. For research design, see Victor H. Vroom, ed., *Methods of Organizational Research* (Pittsburgh: University of Pittsburgh Press, 1967), and James D. Thompson, ed., *Approaches to Organizational Design* (Pittsburgh: University of Pittsburgh Press, 1966). For a comprehensive survey of contemporary developments in the field of organizational studies, see David Dunkerley and Graeme Salaman, eds., *The International Yearbook of Organizational Studies 1979* (Boston: Routledge & Kegan Paul, 1979), which is described as the first volume in a series to portray developments in organizational research.

10. Measures for the three variables believed most important in analyzing correlates between themselves and other variables—size, formalization, and centralization—are selected and reproduced. One social psychological measure, Index of Job-Related Tensions in Organizations, is also introduced.

SIZE 6.D.1

Definition: Size is the scale of operations of an organization. A measure of size might be the number of personnel, the amount of assets, and the degree of expenditures. In organizational research, size is generally expressed as the number of employees, even though the number of employees is not necessarily the best way to measure the scale of operations. A firm may be quite large, but because of a very high degree of mechanization it may have relatively few personnel. Still, as an operating index the number of employees remains the most common measure.

Measurement: Advice to a researcher about the measurement of size would be conditioned by the design of the research. Will it involve few or many organizations? Will these organizations be small, intermediate, or large in size? What breakdowns will be needed? By department, division, total organization? What sensitivity about the data may be involved by the nature of the organizations to be studied—health, governmental, industrial? What resources are available? Only funds to write? Or telephone? Funds to make a personal interview?

Organizations do not usually give out information casually. They make some information public as a matter of custom or law, and needed data may be available from the last annual report of the organization. The researcher should try this first if all he or she needs is figures on total employment.

Numbers of employees in industrial and commercial organizations can be found in the following volumes: *Standard and Poor's Register of Corporations, Directors, and Executives* (Dun and Bradstreet): Vol. 1, *Million Dollar Directory*; Vol. 2, *Middle Market Directory*; and *Moody's Industrial Manuals.*

If needed information is not available publicly, the researcher should send a letter, telephone, or pay a visit to the industrial relations director or personnel director, stating the needs, reasons, and sponsorship of the research. This official may be able to provide what is needed as expressed in department and division breakdowns. (The researcher should be sure to indicate what he or she can do with the data that may be useful to the organization.)

Usually, the employment or personnel department stores personal records and the payroll department has an official payroll printout. The latter record may be the more accurate of the two. Of course, payroll (and personnel) often fluctuate greatly during the course of a year. It is important for the researcher to indicate how his or her computations take this into account.

Validity of Size as an Independent Factor in Organization Structuring and Dynamics

A summary of research on size and its correlates is provided by Richard H. Hall in his *Organizations: Structures and Process.*[1] This summary points out that the size factor has led to rather contradictory conclusions in the determination of the form of the organization. There is, however, growing consensus that larger organizations tend to have more specialization, more standardization, and more formalization than smaller organizations. But a lack of relationship between size and the remaining structural dimensions, that is, concentration of authority and line control of work flows, is equally striking. Hall, Haas, and Johnson, using data on 75 North American organizations, report on the conclusions of their findings:

> The most immediate implication of these findings is that neither complexity nor formalization can be implied from organizational size. A social scientist conducting research in a large organization would do well to question the frequent assumption that the organization under study is necessarily highly complex and formalized. . . . He will need to examine empirically, for each organization, the level of complexity and formalization extant at that time.[2]

Pugh and his associates used size as a "contextual variable," relating it to various aspects of organizational structure in 46 English organizations. Their conclusions are generally supportive of the consensus reported above.[3]

In Hall's review of research on size, conclusions are drawn about correlates with technology, professionalization, work flow, administrative components, the individual, organization, and society.[4] The most important conclusions may be stated as follows:

1. The size factor is greatly modified by the technology or technologies employed by the organization.
2. The administrative component in relation to overall size of the organization displays a curvilinear relationship: the administrative component tends to decrease in size as organizational size increases; however, in very large organizations the relative size of the administrative component again increases with overall size.
3. Large size has an impact on the individuals in the organization. There is more stress, and the depersonalization process can lead to a great deal of discomfort for many members. Negative consequences are partially alleviated by the presence of informal friendship groups found in all organizations.
4. Large size creates difficulties in organizational control, coordination, and communications; at the same time, it gives the organization more power over its environment, more resources for planning, and less dependence on particular individuals.
5. The concentration of power in large organizations may in turn concentrate power in the society, with resulting threats to democratic processes.

Notes

1. Richard H. Hall, *Organizations: Structures and Process* (Englewood Cliffs, NJ: Prentice-Hall, 1972), 112-39.

2. Richard H. Hall, J. Eugene Haas, and Norman J. Johnson, "Organizational Size, Complexity, and Formalization," *American Sociological Review* 32 (December 1967): 111.

3. D. S. Pugh, D. J. Hickson, C. R. Hinings, and C. Turner, "The Context of Organizational Structure," *Administrative Science Quarterly* 14 (March 1969): 98.

4. Hall et al., "Organizational Size," 138.

FORMALIZATION

6.D.2

Definition: Formalization represents the use of rules in an organization. Some organizations carefully describe the specific authority, responsibilities, duties, and procedures to be followed in every job and then supervise job occupants to ensure conformity to the job definitions. A penalty system may be spelled out in writing for impartial monitoring of discipline for infractions. Other organizations have loosely defined jobs and do not carefully control work behavior.

The two dimensions of formalization may be specified as job codification, or the degree of work standardization, and rule leniency, or the measure of the latitude of behavior that is tolerated from standards.

Measurement: Extensive research on formalization has been done by Aiken and Hage, Richard Hall and his associates, and Pugh and Hickson and their colleagues. Aiken and Hage have relied on the traditional type of survey. Both Hall and Pugh have relied more on documentary data. Both approaches are recommended, but for economy the Aiken-Hage measure is reproduced.

Hage and Aiken Formalization Inventory[1]

The data are collected by means of interviews. Fifteen questions are used.

I'm going to read a series of statements that may or may not be true for your job in [name of organization]. For each item I read, please answer as it applies to you and your organization, using the answer categories on this card.

1. definitely true
2. more true than false
3. more false than true
4. definitely false

		Definitely True	More True than False	More False than True	Definitely False
1.	First, I feel that I am my own boss in most matters.	___	___	___	___
2.	A person can make his own decisions here without checking with anybody else.	___	___	___	___
3.	How things are done around here is left pretty much up to the person doing the work.	___	___	___	___
4.	People here are allowed to do almost as they please.	___	___	___	___

(Continued)

	Definitely True	More True than False	More False than True	Definitely False
5. Most people here make their own rules on the job.	____	____	____	____
6. The employees are constantly being checked on for rule violations.	____	____	____	____
7. People here feel as though they are constantly being watched to see that they obey all the rules.	____	____	____	____
8. There is no rules manual.	____	____	____	____
9. There is a complete written job description for my job.	____	____	____	____
10. Whatever situation arises, we have procedures to follow in dealing with it.	____	____	____	____
11. Everyone has a specific job to do.	____	____	____	____
12. Going through the proper channels is constantly stressed.	____	____	____	____
13. The organization keeps a written record of everyone's job performance.	____	____	____	____
14. We are to follow strict operating procedures at all times.	____	____	____	____
15. Whenever we have a problem we are supposed to go to the same person for an answer.	____	____	____	____

Computation: The five following measures are constructed from the 15 questions: job codification (questions 1-5), rule observation (questions 6-7), rule manual (question 8), job descriptions (question 9), specificity of job descriptions (questions 10-15). Replies to these 15 questions are scored from 1 (definitely true) to 4 (definitely false). A mean is constructed for each respondent for each of the five measures of formalization. The higher the mean (4 is the highest mean), the higher the formalization. The researchers report no ranges from the means of the five measures. Each respondent is then classified by "social position," and based on the first mean, a second mean is computed for each social position in the organization for each of the five measures. A social position is defined by the level or stratum in the organization, and the department or type of professional activity. For example, if an agency's professional staff consists of psychiatrists and social workers, each divided into the hierarchical levels, the agency has four social positions: supervisory psychiatrists, psychiatrists, supervisory social workers, and social workers. The organizational scores for each of the five measures are determined by computing an average of all social position means in the organization.

Where published: Michael Aiken and Jerald Hage, "Organizational Alienation," *American Sociological Review* 31 (August 1966): 497-507. Scale and data on reliability and validity are reproduced in James L. Price, *Handbook of Organizational Measurement* (Lexington, MA: D. C. Heath, 1972), 108-11.

Reliability: The study contains no data relevant to reliability.

Validity: Formalization is positively related to alienation. The greater the degree of formalization in the organization, the greater the likelihood of alienation from work. There is great dissatisfaction with work in those organizations in which jobs are rigidly structured. Strict enforcement of rules was strongly related to work dissatisfaction; social relations are also disturbed when rules are strictly enforced. Significant positive relationships are found between routine work and rule manual, job description, and specificity of job descriptions.

Utility: The interview can be conducted in less than five minutes in most cases.

Research applications:

Aiken, Michael, and Jerald Hage. "Organizational Alienation." *American Sociological Review* 31 (August 1966): 497-507.

Hage, Jerald, and Michael Aiken. "Program Change and Organizational Properties." *American Journal of Sociology* 72 (March 1967): 503-19.

———. "Relationship of Centralization to Other Structural Properties." *Administrative Science Quarterly* 12 (June 1967): 72-92.

———. *Social Change in Complex Organizations.* New York: Random House, 1970.

Documentary measures of formalization: The measures developed by Hall and his associates may be found in Richard H. Hall, J. Eugene Haas, and Norman J. Johnson, "Organizational Size, Complexity, and Formalization," *American Sociological Review* 32 (December 1967).

The measures developed by Inkson, Pugh, and Hickson may be found in J. H. K. Inkson, D. S. Pugh, and D. J. Hickson, "Organization Context and Structure: An Abbreviated Replication," *Administrative Science Quarterly* 15 (September 1970): 318-29. The measure and data on reliability and validity are reproduced in James L. Price, *Handbook of Organizational Measurement* (Lexington, MA: D. C. Heath, 1972), 111-15. The serious researcher will examine each of these excellent measures and choose the one that best fits his or her research design.

Note

1. A minor adaptation of this inventory has been made by James L. Price. Used with permission.

CENTRALIZATION   6.D.3

Definition: Centralization is the degree to which power is concentrated in an organization. Power is an important component in every organization. The distribution of power has major consequences for the performance of an organization and the behavior of its members.

An important consideration in dealing with power is the manner in which it is distributed. The maximum degree of centralization would exist if all power were exercised by a single individual; the minimum degree of centralization would exist if all power were exercised equally by all members of the organization. Most organizations fall between these two extremes.

Various problems are generated by the degree of centralized power and the manner in which actors wield their power and influence over superordinate, coordinate, and subordinate members of the organization. The following topics are commonly generated by problems of power stratification: participation-management, industrial democracy, group decision making, employee representation, collective bargaining, alienation, and organizational conflict.

Measurement: As with most measures, centralization may be assessed by the institutional approach, using documents and informants, or by the use of the survey approach, with questionnaires and interview schedules as the principal instruments.

Pugh and his associates relied on data obtained by interviewing one or a few top executives and from documents that organizations (24 manufacturing and 16 services) made available to researchers. Aiken and Hage collected all their data on centralization by interviewing executive directors, department heads, and staff members in 16 social welfare and health organizations.

Johannes Pennings has submitted the measures used by these researchers to validity tests. He contrasts the two research approaches as shown below.

Institutional approach

A₁. Centralization

>   Autonomy: This scale consists of 23 issues to measure whether decisions on these issues are made inside or outside the organization (Pugh et al., 1968, 102-4).
>
>   Chief executive span of control: This indicates the number of subordinates who report directly to the chief executive, regardless of the hierarchical position of the subordinates (Pugh et al., 1968, 104).
>
>   Worker/supervisory ratio: This value indicates the number of subordinates in production departments per first-line supervisor (Pugh et al., 1968, 104).
>
>   Number of direct supervisors (%): This indicates the number of first-line supervisors in production departments, including the assistants and deputies (Pugh et al., 1968, 104).

Questionnaire approach

A₂. Centralization

>   Personal participation in decision making: This is a Likert scale measuring how much the individual participates in decisions about the allocation of resources and the determination of organizational policies (Hage and Aiken, 1967, 78).
>
>   Hierarchy of authority: This scale measures the degree to which the organization member participates in decisions involving the tasks associated with his position (Hage and Aiken, 1967, 78-79).
>
>   Departmental participation in decision making: This Likert scale measures how much an individual "and his colleagues" participate in decisions involving their work and work environment (personal communication).

The organizational researcher should examine these measures carefully in choosing those most suitable to his or her design. Again for economy, only Aiken and Hage's scales of *personal participation in decision making* and *hierarchy of authority* are reproduced.

Aiken and Hage Scale of Personal Participation in Decision Making and Hierarchy of Authority[1]

The questions for the index of actual participation are as follows:

1. How frequently do you usually participate in the decision to hire new staff?

          ____ Never   ____ Often
          ____ Seldom   ____ Always
          ____ Sometimes

2. How frequently do you usually participate in the decisions on the promotion of any of the professional staff?
3. How frequently do you participate in decisions on the adoptions of new policies?
4. How frequently do you participate in the decisions on the adoptions of new programs?

The questions for the scale of hierarchy of authority are as follows:

1. There can be little action taken here until a supervisor approves a decision.

          ____ Definitely false   ____ True
          ____ False   ____ Definitely true

2. A person who wants to make his or her own decisions would be quickly discouraged here.
3. Even small matters have to be referred to someone higher up for a final decision.
4. I have to ask my boss before I do almost anything.
5. Any decision I make has to have my boss's approval.

Computation: The computations differ for the two types of decisions. For the index of actual participation, the five responses are assigned numbers from 1 (low participation) to 5 (high participation). A "never" response receives 1; at the other extreme, an "always" response receives 5. An average score on these five questions is computed for each respondent. Each respondent is then classified by "social position" and a second mean computed for each social position in the organization. "A social position," according to Aiken and Hage, "is defined by the level or stratum in the organization and the department or type of professional activity. For example, if an agency's professional staff consists of psychiatrists and social workers, each divided into two hierarchical levels, the agency has four social positions: supervisory psychiatrists, psychiatrists, supervisory social workers, and social workers." The organizational score is determined by computing the average of all social position means in the organization.

Computations for the hierarchy of authority scale are similar to those for the index of actual participation. The responses are assigned numbers from 1 (definitely false) to 4 (definitely true). As with the index of actual participation, the organizational scores for the hierarchy of authority scale are based on social position means, which in turn are based on the means for each respondent.

Where published: M. Aiken and J. Hage, "Organizational Interdependence and Intraorganizational Structure," *American Sociological Review* 33, no. 6 (1968):

912-30; scales are described in footnotes 6 and 7, p. 924. For measures used by Pugh and associates, see D. S. Pugh, D. J. Hickson, C. R. Hinings, and C. Turner, "Dimensions of Organization Structure," *Administrative Science Quarterly* 13, no. 1 (1968): 65-105; J. H. K. Inkson, D. S. Pugh, and D. J. Hickson, "Organization Context and Structure: A Replication Study," *Administrative Science Quarterly* 15, no. 3 (1970): 318-29.

Reliability: No relevant data are provided by Aiken and Hage.

Validity: Organizations in which the decisions were made by only a few people at the top relied on rules and close supervision as a means of ensuring consistent performance by the workers. These organizations were also characterized by a less professional staff. The presence of a well-trained staff is related to a reduced need for extensive rules. Penning reports that organizations that are highly autonomous tend to have a nonparticipative internal decision structure. The greater the autonomy, the larger the executive's span of control.[2]

Research applications:

Aiken, Michael, and Jerald Hage. "Organizational Alienation." *American Sociological Review* 31 (August 1966): 497-507.

Hage, Jerald, and Michael Aiken. "Program Change and Organizational Properties." *American Journal of Sociology* 72 (March 1967): 503-19.

——— . "Relationship of Centralization to Other Structural Properties." *Administrative Science Quarterly* 12 (June 1967): 72-92.

——— . *Social Change in Complex Organizations.* New York: Random House, 1970.

Hall, Richard H. "An Empirical Study of Bureaucratic Dimensions and Their Relation to Other Organizational Characteristics." Ph.D. dissertation, Ohio State University, Columbus, 1961.

——— . "The Concept of Bureaucracy: An Empirical Assessment." *American Journal of Sociology* 69 (July 1963): 32-40.

Smith, Clagett G., and Arnold S. Tannenbaum. "Organization Control Structure: A Comparative Analysis." *Human Relations* 16 (1963): 299-316.

For a critique of the Tannenbaum Organizational Control Questionnaire, see Lake, Miles, and Earle, *Measuring Human Behavior.* New York: Teachers College Press, 1973, 214-19.

For more recent research, see Section 6.L.1. Also see recent issues of *Administrative Science Quarterly.*

Notes

1. Used by permission.

2. Johannes Pennings, "Measures of Organizational Structures: A Methodological Note." *American Journal of Sociology* 79 (November 1973): 688-89.

6.D.4 INDEX OF JOB-RELATED TENSIONS IN ORGANIZATIONS

Variable measured: This index purports to measure the amount of tension experienced by an individual as a result of his or her job.

Description: The index consists of 15 statements describing what the authors judge to be symptoms of conflict or ambiguity. Respondents are asked to estimate how often they are bothered by each type of symptom on a 5-point Likert scale.

Where published: Robert L. Kahn et al., *Organizational Stress* (New York: John Wiley, 1964), 424-25.

Reliability: No test-retest reliability is indicated, but an intercorrelation analysis of the items was performed on a national sample of 725 employed adults; in addition, an intensive survey was taken of 53 supervisory personnel. On the whole, the average interitem correlation appears to be in the middle .70s. The intercorrelation matrix figures for the intensive sample are quite close to those found in the national sample.

Validity: The survey utilized an open-ended question to elicit information about the number, content, and intensity of job-related worries. These were shown to be closely related to the tension index. Some indirect relationships between tension and satisfaction were found.

Utility: Time required for test administration is estimated at less than 15 minutes. The scale is equally applicable to employees and supervisory personnel. It is a diagnostic instrument as well as a measurement index. The diagnostic capacity of the index to identify major tensions may be its most significant attribute.

Scoring: Respondent answers each item by choosing one of six fixed alternative responses: "never bothered," "rarely bothered," "sometimes bothered," "bothered rather often," "bothered nearly all the time," and "does not apply." Scores of 1 to 5 are assigned to the first five responses. Respondent's total score is his or her average score over all the items, *except* those to which he or she responded "does not apply." A range of scores between 0 and 5 is indicated.

Research application:

Duncan, Robert B. "The Effects of Mobility Orientation on the Manager's Perception of Role Pressure in an Industrial Work Organization." M.A. thesis, Indiana University, 1966.

Index of Job-Related Tensions in Organizations[1]

All of us occasionally feel bothered by certain kinds of things in our work. I am going to read a list of things that sometimes bother people, and I would like you to tell me how frequently you feel bothered by each of them. You are to indicate your response by choosing one of the six alternative answers provided each item.

1. Feeling that you have too little authority to carry out the responsibilities assigned to you.
   1. never bothered
   2. rarely bothered
   3. sometimes bothered
   4. bothered rather often
   5. bothered nearly all the time
   6. does not apply

2. Being unclear on just what the scope and responsibilities of your job are.
   1. never bothered
   2. rarely bothered
   3. sometimes bothered
   4. bothered rather often
   5. bothered nearly all the time
   6. does not apply

3. Not knowing what opportunities for advancement or promotion exist for you.
   1. never bothered
   2. rarely bothered
   3. sometimes bothered
   4. bothered rather often
   5. bothered nearly all the time
   6. does not apply

4. Feeling that you have too heavy a work load, one that you can't possibly finish during an ordinary workday.
    1. never bothered   4. bothered rather often
    2. rarely bothered   5. bothered nearly all the time
    3. sometimes bothered   6. does not apply

5. Thinking that you'll not be able to satisfy the conflicting demands of various people over you.
    1. never bothered   4. bothered rather often
    2. rarely bothered   5. bothered nearly all the time
    3. sometimes bothered   6. does not apply

6. Feeling that you're not fully qualified to handle your job.
    1. never bothered   4. bothered rather often
    2. rarely bothered   5. bothered nearly all the time
    3. sometimes bothered   6. does not apply

7. Not knowing what your supervisor thinks of you, how he evaluates your performance.
    1. never bothered   4. bothered rather often
    2. rarely bothered   5. bothered nearly all the time
    3. sometimes bothered   6. does not apply

8. The fact that you can't get information needed to carry out your job.
    1. never bothered   4. bothered rather often
    2. rarely bothered   5. bothered nearly all the time
    3. sometimes bothered   6. does not apply

9. Having to decide things that affect the lives of individuals, people that you know.
    1. never bothered   4. bothered rather often
    2. rarely bothered   5. bothered nearly all the time
    3. sometimes bothered   6. does not apply

10. Feeling that you may not be liked and accepted by the people you work with.
    1. never bothered   4. bothered rather often
    2. rarely bothered   5. bothered nearly all the time
    3. sometimes bothered   6. does not apply

11. Feeling unable to influence your immediate supervisor's decisions and actions that affect you.
    1. never bothered   4. bothered rather often
    2. rarely bothered   5. bothered nearly all the time
    3. sometimes bothered   6. does not apply

12. Not knowing just what the people you work with expect of you.
    1. never bothered   4. bothered rather often
    2. rarely bothered   5. bothered nearly all the time
    3. sometimes bothered   6. does not apply

13. Thinking that the amount of work you have to do may interfere with how well it gets done.
    1. never bothered   4. bothered rather often
    2. rarely bothered   5. bothered nearly all the time
    3. sometimes bothered   6. does not apply

14. Feeling that you have to do things on the job that are against your better judgment.
    1. never bothered   4. bothered rather often
    2. rarely bothered   5. bothered nearly all the time
    3. sometimes bothered   6. does not apply

15. Feeling that your job tends to interfere with your family life.
    1. never bothered   4. bothered rather often
    2. rarely bothered   5. bothered nearly all the time
    3. sometimes bothered   6. does not apply

Note

1. This index is reprinted by permission.

Section

Community

Measures of community variables are limited. One of the first attempts to secure measures of the "goodness" of a city was made by E. L. Thorndike. His research monograph, *Our City*, published in 1939, provided the first careful attempt to evaluate the quality of American cities.[1] Ratings of 310 American cities with over 30,000 population were made. In his *144 Smaller Cities*, Thorndike applied his "goodness" rating to cities with between 20,000 and 30,000 population. The method requires the gathering of statistics on factors not too easily obtained. Paul B. Gillen, in his *The Distribution of Occupations as a City Yardstick*, presents a shorter technique based on the occupational distribution of the city.[2]

Over the last 20 years there has been a growing interest in what is now called quality of life, or well-being. Numerous researchers and research organizations are seeking to measure quality of life in different communities. Part of this interest reflects the importance of attracting industry to a community by the local chamber of commerce, the state's economic development agency, and numerous other interested parties. Local pride alone is sufficient to provide impetus to the measurement of community achievements. To observe this activity, note the selected bibliography that follows.

Flax, Michael J. "A Study in Comparative Urban Indicators: Conditions in 18 Large Metropolitan Areas." Washington, DC: Urban Institute, April 1972.

Godfrey, Jan, and Jim Weaver. *Community Indicators for Your City.* Austin: University of Texas, Lyndon B. Johnson School of Public Affairs, 1975.

Hughes, James. *Urban Indicators, Metropolitan Evaluation and Public Policy.* New Brunswick, NJ: Rutgers University, Center for Urban Policy Research, 1973.

Johnson, Willard. *An Index of Life Quality: How Does Your Community Stand in Relation to Other Cities of Its Size in the USA?* San Diego, CA: San Diego Urban Observatory, December 1973.

Liu, Ben-Chieh. *Quality of Life Indicators in U.S. Metropolitan Areas.* New York: Praeger, 1976.

National Urban Coalition. *City Profiles: A Statistical Profile of Selected Cities.* 3 vols. Washington, DC: National Urban Coalition, March 1977.

Ontell, Robert. *The Quality of Life in Eight American Cities: Selected Indicators of Urban Conditions and Trends.* NTIS: PB-245 255/5T. Washington, DC: National League of Cities, Urban Observatory Program, March 1975.

Smith, David M. *The Geography of Social Well-Being in the United States: An Introduction to Territorial Social Indicators.* New York: McGraw-Hill, 1973.

Whorton, Joseph W., Jr., and David R. Morgan. *Measuring Community Performance: A Handbook of Indicators.* Norman: University of Oklahoma, Bureau of Government Research, 1975.

Zehner, Robert B. *Indicators of the Quality of Life in New Communities.* Cambridge, MA: Ballinger, 1977.

The measurement of quality of life in communities, comparative evaluations, and trend patterns represents an excellent area for applied sociology. The potential enlargement of this area is promising. Indeed, the scales chosen for this section are chosen for more diagnostic research within a given community. Bosworth's Community Attitude Scale is designed to assess the degree of progressive attitude evidenced by members of a community. Fessler's Community Solidarity Index purports to measure community member solidarity. This scale is useful in determining relationships between community progress and solidarity. The Community Rating Schedule is a useful rating device in ascertaining the different views of such groups as leaders in business and labor, ministers, teachers, welfare workers, and so on. The Scorecard for Community Services Activity can be used to assess participation in the community services of the community. The relationship of community member progressiveness and community service activity might be fruitfully explored. Each scale opens possibilities of studying the impact of such background factors as occupation, social class, education, age, sex, and marital status on community participation and progress.

Notes

1. E. L. Thorndike, *Our City* (New York: Harcourt, Brace, 1939).
2. Paul B. Gillen, *The Distribution of Occupations as a City Yardstick* (New York: Columbia University Press, 1951).

6.E.1 COMMUNITY ATTITUDE SCALE

Variable measured: The degree of progressive attitude evidenced in such areas of community life as general community improvement, living conditions, business and industry, health and recreation, education, religion, youth programs, utilities, and communications.

Description: A cross section of a wide range of groups in various communities defined the meaning of progress by submitting a number of statements that they designated as progressive or unprogressive. These statements provided 364 items that were placed in a 5-point Likert-type format. A representative panel of leaders independently designated each item as progressive or unprogressive. Various tests showed that 60 items were most discriminating. These 60 items were compiled into three subscales with 20 items each. These scales are identified as Community Integration, Community Services, and Civic Responsibilities.

Where published: A Ph.D. dissertation by Claud A. Bosworth, submitted to the University of Michigan, 1954.

Reliability: 60-item scale, $r = .56$.

Validity: Total mean scores discriminated significantly between a progressive and an unprogressive group at the .025 level. It was also found that those citizens who endorsed the scale items designed to measure attitudes toward other phases of community progress also voted for the sewer extension plan.

Utility: The scale is easily administered either in an interview or by questionnaire. Approximate time required is 20 minutes.

Community Attitude Scale

Claud A. Bosworth

	Strongly Agree	Agree	?	Disagree	Strongly Disagree
(Community Services Subscale)					
1. The school should stick to the 3 R's and forget about most of the other courses being offered today.	___	___	___	___	___
2. Most communities are good enough as they are without starting any new community improvement programs.	___	___	___	___	___
3. Every community should encourage more music and lecture programs.	___	___	___	___	___
4. This used to be a better community to live in.	___	___	___	___	___
5. Long-term progress is more important than immediate benefits.	___	___	___	___	___
6. We have too many organizations for doing good in the community.	___	___	___	___	___
7. The home and the church should have all the responsibility for preparing young people for marriage and parenthood.	___	___	___	___	___
8. The responsibility for older people should be confined to themselves and their families instead of the community.	___	___	___	___	___
9. Communities have too many youth programs.	___	___	___	___	___
10. Schools are good enough as they are in most communities.	___	___	___	___	___
11. Too much time is usually spent on the planning phases of community projects.	___	___	___	___	___
12. Adult education should be an essential part of the local school program.	___	___	___	___	___
13. Only the doctors should have the responsibility for the health program in the community.	___	___	___	___	___
14. Mental illness is not a responsibility of the whole community.	___	___	___	___	___
15. A modern community should have the services of social agencies.	___	___	___	___	___
16. The spiritual needs of the citizens are adequately met by the churches.	___	___	___	___	___
17. In order to grow, a community must provide additional recreation facilities.	___	___	___	___	___
18. In general, church members are better citizens.	___	___	___	___	___
19. The social needs of the citizens are the responsibility of themselves and their families and not of the community.	___	___	___	___	___
20. Churches should be expanded and located in accordance with population growth.	___	___	___	___	___

(Continued)

	Strongly Agree	Agree	?	Disagree	Strongly Disagree
(Community Integration Subscale)					
21. No community improvement program should be carried on that is injurious to a business.	—	—	—	—	—
22. Industrial development should include the interest in assisting local industry.	—	—	—	—	—
23. The first and major responsibility of each citizen should be to earn dollars for his own pocket.	—	—	—	—	—
24. More industry in town lowers the living standards.	—	—	—	—	—
25. The responsibility of citizens who are not actively participating in a community improvement program is to criticize those who are active.	—	—	—	—	—
26. What is good for the community is good for me.	—	—	—	—	—
27. Each one should handle his own business as he pleases and let the other businessmen handle theirs as they please.	—	—	—	—	—
28. A strong Chamber of Commerce is beneficial to any community.	—	—	—	—	—
29. Leaders of the Chamber of Commerce are against the welfare of the majority of the citizens in the community.	—	—	—	—	—
30. A community would get along better if each one would mind his own business and others take care of theirs.	—	—	—	—	—
31. Members of any community organization should be expected to attend only those meetings that affect him personally.	—	—	—	—	—
32. Each of us can make real progress only when the group as a whole makes progress.	—	—	—	—	—
33. The person who pays no attention to the complaints of the persons working for him is a poor citizen.	—	—	—	—	—
34. It would be better if we would have the farmer look after his own business and we look after ours.	—	—	—	—	—
35. All unions are full of Communists.	—	—	?	Disagree	—
36. The good citizens encourage the widespread circulation of all news including that which may be unfavorable to them and their organizations.	—	—	—	—	—
37. The good citizen should help minority groups with their problems.	—	—	—	—	—
38. The farmer has too prominent a place in our society.	—	—	—	—	—

	Strongly Agree	Agree	?	Disagree	Strongly Disagree
39. A citizen should join only those organizations that will promote his own interests.	——	——	——	——	——
40. Everyone is out for himself at the expense of everyone else.	——	——	——	——	——

(Civic Responsibilities Subscale)

	Strongly Agree	Agree	?	Disagree	Strongly Disagree
41. Busy people should not have the responsibility for civic programs.	——	——	——	——	——
42. The main responsibility for keeping the community clean is up to the city officials.	——	——	——	——	——
43. Community improvements are fine if they don't increase taxes.	——	——	——	——	——
44. The younger element have too much to say about our community affairs.	——	——	——	——	——
45. A progressive community must provide adequate parking facilities.	——	——	——	——	——
46. Government officials should get public sentiment before acting on major municipal projects.	——	——	——	——	——
47. A good citizen should be willing to assume leadership in a civic improvement organization.	——	——	——	——	——
48. Progress can best be accomplished by having only a few people involved.	——	——	——	——	——
49. Community improvement should be the concern of only a few leaders in the community.	——	——	——	——	——
50. A community would be better if less people would spend time on community improvement projects.	——	——	——	——	——
51. Only those who have the most time should assume the responsibility for civic programs.	——	——	——	——	——
52. Living conditions in a community should be improved.	——	——	——	——	——
53. A good citizen should sign petitions for community improvement.	——	——	——	——	——
54. Improving slum areas is a waste of money.	——	——	——	——	——
55. The police force should be especially strict with outsiders.	——	——	——	——	——
56. The paved streets and roads in most communities are good enough.	——	——	——	——	——
57. The sewage system of a community must be expanded as it grows even though it is necessary to increase taxes.	——	——	——	——	——
58. Some people just want to live in slum areas.	——	——	——	——	——
59. The main problem we face is high taxes.	——	——	——	——	——
60. Modern methods and equipment should be provided for all phases of city government.	——	——	——	——	——

6.E.2   COMMUNITY SOLIDARITY INDEX

Variable measured: Amount of consensus among members of primary rural communities (250-2,000 population).

Description: Eight major areas of community behavior are examined:

1. community spirit
2. interpersonal relations
3. family responsibility toward the community
4. schools
5. churches
6. economic behavior
7. local government
8. tension areas

These eight areas are covered in a series of 40 statements that are rated by respondents on a 5-item scale according to their judgments of how the statements apply to their community. The items range from "very true" to "definitely untrue," with scores ranging from 5 for the "very true" response to 1 for the "definitely untrue" response. The standard deviation of the scores of all the schedules for the community is taken as a measure of the degree of consensus and, therefore, of solidarity in the community. The smaller the S, the greater the solidarity is assumed to be. The mean of the total score is considered to be an index of the members' opinion of the quality of the community. For comparison with other communities an octagonal profile may be used.

Where published: Donald R. Fessler, "The Development of a Scale for Measuring Community Solidarity," *Rural Sociology* 17 (1952): 144-52.

Reliability: Split-half *r* was described as being high but not given.

Validity: Face validity.

Utility: This index measures an important community variable. When relationships are examined between community action programs and community solidarity, this measure may be highly predictive of the success or failure of community efforts.

Research applications: Other scales and efforts to measure community attachment and identification include the following:

Anderson, C. Arnold. "Community Chest Campaigns as an Index of Community Integration." *Social Forces* 33 (October 1954): 76-81.

Angell, Robert C. "The Social Integration of Selected American Cities." *American Journal of Sociology* 47 (January 1942): 575-92.

Fanelli, A. Alexander. "Extensiveness of Communication Contacts and Perceptions of the Community." *American Sociological Review* 21 (August 1956): 439-45.

Kasarda, John D., and M. Janowitz. "Community Attachment in Mass Society." *American Sociological Review* 39 (June 1974): 328-39.

Wilensky, Harold L. "Mass Society and Mass Culture: Interdependence or Independence?" *American Sociological Review* 29 (April 1964): 173-97.

Community Solidarity Index Schedule

Name _____ Community _____

Occupation _____ Married _____ Single _____

If married, number of children in school, if any _____

_____ boys _____ girls _____, number of children out of school _____

Number of years resident in community _____. Location of residence:

in town _____ outside of town _____ how far _____ miles?

Think of each of the statements below as relating to the people of this entire community both in town and on neighboring farms. If you think the statement fits this community very well, after the statement circle *vt* (for very true); if its applies only partially, circle *t* (for true); if you cannot see how it relates one way or another to this particular community, circle *nd* (for not decided); if you think it is not true, circle *u* (for untrue); and if it definitely is not true, circle *du* (for definitely untrue). PLEASE RECORD THE IMPRESSION THAT FIRST OCCURS TO YOU. Do not go back and change your answers.

1. Real friends are hard to find in this community. *vt t nd u du* (2)[1]
2. Our schools do a poor job of preparing young people for life. *vt t nd u du* (4)
3. Local concerns deal fairly and squarely with everyone. *vt t nd u du* (6)
4. The community is very peaceful and orderly. *vt t nd u du* (8)
5. A lot of people here think they are too nice for you. *vt t nd u du* (1)
6. Families in this community keep their children under control. *vt t nd u du* (3)
7. The different churches here cooperate well with one another. *vt t nd u du* (5)
8. Some people here "get by with murder" while others take the rap for any little misdeed. *vt t nd u du* (7)
9. Almost everyone is polite and courteous to you. *vt t nd u du* (2)
10. Our schools do a good job of preparing students for college. *vt t nd u du* (4)
11. Everyone here tries to take advantage of you. *vt t nd u du* (6)
12. People around here show good judgment. *vt t nd u du* (8)
13. People won't work together to get things done for the community. *vt t nd u du* (1)
14. Parents teach their children to respect other people's rights and property. *vt t nd u du* (3)
15. Most of our church people forget the meaning of the word brotherhood when they get out of church. *vt t nd u du* (5)
16. This community lacks real leaders. *vt t nd u du* (7)
17. People give you a bad name if you insist on being different. *vt t nd u du* (2)
18. Our high-school graduates take an active interest in making their community a better place in which to live. *vt t nd u du* (4)
19. A few people here make all the dough. *vt t nd u du* (6)
20. Too many young people get into sex difficulties. *vt t nd u du* (8)
21. The community tries hard to help its young people along. *vt t nd u du* (1)
22. Folks are unconcerned about what their kids do so long as they keep out of trouble. *vt t nd u du* (3)
23. The churches are a constructive factor for better community life. *vt t nd u du* (5)
24. The mayor and councilmen run the town to suit themselves. *vt t nd u du* (7)
25. I feel very much that I belong here. *vt t nd u du* (2)
26. Many young people in the community do not finish high school. *vt t nd u du* (4)

27. The people here are all penny pinchers. *vt t nd u du* (6)
28. You must spend lots of money to be accepted here. *vt t nd u du* (8)
29. The people as a whole mind their own business. *vt t nd u du* (1)
30. Most people get their families to Sunday School or church on Sunday. *vt t nd u du* (3)
31. Every church wants to be the biggest and the most impressive. *vt t nd u du* (5)
32. A few have the town politics well sewed up. *vt t nd u du* (7)
33. Most of the students here learn to read and write well. *vt t nd u du* (4)
34. People are generally critical of others. *vt t nd u du* (2)
35. Local concerns expect their help to live on low wages. *vt t nd u du* (6)
36. You are out of luck here if you happen to be of the wrong nationality. *vt t nd u du* (8)
37. No one seems to care much how the community looks. *vt t nd u du* (1)
38. If their children keep out of the way, parents are satisfied to let them do whatever they want to do. *vt t nd u du* (3)
39. Most of our churchgoers do not practice what they preach. *vt t nd u du* (5)
40. The town council gets very little done. *vt t nd u du* (7)

Note

1. The numbers in parentheses indicate the areas to which the statements belong.

6.E.3 COMMUNITY RATING SCHEDULE

Variable measured: The quality of community life, of "goodness" of the community, is assessed.

Description: Ten institutional areas of community life are rated as good, fair, or poor. The areas selected include education, housing and planning, religion, equality of opportunity, economic development, cultural opportunities, recreation, health and welfare, government, and community organization. Scores range from 0 to 100.

Where published: New York State Citizen's Council, *Adult Leadership* 1 (October 1952): 19.

Reliability: Not known.

Validity: Rests upon face validity.

Standard scores:

good communities = 90-100
fair communities = 80-89
poor communities = 0-69

Utility: The schedule is easy to administer; the time required is about 10 minutes. Raters often have difficulty in making a general judgment and express qualifications. These should be expected. The special advantage of this index is that it permits analysis of individual raters. Individual raters from business, labor, welfare, education, and religion often differ widely in their assessments of the same community.

Research applications: No reported studies. However, the index opens possibilities of examining the patterns of new industrial locations with quality of the community. The relationship of leadership to community quality is an important area that should be explored.

Community Rating Schedule[1]

Ask respondent to rate community as good, fair, or poor as judged by similar communities in the United States.

	Good	Fair	Poor
Standard No. 1 Education Modern education available for every child, youth and adult. Uncrowded, properly equipped schools in good physical conditions. Highly qualified, well-paid teachers.			
Standard No. 2 Housing and Planning Every family decently housed. Continuous planning for improvement of residential areas, parks, highways, and other community essentials. Parking, traffic, and transportation problems under control.			
Standard No. 3 Religion Full opportunity for religious expression accorded to every individual—churches strong and well supported.			
Standard No. 4 Equality of Opportunity People of different races, religions, and nationalities have full chance for employment and for taking part in community life. Dangerous tensions kept at minimum by avoidance of discrimination and injustices.			
Standard No. 5 Economic Development Good jobs available. Labor, industry, agriculture, and government work together to ensure sound economic growth.			
Standard No. 6 Cultural Opportunities Citizens' lives strengthened by ample occasion to enjoy music, art, and dramatics. A professionally administered library service benefits people of all ages. Newspapers and radio carefully review community affairs.			
Standard No. 7 Recreation Enough supervised playgrounds and facilities for outdoor activities. Full opportunity to take part in arts and crafts, photography, and other hobbies.			
Standard No. 8 Health and Welfare Positive approach to improving health of entire community. Medical care and hospitalization readily available. Provision made for underprivileged children, the aged, and the handicapped. Families in trouble can secure needed assistance.			
Standard No. 9 Government Capable citizens seek public office. Officials concerned above all with community betterment. Controversy stems from honest differences of opinion, not from squabbles over privilege.			
Standard No. 10 Community Organizations An organization-community forum, citizen's council, or community federation-representative of entire town is working for advancement of the whole community. Citizens have opportunity to learn about and take part in local affairs. There is an organized, communitywide discussion program. Specialized organizations give vigorous attention to each important civic need.			

Total Score for Your Town

Good _____   10 points for each item   _____

Fair _____   5 points for each item   _____

Poor _____   no points   _____

Total   _____

6.E.4   SCORECARD FOR COMMUNITY SERVICES ACTIVITY

Variable measured: Individual participation in community services.

Description: The scorecard is an arbitrary index to assess individual participation in community services. Fifteen possible behavioral items are presented as those that compose the bulk of community service activity. Scores of 0-15 may be recorded, as each item participation is given a weight of one.

Where published: Unpublished.

Reliability: No tests have been made.

Validity: Rests on face validity.

Standard scores:

10-15, outstanding community member
6-9, average member
0-5, low-participating member

Cutting points were based upon a random sample of 100 adults in a middle-class community.

Utility: Administration of the scorecard takes less than four minutes. It provides for both individual and group assessment.

Research applications: None reported. However, the index opens possibilities of exploring important facets of citizenship, including the importance of background factors such as age, sex, education, race, and social class. Discovering the relations among community service activity, community solidarity, and community rating is a challenging research endeavor.

Scorecard for Community Services Activity[1]

Score one point for each "yes."

FINANCIAL SUPPORT—Did you, in the past year,

_____ contribute money to a community chest campaign?
_____ contribute money to a church?
_____ contribute money for other charitable purposes?

GENERAL ACTIVITY—Did you, in the past year,

_____ serve on any board responsible for civic programs?
_____ serve on any committee working to improve civic life?
_____ assume leadership of any civic action program?

COMMUNITY ISSUES AND PROBLEMS—Did you, in the past year,

_____ inform yourself about civic issues and problems?
_____ discuss civic problems frequently with more than one person?
_____ persuade others to take a particular position?
_____ get advice from others?
_____ speak to key leaders about problems?
_____ visit community organizations or board meetings to inform yourself?
_____ write letters, or circulate literature, or hold home meetings?

GROUP ACTION—Did you, in the past year,

_____ belong to one or more organizations that takes stands on community issues and problems?
_____ make group visits or invite visits of community officials to your organization?

_____ Total Score

10-15 points, an outstanding community member; 6-9 points, an average member; 0-5 points, a low-participating member.

Note

1. Constructed by Delbert C. Miller.

HUNTER'S COMMUNITY LEADERSHIP INDEX   6.E.5

Variable measured: The index measures with some accuracy the power positions of individuals within a local community.

Description: Hunter has created an index as a developmental effort. He seeks to establish a scale that would reflect the normal power position of an individual in community ratings. The information about a given leader may be drawn from anyone who knows this particular individual well, thus making it unnecessary to interview a whole panel of knowledgeables. Hunter believes that if this index seems to have value, others will develop the scale so that it is enhanced with greater rigor and validity.

In its present stage it will readily be seen that the index is more comprehensive in its coverage of factors than the usual device of judging a person to be powerful by naming one or two factors (e.g., mere fame or fortune). It allows for points in relation to business, politics, and professions singly or in combinations. It includes facets of activity and passivity, giving weight or demerit as the case might be. An individual may use the scale to measure his or her own power against that of contemporaries in the same community.

Where published: Floyd Hunter, *Community Power Succession: Atlanta's Policy-Makers Revisited* (Chapel Hill: University of North Carolina Press, 1980).

Reliability: Unknown.

Validity: Validity rests in part on the completeness of the factors assembled to capture the power roles and role performances of leaders who influence community issues and projects. Scoring presents evidence of high validity. Significant scores obtained on Atlanta leaders are as follows:

1. Average score of all Atlanta leaders nominated by others as top power leaders = 94.
2. Range of scores: 30-144.
3. Scores of leaders above 80 include a wide variety of business and political backgrounds, but dominated by the banking interests.
4. White politicians' average score = 72.
5. Black politicians' average score = 56; black businessmen's average score = 58; black professionals' average score = 43.

6. Regional managers likely to be moved from the city by national businesses: average score = 54.
7. Civic lay leaders' average score = 45.
8. Civic professionals' average score = 39.

Other tests made include a comparison of scaled ratings of power structure members with assessments of highly knowledgeable informants and an assessment of the interrelationships among power structure nominees. These tests demonstrate a high validity of the scale scores.

Utility: The index promises to reduce the number of interviews needed to establish the power positions of community leaders and to improve the precision of their identity.

Research applications: Hunter's monograph, *Community Power Succession,* represents the first application. A careful reading will reveal application to problems of leadership continuity and succession. Applications have been made to private power, to political perspective, and to many projects, issues, and policies. An interesting description of leadership in the black community provides a comparative base of community power.

Hunter's Community Leadership Index

Applicable items are graded +1 to +4 or –1 to –4.

1. Rating as a local power (weight by reputation)
2. Independent judgment as member, leading corporation
3. Independent judgment as executive, leading corporation
4. Will to exercise power (public/private)
5. Interest in general policy matters beyond own organization
6. Consulted on policy in own organization
7. Consulted on policy outside own organization
8. Leader recent project affecting body politic
9. Member other recent policy-making committees
10. Member prestige association(s)
11. Officer prestige association(s) or committee(s)
12. Member corporate board(s)
13. Officer corporate board(s)
14. Member prestige club(s)
15. Officer prestige club(s)
16. If extraordinary, institutional rating (education, church, family, welfare)
17. Bridging cultural leader
18. Policymaker beyond local: state to national or multinational
19. Personal qualities:
        peer acceptance
        prime age
        Who's Who listing
        society book listing
        status schools
        church prestige (local standard)
        area residence
        interaction with others
        2nd, 3rd generation
        2nd, 3rd generation ownership establishment

20. Media relations
21. Occupational quarters
22. Wealth:

moderate means	1
$10 million	2
$10 to $100 million	3
above $100 million	4

23. Uses wealth politically
24. Community residence:

relative newcomer	1
long residence	2
most of life	3
life	4

25. If corporate affiliate, control of business

outside owned	1
local and outside	2
local owned	3
local owned and managed	4

26. If corporate affiliate, size of corporation (*Fortune 500* = very large)

small	1
medium	2
large	3
very large	4

27. Family succession in business organization or profession (if yes, +1 to +4)
28. Corporate chain "nomad" (if yes, +1 to +4)
29. Control corporation expenditures
30. Number employees under direction:

under 100	1
100 to 500	2
500 to 1,000	3
over 1,000	4

31. Professional status (besides business/industry)
32. Control finances beyond own organization
33. Run for public office

successful	+1 to +4
unsuccessful	−1 to −4

34. Recent political appointive office, by prestige
35. Political participation, party politics (nonprofessional) (+1 to +4 or −1 to −4)
36. Political popularity (if professional politician in office)
37. Party affiliation by local majority or minority
38. Broker politics/business
39. Other items, by positive or negative weight points

Note on Community Research

The *American Sociological Review* inventory in Section 6.L.1 lists 26 community articles. They reveal the dominant interests of sociologists in the 1980s. Satisfaction with the community ranks as a highly regarded factor. Others have to do with community problems such as zoning, status shifts, suburbanization, population growth, civil disorder, problem-solving strategies, race relations, migration and depopulation of the metropolis, demographic change, locality identity, and interpersonal integration. Generally, authors construct their own individual measures to research their problems.

6.E.6 SELECTED REFERENCES FOR THE ADVANCED STUDENT

Angell, Robert C. "Moral Integration of Cities." *American Journal of Sociology* 57, pt. 2 (July 1951).

Berry, Brian, and Katherine Smith. *City Classification Handbook: Methods and Applications.* New York: Wiley-Interscience, 1972.

Domhoff, G. William, ed. *Power Structure Research.* Beverly Hills, CA: Sage, 1980.

Form, William H., and Delbert C. Miller. *Industry, Labor, and Community.* New York: Harper & Brothers, 1960.

Provides field study guides for assessing industry-community relations, community power structure, and community leadership. Discusses research problems of industry-community relations.

Gibbs, Jack P., ed. *Urban Research Methods.* Princeton, NJ: Van Nostrand, 1961.

Grimes, Michael D., Charles M. Bonjean, Larry J. Lyon, and Robert L. Lineberry. "Community Structure and Leadership Arrangements: A Multidimensional Analysis." *American Sociological Review* 41 (August 1976): 706-25.

Jonassen, Christian T. *The Measurement of Community Dimensions and Elements.* Columbus: Ohio State University, Center for Educational Administration, 1959.

———. "Functional Unities in Eighty-eight Community Systems." *American Sociological Review* 26 (June 1961): 399-407.

Kantner, Rosabeth Moss. *Commitment and Community.* Cambridge, MA: Harvard University Press, 1972.

Levy, Frank S., Arnold J. Meltsner, and Aaron Wildavsky. *Urban Outcomes: Schools, Streets, and Libraries.* Berkeley: University of California Press, 1974.

Provides analysis and measurement of outcomes in Oakland, California, as basis for policy analysis and new ways of understanding decisions that affect cities.

Miller, Delbert C. *International Community Power Structures.* Bloomington: Indiana University Press, 1970.

———. *Leadership and Power in BOS-WASH Megalopolis: Environment, Ecology, and Urban Organization.* New York: John Wiley, 1975.

Shevky, Ershref, and Wendell Bell. *Social Area Analysis.* Stanford, CA: Stanford University Press, 1955.

Contains indexes of social rank, urbanization, and segregation. See also Robert C. Tryon, *Identification of Social Areas by Cluster Analysis* (Berkeley: University of California Press, 1955).

Stein, Barry, A. *Size, Efficiency, Community Enterprise.* Cambridge, MA: Center for Community Economic Development, 1976.

Suttles, Gerald D. *The Social Construction of Communities.* Chicago: University of Chicago Press, 1972.

For measurement of occupational, ethnic, and social class segregation, see the following:

Taeuber, Karl E., and Alma F. Taeuber. *Negroes in Cities.* Chicago: Aldine, 1965, 195-245.

See also:

Anderson, Theodore R., and Lee L. Bean. "The Shevky-Bell Social Areas: Confirmation of Results and a Reinterpretation." *Social Forces* 40 (December 1961): 119-24.

Cowgill, Donald O. "Segregation Scores for Metropolitan Areas." *American Sociological Review* 27 (June 1962): 400-402.

Duncan, Otis Dudley, and Beverly Duncan. "Measuring Segregation." *American Sociological Review* 28 (February 1963): 133.

Jahn, Julius, and Calvin F. Schmid. "The Measurement of Ecological Segregation." *American Sociological Review* 12 (June 1947): 293-303.

Slatin, Gerald T. "Ecological Analysis of Delinquency: Aggregation Effect." *American Sociological Review* 34 (December 1969): 894-907.

For comprehensive research information on urban problems, see *Index of Current Urban Documents* (Westport, CT: Greenwood), a quarterly index to documents from more than 200 American and Canadian cities.

Researchers can also keep in contact with many new research advances by reading *Comparative Urban Research*, a journal of news and ideas devoted to rapid communication among scholars and others interested in the comparative study of urban areas throughout the world. Sponsored by the City University of New York's Comparative Urban Studies Department, it is the official newsletter of the Comparative Urban Studies Committee of the American Society for Public Administration's Comparative Administration Group and the Committee for Community Research of the International Sociological Association.

Section **F**

Social Participation

This section includes Chapin's Social Participation Scale. It is a general scale of participation in voluntary organizations of all kinds—professional, civic, and social. It is used when the total participation pattern is an important variable. The Leisure Participation and Enjoyment Scale enables the researcher to get a detailed picture of leisure patterns and also to get a score for each respondent on both participation and enjoyment.

A measure of neighborhood participation is included. Wallin's Women's Neighborliness Scale is a Guttman-type scale that has exhibited unidimensionality on the samples of respondents that have been tested. It is designed to be answered by women respondents only.

The Citizen Political Action Schedule is a scorecard for political behavior reported by a community resident. If the respondent reports accurately, the scale can reveal the behavioral acts in the political sphere.

6.F.1 CHAPIN'S SOCIAL PARTICIPATION SCALE, 1952 EDITION

Variable measured: Degree of a person's or family's participation in community groups and institutions.

Description: This is a Guttman-type scale with reproducibility coefficients of .92 or .97 for groups of leaders. High scores of 18 and over represent titular leader achievement. The five components are as follows:

1. member
2. attendance
3. financial contributions
4. member of committees
5. offices held

These components measure different dimensions: 1 measures extent of participation, while 2, 3, 4, and 5 measure intensity of participation. Also, rejection-acceptance in formal groups is measured by 1, 4, and 5, for which the intercorrelations are found to be of the order of r_{14} = .53 to .58, r_{15} = .36 to .40, and r_{45} = .36 to .40. Social participation is measured by 2 and 3, with intercorrelations of r_{23} = .80 to .89. Other intercorrelations among the components have been found to be of the order of r_{12} = .88, r_{13} = .89, r_{24} = .60, r_{34} = .40, r_{35} = .35, and r_{45} = .50 to .58.

Where published: F. Stuart Chapin, *Experimental Designs in Sociological Research* (New York: Harper, 1955), Appendix B, 275-78.

Reliability: r = .89 to .95.

Validity:

With Chapin's social status scale scores, r = .62 to .66.
With income class, r = .52.
With occupational groups, r = .63.
With years of formal education, r = .54.
Between husband and wife, r = .76.

Standard scores: Mean scores for occupational groups are as follows:

1. Professional, 20
2. Managerial and Proprietary, 20
3. Clerical, 16
4. Skilled, 12
5. Semiskilled, 8
6. Unskilled, 4

Utility: One sheet is used for entries on each group affiliation of subject recorded in five entries under five columns by the visitor in reply to questions answered by the subject. It takes 10 to 15 minutes to fill in the subject's answers.

The scale may also be self-administered.

Research applications:

Chapin, F. S. "The Effects of Slum Clearance on Family and Community Relationships in Minneapolis in 1935-1936." *American Journal of Sociology* 43 (March 1938): 744-63.

———— . "Social Participation and Social Intelligence." *American Sociological Review* 4 (April 1939): 157-66.

Erbe, William M. "Social Involvement and Political Activity: A Replication and Elaboration." *American Sociological Review* 29 (April 1964): 198-215.

Evan, William M. "Dimensions of Participation on Voluntary Associations." *Social Forces* 35 (December 1957): 148-53.

Lundberg, G. A., and Margaret Lansing. "The Sociography of Some Community Relations." *American Sociological Review* 2 (June 1937): 318-28.

Martin, Walter T. "A Consideration of Differences in the Extent and Location of the Formal Associational Activities of Rural-Urban Fringe Residents." *American Sociological Review* 17 (December 1952): 687-94.

Nelson, Joel I. "Participation and Integration: The Case of the Small Businessman." *American Sociological Review* 33 (June 1968): 427-38.

Parker, Robert Nash. "Measuring Social Participation." *American Sociological Review* 48 (December 1983): 864-73.

Social Participation Scale, 1952 Edition[1]

F. Stuart Chapin

Directions

1. List by name the organizations with which the husband and wife are affiliated (at the present time) as indicated by the five types of participation No. 1 to No. 5 across the top of the schedule. It is not necessary to enter the date at which the person became a member of the organization. It is important to enter *L* if the membership is in a purely local group, and to enter *N* if the membership is in a local unit of some state or national organization.
2. An organization means some active and organized grouping, usually but not necessarily in the community or neighborhood of residence, such as club, lodge, business or political or professional or religious organization, labor union, etc.; subgroups of a church or other institution are to be included separately *provided they are organized* as more or less independent entities.
3. Record under attendance the mere fact of attendance or nonattendance without regard to the number of meetings attended (corrections for the number attended *have not* been found to influence the final score sufficiently to justify such labor).
4. Record under contributions the mere fact of financial contributions or absence of contributions, and *not the amount* (corrections for amount of contributions *have not* been found to influence the final score sufficiently to justify such labor).
5. Previous memberships, committee work, offices held, etc., should *not be* counted or recorded or used in computing the final score.
6. Final score is computed by counting each membership as 1, each attended as 2, each contributed to as 3, each committee membership as 4, and each office held as 5. If both parents are living regularly in the home, add their total scores and divide the sum by two. The result is the mean social participation score of the family. In case only one parent lives in the home, as widow, widower, etc., the sum of that one person's participation is the score for the family (unless it is desired to obtain scores on children also).

6.F.2   LEISURE PARTICIPATION AND ENJOYMENT

Variable measured: The customary use of and degree of enjoyment of leisure time.

Description: The scale includes 47 items that are activities in which one might be expected to participate. Each item is ranked on two 5-point scales. Leisure participation is scaled according to frequency of participation (1, never; 2, rarely; 3, occasionally; 4, fairly often; 5, frequently) and leisure enjoyment is scaled according to likes (1, dislike very much; 2, dislike; 3, indifferent; 4, like; 5, like very much). The appropriate degree on each scale is circled for each item. No ranking on the like-dislike scale is given for those items in which the individual never participates.

Where published: C. R. Pace, *They Went to College* (Minneapolis: University of Minnesota, 1941). Copyright 1941 by the University of Minnesota.

Reliability: Not known.

Validity: Leisure participation:

With income, $r = .019$.
With sociocivic activities scale, $r = .40$.
With cultural status, $r = .039$.

Social Participation Scale

Address _____   Case No. _____

Husband

Age _____ Education _____ Race or Nationality _____

Occupation _____ Income _____

Name of organization	1. Member[a]	2. Attendance	3. Financial contributions	4. Member of committees (not name)	5. Offices held
1.					
2.					
3.					
4.					
5.					
6.					
7.					
8.					
9.					
10.					
Totals					

(Continued)

433

Wife _____

Age _____ Education _____ Race or Nationality _____

Occupation _____ Income _____

Name of organization	1. Member[a]	2. Attendance	3. Financial contributions	4. Member of committees (not name)	5. Offices held
1.					
2.					
3.					
4.					
5.					
6.					
7.					
8.					
9.					
10.					
Totals _____					

Date _____ Investigator _____

[a]Enter L if purely local group; enter N if a local unit of a state or national organization.

Distribution of total scores from a representative sample of an urban population, a J-curve: skewed to higher scores of 100 and over; mode at 0 to 11 points.

SOURCE: University of Minnesota Press, Minneapolis. Copyright 1938 by the University of Minnesota.

Standard scores: A summary of responses to the questionnaire on the Minnesota study is included on pages 142-45 of the Pace book.

| | 1924-25 | | 1928-29 | |
	Graduates	Nongraduates	Graduates	Nongraduates
Median leisure participation for men	125.00	123.24	132.29	131.72
Median leisure enjoyment for men	169.83	167.53	171.67	170.65
Median leisure participation for women	137.90	137.50	133.97	
Median leisure enjoyment for women	177.73	178.75	180.38	176.87

Utility: This scale is easily administered and may be self-administered. It is equally easy to score. It takes little time to administer. Both leisure participation and leisure enjoyment scores are derived and can be compared.

Research applications: Comparative study of 951 graduates and nongraduates of the University of Minnesota (C. R. Pace, *They Went to College*).

Your Leisure-Time Activities

The use of leisure time is supposed to be an increasingly important social problem. We want to know how people usually spend their leisure time. Here is a list of activities. On the left side of the page put a circle around the number that tells how often you do these things now, using the key at the top of the column. On the right side of the page put a circle around the number that tells how well you like these things, using the key at the top of the column. If you never do the activity mentioned, circle number one in the left column to indicate no participation, and circle no number on the right side of the page. Try not to skip any item.

How Often Do You Do These Things		*How Well Do You Like These Things*
1. Never		1. Dislike very much
2. Rarely		2. Dislike
3. Occasionally		3. Indifferent
4. Fairly often		4. Like
5. Frequently		5. Like very much
1 2 3 4 5	1. Amateur dramatics	1 2 3 4 5
1 2 3 4 5	2. Amusement parks and halls	1 2 3 4 5
1 2 3 4 5	3. Art work (individual)	1 2 3 4 5
1 2 3 4 5	4. Attending large social functions (balls, benefit bridge, etc.)	1 2 3 4 5
1 2 3 4 5	5. Attending small social entertainments(dinner parties, etc.)	1 2 3 4 5
1 2 3 4 5	6. Book reading for pleasure	1 2 3 4 5
1 2 3 4 5	7. Conventions	1 2 3 4 5
1 2 3 4 5	8. Conversation with family	1 2 3 4 5
1 2 3 4 5	9. Card playing	1 2 3 4 5
1 2 3 4 5	10. Church and related organizations	1 2 3 4 5

(Continued)

How Often Do You Do These Things		How Well Do You Like These Things
1. Never		1. Dislike very much
2. Rarely		2. Dislike
3. Occasionally		3. Indifferent
4. Fairly often		4. Like
5. Frequently		5. Like very much

How Often		How Well
1 2 3 4 5	11. Dancing	1 2 3 4 5
1 2 3 4 5	12. Dates	1 2 3 4 5
1 2 3 4 5	13. Entertaining at home	1 2 3 4 5
1 2 3 4 5	14. Fairs, exhibitions, etc.	1 2 3 4 5
1 2 3 4 5	15. Informal contacts with friends	1 2 3 4 5
1 2 3 4 5	16. Informal discussions, e.g., "bull sessions"	1 2 3 4 5
1 2 3 4 5	17. Indoor team recreation or sports—basketball, volleyball	1 2 3 4 5
1 2 3 4 5	18. Indoor individual recreation or sports—bowling, gym, pool, billiards, handball	1 2 3 4 5
1 2 3 4 5	19. Knitting, sewing, crocheting, etc.	1 2 3 4 5
1 2 3 4 5	20. Lectures (not class)	1 2 3 4 5
1 2 3 4 5	21. Listening to radio or TV	1 2 3 4 5
1 2 3 4 5	22. Literary writing—poetry, essays, stories, etc.	1 2 3 4 5
1 2 3 4 5	23. Magazine reading (for pleasure)	1 2 3 4 5
1 2 3 4 5	24. Movies	1 2 3 4 5
1 2 3 4 5	25. Newspaper reading	1 2 3 4 5
1 2 3 4 5	26. Odd jobs at home	1 2 3 4 5
1 2 3 4 5	27. Organizations or club meetings as a member	1 2 3 4 5
1 2 3 4 5	28. Organizations or club meetings as a leader (as for younger groups)	1 2 3 4 5
1 2 3 4 5	29. Outdoor individual sports—golf, riding, skating, hiking, tennis	1 2 3 4 5
1 2 3 4 5	30. Outdoor team sports—hockey, baseball, etc.	1 2 3 4 5
1 2 3 4 5	31. Picnics	1 2 3 4 5
1 2 3 4 5	32. Playing musical instrument or singing	1 2 3 4 5
1 2 3 4 5	33. Shopping	1 2 3 4 5
1 2 3 4 5	34. Sitting and thinking	1 2 3 4 5
1 2 3 4 5	35. Spectator of sports	1 2 3 4 5
1 2 3 4 5	36. Symphony or concerts	1 2 3 4 5
1 2 3 4 5	37. Telephone visiting	1 2 3 4 5
1 2 3 4 5	38. Theater attendance	1 2 3 4 5
1 2 3 4 5	39. Traveling or touring	1 2 3 4 5
1 2 3 4 5	40. Using public library	1 2 3 4 5
1 2 3 4 5	41. Visiting museums, art galleries, etc.	1 2 3 4 5
1 2 3 4 5	42. Volunteer work—social service, etc.	1 2 3 4 5
1 2 3 4 5	43. Writing personal letters	1 2 3 4 5
1 2 3 4 5	44. Special hobbies—stamps, photography, shop work, gardening, and others not included above	1 2 3 4 5
1 2 3 4 5	45. Fishing or hunting	1 2 3 4 5
1 2 3 4 5	46. Camping	1 2 3 4 5
1 2 3 4 5	47. Developing and printing pictures	1 2 3 4 5

WALLIN'S SCALE FOR MEASURING WOMEN'S NEIGHBORLINESS　　　**6.F.3**

Variable measured: The neighborliness of women less than 60 years of age.

Description: This instrument is a unidimensional Guttman scale consisting of 12 items. The scale items can be simply scored for any sample by counting each *GN* (greater neighborliness) answer as 1 and each *LN* (lesser neighborliness) as 0. The possible range of scores is 12 to 0.

Where published: Paul Wallin, "A Guttman Scale for Measuring Women's Neighborliness," *American Journal of Sociology* 59 (1953): 243-46. Copyright 1953 by the University of Chicago.

Reliability: The coefficient of reproducibility of the scale from two samples of women was .920 and .924.

Validity: Face validity.

Utility: A short, easy-to-administer scale that may be used for investigating factors accounting for individual differences in neighborliness. The scale also can be used for testing hypotheses as to intracommunity and intercommunity difference in neighborliness.

Research applications:

Edelstein, Alex S., and Otto N. Larsen. "The Weekly Press's Contribution to a Sense of Urban Community." *Journalism Quarterly* (Autumn 1960): 489-98.

Fava, Sylva F. "Suburbanism as a Way of Life." *American Sociological Review* 21 (1956): 34-37.

Greer, Scott. "Urbanism Reconsidered: A Comparative Study of Local Areas in a Metropolis." *American Sociological Review* 21 (1956): 19-25.

Larsen, Otto N., and Alex S. Edelstein. "Communication, Consensus and the Community Involvement of Urban Husbands and Wives." *Acta Sociologica* (Copenhagen) 5 (1960): 15-30.

For some related research on neighborhood satisfaction and integration, see the following:

Fellin, Phillip, and Eugene Litwak. "Neighborhood Cohesion Under Conditions of Mobility." *American Sociological Review* 28 (June 1963): 364-76.

Fishman, Joshua. "A Sociolinguistic Census of a Bilingual Neighborhood." *American Journal of Sociology* 75 (November 1969): 323-39.

Litwak, Eugene. "Voluntary Associations and Neighborhood Cohesion." *American Sociological Review* 26 (April 1961): 258-71.

Olsen, Marvin E. "Social Participation and Voting Turnout." *American Sociological Review* 37 (June 1972): 317-33.

Sewell, William H., and Michael J. Armer. "Neighborhood Context and College Plans." *American Sociological Review* 31 (April 1966): 159-68.

Stuckert, Robert P. "Occupational Mobility and Family Relationships." *Social Forces* 41 (March 1963): 301-7.

Swinehart, James W. "Socio-Economic Level, Status Aspiration, and Maternal Role." *American Sociological Review* 28 (June 1963): 391-99.

Wallin's Scale for Measuring Women's Neighborliness

1. How many of your best friends who live in your neighborhood did you get to know since you or they moved into the neighborhood? Two or more (*GN*); one or none (*LN*).

2. Do you and any of your neighbors go to movies, picnics, or other things like that together? Often or sometimes (*GN*); rarely or never (*LN*).

3. Do you and your neighbors entertain one another? Often or sometimes (*GN*); rarely or never (*LN*).

4. If you were holding a party or tea for an out-of-town visitor, how many of your neighbors would you invite? Two or more (*GN*); one or none (*LN*).

5. How many of your neighbors have ever talked to you about their problems when they were worried or asked you for advice or help? One or more (*GN*); none (*LN*).

6. How many of your neighbors' homes have you ever been in? Four or more (*GN*); three or less (*LN*).

7. Do you and your neighbors exchange or borrow things from one another such as books, magazines, dishes, tools, recipes, preserves, or garden vegetables? Often, sometimes, or rarely (*GN*); none (*LN*).

8. About how many of the people in your neighborhood would you recognize by sight if you saw them in a large crowd? About half or more (*GN*); a few or none (*LN*).

9. With how many of your neighbors do you have a friendly talk fairly frequently? Two or more (*GN*); one or none (*LN*).

10. About how many of the people in your neighborhood do you say "Hello" or "Good morning" to when you meet on the street? Six or more (*GN*); five or less (*LN*).

11. How many of the names of the families in your neighborhood do you know? Four or more (2); one to three (1); none (0).

12. How often do you have a talk with any of your neighbors? Often or sometimes (*GN*); rarely or never (*LN*).

6.F.4   CITIZEN POLITICAL ACTION SCHEDULE

Variable measured: Individual participation in citizen political action.

Description: This is an arbitrary index to assess individual participation in community services. Twelve possible behavioral items are presented as those that compose the bulk of citizen political activity. Scores of 0-12 may be recorded, as each item participation is given a weight of one.

Where published: League of Women Voters of Pennsylvania, Publication No. 101, Philadelphia, PA.

Reliability: No tests have been made.

Validity: Face validity.

Standard scores:

10-12, an outstanding citizen!
6-9, an average citizen.
0-5, a citizen?

Utility: The schedule may be administered in less than four minutes. It provides a measure suitable for both individual and group assessment.

Research applications: None reported. However, the index opens possibilities of exploring important facets of political behavior, including the importance of background factors of age, sex, education, race, and social class. For selection of alternate scales and related research, see John P. Robinson et al., *Measures of Political Attitudes* (Ann Arbor: University of Michigan, Institute of Social Research, 1968), 427-35.

Scorecard for Citizen Political Action

(*Score one point for each "yes")

VOTING—Did you vote

—Once in the last four years? ____

—Two to five times? ____

—Six or more times? ____

PUBLIC ISSUES—Do you

—Inform yourself from more than one
source on public issues? ____

—Discuss public issues frequently with
more than one person? ____

INDIVIDUAL ACTION ON PUBLIC ISSUES—
Did you

—Write or talk to your Congressman
or any other public official—local,
state or national—to express your
views once in the past year? ____

—Two or more times? ____

GROUP ACTION ON PUBLIC ISSUES—
Do you

—Belong to one or more organizations
that take stands on public issues? ____

PRIMARY ELECTION ACTIVITY—Did you

—Discuss the qualifications needed for
the offices on the ballot? ____

—Work for the nomination of a candidate before the primary election once
in the last four years? ____

GENERAL OR MUNICIPAL ELECTION
ACTIVITY—Did you

—Work for the election of a candidate
once in the last four years? ____

FINANCIAL SUPPORT—
Did you

—Contribute money to a party or candidate once in the last four years? ____

TOTAL SCORE ____

SOURCE: Published by the League of Women Voters of Pennsylvania, Publication No. 101.
*10-12 points—An outstanding citizen!
  6-9 points—An average citizen.
  5-0 points—a citizen?

Section **G**

Leadership in the Work Organization

This section contains two leadership scales that may be widely used in work organizations. The first scale, the Leadership Opinion Questionnaire, is designed to find answers to the question, What *should you* as a supervisor do? The second scale, the Supervisory Behavior Description, is designed to find answers to the question, What does *your own supervisor* actually do? Note that these two scales make it possible to get measures of two levels of leadership in an organization. The relationship of a supervisor to his or her immediate superior has been shown to be a very important one. The use of both questionnaires makes it possible to secure a comparison between the two levels. However, each scale may be used for the specific purpose for which it was designed. Use the Leadership Opinion Questionnaire whenever a measure of a leader's personal orientation is desired. Use the Supervisory Behavior Description when it is desirable to get the perceptions of a supervisor by those who report to him or her. This scale can be given to employees or any group of supervisors or managers. These two scales have been subjected to repeated refinement and may be considered highly reliable and valid in terms of present progress in scale construction.

The Work Pattern Profile is an analysis form that permits a description of work activity patterns. This schedule has its greatest worth as a diagnostic instrument. The relation of the work pattern profile to the leadership orientation of initiation and consideration offers interesting research problems.

Many measures of organizational performance might be included. Space prevents their addition, but the following measures are annotated for the consideration of the organizational researcher.

Executive Position Description. This description contains 191 items to determine the basic characteristics of executive positions in business and industry. Part 1 covers position activities; part 2, position responsibilities; part 3, position demands and restrictions; and part 4, position characteristics.[1]

Responsibility, Authority, and Delegation Scales. These scales were designed to measure different degrees of perceived responsibility, authority, and delegation as exhibited by individuals who occupy administrative or supervisory positions.[2]

Multirelational Sociometric Survey. This survey measures interpersonal variables surrounding work activities. Five dimensions are included: the prescribed, the perceived, the actual, the desired, and the rejected.[3]

A Method for the Analysis of the Structure of Complex Organizations. This is an application of sociometric analysis based on work contacts. The method enables the researcher to depict the organization coordination structure as established through the activities of liaison persons and the existence of the contacts between groups.[4]

Notes

1. See John K. Hemphill, *Dimensions of Executive Positions* (Columbus: Ohio State University Bureau of Business Research, 1960).
2. See Ralph M. Stogdill and Carroll L. Shartle, *Methods in the Study of Administrative Leadership* (Columbus: Ohio State University, Bureau of Business Research, 1955), 33-43.
3. See Robert Tannenbaum, Irving W. Weschler, and Fred Massarik, *Leadership and Organization: A Behavioral Science Approach* (New York: McGraw-Hill, 1961), 346-70.
4. See Robert S. Weiss and Eugene Jacobson, "A Method for the Analysis of the Structure of Complex Organizations," *American Sociological Review* 20 (December 1955): 661-68. Compare with Stogdill and Shartle, *Methods in the Study of Administrative Leadership*, 18-32. For a review of leadership theory and research, see Ralph M. Stogdill, *Handbook of Leadership* (Riverside, NJ: Free Press, 1974).

LEADERSHIP OPINION QUESTIONNAIRE   6.G.1

Variable measured: The questionnaire measures leader's orientation around two major factors: *Structure* and *Consideration.*

Structure (S) reflects the extent to which an individual is likely to define and structure his or her own role and those of subordinates toward goal attainment. A high score on this dimension characterizes individuals who play a more active role in directing group activities through planning, communicating information, scheduling, trying out new ideas, and so on.

Consideration (C) reflects the extent to which an individual is likely to have job relationships characterized by mutual trust, respect for subordinates' ideas, and consideration of their feelings. A high score is indicative of a climate of good rapport and two-way communication. A low score indicates the superior is likely to be more impersonal in relations with group members.

Description: This is a 40-item questionnaire divided into the two factors Structure and Consideration. Each factor is tested by 20 items. The items are presented with a 5-point continuum with scoring weights of 0 to 4, depending on the item's orientation to the total dimension.

Where published: Copyright © 1960, Science Research Associates, Inc., Chicago, IL. The scale is sold as the Leadership Opinion Questionnaire by Edwin A. Fleishman. It was first presented to social scientists in Ralph M. Stogdill and Alvin E. Coons, eds., *Leader Behavior: Its Description and Measurement* (Columbus: Ohio State University, Bureau of Business Research, 1957), 120-33.

Reliability: Test-retest coefficients for 31 foremen after a three-month interval show the following:

$r = .80$ on Consideration
$r = .74$ on Initiating Structure

For 24 Air Force NCOs:

$r = .77$ on Consideration
$r = .67$ on Initiating Structure

Split-half reliability estimates for Consideration and Initiating Structure were found to be .69 and .73, respectively.

Validity: Validity was evaluated through correlations with independent leadership measures, such as merit rating by supervisors, peer ratings, forced choice performance reports by management, and leaderless group situation tests. Relatively low validities were found for the particular criteria employed, although a few statistically significant correlations were found. Correlations with other measures revealed that scores on the Leadership Opinion Questionnaire were independent of the "intelligence" of the supervisor, an advantage not achieved by other available leadership attitude questionnaires.

The questionnaire scores have been found to be sensitive for discriminating reliably between leadership attitudes in different situations as well as for evaluating the effects of leadership training.

Science Research Associates has compiled evidence for validity from recent studies in many different organizational settings. It has been used in a test battery to ascertain effectiveness of sales supervisors. It has been administered to foremen in a large wholesale pharmaceutical company, to first-line supervisors in a large petrochemical refinery, to department managers in a large shoe manufacturing company, and to bank managers. In all instances, significant correlations between the questionnaire and proficiency have been shown. The Leadership Opinion Questionnaire has also shown that leadership patterns are directly related to organizational stress and effectiveness in three hospitals.

Standardized scores: Published in Edwin A. Fleishman, "The Measurement of Leadership Attitudes in Industry," *Journal of Applied Psychology* (June 1953): 156.

Dimension	Level in Organization	Mean	S.D.
Consideration	Superintendents (N = 13)	52.6	8.1
	General Foremen (N = 30)	53.2	7.1
	Foremen (N = 122)	53.9	7.2
	Workers (N = 394)		
Structure	Superintendents (N = 13)	55.5	5.7
	General Foremen (N = 30)	53.6	6.9
	Foremen (N = 122)	53.3	7.8
	Workers (N = 394)	44.2	3.9

Utility: Easily administered and scored. Time of administration, 10-15 minutes. See Edwin A. Fleishman, *A Manual for Administering the Leadership Opinion Questionnaire* (Chicago: Science Research Associates, 1960).

Research applications:

Bass, B. M. "Leadership Opinions as Forecasters of Supervisory Success." *Journal of Applied Psychology* (1956): 345-46.

Fleishman, E. A. *Leadership Climate and Supervisory Behavior.* Columbus: Ohio State University, Personnel Research Board, 1951.

————. "The Measurement of Leadership Attitudes in Industry." *Journal of Applied Psychology* (June 1953): 153-58.

————. "Leadership Climate, Human Relations Training, and Supervisory Behavior." *Personnel Psychology* 6 (1953): 205-22.

————, E. F. Harris, and H. E. Burtt. *Leadership and Supervision in Industry.* Columbus: Ohio State University, Bureau of Educational Research.

Hemphill, J. K. *Leader Behavior Description.* Columbus: Ohio State University, Personnel Research Board, 1950.

Seeman, Melvin. "Social Mobility and Administrative Behavior." *American Sociological Review* 23 (December 1958): 633-42.

For a critique of reliability and validity and additional research references, see Dale G. Lake, Mathew B. Miles, and Ralph B. Earle, Jr., *Measuring Human Behavior* (New York: Teachers College Press, 1972).

Leadership Opinion Questionnaire[1]

This questionnaire contains 40 items when presented as a complete scale. The items that follow exemplify the type found in the longer questionnaire. They are presented here so that the researcher may evaluate them for possible use of the complete scale.

Structure

Assign people in the work group to particular tasks.
    1. always   2. often   3. occasionally   4. seldom   5. never
Stress being ahead of competing work groups.
    1. a great deal   2. fairly much   3. to some degree
    4. comparatively little   5. not at all
Criticize poor work.
    1. always   2. often   3. occasionally   4. seldom   5. never
Emphasize meeting of deadlines.
    1. a great deal   2. fairly much   3. to some degree
    4. comparatively little   5. not at all

Consideration

Put suggestions made by people in the work group into operation.
    1. always   2. often   3. occasionally   4. seldom   5. never
Help people in the work group with their personal problems.
    1. often   2. fairly often   3. occasionally
    4. once in a while   5. seldom
Get the approval of the work group on important matters before going ahead.
    1. always   2. often   3. occasionally   4. seldom   5. never

Note

1. Reprinted by permission from Edwin A. Fleishman, *Leadership Opinion Questionnaire*, copyright © 1960 by Science Research Associates, Inc., Chicago, IL.

6.G.2 SUPERVISORY BEHAVIOR DESCRIPTION

Variable measured: Perceptions of subordinates of the leadership behavior demonstrated by their immediate superior. Factor analysis revealed that Initiating Structure and Consideration items are the most significant factors in distinguishing leadership performance. Initiating Structure reflects the extent to which the supervisor facilitates group interaction toward goal attainment; Consideration reflects the extent to which the supervisor is considerate of the feelings of subordinates. All questions are worded in terms of the question, What does your own supervisor actually do?

Description: This is a 48-item questionnaire divided into two independent areas of leadership: Initiating Structure and Consideration. The first area includes 20 items and the second is made up of 28 items. The items are presented with a 5-point continuum answer scale that has scoring weights of 0 to 4, depending on the item orientation to the total dimension. Highest possible score is 112 on Consideration and 80 on Initiation.

Where published: Edwin A. Fleishman, "A Leader Behavior Description for Industry," in *Leader Behavior: Its Description and Measurement*, ed. Ralph M. Stogdill and Alvin E. Coons (Columbus: Ohio State University, Bureau of Business Research, 1957), 103-19.

Reliability: Test-retest reliability coefficients based on numerous samples range from .46 to .87.

Sample	Time Between Administration	Dimension	
		Consideration *r*	Initiating Structure *r*
Workers describing 18 foremen	11 months	.87	.75
Workers describing 59 foremen	11 months	.58	.46
Workers describing 31 foremen	3 weeks	.56	.53

Split-half reliabilities are reported for samples as between .68 to .98.

Validity: The correlation between Consideration and Initiating Structure was found to be −.02 when based on replies of 122 foremen. The intercorrelation was shown to be −.33 when administered to 394 workers who described the 122 foremen. The correlation between the two scales was shown to be −.05 when administered to 176 Air Force and Army ROTC students who described their superior officers. The independence of the two factors appears to be confirmed.

Correlations have been obtained between descriptions of foremen's behavior and independent indexes of accident rates, absenteeism, grievances, and turnover among the foremen's own work groups. In production departments, high scores on the Consideration scale were predictive of low ratings of proficiency by the foreman's supervisor, but low absenteeism among the workers. A high score on Initiating Structure was predictive of a high proficiency rating, but high absenteeism and labor grievances as well.

Standard scores:

Sample	Dimension				
	Consideration			Initiating Structure	
	M	S.D.		M	S.D.
Descriptions of 122 foremen	79.8	14.5		41.5	7.6
Descriptions of 31 foremen	71.5	13.2		37.5	6.3
Descriptions of 31 foremen	73.0	12.7		40.7	7.3
Descriptions of 8 civil service supervisors	75.1	17.6		37.3	9.6
Descriptions of 60 general foremen	82.3	15.5		51.5	8.8

Utility: The questionnaire may be administered in 10-15 minutes. When used in group applications, it is very efficient. By using this questionnaire in conjunction with the Leader Behavior Description, it is possible to get a view of how a supervisor thinks he or she should lead and compare this view with an assessment by the supervisor's subordinates of his or her actual leadership performance.

Research applications: The best summary of research is found in the Fleishman work cited above. Other references may be found in the publications cited in Section 6.G.1, on the Leadership Opinion Questionnaire. Most of the research has been done by E. A. Fleishman in the plants of the International Harvester Company.

Revised Form of the Supervisory Behavior Description

Item Number	Item
	Consideration: revised key
1.	He refuses to give in when people disagree with him.
2.	He does personal favors for the foremen under him.
3.	He expresses appreciation when one of us does a good job.
4.	He is easy to understand.
5.	He demands more than we can do.
6.	He helps his foremen with their personal problems.
7.	He criticizes his foremen in front of others.
8.	He stands up for his foremen even though it makes him unpopular.
9.	He insists that everything be done his way.
10.	He sees that a foreman is rewarded for a job well done.
11.	He rejects suggestions for changes.
12.	He changes the duties of people under him without first talking it over with them.
13.	He treats people under him without considering their feelings.
14.	He tries to keep the foremen under him in good standing with those in higher authority.
15.	He resists changes in ways of doing things.
16.	He "rides" the foreman who makes a mistake.
17.	He refuses to explain his actions.
18.	He acts without consulting his foremen first.
19.	He stresses the importance of high morale among those under him.
20.	He backs up is foremen in their actions.
21.	He is slow to accept new ideas.
22.	He treats all his foremen as his equal.

(Continued)

Item Number	Item
23.	He criticizes a specific act rather than a particular individual.
24.	He is willing to make changes.
25.	He makes those under him feel at ease when talking with him.
26.	He is friendly and can be easily approached.
27.	He puts suggestions that are made by foremen under him into operation.
28.	He gets the approval of his foremen on important matters before going ahead.
	Initiating Structure: revised key
1.	He encourages overtime work.
2.	He tries out his new ideas.
3.	He rules with an iron hand.
4.	He criticizes poor work.
5.	He talks about how much should be done.
6.	He encourages slow-working foremen to greater effort.
7.	He waits for his foremen to push new ideas before he does.
8.	He assigns people under him to particular tasks.
9.	He asks for sacrifices from his foremen for the good of the entire department.
10.	He insists that his foremen follow standard ways of doing things in every detail.
11.	He sees to it that people under him are working up to their limits.
12.	He offers new approaches to problems.
13.	He insists that he be informed on decisions made by foremen under him.
14.	He lets others do their work the way they think best.
15.	He stresses being ahead of competing work groups.
16.	He "needles" foremen under him for greater effort.
17.	He decides in detail what shall be done and how it shall be done.
18.	He emphasizes meeting of deadlines.
19.	He asks foremen who have slow groups to get more out of their groups.
20.	He emphasizes the quantity of work.

NOTE: Most items were answered as 1, always; 2, often; 3, occasionally; 4, seldom; 5, never.

6.G.3   WORK PATTERNS PROFILE

Variable measured: The roles in the organization as composed of certain activities.

Description: The profile includes 14 descriptions of leadership functions that have been found within leadership jobs: inspection of the organization; investigation and research; planning; preparation of procedures and methods; coordination; evaluation; interpretation of plans and procedures; supervision of technical operations; personal activities; public relations; professional consultation; negotiations; scheduling, routing, and dispatching; technical and professional operations. Through questionnaires and interviews, each person studied in the organization indicates the proportion of time spent on each activity.

Where published: Ralph M. Stogdill and Carroll L. Shartle, *Methods in the Study of Administrative Leadership* (Columbus: Ohio State University, Bureau of Business Research, 1955), 44-53; also Carroll L. Shartle, *Executive Performance and Leadership* (Englewood Cliffs, NJ: Prentice-Hall, 1956), 81-93.

Reliability: Forms were administered to 32 officers in a Naval District Command Staff. One month later, the forms were administered again to the same officers. Test-retest coefficients are shown for the 14 major responsibilities:

inspection	.51
research	.59
planning	.49
preparing procedures	.55
coordination	.60
evaluation	.58
interpretation	.18
supervision	.03
personal functions	.46
professional consultation	.61
public relations	.83
negotiations	.83
scheduling	.38
technical and professional performance	.59

Validity: In a study of a Naval Air Station, 34 officers kept logs of work performance for a period of three days. Results suggest that there is a fairly high degree of correspondence between logged time and estimated time for objectively observable performances. More subjective, less observable performances, such as planning and reflection, are not estimated in terms that correspond highly with time recorded on the log. A number of officers expressed the feeling that their estimates of time spent in planning were more accurate than the log, for the reason that they were not always aware at the moment that what they were doing constituted planning.

Standard scores: The 14 activities are plotted in percentage of time spent in the activities. No standard scores have been developed, because many roles must first be analyzed.

Utility: This instrument will make it possible to compare patterns of performance. Therefore, executive selection may be made more appropriately in relation to the role as defined in the organization.

Research applications:

Stogdill, Ralph M., Carroll L. Shartle, Alvin E. Coons, and William E. Janes. *A Predictive Study of Administrative Work Patterns.* Columbus: Ohio State University, Bureau of Business Research, 1956.

———et al. *Patterns of Administrative Performance.* Columbus: Ohio State University, Bureau of Business Research, 1956, chap. 4.

Work Patterns Profile

The Ohio State University Personnel Research Board

The purpose of this analysis is to determine the relative proportion of your time devoted to major administrative and operative responsibilities, disregarding the methods of accomplishment.

Please consider your entire range of responsibilities from day to day. Attempt to account as accurately as possible for the relative percentage of time devoted to various administrative and technical functions.

Before each item below, please write the approximate percentage of time spent in the responsibility described.

(%)   1. *Inspection of the Organization*—Direct observation and personal inspection of installations, buildings, equipment, facilities, operations, services or personnel—for the purpose of determining conditions and keeping informed.

(%)   2. *Investigation and Research*—Acts involving the accumulation and preparation of information and data. (Usually prepared and presented in the form of written reports.)

(%)   3. *Planning*—Preparing for and making decisions that will affect the aims or future activities of the organization as to volume or quality of business or service. (Including thinking, reflection, and reading, as well as consultations and conferences with persons relative to short-term and long-range plans.)

(%)   4. *Preparation of Procedures and Methods*—Acts involving the mapping of procedures and methods for putting new plans into effect, as well as devising new methods for the performance of operations under existing plans.

(%)   5. *Coordination*—Acts and decisions designed to integrate and coordinate the activities of units within the organization or of persons within units, so as to achieve the maximal overall efficiency, economy, and control of operations.

(%)   6. *Evaluation*—Acts involving the consideration and evaluation of reports, correspondence, data, plans, divisions, or performances in relation to the aims, policies, and standards of the organization.

(%)   7. *Interpretation of Plans and Procedures*—Acts involving the interpretation and clarification for assistants and other personnel of directives, regulations, practices, and procedures.

(%)   8. *Supervision of Technical Operations*—Acts involving the direct supervision of personnel in the performance of duties.

(%)   9. *Personnel Activities*—Acts involving the selection, training, evaluation, motivation or disciplining of individuals, as well as acts designed to affect the morale, motivation, loyalty, or harmonious cooperation of personnel.

(%) 10. *Public Relations*—Acts designed to inform outside persons, regarding the program and functions of the organization, to obtain information regarding public sentiment, or to create a favorable attitude toward the organization.

(%) 11. *Professional Consultation*—Giving professional advice and specialized assistance on problems of a specific or technical nature to persons within or outside the organization. (Other than technical supervision and guidance of own staff personnel.)

(%) 12. *Negotiations*—Purchasing, selling, negotiating contracts or agreements, settling claims, etc.

(%) 13. *Scheduling, Routing, and Dispatching*—Initiating action and determining the time, place, and sequence of operations.

(%) 14. *Technical and Professional Operations*—The performance of duties specific to a specialized profession (e.g., practice of medicine, conducting religious services, classroom teaching, auditing records, operating machines, or equipment).

(100%)   Total time spent in major responsibilities.

Section H

Morale and Job Satisfaction

Morale is only one of many words we use to try to express a person's outlook on society and his or her frame of mind. Many scales have been constructed to express the diverse attitudes encompassed by such terms. Karl Schuessler has examined most of these scales and the items appearing in them. *Morale* and other terms seemed too narrow to define the area; Schuessler uses *social life feelings*, a term broad enough to capture what the items have in common. Item correlations indicated significant dimensions that can be seen in the Schuessler Life Feelings Scales, which follow.

The SRA Employee Morale Inventory is a diagnostic tool that was constructed by including dimensions of job morale. This is the most widely used instrument for diagnosis of employee morale problems. Item analysis was used in its construction. The researcher seeking to diagnose morale problems in work organizations might use the SRA Employee Morale Inventory. Norms are available that make possible departmental and interorganizational comparisons. This is probably the best standardized of all sociometric scales.

Nancy Morse and associates have constructed a set of subscales to measure intrinsic job satisfaction, pride in performance, company involvement, and financial and job status. The researcher should use the Morse Scales if short scales are needed to tap these dimensions.[1]

For more information on the reliability and validity of specific questionnaire items, the serious researcher will consult *Some Questionnaire Measures of Employee Motivation and Morale*, by Martin Patchen, with Donald C. Pelz and Craig W. Allen:

> This monograph evaluates the reliability and validity of questionnaire items associated with job motivation, interest in work innovation, willingness to express disagreement with supervisors, attitude toward changes in the job situation, and identification with the work organization.[2]

The Brayfield and Rothe Index of Job Satisfaction has been constructed by applying Thurstone's method of equal-appearing intervals and combining Likert's scoring system, which gives an intensity measure. This scale fits two important criteria: a continuum of interval measures and an intensity measure. The researcher should use the Brayfield and Rothe Index when a precise general measure of job satisfaction is desired.

Notes

1. For a critical review of general job satisfaction scales, see John P. Robinson and Associates, *Measures of Occupational Attitudes and Occupational Characteristics* (Ann Arbor: University of Michigan, Institute for Social Research, 1969), 99-103.

2. Martin Patchen, with Donald C. Pelz and Craig W. Allen, *Some Questionnaire Measures of Employee Motivation and Morale: A Report on their Reliability and Validity* (Ann Arbor: University of Michigan, Institute for Social Research, 1966).

6.H.1 SCHUESSLER'S SOCIAL LIFE FEELINGS SCALES

Variables measured: Doubt about self-determination, doubt about trustworthiness of people, feeling down, job satisfaction, faith in citizen involvement, feeling up, people cynicism, disillusionment with government, future outlook, economic self-determination, feeling demoralized, career concerns.

Social life feelings items were selected from a domain of more than 100 such items appearing in more than 100 scales used in American sociology during the last 50 years. Using Response Analysis, Inc., of Princeton, New Jersey, 187 interviewers tested 237 items with a national sample of adult respondents from 1,522 randomly drawn households.

Based on the highest correlations found in various item clusters, 12 individual scales were identified. Each scale can be considered to represent a common dimension based on high intercorrelations between constituent items as identified using factor analysis.

The findings suggest that the number of social life attitude tests in use is excessive. The Schuessler scales represent the best replacement of scales formerly used.

Where published: Karl F. Schuessler, *Measuring Social Life Feelings* (San Francisco: Jossey-Bass, 1982).

Reliability: General ratings were based on six categories: alpha reliability, Tucker-Lewis reliability, missing response rate, relation to social background, simplicity of measuring, and number of proxies (number of scales dropped in its favor). The following table shows the reliability evaluation sheet. Eight scales were rated as good, and four were rated as fair.

Twelve SLFSs, Evaluation Sheet

SLFS	No. of Items	dα Reliability	T-L Reliability	MR [a]	Largest PEV [b]	Interpretation [c]	Proxies [d]	Summary Evaluation
1	14	.80	.94	3.6	22.8	C	16	good
2	8	.80	.86	3.3	7.3	S	14	good
3	10	.80	.96	1.2	3.5	S	7	good
4	9	.75	.92	2.9	7.8	C	5	good
5	10	.71	.92	5.5	1.5	C	8	fair
6	11	.75	.94	3.5	9.4	S	5	good
7	6	.62	.87	3.2	1.9	S	—	fair
8	9	.71	.96	6.8	6.6	C	—	fair
9	12	.78	.96	4.8	10.0	C	—	good
10	5	.53	.90	4.5	2.0	S	1	fair
11	9	.66	.96	3.5	19.6	C	—	good
12	6	.65	.91	1.4	22.7	S	2	good

SOURCE: Karl F. Schuessler, *Measuring Social Life Feelings* (San Francisco: Jossey-Bass, 1982), 135.
a. Percentage nonscorable responses on base of 1,522.
b. One-factor percentage explained variance.
c. C = complex, S = simple.
d. As between two differently constructed scales with a correlation above 0.60, whichever has the higher reliability is proxy for the other.

Validity: Efforts have been made to establish validity by examining the three best items of each scale, the closest author scale, closest topic scale, and closest subject-class scale; then what Schuessler takes it to be measuring in a word or two, and a rating of that interpretation as simple or complex. Both face and criterion validities were investigated.

Schuessler summarizes the findings as follows:

> None of the twelve SLSFs had face validity in the strict sense that all its items referred directly to the concept it supposedly was measuring. However, some scales approximated this criterion more closely than others. Scales whose interpretations were rated simple generally had more face validity than scales whose interpretations were rated complex. SLFS1 is relatively weak in face validity, since few of its items refer directly to doubt about self-determination; in contrast, SLFS12 is relatively strong, since all its items (with one possible exception) express concern with career.
>
> No SLFS had criterion validity in the strict sense of predicting an independent criterion of that feeling, since in no case was such a criterion available for comparison. The scales did discriminate between social categories (age, race, income, and so on), but those findings do not constitute criterion validity, since they assume what is in question—namely, that social categories differ in their social life feelings. It is sociologically reasonable that social categories would differ in their feelings, and our findings are in line with this expectation. Thus, the finding that SLFS1 discriminates among income groups is in line with expectation that economically successful persons will attach more importance to self-effort than the economically unsuccessful. But such differences are not a demonstration of criterion validity; they would be only if they had been previously established by other means.[1]

Administration: Scales may be utilized in questionnaire form or be administered by interview. The authors worked with Response Analysis, Inc., and set up three ways of presenting scale items. In all three ways the respondent is asked "whether you mostly agree or mostly disagree with each statement." Note below the three ways of administering scale items employed by the researchers:

- *Interview:* "Now I am going to read you some statements that have been made about this country and its government. Please tell me whether you mostly agree or mostly disagree with each statement. Many of these issues are complicated, but we just want your first general impression on each statement."
- *Self:* Interviewer hands respondent questionnaire and pen and then says: "Here are some statements that have been made about this country and its government. Please indicate whether you mostly agree or mostly disagree with each statement on the questionnaire by circling number '1' for 'agree' or number '2' for 'disagree.' " When respondent is finished, interviewer takes back questionnaire.
- *Card:* Interviewer shuffles deck of cards and hands it to respondent along with sort board and then says: "The statements on these cards have been made about this country and its government. Please sort the cards on this board according to whether you mostly agree or mostly disagree with each statement." When respondent is finished, interviewer asks respondent to read the number of cards in each box. Unsorted cards are recorded "don't know." [2]

Method of administration: Each method was applied to each item about 500 times, and to each respondent approximately 67 times. Results indicate that for most items, patterns of responding and techniques of testing were statistically independent.[3]

SLFS1: Doubt About Self-Determination

Statement

1. There are few people in this world you can trust, when you get right down to it.
2. What happens in life is largely a matter of chance.
3. If the odds are against you, it's impossible to come out on top.
4. I have little influence over the things that happen to me.
5. I sometimes feel that I have little control over the direction my life is taking.
6. Nowadays a person has to live pretty much for today and let tomorrow take care of itself.
7. I've had more than my share of troubles.
8. For me one day is no different from another.
9. The world is too complicated for me to understand.
10. I regret having missed so many chances in the past.
11. It's unfair to bring children into the world with the way things look for the future.
12. The future is too uncertain for a person to plan ahead.
13. I find it difficult to be optimistic about anything nowadays.
14. No right or wrong ways to make money, only easy and hard.

SLFS2: Doubt About Trustworthiness of People

Statement

1. It is hard to figure out who you can really trust these days.
2. There are few people in this world you can trust, when you get right down to it.
3. Most people can be trusted.
4. Strangers can generally be trusted.
5. Most people are fair in their dealings with others.
6. Most people don't really care what happens to the next fellow.
7. Too many people in our society are just out for themselves and don't really care for anyone else.
8. Many people are friendly only because they want something from you.

SLFS3: Feeling Down

Statement

1. I feel that I'm not a part of things.
2. I feel somewhat apart even among friends.
3. I sometimes feel forgotten by friends.
4. At times I feel that I am a stranger to myself.
5. I just can't help feeling that my life is not very useful.
6. Very lonely or remote from other people.*
7. Depressed or very unhappy.*
8. Bored.*
9. So restless you couldn't sit long in a chair.*
10. Vaguely uneasy about something without knowing why.*

*O = often; S = sometimes.

SLFS4: Job Satisfaction

Statement

1. There is too little variety in my job.
2. I tend to get bored on the job.
3. There must be better places to work.
4. I would like more freedom on the job.
5. I have too small a share in deciding matters that affect my work.
6. My job means more to me than just money.
7. I am satisfied with the work I do.
8. My job gives me a chance to do what I do best.
9. People feel like they belong where I work.

SLFS5: Faith in Citizen Involvement

Statement

1. The public has little control over what politicians do in office.
2. The average person can get nowhere by talking to public officials.
3. The average citizen has considerable influence on politics.
4. The average person has much to say about running local government.
5. People like me have much to say about government.
6. The average person has a great deal of influence on government decisions.
7. The government is generally responsive to public opinion.
8. I am usually interested in local elections.
9. By taking an active part in political and social affairs the people can control world events.
10. Taking everything into account, the world is getting better.

SLFS6: Feeling Up

Statement

1. I sometimes feel I have little control over the direction my life is taking.
2. When I make plans, I am almost certain that I can make them work.
3. I was happier as a child than I am now.
4. I couldn't be much happier.
5. I get a lot of fun out of life.
6. I am satisfied with the way things are working out for me.
7. The future looks very bright to me.
8. Things get better for me as I get older.
9. I have a great deal in common with most people.
10. I seem to be marking time these days.
11. There is much purpose to what I am doing at present.

SLFS7: People Cynicism

Statement

1. In a society where almost everyone is out for himself, people soon come to distrust each other.
2. Most people know what to do with their lives.
3. Too many people in our society are just out for themselves and don't really care for anyone else.
4. Many people in our society are lonely and unrelated to their fellow human beings.
5. Many people are friendly only because they want something from you.
6. Many people don't know what to do with their lives.

SLFS8: Disillusionment with Government

Statement

1. Most supermarkets are honestly run.
2. We are slowly losing our freedom to the government.
3. Most politicians are more interested in themselves than in the public.
4. I have little confidence in the government today.
5. The government is run by a few people in power.
6. There's little use writing to public officials because they often aren't really interested in the problems of the average man.
7. Public officials work for the people and not just for themselves.
8. Our local government costs the taxpayer more than it is worth.
9. In my opinion, this country is sick.

SLFS9: Future Outlook

Statement

1. We are slowly losing our freedom to the government.
2. I have little confidence in the government today.
3. Many things our parents stood for are going down the drain.
4. Although things keep changing all the time, one still knows what to expect from one day to another.
5. The lot of the average man is getting worse, not better.
6. The future looks very bleak.
7. More people will be out of work in the next few years.
8. Friends are easy to find.
9. The future of this country is very uncertain.
10. The future looks very bright to me.
11. Taking everything into account, the world is getting better.
12. In my opinion, this country is sick.

SLFS10: Economic Self-Determination

Statement

1. Individuals are poor because of the lack of effort on their part.
2. Anyone can raise his standard of living if he is willing to work at it.
3. Most people have a good deal of freedom in deciding how to live.
4. Poor people could improve their lot if they tried.
5. Our country has too many poor people who can do little to raise their standard of living.

SLFS11: Feeling Demoralized

Statement

1. I have little influence over the things that happen to me.
2. I consider myself to be in good physical condition.
3. The world is too complicated for me to understand.
4. Compared to others, my life is not too good.
5. I find it difficult to be optimistic about anything nowadays.
6. I seem to be marking time these days.
7. I can't do much for other people.
8. On top of the world.*
9. Pleased about having accomplished something.*

   *SL = seldom; N = never.

SLFS12: Career Concerns

Question: "How often was each of these things on your mind in the last few weeks?"

1. Money
2. Work
3. Marriage
4. Getting ahead
5. Bringing up children
6. Future

Scoring: All negative statements are scored 1. Negative statements are shown as "agree," "often," or "sometimes." Positive statements answered as "disagree," "seldom," or "never" receive a score of 2.[4]

Utility: These scales represent the best short scales available to measure the given variable. Any single scale can be answered easily in less than two to three minutes. The researcher can use any scales that best fit his or her research design. Use of two or more of these scales can be arranged to establish profiles of individuals and groups. Profiles can show comparative rankings or means.

Norms, means, medians, and standard deviations have been determined for each of the 12 scales on a representative adult U.S. national sample of 1,522 respondents (as carried out by Response Analysis, Inc.). A German sample of 2,003 respondents is also shown. A comparative analysis cannot be made because changes were necessitated in applying the scales in Germany. The same statistics and data are given. (The phrasing of items in German is given on pp. 223-31 of the German monograph; see below.)

Scale	American Sample (N = 1,522)	German Sample (N = 2,003)
1. Doubt About Self-Determination	Scores in the national sample ranged from 0 to 14. They had a mean of 5.69, a median of 5.28 and a standard deviation of 3.57. Number of items = 14	Scores in the national sample ranged from 0 to 12. They had a mean of 5.54 and a standard deviation of 2.84. Number of items = 12
2. Doubt About Trustworthiness of People	Range of scores: 0-8; mean, 3.97; median, 3.94; standard deviation, 2.50. Number of items = 8	Range of scores: 0-6; mean, 4.20; standard deviation, 1.68. Number of items = 6
3. Feeling Down	Range of scores: 0-10; mean, 3.14; median, 2.56; standard deviation, 2.66. Number of items = 10	Range of scores: 0-9; mean, 2.03; standard deviation, 2.23. Number of items = 9
4. Job Satisfaction	Sample: 723 gainfully employed workers. Range of scores: 0-9; mean, 2.29; median, 1.73; standard deviation, 2.21. Number of items = 9	Range of scores: 0-8; mean, 2.54; standard deviation, 1.93. Number of items = 8
5. Faith in Citizen Involvement	Range of scores: 0-10; mean, 5.43; median, 5.71; standard deviation, 2.52. Number of items = 10	Range of scores: 0-7; mean, 5.24; standard deviation, 1.45. Number of items = 7
6. Feeling Up	Range of scores: 0-11; mean, 3.03; median, 2.41; standard deviation, 2.57. Number of items = 11	Range of scores: 0-8; mean, 1.41; standard deviation, 1.56. Number of items = 8
7. People Cynicism	Range of scores: 0-6; mean, 4.00; median, 4.25; standard deviation, 1.58. Number of items = 6	
8. Disillusionment with Government	Range of scores: 0-9; mean, 4.92; median, 5.12; standard deviation, 2.40. Number of items = 9	Range of scores: 0-8; mean, 4.44; standard deviation, 1.93. Number of items = 8
9. Future Outlook	Range of scores: 0-12; mean, 6.97; median, 7.40; standard deviation, 3.13. Number of items = 12	Range of scores: 0-12; mean, 6.47; standard deviation, 2.88. Number of items = 12
10. Economic Self-Determination	Range of scores: 0-5; mean, 1.67; median, 1.47; standard deviation, 1.26. Number of items = 5	Range of scores: 0-5; mean, 2.25; standard deviation, 1.36. Number of items = 5
11. Feeling Demoralized	Range of scores: 0-9; mean, 2.40; median, 2.04; standard deviation, 1.99. Number of items = 9	
12. Career Concerns	Range of scores: 0-6; mean, 4.27; median, 4.58; standard deviation, 1.57. Number of items = 6	

Research applications:

Karl Schuessler. "How Social Background Influences People's Responses." In *Measuring Social Life Feelings*. San Francisco: Jossey-Bass, 73-87.

A total of 31 background variables, both social and demographic, are analyzed for their relation to the 12 Social Life Feelings Scales. Specific attention is given to age, race, family income, education, and marital status.

A comparative study of 9 of the 12 scales was made in Germany in 1984 by Dagmar Krebs and Karl F. Schuessler.[5] A sample of 2,003 German adults was drawn at random. Scales were modified as required to meet scale criteria used in both the American and German samples. Similarities and differences in scale scores and background variables were identified between the Americans and Germans. Ascribed status was more important to the social life feelings of Germans, as shown by the more important role of marital status and age. Achieved status was more important to the Americans, as shown by their scores on the scales especially in relation to income and education.[6]

Notes

1. Karl F. Schuessler. *Measuring Social Life Feelings* (San Francisco: Jossey-Bass, 1982), 132-33.
2. Ibid., 148-49.
3. See Rae R. Newton, David Prensky, and Karl Schuessler, "Form Effect in the Measurement of Feeling States," *Social Science Research* (1982): 301-17.
4. For the rationale of 2-point scales (agree/disagree), see Schuessler, *Measuring Social Life Feelings*, 11-41.
5. Dagmar Krebs and Karl F. Schuessler, *Soziale Empfindungen, Ein interkultureller Skalenvergleich bei Deutschen und Amerikanern*. Mannheim: Zentrum für Umfragen, Methoden, und Analysen, 1987.
6. Ibid., 223-31.

THE SCIENCE RESEARCH ASSOCIATES ATTITUDE SURVEY 6.H.2

Variable measured: The Science Research Associates (SRA) Attitude Survey provides a measure of employee attitudes toward the work environment. It is a diagnostic instrument identifying attitudinal levels for individuals and groups in such areas as job demands, working conditions, pay, employee benefits, friendliness and cooperation of fellow employees, supervisor-employee interpersonal relations, confidence in management, technical competence of supervision, effectiveness of administration, adequacy of communication, security of job and work relations, status and recognition, identification with the company, opportunity for growth and advancement, and, finally, reactions to the inventory itself.[1]

Description: The inventory is not just an opinion survey. It is a kind of "morale audit" for work organizations that provides standard scores in each category based upon more than a million employees in a wide variety of business firms. Practical uses include assessing the general level of morale in an organization, locating the problem departments in the organization, determining satisfactions and dissatisfactions among employees, evaluating supervisory and executive training needs, and providing material for supervisory training programs.

Where published: Science Research Associates, Inc., 259 E. Erie St., Chicago, IL 60611. Copyright 1952 by the Industrial Relations Center of the University of Chicago. All rights reserved. Authors of the survey include Robert K. Burns, L. L. Thurstone, David G. Moore, and Melony E. Baehr.

Reliability: Both individual and group reliability have been determined by the test-retest method, with an interval of one week between the test administrations. A sample of 134 employees shows a product-moment correlation of .89. Group reliabilities range from .96 to .99, with reliability greater for groups of 50 or more employees.

Validity: Good correspondence was found to exist between the inventory results and the considered judgments of experienced observers. In three of the companies surveyed, validity was established by conducting nondirective interviews among a cross section of the employees.[2]

Standard scores: Well-standardized scores are available for comparative analysis of attitude levels in similar business firms and within similar departments. National, industrial, and occupational norms were checked and revised in 1970.

Science Research Associates

SRA Attitude Survey   *Instructions*   *Form A*

Purpose of the Survey

Your company would like to know what you think about your job, your pay, your boss, and the community in general. This inventory is designed to help you tell us your ideas and opinions quickly and easily without signing your name. This booklet contains a number of statements. All you have to do is to mark a cross by each statement to show how you feel. It is easy to do and you can be completely frank in your answers.

How to fill in the Survey

Read each statement carefully and decide how you feel about it. You will agree with some statements, and you will disagree with others. You may be undecided about some. To help you express your opinion, three possible answers have been placed beside each statement:

I would rather work in a large city than in a small town . . . . .
Choose the answer most like your own opinion and mark a cross in the box under it.

For example:

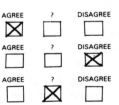

This person feels he wants to work in a large city:
  I would rather work in a large city than in a small town . . . . .

This person wants to work in a small town:
  I would rather work in a large city than in a small town . . . . .

This person can't decide between a large city and a small town:
  I would rather work in a large city than in a small town . . . . .

This is not a test

There are no "right" answers and no "wrong" answers. It is your own, honest opinion that we want.

Work rapidly but answer all statements

Do *not* spend too much time on any one statement. If you cannot decide about a statement, mark the "?" box, and go on to the next statement. If you make a mistake, erase your mark, or fill in the box completely. Then mark a cross in the correct box.

General information

Do *not* sign your name on the booklet. Be *sure* to fill in the blanks for general information such as age, sex, department, etc., that will be asked of you. This information will be used only to make the results more meaningful. It will not be used to identify you in any way.

When you have finished

When you have finished filling out the questionnaire, check to see that you have marked every statement. Then turn to last page where you will find the space to write your comments. In this space we would like you to write anything about your job or the company that is important to you. If something is irritating or trying for you, please comment on it. If something is pleasing or satisfying, please comment on that also. Or if you have a suggestion to help your job or the company, write that also.

PART I. THE CORE SURVEY

	AGREE	?	DISAGREE
1. The hours of work here are O.K..	☐	☐	☐
2. Management does everything possible to prevent accidents in our work.	☐	☐	☐
3. Management is doing its best to give us good working conditions .	☐	☐	☐
4. In my opinion, the pay here is lower than in other companies . . .	☐	☐	☐
5. They should do a better job of handling pay matters here	☐	☐	☐
6. I understand what the company benefit program provides for employees	☐	☐	☐
7. The people I work with help each other out when someone falls behind or gets in a tight spot	☐	☐	☐
8. My boss is too interested in his own success to care about the needs of employees	☐	☐	☐
9. My boss is always breathing down our necks; he watches us too closely	☐	☐	☐
10. My boss gives us credit and praise for work well done.	☐	☐	☐
11. Management here does everything it can to see that employees get a fair break on the job	☐	☐	☐
12. If I have a complaint to make, I feel free to talk to someone up-the-line	☐	☐	☐
13. My boss sees that employees are properly trained for their jobs	☐	☐	☐
14. My boss sees that we have the things we need to do our jobs	☐	☐	☐
15. Management here is really trying to build the organization and make it successful	☐	☐	☐
16. Management here sees to it that there is cooperation between departments	☐	☐	☐
17. Management tells employees about company plans and developments.	☐	☐	☐
18. They encourage us to make suggestions for improvements here	☐	☐	☐

19. I am often bothered by sudden speedups or unexpected slack periods in my work . . . . AGREE ? DISAGREE

20. Changes are made here with little regard for the welfare of employees . . . . AGREE ? DISAGREE

21. Compared with other employees, we get very little attention from management . . . . AGREE ? DISAGREE

22. Sometimes I feel that my job counts for very little in this organization . . . . AGREE ? DISAGREE

23. The longer you work for this company the more you feel you belong. . . . . AGREE ? DISAGREE

24. I have a great deal of interest in this company and its future . . . . AGREE ? DISAGREE

25. I have little opportunity to use my abilities in this organization . . . . AGREE ? DISAGREE

26. There are plenty of good jobs here for those who want to get ahead . . . . AGREE ? DISAGREE

27. I often feel worn out and tired on my job . . . . AGREE ? DISAGREE

28. They expect too much work from us around here. . . . . AGREE ? DISAGREE

29. Poor working conditions keep me from doing my best in my work . . . . AGREE ? DISAGREE

30. For my kind of job, the working conditions are O.K. . . . . . . AGREE ? DISAGREE

31. I'm paid fairly compared with other employees . . . . AGREE ? DISAGREE

32. Compared with other companies, employee benefits here are good. . . . . AGREE ? DISAGREE

33. A few of the people I work with think they run the place . . . . . AGREE ? DISAGREE

34. The people I work with get along well together . . . . AGREE ? DISAGREE

35. My boss has always been fair in his dealings with me . . . . AGREE ? DISAGREE

36. My boss gets employees to work together as a team. . . . . AGREE ? DISAGREE

37. I have confidence in the fairness and honesty of management . . . . AGREE ? DISAGREE

38. Management here is really interested in the welfare of employees . . . . AGREE ? DISAGREE

39. Most of the higher-ups are friendly toward employees . . . . AGREE ? DISAGREE

40. My boss keeps putting things off; he just lets things ride . . . . . . AGREE ? DISAGREE

41. My boss lets us know exactly what is expected of us . . . . AGREE ? DISAGREE

42. Management fails to give clear-cut orders and instructions. . . . . AGREE ? DISAGREE

43. I know how my job fits in with other work in this organization . . . . AGREE ? DISAGREE

44. Management keeps us in the dark about things we ought to know. . . . . AGREE ? DISAGREE

45. Long service means something in this organization . . . . AGREE ? DISAGREE

46. You can get fired around here without much cause . . . . AGREE ? DISAGREE

47. I can be sure of my job as long as I do good work . . . . AGREE ? DISAGREE

48. I have plenty of freedom on the job to use my own judgment . . . . AGREE ? DISAGREE

49. Everybody in this organization tries to boss us around . . . . . . AGREE ? DISAGREE

50. I really feel part of this organization . . . . AGREE ? DISAGREE

51. The people who get promotions around here usually deserve them. . . . . AGREE ? DISAGREE

52. I can learn a great deal on my present job . . . . AGREE ? DISAGREE

53. My job is often dull and monotonous . . . . AGREE ? DISAGREE

54. There is too much pressure on my job . . . . AGREE ? DISAGREE

55. Some of the working conditions here are annoying . . . . AGREE ? DISAGREE

56. I have the right equipment to do my work . . . . AGREE ? DISAGREE

57. My pay is enough to live on comfortably . . . . AGREE ? DISAGREE

58. I'm satisfied with the way employee benefits are handled here . . . . AGREE ? DISAGREE

59. The company's employee benefit program is O.K. . . . . AGREE ? DISAGREE

60. The people I work with are very friendly . . . . AGREE ? DISAGREE

61. My boss really tries to get our ideas about things . . . . AGREE ? DISAGREE

62. My boss ought to be friendlier toward employees . . . . AGREE ? DISAGREE

63. My boss lives up to his promises . . . . AGREE ? DISAGREE

64. Management here has a very good personnel policy . . . . AGREE ? DISAGREE

65. Management ignores our suggestions and complaints . . . . AGREE ? DISAGREE

66. My boss knows very little about his job . . . . AGREE ? DISAGREE

	AGREE	?	DISAGREE
67. My boss has the work well organized.	☐	☐	☐
68. This company operates efficiently and smoothly	☐	☐	☐
69. Management really knows its job	☐	☐	☐
70. They have a poor way of handling employee complaints here	☐	☐	☐
71. You can say what you think around here.	☐	☐	☐
72. You always know where you stand with this company	☐	☐	☐
73. When layoffs are necessary, they are handled fairly	☐	☐	☐
74. I am very much underpaid for the work that I do	☐	☐	☐
75. I'm really doing something worthwhile in my job	☐	☐	☐
76. I'm proud to work for this company	☐	☐	☐
77. Filling in this Inventory is a good way to let management know what employees think.	☐	☐	☐
78. I think some good may come out of filling in an Inventory like this one	☐	☐	☐

PART II. CUSTOM-BUILT SURVEY

This survey consists of up to 21 items designed especially for the client with the advice and assistance of SRA professionals. Responses to these items enable management to learn what needs to be known about situations specific to that company alone. SRA reproduces and collates this set of questions along with the other survey parts to be administered. A few sample items might be:

	STRONGLY AGREE	AGREE	?	DISAGREE	STRONGLY AGREE
79. Our hospital-surgical-medical plan provides good protection	☐	☐	☐	☐	☐
80. My best source of information concerning company plans is through the "grapevine."	☐	☐	☐	☐	☐

General information

1	2	3
4	5	6

PART III. ANONYMOUS COMMENTS

Employees are urged to express feelings on subjects they find most important to them.

Utility: The survey is inexpensive, easily interpreted, quickly scored, and permits use in all kinds of work organizations. Comparative analysis is facilitated by available standard scores. There are two different supplemental surveys available, one for supervisors and one for salespeople.

Research applications:

Ash, Philip. "The SRA Employee Inventory: A Statistical Analysis." *Personnel Psychology* 7 (Autumn 1954): 337-63.

Moore, David G., and Robert K. Burns. "How Good Is Good Morale?" *Factory* (February 1956): 130-36.

The SRA Attitude Survey (originally called Employee Inventory) was prepared by the Employee Attitude Research Group of the Industrial Relations Center, University of Chicago. This group has members from both the university and industry. Thus both the theoretical and practical aspects are well represented in all development work. Further details are given in the *Manual.*

The researcher may wish to compare the SRA Attitude Survey with the newer Survey of Organizations, by James C. Taylor and David G. Bowers (Ann Arbor: University of Michigan, Institute for Social Research, 1974), which is described elsewhere in this volume.

Notes

1. See Zile S. Dabas, "The Dimensions of Morale: An Item Factorization of the SRA Inventory, *Personnel Psychology* 11 (Summer 1958): 217-34.

2. See Robert J. Wherry, "Factor Analysis of Morale Data: Reliability and Validity," *Personal Psychology* 11 (Spring 1958): 78-89.

MORSE INDEXES OF EMPLOYEE SATISFACTION   6.H.3

Variable measured: The degree of satisfaction that individuals obtain from the various roles they play in an organization; specifically, (a) satisfaction with doing the actual content of the work, (b) satisfaction with being in the work group, (c) satisfaction with working in the company, and (d) satisfaction with pay and job status.

Description: These are indexes of employee satisfaction, each of which contains four items developed through a combined logical and empirical method. The items were initially selected from an employee interview on the basis of the definitions of each area of employee satisfaction. Intercorrelations were then computed among all items that logically appeared to belong in each area. Items that showed very low correlations were removed. The items making up each index were not differentially weighed, but were added with unit weights to give a single measure of each type of employee satisfaction. The four indexes are called *intrinsic job satisfaction, company involvement, financial and job status satisfaction,* and *pride in group performance.* Each index has four items that are answered on a 5-point scale ranging from "strong like" to "strong dislike." This gives a range of scores from 4 to 20 on each index.

Where published: Nancy C. Morse, *Satisfactions in the White Collar Job* (Ann Arbor: University of Michigan, Institute for Social Research, 1953).

Reliability: No split-half or test-retest reliabilities are reported. Internal consistency of the scales is attested to by the average intercorrelations of items:

intrinsic job satisfaction, $r = .50$
company involvement, $r = .45$
financial and job status satisfaction, $r = .52$
pride in group performance, $r = .39$

Validity: The intrinsic job satisfaction, company involvement, and financial job status indexes, both from the intercorrelations of the total index scores and from the item analysis, appear to be significantly interrelated (intercorrelations ranging from $r = .35$ to $r = .43$). These three areas can be used to represent a general morale factor. This factor predicts the individual's desire to stay in the company rather than his or her productivity.

Pride in group performance (and its subitems) is, with few exceptions, not significantly related to the items of the other indexes or to the indexes themselves. It must be treated as an independent factor. This index was related to the amount of voluntary help given by members to one another, friendliness in interpersonal relations, and the absence of antiproductivity group norms. It was also correlated with supervisor's identification with employees.

Standard scores:

		Range	N
Intrinsic Job Satisfaction	high group	04-07	717
	medium group	08-11	222
	low group	12-20	181
Financial and Job Status Satisfaction	high group	04-08	160
	medium group	09-12	227
	low group	13-20	248
Company Involvement	high group	04-08	250
	medium group	09-12	255
	low group	13-20	165
Pride in Group Performance	high group	04-08	227
	medium group	09-10	264
	low group	11-20	251

Utility: The indexes consist of easily administered questionnaire items. The time required is about 10 minutes for the administration of all four indexes.

Research applications: In *Satisfactions in the White Collar Job*, Morse reports relationships between the indexes and various supervisory practices, working conditions, and various background factors such as sex, age, length of service, and education.

Company Involvement Index

1. How do you like working here?
   code: 5-point scale ranging from strong like, complete satisfaction to strong dislike
2. Would you advise a friend to come to work for the Company?
   code: 3-point scale including yes, pro-con, and no

3. An overall coder rating of the employee's feelings about the fairness of the company, based on answers to questions throughout the interview.
   code: 3-point scale including feels company fair and generous, feels company fair but very exacting, feels company unfair
4. An overall coder rating of the employee's degree of identification with the company based on answers to questions throughout the interview.
   code: 3-point scale including strong identification, some identification, and no identification

Financial and Job Status Index

1. How well satisfied are you with your salary?
   code: 5-point scale ranging from very well satisfied to very dissatisfied
2. How satisfied are you with your chances of getting more pay?
   code: 5-point scale ranging from very satisfied to very dissatisfied
3. How about your own case, how satisfied are you with the way things have been working for you? (This question was preceded by two questions on "getting ahead here at the Company" and was answered in that context.)
   code: 5-point scale ranging from very satisfied to very dissatisfied
4. Coder overall rating of degree of frustration evidenced by respondent in advancing in his job or in his main vocational objectives. Answers to questions throughout the interview were used to measure the degree to which employee felt his vocational desires were blocked.
   code: 5-point scale ranging from strong frustration to high adjustment, no frustration

Intrinsic Job Satisfaction Index

1. How well do you like the sort of work you are doing?
   code: 5-point scale varying from strong like to strong dislike
2. Does your job give you a chance to do things you feel you do best?
   code: 5-point scale varying from yes (strong) to no (strong)
3. Do you get any feeling of accomplishment from the work you are doing?
   code: 5-point scale varying from strong sense of task completion to no sense of task completion
4. How do you feel about your work, does it rate as an important job with you?
   code: 5-point scale varying from very important to of no importance

Pride in Group Performance Index

1. How well do you think your section compares with other sections in the Company in getting a job done?
   code: 5-point scale ranging from very good, one of best in company, to very poor, one of worst in company
2. Answers to the section comparison question were also coded on the degree of emotional identification with the section that employee showed. (The use of "we" as opposed to "it" or "they" was one of the indications to the coder of identification.)
   code: 3-point scale: strong identification, mild identification, indifference or lack of identification
3. How well do you think your division compares with other divisions in the Company in getting a job done?
   code: 5-point scale ranging from very good, one of best in company, to very poor, one of worst in company
4. Answers to the division comparison question were also coded on degree of emotional identification with the division the employee showed.
   code: 3-point scale: strong identification, mild identification, indifference or lack of identification

6.H.4   BRAYFIELD AND ROTHE'S INDEX OF JOB SATISFACTION

Variable measured: General measure of job satisfaction.

Where published: Arthur H. Brayfield and Harold F. Rothe, "An Index of Job Satisfaction," *Journal of Applied Psychology* 35 (October 1951): 307-11.

Construction: As a working approach for this study it was assumed that job satisfaction could be inferred from the individual's attitude toward his or her work. This approach dictated the methodology of attitude scaling. The following requirements were formulated as desirable attributes of an attitude scale designed to provide a useful index of job satisfaction:

1. It should give an index of "overall" job satisfaction rather than specific aspects of job satisfaction.
2. It should be applicable to a wide variety of jobs.
3. It should be sensitive to variations in attitude.
4. It should contain items of such a nature (interesting, realistic, and varied) that the scale would evoke cooperation from both management and employees.
5. It should yield a reliable index.
6. It should yield a valid index.
7. It should be brief and easily scored.

The construction of this scale was made a class project in personnel psychology for members of a U.S. Army specialized training program in personnel psychology at the University of Minnesota in the summer and fall of 1943. A total of 77 men cooperated. Items referring to specific aspects of a job were eliminated since an "overall" attitudinal factor was desired.

The present index contains 18 items with Thurstone scale values ranging from 1.2 to 10.0 with approximately .5 step intervals. The items are not arranged in the order of magnitude of scale values. The Likert scoring system consisting of five categories of agreement-disagreement was applied to each item, and the Thurstone scoring system of five categories is applied to the items. The Thurstone scale value gives the direction of scoring method so that a low total score would represent the dissatisfied end of the scale and a high total score the satisfied end. The items are selected so that the satisfied end of the scale was indicated by "strongly agree" and "agree," and "disagree" and "strongly disagree" for the other half. The neutral response is "undecided." The Likert scoring weights for each item range from 1 to 5, and the range of possible total scores is 18 to 90 with 54 (undecided) the neutral point.

Reliability: The revised scale (which is the present one) was administered as part of a study of 231 female office employees. The blanks were signed along with other tests. One of the investigators personally administered the tests to employees in small groups. The range of job satisfaction scores for this sample was 35-87. The mean score was 63.8, with an S.D. of 9.4. The odd-even product-moment reliability coefficient computed for this sample was .77, which was corrected by the Spearman-Brown formula to a reliability coefficient of .87.

Validity: Evidence for the high validity of the index rests upon the nature of the items, the method of construction, and its differentiating power when applied to two groups that could reasonably be assumed to differ in job satisfaction. The nature of the individual items is partial, although not crucial, evidence for the validity of the scale. This is an appeal to face validity. Additional evidence is furnished by the method of construction. The attitude variable of job satisfaction is inferred from verbal reactions to a job expressed along a favorable-unfavorable continuum.

The job satisfaction index was administered to 91 adult night school students in classes in personnel psychology at the University of Minnesota during 1945 and 1946. The range of job satisfaction scores for this sample was 29-89. The mean score was 70.4, with S.D. of 13.2. The assumption was made that those persons employed in occupations appropriate to their expressed interest should, on the average, be more satisfied with their jobs than those members of the class employed in occupations inappropriate to their expressed interest in personnel work. The 91 persons accordingly were divided into two groups (personnel and nonpersonnel) with respect to their employment in a position identified by payroll title as a personnel function. The mean of the personnel group was 76.9 with S.D. of 8.6, compared with a mean of 65.4 with S.D. of 14.02 for the nonpersonnel group. This difference of 11.5 points is significant at the 1% level; the difference between the variances also is significant at the 1% level. It might also be mentioned that scores on this index correlated .92 with scores on the Hoppock job satisfaction scale.[1]

Research applications:

Brayfield, Arthur H., Richard V. Wells, and Marvin W. Strate. "Interrelationships Among Measures of Job Satisfaction and General Satisfaction." *Journal of Applied Psychology* 41 (August 1957): 201-5.

Ewen, Robert B. "Weighting Components of Job Satisfaction." *Journal of Applied Psychology* 51 (February 1967): 68-73.

An Index of Job Satisfaction[2]

Some jobs are more interesting and satisfying than others. We want to know how people feel about different jobs. This blank contains 18 statements about jobs. You are to cross out the phrase below each statement that has best described how you feel about your present job. There are no right or wrong answers. We should like your honest opinion on each one of the statements. Work out the sample item numbered (0).

0. There are some conditions concerning my job that could be improved.
   strongly agree, agree, undecided, disagree, strongly disagree
1. My job is like a hobby to me.
   strongly agree, agree, undecided, disagree, strongly disagree
2. My job is usually interesting enough to keep me from getting bored.
   strongly agree, agree, undecided, disagree, strongly disagree
3. It seems that my friends are more interested in their jobs.
   strongly agree, agree, undecided, disagree, strongly disagree
4. I consider my job rather unpleasant.
   strongly agree, agree, undecided, disagree, strongly disagree
5. I enjoy my work more than my leisure time.
   strongly agree, agree, undecided, disagree, strongly disagree
6. I am often bored with my job.
   strongly agree, agree, undecided, disagree, strongly disagree
7. I feel fairly well satisfied with my job.
   strongly agree, agree, undecided, disagree, strongly disagree
8. Most of the time I have to force myself to go to work.
   strongly agree, agree, undecided, disagree, strongly disagree
9. I am satisfied with my job for the time being.
   strongly agree, agree, undecided, disagree, strongly disagree

10. I feel that my job is no more interesting than others I could get.
    strongly agree, agree, undecided, disagree, strongly disagree
11. I definitely dislike my work.
    strongly agree, agree, undecided, disagree, strongly disagree
12. I feel that I am happier in my work than most other people.
    strongly agree, agree, undecided, disagree, strongly disagree
13. Most days I am enthusiastic about my work.
    strongly agree, agree, undecided, disagree, strongly disagree
14. Each day of work seems like it will never end.
    strongly agree, agree, undecided, disagree, strongly disagree
15. I like my job better than the average worker does.
    strongly agree, agree, undecided, disagree, strongly disagree
16. My job is pretty uninteresting.
    strongly agree, agree, undecided, disagree, strongly disagree
17. I find real enjoyment in my work.
    strongly agree, agree, undecided, disagree, strongly disagree
18. I am disappointed that I ever took this job.
    strongly agree, agree, undecided, disagree, strongly disagree

Notes

1. See review of James L. Price, *Handbook of Organizational Measurement* (New York: Heath, 1972), 156-73.

2. Reprinted from Arthur H. Brayfield and Harold F. Rothe, "An Index of Job Satisfaction," *Journal of Applied Psychology* 35 (October 1951): 307-11. This blank containing 18 items with Thurstone scale values ranging from 1.2 to 10.0 with approximately .5 step intervals is not arranged in order of magnitude of scale values. The Likert scoring system of five categories is applied to each item. Thurstone scale values give the direction of scoring method. Likert scoring weights range from 1 to 5 for each item. The range of possible total scores became 18 to 90, with the undecided or neutral point at 54.

Section I

Scales of Attitudes, Values, and Norms

This section includes selected attitude and value scales that revolve around current interests and concerns. In the 1960s and early 1970s, as the counterculture movement gained momentum, much attention was focused on *alienation*. Sociologists responded to demand and research interest increased—using the Srole Anomia Scale, the Neal and Seeman Powerlessness Scale, the Dean Alienation Scale, and many others. Although the interest in alienation has lessened, related feelings of *powerlessness* remain as big government, big business, big religion, big labor, and big cities seem to dominate human life. For this reason, the Neal and Seaman Powerlessness Scale has been selected as representative of one of the dimensions in the alienation of persons and groups from major social institutions.

Achievement orientation has also commanded considerable attention. Kahl's scale has been selected because of its special application to underdeveloped as well as developed societies. The researcher interested in the general factor of aspiration should examine carefully the excellent occupational aspiration scale by Archibald Haller and Irwin Miller listed in the references below.

The measurement of international patterns and norms relates to the growing interest in comparative studies. The author's Battery of Rating Scale is included for such measurements.

Innumerable attitude scales are in existence. Researchers looking for more information on these scales should check the contents tables of *Measures of Occupational Attitudes and Occupational Characteristics, Measures of Political Attitudes,* and *Measure of Social Psychological Attitudes* by John P. Robinson and his coworkers, shown in Section 6.L.6. Note also Shaw and Wright's *Compilation of Scales for the Measurement of Attitudes* in Section 6.L.7. Other sources are listed in Section 6.L.5, "All-Inclusive and Special Compilations of Sources." It would also be helpful to review the attitudes used in the *American Sociological Review* inventory that appears in Section 6.L.1.

Researchers looking for a sourcebook on attitudes that displays trend patterns should see Philip E. Converse, Jean D. Dotson, Wendy J. Hoag, and William H. McGee III, *American Social Attitudes Data Sourcebook, 1947-78* (Cambridge, MA: Harvard University Press, 1980). Also, see Elizabeth Martin and Diana McDuffee, *A Sourcebook of Harris National Surveys: Repeated Questions, 1963-76* (Chapel Hill: University of North Carolina, Institute for Research in Social Science, 1981). This is a compilation of all repeated questions from 121 national surveys conducted by Louis

Harris and Associates and achieved at the Louis Harris Data Center at North Carolina. Almost 14,000 questions are arranged by topic and identified by survey and date.

Interest in the measurement of values is growing. Some important sources of information on this topic follow:

Allport, Gordon W., Phillip E. Vernon, and Gardner Lindzey. *Study of Values*. Boston: Houghton Mifflin, 1950.

Almond, Gabriel A., and Sidney Verba. *The Civic Culture*. Boston: Little, Brown, 1963.

Alwin, D. F., and J. A. Krosnick. "The Measurement of Values: A Comparison of Ratings and Rankings." *Public Opinion Quarterly* 49 (Winter 1985): 535-52.

Cantril, Hadley. *The Pattern of Human Concerns*. New Brunswick, NJ: Rutgers University Press, 1965.

Carter, Roy E. "An Experiment in Value Measurement." *American Sociological Review* 21 (April 1956): 156-63.

Dodd, Stuart C. "Ascertaining National Goals: Project Aimscales." *American Behavioral Scientist* 4 (March 1961): 11-15.

Fallding, Harold. "A Proposal for the Empirical Study of Values." *American Sociological Review* 30 (April 1965): 223-33.

Fave, L. Richard Dells. "Success Values: Are They Universal or Class Differentiated?" *American Journal of Sociology* 80 (July 1974): 153-69.

Haller, Archibald O., and Irwin W. Miller. *The Occupational Aspiration Scale: Theory, Structure and Correlates*. 2nd ed. Cambridge, MA: Schenkman, 1971.

Neal, Sister Marie Augusta. *Values and Interest in Social Change*. Englewood Cliffs, NJ: Prentice-Hall, 1965.

Rokeach, M. *Belief, Attitudes, and Values: A Theory of Organization and Change*. San Francisco: Jossey-Bass, 1968.

———. *The Nature of Human Values*. New York: Free Press, 1973.

Scott, William A. *Values and Organizations*. Chicago: Rand McNally, 1965.

———. "Empirical Assessment of Values and Ideologies." *American Sociological Review* 24 (June 1959): 299-310.

Thurstone, L. L. *The Measurement of Values*. Chicago: University of Chicago Press, 1959.

Vickers, Sir Geoffrey. *Value Systems and Social Processes*. New York: Basic Books, 1968.

Wilson, William J., and F. Ivan Nye. *Some Methodological Problems in the Empirical Study of Values*. Washington Agricultural Experiment Station Bulletin No. 672. Pullman: Washington State University, July 1966.

Yankelovich, D. *The Changing Values on Campus*. New York: John D. Rockefeller III Fund, 1972.

The Measurement of Alienation and Anomie

The "rediscovery of alienation," as Daniel Bell puts it, has encouraged scientists to develop scales to measure these phenomena.[1] The research has been demonstrating that a number of independent factors may be identified. In 1959 Melvin Seeman set forth a fivefold classification: powerlessness, meaninglessness, normlessness, isolation, and self-estrangement.[2] The scales that have been produced have sought to isolate such factors and measure them. The first element, powerlessness, was suggested by Hegel, Marx, and Weber in their discussions of the workers' "separation" from effective control over their economic destiny, of their helplessness, of their being used for purposes other than their own. Weber argued that in the industrial society, the scientist, the civil servant, the professor is likewise "separated from control over his work."

The first scale presented is the Neal and Seeman Powerlessness Scale. It is especially useful for the measurement of worker alienation.[3] Other applications in the hospital, reformatory, and ghetto are listed in the section on research applications of the scale. Other scales have sought to tap such variables as anomie or normlessness.

The loss or absence of social norms is seen to bring personal insecurity, the loss of intrinsic values that might give purpose or direction to life. Leo Srole has sought to isolate this variable by measuring self-to-others sense of belonging. His scale consists of five items, each one measuring one aspect of anomie. The unidimensionality of the Srole Anomia Scale was assessed by the procedures of latent structure analysis and found to satisfy the criteria. It has been found that the scale satisfies the requirements of a Guttman-type scale. This scale has had an extensive application to research problems.

Dwight Dean has developed three subscales to measure powerlessness, normlessness, and social isolation. He combined the three subscales to make up an alienation scale. He believes that the pattern of intercorrelations demonstrates that alienation may be treated as a composite concept, but "there appears to be enough independence among the subscales to warrant treating them as independent variables." Neal and Rettig, using factor analysis, have found empirical evidence for the structural independence of powerlessness, normlessness, and Srole's Anomia Scale. At this time, the subscales should be utilized when the greatest precision is desired. There is great variety in the scales being used, and consensus is low.[4]

The researcher wishing to consult the Srole and Dean scales should see Srole's "Social Integration and Certain Corollaries: An Exploratory Study" and Dean's "Alienation: Its Meaning and Measurement."[5] The researcher may wish to examine other scales purporting to measure alienation and anomie, including McClosky and Schaar's "Psychological Dimensions of Anomie" and Nettler's "A Measure of Alienation."[6] For a more thorough listing and appraisal, see John P. Robinson and Phillip R. Shaver's *Measures of Social Psychological Attitudes.*[7]

Notes

1. See, for example, Allan H. Roberts and Milton Rokeach, "Anomie, Authoritarianism, and Prejudice: A Replication," *American Journal of Sociology* 61 (January 1956): 355-58; Gwynn Nettler, "A Measure of Alienation," *American Sociological Review* 22 (December 1957): 670-77; and Leo Srole, "Social Integration and Certain Corollaries: An Exploratory Study," *American Sociological Review* 21 (December 1956): 709-16. The concepts of alienation and anomie have not only become widely used, they are also among the most misused terms of our times. Researchers need to be especially cautious in estimating the size of the alienated segment of the population when using the scales.

2. Melvin Seeman, "On the Meaning of Alienation," *American Sociological Review* 24 (December 1959): 783-91.

3. Arthur G. Neal and Solomon Rettig, "Dimensions of Alienation Among Manual and Non-Manual Workers," *American Sociological Review* 26 (August 1963): 599-608.

4. See J. L. Simmons, "Some Inter-correlations Among 'Alienation' Measures," *Social Forces* 44 (March 1966): 370-72.

5. Leo Srole, "Social Integration and Certain Corollaries: An Exploratory Study," *American Sociological Review* 21 (December 1956): 709-16; Dwight G. Dean, "Alienation: Its Meaning and Measurement," *American Sociological Review* 26 (October 1961): 753-58.

6. Herbert McClosky and John H. Schaar, "Psychological Dimensions of Anomie," *American Sociological Review* 30 (February 1965): 14-40; Gwynn Nettler, "A Measure of Alienation," *American Sociological Review* 22 (December 1957): 670-77.

7. John P. Robinson and Phillip R. Shaver, *Measures of Social Psychological Attitudes*, rev. ed. (Ann Arbor: University of Michigan, Institute for Social Research, 1973), 254-94.

6.I.1   NEAL AND SEEMAN'S POWERLESSNESS SCALE

Variable measured: Basically measures the subjectively held probabilities that the outcome of political and economic events cannot be adequately controlled by oneself or collectively by persons like oneself. The authors define powerlessness as "low expectancies for control of events," as lack of control over the political system, the industrial economy, and international affairs.

Description: This instrument is a unidimensional seven-item scale that presents a choice between mastery and powerlessness. Like most powerlessness scales, this scale is an adaptation of the forced-choice instrument developed by the late Professor Shephard Liverant and his colleagues at the Ohio State University.[1]

Where published: Arthur G. Neal and Melvin Seeman, "Organizations and Powerlessness: A Test of the Mediation Hypothesis," *American Sociological Review* 29 (April 1964): 216-26.

Reliability: The seven items yielded a reproducibility coefficient of .87 on the sample used by Neal and Seeman. An early version of the scale shows that the split-half reliability coefficient was .70.[2]

Validity: The mean difference of alienation scores of organized and unorganized workers is significant at the .01 level. The difference of means for mobility-oriented and nonmobility-oriented nonmanual workers is significant at the .001 level. Correlation between anomie and powerlessness $r = .33$. Seeman and Evans found a negative relation between powerlessness and objective information concerning nature of illness among patients in hospital settings.[3] They report the following correlations between powerlessness and anomie for nonmanual workers and manual workers in Sweden:

	manual workers	*nonmanual workers*
anomie	.37 $p < .01$	.39 $p < .01$
expert orientation	.13 $p < .05$	.29 $p < .01$
mobility attitude	.15 $p < .05$	.14 $p < .05$
prejudice	.24 $p < .01$	.29 $p < .01$

Each of the seven items is scored dichotomously and the scores are summed. The powerlessness response is scored as 1 and the alternate response is scored as 0. A reproducibility coefficient of .87 (Guttman scalogram technique) was obtained for a communitywide sample (Columbus, Ohio) of 604 respondents.

Research applications:

Bullough, Bonnie. "Alienation in the Ghetto." *American Journal of Sociology* 72 (March 1967): 469.

Groat, Theodore, and Arthur G. Neal. "Social Psychological Correlates of Urban Fertility," *American Sociological Review* 32 (December 1967): 945-49.

Neal, Arthur G. "Stratification Concomitants of Powerlessness and Normlessness: A Study of Political and Economic Alienation." Ph.D. dissertation, Ohio State University, Columbus, 1959.

———— and Solomon Rettig. "Dimensions of Alienation Among Manual and Non-Manual Workers." *American Sociological Review* 28 (August 1963): 599-608.

————. "On the Multi-Dimensionality of Alienation." *American Sociological Review* 32 (February 1967): 54-63.

Seeman, Melvin. "On the Personal Consequences of Alienation in Work." *American Sociological Review* 32 (April 1967): 273-85.

————. "Alienation and Social Learning in a Reformatory." *American Journal of Sociology* 69 (November 1963): 270-84.

———— and John Evans. "Alienation and Learning in a Hospital Setting." *American Sociological Review* 27 (December 1962): 772-82.

The Powerlessness Scale[4]

(Respondent chooses between the pairs of statements.)

1. _____ I think we have adequate means for preventing runaway inflation.
   _____ There's very little we can do to keep prices from going higher.
2. _____ Persons like myself have little chance of protecting our personal interests when they conflict with those of strong pressure groups.
   _____ I feel that we have adequate ways of coping with pressure groups.
3. _____ A lasting world peace can be achieved by those of us who work toward it.
   _____ There's very little we can do to bring about a permanent world peace.
4. _____ There's very little persons like myself can do to improve world opinion of the United States.
   _____ I think each of us can do a great deal to improve world opinion of the United States.
5. _____ This world is run by the few people in power, and there is not much the little guy can do about it.
   _____ The average citizen can have an influence on government decisions.
6. _____ It is only wishful thinking to believe that one can really influence what happens to society at large.
   _____ People like me can change the course of world events if we make ourselves heard.
7. _____ More and more, I feel helpless in the face of what's happening in the world today.
   _____ I sometimes feel personally to blame for the sad state of affairs in our government.

Notes

1. For further description of this method see Julian B. Rotter, Melvin Seeman, and Shephard Liverant, "Internal vs. External Control of Reinforcements: A Major Variable in Behavior Theory," in *Decisions, Values and Groups,* vol. 2, ed. Norman E. Washburne (London: Pergamon, 1962), 473-516.

2. See Melvin Seeman and John Evans, "Alienation in a Hospital Setting," *American Sociological Review* 27 (December 1962): 772-82.

3. M. Seeman and J. Evans, "On the Personal Consequences of Alienation in Work," *American Sociological Review* 32 (April 1967): 273-85.

4. These seven items were derived from a larger "internal-external control" scale by Neal and Seeman; see J. B. Rotter, "Generalized Expectancies for Internal vs. External Control of Reinforcements," *Psychological Monographs* 80, 1 (Whole No. 609, 1966): 1-28.

6.I.2   KAHL'S ACHIEVEMENT ORIENTATION SCALE

Variable measured: According to Kahl, "an index of a generalized motivation to do well, to excel in a variety of tasks."

Description: The scale is composed of four scales derived through the use of factor analysis from a series of studies in the United States, Mexico, and Brazil. The four scales are as follows:

1. Occupational primacy: "Occupational success [is placed] ahead of alternative possibilities." In Mexico and Brazil this scale was used with three items.
2. Trust: "Belief in the stability of life and the trustworthiness of people." This scale is composed of six items.
3. Activism: "Emphasizes planning for a controllable future." This scale is composed of seven items.
4. Integration with relatives: "Loyalty to parents instead of to self or to career." This scale is composed of three items.

Where published: Joseph A. Kahl, "Some Measurements of Achievement Orientation," *American Journal of Sociology* 70 (May 1965): 669-81; and his book, *The Measurement of Modernism: A Study of Values in Brazil and Mexico* (Austin: University of Texas Press, 1968).

Reliability: Not known from the original study, but inferred from Michael A. LaSorte's Ph.D. dissertation, which used similar scales (see listing under Research Applications, below). Applying the Spearman-Brown prophecy formula for correction, the reliability coefficients were occupational primacy, .81; trust, .94; mastery (activism), .94; and familism (which departs significantly from the integration with relatives), .86.

Validity: Trust, activism, and independence from family scales are positively correlated with an index of socioeconomic status (based on occupation, education, and self-identification); occupational primacy is negatively correlated with the others and with status:

	Brazil	Mexico
trust	.30	.26
activism	.42	.49
occupational primacy	−.20	−.09
integration with relatives	−.30	−.46

Administration: Positive and negative items should be intermingled to avoid halo or acquiescence effects.

Utility: Can be administered in 15 minutes. Although Kahl constructed the scale for use in developing countries, it may be applied widely in developed countries with many different age or minority groups.

Scoring: All questions have four possible answers as stated on the scale form when administered: "agree very much," "agree a little," "disagree a little," and "disagree very much." Each of the answers is scored in the order shown as 4, 3, 2, 1 whenever a factor loading is positive (e.g., items 4, 12, 13, 14, 15, 16, 17, 18, 19, 20). The scoring is reversed to 1, 2, 3, 4 when factor loadings are negative (e.g., items 1, 2, 3, 5, 6, 7, 8, 9, 10, 11).

Each number is weighted by the loading shown by the factor analysis for that particular scale. This gives the most weight to the "best" items—those most closely related to the underlying dimension. In *The Measurement of Modernism* (pp. 29-35) Kahl reports that *unweighted scores would not change* the rank order of respondents by much.

Research applications:

Cox, Henrietta. "Study of Social Class Variations in Value Orientations in Selected Areas of Mother-Child Behavior." Ph.D. dissertation, Washington University, St. Louis, 1964.

Kahl, Joseph A. "Urbanizacão e Mudancas Occupacionais no Brasil." *America Latina* 5 (October 1962): 21-30.

———. "Some Measurements of Achievement Orientation." *American Journal of Sociology* 70 (May 1965): 669-81.

LaSorte, Michael Antonio. "Achievement Orientation and Community of Orientation." Ph.D. dissertation, Indiana University, Bloomington, 1967.

Scanzoni, John. "Socialization, Achievement, and Achievement Values." *American Sociological Review* 32 (June 1967): 449-56.

Sewell, William H., Robert M. Hauser, and David L. Featherman, eds. *Schooling and Achievement in American Society.* New York: Academic Press, 1976.

The serious student should read the communication among Wallace D. Loh, Harry J. Crockett, Jr., Clyde Z. Nunn, and John Scanzoni over the relation of socialization practices and occupational achievement values. See *American Sociological Review* 33 (April 1968): 284-91.

For another important scale that incorporates occupational aspiration, see David Horton Smith and Alex Inkeles, "The OM Scale: A Comparative Socio-Psychological Measure of Individual Modernity," *Sociometry* 29 (December 1966): 353-77. See also A. O. Haller and I. W. Miller, *The Occupational Aspiration Scale: Theory, Structure, and Correlates,* 2nd ed. (Cambridge, MA: Schenkman, 1971); and Murray A. Straus, "Deferred Gratification, Social Class, and the Achievement Syndrome," *American Sociological Review* 27 (April 1962): 552-53.

KAHL'S INDEX OF ACHIEVEMENT ORIENTATION

(Scale Items Show Factor Loadings)

TRUST

	Mexico	Brazil	
1.	−.66	−.78	It is not good to let your relatives know everything about your life, for they might take advantage of you.
2.	−.71	−.74	It is not good to let your friends know everything about your life, for they might take advantage of you.
3.	−.67	−.55	Most people will repay your kindness with ingratitude.
4.	+.38		Most people are fair and do not try to get away with something.
5.	−.62		People help persons who have helped them not so much because it is right but because it is good business.
6.	−.40		You can only trust people whom you know well.

ACTIVISM

	Mexico	Brazil	
7.	−.63	−.74	Making plans only brings unhappiness because the plans are hard to fulfill.
8.	−.58	−.65	It doesn't make much difference if the people elect one or another candidate for nothing will change.
9.	−.67	−.63	With things as they are today an intelligent person ought to think only about the present, without worrying about what is going to happen tomorrow.
10.	−.54	−.57	We Brazilians (Mexicans) dream big dreams, but in reality we are inefficient with modern industry.
11.	−.61	−.47	The secret of happiness is not expecting too much out of life, and being content with what comes your way.
12.	+.46		It is important to make plans for one's life and not just accept what comes.
13.	+.41		How important is it to know clearly in advance your plans for the future? (*Very important* is coded positively.)

OCCUPATIONAL PRIMACY

	Mexico	Brazil	
14.	+.59	+.69	The job should come first, even if it means sacrificing time from recreation.
15.	+.64	+.59	The best way to judge a man is by his success in his occupation.
16.	+.80	+.62	The most important qualities of a real man are determination and driving ambition.
17.		+.46	The most important thing for a parent to do is to help his children get further ahead in the world than he did.

INTEGRATION WITH RELATIVES

	Mexico	Brazil	
18.	+.73	+.76	When looking for a job, a person ought to find a position in a place located near his parents, even if that means losing a good opportunity elsewhere.
19.	+.78	+.75	When you are in trouble, only a relative can be depended upon to help you out.
20.	+.65	+.64	If you have the chance to hire an assistant in your work, it is always better to hire a relative than a stranger.

MILLER'S SCALE BATTERY OF INTERNATIONAL PATTERNS AND NORMS 6.I.3

Variable measured: Norms and patterns of national cultures.

Description: This scale battery consists of 20 rating scales to ascertain important norms and patterns within national cultures: (1) social acceptance; (2) standards of personal and community health; (3) concern for and trust of others; (4) confidence in personal security and protection of property; (5) family solidarity; (6) independence of the child; (7) moral code and role definitions of men and women; (8) definition of religion and moral conduct; (9) class structure and class consciousness; (10) consensus on general philosophy and objectives of the society; (11) labor's orientation to the prevailing economic and social system; (12) belief in democratic political system; (13) definition of work and individual achievement; (14) civic participation and voluntary activity; (15) definition of the role of private and public ownership of property. Five more scales are under development, with tests in the United States, England, and Spain already completed. All rating scales have six positions ranging between two contrasting poles.

Where published: Delbert C. Miller, "The Measurement of International Patterns and Norms: A Tool for Comparative Research," *Southwestern Social Science Quarterly* 48 (March 1968): 531-47; Delbert C. Miller, "Measuring Cross National Norms: Methodological Problems in Identifying Patterns in Latin American and Anglo-Saxon Cultures," *International Journal of Comparative Sociology* 13 (September-December 1972): 201-16. See also D. C. Miller, *International Community Power Structures, Comparative Studies of Four World Cities* (Bloomington: Indiana University, 1970).

Reliability: Test-retest correlations for the 15 scales range from .74 to .97 as tested in the United States and Peru. Most scales have reliabilities of .90 and above.

Validity: Three criteria for validity have been met: (a) The mean difference on each rating scale is 2.00 or more when the United States and Peru are rated and compared; (b) average deviation of each scale shows a dispersion less than 1.00 when the United States and Peru are rated; and (c) judges' rankings permit a structuring of significant variations in the social patterning of the United States and Peru. Extended research in Argentina, Spain, England, and the United States reinforces these tests of validity.

Utility: Scales are rated by qualified judges who have experience in two or more national cultures. The rating requires approximately 30 minutes. The scales may be applied to numerous problems of cross-cultural research, including the impact of a foreign culture on the stranger. The use of foreign and native judges rating the same two national cultures in which they have both had extensive experience reveals the significance of cross-cultural differences. Ratings can be made of national cultures by raters who have no previous experience to examine stereotyping. The relation of the class position of the respondent offers the possibility of revealing international differences when viewed from varying class or racial positions occupied by the respondent in the national society.

Comparative scores: The mean scores shown in Table 6.7 for the rating scales on the seven samples may be used for comparative study.

Research applications: Delbert C. Miller, *International Community Power Structures, Comparative Studies of Four World Cities* (Bloomington: Indiana University

TABLE 6.7 Mean Scores for the Rating Scales on the Seven Samples

Scale of International Patterns and Norms	United States [a] (1966) (N = 21)	United States [b] (1968) (N = 32)	Spain [c] (1968) (N = 17)	Argentina [d] (1967) (N = 15)	Peru [e] (1966) (N = 21)	England [f] (1968) (N = 15)	Colombia [g] (1969) (N = 10)
1. Social Acceptance	1.7	1.6	3.1	3.2	4.5	4.0	4.2
2. Personal and Community Health	1.4	1.9	3.2	2.9	4.7	33.1	4.4
3. Concern and Trust of Others	1.8	2.7	4.1	3.3	4.9	2.0	4.3
4. Personal Security and Protection of Property	2.3	3.7	2.2	3.5	5.0	2.1	5.7
5. Family Solidarity	5.4	4.0	2.3	2.7	1.9	2.9	1.8
6. Independence of the Child	1.3	2.1	4.5	2.8	4.4	2.1	4.4
7. Moral Code and Role Definition	2.0	2.3	4.6	2.8	4.9	3.4	4.9
8. Religion and Moral Conduct	4.6	4.3	2.6	3.7	2.1	4.6	2.6
9. Class Structure and Consciousness	5.0	4.9	2.1	3.1	1.4	3.1	1.8
10. Societal Consensus	1.6	2.1	5.0	3.9	4.6	2.1	3.9
11. Labor's Orientation	5.3	5.4	2.3	2.7	3.1	4.0	2.7
12. Democratic Belief	1.4	1.8	4.6	2.8	3.7	2.1	3.8
13. Work and Achievement	1.5	2.1	4.0	3.1	4.8	3.1	4.2
14. Civic Participation	1.2	1.9	4.8	3.6	4.8	3.1	4.2
15. Role of Property	1.2	1.7	3.1	3.6	3.3	3.3	2.7
16. Honesty of Government Officials		1.8	3.5			1.3	
17. Political Influence of Foreign Enterprise		5.2	3.8			5.3	
18. Encouragement of Foreign Enterprise		2.2	2.5			2.3	
19. Nepotism in Organizations		4.8	1.5			4.0	
20. Reciprocity of Favors		3.9	1.5			5.0	

a. American raters.
b. American raters.
c. Spanish raters in Madrid, Barcelona, and Seville.
d. Argentine raters. (Data gathered by Judson Yearwood.)
e. American raters living in Peru.
f. Englishmen living in London, Liverpool, and Bristol, England.
g. Colombian raters. (Data gathered by Dr. Teresa Camacho de Pinto.)

Press, 1970), 228-56. Chapter 14, "The Role of Values in International Decision Making: Anglo-American vs. Latin American Differences," reports on a test of the hypothesis that respondent exposures to any two countries in Latin America are more alike in cultural patterning than any Latin American country compared with the United States. Comparisons with samples in Spain and England are also reported to establish identity of Anglo-Saxon and Ibero-Latin American cultures. Ratings were made using panels of judges, both foreign and native, in Peru, Argentina, the United States, Spain, and England. Studies have been made also with U.S. university students who have gone abroad to study. Before-and-after ratings of their own country and the host country have been secured.

Teresa Camacho de Pinto has completed research on Colombia; her report of respondent ratings is shown in Table 6.7. Paul D. Starr has completed a study in Lebanon to provide a valuable Middle East comparison and perspective.[1]

New scales have been added to the original 15; these include degree of honesty and integrity in government; degree of nepotism in business, governmental, and organizational life generally; degree of expected reciprocity in favors and rewards; encouragement of foreign enterprise; and degree to which foreign enterprise is believed to influence the host government. The scales and scores are shown for the United States and Spain in the following test battery.

Applying Scales: Instructions to the Judge

The following instructions were given to judges. A qualified judge is a college graduate, specially trained to appraise his or her own country and with six months or more consecutive experience with the host country. A qualified judge must be able to read and speak the language of the host country.

Each characteristic has been placed on a scale of six points. The descriptions defining the scale are shown at 1 and 2, 3 and 4, 5 and 6. Thus the first characteristic, social acceptance, attributes highest social acceptance to the number 1 position and lowest social acceptance to the number 6 position. The range between represents a continuum of different degrees of the characteristic.

Task 1. Establish anchor points for each scale by selecting countries from anywhere in the world that reflect the extreme positions of the scale for social acceptance. These countries may or may not be known to you personally. In making a selection *think of the way the pattern appears on the average throughout the country and as it is experienced by a person in the middle sector of society*—that is, omitting the very rich and the very poor. When the selection has been made, write the names of the countries in the answer sheets. Proceed to select countries representing the extremes of all 19 remaining characteristics— that is, standards of health, standards of personal and community health, and so on. Write the names on the answer sheets.

Task 2. Now place the two countries in their proper positions on all 20 characteristics. Again, think of the pattern as it appears on the average throughout the country and as it is experienced by a person in the middle sector of society—that is, omitting the very rich and the very poor. Write answers on answer sheet.

Task 3. Place a third country on the scale if you have lived six months or more within it. Write answers on answer sheet.

Note

1. Paul D. Starr, "Social Patterns and Norms in Lebanon and the United States," *Human Relations* 26, no. 4 (1976): 357-66.

MILLER'S SCALE BATTERY OF INTERNATIONAL PATTERNS AND NORMS

Respondent: Kindly check if you are male or female and indicate years lived in native country and in other countries. Sign your name and give your address if you wish a final report. Read the accompanying directions carefully before you begin. Thank you.

Check: Male ___ Female ___

Years lived in:

Native Country _____

Other Countries _____

_____

_____

(Optional)

Name: _____

Address: _____

_____

_____

1. Social acceptance

1	2	3	4	5	6

High social acceptance. Social contacts open and nonrestrictive. Introductions not needed for social contacts. Short acquaintance provides entry into the home and social organizations.	Medium social acceptance. Ready acceptance in neighborhood and in community organizations but not in family and social life. Friendly in business and other public contacts.	Low social acceptance. Acceptance in specifically designated groups in which membership has been validated. Sponsored introduction is needed for social contacts in all parts of community life.

2. Standards of personal and community health

1	2	3	4	5	6

High standards of personal and community hygiene. Hygienic habits valued in all parts of society.	Varied. High community standards for water and sewage. Personal habits and community standards for cleanliness and hygiene vary widely across the community.	Personal and community standards of hygiene are not valued highly.

3. Concern for and trust of others

1	2	3	4	5	6

High concern for others. Respect for the motives and integrity of others. Mutual trust prevails.	Moderate or uneven pattern of concern for and trust of others.	Lack of concern for others and lack of trust.

4. Confidence in personal security and protection of property

1	2	3	4	5	6

High confidence in personal security. Free movement, night and day, for both sexes. High sense of security of property. Locking of homes is optional.	Moderate confidence in personal security. Confidence of men is high in personal security but women are warned to take precautions. Movements of women restricted to daytime. Simple property precautions essential.	Low confidence in both personal security and protection of property. Men and women restrict all movement at night to predetermined precautions. Many property precautions obligatory. Extensive use of locks, dogs, and guards.

5. Family solidarity

1	2	3	4	5	6

High solidarity with many obligations of kinship relations within large, extended family system.	Relations of solidarity within a limited kinship circle with specified obligations only.	Small, loosely integrated, independent family with highly specific individual relations.

6. Independence of the child

1	2	3	4	5	6

Child is raised to be self-reliant and independent in both thought and action.	Child is given specified areas of independence only.	Child is raised to be highly dependent and docile.

7. Moral code and role definitions of men and women

1	2	3	4	5	6

Single code of morality prevails for men and women. Separate occupational and social roles are not defined for men and women. Similar amounts and standards of education prevail.	Variations between moral definitions for men and women exist for certain specified behaviors. Occupational and social role definitions vary in degree. Varying educational provisions for the sexes.	Double code of morality prevails. Separate occupational and social roles for men and women exist and are sharply defined. Amount and standards of education vary widely between the sexes.

8. Definition of religion and moral conduct

1	2	3	4	5	6

Belief in the sacred interpretation of life as primary explanation of purpose of life and role of death. Emphasis is placed on importance of worshiper role in fulfilling spiritual obligations and duties.	Belief in supreme being a sacred purpose for life. Emphasis is placed on secular interpretation of moral values and importance of applying them to daily conduct.	Belief in secular interpretation of life. Emphasis on importance of achieving the good society for achieving the good life. Moral values prescribed by social and scientific definitions of human well being in the society. Emphasis on social conduct as moral conduct.

9. Class structure and class consciousness

1	2	3	4	5	6

Highly conscious of class differences. Extensive use of status symbols. Social classes and social circles rigidly defined. Very small upward class movement. Contacts between classes limited by social distinctions. Private schools predominate for upper social groups.	Class consciousness prevails moderately. Upward class movement occurs but definite characteristics mark off and limit contact between classes.	Class consciousness low. Class differences devalued. Minimal use of status symbols. Considerable upward class movement. Relatively free social contacts between social classes. Public schools dominate for all social classes.

10. Consensus over general philosophy and objectives of the society

1	2	3	4	5	6

High consensus over philosophy and objectives of the society as achieved either through evolution or revolution. Competition and conflict between parties takes place within generally accepted goals of the society. Stable governments usually prevail.	Consensus is partial. Differing ideological systems conflict. Stable government may be maintained but under threat of overthrow.	Absence of consensus (or very low) over philosophy and objectives of the society. Conflicting and splinter parties may represent the divergent ideologies and cleavages. Unstable governments prevail.

11. Labor's orientation to the prevailing economic and social system

1	2	3	4	5	6

Highly alienated. Ideologically opposed to the prevailing economic and social system. Revolutionary in orientation.	Antagonistic. Partly alienated with some unions ideologically in support and some in opposition to prevailing economic and social system.	Highly assimilated. Ideologically in agreement with prevailing economic and social system. Labor disputes over distribution shares of goods and services to working people but accepts on-going system.

12. Belief in democratic political system

1	2	3	4	5	6

Strongly committed. Deep and persistent belief in the democratic processes regardless of problems or crisis.	Reserved commitment. Belief in democracy as process requiring careful control against mass abuse. Accepts necessity of dictatorial intervention in crisis situations or special safeguard such as one-party systems, relinquishing freedoms in internal crises, etc.	Lack of belief in democracy as political system. Regarded as weak and ineffectual in the solving of problems and improving the lot of the average man. Generally regarded as dangerous because it exposes government to mob psychology.

13. Definition of work and individual achievement

1	2	3	4	5	6

A belief in hard work as obligation to self, employer, and God. Efficiency values accepted. Individual is expected to progress in his work life.	Work is important to the advancement of self and family. Efficiency values accepted. Achievement expectations vary.	Lack of belief in hard work. Work is regarded as necessary, but involves no obligation beyond delivery of minimum services. Efficiency values rejected. Individual is expected only to maintain family status at his inherited level.

14. Civic participation and voluntary activity

1	2	3	4	5	6

High civic activity. People work together to get things done for the community. High identity with volunteer groups. Civic participation and volunteer activity in groups is an important source of social prestige. Moral and altruistic motives are important sources of motivation.	Moderate activity in special areas. Organized participation exists for economic or political self-interest but often is lacking for a general community need.	Low civic activity, often deliberately avoided with no social sanctions. Low identity with volunteer groups. Civic participation is not an important source of prestige. Mistrust of motives is common since self-interest is generally assumed as the principal motivation for all persons.

15. Definition of the role of private and public ownership of property

1	2	3	4	5	6

Strong belief in the right of private property for all persons in all types of goods. Private ownership and control of means of production is accepted for all industries and services except for a few natural monopolies (i.e., water, post office, etc.)	Belief in the wide mixture of private ownership and public ownership in all industries and services. Public ownership of large basic industries (steel, coal, electricity, etc.) and services (transport and communication) is especially common.	Strong belief in the public ownership and governmental controls of all industries and services except for small enterprises. Private ownership accepted in the ownership of personal goods.

16. Standards of honesty and integrity of government officials

1	2	3	4	5	6

Government officials at all levels have a high standard of honesty and integrity. Violations are prosecuted vigorously and punished with appropriate penalties.	Government officials are generally honest but there are differences in the honesty of officials at different levels. Violations do occur and are prosecuted. The certainty of detection and the severity of penalty varies according to differing practices.	Government officials at all levels commonly engage in various kinds of corrupt practices. Most violations are seldom prosecuted. Occasionally token prosecutions are made when abuse becomes excessive.

17. Political influence of foreign enterprise on host government

1	2	3	4	5	6

Foreign enterprise has marked political influence on major economic and political policies of the nation. It can resist attempted nationalization of its own enterprises and enforce favorable trade and political relations.	Foreign enterprise does have significant political influence over certain economic conditions of its special concern, but it has no real influence over political policy and process within the host country.	Foreign enterprise has no real influence over national policies—economic or political. Host government may enforce strict control over all foreign enterprise but often permits foreign enterprise to operate within same set of guidelines as domestic firms.

18. Encouragement of foreign enterprise

1	2	3	4	5	6

All foreign enterprise is strongly encouraged to invest and operate business of all kinds throughout the country.	Selected forms of foreign investment are encouraged. Use of foreign management personnel may be discouraged.	Foreign investment and operation of enterprise is discouraged by official and unofficial means.

19. Degree of nepotism in organizational life

1	2	3	4	5	6

Family members of owners, managers, clerical, and manual workers are given preferential and sometimes privileged opportunities for employment in all types of organizations.	Family members of owners, managers, and professionals are given priority within organizations owned or managed by their relatives.	Merit and training is the sole basis for selection of all persons in all types of organizations.

20. Degree of expected reciprocity in favors and rewards

1	2	3	4	5	6

Pattern of expected reciprocity in favors prevails in regard to economic or political support given to individual or group. Personal basis of contact is encouraged and reciprocity is expected by a returned favor (or gift) in near future.	Reciprocity is expected only in specific situations when both parties have a written and oral agreement to exchange political and social support for services rendered.	No pattern of expected reciprocity prevails in economic or political life. Favors or special gifts for service and business rendered is regarded as self-serving and "wrong."

Section J

Family and Marriage

Marital adjustment has been one of the most widely used concepts in family research. Contributors to the study of marital adjustment include L. L. Bernard, E. W. Burgess, Leonard S. Cottrell, Paul Wallin, Louis Terman, Harvey Locke, and K. M. Wallace. The earlier volumes of this Handbook presented the Burges and Cottrell Marriage Prediction and Marriage Adjustment Schedules. Since this earlier work, Locke and Wallace were able to develop a 15-item scale based on previous scales. Their scale could be completed in only a minute or two. Researchers found this to be a great advantage when used by either interview of questionnaire. Today, students have tried to improve both conceptual and methodological levels of measurement. Graham B. Spanier and Erik E. Filsinger have developed a Dyadic Adjustment Scale (DAS) to provide a standardized assessment of the relationship of couples both married and unmarried. Although developed out of a family sociological research orientation, the DAS can be used meaningfully within a wide range of therapeutic situations. It has been carefully crafted to achieve high reliability and validity.

6.J.1   THE DYADIC ADJUSTMENT SCALE

Variable measured: Marital adjustment is a process, the outcome of which is determined by the degree of: (a) troublesome marital differences; (b) interspousal tensions and personal anxiety; (c) marital satisfaction; (d) dyadic cohesion; and (e) consensus on matters of importance to marital functioning.

Description: The DAS is a 37-item primarily Likert-style questionnaire utilizing 5-, 6-, and 7-point response. The DAS was drawn from an initial pool format of 300 items, all of which were used in previous scales of marital adjustment. New items were added to tap areas of adjustment ignored in previous measures. Duplicate items were eliminated. Three judges examined the items for content validity against the definition of marital adjustment as given above. By consensus among the judges, numerous items were eliminated. A questionnaire was constructed with 225 items along with some demographic items.

The questionnaire was administered to a purposive sample of 218 married persons in Central Pennsylvania. Questionnaires were also sent to every person who obtained a divorce decree in Centre Country, Pennsylvania, during the 12 months previous to the mailing. Tests were made of the scoring means of the married couples and divorced couples. Items not significantly different at the .001 level were eliminated. Forty remaining variables were factor analyzed. A final 32 items remained. These make up the Dyadic Adjustment Scale that follows.

Factor analysis produced four interrelated dimensions: Dyadic Consensus (the degree to which the couple agrees on matters of importance to the relationship); Dyadic Cohesion (the degree to which the couple engages in activities together); Dyadic Satisfaction (the degree to which the couple is satisfied with the present state of the relationship and is committed to its continuance); and Affectional Expression (the degree to which the couple is satisfied with the expression of affection and sex in the relationship). The subscales are also indicated in the DAS as shown. More than 1,000 reported studies have used the DAS. Over 90% of these studies have involved married persons.

Where published: Graham Spanier and Erik E. Filsinger, Chapter 8, "The Dyadic Adjustment Scale," in Erik E. Filsinger, ed., *Marriage and Family Assessment: A Source Book for Family Therapy* (Beverly Hills, CA: Sage, 1983). The DAS is also available in paper-and-pencil and computer versions from Multi-Health Systems, Inc., 95 Thorncliffe Park Dr., Suite 100, Toronto, Ontario, Canada M4H 1L7.

Reliability: Coefficient alphas for internal consistency reliability have been reported by Spanier as Dyadic Adjustment, .96; Dyadic Consensus, .90; Dyadic Cohesion, .86; Dyadic Satisfaction, .94; and Affectional Expression, .73. Cronbach's alpha is reported to be .96 for the overall DAS.

Similar coefficient alpha were reported by Filsinger and Wilson for husbands and wives, respectively: Dyadic Adjustment, .94, .93; Dyadic Consensus, .91, .88; Dyadic Cohesion, .85, .80; Dyadic Satisfaction, .82, .84; and Affectional Expression, .73, .73.

Validity: Judges determined content validity based on the theoretical dimensions.

The scale discriminated between married and divorced samples. Mean scale scores reported by the author for married and divorced samples were 114.8 and 70.7, respectively.

The scale discriminated between distressed and nondistresed samples.

The DAS has the construct validity conforming to a theoretical structure. The correlation between the DAS and the Locke-Wallace Marital Adjustment Scale (1959) is reported by the author to be .86 among married couples and .88 among divorced respondents.

Utility: The DAS is a measure of the individual's adjustment to marriage but also has been used to study the adjustment of the couple to marriage. The scale can also be used to measure the adjustment of persons in nonmarried dyads. It can be used in diagnosing relationships as distressed or not, in identifying potential problems in the relationship, and in evaluating the effectiveness of treatment by comparing intake scores with posttreatment scores. It also can be used for long-term follow-up. The DAS has been translated into several languages for use with various nationalities and cultured groups.

Administration: The DAS can be given to the couple anytime; however, it probably would be useful to have them fill it out at intake or during an early session. The clients should complete the form separately and should not discuss their answers with each other before completing the scale. The form also should not be discussed with the therapist until he or she has the opportunity to examine and score it.

Scoring: The DAS is scored by assigning numbers to each response as indicated on the scale, which follows. The score for the individual is the sum of the numbers for each item. The total scale score is the most meaningful indicator for both researchers and therapists, but the responses to the subscales and to individual items can also be examined for clues as to the origins of problems.

Couple scores can be derived in a number of ways, for example, by adding the individual scores, taking the difference between them, and/or averaging them, but this practice is not empirically or theoretically justified in previous studies. At this point in time there are no aids to interpreting couple scores as normal or distressed.

Mean scale scores reported by the author for married and divorced couples were, respectively, 114.8 and 70.7.

Examples of Means for the Dyadic Adjustment Scales and Subscales from Selected Studies

Study	Sample	Dyadic Adjustment	Dyadic Consensus	Dyadic Cohesion	Dyadic Satisfaction	Affectional Expression
Burger and Jacobson, 1979	60 married and co-habiting	109.62 (110.12)[a]				
Cyr, 1979	200 Marriage Encounter participants, French Canada	114.68	51.38	15.15	39.43	8.91
Dailey, 1979	28 married	116.7	50.2	17.8	39.9	8.8
	24 cohabiting	115.5	48.4	18.5	39.8	8.8
	20 homosexual	109.5	46.5	17.3	37.4	8.3
Filsinger and Wilson, in press	190 married, church-based	117.04 (117.63)	49.22 (50.11)	16.32 (16.45)	40.83 (40.38)	10.66 (10.69)
Laurich, 1980	20 Marriage Encounter, pretest	95.55				
	14 married controls, pretest	115.71				
Maurer, Note 1	74 married, community	108.6 (107.7)	45.9 (47.5)	15.5 (15.5)	39.0 (35.8)	8.2 (8.7)
Romig, 1979	32 beginning seminary, married	121.41 (122.44)				
	27 returning seminary, married	116.19 (118.44)				
Spanier, 1976	218 married	114.18	51.9	13.4	40.5	9.0
	94 divorced	70.7	35.4	8.0	22.2	5.1

a. Scores in parentheses indicate wives' (females') scores. The scores that precede them are the husbands' (males') scores.

The Dyadic Adjustment Scale and Subscales

Items	Responses[a]						Subscale
	Always agree	Almost always agree	Occasionally disagree	Frequently disagree	Almost always disagree	Always disagree	
Handling family finances	5	4	3	2	1	0	Dyadic Consensus
Matters of recreation	5	4	3	2	1	0	Dyadic Consensus
Religious matters	5	4	3	2	1	0	Dyadic Consensus
Demonstrations of affection	5	4	3	2	1	0	Affectional Expression
Friends	5	4	3	2	1	0	Dyadic Consensus
Sex relations	5	4	3	2	1	0	Affectional Expression
Conventionality (correct or proper behavior)	5	4	3	2	1	0	Dyadic Consensus
Philosophy of life	5	4	3	2	1	0	Dyadic Consensus
Ways of dealing with parents or in-laws	5	4	3	2	1	0	Dyadic Consensus
Aims, goals, and things believed important	5	4	3	2	1	0	Dyadic Consensus
Amount of time spent together	5	4	3	2	1	0	Dyadic Consensus
Making major decisions	5	4	3	2	1	0	Dyadic Consensus
Household tasks	5	4	3	2	1	0	Dyadic Consensus
Leisure-time interests and activities	5	4	3	2	1	0	Dyadic Consensus
Career decisions	5	4	3	2	1	0	Dyadic Consensus

(Continued)

487

The Dyadic Adjustment Scale and Subscales (Continued)

Items	Responses [a]						Subscale
	All the time	Most of the time	More often than not	Occasionally	Rarely	Never	
How often do you discuss or have you considered divorce, separation, or terminating your relationship?	0	1	2	3	4	5	Dyadic Satisfaction
How often do you or your mate leave the house after a fight?	0	1	2	3	4	5	Dyadic Satisfaction
In general, how often do you think that things between you and your partner are going well?	5	4	3	2	1	0	Dyadic Satisfaction
Do you confide in your mate?	5	4	3	2	1	0	Dyadic Satisfaction
Do you ever regret that you married? (or lived together)	0	1	2	3	4	5	Dyadic Satisfaction
How often do you and your partner quarrel?	0	1	2	3	4	5	Dyadic Satisfaction
How often do you and your mate "get on each other's nerves"?	0	1	2	3	4	5	Dyadic Satisfaction
Do you kiss your mate?		Every day — 4	Almost every day — 3	Occasionally — 2	Rarely — 1	Never — 0	Dyadic Satisfaction
Do you and your mate engage in outside interests together?		All of them — 4	Most of them — 3	Some of them — 2	Rarely — 1	Never — 0	Dyadic Cohesion

Items	Responses [a]						Subscale

How often would you say the following events occur between you and your mate?

Items	Never	Less than once a month	Once or twice a month	Once or twice a week	Once a day	More often	Subscale
Have a stimulating exchange of ideas	0	1	2	3	4	5	Dyadic Cohesion
Laugh together	0	1	2	3	4	5	Dyadic Cohesion
Calmly discuss something	0	1	2	3	4	5	Dyadic Cohesion
Work together on a project	0	1	2	3	4	5	Dyadic Cohesion

These are some things about which couples sometimes agree and sometimes disagree. Indicate if either item below caused differences of opinions or were problems in your relationship during the past few weeks (check yes or no).

	Yes	No		Subscale
	0	1	Being too tired for sex	Affectional Expression
	0	1	Not showing love	Affectional Expression

The dots on the following line represent different degrees of happiness in your relationship. The middle point, "happy," represents the degree of happiness of most relationships. Please circle the dot which best describes the degree of happiness, all things considered, of your relationship.

0	1	2	3	4	5	6
Extremely *unhappy*	Fairly *unhappy*	A little *unhappy*	Happy	Very happy	Extremely happy	Perfect

Which of the following statements best describes how you feel about the future of your relationship?

		Subscale
5	I want desperately for my relationship to succeed, and would go to almost *any length* to see *that it does.*	
4	I want very much for my relationship to succeed, and *will do all I can* to see that it does.	
3	I want very much for my relationship to succeed, and *will do my fair share* to see that it does.	
2	It would be nice if my relationship succeeded, *but I can't do much more than I am doing* now to keep the relationship going.	
1	It would be nice if my relationship succeeded, but *I refuse to do anymore than I am doing* now to keep the relationship going.	
0	My relationship can never succeed, and *there is no more that I can do* to keep the relationship going.	Dyadic Satisfaction

NOTE: This table is reproduced in modified form from Spanier (1976). Readers who wish to use the scale for noncommercial, research, or education purposes may do so without permission from the author.
a. The numbers presented herein are for scoring and should not appear on the form the individual fills out. The individual places a checkmark to indicate the correct response.

rest

Research applications:

Filsinger, E. E. "Love, liking and individual marital adjustment: A pilot study of relationship changes within one year." *International Journal of Sociology of the Family, 13,* 1 (Spring 1983).

Filsinger, E. E. (Ed.). *Biosocial Perspectives on the Family.* Newbury Park, CA: Sage, 1988.

Filsinger, E. E., & Wilson, M. R. "Social anxiety and marital adjustment." *Family Relations, 32* (1983): 513-519.

Filsinger, E. E., & Wilson, M. R. "Religiosity, socioeconomic rewards, and family development: predictors of marital adjustment." *Journal of Marriage and the Family, 46* (August 1984): 663-670.

Hamilton, G. A. *Research in marriage,* New York: Boni, 1929.

Haynes, S. N., Follingstad, D. R., & Sullivan, J. C. "Assessment of marital satisfaction and interaction." *Journal of Consulting and Clinical Psychology, 47* (1979): 789-791.

Kazak, A. E., Jarnas, A., & Snitzer, L. "The assessment of marital satisfaction: An evaluation of the Dyadic Adjustment Scale." *Journal of Family Psychology, 2* (1988): 82-91.

Lewis, R. A., Filsinger, E. E., Conger, R. A., & McAvoy, P. "Love relationships among heroin-involved couples: Traditional self-report and behavioral assessment." In E. E. Filsinger & R. A. Lewis (Eds.), *Assessing marriage: New behavioral approaches.* Beverly Hills, CA: Sage, 1981.

Margolin, G. "Relationships among marital assessment procedures." *Journal of Consulting and Clinical Psychology, 46* (1978): 1556-1558.

Margolin, G. "Behavioral exchange in happy and unhappy marriages: A family life cycle perspective." *Behavior Therapy, 12* (1981): 329-343.

Spanier, G. B. "Measuring dyadic adjustment: New scales for assessing the quality of marriage and similar dyads." *Journal of Marriage and the Family, 38* (1976): 15-28.

Spanier, G. B. "The measurement of marital quality." *Journal of Sex and Marital Therapy, 5* (1979): 288-300.

Spanier, G. B., & Cole, C. L. "Toward clarification and investigation of marital adjustment." *International Journal of Sociology of the Family, 6* (1976): 121-146.

Spanier, G. B., & Thompson, L. A. "A confirmatory analysis of the Dyadic Adjustment Scale." *Journal of Marriage and the Family, 44* (1982): 731-738.

6.J.2 BURGESS MARRIAGE ADJUSTMENT SCHEDULE

This earlier schedule developed by Ernest W. Burgess and his associates has been used by family researchers over many years.[1] It is reproduced for researchers who wish to continue to build on this schedule.

The schedule was first tested on a total of 526 Illinois couples who had been married one to six years. Marriage adjustment was defined as (a) agreement between husband and wife upon matters that might be made critical issues; (b) common interests and joint activities; (c) frequent overt demonstrations of affection and mutual confidence; (d) few complaints; (e) few reports of feeling lonely, miserable, irritable, and so on. Items classified under these five headings show a measurable relationship to the ratings given by the couples to their expressed happiness rating of their marriage.

Where published: Ernest W. Burgess and Harvey J. Locke, *The Family,* 2nd ed. (New York: American Books, 1960), 693-716. (Contains the refined version of the schedules based upon approximately 25 years of research.)[2]

Reliability: Husband-wife adjustment scores correlated with $r = .88$ ($N = 526$ couples).

Validity: Happiness ratiangs and adjustment scores correlated .92 ($N = 526$ couples). A second sample of 63 cases showed correlation between happiness ratings and adjustment scores of .95.

Correlation between happiness ratings and absence of marital disorganization, divorce, separation, and contemplation of divorce or separation, $r = .89$.

Harvey Locke computed Burgess-Cottrell adjustment scores for divorced men, divorced women, happily married men, and happily married women. Correlations between scores attained in this way and scores from the 29 questions in his test were, respectively, .83, .87, .85, and .88.

Burgess and Wallin gave an adjustment test to 1,000 engaged couples, and then, three years after marriage, gave a marital adjustment test to as many of the couples as could be recontacted. Correlation between adjustment scores of engaged couples was .57; three years after marriage, marital adjustment scores of 505 husbands and wives correlation .41.[3]

Scoring the Marriage Adjustment Schedule

The narrow columns at the right side of each page of the Marriage Adjustment Schedule are provided for scoring the replies to the questions. The score values assigned are arbitrary in the sense that usually each gradation in reply differs by one point. Although arbitrary, the score values are in general conformity with the findings of the studies in this field, particularly those of E. W. Burgess and L. S. Cottrell, *Predicting Success or Failure in Marriage*; L. M. Terman et al., *Psychological Factors in Marital Happiness*; E. W. Burgess and Paul Wallin, *Engagement and Marriage*; and Harvey J. Locke, *Predicting Adjustment in Marriage: A Comparison of a Divorced and a Happily Married Group*.[4]

The two-digit numbers after each subdivision of the questions provide the codes for scoring the replies. The score value of each response is obtained simply by adding together the two digits in the number that is a subscript under the last letter of the final word of the response that has been checked. For example, if a response is checked at number 42, the score for that item is $4 + 2 = 6$. To obtain total score, follow these steps:

1. For each item, enter in Column 1 at the right-hand side of each page the two-digit number that appears as a subscript under the last letter of the final word of the answers to each question.
2. Enter in Column 2 the sum of the two digits appearing in Column 1 for each item. For each part of the questionnaire, compute the total of the values appearing in Column 2, and enter that figure in the space provided at the end of that section.
3. In scoring Part Two of the Marriage Adjustment Schedule, multiply the total number of check marks in each of the four columns as follows:

   Column A by 6   Column C by 4
   Column B by 5   Column D by 6

   Add together the four figures obtained in the four columns. This sum equals your total score for Part Two.
4. Enter the total score for each part in the spaces provided at the end of the questionnaire. Your total score on the inventory equals the sum of the total scores of the separate parts and is your marriage adjustment score.

In evaluating the total score secured on the Marriage Adjustment Schedule, refer to the following table:

Marital-adjustment scores	Adjustment in marriage
720 and over	Extremely well adjusted
700 to 719	Decidedly well adjusted
680 to 699	Fairly adjusted
660 to 679	Somewhat adjusted
640 to 659	Indifferently adjusted
620 to 639	Somewhat unadjusted
600 to 619	Unadjusted
580 to 599	Decidedly unadjusted
579 and under	Extremely unadjusted

Marriage Adjustment Schedule[5]

To Be Filled Out by Married Persons.

This schedule may be filled out by either the husband or the wife. Frank and sincere replies are of the highest importance if the findings are to be of value to the person filling it out or for research purposes. There are no right or wrong answers. The following points are to be kept in mind in filling out the schedule:

- Be sure to answer all questions.
- Do not leave any blanks, as is sometimes done, to signify a "no" reply.
- The word "spouse" is used to refer to your husband or wife.
- Do not confer with your spouse in answering these questions or show your answers to your spouse.

Your Present Marital Status:

1. Are you now (check): married ____? divorced ____? separated ____? widowed ____?

2. If divorced or separated, how long have you been separated? months _____ (If you are divorced or separated, answer the questions as of the time of your separation.)

Utility: Each form may be filled out in approximately 30 minutes. The measure may be used for both research and counseling purposes. Short marital adjustment and prediction tests are now available. It is claimed that "with the short tests, measurement or prediction can be accomplished with approximately the same accuracy in a few minutes as ordinarily would require an hour or more with the longer ones."

	1	2

Part One

1. Present occupation of husband (be as specific as possible) _____
_____ If unemployed, check here ____
How satisfied are you, on the whole, with present occupation of husband? If unemployed, answer this question about his usual occupation:
extremely satisfied (26)____; very much satisfied (34)____; satisfied
(14)____; somewhat satisfied (40)____; somewhat dissatisfied (3)____;
dissatisfied (21)____; very much dissatisfied (30)____; extremely
dissatisfied (12)____

2. To what extent were you in love with your spouse before marriage?
"head over heels" (17)____; very much (25)____; somewhat (32)
____; a little (22)____; not at all (13)____

3. To what extent was your spouse in love with you before your marriage?
"head over heels" (26)____; very much (43)____; somewhat (23)
____; a little (40)____; not at all (22)____

4. How much conflict (arguments, etc.) was there between you before
your marriage? none at all (35)____; a little (43)____; some (5)____;
considerable (31)____; very much (13)____

5. To what extent do you think you knew your spouse's faults and weak
points before your marriage? not at all (44)____; a little (52)____;
somewhat (32)____; considerably (40)____; very much (4)____

6. To what extent do you think your spouse knew your faults and weaknesses before your marriage? not at all (17)____; a little (43)____;
somewhat (41)____; considerably (22)____; very much (13)____

7. What is your attitude toward your father-in-law? like him very much
(61)____; considerably (15)____; somewhat (50)____; a little (4)____;
dislike him a little (30)____; dislike him somewhat (12)____; dislike
him considerably (3)____; dislike him very much (21)____; no attitude, as he is dead (24)____

8. What is your attitude toward your mother-in-law? like her very much
(25)____; like her considerably (42)____; like her somewhat (32)____;
like her a little (22)____; dislike her a little (12)____; dislike her somewhat (30)____; dislike her considerably (3)____; dislike her very much
(21)____; no attitude, as she is dead (51)____

9. What is your attitude to having children? desire children very much
(16)____; desire children a good deal (62)____; desire children somewhat (33)____; desire children a little (5)____; desire no children
(31)____

10. If children have been born to you, what effect have they had on your
happiness? added to it very much (27)____; added to it considerably
(61)____; added to it somewhat (14)____; added to it a little (40)
____; have had no effect (30)____; have decreased it a little (12)____;
have decreased it somewhat (21)____; have decreased it considerably
(3)____; have decreased it very much (30)____; no children (24)____

11. In leisure-time activities: we both prefer to stay at home (26)____;
we both prefer to be "on the go" (41)____; one prefers to be "on the
go" and the other to stay at home (22)____

12. Do you and your spouse engage in outside interests together? all of
them (44)____; most of them (51)____; some of them (14)____; a
few of them (40)____; none of them (22)____

13. Do you kiss your spouse? every day (62)____; almost every day (70)
____; quite frequently (24)____; occasionally (32)____; rarely (13)
____; almost never (40)____

	1	2

14. Do you confide in your spouse? about everything (17)____; about most things (52)____; about some things (5)____; about a few things (13) ____; about nothing (40)____

15. Does your spouse confide in you? about everything (26)____; about most things (52)____; about some things (41)____; about a few things (4)____; about nothing (31)____

16. Are you satisfied with the amount of demonstration of affection in your marriage? yes (25)____; no: (desire less (22)____; desire more (13) ____)

17. Is your spouse satisfied with the amount of demonstration of affection? yes (16)____; no: (desires less (40)____; desires more (31)____)

18. How frequently do you "humor" your spouse? frequently (4)____; occasionally (32)____; rarely (51)____; never (16)____

19. Has your spouse ever failed to tell you the truth? often (22)____; a few times (14)____; once (33)____; never (25)____

20. If until now your marriage has been at all unhappy, how confident are you that it will work out all right in the future? very confident (32) ____; confident (13)____; somewhat uncertain (21)____; very uncertain (30)____; marriage has not been at all unhappy (15)____

21. Everything considered, how happy has your marriage been for you? extraordinarily happy (45)____; decidedly happy (16)____; happy (50)____; somewhat happy (13)____; average (31)____; somewhat unhappy (3)____; unhappy (12)____; decidedly unhappy (30)____; extremely unhappy (21)____

22. If your marriage is now at all unhappy, how long has it been so (in months)? less than 3 (23)____; 3 to 11 (31)____; 12 or more (12)____; marriage has not been at all unhappy (33)____

23. Everything considered, how happy has your marriage been for your spouse? extraordinarily happy (36)____; decidedly happy (43)____; happy (32)____; somewhat happy (4)____; average (21)____; somewhat unhappy (30)____; unhappy (12)____; decidedly unhappy (3)____; extremely unhappy (21)____

24. Indicate your approximate agreement or disagreement with your spouse on the following things. Do this for each item by putting a check in the column that shows extent of your agreement or disagreement.

Check one column for each item below	Always agree (35)	Almost always agree (16)	Occasionally disagree (42)	Frequently disagree (23)	Almost always disagree (22)	Always disagree (12)		
Handling family finances								
Matters of recreation								
Religious matters								
Demonstration of affection								
Friends								
Table manners								

Check one column for each item below	Always agree (35)	Almost always agree (16)	Occasionally disagree (42)	Frequently disagree (23)	Almost always disagree 22)	Always disagree (12)		
Matters of conventionality								
Philosophy of life								
Ways of dealing with your families								
Wife's working								
Intimate relations								
Caring for the baby								
Sharing of household tasks								
Politics								

25. When disagreements arise between you and your spouse they usually result in: agreement by mutual give and take (44)____; your giving in (52)____; your spouse giving in (33)____; neither giving in (40)____

26. Have you ever considered either separating from or divorcing your spouse? have never consider it (26)____; not seriously (61)____; somewhat seriously (40)____; seriously (22)____

27. How many serious quarrels or arguments have you had with your spouse in the past twelve months? none (27)____; one (42)____; two (32) ____; three (13)____; four or more (30)____

28. Indicate to what extent you are in love with your spouse by placing a check in one square on the boxed line below, which ranges from extraordinarily in love to somewhat in love:

Extraordinarily in love	A	B	C	D	E	F	G	H	I	J	Somewhat in love
	36	17	25	43	15	33	23	41	40	13	

Indicate by a cross in the above scale the extent to which you think your spouse is in love with you.

29. How does your present love for your spouse compare with your love before marriage? very much stronger (27)____; considerably stronger (52)____; somewhat stronger (24)____; a little stronger (14)____; a little weaker (30)____; somewhat weaker (12)____; considerably weaker (3)____; very much weaker (21)____

30. If you had your life to live over, what do you think you would do? marry the same person: (certainly (35)____; possibly (41)____;) marry a different person (22)____; not marry at all (31)____

31. If your spouse could do it over again, do you think your spouse would marry you? (certainly (44)____; possibly (50)____); marry a different person (13)____; not marry at all (40)____

32. How satisfied, on the whole, are you with your marriage? entirely satisfied (18)____; very much satisfied (52)____; satisfied (23)____; somewhat satisfied (31)____; somewhat dissatisfied (3)____; dissatisfied (12)____; very much dissatisfied (30)____; entirely dissatisfied (21) ____

	1	2
T		

33. How satisfied, on the whole, is your spouse with your marriage? entirely satisfied (45)____; very much satisfied (34)____; satisfied (41)____; somewhat satisfied (22) ____; somewhat dissatisfied (21)____; dissatisfied (30)____; very much dissatisfied (12)____; entirely dissatisfied (3)____

34. Have you ever been ashamed of your spouse? never (44)____; once (14)____; a few times (31)____; often (40)____

35. Even if satisfied with your spouse, have you ever felt that you might have been at all happier if married to another type of person? never (26)____; rarely (41)____; occasionally (22)____; frequently (13)____

36. Do you ever regret your marriage? never (17)____; rarely (50)____; occasionally (13)____; frequently (40)____

Part Two

In responding to the following items, place a check in the appropriate column to the right of each item below.

Check Column A to indicate the things that have occurred in your marriage but have not interfered with your happiness.

Check Column B to indicate those things that have made your marriage less happy than it should have been.

Check Column C to indicate those things that have done most to make your marriage unhappy.

Check Column D if the item was not present in your marriage.

For the husband or wife to fill out	A 24	B 32	C 13	D 33
Insufficient income				
Poor management of income				
Lack of freedom due to marriage				
Spouse considerably older than I				
Spouse considerably younger than I				
Matters relating to in-laws				
My spouse and I differ in: Education				
Intellectual interests				
Religious beliefs				
Choice of friends				
Preferences for amusements and recreation				
Attitude toward drinking				
Tastes in food				
Respect for conventions				
My spouse: is argumentative				

For the husband or wife to fill out	A 24	B 32	C 13	D 33
My spouse: is not affectionate				
is narrow-minded				
is not faithful to me				
complains too much				
is lazy				
is quick-tempered				
criticizes me				
spoils the children				
is untruthful				
is conceited				
is easily influenced by others				
is jealous				
is selfish and inconsiderate				
is too talkative				
smokes				
drinks				
swears				

For the husband to fill out (cont.)	A 24	B 32	C 13	D 33
For the husband to fill out				
My wife:				
is slovenly in appearance				
has had much poor health				
is interested in other men				
is nervous or emotional				
neglects the children				
My wife:				
is a poor housekeeper				
is not interested in my business				
is extravagant				
lets her feelings be hurt too easily				
is too interested in social affairs				
has annoying habits and mannerisms				
is a poor cook				
interferes with my business				
For the wife to fill out				
My husband:				
pays attention to other women				
is nervous or impatient				
takes no interest in the children				
is untidy				
is always wrapped up in his business				
gambles				
is touchy				
is not interested in the home				
has vulgar habits				
dislikes to go out with me evenings				
is late to meals				
is harsh with the children				
has poor table manners				

For the husband to fill out (cont.)	A 24	B 32	C 13	D 33
For the husband to fill out				
My wife:				
wants to visit or entertain a lot				
does not have meals ready on time				
interferes if I discipline the children				
tries to improve me				
My wife:				
is a social climber				
is too interested in clothes				
is insincere				
gossips indiscreetly				
nags me				
interferes with my hobbies				
works outside the home				
is fussy about keeping the house neat				
For the wife to fill out				
My husband:				
is tight with money				
has no backbone				
does not talk things over freely				
is rude				
is bored if I tell him of the things that happen in my everyday life				
is unsuccessful in his business				
does not show his affection for me				
gets angry easily				
drinks too much				
has friends I do not approve of				
is constantly nagging and bickering				
lacks ambition				
T				

Part I _____, Part II _____, Total _____

Research applications:

Bowerman, Charles. "Adjustment in Marriage, Overall and in Specific Areas." *Sociology and Social Research* 41 (March-April 1957): 257-63.

Burgess, E. W., and Paul Wallin. "Predicting Adjustment in Marriage from Adjustment in Engagement." *American Journal of Sociology* 49 (1944): 324-30.

Hurvitz, Nathan. "The Measurement of Marital Strain." *American Journal of Sociology* 65 (May 1960): 610-15.

Karlsson, Georg. *Adaptability and Communication in Marriage: A Swedish Predictive Study of Marital Satisfaction.* Uppsala, Sweden: Almquist & Wiksell, 1951.

King, Charles. "The Burgess-Cottrell Method of Measuring Marital Adjustment Applied to a Non-White Southern Urban Population." *Marriage and Family Living* 14 (November 1952): 280-85.

Locke, Harvey J. *Predicting Adjustment in Marriage: A Comparison of a Divorced and a Happily Married Group.* New York: Henry Holt, 1951.

———and Georg Karlsson. *Marital Adjustment and Prediction in Sweden and the United States.* " *American Sociological Review* 17 (February 1952): 10-17.

Locke, Harvey J., and William J. Klausner. "Marital Adjustment of Divorced Persons in Subsequent Marriages." *Sociology and Social Research* 33 (1948): 97-101.

Locke, Harvey J., and Muriel Mackerprang. "Marital Adjustment and the Employed Wife." *American Journal of Sociology* 54 (1949): 536-38.

Locke, Harvey J., and Vernon A. Snowbarger. "Marital Adjustment and Predictors in Sweden." *American Journal of Sociology* 60 (July 1954): 51-53.

Locke, Harvey J., and Robert C. Williamson. "Marital Adjustment: A Factor Analysis Study." *American Sociological Review* 23 (October 1958): 562-69.

Luckey, Eleanore Braun. "Marital Satisfaction and Congruent Self-Spouse Concepts." *Social Forces* 39 (December 1960): 153-57.

Nimkoff, Meyer F., and C. M. Grigg. "Values and Marital Adjustment of Nurses." *Social Forces* 37 (October 1958): 67-70.

Schnepp, Gerald J. "Do Religious Factors Have Predictive Value?" *Marriage and Family Living* 14 (1952): 301-4.

Williamson, Robert C. "Socio-Economic Factors and Marital Adjustment in an Urban Setting." *American Sociological Review* 19 (April 1954): 213-16.

Winch, Robert F. "Personality Characteristics of Engaged and Married Couples." *American Journal of Sociology* 46 (1941): 686-97.

Notes

1. For the development of the Marriage Adjustment Schedule, see E. W. Burgess and Leonard S. Cottrell, *Predicting Success or Failure in Marriage* (Englewood Cliffs, NJ: Prentice-Hall, 1939). See also Nathan Hurvitz, "The Measurement of Marital Strain," *American Journal of Sociology* 65 (May 1960): 610-15.

2. For the development of the Marriage Prediction Schedule, see Ernest W. Burgess and Paul Wallin, *Engagement and Marriage* (Philadelphia: Lippincott, 1953).

3. See Lewis M. Terman and Paul Wallin, "The Validity of Marriage Prediction and Marital Adjustment Tests," *American Sociological Review* 14 (August 1949): 497-504; Harvey J. Locke and Robert C. Williamson, "Marriage Adjustment: A Factor Analysis Study," *American Sociological Review* 23 (October 1958): 562-69.

4. Harvey J. Locke and Karl M. Wallace, "Short Marital-Adjustment and Prediction Tests: Their Reliability and Validity," *Marriage and Family Living* 21 (August 1959): 251-55.

5. The following schedule is reproduced by permission of Ernest W. Burgess, Leonard S. Cottrell, Paul Wallin, and Harvey J. Locke.

THE PREPARE AND ENRICH INVENTORIES

Variables measured: Major problems related to personal, interpersonal, and external issues in relationships among premarital (PREPARE) and marital (ENRICH) couples.

Description: The instruments called PREPARE and ENRICH are self-report questionnaires. Both contain 115 Likert-style items and utilize 5-point response formats ranging from "strongly disagree" to "strongly agree." The main purpose of each instrument is to serve as a diagnostic tool in assessing relationship problems.

PREPARE was developed first and was designed for use with premarital couples. ENRICH is used to assess relationship difficulties among married couples. Categories evaluated by ENRICH are idealistic distortion, marital satisfaction, personality issues, communication, conflict resolution, financial management, leisure activities, sexual relationship, children and marriage, family and friends, equalitarian roles, and religious orientation. Of these 12 categories, 11 are also measured by PREPARE. The only category not shared by the two instruments is marital satisfaction. A set of questions assessing realistic expectations is substituted in its place for use with PREPARE. Although the two instruments evaluate similar relationship issues, many PREPARE items needed to be rewritten in order to be appropriate for use in the marital instrument. Approximately 40% of the items on the two instruments are identical. The remainder have changes ranging from minor rewording to complete revisions. Items within each subscale are summed, and individual subscales are evaluated separately.

Sample items:[1]

My partner and I understand each other completely.
I am not pleased with the personality characteristics and personal habits of my partner.
My partner is too critical or often has a negative outlook.

PREPARE and PREPARE-MC help engaged couples identify issues unique to their own relationships so that they may begin more realistic assessment of their upcoming marriages. ENRICH is intended to assist married couples in focusing on their marital strengths and to summarize topic areas that are most troublesome and may be faced in future counseling or enrichment programs.

Where published: The manual and materials for PREPARE-ENRICH are available from PREPARE-ENRICH, Inc., P.O. Box 190, Minneapolis, MN 55440. For a full description, see David G. Fournier, David H. Olson, and Joan M. Druckman, "Assessing Marital and Premarital Relationships," in *Marriage and Family Assessment*, ed. Erik E. Filsinger (Beverly Hills, CA: Sage, 1983).

Reliability: Cronbach's alpha for a nationwide sample of 5,718 individuals for PREPARE ranged from .49 to .88. For the 12 ENRICH scales, the authors report Cronbach's alpha, based on a study of 672 couples (1,344 individuals) as averaging .74 with a range of .48 to .92. Test-retest reliability over a four-week period, based on a study of 115 individuals, is reported to have ranged from .77 to .92 with a mean of .87.

Norms and reliability statistics are shown in Table 6.8.

TABLE 6.8 Statistical Summary of PREPARE-ENRICH Norms and Reliability

PREPARE-ENRICH Categories	Number of Items	Descriptive Statistics Raw Scores						Reliability Estimates			
		PREPARE (N = 5,718)			ENRICH (N = 1,344)			PREPARE		ENRICH	
		$\bar{X}$	SD	Range	$\bar{X}$	SD	Range	(N = 5,718) Alpha	(N = 36) Retest	(N = 1,344) Alpha	(N = 115) Retest
Idealistic Distortion	15 (PREPARE) 5 (ENRICH)	229.3	67.9	0-388	13.7	4.6	5-25	.88	.79	.92	.92
Realistic Expectations (PREPARE)	10	32.5	6.5	10-50	—	—	—	.75	.82	—	—
Marital Satisfaction (ENRICH)	10	—	—	—	37.2	6.7	10-50	—	—	.81	.86
Personality Issues	10	36.0	6.9	10-50	34.5	6.2	16-49	.74	.78	.73	.81
Communication	10	38.0	6.1	13-50	34.5	6.5	14-50	.70	.79	.68	.90
Conflict Resolution	10	37.6	6.0	14-50	33.9	6.1	11-50	.72	.76	.75	.90
Financial Management	10	35.6	5.7	11-50	37.4	6.6	12-50	.67	.81	.74	.88
Leisure Activities	10	38.7	5.2	14-50	34.4	4.1	21-47	.51	.79	.76	.77
Sexual Relationship	10	37.9	4.7	17-50	37.4	6.8	14-50	.50	.64	.48	.92
Children and Marriage	10	37.8	4.5	20-50	38.3	5.7	19-50	.49	.74	.77	.89
Family and Friends	10	38.2	6.2	13-50	38.0	5.8	15-50	.70	.73	.72	.82
Equalitarian Roles	10	36.1	6.8	12-50	28.5	5.6	13-48	.77	.83	.71	.90
Religious Orientation	10	35.7	6.9	10-50	39.5	6.4	13-50	.82	.93	.77	.89
Marital Cohesion (ENRICH)	5	—	—	—	—	—	—	—	—	.76	.75
Marital Adaptability (ENRICH)	5	—	—	—	—	—	—	—	—	.80	.72

Validity: The content of the inventories was specifically selected to represent a diverse range of topic areas most relevant to marital and premarital relationships. Items were specifically developed to identify interpersonal processes that become problematic for many couples. Practitioners rated the relevance of the inventory for engaged and married couples.

The methodological procedures included correlational analysis of the relationship between PREPARE-ENRICH scale scores and more than 100 previously established scales assessing individual and marital topics, and factor analysis on the entire scale, each category separately, and each category combined with an assessment of social desirability.

All 12 scales are significantly correlated with the Locke-Wallace Marital Adjustment Scale. In addition, significant relationships were established between PREPARE-ENRICH scales and existing measures of relationship conflict, esteem, communication, empathy, equalitarianism, assertiveness, temperament, cohesion, and independence, among others.

Factor analysis revealed 11 unique factors matching the 12 significant factors that mirror the titles of the scale categories. Personality Issues and Communication Issues merged to account for the one discrepancy. Intrascale factor analysis revealed that most categories contained only one significant factor.

The PREPARE-ENRICH inventories have been used successfully with thousands of couples. Norms are regularly updated to ensure a representative sample for marriage enrichment. Follow-up studies indicate that many couples are profoundly affected by the procedures and that counselors are highly satisfied with the overall usefulness and clarity of the materials.

Materials and procedures: The PREPARE-ENRICH inventories are part of a comprehensive package of materials and procedures designed to meet the needs of professionals engaged in marriage preparation, marriage enrichment, and marriage counseling. The inventories are flexible diagnostic and discussion tools and can be used in group settings with 50 or more couples as well as with a single couple in private sessions. In addition to the item booklets for PREPARE, PREPARE-MC, and ENRICH, numerous other printed and computer-generated documents have been developed to facilitate use of the inventories, including a recently revised *Counselor's Manual* (Olson et al., 1982).

The PREPARE-ENRICH inventories are made up of eight-page booklets that contain 125 items pertaining to marital issues. The items relate to the individual, the partner, and/or the relationship rather than to marriage in general. All items (excluding the final 10 on ENRICH) are answered on a 5-point Likert-type scale: 1, strongly agree; 2, moderately agree; 3, neither agree nor disagree; 4, moderately disagree; and 5, strongly disagree. The extended 5-point response format allows for variation and never forces couples to agree or disagree with strongly worded items. These choices are clearly displayed at the top of each page of the booklet and on the specially designed computer answer sheet.

PREPARE-ENRICH scoring includes a 15-20 page computer printout specially designed to highlight individual and couple scores, national norm scores, and clearly labeled listings of each person's responses to all inventory items. In addition, other sections have been designed to identify unique aspects of each couple's relationship and to help facilitate discussion. Table 6.9 summarizes the sections of the computer printout.

TABLE 6.9 Components of the PREPARE-ENRICH Computer Printout

Title	Description/Purpose	Length
Cover page	Identifies inventory used, couple ID, user ID, and date.	1 page
Background page	Summarizes 18 couple demographics.	1 page
Summary analysis	Summarizes all individual scores, couple scores, and item scores; individual scores (54 for ENRICH, 48 PREPARE), couple scores (80 for ENRICH, 68 for PREPARE).	1 page
Couple profile	Provides a visual chart of couple scores.	1 page
Expanded couple profile	Provides summary of key scores for each category plus a tentative relationship description to be explored with couple.	2 pages
Item summary: Issues for discussion	Provides comprehensive listing of items by content category and indicates how each partner responded to the item.	8-10 pages
Couple feedback sheets	Provides a condensed summary that can be given to couples.	1-2 pages

Table 6.10 shows individual score trends, item summary, and percentage of positive agreements by the couple. National couple averages are also shown.

Utility: The PREPARE-ENRICH inventories were designed for relationship diagnosis and contain procedures that are both methodologically sound and conceptually consistent with theoretical notions about marital systems. The combination of objective computer processing, relevant item content, and exhaustive couple response summaries provides a solid basis for descriptions of personal and couple issues. Couples find the procedures to be meaningful to their relationships and usually look forward to receiving and discussing the computer-processed results. Counselors enjoy the flexibility and comprehensiveness of the information and the range of diagnostic situations suitable for evaluation with the inventories. Hours of interview time can be condensed by using the inventories to identify the areas likely in need of attention.

Research applications:

Druckman, J. M., D. G. Fournier, B. Robinson, and D. H. Olson. "Effectiveness of Five Types of Pre-Marital Preparation Programs." Unpublished technical report. University of Minnesota, Minneapolis-St. Paul, Department of Family Social Science, 1979.

Fournier, D. G. "Validation of PREPARE: A Premarital Counseling Inventory." Ph.D. dissertation. *Dissertation Abstracts International* 40 (1979): 2385-86B.

———. *A Framework for the Evaluation of a Systemic Diagnostic Battery.* Paper prepared for the preconference Workshop on Family Therapy Assessment, annual meeting of the National Council on Family Relations, Washington, DC, 1982.

———, D. H. Olson, and J. M. Druckman. "Assessing Marital and Premarital Relationships: The PREPARE-ENRICH Inventories." In *Marriage and Family Assessment,* ed. E. E. Filsinger. Beverly Hills, CA: Sage, 1983.

Fournier, D. G., J. S. Springer, and D. H. Olson. "Conflict and Commitment in Seven Stages of Marital and Premarital Relationships." Unpublished technical report. University of Minnesota, Minneapolis-St. Paul, Department of Family Social Science, 1978.

Fowers, B. J., and D. H. Olson. "Predicting Marital Success with PREPARE: A Predictive Validity Study. *Journal of Marriage and Family Therapy* 12 (1986): 403-13.

TABLE 6.10 Summary Analysis Page from ENRICH Computer Printout

	ENRICH Summary Analysis									
	Individual Score Trends				Item Summary				Percent Positive Couple Agreement	
	Male Partner		Female Partner							
ENRICH Categories	Pct	Rev	Pct	Rev	Disagree	Neg Agree	Undecided	Pos Agree	Couple Positive Agreement	National Couple Averages
IDEALISTIC DISTORTION	** 29. **		** 12. **							
Marital Satisfaction	10.	10.	10.	10.	2	7	1	0	0.	34.
Personality Issues	8.	7.	15.	14.	3	6	1	0	0.	46.
Communication	48.	43.	18.	17.	4	3	0	3	30.	34.
Conflict Resolution	9.	8.	11.	10.	4	6	0	0	0.	30.
Financial Management	19.	17.	9.	8.	4	5	0	1	10.	44.
Leisure Activities	17.	16.	17.	16.	3	4	0	3	30.	35.
Sexual Relationship	8.	7.	14.	13.	2	5	1	2	20.	47.
Children and Marriage	10.	10.	8.	7.	2	6	1	1	10.	47.
Family and Friends	31.	29.	13.	12.	5	1	2	2	20.	47.
**Equalitarian Roles	66.	65.	92.	91.	4	0	1	5	50.	44.
**Religious Orientation	10.	10.	6.	5.	2	0	4	4	40.	56.
**Marital Cohesion	46.	43.	42.	41.	4	0	0	1	20.	54.
**Marital Adaptability	82.	80.	66.	65.	3	0	0	2	40.	47.
						Average Couple Positive Agreement			21.	43.
Norms Based on 1200 Couples										

Individual percent scores "PCT" range from 0 to 100 and average 50. Revised scores "REV" adjust PCT scores based on a person's tendency to describe their relationship in an overly idealistic manner. Item summary is based on 10 items per category and matches items listed in the issues for discussion section. The positive couple agreement score is percent positive agreement on 10 items. ** Categories are specially scored.

503

————. "ENRICH Marital Inventory: A Discriminant Validity and Cross-Validation Assessment." *Journal of Marriage and Family Therapy* 15 (1989): 65-89.

Kitson, G. C., and M. B. Sussman. "Marital Complaints, Demographic Characteristics and Symptoms of Mental Distress Among the Divorcing." Paper presented at the meeting of the Midwest Sociological Society, Minneapolis, April 1977.

Microys, G., and E. Bader. "Do Premarriage Programs Really Help?" Unpublished manuscript. University of Toronto, Department of Family and Community Medicine, 1977.

Olson, D. H., H. I. McCubbin, H. Barnes, A. Larsen, M. Muxem, and M. Wilson. *Family Inventories.* St. Paul: University of Minnesota, Department of Family Social Science, 1985.

Olson, D. H., and R. Norem. "Evaluation of Five Pre-Marital Programs. Unpublished manuscript. University of Minnesota, Department of Family Social Science, 1977.

Note

1. All items are taken from the ENRICH questionnaire.

Section K

Personality Measurements

Of the hundreds of existing personality inventories, only two are selected for presentation here. These two measures are probably the most widely used personality measures in research today. The Minnesota Multiphasic Personality Inventory (MMPI) is described but not reproduced. It is a battery of scales containing 550 statements. It is thorough and so well constructed that it has generally won the confidence of researchers as the best scale to use in probing the personality. The research applications included in the description of the instrument attest to its use.[1]

The California F-Scale to measure the authoritarian personality has also won high acceptance and has stimulated wide research application.[2]

Of all the personality measures available, social researchers will likely find these two scales to be the most useful for their purposes. For a compilation of other measures of personality, consult the following:

Anderson, Harold H., and Gladys L. Anderson. *An Introduction to Projective Techniques and Other Devices for Understanding the Dynamics of Human Behavior.* Englewood Cliffs, NJ: Prentice-Hall, 1951.
Cattell, R. B. *Personality and Motivation Structure and Measurement.* New York: World Book, 1957.
Greene, Edward B. *Measurements of Human Behavior.* Rev. ed. New York: Odyssey, 1952.
Krech, David, Richard S. Crutchfield, and Egerton L. Balachey. *Individual in Society.* New York: McGraw-Hill, 1962.
Megaree, E. I. *The California Psychological Inventory Handbook.* San Francisco: Jossey-Bass, 1972.

The Psychological Corporation produces a catalogue of personality and other psychological tests. This organization distributes such widely used tests as the Minnesota Multiphasic Personality Inventory; California Psychological Inventory; Edward's Personal Preference Schedule; Bernreuter Personality Inventory; Allport, Vernon, and Lindzey's Study of Values; Rorschach Technique; and Murray's Thematic Apperception Test. For a catalogue from the Test Division, write Psychological Corporation, 304 E. 45th St., New York, NY 10017.

Also consult Section 6.L.5 for encyclopedic sources of psychological tests.

For General Compilations of MMPI

Hedlund, D. E. "A Review of the MMPI in Industry." *Psychological Reports* 17 (1965): 875-89.
Kleinnuntz, B. "Annotated Bibliography of MMPI Research Among College Populations." *Journal of Counseling Psychology* 9 (1962): 373-96.

Swenson, W. M., J. S. Pearson, and D. Osborne. *An MMPI Source Book: Basic Items, Scale, and Pattern Data on 50,000 Medical Patients*. Minneapolis: University of Minnesota Press, 1973.

For Cross-Cultural MMPI Research

Butcher, James N., and Paolo Pancheri. *A Handbook of Cross-National MMPI Research*. Minneapolis: University of Minnesota Press, 1976.

Report of extensive international research using the MMPI. The authors discuss basic issues in cross-national research, the adaptation of objective personality instruments for such research, and the cross-national validation of the MMPI. For an extensive bibliography of MMPI research, see pp. 415-51.

Newer Developments

Butcher, J. N., ed. *MMPI: Research Developments and Clinical Applications*. New York: McGraw-Hill, 1969.

Carkhuff, R. R., L. Barnett, Jr., and J. N. McCall. *The Counselor's Handbook: Scale and Profile Interpretation of the MMPI*. Urbana, IL: Parkinson, 1965.

Carson, R. C. "Interpretative Manual to the MMPI." In *MMPI: Research Developments and Clinical Applications*, edited by J. N. Butcher. New York: McGraw-Hill, 1969.

Dahlstrom, W. G., G. S. Welsh, and L. E. Dahlstrom. *An MMPI Handbook*. Vol. 2, *Research Applications*. Minneapolis: University of Minnesota Press, 1975.

Duckworth, Jane. *MMPI: Interpretation Manual for Counselors and Clinicians*. 2nd ed. Muncie, IN: Accelerated Development, 1979.

Notes

1. Another excellent option is the California Psychological Inventory, by Harrison G. Gough, which is sold by Consulting Psychologists Press, Inc., 577 College Ave., Palo Alto, CA 94306. Convincing evidence exists to validate each of the 18 scales. The CPI has been carefully standardized. It stresses social functioning, in contrast to the more clinical tone of the MMPI. For a critique of CPI, see Dale G. Lake, Mathew B. Miles, and Ralph B. Earle, Jr., eds., *Measuring Human Behavior* (New York: Teachers College Press, 1973), 37-40.

2. Many researchers prefer the Dogmatism Scale by Milton Rokeach; see his *The Open and Closed Mind* (New York: Basic Books, 1960). Rokeach has sought to devise a measure of general authoritarianism (regardless of ideological content) and general intolerance of those with differing belief systems. The scale has good validity and moderate reliability. It can be recommended for nonclinical use. See Lake et al. *Measuring Human Behavior*, 63-68.

6.K.1   MINNESOTA MULTIPHASIC PERSONALITY INVENTORY

Variable measured: Measures 26 areas of personality traits and attitudes.

Description: The MMPI is primarily designed to provide, in a single test, scores on all the more clinically important phases of personality. The instrument itself comprises 550 statements covering a wide range of subject matter, from the physical condition of the individual being tested to his or her morale and social attitude. For administration of the inventory the subject is asked to respond to all statements, which are in the first person, with "true," "false," or "cannot say." The MMPI yields scores on nine scales of personality characteristics indicative of clinical syndromes.

Where published: Starke R. Hathaway, *The Minnesota Multiphasic Personality Inventory* (Minneapolis: University of Minnesota, 1942); Starke R. Hathaway and

J. Charley McKinley, *Manual for the Minnesota Multiphasic Personality Inventory*, rev. ed. (New York: Psychological Corporation, 1951); W. Grant Dahlstrom and George Schlager Welsh, *An MMPI Handbook: A Guide to Use in Clinical Practice and Research* (Minneapolis: University of Minnesota, 1960).

Reliability: r = .71 to .83.[1]

Validity: Hathaway and McKinley maintain that "the chief criterion of excellence has been the valid prediction of clinical cases against the neuropsychiatric staff diagnosis, rather than statistical measures of reliability and validity."[2]

See also the following works:

Altus, W. D., and T. T. Tafejian. "MMPI Correlates of the California E-F Scale." *Journal of Social Psychology* 38 (August 1953): 145-49.

Benton, A. L., and K. A. Probst. "A Comparison of Psychiatric Ratings with Minnesota Multiphasic Personality Inventory Scores." *Journal of Abnormal and Social Psychology* 41 (January 1946): 75-78.

Ellis, A. "The Validity of Personality Questionnaires." *Psychological Bulletin* 43 (September 1946): 385-440.

Lough, Orpha M., and Mary E. Green. "Comparison of the Minnesota Multiphasic Personality Inventory and the Washburne S-A Inventory as Measures of Personality of College Women." *Journal of Social Psychology* 32 (August 1950): 23-30.

Meehl, Paul E., and Starke R. Hathaway. "The K Factor as a Suppressor Variable in the Minnesota Multiphasic Personality Inventory." *Journal of Applied Psychology* 30 (1946): 525-64.

Utility: The inventory is easily administered. The time required varies from 30 to 90 minutes. No supervision is needed beyond that required for the subject to understand clearly the nature of his or her task and to assure optimal cooperation.

Research applications:

Altus, William D. "A College Achiever and Non-Achiever Scale for the Minnesota Multiphasic Personality Inventory." *Journal of Applied Psychology* 32 (August 1948): 385-97.

——— and T. T. Tafejian. "MMPI Correlates of the California E-F Scale." *Journal of Social Psychology* 38 (August 1953): 145-49.

Benton, Arthur L., and Kathryn A. Probst. "A Comparison of Psychiatric Ratings with Minnesota Multiphasic Personality Inventory Scores." *Journal of Abnormal and Social Psychology* 41 (January 1946): 75-78.

Brower, Daniel. "The Relation Between Intelligence and Minnesota Multiphasic Personality Inventory Scores." *Journal of Social Psychology* 25 (May 1947): 243-45.

———. "The Relations Between Minnesota Multiphasic Personality Inventory Scores and Cardio-Vascular Measures Before and After Experimentally Induced Visuo-Motor Conflict." *Journal of Social Psychology* 26 (August 1947): 55-60.

Burton, Arthur. "The Use of the Masculinity-Femininity Scale of the Minnesota Multiphasic Personality Inventory as an Aid in the Diagnosis of Sexual Inversion." *Journal of Psychology* 24 (July 1947): 161-64.

Carp, Abraham. "MMPI Performance and Insulin Shock Therapy." *Journal of Abnormal and Social Psychology* 45 (October 1950): 721-26.

Carpenter, Lewis G., Jr. "An Experimental Test of an Hypothesis for Predicting Outcome with Electroshock Therapy." *Journal of Psychology* 36 (July 1953): 131-35.

Clark, Jerry H. "Application of the *MMPI* in Differentiating A.W.O.L. Recidivists from Non-Recidivists." *Journal of Psychology* 26 (July 1948): 229-34.

———. "Grade Achievement of Female College Students in Relation to Non-Intellective Factors: MMPI Items." *Journal of Social Psychology* 37 (May 1953): 275-81.

Cofer, C. N., June Chance, and A. J. Judson. "A Study of Malingering on the Minnesota Multiphasic Personality Inventory." *Journal of Psychology* 27 (April 1949): 491-99.

Cook, Ellsworth B., and Robert J. Wherry. "A Factor Analysis of MMPI and Aptitude Test Data." *Journal of Applied Psychology* 34 (August 1950): 260-66.

Cottle, William C. "Card Versus Booklet Forms of the MMPI." *Journal of Applied Psychology* 34 (August 1950): 255-59.

Daniels, E. E., and W. A. Hunter. "MMPI Personality Patterns for Various Occupations." *Journal of Applied Psychology* 33 (December 1949): 559-65.

Drake, Lewis E. "A Social *I.E.* Scale for the Minnesota Multiphasic Personality Inventory." *Journal of Applied Psychology* 30 (1946): 51-54.

——— . "Differential Sex Responses to Items of the MMPI." *Journal of Applied Psychology* 37 (February 1953): 46.

Engelhardt, Olga E. de C., and William D. Orbison. "Comparison of the Terman-Miles M-F Test and the Mf Scale of the MMPI." *Journal of Applied Psychology* 34 (October 1950): 338-42.

Fry, Franklin D. "A Study of the Personality Traits of College Students and of State Prison Inmates as Measured by the Minnesota Multiphasic Personality Inventory." *Journal of Psychology* 28 (October 1949): 439-49.

——— . "A Normative Study of the Reactions Manifested by College Students and by State Prison Inmates in Response to the Minnesota Multiphasic Personality Inventory, the Rozenweig Picture-Frustration Study, and the Thematic Apperception Test." *Journal of Psychology* 34 (July 1952): 27-30.

Gough, Harrison. "Simulated Patterns on the Minnesota Multiphasic Personality Inventory." *Journal of Abnormal and Social Psychology* 42 (April 1947): 215-25.

——— . "A New Dimension of Status: I. The Development of a Personality Scale." *American Sociological Review* 13 (August 1948): 401-9.

——— . "A New Dimension of Status: II. Relationship of the St Scale to Other Variables." *American Sociological Review* 13 (October 1948): 534-37.

——— . "A New Dimension of Status: III. Discrepancies Between the St Scale and 'Objective' Status." *American Sociological Review* 14 (April 1949): 275-81.

Greenberg, Paul, and A. R. Gilliland. "The Relationship Between Basal Metabolism and Personality." *Journal of Social Psychology* 35 (February 1952): 3-7.

Guthrie, George M. "Six MMPI Diagnostic Profile Patterns." *Journal of Psychology* 30 (October 1950): 317-23.

Hampton, Peter J. "The Minnesota Multiphasic Personality Inventory as a Psychometric Tool for Diagnosing Personality Disorders Among College Students." *Journal of Social Psychology* 26 (August 1947): 99-108.

Harmon, Linksey R., and Daniel N. Wiener. "Use of the Minnesota Multiphasic Personality Inventory in Vocational Advisement." *Journal of Applied Psychology* 29 (April 1945): 132-41.

Hathaway, Starke R., and Elio D. Monachesi. "The Minnesota Multiphasic Personality Inventory in the Study of Juvenile Delinquents." *American Sociological Review* 17 (December 1952): 704-10.

——— . *Analyzing and Predicting Juvenile Delinquency with the MMPI.* Minneapolis: University of Minnesota Press, 1953.

Lough, Orpha M. "Teachers College Students and the Minnesota Multiphasic Personality Inventory." *Journal of Applied Psychology* 30 (June 1946): 241-47.

——— . "Women Students in Liberal Arts, Nursing, and Teacher Training Curricula and the Minnesota Multiphasic Personality Inventory." *Journal of Applied Psychology* 31 (August 1947): 437-45.

——— and Mary E. Green. "Comparison of the Minnesota Multiphasic Personality Inventory and the Washburne S-A Inventory as Measures of Personality of College Women." *Journal of Social Psychology* 32 (August 1950): 23-30.

MacLean, A. G., et al. "F Minus K Index on the MMPI." *Journal of Applied Psychology* 37 (August 1953): 315-16.

Maslow, A. H., et al. "A Clinically Derived Test for Measuring Psychological Security-Insecurity." *Journal of General Psychology* 33 (1945): 21-41.

Meehl, Paul E., and Starke R. Hathaway. "The *K* Factor as a Suppressor Variable in the Minnesota Multiphasic Personality Inventory." *Journal of Applied Psychology* 30 (1946): 525-64.

Michaels, John U., and Fred T. Tyler. "MMPI and Student Teaching." *Journal of Applied Psychology* 35 (April 1951): 122-24.

Monachesi, Elio D. "Some Personality Characteristics of Delinquents and Non-Delinquents." *Journal of Criminal Law and Criminology* 37 (January-February 1948): 487-500.

Norman, Ralph D., and Miriam Redlo. "MMPI Personality Patterns for Various College Major Groups." *Journal of Applied Psychology* 36 (December 1952): 404-9.

Schmidt, Hermann O. "Test Profiles as a Diagnostic Aid: The Minnesota Multiphasic Inventory." *Journal of Applied Psychology* 29 (April 1945): 115-31.

Schofield, William. "A Further Study of the Effects of Therapies on MMPI Responses." *Journal of Abnormal and Social Psychology* 48 (January 1953): 67-77.

————. "A Study of Medical Students with the MMPI: I. Scale Norms and Profile Patterns." *Journal of Psychology* 36 (July 1953): 59-65.

————. "A Study of Medical Students with the MMPI: II. Group and Individual Changes After Two Years." *Journal of Psychology* 36 (July 1953): 137-41.

————. "A Study of Medical Students with the MMPI: III. Personality and Academic Success." *Journal of Applied Psychology* 37 (February 1953): 47-52.

Sopchack, Andrew L. "Parental 'Identification' and 'Tendency Toward Disorders' as Measured by the Minnesota Multiphasic Personality Inventory." *Journal of Abnormal and Social Psychology* 47 (April 1952): 159-65.

Tydlaska, M., and R. Mengel. "Scale for Measuring Work Attitude for the MMPI." *Journal of Applied Psychology* 37 (December 1953): 474-77.

Tyler, Fred T., and John U. Michaels. "Comparison of Manual and College Norms for the MMPI." *Journal of Applied Psychology* 37 (August 1953): 273-75.

Verniaud, Willie Maude. "Occupational Differences in the Minnesota Multiphasic Personality Inventory." *Journal of Applied Psychology* 30 (December 1946): 604-13.

Weisgerber, Charles A. "The Predictive Value of the Minnesota Multiphasic Personality Inventory with Student Nurses." *Journal of Social Psychology* 33 (February 1951): 3-11.

Winfield, Don L. "The Relationship Between IQ Scores and Minnesota Multiphasic Personality Inventory Scores." *Journal of Social Psychology* 38 (November 1953): 299-300.

For a few more recent applications, see Section 6.L.1.

Contents of Minnesota Multiphasic Personality Inventory[3]

1. general health (9 items)
2. general neurologic (19 items)
3. cranial nerves (11 items)
4. motility and coordination (6 items)
5. sensibility (5 items)
6. vasomotor, trophic, speech, secretory (10 items)
7. cardio-respiratory system (5 items)
8. gastro-intestinal system (11 items)
9. genito-urinary system (5 items)
10. habits (19 items)
11. family and marital (26 items)
12. occupational (18 items)
13. educational (12 items)
14. sexual attitudes (16 items)
15. religious attitudes (19 items)
16. political attitudes—law and order (46 items)
17. social attitudes (72 items)
18. affect, depressive (32 items)
19. affect, manic (24 items)
20. obsessive and compulsive states (15 items)
21. delusions, hallucinations, illusions, ideas of reference (31 items)
22. phobias (29 items)
23. sadistic, masochistic trends (7 items)
24. morale (33 items)
25. items primarily related to masculinity-femininity (55 items)
26. items to indicate whether the individual is trying to place himself in an acceptable light (15 items)

Notes

1. See Starke R. Hathaway and J. Charnley McKinley, *Manual for the Minnesota Multiphasic Personality Inventory,* rev. ed. (New York: Psychological Corporation, 1951). See also Harrison G. Gough, "Simulated

Patterns on the Minnesota Multiphasic Personality Inventory," *Journal of Abnormal and Social Psychology* 42 (April 1947): 215-25; Charles A. Weisgerber, "The Predictive Value of the Minnesota Multiphasic Personality Inventory with Student Nurses," *Journal of Social Psychology* 33 (February 1951): 3-11.

    2. Hathaway and McKinley, *Manual for the Minnesota Multiphasic Personality Inventory.*

    3. Reproduced by permission of Starke R. Hathaway and J. Charnley McKinley and the University of Minnesota Press.

6.K.2   AUTHORITARIAN PERSONALITY (F) SCALE, FORMS 45 AND 40

Variable measured: "Authoritarianism" or antidemocratic potential.

Description: The scale consists of 30 items grouped into nine attitudinal categories considered as variables in a personality syndrome. The items are rated on a 7-point scale, from +3 to –3, according to the subjects' agreement or disagreement with the statement.

Where published: T. W. Adorno, Else Frenkel-Brunswik, D. J. Levinson, and R. N. Sanford, *The Authoritarian Personality* (New York: Harper, 1950).

Reliability: Authors' report on studies—mean r = .90, range .81 to .97.

Correlation with Ethnocentrism Scale—mean r = .75 with a range from r = .59 to r = .87.

Using Fisher's Z_r, each item was correlated with every other item—mean r = .13 and the range was from r = –.05 to r = .44. In addition, each item was correlated with the remainder of the scale, the mean r being .33, the range .15 to .52. See also the following:

Christie, Richard, Joan Havel, and Bernard Seidenberg. "Is the *F* Scale Irreversible?" *Journal of Abnormal and Social Psychology* 56 (1958): 143-59.

Christie, Richard, and Marie Jahoda, eds. *Studies in the Scope and Method of "The Authoritarian Personality."* Glencoe, IL: Free Press, 1954.

Validity: The authors used the case study method to validate the scale. The scale has been correlated with the Campbell xenophobia: r = .60. See also the following:

Bass, Bernard M. "Authoritarianism or Acquiescence?" *Journal of Abnormal and Social Psychology* 51 (November 1955): 616-23.

Camilleri, Santo F. "A Factor Analysis of the *F*-Scale." *Social Forces* 37 (May 1959): 316-23.

Christie, Richard, and Marie Jahoda, eds. *Studies in the Scope and Method of "The Authoritarian Personality."* Glencoe, IL: Free Press, 1954.

Himmelhoch, Jerome. "Tolerance and Personality Needs: A Study of the Liberalization of Ethnic Attitudes Among Minority Group College Students." *American Sociological Review* 15 (February 1950): 79-88.

Kirscht, J. P., and R. C. Dillehay. *Dimensions of Authoritarianism: A Review of Research and Theory.* Lexington: University of Kentucky Press, 1967.

Prothro, E. Terry, and Levon Melikian. "The California Public Opinion Scale in an Authoritarian Culture." *Public Opinion Quarterly* 17 (1953): 115-35.

Utility: The test may be administered either in interviews or by questionnaire.

Research applications:

Adelson, Joseph. "A Study of Minority Group Authoritarianism." *Journal of Abnormal and Social Psychology* 48 (October 1953): 477-85.

Bass, Bernard M. "Authoritarianism or Acquiescence?" *Journal of Abnormal and Social Psychology* 51 (November 1955): 616-23.

Brown, Roger W. "A Determinant of the Relationship Between Rigidity and Authoritarianism." *Journal of Abnormal and Social Psychology* 48 (October 1953): 469-76.

Camilleri, Santo F. "A Factor Analysis of the *F*-Scale." *Social Forces* 37 (May 1959): 316-23.

Campbell, Donald T., and Thelma H. McCormack. "Military Experience and Attitudes Toward Authority." *American Journal of Sociology* 62 (March 1957): 482-90.

Christie, Richard. "Changes in Authoritarianism as Related to Situational Factors." *American Psychologist* 8 (1952): 307-8.

—— and Peggy Cook. "Guide to Published Literature Relating to the Authoritarian Personality." *Journal of Psychology* 45 (1958): 171-99 (bibliography).

Christie, Richard, and Garcia, John. "Subcultural Variation in Authoritarian Personality." *Journal of Abnormal and Social Psychology* 46 (October 1951): 457-69.

Christie, Richard, Joan Havel, and Bernard Seidenberg. "Is the *F*-Scale Irreversible?" *Journal of Abnormal and Social Psychology* 56 (1958): 143-59.

Christie, Richard, and Marie Jahoda, eds. *Studies in the Scope and Method of "The Authoritarian Personality."* Glencoe, IL: Free Press, 1954.

Davids, Anthony. "Some Personality and Intellectual Correlates of Intolerance of Ambiguity." *Journal of Abnormal and Social Psychology* 51 (November 1955): 415-20.

Gelbmann, Frederick John. *Authoritarianism and Temperament.* Washington, DC: Catholic University of America Press, 1958.

Gough, Harrison G. "Studies of Social Intolerance: I. Some Psychological and Sociological Correlates of Anti-Semitism." *Journal of Social Psychology* 33 (May 1951): 237-46.

——. "Studies of Social Intolerance: II. A Personality Scale for Anti-Semitism." *Journal of Social Psychology* 33 (May 1951): 247-55.

——. "Studies of Social Intolerance: III. Relationship of the *Pr* Scale to Other Variables." *Journal of Social Psychology* 33 (May 1951): 257-62.

Greenberg, Herbert, and Dolores Hutto. "The Attitudes of West Texas College Students Toward School Integration." *Journal of Applied Psychology* 42 (October 1958): 301-4.

Haythorn, William, Arthur Couch, Donald Faefner, Peter Langham, and Launor F. Carter. "The Behavior of Authoritarian and Equalitarian Personalities in Groups." *Human Relations* 9 (February 1956): 57-73.

Himmelhoch, Jerome. "Tolerance and Personality Needs: A Study of the Liberalization of Ethnic Attitudes Among Minority Group College Students." *American Sociological Review* 15 (February 1950): 79-88.

Jones, Edward E. "Authoritarianism as a Determinant of First-Impression Formation." *Journal of Personality* 23 (September 1954): 107-27.

Kates, Solis L. "First-Impression Formation and Authoritarianism." *Human Relations* 12 (August 1959): 277-85.

—— and Lufty N. Diab. "Authoritarian Ideology and Attitudes in Parent-Child Relationships." *Journal of Abnormal and Social Psychology* 51 (July 1955): 13-16.

Kaufman, Walter C. "Status, Authoritarianism, and Anti-Semitism." *American Journal of Sociology* 62 (January 1957): 379-82.

MacKinnon, William J., and Richard Centers. "Authoritarianism and Urban Stratification." *American Journal of Sociology* 61 (May 1956): 610-20.

Martin, James G., and Frank R. Westie. "The Tolerant Personality." *American Sociological Review* 24 (August 1959): 521-28.

Meer, Samuel J. "Authoritarianism Attitudes and Dreams." *Journal of Abnormal and Social Psychology* 51 (July 1955): 74-78.

Mishler, Elliot G. "Personality Characteristics and the Resolution of Role Conflicts." *Public Opinion Quarterly* 17, no. 1 (1953): 115-35.

O'Neil, William M., and Daniel J. Levinson. "A Factorial Exploration of Authoritarianism and Some of Its Ideological Concomitants." *Journal of Personality* 22 (June 1954): 449-63.

Prothro, E. Terry, and Levon Melikian. "The California Public Opinion Scale in an Authoritarian Culture."
    Public Opinion Quarterly 17, no. 3 (1953): 353-62.
Roberts, Alan H., and Milton Rokeach. "Anomie, Authoritarianism, and Prejudice: A Replication." *American Journal of Sociology* 61 (January 1956): 355-58.
Sanford, Nevitt. "Recent Developments in Connection with the Investigation of the Authoritarian Personality." *Sociological Review* 2 (July 1954): 11-13.
Scodel, Alvin, and Paul Mussen. "Social Perceptions of Authoritarians and Nonauthoritarians." *Journal of Abnormal and Social Psychology* 48 (April 1953): 181-84.
Smith, Charles U., and James W. Prothro. "Ethnic Differences in Authoritarian Personality." *Social Forces* 35 (May 1957): 334-38.
Srole, Leo. "Social Integration and Certain Corollaries: An Exploratory Study." *American Sociological Review* 21 (December 1956): 709-16.
Thibaut, John W., and Henry W. Riecken. "Authoritarianism, Status, and the Communication of Aggression." *Human Relations* 8 (May 1955): 95-120.

For a few more recent applications, see Section 6.L.1.

F-Scale Clusters: Forms 45 and 40[1]

A. Conventionalism: Rigid adherence to conventional, middle-class values.
    1. Obedience and respect for authority are the most important virtues children should learn.
    12. A person who has bad manners, habits, and breeding can hardly expect to get along with decent people.
    37. If people would talk less and work more, everybody would be better off.
    41. The businessman and the manufacturer are much more important to society than the artist and the professor.
B. Authoritarian Submission: Submissive, uncritical attitude toward idealized moral authorities of the in-group.
    1. Obedience and respect for authority are the most important virtues children should learn.
    4. Science has its place, but there are many important things that can never possibly be understood by the human mind.
    8. Every person should have complete faith in some supernatural power whose decisions he obeys without question.
    21. Young people sometimes get rebellious ideas, but as they grow up they ought to get over them and settle down.
    23. What this country needs most, more than laws and political programs, is a few courageous, tireless, devoted leaders in whom the people can put their faith.
    42. No sane, normal, decent person could ever think of hurting a close friend or relative.
    44. Nobody ever learned anything really important except through suffering.
C. Authoritarian Aggression: Tendency to be on the lookout for, and to condemn, reject, and punish, people who violate conventional values.
    12. A person who has bad manners, habits, and breeding can hardly expect to get along with decent people.
    13. What youth needs most is strict discipline, rugged determination, and the will to work and fight for family and country.
    19. An insult to our honor should always be punished.
    25. Sex crimes, such as rape and attacks on children, deserve more than mere imprisonment; such criminals ought to be publicly whipped, or worse.
    27. There is hardly anything lower than a person who does not feel a great love, gratitude, and respect for his parents.
    34. Most of our social problems would be solved if we could somehow get rid of the immoral, crooked, and feebleminded people.
    37. If people would talk less and work more, everybody would be better off.
    39. Homosexuals are hardly better than criminals and ought to be severely punished.
D. Anti-intraception: Opposition to the subjective, the imaginative, and tender-minded.
    9. When a person has a problem or worry, it is best for him not to think about it, but to keep busy with more cheerful things.

31. Nowadays more and more people are prying into matters that should remain personal and private.
37. If people would talk less and work more, everybody would be better off.
41. The businessman and the manufacturer are much more important to society than the artist and the professor.

E. Superstition and Stereotypy: The belief in mystical determinants of the individual's fate; the disposition to think in rigid categories.
    4. Science has its place, but there are many important things that can never possibly be understood by the human mind.
    8. Every person should have complete faith in some supernatural power whose decisions he obeys without question.
    16. Some people are born with an urge to jump from high places.
    26. People can be divided into two distinct classes: the weak and the strong.
    29. Someday it will probably be shown that astrology can explain a lot of things.
    33. Wars and social troubles may someday be ended by an earthquake or flood that will destroy the whole world.

F. Power and "Toughness": Preoccupation with the dominance-submission, strong-weak, leader-follower dimension; identification with power figures; overemphasis upon the conventionalized attributes of the ego; exaggerated assertion of strength and toughness.
    2. No weakness or difficulty can hold us back if we have enough willpower.
    13. What youth needs most is strict discipline, rugged determination, and the will to work and fight for family and country.
    19. An insult to our honor should always be punished.
    22. It is best to use some prewar authorities in Germany to keep order and prevent chaos.
    23. What this country needs most, more than laws and political programs, is a few courageous, tireless, devoted leaders in whom the people can put their faith.
    26. People can be divided into two distinct classes: the weak and the strong.
    38. Most people don't realize how much our lives are controlled by plots hatched in secret places.

G. Destructiveness and Cynicism: Generalized hostility, vilification of the human.
    6. Human nature being what it is, there will always be war and conflict.
    43. Familiarity breeds contempt.

H. Projectivity: The disposition to believe that wild and dangerous things go on in the world; the projection outward of unconscious emotional impulses.
    18. Nowadays when so many different kinds of people move around and mix together so much, a person has to protect himself especially carefully against catching an infection or disease from them.
    31. Nowadays more and more people are prying into matters that should remain personal and private.
    33. Wars and social troubles may someday be ended by an earthquake or flood that will destroy the whole world.
    35. The wild sex life of the old Greeks and Romans was tame compared to some of the goings-on in this country, even in places where people might least expect it.
    38. Most people don't realize how much our lives are controlled by plots hatched in secret places.

I. Sex: Exaggerated concern with sexual "goings-on."
    25. Sex crimes, such as rape and attacks on children, deserve more than mere imprisonment; such criminals ought to be publicly whipped, or worse.
    35. The wild sex life of the old Greeks and Romans was tame compared to some of the goings-on in this country, even in places where people might least expect it.
    39. Homosexuals are hardly better than criminals and ought to be severely punished.

Note

1. From T. W. Adorno, Else Frenkel-Brunswik, D. J. Levinson, and R. N. Sanford, "F-Scale Clusters: Forms 45 and 40." In *The Authoritarian Personality* (New York: Harper, 1950). Reprinted by permission.

Section L

Inventories of Sociometric and Attitude Scales and Evaluation of Research Continuity

Researchers who have not found scales in this volume to fit their particular problems should carry out the following search. First, review the inventory that follows of the *American Sociological Review* for the years 1981-87. Check on scales and related research in sections most relevant. Scales appearing in Section 6.L.1 include those for measuring the following:

1. social status
2. group structures and group dynamics
3. social indicators
4. community factors
5. social participation and alienation
6. attitudes and values
7. family and marriage factors
8. personality and leadership factors
9. intelligence and achievement
10. identification

Some miscellaneous scales are also listed, following those in these categories. There is some overlap in categories, and this should be taken into account.

Following the inventory, Section 6.L.2 presents a listing of the most used scales in major sociological journals over the years 1965-87.[1] Researchers should evaluate these carefully, because instrument development and standardization are relatively rare; simple indices are being constructed de novo for particular problems, while scales with far more validity and stability languish unused. The disappointing fact is that few researchers are willing to search for and to examine measuring instruments that are essential to scientific cumulation of knowledge. It is apparent that editors everywhere are failing to establish these requirements for acceptance of research. This does not relieve researchers of the responsibility to use standardized instruments with demonstrated reliability and validity if they wish their work to establish a place in cumulative knowledge. A wealth of information on scales is now available, if only researchers will take the effort to *search*. Researchers who do not find suitable scales in the *American Sociological Review* inventory should continue to examine the various compilations presented here. They report on a great number of scales and, in most instances, offer evaluations to aid in selection.

Note

1. The fourth edition of the *Handbook of Research Design and Social Measurement* (Longman, 1982) has an inventory of all scales used in the *American Sociological Review*, 1965-80 (see pp. 495-540 of that volume).

AN INVENTORY OF MEASURES UTILIZED IN THE *AMERICAN SOCIOLOGICAL REVIEW*, 1981-87[2]

6.L.1

Scales for Measuring Social Status

Duncan's Index of Socioeconomic Status

Authors used two social resource measures based on Duncan's SEI for contact's status for first and current jobs; respondent-contact tie indexed as weak/strong; contact's tie to hiring company; job seeker's education.

Nan Lin, Walter M. Ensel, and John C. Vaughn, "Social Resources and Strength of Ties: Structural Status Attainment," 46 (August 1981): 393-405.

Duncan's SEI scores used to determine respondents' socioeconomic origins and destinations. Three fertility measures were constructed. (Author constructed.)

Gillian Stevens, "Social Mobility and Fertility: Two Effects in One," 46 (October 1981): 573-84.

A measure of occupational mobility was constructed from a 17-category occupational status order classification (Blau and Duncan, 1967; Hauser and Featherman, 1977; Featherman and Hauser, 1978; Breiger, 1981). Mobility measures were constructed from Goodman's (1981) methods based on Hauser's (1978, 1979) measures of occupational mobility. These measures were then subjected to Guttman-Lingoes smallest space analysis (1972).

C. Matthew Snipp, "Occupational Mobility and Social Class: Insights from Men's Career Mobility," 50 (August 1985): 475-93.

Measures were constructed for job involvement, income, occupational status (revised Duncan SEI; Featherman and Stevens, 1977), and work autonomy. Derived from quality of employment surveys (1972-73 and 1977). (Author adapted.)

Jon Lorence and Jeylan T. Mortimer, "Job Involvement Through the Life Course: A Panel Study of Three Age Groups," 50 (October 1985): 618-38.

Four status measures were constructed. Two pertain to education: average school years completed and proportion who finished at least one year of college. Earnings measured as per capita household income. Socioeconomic occupational score (Duncan, 1961; Blau and Duncan, 1967; Featherman and Hauser, 1978). Derived from November 1979 *Current Population Survey*.

Lisa J. Neidert and Reynolds Farley, "Assimilation in the United States: An Analysis of Ethnic and Generation Difference in Status and Achievement," 50 (December 1985): 840-50.

A measure of minority group occupational distribution was constructed as a five-category scheme (upper and lower manual and nonmanual; farm). A measure of occupational differences was constructed as the dissimilarity of majority and minority distributions within occupational groups. SES scores were constructed (Irish Mobility Study and Hout, 1984). (All measures author constructed except SES measures.)

Michael Hout, "Opportunity and the Minority Middle Class: A Comparison of Blacks in the United States and Catholics in Northern Ireland," 51 (April 1986): 214-23.

Featherman and Hauser's (1975, 1978) measures of son's schooling were used.

Robert D. Mare and Meicher D. Chen, "Further Evidence on Sibship Size and Educational Stratification," 51 (June 1986): 403-12.

A measure of homophily was constructed from respondents' replies to sociometric questions. All persons were then compared in terms of occupational prestige (Duncan's SEI), years of education and age, and sex.

J. Miller McPherson and Lynn Smith-Lovin, "Homophily in Voluntary Organizations: Status Distance and the Composition of Face-to-Face Groups," 52 (June 1987): 370-79.

Featherman and Hauser's (1978) occupational mobility scale (revision of Duncan SEI scores).

Kazuo Yamaguchi, "Models for Comparing Mobility Tables: Toward Parsimony and Substance," 52 (August 1987): 482-94.

Occupational Prestige

NORC Occupational Prestige Scale

Respondents rated social standings of persons on occupational cards broken down by sex (M/F) or no sexual indication. Ratings of 1 to 9 were converted into standard NORC prestige metric ranges.

Christine E. Bose and Peter H. Rossi, "Gender and Jobs: Prestige Standings of Occupations as Affected by Gender," 48 (June 1982): 316-30.

Treiman Prestige Scale

Occupational prestige measured on the 7-category International Standard Classification of Occupations (ISCO). A summary measure of occupational attainment obtained with an occupational wage rate scale based on Treiman's (1977) 14-category classification of occupational earnings.

Patricia A. Roos, "Marriage and Women's Occupational Attainment in Cross-Cultural Perspective," 48 (December 1982): 852-64.

Two measures of schizophrenia were constructed from the Psychiatric Epidemiology Research Interview (Dohrenwend et al., 1980) and NIMH's Diagnostic Interview Schedule (Robins et al., 1981). An expanded Cain and Treiman (1981) "undesirable working conditions" scale was constructed. Treiman's occupational prestige scores were used as a measure of occupational mobility.

Bruce G. Link, Bruce P. Dohrenwend, and Andrew E. Skodol, "Socio-Economic Status and Schizophrenia: Noisome Occupational Characteristics as a Risk Factor," 51 (April 1986): 242-58.

Hollingshead Occupational Scale

Measures of social stratification were developed from formal education, job income, and occupational status. The American sample uses Hollingshead Occupational Scale. (Most indices author constructed.)

Kazimierz M. Slomczynski, Joanne Miller, and Melvin L. Kohn, "Stratification, Work, and Values: A Polish-United States Comparison," 46 (December 1981): 720-44.

Diverse Uses of Occupational Classifications

Blau-Duncan occupational status attainment model used. (Author adapted.)

Hugh A. McRoberts and Kevin Selber, "Trends in Occupational Mobility in Canada and the United States: A Comparison," 46 (August 1981): 406-21.

Preexisting occupational ranking used as a measure of occupational prestige and change. Existing historical scale used.

Michael C. Burrage and David Cory, "At Sixes and Sevens: Occupational Status in the City of London from the 14th to the 17th Century," 46 (August 1981): 375-93.

Keith Hope, "Vertical and Nonvertical Class Mobility in Three Countries," 47 (February 1982): 99-113.

Measures were constructed for the probability of (a) moving out of the competitive economic sector (Hodson's 1978 economic sector categorization), (b) moving out of a sex-typical occupation (based on census data), and (c) moving up in wages (shift in wages up or not). (Items b and c author adapted.)

Rachel A. Rosenfeld, "Sex Segregation and Sectors: An Analysis of Gender Differences in Returns from Employer Changes," 48 (October 1982): 637-55.

Lieberson's (1975) Index of Net Difference used as a measure of rank inequality between two groups. Also, an odds ratio was computed for white-collar/blue-collar occupation distribution of blacks and whites. (Author constructed.)

Mark Fossett and Gray Swicegood, "Rediscovering City Differences in Racial Occupational Inequality," 47 (October 1982): 681-89.

Marxian Class Scale Measures were constructed for (a) bourgeoisie and small employers, (b) managers and supervisors, (c) semiautonomous employees, (d) petty bourgeoisie, and (e) working class. (Author constructed.)

Erik Olin Wright, David Hachen, Cynthia Costello, and Joey Sprague, "The American Class Structure," 49 (December 1982): 709-26.

Career mobility was measured by moves made from a job held in one economic sector to a job held in a different economic sector. (Author constructed.)

Jerry Jacobs, "Industrial Sector and Career Mobility Reconsidered," 48 (June 1983): 415-21.

A measure of employment status was constructed from March *Current Population Surveys* (1964-81) as a binary item: employed/not employed. (Author adapted.)

Robert D. Mare and Christopher Winship, "The Paradox of Lessening Racial Inequality and Joblessness Among Black Youth: Enrollment, Enlistment, and Employment, 1964-1981," 49 (February 1984): 39-55.

Mobility and immobility were measured by constructing 3 × 3 classifications of son's by father's occupation for 16 countries. (Author constructed.)

David B. Grusky and Robert M. Hawser, "Comparative Social Mobility Revisited: Models of Convergence and Divergence in 16 Countries," 49 (February 1984): 19-38.

Son's class was measured by Wright and Perrone (1977) four-class model, using three classes: capitalist; petty bourgeoisie; and manager, supervisor, and foreman. Worker category was omitted.

Robert V. Robinson, "Reproducing Class Relations in Industrial Capitalism," 49 (April 1984): 182-96.

Measures of inter- and intragenerational occupational mobility were constructed by using census procedures to code occupational categories (five) for respondent's father and for respondent's present and 1962 occupations. Also included in Census Bureau's "class of worker" measure as an indicator of the economic sector respondents were employed in.

Michael Hout, "Occupational Mobility of Black Men: 1962 to 1973," 49 (June 1984): 308-22.

Albert Simkus, "Structural Transformation and Social Mobility: Hungary 1938-1973," 49 (June 1984): 291-307.

A classification of 24 occupational groups was constructed to measure career mobility shifts within and between economic-sectoral groupings. Measures were constructed for total amount of career mobility, structural and circulation mobility, and upward and downward mobility. (Author constructed.)

Max Haller, Wolfgang Konig, Peter Krause, and Karin Kurz, "Patterns of Career Mobility and Structural Positions in Advanced Capitalist Societies: A Comparison of Men in Austria, France, and the United States," 50 (October 1985): 579-603.

A measure of social mobility was constructed as the change in a five-item occupational category. Fertility was measured as number of children ever born. Derived from Blau and Duncan (1967) 1962 "Occupational Changes in a Generation" survey.

Michael Sobel, "Social Mobility and Fertility Revisited: Some New Models for the Analysis of the Mobility Effects Hypothesis," 50 (October 1985): 699-712.

A measure of occupational mobility was constructed: individual's movement from lower-level (clerical/technical) to upper-level (administration/professional). (Author constructed.)

Thomas A. DiPrete and Whitman T. Soule, "The Organization of Career Lines: Equal Employment and Status Advancement in a Federal Bureaucracy," 51 (June 1986): 295-309.

A measure of ethnic occupational mobility was constructed using 10 occupational categories ordered by status. (From Israel Central Bureau of Statistics in 1969 and 1982). (Author adapted.)

Noah Lewin-Epstein and Moshe Semyonov, "Ethnic Group Mobility in the Israeli Labor Market," 51 (June 1986): 342-51.

A measure of circulation mobility was constructed as exchanges among occupational categories. Patterns of observed and circulation mobility were operationalized as matrices of quantities that allow one to retrieve mobility frequencies up to a scaling factor. (Author constructed.)

Kazimierz M. Slomczynski and Tandensz K. Krauze, "Cross-National Similarity in Social Mobility Patterns: A Direct Test of the Featherman-Jones-Hauser Hypothesis," 52 (October 1987): 598-611.

Miscellaneous Measures of Prestige

Two indicators of current social position were used: respondent's educational attainment (years of schooling) and occupational prestige, coded in the Japanese Occupational Prestige Scale.

David B. Grusky, "Industrialization and the Status Attainment Process: The Thesis of Industrialism Reconsidered," 48 (August 1982): 494-506.

A measure of scholarly recognition was constructed from the number of authors' citations appearing in *Journal Citations Reports, Science Citation Index,* and *Social Science Citation Index.*

Lowell L. Hargens and Diane H. Felmlee, "Structural Determinants of Stratification in Science," 49 (October 1984): 685-97.

Eminence of black Americans was measured as appearance in *Who's Who Among Black Americans.* (Author constructed.)

Elizabeth I. Mullins and Paul Sites, "The Origins of Contemporary Eminent Black Americans: A Three-Generation Analysis of Social Origin," 49 (October 1984): 672-85.

A measure of formal status recognition was constructed from the receipt of state and social honors as interval-level variables (0-9 and 0-6, respectively). (Author constructed.)

Patricia A. Taylor, "The Celebration of Heroes Under Communism: On Honors and the Reproduction of Inequality," 52 (April 1987): 143-54.

Roose and Andersen's (1970) Rating of Graduate Programs scale was employed to measure prestige attainments.

Paul D. Allison and J. Scott Long, "Interuniversity Mobility of Academic Scientists," 52 (October 1987): 643-52.

Use of Income as Measure of Status

Measures were constructed for income and work status (two-item measure). (Author adapted.)

Bruce Link, "Mental Patient Status, Work, and Income: An Examination of the Effects of a Psychiatric Label," 47 (April 1982): 202-15.

A measure of the earnings determination process as an outcome of economic segmentation was constructed by using the natural logarithm transformation of earnings. Other central labor force outcome measures constructed: gender, years of education completed, months of tenure with current employer, class position based on authority in workplace (Wright's workplace control scale, 1978), occupational prestige (Siegal scale, 1971), union membership, hours worked last week, and weeks worked last year.

Randy Hodson, "Companies, Industries, and the Measurement of Economic Segmentation," 49 (June 1984): 335-48.

Measures of income, occupation, and industrial sector were constructed for two years, 1962 and 1972/73, and compared. Derived from Survey of Occupational Changes in a Generation, 1973.

Marshall I. Pomer, "Labor Market Structure, Intragenerational Mobility, and Discrimination: Black Male Advancement Out of Low-Paying Occupations, 1962-1973," 51 (October 1986): 650-59.

A measure of annual earnings was constructed from wage and salary income reports in Public Use Microdata Sample Files, 1970-80.

Marta Tienda, Shelley A. Smith, and Vilma Ortiz, "Industrial Restructuring, Gender Segregation, and Sex Differences in Earnings," 52 (April 1987): 195-210.

The primary outcome measure of status influence in task groups was constructed from the difference between the subject's initial and final award levels on a $0-$25,000 scale. Measures of target's apparent task capacity, dominance, and group- versus self-motivation were constructed from responses to a series of 7-point Likert and semantic differential items. Subjects also rated target's degree of leadership ability and apparent high and low status. (Nemeth and Wachtler, 1974; Lee and Ofshe, 1981, measures.)

Cecilia L. Ridgeway, "Nonverbal Behavior, Dominance, and the Basis of Status in Task Groups," 52 (October 1987): 683-94.

Individual Efforts to Measure Status

Extant nineteenth-century marriage records were used as an index of interclass mobility patterns.

Ronald Aminzade and Randy Hodson, "Social Mobility in a Mid-Nineteenth Century French City," 47 (August 1982): 441-57.

An "outflow" coefficient or transition probability of occupational mobility was computed. (Author constructed.)

Charles M. Tolbert, "Industrial Segmentation and Men's Career Mobility," 47 (August 1982): 457-77.

Criminal involvement was measured using 6 measures for juveniles and adults (12 measures overall). Based on self- and official reports. (Author adapted.)

Terence P. Thornberry and Margaret Farnworth, "Social Correlates of Criminal Involvement: Further Evidence on the Relationship Between Social Status and Criminal Behavior," 47 (August 1982): 505-18.

Scales for Measuring Group Structures and Group Dynamics

Index of Ethnic Diversity (Taylor and Hudson, 1971): "This index gives the probability that two individuals from a country sampled at random belong to the same ethnolinguistic group."

Michael T. Hannan and Glenn R. Carroll, "Dynamics of Formal Political Structure: An Event-History Analysis," 46 (February 1981): 19-35.

Type of Control Scale: A type of management control scale was constructed based on factors of nine previous studies.

David R. James and Michael Soret, "Profit Constraints on Managerial Autonomy: Managerial Theory and the Unmaking of the Corporation President," 46 (February 1981): 1-18.

(a) Influence was measured by the number of trials in which confederate's choice was adopted as group choice; a four-item postexperimental questionnaire provided subjective ratings of other's influence in group decision. (b) Attention was measured by subject's impressions of others in group. (c) Motivation was measured by subject's rating of others' motivations on a three-item measure. (Author constructed.)

Cecilia L. Ridgeway, "Nonconformity, Competence, and Influence in Groups: A Test of Two Theories," 46 (June 1981): 333-47.

Network analysis technique.

Joseph Galaskiewicz and Stanley Wasser, "A Dynamic Study of Change in a Regional Corporate Network," 46 (August 1981): 475-84.

Nielson and Hannan (1977) structure of educational organization forms—primary, secondary, and tertiary—was used as a measure of organizational expansion.

Glenn R. Carroll, "Dynamics of Organizational Expansion in National Systems of Education," 46 (October 1981): 585-99.

Subjects ranked group members for influence, competence, likability, and group leadership to measure influence and status in task-oriented groups. (Author constructed.)

Cecilia Ridgeway, "Status in Groups: The Importance of Motivation," 47 (February 1982): 76-88.

Scales for assessing responsibility, sanctions, and manipulation checks on experimentally manipulated variables were constructed to measure respondents' judgments of wrongdoing on one of four core fictional vignettes (16 variants). Replication of earlier study.

V. Lee Hamilton and Joseph Sanders, "Universals in Judging Wrongdoing: Japanese and Americans Compared," 48 (April 1982): 199-211.

Measures for status integration, labor force integration, marital integration, and parental integration. Suicide rates were from U.S. Public Health Service and Bureau of the Census. (Author constructed, except for suicide rates.)

Jack P. Gibbs, "Testing the Theory of Status Integration and Suicide Rates," 47 (April 1982): 227-37.

Measures were constructed for agreement on (a) agenda within a class of documents, (b) agenda between two classes of documents, (c) a program for an institution within a class of documents, (d) a program for an institution between two classes of documents, and (e) a program for a class of institutions. (Author constructed.)

John Markoff, "Suggestions for the Measurement of Consensus," 47 (April 1982): 290-98.

Measures used consisted of two continuation ratios that were dichotomous contrasts between early and late retirement. Based on timing of retirement and age of permanent withdrawal from labor market. Yielded four mutually exclusive groups. (Author constructed.)

Angela M. O'Rand and John Henretta, "Delayed Career Entry, Industrial Pension Structure, and Early Retirement in a Cohort of Unmarried Women," 47 (June 1982): 365-73.

Two measures of intergroup interaction were constructed: Frequency of Contact with Coworkers (three items) and Encouragement for Promotion from Coworkers. (Author constructed.)

Scott J. South, Charles M. Bonjean, William T. Markham, and Judy Corder, "Social Structure and Intergroup Interaction: Men and Women of the Federal Bureaucracy," 47 (October 1982): 587-99.

Four measures of the effects of early desegregation conflict were constructed: academic self-esteem, racial attitudes, liking school, and racial tension (multiple items). (Author constructed.)

Robert L. Crain and Rita E. Mahard, "The Consequences of Controversy Accompanying Institutional Change: The Case of School Desegregation," 47 (December 1982): 697-708.

Measures were constructed to index conversational ties and strength of those ties (importance, frequency, and tenure). Flow of information, efficiency of flow, and flow of influence were also indexed. (Author constructed.)

Gabriel Weimann, "On the Importance of Marginality: One More Step into the Two-Step Flow of Communication," 47 (December 1982): 764-73.

A measure of acoustic frequency-level adaptation to dyadic conversational interaction was used. (Author constructed.)

Stanford W. Gregory, Jr., "A Quantitative Analysis of Temporal Symmetry in Microsocial Relations," 48 (February 1983): 129-35.

Industry-by-industry matrices were constructed of overlapping directorships. Each industry and an overall centrality score were computed to measure interindustry interlocks. (Author constructed.)

William G. Roy, "The Unfolding of the Interlocking Directorate Structure of the United States," 48 (April 1983): 248-57.

A measure was constructed to show to what extent the effects of a status intervention will persist beyond the situation in which it was administered. A four-condition, dual group-task experiment was designed. The probability of the subject's staying with an initial choice given disagreement, P(S), from Time, to Time, Modified version of Berger et al. (1974, 1977) expectation states program experimental situation.

Barry Markovsky, LeRoy F. Smith, and Joseph Berger, "Do State Interventions Persist?" 49 (June 1984): 373-82.

Measures for three separate dependent variables were created to measure the evaluation of perceptions of social distance and discrimination by creating dichotomous measures for three items: perceptions of discrimination against Cubans, perceptions of social relations between Cubans and Anglos, perceptions of Anglo self-evaluations. (Author constructed.)

Alejandro Portes, "The Rise of Ethnicity: Determinants of Ethnic Perceptions Among Cuban Exiles in Miami," 49 (June 1984): 383-97.

Two measures of delinquency were constructed: Antisocial Behavior, a 25-item scale of frequency; and Association with Delinquent Peers, based on Elliott and Voss's (1974) 3-item scale. (Antisocial Behavior author constructed.)

David C. Rowe and D. Wayne Osgood, "Heredity and Sociological Theories of Delinquency: A Reconsideration," 49 (August 1984): 526-40.

Measures of esteem (prestige) and disesteem (aversion) were constructed through the use of sociometric nominations: (a) who are most skilled (prestige) and (b) who are unenjoyable partners (aversion). (Author constructed.)

Bonnie H. Erickson and T. H. Nosanchuk, "The Allocation of Esteem and Disesteem: A Test of Goode's Theory," 49 (October 1984): 648-58.

NORC General Social Survey's three tolerance measures were used: Should members of various groups (e.g., homosexuals, communists) be allowed (a) to speak publicly, (b) to teach, and (c) to have books in library?

Thomas C. Wilson, "Urbanism and Tolerance: A Test of Some Hypotheses Drawn from Wirth and Stouffer," 50 (February 1985): 117-23.

Group consensus.

Peter H. Rossi and Richard A. Berk, "Varieties of Normative Consensus," 50 (June 1985): 333-47.

A measure of organizational structure was constructed by noting whether (coded 1) or not (coded 0) firm switched to multidivisional form. Derived from Moody's, Chandler (1962), and Rumelt (1974). (Author constructed.)

Neil Fligstein, "The Spread of the Multidivisional Form Among Large Firms, 1919-1979," 50 (June 1985): 377-91.

Network analysis.

Joseph Galaskiewicz, "Professional Networks and the Institutionalization of a Single Mind Set," 50 (October 1985): 639-58.

A measure of sex segregation was constructed from self-reports on sex composition of voluntary, face-to-face local community groups. (Author constructed.)

J. Miller McPherson and Lynn Smith-Lovin, "Sex Segregation in Voluntary Associations," 51 (February 1986): 61-79.

An aggregate measure of business political unity was constructed from Pragmatic (Company Rationality) Scores, proportion of money given to incumbents; and Ideological (Classwide Rationality) Scores, weighted average conservatism rating of candidates to which contributions were made. Three-item measure of unity at individual race level was constructed as (a) unified and (b) predominant business support and (c) business division. (Author constructed.)

Dan Clawson, Alan Neustadtl, and James Bearden, "The Logic of Business Unity: Corporate Contributions to the 1980 Congressional Elections," 51 (December 1986): 797-811.

1985 General Social Survey network instruments were employed to construct measures of the relationship, size, density, and heterogeneity of respondents' interpersonal networks.

Peter V. Marsden, "Core Discussion Networks of Americans," 52 (February 1987): 122-31.

Measures of changes in the proportion of group membership and proportion of liaisons among primary and secondary school children were constructed from three items: (a) Who are your best friends? (b) Who would you like to be your friend? (c) Who do you spend most time with? Respondents were assigned to discrete role categories (isolates, liaisons, or group members). (Author constructed.)

Wesley Shrum and Neil H. Cheek, Jr., "Social Structure During the School Years: Onset of the Degrouping Process," 52 (April 1987): 218-23.

Two measures of party membership were derived from Way of Life, Quality of Life, and Values Survey, 1977 (Institute of Sociology in the Hungarian Academy of Sciences). Dichotomous Membership Index (never/ever member) and Membership in 1977 (active/not active) for entire sample and ever members only.

Szonja Szelenyi, "Social Inequality and Party Membership: Patterns of Recruitment into the Hungarian Socialist Workers' Party," 52 (October 1987): 559-73.

A measure of interracial friendship stability was constructed from a sociometric questionnaire (respondents categorized classmates according to a 5-point scale). The final outcome measure was the termination of P's choice of O, coded unity if friendship dissolved and zero if continued. (Author constructed.)

Maureen T. Hallinan and Richard A. Williams, "The Stability of Students' Interracial Friendships," 52 (October 1987): 653-64.

Scales for Measuring Social Indicators

Work force size was used as an indicator of differentiation within the U.S. capitalist class.

Howard Aldrich and Jane Weiss, "Differentiation Within the United States Capitalist Class: Workforce Size and Income Differences," 46 (June 1981): 279-90.

Numerous indicators were employed to detect influence on municipal police expenditures: race, riots, and black mobilization; racial inequality (ratio of black to white median family income); city population and size; poverty and revenues; crime rate; household activity ratio.

Pamela Irving Jackson and Leo Carroll, "Race and the War on Crime: The Sociopolitical Determinants of the Municipal Police Expenditures in 90 Non-Southern U.S. Cities," 46 (June 1981): 290-305.

Phillips and Feldman Scale (1973) was used to determine mortality levels for suicides and nonsuicides during September and October of presidential election years.

Myron Boor, "Effects of U.S. Presidential Elections on Suicide and Other Causes of Death," 46 (October 1981): 616-18.

Bollen Index (1980) of political democracy was tested for bi- or unidimensionality.

Kenneth A. Bollen and Burke D. Grandjean, "The Dimension(s) of Democracy: Further Issues in the Measurement and Effects of Political Democracy," 46 (October 1981): 651-59.

A measure of major violent crime per 100,000 was constructed from the *Uniform Crime Reports* (FBI, 1971).

Judith R. Blau and Peter M. Blau, "The Cost of Inequality: Metropolitan Structure and Violent Crime," 47 (February 1982): 114-29.

Compound Growth Rates: Average annual rate of growth of income or product per capita for 1950-77 was constructed to measure national economic growth rates. (Author adapted.)

Glenn Firebaugh, "Scale Economy or Scale Entropy? Country Size and Rate of Economic Growth, 1950-1977," 48 (April 1982): 257-69.

Crime rates and police strength were derived from annual reports of Detroit Police Department and examined through the cross-correlation function. (Author constructed.)

Colin Loftin and David McDowall, "The Police, Crime, and Economic Theory: An Assessment," 47 (June 1982): 393-401.

Gross national product per capita was used as a measure of economic growth.

Randall Stokes and David Jaffee, "Another Look at the Export of Raw Materials and Economic Growth," 47 (June 1982): 402-7.

Six indicators of political democracy used: three measures of popular sovereignty and three measures of political liberties.

Kenneth Bollen, "World System Position, Dependency, and Democracy: The Cross-National Evidence," 48 (August 1982): 468-79.

Measure of homicide was constructed from National Center for Health Statistics data.

David P. Phillips, "The Impact of Mass Media Violence on U.S. Homicides," 48 (August 1982): 560-68.

Economic inequality was measured with the standard deviation of logged incomes (S lag) computed on data taken from the census population.

David Jacobs, "Competition, Scale and Political Explanations for Inequality: An Integrated Study of Sectoral Explanations at the Aggregate Level," 47 (October 1982): 600-614.

A wage inequality measure was constructed from self-reported yearly total job earnings, later converted to a weekly measure and, finally, to the natural log of wages. (Author adapted from Quality of Employment Survey, 1977).

Shelley Coverman, "Gender, Domestic Labor, Time, and Wage Inequality," 48 (October 1982): 623-37.

A measure of organizational death rates was constructed from organizational life histories and industry guides by coding births, mergers, and deaths of organizations. (Author adapted.)

John Freeman, Glenn R. Carroll, and Michael T. Hannan, "The Liability of Newness: Age Dependence in Organizational Death Rates," 48 (October 1982): 692-710.

A measure of suicide rates was constructed from U.S. daily mortality statistics. (Author adapted from U.S. National Center for Health Statistics data.)

Kenneth A. Bollen and David P. Phillips, "Imitative Suicides: A National Study of the Effects of Television News Stories," 47 (December 1982): 802-9.

Three measures of economic output were used: output of all goods and services produced, indexed in 1958 dollars; labor input based on Kendrick's index of total person-hours worked per year in private domestic economy; and capital input based on Kendrick's capital input index, a measure of real net capital stock in the private domestic economy.

Pamela Barnhouse Walters and Richard Rubinson, "Educational Expansion and Economic Output in the United States, 1890-1969: A Production Function Analysis," 48 (August 1983): 480-93.

A measure of Labor-Capital Income Ratio (Employee Compensation/Property Income) was constructed. This ratio is an index of the relative share of national income going to particular factor shares of production. (Author constructed.)

Monthly mortality and suicide rates obtained from U.S. Census and Public Health Service data.

Black Civil Rights Insurgency Scale was conducted from synoptic entries in the *New York Times Index* for years 1955-70. (Author constructed.)

Two measures of government repression were used: negative sanctions imposed by government and frequency of protest demonstrations (from *World Handbook of Political and Social Indicators*, Taylor and Jodice, 1983). Political exclusion was measured using Gastril's political rights index (values from Taylor and Jodice).

A measure of federal budget surplus/deficit was constructed from observed values as proportions of GNP. (Author constructed.)

Homicide rates were computed from the FBI's *Uniform Crime Reports*, as the number of murders and nonnegligent manslaughters per 100,000 population, following Messner (1982, 1983) and Blau (1982).

Measures for criminal involvement and unemployment were constructed. Frequency of criminal involvement measures obtained from police and FBI files; measure of unemployment based on an interview item. (Author constructed.)

Leontief input-output matrices of intersectoral flows of commodities were used to measure the disruptive potential of production cessation in one economic sector on another. Other measures constructed were (a) wages, total wage and salary bill in a sector divided by number of employers; and (b) strikes, measured as person-hours lost due to strikes. (Author constructed.)

A measure of suicide rates was constructed from monthly figures published by the U.S. Public Health Service (standardized per 100,000).

Joel A. Devine, "Fiscal Policy and Class Income Inequality: The Distributional Consequences of Governmental Revenues and Expenditures in the United States, 1939-1976," 48 (October 1983): 606-22.

Ira M. Wasserman, "Political Business Cycles, Presidential Elections, and Suicide and Mortality Patterns," 48 (October 1983): 711-20.

Doug McAdam, "Tactical Innovation and the Pace of Insurgency," 48 (December 1983): 735-54.

Michael Timberlake and Kirk R. Williams, "Dependence, Political Exclusion, and Government Repression: Some Cross-National Evidence," 49 (February 1984): 141-46.

Alexander Hicks, "Elections, Keynes, Bureaucracy and Class: Explaining U.S. Budget Deficits, 1961-1978," 49 (April 1984): 165-82.

Kirk R. Williams, "Economic Sources of Homicide: Reestimating the Effects of Poverty and Inequality," 49 (April 1984): 283-89.

Terence P. Thornberry and R. L. Christenson, "Unemployment and Criminal Involvement: An Investigation of Reciprocal Causal Structures," 49 (June 1984): 398-411.

Luca Perrone, "Positional Power, Strikes and Wages," 49 (June 1984): 412-26.

Ira M. Wasserman, "Imitation and Suicide: A Reexamination of the Werther Effect," 49 (June 1984): 427-36.

Multiple items were constructed to measure organizational (a) environments and (b) forms. Five measures were constructed to measure variations in work organization: occupational composition, technology and skills, division of labor, gender composition, and labor market structure. (Author constructed.)

James N. Baron and William T. Bielby, "The Organization of Work in a Segmented Economy," 49 (August 1984): 454-73.

Two measures of educational expansion were constructed: (a) secondary enrollments (number of students enrolled in public secondary schools) and (b) tertiary enrollments (number of students enrolled in institutions of higher education for degree credit). Derived from *Historical Statistics of the U.S.* (Author adapted.)

Pamela Barnhouse Walters, "Occupational and Labor Market Effects of Secondary and Post-Secondary Educational Expansion in the United States: 1922 to 1979," 49 (October 1984): 659-71.

A measure of industrial productivity was constructed as the value added by manufacture, divided by total labor hours for production workers. Figures from Census of Manufactures. (Author constructed.)

Omer R. Galle, Candace Hinson Wiswell, and Jeffrey A. Burr, "Racial Mix and Industrial Productivity," 50 (February 1985): 20-33.

Measures of regime repressiveness were taken from the *World Handbook III* data set, the Political Rights Index, and the Civil Rights Index (Taylor and Jodice). Political violence was measured by deaths occurring from domestic political conflict (Taylor and Jodice).

Edward N. Muller, "Income Inequality, Regime Repressiveness, and Political Violence," 50 (February 1985): 47-61.

Two measures of state expenditures were constructed: social investment and social consumption as proportions of GNP (Wilensky, 1975; Griffin et al., 1982, 1983).

Joel A. Devine, "State and State Expenditure: Determinants of Social Investment and Social Consumption Spending in the Postwar United States," 50 (April 1985): 150-65.

A measure of income inequality was constructed as the standard deviation of logged incomes (S log) computed on data from the census of the population (Jacobs, 1982).

David Jacobs, "Unequal Organizations or Unequal Attainments? An Empirical Comparison of Sectoral and Individualistic Explanations for Aggregate Inequality," 50 (April 1985): 166-80.

Three measures of development were constructed: (a) economic growth (natural logarithms of GNPs), (b) development of the modern sector of the economy (percentage of labor force in nonagricultural work), and (c) domestic turmoil (Taylor and Jodice measures).

York W. Bradshaw, "Dependent Development in Black Africa: A Cross-National Study," 50 (April 1985): 195-207.

Measures of crime rates were constructed from FBI's *Uniform Crime Reports* Index Crimes.

David Cantor and Kenneth C. Land, "Unemployment and Crime Rates in the Post-World War II United States: A Theoretical and Empirical Analysis," 50 (June 1985): 317-32.

A measure of economic growth was constructed as percentage change in gross domestic product. Derived from published reports. (Author adapted.)

Roger Friedland and Jimy Sanders, "The Public Economy and Economic Growth in Western Market Economics," 50 (August 1985): 421-37.

A measure of income inequality was constructed from the distributions of national posttax cash and in-kind income. A summary measure was given as the simple ratio of incomes received by wealthiest 20% to poorest 40% of population. Bollen's (1980, 1979) index of political democracy for 1965 was used. (Income inequality measure author constructed.)

Kenneth A. Bollen and Robert W. Jackman, "Political Democracy and the Size Distribution of Income," 50 (August 1985): 438-57.

Four measures were constructed for labor market sector: primary, secondary, enclave, and informal. Measures of employment and economic situation were length of unemployment, tenure in job, household income, and time on welfare. Dummy variable measures were constructed for employment/unemployment and formal/informal employment.

Alejandro Portes and Alex Stepick, "Unwelcome Immigrants: The Labor Market Experiences of 1980 (Mariel) Cuban and Haitian Refugees in South Florida," 50 (August 1985): 493-514.

Two measures of public pension expenditures were constructed: pension expenditures divided by GNP (times 100) and pension expenditures per person age 65 and over divided by the GNP per capita (times 100). (Author constructed.)

Fred C. Pampel and John B. Williamson, "Age Structure, Politics, and Cross-National Patterns of Public Pension Expenditures," 50 (December 1985): 782-99.

A measure of suicide rates was constructed from 1970 National Center for Health Statistics data and 1970 Census Public Use Sample.

Bernice A. Pescosolido and Robert Mendelsohn, "Social Causation or Social Construction of Suicide? An Investigation into the Social Organization of Official Rates," 50 (February 1986): 80-101.

Measures of payment systems were constructed from interviews providing information on hourly and monthly earnings. (Author constructed.)

Kyu Han Bae and William Form, "Payment Strategy in South Korea's Advanced Economic Sector," 51 (February 1986): 120-31.

A large number of measures were culled and constructed from preexisting historical records and studies: industrial productivity (output per person hour); four wage measures from Douglas (1930); annual earnings for union-nonunion industrial sectors; measures of business failures and business failure rate; trade union growth, membership (Wolman, 1936), and density.

Larry J. Griffin, Michael E. Wallace, and Beth A. Rubin, "Capitalist Resistance to the Organization of Labor Before the New Deal: Why? How? Success?" 51 (April 1986): 147-67.

A measure of economic growth was constructed as time-series changes in GNP. Derived from National Income and Expenditure Accounts 1965-82 data for Canada. Change in aggregate American direct investment was a measure of American economic control. Derived from Canada's International Investment Position 1926-77.

Heather-Jo Hammer and John W. Gartrell, "American Penetration and Canadian Development: A Case Study of Mature Dependency," 51 (April 1986): 201-13.

Two measures of racial occupational inequality were used: Index of Dissimilarity (Duncan and Duncan, 1955) and Index of Net Difference (Lieberson 1975).

Mark A. Fossett, Omer R. Galle, and William R. Kelly, "Racial Occupational Inequality, 1940-1980: National and Regional Trends," 51 (June 1986): 421-29.

Gini coefficient of concentration for the distribution of agricultural capital across households was used as the index of inequality. Also used was the Gini coefficient for the distribution of crop income across households as a measure of income inequality.

John W. Gartrell, "Inequality Within Rural Communities of India," 46 (December 1986): 768-82.

Four measures of black insurgency were constructed as annualized time series: (a) organization of acting unit (five items) and issues (five items), (b) incidence of black urban riots (Isaac and Kelly scale, 1981, 1983; Limberg Center files; *New York Times* and other newspapers), (c) foundation grants to social movements (three items), and (d) three indicators of McCarthy-Zald's structural facilitation and entrepreneurial factors. (Items a, c, and d author constructed.)

J. Craig Jenkins and Craig M. Eckert, "Channeling Black Insurgency: Elite Patronage and Professional Social Movement Organizations in the Development of the Black Movement," 51 (December 1986): 812-29.

A measure of corporate antitrust crime was constructed from Federal Trade Commission case decisions and trade cases.

Sally S. Simpson, "The Decomposition of Antitrust: Testing a Multi-Level, Longitudinal Model of Profit-Squeeze," 51 (December 1986): 859-75.

The *World Handbook of Political and Social Indicators* (1971-83), U.N.'s *Pattern of Population Growth* (1980), and *World Development Report* (1985) were used to construct three measures of urban growth; Kentor's (1981) overurbanization measure and Walter's (1985) and Smith's (1985) measure of change in a nation's level of urban primacy.

Bruce London, "Structural Determinants of Third World Urban Change: An Ecological and Political Economic Analysis," 52 (February 1987): 28-43.

An outcome measure of ethnic endogamy was constructed as whether or not the respondent was married to a spouse of matching ethnic decent. Derived from 1976 Survey of Income and Education. (Author adapted.)

Gillian Stevens and Gray Swicegood, "The Linguistic Context of Ethnic Endogamy," 52 (February 1987): 73-82.

A measure of aggregate voter shift was constructed as proportions of the population that support the rightists, centrists, or leftists, or are nonvoters over time. (Author constructed.)

Courtney Brown, "Voter Mobilization and Party Competition in a Volatile Electorate," 52 (February 1987): 59-72.

A measure of industrialization was constructed through the use of smallest space analysis comparing the level of labor force diversity across industrial sectors in different nations. (Author constructed.)

William Rau and Dennis W. Roncek, "Industrialization and World Inequality: The Transformation of the Division of Labor in 59 Nations, 1960-1981," 52 (June 1987): 359-69.

Suicide measure was constructed as suicides per 100,000 population. From U.S. Public Health Service and National Center of Health Statistics data.

Steven Stack, "Celebrities and Suicide: A Taxonomy and Analysis, 1948-1983," 52 (June 1987): 401-12.

A measure of monthly homicide counts was constructed from *Vital Statistics of the U.S., 1952-84*, standardized per 100,000. A measure of nationally publicized executions was constructed from *Facts on File* (coded as dummy variable, 1 = month with publicized execution story, 0 = month without). (Author constructed.)

Steven Stack, "Publicized Executions and Homicide, 1950-1980," 52 (August 1987): 532-40.

Measures of imprisonment rates were constructed from prison and jail inmate enumerations drawn from U.S. Census figures.

John R. Sutton, "Doing Time: Dynamics of Imprisonment in the Reformist State," 52 (October 1987): 612-30.

Two measures of the relative criminality of youth ages were constructed from *Uniform Crime Reports* (1953-84): proportionate age involvement and proportionate involvement in youth crime. (Author constructed.)

Darrell Steffensmeier, Cathy Streifel, and Miles D. Harer, "Relative Cohort Size and Youth Crime in the United States, 1953-1984," 52 (October 1987): 702-10.

Three measures of political partisanship were constructed from corporate PAC contributions to congressional candidates in 1982 elections: percentage to incumbents, percentage to Republicans, and percentage to New Right. (Author constructed.)

Val Burris, "The Political Partisanship of American Business: A Study of Corporate Political Action Committees," 52 (December 1987): 732-44.

A measure of earning returns to labor market (enclave versus primary) experience was constructed as the natural logarithm of the sum of wages and salaries for Cubans and Chinese. (Author constructed.)

Jimy M. Sanders and Victor Nee, "Limits of Ethnic Solidarity in the Enclave Economy," 52 (December 1987): 745-67.

The outcome measure (transition to parenthood) was constructed from a dichotomous item: whether the respondent (not yet a parent) becomes a parent during the year. A measure of ordered and disordered lifecourse patterns was constructed from lifecourse sequences over an eight-year period. Derived from the National Longitudinal Survey of the High School Class of 1972.

Ronald R. Rindfuss, C. Gray Swicegood, and Rachel A. Rosenfeld, "Disorder in the Life Course: How Common and Does It Matter?" 52 (December 1987): 785-801.

Racial segregation was measured using Duncan and Duncan's (1955) Index of Dissimilarity and Lieberson's (1980, 1981) Measure of Exposure (P index).

Douglas S. Massey and Nancy A. Denton, "Trends in the Residential Segregation of Blacks, Hispanics, and Asians: 1970-1980," 52 (December 1987): 802-25.

Scales for Measuring Community Factors

Median household income was used as indicator of community status.

John R. Logan and Mark Schneider, "The Stratification of Metropolitan Suburbs, 1960-1970," 46 (April 1981): 175-86.

Three measures of economic dependence were used. (Author constructed.)

Jeffrey Kentor, "Structural Determinants of Peripheral Urbanization: The Effects of International Dependence," 46 (April 1981): 201-11.

Urbanism logged scale based on two standardized subscales was used: the 1970 population of the municipality and a measure of "population potential."

Claude S. Fischer, "The Public and Private Worlds of City Life," 46 (June 1981): 306-16.

A measure was created to index overall administrative structure of communities. This measure decomposed into Managerial and Supervisory Index, Communication Structure (clerical) Index, and Professional and Technical Structure Index. (Author constructed.)

Glenn V. Fuguitt and John D. Kasarda, "Community Structure in Response to Population Growth and Decline: A Study in Ecological Organization," 46 (October 1981): 600-615.

An Exclusionary Zoning Index was constructed based on a standard residential zoning levels code. The index was computed to range from 0 to 77, where 77 is the most exclusive tract conceivable. (Author constructed.)

Anne B. Shlay and Peter H. Rossi, "Keeping Up the Neighborhood: Estimating Net Effects of Zoning," 46 (December 1981): 703-19.

Scores for relative status for community areas were constructed, following Choldin et al. (1980), by computing scores based upon educational attainment, occupation, and income level.

Harvey M. Choldin and Claudine Hanson, "Status Shifts Within the City," 47 (February 1982): 129-41.

Two measures of occupational composition were constructed: percentage skilled manual and clerical occupations. Also, three measures of the distribution of family income were constructed: equal-share coefficient, half-share coefficient, and double-share coefficient. (Author constructed.)

Leonard E. Bloomquist and Gene T. Summers, "Organization of Production and Community Income Distributions," 47 (June 1982): 325-38.

Census statistics were used to measure community population growth rates. Community satisfaction measured on a seven-item growth control scale, five-item local concern scale, one-item antigrowth philosophy scale, and seven-item community satisfaction scale. (Author constructed.)

Mark Baldassare and William Protash, "Growth Controls, Population Growth, and Community Satisfaction," 47 (June 1982): 339-46.

AFDC roll growth from 1969 to 1972 served as a measure of urban rooting's impact on the welfare explosion.

Sanford F. Schram and J. Patrick Turbett, "Civil Disorder and the Welfare Explosion: A Two-Step Process," 48 (June 1982): 408-14.

Respondents were asked to card sort individual suburbs into groups of similar places. Using a standard multidimensional scaling technique (Kruskal and Wish, 1978), a similarity matrix was constructed from respondents' groupings.

John R. Logan and O. Andrew Collver, "Residents' Perceptions of Suburban Community Differences," 48 (June 1982): 428-33.

Constructed county railway mileage was used as a measure of a peripheral culture effect on railway capitalization. (Author constructed.)

Samuel Cohn, "Michael Hechter's Theory of Regional Underdevelopment: A Test Using Victorian Railways," 47 (August 1982): 477-88.

Classified real estate ads were used as an index of neighborhood locality identification stability. (Author constructed.)

Avery M. Guest, Barrett A. Lee, Lynn Staeheli, "Changing Locality Identification in the Metropolis: Seattle, 1920-1978," 47 (August 1982): 543-49.

Two indicators (desired and expected) of residential preferences were constructed from two four-item questions in Southern Youth Survey's four-wave panel study. (Author adapted.)

Frank M. Howell and Wolfgang Frese, "Size of Place, Residential Preferences and the Life Cycle: How People Come to Like Where They Live," 48 (August 1982): 569-80.

Four measures of community satisfaction were constructed: (a) support for energy development (5-point scale), (b) satisfaction with locality (5-point scale), (c) overall quality of life (7-point scale), and (d) alienation (9-point scale; from McClosky and Schaar, 1965). (Measures a, b, and c author adapted.)

William R. Freudenburg, "Boomtown's Youth: The Differential Impacts of Rapid Community Growth on Adolescents and Adults," 49 (October 1984): 697-705.

A measure of demographic change was constructed from age- and race-specific rates of interregional migration and intrametropolitan mobility incidence for SMSAs. Based on Rogers (1975) and Frey (1978, 1983) cohort-component projection methodology.

William H. Frey, "Lifecourse Migration of Metropolitan Whites and Blacks and the Structure of Demographic Change in Large Central Cities," 49 (December 1984): 803-27.

Two measures of community problem solving were constructed. One set of questions concerned respondents' identifying community actors in problem solving. The second measure was a 4-point scale concerned with the effectiveness of the above actors. (Author constructed.)

Avery M. Guest and R. S. Oropesa, "Problem-Solving Strategies of Local Areas in the Metropolis," 49 (December 1984): 828-40.

Measures of spatial assimilation were constructed from probabilities of black, Hispanic, and Anglo contact within neighborhoods and census tracts. Adapted from Massey and Mullan (1984). (Author adapted.)

Douglas S. Massey and Nancy A. Denton, "Spatial Assimilation as a Socio-Economic Outcome," 50 (February 1985): 94-106.

A measure of the suburbanization of the elderly was constructed: extent of growth in suburban elderly population among suburbs, 1960-80. Derived from Census of Housing and Population. (Author constructed.)

Kevin M. Fitzpatrick and John R. Logan, "The Aging of the Suburbs, 1960-1980," 50 (February 1985): 106-17.

A measure of black suburbanization was constructed from Census of Population reports as suburban percentage black in 1950s, 1960s, and 1970s.

John M. Stahura, "Suburban Development, Black Suburbanization and the Civil Rights Movement Since World War II," 51 (February 1986): 131-44.

Measures of suburban employment patterns were constructed as a trade ratio (number of wholesale and retail employees divided by population) and a manufacturing ratio (number of manufacturing employees divided by population). (Author constructed.)

John R. Logan and Reid M. Golden, "Suburbs and Satellites: Two Decades of Change," 51 (June 1986): 430-37.

Four measures of integration and settlement were constructed: (a) interpersonal integration (acquisition of personal ties), (b) institutional integration (involvement with organizations), (c) economic integration (regularization of employment), and (d) settlement process (length of stay, total amount of time accumulated, and total years of experience). (Author constructed.)

Douglas S. Massey, "The Settlement Process Among Mexican Migrants to the United States," 51 (October 1986): 670-84.

A multitude of previously constructed measures of urbanization and underdevelopment were employed: GNP per capita 1960 and 1980; relative urbanization, 1960 and 1980; relative service employment, 1960 and 1980; industrial employment, 1960; rural-urban disparity, 1960; all investment variables; concentration of agricultural exports, 1962; gross domestic investment, 1960; and total population, 1960 and 1980.

York W. Bradshaw, "Urbanization and Underdevelopment: A Global Study of Modernization, Urban Bias, and Economic Dependency," 52 (April 1987): 224-39.

Measures of changes in the migration process and its redistributive tendencies were constructed from U.S. Census migration streams for 1965-70 and 1975-80. Comparisons were made across metropolitan and geographic areas. A final measure compared postcensal 1980-84 population change with change data of 1960s and 1970s.

William H. Frey, "Migration and Depopulation of the Metropolis: Regional Restructuring or Rural Renaissance," 52 (April 1987): 240-57.

A measure of metropolitan dominance was constructed from an organizational network prominence indicator (Burt and Minor, 1983) expressed as the sum of the control links between an industrial corporation and all industrial corporations in the system weighted by the prominence of those industrial corporations. *Moody's Industrial Manual*, 1956 and 1976, indices.

Christopher O. Ross, "Organizational Dimensions of Metropolitan Dominance Prominence in the Network of Corporate Control, 1955-1975," 52 (April 1987): 258-67.

Multiple indicators of suburban status were employed: change in education (percentage completing high school or more education), income (median income), and occupation (percentage white-collar) characteristics (Collver and Semyonov, 1979; Stahura, 1979). Bohrnstedt's (1969) residualized change scores were employed.

John M. Stahura, "Suburban Socioeconomic Status Change: A Comparison of Models, 1950-1980," 52 (April 1987): 268-77.

Duncan and Duncan's (1955) Index of Dissimilarity was employed to construct a measure of occupational sex segregation in each metropolitan statistical area.

Mark Abrahamson and Lee Sigelman, "Occupational Sex Segregation in Metropolitan Areas," 52 (October 1987): 588-97.

Scales for Measuring Social Participation and Alienation

Member support *for* voluntary organizations was measured by a Commitment (Likert) Scale and a Detachment (Likert) Scale. A decision participation measure of decentralization was constructed from information about members' involvement in a recent important decision. A total influence variable was measured following Tannenbaum's control-graph procedure. (All measures author constructed.)

David Knoke, "Commitment and Detachment in Voluntary Associations," 46 (April 1981): 141-58.

Summed indices of psychophysiological symptoms were created from *Americans View Their Mental Health* surveys. (Author derived self-report scale of psychological distress.)

Ronald C. Kessler and James A. McRae, Jr., "Trends in the Relationship Between Sex and Psychological Distress: 1957-1976," 46 (August 1981): 443-52.

Three measures of cultural capital were constructed dealing with attitudes, activities, and information surrounding art, music, and literature. (Author constructed.)

Paul DiMaggio, "Cultural Capital and High School Success: The Impact of Status Culture Participation on the Grades of U.S. High School Students," 47 (April 1982): 189-201.

Five social psychological variables were measured: (a) belief in external control, with modified Rotter's (1966) internal-external locus of control scale; (b) tendency toward yeasaying, index constructed on items in Rotter control scale; (c) tendency to give socially desirable responses, by shortened 15-item Marlowe-Crowne (1964) social desirability scale; (d) mistrust, by average response to two questions; (e) paranoia, measured by four questions. (Measures d and e author constructed.)

John Mirowsky and Catherine E. Ross, "Paranoia and the Structure of Powerlessness," 48 (April 1982): 228-39.

Elites were identified in policy-making and politically influential institutional sectors. The representation and influence of ethnicity were measured through interviews with elites and supplemental standard references. (Author constructed.)

Richard Alba and Gwen Moore, "Ethnicity in the American Elite," 47 (June 1982): 373-83.

A measure of participation in instrumental and expressive organizations was computed from NORC's 1967 Political Participation in America Survey. Also, Verba and Nie's typology of political participation (four standardized indexes) was used, as well as a summary participation score from Verba and Nie. (First measure author adapted.)

Thomas M. Guterbock and Bruce London, "Race, Political Orientation, and Participation: An Empirical Test of Four Competing Theories," 48 (August 1982): 439-53.

The 1977-78 NORC survey was used to construct measures of (a) job dissatisfaction; (b) political leftism—political party identification, self-identification as liberal or conservative, and support for state welfare spending; (c) political alienation on a six-item scale; and (d) stratification ideology on a three-item scale. (Author adapted.)

Val Burris, "The Social and Political Consequences of Overeducation," 48 (August 1982): 454-67.

Three measures of political alienation were constructed. Taken from American National Election Studies. (Author adapted.)

Willard L. Rodgers, "Estimable Functions of Age, Period, and Cohort Effects," 47 (December 1982): 774-87.

Voluntary participation rates measured using 22 items were taken from Chapin's (1928, 1939) social participation scale and Indianapolis Area Project survey (1977). (Non-Chapin items author adapted.)

Robert Nash Parker, "Measuring Social Participation," 48 (December 1983): 864-73.

A measure of willingness to take action in a social movement was constructed: binary (moderate/militant) four-item measure. (Author constructed.)

Bert Klandermans, "Mobilization and Participation: Social-Psychological Expansions of Resource Mobilization Theory," 49 (October 1984): 583-600.

Three measures of social movement participation were constructed: (a) membership, (b) activism (active/not active), and (c) leadership. Derived from 1969 Detroit neighborhood study. (Author adapted.)

Pamela Oliver, " 'If You Don't Do It Nobody Else Will': Active and Token Contributors to Local Collective Action," 49 (October 1984): 601-10.

Policy event participation was measured by respondents' reports of organization's involvement or noninvolvement. Events were classified in terms of five formal attributes: (a) decision-making locus, (b) public visibility, (c) controversiality, (d) functional focus, and (e) type of decision cycle (Laumann and Knoke, 1982). (All measures except for e author constructed.)

Edward O. Laumann, David Knoke, and Yong-Hak Kim, "An Organizational Approach to State Policy Formation: A Comparative Study of Energy and Health Domains," 50 (February 1985): 1-19.

Five measures of support for workplace participation were constructed: meaningfulness, autonomy, extrinsic rewards, union support, and workplace participation (five observable variables). Derived from Quality of Employment Survey, 1977.

Rudy Fenwick and Jon Olson, "Support for Worker Participation: Attitudes Among Urban and Non-Union Workers," 51 (August 1986): 505-22.

No Say/Don't Care Index from Michigan National Election Surveys was used as a measure of political alienation.

Joan R. Kahn and William M. Mason, "Political Alienation, Cohort Size, and the Easterlin Hypothesis," 52 (April 1987): 155-69.

The primary church attendance measure was culled from American Institute of Public Opinion time-series surveys: Did you happen to attend church or synagogue during the last seven days? Other measures include probability of attending church in past seven days for each combination of age, period, and religion, transformed into a log-odds. Also, log-odds on weekly attendance relative to each of the other three outcomes: never, yearly, or monthly.

Michael Hout and Andrew M. Greeley, "The Center Doesn't Hold: Church Attendance in the United States, 1940-1984," 52 (June 1987): 325-45.

A measure of participation in a social movement was constructed from a follow-up interview (did go/did not go). (Author constructed.)

Bert Klandermans and Dirk Oegema, "Potentials, Networks, Motivations, and Barriers: Steps Towards Participation in Social Movements," 52 (August 1987): 519-31.

Scales for Measuring Attitudes and Values

Rosen's (1959) three-component conceptualization of achievement orientation was used: achievement motivation, value orientation, educational-vocational aspiration levels.

Robin Stryker, "Religio-Ethnic Effect on Attainments in the Early Career," 46 (April 1981): 212-36.

Two measures were used to index attitude shifts on female roles in work and politics. Derived from NORC General Social Survey. (Author adapted.)

Andrew Cherlin and Pamela Barnhouse Walters, "Trends in U.S. Men's and Women's Sex-Role Attitudes: 1977-1978," 46 (August 1981): 453-60.

Tolerance was measured according to whites' responses to replicated survey questions (1954-78) on school integration. Derived from American Institute of Public Opinion and NORC surveys. (Author adapted.)

A. Wade Smith, "Racial Tolerance as a Function of Group Position," 46 (October 1981): 558-73.

A five-item index was constructed: (a) frequency of prayer, (b) reading Bible, (c) attending religious services, (d) beliefs about Ten Commandments, and (e) beliefs about biblical literalism. Summed in composite measure. (Author constructed.)

Hart M. Nelson, "Religious Conformity in an Age of Disbelief: Contextual Effects of Time, Denomination, and Family Processes upon Church Decline and Apostasy," 46 (October 1981): 632-40.

Judd and Milburn (1980) Political Attitude Scale: 3 involvement measures were isolated from 11 involvement variables in election panel sample—national affairs interest, campaign interest, effort to persuade others. Three attitude measures were constructed: busing children, government guarantee of job and standard of living, and government aid to minorities. (Author constructed.)

Charles M. Judd, Jon A. Krosnick, and Michael A. Milburn, "Political Involvement and Attitude Structure in the General Public," 46 (October 1981): 660-69.

Indices were developed from questions pertaining to parental values, self-conceptions, and social orientations as well as to occupational self-direction.

Kazimierz M. Slomczynski, Joanne Miller, and Melvin L. Kohn, "Stratification, Work, and Values: A Polish-United States Comparison," 46 (December 1981): 720-44.

Delinquency measures were derived from Gold's (1966) scales of self-reported delinquent behavior.

Michael D. Wiatrowski, Stephen Hansell, Charles R. Massey, and David L. Wilson, "Curriculum Tracking and Delinquency," 47 (February 1982): 151-60.

Gurin Scale of psychological distress, Zung Depression Scale, and Rosenberg Self-Esteem Scale were used.

Ronald C. Kessler and James A. McRae, Jr., "The Effect of Wives' Employment on the Mental Health of Married Men and Women," 47 (April 1982): 216-27.

Three measures were constructed for weeks employed, economic adjustment, and affective well-being. Derived from official prison, arrest, and payment records, prerelease and postprison interviews. (Author adapted.)

Jeffrey K. Liker, "Wage and Status Effects of Employment on Affective Well-Being Among Ex-Felons," 47 (April 1982): 264-83.

Measures were constructed for relative terms of exchange (exchange ratio), subject's perceived self-sufficiency based upon potency dimension of the semantic differential scale (Osgood et al., 1957), and subject's judgment of the fairness of person's own terms of exchange based upon semantic differential. (First measure author constructed.)

John F. Stolte, "The Legitimation of Structural Inequality: Reformulation and Test of the Self-Evaluation Argument," 48 (June 1982): 331-42.

Intolerance ratios were computed on homosexuality, extramarital sex, premarital sex, and pornography. (Author constructed.)

G. Edward Stephan and Douglas R. McMullin, "Tolerance of Sexual Nonconformity: City Size as a Situational and Early Learning Determinant," 47 (June 1982): 411-15.

Following Hirschi and Jensen, measure of delinquency was an index of self-reported delinquent acts committed in the year prior to questionnaire.

Ross L. Matsueda, "Testing Control Theory and Differential Association: A Causal Modeling Approach," 47 (August 1982): 489-504.

Seven measures on whites' perspectives on blacks' opportunity were constructed. (Author constructed.)

James R. Kluegel and Eliot R. Smith, "Whites' Beliefs About Blacks' Opportunity," 47 (August 1982): 518-32.

Subjectively experienced distress was measured by psychiatric (symptom) screening scales: measure of depressed mood and measure of psychophysiological distress.

Nine measures were created to measure postaccident attitudes and behaviors: (a) public meetings, (b) nuclear attitudes, (c) Krypton opposition, (d) Krypton evacuation, (e) political solidarity, (f) political ideology, (g) TMI in 1981, (h) civil disobedience attitude, and (i) move residence. (Author constructed.)

Depression was measured using a modified form (12 items) of the Center for Epidemiological Studies Depression Scale (CES-D).

A five-item job satisfaction scale, a job rewards measure, and three indicators of work values were used. Items taken from Quality of Employment Survey. (Author adapted.)

The shift from personal opinion to public norm (norm of evenhandedness) was measured as the differential response to questions as a function of the order of appearance in a survey. (Author constructed.)

Psychological distress was measured using an instrument developed by Macmillan (1957) and Gurin et al. (1960) that consists of 20 psychological and psychosomatic symptoms requiring Likert-type responses.

Three measures were used to scale stress based upon a 22-symptom checklist in the posttraumatic stress disorder diagnosis in the *Diagnostic and Statistical Manual* (3rd ed.) of the American Psychiatric Association (1980).

An additive scale of attitudes on three pornography items was constructed from three items in the General Social Survey. Pornography (a) leads to moral breakdown, (b) leads to rape, and (c) should be legally available. (Author adapted.)

Several standardized measures of psychological distress are used: Center for Epidemiologic Studies Depression Scale (Radloff, 1977), Gurin Scale (Myers et al., 1974), Psychophysiological/Physical Subscales of the Langner Scale (Langner, 1962), Study-Specific Scale (Weissman and Myers, 1978), and Modified Zung Scale (Zung, 1965).

Ronald C. Kessler, "A Disaggregation of the Relationship Between Socioeconomic Status and Psychological Distress," 47 (December 1982): 752-64.

Edward J. Walsh and Rex H. Warland, "Social Movement Involvement in the Wake of a Nuclear Accident: Activists and Free Riders in the TMI Area," 48 (December 1982): 764-80.

Catherine E. Ross, John Mirowsky, and Joan Huber, "Dividing Work, Sharing Work, and In Between: Marriage Patterns and Depression," 48 (December 1982): 809-23.

Arne L. Kalleberg and Karyn Loscocco, "Aging, Values, and Rewards: Explaining Age Differences in Job Satisfaction," 48 (February 1983): 78-90.

Howard Schuman and Jacob Ludwig, "The Norm of Even-Handedness in Surveys as in Life," 48 (February 1983): 112-20.

Peggy A. Thoits, "Multiple Identities and Psychological Well-Being: A Reformulation and Test of the Social Isolation Hypothesis," 48 (April 1983): 174-87.

Charles Kadushin, "Mental Health and the Interpersonal Environment: A Reexamination of Some Effects of Social Structure on Mental Health," 48 (April 1983): 188-98.

Michael Wood and Michael Hughes, "The Moral Basis of Moral Reform: Status Discontent vs. Culture and Socialization as Explanations of Anti-Pornography Social Movement Adherence," 48 (February 1984): 86-99.

Ronald C. Kessler and Jane D. McLeod, "Sex Differences in Vulnerability to Undesirable Life Events," 49 (October 1984): 620-31.

Six broad measures of multiple items were constructed to measure intergroup beliefs, feelings, predispositions for personal contact, and policy orientations of (a) men toward women, (b) whites toward blacks, and (c) nonpoor toward poor. Derived from a survey by the Survey Research Center of the University of Michigan (1975). (Author adapted.)

Mary R. Jackman and Michael J. Muha, "Education and Intergroup Attitudes: Moral Enlightenment, Superficial Democratic Commitment, or Ideological Refinement?" 49 (December 1984): 751-69.

Measures of work role perceptions were constructed from postexperiment questionnaires. Subjects rated selves and others on multiple-item measures of a variety of role- and nonrole-related personality traits. Respondents also completed a 9-point sociogram on motivation. (Author constructed.)

Ronald Humphrey, "How Work Roles Influence Perception: Structural-Cognitive Processes and Organizational Behavior," 50 (April 1985): 242-52.

A six-measure anti-Semitism scale and three non-anti-Semitism scales (liberal democratic values, xenophobic, and Christian traditionalism) were constructed from published (national and international) survey results (e.g., Roper, Harris, Sandager [French], *Allensbach Jahrhücher für Demoskipie* [German]).

Frederick D. Weil, "The Variable Effects of Education on Liberal Attitudes: A Comparative-Historical Analysis of Anti-Semitism Using Public Opinion Survey Data," 50 (August 1985): 458-74.

A measure of racial occupational equality was constructed from the comparison of the proportion of black occupational incumbents at different times and compared to overall racial composition of the labor force. A measure of the annual vacancy rate was also constructed. (Author constructed.)

William E. Feinberg, "Are Affirmative Action and Economic Growth Alternative Paths to Racial Equality?" 50 (August 1985): 561-71.

A measure of distributive justice was constructed from responses to experimental treatments: Respondents could complain of allocations (worker or office complaints) by button pushes and written complaint questionnaire asking about pay satisfaction. (Author constructed.)

Barry Markovsky, "Toward a Multilevel Distributive Justice Theory," 50 (December 1985): 822-39.

A measure of beliefs about the determination of income was constructed from a vignette measurement strategy (respondents estimated vignette families' incomes). Income and reaction to income measures were also constructed: income, fair income, over-underpaid, income satisfaction, relative income, and just income (Jasso and Rossi, 1977; Jasso, 1978). (All items author constructed except just income.)

Norma J. Shepelak and Duane F. Alwin, "Beliefs About Inequality and Perceptions of Distributive Justice," 51 (February 1986): 30-46.

A measure of the effect of gender-based status expectancies on task behavior was constructed from experimental treatments providing a subject's P(S) score (i.e., the proportion of times subject stayed with initial choice, given a disagreement) (Berger et al., 1977, chap. 5).

David G. Wagner, Rebecca S. Ford, and Thomas W. Ford, "Can Gender Inequalities Be Reduced?" 51 (February 1986): 47-61.

Four measures of tolerance were identified and employed from repeated national surveys (e.g., Roper, Gallup): a Guttman scale on civil liberties (four items), a single-item euthanasia measure, a single-item attitude measure on epileptic workers, and a single-item attitude measure on prohibition.

Mark Abrahamson and Valerie J. Carter, "Tolerance, Urbanism, and Region," 51 (April 1986): 287-94.

A measure of educational self-direction was constructed from two indicators: (a) complexity of schoolwork (four items) and (b) closeness of supervision (four items). Measures of self-directedness of orientation and sense of distress were constructed from multiple-item indicators of authoritarian conservatism, personally responsible standards of morality, fatalism, trustfulness and anxiety, self-confidence and self-deprecation, and idea conformity. All items were adapted from Kohn and Schooler's (1969, 1983) occupational self-directedness indices.

Karen A. Miller, Melvin L. Kohn, and Carmi Schooler, "Educational Self-Direction and Personality," 51 (June 1986): 372-90.

A four-item measure of medical care preference was constructed. Derived from Grichting's (1970) data from Taiwan.

Bernice A. Pescosolido, "Migration, Medical Care Preferences and the Lay Referral System: A Network Theory of Role Assimilation," 51 (August 1986): 523-40.

Numerous measures of protest attitudes were taken from various surveys. The final dependent outcome measure was the magnitude of the correlation between educational attainment and each survey item concerning protest attitudes, each r converted to Fischer's z.

Robert L. Hall, Mark Rodighier, and Bert Useem, "Effects of Education on Attitude to Protest," 51 (August 1986): 654-73.

Three scales measuring three substantive areas were used: Gender Ideology Scale, Religious Ideology Scale, and Political Ideology Scale. Scale items were forced-choice, Likert-type questions with four response options. From 1973 Southern California self-administered, mailed questionnaire.

Jennifer Glass, Vern L. Bengtson, and Charlotte Chorn Dunham, "Attitude Similarity in Three-Generation Families: Socialization, Status Inheritance, or Reciprocal Influence?" 51 (October 1986): 685-98.

A measure of evolving organization in disaster events was constructed as the presence/absence of four elements: domains, tasks, resources, and activities. Four items were constructed to measure role-making and role-playing: inconsistency vs. consistency, discontinuity vs. continuity, unique role performance vs. role boundary expansion, and homogeneity vs. heterogeneity.

Susan Lovegren Bosworth and Gary A. Kreps, "Structure as Process: Organization and Role," 51 (October 1986): 699-716.

Six measures of psychological well-being were culled from the NORC General Social Survey: a general life satisfaction scale, trust-in-people scale, anomie scale, general happiness item, marital happiness item, and a self-report item on physical health.

Melvin E. Thomas and Michael Hughes, "The Continuing Significance of Race: A Study of Race, Class, and Quality of Life in America, 1972-1985," 51 (December 1986): 830-41.

Self-report scales of delinquency were employed as indicators of delinquent behavior: Serious Delinquency, Drug and Alcohol Offenses, and Family/School Offenses. Delinquency prevalence measures were constructed from respondent reports (yes/no) and incidence measures from yes responses (How many times?). Derived from Seattle Youth Study.

Robert J. Sampson, "Effects of Socioeconomic Context on Official Reaction to Juvenile Delinquency," 51 (December 1986): 876-85.

Campbell and Converse's (1980) Quality of Life Indicators were employed to construct two material satisfaction measures and one distributive justice measure (just family income).

Duane F. Alwin, "Distributive Justice and Satisfaction with Material Well-Being," 52 (February 1987): 83-95.

Dohrenwend et al.'s (1980) 27-item Demoralization Scale was employed. Income was measured as respondent's earned income and unemployment as respondent's reported number of weeks unemployed.

Bruce G. Link, "Understanding Labeling Effects in the Area of Mental Disorders: An Assessment of the Effects of Expectations of Rejection," 52 (February 1987): 96-112.

Eight measures of German political attitudes were employed from various preexisting surveys: (a) More good than evil in National Socialism; (b) authoritarianism best for Germans; (c) Hitler greatest German statesman; (d) would favor new National Socialist party; (e) would vote again for man like Hitler; (f) disapproval of Parliament; (g) do not really need Parliament; (h) better to have one party.

Frederick D. Weil, "Cohorts, Regimes, and the Legitimation of Democracy: West Germany Since 1945," 52 (June 1987): 308-24.

Three measures of self-attitudes toward just rewards were culled from the 1979 Indianapolis Area Project Survey: equity evaluation (Were you overpaid? 5-point scale), self-explanation (How important was your effort? 4-point scale), and self-evaluation index (four-item composite of individual's assessment of self-esteem).

Norma J. Shepelak, "The Role of Self-Explanations and Self-Evaluations in Legitimating Inequality," 52 (August 1987): 495-503.

Six questions from NORC's General Social Surveys (1972, 1977, 1982, 1985) were employed to construct a measure of prejudice toward blacks.

Steven A. Tuch, "Urbanism, Region, and Tolerance Revisited: The Case of Racial Prejudice," 52 (August 1987): 504-10.

A sex-role attitude measure was constructed from seven questionnaire items from the National Longitudinal Study of the High School Class of 1972 with subsequent follow-ups. Also included were personal life-style and aspiration measures. Five items were used— How important are success, time, family, class, and promotion?—each as a 3-point scale.

S. Philip Morgan and Linda J. Waite, "Parenthood and the Attitudes of Young Adults," 52 (August 1987): 541-47.

A measure of the effect of work-setting gender composition on males' psychological orientations to work was constructed from several attitudinal scales developed by the University of Michigan's Institute for Social Research and used in 1973 Quality of Employment Survey: (a) general job satisfaction (five job satisfaction questions), (b) job depression, and (c) job-related self-esteem.

Amy S. Wharton and James N. Baron, "So Happy Together? The Impact of Gender Segregation on Men at Work," 52 (October 1987): 574-87.

Scales for Measuring Family and Marriage Factors

Two measures were constructed: outmarriage rate for particular groups and intermarriage rates for the entire population. (Author constructed.)

Peter M. Blau, Terry C. Blum, Joseph E. Schwartz, "Heterogeneity and Intermarriage," 47 (February 1982): 45-62.

Preexisting measures from the Berkeley Guidance Study (1929-33) were used to measure marital tension on a 5-point scale, financial conflicts of couples on a 5-point scale, and personal instability on three 5-point scales.

Jeffrey K. Liker and Glen H. Elder, Jr., "Economic Hardship and Marital Relations in the 1930's," 48 (June 1982): 343-59.

Family well-being modeling technique was used.

Sandra L. Hoffarth, "Childbearing Decision Making and Family Well-Being: A Dynamic, Sequential Model," 48 (August 1982): 533-45.

Family pretax income was used as an inequality measure, and relative inequality was reported as a Thail's measure.

Judith Treas, "Trickle Down or Transfer? Postwar Determinants of Family Income Inequality," 48 (August 1982): 546-59.

Multiple-item interview questions and standard scales measuring maladaptive and prosocial behavior were used to examine incidence of marital disruption in children's lives, types of living arrangements children experience following a disruption, and amount of contact children maintain with the outside parent. (Author constructed, adapted, and standard measures used.)

Frank F. Furstenberg, Jr., Christine Winquist Nord, James L. Peterson, and Nicholas Zill, "The Life Course of Children of Divorce: Marital Disruption and Parental Contact," 48 (October 1982): 656-68.

Measures were constructed for proximate employment (number of months employed prior to birth), interval fertility (whether or not birth occurred during interval), and subsequent employment (number of months employed after birth). (Author adapted.)

Douglas T. Gurak and Mary M. Kritz, "Female Employment and Fertility in the Dominican Republic: A Dynamic Perspective," 47 (December 1982): 810-18.

Four items were derived from NORC's General Social Survey as measurements of feminist outlook. These items referred to women in home, at work, as president, and in politics. (Author adapted.)

H. Edward Ransford and Jon Miller, "Race, Sex and Feminist Outlooks," 48 (February 1983): 46-59.

General fertility rate was the number of births in a community area per 1,000 women aged 15 to 44 in the same area.

Collin Loftin and Sally K. Ward, "A Spatial Autocorrelation Model of the Effects of Population Density on Fertility," 48 (February 1983): 121-28.

The intergenerational shift in sex-role attitudes (1962, 1977, 1980) was measured by eight items summed into four variable indices (Sex-Role Index 4) and eight variable indices (Sex-Role Index 8). The coefficients for sex-role attitudes were also used as indicators of sex-role attitude effects (from 1962 to 1977) on education, work, fertility, church attendance, and divorce of respondents.

Arland Thornton, Duane F. Alwin, and Donald Camburn, "Causes and Consequences of Sex-Role Attitudes and Attitude Change," 48 (April 1983): 211-27.

Measures were constructed to show impact of extended family residence on (a) timing of marriage and first birth, (b) intent to have more children, (c) employment patterns, (d) housework duties, and (e) residential preferences and satisfaction. Items from Japanese Institute of Population Problems survey. (Author adapted.)

S. Philip Morgan and Kiyosi Hirosima, "The Persistence of Extended Family Residence in Japan: Anachronism or Alternate Strategy?" 48 (April 1983): 269-81.

Six measures were constructed from a National Council on Aging (1974) survey: (a) adult child confidant, (b) receiving aid (c) getting help (six indicators for b and c), (d) community activities (two indicators for this item—leisure and active social participation scales), and two measures of psychological well-being—(e) positive affect and (f) negative affect (each a five-item measure). (Author adapted.)

Elizabeth Mutran and Donald C. Reitzes, "Intergenerational Support Activities and Well-Being Among the Elderly: A Convergence of Exchange and Symbolic Interaction Perspectives," 49 (February 1984): 117-30.

Two outcome measures were constructed as follow-ups in cases of police intervention into domestic violence. These measures were based closely on instruments designed for a NIMH-funded study of spousal violence. Measures were designed to measure frequency and seriousness of victimizations caused by suspect after police intervention. Outcome measures were (a) police-recorded "failure" of offender to reach six-month follow-up interview and (b) interviews with victims of repeat assaults.

Lawrence W. Sherman and Richard A. Berk, "The Specific Effects of Arrest for Domestic Assault," 49 (April 1984): 261-72.

A measure for the main dependent variable was constructed as a dichotomous indicator (in/out of labor force). An eight-item Likert-type scale was constructed to measure respondent's work attitudes, and a 5-point index was constructed to measure respondent's perceptions of husband's attitudes toward wife's working. (Author constructed.)

Cynthia Rexroat and Constance Shehan, "Expected Versus Actual Work Roles of Women," 49 (June 1984): 349-58.

A series of conditional first-birth probabilities were constructed as a set of dependent variables to be explained. (Author constructed.)

Ronald R. Rindfuss, S. Philip Morgan, and C. Gray Swicegood, "The Transition to Motherhood: The Intersection of Structural and Temporal Dimensions," 49 (June 1984): 359-72.

A measure of the historical variation of adult women's gainful employment was constructed from Census Public Use Samples. (Author adapted.)

Christine E. Bose, "Household Resources and U.S. Women's Work: Factors Affecting Gainful Employment at the Turn of the Century," 49 (August 1984): 474-90.

Two items were constructed to measure the reciprocal impact of (a) educational attainment (years of schooling completed) and (b) age at first birth. (Author constructed.)

Margaret Mooney Marini, "Women's Educational Attainment and the Timing of Entry into Parenthood," 49 (August 1984): 491-511.

Five measures of the sexual division of labor in conversation were constructed: (a) total number of seconds spent talking, (b) number of overlaps, (c) number of interruptions, (d) number of minimal responses used as a turn, and (e) number of backchannels. (Author constructed.)

Peter Kollock, Philip Blumstein, and Pepper Schwartz, "Sex and Power in Interaction: Conversational Privileges and Duties," 50 (February 1985): 34-46.

Mother-tongue shift was measured as the intergenerational retention of a non-English language versus a shift toward English. (Author constructed.)

Gillian Stevens, "Nativity, Intermarriage, and Mother-Tongue Shift," 50 (February 1985): 74-83.

A measure of parenthood's effect on employment activities was constructed from comparing actual outcomes over time with estimated outcomes in absence of parenthood: (a) employment status, (b) full-time employment status, (c) number of hours worked per week for workers only, and (d) number of hours worked per week for all respondents. Taken from National Longitudinal Survey. (Author constructed.)

Linda J. Waite, Gus W. Haggstrom, and David E. Kanouse, "Changes in the Employment Activities of New Parents," 50 (April 1985): 263-72.

Measure of coital frequency was obtained from self-report item on National Fertility Studies.

Guillermina Jasso, "Marital Coital Frequency and the Passage of Time: Estimating the Separate Effects of Spouses' Ages and Marital Duration, Birth and Marriage Cohorts, and Period Influences," 50 (April 1985): 224-41.

The effects of arrest threat on deterrence of wife abuse were measured by a propensity score giving an unbiased estimate of treatment effects. Taken from police-recorded wife-battery incidents. (Author constructed.)

Richard A. Berk and Phyllis J. Newton, "Does Arrest Really Deter Wife Battery? An Effort to Replicate the Findings of the Minneapolis Spouse Abuse Experiment," 50 (April 1985): 253-62.

Nine dependent events reflecting entry or exit from specific states were analyzed: four pertain to cohabitation, five to drug use. (Author constructed.)

Kazuo Yamaguchi and Denise B. Kandel, "Dynamic Relationships Between Premarital Cohabitation and Illicit Drug Use: An Event-History Analysis of Role Selection and Role Socialization," 50 (August 1985): 530-46.

Two multiple-item measures (parent-adolescent communication and affectivity) were constructed for parental attachment. School attachment was measured using two composite measures of school satisfaction. Two seven-item measures (Gold, 1970) of interpersonal violence and theft/vandalism were constructed for juvenile delinquency. (First two measures author constructed.)

Allen E. Liska and Mark D. Reed, "Ties to Conventional Institutions and Delinquency: Estimating Reciprocal Effects," 50 (August 1985): 547-60.

Five measures of marital quality were constructed: marital happiness (11 items), marital interaction (5 items), amount of disagreement (sum of 4 z-scored items), marital tensions, and divorce or permanent separation. Derived from U.S. National Center for Health Statistics probability sample survey, 1984.

Lynn K. White and Alan Booth, "The Quality and Stability of Remarriages: The Role of Stepchildren," 50 (October 1985): 689-98.

A measure of marital stability was constructed by contrasting the observed marital dissolution rates for sample of parents with predicted rates in the absence of parenthood. Sample derived from National Longitudinal Study of the High School Class of 1972. (Author constructed.)

Linda J. Waite, Gus W. Haggstrom, and David C. Kanouse, "The Consequences of Parenthood for the Marital Stability of Young Adults," 50 (December 1985): 850-57.

Two instruments of experienced psychological distress were employed: depression subscale of the Johns Hopkins Symptom Checklist (anxiety, 12 symptoms; depression, 11 symptoms) and Gurin et al. (1960) scale of psychological and psychosomatic symptoms.

Peggy A. Thoits, "Multiple Identities: Examining Gender and Marital Status Differences in Distress," 51 (April 1986): 259-72.

Multiple outcome measures on a wide range of young adults' family- and sex-role-related attitudes, plans, and expectations were constructed: two measures on women's mother and worker role expectations; three measures (one a 5-point Likert scale) on attitudes toward balance of women's worker/mother roles; two general indices of sex-role attitudes (Likert-type questions). Derived from National Longitudinal Surveys of Young Women and Men.

Linda J. Waite, Frances K. Goldscheider, and Christina Witsberger, "Nonfamily Living and the Erosion of Traditional Family Orientations Among Young Adults," 51 (August 1986): 541-54.

An outcome measure was constructed for still married at the end of a two-year period or divorced/separated. Derived from National Longitudinal Survey.

Scott J. South and Glenna Spitze, "Determinants of Divorce over the Marital Life Course," 51 (August 1986): 583-90.

Age-specific fertility rates (not marital), by race and residence, were employed; estimated by the U.S. Census Bureau for 1905-10 and 1935-40.

Stewart E. Tolnay, "The Decline of Black Marital Fertility in the Rural South: 1910-1940," 52 (April 1987): 211-17.

An outcome measure of expectations about premarital residential independence was constructed from two High School and Beyond (1980) questions: (a) At what age do you expect to get married? (b) At what age do you expect to live in your own home or apartment?

Calvin Goldscheider and Frances K. Goldscheider, "Moving Out and Marriage: What Do Young Adults Expect?" 52 (April 1987): 278-85.

Two measures of changing number of years spent in family roles were constructed from a simulation model: (a) proportion occupying a particular family status (or combination of statuses) at a particular age and (b) number of years spent in various family statuses (Bongaarts's 1984 model). Model calculates number of survivors of the original cohort who are in a particular family status s at age x, where s can be a combination of overlapping statuses.

Susan Cotts Watkins, Jane A. Menken, and John Bongaarts, "Demographic Foundations of Family Change," 52 (June 1987): 346-58.

A measure of dual-earning couples' time spent together was constructed from measuring time spent together in seven broad categories of activities: (a) child related, (b) recreation, (c) homemaking and personal care, (d) service/helping, (e) watching television, (f) eating meals, and (g) talking. Also recorded was total time spent together. A Marital Quality Index was constructed from four Likert-type items. (Author constructed.)

Paul William Kingston and Steven L. Nock, "Time Together Among Dual-Earner Couples," 52 (June 1987): 391-400.

A measure of respondent's experience with intercourse was constructed from 1976 and 1981 National Survey of Children: ever had intercourse (yes/no).

Frank F. Furstenberg, Jr., S. Philip Morgan, Kristin A. Moore, and James L. Peterson, "Race Differences in the Timing of Adolescent Intercourse," 52 (August 1987): 511-18.

Measures of child well-being were constructed from three sources: mother's report on delinquency (five items), problem behavior (four items) and distress (five items); teacher's report on problem behavior (four items) and academic difficulty (three items); and child's report on delinquency (five items), dissatisfaction (five items), and distress (four items) (Furstenberg and Allison, 1985; Furstenberg and Seltzer, 1986).

Frank F. Furstenberg, Jr., S. Philip Morgan, and Paul D. Allison, "Paternal Participation and Children's Well-Being After Marital Dissolution," 52 (October 1987): 695-701.

A six-item delinquency measure was constructed from 1965 Richmond Youth Project Survey Delinquency Index: battery, car theft, theft (less than $2), theft ($2-$50), theft (over $50), and vandalism.

Ross L. Matsueda and Karen Heimer, "Race, Family Structure, and Delinquency: A Test of Differential Association and Social Control Theories," 52 (December 1987): 826-40.

A transition to intercourse measure was constructed from a 3-point scale asking respondent to indicate whether he or she had had sex (never or 2/more than 2). (Author constructed.)

J. Richard Udry and John O. G. Billy, "Initiation of Coitus in Early Adolescence," 52 (December 1987): 841-55.

Scales for Measuring Personality and Leadership Factors

Summed indices of psychophysiological symptoms created from *Americans View Their Mental Health* surveys. Author derived self-report scale of psychological distress.

Ronald C. Kessler and James A. McRae, Jr., "Trends in the Relationship Between Sex and Psychological Distress: 1957-1976," 46 (August 1981): 443-52.

Subjects ranked group members for influence, competence, likability, and group leadership to measure influence and status in task-oriented groups. (Author constructed.)

Cecilia Ridgeway, "Status in Groups: The Importance of Motivation," 47 (February 1982): 76-88.

Measures were constructed for income and work status (two-item measure). (Author adapted.)

Bruce Link, "Mental Patient Status, Work, and Income: An Examination of the Effects of a Psychiatric Label," 47 (April 1982): 202-15.

Gurin Scale of psychological distress, Zung Depression Scale, and Rosenberg Self-Esteem Scale are used.

Ronald C. Kessler and James A. McRae, Jr., "The Effect of Wives' Employment on the Mental Health of Married Men and Women," 47 (April 1982): 216-27.

Three measures were constructed for weeks employed, economic adjustment, and affective well-being. Derived from official prison, arrest, and payment records, prerelease and postprison interviews. (Author adapted.)

Jeffrey K. Liker, "Wage and Status Effects of Employment and Affective Well-Being Among Ex-Felons," 47 (April 1982): 264-83.

Criminal involvement was measured using 6 measures for juveniles and adults (12 measures overall). Based on self- and official reports. (Author adapted.)

Terence P. Thornberry and Margaret Farnworth, "Social Correlates of Criminal Involvement: Further Evidence on the Relationship Between Social Status and Criminal Behavior," 47 (August 1982): 505-18.

A measure of suicide rates was constructed from U.S. daily mortality statistics. From U.S. National Center for Health Statistics data. (Author adapted.)

Kenneth A. Bollen and David P. Phillips, "Imitative Suicides: A National Study of the Effects of Television News Stories," 47 (December 1982): 802-9.

Self-report measures of drinking behavior were used: frequency of drinking and modal quantity. Also used was a six-item self-report measure of drinking problems focusing on social behavior impairment. (All author adapted.)

Melvin Sieman and Carolyn S. Anderson, "Alienation and Alcohol: The Role of Work, Mastery, and Community in Drinking Behavior," 48 (February 1983): 60-77.

Psychological distress was measured using an instrument developed by Macmillan (1957) and Gurin et al. (1960) that consists of 20 psychological and psychosomatic symptoms requiring Likert-type responses.

Peggy A. Thoits, "Multiple Identities and Psychological Well-Being: A Reformulation and Test of the Social Isolation Hypothesis," 48 (April 1983): 174-87.

Three measures were used to scale stress based upon a 22-symptom checklist in the posttraumatic stress disorder diagnosis in the *Diagnostic and Statistical Manual* (3rd ed.) of the American Psychiatric Association (1980).

Charles Kadushin, "Mental Health and the Interpersonal Environment: A Reexamination of Some Effects of Social Structure on Mental Health," 48 (April 1983): 188-98.

Five social psychological variables were measured: (a) belief in external control, with modified Rotter's (1966) internal-external locus of control scale; (b) tendency toward yeasaying, index constructed on items in Rotter control scale; (c) tendency to give socially desirable responses, by shortened 15-item Marlowe-Crowne (1964) social desirability scale; (d) mistrust, by average response to two questions; (e) paranoia, measured by four questions. (Measures d and e author constructed.)

John Mirowsky and Catherine E. Ross, "Paranoia and the Structure of Powerlessness," 48 (April 1983): 228-39.

Multiple-item interview questions and standard scales measuring maladaptive and prosocial behavior were used to examine incidence of marital disruption in children's lives, types of living arrangements children experience following a disruption, and amount of contact children maintain with the outside parent. (Author constructed, adapted, and standard measures used.)

Frank F. Furstenberg, Jr., Christine Winquist Nord, James L. Peterson, and Nicolas Zill, "The Life Course of Children of Divorce: Marital Disruption and Parental Contact," 48 (October 1983): 656-68.

Measure of homicide was constructed from National Center for Health Statistics data.

David P. Phillips, "The Impact of Mass Media Violence on U.S. Homicides," 48 (August 1983): 560-68.

Measures of esteem (prestige) and disesteem (aversion) were constructed through the use of sociometric nominations: (a) who are most skilled (prestige) and (b) who are unenjoyable partners (aversion). (Author constructed.)

Bonnie H. Erickson and T. A. Nosanchuk, "The Allocation of Esteem and Disesteem: A Test of Goode's Theory," 49 (October 1984): 648-58.

Two measures of schizophrenia were constructed from Psychiatric Epidemiology Research Interview (Dohrenwend et al., 1980) and NIMH's Diagnostic Interview Schedule (Robins et al., 1981). An expected Cain and Treiman (1981) "undesirable working conditions" scale was constructed. Treiman's occupational prestige scores were used as a measure of occupational mobility.

Bruce G. Link, Bruce P. Dohrenwend, and Andrew E. Skodol, "Socio-Economic Status and Schizophrenia: Noisome Occupational Characteristics as a Risk Factor," 51 (April 1986): 242-58.

Two instruments of experienced psychological distress were employed: depression subscale of the Johns Hopkins Symptom Checklist (anxiety, 12 symptoms; depression, 11 symptoms) and Gurin et al. (1960) scale of psychological and psychosomatic symptoms.

Peggy A. Thoits, "Multiple Identities: Examining Gender and Marital Status Differences in Distress," 51 (April 1986): 259-72.

Dohrenwend et al.'s (1980) 27-item Demoralization Scale was employed. Income was measured as respondent's earned income and unemployment as respondent's reported number of weeks unemployed.

Bruce G. Link, "Understanding Labeling Effects in the Area of Mental Disorders: An Assessment of the Effects of Expectations of Rejection," 52 (February 1987): 96-112.

The primary outcome measure of status influence in task groups was constructed from the difference between the subject's initial and final award levels on a $0-$25,000 scale. Measures of target's apparent task capacity, dominance, and group- versus self-motivation were constructed from responses to a series of 7-point Likert and semantic differential items. Subjects also rated target's degree of leadership ability and apparent high and low status. (Nemeth and Wachtler, 1974; Lee and Ofshe, 1981, measures.)

Cecilia L. Ridgeway, "Nonverbal Behavior, Dominance, and the Basis of Status in Task Groups," 52 (October 1987): 683-94.

Measures of child well-being were constructed from three sources: mother's report on delinquency (five items), problem behavior (four items) and distress (five items); teacher's report on problem behavior (four items) and academic difficulty (three items); and child's report on delinquency (five items), dissatisfaction (five items), and distress (four items) (Furstenberg and Allison, 1985; Furstenberg and Seltzer, 1986).

Frank F. Furstenberg, Jr., S. Philip Morgan, and Paul D. Allison, "Paternal Participation and Children's Well-Being After Marital Dissolution," 52 (October 1987): 695-701.

The outcome measure (transition to parenthood) was constructed from a dichotomous item: whether the respondent (not yet a parent) becomes a parent during the year. A measure of ordered and disordered life-course patterns was constructed from life-course sequences over an eight-year period. Derived from the National Longitudinal Survey of the High School Class of 1972.

Ronald R. Rindfuss, C. Gray Swicegood, and Rachel A. Rosenfeld, "Disorder in the Life Course: How Common and Does It Matter?" 52 (December 1987): 785-801.

Scales for Measuring Intelligence and Achievement

Social Misfit Index and Low Achievement Index used. (Both author constructed.)

Richard A. Berk, William P. Bridges, and Anthony Shih, "Does IQ Really Matter? A Study of the Use of IQ Scores for the Tracking of the Mentally Retarded," 46 (February 1981): 58-71.

Multiple self-report questionnaire items and objective test scores were used to measure educational direction. (Author adapted.)

Karl L. Alexander, Aaron M. Pallas, and Martha A. Cook, "Measure for Measure: On the Use of Endogenous Ability Data in School-Process Research," 46 (October 1981): 619-31.

Four measures of occupational attainment were used: Hope-Goldthorpe Occupational Prestige Scale, self-reported earnings, occupational authority, and occupational control measures. (First three measures author constructed.)

Alan C. Kerckhoff, Richard T. Campbell, and Jerry M. Trott, "Dimensions of Educational and Occupational Attainment in Great Britain," 47 (June 1982): 347-64.

Two subtests of Wechsler Intelligence Scale were used to measure verbal and nonverbal intelligence.

James A. Mercy and Lala Carr Steelman, "Familial Influence on the Intellectual Attainment of Children," 47 (August 1982): 532-42.

Forty-nine measures were constructed on a variety of attitudes and behaviors. Derived from NORC's General Social Survey. (Author adapted.)

James A. Davis, "Achievement Variables and Class Cultures: Family, Schooling, Job, and Forty-Nine Dependent Variables in the Cumulative GSS," 47 (October 1982): 569-86.

Seven twelfth-grade outcome measures were used to index track placement effects: college plans, application to college, GPA, Scholastic Aptitude Test or PSAT scores (verbal and quantitative), College Boards, achievement test scores in English and American history adapted from author's earlier study.

Karl L. Alexander and Martha A. Cook, "Curricula and Coursework: A Surprise Ending to a Familiar Story," 47 (October 1982): 626-40.

Peer influence on college aspirations.

Jere Cohen, "Peer Influence on College Aspirations with Initial Aspirations Controlled," 48 (October 1982): 728-34.

Log-linear odds computed for eight educational progressions. (Author constructed.)

Albert Simkus and Rudolf Andorka, "Inequalities in Educational Attainment in Hungary, 1923-1973," 47 (December 1982): 740-51.

Two measures for educational attainment were constructed: highest grade attended in secondary school and dummy variable for reception of matriculation diploma. (Author adapted.)

Yossi Shavit, "Tracking and Ethnicity in Israeli Secondary Education," 49 (April 1984): 210-20.

A measure of self-reported grades for sixth-, eighth-, tenth-, and twelfth-grade students was constructed. (Author constructed.)

Thomas Ewin Smith, "School Grades and Responsibility for Younger Siblings: An Empirical Study of the 'Teaching Function,'" 49 (April 1984): 248-60.

Four measures of educational attainment were used: verbal achievement (24-item subtest of Wechsler Adult Intelligence Test), high school grade point average (self-report), high school curriculum (self-report of school track), and length of schooling (self-report).

Duane F. Alwin and Arland Thornton, "Family Origins and the Schooling Process: Early Versus Late Influence of Parental Characteristics," 49 (December 1984): 784-802.

A single measure of educational expectation was constructed: Respondents were coded 1 if expressing an expectation to attend an academic high school and 0 for all other responses. Derived from previous survey data. (Author adapted.)

Yossi Shavit and Richard A. Williams, "Ability Grouping and Contextual Determination of Educational Expectations," 50 (February 1985): 62-73.

Three measures of son's educational attainment were constructed: total years of education, total years of graded schooling, and proportion of high school graduates going to college. (Featherman and Hauser, 1978, indicators.)

Judith Blake, "Number of Siblings and Educational Mobility," 50 (February 1985): 84-94.

Measures of cognitive performance were constructed from the High School and Beyond battery of tests in vocabulary (21 items), reading (20 items), mathematics (38 items), science (20 items), writing (17 items), and civics education (10 items).

Karl L. Alexander, Gary Natriello, and Aaron M. Pallas, "For Whom the School Bell Tolls: The Impact of Dropping Out on Cognitive Performance," 50 (June 1985): 409-20.

Measures of differential corporate management attainment were constructed as senior-most management (whether manager has attained highest administrative spot), corporate governance (number of corporate directorships held: single and multiple directors), and business representative (membership in trade associations: none and political activists). (Author constructed.)

Michael Useem and Jerome Karabel, "Pathways to Top Corporate Management," 51 (April 1986): 184-200.

Two measures of reading achievement were constructed: word learning (number of words learned) and reading achievement (Calfee and Calfee, 1982, Interactive Reading Assessment System). (Word learning author constructed.)

Robert Druben and Adam Gamoran, "Race, Instruction, and Learning," 51 (October 1986): 660-69.

Outcome measures of educational achievement were taken from reading and mathematics tests administered by National Children's Bureau of London.

A measure of educational attainment was constructed from a 5-point scale on the National Longitudinal Study of the High School Class of 1972 indicating level of education attained from high school graduation and beyond.

Students' performance outcomes measures were constructed from reading and mathematics marks (4-1 scale), conduct (satisfactory/needs improvement), and California Achievement Test scores. Measures of teachers' perceptions of students and affective orientations were constructed from a three-question scale (taken twice) of classroom/school climate and 14 items from 1976 National Survey of Children to evaluate students' personal maturity. (Unless specified, items derived from Beginning School Study 1982, Baltimore City.)

Alan C. Kerckhoff, "Effects of Ability Grouping in British Secondary Schools," 51 (December 1986): 842-58.

Jay D. Teachman, "Family Background, Educational Resources, and Educational Attainment," 52 (August 1987): 548-57.

Karl L. Alexander, Doris R. Entwisle, and Maxine S. Thompson, "School Performance, Status Relations, and the Structure of Sentiment: Bringing the Teacher Back In," 52 (October 1987): 665-82.

Scales for Measuring Identification

Delinquency index: Guided by Hirschi's (1969) study, equally weighted composite scales were created for attachment, commitment, involvement, and belief. Delinquency was measured by a 26-item index adapted from Gold's (1966) self-report measure of delinquency. (Author adapted indices.)

A three-category respondent's self-placement ethnic identification scale was constructed from NORC's General Social Survey. (Author adapted.)

Affiliation identification.

Six measures of work commitment and five measures of sex-role attitudes were derived from NORC survey data. (Author adapted.)

Measure of work satisfaction was constructed from four often-used items (e.g., How satisfied are you with your job?) (Cole, 1979). Organizational commitment items (six) were drawn from Porter organizational commitment scale (Steers, 1977).

Michael D. Wistrowski, David B. Griswald, and Mary K. Roberts, "Social Control Theory and Delinquency," 46 (October 1981): 525-41.

Richard D. Alba and Mitchell B. Chamblin, "A Preliminary Examination of Ethnic Identification Among Whites," 48 (April 1982): 240-47.

Miller McPherson, "An Ecology of Affiliation," 48 (August 1983): 519-32.

Denise Del Vento Bielby and William T. Bielby, "Work Commitment, Sex-Role Attitudes, and Women's Employment," 49 (April 1984): 234-47.

James R. Lincoln and Arne L. Kalleberg, "Work Organization and Workforce Commitment: A Study of Plants and Employees in the U.S. and Japan," 50 (December 1985): 738-60.

Measures of educational achievement were constructed from English and arithmetic O-grade examination results and an overall measure of Scottish Certificate of Education examination scores. An SES segregation measure was given as the "correlation ratio" (Burstein, 1980) for the summary SES measure and for two dummy variables indicating class.

J. Douglas Williams, "Social Class Segregation and Its Relationship to Pupils' Examination Results in Scotland," 51 (April 1986): 224-41.

Two measures of worker attachment were constructed: propensity to accept job offer from another employer (4-point scale) and propensity to search for another contract with another employer (multiple-point scale). Derived from preexisting survey data: Quality of Employment Survey, 1977.

Charles N. Halaby, "Worker Attachment and Workplace Authority," 51 (October 1986): 634-49.

A single outcome measure was constructed: reconstitution—whether interlock partners created at least one new interlock with each other after their tie was disrupted. (Author constructed.)

Donald Palmer, Roger Friedland, and Jitendra V. Singh, "The Ties That Bind: Organizational and Class Bases of Stability in a Corporate Interlock Network," 51 (December 1986): 781-96.

Religious commitment was measured along four dimensions: church attendance, religious commitment (two items), belief (five fundamentalist religious beliefs), and religious revelation. Taken from Australian Value Survey, 1983.

David De Vaus and Ian McAllister, "Gender Differences in Religion: A Test of the Structural Location Theory," 52 (August 1987): 472-81.

Miscellaneous Scales

Two differential equation models were used: political mobilization model and intragenerational mobility model. (Author constructed.)

Francois Nielsen and Rachel A. Rosenfeld, "Substantive Interpretation of Differential Equation Models," 46 (April 1981): 159-74.

Scientific productivity scale was based on *Chemical Abstracts* and *Science Citation Index.*

J. Scott Long and Robert McGinnis, "Organizational Context and Scientific Productivity," 46 (August 1981): 422-42.

Incidence rates of personal crime victimization, derived from self-reports in National Crime Survey, were employed. (Author adapted.)

Michael A. Hindelang, "Variations in Sex-Role Specific Incidence Rates of Offending," 46 (August 1981): 461-74.

Three measures were constructed: criminal victimization, exposure and guardianship, and proximity. (Author constructed.)

Lawrence Cohen, James R. Kluegel, and Kenneth C. Land, "Social Inequality and Predatory Criminal Victimization: An Exposition and Test of a Formal Theory," 46 (October 1981): 505-24.

Six measures were constructed: skill and variety, physical mobility, diversity, integration or technical interdependence, control over workplace, and intensity. (Author constructed.)

James N. Baron and William T. Bielby, "Workers and Machines: Dimensions and Determinants of Technical Relations in the Workplace," 47 (April 1982): 175-88.

Three measures of strike outcomes were constructed: success (totally in workers' favor), compromise (any compromise), and gain (totally in workers' favor or compromise). (Author constructed.)

Job deskilling was measured through eight different skill ratios based on hourly wage rates. (Author constructed.)

Measures for bomb threats were obtained from U.S. Nuclear Regulatory Commission and an index of media coverage of nuclear power was obtained from *Readers' Guide to Periodical Literature, Television News: Index and Abstracts, New York Times Index,* and *Time* and *Newsweek.* (Author adapted.)

Three measures of response quality were constructed: overall response rate to the survey, response rates to individual questions, and response quality to indicate effect of varied telephone survey strategies. (Author constructed.)

Science Citation Index and *Chemical Abstracts* were used to construct measures of annual publications and counts of citations. (Author adapted.)

Two measures of sentencing were constructed: in/out binary judicial decisions (to imprison or not imprison) and length of prison measured in months. (Author constructed.)

A measure of the extent of age homophily was constructed as the proportion of "same-age" associates. (Author constructed.)

Self-report measures of drinking behavior were used: frequency of drinking and modal quantity. Also used was a six-item self-report measure of drinking problems focusing on social behavior impairment. (All author adapted.)

Two separate analytic measures were constructed: persons labeled and labeled symbols per cartoon as indicators of public figures and political symbols recognition. (Author constructed.)

College athletic coach job mobility patterns were measured by comparing job vacancies appearing in the *National Directory of College Athletics* between 1977-78 and 1978-79. (Author constructed.)

Charles C. Ragin, Shelley Coverman, and Mark Hayward, "Major Labor Disputes in Britain, 1902-1938: The Relationship Between Resource Expenditure and Outcome," 47 (April 1982): 238-52.

Michael Wallace and Arne L. Kalleberg, "Industrial Transformation and the Decline of Craft: The Decomposition of Skill in the Printing Industry, 1931-1978," 47 (June 1982): 307-24.

Allan Mazur, "Bomb Threats and the Mass Media: Evidence for a Theory of Suggestion," 47 (June 1982): 407-11.

Eleanor Singer and Martin R. Frankel, "Informed Consent Procedures in Telephone Interviews," 47 (June 1982): 416-27.

Paul D. Allison, J. Scott Long, and Tad K. Krauze, "Cumulative Advantage and Inequality in Science," 47 (October 1982): 615-25.

Stanton Wheeler, David Weisburd, and Nancy Bode, "Sentencing the White-Collar Offender: Rhetoric and Reality," 47 (October 1982): 641-59.

Scott L. Field, "Social Structural Determinants of Similarity Among Associates," 47 (December 1982): 797-801.

Melvin Seeman and Carolyn S. Anderson, "Alienation and Alcohol: The Role of Work, Mastery, and Community in Drinking Behavior," 48 (February 1983): 60-77.

James R. Beniger, "Does Television Enhance the Shared Symbolic Environment? Trends in Labeling of Editorial Cartoons, 1948-1980," 48 (February 1983): 103-11.

D. Randall Smith, "Mobility in Professional Occupational-Internal Labor Markets: Stratification, Segmentation, and Vacancy Chains," 48 (June 1983): 289-305.

Two measures of sentencing outcome were created: A probit equation estimates whether a drug offender receives an institutional sentence; length of sentence is measured in months. (Author constructed.)

Measures of home ownership and value were constructed from 1980 Panel Study of Income Dynamics. Measures were self-reported items of home ownership and value. Mortgage balance and home equity were examined to aid interpretation of home value results. (Author adapted.)

A measure of workplace size was constructed by establishing the proportion of workers in organizations of various sizes from 1904 to 1977. (Author constructed.)

Two measures were constructed for courtroom outcomes: Pretrial release status was measured by a three-item ordinal level of measurement, and in/out decision was measured as a binary outcome (probation/prison). (Author constructed.)

A measure of severity of sentence was constructed from an 11-point scale. (From Tiffany et al., 1975; Diamond and Zeisel, 1975.)

Dichotomous endogenous variables in simultaneous equations model were constructed for language retention, labor force participation, high school graduation, and nonretaining occupation. Derived from Canadian Public Use Sample Tape (1971). (Author adapted.)

Two measures of influence on organizational structure were constructed: control over work units and control over organizational structure. Control over monetary resources was measured by three questions. Earnings were measured in thousands of dollars. Also included were Wright's class scale, Duncan SEI, Kluegel's authority scale, and Robinson and Kelley's authority scale. (Organizational influence and monetary resource measures author constructed.)

Measures of opportunities for, returns from, and evaluations of legal and illegal activities were constructed. Minimum pay, relative earnings, crime opportunity, and job measured respondent's criminal involvement; self-reports of crime/arrest. Derived from 1975 and 1979 evaluations of National Supported Work Demonstration projects. (Author adapted.)

Ruth D. Peterson and John Hagan, "Changing Conceptions of Race: Towards an Account of Anomalous Finding of Sentencing Research," 49 (February 1984): 56-70.

John C. Henretta, "Parental Status and Child's Home Ownership," 49 (February 1984): 131-40.

Mark Granovetter, "Small Is Bountiful: Labor Markets and Establishment Size," 49 (June 1984): 323-34.

Candace Kruttschnitt and Donald E. Green, "The Sex-Sanctioning Issue: Is It History?" 49 (August 1984): 541-51.

John Hagan and Patricia Parker, "White-Collar Crime and Punishment: The Class Structure and Legal Sanctioning of Securities Violations," 50 (June 1985): 302-16.

Patricia Robinson, "Language Retention Among Canadian Indians: A Simultaneous Equations Model with Dichotomous Endogenous Variables," 50 (August 1985): 515-29.

Joe L. Spaeth, "Job Power and Earnings," 50 (October 1985): 603-17.

Irving Piliavin, Rosemary Gartner, Craig Thornton, and Ross L. Matsueda, "Crime, Deterrence, and Rational Choice," 51 (February 1986): 101-19.

The measure of the differential distribution of black and white men across labor market positions was given as a log-odds ratio (Goodman, 1972; Page, 1977; Fienberg, 1980; Daymont and Kaufman, 1979), contrasting odds of a black gaining employment in a particular labor market position versus employment elsewhere to the odds of a white doing the same. Actual employment measure was constructed as a dichotomy of whether individual was employed in that particular labor market position or elsewhere.

Robert L. Kaufman, "The Impact of Industrial and Occupational Structure on Black-White Employment Allocation," 51 (June 1986): 310-23.

A measure of job-shift patterns was constructed from retrospective career histories. Respondents reported monthly beginning and ending dates of each job held. They also indicated whether shifts occurred across or within firm, occupation, industrial location, size of the firm, and beginning and ending wages.

Glenn R. Carroll and Karl Ulrich Mayer, "Job-Shift Patterns in the Federal Republic of Germany: The Effects of Social Class, Industrial Sector, and Organizational Size," 51 (June 1986): 323-41.

A measure of collective and velocity of footfalls of two or more adjacent persons was constructed from indicators of Initiation, Connectivity, In-Step, and Coordination Index. Wohlstein and McPhail (1979) collective locomotion scale.

Clark McPhail and Ronald T. Wohlstein, "Collective Locomotion as Collective Behavior," 51 (August 1986): 447-63.

A measure of political consensus was constructed from data on campaign contributions of corporate political action committees. (Author constructed.)

Mark S. Mizruchi and Thomas Koenig, "Economic Sources of Corporate Political Consensus: An Examination of Interindustry Relations," 51 (August 1986): 482-91.

A four-category measure of means of job finding was constructed. Nonpersonal measure was subdivided into formalized and direct application. Personal measure was subdivided into weak versus strong ties and work-related versus communal ties. Income was given as yearly earnings (reported by respondents). Measures derived from Metropolitan Employer-Worker Survey.

William P. Bridges and Wayne J. Villemez, "Informal Hiring and Income in the Labor Market," 51 (August 1986): 574-82.

A strike outcome measure was constructed as the percentage rate of change of money compensation for all nonsupervisory production workers in the aggregate economy. (Author constructed.)

Beth A. Rubin, "Class Struggle American Style: Unions, Strikes, and Wages," 51 (October 1986): 618-33.

An employment outcome measure was constructed as four nominal categories: layoff, fired, quit, and employed. From March Current Population Surveys (1969-1978).

Robert L. Kaufman and Paul G. Schervish, "Using Adjusted Crosstabulations to Interpret Log-Linear Relationships," 51 (October 1986): 717-33.

The outcome measure employed was the origin of the president in the firm. Four categories—manufacturing, sales and marketing, finance, and other—were employed to trace how president came up through firm. (Author constructed.)

Neil Fligstein, "The Intraorganizational Power Struggle: Rise of Finance Personnel to Top Leadership in Large Corporations, 1919-1979," 52 (February 1987): 44-58.

Motor vehicle theft and nonnegligent homicide rates were constructed from FBI's *Uniform Crime Reports*.

Lawrence C. Cohen and Kenneth C. Land, "Age Structure and Crime: Symmetry Versus Asymmetry and the Projection of Crime Rates Through the 1990's," 52 (April 1987): 170-83.

The outcome measures of crime victimization constructed were whether or not a respondent was a victim of a violent crime and whether or not a property victimization was reported by the head of the household during 1974. Derived from National Crime Survey, 1975.

Terance D. Miethe, Mark C. Stafford, and J. Scott Long, "Social Differentiation in Criminal Victimization: A Test of Routine Activities/Lifestyle Theories," 52 (April 1987): 184-94.

A measure of publication of positive utopian novels from years 1883-1975 was constructed for Britain and the United States. (Author constructed.)

Edgar Kiser and Kriss A. Drass, "Changes in the Core of the World-System and the Production of Utopian Literature in Great Britain and the United States, 1883-1975," 52 (April 1987): 286-99.

An artistic classification system was constructed from four dimensions: (a) differentiation (institutionally bounded genres), (b) hierarchy (prestige), (c) universality (differ among subgroups of members), and (d) boundary strength (ritualization). (Author constructed.)

Paul DiMaggio, "Classification in Art," 52 (August 1987): 440-55.

Birthrate and death rate measures of state bar associations were constructed from American Bar Association Reports, 1887-1930. Active associations were listed in directory and if one or both officers had changed from previous year. Also listed as active in years during which meetings were held. Seven years of continuous inactivity was required to register death. (Author constructed.)

Terence C. Halliday, Michael J. Powell, and Mark W. Granfors, "Minimalist Organizations: Vital Events in State Bar Associations, 1870-1930," 52 (August 1987): 456-71.

The final outcome measure of manuscript review process was constructed as an ordinal scale (7 points). Also employed was an averaged recommendation measure (summed reviewers' recommendations divided by number of reviewers) and a number of revisions measure (number of times manuscript went through review process). (Author constructed.)

Von Bakanic, Clark McPhail, and Rita J. Simon, "The Manuscript Review and Decision-Making Process," 52 (October 1987): 631-42.

Research articles were cross-classified by research method (quantitative, qualitative, and other) and gender (focus—study topic gender related—and authorship). Ward and Grant, 1985, Gender/Methods Relational Classification Scheme.

Linda Grant, Kathryn B. Ward, and Xue Lan Rong, "Is There an Association Between Gender and Methods in Sociological Research?" 52 (December 1987): 856-62.

Note

1. I am indebted to Charles Zoltac and Jiangong Lei for assistance with compiling this inventory.

A BRIEF HISTORY OF SOCIOLOGICAL MEASURES UTILIZED BY RESEARCHERS IN MAJOR JOURNALS

6.L.2

The most thorough inventory of sociological measures was made between January 1954 and the end of 1965 by Charles M. Bonjean, Richard J. Hill, and S. Dale McLemore.[1] The *American Sociological Review, American Journal of Sociology, Social Forces,* and *Sociometry* (now *Social Psychology Quarterly*) were taken to be representative of the main research currents in American sociology. Every article and research note published in these four journals from 1954 through 1965 was examined carefully. For each article or research note the compilers listed (a) a complete reference to the article in which the measure appeared, (b) the concept indicated by the measure employed, (c) the technique(s) of measurement employed, and (d) other uses and users of the same or similar techniques.

Table 6.11, which shows the most frequently used and cited measures, reveals the findings of the inventory. Note that the socioeconomic grouping of occupations devised by Alba M. Edwards of the U.S. Census leads the list with 91 uses and citations. In addition to use of the Edwards scale as a status measure, it is employed as a related measure (16 mentions) and in studies of occupational mobility (12 mentions). The North-Hall (NORC) prestige rating of occupations has 53 mentions; it is also used as an occupational mobility measure (10 mentions).

The central importance of social status in sociological research is underscored by the use of Hollingshead's Index of Social Position (30 mentions); another of his measures of occupational status has 8 mentions. W. L. Warner's Index of Status Characteristics receives 27 mentions; another of Warner's status measures adds 16 mentions. Duncan's Occupational Status Index (SEI) is just beginning to receive recognition for his 1961 measure (9 mentions). In the four journals reviewed, 435 attempts to measure socioeconomic status were noted.

Measures that have won wide acceptance include the California F-Scale; Shevky, Williams, and Bell's measures of Urban Rank, Urbanization, and Segregation; Burgess, Cottrell, and Locke's Marital Adjustment; Bogardus's Social Distance; and Chapin's Social Participation.

The repeated uses of these measures suggest that social researchers are using standard instruments in many replicated designs under controlled conditions. Unfortunately, the inventory does not reveal this most desired outcome. Indeed, the compilers report that "fragmentation, rather than continuity, is the important characteristic of measurement in social research: a comparison of the number of measures found for each conceptual class indicates that *most measures* used and cited in the journals examined were developed or modified by the investigator for the specific research reported." [2] Continuity may be measured by the following data from the inventory:

1. A total of 3,609 attempts were made to measure various social variables. Of these, 2,080 different measures were used. Only 589, or 28.3%, of the total number of scales and indices were used more than *once*.
2. Of the 2,080 scales and indices appearing in the journals over the 12-year period covered by the analysis, only 47, or 2.26%, were used more than five times.[3]

TABLE 6.11 Most Frequently Used and Cited Measures from All Articles and Research Notes in the *American Sociological Review, American Journal of Sociology, Social Forces, and Sociometry* (now *Social Psychology Quarterly*) from January 1954 Through December 1965

Measure	Frequency of Use and Citations
1. Occupational Status (Census, Edwards)	91
2. California F Scale and Modifications	53
3. Occupational Prestige (North, Hatt)	53
4. Leadership (reputational approach)	35
5. Stereotype Check List (Katz, Braly)	33
6. Indexes of Social Position (Hollingshead)	30
7. Anomia (Srole)	28
8. Social Rank (Shevky, Williams, Bell)	28
9. Index of Status Characteristics (Warner)	27
10. Urbanization (Shevky, Williams, Bell)	26
11. Segregation (Shevky, Williams, Bell)	25
12. Sociometric Status and Structure (various measures)	19
13. Marital Adjustment (Burgess, Cottrell, Locke)	18
14. Social Distance (Bogardus)	18
15. Social Participation (Chapin)	17
16. Achievement Motivation (Murray, McClelland, Atkinson)	16
17. Occupational Status (Census, Edwards related)	16
18. Occupational Status (Warner)	16
19. Ethnocentrism (California E Scale)	15
20. Segregation (Duncan, Duncan)	15
21. Occupational Mobility, Intergenerational (Census, Edwards related)	12
22. Occupational Mobility, Intergenerational (North, Hatt related)	10
23. Social Class: Judges or Informants	10
24. Occupational Status (Duncan)	9
25. Socioeconomic Status (Sewell)	8
26. American Council on Education Psychological Examination	8
27. Centralization	8
28. Consideration (Ohio State Leader Behavior Description Questionnaire and related measures)	8
29. Delinquency Proneness, Social Responsibility (Gough)	8
30. Initiating Structure (Ohio State Leader Description Questionnaire and related measures)	8
31. Occupational Status (Hollingshead)	8
32. Status Crystalization (Lenski)	8
33. Dogmatism (Rokeach)	7
34. Segregation (Cowgill, Cowgill)	7
35. Segregation (Jahn, Schmid, Schrag)	7
36. Social Distance, Summated Differences Technique (Westie)	7
37. Achievement Training (Winterbottom)	6
38. Administrative Rationality (Udy)	6
39. Alienation (Nettler)	6
40. Alienation, Powerlessness (Neal)	6
41. California Test of Personality (Tiegs, Clark, Thrope)	6
42. Conservatism (McClosky)	6
43. Delinquent Behavior Checklist (Nye, Short)	6
44. Edwards Personal Preference Schedule	6
45. Marital Satisfaction (Burgess, Wallin)	6
46. Religious Orthodoxy (Putney, Middleton)	6
47. Social-Emotional Reactions (Bales)	6
48. Status Concern (Kaufman)	6
49. Urbanization (Davis)	6
50. Values (Allport, Vernon, Lindzey)	6

SOURCE: Charles M. Bonjean, Richard J. Hill, and S. Dale McElmore, *Sociological Measurement: An Inventory of Scales and Indices* (San Francisco: Chandler, 1967), 13–14.

3. Continuity is most characteristic among investigations dealing with occupational status, authoritarianism, racial and ethnic stereotypes, community leadership, reputational status, and residential segregation.
4. Little or no continuity is observed in regard to the measurement of achievement, authority, community characteristics, attitudes toward and perceptions of complex organizations, consensus, and characteristics of education.[4]

Bonjean et al. explain that when investigators try to build continuity in their research, they are faced with a double difficulty: First, so many different measures are available for some phenomena that the selection of a scale or index may itself be a research problem of large magnitude; second, in other cases an extensive search through the literature may yield no scale or measure of the variable(s) that concern the investigators.[5] But I believe that there are other, more important reasons for the lack of continuity in research. The further explanation awaits another query: What has happened since 1965? Has continuity increased or has fragmentation continued to dominate? A partial answer may be found by examining the summary review of articles in the *American Sociological Review* from 1965 through 1980 (in the fourth edition of this *Handbook*) and the inventory of *ASR* 1981-87 presented in Section 6.L.1, above.

The data on which to judge research continuity from 1965 through the present rest on a narrower base than the data from 1954 through 1965. This inventory is restricted to the *American Sociological Review*, but this is probably the best single sociological journal that could be chosen. It is the official organ of the American Sociological Association. All members of the association receive it, and with such a guaranteed audience, it becomes the most prestigious and sought-after publication source for sociologists. In 1980, 404 manuscripts were submitted to *ASR*. All papers were refereed. In 26% of reviews, three referees were involved; in 16% of reviews, four or more reviewers were required. In at least two cases, a manuscript was sent to seven different referees. The acceptance rate for 1980 was 15%; for 1979, 14%; and for 1978, 11%.[6] The acceptance rate has remained remarkably stable for the *American Sociological Review* over the last 25 years.[7]

A summary of measures most frequently used and cited in the *American Sociological Review* from 1965 through 1980 is presented in Table 6.12. Again, the high interest in social status is repeated, with 59 measures used to measure the socioeconomic standing of persons in the various studies (see 1, 2, 3, 4, and 12). Duncan's Occupational Status measure (SEI) is easily the most frequently employed scale.

After the social status measures are removed, the number of scales that appear two to five times is narrowed to only nine! What this means can be explained by the number of measures that are either author constructed or data adaptations. Data adaptation measures use data to express a factor or variable, such as percentage of high school graduates, relative earnings of men compared with women, or education of the father. Author-constructed scales are usually a selection of two to five items made by the author and scored to give an index value. Reliability and validity are rarely determined. Face validity is assumed.

Of 461 articles cited in the 1965-80 *ASR* inventory (theoretical and opinion articles, research notes, and comments were not included), 267 were author constructed or data defined (i.e., 58% were measures with no previous utilization). This figure underestimates the actual lack of continuity because at least another 15% represent measures in which the author selects a limited number of items that might serve his or her purpose from previous scales. It may be concluded that research built on

TABLE 6.12 Most Frequently Used and Cited Measures in the *American Sociological Review* 1965–80

	Frequency of Use and Citations
1. Occupational Status (SEI) (Duncan)	30
2. NORC 1964 Prestige Scores (Siegel)	9
3. Two Position Index of Social Position (Hollingshead)	9
4. Occupational Census Classifications (Edwards)	8
5. Anomia Scale (Srole)	5
6. Index of Income Inequality (Gini)	5
7. Self-Esteem (Rosenberg and Simmons)	4
8. Index of Dissimilarity (Duncan and Duncan)	4
9. Powerlessness Scale (Neal and Seeman)	4
10. Occupational Aspiration Scale (Haller)	3
11. Minnesota Multiphasic Personality Inventory	3
12. Occupational Status (Nam and Powers Census Scores)	3
13. Interaction Categories (Bales)	2

established scales and indices is in the distinct minority—about 20-25%. On this basis I have drawn the conclusions elaborated in Section 6.L.4.

The trend did not change from 1981 through 1987. Table 6.13 shows the most frequently cited scales in the *American Sociological Review* during recent years. Only Duncan's SEI and the NORC Prestige Scale remain in the first two positions. Other scales have crowded all others off the list. Again, author-constructed or -adapted scales have remained dominant, reaching a 70% majority. There is no reason to revise the conclusions in Section 6.L.4; the section remains as published in 1983.

TABLE 6.13 Most Frequently Used and Cited Measures in the *American Sociological Review* 1980–87

	Frequency of Use and Citations
1. SEI (Duncan)	6
2. NORC Prestige Scores	6
3. Featherman and Hauser 1978 Occupational Mobility Scale	5
4. Index of Dissimilarity (Duncan and Duncan)	4
5. Taylor and Jodice Measure of Political Attitude	3
6. Bollen's (1980, 1987) Index of Political Democracy for 1965	2
7. Participation Measure (Likert)	2
8. Nielson and Hannan's Structure of Educational Organization	2

	Author-Constructed or Data-Adaptation Measures				
	1965–68	1968–74	1975–80	1965–80	1981–87
Number of author developed	52	88	127	267	227
Total number of articles reviewed	83	165	213	461	323
Percentage of author-developed scales	61	54	60	58	70

Notes

1. Charles M. Bonjean, Richard J. Hill, and S. Dale McLemore, *Sociological Measurement: An Inventory of Scales and Indices* (San Francisco: Chandler, 1967), 4.

2. Ibid., 8.

3. Ibid., 9.

4. Ibid., 7-8.

5. Ibid., 1.

6. William Form, ed. *Footnotes* of the American Sociological Association (March 1981), 14.

7. Lowell R. Hargens, "Scholarly Consensus and Journal Rejection Rates," *American Sociological Review* 53 (February 1988), 150.

CAUSES FOR THE LACK OF STANDARD SCALES IN BEHAVIORAL RESEARCH   6.L.3

A *standard scale* can be defined as a scale whose use is assumed in a given line of research (measurement of social status, job satisfaction, group cohesiveness, and so on) unless special conditions prevail. Karl Schuessler has described two reasons why such standard scales have not been more easily obtained.

Causes for the Lack of Standard Scales in Behavioral Research

Karl F. Schuessler[1]

The variety of scaling methods is one circumstance; uncertainty in the meaning of scale items is another—items may differ in meaning between populations and/or change in meaning within populations.

The variety of scaling methods has multiplied since Thurstone and Chave (1929) first proposed their equal-appearing interval scale in the late 1920s. In the early 1930s, Likert (1932) suggested a change in procedure that would make scaling less costly in time and energy. In the late 1930s, Guttman (1941) came up with a radically different model—the Guttman scale—and a method for fitting it. And in the middle 1940s Lazarsfeld (1950) formulated his latent-structure model with the Guttman scale as a special case. All of these added to the variety of scaling methods.

Just now structural equation models are in the spotlight. The method (LISREL) of Jöreskog and Sörbom (1978) is used in sociology today both to measure the relation of multiple indicators to the latent variable and the relation to its prior causes. A recent study by J. Miller and others (1979) supplies an example. Muthén (1979) has extended this method to the special case of dichotomous indicators, similar to those in our research. His broad strategy is to introduce the latent variable as an explicit term in the classical probit model (Finney, 1951) and then to incorporate that equation in a structural model.

At present, several investigators (Duncan, 1982; Reiser, 1981) are exploring the potentialities of the Rasch model (Lord and Novick, 1968, chap. 21) for measuring social attitudes and the like. But Muthén is the only researcher who has treated the latent variable as both the cause of its dichotomous indicators and the effect of its antecedent causes.

The structural equation approach has significantly changed the form of contemporary sociology; however, its promise for social measurement has yet to be demonstrated. If history repeats itself, it will be in demand for a time, only to be superseded by still later developments. To date the theory and method of scaling (Torgerson, 1967) has been in a state of flux. Although most observers would regard this flux as healthy, they would probably also concede that it has been a factor working against the emergence, possibly premature, of a few standard scales.

But probably a more basic factor working against standard social life feeling scales is the uncertain meaning of scale items, particularly their tendency to change in meaning from time to time and, in consequence, to change in the pattern of their interrelations. An item may lose all meaning in time; or it may reflect two feelings where before and when analyzed for the first time it reflected only one. As a result of such shifts, a scale by definition at the time of construction may be that in name only after a longer or shorter period. Items that scaled soldiers in World War II may not work on the soldiers in the next war.

The prospect of such breakdowns in scale patterns, attributable to the instability of items, has doubtless contributed to the tendency of sociologists to modify existing scales so as to better suit their purposes. That modification may consist in adding items or dropping items or both; and when items are both added and dropped, the modified scale may bear practically no resemblance to the original.

Note

1. From Karl F. Schuessler, *Measuring Social Life Feelings* (San Francisco: Jossey-Bass, 1982), 136-37. Reprinted by permission.

References

Duncan, L. D. "Rasch Measurement in Survey Research: Further Examples and Discussion." In *Survey Measurement of Subjective Phenomena*, edited by C. F. Turner and E. Martin. Washington, DC: National Research Council, 1982.

Finney, D. J. *Probit Analysis.* 2nd ed. Cambridge: Cambridge University Press, 1951.

Guttman, L. "The Quantification of a Class of Attributes." In *The Prediction of Personal Adjustment*, edited by P. Horst. New York: Social Science Research Council, 1941.

Jöreskog, K. G., and D. Sörbom. *LISREL IV: A General Computer Program for Estimation of Linear Equation Systems by Maximum Likelihood Methods.* Uppsala, Sweden: University of Uppsala, 1978.

Lazarsfeld, P. F. "The Logical and Mathematical Foundation of Latent Structure Analysis." In *Measurement and Prediction*, edited by S. A. Stouffer. Princeton, NJ: Princeton University Press, 1950.

Likert, R. "A Technique for the Measurement of Attitudes." *Archives of Psychology* 140 (1932).

Lord, F. M., and M. R. Novick. *Statistical Theories of Mental Test Scores.* Reading, MA: Addison-Wesley, 1968.

Miller, J., et al. "Women and Work: The Psychological Effects of Occupational Conditions." *American Journal of Sociology* 85 (1979): 66-94.

Muthén, B. "A Structural Probit Model with Latent Variables." *Journal of the American Statistical Association* 74 (1979): 807-11.

Reiser, M. "Latent Trait Modeling of Attitude Items." In *Social Measurement: Current Issues*, edited by G. W. Bohrnstedt and E. F. Borgatta. Beverly Hills, CA: Sage, 1981. Thurstone, L. L., and E. J. Chave. *The Measurement of Attitude.* Chicago: University of Chicago Press, 1929.

Torgerson, W. S. *Theory and Methods of Scaling.* New York: John Wiley, 1967.

CONCLUSIONS BASED ON A REVIEW OF RESEARCH PUBLISHED IN THE *AMERICAN SOCIOLOGICAL REVIEW*, 1964-80   6.L.4

Diagnosis

1. High attention is usually given to ties between theory and research methodology.
2. High attention is given to cause-and-effect relationships with numerous applications of path analysis and structural equation models.
3. High attention is given to methodological sophistication. There is an application of many new modeling and statistical techniques.
4. Measures of dependent variables are usually self-constructed, employing one to five items and showing little concern with the reliability and validity of the measures.
5. The numbers of variables, dependent and independent, introduced into the design are increasing in number.
6. Only a limited number of articles deal with the examination of social scales.
7. Articles dealing solely with the accumulating evidence from other studies are almost nonexistent. One or two appear in a three-year period.
8. The overall conclusion is that sociological research lacks the essential attributes of a science that is building cumulative evidence in spite of the significant methodological advances shown in almost all the articles employing quantitative analysis.
9. Sociological research may be viewed as going through a transitional period, when new methodology is being tested on social data. But utilization of scientific techniques alone does not build a science of society.

Prognosis

1. The direction of sociological research toward a science of sociology will not take place until standard measures of important social variables are in place.
2. This direction is not likely to be established until the accumulation of tested findings has been given the highest priority by scholars and students—and especially by publishers, editors, and reviewers, who determine what should be published.

Action

1. To further the accumulation of social knowledge, many of the most prestigious researchers and their students will be replicating the best available research with the same design and standard measures on different populations, holding constant the conditions of prior research.
2. Others will be giving increasing attention to prediction studies, social forecasting, and policy-making research to provide definitive tests against societal needs and demands.

I asked 10 professors on the sociology faculty of Indiana University to comment on each of the above statements. In general there was agreement on all conclusions, but there were some important reservations. A few stressed that the *American Sociological Review* is not necessarily a good testing standard because many subareas of sociology are not included in the journal in sufficient scope. Some stress that in an area such as social stratification, where standard measures have almost always been employed, cumulative research can be observed. Two reviewers said that measures of dependent variables should be judged according to the problem: "Most macro measures (e.g., percent urban, gross national product, literacy), do not need a lot of discussion. Attitudes, values, and other constructs in the 'black box' of social psychology are often self-constructed and are never again seen in the literature."

My conclusion that sociological research lacks the essential attribute of a science in building cumulative evidence (point 8 under "Diagnosis", above) received some objection; my first three points were said to provide opposite evidence. All of these reservations deserve consideration before there is an acceptance of the conclusions. Yet it must be noted that all reviewers agreed that sociological research must face up to more stringent standards of continuity.[1]

Why has the present situation developed? It will be remembered that Bonjean and his coworkers say it is because of the dual problem: too many scales to choose from, and no scales available for many problems. Schuessler has added that uncertainty in the meaning of scale items produces a need for changes of the scale, especially as changes over time distort the meaning of items.

Blalock sees the problem in the proliferation of interests that excite sociologists. He reports:

> I see—a horrifying tendency to move in every possible "interesting" direction to develop new sociologies of X's for each new dependent variable that comes of age without fully exploring our old fields, and a proliferation of new concepts that differ from each other only slightly. In short, I see very little discipline.[2]

Personally, as one who has examined each *ASR* research article carefully from 1965 to 1987, I find the same persistent pattern reported by Blalock, and I believe the reasons go deeper than any mentioned. They begin with a lack of value structure that gives high priority to continuity and accumulation of consistent evidence for the validity of propositions. This lack of continuity values extends to most researchers, the referees of papers, and the editors who publish them. As one reviewer wrote: "Replicating the best available research would be good for sociology in general, but this is not high-status seminal research. The reward structure discourages replications." It might follow that editors of journals and monographs are not receptive to publishing replications of research.

Bollen and Phillips have written one of the few articles published as a *replication* in a major journal. They suggest that one reason replication in sociology is "very rare" is because replication, like most research, is expensive. "This expense may not be justified unless the research to be replicated has substantial implications or produced counterintuitive results." [3]

Moreover, there is some evidence that the computer is now the tail that wags the sociologist. This powerful instrument can take large masses of data and analyze many factors and their various relationships and interrelationships. Secondary use of data gathered by agencies tends to replace the firsthand gathering of data with standard scales selected to fit the design the researcher has formulated. Well-designed quantitative studies developing large matrices of correlations appear to have some exceptional merit often not justified by their ability to build cumulative evidence affirming or rejecting general propositions.

This is the important story of the scales and the inventories. The published research cries out for researchers to build upon it or, failing that, to improve it with standardization of appropriate measures. One lesson is that the researcher should first *search* for the appropriate measures that have been developed previously. The storehouse is bulging with thousands of social and psychological measures, as the numerous compilations attest. Most of them lie unused while social researchers of today are busily constructing new 3-, 4-, and 5-point items and calling them "scales" with unknown reliability and validity. Bohrnstedt has warned of the destructive character of this practice. He writes:

> Careful thought is needed in writing the items. Then extensive analyses need to be done in order to refine and validate the items. The process can literally take *years* if done well. In retrospect, perhaps we have overemphasized the importance of techniques and under-emphasized the role of good theory and reflective thinking in the measure process. Without the techniques one would probably never know how good or poor one's items were. But the fact remains that too often far too little time goes into the writing of the items, and once written and employed in the field, no technique, no matter how "fancy" or sophisticated, can salvage a set of lousy items.[4]

Notes

1. See Chris Argyris, *Inner Contradictions of Rigorous Research* (New York: Academic Press, 1980).
2. H. M. Blalock, Jr., "Thoughts on the Development of Sociology," *Footnotes* of the American Sociological Association 1 (March 1973): 2.
3. Kenneth A. Bollen and David P. Phillips, "Suicidal Motor Vehicle Fatalities in Detroit: A Replication," *American Journal of Sociology* 87 (September 1981): 404-12. See also Blalock, "Thoughts on the Development of Sociology," 2.
4. George W. Bohrnstedt, "Measurement," in *Handbook of Survey Research*, ed. Peter H. Rossi, James D. Wright, and Andy B. Anderson (New York: Academic Press, 1983), 115.

ALL-INCLUSIVE AND SPECIAL COMPILATIONS OF SCALE SOURCES 6.L.5

Following is a list of major sources for scale information and appraisal.

All-Inclusive Compilations

Bonjean, Charles M., Richard J. Hill, and S. Dale McLemore. *Sociological Measurement: An Inventory of Scales and Indices.* San Francisco: Chandler, 1967.

This book is essentially an extensive bibliography that references 3,609 uses of citations of 2,080 separate scales or indexes. Scales are not generally analyzed for reliability and validity. Although limited to research up to 1965, this is still the most comprehensive bibliography. Use this book to locate various scales and research in which the scale was used.

Lake, Dale G., Mathew B. Miles, and Ralph B. Earle, Jr. *Measuring Human Behavior.* New York: Teachers College Press, 1973.

A selection of 84 different instruments meeting stringent criteria, including reasonably current information on reliability and validity. Included are 38 measures of personal variables, 24 interpersonal, 10 group, and 12 organizational. Information is provided for availability, variables measured, description of the instrument, administration and scoring, development, critique, and general comment. Truly a model for scale evaluation!

Maranell, Gary M., ed. *Scaling: A Sourcebook for Behavioral Scientists.* Hawthorne, NY: Aldine, 1974.

Includes a compilation of outstanding position papers on scaling. See Part II for a complete list of papers.

Lantz, Judith C. *Cumulative Index of Sociology Journals, 1971-1985.* Washington, DC: American Sociological Association, 1987.

See the following classifications for research citations: Scales (pp. 640-641), Attitudes (pp. 303-305), Indexes (pp. 468-469), Indicators (p. 470). For a specific research interest see appropriate classification. The journals include *American Journal of Sociology, American Sociological Review, American Sociologist, Contemporary Sociology, Journal of Health and Behavior, Social Forces, Social Psychology Quarterly, Sociological Methodology, Sociological Theory,* and *Sociology of Education.*

Special Compilations

Shaw, Marvin E., and Jack W. Wright. *Scales for the Measurement of Attitudes.* New York: McGraw-Hill, 1967.

Thorough information on 176 attitude measures. Entries are reasonably complete, with criticism of the adequacy of the scales. A bibliography of more than 600 attitude scales is appended. The list of attitude scales appears in Section 6.L.7 of this volume for researcher seeking particular attitude scales.

Occupational Attitudes and Characteristics

Robinson, John P., Robert Athanasiou, and Kendra B. Head. *Measures of Occupational Attitudes and Occupational Characteristics.* Ann Arbor: University of Michigan, Institute for Social Research, 1969.

Reviews a total of 77 test instruments and provides accurate assessments of the form and scope. The author's criteria include sample adequacy, norms, reliability, homogeneity, and discrimination of known groups. Typical items and ease of administration and scoring are indicated. (Contents reproduced in Section 6.L.6.a.)

Political Attitudes

Robinson, John P., Jerrold G. Rusk, and Kendra B. Head. *Measures of Political Attitudes.* Ann Arbor: University of Michigan, Institute for Social Research, 1969.

A total of 95 measures of political attitudes are reviewed with similar criteria to that of the companion volume cited above. Accurate assessments of the form and scope of each study are made. (Contents reproduced in Section 6.L.6.b.)

Social Psychological Attitudes

Robinson, John P., and Phillip R. Shaver. *Measures of Social Psychological Attitudes.* Ann Arbor: University of Michigan, Institute for Social Research, 1969. Revised 1973, with expanded sections on internality-externality and self-esteem.

A total of 106 measures of social psychological attitudes are reviewed. There is a long review of the major attempts to measure "life satisfaction" and "happiness" over the past 15 years. As with its companion volumes, accurate assessments are made using the criteria cited. (Contents reproduced in Section 6.L.6.c.)

Family Measurement

Straus, Murray A. *Family Measurement Techniques.* Minneapolis: University of Minnesota Press, 1969. Updated to 1974, University of Minnesota Press, 1978.

Abstracts of 319 instruments focusing on one or more of the following domains: adolescent, 20; child, 75; family, 63; parent, 129; premarital, 20; and spousal, 81. Criteria used include validity evidence, reliability, norms, availability, and references. Well-organized collection of measures. Discusses problems of scales with lack of reliability and validity—roughly 56% of measures abstracted.

Filsinger, Erik E., ed. *Marriage and Family Assessment: A Sourcebook for Family Therapy.* Beverly Hills, CA: Sage, 1983.

Contains a wide array of scales, inventories, and their proven assessment techniques. Abridged contents: "Assessment: What It Is and Why It Is Important," E. E. Filsinger; "The Interview in the Assessment of Marital Distress," S. N. Haynes and R. E. Chavez; "Capturing Marital Dynamics: Clinical Use of the Inventory of Marital Conflict," A. Hudgens et al.; "The Spouse Observation Checklist," R. L. Weiss and B. A. Perry; "Marital Interaction Coding

System-III," R. L. Weiss and K. J. Summers; "Couples Interaction Scoring System," C. I. Notarius et al.; "Behavioral Assessment for Practitioners," R. D. Conger; "The Dyadic Adjustment Scale," G. B. Spanier and E. E. Filsinger; "Clinical and Research Applications of the Marital Satisfaction Inventory," D. K. Snyder; "The Marital Communication Inventory," W. R. Schumm et al.; "The Marital Agendas Protocol," C. I. Notarius and N. A. Vanzetti; "Assessing Marital and Premarital Relationships: The PREPARE-ENRICH Inventories," D. G. Fournier et al.; "Clinical Applications of the Family Environment Scale," R. H. Moos and B. S. Moos; "The Family Inventory of Life Events and Changes," H. I. McCubbin and J. M. Patterson; "Family Adaptability and Cohesion Evaluation Scales," D. H. Olson and J. Portner; "Other Marriage and Family Questionnaires," G. Margolin and V. Fernandez.

Organizational Measurement

Price, James L. *Handbook of Organizational Measurement.* Lexington, MA: D. C. Heath, 1972.

Describes measures for 22 concepts about which there is the greatest agreement among organizational researchers. Selection of the measures was derived from seven criteria that include reliability, validity, and ease of administration. Each measure is discussed under such headings as description, definition, data collection, computation, validity, reliability, comments, source, and further sources. Additional readings are appended. This is the book that organizational researchers should consult first in designing their research.

Kegan, Daniel L. *Scales/RIQS: An Inventory of Research Instruments.* Evanston, IL: Northwestern University, Technological Institute, 1970.

This inventory contains 360 instruments measuring variables relevant to organizational theory. For each instrument the information is fully computer stored and retrievable. Requests from users can be handled without charge or at minimum cost. The following information is stored: author, reference, date, where instrument was used, reliability and validity, variables measured, comments by author or person depositing the item in Scales/RIQS. Total length of entries is usually 100 to 150 words. A useful working tool for researchers prepared to make their own judgments of adequacy.

Indik, B. P., M. Hockmeyer, and C. Costore. *A Compendium of Measures of Individuals, Groups and Organizations Relevant to the Study of Organizational Behavior.* Technical Report No. 16, Nour-404. New Brunswick, NJ: Rutgers, The State University, 1968.

A file of several hundred measures can be assessed by writing Dr. Bernard P. Indik, Graduate School of Social Work, Rutgers University, New Brunswick, NJ 08903. A nominal fee is charged to cover photocopying and other costs. The variables covered are reviewed in B. P. Indik and F. K. Berrien, *People, Groups, and Organizations* (New York: Teachers College Press, 1968).

Personality and Motivation

Buros, Oscar Krisen. *The Eighth Mental Measurements Yearbook.* Highland Park, NJ: Gryphon, 1978.

The Buros Series of Mental Measurements Yearbooks dates from 1938 and has become the reference work in the field. The reader with particular interest in personality measures should consult *Personality Tests and Review* (Highland Park, NJ: Gryphon, 1970), which includes 513 personality measures. Each test is briefly described with a complete bibliography. A variety of supporting indexes makes the user's task easy. Historical trend data are provided showing numbers of published references for each test over the last 30 years. Numerous other compendia of special instruments are described and analyzed by Dale G. Lake, Mathew B. Miles, and Ralph B. Earle, Jr., in *Measuring Human Behavior* (pp. 341-87). These should be consulted especially by researchers in education and personality.

Chun, Ki-Taek, Sydney Cobb, and John R. P. French, Jr. *Measures for Psychological Assessment: A Guide to 3000 Original Sources and Their Applications.* Ann Arbor: University of Michigan, Institute for Social Research, 1975.

Compilation of annotated references to social science measures. The work grew out of an effort to build a comprehensive, computerized national repository of social science measures. The first of the volume's two major sections lists the original sources for each of 3,000 instruments of attitude measurement. The applications section cites and annotates all studies in which each measure was subsequently used. The entries were obtained through a search of 26 measurement-related journals in psychology and sociology from the period 1960-70. Author and descriptor indices are included to facilitate the use of these major sections.

Webb, Eugene J., Donald T. Campbell, Richard D. Schwartz, and Lee Sechrest. *Unobtrusive Measures: Nonreactive Research in the Social Sciences.* Chicago: Rand McNally, 1966.

Discusses measures not obtained by interview or questionnaire. The measures are observational in nature, and thus do not require the cooperation of a respondent and do not themselves contaminate the response.

Child Development

Johnson, Orval G. *Tests and Measurements in Child Development: Handbook II.* San Francisco: Jossey-Bass, 1976.

Very comprehensive (1,327 pages) inventory of psychological tests for children.

Walker, Deborah K. *Socioemotional Measures for Preschool and Kindergarten Children.* San Francisco: Jossey-Bass, 1973.

A specialized inventory of measures for children of kindergarten age and younger.

Mental Measures

Buros, O. K. *Tests in Print II.* Highland Park, NJ: Gryphon, 1974.

A comprehensive bibliography of tests for use in education, psychology, and industry. Updated from 1961 printing.

Comrey, A. L., T. E. Backer, and E. M. Glaser. *A Sourcebook for Mental Health Measures.* Los Angeles: Human Interaction Research Institute, 1973.

Goldman, B. A., and J. C. Busch. *Directory and Unpublished Experimental Mental Measures.* Vol. 2. New York: Human Sciences Press, 1978.

Mental and personality tests, with bibliographies for both. Updated from 1974 printing by Behavioral Publications, New York.

Drug Abuse

Ferneau, E. W., Jr. *Drug Abuse Research Instrument Inventory.* Cambridge, MA: Social Systems Analysts, 1973.

Aids in locating measures relevant for drug abuse studies. The inventory contains a list of instruments with no descriptive or psychometric information. Six categories of instruments classify attitudes, effects of drugs, characteristics of abusers, access and extent, knowledge about drugs, and drug program evaluation.

Gerontology

Mangen, David J., and Warren A. Peterson, eds. *Research Instruments in Social Gerontology.* Vol. 1, *Clinical and Social Psychology*; Vol. 2, *Social Roles and Social Participation*; Vol. 3, *Health, Program Evaluation, and Demography.* Minneapolis: University of Minnesota Press, 1982-83.

Marquis Academic Media. *Sourcebook on Aging.* 2nd ed. Chicago: Marquis Who's Who, 1979.

Contains a wide range of source material.

Women and Women's Issues

Beere, Carole A. *Women and Women's Issues: A Handbook of Tests and Measures.* San Francisco: Jossey-Bass, 1979.

The recent explosion of interest in the study of women and women's issues has produced literally hundreds of new tests and measures—instruments for investigating sex roles; sex stereotypes; women's roles as spouse, parent, and employee; attitudes toward women including equal rights, abortion, and sexuality. This encyclopedic handbook contains 235 tests selected for reliability, validity, extent of use, and ease of administration. Each test has the following description: title and author of the instrument, year first published, what the instrument measures, with whom it can be used, sample items from the test, directions for administering and scoring, background or test development, data on reliability and validity, source from which the complete instrument is available, notes and comments on the use of the test, and bibliographic data on studies that have used the instrument.

Shaver, Phillip and Clyde Hendrick. *Review of Personality and Social Psychology Annual.* Vol. 7, *Sex and Gender.* Newbury Park, CA: Sage, 1987.

Follows research of Sandra L. Bem, *Gender Scheme Theory and the Romantic Tradition* (pp. 251-271). Bem is the author of the *Sex Role Inventory Professional Manual* (Palo Alto, CA: Consulting Psychologists Press, 1981). This is a 60-item self-report instrument used to assess both sex typing and androgyny. Considerable research has been carried out by Bem and others. A bibliography appears in *Sex and Gender.* See especially S. L. Bem, "Gender Schema Theory: A Cognitive Account of Sex Typing," *Psychological Review* 88: 354-364.

Warren, Carol A. B. *Gender Issues in Field Research.* Newbury Park, CA: Sage, 1988.

Specialized Journal

Gender & Society, official publication of Sociologists for Women in Society. Editor: Judith Lorber, Graduate Center and Brooklyn College, CUNY.

This journal emphasizes theory and research and aims to advance both the study of gender and feminist scholarship. Published by Sage Publications, 2455 Teller Rd., Newbury Park, CA, 91320.

CONTENT TABLES FOR MICHIGAN INSTITUTE FOR SOCIAL RESEARCH ON OCCUPATIONAL, POLITICAL, AND SOCIAL PSYCHOLOGICAL SCALES   6.L.6

6.L.6.a. Contents of John P. Robinson, Robert Athanasiou, and Kendra B. Head, *Measures of Occupational Attitudes and Occupational Characteristics* [1]

1. Introduction
2. Research on Work and Worker in the United States (Kimmel)
3. Occupational Norms and Differences in Job Satisfaction: A Summary of Survey Research Evidence (Robinson)
   - Blauner's Review
   - Gurin, Veroff and Feld Mental Health Study
   - Kilpatrick, Cummings and Jennings Study
   - Wilensky's Labor-Leisure Study of Detroit
   - Converse and Robinson Meaning-of-Time Study
   - Some Further Data on Related Issues
   - Summary and Conclusions
4. Job Attitudes and Occupational Performance: A Review of Some Important Literature (Athanasiou)
   - Relation Between Attitudes and Performance
   - Previous Literature Reviews
   - Effects of Specific Factors on Satisfaction as a Dependent Variable
   - Organizational Structure Variables
   - Satisfaction as an Independent Variable
   - The Use of Occupational Interest Inventories
   - Conclusions
5. General Job Satisfaction Scales
   1. Job Description Index (Smith et al. 1963)
   2. Index of Job Satisfaction (Kornhauser 1965)
   3. Factors for Job Satisfaction and Job Dissatisfaction (Dunnette et al. 1966)
   4. SRA (Employee) Attitude Survey (1951 and 1966)
   5. IRC Employee Attitude Scales (Carlson et al. 1962)
   6. Index of Employee Satisfaction (Morse 1953)
   7. Job Satisfaction Scale (Johnson 1955)
   8. Job Dimensions Blank (Schletzer 1965)
   9. Job Satisfaction Index (Brayfield and Rothe 1951)
   10. Job Satisfaction (Hoppock 1935)

      11. Tear Ballot (Kerr 1948)
      12. Employee Morale Scale (Woods 1944)
      13. Work Satisfaction and Personal Happiness (Noll and Bradburn 1968)
  6. Job Satisfaction for Particular Occupations
      1. Need Fulfillment Questionnaire for Management (Porter 1962)
      2. Managerial Job Attitudes (Harrison 1960)
      3. Job Attitudes and Job Satisfaction of Scientists (Hinrichs 1962)
      4. Attitudes of Scientists in Organizations (Pelz and Andrews 1966)
      5. Job Satisfaction Inventory (Twery et al. 1958)
  7. Satisfaction with Specific Job Features
      1. Supervisory Behavior Description (Fleishman 1957)
      2. Attitude toward the Supervisor (Nagle 1953)
      3. Satisfaction with Supervisor (Draper 1955)
      4. Attitudes toward the Supervisor (Schmid et al. 1957)
      5. Employee Opinion Survey (Bolda 1958)
      6. Need Satisfaction in Work (Schaffer 1953)
      7. About Your Company (King 1960)
      8. Group Morale Scale (Goldman 1958)
  8. Factors from Some Multidimensional Analysis of Job Satisfaction (Peay and Wernander)
  9. Concepts Related to Job Satisfaction
      1. Indices of Alienation (Aiken and Hage 1966)
      2. Alienation from Work (Pearlin 1962)
      3. Job-Related Tension (Kahn et al. 1964)
      4. Job Motivation Index (Patchen 1965)
      5. Identification with the Work Organization (Patchen 1965)
      6. Defining Dimensions of Occupation (Pearlin and Kohn 1966)
      7. Meaning of Work Scales (Guion 1965)
      8. Meaning of Work (Tausky 1968)
  10. Occupational Values
      1. Occupational Values Scales (Kilpatrick et al. 1964)
      2. Occupational Values (Rosenberg 1957)
      3. Faith-in-People Scale (Rosenberg 1957)
      4. Scale of Inner- and Other-Directedness (Bowers 1966)
      5. Inner-Other Social Preference Scale (Kassarijian 1962)
      6. Career-Oriented Occupational Values (Marvick 1954)
      7. Career Orientation in the Federal Service (Slesinger 1961)
  11. Leadership Styles
      1. Leadership Opinion Questionnaire (Stogdill and Coons 1957)
      2. The SRA Supervisory Index (Schwartz 1956)
      3. Leadership Practices Inventory (Nelson 1955)
      4. How Supervise? (File and Remmers 1948)
      5. A Proverbs Test for Supervisor Selection (Reveal 1960)
      6. A Managerial Key for the CPI (Goodstein and Schrader 1963)
      7. Managerial Scale for Enterprise Improvement
      8. Organizational Control Graph (Tannenbaum 1966)
      9. Profile of Organizational Characteristics (Likert 1967)
  12. Other Work-Relevant Attitudes
      1. Union and Management Attitudes toward Each Other (Stagner et al. 1958)
      2. IRC Union Attitude Scale (Uphoff and Dunnette 1956)
      3. Index of Pro-Labor Orientation (Kornhauser 1965)
      4. Pro-Labor Attitude Error-Choice Tests (Hammond 1948)
      5. Attitudes toward Labor and Management (Wechsler 1950)
      6. Attitudes toward Working for the Government (Aalto 1956)
      7. Attitudes toward Working for the Government (Kilpatrick et al. 1964)
      8. Attitude toward Automation (Rosenberg 1962)
      9. Attitude toward Employment of Older Persons (Kirchner 1954)
      10. Opinions about Work of the Mentally Ill (Streuning and Etron 1965)
  13. Vocational Interest Measures
      1. Selective Word Memory Test (Edel and Tiflin 1965)
      2. Job Analysis and Interest Measure (Walther 1961)
      3. Sales Attitude Check List (Taylor 1960)
      4. Work Attitude Key for the MMPI (Tydlaska and Mengel 1953)

Note

1. Published by the Institute for Social Research, University of Michigan, 1969.

6.L.6.b Contents of John P. Robinson, Jerrold G. Rusk, and Kendra B. Head, *Measures of Political Attitudes* [1]

Age
Sex
Religion
Ethnic and Racial Groups
Geographic Region
Voting Behavior and Partisan Affiliation

3. Liberalism-Conservatism
    1. Ideological Agreement with Goldwater (Selznick and Steinberg 1966)
    2. Conservatism Scale (McClosky 1958)
    3. Social Attitudes Scales (Kerlinger 1963)
    4. Conservatism-Radicalism Battery (Centers 1949)
    5. Political-Economic Conservatism (PEC) Scale (Adorno et al. 1950)
    6. Inventory of Social Attitudes (Eysenck 1947)
    7. Radicalism-Conservatism Scale (Nettler and Huffman 1957)
    8. Liberalism-Conservatism Scale (Wright and Hicks 1966)
    9. Liberalism-Conservatism Scale (Kerr 1952)
    10. Liberalism-Conservatism Scale (Hartmann 1938)
    11. C-R Opinionnaire (Lentz 1935)
    12. Personage Admiration (Lentz 1939)
    13. Situation-Response Survey (Pace 1939)
    14. Harper's Social Beliefs and Attitudes Test (Boldt and Stroud 1934)
    15. Politico-Economic Radicalism-Conservatism (Sanai and Pickard 1949)
    16. Radicalism-Conservatism and Social Mobility (Hetzler 1954)
    17. Concern with Progress (Morgan, Sirageldin, and Baerwaldt 1966)

4. Democratic Principles
    1. Willingness to Tolerate Nonconformists (Stouffer 1955)
    2. Scale of Perception of Internal Communist Danger (Stouffer 1955)
    3. Democratic and Anti-Democratic Attitudes (McClosky 1964)
    4. Attitude toward Democratic Principles (Prothro and Grigg 1960)
    5. Attitude toward Communists (Schonbar 1949)
    6. Attitude toward Civil Liberties (Noble and Noble 1954)

5. Domestic Government Policies
    1. Domestic Social Welfare Scale (Campbell et al. 1960)
    2. Attitude toward Government (Opinion Research Corporation 1960)
    3. Big Business-Minded Scale and Socialism-Planning Scale (Rosenberg 1957)
    4. Attitude toward Socialized Medicine (Kubany 1953)
    5. Attitude toward Government (Banerjee 1962)

6. Racial and Ethnic Attitudes
    1. Prejudice and Rationality (Schuman and Harding 1964)
    2. Identification with the Underdog (Schuman and Harding 1963)
    3. Pro-Integration Scale (Sheatsley 1966)
    4. Multifactor Racial Attitude Inventory (Woodmansee and Cook 1967)
    5. Social Distance Scale (Bogardus 1959)
    6. Ethnocentrism Scale (Adorno et al. 1950)
    7. Racial Stereotype Index (Matthews and Prothro 1966)
    8. Racial Identification Index (Matthews and Prothro 1966)
    9. Community Race Relations Ratings (Matthews and Prothro 1966)
    10. Dimensional Attitude Measure toward Negroes (Wrightsman 1962)
    11. Prejudice toward Negroes (Westie 1953)
    12. Paired Direct and Projective Questionnaires (Getzels and Walsh 1958)
    13. Attitude toward the Negro (Hinckley 1932)

7. International Affairs
    1. Foreign Policy Goals and Personal Values (Scott 1960)
    2. Isolationism Scale (McClosky 1967)
    3. Internationalism Scale (Campbell et al. 1960)
    4. Interpretations of Government Policy Scale (Wrightsman 1963)
    5. World-Minded Attitudes (Sampson and Smith 1957)
    6. Internationalism-Nationalism Scale (Levinson 1951)
    7. Attitude toward United States and Russian Actions (Oskamp and Hartry 1965)
    8. Problems and Goals of the U.S. Government (Hefner and Robinson 1964)

9. Criteria for Foreign Aid (Hefner and Robinson 1964)
10. Internationalism (Lutzker 1960)
11. Attitudes toward World Affairs (Schimberg 1949)
12. Pro-Russia Error-Choice Test (Hammond 1948)

8. Hostility-Related National Attitudes
   1. International Reactions Scale (Christiansen 1959)
   2. National Patriotism Scale (Christiansen 1959)
   3. International Hostility Inventory (Grace 1949)
   4. Attitudes toward War (Putney 1962)
   5. Vietnam Policy Scales (Verba et al. 1967)
   6. Ideological Militancy-Pacifism Scale (Dombrose and Levinson 1950)
   7. Hostility in International Relations (Helfant 1952)
   8. Nationalism (Ferguson 1942)
   9. Nationalistic Attitude Changes (Stagner and Osgood 1946)
   10. Attitude toward War (Day and Quackenbush 1942)
   11. Attitude toward War (Stagner 1942)

9. Community-Based Political Attitudes
   1. Community Attitude Scale (Bosworth 1954)
   2. Local-Cosmopolitan Scale (Dye 1966)
   3. Cosmopolitanism Scale (Jennings 1965)
   4. Localism-Cosmopolitanism Scale (Dobriner 1958)
   5. Acquaintanceship Scale (Schultze 1961)
   6. Attitude toward Sources of Power (Haer 1956)

10. Political Information
    1. Political Information Scale (Matthews and Prothro 1966)
    2. Information about Foreign Countries (Robinson 1967)
    3. Information about the Far East (Robinson 1967)
    4. Index of Issue Familiarity (Campbell et al. 1960)

11. Political Participation
    1. Political Participation Scale (Matthews and Prothro 1966)
    2. Political Activity Index (Woodward and Roper 1950)
    3. Index of Political Participation (Campbell et al. 1954)
    4. Political Participation (Robinson 1952)
    5. Public Affairs Opinion Leadership (Katz and Lazarsfeld 1955)
    6. Opinion Leadership (Lazarsfeld, Berelson, and Gaudet 1944)
    7. Opinion Leadership Scale (Rogers 1962)

12. Attitudes toward the Political Process
    1. Subjective Political Competence Scale (Almond and Verba 1963)
    2. Various Other Attitudes about the Political System (Almond and Verba 1963)
    3. Index of Ratio of Support (McClosky et al. 1960)
    4. Political Involvement (Campbell et al. 1960)
    5. Political Efficacy (Campbell et al. 1954)
    6. Sense of Citizen Duty (Campbell et al. 1954)
    7. Extent of Issue Orientation (Campbell et al. 1954)
    8. Issue Involvement (Campbell et al. 1954)
    9. Issue Partisanship (Campbell et al. 1954)
    10. Overall Index of Psychological Readiness for Participation (Matthews and Prothro 1966)
    11. Sense of Civic Competence Index (Matthews and Prothro 1966)
    12. Party Image Score (Matthews and Prothro 1966)
    13. Attitude Dimension of Political Norms (Litt 1963)
    14. Political Cynicism and Personal Cynicism (Agger, Goldstein, and Pearl 1961)

13. Individual Questions from Survey Research Center Election Studies
    1. Party Identification
    2. Attitudes toward Government Principles
    3. Domestic Policy
    4. Civil Rights and Racial Attitudes
    5. International Attitudes
    6. War-Related Attitudes

Note

1. Published by the Institute for Social Research, University of Michigan, 1969.

6.L.6.c Contents of John P. Robinson and Phillip R. Shaver, *Measures of Social Psychological Attitudes* [1]

20. Body Cathexis Scale (Second and Jourard 1953)
21. Self-Report Inventory (Bown 1961)
22. Twenty Statements (Who Am I? Who Are You?) Test (Kuhn and McPartland 1954; Bugental and Zelen 1950)
23. Social Self Esteem (Ziller 1969)
24. Personal Orientation Inventory (Shostrum 1968)
25. Barclay Classroom Climate Inventory (Barclay 1972)
26. Self-Concept Stability (Brownfain 1952)
27. Measure of Self-Consistency (Gergen and Morse 1967)
28. Personality Integration Scale (Duncan 1966)
29. Inferred Self-Concept Scale (McDaniel 1969)
30. Unconscious Self-Evaluation Technique (Beloff and Beloff 1959)
31. Other Self-Concept Measures

4. Internal-External Locus of Control (A. P. MacDonald, Jr.)
   1. Intellectual Achievement Responsibility Questionnaire (Crandall et al. 1965)
   2. Modified Intellectual Achievement Responsibility Questionnaire (Ringelheim et al. 1970)
   3. Locus of Control Scale for Children (Nowicki and Strickland 1972)
   4. Bialer-Cromwell Children's Locus of Control Scale (Bialer 1960)
   5. Multidimensional IE Scale (Gurin et al. 1969)
   6. Rotter's Internal-External Locus of Control Scale (Rotter 1966)
   7. Abbreviated 11-Item Rotter IE Scale (Valecha 1972)
   8. James' Internal-External Locus of Control Scale (James 1957)

5. Alienation and Anomia (John Robinson)
   1. Anomy Scale (McClosky and Schaar 1956)
   2. Anomia Scale (Srole 1956)
   3. Powerlessness (Neal and Seeman 1962)
   4. Political Alienation (Olsen 1969)
   5. Alienation via Rejection (Streuning and Richardson 1965)
   6. Purpose-in-Life Test (Crumbaugh 1968)
   7. Alienation Scale (Dean 1961)
   8. Alienation (Middleton 1963)
   9. Political Alienation (Horton and Thompson 1962)
   10. Alienation (Nettler 1957, 1964)
   11. Anomie Scale (Hyman et al. 1960)
   12. Helplessness (Gamson 1961)
   13. Alienation (Davids 1955)
   14. Alienation within a Social System (Clark 1959)

6. Authoritarianism, Dogmatism, and Related Measures (Phillip Shaver)
   1. The California F Scale (Adorno et al. 1950)
   2. A New F Scale (Webster et al. 1955)
   3. Forced Choice F Scale (Berkowitz and Wolkon 1964)
   4. Forced Choice F Scale (Schuman and Harding c. 1962)
   5. Balanced F Scale (Athanasiou 1968)
   6. Shortened F for Political Surveys (Janowitz and Marvick 1953)
   7. Four-Item F Scale (Lane 1955)
   8. Ten-Item F Scale (Survey Research Center 1952)
   9. Pensacola Z Scale (Jones 1957)
   10. Fascist Attitudes Scale (Stagner 1936)
   11. Unlabeled Fascist Attitudes (Edwards 1941)
   12. Anti-Semitism (Levinson and Sanford 1944)
   13. Traditional Family Ideology (Levinson and Huffman 1955)
   14. Status-Concern Scale (Kaufman 1957)
   15. Rigidity Scale (Rehfisch 1958)
   16. RAPH Scale (Meresko et al. 1954)
   17. Rigidity Scale (Wesley 1953)
   18. Intolerance of Ambiguity (Budner 1962)
   19. Intolerance of Ambiguity (Martin and Westie 1959)
   20. Desire for Certainty Test (Brim 1955)
   21. Ethnocentric Democracy Scale (Hyman et al. 1962)

Note

1. Published by the Institute for Social Research, University of Michigan; revised edition, 1973.

SHAW AND WRIGHT COMPILATION OF SCALES FOR THE MEASUREMENT OF ATTITUDES

6.L.7

The following list of 175 attitude inventories and scales has been arranged so that researchers may examine common areas of interest. Categories include family and child, education, work and occupations, economics, religion, welfare, politics and law, nationalism and internationalism, war, mass media, race and ethnicity, health and medicine, and personal interaction and customary behavior. All scales may be examined in Marvin E. Shaw and Jack M. Wright, *Scales for the Measurement of Attitudes* (New York: McGraw-Hill, 1967).

Family and Child

A Survey of Opinions Regarding the Bringing Up of Children (Itkin 1952)
A Survey of Opinions Regarding the Discipline of Children (Itkin 1952)
Attitude Toward Discipline Exercised by Parents (Itkin 1952)
Attitude Toward the Freedom of Children (Koch, Dentler, Dysart, and Streit 1934)
Attitude Toward Parental Control of Children's Activities (Stott 1940)
Attitude Toward Self-Reliance (Ojemann 1934)
Attitude Toward the Use of Fear as a Means of Controlling the Behavior of Children (Ackerley 1934)
Attitude Toward Parents Giving Sex Information to Children Between the Ages of Six and Twelve (Ackerley 1934)
Attitude Toward Older Children Telling Lies (Ackerley 1934)
The Traditional Family Ideology (TFI) Scale (Levinson and Huffman 1955)
Familism Scale (Bardis 1959)
The Family Scale (Rundquist and Sletto 1936)
Attitudes Toward Parents (Form F) (Itkin 1952)
Parents' Judgment Regarding a Particular Child (Itkin 1952)
Attitudes Toward Feminism Belief Patterns Scale (Kirkpatrick 1936)
The Open Subordination of Women (OSW) Scale (Nadler and Morrow 1959)
Attitude Toward Divorce (Thurstone 1929-34)
A Divorce Opinionnaire (Hardy 1957)
Attitude Toward Birth Control (Wang and Thurstone 1931)
Birth Control (Scale BC) Scale (Wilke 1934)
[Panos D. Bardis has constructed "A Pill Scale: A Technique for the Measurement of Attitudes Toward Oral Contraception," *Social Science* (January 1969): 35-42.]

Education

Attitude Toward Teaching (F. D. Miller 1934)
Attitude Toward Teaching as a Career (Merwin and DiVesta 1960)
Attitude Toward Physical Education as a Career for Women (Drinkwater 1960)
Attitude Toward Education (Mitchell 1941)

Opinionnaire on Attitudes Toward Education (Lindgren and Patton 1958)
Education Scale (Kerlinger and Kaya 1959)
Attitude Toward Intensive Competition in Team Games (McCue 1953)
Attitude Toward Intensive Competition for High School Girls (McGee 1956)
The Education Scale (Rundquist and Sletto 1936)
Attitude Toward Education (Glassey 1945)
Attitudes Toward Mathematics (Gladstone, Deal, and Drevdahl 1960)
Revised Math Attitude Scale (Aiken and Dreger 1961)
Physical Education Attitude Scale (Wear 1955)
Counseling Attitude Scale (Form 1955)
Problem-Solving Attitude Scale (Carey 1958)
High School Attitude Scale (Remmers 1960)
Knowledge About Psychology (KAP) Test (Costin 1963)
An Attitude Scale for Measuring Attitude Toward Any Teacher (Hoshaw 1935)
Attitude Toward Any School Subject (Silance and Temmers 1934)
A Scale to Study Attitudes Toward College Courses (Hand 1953)
Attitudes Toward School Integration (IA) Scale Form I (Greenberg, Chase, and Cannon 1957)
Faculty Morale Scale for Institutional Improvement (AAUP 1963)
Attitude Toward College Fraternities (Banta 1961)

Work and Occupations

Attitude Toward Labor Scale (Newcomb 1939)
IRC (Industrial Relations Center) Union Attitude Questionnaire (Uphoff and Dunnette 1956)
Scale for Management Attitude Toward Union (Stagner, Chalmers, and Derber 1958)
About Your Company (Storey 1955)
Scales to Measure Attitudes Toward the Company, Its Policies, and Its Community Contribu-
    tions (Riland 1959)
Attitude Toward Earning a Living (Hinckley and Hinckley 1939)
Attitude Toward Work Relief as a Solution to the Financial Depression (Hinckley and Hinckley
    1939)
Attitude Toward Farming (Myster 1944)
Attitude Toward Any Practice (Bues 1934)
Attitude Toward Any Home-Making Activity (Kellar 1934)
Attitude Toward Any Occupation (H. E. Miller 1934)
Attitude Toward the Supervisor (AS) Scale (Schmid, Marsh, and Detter 1956)
The Superior-Subordinate (SS) Scale (Chapman and Campbell 1957)
Attitude Toward the Supervisor (Nagle 1953)
Attitude Toward Employment of Older People (Kirchner, Lindblom, and Patterson 1952)
The (Work Related) Change Scale (Trumbo 1961)
Attitudes Toward Dependability: Attitude Scale for Clerical Workers (Dudycha 1941)
Attitudes Toward Legal Agencies (Chapman 1953)
Older Workers Questionnaire (Tuckman and Lorge, 1952)

Economics

Attitude Toward the Tariff (Thurstone 1929-34)
Distribution of the Wealth (DW) Scale (Wilke 1934)

Religion

Religionism Scale: Scale I (Ferguson 1944)
Belief Pattern Scale: Attitude of Religiosity (Kirkpatrick 1949)
Religious Ideology Scale (Putney and Middleton 1961)

The Religious Attitude Inventory (Ausubel and Schpoont 1957)
The Religion Scale (Bardis 1961)
Religious Belief Scale (Martin and Nichols 1962)
A Survey of Attitudes Toward Religion and Philosophy of Life (Funk 1958)
The Existence of God Scale (Scale G) (Wilke 1934)
Attitude Toward God: The Reality of God (Chave and Thurstone 1931)
Attitude Toward God: Influence on Conduct (Chave and Thurstone 1931)
Attitude Toward the Church (Thurstone 1931)
Attitudes and Beliefs of LDS Church Members Toward Their Church and Religion (Hardy 1940)
Attitude Toward Sunday Observance (Thurstone 1929-34)
An Attitude Scale Toward Church and Religious Practices (Dynes 1955)
Relation Between Religion and Psychiatry Scale (Webb and Kobler 1961)
Attitudes Toward Evolution (Thurstone 1931)
Death Attitudes Scale (Kalish 1963)

Welfare

Attitude Toward Receiving Relief (Hinckley and Hinckley 1939)
Humanitarianism Scale: Scale II (Ferguson 1944)
Belief Pattern Scale: Attitude of Humanitarianism (Kirkpatrick 1949)
Attitudes Toward Any Proposed Social Action (Remmers 1934)

Politics and Law

The Conservatism-Radicalism (C-R) Opinionnaire (Lentz 1935)
The Florida Scale of Civic Beliefs (Kimbrough and Hines 1963)
The Economic Conservatism Scale (Rundquist and Sletto 1963)
Questionnaire on Politico-Economic Attitudes (Sanai 1950)
Conservatism-Radicalism (C-R) Battery (Centers 1949; Case 1963)
Tulane Factors of Liberalism-Conservatism Attitude Value Profile (Kerr 1936)
The Social Attitudes Scale (Kerlinger 1965)
Political and Economic Progressivism (PAP) Scale (Newcomb 1943)
Public Opinion Questionnaire (Edwards 1941)
Attitude Toward the Law (Katz and Thurstone 1931)
The Law Scale (Rundquist and Sletto 1936)
The Ideological and Law-Abidingness Scale (Gregory 1939)
Attitudes Toward Law and Justice (Watt and Maher 1958)
Attitude Toward the Constitution of the United States (Rosander and Thurstone 1931)
Attitude Toward Capital Punishment (Balogh and Mueller 1960)
Attitude Toward Capital Punishment (Thurstone 1932)
Attitude Toward Punishment of Criminals (Wang and Thurstone 1931)
Attitude Toward the Police (Chapman 1953)
Attitude Toward Probation Officers (Chapman 1953)
Juvenile Delinquency Attitude (JDA) Scale (Alberts 1962)
The Academic Freedom Survey (Academic Freedom Committee, American Civil Liberties Union 1954)

Nationalism and Internationalism

Internationalism Scale (Likert 1932)
Nationalism Scale: Scale III (Ferguson 1942)
A Survey of Opinions and Beliefs About International Relations (Helfant 1952)

The Internationalism-Nationalism (IN) Scale (Levinson 1957)
The Worldmindedness Scale (Sampson and Smith, 1957)
The Patriotism (NP) Scale (Christiansen 1959)
Attitude Toward Patriotism Scale (Thurstone 1929-34)
Attitude Toward Communism Scale (Thurstone 1929-34)

War

The Peterson War Scale (Thurstone 1929-34)
A Scale of Militarism-Pacifism (Droba 1931)
Attitude Toward Defensive, Cooperative, and Aggressive War (Day and Quackenbush 1942)
Attitude Toward War (Scale W) (Wilke 1934)
A Scale for Measuring Attitude Toward War (Stagner 1942)
A M-P Opinion Scale (Gristle 1940)

Mass Media

Attitude Toward Newspapers (Rogers 1955)
Attitude Toward Freedom of Information (Rogers 1955)
Attitude Toward Movies (Thurstone 1930)
Semantic Distance Questionnaire (Weaver 1959)

Race and Ethnicity

Attitude Toward the Negro (Hinckley 1932)
Attitude Toward Segregation Scale (Rosenbaum and Zimmerman 1959)
The Segregation Scale (Peak, Morrison, Spivak, and Zinnes 1956)
The Desegregation Scale (Kelly, Ferson, and Holtzman 1958)
Attitude Toward Accepting Negro Students in College (Grafton 1964)
Attitude Toward Negroes (Thurstone 1931)
Attitude Toward the Negro Scale (Likert 1932)
The Anti-Negro Scale (Steckler 1957)
Negro Behavior Attitude Scale (Rosander 1937)
Experiences with Negroes (Ford 1941)
The Social Situations Questionnaire (Kogan and Downey 1956)
The Anti-Semitism (A-S) Scale (Levinson and Sanford 1944)
Attitude Toward Jews Scale (Harlan 1942)
Opinions on the Jews (Eysenck and Crown 1949)
The Anti-White Scale (Steckler 1957)
Attitude Toward the German People (Thurstone 1931)
Attitude Toward the Chinese (Thurstone 1931)
A Survey of Opinions and Beliefs About Russia: The Soviet Union (Smith 1946)
Ethnocentrism Scale (Levinson 1949)
Intolerant-Tolerant (IT) Scale (Prentice 1956)
The Social Distance Scale (Bogardus 1925)
Scale to Measure Attitudes Toward Defined Groups (Grice 1935)

Health and Medicine

Attitudes Toward Physical Fitness and Exercise (Richardson 1960)
Opinions About Mental Illness (Cohen and Struening 1959)
The Socialized Medicine Attitude Scale (Mahler 1953)

Attitude Toward Censorship Scale (Rosander and Thurstone 1931)
Attitudes Toward Mentally Retarded People (Bartlett, Quay, and Wrightsman 1960)
The Custodial Mental Illness Ideology (CMI) Scale (Gilbert and Levinson 1956)
The Psychotherapy-Sociotherapy Ideology (PSI) Scale (Sharaf and Levinson 1957)
Medication Attitudes (Gorham and Sherman 1961)
Attitude to Blindness Scale (Cowen, Underberg, and Verrillo 1958)
Attitude Toward Disabled People (ATDP) Scale (Yuker, Block, and Campbell 1960)
Medical Information Test (Perricone 1964)
Attitude Toward Menstruation (McHugh and Wasser 1959)
The Vivisection Questionnaire (Molnar 1955)
Attitudes Toward Mental Hospitals (Souelem 1955)
Attitudes Relating to the State Hospital (Pratt, Giannitrapani, and Khanna 1960)

Personal Interaction and Customary Behavior

The Self-Others Questionnaire (Phillips 1951)
Acceptance of Self and Others (Berger 1952)
People in General (Banta 1961)
An Intimacy Permissiveness Scale (Christensen and Carpenter 1962)
Old People (OP) Scale (Kogan 1961)
The "CI" Attitude Scale (Khanna, Pratt, and Gardiner 1962)
The Chivalry (C) Scale (Nadler and Morrow 1959)
Attitudes Toward Old People (Tuckman and Lorge 1953)
Attitude Toward Any Institution (Kelley 1934)
Attitude Toward the Aesthetic Value (Cohen 1941)
The Competitive Attitude (CA) Scale (Lakie 1964)
The "Value Inventory" (Jarrett and Sherriffs 1953)
Attitude Toward Safe Driving: Siebrecht Attitude Scale (Siebrecht 1941)

HOW RESEARCHERS MAKE THEIR OWN SCALES: AN ACTIVITY OF LAST RESORT

6.L.8

A researcher constructs a new scale if, (a) after a literature search, he or she does not find a scale that fits the problem, or (b) the available scale is poorly constructed. Any constructed scale should be good enough to invite future researchers to use it in the ongoing process of accumulating research findings. Putting some items together and assigning arbitrary weights to them does not produce this kind of scale. The acceptable scale will cover an important theoretical construct and meet the following evaluative criteria.

Checklist of Evaluative Criteria for Assessing a Scale[1]

I. Item Construction Criteria
   1. Selected items reflect accurately the universe of items encompassed by the variable to be measured.
   2. Items are simply worded so that they can be easily understood by the population to whom the scale is to be given.

3. Item analysis demonstrates that each item is closely related to the selected variable. Techniques of item analysis include the following:
   a. Item-intercorrelation matrix.
   b. Factor analysis.
   c. Complex multidimensional analysis.
   d. Item correlation with external criteria.
4. Pretest and eliminate or revise undesirable items.

II. Response Set Criteria
   1. Avoid response set due to acquiescence (subservient syndrome).
      Techniques:
      a. Discard simple affirmative items.
      b. Switch occasional response alternatives between positive and negative.
      c. Use "forceful choice" items: Two or more replies to a question are listed, and the respondent is asked to choose only one.
   2. Avoid response set due to social desirability (good impression syndrome).
      Techniques:
      a. Use forced-choice items in which the alternatives have been equated on the basis of social desirability ratings.
      b. Pretest items in social desirability, and drop or revise alternative pairings (or item pairings) that do not prove to be equated.
   3. Analyze and eliminate efforts of respondents to fake responses according to some image that the respondent wishes to convey.
   4. Analyze and eliminate spurious replies due to respondent's wanting to appear too consistent, to use few or many categories in replies, or to choose extreme alternatives.

III. Scale Metric Criteria
   1. Representative sampling: Sampling methods accurately produce a miniature population that reflects the universe under study.
   2. Adequate normative information: To understand the meaning of responses secured in research the constructed scale should provide the following:
      a. Mean scale score and standard deviation for the sample on which it was constructed.
      b. Means and standard deviations for certain well-defined groups.
      c. Item means and standard deviations.
   3. Reliability: A reliable scale measures consistently what it is supposed to measure. The term refers to three major criteria: (a) the correlation between the same person's score on the same items at two separate points in time; (b) the correlation between two different sets of items at the same time (these sets may be presented as "parallel forms" with items in a separate format or as a "split half" when all items are presented together); (c) the correlation between the scale items for all people who answer the items.

      It is widely agreed by experts that the test-retest index is the best measure of reliability. Many insist that measures b and c are actually indices of homogeneity and not *reliability*, which is a term commonly used in an ambiguous fashion. The test-retest reliability level may be approximated from indices of homogeneity, but there is no substitute for actual test-retest data.
   4. Homogeneity: A homogeneous scale "agrees with itself." The term refers to the internal consistency of a scale. This property is crucial in scale construction. Only a homogeneous scale presents a common attribute.
      Techniques:
      a. Split-half correlation.
      b. Parallel forms and interitem indices of internal homogeneity (Cronbach's alpha).
      c. Interitem correlation matrix.
      d. Guttman scaling technique.
   5. Validity: A valid scale measures what it is supposed to measure. Validity implies a predictive power beyond the immediate range of factors in the scale. The best test is the correlation achieved with an external criterion.
      Techniques:
      a. Discrimination of known groups.
      b. Double cross-validation.
      c. Multitrait, multimethod matrix.

d. Correlation of scale scores with one or more independent criteria of the phenomena being measured.

Note

1. These criteria are drawn largely from John P. Robinson, Robert Athanasiou, and Kendra B. Head, *Measures of Occupational Attitudes and Occupational Characteristics* (Ann Arbor: University of Michigan, Survey Research Center, 1969), 4-13.

MODELS OF MASTER SCALE CONSTRUCTION   6.L.9

Bureau of the Census. *Methodology and Scores of Socioeconomic Status.* Working Paper No. 15. Washington, DC: Government Printing Office, 1963.

Burgess, E. W., and Leonard Cottrell. *Predicting Success or Failure in Marriage.* Englewood Cliffs, NJ: Prentice-Hall, 1939.

Haller, Archibald O., and Irwin W. Miller. *The Occupational Aspiration Scale: Theory, Structure, and Correlates.* 2nd ed. Cambridge, MA: Schenkman, 1971.

Hemphill, John K. *Group Dimensions: A Manual for Their Measurement.* Research Monograph No. 87. Columbus: Ohio State University, Bureau of Business Research, 1956.

Inkeles, Alex, and Karen A. Miller. "Construction and Validation of a Cross-National Scale of Family Modernism." *International Journal of Sociology of the Family* 4 (August 1974): 127-47.

Inkeles, Alex, and David H. Smith. *Becoming Modern.* Cambridge, MA: Harvard University Press, 1974.

Newcomb, Theodore M. *Personality and Social Change: Attitude Formation in a Student Community.* New York: Dryden, 1943.

Reiss, Albert J., with O. D. Duncan, Paul K. Hatt, and C. C. North. *Occupations and Social Status.* Glencoe, IL: Free Press, 1961.

Rundquist, Edward A., and Raymond F. Sletto. *Personality in the Depression.* Minneapolis: University of Minnesota Press, 1936.

Schuessler, Karl. *Measuring Social Life Feelings.* San Francisco: Jossey-Bass, 1982.

Sewell, William H. *The Construction and Standardization of a Scale for the Measurement of the Socio-Economic Status of Oklahoma Farm Families.* Technical Bulletin No. 9. Stillwater: Oklahoma A&M College, Agricultural Experiment Station, 1940.

Thorndike, E. L. *Your City.* New York: Harcourt, Brace, 1939.

Treiman, Donald J. *Occupational Prestige in Comparative Perspective.* New York: Academic Press, 1977.

Warner, W. Lloyd, Marcia Meeker, and Kenneth Eells. *Social Class in America: A Manual of Procedure for the Measurement of Social Status.* Chicago: Science Research Associates, 1949.

Part 7

Research Proposal, Funding, Costing, Reporting, and Career Utilization

THE END PRODUCT OF RESEARCH designing is a proposal. The student setting forth on his or her first independent research and the professional with a lifetime of research achievement both face the same requirement. They must produce an acceptable proposal. Other professionals will critically examine the proposal and decide if it is acceptable. The planning and submission of proposals may take a year or more—always longer than expected. The competition for funds is often intense. In general, more proposals are rejected than accepted because of the quality of the proposals or the limited amount of funds. The researcher must know where the money is and develop the skill of research negotiation.

Section A, "The Research Grant Proposal," describes the preliminary planning of a proposal and offers a few useful hints that are especially appropriate to the evaluations of judges. A general outline of a research proposal follows.

Section B, "Research Funding," lists various guides to research agencies. Section B.1 lists major financing agencies of social science research and information providing guides to a search for research funding. Section B.2 is a description of current federal funding policy and behavioral science reactions. Section B.3 presents a selected list of federal government and private organizations offering fellowships and grants, with sources of more comprehensive listings. Section B.4 describes programs of particular relevance, including predoctoral and postdoctoral fellowships offered by the National Science Foundation, National Institute of Mental Health, Social Security Administration, and the U.S. Office of Education. Aside from university fellowships, the National Science Foundation and the U.S. Department of Health and Human Services are the major sources of competitive fellowships in the social sciences.

Section C, "Research Costing," discusses a difficult task. Most researchers have never had training in this aspect of research, and they acquire their knowledge by trial and error. Most researchers drastically underestimate the time and effort required to complete their proposals. There are many unforeseen hindrances and delays.

The "Guide to Research Costing," Section C.1, requires detailed cost data before it can be used. The researcher must secure the going wage rate for interviewers, the cost of transportation, the rates for machine calculation, and so forth. These cannot be provided here, since they vary by time and place. However, the guide alerts the social scientist to factors that must be taken into account in planning the cost of the research. It should be remembered that overhead costs are not shown. Universities usually demand substantial overhead costs, ranging from 30% to 50% of the total contract.

Guides C.2 and C.3 provide costing estimates for the mail questionnaire, the telephone survey, and the personal interview. The Guide to Research Budgeting in Section C.4 is the form used by the National Science Foundation. This guide provides all items in the budget that may be required in a research project. If the college or university has a contract research officer, the researcher should seek that person's help. The researcher can easily overlook some important items or misjudge the expenditures required. Most universities have strict regulations governing all expenditures, and the researcher must learn about them and follow them.

Finally, Section D, "Research Reporting," discusses plans for the report. This is the "payoff" for the researcher. Section D.1 indicates criteria that judges will commonly use in appraising the publishing possibilities of the report. Section D.2 provides a final check on the research design at the point where it counts—transmission to the profession.

Generally, two or three professional examiners will be using similar criteria in determining their recommendations for acceptance or rejection of the research report. Recently the editors of the five journals sponsored by the American Sociological Association reported an average acceptance of 15%. How to handle rejection, the most common experience, is something that is never taught to researchers. It is probably one of the most significant adjustments they must make. They must learn to utilize the criticism of their work and try to meet objections if possible. Often what is needed is better writing. The best advice for all researchers is to rewrite and resubmit. There are scores of journals. Try to get in the best, but above all, try to get published.

Bettina J. Huber has updated a compilation of sociological journals. The list has been supplemented with Ulrich's *International Periodicals Directory.* This is the "Guide to Sociological Journals" presented in Section D.3.

Section D.4 is devoted to publishing in books and journals. Norval Glenn lists, according to prestige, 63 journals used frequently by sociologists. Section D.5 describes where sociologists get published; D.6 explains how sociologists get published.

A professional research life includes professional communication and reporting to professional meetings. Section D.7 describes the leading sociological associations and the role they play in professional socialization. Section D.8 presents a calendar of annual meetings of various sociological societies and some related societies in the social sciences. Although these meetings change officers and meeting places each year, the national offices can supply current information. Common patterns of topical sections for sociology, psychology, and anthropology are shown.

Guides D.9 and D.10 list journals sponsored by the American Sociological Association and the American Psychological Association, respectively. Sections D.11

through D.15 are guides to major journals in political science and public administration, anthropology, education, and business, and those used by journalism and communication researchers.

Section E, "Career Utilization," describes the final act of research activity—research put into practice. A selected bibliography is appended. Sections E.1, E.2, and E.3 provide guides to sociology job applicants and other behavioral science applicants facing the job market.

The Research Grant Proposal

Preliminary Planning

The purpose of a research proposal is to provide a statement establishing the objectives and scholarly significance of the proposed activity, the technical qualifications of the project director/principal investigator and his or her organization, and the level of funding required.

The proposal should contain sufficient information to persuade both the professional staff of the agency and members of the scholarly community that the proposed activity is sound and worthy of support under the agency's criteria for the selection of projects or under specific criteria specified in the applicable proposal-generating mechanism. The proposal should be both succinct and complete.

Writing a proposal, like writing any other request, is a challenge in effective persuasion. Every agency has its own method for selecting proposals it wants to fund. Whatever the method used, individuals at the agency will be reading the proposal to determine how it fits into their funding pattern and how cogently the applicant has presented it.

There are a few hints that are especially appropriate to the evaluations of judges:

1. A clearly written abstract is especially helpful. The review committee may be examining many proposals over a busy weekend. An abstract makes it possible to grasp, define, and retain the proposal for a comparative judgment.
2. A statement of previous work serves to validate the ability of the applicant to get into his or her research quickly without false starts and to carry out the proposed research successfully.
3. The availability of the research population is important. An indication from pretests that show that the population is responsive adds weight.
4. The availability of research facilities is also important. If matching funds or supporting facilities are needed, it is important for the committee to know that they are forthcoming.
5. Clear, professionally defined budgets over the time period are imperative. The committee must be convinced that the size of the grant is appropriate and that the money will be spent wisely. They want to know if the applicant is realistic.
6. Supporting evidence that convinces the committee the applicant is able and will carry the research to completion is especially important. Such evidence may include a biographical sketch, a statement of ongoing research, current support letters of recommendation, and published material relevant to the proposal. (See Sections 7.C.1 and 7.C.4.)

Each funding agency has its own rules for grant applications. Some seek very short statements, perhaps limited to 5-10 pages; others prefer longer statements. Some provide forms that prescribe precisely what is wanted; others encourage latitude. The researcher must bend to meet the requirements.

Whatever the differences between agencies or foundations, all are greatly concerned with elements of the research design. In general, they include those shown in this volume in Section 2.1, "Basic Research Outline Guide for the Design of a Social Research Problem."

Guide for a Research Grant Proposal

Writing the Proposal

When an agency has a set of instructions and/or forms, the researcher should use them and follow them rigorously. In the absence of any instructions, this general outline of parts of a proposal may be helpful:

1. title page
2. abstract
3. table of contents
4. introduction
5. background
6. description of proposed research
7. evaluation
8. description of relevant institutional resources
9. list of references
10. vitae
11. personnel
12. budget
13. other items

Title page. Many sponsoring agencies have their own format for the title page, which is usually self-explanatory. In the absence of that requirement, the face page should include most of the following items: the agency to which the proposal is to be submitted; the name and address of the institution submitting the proposal; the title of the proposed work; the name, title, phone number, and address of the project director; the period of time; the requested amount; the date of the proposal and endorsements. Minimum endorsement should be arranged for signature of the project director and the authorizing official of the submitting institution.

Abstract. Though the abstract appears at the front of the proposal, it is written last, as a concise summary of the material presented in the proposal. The abstract usually includes the major objectives of the proposal and the procedures to be used to meet these objectives. These materials are condensed to a page or less (specific lengths are sometimes given in guidelines), and if the proposal is awarded, the abstract will be printed in national data banks. The abstract serves several purposes: (a) The reviewer usually reads it first to gain a perspective of the study and its expected significance; (b) the reviewer uses it as a reference to the nature of the study when the project comes up for discussion; (c) it will sometimes be the only part of the proposal that is read by those reviewing a panel's recommendation or the field readers' consensus. With these many uses, it is important that the abstract be prepared with the utmost care and that objectives and procedures are paraphrased using general but precise statements. Key concepts presented in the body of the proposal are highlighted in the abstract to alert the reviewer to look for them in the body of the proposal.

Table of contents. A brief proposal does not necessarily need a table of contents. The convenience of the reader should be the guiding consideration. When included, the table of contents should list all major parts and divisions of the proposal.

Introduction. The introduction should be clear to the layperson, should give enough background to enable the reader to place the proposal in a context of common knowledge, and should show how the proposed activities will advance the field or be important to the solution of the problem.

Background. Information should be presented here to review what has been accomplished in the field, to demonstrate the researcher's competence in connection with the problem, and to show what he or she will add to the existing field of knowledge.

Description of proposed research. The proposal should present a detailed description of the work to be undertaken. The objectives and significance should be clearly and specifically stated. Research methods or operating procedures should be detailed, and the general plan of work, including the broad design of experiments, should be outlined.

Evaluation. The proposal should provide an evaluation component designed to determine how effective the program is in reaching the objectives established and in solving the problems dealt with. If possible, the evaluation should also be designed to allow for appropriate changes and adjustments in a program as it proceeds.

Description of relevant institutional resources. Available facilities and major items of equipment especially adapted to the proposed project should be described. These facilities could include libraries, computer centers, other recognized centers, and any special but relevant equipment.

List of references. This list is desirable only if the proposal contains six or more references. Otherwise, references can be inserted in the text.

Vitae. Most sponsoring agencies require a curriculum vitae and list of publications for each faculty member and senior professional staff member in the project.

Personnel. All personnel who will participate in the proposed project should be identified by name, title, and the expected amount of time to be devoted to the project. Unfilled positions should be marked "vacant" or "to be selected." If the individuals involved have exceptional qualifications that would merit consideration in the evaluation of the proposal, this information should be included.

Budget. A checklist for budget items should include the following:[1]

salaries and wages
  academic personnel during academic year
  academic personnel during summer
  research associates
  research assistants
  technicians
  secretarial staff
  hourly help
fringe benefits
consultants
  fees
  travel expenses
equipment, including installation and freight
supplies
  chemicals and glassware
animals and animal supplies
photocopying costs
office supplies
film
travel
  domestic
  foreign
alterations and renovation
other costs
trainee costs
publication of reports
telephone and telegraph
equipment rental
data processing
postage
subcontracts
indirect costs

For further assistance, see the NSF research grant proposal budget in Section 7.C.4.

If a grant research officer is available in the researcher's organization, his or her help and counsel should be sought. The preparation of a budget requires all the planning skill that can be mustered. Nothing but problems await for failures at this phase of the research.

Other items. Space does not permit the publication of a complete proposal. Those interested in more detailed advice on proposal writing are referred to D. R. Krathwohl's *How to Prepare a Research Proposal.*[2]

After writing the proposal, the researcher should imagine that he or she is a member of a review board. What questions would the proposal raise? The researcher should review the specifications for sociological report rating presented in Section 7.D.1 and ask, Would I receive a superior rating on all specifications? If not, he or she should start again.

Pitfalls and What You Can Do About Them

No one can foresee all the contingencies and conflicts that may arise in a research project. The sociology of research is a neglected area of study. There is not enough space in journals to detail all the problems encountered in each piece of published research, but it can be assumed that every researcher encounters unanticipated problems. Some problems can be so severe that it is not possible to complete the research. In other cases the end result is agonizing conflict until a resolution is reached. A few writings are now available to provide the kind of forewarnings that may be helpful.[3] And certain procedures can be followed to protect the researcher when dealing with a granting agency.

One important matter is the protection of the researcher against the claims of the granting or monitoring agent after the research is under way. For example, there is the issue of confidentiality of the data. One researcher found himself pressed by a granting agency to display his data after he had promised complete confidentiality to his respondents. He will not accept future grants without an explicit legal statement on confidentiality.[4]

The use of respondents in the research design may cause special problems when the research calls for concealing from the respondents certain treatments needed to conduct a successful test of the hypotheses. This has usually emerged as a legal question in the last decade because of abuses with research on the physical and psychological effects of drugs. Even in sociological research, however, the question of psychological injury may arise in such areas as role playing, group dynamics, and stress research. Criminologists and educational sociologists are directly involved because of their work with special groups. Sex researchers are also on warning. The U.S. Department of Health and Human Services has expressed its concern with research on human subjects in areas involving their privacy, the need for informed consent, and protection against physical, psychological, sociological, or legal risks. If the grant proposal involves human subjects, the research applicant is required to do the following:

1. Describe the requirements for a subject population and explain the rationale for using in this population special groups such as prisoners, children, the mentally disabled, or groups whose ability to give voluntary informed consent may be in question.
2. Describe and assess any potential risks—physical, psychological, social, legal, or other—and assess the likelihood and seriousness of such risks. If methods of research

create potential risks, describe other methods, if any, that were considered and why they will not be used.

3. Describe consent procedures to be followed, including how and where informed consent will be obtained.
4. Describe procedures (including confidentiality safeguards) for protecting against or minimizing potential risks and an assessment of their likely effectiveness.
5. Assess the potential benefits to be gained by the individual subject, as well as benefits that may accrue to society in general as a result of the planned work.
6. Analyze the risk-benefit ratio.[5]

Statements submitted by the applicant are subject to review by the local organization's review committee. The responsibility then shifts to the organizational review committee and the HHS staff and advisory committees. Any changes in the researcher's procedures must be reported.[6] Obviously, this means that all parties should get their agreements in hand so that no barriers can be thrown in the path of the researcher once the work is under way.

A guarantee of publication rights should be clearly spelled out. The problem can arise with any contract research agency of the federal government. Most applied research contracts contain either a "rights in data" clause or a copyright clause. Two propositions, partially incompatible, must be reconciled. One states that everything done under a government contract belongs to the government, to do with as it sees fit. The second holds that the work done under a government contract should be freely available to the public. In actual practice this usually means that the government reserves exclusive license over the product of the study but interposes no objection to the publishing of results by the investigator as long as he or she *first secures the permission of the contracting officer.*

Academic researchers must recognize that grants and contracts have two different sets of rules with respect to publication. The grant carries the right of publication; indeed, the National Science Foundation assures researchers that it encourages publication and distribution of the results of research conducted under its grants. Under contract research, investigators cannot go off on their own and publish articles from their studies.[7] Many applied research agencies are uninterested in generating publications. Instead, the agency will insist upon reports that fit the specifications that meet its internal needs. It is up to the investigator to work out an understanding on publication rights. In dealing with a military funding agency, this is especially important; it is possible that the military will clamp a censorship or restraining order on research publication as the uncertain winds of military security blow across the Pentagon.

If none of the possible sources of conflict has frightened you against the research life, you are ready to enter or renew the exciting quest for knowledge. If you are an "academic," you will probably seek "clean" money—that is, a grant to do basic research with no strings attached. But you may find such a posture automatically removes you from many research opportunities. Basic research amounts to only about one-third of federal spending for applied research.[8]

Notes

1. Office of Research and Graduate Development, *Research Policy Manual* (Bloomington: Indiana University, July 1978).

2. D. R. Krathwohl, *How to Prepare a Research Proposal*, 2nd ed. (Syracuse, NY: Syracuse University Book Store), 1977.

3. Margaret Archer, ed., *Problems of Current Sociological Research*, vol. 22. *Current Sociology: The Journal of the International Sociological Association* (special issue) (1974); Gunnar Boalt, *The Sociology of Research* (Carbondale: Southern Illinois University Press, 1969); Richard O'Toole, ed., *The Organization, Management, and Tactics of Social Research* (Cambridge, MA: Schenkman, 1971). Refer also to Section 3.5 of this volume, "The Shaping of Research Design in Large-Scale Group Research."

4. Robert F. Boruch and Joe S. Cecil, *Assuring the Confidentiality of Social Research Data* (Philadelphia: University of Pennsylvania Press, 1979); Sandra C. Reese, "Retention of Raw Data: A Problem Revisited," *American Psychologist* (August 1973): 723; R. W. Johnson, "Retain the Original Data," *American Psychologist* 19 (1964): 350-51; L. Wolins, "Responsibility for Raw Data," *American Psychologist* 17 (1962): 657-58.

5. These regulations follow from sec. 212 of the National Research Act, Public Law 93-348, and were made effective July 1, 1974.

6. Robert T. Bower and Priscilla de Gasparis, *Ethics in Social Research: Protecting the Interests of Human Subjects* (Washington, DC: Bureau of Social Science Research, 1978); Paul Davidson Reynolds, *Ethical Dilemmas and Social Science Research: An Analysis of Moral Issues Confronting Investigators in Research Using Human Participants* (San Francisco: Jossey-Bass, 1979); Tom A. Beauchamp, Roth R. Faden, R. Jay Wallace, Jr., and LeRoy Walters, *Ethical Issues in Social Research* (Baltimore: Johns Hopkins University Press, 1982).

7. Keith Baker, "A New Grantsmanship," *American Sociologist* 10 (November 1975): 212-13.

8. Ibid., 206.

Research Funding

MAJOR FINANCING AGENCIES OF SOCIAL SCIENCE RESEARCH   7.B.1

Federal Agencies

National Science Foundation
National Research Council
2101 Constitution Ave.
Washington, DC 20418

U.S. Department of Justice
633 Indiana Ave., NW
Washington, DC 20531

U.S. Department of Health and Human Services
National Institute on Aging
NIH Bldg. 31, Rm. 4C32
9000 Rockville Pike
Bethesda, MD 20892

National Endowment for the Humanities
1100 Pennsylvania Ave., NW
Washington, DC 20506

U.S. Department of Health and Human Services
National Institute of Mental Health
Parklawn Bldg., 5600 Fisher's Ln.
Rockville, MD 20857

U.S. Department of Education
555 New Jersey Ave., NW
Washington, DC 20209

U.S. Department of Labor
8000 Patrick Henry Bldg.
601 D St., NW
Washington, DC 20213

U.S. Department of Defense
5001 Eisenhower Ave.
Alexandria, VA 22333

Private Foundations

Social Science Research Council
230 Park Ave.
New York, NY 10017

Rockefeller Foundation
1153 Avenue of the Americas
New York, NY 10036

Russell Sage Foundation
633 Third Ave.
New York, NY 10017

Ford Foundation
320 E. 43rd St.
New York, NY 10017

Carnegie Corporation of NY
437 Madison Ave.
New York, NY 10022

The Big Five by Staff Size and Assets[1]

- Ford Foundation: staff members, 560; assets, $5.3 billion
- PEW Charitable Trusts: staff members, 50; assets, $2.3 billion
- Robert Wood Johnson Foundation: staff members, 103; assets, $1.9 billion
- Lilly Endowment: staff members, 21; assets, $1.7 billion
- Carnegie Corporation of New York: staff members, 53; assets: $637 million

Note

1. Sources: Chronicle Reporting and *The Foundation Directory*.

7.B.2   FOUR MAJOR SOURCES OF FUNDING INFORMATION

Guide to Federal Funding for Social Scientists

This book was researched and written by the Consortium of Social Science Associations (COSSA), a Washington advocacy group serving the major professional associations in the social and behavioral sciences. The book was edited by Susan D. Quarles and published by the Russell Sage Foundation in 1986.

Social scientists now have an important new resource to aid them in locating scarce federal research dollars. The myriad offices, agencies, and departments of the federal government are major supporters of research in the social sciences, but until now, no comprehensive guide to federal grants, contracts, and fellowships in these fields has been available.

COSSA's *Guide to Federal Funding* describes more than 300 federal programs of interest to researchers in the social and behavioral sciences and related areas of the humanities, including funding priorities, application guidelines, and examples of funded research. The book is based on extensive interviews with federal research managers and has been carefully tailored for the greatest possible relevance to the concerns of social and behavioral scientists.

The *Guide* is useful for both new scholars and experienced researchers. Of particular interest for sociologists are descriptions of numerous funding sources in the Departments of Education and Justice, lesser known programs in the Departments of Health and Human Services and Commerce, and fellowships and research opportunities in the independent agencies. In addition, an entire chapter is devoted to discussion of the federal statistical agencies.

Introductory essays include "Structure and Organization of the Social Sciences in the Federal Funding Arena," "Academics and Contract Research," "Social and Behavioral Science Support at NSF: An Insider's View," and "The National Institutes of Health: Extramural Funding and the Peer Review Process," all written by experts in these areas.

This guide is now available at COSSA, 1200 17th St., NW, Ste. 520, Washington, DC 20036 ($19.95). Or consult the reference department at your library.

Guide to Research Support

The third edition of this volume, published by the American Psychological Association, appeared in 1987; it was edited by E. Ralph Dusek, Virginia E. Holt, Marti E. Burke, and Alan G. Kraut. This is a comprehensive handbook of behavioral science research funding covering 180 federal programs and 55 nonfederal organizations that support behavioral science research. Application procedures are specified clearly, and the book gives practical advice on how to prepare successful proposals. Research interests of each program are well indexed, and a telephone directory for all federal employees is included.

This guide is available from the American Psychological Association, P.O. Box 2710, Hyattsville, MD 20784 ($30.00). Or consult the reference department at your library.

Annual Register of Grant Support

This is a definitive reference book that is published annually. The volume for 1987-88 has 2,679 entries representing billions of dollars to potential grant seekers. It is published by National Register Publishing Co., Wilmette, IL 60091. It is a very expensive volume—consult your reference library.

The Foundation Directory and Supplements

Information compiled by the Foundation Center is available to the public through national collections in three cities, regional collections in 39 states, publications and services, and membership in an associates program.

The national collections of source materials on the foundations and their grant-making activities includes the basic records filed by every private foundation with the Internal Revenue Service, annual reports, and the Foundation Center's standard reference works. Also available are books, reports, and guides relating to the foundation field. Information has been compiled on about 26,000 American foundations.

The New York collection also includes reference materials on foundations in other countries, as well as information on the international activities of American foundations.

The national collections are located at the following addresses:

The Foundation Center	The Foundation Center	Donors' Forum
888 Seventh Ave.	1001 Connecticut Ave., NW	208 South LaSalle St.
New York, NY 10019	Washington, DC 20036	Chicago, IL 60604

In addition, 49 regional collections are located in 39 states. These collections contain the Center's standard reference works, some recent books and reports on foundations, foundation annual reports on film, and a smaller collection of foundation information returns limited usually to the state in which the collection is located. Selected computer listings of grants data on topics of broad general interest are available for consultation. A listing of the regional collections is available from the New York office.

Anyone who visits the national or regional collections may consult all of the published sources and film records, including subject lists of recent foundation grants, without charge. Reference staff is available to assist visitors.

In addition to the collections, the Foundation Center produces the publications listed below, which are available in the reference sections of many college, university, and public libraries. They may also be purchased from the Columbia University Press.

- *The Foundation Directory and Supplements* contain information on the more than 4,000 largest foundations in the country. These foundations account for about 90% of all foundation assets and 80% of all grants given in this country. The Foundation Center also plans to publish regional directories in order to provide information on smaller foundations.
- *The Foundation Grants Index* is published bimonthly in *Foundation News*. The *Index* reports grants by state in which foundation is located, by recipient, and by subject matter.
- *Corporate Foundation Profiles* also provides valuable information about recent foundation interests and awards.
- *Foundation News* is published by the Council on Foundations, Inc., 888 Seventh Ave., New York, NY 10019.

7.B.3   THE ART AND SCIENCE OF GRANTSMANSHIP

The procurement of grants and contracts is a game that many universities and research institutes play. For many of these organizations, research funding is big business, amounting to millions of dollars yearly. A large part of the funding of graduate students rests upon a steady flow of federal research grants.

The term *grantsmanship* is sometimes used to refer to a personality attribute (like *showmanship*): the ability to persuade and influence others to trade their research dollars for a promised performance. At other times, it refers to an elaborate institutional mechanism (e.g., a Division of Research and Development) erected solely to influence the flow of research dollars to a given institution. Prestige and power are thrown into the operation in a competitive game to get more and more. Individual researchers who stay outside these contests often pay the price: underfunding. Those who get in pay another kind of price: large amounts of time and energy expended in cultivating contacts and writing proposals. It is also not commonly understood that the recipient of a large research grant is almost automatically converted from a research investigator to a research administrator. He or she gives up field research for the recruiting of personnel, drafting of reports, and supervision of professional and staff members and the endless flow of paper between the financial offices of the university and the granting agency. (Of course, well-funded researchers get the right people to assume much of the administrative responsibility.)

Since grantsmanship is part art and part management, no one can teach it with high efficiency. Experience is the best teacher. And it is necessary to have experience in both grants and contracts. Clive Veri provides experienced guidance for successful pursuance of grants.[1] Keith Baker describes ways to get a contract that he calls "the new grantsmanship" and by which he means "contractmanship."[2] Dave Krathwohl and George R. Allen provide detailed advice for proposal writing in general.[3] Craig Smith and Eric Skjei have produced a creative guide to the grants system promising to reveal how to find funders, how to write convincing proposals, and how to make grants work.[4] All successful grantsmen agree that it is not feasible to wait until a request for applications is published to begin formulating a research proposal.

Scientists should familiarize themselves with a variety of agencies that could have an interest in their research, in anticipation of future funding competition. There is no substitute for developing and maintaining good contacts with experienced researchers, disciplinary and other professional associations, and federal program managers.

Federal Government Contract Research

Any academic institution seriously interested in contract research should have somebody who reads *Commerce Business Daily* and refers relevant announcements to interested faculty immediately. Subscriptions to *Commerce Business Daily* may be obtained from the Superintendent of Documents, U.S. Government Printing Office, Washington, DC 20402. The *Federal Register* is an excellent secondary resource.

Other Sources on Grantsmanship and Proposal Writing

Grantsmanship

Durek, E. Ralph, V. Holt, M. E. Burke, and Alan G. Kraut. *Guide to Research Support.* 2nd ed. Hyattsville, MD: American Psychological Association, 1988.

Lauffer, Armand. *Grantsmanship.* 2nd ed. Beverly Hills, CA: Sage, 1983.

———. *Grantsmanship and Fund Raising.* Beverly Hills, CA: Sage, 1984.

Leskes, Andrea, ed. *Peterson's Grants for Graduate Students 1986-88.* Princeton, NJ: Peterson's Guides, 1986.

Margolin, Judith. *The Individual's Guide to Grants.* New York: Plenum, 1983.

Marquis Academic Media. *Grantsmanship: Money and How to Get It.* 2nd ed. Chicago: Marquis Academic Media, 1978.

Read, Patricia E., ed. *Foundation Fundamentals: A Guide for Grantseekers.* 3rd ed. New York: Foundation Center, 1986.

Shellow, Jill R. *The Grantseekers Guide: A Directory for Social and Economic Justice Projects.* Chicago: National Network of Grantmakers, 1982.

Western Center on Domestic Violence. *Dollars and Sense: A Community Fundraising Manual for Women's Shelters and Other Non-Profit Organizations.* San Francisco: Western Center on Domestic Violence, 1983.

White, Virginia P. *Grants: How to Find Out About Them and What to Do Next.* New York: Plenum, 1975.

Proposal Writing

Coleman, William, et al. *A Casebook of Grant Proposals in the Humanities.* New York: Neal-Schuman, 1982.

Kalish, Susan E., ed. *The Proposal Writer's Swipe File: 15 Winning Fund Raising Proposals—Prototypes of Approaches, Styles and Structures.* 3rd ed. Washington, DC: Taft Corp., 1984.

Kiritz, Norton J. *Program Planning and Proposal Writing.* Expanded version. Los Angeles: Grantsmanship Center, 1980.

Locke, Lawrence F., Warren W. Spirduso, and Stephen Silverman. *Proposals That Work: A Guide for Planning Dissertations and Grant Proposals.* Newbury Park, CA: Sage, 1987.

White, Virginia, ed. *Grant Proposals That Succeeded.* New York: Plenum, 1983.

Notes

1. Clive C. Veri, "How to Write a Proposal and Get It Funded," *Adult Leadership* 16 (March 1968): 318-20, 343-44.
2. Keith Baker, "A New Grantsmanship," *American Sociologist* 10 (November 1975): 206-18.

3. David R. Krathwohl, *How to Prepare a Research Proposal,* 2nd ed. (Syracuse, NY: Syracuse University Bookstore, 1977): George R. Allen, *The Graduate Student's Guide to Theses and Dissertations: A Political Manual for Writing and Research* (San Francisco: Jossey-Bass, 1973).

4. Craig W. Smith and Eric W. Skjei, *Getting Grants* (New York: Harper & Row, 1980).

7.B.4   PROGRAMS OF PARTICULAR RELEVANCE, INCLUDING PREDOCTORAL AND POSTDOCTORAL FELLOWSHIPS

7.B.4.a The National Science Foundation

Information may be obtained by writing to the foundation, and informal communication with the foundation's staff is encouraged prior to formal submission of a proposal. Among a variety of forms of foundation support, the activities of greatest interest to sociologists follow:

1. Grants for *basic scientific research,* or for related activities, such as research conferences, construction of specialized research facilities, and travel to selected meetings of international scientific organizations of major importance. In addition, social science dissertation research grants provide funds for research expenses (not stipends) in order to improve the quality and significance of dissertations and reduce the time required for their completion. All of these programs seek basic scientific understanding of behavioral and social processes and improved research methods. Support is provided for research that seeks to discover and test scientific generalizations. Criteria for the selection of research projects as approved by the National Science Board August 21, 1981, include (a) competent performance of the research, (b) intrinsic merit of the research, (c) utility or relevance of the research, and (d) effect of the research on the infrastructure of science and engineering.

2. *Computer research* including theoretical computer science, software systems, intelligent systems, and societal issues in computer science, including privacy and security, social and economic impact, and new directions in computer science and applications.

3. *Measurement methods and data resources.* Survey operations research; methods and models for the quantitative analysis of social data; improvements in the scientific adequacy and accessibility of social statistical data, including those generated by government as well as the academic research community; development and testing of new social indicators.

4. *Institutional programs.* NSF programs include support of small college faculty in research at large institutions; support for research workshops, symposia, publications and monographs, conferences, the purchase of scientific equipment for research purposes, the operation of specialized research facilities, and the improvement of research collections. For the past seven years the foundation has been encouraging working linkages between industry and universities in research activity (university cooperative research center).

5. *International cooperative research programs.* The areas of research supported are health sciences, natural sciences, energy, and social and behavioral sciences.

6. *Socioeconomic aspects of science and technology* are supported under the Division of Policy Research and Analysis. A special program of interest is Ethics and Values in Science and Technology (EVIST).

Social and Behavioral Science Support at NSF: An Insider's View

Felice J. Levine, Program Director, Law and Social Sciences Program, National Science Foundation [1]

The National Science Foundation is the most comprehensive source of federal support for research in the social and behavioral sciences in the United States. Whether based in universities, colleges, or research institutes, scholars pursuing the scientific study of social phenomena are encouraged to seek funding from NSF. No doubt, in an inherently competitive situation, applying for a grant can be quite a formidable task. The difficulty can be compounded, however, if there is an informational vacuum regarding how the system works, what is expected, what actually happens along the way, and why. The purpose of this essay is to minimize this source difficulty by providing an insider's view of the social and behavioral sciences at the Foundation and thus making more understandable what is inside the "black box."

The Role of NSF in Federal Research and Development

Mandated purpose. The National Science Foundation is unique among federal agencies in its singular commitment to the advancement of science. Established in 1950 as an independent agency in the Executive branch of the federal government, its primary mission is to encourage and preserve the health of all fields of science, including the social and behavioral sciences. Despite limited resources (commanding less than 5% of the total NSF budget), the social and behavioral sciences play a significant and vital role within the NSF family of science. With all programs having an "open window" for investigator-initiated research and with decisions based on full peer review, in large measure the strength of the social and behavioral science programs at NSF depends heavily on the richness of the ideas that are proposed for funding and the commitment of intellect and time exhibited by the scholarly community. In essence, while NSF is an agency of the federal government, its mandated purpose places it in and of the science community.

Structure of funding. The social and behavioral sciences are funded primarily through programs in the Divisions of Social and Economic Science, Behavioral and Neural Sciences, and Information Science and Technology—all in the Directorate for Biological, Behavioral, and Social Sciences. All programs are directed by program officers who are scholars in their respective fields. At NSF programs are the central vehicle for recommendations on the support of research. This substantial delegation of responsibility to programs embodies NSF's philosophy that the agenda of funding in science can best be set by active scientists in an area (i.e., by program officers' making funding recommendations based on the expert counsel of peer reviewers). Each fiscal year, once an appropriations bill or continuing resolution for NSF has been passed by Congress and signed by the President, programs are allocated operating budgets and each program director knows approximately what resources are available. Other, generally modest, opportunities for expansion of a program's resources include special initiatives, joint funding with other programs, other agency support via inter-agency transfers, and funds held in reserve at the division director level. Once program budgets are set by the division director, however, program directors generally know the parameters within which they can navigate for their fields.

Why Submit a Proposal?

Research costs money, and sometimes it is quite expensive. Therefore, scientists typically require additional resources to pursue their theoretical and empirical strands of research. In large measure, this is the fundamental reason for applying to NSF. Beyond this material "why," however, there are more subtle "whys" that deserve consideration. Drafting a proposal is itself part of the research process, for most people explicate their concepts, questions, and plans more fully when they are presenting them for others to examine. Also, the peer review system is an institutionalized vehicle for providing expert opinion on the strengths and weaknesses of a line of work before its initiation. The comments and critiques received by the applicant are usually informative and are important indicators of how the work may be received. Even reviews that seem unhelpful may reveal areas in the proposed work that are prone to confusion or open to misinterpretation. Thus, while from one vantage the peer review process seems to be a hurdle (i.e., something to be transcended as a predicate to funding), from another it is an important opportunity for the investigator to gain genuine feedback from other scholars.

Guidance for the Preparation of Unsolicited Proposals to NSF

An "unsolicited proposal" is prepared by a principal investigator and submitted by an institution on its own initiative without a formal written solicitation from NSF. Contact with NSF program personnel prior to proposal preparation is encouraged to help determine if preparation of a formal submission is appropriate.

The provisions apply to all programs and related activities, such as foreign travel, conferences, symposia, and research or education equipment and facilities. Sources of additional information on these related activities are available from appropriate NSF programs.

Formal application blanks are not used in the research grants program. However, a desired cover page is requested as given in Appendix I of the NSF *Guide to Grants for Scientific Research*. Information to be included is as follows:

1. name and address of institution
2. name, address (if different), and department of principal investigator(s) (telephone numbers helpful)
3. title of proposed research project
4. desired starting date (the earliest date on which funds would be required)
5. time period for which support is requested
6. abstract of description of proposed research project
7. description of proposed research project, including objectives and research design
8. bibliography of related research
9. description of facilities available for the research
10. biographical information for senior personnel, and for junior personnel when appropriate, including bibliographies
11. budget
12. statement of current support and pending applications for this and other research by the principal investigator(s)

This should be used as a checklist when submitting an application. Twenty complete copies of the proposal are necessary. One copy should be signed by the principal investigator, by the department head, and by an official authorized to sign for the institution.

Information about program deadlines and target dates for proposals appears in the *NSF Bulletin*, issued monthly except July and August; copies may be obtained from the Editor, *NSF Bulletin*, NSF, Washington, DC 20550. General information about NSF programs may be found in *Guide to Programs*, available from the Forms and Publications Unit of NSF.

Additional information about special requirements of other NSF programs may be obtained from the appropriate Foundation program offices.

For information about the NSF grant process, proposers and grantees should refer to the NSF *Grant Policy Manual*, NSF 77-47 (as revised), or to Chapter VI of Title 45 of the *Code of Federal Regulations*. The manual is a compendium of basic NSF policies and procedures for use by the grantee community and NSF staff. NSF grants are subject to the specific provisions contained in the grant instruments, including Grant General Conditions. The manual is available only by subscription (currently $13.00 domestic and $16.25 foreign) from the Superintendent of Documents, Government Printing Office, Washington, DC 20402. GPO subscription prices and terms are subject to change without notice.

Copies of the Grant General Conditions may be obtained from Forms and Publications, National Science Foundation, Washington, DC 20550.

NSF Publications of General Interest

1. "About the National Science Foundation" (brochure)
2. *NSF Bulletin* (published monthly except in July and August)
3. *Publications of the National Science Foundation*
4. *NSF Annual Report*
5. *Guide to Programs*
6. *NSF Films* (booklet)
7. *Mosaic* (magazine)

Single copies of these publications are available from Forms and Publications, NSF, Washington, DC 20550; phone (202) 357-7861.

Further information on proposals, target dates, and review may be obtained from individual program staff listed below.

NSF Staffing and Programming, Social and Economic Science Division

Director, Roberta Balstad Miller: (202) 357-7966
Deputy Director, James H. Blackman: (202) 357-7966
Senior Scientist, Murray Aborn: (202) 357-7913
Administrative Officer, Geraldine E. Griffin: (202) 357-7930
Center Manager/Staff Assistant, Bonney H. Sheahan: (202) 357-7697

Program Directors

Decision, Risk & Management Science, Arie Y. Lewin: (202) 357-7569
Economics, Daniel H. Newlon and Lynn A. Pollnow: (202) 357-9675
Geography & Regional Science, Ronald F. Abler: (202) 357-7326

History & Philosophy of Science, Ronald J. Overmann: (202) 357-9677

Law & Social Sciences, Felice J. Levine: (202) 357-9567

Measurement Methods & Data Improvement, Murray Aborn: (202) 357-7913

Political Science, Frank P. Scioli, Jr.: (202) 357-7534

Risk Assessment, Vincent T. Covello: (202) 357-7417

Sociology, Murray A. Webster, Jr.: (202) 357-7802

NSF Directorate for Biological, Behavioral, and Social Sciences

Division of Social and Economic Science

The Division of Social and Economic Science supports fundamental research in economics, geography and regional science, history and philosophy of science, law and social sciences, political science, sociology, and measurement methodology. Interdisciplinary studies also are eligible. The goal of the division is to support research that will contribute to the basic understanding of how social organizations and institutions function and change and how human interaction and decision making are influenced by social conditions and institutional arrangements.

Programs within the division also consider proposals for doctoral dissertation support, research conferences, the acquisition of specialized research equipment, and data resource development.

The programs of widest concern to social and behavioral scientists are discussed in turn below.

The *Political Science Program* supports research designed to understand the political processes by which societies coordinate their activities through governments. Research areas supported include studies of governmental institutions and their effects on social life, investigations of the effects of structural factors on political participation and effectiveness, and explorations of how political processes are modified in response to economic and social change. Frank P. Scioli, Jr., and Lee Sigelman are program directors; (202) 357-9406.

The *Sociology Program* supports research on problems of human social organization, demography, and the processes of institutional change. The program provides support for theoretical investigations aimed at improving the explanation of fundamental social processes. Included is research on decision making, organization change, social movements, urban development, resource allocation, reward distribution, and the social construction of norms. Target dates for regular proposals are August 15 and January 15. For information, program announcements, and application forms, contact Program Director Murray A. Webster, Jr., Sociology Program, National Science Foundation, 1800 G St., NW, Washington, DC 20550; (202) 357-7802.[2]

The *Anthropology Program* supports all topics, geographic areas, and methodologies involving research in cultural and social anthropology, archaeology, and physical anthropology. Included are studies of human origins and the interactions of population culture, and environment. John E. Yellen is program director of Archaeology and Physical Anthropology; Stuart M. Plattner is associate program director of Social and Cultural Anthropology; (202) 347-7804.

The *Law and Social Sciences Program* funds social scientific research on law and lawlike systems of rules. Illustrative of the areas receiving support are studies of the processes that enhance or diminish the impact of law; causes and consequences of variations and changes in legal institutions; personal, social, and cultural factors affecting the use of law; dynamics and effects of dispute processing and alternative means of dispute resolution; determinants of decision making in legal forums and contexts; and conditions and processes that create transformations between formal legal rules and law in action. The program encourages theoretical development, empirical study, and methodological improvements aimed at advancing scientific knowledge about law, human behavior as it relates to law, and the dynamics of normative ordering in complex societies. Felice J. Levine is the program director; (202) 357-9567.

The *Measurement Methods and Data Improvement Program* supports projects to improve the scientific adequacy and accessibility of social data, with emphasis on improving survey data and on increasing the research usefulness of federal statistical data. Projects designed to enhance the reliability, validity, or accessibility of existing data sources, to develop and make available new data sources, and/or to create analytic tools of broad utility are considered. The program also includes measurement and data projects focused on the development of social indicators and systems of social accounts. Murray Aborn is the program director; (202) 375-7913

The *Decision and Management Science Program* at NSF supports basic research on decision making, management, and processes for improving practice. The focus is on the social and behavioral aspects of sociotechnical systems. Arie Y. Lewin is the program director; (202) 357-7569.

Division of Behavioral and Neural Sciences

The *Social and Developmental Psychology Program* supports laboratory and field research in all areas of human social behavior, including social perception, attitude formation and change, and social influence. The program includes research on developmental processes in children and adults, with emphasis on social, personality, and emotional development. Research to improve the conceptual and methodological base of social and developmental psychology is encouraged. Jean B. Intermaggio is the program director; (202) 347-9485.

Fellowships and Other NSF Programs

Graduate Fellowship Program

NSF graduate fellowships are awarded for study or work leading to master's or doctoral degrees in the mathematical, physical, biological, engineering, and social sciences, and in the history and philosophy of science. Awards are not made in law, education, or business fields; in history or social work; for work leading to medical, dental, or public health degrees; or for study in joint science-professional degree programs. Applications are encouraged from minorities, women, the physically handicapped, and members of other groups underrepresented in science and engineering.

Graduate Fellowships

Address and Phone
National Science Foundation Fellowship Office
National Research Council
2101 Constitution Ave.
Washington, DC 20418
(202) 334-2872

Program Description

Approximately 540 three-year graduate fellowships, carrying yearly stipends of $11,100 plus a $6,000 institutional allowance to cover tuition and fees, are awarded annually for full-time study. Selection is based on academic achievement, recommendations, and GRE scores. The fellowships are tenable both in the United States and abroad. No allowances are provided for dependents or travel.

Eligibility

Applicants may be from the following fields: mathematics; physical, biological, chemical, and social sciences; the history and philosophy of science; and engineering.

Applicants must be at or near the beginning of their graduate study. They must not have completed more than 20 semester hours of graduate study in science or engineering by the time of application. Students may be enrolled in either master's or Ph.D. programs.

NSF strongly encourages women to apply.

The program is limited to citizens and nationals of the United States.

Application Procedure

Application forms are available from the above address or from campus representatives. Part I of the application must be returned by the deadline date below. NSF will then forward the remaining forms to each applicant. The December Graduate Record Exams date is the last one acceptable for fellowship applicants. A special GRE registration form is included in Part I of the application packet.

Deadline

November 15.

Minority Graduate Fellowships

Address and Phone

National Science Foundation Fellowship Office
National Research Council
2101 Constitution Ave.
Washington, DC 20418
(202) 334-2872

Program Description

Approximately 60 three-year graduate fellowships, each carrying a yearly stipend of $11,100 plus a $6,000 institutional allowance to cover tuition and fees, are awarded annually for full-time study. Selection is based on academic achievement, recommendations, and GRE scores. The fellowships are tenable both in the United States and abroad. No allowances are provided for dependents or travel.

Eligibility

Applicants may be from the following fields: mathematics; physical, biological, chemical, and social sciences; the history and philosophy of science; and engineering.

Applicants must be at or near the beginning of their graduate study. They must not have completed more than 20 semester hours of graduate study in science or engineering by the time of application. Students may be enrolled in either master's or Ph.D. programs.

NSF strongly encourages women to apply.

The program is limited to citizens and nationals of the United States.

Only members of the following ethnic minorities may apply: Native Americans, blacks, Hispanics, and Pacific Islanders.

Application Procedure

Application forms are available from the above address or from campus representatives. Part I of the application must be returned by the deadline date below. NSF will then forward the remaining forms to each applicant. The December Graduate Record Exams date is the last one acceptable for fellowship applicants. A special GRE registration form is included in Part I of the application packet.

Deadline

November 15.

Contents of the Proposal

The proposal should have the same format as proposals by faculty members for support of their own research (see *Grants for Scientific Research,* NSF). A 200-word project summary of the proposed research, suitable for publication, is required. The main body of the proposal should not exceed eight single-spaced typewritten pages and should include (a) a description of the scientific significance of the work and the design of the project in sufficient detail to permit evaluation; (b) presentation and interpretation of progress to date if the research is already under way; (c) a statement of the items for which funds are requested and their estimated costs with an explanation of their necessity for the research; and (d) a schedule for the research, including the date funds will be required.

Biographical data should be included for the student and the dissertation adviser, including educational background, training, and experience directly relevant to the dissertation, together with a list of other financial aid received, applied for, or anticipated during the award period. Transcripts are not required, but lists of relevant courses and grades may be included. Statements from faculty members or other references concerning the student are optional. If survey questionnaires or interviews are to be used, the proposal should contain a copy of the questionnaire, if available, or sample questions, and information on who will conduct the interviews.

Submission Procedures and Grant Administration

Proposals should be submitted by the university to the Central Processing Section, National Science Foundation, Washington, DC 20550. Six copies of doctoral dissertation research proposals are necessary, one of which should be signed by the student, the dissertation adviser, and an official authorized to sign for the university. Formats for the cover page, project summary, and summary proposal budget are contained in the appendixes of *Grants for Scientific Research.* Proposals may be submitted at any time. Up to six months should be allowed for normal processing. The Foundation's decision will be announced as promptly as possible.

Awards will be made to the institution, with the student's dissertation adviser designated as "project director." Grants will be awarded for periods up to 24 months. The grant is to be administered in accordance with the applicable policies and procedures contained in the NSF *Grant Policy Manual* (NSF 77-47). *Grants for Scientific Research* (NSF 78-41) summarizes the salient provisions of interest to the project director and to the student. A final project report (in the general format of Appendix VI to NSF 78-41) is required within 90 days after the expiration of the grant. A copy of the dissertation abstract or other publication deriving from it may be submitted with the final project report. NSF does not reimburse grantee institutions for the indirect costs associated with doctoral dissertation research and considers this as satisfaction of the cost-sharing requirement.

According to an official NSF program description, "four criteria are key to securing . . . support" in addition to "overall quality":

1. The issue investigated must be theoretically grounded.
2. The research design must be appropriate to the hypotheses posed or the questions asked.
3. The proposed research must have cumulative value, building on previous work in the same area.
4. The principal investigator must be demonstrably qualified to carry out the study.

The NSF officials with whom I talked mentioned one further criterion—that research findings should be replicable by a different researcher using the same methods.

National Science Foundation Directorate for Biological, Behavioral, and Social Sciences: Division of Environmental Biology, Division of Behavioral and Neural Sciences, and Division of Social and Economic Science

Grants are awarded in support of doctoral dissertation research in the environmental, behavioral, neural, and social sciences in order to improve the overall quality of dissertation research in these sciences. The grants allow doctoral candidates opportunities for greater creativity in the gathering and analyzing of data than would otherwise be possible. Proposals are judged on the basis of scientific content, importance, and originality. Dissertation proposals compete for research grant funds with proposals for regular research projects. Awards will be made only when it is clear that the dissertation to be produced will be of the highest scientific merit.

The grants are intended to provide funds for items not normally available from the student's university or other sources. Allowable items include travel to specialized facilities or field research locations, sample survey costs, specialized research equipment and services not otherwise available, supplies, microfilm and other forms of unique data, payments to subjects or informants, rental of environmental chambers or other research facilities, and computer time only when not available at the institution. A request for per diem allowance for time away from a home base to conduct research should be carefully justified in terms of living costs in excess of those in the vicinity of the home base.

Funds may not be used as a stipend for the student, for tuition, or for dependents of students. Textbooks and journals cannot be purchased with dissertation research grant funds, and funds may not be used for typing or reproduction of the student's dissertation. In special circumstances and with special justification, funds may be requested for research assistants.

Who May Submit

A proposal should be submitted through regular university channels by the dissertation adviser on behalf of a graduate student who is at the point of initiating dissertation research. A proposal may be submitted while the student is completing other requirements for the doctorate. Only students enrolled at U.S. institutions are eligible. Academic departments should limit the applications submitted to outstanding dissertation proposals with unusual financial requirements that cannot be met by the university.

Division of Social and Economic Sciences

The target dates for NSF proposals this year are January 15 and August 15. In past years, NSF has accepted proposals up to two weeks after the target date, but it would be a good idea to call NSF (Sociology Program: [202] 357-7802) to check on willingness to accept late applications.

Doctoral Dissertation Research Improvement Grants

Address

National Science Foundation
Washington, DC 20550

Program Description

Grants for periods up to two years are awarded to improve the overall quality of dissertation research and to allow doctoral candidates opportunities for greater creativity in the collection and analysis of data than would otherwise be possible. Proposals are judged on the basis of scientific content, importance and originality.

Eligibility

Students in the environmental, behavioral, neural, and social sciences may apply.

Ph.D. candidates who are at the dissertation stage are eligible. Application may be made while the student is completing other requirements for the degree or when the student is about to begin research.

Application Procedure

Applications are submitted through regular university channels by the dissertation adviser on behalf of the graduate student. The proposal should have the same format as NSF faculty proposals. A 200-word summary is required. The main body of the proposal should not exceed the equivalent of eight single-spaced typed pages and should include a description of the project, its significance, and design; summary of progress to date; budget and explanation; and schedule for research. Biographical data on the student and adviser should include educational background, training, and experience as well as financial support applied for, received, or anticipated. Transcripts are not required, but a list of relevant courses and grades may be included. Letters of reference are optional. Six copies of the dissertation proposal are required—one copy must be signed by the student, the dissertation adviser, and an official authorized to sign for the university. For information on the format to be used, see the NSF publication *Grants for Scientific and Engineering Research*. Approximately six months is required for processing. For additional information contact the Division of Social and Economic Science, (202) 357-7966.

Deadline

Applications accepted continuously.

Ethics and Values in Science and Technology Dissertation Research Awards

Address and Phone

Ethics and Values in Science and Technology
National Science Foundation
Washington, DC 20550
(202) 357-7552

Program Description

The EVIST program supports research and related activities to improve professional and public consideration of the ethical and value aspects of contemporary issues that involve science and technology. Proposals submitted for consideration should illustrate to scientists and engineers the ethical and value implications of their work, address issues of importance to nonspecialists, facilitate discussion among a broad range of individuals, and contribute to the formulation of improved policy or practice.

Eligibility

The program will support work by students who are in the fields of science, engineering, humanities, or social sciences as long as they are concerned with science and ethics and are addressing a problem relevant to the aims of EVIST. Interdisciplinary studies are also supported.

Applicants must be Ph.D. candidates enrolled in doctoral programs and entering the dissertation stage. Application may be made while the student is completing other requirements for the doctorate.

Application Procedure
Application should be made through regular university channels by dissertation advisers on behalf of the student. Preliminary proposals are requested and are due three months before the deadlines noted below for final proposals. They will be evaluated within four to six weeks after delivery. These preliminary proposals should identify both the topic and its significance, the research design and items for which funds are requested, the qualifications of the adviser and the applicant, and the cost. Final proposals will be evaluated within six months by the EVIST program officer and 3 to 10 other experts in the field.

Deadlines
February 1/August 1.

Notes

1. This section is an excerpt from a longer statement regarding the application and processing of grant proposals to NSF. As shown, Felice J. Levine is program director of the Law and Social Sciences Program. Researchers specifically interested in the sociology of law should contact the program director. A brief statement follows, with descriptions of other social science programs. This essay can be found in its entirety in the COSSA guide discussed in Section 7.B.2.

2. See Phyllis Moen, "A Newcomer's View of NSF," *Footnotes* of the American Sociological Association (January 1988). Director Moen writes that she is willing to talk about proposals as they are being developed. All decisions on particular proposals are based on input from peer reviews.

7.B.4.b U.S. Public Health Service: Alcohol, Drug Abuse, and Mental Health Administration

Program Staff

Applicants are encouraged to contact the program staff listed below to determine priorities within various program areas and to obtain further information about application procedures.

National Institute on Alcohol Abuse and Alcoholism

Helen Chao, Ph.D., Chief
Biomedical Research Branch
Division of Extramural Research
Room 14C-17
(301) 443-4223

National Institute on Drug Abuse

Beatrice Rouse, Ph.D., Research Sociologist
Division of Epidemiology and Statistical Analysis
Room 11A-55
(301) 443-2974

John Boren, Ph.D., Research Psychologist
Division of Clinical Research
Room 10A-16
(301) 443-1263

Charles Sharp, Ph.D., Biochemist
Division of Preclinical Research
Room 10A-31
(301) 443-6300

National Institute of Mental Health

Thomas Lalley, M.A., Chief
Biometric and Clinical Applications Branch
Division of Biometry and Applied Sciences
Room 18C-14
(301) 443-3364

Leonard Lash, Ph.D., Associate Director
Research Training and Research Resources
Division of Clinical Research
Room 10-95
(301) 443-3264

Stanley Schneider, Ph.D., Associate Director
Research Training and Resource Development
Division of Basic Sciences
Room 11-95
(301) 443-4347

The mailing address for all of the above individuals is 5600 Fishers Ln., Rockville, MD 20857.

Program descriptions for NIMH are included in the general announcement for research support programs, which may be obtained from Anne Cooley, Division of Extramural Activities, 5600 Fishers Ln., Rm. 9-95, Rockville, MD 20857; (301) 443-4673.

National Institute on Alcohol Abuse and Alcoholism

The National Institute on Alcohol Abuse and Alcoholism (NIAAA) provides support for basic and applied alcohol research. The long-range goal of the research program is to develop new knowledge that will facilitate the achievement of two broad objectives: to reduce the incidence and prevalence of alcohol abuse and alcoholism and to reduce the morbidity and mortality associated with alcohol use, alcohol abuse, and alcoholism.

NIAAA supports alcohol-relevant research in many disciplines, including anthropology, economics, epidemiology, psychology, and sociology. Studies must be clearly related to the etiology, prevalence, prediction, diagnosis, prognosis, treatment, management, or prevention of alcoholism or other alcohol-related problems.

Most proposals funded by NIAAA are submitted in response to a general program announcement. In addition, NIAAA issues announcements of special research interests, as well as joint program announcements with the National Institute on Drug Abuse, the National Institute of Mental Health, and the National Institutes of Health. Two special program announcements concern the prevention of alcohol, drug abuse, and mental health disorders at the work site, and community prevention research in alcohol and drug abuse.

The research program of NIAAA is administered through the Extramural Research Division, the Biometry and Epidemiology Division, and the Intramural Clinical and Biological Research Division. Most social and behavioral science research is located in the Clinical and Psychosocial Research Branch of the Extramural Research Division:

Ernestine Vanderveen, Chief
Clinical and Psychosocial Research Branch
14C-17 Parklawn Bldg.
5600 Fishers Ln.
Rockville, MD 20857
(301) 443-4223

Individual National Research Service Awards

Address and Phone
Alcohol, Drug Abuse, and Mental Health Administration
National Research Service Awards Individual Fellowships
5600 Fishers Ln.
Rockville, MD 20857
(301) 443-3855

Program Description
Awards are offered for full-time biomedical and behavioral research and training directly related to alcoholism and other alcohol-related problems, drug abuse, and mental health/ mental illness. Research in the following areas will be considered: basic processes; incidence and prevalence; etiology, description, diagnosis, and pathogenesis; treatment development, assessment, and evaluation; and public health/prevention. The award is renewable up to a maximum of five years of support for predoctoral applicants and up to three years of support for postdoctoral applicants. The annual predoctoral stipend is $6,552, while the annual postdoctoral stipend ranges from $15,996 to $30,000, depending on years of experience. The award also includes an institutional allowance to cover tuition, fees, research supplies, medical insurance, and travel to professional meetings. Additional allowance may be requested for field research travel and travel to a foreign site. The award, which is intended as fellowship rather than research grant funds, may be supplemented with nonfederal money. All support beyond the initial 12 months of postbaccalaureate support is subject to a payback service, which can be in terms of health-related biomedical or behavioral research, teaching, or a combination of these. With proper justification, the award may be used to support research or training abroad. Selection is based on background, clearly focused research interests, ability to think and write clearly, strong and appropriate recommendations, and a clearly written application. In 1980, out of the 135 new or competing continuation grants awarded, approximately 45 were predoctoral and 90 postdoctoral. Support will not be provided for general cultural and sociological problems unless explicitly related to the areas of interest of the administration. No service training is funded.

Eligibility
Applicants may be from the biological, behavioral, or social sciences, including sociology, psychology, biomedical sciences, and physiology, or from the areas of public health, mental health, or education.
Predoctoral students must be enrolled in Ph.D. programs and have completed at least two years of graduate work by the proposed activation date of the fellowship. Postdoctoral applicants must possess a Ph.D., M.D., or equivalent degree or must have completed all requirements for the degree.
Only citizens, nationals, or permanent residents of the United States may apply.

Application Procedure
Request form PHS 416-1 and guidelines from the appropriate division of ADAMHA, National Institute on Alcohol Abuse and Alcoholism, National Institute on Drug Abuse, or National Institute of Mental Health, at the above address. State actual date doctorate granted or expected date, plus discipline. Processing takes six to nine months and involves an initial peer review and a secondary staff review.

Deadlines
September 10/January 10/May 10.

First Independent Research Support and Transition (FIRST) Award:
National Institute on Alcohol Abuse and Alcoholism,
National Institute on Drug Abuse, National Institute of Mental Health

The purpose of the FIRST Award is to provide a sufficient initial period of research support for highly promising newly independent behavioral, psychosocial, and biomedical investigators to develop the merit of their research ideas in the alcohol, drug abuse, and mental health fields. These grants are intended to underwrite the first independent investigative efforts of an individual; to provide a reasonable opportunity for the investigator to demonstrate creativity, productivity, and further promise; and to help effect a transition toward the traditional types of ADAMHA research project grants. FIRST Awards will provide funds for up to five years, during which time the newly independent investigator can provide evidence of significant and innovative contributions to behavioral, psychosocial, or biomedical research.

National Institute of Mental Health: General Funding Statement, Research Support Programs

The National Institute of Mental Health supports programs designed to increase knowledge and improve research methods on mental and behavioral disorders; to generate information regarding basic biological and behavioral processes underlying these disorders and the maintenance of mental health; and to develop and improve mental health services, including prevention and treatment.

Address and Phone
  Division of Extramural Research Activities
  5600 Fishers Ln.
  Rockville, MD 20857
  (301) 443-4347
Areas of Interest
  Mental health research and research training.

Type
  Research grants, program project grants, cooperative agreements, clinical research center grants, small grants, research conference grants, small business innovation research grants, research scientist development awards, physician scientist awards, and clinical investigator awards for support of mental health research.
  Research training support provided through National Research Service Awards (NRSA) of two types: institutional research training awards and individual fellowships. In addition, the Minority Research Resources Branch provides support for research and research training at predominantly minority institutions.
  Research and research training supported by the NIMH may employ theoretical, laboratory, clinical, methodological, and field studies, any of which may involve clinical, subclinical, and normal subjects and populations of all age ranges, as well as animal models appropriate to the system or disorder being investigated and to the state of the field.
  Among the divisions providing support are the following:
    Division of Basic Sciences, which provides support for research and research training in the neurosciences, behavioral sciences, and the area of health and behavior.
    Division of Clinical Research, in which the study of distinct mental disorders is supported by research and research training on epidemiology, etiology, diagnosis, treatment and prevention. This problem-oriented approach gives precedence to the study of specific clinical entities over methodologically specific research so that attention can be focused on diagnostic categories and on the special mental health needs of children, adolescents and older people.

Division of Biometry and Applied Sciences, which supports research and research training on service delivery within the mental health system; the provision of mental health services in other types of health care settings; economic factors influencing supply, demand, and costs of mental health services; mental health issues and problems related to antisocial and violent behavior, rape and sexual assault, and law and mental health interactions; and mental health status and mental health services for minority populations.

Application Information

Further information and application materials are available upon request. When requesting forms, prospective applicants should specify the field or area for which support is sought. Individuals interested in traineeships should apply directly to institutions receiving support under these programs.

Duration

Varies according to the terms of the grant or award.

Deadline

Varies depending upon the program.

Address inquiries to Anne Cooley, Division of Extramural Research Activities, National Institute of Mental Health, Parklawn Bldg., Rm. 9-95, 5600 Fishers Ln., Rockville, MD 20857.

Persons specifically interested in behavioral science research should contact Joy G. Schulterbrandt, Chief, Behavioral Sciences Research Branch, National Institute of Mental Health, Parklawn Bldg., Rm. 11C-10, 5600 Fishers Ln., Rockville, MD 20857; (301) 443-3942. Research support is provided for projects with mental health relevance in anthropology, sociology, and social psychology in such areas as socialization process, the changing nature of family structure and function, sex-role behavior, social structure and dynamics, social change, group processes, social perception and attitudes, and belief systems.

For specific interests and opportunities for funding, see the following statements.

Small Grant Program

The Alcohol, Drug Abuse, and Mental Health Administration Small Grant Program provides research support of up to $15,000 (direct costs). Support is limited to a one-year period and is not renewable.

The ADAMHA Small Grant Program accepts applications that fall within the program interests of the National Institute of Mental Health, the National Institute on Alcohol Abuse and Alcoholism, and the National Institute on Drug Abuse. Each institute makes awards for small grants relevant to its mission.

Purpose

The ADAMHA Small Grant Program provides relatively rapid financial support that is principally intended for

1. newer, less experienced investigators and those at small colleges; and
2. more experienced investigators, for pilot studies for the development/testing of new methods and techniques or exploratory studies in areas significantly different from previous work.

Applications may be made for support of research in any scientific area relevant to mental health or to drug or alcohol abuse. While proposals may involve a wide variety of biomedical, biobehavioral, behavioral, or clinical disciplines, relevance to the missions of the ADAMHA institutes must be present. Applications for studies aimed at problems outside these areas will not be accepted. Programmatic areas of interest are described in program announcements available from offices listed. Behavioral scientists should consult

Division of Basic Sciences
Joy Schulterbrandt, Chief
Behavioral Sciences Research Branch
Parklawn Bldg., Rm. 11C-10
5600 Fishers Ln.
Rockville, MD 20857
(301) 443-3942

7.B.4.c Department of Health and Human Services

Office of the Assistant Secretary for Planning and Evaluation

Gerald Britten
Deputy Assistant Secretary for Planning and Evaluation
Office of Program Systems
447-D HHH Bldg.
200 Independence Ave., SW
Washington, DC 20201
(202) 245-9774

Program

In addition to the principal function of policy development, the Office of the Assistant Secretary for Planning and Evaluation (ASPE) has two support functions within the Department of Health and Human Services: the conduct of research on policy issues of interest to both the executive and legislative branches and evaluations of HHS programs and policies. Evaluations are performed by this office usually in cross-cutting areas germane to more than one program, in cases where an agency does not have sufficient staff or resources to conduct its own evaluation, or in cases where an objective, external evaluation of a program is necessary.

The ASPE policy research program has moved from long-term, high-cost projects to smaller and more targeted studies. This change in the nature of ASPE research has occurred concurrently with the steady decline in its research budget. The FY 1986 budget represents a 75% decrease from its FY 1980 level. A number of ASPE research projects are mandated or suggested by the Congress; in some cases the performer of the research is also mandated.

Most ASPE research interests fall into one of four broad categories:

1. income security and employment (principally welfare and retirement policy, addressing questions such as the following: What is the nature of welfare dependency and how is it affected by such factors as female-headed households, minorities, adolescent pregnancy? What are appropriate public and private sector interventions? How effective are employment programs for minorities? Do family issues and a history of family welfare dependency contribute to its perpetuation? What is the proper balance between social security

and private pensions? How could federal policies encourage or stimulate increased private sector participation?)

2. health policy (principally to explore changes in the health care system and the impact of HHS policies on that system, addressing questions such as: What incentives will encourage prudent "buying" of health care? What are the benefits of free enterprise? What geographic variances occur in health care costs/delivery? What effect do preventive efforts such as antismoking campaigns and prenatal care have on health care costs?)

3. social services policy (examining questions such as: What incentives found effective in the private sector can be introduced in the public sector? How can increased private sector service provision, such as employer-provided day care, be encouraged? How can social services be made more effective and efficient? What are the effects of voucher systems and competitive bidding?)

4. long-term care policy (addressing questions such as: What are the policy implications and costs of alternative long-term care systems, e.g., home-delivered care and case management? What are possible new ways to organize/deliver long-term care? What are the barriers to/incentives for private insurance?)

Application/Review Process

ASPE issues very specific requests for proposals in each of the four priority areas, usually in the *Federal Register* or the *Commerce Business Daily*. Proposals are reviewed by ad hoc panels convened according to topic and generally composed of federal staff. Review panel recommendations are only advisory; final funding decisions are made by the program officers and the assistant secretary.

ASPE has a fairly well-defined grantee network. Because research dollars are scarce, awards are most likely to go to researchers known for the quality of their work. Contact with program staff prior to submitting proposals is encouraged.

Funding Mechanisms

ASPE awards grants, contracts, and task orders (competitively awarded purchase orders, usually up to $600,000 each, which contract for multiple short-term studies in a particular subject area).

Examples of Funded Research

1. "Causes of Growth in Payments for Medicare Part B, Physician Services" (awarded $222,000 in FY 1985)
2. "Poverty and Family Structure" (awarded $50,000 in FY 1985)
3. "Factors in AFDC Participation Rates" (awarded $77,000 in FY 1985)
4. "Study of Preferred Provider Organizations as Alternative Financing and Delivery System Models" (awarded $638,000 in FY 1985)
5. "Hospital Capital Financing Practices in a Variety of Settings" (awarded $340,000 in FY 1985)

National Institute of Child Health and Human Development

Social and Behavioral Sciences Branch Center for Population Research

Research problem areas for which grants are available include the following:

fertility of human population groups
family planning in developed societies

social acceptability of measures for the biological regulation of human fertility

household formation, family structure, fertility, and migration

marriage, divorce, and fertility

age at marriage, child spacing, family size, and fertility

status and roles of women in relation to fertility, with special reference to implications for the United States

nutrition and fertility

relation of economic development to population growth and decline

antecedents and consequences of stability or change in the size of U.S. population

population modeling for the projection and/or prediction of human population change in the United States

migration of human population groups

population redistribution in the United States

human population density and crowding as factors in population change

population composition and structure in the United States

mortality of human population groups

Other outlines are available. Interested researchers should write for outlines on demographic effects and psychological aspects of population. Areas for which outlines are being developed include population sociology, population economics, population geography and population aspects of political science.

National Institute of Child Health and Human Development

Wendy Baldwin, Branch Chief
Social and Behavioral Sciences Branch Center
  for Population Research
Bethesda, MD 20014
(301) 496-1174

National Institute on Aging: Behavioral Sciences Research Program

Matilda White Riley, Associate Director
NIH Bldg. 31, Rm. 4C32
9000 Rockville Pike
Bethesda, MD 20892
(301) 496-3136

Program

The Behavioral Sciences Research (BSR) Program is concerned with the social, cultural, economic, and psychological factors that affect both the process of growing old and the place of older people in society. A broad range of basic research topics in psychology, sociology, anthropology, economics, political science, and social epidemiology fall within the purview of BSR. The BSR Program is divided into three broad categories: cognitive and biopsychological aging, social psychological aging, and older people and society.

1. cognitive aging (mechanisms of age-related changes in intelligence, learning ability, memory, and sensorimotor function, including visual perception and hearing)
2. biopsychology of aging (relationships between behavioral aging and the neural and other physiological aspects of aging)
3. behavioral geriatrics research (broad questions on the relationships among health, behavior, and aging; health-related attitudes and behaviors of older people and their families and friends; the social context of daily living; change with age; means for positive modification)
4. effects of gender on health and longevity (sources of gender differences; implications for the quality of life for both sexes; ability to function independently; societal costs)

5. oldest old—those over 85 (morbidity, mortality, and causes of death; changes in social structures to accommodate their needs; social and economic conditions; psychological functioning)
6. changing age composition of the population (modeling the societal impact on the health and status of older people, including migration patterns)
7. economic well-being of the elderly (accurate estimations of the impact of taxation; monetary and nonmonetary public benefits; cross-generational transfers; sources of income)
8. influences of social institutions on health and functioning (formal health care systems; patient-provider interactions)
9. research methods and data resources (development and application of social science research methods to research on aging; identification and support of human study populations and data archives; cross-national comparisons)
10. productivity in the middle and later years (relationships among age, work incentives, health, and productivity; motivation; cognitive and sensorimotor abilities and job skills; phased retirement and flexible work schedules; health and early retirement)

BSR has traditionally supported studies of social networks, interpersonal relations, and social support. Other topics currently undersupported because of the lack of applicants include personality, coping, and attitude formation and change. Special emphasis is given to research and training on the role of social and behavioral factors in health and effective functioning in the middle and later years of life.

Office of Population Affairs

The Office of Population Affairs (OPA), directed by a deputy assistant secretary of population affairs, was established by Congress in 1970 as a policy-coordinating office to advise the secretary of HHS on population research and family planning services.

The OPA has two divisions: the Office of Family Planning and the Office of Adolescent Pregnancy Programs. Both divisions award grants and contracts for research appropriate for social and behavioral scientists.

The Office of Population Affairs also sponsors a Data Archive on Adolescent Pregnancy and Pregnancy Prevention at Sociometrics Corporation in Palo Alto, California. Through the archive, researchers, practitioners, administrators, and policymakers have access to large-scale data on important issues in the fields of adolescent pregnancy, pregnancy prevention, and family planning.

Office of Family Planning

Patricia Thompson, Director of Research
731-E HHH Bldg.
200 Independence Ave., SW
Washington, DC 20201
(202) 245-1181

Program

The Office of Family Planning (OFP) administers the federal Title X program aimed at improving the efficiency and effectiveness of family planning projects, keeping the cost per unit of service to a minimum, and encouraging the involvement of the family in the provision of family planning services. OFP provides funds to over 4,000 community family planning clinics across the country. A small portion of the budget is retained to support applied research on the improvement of family planning services delivery for low-income women, adolescents, and others in need of such services.

OFP first issued solicitations for competitive, peer-reviewed research proposals in FY 1983 and moved to a more routinized system in FY 1986. The office now issues a general research announcement, which is published in the *Federal Register* and the *NIH Guide for Grants and Contracts*. Preference is given to proposals in the priority areas announced by the agency. The office will continue to issue requests for applications on specific topics on occasion.

The FY 1986 research announcement contained 10 priority areas: family planning client behavior; adolescent family planning clients; male family planning clients; targeting of family planning services to subgroups with special needs (i.e., low-income families, minorities, handicapped); clinic personnel behavior; organization and management of family planning services; the role of private physicians; natural family planning; infertility services; and counseling services (evaluation of role and effectiveness).

OFP encourages proposals from a variety of social and behavioral science disciplines. To date, most support has gone to sociologists, anthropologists, psychologists, economists, and epidemiologists. Proposals that are primarily studies of federal policies are not encouraged, although there is some interest in analyses of state and local policies. Proposals for historical studies could be considered, although, to date, few have been submitted.

Budget

OFP awarded approximately $1.5 million for extramural research in FY 1985. Approximately $1 million in new starts per year is now expected.

Application/Review Process

OFP staff invite preliminary contact by phone from prospective applicants to discuss research ideas, but will not review preliminary proposals or give technical assistance to applicants.

Grant applications are submitted on PHS Form 398 to the Division of Research Grants at the National Institutes of Health. Deadlines are February 1, June 1, and October 1. After scientific review by DRG study sections, final funding decisions are made by the deputy assistant secretary for population affairs with assistance from staff.

Funding Mechanisms

Researchers may apply for individual research project grants or New Investigator Research Awards (NIRA). Direct costs for investigator-initiated research projects should not exceed $100,000 per year. NIRA awards are limited to $37,500 per year. Awards can be made for a maximum of three years.

Office of Adolescent Pregnancy Programs

Eugenia Eckard, Acting Director of Research
731-E HHH Bldg.
200 Independence Ave., SW
Washington, DC 20201
(202) 245-1181

Program

The Office of Adolescent Pregnancy Programs (OAPP) was established in 1978 and began awarding research grants in FY 1982. Like the Office of Family Planning, OAPP has begun issuing a general research announcement to stimulate investigator-initiated proposals in areas of agency interest. OAPP is primarily responsible for administering the Adolescent Family Life Act (AFL) enacted by Congress in 1981. Language contained in the act permits OAPP to spend up to one-third of AFL funds for research, although the agency has not chosen to utilize that amount to date.

OAPP supports demonstration and evaluation projects for delivery of services to prevent adolescent pregnancy and to care for pregnant adolescents, and research on topics including adolescent sexual activity, parenting, and childbearing. A fundamental basis of the AFL (and thus of the research program) is to encourage the delay of sexual activity among adolescents, rather than to promote contraceptive use.

Five research topics of interest identified by OAPP are as follows:

1. influences on adolescent premarital sexual behavior (demographic, economic, social, and psychological characteristics; family, peer, and media influence; adolescent decision-making processes; different patterns of influence for males and females)
2. consequences of adolescent premarital sexual behavior (differing effects on development of males and females, including psychological, social, educational, moral factors; differing consequences for major population subgroups)
3. adoption option for unmarried adolescent mothers (social, psychological, legal, and service factors; role of counseling; social attitudes toward single parenthood; family involvement)
4. parenting by unmarried adolescent mothers (role of the extended family; factors influencing parenting behavior; role of the father)
5. adolescent pregnancy services (scope and impact of public and private sector services and policies; evaluations of strategies to eliminate adolescent premarital sexual relations; evaluations of strategies that might enhance service delivery)

Budget

OAPP spent about $1.5 million for extramural research in FY 1985. Approximately $1 million in new starts per year is now expected.

Application/Review Process

Grant applications are submitted on PHS Form 398 to the Division of Research Grants at the National Institutes of Health. Deadlines are February 1, June 1, and October 1. After scientific review by DRG study sections, final funding decisions are made by the deputy assistant secretary for population affairs with assistance from staff.

Funding Mechanisms

Researchers may apply for individual research project grants or New Investigator Research Awards. Direct costs for investigator-initiated research projects should not exceed $100,000 per year. NIRA awards are limited to $37,500 per year. Awards can be made for a maximum of three years.

Examples of Funded Research

1. "Short-Term Consequences of Adolescent Sexual Behavior" (one-year project; total costs, $130,576)
2. "Sex and Pregnancy Among Mexican-American Adolescents" (three-year project; total costs, $420,084)
3. "The Antecedents of Early Premarital Intercourse" (two-year project; total costs, $116,945)
4. "Adoption Behavior and the Propensity to Adopt in the U.S." (two-year project; total costs, $66,930)
5. "Fathers of Infants of Adolescent Mothers" (four-year project; total costs, $352,399)

7.B.4.d Social Security Administration

Office of Research, Statistics, and International Policy

Dan Graham, Program Analyst
Altmeyer Bldg., Rm. 138
6401 Security Blvd.
Baltimore, MD 21235
(301) 597-2927

The Social Security Administration (SSA) conducts an integrated program of intramural and extramural research activities designed to provide accurate information and analyses concerning the major programs of SSA responsibility—Old Age and Survivors Insurance (OASI), Disability Insurance (DI), Supplemental Security Income (SSI), and Aid to Families with Dependent Children (AFDC). Research and statistical data are used to provide cost, revenue, and work-load estimates, and to enhance program management and efficiency. They are also used to provide cost estimates and analyses for legislative initiatives.

The SSA is interested in research projects that develop and implement analytical models for comparing the merits of alternative methods for carrying out income security goals. Priority areas for research funding include (a) labor force participation of women; (b) factors that affect the social, psychological, occupational, and financial situations of the aged; (c) impacts of immigration and immigration policy on social security and related programs; (d) analysis of need for income support, health services, retraining, or relocation assistance in relation to disability; (e) comparative studies and analysis of other countries' social security concepts and programs; (f) research that uses available SSA data bases such as the Retirement History Study.

7.B.4.e Minority Research Resources Branch

James R. Ralph, Chief
Parklawn Bldg., Rm. 18-101
5600 Fishers Ln.
Rockville, MD 20857
(301) 443-2988

Program

The Minority Research Resources Branch (MRRB) provides support for research and research training. Small grant applications dealing with minority issues are funded by the MRRB, as are the Minority Fellowship Program, Minority Access to Research Careers (MARC) Program, the Minority Biomedical Research Support Program, research and development centers for minority research, and conference grants.

The MARC Program consists of two training activities: the Honors Undergraduate Research Training Program and the Faculty Fellowship Research Training Program. The objectives of this program are (a) to increase the number of well-prepared students from institutions with substantial minority enrollment who can compete successfully for entry into Ph.D. degree programs in disciplines related to mental health, alcoholism, and drug abuse; and (b) to develop and strengthen biological, psychological, behavioral, and/or public health sciences curricula and research training opportunities in these academic institutions. Currently, support is provided to 11 minority-based institutions throughout the nation, including 4 historically black colleges and universities. The objective of the MARC Faculty Fellowship Program is to enhance research capabilities of faculty at institutions with substantial minority enrollment by providing fellowships for selected individuals for advanced research training in specified areas of research related to alcoholism, drug abuse, and mental health. It is intended that the recipients of these awards will return to their home institutions following such training, to teach and conduct research, and to inspire and assist students in preparing for research careers in these areas.

The Minority Fellowship Program (MFP) provides predoctoral support for research training to minority students through four professional associations: the American Psychological Association, American Sociological Association, American Nurses Association, and Council on Social Work Education.

The Minority Biomedical Research Support Program (MBRS) provides support to minority faculty conducting mental health research and to undergraduate and graduate students obtaining research experience through a Reimbursable Agreement with the Division of Research Resources, NIH. The objectives of the program are to increase the numbers and quality of minority health and mental health scientists and to strengthen the capability of minority (eligible) institutions to provide health and mental health research career opportunities to their students and to conduct research in the health and mental health sciences. This program is currently funding 45 undergraduates and 15 graduate students in 16 separate academic institutions having a substantial percentage of minority enrollment.

National Institutes of Health Pre- and Postdoctoral Fellowships

The National Research Service Award Act of 1974 (NRS) authorizes the National Institutes of Health and the Alcohol, Drug Abuse, and Mental Health Administration to have predoctoral and postdoctoral research training programs—individual fellowships and institutional fellowships (training grants).

Although NIH has this authorization, it has been determined (new legislation pending) that individual support would be available only at the postdoctoral level and that predoctoral support would be available only through the institutional fellowship program. Some institutional support at this level may possibly be available through existing NIH training grants, and inquiries concerning this kind of support should be directed to the graduate or medical dean of the institution where the applicant would like to study.

Institutional National Research Service Awards

A domestic public and nonprofit private institution may apply for a grant for a research training program in a specified area of research from which a number of awards will be made to individuals selected by the training program director at the institution. Grants may also be made to federal institutions that are eligible under Section 507 of the Public Health Service Act. Support for both predoctoral and postdoctoral trainees may be requested. Each applicant institution must submit an application according to instructions, using forms provided by NIH or ADAMHA.

The applicant institution must have or be able to develop the staff and facilities required for the proposed program. The training program director at the institution will be responsible for the selection and appointment of trainees and the overall direction of the training program. In selecting trainees, the program director must make certain that individuals receiving support meet the eligibility requirements set forth in these guidelines and that they will submit a signed Payback Agreement at the time of appointment and prior to receiving any stipend or other allowance from the grant.

The stipends for predoctoral and postdoctoral trainees are the same as for the individual award. In addition to stipends, the applicant institution may request and be provided with tuition, fees, and travel costs for predoctoral trainees; an allowance of up to $1,000 for each postdoctoral trainee (in lieu of tuition, fees, and travel); actual indirect costs or 8% of the total award for related institutional costs such as salaries, equipment, and supplies.

A Statement of Appointment Form (PHS-2271) and a Payback Agreement signed by the trainee indicating his or her intent to meet the service or payback requirements must be submitted to the awarding unit at the time the training begins for each appointment or reappointment of a trainee on the grant. Subsequent changes in the terms and conditions of appointments will require amended appointment forms. Any change in training status that will affect the payback requirement must be reported to the awarding unit by the grantee institution.

Selected NIH Extramural Behavioral Training Opportunities

1. *National Research Service Award (NRSA) Institutional Training Grants.* These grants allow eligible institutions to develop or enhance pre- and post-Ph.D. and post-M.D. research training opportunities for individuals who want to prepare for careers in biomedical or behavioral research. Applications for such grants are subjected to rigorous peer review in national competition. The training program director at the grantee institution is responsible for the selection and appointment of trainees and for the overall direction of the program. Postdoctoral trainees must have received recognized doctoral degrees before beginning the appointment.
2. *National Research Service Award Individual Fellowships.* These awards finance full-time research training in areas that reflect national needs in biomedical and behavioral research. This award permits the applicant to exercise creativity in developing a research training project that will best serve his or her research goals. The candidate's application is subject to national competition. As of the beginning date of the proposed fellowship, an applicant must have received a doctoral degree and arranged to work with a particular sponsor affiliated with an institution that has the appropriate staff and facilities.
3. *National Research Service Award Senior Postdoctoral Fellowships.* These awards are designed to permit experienced scientists to make major changes in the direction of their

research capabilities. As of the beginning date of the proposed fellowship, an applicant must have at least seven years of relevant experience.

4. *Research Career Development Award (NIH)*. The purpose of the RCDA is to provide five years of salary support to investigators who have demonstrated outstanding research potential. In order to enable these investigators to develop this potential, the award guarantees them the ability to devote at least 80% of their time to research for five years. Investigators should already have five years of postdoctoral research experience. New guidelines went into effect as of February 1, 1988. Deadlines are October 1, February 1, and June 1.

The regular research grant application Form PHS 398 (Rev. 5/82) must be used in applying for the RCDA/NRSA awards. Supplemental instructions prepared especially for these programs are included with the application kit, which can be obtained by contacting the ADAMHA institute to which the researcher intends to apply for funding.

| National Clearinghouse for Alcohol Information P.O. Box 2345 Rockville, MD 20852 | National Institute on Drug Abuse Grants Management Officer, NIDA 5600 Fishers Ln. Rockville, MD 20857 | National Institute of Mental Health RCDA/NRSA Program Division of Extramural Research Programs, NIMH 5600 Fishers Ln. Rockville, MD 20857 |

Completed application forms are submitted to the Division of Research Grants, 5333 Westbard Ave., Bethesda, MD 20205. To avoid delays in assignment and review, complete applications should be submitted as early as possible. The PHS uses the review and award schedule shown in Table 7.1.

Applications must be *received* by the dates shown in the table. To ensure against problems caused by carrier delays, the applicant should retain a legible proof-of-mailing receipt from the carrier, dated no later than one week prior to the receipt date. If the receipt date falls on a weekend, it will be extended to Monday; if the date falls on a holiday, it will be extended to the following business day. The receipt date will be waived only in extenuating circumstances. To request such a waiver, the applicant must include an explanatory letter with the signed, completed application. *No request for a waiver will be considered prior to receipt of the application.*

As soon as possible after the receipt date, usually within six weeks, the PHS will send the principal investigator/program director and the applicant organization the application's number and the name, address, and telephone number of the executive secretary of the initial review group to which it has been assigned. If this information is *not* received within that time, the applicant should contact the Referral Office, Division of Research.

7.B.4.f Department of Education

Office of Research

The mission of the Office of Research (OR) is to generate knowledge that will increase understanding of the education system and contribute to improvements in

TABLE 7.1

Application Receipt Dates (unless specified differently in additional instructions, a program announcement, or a request for applications)			Initial Review Group Dates	National Advisory Council or Board Dates	Earliest Possible Beginning Dates
Jan. 10	Feb. 1	Mar. 1	June-July	Sept.-Oct.	Dec. 1
May 10	June 1	July 1	Oct.-Nov.	Jan.-Feb.	Apr. 1
Sept. 10	Oct. 1	Nov. 1	Feb.-Mar.	May-June	July 1
for all [a] Institutional National Research Service Award applications	for all *new* grant and Research Career Development Award applications all [a] Program Project and Center grant applications	for *competing,* continuation, and *supplemental* research grant applications			

a. Includes new, competing, continuation, and supplemental.

the quality of education. OR supports research on fundamental educational processes at all levels and in all settings. The emphasis of OR research is on factors that contribute to, or detract from, the achievement of excellence in education for all individuals. Research is also designed to strengthen the scientific and technological foundations of education with the intent of advancing the practice of education as an art, science, and profession. Research is conducted primarily by scholars outside of government. It may be initiated by the field or solicited, or some combination of these processes. The Office of Research has four divisions: Learning and Instruction, Schools and School Professionals, Higher Education and Adult Learning, and Education and Society. Sociologists and anthropologists will find special interests in the Education and Society Division.

Program

The Education and Society Division supports basic and applied research and analytic activities that focus on the interaction between education and the community at large. Topics of inquiry range from the involvement of parents in the education of their children to the influence of parents and communities on local schools, the social context of education, and state and local responsibilities of education. Methods of inquiry range from contemporary empirical investigations to historical studies and philosophical analyses.

Persons interested in the department's research and development program should direct inquiries to officials shown below.

Director, Sally Kilgore: (202) 357-6079
Senior Program Manager, Emmett Fleming: (202) 357-6239
Senior Program Coordinator, Arthur Sheekey: (202) 357-6079
Special Studies Staff Director, Chapter, Bea Bieman: (202) 357-6161

Special Studies Staff Director, Japan, Robert Leestma: (202) 357-6090

Education & Society Division Director, James Carper: (202) 357-6223

Higher Education & Adult Learning Division Director, Sal Corrallo: (202) 357-6243

Learning & Instruction Division Director, John Taylor: (202) 357-6021

Schools & School Professionals Division Acting Director, Conrad G. Katzenmayer: (202) 357-6207

Persons interested in participating in the department's research and development program should request a copy of the *Guide to Programs*. Write to Public Affairs Services, U.S. Department of Education, Washington DC 20202.

The Bureau also operates the Educational Resources Information Center (ERIC), which provides direct access to research literature in behavioral sciences and education. Monthly issues of *Research in Education* (available from the Government Printing Office) abstract and index over 700 documents—the latter available from the ERIC Document Reproduction Service, National Cash Register Company, 2926 Fairmont Ave., Bethesda, MD 20014.

7.B.4.g Department of Justice

National Institute of Justice

The National Institute of Justice (NIJ) is a research branch of the Department of Justice. NIJ's mission is to develop knowledge about crime, its causes, and its control. Priority is given to policy-relevant research that can yield approaches and information that state and local agencies can use in preventing and reducing crime. NIJ reorganized its extramural program somewhat in FY 1986 in an effort to provide a more sustained, coordinated support base. The new Sponsored Research Program solicits proposals in several broad areas, with specific priorities established in each area. In addition, support is available through the visiting fellowships, graduate research fellowships, and summer research fellowships programs. Unsolicited proposals may be submitted, but because the targeted priority areas are so broad, most unsolicited proposals can be placed in one or more of the designated programs. All NIJ programs are appropriate for social and behavioral scientists.

Sponsored Research Program

John Pickett, Director of Planning and Management
633 Indiana Ave., NW
Washington, DC 20531
(202) 724-2945

Program

The Sponsored Research Program funds both basic and applied studies intended to bridge the gap between criminal justice theory and practice. All research is directed at improving the nation's ability to control crime and criminal behavior. Several topics have been established as ongoing priority areas, although specific topics within each may be designated each year.

Ongoing areas of interest are as follows:

1. controlling the serious offender (including crime control theory and policy; offender classification and prediction of criminal behavior; violent criminal behavior; and drugs, alcohol, and crime)
2. aiding the victims of crime (including legislation and other changes affecting victims; police assistance to victims; and family violence and child sex abuse)
3. crime prevention (including partnerships between police; neighborhood actions against crime; and the private sector and prevention of specific crimes)
4. improving the criminal justice system (including police efficiency and effectiveness; police response to spouse assault; court effectiveness; corrections; and the system of criminal justice).

Office of Juvenile Justice and Delinquency Prevention, Research and Program Development Division

Pamela Swain, Director
Indiana Bldg., Rm. 780
633 Indiana Ave., NW
Washington, DC 20531
(202) 724-7560

Program

The Office of Juvenile Justice and Delinquency Prevention (OJJDP) supports research that will contribute to the prevention and treatment of juvenile delinquency. The Research and Program Development Division is organized in three major topical areas: prevention of delinquent behavior and child exploitation, improvement of the juvenile justice system, and development of alternatives to traditional juvenile justice systems. The majority of resources in each area are focused on serious juvenile crime and protection of abused and exploited children. Support is available for basic research, policy studies, and program evaluation.

Different priorities are established for the three research areas each year, with requests for applications issued for specific topics. Current priorities include (a) research on the causes and correlates of delinquency, (b) school crime and discipline, (c) legal issues involving juvenile justice, (d) law enforcement agencies' policies and practices for handling missing children and homeless youth, (e) statistics on missing children, and (f) programs and services for children and youth abusing drugs and alcohol.

Future topics of interest to OJJDP include missing children, child victims as witnesses, drug abuse among inner-city minority youth, longitudinal studies of causes of delinquency, and the impact of deinstitutionalization of status offenders.

Program priorities are decided internally by OJJDP staff, but public and congressional interests are considered. Although Congress seldom mandates specific studies to be undertaken by OJJDP, it does suggest particular research themes for the agency to pursue.

Grantees in this program have traditionally included sociologists, psychologists, and political scientists. More proposals from anthropologists, economists, and psychiatrists are particularly encouraged. Program evaluations are more frequently being funded by the state agencies that receive juvenile justice formula (block) grants. Since evaluations are generally contracted out, interested researchers are encouraged to contact their appropriate state agencies.

Examples of Funded Research

1. "The Impact of Residential Treatment: Adaptation in the Community Five Years Later"
2. "Dropping Out and Delinquency Among Puerto Rican Youths"
3. "The Young Criminal Years of the Violent Few"
4. "High Risk Early School Behavior for Later Delinquency"
5. "Delinquency in a Birth Cohort Replication"
6. "Juvenile Arrest Trends in the United States: The Years Between 1970 and 1981"
7. "Evaluation of the Habitual Juvenile Offender Program"

7.B.4.h Department of Labor

Employment and Training Administration, Performance Management and Evaluation Division

Raymond Uhalde, Chief
8000 Patrick Henry Bldg.
601 D St., NW
Washington, DC 20213
(202) 376-6660

Program

The Employment and Training Administration (ETA) supports research and evaluation projects related to the Job Training Partnership Act, the Employment Service, the Job Corps, labor markets, and the technology of training. In addition, it continues to support the Job Training Longitudinal Survey and the National Longitudinal Survey of Labor Market Experiences and is conducting three experiments related to youth and adult training. Because most ETA research funds are earmarked for these and other departmental projects, little money is available for discretionary funding.

Application/Review Process

Notices for competitive contracts are published in the *Commerce Business Daily.* Unsolicited proposals are accepted, but limited resources make funding unlikely.

Funding Mechanisms

All awards are made through contracts.

Employment and Training Administration

The Department of Labor has a number of research programs administered by its Office of Research and Development. These include institutional grants, doctoral dissertation fellowships, and small-grant research projects. The proposed projects should focus on potential solutions to significant employment and training problems. These programs are described in detail in U.S. Department of Labor, *Research and Development Projects*. For information, write Employment and Training Administration, Office of Research and Development, Washington, DC 20213.

7.B.4.i National Endowment for the Humanities

The National Endowment for the Humanities (NEH) supports scholarship, research, education, and public programs in the humanities. The 1965 act of Congress establishing the Endowment defines the humanities as the study of

> language, both modern and classical; linguistics; literature; history; jurisprudence; philosophy; archaeology; comparative religion; ethics; the history, criticism, and theory of the arts; those aspects of the social sciences which have humanistic content and employ humanistic methods; and the study and application of the humanities to the human environment with particular attention to the relevance of the humanities to the current conditions of national life.

Within the terms of the NEH mandate, social science studies that have been awarded NEH support tend to be historical or philosophical in approach or attempt to cast light on questions of interpretation or criticism traditionally identified with the humanities. NEH also supports studies that use the disciplines of the humanities to interpret, analyze, or assess science and technology. Thus, within these constraints, social scientists are eligible for nearly all of the programs of the Endowment.

7.B.4.j Department of Defense

The Department of Defense (DOD) research program includes basic research, exploratory development, advanced development, and operations systems development. Most social and behavioral science research is conducted in the first two categories at the Office of the Chief of Naval Research, the Army Institute for the Behavioral and Social Sciences, and the Air Force Office of Scientific Research. Some exploratory development particularly of interest to behavioral scientists is conducted at the technical laboratories supported by the U.S. Navy and the Air Force. Policy research of interest to political scientists, economists, sociologists, and others is supported by the Office of the Undersecretary for Policy. Although much of DOD's research and development is mission related, unsolicited proposals are accepted by most offices. For social and behavioral scientists interested in DOD-sponsored research it is important to make informal contacts with program directors first. Another avenue of garnering support for research is to make contact with major contractors that often subcontract portions of their research contracts.

Secretary of the Army, Army Research Institute for the Behavioral and Social Sciences

Milt Katz, Director, Office of Basic Research
5001 Eisenhower Ave.
Alexandria, VA 22333
(202) 274-8641

The Army Research Institute for the Behavioral and Social Sciences (ARI) is the U.S. Army's focal point for research and development efforts in these fields. ARI is problem and product oriented, responding to and working with agencies and commands throughout the Army. The core program is divided into three major areas: manpower and personnel research, systems research, and training research. Three specialized laboratories associated with each technical area administer the research program. The Office of Basic Research conducts an extramural program that cuts across all three areas.

7.B.5   SELECT LIST OF FEDERAL GOVERNMENT AGENCIES AND PRIVATE ORGANIZATIONS OFFERING FELLOWSHIPS AND GRANTS

American Council of Learned Societies: Several categories of fellowships and grants for which scholars in various fields whose research programs have predominantly humanistic emphasis may apply. (Address: 800 Third Ave., New York, NY 10022.)

American Philosophical Society: Grants averaging $800 and not exceeding $2,000 to individuals for expenses of research in all fields, including the social sciences. Awards made on the first Fridays of October, December, February, April, and June; applications due eight weeks in advance; the Society does not offer fellowships or predoctoral grants. (Address: 104 S. Fifth St., Philadelphia, PA 19106.)

American Association of Retired Persons Andrus Foundation: Grants for applied research in gerontology (behavioral, social and health sciences, policy, planning, or practice). Special interest in studies (a) pertinent to claimants under the Age Discrimination in Employment Act, (b) on the impact of older-employee benefits on employer decisions concerning older workers, (c) on the effect of retirement on the income of recent retirees, and (d) concerning part-time employment of older workers. Awards up to $50,000 for 12 months. Deadline: December 1.

American Sociological Association (ASA): Small grant awards offered jointly by ASA and NSF for postdoctoral research in sociology. The nature of the request may include but is not limited to the following: an exploratory study, a small conference, travel to consult with specialists, a program of study at a major research center, and projects not ordinarily supported by other sources of funds. Deadlines: November 15, June 30.

American Association of University Women Educational Foundation: Research and project grants offer women the opportunity to foster equity and positive societal change through projects, research, or study. Individual grants to conduct research in the public interest, implement community service projects, or prepare literary works for publication ($500 to $2,500). Issue focus grants offer assistance to encourage active participation in the following topics: promoting individual liberties, women's work/women's worth, public support for public education ($500 to $5,000). Deadline all programs: February 1.

American Association of University Women Educational Foundation: Seven postdoctoral fellowships, each for a 12-month period beginning July 1, to women who will be devoting full time to the project: Founders Fellowship ($20,000) for distinguished scholars in any field; Palmer Fellowship ($15,000) in any field; Cuneo Fellowship ($15,000) in any field. Dissertation fellowships to women for 12 months beginning July 1. Stipend is $10,000 for the final year of doctoral work. Deadline all programs: November 15.

The Lynde and Harry Bradley Foundation, Inc.: Support for projects in two main areas: public affairs—national public policy research, and also international and strategic policy research; and education—higher education and gifted children. A variety of activities are supported: research, institutional support, fellowships, professorships, lectures and lecture series, books, scholarly journals, conferences and seminars, and, occasionally, television and radio programs. No deadlines.

Congressional Science Fellowships in Child Development: These fellowships provide a unique opportunity for scholars in child development and related fields to learn about the intersection of research and public policy. Serving as special legislative assistants in congressional offices, fellows gain firsthand experience in federal policy formation. The fellowship year enables fellows to identify productive directions for future research, to perceive new applications for existing research, and to contribute their knowledge and expertise to the policy process. Midcareer individuals are especially encouraged to apply. Stipends have ranged from $25,000 to $31,000 (with a moving allowance to Washington). Deadline: November 9.

Danforth Foundation: Several fellowship programs for men and women at various stages of graduate study. Applicants must be planning for careers in college teaching or administration; fields of study common to the undergraduate liberal arts curriculum in the United States. (Address: 222 S. Central Ave., St. Louis, MO 63105.)

Educational Foundation of America: Grants in the broad area of undergraduate higher education, with limited support in the medical field, particularly dealing with cancer and heart disease and care. Recent grants have been in the areas of population planning, medical education and research, health, higher education, children's education, cultural education, philanthropy, energy and environment, and Native Americans. Letters of inquiry; no deadlines.

The Ford Foundation: (a) Postdoctoral grants for research in Southeast Asia in the social sciences and humanities: address inquiries to Southeast Asia Regional Council, Box 17, 5828 S. University Ave., Chicago, IL 60637. (b) Graduate Fellowship Program for black Americans, Mexican-Americans, Native Americans (American Indians), and Puerto Ricans planning a career in higher education and enrolled in or planning to enter an accredited U.S. graduate school in the social sciences, natural sciences, or humanities: black American students address inquiries to Graduate Fellowships for Black Americans, National Fellowships Fund, 795 Peachtree St., NE, Ste. 484, Atlanta, GA 30308; Mexican-American and Native American students address inquiries to Educational Testing Service, Box 200, Berkeley, CA 94704; Puerto Rican students address inquiries to Graduate Fellowships for Puerto Ricans, Educational Testing Service, Box 2822, Princeton, NJ 08540.

Fulbright-Hays and other U.S. government awards for predoctoral study and postdoctoral research in certain foreign countries: Address inquiries concerning predoctoral applications to Institute of International Education, 809 United Nations Plaza, New York, NY 10017; postdoctoral applications to Council for International Exchange of Scholars, 2101 Constitution Ave., NW, Washington, DC 20418.

The Harry Frank Guggenheim Foundation: Support for individual projects of research and/or study designed to promote understanding of human social problems growing out of dominance, aggression, and violence. Awards restricted to projects with well-defined aims clearly germane to the human case (but not necessarily restricted to studies of humans). Grants average $20,000 for one to two years. Deadlines: February 1/August 1.

John Simon Guggenheim Memorial Foundation: Postdoctoral fellowships in social sciences and other fields. (Address: 90 Park Ave., New York, NY 10016.)

Alexander von Humboldt Foundation: Research fellowships for young scholars (up to age 40) for 6-24 months in Germany. Stipend from DM 2,700 to DM 3,500 per month plus family allowance, travel expenses, and grants for language courses. Suggested deadlines: five to six months before committee meetings in March, July, and November.

IREX: Grants for senior scholars who need to make brief visits to Eastern Europe or the Soviet Union in connection with ongoing research and who do not require academic or administrative assistance in carrying out their proposed projects. Deadline: April 1.

Japan Foundation: Postdoctoral grants and dissertation fellowships for research conducted in Japan in the social sciences, the humanities, and professional fields. (Address: 1302 18th St., NW, Ste. 704, Washington, DC 20036.)

Lilly Endowment Faculty Open Fellowships: Lilly offers support to college and university faculty of ability whose aspirations and needs cannot be served by conventional fellowships for study and research. The Endowment is particularly interested in teacher/ scholars in midcareer who seek a break from the academic routine through which they can hope for enrichment as persons and as teachers. The maximum award is $25,000. To be eligible, the candidate must have been a member of the faculty at his or her institution for a minimum of five years.

The Josiah Macy, Jr., Foundation: Primary interest is in medical education, clinical medicine, and medical research. Grants are made to universities for programs designed to recruit and prepare minority students for careers in medicine, biomedical science, and related health professions. Also grants for new academic programs in pathobiology, to improve the academic experience in medical schools, for conferences, improved communication of medical and medical science to the public, and sociological studies on women's careers in science and medicine. Preliminary letter suggested. No deadlines; board meets in January, May, and September.

National Science Foundation: Research grants and fellowships in anthropology, economics, geography, history and philosophy of science, linguistics, political science, psychology, and sociology. Also included are interdisciplinary areas composed of two or more overlapping fields, and work in the field of law that employs the methodology of the social sciences or that interrelates with research in the natural or social sciences and research on science policy. Not supported is research or study in business administration, clinical psychology, or social work. Predoctoral fellowships are open only to students who have completed not more than one year of graduate study. The NSF also administers NATO Postdoctoral and Senior Fellowships, in cooperation with the U.S. State Department. Research grants are intended primarily for established scholars. A special program of doctoral dissertation research grants provides assistance toward the expenses of research but does not include a stipend. The target dates for NSF proposals are January 15 and August 15. (Address: 1800 G St., NW, Washington, DC 20550.)

Population Council: Fellowships and grants for training and research in demography and in family planning. (Address: One Dag Hammarskjold Plaza, New York, NY 10017.)

National Endowment for the Humanities: Research grants and fellowships for humanists and certain social scientists whose projects will strengthen the humanistic aspects of a social science. (Address: 806 15th St., NW, Washington, DC 20506.)

National Institutes of Health: NIH offers research and research-training grants and awards in the biomedical and health-related sciences. For information, write Division of Research Grants, National Institutes of Health, Bethesda, MD 20014.

National Institute of Mental Health: For information on research grants, address Social Sciences Section, Behavioral Sciences Research Branch, Division of Extramural Research Programs, NIMH, Parklawn Bldg., 5600 Fishers Ln., Rockville, MD 20852.

Other U.S. agencies: Grants for research relevant to their respective responsibilities are available from the following: Office of Education, Social Security Administration, Vocational Rehabilitation Administration, Welfare Administration.

Radcliffe College: Research Support Program for postdoctoral research in the humanities and the social and behavioral sciences. Researchers must use the Arthur and Elizabeth Schlesinger Library on the History of Women in America and/or the Henry A. Murray Research Center at Radcliffe College. Awards range from $100 to $2,000; additional funds of up to $2,500 may be budgeted for expenses such as computer time, transcribing, or research assistance. Deadlines: May 12, October 15, March 30.

Research Career Development Award (NIH): The purpose of the RCDA is to provide five years of salary support to investigators who have demonstrated outstanding research potential. In order to enable these investigators to develop this potential, the award guarantees them the ability to devote at least 80% of their time to research for five years. Investigators should already have five years of postdoctoral research experience. New guidelines went into effect as of February 1, 1988. Deadlines: October 1, February 1, and June 1.

The Rockefeller Foundation: Several categories of research fellowships and grants, including a fellowship program in environmental affairs, fellowships in conflict in international relations, and the Rockefeller Foundation and Ford Foundation program in support of population policy research in the social sciences. (Address: 1133 Avenue of the Americas, New York, NY 10036.)

Russell Sage Foundation: Grants to visiting scholars who wish to collaborate on joint projects. Foundation has three principal programs: (a) social analysis of poverty (fosters new analytic strategies that offer insights into the nature of poverty and the reasons for its persistence), (b) behavioral economics (interdisciplinary effort to examine the consequences of introducing into economics information from neighboring social sciences about the nature of human motivation and decision making, as well as the complexities of economic institutions), and (c) research synthesis (provides financial support and technical assistance designed to encourage effective use of statistical methods for detecting the significant generalizations that can be derived from multiple studies of the same social problem or program). No deadline; letter of inquiry requested.

The Spencer Foundation: Small Grants Program for research in the field of education for investigators who have earned doctorates in academic disciplines or in the field of education and hold appointments in colleges or universities. One-year grants range from $1,000 to $7,500. This grant replaces the annual competition Seed Grants for Young Scholars, which was managed by the School of Education. No deadline. Also, the foundation provides support for research in the social and behavioral sciences aimed at the improvement of education. Brief preliminary proposals, with a copy of the investigator's curriculum vitae, are strongly recommended. No deadlines; proposals to be considered during a particular review cycle must reach foundation by November 15, July 15, March 15.

Society for the Psychological Study of Social Issues: Grants-in-aid (up to $1,000) for scientific research in social problem areas, including sexism and racism. Also funding up to $500 on a 1:1 match with university funds for doctoral dissertation research. Deadlines: November 1, February 1, and May 1. Also, the Society awards the Gordon Allport Intergroup Relations Prize ($500) for the best paper or article of the year on intergroup relations. Deadline: December 1.

Social Science Research Council: Several categories of research fellowships and grants, including postdoctoral research training fellowships, grants to minority scholars for research on racism and other social factors in mental health, postdoctoral fellowships in criminal justice indicators, fellowships for international doctoral research, postdoctoral grants for research on foreign areas, and grant programs for training and travel in foreign countries. The last three programs mentioned are sponsored jointly with the American Council of Learned Societies. (Address: 605 Third Ave., New York, NY 10016.)

Twentieth Century Fund: Support for analytical studies of contemporary public policy issues in one of the following four areas: domestic policies, politics, and economics; communications, science, and technology; urban economic and social issues; and U.S. policy in the international arena. Projects are expected to result in book-length manuscripts. No deadlines; board meets early in May and November.

7.B.6   INFORMATIONAL SOURCES THAT LIST OTHER FELLOWSHIPS AND GRANT OPPORTUNITIES

General

Annual Register of Grant Support. 19th ed. (1985-86). Chicago: Marquis, 1985.

Part of the section on educational research is devoted to Scholar Aid Programs (all disciplines). Typical entries include name, address, and phone number of the grant-making organization and a description of the aid program, including eligibility and application requirements, average amount of financial support awarded, number of applications received (for the most recent year for which statistics are available), and the number of awards made annually.

Catalog of Federal Domestic Assistance. Washington, DC: U.S. Office of Management and Budget, current year, with updates.

A comprehensive listing and description of federal programs that provide benefits to the American public. Gives information on grants, loans, scholarships, and other types of financial assistance, with addresses for offices to contact for additional information and application procedures. Several indexes are provided. Look in the Subject Index under such headings as Fellowships, Scholarships, Traineeships, and Education. Kept reasonably current by annual editions updated six months after publication.

Chronicle Student Aid Annual. Rev. ed. Moravia, NY: Chronicle Guidance Publication, 1985.

Contains information on award programs offered in the United States, nationally or regionally, primarily by noncollegiate organizations, public and private. The scope of these programs ranges from incoming freshmen through postdoctoral students. Descriptions provided for each program indicate eligibility requirements, amount of the award, selection criteria, and application procedures. Well indexed.

The College Blue Book. 19th ed., 5 vols. New York: Macmillan, 1983; published irregularly.

The volume titled *Scholarships, Fellowships, Grants & Loans* lists and describes awards offered by corporations, labor unions, foundations, professional societies, and federal and state governmental agencies. Several indexes are provided: by title of the award, by name of the sponsoring organization, by level of the award (e.g., paraprofessional, community college, college, professional, postdoctoral, seminary), and by subject. Addresses of persons to contact for further information are given.

DRG: Directory of Research Grants. Scottsdale, AZ: Oryx, annual.

Describes more than 4,000 potential sources of funding for research-related projects within specific disciplines and subject areas. Awards for graduate study not limited by subject area are indexed under Dissertations and Scholarships. Others are under specific subjects, for instance, art (dissertation support), economics (scholarships and fellowships).

Fellowship Guide to Western Europe. 6th ed. New York: Council for European Studies, 1985.

Lists many fellowships and grants for study and travel in Europe. Provides details concerning eligibility requirements and procedures for applications. Entries are categorized as follows: general (broad qualifications), fellowships for women, fellowships for specific fields of study, fellowships tenable in specific countries.

Foundation Grants to Individuals. 4th ed. New York: Foundation Center, 1984.

Identifies foundations that give grants to individuals for various purposes, including scholarships and loans, fellowships, internships, and residencies. Descriptive entries include addresses of persons to contact for further information. A very useful bibliographic essay describing additional printed sources of information on grants to individuals is included in the preface.

Graduate Study in Psychology and Associated Fields. Rev. ed. Washington, DC: American Psychological Association, 1985.

The Grants Register. 9th ed. (1985-87). Edited by Normal Frankel. London: Macmillan, 1984; biennial.

An international directory of scholarships, fellowships, and research grants, exchange opportunities, support for creative work, and so on. Intended primarily "for students at or above the graduate level, and for all who require further professional or advanced vocational training" (editor's note). This directory is updated less frequently than the *Annual Register of Grant Support*, but its international coverage is broader.

Need a Lift? To Educational Opportunities, Careers, Loans, Scholarships, Employment. 34th ed. American Legion Education Program. Indianapolis: American Legion, 1985.

An annually revised guide of interest to any student in need of aid for postsecondary education. Sources of funds are listed and described in separate sections titled "For Undergraduates Only," "For Graduates," and "For Both." Other units contain information relative to state educational benefits, financial assistance for veterans and their dependents, sources of loans, and more.

Peterson's Grants for Graduate Students, 1986-88. Edited by Andrea Leakes. Princeton, NJ: Peterson's Guides, 1986.

The Student Guide to Fellowships and Internships. The Students of Amherst College. New York: E. P. Dutton, 1980.

Contains two kinds of information: advice on internship and fellowship hunting and descriptions of individual programs. The chapter on fellowships is devoted to the so-called national fellowships, which are open to students anywhere in the nation on a competitive basis: Fulbright-Hays, Luce Scholar's Program, Marshall Scholarship, Rhodes Scholarship, Rotary Educational Awards, Thomas J. Watson Fellowship Program, English-Speaking Union Study Grant, and Intercollegiate Studies Institute Weaver Fellowship.

Scholarships, Fellowships, and Loans. Vols. 6-7. S. Norman Feingold and Marie Feingold. Arlington, MA: Bellman, 1982.

Contains data on more than 1,800 funding sources available to researchers and students at all levels of post-secondary education.

Study Abroad: International Directory of Fellowships, Scholarships and Awards. 24th ed. Paris: UNESCO, 1983; biennial.

This edition was intended for use in 1984-85 and 1985-86. It is arranged in two parts: Part One lists international scholarships and other forms of financial aid for study abroad; Part Two lists international courses and study programs, some of which also have scholarships attached. An index to subjects of study is provided.

Specific Population Groups

Directory of Financial Aids for Minorities 1986-1987. Gail Ann Schlachter. Santa Barbara, CA: Reference Service Press, 1986.

Describes scholarships, fellowships, loans, grants, awards, internships, and state sources of educational benefits for minorities in general, Asian Americans, black Americans, Hispanic Americans, and Native Americans.

Directory of Financial Aids for Women. 2nd ed. Gail Ann Schlachter. Los Angeles: Reference Service Press, 1982.

A listing of scholarships, fellowships, loans, grants, awards, and internships designed primarily or exclusively for women. Indexed by sponsoring organization, geographic area, and subject.

A Foreign Student's Selected Guide to Financial Assistance for Study and Research in the United States. Garden City, NY: Adelphi University Press, 1983.

Provides information about awards specifically reserved for foreign nationals at 232 undergraduate schools and 173 graduate schools in the United States. Awards offered by other institutions and foundations are described on pp. 288-313. Note: Foreign students should also consult the indexes found in the general directories, such as the *Chronicle Student Aid Annual*, under the subject heading "foreign students."

A New Newspaper Devoted to Philanthropy

The Chronicle of Philanthropy. 1255 23rd St., NW, Ste. 700, Washington, DC 20037. $47.50 one year, 24 issues.

In the fall of 1988, this periodical began coverage of all the news of corporate and individual giving, foundations, fund-raising, taxation, regulation, management, and many more topics. It is published every other week and is timely, authoritative, and easy to read. Its publication is directed by the same organization that issues the well-known *Chronicle of Higher Education.*

Section C

Research Costing

How much does it cost to conduct a research project? One writer says that such a question can no more be answered than a question about how much it costs to go on a vacation. One major cost can be the overhead charges of the sponsoring agency. The overhead or indirect costs charged by universities to grants (especially federal grants) are commonly in the 40-50% range of the total grant. Other major cost variables include the size of population or sample involved, the mode of collecting data, the amount of assistance required, and the size of salaries needed for the principal investigator(s) and assistants. The motivation and efficiency of each member of the research team is a hidden variable.

Frequently, when the cost question is asked, researchers want to know all costs for every single aspect of planning and conducting a project, analyzing the data, and writing a final report. In other instances, they assume that researchers' salaries, typewriters, clerical staff, and even the graphic illustrator are fixed costs of the sponsoring organization; their only interest is in the out-of-pocket costs that will be incurred for data collection. Sometimes even computer costs are underwritten by the sponsoring organization. It is not surprising, therefore, that costs reported by one researcher are likely to be double or triple those reported by another.

Our purpose here is to enable various researchers working under different conditions to make cost estimates that apply to their own designs. In this section the first guide is a general form to apply to any research project. The "Guide to Research Costing" is a budget-time schedule summary setting forth all the major activities that are necessary and that will incur costs. To utilize this guide one of the principal needs is information about the costs associated with various modes of collecting data. Section 7.C.2 presents a guide to costs associated with the mail questionnaire. This is followed by a guide to comparative costs of telephone surveys and personal interviews (7.C.3). A subsection devoted to research budgeting (7.C.4) places the cost data in the format of a research proposal.

7.C.1 GUIDE TO RESEARCH COSTING

Activity	Total	Week ending _____	Week ending _____	Week ending _____	_____
1. Total 　a) Man hours 　b) Cost ($) 　c) % of total completed					
2. Planning 　a) Man hours 　b) Cost ($) 　c) % of total completed					
3. Pilot Study and Pretests 　a) Man hours 　b) Cost ($) 　c) % of total completed					
4. Drawing Sample 　a) Man hours 　b) Cost ($) 　c) % of total completed					
5. Preparing Observational Materials 　a) Man hours 　b) Cost ($) 　c) % of total completed					
6. Selection and Training 　a) Man hours 　b) Cost ($) 　c) % of total completed					
7. Trial Run 　a) Man hours 　b) Cost ($) 　c) % of total completed					
8. Revising Plans 　a) Man hours 　b) Cost ($) 　c) % of total completed					
9. Collecting Data 　a) Man hours 　b) Cost ($) 　c) % of total completed					
10. Processing Data 　a) Man hours 　b) Cost ($) 　c) % of total completed					
11. Preparing Final Report 　a) Man hours 　b) Cost ($) 　c) % of total completed					

SOURCE: Russell K. Ackoff, *Design for Social Research* (Chicago: University of Chicago, 1953), 347. By permission of the University of Chicago Press. Copyright 1953 by the University of Chicago.

NOTE: Suggested form for budget-time schedule summary. (There is nothing necessary or sufficient about this listing of activities, nor is the order absolute in any sense.)

7.C.2 GUIDE TO COSTS OF THE MAIL QUESTIONNAIRE

Dillman studied mail questionnaire costs over a 10-year period. The minimum first-class mailing rate was 6 cents in 1970, 8 cents in 1971, 13 cents in 1977, 15 cents in 1980, and 20 cents in 1981—a 333% increase in just over a decade. The first-class mailing rate went to 25 cents in 1988, and to 29 cents in 1991.

Other costs continue to rise as well. The average rate of increase between 1982 and 1991 has been about 8% per annum.

In this situation the researcher must make projections of costs from the base date (1982). Dillman has provided itemized costs for questionnaire surveys using his total design method (TDM; see his article in Section 4.10 of this volume). The costs are shown for general public surveys of Washington residents in 1977, which has been updated to 1982. The cost specifications include the following:

- 12-page questionnaires mailed for the minimum first-class postage in 1982 (20 cents)
- no keypunching or computer processing costs
- labor costs calculated at the prevailing rate ($4.50 per hour) for part-time clerical help, the type of labor normally used in studies
- professional supervision costs based on the number of hours actually spent by the principal investigator providing direct supervision of data collection activities

Table 7.2 shows costs by general expenditure area followed by phases of the study. The reader will note that costs are shown for one large statewide survey of the general public (450). The bottom line is a mean cost for each potential respondent of $4.33 for the larger sample and $6.86 for the smaller—a difference of $2.53.

Elimination of the cost for professional supervision (often considered a fixed cost) brings the difference down by 50 cents for the larger sample and $1.11 for the smaller; with free access to an existing clerical staff, the mean cost per interview drops to $1.85 and $2.81 for the two samples, respectively. Economies of scale make the difference; nearly all aspects of surveying can be achieved with lower cost as size increases. Getting both professional and clerical services free is seldom attained.

The variation in costs reported by different researchers can now be more fully understood. The costs shown in Table 7.2 cannot be transferred to any other survey. Dillman reports TDM surveys cited by other researchers in which researchers felt that such things as consultant fees, expensive computer equipment, and professional time spent drafting and redrafting the questionnaire should be charged to the survey budget. It is not unusual for the computer cost of data analysis to far exceed that reported in the table for data collection alone.

The researcher seeking estimates for a proposed mail questionnaire survey can utilize the table shown by estimating the percentage of expenditure required using the data given in the survey more nearly comparable to his or her own sample. A determination of inflationary costs since 1982 must be projected to the year of administration selected.

Conclusion. Data collection by mail is relatively inexpensive; in general, costs will be substantially lower than those encountered for personal interview or telephone surveys. Although all costs shown in the tables have shown significant increases, the relative costs of mail, personal interview, and telephone survey methods remain relatively stable.

TABLE 7.2 Sample Budgets for TDM Mail Surveys

	Large Statewide Survey of General Public (N = 4,500)	Small Statewide Survey of General Public (N = 450)	Your Survey?
General Costs			
Draw systematic sample from telephone directories or other sample source	$ 1,350	$ 150	____
Purchase mailout envelopes	210	40	____
Purchase business reply envelopes	160	30	____
Print questionnaires	775	275	____
Graphics design for cover	125	125	____
Telephone (toll charges)	200	20	____
Supplies (miscellaneous)	400	60	____
Type, proof, and store names in automatic typewriters	1,500[a]	190[a]	____
Subtotal	$ 3,260	$ 665	____
First Mailout			
Print cover letter	$ 150	$ 30	____
Address letters and envelopes	1,500[a]	165[a]	____
Postage for mailout	910	95	____
Prepare mailout packets	825[a]	115[a]	____
Postage for returned questionnaires (business reply envelopes)	250	25	____
Process and precode returns	375[a]	55[a]	____
Subtotal	$ 4,010	$ 485	____
Postcard Follow-Up			
Purchase postcards	$ 585	$ 60	____
Print postcards	220	30	____
Address postcards	675[a]	75[a]	____
Prepare mailout	225[a]	30[a]	____
Process and precode returns	375[a]	55[a]	____
Postage for returned questionnaires (business reply envelopes)	250	25	____
Subtotal	$ 2,330	$ 275	____
Third Mailout			
Print cover letter	$ 125	$ 25	____
Address letters and envelopes	1,425[a]	150[a]	____
Prepare mailout packets	600[a]	75[a]	____
Postage for mailout	500	50	____
Process and precode returns	375[a]	50[a]	____
Postage for returned questionnaires	170	17	____
Subtotal	$ 3,195	$ 367	____
Fourth Mailout			
Print cover letter	$ 75	$ 20	____
Address letters and envelopes	375[a]	40[a]	____
Prepare mailout packets	450[a]	50[a]	____
Postage for mailout (certified)	1,700	170	____
Process and precode returns	225[a]	25[a]	____
Postage for returned questionnaires	170	17	____
Subtotal	$ 2,995	$ 322	____
Professional Supervision			
Clerical staff	$ 2,250	$ 750	____
Grand Total	$19,500	$3,089	____

(Continued)

TABLE 7.2 (Continued)

	Large Statewide Survey of General Public (N = 4,500)	Small Statewide Survey of General Public (N = 450)	Your Survey?
Mean cost potential respondent	$4.33	$6.86	____
Mean cost, omitting professional supervision	$3.83	$5.75	____
Mean cost, assuming free access to existing clerical staff	$1.85	$2.81	____

SOURCES: Reprinted from Don A. Dillman, "Mail and Other Self-Administered Questionnaires," in *Handbook of Survey Research,* ed. Peter Rossi, James Wright, and Andy Anderson (New York: Academic Press, 1982), chap. 12.
a. Costs calculated on 1977 bases of clerical labor at $4.50 per hour and first-class postage at 20 cents per ounce. (First-class postage was raised to 20 cents per ounce in November 1981.) All operations involving typing of names and addresses onto letters, envelopes, and postcards included an additional charge for use of memory typewriters.

7.C.3 GUIDE TO COMPARATIVE COSTS OF THE TELEPHONE SURVEY AND PERSONAL INTERVIEW

Groves and Kahn of the Survey Research Center of the University of Michigan undertook a study in 1976 to identify certain basic characteristics of telephone surveys and compare them to corresponding features of personal interview surveys. A comparison of costs was an important objective.

The cost data shown in Table 7.3 are based on two national surveys: a telephone survey sample of 1,618 persons using random digit dialing, and a personal interview sample of 1,548 persons. These surveys include the following cost items:

1. All cost factors in sampling, pretest, training of interviewers, materials, field salaries, field travel, communication costs, control functions, and postinterview activities (interview-evaluation/debriefing, verification, and final report to respondents). This is a cost package in which the salaries of a large staff constitute a sizable component of the expense. But it still does not include various analyses made with the data collected.
2. The overall expenses of sampling and field costs for the telephone survey come to $37,939; for the personal survey, $84,864. This makes the telephone survey 45% less expensive for a roughly similar size sample of personal interviews.
3. The per-completed-interview cost for sampling and fieldwork is $23 using telephone interviews and $55 using personal interviews. This involves an average of 3.3 person-hours per telephone interview and 8.7 person-hours per personal interview.

Dillman has conducted extensive studies of the comparative costs of mail questionnaires and telephone surveys.[1] In responding to my request for his current experience with telephone survey costs, he wrote on October 1, 1980:

> I have resorted to using a rule of thumb. There are two major costs components: toll charges and interviewer time. I multiply the average length of interview times the per minute telephone cost. On in-state surveys, we have a standard per minute rate, and it's quite simple. On national surveys, one has to do some rough estimates as to how many calls will be in each zone. I then increase that value by about 20 percent to cover callbacks, wrong numbers and other connections that do not result in interviews. The other major component

of cost is interviewer time. Based on experience using my methods, I have concluded that the time required per completed interview is about twice the length of that interview. In other words, if my interviews are averaging 30 minutes, I allocate about 60 minutes of interviewer time per interview. The excess time is used for editing, coffee breaks, wrong numbers, callbacks, etc. To the minutes associated with each completed interview, I then allocate hourly wages. Adding together toll charges and interviewer costs gives me most of the costs of doing the surveys. Using the methods outlined in the book, I usually end up with about $1.50 per interview of additional cost: e.g., supervision and paper. So for a 30-minute instate interview, I figure [30 mins. × .09¢ (current toll charge)] $1.20 + $4.00 for wages plus $1.50 for supervision = $9.40. Costs vary tremendously depending upon geographic area, sampling method, and callback requirements.

It is interesting to observe the difference between the $23.45 reported by Groves and Kahn per completed telephone interview and the $9.40 given by Dillman. These figures substantiate my earlier statement that great variation can be observed in the reports of different researchers.

Total costs for a completed study are subject to wide variation depending on the amount of developmental work and analysis performed. Here is where computer time and salaries can incur very large costs.

There is considerable variation in the costs of operating phases of the two modes. Five areas exhibit the largest differences. Table 7.3 shows these to be sampling, prestudy, training, travel, and communication costs.

Conclusion. The telephone survey is substantially less expensive in time and money than the personal interview.[2] Nevertheless, selection of the more appropriate mode depends on a total evaluation of the advantages and disadvantages. See Section 4.14, "Choosing Among the Mail Questionnaire, Personal Interview, and Telephone Survey."

Notes

1. Don A. Dillman, *Mail and Telephone Surveys.* New York: Wiley-Interscience, 1978.
2. On August 30, 1982, Dillman wrote to me as follows:

> In response to your question about shifting costs relative to mail and telephone, I think the gap has narrowed a bit, but telephone surveys remain considerably more expensive. The changes in postage and labor costs are the reasons. Comparing of mail and telephone costs is confounded by the different way that greater length affects cost. For telephone surveys, costs go up in fairly direct proportion to length. But for mail, the difference in cost between administering a four- and a twelve-page questionnaire is fairly insignificant. The first "jump" comes when one goes beyond the maximum weight for the 20-cent stamp, which for the TDM usually occurs after twelve pages.

GUIDE TO RESEARCH BUDGETING   7.C.4

This guide includes all items that are required in the NSF research grant proposal budget.[1] If the researcher has carefully followed the guide to research costing presented in Section 7.C.1, the preparation of the grant proposal budget will be more accurate.

TABLE 7.3 A Comparative Summary of Costs for Two Large Sample Studies and a Design Utilizing Telephone Survey and Personal Interview as Modes of Data Collection (1976)

Major Division of Work	Telephone Survey (N = 1,618)		Personal Interview (N = 1,548)	
	$	%	$	%
1. Sampling costs	955.27	2.5	8,547.15	10.1
2. Pretesting	723.45	1.9	1,113.10	1.3
3. Training and prestudy work	2,066.34	5.4	9,523.61	11.2
4. Materials	1,374.96	3.6	3,660.15	4.3
5. Ann Arbor headquarters field office salaries: administrative and clerical (typing)	1,394.74	3.7	4,159.42	4.9
6. Field salaries: supervisory and interviewer	12,544.69	33.1	32,277.92	38.0
7. Field staff travel		0.0	16,815.11	19.8
8. Communications	15,793.60	41.6	5,980.31	7.0
9. Control function	1,202.55	3.2	883.22	1.0
10. Postinterview activities				
a. Interviewer evaluation/debriefing	246.72	0.6	281.29	0.3
b. Verification	507.53	1.3	876.38	1.0
c. Report to respondents	1,129.94	3.0	746.26	0.9
Total	$37,929.79		$84,863.92	
Per interview costs	$ 23.45		$ 54.82	
Per interview average hours required	3.3		8.7	

SOURCE: Adapted from Robert M. Groves and Robert L. Kahn, *Surveys by Telephone: A National Comparison with Personal Interviews* (New York: Academic Press, 1979), 189, 193.

Budget Format

Proposals for research grants should include budgets in the format shown on the following page for each year of support requested. It is important to note that the use of a budget summary does not eliminate the need for an itemized explanation of proposed costs when required.

Note

1. National Science Foundation, *Grants for Scientific Research*, NSF73-12 (Washington, DC: National Science Foundation), Appendix III, 34-39. For a copy, write National Science Foundation, Washington, DC 20550.

RESEARCH GRANT PROPOSAL BUDGET
Year Beginning _____

Budget Category	NSF funded Man-months			Proposed amount
	Cal	Acad	Sum	
A. Salaries and Wages				
1. Senior personnel				
a. (Co) Principal investigator				
(list by name)	____	____	____	_____
b. Faculty associates				
(list by name)	____	____	____	_____
Subtotal				_____
2. Other personnel (nonfaculty)				
a. Research associates (postdoctoral)				
(list separately by name if available,				
otherwise give numbers)				
. . . .	____	____	____	_____
. . . .	____	____	____	_____
b. Nonfaculty professionals				
(list separately, by category, giving				
number, e.g., one computer				
programmer)				
. . . .	____	____	____	_____
c. (number) Grad. students				
(Res. Asst.)				_____
d. (number) Prebaccalaureate				
students.				_____
e. (number) Secretarial-clerical				_____
f. (number) Technical, shop, and				
other				
Total salaries and wages				_____
B. Staff Benefits				_____
C. Total Salaries, wages and staff				
Benefits (A + B)				_____
D. Permanent Equipment				
(list as required)				
1.				_____
2.				_____
Total permanent equipment				_____
E. Expendable Supplies and Equipment . . .				
F. Travel				
1. Domestic.				_____
2. Foreign (list as required).				_____
Total travel				_____
G. Publication Costs				_____
H. Computer Costs (if charged as direct costs)				_____
I. Other Costs				
(itemize by major type)				
1.				_____
2.				_____
3.				_____
Total other costs				_____
J. Total Direct Costs (C through I)				_____
K. Indirect Costs				
1. On campus. . . . . .% of				_____
2. Off campus . . . . .% of				_____
Total indirect costs				_____
L. Total Costs (J plus K)				_____
M. Total Contributions from Other				
Sources				_____
N. Total Estimated Project Cost				_____

Section **D**

Research Reporting

Within the professional code, the reporting of research is one of the mores. Beyond the mundane pressures to publish, there is an underlying normative prescription: *Let the world know what you have found. Add to the storehouse of knowledge. Try to write so that you connect past research with your findings and so that other scholars may build upon your work in the future.*

In this section both oral and written reporting are described. Research reporting usually takes place in a rather closed world, where professionals interact with one another either in professional meetings or through learned journals. Some important attributes of this subculture will be described.

The subsections that follow include material on specifications for sociological report rating, a form for sociological report rating, and a guide to sociological journals and related journals. Also discussed are where and how (and why) sociologists publish their findings, information on professional communication and reporting, and annual meetings held by various sociological and kindred societies.

Lists are provided of journals sponsored by the American Sociological Association and the American Psychological Association, as well as major journals in political science and public administration, anthropology, and education, and those used by organizational and behavioral researchers in business and by journalism and communication researchers.

7.D.1 SPECIFICATIONS FOR SOCIOLOGICAL REPORT RATING

	Defective	*Substandard*	*Standard*	*Superior*
Statement of Problem				
1. Clarity of statement	Statement is ambiguous, unclear, biased, inconsistent, or irrelevant to the research.	Problem must be inferred from incomplete or unclear statement.	Statement is unambiguous and includes precise description of research objectives.	Statement is unambiguous and includes formal propositions, and specifications for testing them.

	Defective	*Substandard*	*Standard*	*Superior*
2. Significance of problem	No problem stated, or problem is meaningless, unsolvable, or trivial.	Solution of the problem would be of interest to a few specialists.	Solution of the problem would be of interest to many sociologists.	Solution of the problem would be of interest to most sociologists.
3. Documentation	No documentation to earlier work, or documentation is incorrect.	Documentation to earlier work is incomplete or contains errors of citation or interpretation.	Documentation to earlier work is reasonably complete.	Documentation shows in detail the evolution of the research problem from previous research findings.
Description of Method				
4. Appropriateness of method	Problems cannot be solved by this method.	Only a partial or tentative solution can be obtained by this method.	Solution of the problem by this method is possible, but uncertain.	Problem is definitely solvable by this method.
5. Adequacy of sample or field	Sample is too small, or not suitable, or biased, or of unknown sampling characteristics.	The cases studied are meaningful, but findings cannot be projected.	Findings are projectable, but with errors of considerable, or of unknown, magnitude.	Results are projectable with known small errors, or the entire universe has been enumerated.
6. Replicability	Not replicable.	Replicable in substance, but not in detail.	Replicable in detail with additional information from the author(s).	Replicable in detail from the information given.
Presentation of Results				
7. Completeness				
8. Comprehensibility	Results are incomprehensible, or enigmatic.	Comprehension of results requires special knowledge or skills.	Relevant results are presented, partly in detail, partly in summary form.	Relevant details are presented in detail.
9. Yield	No contribution to solution of problem.	Useful hints or suggestions toward solution of problem.	Tentative solution of problem.	Definitive solution of problem.
Interpretation				
10. Accuracy	Errors of calculation, transcription, dictation, logic, or fact detected.	Errors likely with the procedures used. No major errors detected.	Errors unlikely with the procedures used. No errors detected.	Positive checks of accuracy included in the procedures.
11. Bias	Evident bias in presentation of results and in interpretation.	Some bias in interpretation, but not in presentation of results.	No evidence of bias.	Positive precautions against bias included in procedures.
12. Usefulness	Not useful.	Possible influence on some future work in this area.	Probable influence on some future work in this area.	Probable influence on all future work in this area.

SOURCE: Theodore Caplow designed this form. It was tested by the Committee on Research, American Sociological Society. See "Official Reports and Proceedings," *American Sociological Review* (December 1958): 704–11. See Stuart C. Dodd and Louis N. Gray, "Scient-Scales for Measuring Methodology," Institute for Sociological Research, University of Washington, Seattle, 1962. Mimeograph copies available on request.

7.D.2 FORM FOR SOCIOLOGICAL REPORT RATING

Author _____

Title _____

Publication Reference _____

Rater _____

Date _____

Check (✓) Appropriate Columns	Defective 0	Substandard 1	Standard 2	Superior 3
Statement of problem:				
1. Clarity of Statement	____	____	____	____
2. Significance of Problem	____	____	____	____
3. Documentation	____	____	____	____
Description of method:				
4. Appropriateness of Method	____	____	____	____
5. Adequacy of Sample or Field	____	____	____	____
6. Replicability	____	____	____	____
Presentation of results:				
7. Completeness	____	____	____	____
8. Comprehensibility	____	____	____	____
9. Yield	____	____	____	____
Interpretation:				
10. Accuracy	____	____	____	____
11. Bias	____	____	____	____
12. Usefulness	____	____	____	____

Enter number of checks in each column in appropriate blanks; weight as indicated, and add for Total Rating

__ X 0 = 0   __ X 1 = __   __ X 2 = __   __ X 3 = __

[*Total Rating*]
[ ]

SOURCE: Theodore Caplow designed this rating form. Test reliabilities appear in "Official Reports and Proceedings," *American Sociological Review* 23 (December 1958): 704–11. See also the reports of the Educational Testing Service, Princeton, NJ, for ingenious rating scales on a large variety of subjects.

7.D.3 GUIDE TO SOCIOLOGICAL JOURNALS[1]

Acta Sociologica. Scandinavian Sociological Association, Norwegian University Press, Kolstadgt, 1 Box 2959 Toegen, 0608, Oslo 6, Norway; or Publications Expediting, Inc., 200 Meachen Ave., Elmont, NY 11003.

1955. Quarterly.

American Journal of Economics and Sociology. 5 E. 44th St., New York, NY 10017.

1941. Quarterly.

American Journal of Sociology. University of Chicago Press, Journals Division, P.O. Box 37005, Chicago, IL 60637.

1895. Bimonthly. Abstracts. Book reviews. Annual index. Cumulative index for volumes 1-80.

American Sociological Review. American Sociological Association, 1722 N St., NW, Washington, DC 20036.

1936. Bimonthly. Abstracts. Book Reviews. Annual index. Cumulative index for volumes 1-50. Official journal of the American Sociological Association; distributed free to members.

American Sociologist. Department 4010, Transaction Periodicals Consortium, Rutgers University, New Brunswick, NJ 08903.

1966. Quarterly. Devoted primarily to discussion of professional concerns and includes employment bulletins and announcements of professional meetings. Official journal of the American Sociological Association and distributed free to members.

Annual Review of Sociology. American Sociological Association, 1722 N St., NW, Washington, DC 20036.

1975. Bimonthly. Progress reports of developments in various fields of sociology. Official journal of the American Sociological Association.

Archives Européens de Sociologie (European Journal of Sociology). Muséee de l'Homme, Palais de Chaillot, F.-75, Paris XVI, France.

1960. Semiannually. Annual index. Text in English, French, and German.

Australian and New Zealand Journal of Sociology. La Trobe University Bookshop, Bundoorh, Victoria, 3085 Australia.

1965. Semiannually. Abstracts. Book reviews. Annual index. Official journal of the Sociological Association of Australia and New Zealand.

British Journal of Sociology. Routledge & Kegan Paul, Ltd., Broadway House, Newton Rd., Henley-on-Thames, Oxon RG9 1EN, England.

1950. Quarterly. Book reviews. Annual index. Cumulative index of volumes 1-10.

California Sociologist: A Journal of Sociology and Social Work. Department of Sociology, California State University, Los Angeles, CA 90032.

1978. Semiannually.

Canadian Journal of Sociology/Cahiers Canadiens de Sociologie. Department of Sociology, University of Alberta, Edmonton, Alberta, Canada T6G 2H4.

Canadian Review of Sociology and Anthropology. Department of Sociology and Anthropology, Concordia University, 1455 de Maisonneuve Ouest. N-317, Montreal, Quebec, Canada H3G 1M8.

1964. Quarterly. Official journal of the Canadian Sociological Anthropology Association.

Chinese Sociology and Anthropology: A Journal of Translations. M. E. Sharpe, Inc., 80 Business Park Dr., Armonk, NY 10504.

1968. Quarterly.

Clinical Sociology Review. Clinical Sociology Association, Department of Sociology, Rhode Island College, Providence, RI 02908.

1981. Annually.

Comparative Social Research. Department of Sociology, University of New Mexico, Albuquerque, NM 87131.

1978. Annually.

Contemporary Sociology: A Journal of Review. American Sociological Association, 1722 N St., NW, Washington, DC 20036.

1972. Bimonthly. Book reviews. Book notes. Letters. Official journal of the American Sociological Association.

Contributions to Indian Sociology. Mouton & Company, Herderstraat 5, The Hague, Netherlands.

1957. Irregularly. Book reviews. Annual index.

The Cornell Journal of Social Relations. Sociology Department, Uris Hall, Cornell University, Ithaca, NY 14850.

1966. Semiannually. Publishes especially, but not exclusively, the work of young scholars.

Current Perspectives in Social Theory. Department of Sociology. University of Kansas, Lawrence, KS 66045.

1980. Annually.

Current Sociology: A Journal of the International Sociological Association. Sage Publications, 2455 Teller Rd., Newbury Park, CA 91320.

1952. Triannually. Each issue contains an analysis of trends in, and an annotated bibliography on, some aspect of sociology.

European Journal of Sociology. Journal Department, Cambridge University Press, 32 E. 57th St., New York, NY 10022.

G.S.S. Journal. Columbia University Graduate Sociology Club, Department of Sociology, Columbia University, 605 W. 115th St., New York, NY 10025.

1961. Triannually. Official journal of the Columbia University Graduate Sociology Club.

Free Inquiry in Creative Sociology. Department of Sociology, Oklahoma State University, Stillwater, OK 74078.

1972. Biannually.

Ghana Journal of Sociology. Department of Sociology, University of Ghana, Legon, Ghana, West Africa.

1963. Semiannually. Book reviews. Official publication of the Ghana Sociological Association.

Humanity and Society. Association for Humanist Sociology, Department of Sociology, Howard University, Washington, DC 20059.

1977. Quarterly.

India Journal of Sociology. Sociology House, Hauz Khas Enclave, New Delhi, India 110016.

1970. Triannually. Official journal of India Academy of Social Sciences.

The Insurgent Sociologist. Department of Sociology, University of Oregon, Eugene, OR 97403.

1969. Quarterly. Devoted to development of new sociology with Marxist orientation.

International Journal of Comparative Sociology. Department of Social Anthropology, Karnataka University, Dharwad 580003, Karnataka, India.

1960. Semiannually.

International Journal of Contemporary Sociology (Indian Sociological Bulletin). Dr. Raj P. Mohan, Department of Sociology, Auburn University, Auburn, AL 36849.

1963. Biannually.

International Journal of Critical Sociology. Editor: T.K.N. Unnithan, Department of Sociology, Jaipur, India.

1973. Biannual publication of Jaipur Institute of Sociology. Publishes articles critical of present type of sociology and critical appraisals of social issues and policies.

International Journal for the Sociology of Law. Editors: Maureen Cain, Department of Sociology, Brunel University, Uxbridge, England; Kit Carson, Department of Criminology, University of Edinburgh, Scotland; and Paul Wiles, Department of Law, University of Sheffield, England. Publisher: Academic Press, Inc. (London) Ltd., Journal Subscription Department 24-28, Oval Rd., London NW2 70X, England.

International Review of Modern Sociology. International Journals, Inc., Department of Sociology, Northern Illinois University, De Kalb, IL 60115.

1971. Semiannually.

Jewish Journal of Sociology. 187 Gloucester Place, London NW1 6BU, England.

1959. Semiannually. Book reviews. Annual index.

Journal of Health and Social Behavior. American Sociological Association, 1722 N St., NW, Washington, DC 20036.

1967. Quarterly. Book reviews. Annual index. Official publication of the American Sociological Association. 1960-66, volumes 1-7, published as the *Journal of Health and Human Behavior.*

Journal of Historical Sociology. Basil Blackwell, Box 1320, Murray Hill Station, New York, NY 10156.

Journal of Mathematical Sociology. Gordon and Breach, Science Publishers, Inc., P.O. Box 197, London WC2E 9PX, England.

1971. Biannually.

International Journal of Sociology. M. E. Sharpe, Inc., 80 Business Park Dr., Armonk, NY 10504.

1971. Quarterly.

International Journal of Sociology of the Family. Department of Sociology, Northern Illinois University, De Kalb, IL 60115.

1971. Semiannually.

International Review of Modern Sociology. Department of Sociology, Northern Illinois University, De Kalb, IL 60115.

1971. Semiannually.

International Sociology. International Sociological Association, University College, Cardiff Press, P.O. Box 78, Cardiff CF1 1XL, Wales.

Journal of Political and Military Sociology. Department of Sociology, Northern Illinois University, De Kalb, IL 60115.

1973. Biannually.

Journal of Sociology and Social Welfare. School of Social Work, Western Michigan University, Kalamazoo, MI 49008.

1973. Quarterly.

Mid-American Review of Sociology. Department of Sociology, University of Kansas, Lawrence, KS 66045.

Philippine Sociological Review. Philippine Sociological Society, Central Subscriptions Service, Box 154, Manila 2801, Philippines.

1953. Quarterly. Cumulative index for volumes 1-13. Official journal of the Philippine Sociological Society.

Polish Sociological Bulletin. Publishing House of the Polish Academy of Sciences, Rynek 9, 50-106, Wroclaw, Poland.

1961. Semiannually. Official publication of the Polish Sociological Association.

Qualitative Sociology. Human Sciences Press, 72 Fifth Ave., New York, NY 10011.

1977. Quarterly. Devoted to the qualitative interpretation of social life.

Revista Mexicana de Sociologia. Facultad de Ciencias Politicas y Sociales, Ciudad Universitaria, Mexico 20, D.F.

1938. Quarterly.

Revista de Sociologia. Facultad de Sociologia, Universitaria Pontificia Boliviana, Av. de La Playa, 40-88, Apdo. 1178, Medellin, Colombia.

1968. Semiannually.

Revue Internationale de Sociologie (International Review of Sociology). University of Rome, 00/00 Rome, Italy.

1964. Triannually. Covers proceedings of International Institute of Sociology.

Rivista Di Sociologia. Instituto Di Sociologia, Libera Universita, Viale Pola, 12, Roma, Italy.

1963. Quarterly.

Rural Sociology. 325 Morgan Hall, University of Tennessee, Knoxville, TN 37916.

1936. Quarterly. Abstracts. Book reviews. Annual index. Cumulative indexes for volumes 1-20 and 21-30. Official journal of the Rural Sociological Society.

Social Forces. University of North Carolina Press with Southern Sociological Society, 168 Hamilton Hall, University of North Carolina, Box 2288, Chapel Hill, NC 27514.

1925. Quarterly. Abstracts. Book reviews. Annual index. 1922-25, volumes 1-3, published as the *Journal of Social Forces.*

Social Problems. HB 208 State University College, 1300 Englewood Ave., Buffalo, NY 14222.

1953. Quarterly. Book reviews. Annual index. Official journal of the Society for the Study of Social Problems.

Social Research. Manuscripts: Boyd Printing, 65 Fifth Ave., Rm. 354, New York, NY 10003.

1934. Quarterly.

Social Science Journal. Department of Sociology, Colorado State University, Fort Collins, CO 80526.

1964. Quarterly. Journal of Western Social Science Association.

Social Science Quarterly. Will C. Hogg Building, University of Texas, Austin, TX 78712.

1920. Quarterly. Journal of Southwestern Social Sciences Association.

Social Science Research. Editors: James D. Wright and Peter H. Rossi, University of Massachusetts, Amherst. Academic Press, 111 Fifth Ave., New York, NY 10003.

1972. Quarterly. Multidisciplinary journal emphasizing quantitative and methodological techniques.

Sociological Bulletin. Indian Sociological Society, Center for the Study of Social Systems, Jawaharlal Nehru University. New Delhi, India 110057.

1951. Semiannually. Official publication of the Indian Sociological Society.

Sociological Focus. North Central Sociological Association, Department of Sociology, Kent State University, Kent, OH 44242.

1967. Quarterly. Official journal of the North Central Sociological Association.

Sociological Forum. Department of Sociology, Cornell University, Ithaca, NY 14853.

1989. Quarterly. Editor: Robin Williams. Official journal of the Eastern Sociological Society.

Sociological Inquiry. OIES, University of Texas Press, Journals Department, P.O. Box 7819, Austin, TX 78712.

1961. Semiannually. Annual index. Each issue devoted to a single topic. Official journal of Alpha Kappa Delta. 1930-60, volumes 1-30, published as *Alpha Kappa Deltan.*

Sociological Methods and Research. Sage Publications, 2455 Teller Rd., Newbury Park, CA 91320.

1974. Quarterly. Devoted to sociology as a cumulative empirical science, focused on the assessment of the scientific status of sociology.

Sociological Quarterly. Department of Sociology, Southern Illinois University, Carbondale, IL 61761.

1960. Quarterly. Journal of the Midwest Sociological Society.

Sociological Review. University of Keele, Keele, Staffordshire ST5 5BG, England.

1953. Triannually. Book reviews. Annual index.

Sociological Spectrum. Mid-South Sociological Association, Hemisphere Publishing, 79 Madison Ave., New York, NY 10016.

1980. Quarterly.

Sociologie et Societies. Department de Sociologie, Universite de Montreal, Montreal, Canada.

1969. Semiannually. Cross-cultural journals in sociology in French.

Sociologiske Meddelelser. Sociological Institute, University of Copenhagen, Rosenborggrade 15, Copenhagen K, Denmark.

1952. Semiannually. Book reviews. Annual index. Cumulative index for volumes 1-10.

Sociologisk Forskning. Swedish Sociological Association, Stockholm Universitet, S10691 Stockholm, Sweden.

Sociological Theory. American Sociological Association, 1722 N St., NW, Washington, DC 20036.

Semiannually.

Sociologus: New Series. Duncker and Humbolt, Dietrich-Schafer-Weg 9, Berlin 41, West Germany.

1951. Semiannually. Abstracts. Book reviews. Text in English and German.

Sociology. British Sociological Association, 351 Station Rd., Dorridge Solihull, W. Midland B93 8EY, England.

1967. Triannually. Official publication of the British Sociological Association.

Sociology of Education. American Sociological Association, 1722 N St., NW, Washington, DC 20036.

1963. Quarterly. Abstracts. Annual index. Official publication of the American Sociological Association. 1927-62, volumes 1-36, published as the *Journal of Educational Sociology.*

Sociology and Social Research. University of Southern California, University Park, Los Angeles, CA 90089-0032.

1927. Quarterly. Abstracts. Book reviews. Annual index. Cumulative index for volumes 1-30. 1916-21, volumes 1-5, published as *Studies in Sociology;* 1921-27, volumes 6-11, published as *Journal of Applied Sociology.*

Work and Occupations: An International Journal. Sage Publications, 2455 Teller Rd., Newbury Park, CA 91320.

1974. Quarterly.

Social Psychology Quarterly (formerly *Sociometry*). American Sociological Association, 1722 N St., NW, Washington, DC 20036.

1937. Quarterly. Abstracts. Annual index. Official publication of the American Sociological Association.

Teaching Sociology. American Sociological Association, 1722 N St., NW, Washington, DC 20036.

1973. Quarterly.

Theory and Society. P.O. Box 1113, Washington University, St. Louis, MO 63136.

1974. Bimonthly.

The West African Journal of Sociology and Political Science. Editor: Justin Labinjoh, University of Ibadan, Department of Sociology, Ibadan, Nigeria.

Note

1. Two earlier guides have prepared the way for this latest guide to sociological journals. They are Lawrence J. Rhoades, *The Author's Guide to Selected Journals* (Washington, DC: American Sociological Association, 1975), and Marvin Sussman, *Author's Guide to Journals in Sociology and Related Fields* (New York: Haworth, 1978). Bettina J. Huber has updated the listing of journals with her *Publishing Options: An Author's Guide to Journals, 1982* (Washington, DC: American Sociological Association, 1982). In 1981 she sent questionnaires to 390 North American journals that appeared to deal with topics of interest to sociologists. Considerable information was received from those answering. The guide contains a list of subject areas covered by the journals, article types, abstracting and indexing services, and a list of previous journal titles for journals changing their names. The listing in this section has been checked using *Sociological Abstracts*, 1987-88, and *Ulrich's International Periodicals Directory*, 1987-88. Both directories have extensive information about each journal.

GUIDE TO RELATED SOCIOLOGICAL JOURNALS   7.D.4

The following journals were identified by Lawrence J. Rhoades, Marvin Sussman, or Bettina J. Huber in their various guides to journals in sociology and related fields.

Academy of Management Review
Acta Criminologica
Administration & Society
Administration in Mental Health
Administrative Science Quarterly
Administrative Science Review
Adolescence
Africa Today
African Studies Review
Altered States of Consciousness
Alternative Lifestyles
American Demographics
American Educational Research Journal
American Journal of Community
    Psychology
American Journal of Political Science
American Psychologist
American Statistician
Asian Survey
AV Communication Review
Behavior Research Methods &
    Instrumentation
Behavior Science Research
California Journal of Educational Research
Catalyst
Character Potential: A Record of Research
Child Care Quarterly
Child Psychiatry and Human Development
Child Welfare
Cleveland State Law Review
Clinical Social Work Journal
Cognition
Colorado Quarterly
Communication Research

Community College Social Science
    Quarterly
Community Mental Health Journal
Comparative Political Studies
Compensation Review
Continuity and Change
Crime and Delinquency
Crime and Social Justice
Criminal Justice and Behavior
Criminology
Cybernetica
Cycles
Day Care and Early Education
Demography
Drug Forum
Economic and Social Review
Education and Urban Society
Environment and Behavior
et al.
ETC.: A Review of General Semantics
Ethnicity
European Journal of Social Psychology
Evaluation
Exceptional Children
Family Coordinator
Family Planning Digest
Family Planning Perspectives
Family Process
Federal Probation
Feminist Issues
Feminist Studies
Free Inquiry in Creative Sociology
The Futurist
Gender and Society

Georgia Social Science Journal
The Gerontologist
The Green Revolution
Group Psychotherapy & Psychodrama
Growth and Change
Handbook of International Sociometry
Harvard Business Review
Health Services Research
Hospital Administration
Human Behavior Magazine
The Human Context
Human Mosaic
Human Resource Management
Humanitas
Improving College & University Teaching
The Indian Historian
Industrial and Labor Relations Review
Industrial Relations: A Journal of
    Economy & Society
Intellect
International Development Review
International Interactions
International Journal of Aging & Human
    Development
International Journal of Cooperative
    Development
International Journal of Ethnic Studies
International Journal of Offender
    Therapy & Comparative Criminology
International Journal of Politics,
    Culture, and Society
International Journal of Symbology
International Journal of the Addictions
International Migration Review
International Review of Administrative
    Sciences
International Studies Quarterly
Issues in Criminology
Journal for the Theory of Social Behavior
Journal of Black Studies
Journal of Aging Studies
Journal of American Folklore
Journal of Applied Behavioral Science
Journal of Applied Communications
    Research
Journal of Applied Social Psychology
Journal of Applied Social Sciences
Journal of Black Studies
Journal of Broadcasting
Journal of Communication
Journal of Conflict Resolution
Journal of Consumer Affairs
Journal of Contemporary Ethnography
Journal of Criminal Law & Criminology
Journal of Cross-Cultural Psychology
Journal of Developing Areas
Journal of Educational Psychology
Journal of Educational Thought
Journal of Emotional Education
Journal of Ethnic Studies
Journal of Forecasting
Journal of General Psychology
Journal of Higher Education

Journal of Homosexuality
Journal of Human Resources
Journal of Interamerican Studies &
    World Affairs
Journal of Law and Society
Journal of Leisure Research
Journal of Marketing Research
Journal of Marriage and the Family
Journal of Negro Education
Journal of Personality & Social
    Psychology
Journal of Personality Assessment
Journal of Popular Culture
Journal of Psychology
Journal of Research in Crime and
    Delinquency
Journal of School Psychology
Journal of Sex Research
Journal of Social and Personal
    Relationships
Journal of Social Issues
Journal of Social Policy
Journal of Social Psychology
Journal of Socio-Economic Planning
    Sciences
Journal of the American Geriatrics Society
Journal of the American Institute
    of Planners
Journal of the Association for the Study
    of Perception
Journal of the Community Development
    Society
Journal of the Scientific Study of Religion
Journal of Thought
Journal of Urban Affairs
Journal of Vocational Behavior
Law and Society Review
Leisure Sciences
Leisure Studies
Manpower
Methods of Information in Medicine
Milbank Memorial Fund Quarterly/Health
    and Society
Multivariate Behavioral Research
The New Scholar
Opinion
Organization Science
Peace and Change: A Journal of Peace
    Research
People Watching
Personnel
The Personnel Administrator
Personnel and Guidance Journal
Political Science Quarterly
Population Review
Population Studies
Public Opinion Quarterly
Prison Journal
Psychiatry
Psychological Bulletin
Psychological Record
Psychological Review
Psychology

Psychometrika
Public Administration Review
Public Welfare
Quarterly Journal of Economics
Quarterly Journal of Speech
Race
Review of Religious Research
Religious Humanism
Research on Aging
Research on Consumer Behavior
Review of Educational Research
Review of Public Data Use
Review of Social Theory
Rocky Mountain Social Science Journal
Rural Sociologist
Sage Family Studies Abstracts
S.A.M. Advanced Management Journal
Science & Society
*Signs: Journal of Women in Culture
  and Society*
Simulation & Gaming
Small Group Behavior
Social Action
Social Biology
Social Compass
Social Policy

Social Science Quarterly
Social Work
Sociological Analysis
Sociological Forum
Sociological Perspectives
Sociology of Sport
Sociology of Sport Journal
Soundings: An Interdisciplinary Journal
Southeastern Review
Southern Speech Communication Journal
Studies in Family Planning
Suicide & Life-Threatening Behavior
Symbolic Interaction
Technology and Culture
Technology Assessment
Town Planning Review
Trans-Action
University of Chicago School Review
Urban Affairs Quarterly
Urban and Social Change Review
Urban Education
War on Hunger
War/Peace Report
Women's Studies
World Politics
Youth & Society

Supplementary List of Related Sociological Journals

This is a list of journals that publish work of interest to sociologists who have specialized interests. Some are new in the last five to seven years and express increased concern with drugs, crime, family, health, and environmental problems. Even this supplementary list does not begin to exhaust the array of journals with some relationship to sociology. Many journals related to education, law, communication, politics, and the economy are not listed. Those that are listed fall most closely within the "sociological orbit."

Advances in Alcohol and Substance Abuse
Aging and Society
Alternative Higher Education
American Behavioral Scientist
American Journal of Police
*Annals of the American Academy of
  Political and Social Science*
Armed Forces and Society
Behavior Today
Behavioral and Brain Sciences
Bioethics Quarterly
The Black Scholar
Caribbean Review
Case Analysis
Child and Adolescent Social Work Journal
Children and Youth Services Review
Comparative Education Review
Comparative Studies in Society and History
*Contemporary Crisis, Crime, Law, and
  Social Policy*
Contemporary Psychology

Current Anthropology
Decision Sciences
Economy and Society
Energy and Society
Ethnic and Racial Studies
*Evaluation: A Forum for Human Service
  Decision Centers*
Evaluation Quarterly
Evaluation Review
Family Relations
Family Therapy
Focus on Poverty Research
Group
Health and Social Work
Health Policy Quarterly
Home Health Care Services Quarterly
Housing and Safety
Human Communication Research
Human Ecology
Human Sexuality Update
Human Studies

Humanity and Society
International Journal of Aging and Human Development
International Journal of Group Tensions
International Journal of Health Services
International Journal of Urban and Regional Research
International Quarterly of Community Health Education
International Social Science Journal
Journal of American Statistical Association
Journal of Business
Journal of Community Health
Journal of Comparative Health Studies
Journal of Consumer Research
Journal of Divorce
Journal of Drug Education
Journal of Family History
Journal of Family Issues
Journal of Homosexuality
Journal of Housing for the Elderly
Journal of International and Comparative Social Welfare
Journal of Interpersonal Violence
Journal of Nonverbal Behavior
Journal of Organizational Behavior and Performance Management
Journal of Religion
Journal of Religion and Health
Journal of Research in Personality
Journal of Social Service Research
Journal of the History of the Behavioral Sciences
Knowledge: Creation, Diffusion, Utilization
Language in Society
Marriage and Family Review

Merrill-Palmer Quarterly of Behavior and Development
Mexican Studies/Estudios Mexicanos
Migration Review
Multivariate Behavioral Research
Offender Rehabilitation
Omega: Journal of Death and Dying
Organizational Behavior and Human Performance
Organizational Studies
New Human Services Review
Population: Behavioral, Social, and Environmental Issues
Population and Environment
Psychology of Women Quarterly
Quarterly Journal of Ideology
Social Analysis
Social Behavior
Social Indicator Research
Social Science History
Social Science Journal
Social Science Review
Social Work in Health Care
Social Work Research and Abstracts
Society Magazine
Sociology of Health and Illness
Survey Research
Symbolic Interaction
Topics in Strategic Planning for Health Care
Women and Criminal Justice
Women and Health
Women and Politics
Women Studies Abstracts
Work, Employment, and Society
Work and Organizations

7.D.5   WHERE SOCIOLOGISTS PUBLISH: WHERE PRESTIGIOUS SOCIOLOGISTS PUBLISH AND WHY

Sociologists publish research monographs with numerous publishing companies and university presses and research articles in 300 or more journals. A directory of publishers lists more than 260 publishing outlets in the United States. The "Guide to Sociological Journals" (Section 7.D.3) includes 72 journals, and the list of related journals in Section 7.D.4 extends that number to almost 200. Other outlets include many well-known periodicals that print sociological articles, including *Harper's Magazine, The Atlantic, Commentary,* and *New Republic.* Sociologists write in newspapers, prepare pamphlets, and distribute mimeographed and printed materials to selected audiences.[1] They write to secure tenure and promotion, to gain merit increases, to increase their status, and because they just like to write and "get their work out." They are driven by an ethic that impels them to "make their work known" so that their knowledge will be preserved and transmitted.

Of all the motives that drive the scholar to write, the most universal and persistent is the desire for status. This is expressed first as a desire to become "known" and then as the desire to rank even higher in prestige. It is appropriate therefore to find out which journals rank high in prestige.

Where Do Prestigious Sociologists Publish and Why?

Ideally, every writer would be judged by the intrinsic worth of his or her research, in whatever journal it appeared. In fact, no scholar, no matter how thorough, can read all or even a substantial part of the available journals. The result is that each sociologist who publishes is evaluated in part (in large part?) by the reputations of the journals in which he or she publishes. The degree to which most articles are noticed, read, and cited depends to a great extent on the kinds of journals in which the articles are published.

Norval D. Glenn undertook investigations of American sociologists' evaluations of 63 journals in which sociologists frequently publish.[2] In February 1970, he mailed a questionnaire to a randomly drawn sample of 250 professors and associate professors in departments with sociology Ph.D. programs listed in the *Guide to Graduate Departments of Sociology, 1969*. He asked his respondents to assign weights to the list of 63 journals in accordance with their judgment of the average importance of their contributions to the field. They were asked to use articles in the *American Sociological Review* as a standard for reference, using a weight of 10 for an article in that journal.[3] A publication judged only half as important was to be assigned a weight of 5. Using relative weights in this manner, judges produced the mean weights shown in Table 7.4.

Glenn describes some of his conclusions to the findings as each column is analyzed:

> The data in the first column of [Table 7.4] indicate two major dimensions of the reputations of the journals. The mean weight is essentially an indicator of the *intensity* of prestige, whereas the number of respondents who assigned weights (shown in parentheses) is a rough indicator of how well the journal was known among the respondents, or of the *extensity* of the journal's prestige. The extent of being known and the extensity of prestige are not the same, of course, unless all of those who know an object grant it some prestige.[4]
>
> If the measure of extensity were exact, total prestige could be arrived at by multiplying the measure of extensity by the measure of intensity. However, since no measure of total prestige can be derived from the data at hand, and since the measures of intensity and extensity are imperfectly correlated ($r = +.73$), the journals can be only partially ordered as to their prestige.[5]
>
> The reader must be cautioned that citation data indicate that the prestige of the journals does not closely correspond with the average impact their articles have on the discipline. For instance, Lin and Nelson (1969) found substantial differences in the frequency of citation of articles in the *ASR*, the *AJS*, and *Social Forces*; yet my data indicate that those three journals were very similar in prestige. A major reason for this discrepancy may be that variation in circulation of the three journals (16,584 for the *ASR*, 9335 for the *AJS*, and about 4000 for *Social Forces* in 1969 and 1970); authors probably are more likely to cite an article if the journal is in their personal library.[6]

It is important to direct the reader's attention to the considerable dissensus in the evaluations of the journals, as roughly indicated by the standard deviations in the third column of the table.

TABLE 7.4 Means of the Weights Assigned to 63 Journals by a Sample of American Sociologists

| | | | | Category of Respondent | | | |
| | | | | Had Published in Journal | | Relevant Specialists [a] | |
Journal	Mean Weight	N	Standard Deviation	Mean	N [b]	Mean	N [b]
American Sociological Review	10.0[c]	—	—	—	—		
American Journal of Sociology	9.6	129	1.2	9.6	35	—	—
Social Forces	8.1	127	1.9	8.1	41	—	—
Sociometry	7.8	119	2.2	8.6	8	8.1	34
British Journal of Sociology	7.8	115	2.1	—	—	—	—
American Anthropologist	7.7	118	2.3	—	—	—	—
Social Problems	7.6	113	2.2	8.7	15	—	—
American Political Science Review	7.5	110	2.2	—	—	8.0	9
Demography	7.4	90	2.2	8.8	5	9.1	13
Annals of the American Academy of Political and Social Science	7.2	126	2.3	8.1	10	—	—
Public Opinion Quarterly	7.1	116	2.1	7.4	14	7.2	14
American Economic Review	7.1	99	2.9	—	—	—	—
Journal of Personality and Social Psychology	7.1	81	2.2	—	—	7.1	26
European Journal of Sociology	6.9	69	2.4	—	—	—	—
Behavioral Science	6.8	87	2.3	—	—	—	—
Rural Sociology	6.7	109	2.2	7.2	18	7.8	8
Human Organization	6.7	104	2.0	7.4	5	—	—
Journal of Social Psychology	6.7	102	2.1	5.3	6	6.8	33
Administrative Science Quarterly	6.7	98	2.4	6.5	5	—	—
Milbank Memorial Fund Quarterly	6.7	97	2.4	—	—	7.1	14
International Journal of Comparative Sociology	6.7	77	2.4	—	—	—	—
American Behavioral Scientist	6.6	110	2.4	—	—	—	—
Journal of Social Issues	6.6	108	2.0	—	—	—	—
Social Research	6.6	88	2.2	—	—	—	—
Daedalus	6.5	111	2.8	—	—	—	—
Human Relations	6.5	91	2.2	6.4	5	—	—
Population Studies	6.5	74	2.2	—	—	7.3	12
Harvard Educational Review	6.4	93	2.9	—	—	6.0	7
Current Sociology	6.4	78	2.4	—	—	—	—
Canadian Review of Sociology and Anthropology	6.4	77	2.1	—	—	—	—
Sociological Review	6.3	68	2.0	—	—	—	—
International Social Science Journal	6.3	65	2.2	—	—	—	—
American Sociologist	6.2	123	2.4	7.9	8	—	—
Journal of Marriage and the Family	6.2	108	2.4	6.4	14	6.5	21
Journal of Conflict Resolution	6.2	86	2.6	—	—	—	—
Journal of Health and Social Behavior	6.2	83	2.4	8.8	6	8.3	12
Sociology of Education	6.1	93	2.0	6.4	5	6.1	8
Sociological Quarterly	6.1	83	1.9	6.6	11	—	—
Acta Sociologica	6.1	71	2.1	—	—	—	—
Social Science Quarterly	6.0	64	2.0	—	—	—	—
Southwestern Journal of Anthropology	6.0	54	2.2	—	—	—	—

| | | | | Category of Respondent | | | |
| | | | | Had Published in Journal | | Relevant Specialists [a] | |
Journal	Mean Weight	N	Standard Deviation	Mean	N [b]	Mean	N [b]
Sociology and Social Research	5.9	107	1.9	6.0	10	—	—
Sociology	5.9	33	2.0	—	—	—	—
Sociological Inquiry	5.8	86	1.9	6.7	13	—	—
Transaction	5.7	118	2.7	5.0	8	—	—
Pacific Sociological Review	5.7	94	2.2	5.7	7	—	—
Law and Society Review	5.7	62	2.3	—	—	8.0	5
Sociological Analysis	5.7	57	1.7	6.2	5	5.7	7
Journal of Gerontology	5.4	51	2.2	6.5	6	—	—
Journal of Research in Crime and Delinquency	5.4	46	1.9	—	—	6.6	14
American Journal of Economics and Sociology	5.3	96	2.0	—	—	—	—
British Journal of Criminology	5.3	61	1.8	—	—	6.7	14
Gerontologist	5.3	57	2.1	—	—	—	—
Crime and Delinquency	5.2	58	1.9	—	—	5.6	16
Science and Society	5.2	51	2.1	—	—	—	—
Journal of Criminal Law, Criminology, and Police Science	5.1	64	1.9	—	—	5.9	15
Phylon	5.0	82	2.1	5.4	8	5.4	12
Eugenics Quarterly [d]	5.0	51	2.3	—	—	—	—
Jewish Journal of Sociology	4.9	43	1.8	—	—	—	—
American Journal of Correction	4.8	73	2.0	—	—	5.3	15
Eugenics Review	4.7	41	2.2	—	—	—	—
Journal of Negro Education	4.5	57	2.2	—	—	5.5	11
New Society	4.5	37	2.0	—	—	—	—
Federal Probation	3.8	57	1.8	—	—	4.5	15

SOURCE: Norval D. Glenn, "American Sociologists' Evaluation of 63 Journals," *TAS* 6 (November 1971): 300–301. Used by permission of the American Sociological Association.
a. The relevant specialists for a specialized journal are the respondents with a specialty in the same area as that of the old journal.
b. Means are shown only where the *N* is five or more.
c. The weight for the *ASR* was given on the questionnaire and was not assigned by the respondents.
d. This journal is now called *Social Biology*.

These data, plus data not shown, make it clear that there is not a highly integrated system of prestige in sociology. Therefore, the best outlets for the writings of a particular sociologist depend on who are his or her significant others and who is likely to judge and reward him or her. Only the highest-prestige general journals seem to be very good outlets for almost any sociologist.[7]

One might suspect that respondents would tend to overevaluate journals in which they had published or with which they were otherwise identified, but in the case of the general journals, the means of the weights given by respondents who had and who had not published in them were invariably similar and in some cases identical (see the fourth column in the table). There was, however, a tendency for persons to assign unusually high weights to the lower-prestige journals if they had published in them but not in the higher-prestige journals.

Although articles in prestigious journals rank high, the highest weights are given to research and theoretical monographs (mean weight = 33.8), textbooks (18.1), and edited books (11.2).[8]

Notes

1. For a comprehensive guide to publishing opportunities, see *Directory of Publishing Opportunities*, 3rd ed. (Chicago, IL: Marquis Who's Who, 1975).

2. Norval D. Glenn, "American Sociologists' Evaluations of Sixty-Three Journals," *American Sociologist* 6 (November 1971): 298-303.

3. The *American Sociological Review* is the official journal of the American Sociological Association and is received by all members.

4. Glenn, "American Sociologists' Evaluations," 300.

5. Ibid., 301.

6. Ibid., 302.

7. Ibid.

8. Glenn and Villemez have derived a weighting scheme for the different types of publications. It yields a useful index of "importance to the discipline." The Glenn-Villemez Comprehensive Index (GVCI) generates six distinct indices of publication productivity: number of articles, number of books, total publications (articles plus books), article points, book points, and total points. See Norval D. Glenn and Wayne Villemez, "The Productivity of Sociologists at 45 American Universities," *American Sociologist* 5 (August 1970): 244-52.

7.D.6   HOW SOCIOLOGISTS GET PUBLISHED: HOW TO TAKE REJECTION

Few academics know all the ins and outs of publishing because the rules governing this activity are not a few, easily learned principles, but rather a multitude of various considerations, any one of which can work for or against the researcher. Each form of publishing has its own set of particular requirements.

Finding a Publisher for Articles

Each journal has its own goals and its own preferred style. It may have its own definition of "appropriate length" as well. Most important will be the standards of quality the journal's editors impose upon their acceptance of articles received. The more accurately the writer gauges these considerations, the greater his or her chance of acceptance. The way to gain such a background is to become thoroughly familiar with the journal in which you hope to publish. If you want to publish in the most prestigious journals you should not send them any work that fails to meet the standards exhibited in those journals. You must be aware that the competition is intense, and that the acceptance rate ranges each year between 10% and 20% of the articles received. And this rate includes articles often rejected until substantial revisions have been made to meet editors' criticisms. Each article is read by two or more professional readers, whose evaluations are subsequently weighed by the editor.

The younger scholar might be advised to choose among journals where the competition is less intense. Specialized journals in the area of interest may more readily accept an article if it conforms to their interest pattern. Many journals look for theoretical or opinion material and do not impose patterns of design and statistical rigor. They are more interested in well-written material that treats matters of concern to their journal readers.

The writer who gets published usually makes tentative drafts and asks for the advice of colleagues. He or she is willing to accept criticism and willing to rewrite,

rewrite, and rewrite if necessary. The final draft is a perfect copy as far as possible. This means good paper, clear and correct typing, with footnoting and all style requirements matched against the format of the given journal.

Whatever the fate of the papers submitted, it must be remembered that writing is an art even for scientific work. The writer who wants to be published keeps writing and submitting work. There are numerous journals, and most work of reasonable quality can be published somewhere. This is a wonderful opportunity that is offered. In the exercise of the art the writer learns the ins and outs of both writing and the placement of work. If a writer seeks prestige, he or she will aim for the prestigious journals only when the work merits it and when the writing commends it.[1]

Finding a Publisher for Books

It will be recalled that Norval Glenn has reported that, although articles in prestigious journals rank high, the greatest weights are given to research and theoretical monographs, textbooks, and edited books. In addition to gaining the writer higher prestige, books may make money. Royalties for best-selling texts and books of readings can be relatively substantial. All books have the prospect of making some money, but research monographs ordinarily yield only prestige. The monograph has a long and durable life, however, and the writer may be remembered for it long after his or her other writings are forgotten. Decisions about whether to publish monographs, texts, or readings require a balance of motives and skills—all timed according to appropriate stages in the professional career. A few general rules for finding a publisher for books have been set forth by Carolyn Mullins:

When and How?

The ideal time to begin interesting publishers in a research monograph is when you begin the research or receive funds to support it. If a text or trade book is on your mind, start looking for a publisher as soon as you get the idea for it.

Texts are usually intended for classroom use only. Rarely do they have scholarly interest. Trade books—e.g., Vance Packard's books and Riesman's *The Lonely Crowd*—have a nonacademic market in addition to whatever student or professional market they may have. Monographs are usually intended for faculty use; many have some utility in graduate seminars, and a few are useful in advanced undergraduate courses. Publishers, naturally, are delighted when a genuine research monograph also has obvious text and/or trade markets. Publishers (some university presses excepted) usually show greater interest in texts and trade books than in monographs because the former are more likely to make money. It follows, then, that competition is more likely to develop if you are trying to interest publishers in a text or trade book than if a monograph is your intended product.

Edited collections—whether of previously published papers or of unpublished papers— can fall into any category. They present many different and specialized problems. These have to do with obtaining permissions, pricing, keeping them within reasonable size limits, getting several contributors to cooperate and meet deadlines, trying to set contract obligations and rewards equitably, and so forth. They are also less popular now than they used to be, partly because of the high permission cost that is often involved.[2]

Charles Kadushin explains that he has been besieged for advice since the publication of Lewis A. Coser, Charles Kadushin, and Walter W. Powell's *Books: The Culture and Commerce of Publishing* (Chicago: University of Chicago Press, 1982):

Colleagues want to know how to deal with editors and publishers, what different kinds of publishers there are, how to get editors and publishers to pay attention to your work, what kinds of manuscripts are appropriate for whom, how to negotiate a contract, and one hundred and one tactical and practical questions about scholarly communications in print. I now have an immediate answer to almost any question. First read *Scholarly Writing and Publishing*. Chances are that your question is answered in that slim volume.[3]

Words of wisdom from Kadushin include the following:

- The kind of organization, style, and presentation of a dissertation are anathema to publishers and journal reviewers.
- Potential authors of college texts should be forewarned that they are about to enter into a complex system that has more in common with mass media business than with academic scholarship.
- The major means of communication among scholars remains, for better or worse, the journal article.
- Amatai Etzioni once said that the way to reach your colleagues is to write them a letter.
- Authors need to take a much more active role in the publishing process, especially in book promotion. If the scholarly author does not know, by name, the 3,000 or so persons who *must* read her book, then she does not know enough to have written it.[4]

Notes

1. For assistance, the following may prove helpful: Jacques Barzun and Henry F. Graff, *The Modern Researcher*, 3rd ed. (New York: Harcourt Brace Jovanovich, 1977); chap. 16 is excellent for revising writing; David W. Ewing, *Writing for Results in Business, Government, the Sciences, and the Professions*, 2nd ed. (New York: John Wiley, 1979); Oliver Holmes, "Thesis to Book: What to Get Rid Of," *Scholarly Publishing* 5 (July 1974): 339-49. C. P. Lee, *Library Resources: How to Research and Write a Paper* (Englewood Cliffs, NJ: Prentice-Hall, 1971).
2. Carolyn J. Mullins, "Everything You Always Wanted to Know About Book Publishing," paper presented at Indiana University (February 1, 1975), 2-3. Quote used by permission of author. Writing books and finding a publisher for monographs and textbooks is discussed more fully in C. J. Mullins, *Writing and Publishing in the Social and Behavioral Sciences* (New York: Wiley-Interscience, 1977).
3. Charles Kadushin, "How Not to Perish in the Publishing Process," *Contemporary Sociology* 16 (November 1987): 857-58. The work Kadushin cites is Mary Frank Fox, ed., *Scholarly Writing and Publishing: Issues, Problems, and Solutions* (Boulder, CO: Westview, 1985).
4. Kadushin, "How Not to Perish," 858.

Other Literature

Carter, Sylvester P. *Writing for Your Peers: The Primary Journal Paper.* Westport, CT: Praeger, 1987.
Cummings, L. L., and Peter J. Frost. *Publishing in the Organizational Sciences.* Homewood, IL: Richard D. Irwin, 1985.
Powell, Walter W. *Getting into Print.* Chicago: University of Chicago Press, 1985.

How To Take Rejection

Rejection Comes Naturally

The probability is far higher that your learned paper will receive a rejection from a major journal than that it will be awarded acceptance for publication. There are many reasons for this, including the ones discussed below.

Lack of space. The *American Sociological Review* receives approximately 400 papers a year (1980); the *American Journal of Sociology*, 350. Even a specialized journal like *Social Psychological Quarterly* may get 200. Obviously, only a fraction of the submitted papers can be accepted. The four major journals in sociology accept about 16% of the papers submitted to them.

Errors of judgment made by competent reviewers and editors. Let us assume that no biases exist in the review process and that the same level of measurement efficiency exists as in other measurement processes based on coding of qualitative materials. Given these assumptions, Stinchcombe and Ofshe estimate the validity of a judgment of article quality to be about .70. They then set forth a model providing an estimate of the proportion of acceptance of papers of different quality at the acceptance level of 16%. If the quality of the papers is approximately normal, we can say papers *judged* to be one standard deviation or more above the mean of the papers submitted will be accepted. For papers at different points of *true quality*, the researchers calculate what proportion will be judged to be above the acceptance level of one standard deviation above the mean. They compute the conditional distribution of *judged* quality for a given value of *true* quality. They apply the resulting model to a random 100 papers submitted for publication with the following results: of 84 submitted papers that were truly below the acceptance level, 77 (92%) were rejected and only 7 (8%) were accepted. Of 16 papers truly above the cutoff point, 9 (56%) were accepted and 7 (44%) were rejected. "In terms of numbers of papers, there are about equal numbers of distinguished papers mistakenly rejected and mediocre papers mistakenly accepted." [1]

Many editors would dispute this finding and would contend that good reviewers and editors are better judges than the validity coefficient (.70) allows. Stinchcombe and Ofshe contend that the virtue of their model does not "take a conspiracy theory of journal editing to account for the rejection of a great many good papers and the publishing of a large number of mediocre papers." [2] And, of course, since the cutoff level is 16%, 84 out of every 100 papers are, on the average, rejected.

Reviewer and editor incompetence and bias. There is a widespread suspicion (but no proof) that considerable incompetence exists among referees and editors.[3] It is possible that such suspicion is based on the understandable reaction that "*my* paper was of such high quality that only poor reviewing failed to discern its merit." But wounded ego aside, it must be remembered that most reviewers are *volunteer workers* (the exceptions are paid editorial assistants, when they exist) and that they sometimes give their valuable time grudgingly and unevenly. Almost none has been specifically trained to review. It is like college teaching; they are expected to learn this as a by-product of other training. Some reviewers get an "ego trip" out of overcritical behavior; some just do a lazy "once over"; some are simply not competent to handle particular papers. And some react with ideological or methodological bias rather than give a decision based on balanced judgment.

It is up to the editor to catch this kind of crime, but editors, too, have human frailties. And as professionals, editors must budget their time. There is just so much time to give to the reviewing process of the journal. In defense of editors, the following may be said:

- Editors often lack information about many reviewers' work and lack resources to identify the ablest reviewers.
- Editors must persuade busy professionals to give up valuable productive time in order to get the best reviews; failing to get the best, editors often must take second or third best if a review is to be made at all.
- Editors cannot read every paper and every review if their journals command large numbers of papers.

TABLE 7.5 A Typology of Reviewers

The Lazy	The Ego Aggrandizer	The Ego Projectionist	The Competent	The Compassionate
Gives the paper a hasty examination.	Wants to parade his or her critical and superior faculties.	Wants the author to write just as he or she, the reviewer, would do it.	Studies carefully and conscientiously prepares a balanced critique.	Does a competent review and takes added care in pointing out ways of improving the article.

- Most editors are specialists in particular fields and cannot be expected to judge wisely on papers in a large number of fields.

Inherent difficulty of judging social research. Finally, for editor and reviewer alike, ascertaining the "quality" of a paper is more difficult in sociology and the other social sciences than in the physical sciences. Standards are difficult to apply. In the physical sciences criteria for quality can be established more easily, and rejection rates in physical science journals are proportionally much lower than in the major sociological journals.

Don't Blow Your Cool

There are sensitive egos in any profession. Professionals have worked many years and have surmounted many barriers to prove their right to hold degrees and to practice. The ego gets a jolt when an "excellent" paper fares badly. The range of emotions runs from *disappointment and despondence to humiliation to anger and explosive vehemence.* One editor writes

> In my judgment, authors' distress with the review process is more a function of the rejection of submitted articles than the quality of reviews; the two are not necessarily related. . . . Nothing so infuriates an author as to be told that little fault can be found with an article but that it cannot be accepted for publication.[4]

In the world of "publish or perish," with tenure, promotion, and merit increases at stake, there is ample impetus to raise both adrenalin and blood pressure in the human organism.

The Adaptive Response

You can "stew in your juices" or take a new look at your paper and at the reviews. (Ordinarily the editor will send copies of the review in whole or in part.) Maybe you will be asked to revise and resubmit. Now is the time to apply some social insight. What kind of reviewers did you have? A typology of reviewers is provided (Table 7.5) so that you can make a judgment.

This typology may give you some clues as to the quality of your reviewers and help you make up your mind as to the worth and future prospects for your paper. You may want to dig deeper into the motivations of the anonymous persons who judged your paper. To do this it is suggested that you examine some basic orientations of social researchers. This is the age of diversity, and professionals come in all colors. Look at the classification in Table 7.6 and examine carefully the radicals, the

TABLE 7.6 Orientations of Reviewers

Radical			*Humanist*			*Positivist*	
(personality and organizational change oriented)			*(historical, theoretical, value-oriented)*			*(measurement oriented)*	
Concern with Rapid Social Change			*Concern with Current Social Problems*			*Concern with Sociological Problems*	
Marxist ideologist.	Ideologically uncommitted but critical of established institutions.	Active intervention in social problems.	Monitoring of crisis.	Eschews any interest in applied work. Concerned only with theoretical and value implications.		Favors placing method secondary to the cumulation of new knowledge around central persistent sociological themes.	Favors rigorous empirical treatment with emphasis on sophisticated mathematical statistical methods.

humanists, and the positivists. Did you get caught in an ideological bias that helped to reject your paper? Where do you fit in these orientations? What is the dominant orientation of the journal to which you offered your paper?

It is entirely possible that your reviewers may have "liked your paper but found weaknesses in your method." This may mean that their methodological biases are showing. A look at methodological bias is in order (see Table 7.7).

Make Decisions, Then Act

You are now ready to reevaluate your paper. Go over the reviewer's criticisms and look at your paper as if you are a critic. Your choices are these:

1. Submit a revised version of your paper with an accompanying letter to the editor setting out your dispute with points used in the initial rejection. Ask the editor to bring your revised paper and notes to the attention of the previous reviewers in order to get a reappraisal.
2. Try another publication channel. They are numerous. Look at Section 7.D.3, which lists journals not only in sociology but also in related fields.[5] If your paper has something to offer, it will get published. Keep trying.
3. Have the guts to admit that the paper is seriously flawed and get on with new work.[6]

Notes

1. Arthur L. Stinchcombe and Richard Ofshe, "On Journal Editing as Probabilistic Process," *American Sociologist* 4 (May 1969): 116.

2. Ibid., 117. A symposium in *Contemporary Sociology* reviews in detail the *American Journal of Sociology, American Sociological Review,* and *Social Forces* for 1975-79; see *Contemporary Sociology* 8 (November 1979): 789-824 (includes discussions by Jerry Gaston, Norbert Wiley, Walter B. Grove, Everett K. Wilson, Morris Zelditch, Jr., James L. McCartney, Samuel A. Mueller, and Duncan Lindsey). Critiques and suggestions for improvement of the review process abound. This symposium is the most thorough analysis made to date.

For further research and discussion, see Lowell L. Hargens, "Scholarly Consensus and Journal Rejection Rates," *American Sociological Review* 53 (February 1988): 139-51 (note Appendix, p. 150, showing annual acceptance rates and submissions for 30 journals during the late 1960s and early 1980s). This is followed

TABLE 7.7 Methodological Predispositions of Reviewers

Introspection	Theory	Observation	Measurement
Likes evidence of capable intuitive identification of personal and social processes.	Likes demonstration of interrelated theoretical propositions ranging from global to middle range according to reviewer's preference.	Gives special significance to the manner of observation, ranging from archival and documentary work to field work to laboratory work.	Gives favor to the rigor of measurement, ranging from qualitative to quantitative methodology.

by a provocative paper by Stephen Cole, Jonathan R. Cole, and Gary Simon, "Do Journal Rejection Rates Index Consensus?" *American Sociological Review* 53 (February 1988): 152-56. A reply by Hargens follows on pp. 157-60.

3. Lee Freese, "On Changing Some Role Relationships in the Editorial Review Process," *American Sociologist* 14 (November 1979): 231-38.

4. Sheldon Stryker, "On the Editorial Review Process," *American Sociologist* 14 (November 1979): 238. See other comments by Rita James Simon, Duncan Lindsey, Helen MacGill Hughes, and George W. Bohrnstedt.

5. For a broader view, see Duncan Lindsey, *The Scientific Publication System in Social Science: A Study in the Operation of Leading Professional Journals in Psychology, Sociology and Social Work* (San Francisco: Jossey-Bass, 1978); John S. Harris and Reed H. Blake, *Technical Writing for Social Scientists* (Chicago: Nelson-Hall, 1979).

6. For a discussion of behavioral response to the failure, see Kathleen S. Crittenden and Mary G. Wiley, "Causal Attribution and Behavioral Response to Failure," *Social Psychology Quarterly* 43 (September 1980): 353-58. Authors' attributions to rejections in the referred journals *Sociology of Work* and *Sociological Quarterly* are studied using regression procedures. They find the behavioral response is directly influenced by past experience. It makes a difference in confidence whether one attributes the rejection to variable causes or to stable causes. Women, especially, are prone to attribute rejection to stable causes.

7.D.7   PROFESSIONAL COMMUNICATION AND REPORTING

A professional research life is an ongoing process of research investigation, reading research journals, preparing scientific papers and reading them before professional audiences of various learned societies, and finally publishing articles and monographs.[1] In order to command attention, it is necessary for researchers to make themselves and their work known to colleagues in local, state, regional, national and international circles.

The North American sociologist who wishes to be known in national and international circles will join the American Sociological Association and may affiliate with one or both of the leading international sociological associations: International Sociological Association and Institut International de Sociologie.

Of all the many circles in which the researcher may move and find outlets, no forums are more important than reports at annual meetings of the American Sociological Association and publication in the *American Sociological Review*. If you are a young sociologist, you should join the American Sociological Association as soon as you make a commitment to professional life. You should begin reading the *ASR*, which will provide research examples of high-quality work as well as names of leaders in the field. For the aspiring sociologist, the *ASR* should stimulate participation in the annual meetings and encourage growth of research interests. One of the first steps to professionalization is to know the research in your fields of interest and the leading researchers who are at the cutting edge of the discipline. The second and most important step is to join this circle by participation, achievement, and recognition.

The American Sociological Association is a voluntary association of individual members. Many categories of membership exist. Full membership in the ASA requires the holding of a Ph.D. degree in sociology or in some related field, or the completion of three years of graduate study in such field. Students are encouraged to join as associates at low fees. There were 12,400 members of all categories in 1988. An earlier survey showed that 8 out of 10 members are employed in colleges and universities and another 2 out of 10 members work in nonacademic settings. Of the total membership, 11,000 come from the United States and 1,400 come from outside the United States. Approximately 30% of the members are women. The proportion of women has risen steadily over the last decade. The growth of the ASA is indicated by a membership of 115 in 1906, the year of founding, to membership of 12,400 in 1988.

Regional associations are part of the contact and communication pattern and often represent the first professional experience of the young scholar. Regional meetings are smaller, and the competition for acceptance of papers is less intense. This is a good place for the young scholar to start becoming a professional. There are associations in every region; their names are listed in Section 7.D.8.

Note

1. Acutely sensitive to the anxieties that plague social science writers, Howard S. Becker has written *Writing for Social Scientists: How to Start and Finish Your Thesis, Book, or Article* (Chicago: University of Chicago Press, 1986).

ANNUAL MEETINGS HELD BY VARIOUS SOCIOLOGICAL AND KINDRED SOCIETIES WITH COMMON SECTION TOPICS IN SOCIOLOGY, PSYCHOLOGY, AND ANTHROPOLOGY   7.D.8

For information about annual meetings of the American Sociological Association and the other sociological societies, contact:

American Sociological Association
1722 N St., NW
Washington, DC 20036
(202) 833-3410

Other Major Sociological Associations

American Catholic Sociological Society
District of Columbia Sociological Society
Eastern Sociological Society
International Sociological Association
Institut International de Sociologie
Midwest Sociological Society

North Central Sociological Association
Pacific Sociological Association
Rural Sociological Society
Society for the Study of Social Problems
Southern Sociological Society
Southwestern Sociological Association

Kindred Social Science and Allied Societies Holding Annual Meetings

American Anthropological Association
Executive Offices
1703 New Hampshire Ave., NW
Washington, DC 20009

*American Association for the Advancement
of Science*
1515 Massachusetts Ave., NW
Washington, DC 20005

American Political Science Association
1527 New Hampshire Ave., NW
Washington, DC 20036

American Psychological Association
1200 17th St., NW
Washington, DC 20036

American Public Health Association
1015 15th St., NW
Washington, DC 20005

American Statistical Association
Executive Director
806 15th St., NW, Ste. 640
Washington, DC 20005

*Canadian Sociology and Anthropology
Association*
Postal Box 878
Montreal, Quebec, Canada

Population Association of America
P.O. Box 14182
Benjamin Franklin Station
Washington, DC 20044

Annual sociological meetings are commonly organized around the following topics:

Methodology and Research
Technology
  methodology (social science and be-
    havior)
  research technology
  statistical methods
Sociology: History and
Theory
  of professional interest
  history and present state of sociology
  theories, ideas, and systems
Social Psychology
  personality and culture
  interaction within (small) groups
  leadership
Group Interactions
  interaction between (large) groups
  (race relations, group relations, etc.)
Culture and Social Structure
  social organization
  culture (evolution)
  social anthropology (and ethnology)
Complex Organizations
(Management)
  industrial sociology (labor)
  military sociology
  bureaucratic structures

  market structures and consumer be-
    havior
Mass Phenomena
  social movements
  public opinion
  communication
  collective behavior
  sociology of leisure
  mass culture
Political Interactions
  interactions between societies, na-
    tions and states
  political sociology
Social Differentiation
  social stratification
  sociology of occupations and pro-
    fessions
Rural Sociology and
Agricultural Economics
  rural sociology (village, agriculture)
Urban Structures and
Ecology
  urban sociology and ecology
Sociology of the Arts
  sociology of language and literature
  sociology of art (creative and per-
    forming

Social Change and Economic
Development
   social change and economic development
Social Control
   sociology of law
   penology and correctional problems
Sociology of Science
   sociology of science and technology
Demography and Human
Biology
   demography (population study)
   human biology
The Family and
Socialization
   sociology of the child and socialization
   adolescence and youth
   sociology of sexual behavior
   sociology of the family
Sociology of Education
   sociology of education

Sociology of Religion
   sociology of religion
Sociology of Health and
Medicine
   sociology of medicine (public health)
   social psychiatry (mental health)
Social Problems and Social
Welfare
   social gerontology
   social disorganization (crime)
   applied sociology (social work)
   delinquency
Sociology of Knowledge
   sociology of knowledge
   history of ideas
Community Development
   sociology of communities and regions
Planning, Forecasting, and
Speculation
   planning, forecasting, and speculation

The specialized sections listed below meet concurrently with those above:

undergraduate education
methodology
medical sociology
criminology
sociology of education
family
organizations and occupations
theoretical sociology
sex and gender
community
social psychology
peace and war
environmental sociology

Marxist sociology
sociological practice
sociology of population
political economy of the world-system
sociology of aging
collective behavior/social movements
racial and ethnic minorities
comparative historical sociology
political sociology
Asia and Asian America
sociology of emotions
sociology of culture

Meetings of the International Sociological Association are developed around 34 research committee sections. These divisions of interest represent a good statement of what modern sociologists are doing around the world.

1. Armed Forces and Society
2. Aspirations, Needs and Development
3. Community Research
4. Sociology of Education
5. Ethnic, Race and Minority Relations
6. Family Research
7. Futures Research
8. History of Sociology
9. Innovative Processes in Social Change
10. Sociology of International Relations
11. Sociology of Aging
12. Sociology of Law
13. Sociology of Leisure
14. Sociology of Mass Communications

15. Sociology of Medicine
16. Sociology of National Movements and Imperialism
17. Sociology of Organization
18. Political Sociology
19. Sociology of Poverty, Social Welfare and Social Policy
20. Sociology of Mental Health
21. Regional and Urban Development
22. Sociology and Religion
23. Sociology of Science
24. Social Ecology
25. Sociolinguistics
26. Sociotechnics
27. Sociology of Sport
28. Social Stratification
29. Deviance and Social Control
30. Sociology of Work
31. Sociology of Migration
32. Sex Roles in Society
33. Logic and Methodology in Sociology
34. Sociology of Youth

A series of sociological studies has recently been sponsored by the International Sociological Association (ISA). The series represents a collection of outstanding and original research in sociology that has emerged from presentations of World Congresses of Sociology held in Toronto (1974) and Uppsala (1978). They provide a forum for intellectual exchange among internationally respected sociologists and demonstrate intellectual frontiers, disciplinary challenges, and professional controversies with international perspectives. The Sage Studies in International Sociology are published by Sage Publications, Inc., 2455 Teller Rd., Newbury Park, CA 91320. The current list includes the following:

Crisis and Contention in Sociology, edited by Tom Bottomore
The Military and the Problem of Legitimacy, edited by Gwyn Harries-Jenkins and Jacques van Doorn
Sociological Praxis: Current Roles and Settings, edited by Elisabeth Crawford and Stein Rokkan
Internal Migration: The New World and the Third World, edited by Anthony H. Richmond and Daniel Kubat
The Intelligentsia and the Intellectuals: Theory, Method and Case Study, edited by Aleksander Geila
Power and Control: Social Structures and Their Transformation, edited by Tom R. Burns and Walter Buckley
Beyond the Nuclear Family Model: Cross-Cultural Perspectives, edited by Luis Lenero-Otero
Scientific Technological Revolution: Social Aspects, by R. Dahrendorf et al.
Power, Paradigms, and Community Research, edited by Roland J. Liebert and Allen W. Imershein
Work and Technology, edited by Marie R. Haug and Jacques Dofny
Education in a Changing Society, edited by Antonia Kloskowska and Guido Martinotti
Organization and Environment: Theory, Issues and Reality, edited by Lucien Karpik
Disasters: Theory and Research, edited by E. L. Quarantelli
Social Policy and Sex Roles, edited by Jean Lipman-Blumen and Jessie Bernard
The Social Ecology of Change: From Equilibrium to Development, edited by Zdravko Mlinar and Henry Teune

Identity and Religion: International, Cross-Cultural Approaches, edited by Hans Mol
Gender Inequality: A Comparative Study of Discrimination and Participation, by Mino Vianello and Renata Siemienska
Comparative Methodology: Theory and Practice in International Social Research, edited by Else Øyen

Common Section Topics for Psychology at Annual Meetings

Clinical Psychology
  behavior problems
  community mental health
  crime and delinquency
  experimental psychopathology
  group therapy
  individual diagnosis
  mental deficiency
  objective tests
  projective techniques
  psychotherapy
  speech pathology
Counseling and Guidance
  educational counseling
  nondirective therapy
  personal adjustment
  rehabilitation
  vocational counseling
Developmental Psychology
  childhood and adolescence
  infancy
  maturity and old age
  nursery and preschool
Personality
  development
  measurement
  personality and body
  personality and learning
  personality and perception
  personality theory
  structure and dynamics

School Psychology
  anthropological linguistics
  physical anthropology
  social/cultural anthropology
Specialties
  anthropological folklore
  cultural ecology
Education Psychology
  educational measurement
  programmed learning
  school adjustment
  school learning
  special education
  student personnel
  teacher personnel
Engineering Psychology
General Psychology
  history and biography
  theory and systems
Industrial and Personnel Psychology
  employee and executive training
    and development
  job analysis and position
    classification
  labor-management relations
  market research, advertising
  organizational behavior
  performance evaluation, criterion
    development
  recruiting, selection, placement
  safety research and training
  salary and pay plans

Systems, Methodologies and Issues

apparatus/equipment
computer applications and programming
experimentation and observation,
  experimental design
factor analysis and related techniques
history and systems of psychology

models and mathematical models
operations research
professional issues in psychology
program evaluation
psychometrics
statistics

Physiological Psychology

behavior genetics
biochemistry
brain lesions
brain stimulation, chemical
brain stimulation, electrical
cardiovascular processes
electrical activity
electrophysical psychology

gastrointestinal processes and
  nutrition
motivation and emotion
neurology
personality correlates
psychophysiology
sensory physiology
sexual physiology

Community Psychology

community development	rehabilitation administration
community mental health	research and training in
counselor education	community psychology

Common Section Topics for Anthropology at Annual Meetings

Major Divisions

archaeology	human paleontology
economic anthropology	methodology
ethnology	museology
ethnomusicology	primatology
history of anthropology	psychological anthropology

7.D.9   GUIDE TO JOURNALS SPONSORED BY THE AMERICAN SOCIOLOGICAL ASSOCIATION

American Sociological Review is the official journal of the American Sociological Association, publishing articles of major concern to social scientists. New trends and developments in theory and research are reported. Comments from readers and authors are printed relevant to articles previously published. The *Review* is sent to all members and is the journal most widely read by sociologists. Bimonthly.

Contemporary Sociology: An International Journal of Reviews is devoted entirely to book reviews and is designed to give new thrust and style to book reviewing. Besides reviews of specific books it features survey essays, symposium essays, review essays, and letters. Bimonthly.

Journal of Health and Social Behavior is distinctive for a sociological approach to the definition and analysis of problems bearing on human welfare. Articles range from drugs and smoking to health care organizations and costs, professional and nonprofessional role conflicts, and various topics related to women. Quarterly.

Social Psychology Quarterly is a journal of research in social psychology. It is genuinely interdisciplinary in the publication of works by both sociologists and psychologists. Quarterly. (Formerly called *Sociometry*.)

Sociological Methodology is an official publication of the American Sociological Association. It is an annual series that began in 1969 and was designed to keep social scientists abreast of methodological changes and innovations in all areas of sociological inquiry.

Sociological Practice Review features articles that rely on sociological methods and challenges associated with practicing sociology in administrative, policy-making, and therapeutic settings. It encourages articles that rely on sociological methods and insights to deal with practical and policy problems as well as theoretical and methodological dimensions of practice. Originated in 1989.

Sociological Theory publishes papers in all areas of sociological theory, including new substantive theories, history of theory, metatheory, formal theory construction, and syntheses of existing bodies of theory. Semiannually.

Sociology of Education is a forum for educators and social scientists seeking to advance sociological knowledge about education. The journal serves as a significant medium for the application of this knowledge to major issues of educational policy and practice. Quarterly.

Teaching Sociology publishes articles of analysis that synthesize the issues in an area and highlight the implications for teaching sociology. Articles on practice report on specific strategies for teaching sociology. Research articles report on studies of specific aspects of teaching sociology. Quarterly.

ASA Journals: Editors and Months of Publication

American Sociological Review: Gerald Marwell, Department of Sociology, University of Wisconsin, Madison, WI 53706; (608) 262-7458. Bimonthly: February, April, June, August, October, December. $15 manuscript submission fee.

Contemporary Sociology: Ida Harper Simpson, Department of Sociology, Duke University, Durham, NC 27706; (919) 684-2915. Bimonthly: January, March, May, July, September, November.

Footnotes: William D'Antonio (Executive Officer), ASA, 1722 N St., NW, Washington, DC 20036; (202) 833-3410. Monthly, except June, with a combined July-August issue. Contributions to "Open Forum" limited to 800 words; "Obituaries," 500 words; "Letters to the Editor," 400 words. News items and announcements are due the first of the month preceding publication and are printed only once on a space-available basis.

Journal of Health and Social Behavior: Mary Finnell, Department of Sociology, Pennsylvania State University, 201 Liberal Arts Tower, University Park, PA 16802; (814) 865-4812. Quarterly: March, June, September, December. $15 manuscript submission fee.

Rose Monograph Series: Teresa A. Sullivan, Department of Sociology, University of Texas, Burdine Hall 436, Austin, TX 78712-1088. Occasional publication of monographs.

Social Psychology Quarterly: Karen S. Cook, Department of Sociology, University of Washington, Seattle, WA 98195; (206) 545-2769. Quarterly: March, June, September, December. $15 manuscript submission fee.

Sociological Methodology: Clifford Clogg, Department of Sociology, Pennsylvania State University, University Park, PA 16802; (814) 865-6802. Annual (August). $15 manuscript submission fee.

Sociological Practice Review: Robert Dentler, Department of Sociology, University of Massachusetts, Harbor Campus, Boston, MA 02125-3903; (617) 929-7450. Quarterly. $15 manuscript submission fee.

Sociological Theory: Alan Sica, Department of Sociology, University of California, Riverside, CA 92521; (714) 787-3935. $15 manuscript submission fee.

Sociology of Education: Philip Wexler, Graduate School of Education, 309 Lattimore Hall, University of Rochester, Rochester, NY 14627; (716) 275-3958. Quarterly: January, April, July, October. $15 manuscript submission fee.

Teaching Sociology: Theodore C. Wagenaar, Department of Sociology, Miami University, Oxford, OH 45056; (513) 529-3437. Quarterly: January, April, July, October. $15 manuscript submission fee.

Cumulative Index of Sociology Journals, 1971-85

The *Cumulative Index of Sociology Journals*, compiled by Judith C. Lantz, represents the American Sociological Association's first attempt to compile an index for ten major journals in sociology. The journals are as follows:

American Journal of Sociology
American Sociological Review
The American Sociologist
Contemporary Sociology
Journal of Health and Social Behavior
Social Forces
Social Psychology Quarterly
Sociological Methodology
Sociological Theory
Sociology of Education

An author and subject index is available for all journals. Each entry contains name of journal, volume year, month of issue, and article page numbers. Author entries contain the first and last names of article authors.

The *Cumulative Index* was published by the American Sociological Association in 1987. It may be ordered from American Sociological Association, 1722 N St. NW, Washington, DC 20036. ASA members, $37.50; nonmembers, $48.50; institutions, $65.00.

Other Important Publications Issued Regularly

Footnotes of the American Sociological Association is the organ for the official reports and proceedings of the association. It invites opinion on such matters as the state of undergraduate education, the future employment of sociologists, the status of women and minorities in sociology, the linkage of sociology to social policy, alternative modes of graduate training, broadening the world perspective of American sociology, and adding to the knowledge base of the discipline.

Arnold Rose Monograph Series provides an opportunity for members and student members of the ASA to publish short research monographs (100-300 typed pages) in any subject-matter field in sociology that normally is beyond the scope of publication in regular academic journals. Numerous volumes have been published since its establishment in 1968.

Employment Bulletin is published monthly and contains current position vacancies.

Annual Review of Sociology summarizes progress of development in various fields of sociology. Established in 1975.

ASA-Sponsored Publications Available from Other Sources

The following publications must be ordered directly from the publishers; do *not* send orders or payments to the ASA.

Sociological Methodology. Vols. 1970-88. Publisher: Jossey-Bass, Inc., 433 California St., San Francisco, CA 94104.

Issues and Trends Series: *The Formal Organization*, edited by Richard H. Hall; *Neighborhood and Ghetto*, edited by Scott Greer and Ann Lennarson Greer. Publisher: Basic Books, Inc., 10 East 53 St., New York, NY 10022.

Social Policy and Sociology, edited by N. J. Demerath III, Karl F. Schuessler, and Otto N. Larsen. Publisher: Academic Press, 111 Fifth Ave., New York, NY 10003.

Sociology and the Public Policy: The Case of the Presidential Commissions, edited by Mirra Komarovsky. Publisher: Elsevier Scientific Publishing Company, Inc., 52 Vanderbilt Ave., New York, NY 10017.

Sociology and Rehabilitation, edited by Marvin B. Sussman. Publisher: University Microfilms, Books Editorial Department, 300 N. Zeeb Rd., Ann Arbor, MI 48106.

Sociological Theory. Jossey-Bass, Inc., 433 California St., San Francisco, CA 94104. 1983 and 1984 volumes are available in hardcover format. This publication is now a semiannual ASA journal. See list of ASA publications, above, for information.

Applied Sociology: Roles and Activities of Sociologists in Diverse Settings, edited by Howard E. Freeman, Russell R. Dynes, Peter H. Rossi, and William Foote Whyte. Jossey-Bass, Inc., 433 California St., San Francisco, CA 94104.

Social Policy and Sociology, edited by N. J. Demerath III, Karl F. Schuessler, and Otto N. Larsen. Academic Press, 465 S. Lincoln Dr., Troy, MO 63379.

Social Psychology: Sociological Perspectives, edited by Morris Rosenberg and Ralph H. Turner. Basic Books, 10 E. 53rd St., New York, NY 10022.

Research Annuals in Sociology and Related Fields

The research annuals shown below are all publications that have appeared since 1979. They are usually under the editorship of specialists who change with each issue. For current information, write the publisher, JAI Press, Inc., P.O. Box 1678, 165 W. Putnam Ave., Greenwich, CT 06830.

Advances in Early Education and Day Care
Advances in Special Education
Advances in Substance Abuse
Comparative Social Research
Contemporary Studies in Sociology
Current Perspectives in Social Theory
Political Power and Social Theory
Research in Community and Mental Health
Research in Economic Anthropology
Research in Law and Sociology
Research in Organizational Behavior
Research in Race and Ethnic Relations
Research in Social Movements

Research in Social Problems and
  Public Policy
Research in Social Stratification and
  Mobility
Research in Sociology of Education and
  Socialization
Research in Sociology of Knowledge
Research in the Interweave of Social
  Roles: Women and Men
Research in the Sociology of Health Care
Research in the Sociology of Work
Studies in Communication Research
Studies in Symbolic Interaction

Current Information About Published Work

Current Contents in the Social and Behavioral Sciences is a weekly listing of the contents of journals and some books in the social and behavioral sciences. It also includes an index by first author and principal words in the titles of articles.

The Educational Resources Information Center (ERIC) of the National Institute of Education (NIE) publishes a monthly abstract journal, *Resources in Education* (RIE), which announces research reports and other nonjournal literature of interest to the educational community. These documents are cataloged, abstracted, and indexed by subject, author or investigator, and responsible institution.

Resources in Education started publication in November 1966 and can be purchased in single copies or on subscription from the Superintendent of Documents, U.S. Government Printing Office, Washington, DC 20402. Annual cumulative sets have been reprinted and can be obtained from Macmillan Information, 216R Brown St., Riverside, NJ 08075.

Macmillan Information also publishes *Current Index of Journals in Education* (CIJE), which indexes articles in more than 700 journals. These journals represent the core of the periodical/serial literature in the field of education.

Individual monthly volumes and yearly cumulations of *Resources in Education* and *Current Index to Journals in Education* are available in many college and university libraries, as well as some special libraries. Most of these libraries are open to the public for on-site reference and many also have complete ERIC microfiche collections. *Resources in Education* is also available in the offices of many school systems at the state and local levels. All routine searches for documentary material should begin with *Resources in Education.*

ERIC was originally conceived in the U.S. Office of Education in the mid-1960s as a system for providing ready access to recent educational research and other education-related literature. The ERIC Processing and Reference Facility is a centralized information processing facility serving Central ERIC and 16 decentralized clearinghouses, each specializing in a branch of knowledge. For further information, contact ERIC Processing and Reference Facility, 4833 Rugby Ave., Ste. 303, Bethesda, MD 20014; (301) 656-9723.

ASA Presidential Series

Volumes in this series are edited by successive presidents of the American Sociological Association and are based upon sessions at the annual meetings of the organization. The series is currently published by Sage Publications, Inc., 2455 Teller Rd., Newbury Park, CA 91320.

Approaches to the Study of Social Structure, Peter M. Blau (1975; out of print)
The Uses of Controversy in Sociology, Lewis A. Coser and Otto N. Larsen (1976; out of print)
Major Social Issues: A Multidisciplinary View, J. Milton Yinger (1978; out of print)
Societal Growth: Processes and Implications, Amos H. Hawley (1979; out of print)
Sociological Theory and Research: A Critical Approach, Hubert M. Blalock (1980; out of print)
Gender and the Life Course, Alice S. Rossi (1985; available from Aldine Publishing Company)
The Nature of Work: Sociological Perspectives, Kai Erikson and Steven Peter Vallas (1990; available from Yale University Press)
The Social Fabric: Dimensions and Issues, James F. Short, Jr. (1986; available from Sage Publications)
Social Structures and Human Lives: Social Change and the Life Course, Volume 1, Matilda White Riley, in association with Bettina J. Huber and Beth B. Hess (1988; available from Sage Publications)
Sociological Lives: Social Change and the Life Course, Volume 2, Matilda White Riley (1989; available from Sage Publications)
Cross-National Research in Sociology, Melvin L. Kohn (1989; available from Sage Publications)
Sociology in America, Herbert J. Gans (1990; available from Sage Publications)
Macro-Micro Linkages in Society, Joan Huber (1991; available from Sage Publications)
The Social Context of AIDS, Joan Huber and Beth E. Schneider (1991; available from Sage Publications)

ASA Publications

The list that follows includes publications of professional interest to sociologists and students majoring in sociology. All are available from the American Sociological Association, 1722 N St., NW, Washington, DC 20036.

Majoring in Sociology: A Guide for Students
Careers in Sociology
Guidelines for Initial Appointments in Sociology
Sociologists in Non-Academic Employment
Report: Status of Women in Sociology, 1934
Federal Funding Program for Social Scientists
Directory of Members
Directory of Departments of Sociology
Guide to Graduate Departments of Sociology, 1977

GUIDE TO JOURNALS SPONSORED BY THE AMERICAN PSYCHOLOGICAL ASSOCIATION

7.D.10

American Psychologist, the official journal of the American Psychological Association, publishes the official papers of the association and substantive articles on psychology. Monthly.

Contemporary Psychology is a journal of reviews—critical reviews of books, films, and other material in the field of psychology. Monthly.

Journal of Abnormal Psychology is devoted to basic research and theory in the broad area of abnormal behavior. Bimonthly.

Journal of Applied Psychology gives primary consideration to original quantitative investigations of value of those people interested in the following broad areas: personnel research; industrial working conditions; research on opinion and morale factors; job analysis and classification research; marketing and advertising research; vocational and educational prognosis, diagnosis, and guidance at the secondary and college levels. Bimonthly.

Journal of Comparative and Physiological Psychology publishes original research reports in the field of comparative and physiological psychology, including animal learning, conditioning, and sensory processes. Bimonthly; two volumes per year.

Journal of Consulting and Clinical Psychology is devoted to the area of clinical psychology, both child and adult. Bimonthly.

Journal of Counseling Psychology serves as a primary publication medium for research on counseling theory and practice.

Journal of Educational Psychology publishes original investigations and theoretical papers dealing with problems of learning and teaching, and with the psychological development, relationships, and adjustment of the individual. Monthly; three volumes per year.

Journal of Personality and Social Psychology is devoted to basic research and theory in the broad areas of social interaction and group processes. Specifically, it deals with interpersonal perception and attitude change, the psychological aspects of formal social systems and less structured collective phenomena, the socialization process at both child and adult levels, social motivation and personality dynamics, the structure of personality, and the relation of personality to group process and social systems. Monthly; three volumes per year.

Psychological Abstracts publishes concise abstracts of the world's literature in psychology and pertinent allied subjects. All titles and abstracts of foreign material are translated into English. Monthly.

Psychological Bulletin is concerned with research reviews and methodological contributions in the field of psychology. One of the principal functions of this journal is to publish critical, evaluative summaries of research. The methodological articles are directed toward people who might or do make practical use of such information, and are intended to bridge the gap between the technical statistician and the typical research psychologist. Articles feature the application of new methodology as well as the creative application of more familiar methodology. Monthly; two volumes per year.

Psychological Review is the major psychological journal of articles of theoretical significance to any area of scientific endeavor in psychology. Bimonthly.

7.D.11   GUIDE TO MAJOR JOURNALS IN POLITICAL SCIENCE AND PUBLIC ADMINISTRATION

American Political Science Review. American Political Science Association, 1527 New Hampshire Ave., NW, Washington, DC 20036.

Official journal of the American Political Science Association. Offers scientific studies, essays, bibliographies, and news and notes on contemporary matters in the profession. Founded 1903.

Annals of the American Academy of Political and Social Science. Sage Publications, Inc., 2455 Teller Rd., Newbury Park, CA 91320.

Founded in 1890 by the American Academy of Political and Social Science in Philadelphia.

Foreign Affairs. Council on Foreign Relations, Inc., 58 E. 68th St., New York, NY 10021.

A nonpartisan review of current ideas and policies affecting U.S. relations in all parts of the world, including international, political, commercial, and business communities. Founded 1922.

Journal of Politics. Southern Political Science Association, University of Florida, Gainesville, FL 32601.

Interpretative articles covering all of the various subfields of political science by leading United States and foreign scholars. Scholarly review of new publications. Founded 1938.

Midwest Journal of Political Science. Wayne State University Press, 5980 Cass Ave., Detroit, MI 48202.

Scholarly publication of the Midwest Conference of Political Science. Founded 1957.

Political Science Quarterly. Academy of Political Science, Fayerweather Hall, Columbia University, New York, NY 10027.

Studies in the field of political science and economics of interest to scholars and lay readers. Founded 1886.

Public Administration Review. American Society for Public Administration, 1225 Connecticut Ave., NW, Washington, DC 20036.

Publishes material representative of all interests and opinions among practitioners, teachers, researchers, and students of public administration. Founded 1939. Bimonthly.

Review of Politics. University of Notre Dame, Notre Dame, IN 46556.

Political theory, contemporary social movements, international relations, cultural developments, and politics. Founded 1939.

Social Research. Graduate Faculty of New School for Social Research, 66 W. 12th St., New York, NY 10011.

International quarterly of political and social science. Founded 1934.

World Politics. Center of International Studies, Princeton University, Crown Hall, Princeton, NJ 08540.

Problems of international relations of a general and theoretical nature, emphasizing social change and employing multidisciplinary methods and concepts. Founded 1948.

Other journals to which political scientists contribute and that they read are the *Western Political Quarterly, The Public Interest,* and *Commentary.* A great number of specialized journals exist.

7.D.12   GUIDE TO MAJOR JOURNALS IN ANTHROPOLOGY

There are many specialized fields in anthropology, and journals exist that specialize in physical anthropology, ethnology, archaeology, and linguistics. The three journals of most general interest to social scientists generally are probably the following:

American Anthropologist. American Anthropological Association, 1530 P St., NW, Washington, DC 20005.
  Founded 1899.
Current Anthropology. University of Chicago Press, 5750 Ellis Ave., Chicago, IL 60637.
  Founded 1953.
Human Organization. Society for Applied Anthropology, Lafferty Hall, University of Kentucky, Lexington, KY 40506.
  Founded 1941.

GUIDE TO MAJOR RESEARCH JOURNALS IN EDUCATION 7.D.13

Education represents a field of great breadth and scope, given that it extends from nursery school to adult education and encompasses a wide variety of subjects. The journals listed below are the research journals that have the broadest scope.

  American Educational Research Journal
  Child Development
  Educational and Psychological Measurement
  Journal of Education Psychology
  Journal of Educational Measurement
  Journal of Experimental Education
  Review of Educational Research

Other more specialized research journals include *American Journal of Mental Deficiency, The Educational Psychologist, Journal of Reading Behavior, Journal of Research in Science Teaching,* and *Reading Research Quarterly.*

GUIDE TO MAJOR JOURNALS USED BY ORGANIZATIONAL AND BEHAVIORAL RESEARCHERS IN BUSINESS 7.D.14

  Academy of Management Journal
  Administrative Science Quarterly
  Decision Sciences
  Human Relations
  Journal of Applied Psychology
  Organization and Administrative Sciences
  Organizational Behavior and Human Performance
  Social Psychology Quarterly

7.D.15 GUIDE TO MAJOR JOURNALS USED BY JOURNALISM AND COMMUNICATION RESEARCHERS

Communication Research
Journal of Communication
Journalism Quarterly
Newspaper Research Journal
Public Opinion Quarterly

There are hundreds of journals in anthropology, economics, education, law, business, social work, and so on. Directories of world journals include *Documentation in the Social Sciences: World List of Social Science Periodicals*, 5th ed., by the International Committee for Social Sciences (Paris: UNESCO, 1980) and *The Standard Periodical Directory*, 7th ed. (New York: Oxbridge, 1980).

Section E

Career Utilization

CAREERS FOR SOCIOLOGY DEGREE HOLDERS IN ACADEMIC AND   7.E.1
NONACADEMIC MARKETS

Each of the three degrees in sociology—the B.A., the M.A., and the Ph.D.—offers a varying range of opportunities. Usually the Ph.D. degree is required for full-time teaching in a college or university. No degree holders can teach in public elementary or secondary schools without a degree in education and state certification.

Careers for Students with a B.A. Degree

The B.A. is not considered a professional degree in any of the social studies fields (history, political science, economics, human geography, social psychology, or social anthropology). The B.A. holder in sociology usually seeks entry-level jobs in social work; in nonprofit or religious organizations; in federal, local, or state government; or in business and industry. The American Sociological Association states:

> There are still very few employers who are looking for sociology BA's in the same sense in which they might look for BA's in engineering, nursing, accounting, etc. Sociology BA's will often find themselves competing with other liberal arts students who have majored in English, history, psychology, etc. Here, a strong undergraduate program in sociology can conceivably produce a competitive advantage. For example, students interested in business careers after the BA might emphasize courses in industrial sociology and complex organization; students seeking work with public welfare agencies might concentrate their course work in areas such as stratification, race and ethnic relations, sociology of the family, and urban sociology.
>
> Regardless of one's special interests, many students would do well to emphasize research methods and statistics. It is precisely these courses that are cited as most valuable by persons already employed in non-academic jobs who are asked to reconsider their education with the wisdom of hindsight. Statistics is not as difficult as many students fear and it often provides the most valuable and marketable career skills. This is especially true for the student who plans to stop with the BA.[1]

By combining data from several surveys, it proved possible to arrive at a general overview of the initial occupational positions held by B.A. graduates in sociology.

TABLE 7.8 Frequency of Selected Position Titles Held by B.A. Graduates

Employer	Percentage
Professions	33.7
Social work	9.9
Counseling	5.4
Researcher	5.4
Elementary/secondary teacher	4.7
Nursing	1.1
Management/administration,	
Sales	
Retail sales	7.4
Insurance	1.6
Service occupations	23.5
Restaurant service	2.2
Planning	2.1
Parole/probation agent/officer	1.9
Police Officer	1.4
Day-care/child-care worker	1.8
Clerical	11.3
Secretary	2.6
Construction and trades	3.2
Miscellaneous	2.4
Total	100.0
Number of cases	759

SOURCE: Bettina J. Huber, "Career Possibilities for Sociology Graduates," *Footnotes* of the American Sociological Association (December 1984): 6–7.

Table 7.8 shows the frequency of these positions. Note that sociologists are employed in all sectors of the economy, and in a diverse array of positions.

Careers for Students Who Hold the M.A. Degree

The holder of an M.A. or M.S. degree in sociology often teaches in a junior or other two-year college. Thus educational background offers occupations with public agencies and private businesses. The M.A. is often sought for technical skill in social research.

Careers for Students Who Hold the Ph.D. Degree

The "best" job usually goes to the holder of a Ph.D. in sociology. Teaching in the university is possible at undergraduate and graduate levels. Research and administration jobs at higher levels become available as experience is gained and competence is demonstrated. (This can be seen in Table 7.11 in Section 7.E.3, which reports on the occupations of sociologists with earned doctorates.) A sociology Ph.D. finds a place in the wider market of behavioral scientists from many disciplines.

Note

1. American Sociological Association, *Careers in Sociology* (Washington, DC: ASA, 1975), 14.

THE BEHAVIORAL SCIENTIST MARKET IN THE UNITED STATES   7.E.2

More than a fourth of all doctoral scientists and engineers in the United States are social and behavioral scientists. Social and behavioral scientists were 29% of the 424,616 doctoral scientists and engineers in 1985. (Other categories of scientists and engineers are life sciences, 25.9%; physical sciences, 17.2%; engineers, 16.0%; environmental sciences, 4.2%; mathematical sciences, 4.1%; computer/information sciences, 3.5%.) The percentage of social and behavioral scientists has increased from 1975, when they constituted 25.9% of the 270,355 scientists and engineers.[1]

Of the 390,930 scientists and engineers who received Ph.D.s from 1960 to 1985, 30.1% or 117,580 were in social and behavioral sciences. In terms of recency of training, they are about the same as all scientists and engineers: 30% of them received their Ph.D.s between 1980 and 1985, whereas 27.3% of all scientists and engineers received their Ph.D.s during those years. In terms of actual age, they are collectively older than other employed scientists and engineers: A third (33.7%) are under 40, whereas almost half (46.6%) of all scientists and engineers are under 40.

Women social scientists are proportionally greater in number than in the other sciences. One-fourth (24.9%) of 123,344 doctoral holders in social and behavioral sciences are women, whereas less than a fifth (17.7%) of the 424,616 doctoral holders in all fields of science and engineering are women.

There has been somewhat of a shift in employment trends of social scientists in recent years. In 1975, more social and behavioral scientists (69.2%) were employed by educational institutions than other scientists and engineers (58.2%). In 1985, the percentage difference had narrowed so that the number of social and behavioral scientists (59.5%) employed by educational institutions was very close to the number of all other scientists and engineers (52.9%). Instead, more social and behavioral scientists are going into business and industry. In 1975, 9.9% of social and behavioral scientists were employed by business and industry, compared with 25.2% of all scientists and engineers. In 1985, 20.7% of social and behavioral scientists were employed by business and industry, compared with 31.4% of all scientists and engineers. The number of social and behavioral scientists working for the federal government essentially remained constant between 1975 and 1985. In 1975, 4.9% of social and behavioral scientists worked for the federal government, compared with 7.4% of all scientists and engineers. In 1985, 4.6% of social and behavioral scientists worked for the federal government, compared with 6.6% of all scientists and engineers.

Recognition has been achieved in major scientific bodies. Social and behavioral scientists are a formally recognized part of the major national science institutions. Since 1973 the Assembly of Behavioral and Social Sciences has been coequal to the Assemblies of Engineering, Life Sciences, and Mathematical and Physical Sciences in the National Academy of Sciences. In the early 1980s the Commission on Behavioral and Social Sciences and Education was accepted as a member with full status to the Academy of Sciences. During this period, the number of social and behavioral scientists elected to the National Academy more than doubled, and today 182 out of the 1,505 members are from these disciplines. In 1968 the public law that governs the National Science Foundation was amended to include the social sciences explicitly in the authority that directs NSF to initiate and support basic science research.

Note

1. I am indebted to Roberta Balstad Miller, director of the Division of Social and Economic Science, National Science Foundation, for assistance in locating some of the data reported here in *Characteristics of Doctoral Scientists and Engineers in the United States in 1985*, Surveys of Science Resource Series (Washington, DC: National Science Foundation, 1986).

7.E.3 ROLES OF ACADEMIC AND NONACADEMIC MARKETS

Professional sociologists with Ph.D.s have usually trained for college or university teaching and hope to find opportunity for their own research as a part of their total responsibilities. In fact, two out of three (68.5%, according to a 1977 National Research Council survey) do just that. Research and its publication actually become obligatory for tenure and promotions at major universities.

With teaching opportunities becoming increasingly restricted, the nonacademic market is an ever more important outlet. It is the nonacademic market that has provided most of the jobs for B.A. and M.A. degree holders in sociology. In terms of number, this is the major market. For this reason, the remainder of this section is devoted to it. A simple graph would depict the relationship between the academic and nonacademic markets for the three degree holders as shown in Figure 7.1.

Education That Facilitates Entry into the Nonacademic Market

1. *Master existing knowledge.* Acquire a substantial store of knowledge about social problems and theories. This is the resource that will provide the best source for attacking problems. Many nonacademic researchers are not scholars; some are little more than technicians. The majority of administrators in nonacademic institutions have limited opportunities to do systematic reading in the broad field of social knowledge. Someone who is able to provide needed knowledge may have an immediate value. The three degree holders—of the B.A., M.A., and Ph.D.—have opportunities for more important responsibilities.
2. Do everything possible to *improve your basic writing and quantitative skills.* Seek opportunities to write papers for credit. Select courses in statistics and computer science that can give you marketable skills for many entry-level positions.
3. *Consider a double major* and interdisciplinary programs such as sociology and communications (or economics, urban planning, statistics, computer science, journalism, or business administration).
4. *Seek opportunities for student-originated research* at the undergraduate level and research support at the graduate level.
5. *Locate opportunities for internships and work experience.* Make your summer and college work count. If at all possible, find work that can be used later as "good experience for an entry-level job."
6. *Develop an understanding of the job market* in your college town as well as your home community. Talk with professionals about careers and technical expertise such as writing and editorial skills, experience in computer programming, statistical knowledge, graphic skills, and interviewing.

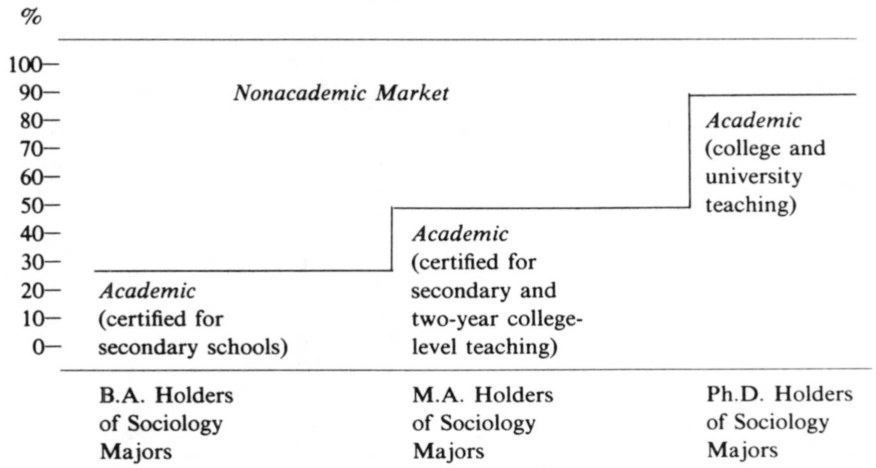

%

Figure 7.1 The Academic and Nonacademic Markets for Sociology Degree Holders

7. Remember, regardless of whether your degree is a B.A., M.A., or Ph.D., the nonacademic market has *not* been structured to fit your social science major. You must *fit your major study to the market* under whatever name you find a job related to your knowledge and skills.

Understanding the Nonacademic Job Market

Most nonacademic sociologists are in research or administration. Table 7.9 shows the main work activities of men and women. The jobs include research, administration, consultation, program planning, writing and editing, counseling, and computer programming. Table 7.10 locates employers and lists them in order of frequency as nonprofit organizations, federal government, state or local government, self-employed, business and industry, and religious organizations.[1]

In early 1978, Doris Wilkinson of Howard University sought information from sociologists in business, industry, and government on positions held and tasks performed. Of those responding (N = 191), the majority held administrative positions (e.g., program manager, research director, chief of law enforcement); 46% of the males (N = 133) and nearly 30% of the females (N = 58) were in this general category. (It may be noted that this gives females a marked increase over the 14.3% shown in the 1975 report.)

The agencies in which these sociologists were employed as administrators/managers included hospitals and health systems agencies, research councils, housing organizations, departments of corrections, state planning bureaus, and the federal government. The occupational group with the second largest number of respondents (males, 19.5%; females, 36.3%) was that of researcher/research assistant (e.g., research analyst, public health analyst, behavioral research associate). Of those who held positions as sociologists, 12% were females and 4% were males. All others in the survey held job titles such as statistician/statistical analyst, consultant, fellow, planner, clinical counselor, project director, equal opportunity specialist, higher education organizer, minister, community development specialist, consultant, and

TABLE 7.9 Main Work Activity of Sociologists in Nonacademic Employment, 1975

Nature of Work	Total Frequency	%	Females Frequency	%	Males Frequency	%
Research	63	52.5	18	64.3	44	48.9
Administration	26	21.7	4	14.3	22	24.4
Consultation	11	9.2	3	10.7	7	7.8
Program planning	8	6.7	2	7.1	6	6.7
Writing and editing	6	5.0	1	3.6	5	5.6
Counseling	3	2.5	0	0.0	3	3.3
Training or teaching	0	0.0	0	0.0	0	0.0
Computer programming	1	.8	0	0.0	1	1.1
Public relations	0	0.0	0	0.0	0	0.0
Other	2	1.7	0	0.0	2	2.2
No information	1		3			
Totals	121		28		90	

assistant representative to the U.N. It should be noted that not all respondents to this survey held doctorates.[2]

More recent surveys indicate that the trend to nonacademic employment continues. The 1981 survey of the 9,977 responding members of the American Sociological Association revealed that the proportion of Ph.D. sociologists in nonacademic employment had increased 10% between 1975 and 1981. The proportion of Ph.D. sociologists employed by business and industry increased fourfold between 1975 and 1981, while the proportion working for nonprofit organizations just about doubled and that working for the government increased by 50%.[3] Table 7.11 shows the distribution of ASA members by type of employer and years of experience.[4]

Getting In and Staying In

Put your skills front and center. For the nonacademic market it is not sufficient simply to itemize areas of specialization. Employers want to know, What can a sociologist do? Applicants for positions must specify skills beyond those of subject-

TABLE 7.10 Employers of Sociologists in Nonacademic Employment, 1975

Employers	Total Frequency	%	Females Frequency	%	Males Frequency	%
Nonprofit organization (nonreligious)	51	42.5	15	53.6	36	40.0
Federal government agency	33	27.5	5	17.9	27	30.0
State, local government agency	13	10.8	2	7.1	10	11.1
Self-employed	11	9.2	3	10.7	8	8.9
Business and industry	6	5.0	1	3.6	5	5.6
Religious organization	4	3.3	1	3.6	3	3.3
Nonprofit organization, business and industry	2	1.7	1	3.6	1	1.1
No information	1		3			
Totals	121		28		90	

TABLE 7.11 Ph.D. Sociologists, by Type of Employer and Years of Experience

Years of Experience: Type of Employer	Less than 5 Years	5-9 Years	10-19 Years	20-29 Years	30+ Years
1975					
Educational institutions	90.0	90.9	87.8	86.1	69.8
Business/industry	1.8	1.0	0.4	2.1	2.3
Nonprofit organizations[a]	3.2	3.3	3.3	3.5	3.2
Government	3.2	2.3	6.8	5.8	5.6
Not employed	1.8	2.6	1.7	2.5	19.1
Total	100.0	100.0	100.0	100.0	100.0
Number of cases	602	1,505	2,246	1,752	748
1981					
Educational institutions	68.8	72.2	80.3	76.8	66.1
Business/industry	8.2	3.5	4.9	2.7	5.3
Nonprofit organizations[a]	9.9	8/2	5.7	6.5	2.8
Government	3.9	12.5	7.9	6.4	3.3
Not employed	9.2	3.5	1.1	7.6	22.5
Total	100.0	100.0	100.0	100.0	100.0
Number of cases	805	2,006	3,156	1,507	1,218

SOURCE: The data are drawn from the Survey of Doctorate Recipients maintained by the National Research Council.
a. This category includes hospitals and clinics.

matter expertise. In the Wilkinson survey of nonacademic sociologists, the following skills were listed by practitioners:

advising, academic
advertising
community service
computer programming
consulting
counseling
curricula development
designing and conducting training
   programs
developing and administering
   educational programs
directing and implementing research projects

editing
market research
policy administration and analysis
program evaluation
providing informed testimony
public opinion polling
reviewing grant proposals
survey design and research
technical writing
testing and measurement
urban planning[5]

Job Titles for Sociology Trainees

An academic degree holder enters the nonacademic market as an innocent. No matter the degree held, there is much to learn about the goals of the department and the distinctive cultural world in which the work is set.

A number of factors will determine whether you get the particular job you want. These factors include, among others, demand for the applicant's skills and training, number of persons applying for the same position, qualifications of the applicant, and the applicant's success in the interviewing session. The list that follows is of selected positions for which the study of sociology, supplemented with relevant training, is useful. Most of the occupational titles are found in nonacademic outlets—business, industry, government—and do not carry the label "sociologist." Many of these jobs require advanced training and previous work experience. Each job seeker must inventory his or her own skills objectively.

admission counselor/director of admissions
affirmative action coordinator
alumni relations coordinator
audiovisual supervisor/specialist
bank teller
book salesperson
Boy Scouts professional worker
camp counselor
card punch operator
college placement officer
community planner
computer aide/programmer
computer analyst/computer specialist
correctional officer
correctional program assistant
counselor (alcoholism, career, drug abuse, handicapped)
day-care worker
demographer
department store manager
editor/editorial assistant
educational therapist/educational therapy assistant
employment counselor/interviewer
environmental analyst/planner
equal opportunity specialist (employment)
foreign service worker
forestry aide/environmental specialist
Girl Scouts professional worker
grants officer or assistant
group worker (in social service agency or hospital)
guidance counselor
health planner
hospital aide/hospital director
journalist/reporter

keypunch operator
labor relations specialist
legal assistant
management trainee (department stores and corporations have training programs)
marketing researcher/assistant
medical records librarian/medical records administrator/assistant
parks and recreation program planner
Peace Corps volunteer
personnel management/personnel relations assistant
photographer
police officer
policy analyst/policy evaluator
probation officer
proofreader[6]
program analyst
public information specialist
public relations supervisor
recreation director/aide
Red Cross worker
registrar
rehabilitation counselor
research analyst/assistant
resident director
salesperson (pharmaceutical, computer, etc.)
social science analyst
social science research assistant
social service worker or aide
statistician/statistical assistant
urban planner/urban analyst
vocational development specialist
writer/editor
writing skills teacher

In my own career, I have had the following nonacademic titles:

supervisor of supervisory training (Sperry Gyroscope Co.)

senior economist and policy appraisal specialist (National War Labor Board)

labor relations consultant (Fisher Flouring Mills, Boeing, and others)

supervisory trainer consultant (Fort Benjamin Harrison Army Post, Wright Patterson Air Force Base, U.S. Chamber of Commerce, Yale University, and others)

labor arbitrator (American Arbitration Association, State of Indiana, Hoover Vacuum Sweeper Co., American Smelting and Refining Co., Indiana State Reformatory, and others)

wage stabilization commissioner (Pacific Region)

labor mediator (Indiana Employment Relations Board)

public relations adviser (American Public Relations Association)

Of these positions, only two were full-time; all the others were practiced in tandem with full-time university teaching. I list them here to call attention to the job variety. Note that not one job carries the title *sociologist*, although my specialized area is industrial sociology.

Finding Where the Jobs Are

In the early stages of a career the applicant may have to search hard and long for jobs. Later, jobs may come to the experienced worker. It is entirely possible that the first job is the only one that must be seriously searched for. For the young worker anxious for employment this is little consolation, but people are willing to help. The applicant must find these helpers and find the available jobs. What follows are some step-by-step hints.

Step 1: Use the resources of your college's sociology department. Provide faculty members with good résumés and ask their counsel.

Step 2: Use your college's employment office. Find out which interviewers are coming to the college and talk with as many as possible.

Step 3: Attend the annual meetings of your Regional Sociological Society and the American Sociological Association. All have employment services where registrants seeking jobs and employers seeking applicants can get together. The ASA has a nonacademic roster. Ask to see this, and use employed sociologists to assist you in locating jobs and arranging interviews. Try to get face-to-face contact with possible employers. Employers want to see you in person!

Step 4: Read the *Bulletin Board of the Chronicle of Higher Education*. This weekly newspaper, widely read in higher-education circles, has an extensive listing of available college and university teaching, research, counseling, and administrative positions. Ordinarily, 40-50 pages of each issue are devoted to the paid advertisements of college employers. Positions available are indexed by occupational titles and also by geographic location. A subscription could be a valuable job seeking tool. Address: The Chronicle of Higher Education, 1255 23rd St., NW, Ste. 700, Washington, DC 20037.

Step 5: Utilize any relevant job bank, information or employment services. Suggested options:

1. *Evaluation Research Society Job Bank.* The Society has established a job bank for individuals seeking new positions and employers looking for qualified job applicants in the fields of program evaluation, evaluation research, and applied social research. For further information, contact Dr. Ann Majchrzak, Chair, Employment Committee, Evaluation Research Society, c/o Westat, Inc., 11600 Nebel St., Rockville, MD 20854; (301) 881-5310, ext. 245.

2. *Federal Employment Information Services of the U.S. Civil Service.* The Civil Service Commission offers federal employment information through a nationwide network of Federal Job Information Centers. For a directory of these centers, as well as for job announcements, write or phone the Civil Service Office in your area. The address for the U.S. Civil Service Commission in the District of Columbia is 1900 E St., NW, Washington, DC 20415.

3. *Register for International Service in Education* (RISE) is a computer-based referral service that matches teaching, research, and consulting assignments in other countries to the qualifications and interests of registered scholars. RISE is administered by the Institute of International Education. A $35 registration fee keeps your application active for two years. For more detailed information and registration forms, write RISE, Institute of International Education, 809 United Nations Plaza, New York, NY 10017.

4. *Occupational Outlook Handbook, 1980-81* (Washington, DC: Bureau of Labor Statistics). Copies may be ordered from the U.S. Superintendent of Documents, Dept. 34, U.S. Government Printing Office, Washington, DC 20402. It provides excellent coverage of current occupational opportunities.

5. *Alternative Careers for Academics Bulletin.* According to Department of Labor projections, between 1972 and 1985 about 583,000 Ph.D.s were granted in all fields. But 396,000 of these degree holders will not find academic employment. The *Alternative Careers Bulletin* is a monthly periodical that discusses openings suitable for professionals with advanced degrees. For example, a typical recent issue dealt with political action to create new jobs, discussed different government positions with hundreds of openings annually, described a career for which most sociologists would be eligible and in which experienced people average $44,000 a year, told where to apply for some excellent overseas posts, and suggested practical ways to start your own consulting or other business. Write: Creative Center Services, A Division of Intellect Corp., P.O. Box 6405-G2, Mobile, AL 36606.

6. Consult Ronald B. Uleck, *Social and Behavioral Sciences Jobs Handbook* (write to R. B. Uleck, Box 3069, Diamond Farms Branch, Gaithersburg, MD 20760). The book includes the following useful materials:
   a. A periodicals matrix showing periodicals that contain job listings for the social and behavioral sciences. There is a description of each periodical, stating address and type of job listings.
   b. A list of city newspapers with circulations over 100,000 that are the focus of activity in a state. Addresses are given.
   c. A list of placement services, with addresses and statements of services rendered.
   d. A list of federal agencies with responsibility for activities in the social and behavioral sciences classified by subject focus: community development, culture and cultural exchange programs, and so on. State and local agencies are also listed, with their addresses.
   e. A list of consulting firms, classified by function.
   f. A description of professional help and various career guides.

7. *Consider a private employment agency.* Agencies work for you and in many cases charge a fee only if they find you a job. Make sure that you use an agency that has a good record for results and integrity.

8. *Try the shotgun approach.* Write to any organization you would be willing to work for and state your assets in the best possible way. Learn to write a résumé that sells *you*.[7] A useful book is *Resume Writing: A Comprehensive How-to-Do-It Guide*; it includes the following:
   a. How to prepare a résumé that will bring your goals, personality, and attributes to the fore and will make the most of your vocational experiences.
   b. When, how, and where to use your résumé for maximum effect, and what employers want to see in your résumé.
   c. A glossary of motivating words, phrases, sentences, and paragraphs, and instruction on items to omit from your résumé.
   d. Valuable source lists of companies.

Staying in the Upstream

This discussion would require a book[8] and a self-analysis: How hard and how long are you willing to work? What kind of a record do you have? What references can you get? What creative skills do you have? What technical skills do you have? Are you keeping up with new developments? What human relations skills do you possess? Are you a good team worker? Have you political savvy? Can you play internal politics successfully? Have you developed a reputation for integrity and compassion? Have you an advancement plan with goals and targets? Are you willing to take risks—to move when opportunity knocks?

You must find the answers to these questions. No one can make predictions without data, but keeping steady and on course should give you a marked advantage.

Notes

1. Sharon K. Panian and Melvin L. De Fleur, *Sociologists in Non-Academic Employment* (Washington, DC: American Sociological Association, 1975), tables 6 and 7.

2. Doris Wilkinson, "Skills Assessment: Market Our Assets," *Footnotes* of the American Sociological Association (October 1980): 3.

3. Bettina Huber, "Sociological Practitioners: Their Characteristics and Role in the Profession," *Footnotes* of the American Sociological Association (May 1983): 1, 6-8.

4. Ibid., 6.

5. Wilkinson, "Skills Assessment," 3.

6. *Footnotes* (August 1978): 7.

7. *Resume Writing: A Comprehensive How-to-Do-It Guide* (New York: Wiley-Interscience, 1976).

8. A good choice would be Jeanne Curran and Carol Telesky, *Up the Job Market: Controlling the Ascent.* It is available at ASA Teaching Resources Center, 1722 N St., NW, Washington, DC 20036. Chapter titles include "The Array of Career Opportunities: Evaluating Trends in the Job Market"; "Social Problem Issues: Indicators of Job Market Trends"; "Penetrating Organizational Boundaries: Probing the Career Path"; "Organizational and Self-Identity"; "Individual Fit with the Organization"; and "Definition of Self and Career: Controlling and Social Context of Identity."

EVALUATION CHECKLIST FOR UNIVERSITY FACULTY JOB SEEKERS WHO MAKE RESEARCH A HIGH PRIORITY   7.E.4

1. Research.
   a. Research/teaching/service orientation of the department and the institution generally.
   b. Types and scopes of research encouraged.
   c. Research budget for department or division (dollars per faculty member).
   d. Assistance available in securing grants.
   e. Research facility—computer capabilities, editorial or computer assistance, a supportive institute of social research.
   f. Number of hours per week per professor of secretarial help. Research atmosphere implies great secretarial support.
   g. Reproduction support (access to machines, type and number of machines).
   h. Machine availability (dictating, electric typewriter, photocopy, computer type, and programming assistance).
   i. Number of research assistants (criteria for obtaining assistants).
   j. Grading help (number of hours per week per professor). Research atmosphere implies grading help.
   k. Relief time for research; sabbatical program.
   l. Teaching demands on time: class size to expect; number of preparations per term; number of *new* preparations per term; number of courses per term; summer course load; day/night schedule; travel time committed to teaching.
   m. Graduate program: seminar teaching opportunities; number and quality of graduate students.
   n. Fellow faculty members, especially in area of interest; research emphasis, compatibility, competence of faculty.
   o. Travel money for professional conferences.

2. Salary offered: Check *Bulletin of American Association of University Professors* for most recent report on the economic status of the profession showing salary rating of the institution. Also check to see if it is among "Censured Institutions."

   a. Summer salary available; moving expenses provided; life insurance; health insurance.

3. Faculty housing available; cost of housing and other living expenses in the area.
4. Office space and equipment.
5. Library facility; extent and quality of holdings.
6. Number of undergraduate and graduate majors in the department.
7. Tenure rules.
8. Promotion procedures.
9. Retirement program.
10. Morale of the faculty; history of faculty mobility in the department.
11. Relationships across departments and schools.
12. Quality and character of the administration, especially the chair of the department and the dean.
13. History and current status of the financing of the institution.
14. Faculty governance and rules (ask for faculty handbook).

7.E.5   SELECTED BIBLIOGRAPHY OF NONACADEMIC CAREERS

The American Sociological Association has a general career booklet for undergraduates titled *Embarking upon a Career with an Undergraduate Sociology Major*. Its primary purpose is to assist students in the process of finding employment. A more specialized booklet is also available from ASA: Delbert C. Miller, *The Sociology Major as Preparation for Careers in Business*. See the following description for guides directed to undergraduate and graduate students.

Foote, Nelson. "Putting Sociologists to Work." *American Sociologist* 9 (August 1974): 125-34.

Gelfand, Donald E. "The Challenge of Applied Sociology." *American Sociologist* 10 (February 1975): 13-18.

Huber, Bettina. "Sociological Practitioners: Their Characteristics and Role in the Profession." *Footnotes* of the American Sociological Association 11 (May 1983): 1, 6-8.

Lyson, Thomas, and Gregory D. Squires. "Sociologists in Non-academic Settings: A Survey of Employers." *SSSP Newsletter* 13 (Winter 1982): 16-18.

Montoya, Marco. *The Sociologist in Government.* Severn, MD: Resource Development Center, 1976.

———. "The Federal Government: Getting In and Staying In." Paper presented at annual meeting of the American Sociological Association, Chicago (September 6, 1977).

Panian, Sharon K., and Melvin L. De Fleur. *Sociologists in Non-Academic Employment.* Washington, DC: American Sociological Association, 1975.

Rice, Thomas J. "Life on the Applied/Clinical Side." *Footnotes* of the American Sociological Association (November 1986): 8.

Rossi, Peter H. "The Challenge and Opportunities of Applied Social Research." *American Sociological Review* 45 (December 1980): 889-904.

Scott, Robert A., and Arnold Shore. "Sociology and Policy Analysis." *American Sociologist* 9 (May 1974): 51-59.

Tuchfeld, Barry S. "Putting Sociology to Work: An Insider's View." *American Sociologist* 11 (November 1976): 188-92.

Career Bulletins Designed for Applicants in Business
at the B.A., M.A., and Ph.D. Levels

The Sociology Major as Preparation for Careers in Business, by Delbert C. Miller, provides information on the options available to sociology majors interested in pursuing careers in business or industry. The booklet includes sections on roles of practitioners and academics, job prospects, post-B.A. education, and advice for the student interested in practicing sociology in the context of a business career. Single copies are free from the American Sociological Association with a self-addressed, stamped envelope.

Another work of interest is *Academic and Practitioner Roles of Industrial Sociologists: A Career Bulletin for Graduate Students*, edited by Delbert C. Miller. This publication describes in some detail the career options available to sociologists with a special interest in industrial relations and the sociology of business. Roles of teachers, trainers, consultants, mediators, arbitrators, divisional staff, owners, and managers are described by industrial sociologists who have held those positions. This work should be especially useful to undergraduates planning to pursue graduate training and to those who want additional information about industrial sociology. Price is $6.00 to ASA members; $4.00 for students.

For additional information, write for the *1989 Catalogue of Materials Available in Career Resources and Professional Development*, Professional Development Program, American Sociological Association, 1722 N St., NW, Washington, DC 20036.

Subject Guide

Index of Names

About the Author

Delbert C. Miller is Professor of Sociology and Business Administration at Indiana University, Bloomington. He is the author of numerous research articles in scholarly journals, and his books include *Industrial Sociology* (1st, 2nd, and 3rd eds.) and *Industry, Labor, and Community* (both with William H. Form). His research monographs, *International Community Power Structures* and *Leadership and Power in Bos-Wash Megalopolis*, describe large-scale team research projects that he has directed. He has served for many years as a Supervisory Training Specialist and as Arbitrator for the American Arbitration Association and the State of Indiana. The history of the five editions of the *Handbook of Research Design and Social Measurement* is described in the Preface to this book.